Praise for **GUITA**

“Encyclopedic . . . packed with enough info to
joy . . . [a] rich, resonant, detailed account . . . this book draws you in the way a novel does, one by Dostoyevsky, say, in which the hero is part genius, part stumblebum, a flawed artist making his way half-aware through a world of joys and pitfalls—someone very much like most of us, in other words, if a lot more talented and a little more careless.”

Wall Street Journal

“Thanks to new interviews with associates and animated descriptions of [his] playing, motor-mouth way of talking, and scholarly music knowledge, [Bloomfield’s] tug of war between the commercial and the uncompromised makes for an absorbing read. Guitar King isn’t the first book on Bloomfield but is most fleshed out, and it also feels like one of the last great untold classic-rock tales, right up through Bloomfield’s mysterious passing. . . . Guitar King gives you its own version of the blues.”

Rolling Stone

“Bloomfield hated stardom, and what unfolds is the story of a genius ‘relegated to footnote status’ by a self-sabotaging streak Dann lays out in tragic, vivid detail.”

Rolling Stone, “Best Music Books of 2019”

“A compelling narrative of a young blues fanatic whose problems with drugs and mental instability pre-dated his fame. . . . Those with a passion for the music will enjoy revisiting a time when Bloomfield’s influence exceeded even Stevie Ray Vaughn’s.”

Kirkus

“This monumental book illuminates the legacy of a musician who has been overshadowed by other Sixties luminaries but who helped bring the vernacular of the blues to rock and whose playing influenced thecourse of rock and roll.”

Library Journal, starred review

"Exhaustive and engaging."

Largehearted Boy

"Guitar King is voluminous in size, as befits a man whose contribution to modern music is greater than history has ever acknowledged. It is clear that Dann, drawing from his deep research and numerous interviews, put tremendous effort into this book. It is a biography that puts Bloomfield back in his rightful place on the roster of rock and blues greats. The result is a tremendous and magnificent work."

CounterPunch

"[Dann] restores Bloomfield to the prominence he once enjoyed, careful to avoid hagiography as he documents the musician's rise to glory and swift, heartbreaking (but seemingly inevitable) demise."

MOJO

"Essential reading for serious rock and blues fans."

Goldmine Magazine

"[Guitar King] goes beyond previous Bloomfield books to examine his music and turbulent life at a near-molecular level. . . . [Dann] reveals the depths of Bloomfield's musical passions, genius, and personal despair. . . . Guitar King establishes his pivotal role in American music history."

Pittsburgh Post-Gazette

"This is the definitive book on Michael Bloomfield. . . . Guitar King reads like a novel with stunning points of new information and a great compassion for the vagaries of Bloomfield's life . . . one of the greatest books written about any musician, of any genre."

PolitiChicks

"[A] rich and definitive presentation that will enhance the converted and convert the unfamiliar."

Oakland Press

"No matter how much knowledge you may already have about Michael Bloomfield, reading Dann's biography will certainly add multiple layers of understanding about his life and the extent of his influence on the lineage of blues guitar playing. . . . [A] magnificent tribute to a man who undoubtedly was a 'Guitar King,' making this book a highly recommended addition to any musical library!"

Blues Blast Magazine

"Compelling reading from start to finish . . . only this prolific artist's music itself could be a more vivid act of advocacy."

All About Jazz

"Without doubt, David Dann has the goods on the person who could well be the most exciting electric guitarist to come out of all the '60s musical machinations. And though the '70s were pretty much a bust for Bloomfield, the decline and eventual sad demise of this nonpareil bluesman holds so many intriguing what-could-have-beens that for anyone who is super-interested in how the modern musical landscape was born and why it went so far south during the '70s for such a pivotal original, this is the tome that tells the tale."

Americana Highways

"An important and compelling book about an important and compelling artist. Bloomfield's peers—Hendrix, Clapton, Joplin, the Rolling Stones, and of course Dylan—have had their lives chronicled in exhaustive detail, and this biography is long overdue. Dann's research is excellent, and the writing strong and engaging, tracing Bloomfield's journey and telling his story with skill and understanding."

Elijah Wald, author of *Escaping the Delta* and *Dylan Goes Electric!*

"David Dann has restored bluesman Michael Bloomfield's premier place in the pantheon as the very first American rock guitar god. The author brings the excitement of Michael's searing licks to the written word and paints a poignant portrait of a man who was unequipped for and uninterested in playing the games that the entertainment-industrial complex demands of artists. This soulful bio reminds us of one man's dedication to excellence at the expense of fame and fortune."

Michael Simmons, contributor to *MOJO* and author of liner notes to *Michael Bloomfield: From His Head To His Heart To His Hands*

"I love this book. It's the best thing I've read about Mike Bloomfield and about the whole era."

Charlie Musselwhite, Grammy Award–winning blues harmonica player and bandleader

"Michael Bloomfield was a heart-to-hand guitar player who was able to take everything he learned from B. B. King, Hubert Sumlin, and everyone else he ever encountered—including the piano style of Little Brother Montgomery—and turn it all inside out and make it his own. He is still the well I draw from for inspiration in the blues, and I drink from it daily. Written from heart to hand just like Bloomfield played his music, Guitar King is a must-read book for all guitar players and music fans alike. It should be the final word on Michael Bloomfield's journey and his legacy."

Jimmy Vivino, music director on *Conan* and leader of Jimmy Vivino and the Basic Cable Band

GUITAR KING

MICHAEL BLOOMFIELD'S LIFE IN THE BLUES

DAVID DANN

University of Texas Press
Austin

Printed in the United States of America
First edition, 2019
First paperback printing, 2021

Permissions
University of Texas Press
P.O. Box 7819
Austin, TX 78713–7819
utpress.utexas.edu/rp-form

♾ The paper used in this book meets the minimum requirements of ANSI/NISO Z39.48–1992 (R1997) (Permanence of Paper).

Library of Congress Cataloging-in-Publication Data
Names: Dann, David, author.
Title: Guitar king : Michael Bloomfield's life in the blues / David Dann.
Description: Austin : University of Texas Press, 2019. | Includes bibliographical references and index.
Identifiers: LCCN 2019012699 | ISBN 978-1-4773-2367-0 (pbk. : alk. paper) | ISBN 978-1-4773-1892-8 (library e-book) | ISBN 978-1-4773-1893-5 (nonlibrary e-book)
Subjects: LCSH: Bloomfield, Michael. | Guitarists—United States—Biography. | Blues musicians—United States—Biography.
Classification: LCC ML419.B58 D35 2019 | DDC 787.87/1643092 [B] —dc23
LC record available at https://lccn.loc.gov/2019012699

doi:10.7560/318775

View from the Guitarist

The audience glistens a strange love;

listens

to the old voices in

the season to be released from

disease and freedom

ROY (LANDES) RUBY, "Come to This" (1968)

CONTENTS

GUITAR KING

PROLOGUE

Bob Dylan stared at the menu, trying to make sense of it. There were a few odd French entrées, but the specialty of the house seemed to be "peanut butter sandwiches, served under glass bells, flaming!" He looked up at the waiter, then at the bill of fare, then back at the waiter. "Uh, I guess I'll just have coffee," he said. "Un café," *the man said flatly. He turned and disappeared through a side door.*

The folksinger looked around the room. Though thick drapes hung over its floor-length windows, there was enough afternoon light coming in to show paint peeling in places on the walls. An ornate rosette on the ceiling was stained with water spots, and there were wide swaths in the carpet that years of traffic had worn nearly bare. A musty odor pervaded, suggesting glories that had long since faded. It was the room's funereal silence, though, that spoke most prominently of decay.

It was a silence that was suddenly broken.

Startled, Dylan turned to see a young man with a guitar case standing in the hallway. He was loudly arguing with the maître d'.

"No, man, <u>no</u>, we don't want a table," he said, talking fast. "We don't wanna eat. I'm looking for the folksinger—the guy who's working here. <u>That</u> guy." He pointed to a chalkboard on an easel in the archway.

Welcome to The Bear
A Different Kind of Nightclub
Presenting
Gospel Great Bessie Griffin
And the Gospel Pearls
Plus—One Night Only
Special Guest Star
Bob Dylan

"I just wanna talk to this Dylan guy," the man continued. "You know where he is?"

"That's me," Bob said quietly. The man in the doorway turned, stared for a moment, and then smiled.

"Oh, yeah, that is you," he said affably. "Nice to meet you. I'm Mike Bloomfield. This is Susie, my wife."

Dylan stood as the couple entered the room. Though the man was tall, he walked with a peculiar stoop and took great splayed strides. What was most striking about him was his giant beehive of unruly black hair. His wife, by contrast, was a petite woman, an attractive blonde with a dimpled smile.

"Yeah, hi, I'm Bob," Dylan replied. He gestured to the empty chairs at the table. "Uh, what can I do for you?"

"Well, I'll tell you, now. I heard you're a real hot guitar player," Bloomfield began, leaning the case up against the table and pulling out a chair. "I thought maybe we could play a little, you know? Jam or something."

"I, uh, well . . ." Bob stammered. "I don't know. I mean, I've gotta play tonight. And I'm really more a poet than a guitar player—"

"We got your album," Susie interrupted. "You played guitar on that. Blind Lemon Jefferson, Bukka White, Jesse Fuller—you played blues tunes by them."

"Yeah," said Michael. "The back of the record says you're one of the best white blues players ever to be recorded. I sure would like to hear you play some blues." He smiled broadly and leaned in for the kill. "I mean, I've been hanging out with my friend Big Joe and he's a pretty good blues picker. But you're the best—hell, man, I'd really like to hear that!"

"Big Joe?" Dylan quietly. "You mean Big Joe Williams? Well, I recorded with him. But that was on harmonica."

"You recorded—?" Bloomfield suddenly sat back. He looked at Susie and then at his host. "You know Big Joe? 'Baby Please Don't Go'—that Big Joe?"

"Yeah," said Bob. "I met him in New York. We shared a bottle of schnapps and made a record. But I'm not much of a harp player, either."

Dylan smiled at the couple, and for a moment no one said anything. Then all three burst out laughing.

"Man, you know Big Joe," Michael said, chortling. "I'll bet you know now never to have a drink with him! So who else do you know?"

By the time Dylan's coffee arrived, the folksinger and his two guests were in the midst of a private hootenanny. Bloomfield had his guitar out and was running through a few numbers by Big Joe. Bob was improvising comic verses, trying to follow along on his guitar, while Susan sang harmony. All three laughed and joked as Michael moved on to blues by Rev. Gary

Davis, Son House, Tampa Red, and Big Bill Broonzy. Soon they were singing Woody Guthrie songs, re-creating hollers by Lead Belly and picking country ballads by Hank Williams. It seemed that Dylan knew every song Bloomfield could name and that Michael could play every style Bob could name. An hour flew by and then another, and by the time Dylan had to prepare for the evening's performance, he and Michael Bloomfield were rocking through tunes by Chuck Berry, Little Richard, and the King, Elvis Presley.

"Hell, man," Bob said to his new friend as he stood up. "You are just about the best damn guitar player I have ever heard!"

Though the foregoing scenario is a dramatization, the basic facts surrounding Michael Bloomfield's first encounter with Bob Dylan are not fiction. When Bloomfield went down to the Bear on Ontario Street on Thursday, May 2, 1963, he fully intended to cut one of the rising stars of the New York folk revival. Dylan was just about to release his second album on Columbia to great critical acclaim, but Bloomfield couldn't understand what all the fuss was about. He had heard the folksinger's debut recording and found it laughable—the man couldn't sing, and he couldn't play guitar. *Time to teach this upstart a lesson*, Michael thought. As one of Chicago's finest young guitarists, someone who'd played with Muddy Waters, Howlin' Wolf, and countless other blues masters as well as Big Joe Williams, Bloomfield knew he had the bonafides to do it.

It was opening week for the Bear, a nightclub in a run-down Chicago mansion that had formerly been a French restaurant called L'Aiglon. A warren of dusty Victorian rooms, the venue offered its patrons "weirdness accompanied by Holy Rollers, sexologists and occasionally musicians" and was described as "the dream residence of a Charles Addams couple." The creation of Second City founder Howard Alk, the Bear featured an eclectic roster of entertainment that first week, with gospel singer Bessie Griffin headlining. Dylan was included in the Thursday night show because his manager, Albert Grossman, was the club's primary investor. He hoped the folksinger would attract an audience.

He did attract Mike Bloomfield. And two things happened when Bloomfield found Dylan in one of the club's dingy dining rooms. First, Michael was completely disarmed by Bob's affability. The folksinger's quiet charm, quick wit, and self-effacing modesty easily won Bloomfield over. Any desire to humiliate the folk star was forgotten. The two became fast friends and remained so throughout Michael's life.

The second thing that happened was that Bob Dylan, who would become one of the great influences on American pop culture in a career spanning more than half a century, encountered a guitar player whose virtuosity astonished him. Michael Bloomfield's intelligence, knowledge of music, and mastery of its many styles made a powerful and lasting impression. In a few years, Bloomfield would help Dylan reshape his own music, leading to a pop revolution that would define much of the music of the 1960s and 1970s. Nearly five decades after they first met, Bob was still in awe of his friend's artistry. "He could just flat out play. He had so much soul. And he knew all the styles, and he could play them so incredibly well," Dylan told *Rolling Stone*. Bloomfield was the one guitarist who, for Bob Dylan, set the standard for all the others. Michael was the one he never forgot.

Today, though, many people seem to have forgotten Mike Bloomfield.

It wasn't always so. Bloomfield was a big star in his day—for a brief period, the biggest when it came to electric guitar. Everyone from folk diva Joan Baez to rhythm and blues (R&B) rocker Mitch Ryder to jazz trumpeter Don Ellis wanted to work with him. But then Eric Clapton crossed the Atlantic with Cream and Jimi Hendrix's "Wild Thing" ignited Monterey, and every other week it seemed like there was another hot guitar player grabbing music headlines. That was when Bloomfield decided he had had enough. As he later said, "I didn't relate to being a rock star at all." He dropped off the scene, played locally, and toured only when he needed cash. Popular music, preoccupied with stardom, moved on, becoming a massive and influential industry capable of manufacturing rock stars the way Detroit stamps out cars for each new model year. Record companies quickly forgot about Michael Bloomfield, as did the pop media, the critics, and many of the guitarist's fans and followers. Not long after his death in 1981, Bloomfield had been relegated to footnote status: the guy who accompanied Bob Dylan when Dylan plugged in at Newport.

But Dylan knew how important Mike Bloomfield had been to the development and expansion of American popular music at a time when Top 40 radio was preoccupied with British invaders, surfer dudes, and lemon twisters. Michael was not only a startlingly original and brilliant player, but also pivotal in introducing a generation to the blues and to those masters who originated it. He helped create folk-rock, inspired the psychedelic rock craze, was the first to experiment with brass-rock, and arguably laid the groundwork for jazz fusion. His influence unquestionably affected the direction popular music took in the 1960s. But following his death in 1981, that fact seemed to get lost as critics scrambled to laud glam rock, punk rock, grunge rock, indie rock—*whatever* rock—in the decades that followed.

It has been thirty-eight years since Michael Bloomfield died of an overdose, a period slightly longer than the duration of the guitarist's short life. For many decades, he was American pop music's forgotten man. But in recent years, that condition has shown signs of a correction. Authors Jan Mark Wolkin and Bill

Keenom sparked renewed interest in Bloomfield when they published their fine oral biography *Michael Bloomfield: If You Love These Blues* in 2000. A decade later, Gibson introduced the Michael Bloomfield 1959 Les Paul Standard—a signature model created by their custom shop—and suddenly contemporary guitar players were seeking out Bloomfield's recordings and rediscovering his extraordinary virtuosity. With the release in 2014 of *Michael Bloomfield: From His Head to His Heart to His Hands*, Sony Legacy's box set tribute to Michael, many new listeners could hear that virtuosity for themselves.

And now comes this biography. The story of Michael Bloomfield's life is a fascinating tale of musical genius and artistic innovation, a saga punctuated by unorthodox adventures and wild excesses. Its arc parallels a time in American history when pop culture was undergoing a radical change, when politics, drugs, sex, and rock 'n' roll were growing up. Bloomfield grew with them and contributed to their maturation. His musical ideas, coupled with his extraordinary personality and boundless energy, proved to be irresistible for a generation of young musicians. Certainly they were for Bob Dylan.

So it seems that Michael Bloomfield's time may finally be at hand, a time when he'll assume his rightful place among those guitar players whose artistry has shaped the evolution of American popular music and culture. About time, I say. And it's my sincere hope that this volume will in some way contribute to that worthy eventuality.

PART I

GUITAR KING

CHAPTER 1

SOCIAL MISFIT

CHICAGO AND GLENCOE, 1943–1958

In 1958 the verdant bedroom community of Glencoe, Illinois, was an ideal repository for the American Dream. A wealthy village on Chicago's North Shore, it was home to successful professionals who had escaped the growing urban blight of the big city to the south. Glencoe's stately homes with expansive lawns, tree-lined streets, excellent schools, charming shops, and country club exclusivity were a magnet for the Windy City's upwardly mobile. Families with means invariably decamped to the North Shore, and Glencoe was a favored destination.

Sheridan Road was the village's main residential thoroughfare. One block west, and three blocks from the sandy beaches of Lake Michigan, lay Greenleaf Avenue. A quiet lane of suburban domesticity, the street was flanked by landscaped manses set at a tasteful distance from the curb—and from one another. One, a six-bedroom house in the Spanish style, occupied a manicured corner lot at the north end of the street. It was home to a family recently arrived from Chicago's North Side, a husband and wife and their two adolescent sons. Harold and Dorothy Bloomfield were an attractive couple, and they easily fit the village's ideal demographic. Their boys—Michael Bernard, born on July 28, 1943, and Allen, born eighteen months later—were typical American adolescents, bright and engaging. They attended the local secondary school and, with their parents, regularly worshipped at North Shore Congregation Israel, the village's reform temple. In all respects, the Bloomfields were a conventional, well-to-do Glencoe family.

In all respects, that is, except one. The couple's elder son, fourteen-year-old Michael Bloomfield, had developed a passion for music. Like many teens his age, he was enthralled by the new sounds he was hearing on the radio, music the newspapers were calling "rock 'n' roll." He was a big fan of Jerry Lee Lewis, Chuck Berry, Little Richard, and Gene Vincent. The star singer from Memphis, Elvis Presley, was a particular favorite. But Michael's musical tastes weren't limited to the current hit parade. In that way, he was different from other kids in Glencoe.

Michael Bloomfield was obsessed with the blues.

It was music he had first heard under the covers at night, music he secretly tuned in on a pocket transistor radio he had been given as a bar mitzvah gift. That same year, his thirteenth, he talked his parents into buying him a guitar, largely because his cousin had been given one. Lessons with Tony Tenaglia, his mother's hairdresser, followed, and soon young Michael was spending hours alone in his room, practicing chords and running scales with an enthusiasm he rarely exhibited for his schoolwork. Though he was left-handed, he never bothered to restring his Harmony to accommodate his natural preference. He simply forced himself to learn right-handed. Even so, it wasn't long before he was picking out the guitar parts to his favorite rock 'n' roll songs.

That was two years earlier. Since that time, Michael had purchased a *real* guitar—a Gibson ES-175, an archtop electric with two pickups—and a heavy amplifier to plug it into. He had become proficient enough on the big instrument to begin playing in public, comping along as part of an adult accordion quartet or running down raucous rock 'n' roll licks with other teens at weekend beer parties at an abandoned shopping center in neighboring Wilmette. He would play with anybody, and he would play anything. But what he wanted to play most was blues.

Not that he really understood what the blues were. He heard songs at night on his transistor radio that DJs described as "blues," songs that were regularly featured on stations like WDIA out of Memphis or on Nashville's WKDA. He heard some of those same tunes during the day as the family's live-in housekeeper, an African American woman named Mary Williams, went about her duties. When her employers were not at home, Mary tuned in to WGES and WVON, stations broadcasting from Chicago's South Side, and passed the time listening to the latest releases by Muddy Waters or Howlin' Wolf. Michael soon learned their names and the names of other blues musicians—players with exotic-sounding monikers like Lightnin' Hopkins and T-Bone Walker. He began searching for their records and trying to learn the guitar parts to their tunes.

Over those same stations, Michael also heard ads for clubs that featured bluesmen. With Mary Williams's help, he had even gotten into one venue north of the Loop, a folk club called the Gate of Horn, to see the legendary Josh White. He had met the blues singer before the show and had been thrilled by his performance. It was an experience that convinced the young guitarist that he had to see some of Chicago's other blues stars. But that meant he would have to travel deep into the city's black ghetto, the South Side neighborhood that ran along the lake from Roosevelt Road to Sixty-Third Street, a stretch known as "Bronzeville." It was a part of Chicago that few whites would ever think of visiting, and it was certainly no place for a suburban teenager. But

Michael was determined to go, even though he knew his parents—especially his father—would disapprove.

It wasn't that Harold Bloomfield was averse to taking risks. As a highly successful businessman, he understood that necessity. His father, Samuel Bloomfield, had given him a gas station to manage when he was only fourteen, and now, at forty-four, he ran the production side of one of the fastest-growing hotel and restaurant supply companies in the country. Bloomfield Industries, started in 1933 as a purveyor of dessert display cases for diners and roadside eateries by the elder Bloomfield, had grown under Harold's guidance in partnership with his brother, Daniel, into a multimillion dollar company occupying six acres of Archer Heights, a southwest Chicago neighborhood near suburban Cicero, and employing nearly one thousand workers. Michael Bloomfield's father was nothing if not a risk taker.

But Harold strongly disapproved of his elder son's obsession with music. He was a consummate businessman, driven by personal discipline and a determination to succeed, and he devoted nearly all his waking hours to that objective. That Michael could spend entire days in his room listening to music—if that *noise* could even be called music—while playing along on a buzzy, loud electric guitar was alarming. Time that should have been devoted to schoolwork was instead squandered on a frivolous hobby. Mr. Bloomfield could see no future in rock 'n' roll for his son. In his eyes, Michael was destined to join him in the family business, just as he had done with his father. The boy would be a businessman like the Bloomfield men before him.

But Michael Bloomfield had no interest in business. He had found something he was good at—playing guitar—and had discovered a world of sound in rock 'n' roll, R&B, and blues—especially blues—that excited him like nothing else. He had to know more about it, and about its creators. Many of them lived and worked in the vast metropolis just twenty miles to the south. Why couldn't he go see them? Michael had been listening to the big stars of Chicago blues on the radio for many months, and now he decided he would go see the biggest. He would go see Muddy Waters.

Muddy Waters, in 1958, was Chicago blues royalty. A string of hits for the city's Chess label, beginning in the late 1940s, had made the forty-four-year-old Mississippi native famous. Tunes such as "Rollin' and Tumblin'," "I'm Your Hoochie Coochie Man," and "I'm Ready" had become blues standards by the middle of the decade, and "Got My Mojo Working," Muddy's latest single, was the current favorite on many of Chicago's R&B radio stations. Waters had a regular Thursday night gig at Johnny Pepper's modest club on Forty-Third Street, six blocks east of the Forty-Third Street L stop. Called Pepper's Lounge, the joint provided setups for its customers and charged thirty-five cents at the door.

Pepper's was not exactly a place one would expect to find a fourteen-year-old white boy from the suburbs. But one Thursday after school, Michael caught a bus on Green Bay Road. With him was his closest friend, a schoolmate named Roy Ruby whose stepfather was a professor of logic at Chicago's Roosevelt University. A bright, inquisitive teenager who fancied himself a poet, Roy, too, had gotten caught up in the blues. He had no qualms about joining Michael in his unprecedented sojourn, and the two boys rode the bus through the villages of Winnetka, Kenilworth, Wilmette, and Evanston, then on into Chicago, where they switched to an L train at the line's northernmost terminus at Howard Street. From there they rode down through the city's North Side neighborhoods, descending into the subway tunnel after the Fullerton Parkway stop for the ride into the Loop.

Even though rush hour was nearly over, the subway's downtown platforms were still crowded with commuters. There were businessmen in heavy overcoats, their hats pulled down against the city's notorious wind; shop girls checking their makeup one last time in a vending machine mirror; day laborers with tool belts and lunch pails; and book-laden school kids heading home from after-school programs. It was a cross section of Chicago's diversity—a healthy mix of race, gender, and age, all waiting for the next train.

With each station stop, Michael and Roy were buffeted as passengers pressed in through the open car doors. They shared a strap, swaying each time the train lurched forward and shifting their feet to keep their balance. The trip was beginning to feel like a real adventure, and they both were excited.

When the cars pulled into the Jackson Boulevard station, many of the seated riders stood and most of the straphangers reached for the aisle poles. After a moment, the doors opened and the commuters streamed out onto the platform. Most were transferring to the Cermak Road line, heading for the Southwest Side suburbs. But Michael and Roy stayed on the train and rode to Roosevelt Road. There they went upstairs to the L platform and switched to a Jackson Park train headed for Bronzeville. The car was comfortably empty compared to the Howard, and the boys slid into one of the vacant seats as the train picked up speed. Michael gazed drowsily out the window as signal lights flashed by, but Roy, glancing around, suddenly felt uneasy. He realized that he and Michael were the only white people in the car.

The Jackson Park train passed by the lighted windows of apartment buildings and over cross streets busy with evening traffic. When it reached the Forty-Third Street stop, the boys stepped out of the car into the cold night air and clambered down the platform steps to the darkened street below. It felt good to stretch their legs—the trip had taken the better part of two hours.

Though they were strangers in a strange land, Michael and Roy found Pepper's without mishap. It was early yet, but there was already a crowd of people standing around the door, waiting to get in. Michael saw why—an old gent seated on a stool was taking money just inside the entrance. He was holding a silver chain across the doorway and letting in only one person at a time. Once he had the money in hand and had given the patron a visual once-over, he would drop the chain and allow him to pass. Then the process would begin again.

Michael and Roy stood in line, waiting their turn. They hadn't attracted much attention beyond a few curious stares from people passing by on the street. But when they stood before the doorman, they suddenly stuck out.

"Where you boys think you're going?" asked the man on the stool, more than a little surprised.

"Uh, we're here to see Muddy Waters. We, uh . . . we just want to see the band," stammered Michael.

"Muddy *Waters*?" barked the doorman. "How old are you, boy? Your mama know where you are? Go on now, you boys better move on away from here."

Some in the crowd began to laugh. "What they doin' here?" one man said. "Probably lookin' for some brown sugar," said another, inspiring snickers. Roy suddenly felt uncomfortable again. What *were* they doing there?

But Michael was undeterred. He could see there was no point in arguing with the doorman—they were not going to get in. But he could hear the band tuning up inside Pepper's, and the young guitarist grabbed his friend's arm. The teenagers moved over to the adjacent storefront and listened. Soon they heard Muddy being introduced, and then the band launched into "Forty Days and Forty Nights." Muddy's amplified voice boomed out over the driving sound of bass and drums while the piercing keen of his slide guitar rattled the club's big plate glass windows. In the spaces between the words cascaded the notes of a piano. Mike knew that had to be Otis Spann. He was absolutely thrilled.

The boys spent the better part of an hour outside of Pepper's transfixed, listening to the great Muddy Waters perform and catching glimpses of the band through the few unpainted portions of the storefront window. They wouldn't get home until after midnight, and they hadn't gotten into the club to actually *see* the star bluesman. But the trip was a success anyway, and Michael knew he would be back.

* * *

Michael Bloomfield's early years were spent in Chicago. He had been born in the city and lived with his family in a high-rise apartment building on Melrose Street, a few quiet residential blocks on the city's North Side. He attended the Nettelhorst School around the corner, and his days were filled with childhood pleasures—Duncan yo-yo demonstrations at ABC Toyland, frolics in Lake Michigan at nearby Montrose Beach, the latest Hollywood Western at the Diversey Theater, trick-or-treating in homemade costumes, walking to and from school with classmates. Michael was an integral part of life in the neighborhood and had a deep enthusiasm for Chicago's many attractions. He was a real city kid.

But then, in the middle of Michael's sixth-grade year, the Bloomfields abruptly moved. Dorothy, known in the family as "Dottie," decided her boys would receive a better education in the North Shore's prestigious schools. Harold agreed but had his own reasons for relocating. His brother and business partner, Daniel, had recently built a grand house in the suburbs, becoming the first member of the Bloomfield family to own his own home. Unwilling to be outdone, Harold also decided to move north. Because his brother had selected Glencoe for his family's new address, Harold did too. Thus, in the spring of 1955, young Michael Bloomfield found himself transplanted to the woodsy bowers and shady lanes of suburbia.

The change was disorienting.

In their new school, it quickly became apparent that the Bloomfield boys were social outsiders. The prosperous North Shore had unspoken but strictly observed rules of dress and demeanor—especially among its adolescents. The kids in Glencoe's schools all came from similar backgrounds; there was none of the diversity found at Nettelhorst. As a consequence, there was a premium on conformity. Suddenly, the clothes Michael wore mattered. The way he wore his hair and the way he looked and behaved mattered.

Money also mattered. Glencoe was a rich town, and the students at school mostly came from very well-to-do families. Their holidays were spent not at Chicago's Riverview Amusement Park but at resorts in Vale or the Bahamas. Winter tans were de rigueur. That wealth-conferred status was something Glencoe kids understood well, and they arranged their social lives accordingly. Michael lived in one of the wealthiest parts of the village, but he had no notion of status. He quickly became a pariah in the eyes of his peers.

Lack of social status wasn't the boy's only shortcoming. Michael was big for his age and heavy, and his awkwardness made him an easy target for the "jocks" in his class. And because athletic ability was seen by his schoolmates as essential—and Michael had none—he endured many humiliations on the playing field. Very soon he was left isolated and friendless. At times he became so despondent he simply got on his bike and rode home. Dottie, preoccupied with her new life as a suburban housewife, assumed his truancy was because her bright son was bored. She seemed unaware that her elder son had lost his social bearings.

It was then that the guitar and the radio came to the rescue.

But playing and listening to music weren't only a way to fill the lonely hours for Michael Bloomfield. They soon provided him with an identity, a persona apart from that of his peers. "It knocked me out—not just the music but the social-aesthetic thing at that time. I saw myself, in my mind, as this lanky hillbilly, and the radio was a reinforcement of that whole lifestyle," the guitarist later recalled.

Brother Allen agreed. "He wanted to be this tall, slender guy with a gorgeous mane of hair and a surly look, playing music that every girl would adore. It just captivated him."

It was Michael's discovery of the blues that solidified his image of himself as a social rebel. A visceral, aggressive music made by people outside the norms of white society, the blues became Michael's secret strength, conferring a status that set him apart from the other kids his age. It was his entry into an adult world of forbidden pleasures and passions, a world largely unknown to the grown-up residents of suburban Glencoe. And while his obsession with an art form so culturally alien might have raised more than a few eyebrows, it was Michael's determination to experience that art form firsthand—as a *participant*—that was so radical. Despite the North Shore's liberal attitudes toward race and class, integration was seen as an issue largely of concern for the American South. Whites and blacks did *not* mix in the affluent suburbs of Chicago. That Michael Bloomfield might have an African American teenager in his high school rock 'n' roll band was unprecedented enough. That he would soon think nothing of venturing into the city's black ghetto to play blues in gritty neighborhood bars with adult musicians into the early morning hours was all but unheard of. White boys from good families simply did not do that.

But Michael Bloomfield was not like other white boys. He wanted to be a blues musician.

CHAPTER 2

NORTH SHORE HOTSHOT

GLENCOE, 1958–1961

In the fall of 1958, Mike Bloomfield began his sophomore year at New Trier High School. Located several miles south of Glencoe in the equally affluent village of Winnetka, New Trier had an enrollment of nearly four thousand students drawn from four North Shore towns. One of the nation's highest-rated educational institutions, the school employed a unique "tracking system" that divided kids according to their abilities. For a motivated, engaged teenager, New Trier provided a rare and exceptional educational opportunity, a real chance to excel. But Michael Bloomfield had no interest in excelling—not, at least, in the subjects offered at school. Though he was enrolled in all top-tracked classes, he was at best an indifferent student. Music was his focus.

The garrulous young guitarist, eager to share his enthusiasm for music, talked up rock 'n' roll and the blues to anyone at school who would listen. Eventually, he found other students who were tuning into the same radio stations and were as excited about what they heard as he was. One was a teen from Wilmette named Roy Jespersen. Roy was learning to play drums, and Michael asked him to join a band he was forming.

With Jespersen on drums, Bloomfield got his friend Roy Ruby to play rhythm guitar and added Craig Sherman, another New Trier student, on acoustic bass. They rehearsed at Jespersen's home and eventually called themselves the Hurricanes, after a tune that Michael had written called "Hurricane." He and Jespersen also worked out a second instrumental called "Hot Rod," composing both tunes together on one of the pianos in New Trier's practice rooms.

The band was soon playing teen dances at local temples and churches around the North Shore. On the few occasions when they rehearsed at Michael's house on Greenleaf Avenue, they were joined by another New Trier student from Glencoe—a junior named Marshall Chess.

Chess was the son of Leonard Chess and nephew of Phil Chess, the brothers who owned Chess Records. The label had recorded Muddy Waters, Howlin' Wolf, Sonny Boy Williamson, and many of the other Chicago blues greats whom Michael Bloomfield idolized, and Marshall was well known at New Trier as the scion of a record industry family. Though the boys didn't particularly like him, they saw their schoolmate as a direct connection to the blues—and to the music business. With Marshall's help, they thought, the Hurricanes might get to make a record.

Young Chess did eventually get the quartet into the recording studio, but the session wasn't at his father's facilities at 2120 South Michigan Avenue. It was held at a small rental studio in downtown Chicago, and Marshall simply arranged for the band to make a demo there. The boys each put in ten dollars to cover the cost of cutting a single 45 rpm acetate disc, and they recorded "Hurricane" backed with "Hot Rod." They were thrilled with the result and passed the record around, each taking turns listening to it. The disc was even heard at school because the cafeteria programed music during lunch period and Michael was able to get "Hurricane" played repeatedly. The band was soon known all over New Trier, and Bloomfield, not one to miss an opportunity to make a good story even better, told everyone they had signed a recording contract with Chicago's Mercury Records.

It was that demo recording that further complicated Michael Bloomfield's already difficult relationship with the authorities at school. In the week before New Trier's Christmas holiday break, the sophomore class was scheduled to hold a gala. It was to be a Saturday evening affair, winding up with a dance to music provided by a twelve-piece orchestra. The festivities would start off with a sophomores-only talent showcase.

Mike and the band decided they would try out for the talent show. They had to pass an audition first and were cautioned against playing "rock 'n' roll." The Hurricanes decided they could play a Chet Atkins tune that Michael knew, and they were informed that there were to be no encores.

On December 13, the day of the party, students arrived to find the school's auditorium transformed for a fantasy-themed extravaganza titled Shangri-La. There was a festive holiday mood in the air, and everybody was excited about the upcoming winter break. The students were ready to enjoy themselves.

Michael and the band unloaded their equipment and set up backstage. He had brought his Gibson electric guitar and amp, and Roy Jespersen had his trap set, Craig Sherman his big upright bass, and Roy Ruby his acoustic guitar. They were scheduled to close the show, and when their moment onstage came, all went smoothly. But at the conclusion of their Chet Atkins number, the students in the auditorium began screaming and stomping their feet, shouting, "More! *More*!"

The Hurricanes had been told they couldn't play an encore, and the curtain had already descended. But their classmates out front were still noisily shouting. The boys looked at one another, not knowing what to do—and then fate stepped in. Someone backstage raised the curtain while they were still standing there, and after a moment's hesitation, Jespersen shouted, "Let's play 'Hurricane'!"

The kids in the audience immediately recognized the tune they had been hearing for weeks in the lunchroom, and they responded vociferously with unbounded excitement. The entire cast of the talent show rushed out from the wings and began clapping and dancing to the beat. The kids in the seats stood, cheering the quartet on. It was a real struggle for the adult chaperones to clear the stage and restore order in the auditorium. Mike, flushed with the band's triumph, was thrilled by his brief moment as a guitar star.

But the authorities were furious.

Monday morning, the boys were called down to the sophomore dean's office for an official reprimand. Michael bore the brunt of the dean's ire because he had been the loudest member of the quartet and the one who had largely triggered the hysteria with his rock 'n' roll "licks" and wild contortions. The episode put him on the dean's short list as someone who needed watching. But Mike didn't care. All he knew was that he had been a hit onstage and that he could really excite people with the way he played.

That fall, Mike's friend Roy Ruby introduced him to a new sensation. Roy had learned how to use paregoric, an opium derivative intended to relieve the symptoms of diarrhea, for recreational purposes. His family's gardener had explained the process to him, and Roy soon had Michael and their classmate Fred Glazer experimenting with the drug. The boys would pedal to the local Walgreens drugstore, where the tincture could be purchased without a prescription, and buy several bottles. They would then soak cigarettes in the solution, dry them out, and light up. A few puffs would produce a mild high, a pleasurable and exciting euphoria. Before long, they also discovered terpin hydrate, an expectorant meant to suppress coughs that was frequently combined with codeine for pain relief. The friends found that by drinking bottles of the medication, they could experience an even greater high.

The use of intoxicants was nothing new among the teenagers of Glencoe. Alcohol was readily available in nearly every home in the village despite the fact that the town, like most others on the North Shore, was "dry," meaning liquor sales were prohibited. Kids and booze had a long-standing relationship, one that was often winked at by parents.

But Mike Bloomfield and his friends were different. Using narcotics—however innocently—was all but unheard of in Glencoe and most of the surrounding white communities in the 1950s. Hard drugs were the stuff of newspaper police blotters, of criminals and addicts. That the boys were experimenting with opiates would have alarmed their parents. And though the drugs were still legal at the time, they were highly addictive and potent narcotics—not something North Shore kids normally fooled with.

It was, of course, just those dangerous qualities that appealed to Michael. Along with the high, the drug conferred a tacit "outlaw" status. The boys felt themselves part of a hip, adult world completely foreign to that of their parents. And for Mike Bloomfield it gave some substance to the fantasy image he had of himself as a svelte, luxuriously coiffed rock 'n' roll rebel.

By the spring of 1959, the Bloomfields' first son had his driver's license. Suddenly all of the North Shore and Chicago, the city's South and West Sides, were accessible as they had never been before. If Michael could manage to borrow Dottie's new Chevrolet Corvair, he could easily get nearly anywhere he wanted to go. Even though he had already visited South Side blues clubs like Pepper's and Theresa's, a basement club on the corner of Forty-Seventh Street and Indiana Avenue, Michael could now drive himself to many others. Soon he was visiting places like McKie's Disc Jockey Show Lounge, Florence's, and Silvio's Lounge—Howlin' Wolf's regular haunt—on the West Side.

It was in a tavern at Sixty-Third and Saint Lawrence Avenue, a funky blues bar called the Place, that the young guitarist from Glencoe first dared to sit in. With Michael that night was Roy Ruby, and the boys sipped sodas while the club's band warmed up. Onstage were Guitar Junior and his group. Junior—whose given name was Luther Johnson—was fronting a rhythm section that included a female saxophone player, a big woman dressed all in red. During the set, she teased the two white boys down front, eliciting laughter and smirks from the other patrons. Michael and Roy were embarrassed, but the teasing served to break the ice, tacitly involving the Place's two white patrons in the evening's entertainment. Bloomfield had been afraid to ask if he could get up and play, but now he was emboldened. He got his guitar out and got up on the stand.

"[Mike] sat in, and they liked it," Roy recalled later. "We didn't know if they'd like it—he was scared too." But Michael pulled it off, jamming onstage in a South Side club with black blues musicians. He had held his own, and he would be back for more.

There were many budding young musicians around the North Shore in 1959 and, now that he could drive, it was inevitable that Mike Bloomfield would meet them. At a party one evening, he was surprised to see a kid his age playing an unusual five-string upright bass. Mike introduced himself and learned that the bassist's name was Horace Cathcart. Horace went by the nickname "Ace" and was from Lake Forest, a village north of Glencoe. He earned spending money playing gigs on the weekend, and the boys began playing together whenever they could, eventually putting together a quartet with guitar, bass, drums, and organ. They played folk and blues at private parties around Highland Park, Glencoe, and other North Shore towns. Because Ace Cathcart was African American, the fact that he was playing with a white guitarist was something of a shock. An integrated band—especially one composed of teenagers playing for other teens—was all but unknown in white suburbia.

Bloomfield also began playing regularly with another student from New Trier. His name was Gerald Pasternack. Gerry was two years younger than Michael, and he had an unusual arrangement with New Trier High School. The school permitted the freshman to come in late each morning because he worked in the evenings. He had a job playing drums for a professional band that performed on Rush Street in Chicago's nightclub district. Gerry's parents had gotten New Trier to officially let him sleep in. Because Roy Jespersen's family had moved away during the summer of 1959, fourteen-year-old Gerry soon became the drummer for Bloomfield's group. But he and Michael didn't play only high school dances.

"I'd get Mike to come down to Rush Street and jam," said Pasternack. "We played mostly R&B with my band, and then we would go up and down the street and sit in wherever we could."

Sitting in with Gerry's band, Michael got a chance to try out his growing arsenal of hot rock 'n' roll licks. He imitated Chuck Berry and Scotty Moore from Elvis Presley's band, maybe throwing in a few Duane Eddy riffs. On the nights when they visited other clubs, Mike got a chance to play a variety of musical styles. After a late night of jamming, the boys would head back to the Pasternack home in the early morning hours and Michael would find a place to sleep. In the morning, he would head to school with Gerry, leaving his parents to wonder what had become of their elder son.

As the 1950s drew to a close, life in the Bloomfield household had become increasingly stressful. By 1959 the rivalry between Michael and his brother, Allen, a growing problem since the family's departure from Melrose Street, had blossomed into full-scale war. It was exacerbated by the boys' emotional and physical differences. Allen was "small, wiry and introverted," while Michael described himself as "bigger, heavy and endlessly verbose."

A major part of the boys' troubles stemmed from their difficult relationship with their father. Of the two brothers, Allen alone seemed capable of meeting

Harold Bloomfield's expectations, thus winning his father's approval. He was better in school, better on the playing field, more responsible, and much more respectful than his older sibling. Michael often vented his anger over Harold's rejection by goading Allen into fights—something he seemed to relish doing. The younger Bloomfield was the stronger of the two, but because Mike was bigger and bulkier, the boys were about evenly matched. Their battles quickly became physical and ranged throughout the house, often ending with Mike locking himself in the bathroom and Allen snipping the strings on his brother's guitar.

There were other problems too; the tension in the Bloomfield home wasn't only the result of teenage enmity. After a decade and a half of marriage, Harold and Dorothy Bloomfield had grown apart. Their very different personalities and interests had, over the years, created a division. Harold was a taciturn man with a very traditional understanding of marriage; in his view, a wife stayed home, cared for the children, and ran the household. Though the couple tried to play their respective roles, neither spouse found real satisfaction in them or, eventually, in each other. Dottie's friends were theater people, actors, writers, and artists; Harold, the consummate businessman, socialized primarily with his brother and others in the industry. The couple had begun leading separate lives. Mrs. Bloomfield was often in Chicago during the day, visiting with friends, while Mr. Bloomfield was spending more and more time at the office, frequently late into the evening. These divisions were not only physical; they soon became emotional as well.

It was his troubled relationship with his father that underscored many of Mike Bloomfield's difficulties. But the family's emotional and physical turmoil also served to push him further into music. It had become his comfort and solace, a place where he could find acceptance and security—and where he could prove himself better than anybody else. Music offered Michael Bloomfield an unassailable identity—a defense against the harsh judgment of his father, the man he both loved and feared.

School was another sore topic. Throughout his sophomore year at New Trier, Mike Bloomfield continued to flounder academically. His attendance was spotty, and when he made it to class he was often disruptive. His reputation as a hyperactive, fresh-mouthed kid was, by 1959, well earned. His quips frequently earned him stints in detention.

"The teacher would ask, 'What's *Moby Dick*?' and Michael would say, 'It's a disease,' and—*pow!*—he would be booted," said Allen, describing one instance where his brother's mouth got him in trouble.

"There was this story that went around about Michael that will tell you what he was like," said Michael's friend Fred Glazer.

> There was an old teacher named Johnston—he was called "Smoky" Johnston because his job was to prowl around and see if anybody was smoking cigarettes on the school grounds. One day he was in the bathroom looking for smokers, and Mike came in to pee. Well, Bloomfield pisses and turns around and starts to walk out, and Smoky looks at him and says, "Young man, where I come from we wash our hands after we go to the bathroom." And Michael looks back at him and says, "Well, where I come from, sir, we don't pee on our hands." *That* was Michael.

Bloomfield could also be brutally honest. He often said whatever was on his mind, regardless of the repercussions. That trait would play a large role in shaping his destiny, as it did one November day at New Trier, not long after the start of his junior year.

Late that afternoon, Mike was sitting in study hall. Other students in the classroom had their books open on their desks, reading quietly. Some were studiously writing, working on the day's assignment. At the front of the room, behind a big slate-colored desk, a teacher sat silently grading papers from one of his morning classes. Aside from an occasional cough or rustling of papers, the room was silent. The large round clock on the wall audibly ticked off the minutes with martial regularity.

Michael had been staring at his empty desktop, not moving. Time passed. Then he slowly looked up. More time passed. He slowly stood up.

"*Eat* . . . SHIT!" he hollered as loud as he could toward the front of the room.

The teacher dropped his pen as though it had stung him. His mouth opened as if to speak, but no words came. He turned bright red.

The kids in the study hall stared at Michael in horror, and then looked at one another and at the mute authority figure at the front of the room. One girl covered her ears and shut her eyes. A boy in the back let out a low whistle. Then all was silent again. The clock ticked.

Bloomfield shook his head. Without even a glance at the teacher, he walked to the front of the room, opened the door, and stepped into the hallway. In a second he was gone. His battered books were still on the floor by his seat.

He just couldn't stand being there any longer.

And New Trier could no longer deal with Michael Bloomfield. The administration quietly let Mrs. Bloomfield know that they thought it better for all involved if her troublesome son did not return to the school for the 1960 spring semester.

When he learned that Michael had essentially been expelled from one of the finest high schools in the country, Harold Bloomfield decided that it was time to take matters in hand. The boy needed to learn discipline, self-control, and respect for authority. He needed to get serious about something other than music. If Michael was unwilling to do these things for himself, there were places that would do them for him. Harold told Dorothy he wanted to put Michael in a private school—preferably a military-style boarding school. Some place far away from the South Side of Chicago and from rock 'n' roll.

Mr. Bloomfield soon found a suitable prep school in the Berkshire Mountains of western Massachusetts. Located in the rural village of Great Barrington, Cornwall Academy was a small traditional high school with only one hundred students. It sought to improve academic performance with six days of classes each week and supervised study periods in the evening. Kids who enrolled in Cornwall were kids who were having trouble focusing in school at home. The academy seemed to offer a perfect cure for what ailed Michael.

By the end of November, Mike Bloomfield found himself in the snow-covered mountains of the Bay State, sharing a room with another student and sleeping in a military barracks-style bunk bed. He was compelled to attend classes with a regularity he hadn't experienced since grade school and was spending nearly every evening with his books. In his free time, he was essentially grounded with no way to get off campus or into town.

He was miserable.

There were, however, a few things about Cornwall that made boarding school life at least bearable. Michael's best friend, Roy Ruby, was only ten miles away, having been enrolled by his parents that fall in the progressive Windsor Mountain School in Lenox. If he could manage to catch a ride up Route 7, Mike could spend his Sundays hanging out with Roy and playing music.

There was another advantage of being at Cornwall: marijuana was readily available. Unlike most kids at New Trier, many of the boys in Great Barrington knew all about drugs. They came mostly from progressive, permissive families in New York and Boston, and they were far more worldly than their Midwestern counterparts. Michael had heard about marijuana, but he had never smoked any. Always eager for new sensations, he didn't refuse when the opportunity came his way, and it wasn't long before he, too, was rolling joints and lighting up with his classmates. The boys at Cornwall wouldn't have stooped to drinking cough syrup to get high; they were emulating their heroes in the beat community. Grass was hip, and smoking it was an act of rebellion, a rejection of conventional societal norms. It was a way to identify with the liberal, free-thinking artists and musicians of the day.

Smoking marijuana was, of course, also a way to get high. Michael liked the way the drug enhanced his perceptions while quieting his overactive mind, and he liked the notoriety associated with "reefers" and "pot smokers." Politics aside, now he really was the rebel he imagined himself to be—a prep-school Elvis.

The preppies at Cornwall were sophisticated in other ways too. They were well read and knew about progressive authors and their antiestablishment ideas. They introduced Michael to books like J. D. Salinger's *The Catcher in the Rye* and Jack Kerouac's *On the Road*. Because many of Cornwall's students had been raised in an East Coast intellectual environment, they understood the politics of the left. They accepted as gospel the notion that all forms of cultural expression had artistic merit. Folk musicians in particular were to be venerated as great artists and their music given status of the highest order. This was especially true of black artists. It surprised Michael to learn that many of the blues players he had been listening to—and a few he had met—were of great interest not only to his classmates but to learned scholars.

For Michael, black music was not something he had only read about in books or heard on records. He had grown up with African Americans in his home, had befriended and played with black musicians, and knew many black performers personally. Though there were a number of black students at Cornwall, the other white boys had little firsthand experience with African American culture, and they were impressed that the new kid from Chicago was friends with artists like Josh White. Suddenly Mike was regarded as an authority on black music. He regaled the boys with tales of his adventures on the South Side, of meeting Muddy Waters and jamming in black clubs. Then he picked up his guitar and demonstrated. His classmates were further impressed by his ability to play.

Michael was clearly a gifted player. He could frequently be heard late into the evening working on licks or playing along with records in his dorm room. On free afternoons when Roy visited, he organized impromptu jam sessions with whoever was around and could play. Eventually, he put together a little combo with bass and drums that performed for the students.

Yet despite all of this, he was still miserable.

He missed home and his friends, and he missed playing music in his many groups and on the South Side in the blues clubs. He missed being able go wherever he wanted whenever he wanted. He missed buying records and listening to the radio. He even missed his brother.

* * *

Over Christmas break, Mike Bloomfield was back in Glencoe. He immediately let his parents know how much he disliked Cornwall Academy. Even though he knew Harold would be furious, he told them he wasn't going back.

But Mr. Bloomfield was resolute. He insisted that Michael finish the spring term, and then they would see. Michael agreed, but on one condition—that his parents get him a new guitar. It was a bribe of sorts, disguised as a five-hundred-dollar Christmas gift.

A few days later, Bloomfield visited Chicago Musical Instruments in the northwestern suburb of Lincolnwood. The store featured a full range of instruments, from pianos and organs to marching band equipment. It also sold a wide variety of guitars, offering models for students up to professionals. It specialized in Gibsons.

This time, Mike picked out an instrument similar to the one his former teacher had. It was an updated version of Tony Tenaglia's "Fretless Wonder," a jet-black solid body marketed as the Les Paul Custom. One of Gibson's top-of-the-line models, the Custom had three pickups and came with a gadget called a "Bigsby," which allowed the guitarist to create a vibrato effect simply by moving a lever. The guitar was heavy—much heavier than his ES-175—but it had a much punchier sound when fully cranked. And by switching its pickups, Mike found he could make the Custom's tone match nearly any guitar tone he heard on his records. He would be going back to Great Barrington, but his new ebony Gibson made the sacrifice worth it.

During Christmas week, Mike heard an intriguing concert promoted over several of his blues radio stations. The Regal Theater, a South Side venue that frequently showcased the urban blues of B. B. King, Bobby "Blue" Bland, and T-Bone Walker, was hosting a week-long Gala Holiday Show, an all-star jazz program featuring the Miles Davis sextet, Art Blakey's Jazz Messengers, and altoist Sonny Stitt's quartet. Michael was curious about jazz and decided that he and his friends should go. Roy Ruby was also home for the break, and he loved the idea. He suggested they go see the show and then spend the night at his housekeeper's place in Bronzeville.

In Miles's band at the time was tenor saxophonist John Coltrane. By 1959 Coltrane had begun experimenting with extended techniques and modal scales, and his music would directly influence Bloomfield's own musical thinking over the next decade.

In January 1960, Mike Bloomfield returned to Cornwall Academy. He brought along his new Les Paul Custom, but though he loved the way it looked and enjoyed playing it, the guitar did little to ease the day-to-day tedium of the school's classes-and-homework regimen. The newly discovered pleasure of smoking dope offered some relief, and Mike rarely missed an opportunity to partake whenever pot was available. But his life at Cornwall felt like an endless grind.

At the end of the spring term, Bloomfield flew home for the summer break. During the ride from the airport, Michael cautiously pleaded with Harold not to send him back to Cornwall in the fall. He tried to cajole his father into allowing him to return to New Trier by promising to work hard, attend all his classes, and behave himself. Mr. Bloomfield listened to the boy's complaints and pledge to do better without saying much. Unlike his son, Harold was a man of few words. By the time they reached Glencoe, he hadn't agreed to Mike's plan. But he hadn't said no to it either.

Now that he was home again, Bloomfield immediately got in touch with his friends, and he found one of them had been busy in his absence. Bob Greenspan first met Michael in Glencoe when they both were students of Tony Tenaglia, and he, too, had been captivated by the new music. A big fan of rockabilly, Bob occasionally worked in a band at a club in nearby Highwood, the town just north of Glencoe. Because it was adjacent to the US Army's Fort Sheridan on Lake Michigan, Highwood was home to many servicemen and a playground for many more. The town had numerous bars and taverns, and it had the distinction of being one of the few municipalities on the North Shore where it was legal to purchase alcohol. Many of Highwood's bars featured live music and dancing on weekends, and some had resident bands that performed all week long.

One of these groups was led by Hayden Thompson, a rockabilly singer who had recorded for Sun Records in 1956. By 1958 Thompson had moved north and was regularly working at the Tally Ho Club on Highwood's strip, playing a mix of rock 'n' roll, R&B, and country. Bob sometimes played rhythm guitar with Hayden's band.

Greenspan invited Michael to come see Thompson perform, knowing that Bloomfield would be impressed. But though Michael enjoyed the show, he was far more impressed by Highwood. The town's nightlife and preponderance of clubs immediately caught his attention. The strip would be the perfect place for a band of their own to play. The boys only had to find a club that would hire them.

Their connection came through a local musician named Vincent Viti. A twenty-six-year-old boogie-woogie pianist, Viti lived in Highwood and frequently worked on the strip as a solo performer. But he agreed to let Michael, Bob, Gerry Pasternack, and their high school friends back him up, calling the band Vince Viti and Them. They were soon appearing regularly at a bar in Highwood known as PG's Club 7. A veteran showman, Vince covered the front of his all-white Baldwin piano with a mirror and added little mirrors to the upright's ivories. He also had a custom cover made for Pasternack's bass drum with the band's name in fancy logo-styled lettering. Mike Bloomfield loved it, and Vince was equally happy about Bloomfield's participation.

"Mike could really play," Vince recalled. "He'd make you look good—man, could he *play*!"

Vince Viti and Them would perform several sets at Club 7 beginning at about 9:00 p.m., and whatever was collected at the door as admission was the band's to share. They played a mix of rock 'n' roll, boogie-woogie, and blues, and once the music started, Club 7 would quickly fill up. Soldiers on leave from Fort Sheridan, young women looking for dance partners, underage teens with fake IDs, boozy regulars tucking into the bar, townie boys eager to find a date or pick a fight—they all were part of the weekend scene at PG's. When things got really wild, the band had to take precautions. There was often so much spilled beer on the floor, they had to perform standing on chairs to keep from getting shocked.

Over the summer, Michael gained valuable experience playing multiple sets with Viti, and before long the band began to develop a sound. The boys rehearsed regularly at the Pasternack's home, and the guitarist, who had taught himself to play blues on piano, frequently filled in for Vince at the keyboard.

"We had a piano in the living room. Mike wasn't allowed to play the piano at home even though his parents had a big grand piano, so he would play ours," said Gerry. "We brought my drums upstairs so I could accompany him."

They played the hits of the day, but they also performed a few songs of their own. One of the band's originals seemed to be a real crowd-pleaser. The tune—an instrumental—was so good that Gerry Pasternack's dad thought they should record it. He arranged for Vince Viti and Them to do a session at Lyon & Healy, the big music store at Wabash Avenue and State Street in Chicago's Loop.

The resulting demo was successful enough that Mr. Pasternack hoped they might be able to release the tune commercially. He gave a copy of the recording to the studio's engineer for safekeeping and then set up a meeting for the band with a local producer he knew. But before any deal could be made, a band called the Ventures released "Walk, Don't Run," a tune so similar it effectively killed any chances for a release. The boys felt they had been betrayed by the studio's engineer—that he had given their recording to the other group. They were so upset over their missed opportunity that the group soon broke up over it.

Of course, the Ventures, a Seattle-based band that had formed in 1958, never heard the demo by Vince Viti and Them. "Walk, Don't Run" was based on Chet Atkins's version of a Johnny Smith composition by the same name. When it came out in the fall of 1960, it went to number two on the *Billboard* charts and propelled the Ventures to national fame. But Mike Bloomfield and the boys felt their chance for a hit had been stolen from them. Vince Viti and Them never recovered from the disappointment.

In September 1960, Mike Bloomfield went back to New Trier High School. His parents, largely on his mother's insistence, had agreed to re-enroll him. It hadn't been easy to convince the school's administration to give him a second chance, but Michael was now officially a senior at the Winnetka campus. It was tacitly understood that he was there on probation, and he was delighted to be back among his friends. But music was still foremost in his mind.

Highwood had been a fun place to spend the summer, but seventeen-year-old Mike Bloomfield's musical interests lay in the opposite direction. In the fall, he began driving down to the South Side to sit in wherever he could, and on Sunday mornings he would head to Roosevelt Road and South Halsted Street, just west of the Loop, to catch the action at the city's huge, open-air flea market. Known earlier in Chicago's history as "Jew Town" for its preponderance of Jewish retailers, the area encompassed sixteen square blocks filled with wholesale outlets, discount storefronts, street vendors, pushcart operators, and hustlers of every stripe. Since the great African American migration north between the wars, black sellers had become a significant part of the market, and by the early 1960s the area was known generally as "Maxwell Street" for the thoroughfare that bisected it. Because the market's weekend crowds could be enormous, musicians would often set up and perform for passersby, picking up whatever spare change they could. Young musicians just starting out as well as seasoned blues veterans could be seen performing on the market's street corners and vacant lots on any given Sunday.

Michael frequently brought his guitar along on his trips to Maxwell Street so he could jam with whoever happened to be performing. But just as often, he went simply to take in the scene. The market was a remarkably colorful cultural event, filled with sights, sounds, smells, and tastes of every imaginable variety. There were the old-time Jewish retailers, their merchandise hung on ancient sidewalk racks outside dingy shops. There were vendors from the big chain stores out in the suburbs who came to sell off their overstock. There were rural down-staters with beat-up step vans filled with scrap copper and aluminum. There were fast-talking hucksters who kept watch over their shoulders while producing small jewelry cases from under their coats. There were Mexican farmworkers selling skids of fresh eggs in neatly stacked rows of cartons. There was the old black man who each week lined a cyclone fence with hundreds of hubcaps, no two alike. And a novelty pitchman hawking marked poker decks from a tray suspended on a strap around his neck. Lots of people with haunted eyes too, selling off what little they had just to make the rent.

In the midst of it all, there was music. Whether it was the street singer Arvella Gray, who played guitar with a bottleneck on his mangled, three-fingered left hand, or the gospel harmonies of Blind Jim Brewer and his wife, Fanny, or the big city blowing of harmonica master Walter "Shakey" Horton, the blues was everywhere on Maxwell Street. Nearly every corner had its resident musician.

Mike Bloomfield loved it.

But he wasn't catching blues only on street corners. He regularly visited South Side clubs where he was welcome to sit in and jam. Chief among them was Pepper's, the club on Forty-Third Street that featured Muddy Waters. It was the first blues bar that Mike had visited in Bronzeville, and by age seventeen he had been there often enough to have no trouble getting in. He would bring friends along and frequently join Muddy onstage for a number or two, much to the delight of the small club's patrons.

Muddy quickly grew fond of Michael, and before long the young guitarist from Glencoe wasn't just jamming with Waters at Pepper's—he and his friends were visiting Muddy at his home on South Lake Park Avenue and East Forty-Third Street. They would spend the day there, have dinner, and then head downstairs to jam with Otis Spann. Muddy's longtime sideman lived in the house's basement.

Bloomfield grew close to the affable, easygoing Otis Spann, and the pianist often had Michael accompany him on solo gigs. But it was Muddy Waters who became like a second father to the young guitarist. When the great bluesman had business to attend to, Michael would come by and babysit Cookie, one of Muddy's granddaughters. And when Michael decided one afternoon that he needed to find a blues talisman—a John-the-Conqueror root—it was Muddy who took him all over the South Side looking for one.

"Muddy Waters, he was like a god to me," said Michael. With the great Chicago bluesman as his deity, the blues was increasingly becoming Mike Bloomfield's chosen religion.

As the fall progressed, Michael made an effort to keep up with his schoolwork. But his heart was decidedly not in it. His South Side escapades, playing music in Highwood over the summer, and making a recording that could have been a hit had convinced him that he really should become a full-time musician. Very soon it began to feel like his hours at New Trier were standing in the way of that goal. Before long, Mike was again skipping classes and eventually whole school days. His sojourns on the South Side and his bunking in with friends meant that there frequently were nights when his parents had no idea where he was. Housekeeper Mary Williams made excuses for him, and Dottie even tried to cover for his absences, but Harold Bloomfield could see that his son was not living up to his promises. It was clear that Michael hadn't changed—he still cared only about music. And it was that focus that probably caused the revocation of the young guitarist's probation at New Trier for the final time.

After what may have been an all-night jam session on the South Side, Mike and Fred Glazer staggered into high school in less than fit condition. A teacher patrolling the hallways spotted the boys and confronted them. In the exchange, Michael got angry. As was his habit, he didn't mince words, and the altercation resulted in a trip to the office. The authorities quickly surmised that the boys had been drinking, and Fred was immediately suspended. But New Trier booted Michael for violating the terms of his readmittance. He was finished as a student at the school, and he would not be awarded his diploma.

Harold Bloomfield was enraged. He tore into his son verbally and physically. How could Michael let him down once again? Every effort Mr. Bloomfield had made to thwart what he saw as his son's self-destructive behavior had ended in failure. Michael continued to do as he pleased, to shirk his studies, to disrespect his elders, to pursue music—if you could call that *noise* music—with an almost pathological fervor. Indeed, his son's obsession with rock 'n' roll seemed like an illness to Harold Bloomfield—an illness that was placing Michael's future in jeopardy and affecting the well-being of the entire family.

There was also the fact that his son's repeated failures were highly embarrassing. Daniel had no such trouble with his own boy, and in their complex relationship, Harold was loath to appear less accomplished than his elder brother. The humiliation brought on by Michael's second expulsion was more than he could tolerate. He was determined this time to remedy the situation.

If Michael's passion for music *appeared* to be an illness, might it not actually be a medical condition? Harold Bloomfield decided to find out. And in so doing, he would impress upon Michael the consequences of his wild misdeeds. It would serve as a punishment as well as a possible cure.

The father decided to have his son committed.

In the late fall of 1960, Harold Bloomfield signed his elder son into the lockdown ward of Northwestern University Hospital on the university's medical campus in downtown Chicago. He had explained to the staff that his son was experiencing behavioral issues and that he wanted the boy evaluated. At the time, psychiatric institutions routinely took in teens who were delinquent, and the request by a prominent Chicago businessman was taken seriously. Northwestern admitted the rebellious seventeen-year-old.

Michael hated it there. He had been divested of his personal belongings, his street clothes, and even his shoes. He had been locked into a hospital ward with adults suffering from serious maladies ranging from schizophrenia to depression to substance abuse. The hospital required him to meet with a psychiatrist several times a week. He also had to attend regular group therapy sessions with other patients on the ward. The rest of the time he was confined to his room or the lounge and was under observation. His predicament soon became intolerable.

One afternoon, Michael noticed an emergency exit door that had been left open. When no one was looking, he quietly slipped through the doorway and into the stairwell. In a matter of minutes, he was down the eight flights of stairs and out the exit onto Chicago Avenue. Wearing only his pajamas and slippers, he hustled up the busy street and headed for his grandmother's apartment. Phyllis and Max Klein, Dottie's mother and father, lived a few blocks north of the hospital in the Seneca Hotel at 200 East Chestnut Street, and Michael sought refuge there, if only for the afternoon. He was soon back on the ward, and he remained there for another long week of observation.

His stint in Northwestern's psychiatric hospital was Mike Bloomfield's first serious encounter with issues of mental health, and he did not like it. No one had ever paid much attention to his emotional state, and now people were treating him like he was crazy. That he had behavioral problems and had been fooling around with drugs were indeed concerns. But lots of kids in the late 1950s were rebels with similar antisocial tendencies. Michael was one of many in his generation—at worst, another "juvenile delinquent." Having him locked up in a medical facility seemed like an extreme response to what could reasonably be considered adolescent acting out.

But there was a darker side to Harold Bloomfield's decision to have his son evaluated by mental health professionals. He was indeed angry about Michael's obsession with music, expulsion from school, and rebellious behavior, but he was also concerned about a more serious issue: the Bloomfield family had a history of emotional instability. It wasn't discussed, but Harold was well aware of it. He and Daniel had experienced strong mood swings throughout their lives. Their father, Sam, was outwardly a businessman of uncommon ability and drive who had achieved great success in his life. But the elder Bloomfield was also prone to severe bouts of depression. On several occasions, his mood was dire enough to require hospitalization. It was even said within the family that though the official cause of death was listed as a heart attack, Sam Bloomfield had actually taken his own life in 1954.

Harold Bloomfield was worried that his elder son might be suffering from the same disorder of mood regulation. That could explain Michael's impulsiveness and inability to focus on his studies, and it might also explain his all-consuming preoccupation with music. Rock 'n' roll provided a distraction, a way of avoiding whatever was troubling him emotionally.

"I think our dad and his father had what today is called bipolar disorder," said Allen Bloomfield.

> It's a congenital illness, and Michael had it too. It's like a burning fire in your brain, and back then they didn't really understand it. Michael never had the benefit of the drugs they have today to control bipolar disorder. He medicated himself with all sorts of substances, though he never touched speed or coke—he didn't want to stir up the fire.

The fire for Mike Bloomfield was kept well stoked without artificial stimulation. By nature his was a hyperactive personality, and his mind moved rapidly from one thing that interested him to another. His high energy may have been a sign of bipolar disorder, though elevated activity alone would be evidence of only one of the milder forms of the illness. Those less severe conditions weren't well understood in the 1950s. Experiencing emotional highs alternating with immobilizing lows was described at the time as "manic depression," and that state often required hospitalization. Because Bloomfield had never been hospitalized before, it's likely that he had a milder form of bipolar disorder—if, indeed, he had the illness at all. Members of his immediate family—his father and grandfather—suffered from various forms of depression, and that increased the chances that Michael also experienced those symptoms. But because he had poor school performance, a need to be active, and a racing mind much of the time, it was more likely he had what today would be described as attention deficit disorder.

Whatever the case, it was clear that Harold Bloomfield was concerned about his son's mental state. He doubtless hoped a clinical diagnosis would provide a way to change Michael's harmful behavior. But when his son was officially released from Northwestern's psychiatric unit, Harold couldn't bring himself to show that concern.

"I remember my brother came out of the hospital and he wanted to hug my father . . . and my father barely hugged him," recalled Allen Bloomfield. "He was a cold guy."

Mike Bloomfield left Northwestern University's psychiatric hospital with no plan for the future. He no longer had a school, he was not going to get a diploma, he had lost whatever remaining respect his father had for him, and he had come through a medical evaluation with no apparent diagnosis or treatment plan. All he had was his music. And that might have been enough for him.

But his parents thought otherwise.

In the heart of the Loop was a special school, a private institution that had opened in the years following the Civil War to serve Chicago's students who had special needs or whose circumstances prevented them from attending the city's high schools. Located at Lasalle and Madison streets, the school was funded and operated by the Young Men's Christian Association and was known as Central YMCA High School. It offered night classes for working students and special day courses for those seeking a better-quality education than could be found in their neighborhood schools. Central Y, as it was known, was structured more like a college than a conventional high school, with students attending only those classes they needed to graduate. Because Central Y offered an alternative way to receive a quality education, a significant portion of its students came from the poorer African American neighborhoods on the South and West Sides of the city.

Central Y also had a reputation as being the "end of the line" school for misfit white students from the North Side and surrounding suburbs who were in academic trouble of one sort or another. It was the school, everyone knew, where all the "bad" kids went.

Mike Bloomfield began going to Central YMCA High School in the winter of 1960–1961. Things were too tense at home, so he bunked in with his grandparents. The Klein's apartment on Chestnut Street was just a short bus ride from Central Y, and it was also much more convenient for his trips to the South Side. Central Y was a far cry from New Trier, but at least Michael had to be in school only for his assigned classes. The rest of the day was his to do with as he pleased. And he wasn't alone on the downtown campus.

There was another student at Central Y whom Michael knew from gigging around the North Shore. He was a rock 'n' roll keyboard player who was also developing a taste for the blues. His name was Barry Goldberg.

Goldberg had grown up on Chicago's near North Side. His parents had an apartment on Lake Shore Drive, not far from where Bloomfield's grandmother Ida Bloomfield lived. Barry's mother was a talented amateur stride and boogie-woogie pianist, and she had tutored her young son. As he got older, Barry also became fascinated by the music he heard on the radio. He began trying to play like Jerry Lee Lewis and Little Richard, and he would stay up late so he could listen to the blues of Muddy Waters and Howlin' Wolf on WGES and WOPA. In high school he was part of a group called Denny Lee and the Ramblers, and it was at a "sweet sixteen" party they played that Barry first saw Michael, playing with his own band.

The two young musicians ran into each other again in a record shop located downtown in the Roosevelt College building on Roosevelt Road and State Street. The store was owned by a twenty-seven-year-old independent record producer and retailer from St. Louis named Bob Koester. Called the Jazz Record Mart, it stocked a complete line of jazz recordings, as its name implied, but it also carried nearly every available blues record. Koester even sold used and rare recordings, all at reasonable prices. The Jazz Record Mart was a blues enthusiast's paradise.

The store advertised its wares over the radio, and Mike Bloomfield heard those ads on *Jam with Sam* and other Chicago blues and jazz shows. He soon began making the Mart one of his regular musical stops. On one visit, he noticed Barry Goldberg going through the blues bins. The teenagers realized they had seen each other before and struck up a conversation. They quickly discovered they shared a deep enthusiasm for rock 'n' roll and the blues.

Both boys were trying to get their academic lives in order at Central Y. Whenever they saw each other in the halls, they got caught up in a discussion of the latest records and their favorite players. Michael talked of his adventures in the blues clubs on the South and West Sides. One day he told Barry he was going to take him to see Howlin' Wolf.

Goldberg had never been to Chicago's black neighborhoods, and he had never seen Wolf, one of his favorites, in person. The power of the music thrilled him when they arrived at Silvio's late one evening, and when Wolf dismissed his band and invited the boys up onstage play a number, Barry could hardly believe it. But Mike was unperturbed—he knew Howlin' Wolf's routine. Moments later the burly blues singer launched into "Spoonful" with Bloomfield on guitar and Goldberg seated at the piano. The boys navigated the changes successfully and were rewarded with warm applause as they left the stage. For Michael it was only one of many performances with the blues legend, but for Barry it was a life-changing experience.

By the late spring of 1961, Mike Bloomfield had accumulated enough credits to earn an equivalency diploma from Central YMCA High School. His parents and brother attended the graduation ceremony, and though Michael had finally succeeded academically, it was a painful moment for his father.

"They were going up the aisles giving each other high fives when they got their papers," said Allen Bloomfield of Central Y's awarding of diplomas. "My father—I never remember seeing anyone more stoic. It was as if he was watching someone being executed."

Whatever Harold may have thought of his elder son's graduation, Michael saw it as a turning point. For the seventeen-year-old guitarist, the ceremony at Central Y marked the conclusion of his life at home. He had fulfilled his obligation to his father and now was his own man, no longer a child in the

Bloomfield household, free to do whatever he wished. His life on Greenleaf Avenue in Glencoe was drawing to a close. Very soon after finishing up at Central Y, the young musician moved back to Chicago to be closer to the music he loved.

"Mike decided to live alone after he graduated," said Mrs. Bloomfield. "He moved out of the family house and went to live on the South Side."

Michael Bloomfield, having grown to young adulthood in the affluence and cultural conservatism of the North Shore, returned to his home city with his guitar and a few books and clothes stuffed into a suitcase. He was going to be a musician, a *blues* musician, and Chicago was the place for that. His future lay like an open road before him, and he was its inspired traveler.

CHAPTER 3

FOLK FANATIC

CHICAGO, 1961–1963

In the late 1950s, American musical tastes were undergoing a change, especially on college campuses. Interest in traditional forms of music and in acoustic music of varied styles and origins was undergoing a reawakening. As the McCarthy era with its toxic taint receded, a renewed enthusiasm for music of the people—for "folk" music—began to emerge. Then, in 1958 "Tom Dooley," a traditional ballad recorded by a trio of young folksingers from California called the Kingston Trio, became an unexpected hit. Its success helped inspire a renewed interest in traditional American music across the country. Kids who had grown up on Elvis, Jerry Lee Lewis, Fats Domino, and the doo-wop styles of the mid-1950s found they wanted to know more about the origins of rock 'n' roll and R&B. In digging deeper into these and other American popular music forms, they began to uncover a multitude of rich and colorful folk traditions. Suddenly, college students around the country were forming folk music clubs and learning to fingerpick and frail.

The appeal of folk music was obvious—it was music that anyone could play. It required only a simple acoustic instrument and a willingness to learn. There was also the appealing romanticism of the individual songster, the roustabout hoboing around the country with guitar in hand, singing for his supper and living life on the open road. For those whose interest was primarily academic, folk music offered a far more authentic—and thus more valid—alternative to whatever derivative fare the hit parade was serving up.

In Chicago this folk revitalization was centered around an institution that had opened on North Avenue in 1957. Called the Old Town School of Folk Music after its North Side neighborhood, it offered classes in various folk music styles, lectures and demonstrations, group sings, and folk performances by local and nationally known players. Its founders, singers Win Stracke and Frank Hamilton, were both accomplished and schooled musicians with deep roots in Chicago's folk community. They took an all-inclusive approach to instruction—anyone, they believed, could learn to sing and play folk music.

From its modest beginnings, the Old Town School of Folk Music had grown to serve hundreds of eager students by 1960.

On the South Side, the folk movement was situated in the integrated neighborhood of Hyde Park on the campus of the University of Chicago (UC). In the early 1950s, a group of students at the university had formed a club called the Folklore Society. The society's mission was to present folk art of all sorts from around the world, and by the end of the decade a sizeable portion of its members were music enthusiasts. In the fall of 1960, the society planned to host an ambitious, three-day concert of folk music and intended to make the festival an annual event. Inspired in part by the success of the first Newport Folk Festival in 1959, UC's fest would take a more academic approach to its presentation. With dozens of traditional performers drawn from all over the country and numerous instrumental and song workshops, the concert series would be one of the first of its kind in the country and would set a benchmark for many folk festivals to come. The University of Chicago Folk Festival was scheduled for the first weekend in February 1961.

Mike Bloomfield had heard about the university's festival, and he had stopped by the Old Town School of Folk Music on occasion. But until his seventeenth year, he had been mostly interested in making electric music. Blues and rock 'n' roll were his obsession—his lanky, coiffed hillbilly-greaser fantasy. His old acoustic Harmony guitar sat in a closet at home in Glencoe, long unplayed. But something about the burgeoning folk revival caught his attention.

"There was a time when I got older that I was starting to look at music on a more musicological basis," said Michael of his days after high school. "I was more than a player—I was an *analytical* player. I was wondering how the music got this way and where did it come from, things like that. I was really sort of a folklorist."

Because the University of Chicago was the hub of folk music activity on Chicago's South Side, Michael began hanging out there. When the Folklore Society presented its first folk festival on the weekend of February 3, he was in the audience. The roster featured a few blues performers; Mike already knew the music of Willie Dixon and Memphis Slim, and he had heard Arvella Gray many times at Maxwell Street. But during the festival's three days he also saw traditional singer Horton Barker, Appalachian banjo pickers Frank Proffitt and Roscoe Holcomb, bluegrass masters Ralph and Carter Stanley, and many other legendary folk artists. The wide variety of traditional American musical styles and techniques showcased during the event made a deep impression on Mike Bloomfield.

He wasn't the only one who was impressed. There was another young guitarist in the Mandel Hall audience on those evenings who was also caught up in the folk movement. He had come up to Chicago from Yellow Springs, Ohio, where he was a freshman at Antioch College. He introduced himself to Bloomfield as John Hammond.

"I'd heard about the festival, and I went up to Chicago in a friend's car," said Hammond. "I met Michael at the festival and we really hit it off—we were both so into the blues."

Nineteen-year-old Hammond came by his enthusiasm for the blues naturally. His father, also named John Hammond, was a legendary record producer, A&R man, and civil rights activist. The younger Hammond grew up hearing the music of Robert Johnson, Son House, and Charlie Patton, and he had been taken by his father to see Big Bill Broonzy when he was only seven. By 1961 he had decided he, too, wanted to play music. He had just started teaching himself guitar and was trying to re-create the classic blues styles he heard growing up.

Michael recognized the Hammond name right away. When John acknowledged his parentage, Bloomfield wanted to know all about his father and what it was like growing up in New York around so many famous musicians. The normally shy, self-effacing Hammond was awed by the loquacious enthusiasm of his newfound friend, and the two spent the evening comparing notes on blues artists and records while trading stories about players they knew. Mike invited him to his apartment and offered John his couch for the weekend. He also promised that the next time the New Yorker came to Chicago, he would take him around the South Side and introduce him to some of the blues greats. Hammond was thrilled by the prospect.

"He seemed to know *everybody* in the city," John later recalled. He promised Michael he would stay in touch and they would definitely make the rounds of the clubs when he next came to town.

There was plenty of folk music on the UC campus, with lots of young players learning to pick country, bluegrass, and blues tunes. Mike Bloomfield enjoyed being around them, and he was keen to learn whatever he could from the better players. But there was another reason he liked to visit Hyde Park. A university lab technician and collector of old instruments named Peter Leibundguth had opened up an acoustic guitar store called the Fret Shop at 1551 East Fifty-Seventh Street. Leibundguth did repairs, sold strings and accessories, and kept a small stock of new and vintage instruments. His relaxed attitude toward his merchandise meant that anyone with even a modest ability could take down an instrument and try it. As a result, patrons spent long hours in the store playing his guitars, trading licks and gossip, and generally hanging around. Mike soon became a regular, and his growing mastery of numerous styles caught the ears of many. One who was particularly impressed was a UC junior named Norman Dayron. He first met Bloomfield in the fall of 1960.

"One day I went to the shop to get an E-string, and there was this guy sitting on one of those metal folding chairs, and he was playing a guitar," recalled Dayron. "It just struck me immediately that he had a *sound*."

Dayron, who grew up in Mount Vernon, a suburb of New York City, had come to UC that summer as a transfer student from Case Western Reserve University in Cleveland. He had enrolled in the undergraduate college's liberal arts program and was a committed and gifted student majoring in psychology. Though he was primarily a jazz fan, he had developed an interest in folk music along with many of the country's college students. And like many of them, he was learning to play guitar.

After listening to Bloomfield play a few tunes, Norman struck up a conversation with the young guitarist. He learned that Michael had been kicked out of high school and was trying to get his diploma in the Loop, and that he had learned the country tunes he was playing simply by listening to records. Dayron was overwhelmed by the guitarist's skill—and his exuberant demeanor.

"I had heard great blues and jazz artists. But here was a guy my age sitting right in front of me that I'd never heard of, and I didn't expect him to have that sound, and he *had* it. Plus, he had a personality to match."

There was another Hyde Park resident who also discovered Mike Bloomfield at the Fret Shop, a colorful character quite unlike the studious Norman Dayron.

Nicholas Gravenites was a local kid. He had grown up around Thirty-Fifth Street and Archer Avenue in Brighton Park on Chicago's Lower West Side, born into a family of poor immigrant Greeks. Despite a hardscrabble childhood and lackluster performance in school, Gravenites had managed to get into the University of Chicago in 1956. He, too, had gone to Central YMCA High School—a few years before Michael—and had met a teacher there who recognized his ability as a writer. With his mentor's help, Nick was accepted into the university's experimental liberal arts program. He had attended UC for a while but found himself drawn more to the South Side's music and nightlife than to his studies. He was a competent guitar player and a gifted singer, and he was a regular patron of many of Bronzeville's bars and clubs. By 1961 he considered himself musically hip and street-smart.

"I was a pistol-packin' tough guy and I had a reputation," said Gravenites. "I was affecting a 'gangster-type persona.'" Like Michael, Nick had been exploring the South Side's blues venues since the late 1950s. But where Bloomfield used charm and his ability to play to win acceptance, Gravenites relied on an aggressive, threatening demeanor to gain access. Nick knew the music and, as one of the first members of the university's Folklore Society, knew how it should authentically be played. When he walked into the Fret Shop one afternoon, he heard Mike Bloomfield playing guitar with that authenticity. "Most people could get close, but Mike could play it the way it was supposed to be played. He had a real passion for accuracy and authenticity that was lacking in most other people. He was like a student of music."

Michael met other young white blues fans from Hyde Park, too. A UC junior and budding guitar player from Tulsa, Oklahoma, Elvin Bishop had come to the university at age sixteen on a National Merit Scholarship. He was there to study math and English, but he, too, had gotten caught up in the South Side's blues scene, and the guitar had become his main academic focus. One afternoon he traveled to the North Side in search of a new instrument.

"I met Bloomers at a pawn shop on Clark Street," Bishop said.

> I didn't know much about guitars or playing them—I was just in the burning-desire stage. I was checking out a couple of guitars and playing a few pitiful licks on them. Finally, I got one I halfway liked. There was this real hyper, fast-talking kid behind the counter. He was kind of rude and snotty. He looked down his nose at me, picked up this guitar, reeled off some real fast shit, and I just couldn't believe it. It was Michael—his uncle owned the pawnshop.

The pawn shop—in a seedy neighborhood not far from Washington Square Park at 675 North Clark Street—was called Uncle Max's Buy & Sell. It was owned not by Mike Bloomfield's uncle but by his grandfather, Max Klein. Michael frequently worked there on weekends, ostensibly helping customers from behind one of the two long counters that flanked the store's center aisle, but more often just fooling around with Uncle Max's stock of used instruments. By the time he had left home in 1961, Bloomfield was doing a regular Saturday shift at his grandfather's store in an effort to support himself. His hours in the store not only provided him with some much-needed cash, but also gave him access to a variety of stringed instruments and an opportunity to meet other young musicians.

But it wasn't only folk enthusiasts and musicians that Mike Bloomfield was meeting in the spring of 1961. One Saturday afternoon while Michael was still finishing up high school at Central Y, a cute seventeen-year-old girl came into Uncle Max's. She was from the city's far South Side, a lakeside neighborhood nearly ten miles from the Loop called South Chicago. Her name was Susan Smith.

Susan had come to the North Side with a friend who wanted to buy a guitar, and they thought they might find one for a good price at Uncle Max's. Michael came over to help them and immediately was smitten by the demure blonde. In an effort to charm his young customer, Bloomfield began one of his verbal onslaughts. He talked in a rush about guitars, music, life, and himself, all without pausing for breath. Susan and her friend were overwhelmed, unsure what to make of this hyper, animated sales clerk. Michael wound up his pitch with a candid revelation about himself, knowing it was certain to make an impression.

"He told us this crazy story about how he had been a Mouseketeer!" said Susan, laughing. "I believed it for a long time." Michael had acquired a habit of improvising with the truth just as he could improvise with his guitar, and his tall tale about having once been a cast member on the popular Disney TV show had the desired effect. When he asked Susan for her phone number, she gave it to him.

The two girls left Uncle Max's without purchasing a guitar, and both were more than a little surprised by their experience. Susan was intrigued by the aggressive boy behind the counter, but unsure whether she would consent to see him again. "There weren't too many people like him," she said, reflecting on how unusual Michael had seemed. "He was just kind of amazing."

Michael, on the other hand, was greatly encouraged by the encounter. He had never had any luck with girls—he wasn't handsome like his brother, and he was far too direct to navigate the requisite subtleties of small talk with the opposite sex. It was not surprising that throughout his adolescence and teen years he had never really dated.

But Susan Smith was not like the girls he knew in high school. Though she came from working-class Christian family, she grew up in a neighborhood that was predominantly Jewish and had graduated that January from James H. Bowen High School on East Eighty-Ninth Street. While in school she had gotten caught up in the folk movement, and she shared Michael's deep interest in traditional American music and music of other cultures. She had been to Folklore Society events at UC and knew all the folk music haunts in Hyde Park. She was also a student at the Old Town School of Folk Music, taking banjo lessons from Frank Hamilton.

Hamilton, as it happened, played a part in Michael's first date with Susan.

Bloomfield called Susan not long after they had met at Uncle Max's and—after some convincing—got her to agree to go out with him. At the last minute, though, Susan thought the better of it and canceled the date. It was only when Michael called again and asked her to go see *The Subterraneans*, a Hollywood reworking of a Jack Kerouac novel, that they finally got together. The movie had just opened in Chicago, and Susan wanted to see it because it featured a number of prominent musicians along with the actors. One of those musicians was her teacher, Frank Hamilton.

The couple's second date also involved music.

"Michael said, 'Well, I have to go play in these clubs,'" recalled Susan. "I didn't even know what he was talking about. He had his guitar and a big, heavy amplifier. I'd never even seen an amplifier before." The young guitarist had decided to take his new lady friend along on one of his jamming junkets. Despite repeated car trouble and much hefting of equipment, Susan found the evening an entertaining if somewhat perplexing diversion.

"This was the strangest thing I'd ever experienced in my life!" she said. "I didn't know what was going on. I didn't know what he was. He was an odd guy."

Despite that oddness—or perhaps because of it—the teenagers began to see each other regularly. While he was still playing occasional electric gigs with his black Gibson Les Paul Custom, Michael's interest in acoustic music was becoming all-consuming. Susan encouraged his exploration of traditional styles and urged him to get involved in the Hyde Park folk scene. So, in the fall of 1961, Mike moved into a rented room in Hyde Park, where he could be closer to his new girlfriend and more easily hang out with other traditional music enthusiasts. He soon immersed himself in traditional folk, country, and rural blues styles, making an all-encompassing study of American music from the century's early decades.

To better play those styles, Michael traded his top-of-the-line Les Paul Custom for a pair of acoustic guitars—a six- and a twelve-string. The six-string was a vintage 1940s Martin 000-28, an instrument that was extremely popular with fingerpickers. The other guitar was a big twelve-string, a newer model of indeterminate make, good enough for re-creating tunes by twelve-string players like Lead Belly, Barbecue Bob, and Blind Willie McTell.

Michael immediately put both instruments to good use, continuing to work on Delta and ragtime styles, bluegrass picking patterns and runs, and the Travis technique that Norman Dayron had seen him demonstrating at the Fret Shop. Soon he could re-create nearly any traditional style with startling accuracy.

By the early winter of 1961, Michael's relationship with Susan Smith had blossomed into a full-blown romance, and the young couple began spending much of their free time together. They explored the city and its music, and Susan was greatly impressed by Mike's knowledge of Chicago's neighborhoods and cultures. She had enrolled in the Art Institute of Chicago on Michigan Avenue at the end of the summer and was making a half-hearted effort at being an art student. But being with Michael was as unpredictable as it was exciting, and he left her little time for studying. Bloomfield himself may have signed up for classes at Roosevelt College, just a few blocks from the institute, but it's more probable that he just spent time hanging out there.

Marshall Field's, Chicago's huge downtown department store, soon became a favorite place for Mike and Susan to rendezvous. Covering an entire city block on State Street and located conveniently around the corner from the Art Institute, the couple spent many pleasant afternoons wandering among the display counters on the vast store's many floors. They would eventually make their way up to the Walnut Room, the elegant restaurant on the store's top floor, and there Mike and Susan would order food, charging it to the Bloomfield account.

On the days when Susan actually did attend her classes, Mike would take the elevator down from Roosevelt's student lounge and wander into the Jazz Record Mart on the college building's street level. He would kill time sifting through the hundreds of records in the shop's bins, looking for an obscure artist or a rare side. He was also hoping he might run into a blues legend named Big Joe Williams.

Bob Koester, the shop's proprietor, had begun producing blues recordings in 1958 when he was still in St. Louis. One of his first releases was an album called *Piney Woods Blues*. It featured a fifty-eight-year-old itinerant blues guitarist originally from Crawford, Mississippi, named Joe Lee Williams. Big Joe, as he was called, had been a recording artist for the influential Bluebird label back in the mid-1930s, and Koester had revived his career with a session for his Delmar Records label, which he would later rename Delmark. The short, stout Williams played a unique, hand-modified guitar and sang his songs with a ferocity that only increased as each tune progressed. Big Joe was a consummate Delta blues artist who had authored such classics as "Baby Please Don't Go," and he was a walking history lesson for anyone interested in the blues tradition. Mike Bloomfield was seriously interested—and was immediately taken with Joe.

Koester had also been producing occasional concerts at a coffeehouse called the Blind Pig, located in the basement of the Old Town School of Folk Music on North Avenue near North Sedgwick Street. Because Big Joe needed a place to perform his music, Bob frequently featured the Mississippi blues artist. It was at one of those performances that Michael first met Williams.

Big Joe was in Chicago in the fall of 1961 because he had just recorded another album for Koester and was hoping to pick up a few additional gigs. Bob gave Joe odd jobs around the Mart to keep him in spending money, though the singer was at best an irregular employee—working only when it suited him. But whenever Joe and Michael happened to be in the store at the same time, the young guitarist peppered the older man with questions about technique, famous singers Big Joe had known, life on the road, and anything else he could think of. Joe, in turn, was flattered by the young guitarist's attention and was amused by his hyperactive enthusiasm. He took a real liking to Michael and often invited him to sit in whenever Joe was playing around town.

As the fall progressed, Michael and Susan continued to enjoy each other's company, and the guitarist continued to broaden his knowledge of the blues while refining his skill as a player. For the first time in a long while, Mike Bloomfield was enjoying his life. He was out from under his father's judgmental eye, free to pursue the music he loved, in a blossoming relationship, and making a name for himself on Chicago's music scene. And he was a having a very good time doing it.

In Hyde Park, students at the University of Chicago were also having a good time—though only after their classes. One of the university's recently constructed dormitories, a four-story boxy structure called the New Women's Residence Halls or the New Dorms, began having Wednesday evening sock hops. On its first floor was a student lounge, a glassed-in space with cozy alcoves, and it was there that a senior from Minnesota named Ivan Argüelles began playing records from his vast collection of rock 'n' roll and blues 45s. Originally, the gatherings had been set up as "Wednesday night coffee hours," but Argüelles's music trumped the java. The dorm's residents would come down and dance the night away, taking a break from their studies and easing themselves over the mid-week hump. Soon, these Wednesday night hops—known as "twist parties" after the dance craze popularized several years earlier by R&B singer Chubby Checker—began attracting local musicians and bands.

The New Dorms hops soon got Mike Bloomfield's attention too, and he wasted no time checking them out. He brought along Fred Glazer, and the two friends were amazed by what they found. Elvin Bishop was there with his little group playing electric Chicago-style blues, and with them was a young white harmonica player who was *really* impressive. His name was Paul Butterfield.

Seeing a white kid their age play harp with the authority and skill of Junior Wells, James Cotton, or even Little Walter was a revelation. "That was the first time we met another group of people that were into the same type of music we were," said Glazer. "We were flipped out that here were other white people that we didn't know who were playing this music."

Ironically, Paul Butterfield had been playing harmonica for only a few years when he began performing at the New Dorms. Born in Chicago in 1942, Paul had been raised in Hyde Park, where his father was a lawyer and his mother, originally a painter, worked as assistant to the Dean of Students at the university. Butterfield had attended UC's Lab School, a progressive preparatory school, and had studied classical flute for nine years while there. He had a talent for drawing and painting as well as for music, and he practiced both arts with a seriousness that belied his years. After graduating from high school and briefly attending the University of Illinois, he had devoted himself completely to playing the blues.

Butterfield's enthusiasm for the music of the South Side stemmed in part from his close friendship with Nick Gravenites. He and Nick had met at one of the Folklore Society's hootenannies, and Nick had taken him around to all his favorite blues haunts. Paul had fallen in love with the music he heard, and the two friends had formed a duo called Nick and Paul in 1960, with Butterfield playing harmonica behind Gravenites's acoustic guitar and vocals. They performed at various coffeehouses around Hyde Park and at university events, but the twist parties offered Paul a chance to play amplified harp backed by a Chicago-style electric band of his peers for the first time. He became a regular at the Wednesday evening dances, often with Bishop as his rhythm guitarist.

The twist parties at the New Dorms were a real eye-opener for Mike Bloomfield. Though he had largely given up amplified music so he could concentrate on traditional acoustic guitar, the proficiency of Butterfield's playing made a strong impression on him. Not only had he found a community of folk music enthusiasts in Hyde Park who, like himself, were interested in the history and origins of American music, but here was another group of young white players who were as excited about modern blues as he was. Michael decided he would get together a few friends and play for the twist dancers himself. One of his ad hoc groups included Roy Ruby on rhythm guitar, and that evening's twist party was a showcase for young blues talent.

"One balmy spring night, the twist party scene at the New Dorms reached its climax because each alcove had its own band," recalled Mike Michaels, a UC junior and one of the founders of the university's folk festival.

> The lounge was filled with dancers, and the glass walls were pulsating with the music. In one alcove were Paul Butterfield and Nick Gravenites. In another alcove was Elvin Bishop with several black guys, including two brothers who owned a shoe repair shop on Fifty-Third Street and played R&B and blues on the side. In the third alcove was a very manic Michael Bloomfield, backed up by a short, curly-haired, Italian-looking kid. He was playing the fastest rock 'n' roll licks I had ever heard anywhere.

Another musician, a first-year student from Minneapolis, came as often as he could to the twist parties. His name was Mark Naftalin, and he occasionally played piano while Elvin and Paul performed. Mark had played rock 'n' roll in a group called Johnny and the Galaxies while in high school, and at the university he had been taking classes in music. He remembered meeting Mike Bloomfield for the first time in the lounge of the New Dorms.

"I watched him playing on his guitar very, *very* fast," recollected Naftalin. "He was very flashy with the Chuck Berry licks and so on—really a dynamo!"

The third week in February, Michael and a friend from Highland Park named Matt Cushner went to the Gate of Horn on North Dearborn Street to hear some live music. With them was Matt's college friend, Sid Scott. Because Matt's parents were out of town for the week, they drove down to the club in the Cushners' big, luxurious Lincoln Continental. On the ride back to Highland Park, Michael suddenly spoke up. "He said we should drive to Memphis and meet Elvis!" said Sid, laughing. "It was Michael's idea. We hadn't planned anything—it just happened. The car was available, just sitting in the garage, so we thought, 'Why not?'"

The trio packed some clothes at Matt's house, and Michael grabbed his Martin. Even though it was almost 2:00 a.m., they set out for Memphis, some ten hours and six hundred miles away, on a pilgrimage to see the King. Matt took the wheel while Sid rode shotgun. Michael climbed in back, entertaining the travelers with his guitar as they headed out through the western suburbs to connect up with Route 66 in La Grange. As they drove, Bloomfield improvised a running narrative of the trip.

"He made up hilarious songs about us going to Memphis and entertained us the whole way," said Scott. One ditty had a refrain that everybody joined in on: "We're on our way to Memphis, we're going to Memphis to get a piece of ass!"

The rock 'n' roll pilgrims made it to Memphis by early evening the next day. They drove downtown to Beale Street, the thoroughfare legendary for its blues clubs and bars. Though they were tired, they parked the Lincoln and went in search of some entertainment. They were in one of the country's great cities for American music, but it seemed that night there was very little to do on Beale Street.

"We couldn't find anything happening in the clubs. It was pretty quiet," said Sid Scott. "So Mike said we should go see Elvis—right then, in the middle of the night!" Though Sid and Matt were dubious, Michael said he would get them in to see the King. They drove to Graceland, Presley's estate some ten miles south of the city on Route 51, arriving there well after midnight.

"We stood outside the gates at Graceland—the place was all closed up because it was after dark," said Sid. "A guard was there in a jeep, and he asked us what we were doing." Michael explained that they had come all the way from Chicago to see Elvis. The guard laughed and said that wouldn't be possible because the pop music star wasn't at home—he was in Las Vegas, working on a movie. Michael was undeterred.

"Bloomfield had his guitar, and he just started playing one Elvis hit after another," Sid said. "The guard was really impressed, and he decided to let us in and take us around." The sentry was a lover of the King's music too, and he enjoyed Bloomfield's playing so much that he drove the three fans around the grounds of Graceland, showing them the house and its garage with several of Elvis's Cadillacs. After the hour-long tour, he brought them back to the front gate. The three friends were elated even though they hadn't met Presley himself. They climbed into the Lincoln, turned the big sedan around, and headed back up Route 51. Sid and Matt took turns driving all the way back to Highland Park, and all three switched off in the back seat, grabbing a few hours of sleep as the dawn broke in the eastern sky.

Throughout the winter and early spring of 1962, Mike Bloomfield continued to refine and expand his mastery of traditional acoustic guitar techniques while exploring American folk music's rich history. He was shuttling between Hyde Park, the Loop, and Glencoe, spending time with friends and with Susan, occasionally making side trips to South Chicago to visit her at the Smith family home. He went to the second UC Folk Festival in February and saw Doc Watson, Jean Ritchie, the New Lost City Ramblers, and the Staples Singers perform. Rev. Gary Davis also played, and during an afternoon workshop with the blind guitarist, Mike gave an impromptu performance for the audience using Davis's guitar.

But Michael was having trouble making ends meet. His weekend hours at Uncle Max's barely covered his rent, leaving him almost nothing for carfare and gas for Dottie's Corvair—when he could manage to borrow it. And then he had to eat. Bloomfield realized that if he were going to stay in Hyde Park he had to make other arrangements.

Norman Dayron was in his final semester at the university, and he was living in a small apartment at 5319 South Kimbark Avenue, a few blocks from the school. Michael ran into Norman at the folk festival, and the two got to talking. Bloomfield recounted his financial woes, and Norman suggested that Michael move into his place for a few months. Dayron was planning to get married that summer to his high school sweetheart, and the newlyweds were going to make a month-long honeymoon tour of Europe and Greece. After that, Norman and his bride would be living in the apartment. But until then, Michael was welcome to sleep on the couch.

The offer suited Michael's needs perfectly, and he decided to move into Dayron's apartment.

The two roommates spent the spring pursuing their separate interests. Norman was finishing up his coursework in pursuit of his degree while Michael, when not practicing, more often than not was following his heart. He made frequent visits to the Smith family home in South Chicago after the Art Institute's spring semester ended. Susan was less often in the Loop, and Michael worked to ingratiate himself with her family. The Smiths, though, were not impressed. The fast-talking, hyperactive Jewish teenager from the North Shore struck them as odd and more than a bit naïve. Susan's dad was a no-nonsense steel worker, and he found Michael's obsession with the music of the ghetto and its hardscrabble lifestyle foolish.

"I know my father used to think Michael was really stupid and pretentious for wanting to know about eating beans, or that he wanted to know about being poor," said Susan. But Mike was accustomed to having parents disapprove of him, and he was undaunted by Mr. Smith's criticism. Next to music, Susan was the most important thing in his life, and nothing would deter him from pursuing both.

Fred Glazer had been having a romance of his own that spring. After graduating from New Trier in 1961, Fred had tried college at Miami University in Oxford, Ohio, but had dropped out midway through his first year. While at the university he had gotten involved with a girl—and had managed to get her pregnant. Now she and Fred were back in Glencoe, and Fred was faced with a decision. She wanted to get married, and he knew he would probably have to tie the knot. But to put that eventuality off as long as possible, he decided to leave town for a while.

In the last weeks of May, Michael, too, was thinking a change of scene would be good. His feelings for Susan were strong enough that he was seriously thinking about asking her to marry him. But before he settled down, he wanted to have a real adventure, an *On the Road* rite of passage. Fred's dilemma provided Michael with the perfect excuse for an extended road trip. He told Susan he was taking Fred out of town for a while so Fred could clear his head and decide what to do with his life. For Bloomfield, it would be an opportunity to see a bit of the world on his own.

Early one morning, the boys hit the open road. They hitchhiked out of Chicago and headed down Route 66. Both sported backpacks with sleeping bags and a change of clothes, and Michael had his Martin 000-28 in its taped-up cardboard case. They were off on a thousand-mile trek to Colorado, and Mike decided he and Fred would follow in the footsteps of Kerouac's Sal Paradise, the famed hero of Beat literature. They would hobo out to Denver, meet colorful characters, party a little, and have real-life adventures.

They got as far as Manhattan, Kansas, by thumb. There they ran afoul of the local constabulary and were ordered off the road and directed to the town's bus station. A Greyhound provided transportation for the remainder of the trip, and before long the wayfarers made it to the Mile High City. They stayed in Denver for a couple of days with one of Michael's former campmates from his summers at a Colorado resort but soon needed to find a permanent place to stay. They heard that something was happening in nearby Boulder, so after a few days they headed north up the Denver-Boulder Turnpike.

"Boulder was just developing a hip kind of underground scene there," said Fred. "There was some pothead guy that had started a hip student newspaper that summer, and we met him somehow, and he moved us into this house. We just drank wine all day long and smoked pot and got high. And the guy put a band together."

True to form, as soon as Michael Bloomfield met a few musicians in Boulder, he wanted to organize a group. The Chicagoans' newspaper-editor host helped make it happen. He hooked Mike up with Warner Logan, the son of Happy Logan, owner of a number of prominent music stores in the Denver area. Warner gave them access to instruments from his dad's shop in town. Bloomfield got an electric guitar and Fred played harmonica. Warner Logan joined them on drums and, with the addition of a black saxophonist and a few other players, they had what Fred called "a real heavy R&B band."

In town were two bars. One, called Tulagi, was an upscale club that featured Beach Boys–style white rock 'n' roll and drew huge crowds on weekends. The other, located down the block at Thirteenth Street and Pennsylvania Avenue, was Tulagi's scruffy cousin. Called the Sink, it was a burger-and-brew joint that catered to Boulder's University of Colorado students. The owners wanted to add music on the weekends to better compete with their more successful neighbor, and when Michael approached them about playing there, they readily agreed. They said they would give the band one hundred dollars if they could draw a crowd.

Bloomfield's ad hoc group played the sort of music that Michael had been performing around Chicago for years—rock 'n' roll, R&B, and a generous helping of South Side blues. They played hits by Chuck Berry, Little Richard, and Jerry Lee Lewis, and they burned through classic blues by Muddy Waters and Howlin' Wolf. Fred did his best to evoke Little Walter on harmonica, and the addition of a saxophone gave the band a fuller, jazzier sound. They even played the tune that had launched that summer's dance craze—Chubby Checker's

"Limbo Rock." In no time, they filled the Sink with revelers, stealing away most of Tulagi's audience and turning the seedy bar into the street's hot nightspot.

"It was like Big John's would be six or seven years later," Fred remembered fondly. "We created a mini-scene there in Boulder during the summer of 1962."

But even as Michael was working to put an electric band together, he was checking out Boulder's folk scene. Right across the street from the Sink was a drugstore that had a small folk club in its basement. Ironically called the Attic, the subterranean coffeehouse was run by Joe Loop, a musician and folk enthusiast who was not much older than Michael.

"Mike walked in right off the street with a Martin slung upside down over his back, no case," recalled Loop. "We hit it off immediately." Bloomfield hung out quite a bit at the Attic and struck up a friendship there with a young blues and folk singer named Judy Roderick. Roderick was just beginning a music career that would eventually take her to New York and land her recording contracts with Columbia and Vanguard, but in 1962 she was still learning her craft. To help Judy out, the guitar ace from Chicago recorded a few demos with her. Michael backed Roderick up while she sang a few Lightnin' Hopkins tunes and several traditional folk songs into a reel-to-reel. The result was four short duets with Bloomfield demonstrating various strumming patterns and picking techniques while Roderick sang the lyrics in her gutsy contralto.

That recording session led to a second collaboration with the diminutive singer. Leon Bibb, the famed folksinger and Vanguard recording artist, was performing that summer at the Exodus on Lincoln Street in Denver. A producer friend of Judy Roderick's knew Bibb and thought it might help her career if Judy auditioned for the folksinger. The friend arranged for her to do a few tunes for Bibb—with Mike Bloomfield as accompanist.

At forty, Leon Bibb was a veteran stage performer, a singer who had been featured at the first Newport Folk Festival and a friend of Paul Robeson who had been blacklisted in the early 1950s for his political views. He was a seasoned professional, and it was only out of courtesy that he agreed to listen to the young white girl who looked more like an Ivy League sorority sister than anybody's idea of a blues belter.

But one afternoon, Roderick, accompanied by Mike Bloomfield, performed for Bibb at his hotel in downtown Denver. Joe Loop had come along for moral support, and he was greatly amused by Bibb's reaction.

"They performed 'Come Back Baby,'" said Joe. "Mr. Bibb was absolutely slack-jawed. 'Where did you hear that song? Where did you learn to sing like that? And where did you learn to *play* like that?' was all he could say." Leon had been sitting, arms folded, prepared for the worst before Roderick began. But her choice of the slow blues popularized by Ray Charles surprised and pleased him, and Bloomfield's Lightnin' Hopkins–style picking rang with an authority that belied his baby-faced, suburban teenager appearance.

"The look on Leon Bibb's face was priceless!" said Loop.

When they weren't rehearsing or playing at the Sink, Mike and Fred spent their days exploring Boulder and Denver. In the capital city they found a seedy African American neighborhood that reminded them of Chicago's Bronzeville. It was called Five Points, named for an intersection where five city thoroughfares met. Known at one time as the "Harlem of the West" for its community of black artists, musicians, and professionals, Five Points had suffered from neglect since the war years and many of its buildings were abandoned, its vacant lots strewn with garbage. By the time Michael and Fred arrived, Five Points had become a slum with a reputation to match. The one thing it still had in abundance was bars.

"We met this black guy who took us around Denver and showed us this drink called 'shake-'em-ups.' You take a package of frozen lemonade and put it into a big decanter of wine, and you shake up the wine and lemonade," Fred remembered. "We'd sit around in the bars there, drink these shake-'em-ups, sitting on the sidewalks, me and Michael and this black guy who was in the band, who played the sax."

For the first time, the young men were free to indulge in adult vices *as* adults. They were on their own, away from home and away from their parents, making their own way. They were able to do whatever they wished, and that included a lot of experimenting. "It was a little heavier scene than we'd been into in Chicago," acknowledged Fred.

For Michael, though, making friends and being accepted in the black community wasn't about only getting high and having a good time. He was also deeply interested in learning as much as he could about the struggles, passions, loves, and sorrows of America's underclass—life as it was lived on the other side of the tracks. His own experience had been the exact opposite. A child of privilege, Mike Bloomfield had grown up a world apart from the deprivations and indignities experienced by the residents of Chicago's Bronzeville. His fascination with "outsider status"—personified by his lanky-hillbilly-singer fantasy—had expanded to include African Americans and the blues by 1962.

"I was from a very rich family," explained Bloomfield.

> Like many kids in the '50s, I had a real affection, an *afición,* for funk. My aesthetic was based on, like, if I couldn't be tough, if I couldn't be a greaser . . . even funkier than that was to be colored. These people kicked ass and everything, they fought[,] which is something a Jewish kid like me just *never* did. If it was funky to be a Gene Vincent or somebody like that, to be a n***** . . . to play with these black bands and go to all these funky places and hear this music that I loved—I mean, I was living the life, you know? If it was cool to be like Elvis, to be what Elvis thought was cool, well, that was the *coolest* in the world.

Susan Smith's father regarded Bloomfield's obsession with the blues life as foolhardy. From his perspective, a boy like Michael had no business wasting time pursuing some misguided romantic notion about poverty and oppression. His parents had worked hard to provide him with all the advantages he had enjoyed growing up, and only a fool would toss those away in favor of a life of indolence, of scuffling and shake-'em-ups.

The music of the African American community, however, was anything but superficial. It was direct, unsparingly honest, and at times intensely emotional. These qualities resonated with Mike Bloomfield, for they were ones he shared, and they were what drew him in. He could see that the blues was music for adults and, as such, spoke to the struggles and injustices of adult life in the ghetto. The often plaintive, defiant tone of the blues echoed Michael's own conflict with authority. In no small way, the music's assertive nature mirrored the central emotional issue of Bloomfield's own life—namely, his complex relationship with that supreme authority figure, his father.

In an interview given in 1967, Bloomfield was uncharacteristically political on the topic of black oppression and injustice. The anger he clearly felt could easily be heard as emanating from issues he had with his dad.

"[I]n this fucked up country, the black man will forever be down unless a revolution takes place, which it should—an armed revolution," Michael told the interviewer. "Thank [G]od there are Malcolm Xs and Rap Browns around who are finally, finally getting the people together into revolution because this economy and this country will never, ever, ever, ever allow the black man to get anywhere."

Just as Harold Bloomfield, if he had his way, would never allow Michael Bloomfield to get anywhere as a musician and creative artist. Oppression takes many forms, and it makes kindred spirits out of those oppressed.

Of course, many other factors played into Mike's love of the blues and his desire to experience life in the black community. It would be wrong to attribute his fascination with "funk" solely to an armchair psychological assessment of his struggles with his father. But the harsh judgments of Mr. Bloomfield were unquestionably an influence on the course of his son's young life. When asked by a friend years later what she thought had troubled Michael most throughout his life, Susan Smith replied without hesitation: "Harold."

By early June, the boys were growing restless. Mike missed Susan, and Fred, despite the pleasures of carousing and indulging, felt he needed to get home to assume responsibility for his impending fatherhood. They had been having a ball playing music at the Sink, but there was no real possibility of keeping the band together for more than a few weeks, and living out of a backpack and sleeping on the floor had lost its *On the Road* charm. One summer morning, Bloomfield and Glazer bid farewell to their editor host and caught a Greyhound for parts east.

They got as far as Kansas City. Short on funds, the boys found a busy street corner and spent the day playing music for spare change. By that time, the reality of a life on the road without resources or roots had begun to sink in. It was hard to find anything romantic about panhandling and dodging the cops.

"I remember being in Kansas City and thinking, 'Boy, this is a crazy life,'" Fred said. "'What are we doing here, sitting on a street corner with no food and a dime in our pocket?'" The pair had no choice but to hitchhike the remaining five hundred miles back to Chicago.

Back in the Windy City, Michael immediately went to see Susan while Fred informed his girlfriend, Bobbie, that he had decided they should get married. Michael provided moral support as Fred's best man, and the couple took the vows at City Hall in Glen Ellyn, a village some fifteen miles west of Chicago. After the ceremony, the newlyweds and their best man skipped out on the dinner reception Bobbie's parents had planned and headed north toward the lake. They decided to celebrate in Highwood, where they could toast the occasion with a few drinks. Michael took them to the Tally Ho, where he sat in with the band and entertained the new husband and wife with a few blues tunes in fine South Side fashion.

CHAPTER 4

MARRIAGE, THE PICKLE, AND BIG JOE

CHICAGO, 1962–1963

After his month away, Michael was eager to resume his courtship of Susan Smith. They had been seeing each other for more than a year, and the possibility of marriage was on both their minds. Michael was in favor of it. He had helped one of his best friends get married—in fact, he had insisted that Fred take the leap—and now he was giving serious thought to proposing to Susan.

Susan was ambivalent. Though she was unsure what to do with her life, she was tired of living in her parents' home and longed to be out on her own. She knew classes at the Art Institute would be starting up soon, but she had done so poorly her first year that she felt it would be difficult to return for a second. The best alternative—maybe the only alternative—seemed to be marriage.

"I felt like, oh my god, I've got to do *something*," said Susan. "So I said, 'We've got to get married,' and he said, 'OK.' And we did it."

On the warm and hazy Tuesday morning of September 4, the bride- and groom-to-be climbed into the back of Fred and Bobbie Glazer's 1955 Pontiac and drove to Michigan. They had to leave the state because Illinois would issue marriage licenses only to couples at least twenty-one years old. Both Michael and Susan had just turned nineteen, so they had to drive through Indiana and into Michigan, where it was legal to marry at eighteen.

On their way out of town, they made a stop in Bronzeville. Michael's friend from the Jazz Record Mart, Big Joe Williams, had heard about his and Susan's impending nuptials, and he wanted to do something special for them. At a cousin's house, Joe had prepared a basket of his fried chicken for the wedding party, and Michael had Fred stop by to pick the gift up. The still-warm chicken filled the car with an appetizing, savory aroma as the Pontiac left Chicago's city streets and merged onto the Indiana Toll Road.

Fred drove them east to New Buffalo, Michigan, a small beach resort town some seventy miles from Chicago on the opposite shore of Lake Michigan.

Michael and Susan had gone the week before to the courthouse in town to buy a marriage license, and now they drove to the offices of a local justice of the peace. Fred acted as Michael's best man, and he and Bobbie were witnesses to the union. In a matter of minutes, the deed was done. Mike and Susan were now husband and wife. That called for a celebration.

Being a resort town, New Buffalo had a small harbor for pleasure crafts along with a number of concessions where tourists could hire small boats by the hour. The four friends selected a dinghy, paid for a few hours' rental, and rowed out onto Lake Michigan. The afternoon was warm and humid for early fall, but the air was cooler out on the water, and the gentle waves sparkled in the hazy sunshine. The quartet dug into Big Joe's crispy chicken and shared a few bottles of wine.

"We sat in the boat all day on Lake Michigan, drinking Thunderbird wine and eating Big Joe's chicken and smoking pot and floating away into the distance," Fred recalled.

It was an idyllic conclusion to what had been a delightful day. But as the newlyweds rode back to Chicago that evening, they both knew an unpleasant duty awaited them. Neither had told their parents they were getting married. In fact, Michael's mother and father didn't even know he had a girlfriend.

It was Dewey Williams, the Bloomfields' gardener, who passed along the news.

He and his wife, Mary, the family's housekeeper, had heard about Michael's change in marital status—probably from the groom himself. A few days later, Dewey mentioned it to Dottie and Harold, and both were shocked. They couldn't believe it. They had seen no indication from their elder son that he was intending to take such a life-changing step. To his parents, nothing about Michael seemed different.

Truthfully, nothing much was different, at first. After their wedding, Susan and Michael returned to Chicago to resume their lives as they had been. Not knowing what else to do, Susan went back to South Chicago and her parents' home, while Michael spent the weeks shuttling between his hangouts in the Loop, on the South Side, and at Norman Dayron's apartment in Hyde Park. The couple were together as often as they could be, but they had no idea how to proceed next.

Once the secret was out, though, Harold Bloomfield was furious. His foolhardy, irresponsible son, a boy not even out of his teens, had impulsively married some working-class girl from a family that lived somewhere down near Gary. And she wasn't even Jewish! Though the Bloomfields were liberal in their religious views and were not averse to the idea of intermarriage, cultural differences could make such a union problematic. Harold, normally a man of few words, wanted to share more than a few choice ones with his errant son. Michael soon realized he could put it off no longer, and one evening he went up to Glencoe to tell his parents of his marriage. It did not go well.

"There was a *huge* blowout. Dad really beat him up—he was a boxer and he literally smacked Michael around—and I remember Michael yelling," recalled Allen Bloomfield. "He would never raise a hand to his father, but he shouted, 'I'm outta here, you *motherfuckers*!'"

Mrs. Bloomfield got sucked into the scuffle, trying to protect her son, and she separated the two men. But Dottie could see that the damage was done. She knew they needed to do something to make amends. "I bawled my husband out, and I said, 'You'd better have a cocktail party and introduce this girl to our friends or you'll lose a son,'" she recalled.

"That was the weird thing," Allen acknowledged. "A month later my parents gave a huge party for the newlyweds." After the emotional trauma of being attacked by his father, Michael and his bride were welcomed into the family as though nothing had happened. It felt disingenuous at best.

"That was the way it was—Michael desperate for approval and never really getting the real thing. Just the appearance of it," Allen said. "He never really came home again after that."

Once their marriage was public knowledge, Mike and Susan realized they were free to move in together. That October they started looking for a place to live, and they soon found an apartment for a modest fifty dollars a month. It was on Lakeside Avenue near Clarendon Avenue in Uptown, a dingy, working-class neighborhood on Chicago's North Side. Though they had very little money, they set up house with whatever furniture they could scavenge and began a life together as husband and wife—or what they thought the life of a married couple should be.

To support his new wife, the young guitarist took on a succession of improbable jobs. Michael worked briefly as a clerk in a shoe store, and Susan distinctly remembered that for a while he tried selling door-to-door. "We took a stab at being normal," Susan said with a laugh.

Normal or not, the couple needed money, and it was Susan who eventually landed a regular, paying job. She found work at a neighborhood office of the Kemper Insurance Company on North Sheridan Road, not more than a block from their Uptown apartment. The steady income was enough to pay for rent and food, and Mike contributed whatever he could by playing the occasional gig. He also brought in extra cash by visiting the returns windows at the big department stores in the Loop, exchanging wedding gifts the newlyweds had received at their reception in Glencoe.

Mostly, though, Michael spent his days practicing, listening to music, hanging out with friends, and jamming whenever and wherever he could. The Fret Shop in Hyde Park, the Jazz Record Mart, and even the Old Town School of Folk Music were favorite haunts, along with numerous clubs and bars on the South Side.

"He really didn't *do* anything," Susan said, describing Michael's activities during their early married life. "He played music. I worked; I took care of everything. . . . I was his 'mom'; I did everything for him."

Michael was too preoccupied with music to bother about the routine requirements of daily life, and the responsibilities of running the household quickly fell to Susan. She took care of the bills, did the shopping, cooked the meals, kept house—and earned the money. But she didn't mind.

"We were children, but it was wonderful fun," she said. "Wonderful fun."

In the late fall of 1962, Mike Bloomfield made another friend, one who would join him in pursuing a career in the blues. His name was Charlie Musselwhite.

By the end of the summer, owner Bob Koester had decided to move the Jazz Record Mart to a larger space to accommodate his growing stock of jazz and blues recordings. He had begun actively producing records on his own label, and he needed additional room for product storage. In August he rented a storefront at 7 West Grand Street, a little more than a mile north of his original location on Roosevelt Road, and set up shop selling records on the ground floor and warehousing his boxes of Delmark LPs in the shop's spacious basement.

Blues singer Big Joe Williams made the move with Koester to 7 West Grand, occupying a cot in the Jazz Record Mart's basement whenever he was in town. Before long, he was joined there by a young white musician from Memphis.

"One day I was standing on the corner of Grand and State, waiting for a bus, and there was this record shop there," said Charlie Musselwhite. "I'd never seen so many blues records in a store window before. I got to hanging around there . . . and ended up getting a job there, selling records and boxing them up to sell mail order. And I ended up living there in the basement."

Musselwhite was six months younger than Bloomfield, and at age eighteen he had come up to Chicago from Tennessee looking for work. Born in Kosciusko, Mississippi, and raised in Memphis, he knew well the music of the city's street singers and field workers, and he was an avid fan of the blues he heard over local radio stations—the same broadcasters Michael had tuned in to late at night as a teenager in Glencoe. Like Mike, Charlie had taught himself to play guitar. But

Musselwhite had done so purely for his own enjoyment. It had never occurred to him that he might pursue music as a career. On his arrival in Chicago, he had found work as a pest exterminator.

But once he became a clerk at the Jazz Record Mart, Musselwhite soon struck up a friendship with Mike Bloomfield. Though the Tennessean was a blues fan just like Michael, the two young musicians could not have been more different. Charlie was soft-spoken and shy, with the unhurried demeanor and comfortable drawl of a Southern boy raised to address his elders as "sir" or "ma'am." Michael, on the other hand, was impulsive and direct, unafraid to speak his mind, and always in a rush to learn and see and do.

The Jazz Record Mart also served to introduce Michael to another music enthusiast who would become a close friend and mentor. His name was Pete Welding.

The twenty-six-year-old Welding had arrived in Chicago that spring from his native Philadelphia. There he had been a writer and journalist working for publications like *Down Beat* and *Saturday Review*, and a radio producer hosting jazz and folk shows on WHYY. He had come to the Windy City because he had taken a job as *Down Beat*'s assistant editor. But Welding was also interested in starting his own record label. He planned to scout out older Chicago blues players and document their music in a series of albums. He had been inspired by Bob Koester's success with Delmark Records, and he wanted to learn from Koester how to do it. He could frequently be found in the new store on West Grand, and it was there that Pete and Michael met.

Bloomfield knew the writer's name from numerous album liner notes and record reviews that Welding had written, and he could see that Pete was an insightful and highly knowledgeable authority on American music. Welding also had a vast collection of jazz and blues records, and listening sessions at his place eventually became a cram course for Bloomfield on jazz, from its classic New Orleans days to its post-bop, free-jazz present. Michael was eager to learn all he could about the music, and Pete became his tutor.

With Big Joe Williams making the Jazz Record Mart his occasional home, Memphis Charlie Musselwhite clerking behind the counter, and Bob Koester and Pete Welding working to find and record long-lost blues talent, the store at 7 West Grand was not only one of the best purveyors of blues recordings in the country, but also an exciting hub of blues activity in Chicago. Mike began hanging around the Mart so often, many people thought he worked there.

But Michael Bloomfield wasn't thinking only about the history of blues and the legendary musicians who created it. He was also thinking about his own future in music. Young white players, blues guitarists and singers, were beginning to record for nationally known record labels. Mike had heard albums by New York's Dave Van Ronk, Boston's Eric von Schmidt, and Chicago's folk patriarch, Bob Gibson. Even John Hammond, the young blues enthusiast he had befriended at the first University of Chicago Folk Festival, was busy recording an album of classic blues covers. The records were issued by small independent labels like Folkways, Vanguard, and Elektra, all based in New York City, and Michael thought if he could just connect with one of those companies, he, too, might be able to make a record. With a record, he might be able to make a living from his music.

In November he called up Fred Glazer and talked his friend into driving the old Pontiac out to the Big Apple. There, they could check out the scene for a few days while Mike shopped his music around. The two friends drove to New York, leaving Susan and Fred's very pregnant wife, Bobbie, to mind the home fires. In the city, they hooked up with Jim Cain, a former classmate of Fred's from Miami University, and began to explore the folk scene. Cain's living arrangements on Avenue B in the East Village were unlike any the Chicagoans had encountered back home.

"Jim was living there with a black hooker and some bisexual, weird New York kind of guy," said Fred.

> It was surreal, like out of a dream. We were a *little* hip, but we were really both from upper-middle-class, conservative suburban homes. All of a sudden we were living with this black hooker, who was taking guys behind this little curtain in the back, and this other guy who had, like, a fishing tackle box full of dope . . . and everybody was hustling money however they could!

Michael and Fred's first road trip to Colorado had mirrored the adventures of Sal Paradise, but this latest escapade made the two friends feel as though they had been dropped into a scene from *Naked Lunch*.

Neither Chicagoan knew anybody in New York, and they found the city more than a bit overwhelming. Michael had brought his Martin guitar along, but for once he was hesitant to sit in. The folk music scene in Manhattan centered around Washington Square Park and New York University's campus in Greenwich Village. Every Sunday afternoon, amateur pickers and singers would gather in the park by the hundreds to trade songs and licks, entertaining each other and anyone else who might be strolling by. At night, dozens of small clubs and coffeehouses from Bleeker Street to Waverly Place offered a variety of folk music fare, provided by polished professionals and earnest amateurs alike. There were sit-down places with covers and drink minimums, and there were "basket houses," where patrons' donations paid for the music.

It was all very different from Chicago's folk scene. The Windy City's traditional music community was, despite its academic gloss, a grassroots movement. In New York, folk music was a more edgy affair. There were many more players, a greater feeling of competition, and a kind of unspoken snobbery that delineated insider from outsider. Two guys fresh in town from the Midwest were definitely on the outside.

Then there were the record companies. Despite Folkways' populist politics, its offices weren't housed in the basement of a music shop or in the spare room of a neighborhood apartment. They were located amid Midtown's skyscrapers at Seventh Avenue and Forty-Seventh Street, in the heart of Times Square. The address alone was enough to evoke a sense of exclusivity.

But Michael felt Folkways was the ideal label to release the sort of music he was playing. One afternoon, he rode the subway uptown to Forty-Ninth Street and walked his demo tape over to Times Square. There he found the Folkways building, took the elevator up to the label's offices, and left his tape with the clerk behind the desk. He tried to introduce himself, saying he was a guitarist who played traditional music, but the clerk was busy boxing up records and barely acknowledged him. Feeling a twinge of discouragement, Michael took the elevator to the ground floor and headed back to the IRT. His Folkways plan suddenly felt like a bust.

But he and Fred were in New York City, and there was plenty to see and do. They visited Gerde's Folk City on West Fourth Street, the Bitter End on Bleecker, and the Folklore Center, a small music- and bookstore that was a hangout for the city's folk enthusiasts. But it wasn't only folk music the Chicagoans went to see. One night they caught a performance by the legendary jazz pianist Thelonious Monk and his quartet. That evening proved to be a pivotal one for Mike Bloomfield, and not just because of the music.

For the first time in his young life, he got *really* high.

"I remember we went to this place called Googie's, which was a jazz bar in the Village, and we sat there all night listening to Monk," recalled Fred Glazer. "That was the first time we ever shot any kind of dope." Unlike the coffeehouses off the park that presented folk music, Googie's on Sullivan Street was a nightclub that primarily featured jazz performers. One weekend in November, the venue showcased Monk and his group, and Michael, Fred, and Jim Cain found themselves in the audience. The three friends were in a euphoric state.

"Jim Cain was this writer, an ascetic kind of guy," said Glazer. "And he was into shooting sodium pentothal. We all shot up at Cain's place and got *tremendously* high."

Sodium pentothal, or sodium thiopental, was developed in the 1930s as a fast-acting anesthesia, primarily for medical use. It induced a calming, sedated effect and later earned a reputation as a "truth serum" because it reduced a patient's inhibitions. Under its influence, people were likely to say whatever came into their minds. That was one effect it had on Michael.

"He was telling me how much he loved me, and how much he was my friend, you know," Fred said, laughing. "How we were going to hang out together forever and how important my friendship was to him. That was the first time he ever got high on something for real, other than pot. It *really* just turned him on."

Sodium pentothal was never very popular as a recreational drug. Those who experimented with narcotics preferred the longer-lasting effects of heroin. But as a prescription drug, sodium pentothal was easier to get and relatively inexpensive. Michael found that its depressant effect provided welcome relief from his hyperactive, often agitated mental state. Within minutes of the injection, he was flooded with a calming sense of well-being. Fred could see that his friend was strongly attracted to the way the narcotic made him feel.

"Mike loved it—he just went *berserk*," Glazer recounted. "He probably never felt better in his whole life than he did that one night. I think that shot set him up for shooting dope later on."

The two friends stayed in New York for a week and then headed back to Chicago. They had completed another adventure, similar to their Colorado sojourn, and Mike had gotten a first look at the Big Apple's folk scene. Though he had probably struck out at Folkways, Bloomfield could see that New York was the place a musician had to be if he was serious about making it in the music business. And his bohemian host in the East Village had introduced him to an entirely new sensation, one that he would pursue in one form or another for the rest of his life. After Avenue B, Michael would no longer be completely satisfied with marijuana, cough syrup, and shake-'em-ups.

Back in Chicago, things were happening.

Bob Koester was busy recording new music for Delmark. He had released five traditional-style blues records on the label and was planning a sixth featuring Tennessee-born mandolinist Yank Rachell. His occasional Blind Pig concerts had turned into a regular series of "blues nights" at a basement juice bar at 1137 North State Street on the outskirts of Old Town called the Fickle Pickle. He planned to use the shows to promote the artists he issued on Delmark. Big Joe Williams was his featured performer, but he also showcased the blues of Sleepy John Estes, Hammie Nixon, Sunnyland Slim, Washboard Sam, and others. Mike Bloomfield was frequently in the audience and often sat in, especially when Big Joe was onstage.

Because Koester couldn't afford to hire a studio to record Yank Rachell, he let it be known that he was looking for a space to hold the session. Bloomfield volunteered his place, and on March 6 Bob brought Rachell, harmonica player Hammie Nixon, and guitarist Sleepy John Estes to Michael and Susan's Lakeside Avenue apartment. Also there was a friend of Mike's, a photographer named Peter Amft. The son of famed Chicago painter Robert Amft, twenty-one-year-old Peter had just started taking pictures professionally and was looking for work. He began snapping photos as Bob set up the mics and the musicians tuned up. The session proceeded quickly, and in no time Koester recorded half the material he needed for the album.

"Bloomfield soon had to look for a new apartment," Bob later claimed, "because Hammie's foot-stomping dislodged some plaster on the ceiling of the apartment below."

Three weeks later, Yank Rachell's second recording date took place. This time it was in the home of an engineer friend of Bob Koester's. "John, Hammie, and Yank were supposed to meet me at the Jazz Record Mart," Koester said. "Big Joe wanted to come along to the record taping to hear the guys play." Bob and Joe waited for Rachell and his group, but when they didn't appear, Koester left a note in the door with the session's address, and he and Williams went on ahead. At the engineer's place, they met up with Mike Bloomfield, who had come by to help out.

Fearing that the three missing musicians wouldn't arrive in time and not wanting to waste the opportunity to do some taping, Koester decided to record Big Joe with Michael playing second guitar. As soon as they had everything set up, Yank and his accompanists were at the door and ready to play. Bob decided to make the group a quintet, and the expanded band played music that Koester felt was some of the best he had ever recorded.

The serendipitous session with Yank Rachell was also a watershed event for Michael Bloomfield. It marked a debut of sorts: the nineteen-year-old had made his first real record. It wasn't a featured spot, and he appeared only on a portion of the album, but it was for a legitimate label and it was with some of the legends of classic American blues.

Yet because things were happening so fast in the spring of 1963, Michael hardly noticed the achievement.

Bob Koester continued with his Tuesday night blues shows at the Fickle Pickle throughout April and May. The weekly concerts regularly featured Big Joe and other traditional bluesmen. But Koester wasn't very happy with the proceeds from the performances. He couldn't seem to draw much of an audience, and he frequently had to pay the musicians out of his own pocket. Mike Bloomfield volunteered to help with promotion, but even with his efforts, attendance failed to increase.

The Fickle Pickle was a basement venue that billed itself as Chicago's "only non-alcoholic nightclub." It had opened in 1961 and could seat forty to fifty patrons at candle-topped tables covered by standard red-and-white tablecloths, with standing room for nearly as many more. The club was owned by Larry Fleischman, a Cary Grant look-alike who also operated Larry's Bar, one of the Rush Street neighborhood's most successful watering holes. Larry's was on the ground floor at 1137 North State, right above the Fickle Pickle. On weekends, the bar crowd would have a few drinks at Larry's and then head downstairs to catch whoever was onstage at the Pickle. The weekend performers were usually folksingers and comedians, and the comics would serve as emcees for the shows. The Pickle almost always drew a big crowd on Fridays and Saturdays.

But the Tuesday night shows were another story. Audiences frequently consisted of only a few dozen dedicated blues fans. While he usually made enough to break even, Bob Koester didn't have time to waste on a project that wasn't going to help him pay the bills. Even Pete Welding's glowing review of a Sleepy John Estes appearance in the May 5 edition of *Down Beat* magazine failed to improve business. By mid-month, Koester was thinking of tossing in the towel on the weekly Fickle Pickle concerts.

Producing the club's sellout weekend folk shows was an ambitious twenty-year-old music promoter and manager named Joel Harlib. Harlib had gotten involved in Old Town's folk scene while attending Roosevelt College and after graduating had begun organizing the Fickle Pickle's Friday and Saturday performances. He often showcased talent he was managing, and one weekend the club's owner told him someone new was going to be producing the Tuesday night shows.

"Larry Fleischman told me this guy, a guitar player, was going to take over the blues sessions," recalled Harlib. "He said his name was Michael Bloomfield."

Bob Koester's frustration with the poor attendance for his Fickle Pickle shows had reached a tipping point by early May. But Michael Bloomfield didn't want the series to be canceled. He asked Koester if he could take over the performances, and Bob was more than willing to have the exuberant teenager assume his duties. Michael then got the OK from owner Larry Fleischman to continue the series despite its poor turnout by promising he would significantly improve business. He was confident of success because he wouldn't be managing the shows all by himself. A college student he had met through Koester was going to be his partner. His name was George Mitchell.

Mitchell was a nineteen-year-old fan of traditional blues who was in his freshman year at Emory College in Atlanta. He had become interested in documenting the older players he had heard while growing up in the city. George knew the Big Joe Williams recordings Bob Koester had issued on Delmark, and he had written to Koester about possibly coming to work for the label so he could learn about record production. His letter got him an interview with Bob that December and, after Koester offered him a job, George made the move to the Windy City at the end of April.

"I had fantasies of being a big A&R man," said Mitchell, laughing. "But when I got there, Koester had me working behind the counter and making up crates for shipping these 78s he sold by auction. So I was hoping to be able to do something else."

When George encountered Mike Bloomfield, that something else became the Tuesday night shows at the Fickle Pickle.

"My very first day on the job, Bloomfield came into the Jazz Record Mart, and we got to talkin'," Mitchell said. "We decided we'd take over the Fickle job. We agreed two things needed to be done—finding and booking the people to play and then promoting the shows."

George was impressed not only by his new partner's knowledge of the blues but also by the way he could replicate the styles of classic bluesmen on guitar.

"He invited me up to his family's house in Glencoe soon after we first met," recalled Mitchell. "He picked up a guitar and played just like Blind Lemon Jefferson. 'Now let's hear Charlie Patton,' I said, and he did Patton note-for-note. Mike could actually play like *anybody* I could mention—it was unbelievable. I've never, ever heard anybody who could do that. I was astounded!"

George also enjoyed Michael's ebullient personality. He found the guitarist's quick wit and broad sense of humor very entertaining, and the two blues enthusiasts soon became good friends. Over dinner at the Lakeside Avenue apartment, he and Michael decided they would take a different approach to programming the Tuesday night blues shows at the Fickle Pickle. Instead of importing blues talent as Koester had done, they would locate traditional players who lived right there in Chicago and save on travel expenses. Bob had brought performers like Sleepy John Estes and Hammie Nixon all the way from Memphis, and Yank Rachell from Indianapolis, primarily because he wanted to record them. But to present them at the Pickle, he had to find them a place to stay and make sure they were looked after while they were in town. Mike and George wouldn't incur those costs because all their performers would be local. And the prospect of locating long-forgotten but legendary talent living right there in Chicago was an exciting one.

"I was really into discovering blues singers who had been famous in the past—and I mean *famous*. Like guys who were the James Browns of their days," said Bloomfield.

> There was a guy named Washboard Sam who was a big star on Bluebird in his time—he wrote "I'm Gonna Move to the Outskirts of Town" and "Momma Don't Allow No Guitar Playing in Here"—and a guy named Tampa Red, a guy named Tommy McClennan. In black music in the '30s and '40s, these guys were the Sly Stones of their time.

Mike and George scoured the South Side looking for traditional artists to feature at the club. They often enlisted Big Joe's help because the itinerant blues singer seemed to know nearly everybody and where they lived. Through Joe, Mike and George found a number of legendary blues singers right there in the Windy City. Among them were Jazz Gillum and Kokomo Arnold.

"Kokomo's big hit was 'Old Original Kokomo Blues,' about that bright-light city, that seven-light city, sweet old Kokomo. He said the last people that had come to see him were some jazz magazine people from Belgium in the early '50s," Mike later recalled. "I was the first person who had come to see him about his music in years and years." The elderly slide guitarist's singing style had strongly influenced the great Robert Johnson, and the Delta legend had taken some of Arnold's tunes for his own. But even though two young white men had sought him out and were eager to have him perform for a growing audience of folk blues enthusiasts, Arnold wasn't interested. Even the gift of a guitar from Bloomfield wouldn't change his mind. Kokomo was interested only in playing music for his grandkids.

It was different with other traditional players the producers contacted. In the weeks following their takeover of the club's blues night, Bloomfield and Mitchell presented pianists Little Brother Montgomery and Eddie Boyd, blues and gospel singer Blind James Brewer, street singer Arvella Gray, and harp players Billy Boy Arnold and Jazz Gillum. Bloomfield was especially taken with the older musicians. He helped them with money and occasionally brought them home to Susan for a meal. He also never missed a chance to learn whatever he could from them.

As a result, Michael's ever-growing repertoire of traditional blues styles and techniques benefited greatly from his and George's blues discoveries. And over the course of their forays into the South Side and beyond, Bloomfield developed a close friendship with Big Joe Williams. The elderly bluesman became something of a father figure for Michael.

* * *

With Joe's help, the Tuesday night shows at the Fickle Pickle continued unabated. But the first weeks were tough going. Audiences continued to be small, and organizing the shows and performers turned out to require considerable work. The Pickle opened at 7:00 p.m., with the first show scheduled to start at 8:00. There were five shows every Tuesday, the last going on at 1:30 Wednesday morning. To complicate matters, the young men had decided to present two different sets of artists each night, and making sure performers were all present was often a logistical juggling act. They paid the musicians a flat fee and a percentage of the door, and they also had to pay the waitress, all from whatever they were able to make from the cover charge. The proceeds from the modest dollar admission didn't amount to much if they were unable to fill the room. George's day job at the Jazz Record Mart paid him a meager forty dollars a week, and he sometimes used as much as half of it to meet the shows' expenses. Michael himself had no steady income beyond whatever he could make from an occasional gig, and Susan often contributed his share from her salary.

But Mike Bloomfield was determined to make the Fickle Pickle blues nights a success. He had done some promotion work for Bob Koester, but these were now his shows that were on the line. With the business acumen that was his heritage, Michael set to work getting the word out about the legendary players of authentic rural blues who he was presenting every Tuesday night in the heart of Chicago's entertainment district. One of his first stops was the newsroom of the *Chicago Daily News*, where he braced columnist Mike Royko. The newsman was at the time the city's leading political columnist, but he also wrote a weekly music column that followed Chicago's folk scene, and Bloomfield got him to do a piece on the Pickle's blues series. He then talked club owner Fleischman into doing weekly advertisements in the *News* and other papers promoting the shows at the Fickle Pickle. In a few short weeks, attendance on Tuesday nights began to improve.

And Michael wasn't only hyping the shows in the press and with posters. He was often an active participant in them. When pianist Roosevelt Sykes and singer St. Louis Jimmy Oden appeared at the Pickle, Bloomfield joined them onstage, backing them up with his Martin. Between sets, Michael also acted as emcee and, taking a cue from the comedians who hosted the Pickle's weekend folk shows, told stories and jokes in an effort to hold the crowd. It was his timing and quick wit that caught manager Joel Harlib's attention.

"He was bigger than life, a huge talent. I could see that right away," said Harlib. "He'd be up there telling jokes like Henny Youngman, and he was hilarious. Michael was just a *natural* showman." Harlib thought Bloomfield should become a performer himself, that he should develop an act using his music and humor. He and Mike quickly became friends, and Joel talked Bloomfield into joining his growing roster of artists. They signed a contract, and he became the guitarist's first manager.

But Bloomfield's primary focus in the early summer of 1963 was the Tuesday night shows at the Fickle Pickle. His own career was temporarily on hold. Keeping the series going and growing its audience came first. Michael even resorted to Maxwell Street tactics to help defray the shows' costs.

"One way Bloomfield came up with extra money for those first shows was by playin' in the street," said Mitchell. "I'd see him on a corner somewhere, with sunglasses and a cane and a can!" Mike feigned blindness while running through many of the blues and rags he knew, often playing in a variety of styles at wild tempos. If someone stopped to listen or tossed a coin, he would launch into a rap about how if they liked what he was playing, they could hear a lot more of it over at the Fickle Pickle. And they could hear it played by some of the great legends of American traditional music.

"He was so good, sometimes I'd drop a dime in the can too!" George said, chuckling.

In a few weeks, word spread about the shows and audiences began to fill the club. Many of the patrons were college students who were folk music fans, but many were aspiring young musicians eager to learn from the masters. Established blues players frequently came to the performances too, and many sat in with whoever was onstage.

The growing success of the Tuesday blues series even inspired Larry Fleischman. He asked if Michael and George would like to present blues on Mondays as well. The producers readily accepted the owner's offer and soon were running the Fickle Pickle two nights a week. They decided to present Big Joe Williams as a regular on Mondays, along with an opening act. Joe now had a steady gig, which had been Bob Koester's reason for starting the weekly blues nights at the Blind Pig some five months earlier. The bluesman was delighted to have the work and was particularly pleased to see his name featured prominently in the club's weekly newspaper ads.

With so many legendary performers appearing on the Pickle's stage, it seemed important to do something to document the music. George Mitchell had ambitions to become a record producer, and Michael had a friend who was an amateur audio engineer. Norman Dayron had been helping Pete Welding with recording sessions for Welding's nascent record label, and Norman had recently purchased some equipment of his own.

"I had an ancient Telefunken reel-to-reel recorder that I'd found in an Army-Navy store for about fifteen dollars," recalled Dayron. "I'd been tinkering with it, and I was really getting interested in making sound recordings."

The producers asked Norman to make recordings of the Monday and Tuesday night shows. To make the arrangement official, they signed a contract dividing ownership of the recordings equally, and on Monday, June 24, Norman set up his mics at the club to record Big Joe Williams and pianist Eddie Boyd in separate sets. It was the first of seven nights of blues performances over the summer months that Dayron would capture. The artists who performed for Mike and George over those weeks included Big Joe Williams, James Brewer, Billy Boy Arnold, Johnny Jones, Little Brother Montgomery, John Henry Barbee, Sunnyland Slim, J. B. Lenoir, Homesick James, Washboard Sam, Jazz Gillum, Jimmy Walker, Arvella Gray, Daddy Stovepipes, John Lee Granderson, and St. Louis Jimmy Oden.

One artist who appeared wasn't recorded by Dayron. He was a guitarist from Texas, an extraordinary player—and a striking figure visually. Michael told friends about the experience several days later, saying that he had really gotten cut—by an *albino*. That guitarist was nineteen-year-old Johnny Winter, in Chicago for several months while working a show lounge gig at the Scotch Mist, a "twist club" on North Wabash. Johnny had read about the blues shows at the Fickle Pickle, and Michael let him sit in during a set on a Monday night. Mike swapped solos with the white-haired guitarist, and Johnny matched him lick for lick.

It was the first time Michael had encountered another player his own age who was his equal, but any challenge to Bloomfield's unofficial crown as the city's hotshot guitar player was short-lived. The slender Texan left Chicago in October after only a few months in the Windy City, having found the town and its music scene too hard-edged for his liking.

But Johnny Winter wasn't the only talented contemporary Michael encountered during the spring and summer of 1963. Another was a young folksinger—a Midwesterner like himself, but from Minnesota—a poet with a guitar who would eventually change Michael Bloomfield's life.

In the spring of 1963, Mike Bloomfield heard about an unusual new club that was opening on Rush Street. His close friend Roy Ruby had gotten a job playing classical guitar between its various acts. Called the Bear, it was the creation of Howard Alk and John Brent, two members of a popular comedy troupe named Second City. They envisioned the club, situated in a dilapidated Victorian mansion on the corner of Ontario Street and Wabash Avenue, as a surreal cross between a painting by Magritte and an absurdist comedy by Alfred Jarry. Funding the new venue was a Chicago entrepreneur named Albert Grossman, owner of the Gate of Horn. Alk had met Grossman while working as a comedian at the prominent North Dearborn Street night spot, and he had convinced Albert to come in on the new club as a silent partner. Because Grossman not only presented performers at the Gate but also managed many of them, he saw the Bear as a second venue where he might showcase some of his talent—particularly those artists who were just starting out.

Roy, who was living in one of the empty rooms on the mansion's top floor, told Mike the place was going to be really bizarre and that its opening act would be the gospel singer Bessie Griffin. Also on the bill, he said, was a folksinger, a guy from New York with the pretentious-sounding name "Dylan." He was being managed by Albert Grossman, and Grossman had gotten him on the bill for the Bear's opening week.

Michael already knew about this folksinger. He had read about the twenty-two-year-old in *Sing Out!*, the unofficial magazine of the folk movement, and he had even purchased his debut recording. The New York folk scene was buzzing about Bob Dylan, but Bloomfield couldn't see what all the fuss was about.

"His first album had come out, and I bought it and I thought it was just *garbage*!" Bloomfield recalled. When the Bear opened the third week of April, Michael decided he would visit the club and teach Bob Dylan a lesson, Chicago style. "I went down there to cut him, just like I had been doing in black clubs, you know?" said Michael. "Just saying, 'Listen, man, you think you can play and sing? You *fart*, sit down! I'm gonna show you what playing's all about.'"

Mike and Susan visited the Bear one afternoon and found the folksinger at a table in one of the dining rooms. Bloomfield had his Martin with him, and he was out to humiliate the fellow. But it took only a few minutes for Dylan to completely disarm the guitarist from Chicago.

"When I got there, I couldn't believe it," said Mike of his encounter with Dylan. "His personality. He was so nice. I went there with my wife, and we just talked. He was the coolest, nicest cat." Bloomfield had gone to the Bear ready to cut a rising star in the folk world and instead found himself enchanted. He and Bob talked enthusiastically about music and musicians, about styles and recordings. Michael found he had a lot in common with the young singer from Minnesota. They talked about Sleepy John Estes and Elvis's first records and rock 'n' roll. "Here was this genius cat," Bloomfield said. "He was a nervous, crazy guy[,] but he was so nice it was just staggering."

Michael and Susan spent the afternoon with Dylan and then stayed to see his set. Dylan's performance also made a deep impression. The Chicagoan was so taken with the folksinger that he returned to the Bear the next night to see Dylan's show again. This time he brought Fred Glazer and his photographer friend, Peter Amft, along. Amft joined Mike and Bob after the show, when they went back to Dylan's room in the Mark Twain Hotel at Clark and Division Streets.

"We stayed up all night, playing and singing every damn song they ever heard of!" said Amft. "They seemed to get along just great, because Michael had a great memory and knew every song in the world. And so did Dylan. I remember being totally bored sitting in that little room with them, singing all these songs that they knew. Everly Brothers songs all the way down to practically, like, campfire songs!"

Dylan went back to New York at the end of the weekend, but the two musicians promised to keep in touch. Bob said they should get together when Michael was next in the city. The folksinger, too, had been impressed—with Michael's playing and with his knowledge of music and enthusiasm for it. He would remember Mike Bloomfield.

George Mitchell was energized by the success of the shows at the Fickle Pickle. With his plans to become a producer of traditional blues records temporarily sidetracked, he decided he might concentrate on a less ambitious project, one he could easily do while working at the Jazz Record Mart and organizing the Pickle shows. He had brought a camera with him from Atlanta, and he began photographing and interviewing some of the musicians he and Mike were hiring. He thought he might use the material to produce a book. He had taken photos at the Fickle Pickle, at Maxwell Street, and on the South Side, but George was also interested in finding and photographing players outside of Chicago.

"Big Joe had said that Walter Davis and Henry Townsend were in St. Louis," Mitchell said. Pianist Davis and guitarist Townsend had recorded extensively for Bluebird in the 1930s, and Henry Townsend had worked with Tampa Red, Memphis Minnie, Bo Carter, and others—even recording with Big Joe in 1935. But both artists had fallen into obscurity as musical tastes changed, and George was excited that Joe Williams knew where to find them. He was eager to meet them and get a few pictures.

Joe had already helped George and Michael locate older bluesmen in Chicago for the Fickle Pickle shows, and he was glad to lead the two young producers on an expedition out of town in search of a few more. Williams had gone to St. Louis earlier in the year, acting as a talent scout for Pete Welding, and he saw the return trip as a chance to visit a few relatives and renew old acquaintances while helping out his young white friends.

Mitchell and Bloomfield decided they would travel with Joe to St. Louis the first week in July. On Monday night they featured Big Joe and Billy Boy Arnold with Johnny Jones at the club, and on Tuesday night James Brewer and his Maxwell Street gospel group were the headliners. On Wednesday, July 3, they set off on the six-hour ride to St. Louis. Because neither had a car, Michael talked a friend, a young guitar player named Mike Allen who was a regular patron of the Fickle Pickle blues nights, into chauffeuring them to Missouri.

Late that morning they loaded up Allen's car, stowing Michael's Martin and George's big reel-to-reel tape recorder in the trunk. Mitchell thought that if they succeeded in finding Walter Davis and Henry Townsend, he might be able to capture a few tunes on tape while snapping photos. Mike Allen drove them over to the Jazz Record Mart to get Big Joe, and they made room in the trunk for Joe's nine-string Silvertone and his small amp. By early afternoon all preparations had been completed, and George and Joe piled into the back seat while Mike Allen slid behind the wheel and Bloomfield rode shotgun. Allen steered the car west on Grand to Ogden Avenue and then out through the western suburbs. They took Route 66 all the way across Illinois, passing through Joliet, Bloomington, and Springfield. As they traversed the open prairie, the weather turned hot and muggy, but traffic was light, and cruising along with the windows open kept the travelers cool and comfortable. The junket began pleasantly enough.

But it would be a trip to remember.

"We all got in the car and we drove to St. Louis," Michael said of the experience.

> Joe talked about things thirty years [before] as if they were yesterday. He reminisced about Robert Johnson and about Willie McTell, and he reminisced about Blind Boy Fuller. He talked about this singer and that singer as if they had been in his house the other day. . . . It was a wonderful trip. Being with him was like being with a history of the blues.

But there was another side to Big Joe Williams. When sober he could be a paragon of Southern gentility. After a few drinks, though, the blues legend would become someone altogether different. Both Michael and George knew from experience that Big Joe and alcohol didn't mix well. They had seen him become combative and incoherent after a night of boozing more than once. He had even gotten physical with Bob Koester at the Jazz Record Mart on a few memorable occasions.

"Joe was the type of guy that could not drink," Mike said. "When he drank he became really disturbed, *mentally* disturbed—it brought out the Mr. Hyde in him."

The young travelers didn't want to be at the mercy of an intoxicated, befuddled old man while driving around a strange city, so they made a deal with Big

Joe before leaving Chicago: they would make the trip only on the condition that he did not drink. Joe agreed, and he was true to his word—at first.

"Big Joe didn't drink a thing all the way down to St. Louis," Mitchell said. "He kept to the agreement, and we had a great ride." As long as Joe stayed clearheaded, he regaled his young friends with stories of his days on the road and gave succinct directions to Mike Allen behind the wheel. He seemed to know exactly where they were going.

Big Joe got them to East St. Louis by nightfall. He directed them through the city streets, giving Mike Allen concise instructions from the back seat in his thick Mississippi accent. Joe took them deep into the city's sprawling black ghetto, and after a while he had them pull the car up in front of a dilapidated tenement building on a trash-strewn side street. Though the sun had long since set, the temperature was still in the mid-eighties and the air was close and thick with humidity. Heat lightning occasionally illuminated the arc of the western sky. Big Joe announced that they would visit with relatives for a while.

"Chicago has such funky tenements, but I didn't know what funky was until I got to East St. Louis!" Bloomfield recalled of their accommodations that night. "There was just no words for this!"

The travelers collected their things from the car and followed Big Joe up the steps and into the building. Over his shoulder Joe announced that his cousin lived several floors up. She had an apartment with her husband and their family—their *big* family.

"When we got to her place, it was late at night and there were hundreds of little kids sleeping on every surface. There were little kids on the couch and on the floor!" said Michael. "The woman woke up and she rubbed the sleep out of her eyes, and we could see it was too crowded for us to stay there. So Joe sat down in the kitchen and said, 'You know, this boy, Michael, he plays the guitar and I play the guitar, and we'll visit a while.'"

As hot as it was out on the street, it was far hotter in the kitchen of the walk-up apartment. The lingering smell of the day's cooking along with the rank odor of ancient plumbing and the sweat of warm bodies made the room into a fetid steam bath.

"My God, it was *hot*!" said George. A Georgia native, Mitchell knew about heat.

Big Joe, sweat glistening on his forehead, bent down and snapped the clasps on his suitcase. From it he produced three bottles—a fifth of vodka, a pint of peppermint schnapps, and a quart of bourbon. He pushed a chair up to the kitchen table, sat down and placed the bottles in front of him. Bloomfield and Mitchell exchanged worried looks.

"On the way down, Joe must have bought himself a shitload of booze," George remembered. "Somebody brought out a case of beer, and Joe proceeded to make up for his sobriety earlier in the day by getting royally drunk."

"I knew that if we let Joe get drunk that he'd just go completely crazy," said Michael. "He'd be berserk for the entire weekend. His brains would fly right out the window, and we'd have this lunatic-crazy man with us the whole time."

The next twenty-four hours would amount to an adventure like nothing Michael Bloomfield had ever experienced. His sojourns in Boulder and New York City had been memorable, but they couldn't compare. From those few days spent in St. Louis with Big Joe Williams, Bloomfield would weave an epic narrative, a comic tale he would tell and retell in broad and unsparingly candid terms. Friends would come to know parts of it by heart, and interviewers would nearly always get a variation for their readers to marvel over. In time the story would become larger than life, an entertaining saga that spoke to the larger truths of profoundly American issues like race, class, and poverty. It would also speak honestly of relationships, of passions of the human heart—and of one man's love and appreciation for another man despite their great cultural and generational differences.

Michael eventually recorded the narrative and had it transcribed and edited into a short book. By that time the story had become a burnished, cohesive series of vignettes. But in Michael's original telling, the two days in St. Louis were rendered with the immediacy of a stand-up monologue. The rhythm of his language had its own energy, and his satiric descriptions evoked a modern-day, albeit profane, Mark Twain. The veracity of the entire tale remains uncertain. Accounts vary, and many of those variations come from Mike himself, but a story is for the telling. What is true is that on the evening of July 3, Big Joe Williams began to drink.

"Joe said, 'Well, why don't you go ahead and have a drink?'" recalled Bloomfield. "I said, 'Well, I believe I will.' I figured if the guy was going to get drunk and crazy, I was going to get drunk and crazy right along with him."

The elderly bluesman, his three companions, and his cousin, her husband, and a few kids all were crowded into the sweltering kitchen. Joe poured drinks all around, and then he and Michael took out their guitars and began to play. Mike was normally a non-drinker, preferring pot to alcohol, and he soon felt the effects of the booze. George and Mike Allen were less susceptible, but they, too, were soon pleasantly high, the heat making them more than a little groggy. Only Joe showed no signs of slowing down. The more he sang and played, the thirstier he got. The bottles steadily grew lower, and empty beer cans piled up on the table and in the kitchen sink. Before long the family went back to their respective beds, and George and Mike Allen were nodding in their seats at the table. Big Joe was finishing off the peppermint schnapps and starting up another tune when Michael suddenly jumped up and left the room. Moments later the sound of retching could be heard.

"Man, I got sick. I puked all over his cousin's house," Michael said. The drunken nineteen-year-old guitarist stumbled out of the apartment, down the stairs, and out into the hot night, seeking some air. He wandered into the alley next to the tenement and was violently sick again. "I was out in the alley, I was rolling in puke. I was sick, sick, sick!"

Mitchell found Bloomfield passed out in the alley and helped him back up the stairs and into the apartment. Mike Allen had gone to sleep on the sofa, and George and Michael squeezed into an available bed in a back room. They could hear Big Joe singing quietly to himself in the kitchen.

"Mike and I crashed in a big bed with five or six kids in it," said George. The two producers slept fitfully in the crowded bed for three or four hours before they were roused by Big Joe. In his drunken state, the bluesman's speech was so slurred and incoherent that even George had trouble understanding him. But after a few minutes of repeated grunts and gestures, it became clear that Joe wanted them to take him to another relative's place. He said there'd be more room there for sleeping.

The bleary-eyed travelers gathered up their things and loaded them into the car. Bloomfield, still feeling the effects of the alcohol, barely woke long enough to stumble down the stairs and out onto the street. Mike Allen did his best to follow Joe's mumbled directions, and before long they found themselves at the home of another Williams relative. It was still uncomfortably hot.

"Mike and I found an unused bedroom and went to sleep. Mike Allen went to sleep in another room," said Mitchell. Big Joe sat up talking with his relatives—and finishing off whatever was left in his bottles. The dawn—and the start of the Chicagoans' first full day in St. Louis—was just a few short hours away.

The Fourth of July promised to be another hazy day, and hotter still. By 10:00 a.m. the temperature had hit the mid-nineties and the city was already baking under a relentless, blood-colored sun. Mike Bloomfield opened his eyes to find himself alone, his head throbbing.

"I woke up in some bed. And how I woke up was, I felt this hot stuff sputtering on my chest," he said as he told the tale. "I opened my eyes, and Joe was standing there. And he was more than drunk. He was on a bender. He hadn't stopped drinking since we had started drinking that evening.

"It was like looking into the eyes of the devil himself. His eyes were small and they were red and running at the sides, and his nostrils were all flared out," said Michael. Joe had something to tell Mike, something he thought his young friend would be pleased to hear.

"He was holding a barbecue fork, and on it was a pig nose, and it was dripping hot grease on my chest," Michael said, grimacing. "He was breathing that schnapps breath in my face and he was saying, 'Snoots, snoots, we got snoots. I promised you barbecue, we got snoots!'"

Bloomfield took one look at the porcine proboscis and felt his gorge rise. He jumped out of bed and stumbled into the bathroom, retching up whatever was left in his stomach. He realized that for the first time in his life, he was seriously hungover, and he wanted no part of a breakfast of barbecued "snoots." What he wanted was something to settle his stomach and maybe ease his colossal headache. He went looking for George.

"It was so hot, Bloomfield and I decided to find somewhere where it was air-conditioned and we could get out of the heat and get a Coke," said Mitchell. Mike Allen was still sleeping, so George took his keys from the kitchen table, and he and Michael climbed into the car and drove a few blocks over to a pharmacy that had a soda fountain.

"Me and Mitchell went out and found us a drugstore and had some Coca-Cola and bicarbonate," said Michael. "My stomach settled down a little bit, but it never did get any better."

They had been gone less than half an hour, but when Mitchell and Bloomfield returned, they found Big Joe standing on the stoop in front of his relative's building. He was enraged.

"When we got back, Big Joe was furious at us," said Mitchell. "He shouted, 'What you doin' *stealin'* a car?' Somehow he'd got it in his head we'd stolen Mike Allen's car. Then he pulled out a knife and stuck it right in my stomach. I could feel the blade through my shirt and if he'd have moved at all he would have stabbed me!"

George quickly reassured Joe that they had just borrowed the car to go looking for some relief from the heat. Mike Allen was their friend, George pointed out, and he didn't mind if they used his car. The inebriated bluesman eventually pocketed his knife, but he was still angry. They shouldn't go taking another man's car, he admonished the two friends, still unwilling to believe the trip was completely innocent.

The rest of the day proved equally as difficult.

Joe spent the morning out on the stoop, picking his guitar and shouting at passersby.

"Joe was just crazy," said Michael.

> He sat there on the porch, he would strum the guitar for a few minutes and if some young woman passed on the street he'd call her. He'd say, "Sweet mama, say, sweet mama—come over here!" And she'd look back and see a man about seventy years old, weighing three hundred pounds, yelling at her, and this just didn't make any sense to her and she'd just keep on passing.

Finally, an older woman in the building came down and scolded Joe for his lewd behavior.

"She said, 'You can't act this way here. What do you think this is, a whorehouse or something?'" Bloomfield recalled. She told Big Joe she thought it was best for him to move on. Joe's traveling companions agreed. Michael and George were eager to find Henry Townsend and Walter Davis.

"It was hot as hell, and we just got in the car and drove all over St. Louis," recalled Mitchell. Joe made a phone call to Townsend from a phone booth in East St. Louis and told his companions he was taking them over to St. Louis to see the blues legend. They crossed the Mississippi River into Missouri and began making their way through the city's neighborhoods. But after what seemed like hours of aimlessly riding around, it became clear that Big Joe had no intention of finding Henry Townsend or Walter Davis.

"I said, 'Joe, where are we going? Why aren't you taking us to Henry Townsend's house?' and Joe turned around, grabbed my arm over the back of the seat, and said, 'Listen, Mitch, you say *one* more word, I'm gonna knock your teeth down your throat!'" George Mitchell remembered. "After that, I just kept quiet and went along for the ride."

As the car crawled up and down the city's streets, the temperature felt like it had topped one hundred degrees. The sun was high overhead, and heat radiated off the asphalt and surrounding buildings, turning the car's interior into an oven. Everyone was sweat soaked, short-tempered, and miserable. But Big Joe still refused give specific instructions on how to get to their destination.

Suddenly the old bluesman perked up. "Well, now we're gonna *really* find the best blues singer of all," Joe announced. He directed Mike Allen down a few more side streets and out toward the city limits. In the backseat, George and Michael exchanged looks—both were beginning to have serious doubts about the trip.

"He was really like putting us on in a lotta ways," said Michael. "He completely didn't know where they were—all he wanted to do was visit his kin. We drove all the way to St. Louis, man, and I was so furious—it was just a stone burn job!"

It was mid-afternoon when Big Joe told them to stop in front of a three-story frame house. The ramshackle building was even more decrepit than the apartment buildings in East St. Louis had been. Its front steps had rotted away, and the front door was completely inaccessible from the street. The travelers grabbed their things out of the trunk and went around back, looking for a way in. Michael was appalled by what he saw in the backyard.

"It looked like they had been pouring their garbage out back there for fifty years," he said. "There were old mattresses with the springs all sprung out and they were all moldered, and there were pieces of cars that were all rusted and reddened from years and years back, and just about every kind of garbage and filth imaginable!"

Big Joe led them up the steps of the back porch to the third floor and banged on the screen door. Michael was behind him with Joe's heavy amplifier and guitar, followed by George, hefting his bulky tape recorder. Bringing up the rear was Mike Allen, loaded down with suitcases. All three were drenched in sweat. The stench from the festering garbage in the yard below was overpowering.

A middle-aged woman let them in, and the three white men stashed their loads in the kitchen. Joe greeted the house's occupants and introduced his friends. The woman was another of Big Joe's cousins, and the "best blues singer of all" lived with her.

"This famous blues singer of his showed up and he was a crazy old fiddle player named Jimmy," Bloomfield said, laughing. "Jimmy" was Jimmy Brown, a blues fiddler and singer originally from Mississippi. Mike wasn't impressed—Brown also appeared to be drunk, and when he brought out his violin, it had only two of its four strings. But Joe directed George to set up the tape recorder and microphones and had Michael plug in his amplifier. He and Brown were going to record a few tunes, and he produced another bottle of schnapps for inspiration.

"We recorded Joe and the fiddle player," said Mitchell. "They did a few tunes together, and I thought they were pretty good." Mike, who by this time was thoroughly disgusted, thought otherwise.

"He just would saw off a few notes and sing something indecipherable, and Joe would rant and rave for a while, and Jimmy would sing some more indecipherable stuff," said Bloomfield. "I looked over at Mitchell and I said, 'George, this is about enough. I believe we gotta go back to Chicago right now. We gotta cut out.'"

But Big Joe was busy recording and not about to go anywhere. Michael was still feeling the effects of the previous night's drinking, and he asked Joe's cousin if he could use the bathroom. She took him into the front room, where Bloomfield was confronted by a sight that he would never forget.

"The first thing I see is this big old couch, and on the couch is sitting this girl," Michael recalled. "She was around twelve years old, she weighed around four hundred pounds." The obese girl was gnawing on spare-rib bones that she was dipping in a jar of sour-looking mayonnaise. Michael was speechless at the sight.

"I took one look at this thing and said, 'Oh my God almighty, what have I got myself into now?'" Bloomfield said. "I mean, it had been funky before, but this was freak city, daddy!"

The girl's mother led Bloomfield into a hallway and pointed to a closet door. Here was the family's toilet.

"Inside the apartment they didn't have bathrooms. All they had was a closet with a hole in the floor," said Mike. "The downstairs was evicted, so they shat in a hole in the closet!"

That was the final straw for the nineteen-year-old from suburban Glencoe. "Whatever radical chic pretensions I may have had then just flew out the window," Michael remembered with a grimace later. "It was *too* gross for me."

Back in the kitchen, Bloomfield pulled his two friends aside. He told them he didn't care if they hadn't found Henry Townsend or Walter Davis—it was definitely time to go home. Both George and Mike Allen agreed, and Michael went into the kitchen to confront Big Joe.

"I said, 'Joe, pack up. We're going back to Chicago because I can't stand this no more,'" Mike said. "And he said, 'Yeah, you can't stand it, that's right.' And he led me to believe I was just some little white pussy that couldn't take it." But by that point Bloomfield didn't care what his friend and mentor thought of him. He was determined to get out of St. Louis and away from the heat and squalor.

In fact, the experiences of the previous twenty-four hours had taught Michael a lesson about himself. "The sad truth was that I had a bad case of culture shock," said Bloomfield.

> I thought that I could just hang out with these black people and live in their scene and be comfortable, but there was just no way I could do it. I mean, I was a displaced person. I was a stranger in a strange land. I was a young white boy in a place where I shouldn't be. And I felt ashamed of that fact.

Big Joe Williams was just as determined to stay. He was having a fine time scouting for talent and visiting with his kinfolk. If his white friends weren't happy, they could just go back to Chicago for all he cared. "Well, you can just leave me here," Bloomfield remembered him saying.

George and Michael packed up the gear and hauled it down to the car. As Mike Allen was loading the trunk, Big Joe came staggering down the steps.

"No, I don't want you to leave me here," he said to his young friends. "I want you to carry me over to East St. Louis and leave me at someone else's house."

The sun, a ruddy eye in a merciless sky, was beginning to dip toward the western horizon as the car crossed back over the Mississippi into Illinois. The heat was unrelenting, and the passengers were all in a sour mood. Between pulls on his schnapps bottle, Big Joe began to argue with Bloomfield in the back seat. Why didn't they all stay for the weekend as they had planned? He, Big Joe, was in charge of the trip, and he should be the one to say when they would leave. Who were they to tell him where to go? This was *his* city, and *he* was in charge. The elderly bluesman was working himself into an indignant rage.

"He got madder and madder, and he reached into his pocket and pulled out a little old tiny penknife," Bloomfield said. "He said, 'I'm gonna cut you!' I said, 'Oh my God, this guy's gonna cut me with this tiny penknife?' And then I started to giggle!"

That was too much for Big Joe. With a quick jab, he pricked Michael's hand. Bloomfield was momentarily stunned, and then furious as blood appeared on his palm. He struck back at Joe.

"I kicked him as hard as I could in the side of his stomach, and he punched me in the leg," said Mike. "And then we looked at each other and, uh, we both felt real bad. Like *real* bad. It was like hitting my father or something. And he felt real bad for getting drunk and hurting me."

The occupants were mostly silent for the rest of the ride into East St. Louis. Joe occasionally issued directions to Mike Allen as George dozed in the front seat and Bloomfield nursed his hand while staring sullenly out the window. After fifteen minutes, Big Joe said gruffly, "Let me out here."

They were on a residential street in a neighborhood much nicer than the one they had visited the night before. Mike Allen pulled the car over, got out, and opened up the trunk. He hefted out Joe's guitar, amp, and valise and put them on the curb. From the sidewalk, the bluesman leaned in the passenger's side window and asked Mitchell for the tape they made earlier that afternoon. George gave it to him, and Big Joe picked up his things and began walking down the street. The sky was beginning to color red and purple with the sunset.

After he had gone a few steps, Big Joe suddenly turned around and came back to the car. He handed the tape back through the window, saying he thought it would be better if George kept it. To the three friends, the disheveled, overburdened bluesman was a pathetic sight.

"We felt real bad. And we felt real guilty because he was an old man and he was a friend of ours, and we were letting him down," Bloomfield said. They asked Big Joe if he wouldn't reconsider and come back to Chicago with them.

"No, go on," the bluesman said quietly. "Go on back to Chicago. Go on, be with your people. You don't belong here." Bloomfield acknowledged the truth of that statement many years later: "He was right. We left, and beat our asses back to Chicago as fast as we could!"

Back in the Windy City, George Mitchell and Mike Bloomfield had another week of Fickle Pickle shows to organize. Before leaving Big Joe Williams in East St. Louis, George had asked him if he would do his regular Monday night set.

"I said, 'Big Joe, will we see you on Monday?' and he said no, he wasn't going to do the show," said Mitchell. "So I told him I'd wait until 5:00 p.m., but if he didn't come by then I'd have to hire someone else."

By Monday evening they still hadn't heard from Big Joe. As showtime approached, George called pianist Little Brother Montgomery and hired him to fill in. But just as Little Brother was getting ready to start his first set, down the stairs and into the club came Big Joe, guitar case in hand. When he learned that he had been replaced for the evening's series of performances, he became angry.

"He said, 'These people have come to see *me*, Mitch—they don't want to see somebody else. It's my name on the sign out front!'" George recalled. "And he was right; they did want to see Big Joe. So even though he said he wasn't going to play and he hadn't showed up by the time I said, Joe went on and did the show anyway—with Little Brother, and they were great!"

Michael was unsure how Big Joe would react after their two disastrous days in St. Louis. He felt bad for losing his temper and fighting with Joe, and especially for abandoning him on the road. He stayed away from the Pickle that Monday night.

"I was scared to see him," Mike said.

> I thought he would probably be mad at me and be pretty resentful of what went down. Or, if he wasn't mad at me, he'd probably lost all respect for me because I could talk a good game, but when it came right down to living it, I couldn't take it. And I just didn't want to confront that truth in myself or see that in his face.

But Michael knew he couldn't avoid the blues singer forever. Later in the week, he caught the L down to Grand Street and stopped in at the Jazz Record

Mart. He found Big Joe down in the basement, sitting on his bed. Joe looked up as the young guitarist walked in, and after a moment, he spoke.

"We had us a time in St. Louis, didn't we?" Joe said quietly. Michael could see by the bluesman's shy smile that there were no hard feelings. They were still friends.

"The look on his face was so hard to describe," Mike said, feeling relieved. "He almost looked like a little boy, abashed and sort of embarrassed. . . . It wasn't at all this gruff old blues singer, this scarred hobo veteran of so many highways.

"And I looked at him and said, 'That's right, we sure had us a time.'"

CHAPTER 5
OLD TOWN

CHICAGO, 1963–1964

Throughout the summer of 1963, Mike Bloomfield worked to promote and manage the Monday and Tuesday night blues shows at the Fickle Pickle. The rest of his week was spent reading, practicing, hanging out with friends, and maybe visiting the Jazz Record Mart or other record stores during the day, and making the rounds of the clubs in the evening. Susan kept house and paid the rent through her job at the Kemper company. Because of her work schedule, she often skipped club-hopping with her husband.

On a typical evening, Michael would meet up with Charlie Musselwhite after the Jazz Record Mart closed. Sometimes—if he was free—George Mitchell would come along. They might stop in Hyde Park to pick up Norman and anybody else who was around. Then they would go to Silvio's, Theresa's, the Copa Cabana, Pepper's, or any number of other blues venues. If Michael could get his mother's car, he would drive. Or Fred Glazer would pick them all up in his Pontiac. Even Michael's manager, Joel Harlib, would occasionally join the party and ferry them to the South Side in his white Oldsmobile Cutlass.

They would spend the night going from one club to another, and often Michael and Charlie would sit in. Musselwhite had started playing harmonica in 1957, and by 1963 he had developed a big sound reminiscent of Big Walter "Shakey" Horton's. Michael's own understanding of the blues had deepened considerably since he had first joined Guitar Junior onstage at the Place, and his speed and repertoire of licks made him an exciting—and novel—attraction at South Side venues. While the presence of white musicians in Chicago's black clubs wasn't unheard of in 1963, it was rare that black audiences encountered white players who were as good as many of their black counterparts. When Mike or Charlie took the stage, club patrons were often amazed at how well they could play. The fact that they were white made them all the more unusual.

"I could play as good as them—that was always the trip," Mike said of his reception in South Side blues clubs. "That was the trip in Chicago—you had to be *good* to make it. White was not enough. If you were good and white, then you were better than black because you were a 'freak.' The clubs could advertise you as a freak . . . you know, 'Come see our white soul brother!'"

That Michael had the approval and friendship of the great Muddy Waters also worked in his favor. At Pepper's, he and his friends would be given tables down front, where Bloomfield could easily access the stage in case the nod came from Muddy. He would play a few tunes with the band and then share drinks with the musicians between sets. More often than not, they would all step outside into the alley adjacent to the club and pass around a few joints. A truer measure of the social acceptance of Bloomfield and his friends by South Side musicians would be hard to find.

Michael didn't indulge in marijuana only during set breaks in Bronzeville. The drug also played an ever-increasing role in Bloomfield's daily routine. Organizing shows for the Fickle Pickle, hanging out with friends, and jamming in blues clubs frequently involved grass.

"Mike was always smoking pot," recalled George Mitchell. The Georgia college student had never seen marijuana before he met Michael, and he was a bit leery of it. "Bloomfield was always offering me some. I said, 'Mike, if I take one toke of that stuff I'll never quit!'"

Often a portion of Michael's day would be spent visiting friends and acquaintances in an effort to find someone with dope to share. Straight-laced Joel Harlib usually accompanied Bloomfield on these visits. He had become so enamored of his charismatic client that throughout the summer of 1963 he would routinely come by Michael's apartment in the late morning, wake the guitarist up, and spend the day chasing around the city with him. The manager and his client made an improbable pair—the diminutive Harlib with his horn-rimmed glasses and charcoal-colored Madison Avenue suits and lanky Michael in blue jeans with his long, bushy hair.

"I considered him my best friend. When I hung with Mike, every day was an adventure!" recalled Harlib with a laugh. "We were either smoking someone's grass, listening to music, or listening to Mike play guitar. Those were great times of fun and camaraderie!"

Michael's days were filled with camaraderie, to be sure, and packed with exciting musical experiences. His hyperactive nature kept him on the go, moving from one encounter to another, always learning and always eager for more. He seemed to be everywhere at once, resolutely chasing down the next new thing, the next sensation. Pot was one of those sensations, but it also offered a respite from relentless hyperactivity. Michael had grown to depend on it. When he and Joel visited Hyde Park, they would often light up at one of Tommy Walker's places. Walker ran a "reefer house" at Fifty-First Street and Woodlawn Avenue, one of several he had in the neighborhood.

"Mike and I would also visit him to have a smoke," commented Harlib. "Tommy Walker, the 'Old Fox'—a very hip, cool hustler."

Walker was another of Chicago's colorful characters. Michael had first met him when the guitarist was still in high school. The twenty-nine-year-old hipster was one of the first black residents of Old Town, maintaining a huge apartment on North Wells Street. Tommy dressed in elaborate handmade leather outfits and was rarely seen on the street without his pet Siamese cat riding on his shoulders. He was known unofficially as the "Mayor of Old Town," and his apartment was a hangout for artists, musicians, actors, writers, and anybody else who considered himself a part of hip culture. Walker owned a fancy leather shop in Old Town, where he sold the suede capes, vests, and clothing he created. He also supplemented his income by dealing drugs.

While grass couldn't come close to producing the high Bloomfield had experienced in New York when he and Fred Glazer were staying with Jim Cain, smoking it helped him get through the day. Its calming effect took the edge off his overactive mind and left him feeling relaxed and comfortable. It was also true that he really enjoyed being high.

On July 28, Mike Bloomfield turned twenty. He and Susan had been married for nearly a year, and a good portion of their time together was spent living in the dingy Lakeside Avenue apartment in Uptown. The couple had acquired a puppy, a cute Collie-mix mutt that Michael named Harry, and by summer the dog was nearly full grown. The addition of an active young canine made the already cramped apartment feel too small, so the couple began looking for another place to live.

In the summer of 1963, Michael's parents were also planning a move. After brother Allen's graduation from New Trier in the spring, the Bloomfields decided to return to Chicago. They had moved to Glencoe so their sons could get a better education, and now that both boys had finished school, there was no longer any reason to stay in the suburbs. Dottie wanted to be closer to her friends in the city, and a Chicago home would mean a shorter commute to the factory for Harold. They were looking for an apartment in one of the Gold Coast high-rises along Lake Shore Drive so they could also be near Harold's mother, Ida.

When she learned that Mike and Susie also desired to move, Dottie was very pleased. She had never liked the rough neighborhood where her son and daughter-in-law were living, and she urged Harold to help them find a place that would be safer and more suited to their needs. Mr. Bloomfield agreed and began making inquiries. Perhaps a new, more upscale address would inspire Michael to settle down and begin thinking more responsibly about his future.

Mike Bloomfield, of course, was thinking only about music. He had the weekly shows at the Fickle Pickle to promote and produce, and Joel Harlib was urging him to put together a show of his own, something the manager could offer to local clubs. The guitarist's life was entirely taken up with music, and he had little time for anything else. Then, in late August, things got even more complicated. George Mitchell told Michael that he was going back to school in the fall.

George's plan to become a record producer had stalled, and it now appeared that Bob Koester needed only a salesman and shipping clerk at the Jazz Record Mart. It had been fun producing the Fickle Pickle shows with Michael, but George couldn't see a future in that or in ringing up sales at the Mart. So he was heading back to Atlanta in September to finish his degree. Bloomfield was disappointed to see his southern partner and friend leave, but he vowed to keep the Pickle blues nights going. Without George's organizational skills, though, Mike knew it would be a challenge.

Taking on the Fickle Pickle's weekly schedule by himself meant that now Michael had to not only publicize the shows but hustle up all the performers. Big Joe was still the regular Monday night headliner, but Bloomfield had to find an opening act every week. He was soon struggling to fill the Tuesday night slots, too, and was thinking of bringing in Furry Lewis from Memphis despite the extra cost. The blues shows at the Fickle Pickle remained viable for the time being, but even with Michael's best efforts, they were clearly beginning to wind down.

Meanwhile, Joel Harlib was determined to get his talented client's name out as a performer. It was fine for Mike Bloomfield to be known around town as a hotshot guitar player, and it was alright if Michael wanted to sit in on the South Side at Pepper's or Theresa's. But those things did nothing for his career. Harlib knew that if Michael was going to have a career worth managing, the guitarist would have to work up an act and actually perform it somewhere.

"He was a real showman, but he never wanted to be a performer," said Harlib. "After hours at the Pickle, he would sit and play all night for us. All kinds of stuff—blues, country, Merle Travis, Doc Watson. He was fantastic and I could see he had huge potential. But he didn't want to be a professional—he was a total paradox in that way!"

The intense, fast-talking Harlib eventually cajoled Michael into doing a solo act. Joel explained that all Bloomfield had to do was re-create his after-hours sessions and pepper his tunes with a few amusing anecdotes—just the sort of thing he had been doing as emcee at the Fickle Pickle. Bloomfield remained reluctant, but Harlib booked the guitarist into a club in Old Town called Mother Blues. It was Michael's first real solo gig.

Located at 1305 North Wells Street, Mother Blues was run by a former suburban housewife and mother named Lorraine Blue. The club featured folk music, jazz, blues, and comedy on successive nights, and Bloomfield was known there as a musician who would drop by and hang out, occasionally sitting in with whoever was playing. Blue was more than glad to hire him to do a few weekends as a single. But it was the first time Mike would perform for an audience by himself and not as a member of a band. He was petrified, and Harlib had to persuade him to do the show each night.

"He didn't like being an entertainer—he really was shy about getting up onstage by himself," said Harlib. "Mike was so charismatic, and so dynamic, so burning with this kind of luminosity, so entertaining and so funny—that's why I thought he should be a performer. But I think he always considered himself to be an artist and a musician—and *not* a performer." Joel found Bloomfield to be a complete paradox.

> He was really reluctant about performing. He was *not* reluctant about playing, and he would play and put on great shows for me or a few other friends. But it was like pulling teeth to try to get him to go in front of an audience and do that. I think he was shy, but also he was this incredible egotist who really enjoyed attention and adulation and hero-worship. Whatever you could say about him, you know, you could also say the opposite about him.

Michael had the kind of brash confidence that would enable him to get up onstage with Muddy Waters or Howlin' Wolf. But that confidence could fail him when he had to carry a performance by himself. It was an aspect of his personality that would be an issue throughout his career.

In the fall of 1963, Michael and Susan began packing up their Uptown apartment, getting ready to move. Dottie Bloomfield called with the news that Harold had found them a place right in the heart of Old Town. Through his business connections, Mr. Bloomfield had managed to get them into an apartment in a newly opened development just a few blocks from Lake Shore Drive. The complex was called Carl Sandburg Village.

Named for Chicago's famous poet, Sandburg Village was built with city money as a moderate-income housing project, intended to stem the spread of urban blight on the city's Near North Side. Located between Clark and LaSalle streets, and bounded north and south by North Avenue and Division Street, the Village featured a combination of townhouses and high-rises, landscaped plazas, tennis courts, and two public swimming pools. It opened its first units to renters in December 1962 and by the following summer was attracting national attention as an example of successful urban renewal. Harold Bloomfield knew the developer, and he was able to arrange for Michael to rent one of the Village's apartments. Mike was pleased, because the choice location put him within walking distance of the Fickle Pickle, Rush Street, the Jazz Record Mart, and many of his other haunts.

The couple's new address also impressed their friends. They had apartment number 303 at 1360 North Sandburg Terrace—actually a segment of North Clark Street—in a four-story, brick row house–style building. Instead of climbing the stairs, visitors could ride up in one of the building's modern elevators. Windows on the east side of the apartment overlooked a landscaped commons, while on the west side they afforded a view of a private yard for use by residents. The place was a far cry from Mike and Susie's modest walk-up on Lakeside Avenue, and some friends wondered how they could afford it. One even speculated that Michael's wealthy father must have purchased the building.

Mr. Bloomfield, of course, was not his son's landlord. But he soon was Michael's neighbor. He and Dottie returned to the city that fall, renting a grand apartment on the thirty-fourth floor of a new thirty-six-story high-rise building at 1440 North Lake Shore Drive. They put the Glencoe house up for sale and traded suburban greenery for sweeping views of Lake Michigan and the Chicago skyline. Their building was only five blocks and a short walk away from Sandburg Village, and Mrs. Bloomfield could easily visit Michael and Susan whenever she wished. The young couple, in return, could come to brunch or dinner whenever the Bloomfields entertained. Harold helped them with the rent and hoped for the best.

As the fall progressed, Michael Bloomfield continued to gig in a multitude of settings. Along with his South Side blues jamming and UC twist party appearances, he did solo shows at Mother Blues—at the insistence of Joel Harlib—and played rock 'n' roll with his Highwood friends whenever they needed him.

But Bloomfield wasn't playing just blues, folk, and rock. His deep fascination with all varieties of American traditional music led him to join a bluegrass trio that a high school friend from Glencoe named Michael Melford had formed. Melford played mandolin while Michael backed him on guitar. The third member of the group was a banjo and piano player named Ira Kamin.

Bloomfield had met Ira at the Fret Shop in Hyde Park a few years earlier, when Kamin was still a student at Nicholas Senn High School in Chicago. A year younger than Bloomfield, Ira, too, was a fan of the blues, and he and Michael soon became friends. Together with Mike Melford, they played occasional sets at the Fickle Pickle on weekends when folk music was the fare, and Bloomfield did his best Doc Watson impression to the delight of the audience.

In addition to his gigging activities, Michael was usually busy at the start of each week, still working to fill the slots for the Monday and Tuesday blues shows at the Fickle Pickle. He would then host whatever shows he could arrange. But the departure of coproducer George Mitchell had dampened Michael's enthusiasm for the project, and often Big Joe Williams was the only artist to appear. Mitchell's return to Atlanta also put a serious dent in the blues nights' budget. Whenever the take at the door fell short of what was needed to cover expenses, Michael alone now had to make up the difference. Susan was happy to contribute, but her husband wanted to pull his own weight—at least when it came to his productions at the Pickle. Bloomfield was still determined to keep the shows going, so he decided to take a regular paying gig—with a show band.

Michael joined Robby and the Troubadours, a sextet from New York City. They had scored a minor hit in 1961 with a single called "The Lemon Twist," and that success brought them to Chicago for an extended engagement at the Playboy Club. But by 1963 the band had fallen on hard times, with drugs taking a heavy toll. They were working on Rush Street, playing at the Tony Paris Show Lounge and the Scotch Mist, but some of the original members had left and the Troubadours were in need of a lead guitarist. Barry Goldberg was their keyboardist, and he recommended Michael. The guitarist didn't really care for the band's music—and cared even less for their stage act, which involved dying their hair to match their suits—but he needed the steady money. It helped keep the Fickle Pickle shows going—at least for a little longer.

The fall and winter of 1963 were a happy time for Mike Bloomfield. He loved living in Sandburg Village, with its proximity to the Old Town and Rush Street neighborhoods, and he relished being an integral part of the burgeoning Chicago folk and blues scene. He was a familiar and welcome figure in South Side clubs, and his friendship with Muddy Waters complemented the gruff respect proffered him by Howlin' Wolf. He knew everybody and was known throughout the city as one of Chicago's most gifted guitarists, a "hotshot rock 'n' roll player" as he often described himself, and a formidable interpreter of a variety of acoustic folk and traditional music styles. Everything seemed to be going Mike Bloomfield's way.

Except for one thing.

Michael's innate restlessness, overactive mind, and relentless drive kept him continually animated. Friends simply described his personality as "nervous," but Harold Bloomfield had been troubled enough by his son's apparent mania to have him placed under psychiatric observation. Now, as he entered his twenty-first year, those periods of agitation were becoming more pronounced, and Michael was finding it harder and harder to slow down. It was bad enough that he was finding it difficult to sleep.

Never a morning person, Bloomfield's habit was to stay up late reading, practicing, or listening to music, often long after Susan had gone to bed. His clubbing frequently kept him out until the early morning hours, and when he got back to the apartment, he was often too agitated to turn in. Instead, he would read or pace around the living room, quietly picking blues and rags on his Martin until dawn.

This was nothing new. Even from his earliest days, Michael seemed to need little sleep. With his transistor radio, he had spent many a night awake under the covers, listening to the latest sounds from Memphis or Nashville. As he got older, he sometimes snuck out after bedtime to join Fred Glazer or Roy Ruby in a South Side escapade and then would be ready for school the following morning. But when he needed to sleep, Michael always could.

Now, he was having trouble closing his eyes.

"Michael was never an insomniac when he was a child," his mother confirmed. She knew her son was a night owl, but any sleep problems came along later—the result, she asserted, of the pressures of leading a band and the stress of constant performing. Insomnia, though, did run in the Bloomfield family—Michael's grandmother Ida suffered from it. When he stayed at her apartment, Mike often sat up late into the night with his wakeful grandmother, despite the fact that her bedside table was covered with dozens of bottles of prescription sleep medication.

Susan thought such medications might have been the cause of her husband's sleeplessness. "It's always been my theory that Michael didn't get insomnia until he discovered sleeping pills," she said. Sleeping pills came into his life, she recalled, when they were living in Sandburg Village and Bloomfield came down with chicken pox. He itched so terribly, the doctor gave him a prescription so he could sleep. The pills were so effective that in later years, when he needed to rest, Michael would reach for a bottle. As a result, his natural sleep cycle was thrown off, and he found it harder and harder to get to sleep without medication. "I always felt that was the beginning," said Susan. "But he did have insomnia, and it really ruled his life later on."

For the present, Bloomfield's sleeplessness was manageable. But there were times when it felt like he had been awake for days.

In November, Joel Harlib came to his favorite client with a request. He had been managing Michael Bloomfield for nearly six months, but in all that time he had secured only a few gigs at Mother Blues for the guitarist. Someone with Bloomfield's talent needed to be heard, and Joel said it was time for the guitarist to make a record. To make that happen, the manager needed a sample reel.

"We decided we had to do a serious demo," said Harlib. "I asked Mike to put together some of the things he liked to do—blues, ragtime, and folk numbers—you know, show his range. Then we would make a really good-quality recording of them."

Harlib planned to take the tape to New York City himself and shop it around. With his glib manner and buttoned-down appearance, the manager was certain he would have more success than Michael did when he visited Folkways the year before. Norman Dayron was the natural choice to engineer the session, and he readily agreed to set up mics and monitor levels. Norman suggested they do it in his Hyde Park apartment.

Michael was confident that this time he would succeed in connecting with a record company, and for good reason. One Friday evening in December, he had gone with Charlie Musselwhite and Paul Butterfield to see Otis Rush at Pepper's, and Paul had told him about a producer he had met. Butterfield had just returned from a trip to San Francisco, where he had been visiting Nick Gravenites, and while he was there they played a few sets at a local coffeehouse named the Cabal. Paul said the producer, who approached them during a break and introduced himself as Paul Rothchild, was excited about the emerging white blues scene and was looking for talent. He wanted Butterfield to come to New York and make a few "harmonica singles" for Elektra, the label Rothchild was representing. Butterfield said he declined the offer, feeling he wasn't ready yet to record. But when Michael heard the story, he realized that there were record companies in New York City that weren't interested in recording only musicians from Greenwich Village or Cambridge.

He and Norman decided they would wait until after the New Year to record. Once the holidays were out of the way, they set a date for the last week in January. Michael went to work, picking tunes and practicing them until he could execute them flawlessly. But while he was getting them together, he got a request. The fourth annual University of Chicago Folk Festival was coming up at the end of January, and Big Joe Williams asked Bloomfield to accompany him during a portion of a set he was going to do with the Tennessee Jug Busters.

Bob Koester had arranged for Big Joe, Sleepy John Estes, Hammie Nixon, and Yank Rachell to re-create the tunes from *Mandolin Blues*, the record Delmark had issued under Rachell's name the previous spring. But Joe also wanted to do a few numbers at the festival by himself, backed only by Bloomfield—on acoustic bass. Michael borrowed his friend Ace Cathcart's big upright and began working on Joe's tunes as well.

A week before the festival, Bloomfield went to Fickle Pickle owner Larry Fleischman with a request of his own. He wanted to skip that week's blues shows so he could focus on material for the demo session and his appearance with Joe Williams. The Pickle shows hadn't been doing all that well lately, and his last performer, pianist Blind John Davis, hadn't brought in an audience large enough to cover expenses. Michael thought Fleischman wouldn't have a problem with his taking a week off.

But the club's owner disagreed. The way the Pickle's waitress Dorothy Weiss remembered it, Michael and Larry got into a heated argument.

"He said, 'Oh, by the way, Larry, I won't be in next week,'" Weiss recalled. "And Larry said, 'What do you mean, you won't be in next week?' and he said, 'Well, you know, I'm busy, I've got some place to go,' and Larry said, 'This is your job, you *can't* be busy,' . . . and Michael said, 'Well, I *quit*!' And that was that—that was the end of him."

With that brief confrontation, Mike Bloomfield's six-month stint as a music producer and promoter at the Fickle Pickle came to an abrupt end. But the experience while it lasted had been a productive one. Through organizing and hosting the Monday and Tuesday night shows at the Old Town venue, Michael had rediscovered some of the legendary musicians of the classic blues era. He had gotten to know them, learned from them, and provided them with an appreciative audience for the first time in decades. He had also helped popularize authentic traditional blues styles with a new generation of Chicago folk music fans.

But now Bloomfield was moving into a different phase of his musical life. By leaving the Fickle Pickle, he unwittingly gave himself the time to concentrate his enormous energy on his own music-making and his future as a performing artist. Joel Harlib was elated.

On January 28—a cold, snowy Tuesday evening—Michael brought his Martin guitar over to Norman Dayron's apartment at Fifty-Third Street and Kimbark Avenue. As he had done for some of the bluesmen he had recorded for Pete Welding, Norman set up a corner of the living room as a makeshift recording studio. A small desk in an alcove off the main room held a reel-to-reel tape deck—Norman had recently replaced his old Telefunken with an Ampex machine, a smaller recorder that wasn't nearly as heavy. A boom stand was positioned over a small armchair in the corner, and from it Norman hung a bullet-shaped Sony microphone. The snow on the street outside muffled whatever traffic noise there was, and Norman's wife, Betty, had gone to the library for the evening, so the apartment was perfectly quiet for the session.

Michael had prepared a dozen tunes, each representing a particular style of American music. He warmed up with a half-dozen choruses of a Lightnin' Hopkins–style blues and then ran through a few test recordings. When Norman was satisfied with the levels and had positioned the mic to get the best sound, he cued up a new seven-inch reel of quarter-inch Scotch magnetic tape for the first take.

Bloomfield had decided to start off with a novelty number, a minstrel tune written in 1906 with broadly comic lyrics that was anything but a blues. He had heard the New Lost City Ramblers do a version on their 1963 Folkways album, and it always made him laugh. Originally titled "My Name Is Morgan, but It Ain't J. P.," Michael shortened it to "J. P. Morgan" and added his own lyrics to place the saga of the beleaguered William Morgan in downtown Chicago. He sang it with a gusto that evoked a Vaudeville veteran working a boozy hometown crowd, and he nailed it in one quick take.

Then he switched gears and ran through a rag he had composed. Norman described "Bullet Rag" as "something Michael made up to play in Travis style as fast as a human could play it." The complex piece was taken at breakneck speed and was clearly meant to demonstrate the guitarist's technical skill. After a few false starts, Bloomfield sailed through the tune, completing it in a breezy minute-and-a-half.

Next, it was time for the blues.

"Kingpin," another Bloomfield original, probably took inspiration from Slim Harpo's 1957 hit "I'm a King Bee." But Michael's tune wasn't about sexual prowess—it was the assertive boast of an alpha male. Accompanying himself with a rumbling, minor vamp on his Martin and tapping his foot à la John Lee Hooker, Michael affected a gruff, guttural tone as he sang the braggadocio lyrics. He took a brief solo and then returned for one more verse, declaring in a threatening tone, "If you mess with the Kingpin, it's a crying shame!" The piece would have been right at home in a South Side tavern, performed by a raucous electric blues band.

For the next tune, Bloomfield wanted to try something a little different. Both Norman and Michael knew about guitarist Les Paul's experiments with overdubbing, and Norman had heard that if a tape recorder's erase head were disconnected, the machine could add sound to an existing recording. Bloomfield wanted very much to overdub himself playing other parts on a few of the pieces he had prepared, and he talked his friend into cutting the wires to the Ampex's erase head.

"We started overdubbing on the mono recorder," said Dayron. "You could make lots of passes until the first ones would just disappear into the ozone. Michael saw that I could do that, so he added another layer to the original recordings on some of the tunes we did."

"Steel Guitar Rag" was another of Michael's compositions, a bluegrass instrumental with ornate lead and rhythm parts. To create the composite, he first recorded a combination of bass lines and chords, then he had Dayron clip the erase head wires. As Norman ran the tape through the machine again in record mode, Bloomfield listened to the first pass over headphones and added the solo line to it. The technique was crude by studio standards, but it seemed to work. Even so, it was difficult to coordinate playing while listening because of the tune's brisk tempo. "Steel Guitar Rag" had tricky places where both parts had to rhythmically shift gears and hit certain notes in unison—a challenge to execute even for a seasoned studio guitarist. Michael managed the interaction of lead and rhythm perfectly—until the last chorus, when his overdubbed line finished a few bars ahead of the rhythm accompaniment.

"I fucked the whole ending up!" he complained to Norman. But they decided to press on with the remaining tunes because a redo would require rerecording both parts.

"Since I Met You, Baby" by R&B singer Ivory Joe Hunter was Bloomfield's next tune. For this one, he clipped a harmonica into a rack around his neck and accompanied himself on guitar as he blew the melody, doing an instrumental version of the 1956 hit. In the middle of the piece, he played rhythm alone for two choruses, leaving space for a guitar solo. Norman then rewound the tape and Michael dubbed in a T-Bone Walker–style lead over the accompaniment.

Switching to a syncopated finger-picking technique, Michael next played a Delta-style blues based loosely on Mississippi John Hurt's "Got the Blues, Can't Be Satisfied." He did the tune straight through with no overdubbing, urging his fingers to "Play it for a while!" midway through his two solo choruses. His singing, in contrast to the menacing vocal on "Kingpin," was relaxed and personal—a perfect foil for the piece's intricate but mellow counterpoint. Bloomfield called the tune "A Feelin' Called the Blues."

To wrap up the session, Michael decided to do an old American folk song that had roots in a centuries-old English children's poem. He had heard traditional banjo player Buell Kazee's version on a Folkways release, and he liked the repetition of its question-and-answer verses as they built to a dramatic climax. But it was meeting Bob Dylan at the Bear that really brought "Who

Killed Cock Robin?" to Michael's attention. Dylan had taken the tune's nursery rhyme and turned it into a contemporary meditation on the sport of boxing, calling it "Who Killed Davey Moore?" Moore died following a boxing match in March 1963, and Dylan had rewritten the traditional tune to highlight the sport's senseless brutality. He sang it in a performance at the Bear, and later he and Michael played the original together in Bob's hotel room. It seemed like a suitable example of American folk music for the demo, and Bloomfield intuitively knew the association with Dylan wouldn't hurt.

When Michael completed "Cock Robin," he had nearly filled the seven-inch reel of tape—close to thirty minutes of demo material. They had covered a lot of stylistic territory with the six pieces recorded—from hard blues to bluegrass, R&B, old-timey, novelty, and classic blues genres—and he had demonstrated not only his skill with the guitar but also his ability to sing and play harmonica. Norman then edited the tape and dubbed the recording onto a master reel that Joel Harlib was to take to New York. He was happy with the quality of the recording and pleasantly surprised that the overdubbing technique had proven effective. Michael was satisfied with his playing too. It had been a productive evening, and the two friends lit up a joint to celebrate.

Three days later, on January 31, Mike Bloomfield joined his friend Big Joe Williams onstage at Mandel Hall for the University of Chicago Folk Festival. The opening night had been sold out, and the seven-hundred-seat hall was filled to capacity with the overflow of enthusiastic folk fans seated right onstage with the performers.

Mother Maybelle Carter, accompanied by the New Lost City Ramblers, opened the evening with thirty minutes of traditional country ballads. She was followed by banjo player Roscoe Holcomb, guitarists Doc Watson and Furry Lewis, fiddler Gaither Carlton, and a number of other folk performers. Big Joe appeared midway through the concert and began his set with a few solo numbers, introducing Mike Bloomfield as his accompanist. Michael, who had been sitting with the audience onstage, fetched his big upright bass from the wings and took up a position to the right of Joe. Many in the hall already knew Bloomfield from seeing him around campus and at the twist parties, but nobody had seen him play bass before.

Stomping his foot on the stage in rhythmic accompaniment, Big Joe performed a number of his original tunes while Bloomfield gamely followed along. The bluesman's habit of speeding up the tempo as he warmed to the song while making chord changes at irregular intervals would have made it a challenge for any other musician to stay with him, but Michael knew Joe's tunes and their eccentricities well. The journeyman bassist managed to convincingly complement his mentor's performance and even added a few embellishments along the way.

Even though he was performing acoustically, Big Joe's intense singing and raw slide playing electrified the audience. After an hour or more of mostly white folk music, the black Mississippian's Delta blues got the crowd moving. At the conclusion of his short set, the audience rewarded him with loud applause. Joe looked over at Michael and gave him a boyish smile as his young protégé hefted his bass back toward the wings. The other members of the Tennessee Jug Busters made their way to the stage as Bloomfield took his seat back in the audience. He was pleased with his performance and gratified by the reception. It was the first time he had played before a discerning, knowledgeable crowd in an academic setting, and it made him more determined than ever to find a record company willing to showcase his talents and capitalize on his deep appreciation for American musical styles.

One day during the first week of February 1964, Joel Harlib caught a flight to New York City. In his briefcase were several reels of tape containing music by some of his best clients. Chief among them was the recording of Bloomfield's six demo tunes. Joel was determined to convince a major record label to give his guitarist friend a recording contract. Once in the city, he pursued that goal with the brash confidence of a natural-born salesman.

"I decided I might as well start at the top," recalled Harlib. "So I went to see John Hammond. I figured if he had signed Dylan, he might sign Michael."

The elder Hammond had been involved with Columbia Records since the 1930s and had been instrumental in developing its formidable stable of jazz artists during the swing era. He and the label eventually parted ways a decade later, but Hammond had returned to Columbia in 1958 to resume his duties as a senior executive. He was put in charge of acquiring new talent for the label—a task for which he was particularly well suited. Though many of the company's younger producers thought of him as an industry dinosaur, no one disputed the fact that John had great ears.

That was exactly what Joel Harlib was counting on.

"I cold-called him by showing up at his office at the Columbia building. Without an appointment." Joel said. "I was greeted by his secretary, and I sat there in the waiting room, and after a short while, the door opened and out comes John Hammond.

"He took me into his office, and there I was with one of the greatest A&R men in the history of recorded music," said Harlib, still impressed many years later. "So Hammond says to me, 'What do you have?' I showed him Mike's tape and he says, 'Let's give it a listen.'"

Joel cued the tape up on a deck on the producer's desk and ran through several of Bloomfield's tunes. "After a few minutes, he says to me, 'I like it. I'd like to see him in person. Does he have a band?'"

Mike Bloomfield's personal manager was, for a rare moment, speechless. Joel thought he would probably have to leave the demos at Hammond's office, with the possibility that the Columbia producer might find a moment over the next week to listen to them. He never expected to meet Hammond in person, let alone have him listen to a tape right away and then want to see his client.

Harlib was only too happy to tell Hammond all about the young guitar player who was the talk of the Chicago music scene. The legendary producer asked if Bloomfield would be willing to come to New York City to audition for the label—just to demonstrate his talents. Harlib said oh yes, Michael would certainly be willing to do that. He would make arrangements once he was back in Chicago for Michael to be available whenever Hammond wanted him.

In the span of twenty minutes, Harlib had managed to secure Bloomfield's future as a serious musician. What had happened for Bob Dylan might just happen for Bloomfield. Emboldened by this unexpected success, Harlib asked Hammond if he would like to hear some of his other tapes. Hammond patiently listened to several other reels but was unimpressed. It was only the guitar player he was interested in.

As Joel was leaving the office, he turned and asked the producer the obvious question.

"I said to him, 'How come you saw me?'" Harlib remembered with a laugh. "Hammond said that one time a woman folksinger came down from Boston, and he had been too busy to see her. 'Do you know who she was?' he asked me. 'Joan Baez. Now I see everybody who comes to my door.'"

CHAPTER 6

AUDITIONING FOR HAMMOND

CHICAGO AND NEW YORK, 1963–1964

Back in Chicago, Joel Harlib wasted no time in telling his client about his fortuitous connection in the Big Apple. He described how John Hammond had ushered him into his office and had been very impressed with Michael's demo. He explained that the producer wanted Bloomfield to audition for the label in their New York City studios as soon as possible. He also said Hammond was interested in hearing Michael with a band, but that was something they could worry about later. Joel stressed that for now, if the audition went well, it could be Michael's big break—and Harlib's as well.

Bloomfield was thrilled. To play for the man who had signed many of the greatest artists in American music was an exciting prospect—and one that made him more than a little nervous. If Joel was right, a successful audition for Columbia could lead to a recording contract and possibly more.

Harlib felt his brash act had opened the door to Michael's career. But in truth, John Hammond had heard about Mike Bloomfield long before Joel Harlib paid an impromptu call to his office. The producer had learned of Michael from his son. The younger Hammond had talked to his father about the amazing guitar player he had met in Chicago. So Michael Bloomfield may well have been a talent John Hammond wanted to know about even before Joel cued up his demo tape. Harlib's visit served to focus that interest, giving substance to the younger Hammond's glowing reports. All that remained was for the elder Hammond to hear Bloomfield play in person.

To that end, an audition was arranged for the third week in February.

On Monday afternoon, February 17, Michael Bloomfield arrived at John Hammond's office in the Columbia Records building at 799 Seventh Avenue in Manhattan. He had brought with him his Martin guitar, some harmonicas, a neck rack, and Joel Harlib. He shyly introduced himself to the fifty-four-year-old producer and said he was ready to play whatever Mr. Hammond would like to hear.

After exchanging a few pleasantries, Hammond introduced Michael to Len Levy and Sol Rabinowitz of Epic Records, the Columbia subsidiary that Hammond thought might be a fit for Bloomfield's talents. He then escorted the young guitarist and his manager up to Studio A on the building's seventh floor for the audition. Waiting there for them was Bill Lee, an acoustic bass player who frequently did session work for Columbia. Hammond thought he would be a suitable accompanist for Bloomfield. Michael, on the other hand, hadn't expected to work with anyone. He was willing to do whatever John Hammond thought was best, but playing with someone he didn't know might be a challenge. He was already nervous, and Lee's presence only increased Michael's anxiety.

From inside the control room, Hammond asked the musicians to play something so the engineer could set levels. After a few minutes, the producer signaled they were ready and suggested Bloomfield try a tune.

The guitarist's opening selection was "Judge, Judge," Michael's variation on Bessie Smith's 1927 tune "Send Me to the 'Lectric Chair." He knew John Hammond had produced Bessie Smith's last session three decades earlier and was intimately familiar with the Empress's music. Playing one of her songs, Bloomfield reasoned, would demonstrate a broad knowledge of traditional blues and jazz. But in his animated state, Michael sped up the tempo as he worked through the tune's choruses, and "Judge, Judge" came off more like a folk song parody, a bit of Vaudeville hokum.

Over the next twenty minutes, Mike recorded a quick succession of novelty numbers. In his desire to show Hammond that he could play a variety of styles, Bloomfield ran through four tunes he probably played in his one-man shows at Mother Blues. Each was a loose interpretation of a classic piece, with lyrics that only vaguely resembled those of the originals. Though the guitarist's singing became more exaggerated and affected with each performance, Michael seemed to enjoy himself.

Indulging in a bit of ragtime comedy, Bloomfield sang Sam Chatmon's "God Don't Like Ugly" and then did a variation on Blind Boy Fuller's "Truckin' My Blues Away," calling it "Don't Lay That Snake on Me." He also did "J. P. Morgan," trusting that Bill Lee would be able to follow the changes and make the stops. When he brought the comic rag to a conclusion, the studio was suddenly quiet.

"Why don't you try some blues, Mike?" came Hammond's voice over the intercom. The producer had been most impressed with his young prospect's guitar playing on his demo tape, but so far he had only heard him sing.

"Uh, okay, but I'd rather play electric if it's alright with you," said the guitarist. Hammond suggested he try one of the studio's instruments, and Bloomfield selected a big F-hole archtop.

"Let me do a Jimmy Reed tune for you," said Michael, putting a harmonica into the rack around his neck. "It's 'You Got Me Runnin'.'"

A big hit for Jimmy Reed in 1959, "Baby What You Want Me to Do"—the tune's actual title—gave Bloomfield a chance to play a harp solo and get in a few lead licks. He followed that with a variation on "Poor Boy Blues," a traditional tune by "Barbecue Bob" Hicks. Calling it "Country Boy Blues," Michael attempted several takes but became increasingly frustrated with Bill Lee's accompaniment, and John Hammond had to intervene to calm Bloomfield down. When they finally succeeded in recording the song, Hammond finally got a chance to hear a little of what Bloomfield could do with a guitar.

Michael continued the session with Muddy Waters's signature tune, "Got My Mojo Working." He clipped his harp back into the rack and launched into the high-octane shuffle with Bill Lee in hot pursuit. When he brought the tune to a close with Muddy's parting declaration, "It just don't work on *you*!" Joel Harlib, who had been silent throughout the session, let out a joyous whoop and then broke into laughter.

Michael then told the producer he wanted to do a Merle Travis–inspired instrumental, something he had composed himself. Seeming to be nothing more than an afterthought, Michael's last tune was the audition's showstopper. He coyly saluted the producer with its apparently spontaneous title and, after a false start, launched a musical salvo. "Hammond's Rag," a Bloomfield concatenation of complex rhythm patterns, tricky contrapuntal melodies, chord substitutions, and stop-time bass runs, flew by in a breathtaking ninety seconds. Despite its brevity, the piece provided a comprehensive exhibition of Michael's skills.

"Good playing, Mike. That's great!" came the producer's voice over the intercom. "I think we've exploited you enough—I just want you to know I'm signing you."

"Oh, that's *great*!"

Michael was elated. Joel came over and shook his client's hand, clapping him on the back. It was a moment that for nearly a year they had both been waiting for. Instead of being picked up by one of the independent folk labels or by a shoestring operation like Folkways, Mike Bloomfield would be recording for one of the world's great record companies, an industry giant. John Hammond, the man who had discovered Count Basie and Billie Holiday, who had revived interest in the music of Robert Johnson and had brought Pete Seeger and Bob Dylan to Columbia, judged Bloomfield's talent worthy. Hammond was going to record him.

It looked like Michael Bloomfield's career was about to take off.

* * *

But Bloomfield wasn't going to be on Columbia. His contract was going to be with Epic Records, a spin-off label that had been established in 1952 to handle Columbia's classical music overflow. Despite the arrival of rock 'n' roll a few years later, Epic finished the decade primarily as a purveyor of easy listening music and pop singers. But in the early 1960s, the label scored a series of Top 40 hits with singer Bobby Vinton, and by 1962 it was scouting around for artists to add to its growing pop music roster.

The producer had also expressed interest in hearing Michael play with a band. In putting together material for his Dayron demo tape, Bloomfield had focused solely on acoustic performances because he was expecting his manager to take the recording to companies that put out folk music. He tried to select tunes that exhibited a range of styles but were also similar to those being released by other folk artists—such as Dave Van Ronk; Ramblin' Jack Elliott; Eric von Schmidt; and Koerner, Ray, and Glover. That way, Mike reasoned, his chances of connecting with a label like Vanguard or Elektra would be increased.

But something had happened earlier in the month that would profoundly alter the American musical landscape, though few at the time were aware of how profound the coming change would be. On Sunday evening, February 9, the nation's top TV variety program, the Ed Sullivan Show, aired a performance by a British band called the Beatles. Nearly half of all American households were tuned in that night, and within a week "Beatlemania" was rampant throughout the land. That the hirsute quartet from Liverpool had sold more than a million copies of their first American release in a little over two weeks and was currently holding the number-one spot on *Billboard*'s singles chart was a fact not lost on many record company executives. The listening public suddenly seemed to want music by rock-oriented groups. John Hammond, an astute observer of American musical trends, was not about to miss the obvious. After that Sunday broadcast he was looking for bands, and he wanted to hear what Michael could do with one.

Hammond had a copy of the company's standard agreement sent to Joel Harlib once he and Michael were back in Chicago, and Joel began negotiations with the producer, hoping for a better deal. Then, fate stepped in. In early March, on his way to the office, John Hammond was stricken with a major heart attack. He wound up in Lenox Hill Hospital in intensive care. His doctors told him it would take six months of bed rest for him to recuperate.

"That was the end of any deal-making," said Harlib. "I told Michael to go ahead and sign."

The news of Hammond's illness troubled Michael. Without an advocate at Columbia, he was unsure whether anything would really happen with the company. Any interest in recording him might get sidelined. His only alternative, he decided, was to hope for Hammond's speedy recovery, and he signed with Epic Records, agreeing to a one-year contract beginning April 1. He was to get a first-year royalty payment of 6 percent on sales, subject to 1 percent annual increases if the agreement was renewed.

Shortly after his return from auditioning in New York, Bob Koester asked Michael to participate in a recording session with Sleepy John Estes. Bob was hoping to re-create the jug band quintet he had recorded the year before under Yank Rachell's leadership. But Big Joe Williams was in New York and unavailable, so he decided to go ahead with a quartet, using Bloomfield to augment Sleepy John's rudimentary guitar style. Michael was glad to do it, but he cautioned Koester that he had been sent a contract by Columbia and was about to sign with Epic Records. Bob realized that he needed to get into the studio quickly if he wanted to avoid the hassle of obtaining permission to use Michael, so he scheduled a session for March 3 at Sound Studios in the Union Carbide building on North Michigan Avenue.

Of the tunes that were recorded that afternoon, four were issued under Sleepy John Estes's name on *Broke and Hungry*, Delmark 608. Koester's liner notes acknowledged that Bloomfield had signed a "Columbia recording pact." They also announced that Michael's "first LP under his own name is in preparation as this is written"—a claim that no doubt had more in common with Bloomfield's aspirations than it did with the truth. In reality, his first solo album would be more than five years away.

While he was waiting for word from Epic, Bloomfield went about his daily routine. He read and practiced, visited his usual haunts—the Jazz Record Mart and other record stores and music shops—and sat in wherever he could. The great harmonica player Little Walter (Walter Jacobs) had just returned from St. Louis, and Michael spent a week working with him. He also played a string of South Side gigs with guitarist Sam "Magic Sam" Maghett, singer Andrew "BB, Jr." Odom, and guitarist Lee Jackson, and he even substituted for Hubert Sumlin in Howlin' Wolf's band while Sumlin was briefly in jail. He was a regular at coffeehouses and clubs in Old Town and on Rush Street, and he could frequently be found at Mother Blues and even the Fickle Pickle.

Another venue that soon was included in his daily rounds was a small record shop located on the corner of North Wells and West Schiller streets. Called the Old Wells Record Shop, the store was run by an eccentric hipster named Bill Chavers. Chavers had been the proprietor of a major record outlet near the Regal Theater on the South Side in the 1940s and had a remarkable stock of rare and unusual blues and jazz recordings. Though the store was open most days of the week, Bill often seemed less interested in selling albums than in simply hanging out with other hipsters who dropped by. He often locked the store's front door to discourage interruptions by customers, thus creating a vibe at the Old Wells that more closely resembled that of an exclusive party than of a place of business.

There was another reason Michael liked hanging out at the Old Wells Record Shop—Charlie Musselwhite had moved into Bill Chavers's back room. Musselwhite left the basement of the Jazz Record Mart after a run-in with Bob Koester. Koester could be provocative, and one time he pushed Charlie too far. The record clerk grappled with his boss—"started slapping him around" was how Charlie put it—and soon afterward Musselwhite went to work for Chavers. The shop was just a few blocks from Sandburg Village, and Bloomfield came by frequently just to hang out.

Michael also frequented his regular South Side haunts—Silvio's, the Copa Cabana, Pepper's, and Florence's. One evening he and Charlie Musselwhite went down to Theresa's at East Forty-Eighth Street and South Indiana Avenue with Paul Butterfield. Butterfield had been dividing his time between gigging at the Blue Fame with Little Smokey Smothers and playing in a duo with his friend Elvin Bishop at Old Town North, a coffeehouse in Mike's neighborhood. Butterfield brought along his new lady friend, Lisa Kindred, an aspiring blues singer from Buffalo. She had come to town from New York City for a gig at Mother Blues and had hooked up with Paul. It was her first trip to the South Side.

Guitarist Hound Dog Taylor and his band were performing. When Butterfield and his North Side acquaintances came in, Hound Dog seized the opportunity. He invited Mike and Paul to sit in, passed his funky Teisco guitar to Bloomfield, and adjourned to the bar to freshen his drink. Backed by Taylor's rhythm section, Butterfield and Bloomfield finished the set with a series of uptempo blues. Michael hugged the big Japanese guitar, shaking it as he squeezed out runs and jerking his rangy frame from side to side while the beat surged under the changes. Paul, in marked contrast, stood almost motionless, his head cocked to one side and his eyes tightly shut. His hands cupped mic and harp to his mouth as his arcing solos filled the basement club.

A few patrons who were dancing stopped to listen, more than a little surprised that white boys seemed to know the music. Heads bobbed in appreciation in the booths along the wall, and several who had seen Michael and Paul before were whispering to friends. Charlie sat with Lisa at a small table next to the dance floor, impassive and watching his friends closely. His turn was coming up, and Butterfield had set the bar high. One thing was obvious—when Michael and Paul played together, they took the blues to another level, one that transcended race and excited every listener.

* * *

In mid-June, Michael decided he would visit New York. He had been hoping to hear something from John Hammond and the people at Epic Records regarding his future, but so far there had been no word. The producer was still out of the office, at home recuperating from his heart attack. Bloomfield thought he would pay the city a visit and see what was happening anyway. He went over to the Old Wells Record Shop and invited Charlie Musselwhite to come along, and later that day the two friends caught an overnight bus to New York at the Greyhound terminal in the Loop. The Chicagoans arrived the next morning in the Big Apple, and after getting a room in an inexpensive hotel, they made a few calls to friends to say they were around. One of those friends was guitarist John Hammond.

Their timing couldn't have been better, and Hammond issued them an invitation. "John said he was going to be recording and to please come on down," Musselwhite recalled. "We didn't know about the session ahead of time—it was pure chance."

Hammond was about to record his third album for Vanguard and had decided to use an all-electric band. He wanted his next release to be an album of modern Chicago blues. To help him create the Chicago sound, John had assembled a stellar group of musicians. They weren't studio professionals, adept at a variety of watered-down styles, or even seasoned black veterans of the Windy City's blues circuit. With one exception, Hammond's accompanists were all young white men like himself. The odd man out was forty-six-year-old Jimmy Lewis, an African American bassist who had worked with numerous jazz and R&B musicians and had been a member of saxophonist King Curtis's band. Hammond used him on his second album for Vanguard, and the label had invited him back to help make the third. The other sidemen were musicians John had met earlier in the year when he was playing a gig in Toronto. They were from a Canadian band called Levon and the Hawks, a group originally formed to back R&B singer Ronnie Hawkins. Led by drummer Levon Helm, an Arkansas native, and Canadian guitarist Robbie Robertson, the band had recently gone out on its own, trying to develop its own music.

"I was amazed at how well they played American R&B together," said Hammond, recalling his first encounter with the Hawks. When he learned they were playing a two-week gig at the Peppermint Lounge in New York, he took advantage of their availability. Levon, Robbie, and the Hawk's organist and sax player, Garth Hudson, were happy to participate, and Hammond had planned to do the session with a quintet. But Bloomfield's serendipitous call increased the band to a possible septet.

Mike and Charlie met John at Mastertone Studios on West Forty-Second Street in busy Times Square. Bloomfield was pleasantly surprised to encounter Helm and Robertson there, too. He had met them earlier in the year when they visited Chicago, taking them around to hear blues in various South Side clubs and putting them up overnight in his Sandburg Village apartment. He introduced Charlie, who felt an immediate affinity with the Canadians. So that Musselwhite could play amplified harmonica for the session, Hammond found him a microphone. "John loaned me a mic from his Roberts tape recorder to play through," Musselwhite remembered.

The rest of the group was busy setting up and getting miked for recording. Michael watched as Robbie open his case, pulled out a Fender Telecaster and plugged it in. He began warming up with an aggressiveness that was bracing. The cream-colored guitar had a raw, metallic sound. Robertson ran through a series of fast blues licks and then smiled at Michael. Bloomfield nodded, impressed. Though he may have been expecting to play guitar himself, Bloomfield deferred to the Canadian. "He wasn't about to bully his way into taking over the guitar chair," Musselwhite observed. Instead, Michael opted to play keys. "Since there was a piano there, Mike was eager and happy to play it to be part of the session," Charlie said.

Bloomfield sat down at the studio's baby grand and ran through a few twelve-bar choruses to warm up. Hammond, who had been thinking he might get a chance to record with two lead guitars, was a little surprised. But he was willing to let Michael play whatever instrument he wanted.

Vanguard had allotted Hammond a single three-hour recording session, thus tightly limiting the time the musicians had to get the music organized and on tape. The company wasn't too happy with John's choice of sidemen and would have preferred them to be experienced studio musicians. It didn't want to risk wasting valuable studio time—especially on loud blues and rock 'n' roll players. But John was aware that something was happening, that a cultural shift was coming, and he wanted to experiment with its new possibilities. The folk archetype that had predominated through the late 1950s and early 1960s was giving way to something more exciting. Something more akin to rock.

With his electric band that afternoon, John Hammond recorded eight hard blues tunes in quick succession. Two were by Willie Dixon, two by Muddy Waters, one each by Robert Johnson and Bo Diddley, and two more from Jimmy Reed and Billy Boy Arnold. The group's sound was raw and exciting and driven by Robertson's biting guitar. Musselwhite tagged Hammond's wildly emotive vocals with rumbling harp riffs and took brief solos in Big Walter fashion. Even though he was playing through a tape recorder microphone, his harmonica's sound was pure Chicago. Here and there Bloomfield's piano pushed through the surge of electric instruments, making terse comments on the action before receding in support of the beat created by Lewis and Helm. The music had an aggressive swagger and radiated youthful exuberance. Though the songs were all part of the blues canon and some were decades old, they sounded fresh.

Five additional tunes were recorded for the album, and Hammond remembered them all as having been completed in that single session. On those remaining tunes, Garth Hudson joined the group on electric organ and Bloomfield may have been replaced by pianist Donald Cook. But the resulting thirteen songs, all covers of pieces by or associated with contemporary blues artists, constituted a real departure for Hammond. He was known as a solo artist, a blues singer mostly of prewar classics and an acoustic player very much out of the broader folk tradition. The fact that he was fronting an electric band on his latest studio effort—a combo with drums, piano, and organ in addition to amplified guitars and harmonica—was a first for Hammond.

It was also a first in American popular music. The singer's third Vanguard recording session brought together for the first time a group of young white musicians to record an album of blues in the modern style. These musicians were no strangers to modern blues. Both Bloomfield and Musselwhite had years of experience playing with many of Chicago's masters, and the Hawks had been seasoned by life on the road playing R&B and blues in bars across North America. They all knew their business and it showed.

Though a first, Hammond's rocking blues session was not entirely without precedent. Seven weeks earlier, at the end of May, a British group called the Rolling Stones made their American debut with an album accurately titled *England's Newest Hit Makers*. Though they were promoted as a pop act in the wake of the Beatles' huge commercial success, the band, as their name implied, had a deep appreciation for the blues. The Stones' album had five tunes that were in the twelve-bar form, with one by Willie Dixon and another by Jimmy Reed. They played loud electric guitars augmented by harmonica, bass, drums, and keyboards. And they were—no surprise—all young white musicians. The parallels with Hammond's group were striking.

Hammond, of course, was much closer to the real thing. While the Rolling Stones knew blues largely through whatever records they could find, the Americans knew many of the creators of those recordings personally. And Hammond had the amplified harmonica of Charlie Musselwhite. Musselwhite's contribution constituted a major departure from the acoustic suck-and-blow style of many of his white contemporaries. For the first time, true Chicago-style harp had been recorded by a young white player.

John Hammond's electric album, recorded in the summer of 1964, was an important milestone in the development of American blues-rock. Had the record been released that fall as planned, it might have had a profound effect on the popular music landscape. But Vanguard was unsure how to promote it—they were, after all, a folk label—and they were uncomfortable with its raw, electric sound. The company put Hammond's tapes on the shelf and sent him back into the studio. His next release would be another solo acoustic effort, in keeping with the sort of blues performances John was known for. His groundbreaking electric album, titled *So Many Roads*, would not be released by Vanguard for more than a year—and by that time the music world would have already discovered other exciting young electric blues players.

Back in Chicago, the summer was in full swing. Old Town was crowded on weekend afternoons with tourists perusing its exotic clothing, craft, and jewelry shops, and Rush Street was alive at night with revelers in search of exciting entertainment in its many clubs and cabarets. There was plenty of music and plenty of places to play it. Though the Gate of Horn had closed in February, the Fickle Pickle continued to feature folk acts on weekends and blues on Tuesdays, and Mother Blues was open throughout the week. There were clubs like the Rising Moon, Old Town North, the Blind Pig, the Crystal Pistol, and the Oblique around the neighborhood, and coffeehouses on the North Side like the Broken Wall, the Door, and It's Here. It seemed like every storefront eatery and bar with a few tables and room for a little stage was looking for someone to perform.

A little more than a week after Michael Bloomfield and Charlie Musselwhite returned from New York, Charlie began playing with Big Joe Williams at one such tavern down the street from the Old Wells Record Shop. Big Joe had followed Charlie to Bill Chavers's place and was camping out in the record shop's back room too. One afternoon, Joe wandered into the bar and got to talking with the owner.

"The owners of the bar thought Joe was some kind of folksinger," Musselwhite recalled, laughing. "They didn't really know what they were getting into with Joe. Anyhow, they asked him if he would come and play at their bar, and Joe asked me to come with him." The inauspicious watering hole was named Big John's, and the owner wanted to boost business by hiring someone to entertain for the upcoming Fourth of July weekend.

"I remember it was a holiday weekend," Charlie said. "Joe got the gig, and it went so well, they asked us to come back the next night. The bar was selling so many drinks, they asked Joe to just make it into a regular gig."

Big John's, located at 1638 North Wells Street, was big for a bar; it was a boxy room with swinging saloon-style doors at the entrance and a bar running along the left wall with a small kitchen in back. The "bandstand" was a small riser at the end of the bar, barely large enough for drums and a couple of musicians. Behind the kitchen was another room with a pair of pool tables, a favorite hangout for penny-ante hustlers. The decor was neighborhood tavern rustic—a few posters on the walls, faux tiffany lamps suspended from the ceiling, and rows of small round tables with red-checkered tablecloths. Business, until that Fourth of July weekend, was usually limited to a few barfly regulars and the occasional tourist seeking relief from the heat of the day.

But once Big Joe and Charlie began playing at Big John's, Old Town took notice. Big Joe had played many times at the Fickle Pickle and the Blind Pig, but performances there were almost always acoustic affairs. At Big John's, Williams plugged in and played his nine-string Silvertone amplified, and Charlie blew harp through his vintage Gibson Custom amp. Together, accompanied only by Joe's stomping foot, they filled the room with sound. "That was the very beginning of electric blues becoming popular on the North Side," said Musselwhite. "Right there in Old Town." The fact that patrons could buy a beer while listening to the blues didn't hurt business any.

Within a few weeks, other musicians were sitting in with the duo. Big Joe had his friend Jimmy Brown, the two-string fiddler from St. Louis, join them one weekend, and Musselwhite performed with guitarist John Lee Granderson on another Saturday when Joe was elsewhere. Michael Bloomfield got in on the action, too, on piano.

Next to the bandstand, on the floor was a large studio upright. Michael removed its upper and lower panels to expose the soundboard and increase its volume, and he began to regularly play with Joe and Charlie. The trio sounded good together, and their amplified instruments carried well over the din of the crowded bar. When Joe got wound up, he would get the crowd moving and make Big John's feel like a big party.

Soon the bar was being listed in the local papers—and even in *Down Beat* magazine, thanks to Pete Welding—as the place to go on the North Side to hear Chicago blues. Through the first weeks of August, Big Joe headlined, with Michael and Charlie Musselwhite accompanying the Mississippi bluesman. But by mid-month Joe began to feel the call of the open road, and before long he decided to leave Chicago for St. Louis.

On Joe's last Saturday evening at Big John's, Michael was having a smoke on the sidewalk out in front of the bar during a break. He struck up a conversation with a twenty-two-year-old who happened to be passing by, a recent arrival to Old Town named Norman Mayell. Norm had grown up in Chicago and had just returned from attending college in Hawaii. He was living in Old Town and working as a sandal maker in one of the neighborhood's trendy tourist shops.

"Michael was standing there holding a folk guitar, and we just started talking," said Mayell. "He said Big Joe was leaving and he wanted to get a band together. He had to get himself a drummer, and if he could get one, he said he could keep the gig. I said, 'Well, I play drums.'"

Mayell had played in bands during high school, but he hadn't touched a drum kit since he had gone off to college. He didn't even own a set. That didn't matter to Bloomfield. The guitarist told Norm to go rent a kit and he could be in the band. A few days later, the newly enlisted drummer returned with a set of new Slingerlands.

Mayell began performing on weekends at Big John's with Bloomfield and Musselwhite. The trio was frequently joined by whoever happened to stop in, including boogie-woogie pianist Erwin Helfer, who pounded the ivories with them on several successive Saturdays. Michael also invited his friend Roy Ruby to join the group. Roy was a competent classical guitarist—he had been on the payroll as such at the Bear—but he agreed to switch to electric bass for his friend's impromptu band. Another player Bloomfield recruited was guitarist Mike Johnson, nicknamed "Gap" because of a space between his front teeth. Johnson had met Michael at a University of Chicago fraternity party several weeks earlier, and he was conscripted to play rhythm behind Michael's lead. Though Johnson preferred jazz blues to the harder Chicago style, he comped along gamely and even took an occasional solo.

The last member to join the band was a young guitarist and keyboard player from Madison, Wisconsin, named Brian Friedman. The nineteen-year-old had come to Chicago in the summer of 1963 with a group called the Ardells, led by another guitarist—a dropout from the University of Wisconsin named Steve Miller. Friedman had been playing Texas-style blues with Miller, and when he walked into Big John's one Saturday evening, he was impressed by what he heard. When he sat in with the band, Michael was equally impressed by Friedman's ability as a piano player. Brian joined the quintet, and the addition of keys gave the group a distinctive Chicago sound.

With a full band now on the stage, Saturdays at Big John's became even more successful. Management was delighted with the crowds and the increased business at the bar. They kept asking Michael and Charlie back, and soon the band was performing there three and four nights a week. In a little more than a month and a half, Big John's had gone from being a nondescript neighborhood bar to being one of the hottest clubs in Old Town. And by the end of September, the sextet that was its main attraction was beginning to develop a sound—an exciting, freewheeling version of Chicago blues laced with elements of rock and jazz.

"After a while we developed this real rapport. We would get to a place of pure *aura*," recalled Mike Johnson. "The music got really tight. The place would be empty and we'd start playing and it would be wall-to-wall people after one tune!"

The music was indeed tight, and it was also loud. "You could hear them playing two blocks away," remembered Donna Koch Gower. Gower had become a follower of the band and a close friend of Michael's, and she spent so much time at Big John's that she sometimes volunteered to waitress. She recalled that Mike Royko, the famed Chicago columnist, lived down the street from the bar and did not appreciate the group's formidable sound. "He wrote a column that said the two worst things to happen to the city were the Chicago fire and the music at Big John's!" said Donna, laughing.

For Mike Bloomfield, having a band meant he and Charlie could keep the gig at Big John's. It also was a decisive move away from the limitations of folk music. With the backing of a rhythm section, Michael was free to indulge his considerable skills as a soloist. The fact that his friend John Hammond had recorded blues with an electric band and that Paul Butterfield was working with a regular group hadn't escaped Bloomfield's notice. Then there were the British bands, like the Beatles and the Rolling Stones, that were having a profound effect on American audiences. Michael had played with groups before, with show bands like Robby and the Troubadours, but popular musical tastes seemed to be moving away from Rush Street's twist circuit artificiality. The trend was toward bands that played music of a different sort—music that combined the gravity of the blues with the integrity of folk but also added the excitement and energy of rock 'n' roll. Bloomfield sensed the huge potential of a band that could merge those attributes.

He also knew that his producer at Columbia was eager to hear what he could do with a group. Michael had presented himself to the elder Hammond primarily as a conventional folk artist—a solo performer with a guitar—thinking that was what the producer wanted to hear. He now knew better, and he was anxious to prove himself to Hammond and the executives at Epic. A hot electric blues band might do just that.

Things weren't happening only in Old Town for Michael Bloomfield. In August 1964, the guitarist also got himself involved in a groundbreaking project at the Maxwell Street Market. A photographer he knew named Mike Shea planned to make a documentary film about the market and its many colorful characters. Shea asked Michael to act as his musical advisor and help him coordinate the filming of Maxwell's many musicians. Bloomfield was only too happy to assist, especially because he knew most of the market's performers personally.

The thirty-nine-year-old Shea was a veteran news photographer who had worked for all the Chicago dailies as well as *Life*, *Time*, and *Playboy* magazines. He had become interested in the cinema verité style of filmmakers David and Albert Maysles, D. A. Pennebaker, and Richard Leacock, and he wanted to explore the genre's journalistic potential for himself. Shea had purchased a used 16 mm movie camera and was planning to capture Maxwell Street's buyers and sellers as they went about their business within the market's sixteen square blocks. It soon became obvious, however, that the Maxwell Street story was about much more than commerce—it was also very much about music.

"Mike Bloomfield was our connection to the blues musicians," said Gordon Quinn, Shea's soundman and editor. "He'd say, 'This important guy is playing on the street today; you've got to come.'"

Bloomfield's extensive knowledge of Maxwell Street's music resulted in Shea filming many of Chicago's famed street performers and bluesmen, including harmonica player Carey Bell, guitarist and mandolin player Johnny Young, and the legendary slide master Robert Nighthawk. Michael would scout out the musicians who were performing on a particular Sunday, get their OK to be filmed, and then bring in Shea and his crew. The filmmaker captured many extraordinary scenes of Chicago's vibrant blues and gospel tradition as a result. There were impromptu street performances; electric blues bands with large, enthusiastic crowds of writhing dancers; gospel shouters and holy-roller proselytizers; and even a young singer banging out a hambone rhythm on an empty cardboard box.

The filming began in mid-August and continued for sixteen weeks. The team shot hours and hours of footage of eager merchants, pitchmen and their marks, con artists and hustlers, street preachers, food vendors, and bargain hunters of every age, ethnicity, and economic status. With Bloomfield's direction, a substantial portion of those hours captured the market's music.

When Shea finished filming in early December, he had a vast number of exposed reels—far more that he needed for a short documentary. Five of the reels that were shelved and not used in the film comprised a remarkable in-depth interview that Bloomfield did with guitarist Robert Nighthawk. In the interview, which was shot in segments because Shea's reels held only eleven minutes of film, Bloomfield showed his extensive knowledge of blues players and history. He discussed the original Sonny Boy Williamson, Maxwell Street veteran Daddy Stovepipe, pianist Leroy Carr, and Muddy Waters—whom Nighthawk had taught to play slide. As he wound up the interview, Michael candidly asked Robert about white players and the blues.

"They say in the future there'll be a lot of young white kids taking up the blues," Bloomfield said. "Do you think that they'll be able to—?"

"Oh, they'll make it," replied Nighthawk without hesitation. "They just catchin' on to it, and they just really got that feeling right there." The slide guitarist, of course, knew who he was talking to and doubtless was expressing tacit approval of Michael's own playing. The interview finished with Bloomfield asking Nighthawk to play something, and the bluesman responding with a brief version of Jim Jackson's "Kansas City," a 1927 blues tune that would become part of Michael's regular repertoire in later years.

By the summer of 1965, Mike Shea's Maxwell Street documentary was complete. Called *And This Is Free*, a point-of-sale phrase used repeatedly by one of the market's vendors, the film was nearly fifty minutes long and offered an unvarnished portrait of one of Chicago's long-standing traditions. But the nonnarrative structure that Shea used in creating the film, its pastiche of sights and sounds in seemingly random juxtaposition, made the documentary challenging for most audiences. That the Maxwell Street market was seen as an eyesore and a haven for criminal activity by most of the city's civic groups and politicians further tempered enthusiasm for *And This Is Free*. The movie received a few showings but went largely unnoticed by critics and the larger filmmaking community. Its tepid reception discouraged Shea, and he eventually stowed the documentary away and went on to other projects.

But Mike Bloomfield was listed prominently in the opening credits. He was given the title "technical consultant," a role he clearly played. But he was also the reason that Mike Shea was able to capture some of the most remarkable footage of unfiltered blues and gospel music ever filmed. It was Bloomfield's deep love of the music, knowledge of its players, and innate charm and glib tongue that secured a glimpse into the heart of those purely American art forms.

Meanwhile, at Big John's things were cooking. Michael's band, now called by its members the Group for lack of a better name, was listed as playing Thursday through Saturday, with an occasional Sunday thrown in, throughout the month of October. They would start at 9:00 p.m. and play four or five sets, usually finishing up between 1:00 and 2:00 a.m. At the end of the night, they would split up whatever money the management had taken in at the door, and then they would walk home in the cool night air while sharing a few joints. Michael was the tacit leader of the Group, and he had a strong effect on his sidemen both on and off the bandstand.

"Michael was so frenetic; he was an attention-deficit type of guy," said Norm Mayell. Brian Friedman agreed. "When I first met him, he was *so* hyper.

But as I got to know him, we became good friends. He was difficult to *really* get to know, though. That might have been the drugs, but I don't want to say too much about that."

One thing was certain—the Group was the most exciting thing happening in Old Town that fall. People would fill Big John's to actually *listen* to the band—when they weren't dancing in the aisles between the tables. The sound of loud electric music with infectious rhythms, pulsating drums, and hot guitar and harmonica solos was unlike anything many patrons had heard. They were familiar with rock 'n' roll bands' formulaic renditions of pop tunes, and they knew about folk music singers of traditional blues. They had also heard the British blues-rock of groups like the Rolling Stones and the Animals. But here were six musicians who were plugged into a whole new sound. It was aggressive and raw, similar to rock 'n' roll in its swagger and excess, but also like jazz with its emphasis on solos. What the Group was playing was tough, uncompromising South Side blues brought north and interpreted by an entirely new generation of bluesmen.

The band generally had nothing planned when they started to play, but that didn't matter. Their sets inevitably amounted to an evening of spontaneous blues. Bloomfield would start off with a shuffle and just let things evolve from there. "We never practiced," said Johnson. "Mike would just yell, 'E shuffle, from the turnaround!' and we would start."

One evening, a stocky man with a Van Dyke beard came into Big John's, watched the band for a few minutes, and then approached the bandstand. His name was Sidney Warner.

"One day I was walking down Wells Street and I heard this music. What caught my ear was the bass player—he was terrible!" said Warner. "So I went looking for the band and I found Big John's. . . . I walked in and went right up to the bandstand, and there's this guy with this wild, bushy hair up there."

Roy Ruby was still playing bass with the band, struggling to keep up with the rest of the players. He apparently wasn't having a good night when Sid happened by. Warner indicated he wanted to speak to the leader of the band, right in the middle of the performance. The hirsute guitar player—Bloomfield—leaned over, heard Sid's complaint about Roy's playing, and stopped the band cold. When the music started up again, it was Warner who was on bass. "Mike brought me up to play one tune and I wound up staying with the band for a year!" Sid said, laughing.

Unlike the other members of the Group, thirty-one-year-old Sid Warner was a seasoned professional. He had grown up in Lynwood, California, where at age fifteen he had gotten involved with local rhythm-and-blues groups and had spent three years as jump saxophonist Big Jay McNeely's guitarist. In his twenties, Sid had been a member of TV cowboy Roy Rogers's orchestra in Las Vegas and had even played briefly with the great Nat King Cole. He had come to Chicago in an effort to patch up his marriage and had opened a jewelry shop on the corner of North Avenue and Sedgwick Street, near the Old Town School of Folk Music.

Warner had largely given up music by 1964, but when he heard the Group and met Michael Bloomfield, he suddenly found himself pressed into service as a bass player. With Sid anchoring the beat, the rhythm section became tighter and the band's sound measurably improved. Because he was a jeweler by day, the band began calling him "Silver Sid."

"On our best nights, we would get a *monster* groove going," said Norm Mayell. "Sid brought a balance immediately to our group. He knew just what to do and always kept a twinkling eye on the fiery Michael, as if to say, 'He's something, isn't he? We're going to have to focus to keep up!'"

It often was a struggle for the members of the Group to keep up with their leader. Bloomfield's unrestrained enthusiasm for music and boundless energy for playing sometimes seemed to run away with whatever the band was doing. But the crowds at Big John's were enthralled, and they kept coming. It didn't matter that the music was occasionally a little ragged because the sound was so novel.

The energy and excitement generated by the band's shows didn't inspire only the audience. Mike Bloomfield wanted to hear for himself how the band sounded in live performance, so he asked Norman Dayron to set up his recording equipment in the bar to tape the Group as they played. He was especially eager to hear what his own playing sounded like. So on Thursday afternoon, October 15, Norman brought his Ampex tape deck, a few reels of recording tape, and a couple of mics over to North Wells Street. He set up the mid-size deck at the end of the bar near the bandstand and then ran one mic to the riser, taping it to the vocal microphone stand. The other he hung farther back in the room, dangling it over the tables and chairs. While the band warmed up, Norman patiently moved the suspended mic around until he was satisfied that he could capture all the instruments without risk of distorting the recording.

A crowded room would have made Dayron's job more difficult, so he suggested that the band start early. Only a few customers sitting at the bar and Big John's staff were present when he signaled to Michael that he was ready. After some additional tuning and a few false starts, the Group launched into a medium-tempo shuffle in C.

For a conventional blues, the tune was a radical departure.

On all his previous recordings, Michael had limited himself to one or two solo choruses. Now Bloomfield stretched out—*really* stretched out. From the very start of the instrumental until its last chord, Michael spun out chorus after chorus of loud, intense blues improvisation. He burned through twenty-six of them before he brought the shuffle to a close some ten minutes later. It was a tour de force of endurance, if nothing else.

But it was also what made the Group's music so different. In pop music, solos were incidental ornaments, brief interludes before the melody and singer returned. In rock 'n' roll, they were a quick way to energize listeners, to ramp up the excitement. Even in traditional country music, bluegrass, and blues, in which solos were often an essential part of a tune, the soloist was usually limited to a chorus or two. Only in jazz performance—and then only recently—did improvisers have the freedom to develop their ideas for as long as they wished. Michael Bloomfield had an abundance of ideas, and he saw no reason to limit himself. At Big John's, he would play a tune for as long as necessary in order to have his say.

"I remember we'd sometimes play Muddy's 'Got My Mojo Working' for half an hour!" said Sid Warner.

What they played may have been Chicago-style blues, but the Group's approach to soloing had more in common with contemporary jazz. The solo *was* the music, and Michael was the band's chief soloist.

Norman recorded three more selections before Big John's began to get busy. Two were with the band, a quintet with the arrival of Charlie Musselwhite, and one featured Michael accompanying himself on the bar's big upright piano. At the keyboard, Bloomfield played a relaxed version of Ivory Joe Hunter's "The Moon Is Rising," a tune Robert Nighthawk would do with drummer Kansas City Red. Bloomfield improvised his own lyrics over a rolling bass line like one that Otis Spann would use, then soloed with tremolos, triplets in thirds, and simple single-note runs. The performance was engagingly casual, with Michael clearly feeling comfortable in the moment and the music. His vocal was unforced, and his playing, though uncomplicated, was highly effective. The "hotshot" guitar player was clearly a competent blues pianist, though Bloomfield's simple keyboard style hewed closely to traditional blues piano forms and stood in sharp contrast to the pyrotechnic busyness of his six-string work.

The other two tunes Dayron recorded that night again featured the leader's searing solo guitar. One shared a title with a song that Michael had played for his audition with John Hammond, but this version of "Country Boy" was patterned after the 1951 Chess recording by Muddy Waters. Bloomfield again opened with Muddy's slide introduction, nimbly backed by Musselwhite, and then went right into the lyric. Though the tempo was slower than Muddy's original, Bloomfield's solo following his two vocal verses was brimming with staccato bursts of sixteenth notes. Though it was only five choruses, the solo lasted five full minutes and had Michael switching between shrill slide glissandi and blistering fretted lead. The tension between the performance's turgid rhythm and Bloomfield's furious lines was striking.

The quintet's second tune, a slow blues in A that was built around a standard South Side bass line, had Michael again alternating between slide and fretted notes. Over the bump-and-grind rhythm riff played in octaves by Mike Johnson and Sid Warner, the guitarist built a wall of sound that was like a blues assault. Even though his intonation wasn't always accurate and he sometimes rushed the beat, it was easy to hear how Mike Bloomfield could absolutely overwhelm his listeners with the ferocity of his playing. As the tune came to a close, cries of "Yeah, Mike, *yeah*!" could be heard over a smattering of applause—the Thursday night crowd had begun to arrive at Big John's.

Norman tried to tape a few more performances, but the growing audience and the club's happy, boisterous atmosphere soon made it too crowded and noisy to get a clean recording. He packed up his equipment during a break, carefully stowed his reels in their cardboard boxes, and let Michael know that the live session had been a success. He told his friend that the Group—and its star guitarist—had been suitably documented.

On that point, Norman Dayron was absolutely right. The band *had* been captured in all its wild enthusiasm, its indulgences and excesses, and its groundbreaking take on the blues. Behind it all was Michael Bloomfield. His intense devotion to music coupled with his boundless, hyped-up energy was unquestionably the driving force. Almost without knowing it, Michael was pushing himself and his sidemen into experimental territory, redefining the nature of the blues. That intensity, that unfettered need to express himself, would play a central role in his musical career, and it would set him apart from many other young white blues players.

CHAPTER 7

BIG JOHN'S AND THE GROUP

CHICAGO AND NEW YORK, 1964

By late October, people were lining up outside Big John's every night the Group was there. Inside, the place was filled with hipsters of all shades—actors, writers, artists, musicians, people wanting to see and be seen. Michael's leathers-and-drug-dealing friend, Tommy Walker, spent most evenings in the back room, hustling tourists on the pool tables. Out front, members of Second City and the Goodman Theater regularly occupied tables. Students from UC, Northwestern University, DePaul, Loyola, and Roosevelt College lined up along the walls and crowded the bar area. What had begun as a holiday weekend gig with Big Joe Williams had evolved into an extraordinary scene with Mike Bloomfield and his band at its center.

"The crowds at Big John's were huge!" said Sid Warner. "They were a real mixture of people—black, white, all ages. It was *packed*. One night I remember it took me ten minutes to get across the room to the men's room!" On some evenings, other blues players would come by and join the band for a few tunes.

"Paul Butterfield and Elvin Bishop would sit in sometimes," said Mike Johnson. Barry Goldberg also jammed with the Group on at least one occasion.

The little bar on North Wells Street was creating such a stir that Pete Welding reviewed several of the Group's shows for *Down Beat* magazine. After pianist Brian Friedman joined the band, Welding caught two consecutive nights in late October and reported that "the Bloomfield sextet has developed into a tight, cohesive unit that generates a powerful—if a bit thunderous and unsubtle at times—rhythm." He went on to praise Michael:

> The group is built around the gifted guitarist-leader. Recently signed to a recording contract by Columbia, Bloomfield apparently has no limitations within the confines of blues guitar. He offers fleet, supercharged modern R&B guitar pyrotechnics with the same ease with which he re-creates the insinuating, vigorous bottleneck style of Muddy Waters.

> The range of his playing is pretty much confined to postwar blues styles, and it must be admitted that he brings them off with drive, vigor and consummate ease.

He also noted that often Bloomfield "plays too much, for he tends to turn each piece into a virtuosic display, so much so, in fact, that the virtuosity tends to cancel itself out through overstatement." Welding's assessment was accurate on all counts, especially in regard to Michael's habit of overplaying. But in Bloomfield's musical verbosity, his "notey-ness," lay the seeds of what would become a defining characteristic of his later style.

With their success at Big John's and their growing popularity, the Group began to think about compensation. Sharing whatever was taken in at the door had been fine with the band members at first. But now, with business booming, they felt Big John's could afford to be a bit more generous. Sidney Warner decided to intercede with the management. He had recorded with nationally known groups and had worked extensively in Los Angeles and Las Vegas, so he knew how to do business. He took up the matter of pay with Big John's manager and soon negotiated a better deal for the Group.

"When I started with the band, they were each getting four dollars a night," Warner said. "I talked to Michael, I said, 'Man, don't you see all these people here, having a good time? Don't you know why they're here? They could buy a bottle of booze and drink at home. They're here because of you guys!' The following night, everybody in the band got twenty-five dollars, and eventually we were making fifty dollars a night."

While the money might not have been quite that good, Silver Sid did succeed in significantly boosting everyone's salary. After several more weeks of capacity crowds at Big John's, Warner began to think the Group might do even better elsewhere. He knew a pair of brothers named Bill and Terry McGovern who were in the nightclub business, and they seemed to have a lot of money. He had met them at a little Italian café across the street from his jewelry shop. "The McGovern boys were hanging out there and doing shady business," said Sid. He added with a laugh, "Stuff I shouldn't really talk about."

The McGoverns owned several bars out in Chicago's northwestern suburbs and one in town at 5551 North Broadway, just south of Bryn Mawr Avenue. The place wasn't a neighborhood tavern like Big John's—it was more like a small nightclub. Called Magoo's, it was reputed to be a front for mob activity.

"It was a gangster hangout," confirmed Warner. "The McGovern brothers were a couple of guys who either were connected to the Mafia or wanted to be. They had hot merchandise going in and out of the back of Magoo's all the time." Despite his doubts about the brothers' legitimacy, Sid talked them into hiring the Group at a premium, and the first week of November the band left Big John's, exchanging Old Town's bustling, hip scene for staid Edgewater, a neighborhood some forty blocks north. Magoo's wasn't far from where Susan and Michael first lived in Chicago, but it was a long way from where things were happening. Right away, the band knew that they and the club's clientele weren't a match.

Magoo's patrons were far more straitlaced than their counterparts at Big John's. They were the 1960s version of young urban professionals—accountants, lawyers, junior executives. Those involved in shady dealings, whatever they might have been, were there strictly to conduct business. Nobody in the place seemed to be very interested in the music. Even though they were making good money, the members of the band began to feel uncomfortable. Their leader was himself soon dissatisfied.

"Mike *hated* playing there," said Sid. "All the action was at the tables. They didn't really pay any attention to us, even though the bandstand was right behind the bar." Bloomfield felt the lack of response from the listeners acutely, and it took away much of his enthusiasm for playing. The band performed a grueling schedule at the North Broadway club, working five nights a week from Wednesday to Sunday, doing six or seven sets each night, and usually finishing up around 4:00 a.m. Playing at Big John's had been an exciting adventure, but making music at Magoo's quickly felt like going to a job.

There was unfortunately no possibility of returning to Old Town and Big John's. Mike Bloomfield had given the band's gig there away. True to his generous nature, the guitarist had convinced Paul Butterfield to leave his steady job at the Blue Flame and take the Group's spot at the North Wells Street bar.

Paul had been reluctant at first. He had played gigs in Old Town before, but he was leery of committing himself to what seemed like a tourist scene. His hesitation stemmed in part from his reluctance to leave the gritty authenticity of the South Side, but it also likely had something to do with his feelings about Michael. Butterfield undoubtedly respected the guitarist's ability, but he still saw Bloomfield as primarily a rock 'n' roll player, a blues kibitzer who'd only recently gotten serious about the music. From the harp player's perspective, Bloomfield was a North Side guy who occasionally showed up at clubs on the South Side. He would bring along a gaggle of friends, sit at a front row table, and climb up onstage whenever he could to showboat. He lived in cushy Sandburg Village, came from a rich suburban family, and didn't have to work. Even though Butterfield had played with Michael at twist parties and jammed with Bloomfield's band at Big John's, he didn't much like the guitarist, and he had a hard time trusting his judgment.

"He just sort of thought of me as a folky Jew boy," Bloomfield said. "Because, like, Paul was there and I was just sort of a white kid hanging around and not really playing the shit right, but Paul was *there*."

Despite his misgivings about Michael, Butterfield could see that the money at Big John's was good—much better than what he was making on the South Side as a sideman. And an extended gig would allow him to put together a permanent band of his own. After some consideration, he decided he would bring a group into the North Side bar. The newly formed Paul Butterfield Blues Band began working at Big John's four nights a week in mid-November.

Even though Mike Bloomfield was unhappy with the Magoo's gig, things were looking up for the guitarist. The second week in November, he received an unexpected letter from his producer. John Hammond, now fully recovered from his heart attack, was back at work and eager to get Michael into a studio. He had tried to reach Bloomfield at his parents' home on Lake Shore Drive, thinking he might find him there. "I talked to your mother this afternoon and was terribly sorry to have missed you," Hammond wrote in his November 5 letter. "I told her I have plans either to come up to Chicago within the next ten days or make arrangements for you and your group to finally be recorded."

Mrs. Bloomfield informed the producer that Michael and the band had taken a new job at place in Edgewater and that they seemed to be doing very well. She was pleased that Hammond wanted to move ahead with recording her son and was excited for Michael. Hammond, in turn, was enticed by Dottie's enthusiastic report. He was more determined than ever to exploit Michael's talents and felt it might be good to hear the band in person. To get the ball rolling, he wrote a memo to Len Levy and a few of the other executives at Epic.

> This kid is a tremendous talent, has a lot of original material, and I think we should do something about him quickly. Would it be possible either for Carl Davis to get in touch with him in Chicago so that we can set up a session or at least listen to the band that Mike has together which is working at a place called McGoo's [*sic*]"?

The first weekend in December, John Hammond flew out to Chicago. He arranged to see the Group at Magoo's on Friday night and caught one of the band's shows at the club on North Broadway. It may have been nervousness or just an off night, but the Group's performance did not particularly impress Hammond. The band sounded unfocused, and Michael's playing was overly busy and loud. But the producer decided to bring the Group into the studio and record them anyway. He wanted to get Bloomfield on tape with a band so that the management at Epic could hear what he could do. At that point, Hammond reasoned, they could determine how best to utilize his talent.

The producer booked time in Columbia's Chicago studios for the following Monday afternoon. Michael sensed that Hammond had been disappointed with the Friday night performance, so he called a rare rehearsal for the band to prepare.

"We were basically a jam band, and as long as we did it that way it worked," said Mike Johnson. "But we had a practice session before going into the studio, and it didn't go very well. Mike had a foul mouth sometimes, and I remember him cursing and saying that we were *never* going to rehearse again!"

On Monday afternoon, December 7, the members of the Group congregated at Columbia's studios. The facility was in a huge building at 630 North McClurg Court, a few blocks north of the Loop. The company used it primarily for television and radio production, but the building also had a small recording studio space. It had snowed lightly in the morning, and the wet sidewalks, sloppy with ice and slush, made it a chore for the musicians to get their equipment into the building. Michael, Mike Johnson, and Sid Warner were lugging their amps off the freight elevator when Joel Harlib arrived with filmmaker Mike Shea in tow. Shea had been pressed into duty as the session's photographer by Harlib. Bloomfield's manager felt the occasion was going to be a historic one, and he wanted it properly documented. Shea went to work immediately, taking a few shots of the band setting up and then organizing them into a lineup for a group portrait.

The last to appear that afternoon was the session's legendary producer. Wearing dark glasses and carrying a copy of the trade magazine *Record World* and one of the Chicago dailies, John Hammond strode into the studio and greeted the band. He then introduced himself to the engineers in the studio's cramped control room and was dismayed to learn that Columbia's chief Chicago engineer, Carl Davis, would be unavailable for the date. John also wasn't very happy with the studio after looking it over, finding it outdated and ill-equipped compared to the company's New York facilities.

But Hammond was determined to make the best of it. He hung up his coat and had coffee brought in for the musicians and studio crew. He then sat Michael and the rest of the band down in the control room and had them sign the standard American Federation of Musicians recording agreement, as required by the union. Once the legal requirements were completed, Bloomfield gathered his men and began reviewing the tunes they were going to do. John Hammond walked back into the studio with Joel Harlib and began to offer some suggestions. But Michael had his own ideas about how he wanted the session to proceed.

"Hammond came into the studio, and immediately it was clear he was an alpha-guy," remembered Norm Mayell. "So was Michael, and right away there was a clash."

Seeing that arguing wasn't going to move things along, Hammond retreated back into the control room and let Bloomfield handle things his own way. The producer generally liked to step aside and allow an artist he was recording to have free rein, but Michael seemed unfamiliar with the process. To the producer, it appeared the guitarist had no idea how to run a session.

Despite the rocky beginning, the taping got under way a little after 2:00 p.m. as Mike Shea moved about the room, snapping pictures. Michael briefly sat at the grand piano at one end of the studio and demonstrated to Brian Friedman how he wanted a particular riff for one of the tunes to go, and then he showed Sid a turnaround progression to use on another. He next plugged his guitar in, turned up his amp, and began to tune. Michael was using gear he had purchased from his grandfather's pawn shop earlier in the year—a 1956-vintage Fender Duo-Sonic and an old Ampeg guitar amp.

He had gotten the Fender to replace the Les Paul Custom he had traded away in 1961. The guitar was a three-quarter-sized, two-pickup model originally intended for student use, and it had seen some rough treatment, evidenced by its chipped creamy finish and discolored neck. Michael later claimed that it cost him about twenty-three dollars, but it was adequate enough for his plugged-in needs. Its brittle, bright tone and buzzy action made it sonically a challenge, but in Bloomfield's hands it could really wail.

When he was ready, Bloomfield counted off Muddy Waters's "Got My Mojo Working" as a warmup for the band. The tempo was as brisk as the original, but the rhythm was oddly different. Mayell used his snare to punctuate the backbeats in cut time, effectively accentuating the third beat of each measure. But the band knew the number well and played it with confidence.

A listen to the playback revealed that—no surprise—Michael's guitar and vocals were dominant. The bass and drums were clearly present, but Charlie Musselwhite's harp was down in the mix, and Mike Johnson and Brian Friedman were all but inaudible. Hammond suggested the band try another take as the engineer fiddled with the dials in the control room and checked the mic cables. But after three successive run-throughs, the mix remained mysteriously unimproved. The band, though, had tightened up since the first attempt, and it was decided that the fourth take was a keeper.

Next up was an original by Bloomfield. "The First Year I Was Married" was taken at a slow crawl, and the band managed to maintain the tempo as the tune progressed. Bloomfield switched between slide and fretted lead as he sang the plaintive verses and then played a slide duet with Musselwhite for the first four bars of his solo chorus. He returned with the third and fourth verses, punctuating his phrases with fits of lead, and then closed the tune out with a walk down to a final A chord.

A single take was deemed sufficient for Bloomfield's original, so it was on to Little Walter's "Last Night." Originally a feature for solo harmonica, Michael's version of the tune relegated Charlie's harp to a supporting role for the guitar. Taken at a slower pace than Walter's 1954 recording, the piece started off with Mike Johnson's approximation of the bass line. After two bars, the full ensemble joined in, supporting Bloomfield as he sang two verses and played rhythm. His solo chorus mixed knotty pockets of lead with bright triplet clusters; he followed it with another verse before bringing the tune to a close. The band decided to try one more take, giving Michael a chance to improve his singing. On slower songs, the often forced, toneless quality of his tenor vocalizing would become painfully obvious.

The fourth tune the band tackled was another slow blues, a song by St. Louis Jimmy called "Goin' Down Slow." Playing the piece in D, Michael started the band off on the five chord and worked through the turnaround, doing his best B. B. King lead. He continued to play fills as he sang Oden's regret-filled lyrics, stretching notes in a call-and-response duet with himself. The mix, for the first time in the session, seemed more evenly balanced, with Friedman's piano clearly audible in the rhythm section and Musselwhite's harp nearly on a par with Bloomfield's stinging guitar. Because Charlie hadn't brought his amplifier and was playing acoustically into the studio mic, he was at the mercy of the engineer. An adjustment in the control room prior to the take had happily increased his volume.

Michael then played a second original, a tune he called "I've Got You in the Palm of My Hand." An up-tempo rocker, the blues had clever lyrics with stop choruses and was reminiscent of the songs Chess A&R man Willie Dixon liked to compose. Michael counted it off, sang a verse, and then went into the first of two stop choruses. But the stops weren't quite together, and the take faltered as the band tried to come back in for Bloomfield's solo.

They tried it again. And then a third time. But they couldn't seem to hit the stops correctly. When he saw that Michael was becoming frustrated with his bandmates, John Hammond decided to step in. Over the control room speaker he suggested the musicians take a break and listen to some of the playback.

The band piled into the control room as the engineer rolled back a few of the reels and played a sampling of their recordings over the console speakers.

But the mix was hard to hear in the crowded little room, so Michael had it switched to the big speaker cabinets in the studio. He plopped himself down in front of them and listened intently while the other band members milled around, chatting and taking a cigarette break. While the mix still wasn't very balanced, the playing was good and the sound quality was acceptable.

After the break, the musicians reassembled in the studio and took another stab at "I've Got You in the Palm of My Hand." This time there were several false starts, but the final take was completed with the stops executed flawlessly. "Alright!" Bloomfield commented as he began two solo choruses after the first of the stops, doubtless pleased that the rhythm section had negotiated its part successfully. He flew through the changes with a shower of licks, repeatedly using a technique he would later describe as a "roll"—a rapid back-and-forth between two consecutive notes on each string, usually played while ascending a scale across the strings. After the second set of stops and another solo chorus, the song came to a quick end as Michael tagged it with a ninth chord high on the neck. It had required seven takes and nearly forty-five minutes to complete, but everyone was more than happy with the final version of the tune.

Their three-hour studio time was running out, but Bloomfield wanted to try to get one more song on tape. For their final selection, Michael picked a blues by Big Bill Broonzy titled "I Feel So Good." Muddy Waters had done a version in 1959, and the Group's interpretation was patterned after it. An unusual sixteen-bar blues with stops after the first six bars, "I Feel So Good" was a challenging number to both sing and play, and during the first run-through Bloomfield missed a chord change. In frustration—and probably from fatigue—Michael became angry at himself and everybody else. Hammond again had to intervene to calm him down.

The band made another attempt, and this time the take was completed. But Michael was still not satisfied, and he quickly counted off a third take. His playing was flashy and flawless, but the performance ran long and would probably have to be faded to accommodate commercial considerations. Most of the other selections recorded that afternoon were also overlong, and they, too, might have to be shortened.

In all, the Group recorded six tunes during its three-hour session, waxing some seventeen full takes as well as numerous incomplete attempts. Despite the initial confusion, it had been a productive date, and John Hammond seemed satisfied. As the band members were packing up their equipment, the producer joined them in the studio, thanking them and making small talk. He told Michael he would take the tapes back to New York and have them edited and mixed, and that they would be in touch. Nothing was said about going back into the studio to record additional material, and no mention was made of an album. When Bloomfield pressed the issue, Hammond was noncommittal. "We'll see," was all he would say.

That confused Michael Bloomfield. He had waited eight months for something to happen with his contract, and now that he had been officially recorded, he expected Epic to move forward with a record release. If that was the plan, and Michael had no reason to think it wasn't, then more tunes would be needed. But there was no discussion of another session. Hammond was very complimentary of his playing and seemed enthusiastic about the group, but he was tight-lipped about Michael's future. The other band members sensed the producer's reticence too.

"We were really excited about that session," said Silver Sid. "It seemed like a big break for Mike, but then Hammond just left after it. Mike seemed pretty discouraged."

"We were kind of deflated after that," agreed Norm Mayell. "We just went back to playing Magoo's, and nothing seemed to happen with Columbia."

Michael himself felt the band's exotic appearance and unorthodox behavior had intimidated Hammond and caused his hesitancy. "We made wild music and were wild people—that's how we acted," Bloomfield explained to an interviewer many years later. "It made him afraid of us; he just found us too wild and crazy."

John Hammond may indeed have been put off by the Group's demeanor, but it was more likely that after seeing the band perform, he couldn't envision a way to market Bloomfield and his men. Current tastes were trending toward rock bands, yes, but those bands were pop entities like the Beatles. When the Fab Four sang a blues, it was in three-part harmony with recognizable melodies. Even the rougher, more authentic blues of the Rolling Stones seldom strayed from the commercial format and rarely featured solos longer than a single chorus. And none of those blues-based songs had ever charted as a hit. Michael's music was just too close to the source for current tastes.

And then there was his singing. Hammond knew right away when Michael first auditioned that he was not a natural singer. The guitarist would have to develop his voice if he wanted to succeed as a performer. There was no question that Bloomfield was an extraordinary soloist, a player of virtuosic ability, but in the current pop market, that wasn't enough to succeed.

John Hammond flew back to New York, gave the Group's tapes to one of Epic's staff engineers for editing, and went to work on other more pressing projects.

* * *

For the remainder of December, Mike Bloomfield and the Group continued to perform at Magoo's. Michael was hoping for a call from New York, but as the days and weeks passed and no word came, he decided simply to concentrate on his music and let his career take care of itself. He enjoyed playing with his fellow band members and had become good friends with several of them, but the music and camaraderie did little to relieve the tedium of the nightly sets at Magoo's.

The McGovern brothers seemed perfectly fine with the fact that their patrons didn't much care about the Group's music, didn't dance, and came and went regardless of whatever was happening onstage. It seemed that the band's presence was necessary solely to complete the illusion that Magoo's was a bonafide nightclub. Before too long, Michael began coming in late.

"Silver Sid would switch to guitar when Michael wouldn't show up," said Mayell. "After the Hammond session, there was a kind of lull. Sometimes nothing was happening at Magoo's."

Despite their apparent indifference to the Group's music, Bill and Terry McGovern had big plans for the band. They wanted Michael and the group to work a circuit of their suburban clubs. They planned to have the band play a few weeks at each location in a continual rotation. But with Bloomfield's growing antipathy, Silver Sid thought it might be better to make a change. He began actively looking for another gig for the band.

Michael and Charlie Musselwhite began thinking about other jobs too—or at least quitting the one at Magoo's. One evening in mid-January they both decided to not show up. The night before, an argument over admitting one of Bloomfield's friends had led to management shutting the lights off on the band, and Michael left the stage saying, "That's it! We're through." Silver Sid took over playing guitar and leading the band the next night, but without Charlie and Michael the sound wasn't the same. In an attempt to keep the Group together, Sid redoubled his efforts to find other work, and before long he did. But leaving the North Side club wouldn't be as easy as he thought.

"I went to the McGoverns and told them we'd found another job, and they looked at me and said, 'It's *not* a good idea for you to quit.' I'd heard stories about those guys, and the way they said that meant only one thing. So I left Chicago that very week and went back to California. Just like that." Whatever the McGovern brothers were insinuating by their comment, Warner took it to mean that his life was in danger, and he simply cleared out.

Silver Sid's abrupt departure left the Group without a bass player, and Bloomfield's and Musselwhite's disaffection further compounded the band's troubles. The gig at the North Broadway club suddenly became unworkable.

"After a while, nobody was actively trying to book the band," said Mike Johnson. "We just fell apart after Magoo's."

"After Sid left, I sold my drums and bought a car," said Norm Mayell. "Then I decided to go back to school and finish my degree."

By the end of January, the Group was no more.

Mike Bloomfield suddenly found himself with time on his hands. After more than four months of steady work, first at Big John's and then at Magoo's, the guitarist was suddenly without a gig—and bandless. He and Charlie picked up a few jobs here and there, and Michael continued to sit in with other musicians both on the South Side and in Old Town, but without a band steady work was hard to find.

He wasn't alone. Another Chicago blues player was at loose ends too, looking for a musical connection. In the winter of 1963, Nick Gravenites returned to the Windy City after a two-year stay in San Francisco. He had been hoping to restart his folk duo with Paul Butterfield, but the harp player was by then working regularly with Smokey Smothers at the Blue Flame. So Nick had taken work in a South Chicago steel mill by early 1964 to make ends meet. He had left a wife and a baby son back in California and needed to send money out to the West Coast to support them. He was toiling in front of an open hearth by day while living in a Fifty-Third Street rooming house in Hyde Park with Paul. Needless to say, Nick was hoping to find something else to do.

When Butterfield accepted the offer to take over Bloomfield's gig at Big John's, Gravenites came along. Nick would occasionally sit in, singing a few numbers and playing guitar. But mostly he just enjoyed being in Old Town. The thriving scene that had developed around the North Side club amazed him.

"Big John's was my first white blues bar experience," said Nick. "There were other clubs that featured blues, but it was of the folk music variety featuring single artists, not the electrified band music I was used to. . . . The place was filled all the time and became the happening, 'in' place in Chicago." Gravenites soon quit his steel mill job and began hanging out at Big John's all the time.

Michael Bloomfield kept running into Nick at Big John's and everywhere else on the North Side. He respected the baritone's talent as a blues singer, and it occurred to him that Gravenites might provide the solution to an ongoing problem—that of a credible singer for Michael's group. With a real vocalist in the band, there would be no need for the guitarist to sing. While he could handle some tunes convincingly, singing was decidedly not Bloomfield's strength.

Accordingly, one afternoon he came to Nick with a proposition. Would Gravenites like to put together a band? Nick said he would, and Michael rounded up the remaining members of the Group and a few other Chicago players. With Charlie Musselwhite playing harp, Brian Friedman on piano, and a guy named Bennie Ruffin on drums, they had the makings of a first-rate blues and R&B group.

"I had a lot of fun with that band," said Gravenites. "I got to do more than the traditional Chicago blues. I got to develop and perform a lot of originals, my own stuff, my own blues, and Michael Bloomfield, the master interpreter, made it easy, helped give me a voice that I never had."

Two of the tunes Nick developed in his collaborative band with Bloomfield would have a life well beyond the tenure of the group. One, called "Born in Chicago," was semiautobiographical, telling of the composer's hard times on the mean streets of the Windy City. The other, "It's About Time," was a cautionary tale about the dangers of excess that characterized Nick's days laboring in the steel mill while partying at night. Although "It's About Time" is basically built around a single chord, Gravenites and Bloomfield developed it into a jam piece consisting of Nick's verses followed by a series of extended solos. It gave Michael a chance to experiment with exotic scales and extended harmonies, and it would eventually form the basis for one of the most revolutionary pieces in 1960s blues-rock.

Before long, the Bloomfield/Gravenites band found a home. After playing up north in Edgewater for several months with the Group, Michael found himself back in the heart of things—in Old Town. A club near Rush Street named the End hired their six-piece band to perform on its large stage behind the bar. The End didn't have many patrons despite the presence of the band, and Gravenites thought they intentionally discouraged business. But work was work, and Michael, Charlie, and Nick were glad to have a place to play regardless of the End's questionable attitude toward commerce. Michael was particularly pleased to be playing with Nick. The singer, affectionately known as "the Greek," was a gruff, Nelson Algrenesque character with a piercing wit and a heart of gold. He and Michael kept each other in stitches with their wild stories, speed raps, and wry asides.

Though the band was composed of talented musicians, Michael Bloomfield was its star attraction. He was fast becoming Chicago's most talked-about young blues musician, a white boy from the suburbs who could hold his own on the South Side, who had a contract with a major record label, and who had just recorded for no less an industry giant than John Hammond. With those credentials, Bloomfield felt more than a modicum of pride. But he wasn't terribly proud of his guitar. The Duo-Sonic was dirty, discolored, and sometimes too shrill even for Michael. He decided he was going to get a new instrument, one that would be worthy of his skill and stature.

With his steady income from Big John's and Magoo's, Bloomfield had managed to save a little. He also had some money left over from his recent session with John Hammond. With a week's pay from the End added to that, he had nearly two hundred dollars in cash. He could probably get his parents to foot the bill for a new instrument, but Michael didn't want to depend on them any more than he already had. He would buy a new guitar himself.

He had his eye on another Fender, a Telecaster—the same guitar that Robbie Robertson had played so effectively at his friend John Hammond's recording session in June. Its sound had been raw and assertive, perfect for the blend of blues and rock that Michael excelled at. He had played Muddy's red Telecaster many times and he liked the feel and heft of the guitar. He liked its modern look too.

This time, though, Bloomfield wasn't going to pick out a tired veteran from Uncle Max's Buy & Sell. He was going downtown to buy himself a shiny *new* Telecaster, one fresh from the factory with no scratches and dings, one with the intonation properly adjusted and the electronics fully working.

In mid-February, Bloomfield went to one of the big instrument retailers in the Loop, probably Carl Fischer on Wabash Avenue, with every cent he had stuffed into his jacket pockets. He had managed to scrounge an extra $20 from Susie's rent money, making his bankroll close to $220. In the store, he had the clerk take down a pristine 1963 Olympic White Telecaster from the display of guitars on the wall behind the counter so he could try it. The instrument felt cool to the touch, its neck smooth like glass and its strings bright and untarnished. A few strums was all it took. Within minutes, Michael was piling his crumpled bills on the counter as the bemused clerk rang up the sale. The total came to nearly $215 with tax.

"Would you like to pick out a case for the guitar, sir?" the clerk asked his young customer. Bloomfield slid the Telecaster off the countertop and hefted it under one arm.

"No, man, that's all my money," he said. "Can't afford one."

"Not even a . . . bag?"

"Thanks, but I'll just take it like this," said the guitarist over his shoulder as he made for the door.

While Mike Bloomfield was organizing his band with Nick Gravenites, his South Side compatriot was creating a sensation at Big John's. Paul Butterfield's quartet had stormed into Old Town and in a little more than two months established itself as the most exciting group in Chicago. With Paul had come guitarist Elvin Bishop, his friend and frequent accompanist at UC's twist parties. Elvin had mastered the exacting and nuanced art of Chicago-style rhythm guitar and was now a capable blues soloist as well. But the real meat of Butterfield's sound—in addition to Paul's harmonica—was the band's rhythm section.

The harp player had been able to convince the bassist and drummer who were the backbone of Howlin' Wolf's band at Silvio's to join his new group. When Butterfield approached Jerome Arnold and Sam Lay with an offer of steady work in one location, they were tempted. When he mentioned the pay, they were convinced.

"We was looking at the money part of it," said Sam Lay. "We had like a guaranteed four nights a week in one place . . . and the money was like twenty bucks a night. Man, that's a lot of money." Wolf was paying his drummer and bassist only $12.50 for eight hours of work—fair wages on the South Side but significantly less than they could make at Big John's. Sam and Jerome gave notice and headed north with Butterfield.

Lay's powerful way with a shuffle and Arnold's rock-steady beat gave the quartet a solid blues foundation. Bishop added concise chords and rhythm riffs, creating a melodic framework over which Butterfield sang and constructed ringing solos. The band's sound was reminiscent of Little Walter's famed quartet with the Aces, but updated and energized. The effect was stunning. After eight weeks of steady work at Big John's, the Paul Butterfield Blues Band had taken the excitement originally generated by the Group to a whole new level.

One musician from back east who stopped by Big John's one evening in December was deeply impressed. He was Fritz Richmond, a founding member of the Boston-based Jug Band along with its leader, Jim Kweskin. Fritz was amazed at how exciting Butterfield and his band were, and when he got back to Cambridge, he made it a point to talk them up to his friend, producer Paul Rothchild.

Rothchild remembered Butterfield well. A year earlier he had tried in vain to talk the harp player into recording for Elektra. Fritz's enthusiastic report rekindled the producer's interest, and several weeks later he flew to Chicago to see Butterfield for himself. Calling what he heard at Big John's "thrilling, chilling," this time the determined Rothchild succeeded in signing the recalcitrant harmonica player. He wanted to get Butterfield to New York and into Elektra's studios as soon as possible to cut a record. He also wanted to get the band a gig in a Greenwich Village club for a few days so he could show them off to New York City insiders and maybe build a little critical buzz around them. Things were suddenly happening for Paul Butterfield.

Things were suddenly happening for Mike Bloomfield too. Joel Harlib had been pressing John Hammond for an answer regarding his intentions for the material Michael and the Group had recorded in December, and the last week in February he finally got a reply. The Columbia producer informed Harlib that he had arranged another recording session for Bloomfield—this time in Columbia's state-of-the-art studios in New York. Hammond was hoping a more professional studio would be able to better capture Michael's prodigious talent. He was also hoping an additional session might yield a clue for how to best utilize that talent.

News of a second recording date reinvigorated Bloomfield—John Hammond and Epic appeared to be interested in producing an album after all. The guitarist sent off a letter to the producer listing some of the tunes he would like to record and then quickly rounded up the band members who could make the trip to New York. Brian Friedman agreed to go, as did Roy Ruby and Charlie Musselwhite. For transportation, Michael enlisted his old traveling buddy, Fred Glazer. Fred's parents just happened to be out of town on vacation for a few weeks, and Glazer had the keys to the family's station wagon. He knew they wouldn't mind if he borrowed it—especially if they didn't know.

On Saturday, February 27, Fred brought the car over to Sandburg Village and helped Michael load up his equipment. Charlie, Roy, and Brian met them there, and Roy stowed his instruments in the wagon's rear cargo space next to Michael's caseless Telecaster. The three sidemen then crowded into the back seat while Fred took the wheel. The quintet drove over to Lake Shore Drive and cruised down to the South Side, heading for a rendezvous with the Paul Butterfield Blues Band.

Butterfield was also going to New York that week to record for Elektra. He and Michael had decided the two bands would caravan. Paul was anxious about taking the next big step in his career, and he wanted lots of company. He hadn't been back and forth to New York City the way Michael had, and the city was new territory for him. The prospect of recording for a major independent label in the Big Apple had him a bit spooked.

"Paul was really nervous about going to New York City, so he asked all his friends to come along," said Nick Gravenites. "A whole gang went out East for that trip." Gravenites hitched a ride in one of Butterfield's cars, and the caravan made its way onto the Chicago Skyway and headed east toward the Indiana Toll Road. The sun had broken through early morning clouds and the weather had turned mild, boding well for the trip.

The caravan made its way across Indiana, Ohio, and Pennsylvania, rendezvousing at the New Jersey tolls before heading through the Holland Tunnel, under the Hudson River, and into Manhattan. After negotiating downtown traffic for twenty blocks, the cars pulled up in front of a huge Italianate building on the corner of University Place and Eleventh Street in Greenwich Village. The passengers climbed out, stretched themselves after the long ride, and looked around. By coincidence, both bands had been bivouacked by their respective labels at the aging Hotel Albert, home to many famed artists, writers, and musicians over the years.

Michael and Roy, lugging their instruments, pushed through the hotel's lobby doors while Charlie, Brian, and Fred followed them in. As Paul and his men were piling drums and amplifiers on the sidewalk, a cab pulled to the curb and Elektra producer Paul Rothchild climbed out. He greeted the harmonica player and the band, then escorted them into the Albert.

The Hotel Albert—or Albert hotel as it was more commonly known—was, by 1965, on the way down. At one time an elegant residence for the city's well-heeled denizens, by mid-decade the Albert had fallen on hard times and was known for its cheap rooms, questionable tenants, and faded glory. But the seven-story leviathan was a grand palace to the Chicagoans, a colossal warren filled with colorful characters, capricious circumstances, and intriguing possibilities. The hotel also had a full basement with space for band rehearsals, which suited Paul and Michael perfectly. After checking in at the desk, they had their musicians stow their gear in a corner of the hotel's dank, musty lower level. Next, they all went in search of their rooms, hoping to get a little sleep after their long journey.

Early Monday afternoon, March 1, Bloomfield and his men appeared at Columbia's studio facilities on Thirtieth Street ready to record. With Michael, Charlie, Roy, and Brian were two members of the Butterfield's band. The guitarist had talked Sam Lay and Jerome Arnold into coming along, hoping to get them to play drums and bass for the session. Without a rhythm section of his own, Bloomfield thought the studio might provide him with players and, remembering his audition experience with Bill Lee, he wanted to avoid working a second time with musicians unfamiliar with Chicago-style blues.

Also along for the date was Michael's friend, John Hammond. The producer's son had been asked by Bloomfield to sit in on the session and maybe play rhythm on some of the tunes he planned to record. Accordingly, John had brought along his electric guitar, an inexpensive Japanese import that was probably his first plug-in instrument.

Completing the party was Paul Butterfield himself. The harmonica player had asked to come so he could watch the session. He was hoping to get an idea of what to expect during his own recording dates for Elektra later that week.

The receptionist was somewhat nonplussed when Michael's gang trooped in from the lobby and crowded around her desk. But after a few calls, she signed him in and directed the group toward the studio. The elder John Hammond met Michael at the door to the control room and greeted everybody as the rest of the band crowded in. He then called over a dark-haired younger man who was giving instructions to the engineers at the board. Hammond introduced him as Bob Morgan and told Michael he would be supervising the session. Morgan was head of A&R for Epic, an executive on the way up with an ear for the new rock 'n' roll. He had played a role in bringing the Dave Clark Five to America and was currently working on a deal to release recordings on Epic by a little-known British blues-rock band called the Yardbirds.

Michael was a bit relieved that Hammond was turning the reins over to another producer. He had gotten his hair cut and had even worn a nice shirt in anticipation of working with the older man again, hoping to appear less "wild." But with Hammond taking a back seat, Bloomfield's appearance seemed less of a concern. What Michael was now concerned with was getting the music right.

Columbia's facilities on Thirtieth Street were a world apart from their counterpart in Chicago. Housed in a building that had formerly been a church, the huge studio had a ceiling that rose several stories above the musicians' heads and was crisscrossed by massive, ornate arches. The walls were hung with curtains that could be lowered to dampen reverberation, and movable partitions could be used to change the shape of the recording space. Michael and his men, awed by the grandeur of the cavernous studio, stood gaping for a few moments. But they were soon ushered into Studio D, a smaller space off the main room that had been the church's sacristy, and began setting up their equipment.

After the union paperwork had been filled out and release forms signed, Bob Morgan suggested the musicians play something to warm up. That way the engineers could also set levels and make whatever adjustments would be needed. With so many amplified instruments to contend with, Columbia's skilled engineers faced a formidable task. They had vast experience in recording music of all kinds in their state-of-the-art facility, but the volume of sound produced by these musicians from Chicago was daunting.

Then there was the band itself. Epic had expected Bloomfield to be using the same musicians he had recorded with in Chicago—members of the Michael Bloomfield band, the band called the Group. But neither John Hammond nor Bob Morgan seemed to notice that only two musicians of the six in the studio with Mike had been present at the session in December. Bloomfield placed Sam Lay behind the drums, and he gave Roy Ruby's bass-playing role to Jerome Arnold, knowing that Arnold and Lay were used to working together as a unit and that replacing Roy would give the session a tighter ensemble sound. That Michael was using Paul Butterfield's rhythm section as the backbone of his own band—even before Paul had a chance to record with them himself—didn't appear to trouble the harmonica player. Butterfield was absorbed in the studio doings and seemed unconcerned that half of his band was suddenly recording for another label.

After a few sound checks, the twenty-nine-year-old Morgan gave the OK for the band to record. "Whenever you're ready, Mike," he said over the control room intercom.

The guitarist decided to start off with a new tune he had written, a piece called "I'm Cuttin' Out." He hastily demonstrated the bass line he wanted to Jerome and then showed John Hammond the tune's simple rhythm part. The band tried a few choruses while Michael conducted, shouting instructions as the musicians tried to find the groove.

"OK, let's go. Let's try it," said Bloomfield after a few attempts. He nodded toward the control room.

"We're rolling," came the reply over the speaker. "Mike Bloomfield, 'I'm Cuttin' Out,' take 1."

An up-tempo piece, the tune was a classic Chicago blues shuffle in rapid two-beat style. Sam Lay hunched over his drums and drove the song forward with unwavering determination. Arnold outlined the harmonic structure with his bass and Hammond provided chords that were complemented by Friedman's piano. Bloomfield soloed through the first chorus, his Telecaster awash in reverb and overdriven sound. His singing was dramatic but less exaggerated than it had been during the first session for Hammond.

But after the first verse, the rhythm faltered and the song fell apart. Repeated attempts were made, and it was only after eight takes that Bloomfield registered his approval. The final version of "I'm Cuttin' Out" featured excellent guitar work from the leader. Michael's new Fender had a much fuller sound that his old Duo-Sonic. Its tone, while not as raw as Robbie Robertson's had been during the *So Many Roads* date, was richer, with a more vocal quality. Michael's playing easily combined rock and blues vernacular, but the move away from the Duo-Sonic's overly bright, tinny sound brought him closer to the expressiveness of the blues.

Charlie Musselwhite missed the recording of "I'm Cuttin' Out." He had come to the session without a microphone, thinking he would play acoustically into one of the studio vocal mics as he had done during the session in December. But Bloomfield wanted the recording to capture the sound of the band live, and that meant Charlie would have to be amplified. While the group had been working its way through Michael's first tune, Musselwhite was trying out mic-and-amp combinations. Now he joined the rest of the musicians in the vaulted studio while one technician positioned a mic in front of his amp and another moved a partition into place.

They next tackled "Got My Mojo Working." The Group had done a version of Muddy Waters's signature tune back in December, but now with better recording conditions and Arnold and Lay in the rhythm section, the song became a blues juggernaut. Because everyone knew it so well, only three takes were needed to capture an exciting performance. Michael's solo was a fiery display of blues and rock licks, and the addition of Charlie's harp, with its repeated warbles and bent notes, completed the South Side sound.

Next up was another Bloomfield original, a slow drag titled "Lonesome Blues." Sounding largely improvised in the studio, the tune was given only one complete run-through, as the session was fast approaching its three-hour limit. Michael had Roy replace John on rhythm guitar, feeling that his Glencoe friend was more familiar with Chicago-style slow blues accompaniment, and Ruby plugged in his Gretsch archtop and tuned to Friedman's piano. After a tentative start beginning on the fifth and moving through the turnaround, the band found the beat and established the mood. Michael sang the plaintive lyrics in a subdued voice, then began his solo by quoting Muddy Waters. Musselwhite's harp shadowed his friend's lines, emphasizing certain phrases and anticipating the changes. The blues was slow enough that it ran nearly five minutes in length, obviously too long for commercial purposes. But there was no possibility of reworking it—the session had exhausted its allotted time.

John Hammond had already left, but Bob Morgan was in the control room. He seemed satisfied with the material the band had recorded, but he said little to Michael beyond complimenting him on his playing. There was no mention of an additional session to tape more tunes and no discussion of what Epic intended to do with the recordings they already had. A few minutes of playback in the control room made it obvious that the engineers hadn't gotten the mix quite right—Friedman's piano was all but inaudible and Ruby's guitar was too loud in places. But Morgan seemed unconcerned. He just thanked Bloomfield and the other band members. It was clear to the Chicagoans that it was time to pack up and be on their way.

Michael Bloomfield was again confused. Was the session just another audition? Was John Hammond going to listen to it and pass judgment? Would he, Michael, then be brought back into the studio to record a *real* album? What had begun in December as an exciting opportunity, the next step in a career with great potential, now seemed to be no more than an exercise in futility. The young guitarist couldn't help but feel discouraged.

He had reason to be. Bob Morgan, unlike John Hammond, was working directly with bands that were part of the emerging trend in popular music. With the huge success of the Beatles, everything had changed. American audiences were increasingly eager for music by attractive, well-turned-out lads who could sing and play, but who were also easily packaged. Morgan was used to dealing with disciplined, well-managed groups who had long since honed their stage acts into tight professional routines. That the Beatles and other bands wrote their own material, were excellent musicians, and had a deep appreciation for the tradition was only part of the success equation. A band had to be marketable.

What Morgan saw when Mike Bloomfield and his men arrived at the Thirtieth Street studio was something else. The musicians appeared to be unrehearsed and disorganized. The Group seemed to be an ad hoc outfit and not really a working band. Their material was loud and not particularly melodic, and the leader, while clearly an excellent guitarist, was no singer. And then there was the fact that the group in the studio was interracial. While Morgan personally had no problem with mixing races, he knew that configuration could severely limit a pop group's potential.

John Hammond had initially been excited by Michael's guitar playing. He had wanted to hear what the guitarist could do with a band, knowing that Epic was looking for groups, and had arranged a session in Chicago and a second in New York. But after just half an hour in the studio, Bob Morgan could discern no commercial angle to the music he was hearing. Epic was indeed looking for a certain type of band, a certain type of sound. While modern Chicago blues could be exciting, Morgan felt the music alone would not be enough.

As far as he was concerned, Michael Bloomfield's relationship with Epic was probably going nowhere.

CHAPTER 8

BUTTERFIELD BLUES

NEW YORK AND CHICAGO, 1965

Paul Butterfield, unlike Michael Bloomfield, *was* going somewhere. Paul Rothchild had arranged for the Paul Butterfield Blues Band to do three nights at the famous Village Gate in Greenwich Village. The venue, on the corner of Bleecker and Thompson streets, had a reputation as the place to hear the best jazz and Latin music in the city. By the winter of 1964–1965, the club had added a dance space in response to the growing popularity of discotheques. Called the Disc-Au-Gate, the new disco had scheduled jazz flutist Herbie Mann and his group for three nights beginning on March 2, with the unknown Paul Butterfield Blues Band opening. To attract a younger crowd to the performances, the Gate's management had gone so far as to bill Mann's group as his "new Latin-blues band."

Neatly attired in matching blazers, Butterfield and his men—a real blues band—played tight, concise versions of tunes from the South Side repertoire. Onstage at the Disc-Au-Gate, they stormed through standards like "Help Me," "Look over Yonders Wall," "Blues with a Feeling," and "Got My Mojo Working." Paul was the vocalist and primary soloist on nearly all the selections, while Elvin occasionally got in a few lead licks. The relentless, driving rhythm provided by Jerome Arnold and Sam Lay made the quartet sound larger than four pieces, and when the band got going full-bore, the beat was irresistible. New Yorkers had never heard anything like it.

A few days after participating in Mike Bloomfield's Epic recording session, John Hammond dropped by the Village Gate, caught one of the Butterfield Band's sets, and was bowled over. Mark Naftalin, Butterfield's piano-playing acquaintance from the University of Chicago, also saw the band that week at the Gate. He had moved to New York City after graduating from the university and was studying music composition and theory at Mannes College of Music on East Seventy-Fourth Street. He, too, was amazed by how well the quartet played.

Hammond and Naftalin weren't the only musicians in the Big Apple who were overwhelmed by the Paul Butterfield Blues Band. Bob Dylan caught one of their shows and was doubtless affected by the band's powerful electric sound.

With him was Robert Shelton, editor of *Hootenanny* magazine and music critic for the *New York Times*. Shelton was so impressed that he wrote a flattering profile of Paul in the March 11 edition of the *Times*. He noted the growing domestic interest in Chicago-style electric blues, spurred on largely by British bands, and characterized Butterfield and his group as the vanguard of an American response to the English imitation. The critic went on to acknowledge that Butterfield had been "the talk of musical circles here since he came to record a few weeks ago."

Paul Rothchild was eager to capitalize on the Chicago quartet's enthusiastic reception. He and Elektra arranged to get the band into the studio right after their Village Gate gig so they could begin recording. Elektra could then issue a Butterfield Band single and test the marketability of a new sound—the sound of electric Chicago blues played by a new generation of bluesmen. If Rothchild's intuition was right, Elektra would have a hit band on its hands. Within a few days, the label announced to the industry that it had signed a new, exciting group from Chicago, and *Billboard* reported that Paul Butterfield "has been brought to New York from Chicago to record Elektra's first batch of singles."

Having nothing better to do following his March 1 studio date, Michael Bloomfield decided he would return the favor and visit Paul Butterfield's recording sessions for Elektra. During the second week of March, Mike and a few friends stopped by Mastertone Studios on West Forty-Second Street, the same facility where he had recorded with his friend John Hammond the previous June.

When Bloomfield arrived, Butterfield and his men were running through a few tunes while producer Paul Rothchild hovered and made suggestions. With Michael were Roy Ruby, Brian Friedman, and Fred Glazer. Young John Hammond was also there, and Nick Gravenites was bustling about, helping Butterfield work out which tunes they would record.

With all the visitors and the addition of a few of Elektra's engineers, the small studio was suddenly quite crowded. Rothchild managed to keep things moving, though, and the band recorded a few numbers while their friends watched through the control room's picture window. Butterfield had decided to do several blues standards, including one by Chicago's premier harmonica player. He re-created Little Walter's version of the Pete Johnson and Joe Turner song "Piney Brown Blues," turning the fast shuffle into an extraordinary tour de force of rhythmic energy. The beat generated by Sam Lay, sequestered as he was in the studio's drum booth, was breathtaking. He also did a bluesy rendition of "Work Song," a jazz standard by cornetist Nat Adderley, and "Our Love Is Driftin'," a song he and Elvin had composed. A one-chord vamp reminiscent of Howlin' Wolf's "Smokestack Lightning," "Our Love Is Driftin'" consisted of Bishop and Arnold repeating a bass line several octaves apart while Paul sang and soloed. The arrangement was meant to be sparse, but with no chordal part it sounded a little too thin to Rothchild. It's too bad the band doesn't have a piano player, he observed to Butterfield during a break.

"Mike plays piano," Paul replied, indicating Bloomfield sitting in the control room. "Why don't you get him to sit in?"

It seemed like an easy solution. Michael came in and sat at the grand piano in one corner of the studio while engineers set up microphones. When they were ready, Elvin kicked off "Our Love Is Driftin'," and Paul blew a few bars of salty harp before singing the first verse. Bloomfield first comped along, playing the bass line with Elvin and Jerome. But then he began adding little fills in the offbeats and embellishments around Paul's lyrics. The effect was just enough to add some color to the tune's austere sound. Rothchild stood in the control room watching, nodding his head in approval. At the conclusion of the take, Michael sauntered back into the booth and lit a cigarette. He smiled at Rothchild and took a seat next to John Hammond.

The band worked through four more tunes, including Little Walter's "Take Me Back Baby," "It's Too Late, Brother," the instrumental "Off the Wall," and the traditional "Poor Boy." As the session wound up and the musicians were packing their gear, Paul Rothchild pulled Butterfield aside. An idea had occurred to him during the recording of "Our Love Is Driftin'," and he wanted to sound Paul out on it.

Why not use Bloomfield as a backup player on some of the tunes they were going to record? He could play keyboards as needed, and he could also play some guitar. A second guitar might enhance the dynamism of the band, Rothchild suggested. The producer had heard Michael before—Butterfield had taken Rothchild to see the Bloomfield-Gravenites band at the End in January. The Elektra man had been duly impressed, and there had been some talk of Bloomfield joining the harmonica player's group then. But Michael had his own band and a contract with Epic, and he didn't much like the harp player, so the Paul Butterfield Blues Band had remained a quartet.

Now, though, Bloomfield was in New York City with time on his hands. His record deal with Epic seemed to have stalled, and his band, lacking a rhythm section, wasn't really a band at all. What harm would there be in playing on a few of Butterfield's tunes?

"Paul asked me if I wanted to play a little slide for him," Bloomfield said. "I admired Paul incredibly for his singing and his music but I never liked him, so I was kind of reluctant to do it. And finally I said all right, so he took me down and I recorded a whole bunch of stuff in New York."

In successive sessions over the next few days, Bloomfield recorded five more tunes with Butterfield—four of them on piano and a fifth on organ. They did Muddy Waters's "Just to Be with You," Little Walter's "Everything's Gonna Be Alright," B. B. King's "Rock Me, Baby," and Jimmy Rogers's "That's All Right." For "Hate to See You Go," a Little Walter blues vamp, Paul upped the tempo and had Michael play a simple counterpoint to Elvin's lead line on the studio's Hammond B3. The resulting recordings had a fuller, more dynamic sound, giving the band an extra dimension and hewing closer to the initial versions of the tunes. Each one of those originals had a piano in its rhythm section.

Paul Rothchild was pleased with the augmented configuration of the Paul Butterfield Blues Band, but he was also curious about how the band would sound with two guitars. Though Elvin Bishop was the band's guitarist, Rothchild had heard what Michael could do. Adding Bloomfield to the mix could only boost the band's driving appeal and add to its exciting reinvigoration of the blues. When Butterfield was next in the studio, Rothchild decided, he would make sure Michael was there—with his guitar.

Mike Bloomfield wasn't spending all his time in New York City waiting for news from Epic and sitting in on recording sessions. He was also hanging out with his friends and making the rounds of the Village's various clubs and coffeehouses. There were more than a few after-hours get-togethers too.

"I do remember one time at a party in somebody's apartment," said Charlie Musselwhite. He and Michael frequently went to Village gatherings together during their stay in New York. "Bob Dylan was there and Mike wanted to have *all* the attention, so, knowing what keys I could play in because he knew what key harps I had, he avoided playing in any of those keys!" Charlie wasn't offended by his friend's desire to be the focus of the party, though he did share Joel Harlib's opinion of Bloomfield's desire for adulation.

"Oh, Mike had a tremendous ego," Musselwhite said, laughing. "That never bothered me, though. It was amusing, and he could often laugh at himself. . . . One time Mike said to me, 'There's nothing I like better than being in a room full of people and all of them looking at me.' I remember that I physically cringed at that!"

There were many other opportunities for Michael to shine. As happened in Chicago during his teen years, Bloomfield was beginning to make a name for himself in New York. He was in the epicenter of the American music scene, meeting people and playing music at a time when a new generation of gifted musicians and producers was emerging. It was an exciting period with much experimentation, and drugs were increasingly a part of the scene. Marijuana use was pervasive, and Michael and his friends had their own stash. But their indulging wasn't limited just to pot.

"We'd buy cough syrup with codeine in it and walk around Manhattan, laughing a lot," recalled Charlie Musselwhite. As he had done with Michael and Fred Glazer in Glencoe, Roy Ruby was "coasting" on terpin hydrate. He, Charlie, and a friend from Roy's Windsor Mountain School days would purchase a few bottles of the medication and spend a pleasant afternoon on the nod. But that wasn't all the twenty-two-year-old Ruby was into.

"I remember watching Roy shoot up," Charlie Musselwhite said.

Roy Ruby had begun experimenting with heroin in 1963, around the time he was working at the Bear. He would occasionally visit Tommy Walker, Old Town's leather shop owner and resident drug dealer, and Walker soon noticed a change in him. He recalled one evening when he went to his front window to toss the door keys down to a visitor who had rung his bell, and he saw Ruby standing on the pavement below. When Roy climbed the stairs to Tommy's apartment, it was obvious he was in bad shape.

"He came in and was crying-like," Walker said. "He was strung out, you know, real sick. He told me he had been doing it for a year."

Now, in New York with his friends, Roy Ruby was again shooting heroin. One evening, his friends joined him.

"We were in somebody's apartment, somewhere, late at night," remembered Fred Glazer. He, Michael, and a few others were there with Roy. "We had like two bags of dope. We stood around, we cooked it up and we all shot up. It was a big loft somewhere . . . *that* was the first time we ever got into dope."

Michael Bloomfield had thoroughly enjoyed his experience with sodium pentothal a few years earlier, but this new sensation was something altogether different. He knew all about heroin, and he probably knew his friend Roy Ruby "chipped," or occasionally used the drug, but he had never tried it himself. Now Michael was helped to tie off and inject the liquefied powder. What he felt as the narcotic took effect was pure warmth, the satisfying glow of total peace of mind. It was something he had rarely experienced, and it was a revelation.

"I *dug* it!" Michael said enthusiastically of the drug. He was unapologetic about his heroin use. "I always enjoyed it. I have not one moment of regret." For Bloomfield, it was welcome relief from the relentless hyperkinetic static of his waking consciousness.

For Fred Glazer, the drug's appeal lay in its ability to assuage deep personal issues the friends all shared. "We needed it," Glazer explained. "We were sad, unhappy, tragic people, all of us. We needed this artificial substance to mediate our thinking so we could face the world. We couldn't face the world *without* something."

Whether heroin was an emotional palliative as Fred claimed or simply a potent and pleasurable high, the narcotic unquestionably placed its users beyond the pale of polite society. In the public's mind, the drug was the opiate of hard-core, dead-end addicts seeking only to stave off the pain of withdrawal as they spiraled downward. But it was also romanticized by some as a refuge for heroic, tortured artists seeking to transgress the limits of convention. In the frightening consequences of addiction lay heroin's social power—a power conferred on anyone willing to assume its risks. Narcotics users were a breed apart, committed social outlaws.

It was that outlaw status that also appealed to Mike Bloomfield. The fantasy image he had long harbored of himself as a modern-day Elvis, a rock 'n' roll rebel, gained greater credence with heroin added to the picture. Bloomfield was not only a dope-smoking guitar wizard who consorted with black people and played their music as an equal; he was now an initiate to the avant-garde world of hard drugs. His image of himself as a "greaser" and a "hoodlum" was, by conventional measure, no longer an image. It was reality.

And the truth was, Michael *was* different. He was not like others of his generation. He never had been. From his earliest days he sought to push the limits, to test boundaries, to seek out sensation. His creative spark would not be contained, and as a result he was destined to live outside of society's norms. It would make him a visionary, the musical virtuoso who would point the way for a generation of guitar players. And as the supernova of his white-hot genius eventually faded to red-dwarf status in the heavenly vault of popular music, that creative flame would ultimately consume him.

By the third week in March, Michael Bloomfield was back in Chicago. Fred Glazer had driven them all back to the Windy City after it became clear that no additional sessions for Epic were on the horizon. Michael reassembled his band with Nick Gravenites and, with Paul Butterfield still busy recording in New York, managed to reclaim the gig at Big John's. *Down Beat* magazine announced that Mike Bloomfield would be at the North Wells Street club "until further notice."

Since Butterfield's departure for the East Coast, Junior Wells had been filling in at Big John's, and the club had expanded its roster to include performances by Howlin' Wolf on Mondays. Before long, Otis Rush and Buddy Guy were making appearances in Old Town, too. Guitarist Steve Miller and his new band had a nightly spot at the Shrimp Boat on North Wells Street, and the Siegel-Schwall Blues Band was soon playing Big John's as well. By spring, the electric blues scene had exploded on the North Side.

The first week in April, Bloomfield got a call from Paul Rothchild. He asked if Michael would be able to come back to New York for another recording session with the Butterfield Band. The producer was hoping to wrap up taping for a possible album, but he wanted to use Bloomfield's lead on some of the tunes before he did.

Michael was amenable, and he told Nick and the group that he would again be out of town for a while. He caught a bus for New York and joined Paul Butterfield and the band at the Hotel Albert in the Village. The next afternoon, he went with them to Mastertone Studios, Telecaster in hand.

The recording sessions had, up to that point, been grueling. Paul complained to Michael that Elektra appeared to have no idea how to record loud electric music, and that Rothchild was having him do tunes over and over again while the engineers tinkered with the mics and the mix. The producer seemed to be trying to get as many versions of each song as possible on tape, hoping that at least one take would be usable. The harp player said the effort was beginning to hurt his voice.

The truth was, Elektra was completely inexperienced when it came to recording loud music. A band like Butterfield's, with three amplified instruments and the powerhouse drumming of Sam Lay, was far beyond anything the label's audio engineers had ever tackled. They were making it up as they went along.

With Michael Bloomfield in the studio, the volume only increased. Over the course of a few days, Butterfield's quartet and its guest soloist recorded more than a dozen tunes while the engineers continued to experiment with the acoustics. The sound quality varied from take to take as they toyed with the mix, switching instruments to different tracks and moving sound barriers around between the amplifiers. With all the readjusting and multiple takes, the process was a slow one.

But the band had never sounded better. The addition of another instrument greatly increased the depth of the music while releasing Butterfield from duties as the primary soloist. Bloomfield relished playing with Bishop, Arnold, and Lay in the rhythm section and, though he could be intimidated by Paul, he deeply respected Butterfield's skill as a harp player and knowledge of the blues. Despite their mutual antipathy, Michael's and Paul's styles seemed particularly suited to one another. Paul Rothchild was thrilled.

Among the songs the group recorded were "Mellow Down Easy" and "Spoonful," both by Willie Dixon. Michael played spiky fills between Paul's verses on "Mellow Down Easy," then backed the harmonica player's solo lines with uncanny precision. Elvin Bishop stepped out from his accompanying role to take a rare solo on "Spoonful."

Michael alternated between slide and fretted runs for Tampa Red's "It Hurts Me Too" and an original by Paul called "Lovin' Cup." Sonny Boy Williamson's "Help Me" featured Butterfield's harp, while "One More Mile," a tune by James Cotton, was all Bloomfield's. By the time they got to Cotton's slow blues, Michael had turned his amp way up, his sound enveloped in reverb. Bloomfield's lead was so intense that Paul let out an involuntary shout during the guitarist's first of two solo choruses. Elektra's beleaguered engineers were frantically riding the gain knobs in the control room.

"Look over Yonders Wall," a song popularized by bottleneck master Elmore James under the title "Look on Yonder Wall," again showcased Bloomfield's slide. Michael repeatedly burned through James's signature lick during Paul's vocal and then switched between fretted notes and slide for his solo. Toward the end of the week's sessions, the band recorded another original by the leader, this time an instrumental called "Nut Popper #1." As with nearly all the tunes they recorded, Rothchild insisted on multiple takes. By the fifth run-through, Butterfield was becoming annoyed, and when asked by Rothchild for the name of the piece, he repeatedly replied, "Numbpupper #1." The irascible bandleader was clearly messing with his producer.

One of the last tunes Butterfield and the band recorded was a Nick Gravenites original. Michael suggested it because it was one he and Nick had been playing with their group back in Chicago, and he thought it particularly suited Paul. He demonstrated the arrangement he had worked out, and after a few attempts, the band picked it up. Bloomfield scrawled out the lyrics on a piece of paper and handed them to Butterfield, and the harp player tried a few verses. He was hesitant to record the song at first, but as the group warmed to it, Paul gave it a try. After a number of takes, everyone in the studio as well as in the control room was satisfied. Butterfield decided that Gravenites's "Born in Chicago" was a keeper.

With his sessions for Elektra completed, Paul Butterfield returned to Chicago during the second week in April. Within a few days, he and the band were once again working at Big John's. All of Old Town was buzzing about Butterfield's soon-to-be-released album, and hipsters crowded the North Wells Street club, eager to hear the new sound of the blues.

Mike Bloomfield came home that week too. He made a half-hearted attempt to restart his band with Nick Gravenites, but they had lost their gig at Big John's in his absence and now had nowhere to play. So Bloomfield kept himself busy sitting in around town and picking up work wherever he could. He had liked playing with Paul Butterfield in New York, and though Elvin Bishop was Paul's guitar player, there might be possibilities with the band. Butterfield clearly appreciated Michael's playing even though he seemed to have little regard for the guitarist personally—"For a while he thought I was a turkey" is how Bloomfield later described the harp player's attitude. But working regularly with the Paul Butterfield Blues Band—that was something Michael would have to think about.

Then, one day in early May, the guitarist got a call from Paul. The harp player wanted to know if Bloomfield could come down to the South Side for a photo shoot. Elektra was sending its art director, William Harvey, out to Chicago to take some promotional pictures of the Butterfield Band on its home turf. Paul Rothchild wanted Michael to be included in the shots because the guitarist was on ten of the fourteen songs he was considering for the album—and was the featured soloist on several of them. Though he wasn't officially part of Butterfield's group, Bloomfield was a large part of its sound—or at least he would be on its forthcoming Elektra album. It wouldn't be right to omit him.

The day had warmed by mid-afternoon, the bright spring sun breaking through the clouds to dispel the chill of the morning air. The members of the Butterfield Band congregated on the corner of Roosevelt Road and South Halsted Street, the northeastern boundary of the sprawling Maxwell Street Market. With them was Nick Gravenites, invited along by Butterfield to help set up the shots. There they met up with Bill Harvey and immediately began scouting for locations that were suitably bluesy backdrops for a few candids of Chicago's hottest new band. Harvey suggested they find a place that characterized the South Side, somewhere that was common to life in Chicago's black neighborhoods. Maxwell Street would have been perfect, but the market was open only on Sundays. Michael had an idea. They should pose for pictures "in the alley," he said, taking inspiration from the well-known blues expression meaning to play "down and dirty."

Chicago, unlike most eastern cities, was built on a grid with each block of buildings split down the middle by a service alleyway. The alleys allowed for deliveries, trash removal, and parking behind the buildings, and they also provided backyard space. Contractors saved on construction expenses by building external fire escapes in those backyard spaces, and those towering wooden "back porches" were a distinctive Chicago icon.

It was an excellent idea. The photographer and his subjects trooped down an alley off Halsted Street and found a suitable boarded-up building with a three-story set of porches. Harvey sent the band up the porch stairs and directed them to arrange themselves on the first level. The photographer then positioned himself in the alley and took a few long shots as some curious neighborhood kids mugged for the camera. Then he entered the backyard and snapped a few close-ups. The band looked suitably serious, their no-nonsense demeanor underscored by the stark urban setting.

Having gotten the shots he wanted, Harvey signaled to the band that they could come down off the porch. The group then made its way back to Halsted, but the photographer wasn't completely satisfied. He wanted to get a few more photos, preferably horizontal shots that would be suitable for an album cover. As they looked around the neighborhood, Gravenites noticed a storefront on the corner of Maxwell and Newberry streets that had oddities and curios in its windows. It was just the sort of place where one might find a John the Conqueror root or a mojo hand. "That's it, boys," Nick said. "Get over there!"

Harvey thought it was perfect, and the group spread out in front of the shop under the hand-painted legend in one window, which read "Incense, Herbs, Oils." As a little girl played in the shop's doorway, the photographer loaded his camera with a fresh roll of color film. Paul and Elvin were wearing sunglasses against the bright afternoon glare, and Mike, who had arrived in a raincoat, now took it off and draped it casually over one arm. Jerome looked sharp in chinos and a dark sport shirt while Sam, his curly hair "relaxed" and oiled, displayed his huge arms in a white muscle shirt. His pointed-toe, gold-lamé shoes said he meant business.

The Paul Butterfield Blues Band looked like nothing so much as a gang of neighborhood toughs. They weren't dressed in matching blazers and slacks, neatly attired and photogenic in the way pop music groups were supposed to be in 1965. They didn't have cute haircuts and cherubic faces. They looked like the kind of guys who would hang around a pool hall, smoking and drinking and shaking down neighborhood kids for lunch money. They looked like hoodlums.

Harvey took a half dozen frames of the quintet while they joked about being photographed in a "lineup." After fifteen minutes, Bill was satisfied that he had all the images he needed. He thanked Butterfield and his men for their forbearance and then hailed a cab. The musicians waved him off and wandered over to Buck's Redhots. The smells wafting from the Halsted hot dog concession had given everyone an appetite for a Polish with mustard, fried onions, and sport peppers.

The Butterfield photo shoot, as casual as it was, raised real questions for Mike Bloomfield. Was he a member of Paul's band or wasn't he? Was he an Epic recording artist with his own contract, or was he a sideman in someone else's band, recording for Elektra? He was deeply ambivalent about his status. He liked playing with Paul, and he very much liked working with Butterfield's rhythm section. But he still had doubts about the harmonica player.

"[Paul] was the white guy that most had transcended the color line," Bloomfield said. "He carried a gun, he was dangerous. He would kick ass faster than he would shake hands. He would kick *anyone's* ass." Michael sensed that Butterfield's blues "credibility" was far greater than his own, and it made him uncomfortable. "He *chose* from his earliest years to hang out in the toughest, baddest, no-white areas," Bloomfield said of Butterfield. "I mean, a white man would get killed and [Paul] would just do whatever it took to hang out there. He had completely transcended the color line. I never liked Paul, 'cause he was *much* too rough. Much too street for me. Much too dangerous a guy."

Bloomfield's ambivalence only increased his uncertainty about his future. Despite his best efforts, he seemed unable to advance his career in any meaningful way. He was known in Chicago as one of the city's best guitar players, and he was fast acquiring that reputation in New York City as well. But no one seemed interested in recording a hotshot guitarist. Everyone wanted groups.

Or nearly everyone. There was one person who needed an ace guitar player—one who could play electric with edgy, raw energy. Who could blend blues and rock in an exciting way. Who knew the folk tradition.

One afternoon in early June, the phone rang in Michael and Susan's Sandburg Village apartment. On the line was Michael's friend Bob Dylan. Was the guitarist available? Bob wanted to know. Would he be interested in coming to New York to record? On electric guitar? With him?

The folksinger had been amazed by Michael Bloomfield's skill as a player and his encyclopedic knowledge of music when they had first met at the Bear in 1963. The few times he had run into the guitarist since then, he had only become more impressed.

"He was an expert player and a real prodigy, too," Dylan later said of Bloomfield. "He could play like Willie Brown or Charlie Patton. He could play like Robert Johnson way back in the Sixties." Bob was planning to use electric instruments on his next Columbia release, and Michael immediately came to mind. "He could outplay anybody, even at that point. When it was time to bring a guitar player onto my record, I couldn't think of anybody but him. I mean, he just was the best guitar player I'd ever heard."

The offer came as a complete surprise to Bloomfield. As far as he knew, the musician he had befriended at the Bear was an acoustic player. "Then I saw him again in New York at a party, and we played a little," recalled Michael. "Through the strength of those two meetings, he called me to make a record with him."

Despite his warm feelings for Dylan as a friend, Michael's opinion of his playing and singing hadn't changed much. He still thought of Bob as a mediocre musician, and he wasn't too sure that recording with him would be a good career move. As far as Michael was concerned, Dylan—even though he had a few albums out on Columbia—was just another earnest folksinger playing the circuit.

But the pay Columbia was offering for Dylan's sessions was good, and Michael liked the idea that he would be in the label's New York studios again. His presence might not get things moving with Epic, but it couldn't hurt. At least they wouldn't forget him.

After talking it over with Susan and a few friends, Bloomfield decided he would do it. He called Bob back and told him he would see him in New York in a few days.

It was a life-changing decision.

On Saturday, June 12, Mike Bloomfield caught a mid-morning flight to upstate New York out of O'Hare International Airport. He gave his overnight bag to the attendant at the check-in counter but kept his new Telecaster with him, strolling through the terminal concourse with it under one arm. As he made his way to the departure gate, the bushy-haired young man with the caseless electric guitar drew curious stares from more than a few travelers. But Michael was unperturbed. Once he boarded the plane, he simply sat the Telecaster on the vacant seat next to him and settled in for the two-hour flight.

Early that afternoon, Bob Dylan picked Michael up at Albany International Airport in his Ford Galaxie station wagon. During the sixty-minute drive to Woodstock, the folksinger explained that they would spend a few days in the country working out his new songs, and then they would head down to the city for the recording sessions at Columbia's studios. Michael was amenable to that and was eager to see Bob's rural retreat, the place where Dylan would go to temporarily escape the trappings of his growing celebrity.

By the summer of 1965, that celebrity was considerable. Dylan had just returned from a month-long concert tour of England, where he had played the Royal Albert Hall, hung out with the Beatles and the Rolling Stones, been the subject of a documentary film, and famously ended his affair with folk queen Joan Baez. His current single, "Subterranean Homesick Blues," had reached number thirty-nine on *Billboard*'s Hot 100 chart. "Mr. Tambourine Man," one of his songs recorded by a new group based in Los Angeles called the Byrds, was climbing the charts in the United States and Britain, and it would soon reach number one in both countries. By any measure, Bob Dylan was a huge pop music success. It didn't take long for Bloomfield to realize that.

"I knew he was, like, popular," Michael said of his friend. "But I had no idea until I got there that he was like an *enormous* superstar!"

Dylan drove to West Hurley and on up through Woodstock to the tiny hamlet of Bearsville. There he pulled into a long driveway next to an imposing laid-stone mansion partially hidden by fragrant pines and leafy maples. It was Dylan's manager's home, and Michael was stunned.

Albert Grossman, the former owner of Chicago's Gate of Horn and one-time partner in that city's experimental nightclub the Bear, had become a high-powered manager of top-rated musical talent by 1965. His portfolio of artists included folksingers Odetta, Bob Gibson, Gordon Lightfoot, and Hedy West; bluesman John Lee Hooker; and folk ensembles Ian & Sylvia, the Jim Kweskin Jug Band, and Peter, Paul and Mary. Bob Dylan was the thoroughbred in his stable, and he had deftly guided Dylan's career since 1962—making a small fortune in the process. He had used some of that money to purchase the Bearsville estate in 1963 and had moved there permanently a year later. In addition to the main house, the compound had a barn with a living space and several small cabins. Dylan was staying in one of those with his new girlfriend, Sara Lownds.

That evening, when the two musicians got to work on the tunes for the new album, Bob struggled to describe to Michael the sound he was looking for. One thing he *didn't* want was straight-ahead blues. While in England, Dylan had tried to record one of his new tunes with a London-based blues band called the Bluesbreakers, headed by keyboardist John Mayall and powered by a twenty-year-old guitar firebrand named Eric Clapton. When the Bluesbreakers had no idea what to do with Bob's music, the session had turned into a disaster. The folksinger didn't want to repeat that experience. He wanted Michael to come up with another way to put his music across.

At first, Bloomfield was at a loss about what to do.

> The first thing I heard was "Like a Rolling Stone." He wanted me to get the concept of it, how to play it. I figured he wanted blues, string-bending, because that's what I do. He said, "Hey, man, I don't want any of that B. B. King shit." So, OK, I really fell apart. What the hell does he want? We messed around with the song. I played the way that he dug and he said it was groovy.

"Subterranean Homesick Blues" had been recorded with electric guitars and drums, but Dylan now wanted a different sound. He played examples of his songs that other pop artists had recorded, including a version of "All I Really Want to Do" by a young female singer named Cher as well as a just-released rendition of that song by the Byrds. Michael was already familiar with their cover of "Mr. Tambourine Man." Bob especially liked the sound the Byrds got and told Bloomfield that he wanted something similar when they went into the studio.

Over the weekend, Bob and Michael worked out arrangements for each of the songs Dylan had written for the upcoming session. The folksinger's approach to composing, according to Michael, involved sitting at the piano and sketching out his tunes "all on the black keys." As a result, the pieces were often in odd keys, making them difficult to play on guitar. But while Dylan comped away at the piano, Michael improvised, trying chord substitutions and different voicings in an effort to find accompaniment that fit. When he hit on something that Bob liked, he noted it on a scrap of paper so he wouldn't forget. Dylan only had a few new songs, but they were complicated and had verses that went on and on. It quickly became obvious that remembering all the changes, additional chords, and substitutions was not going to be possible without writing them down.

But it wasn't all work that weekend. While Michael was impressed by the folksinger's writing, he very much enjoyed Bob's company. He also enjoyed wandering around the estate's wooded lawns, basking in the fresh country air and majestic quiet of the Catskills setting. Sara and Bob seemed to be very much in love and were busy making plans to buy a home in Bearsville, not far from Grossman's property. At one point, Bob took Michael over to the main house to introduce him to his manager and their host. Even though Bloomfield knew him from Chicago, he was unsure who Grossman was at first.

"I didn't recognize Albert even though I had met him many times before," said the guitarist. "He had short hair before and now he looked like Benjamin Franklin." An imposing physical presence, the taciturn Grossman made a strong impression on Michael. Here was a man who seemed tight lipped and remote while at the same time acutely aware of those around him. To Bloomfield, the manager was an enigma.

"We used to call him 'Cumulus Nimbus,'" said Bloomfield with a laugh, recalling his nickname for Albert. "He was such a vague guy, you know? It was so hard to understand what he was saying, man—the 'Gray Cloud.'"

On Tuesday, June 15, Bob and Michael drove down to New York City. They arrived at Columbia's building at 799 Seventh Avenue early in the afternoon and took an elevator up to Studio A on the top floor. It had been raining lightly for much of the morning, and Bloomfield's naked Telecaster glistened with beads of rainwater. Albert Grossman was in the control room already, having arrived in New York the day before. With him was Columbia's producer for Dylan's last three recordings, Tom Wilson.

The studio was crowded—even more crowded than it had been during Butterfield's Elektra tapings in March. If Michael needed more evidence of Dylan's celebrity, here it was. Along with the manager and the session's producer, there were at various times two studio engineers, several of Grossman's assistants, a pair of staff photographers and famed photo journalist W. Eugene Smith, Bob's estranged girlfriend Suze Rotolo, New York guitarist Danny Kalb, Elektra producer Paul Rothchild, and a steady stream of curiosity seekers from Columbia's offices downstairs. There was a pervasive sense that history was being made, and nobody, it seemed, wanted to be left out.

In the studio proper were half a dozen session musicians waiting for things to get under way. One of them was a songwriter friend of Tom Wilson's, a twenty-one-year-old guitar player and composer from Queens, New York. He had been invited to the session by Wilson. His name was Al Kooper.

"I used to hang out in Tom's office," said Kooper. "I was a big fan of Dylan's, and whenever he'd record something new I'd take home the acetates and listen to them. So Wilson knew I was into Bob and he invited me to come down to the recording session. Just to watch."

Kooper had briefly been a member of the Royal Teens in 1959, touring with them as they performed their hit "Short Shorts," and he had recently penned "This Diamond Ring" for Gary Lewis and the Playboys, a rock 'n' roll lament that had reached number one on the *Billboard* chart in February. Al had come to Dylan's recording date with guitar in hand, determined to play. He was just plugging in when Mike Bloomfield burst into the studio, toweling off his wet Telecaster. When the Chicagoan sat down and began warming up, Kooper quietly put his guitar back into its case.

"I realized then that there was no chance I was going to be the guitarist on the session," Al recalled. "I'd never heard *anybody* play like that. 'Well,' I thought, 'I'm not gonna be able to play on this, so I might as well go back into the control room.'"

The other musicians in the room were sanctioned by Tom Wilson. All were studio professionals who had recorded for Columbia numerous times, and all had been on Dylan's previous album, *Bringing It All Back Home*. Wilson had selected them to back Dylan for that recording in an experiment to see how the folksinger sounded with electric instruments and drums. As a result, seven of that album's eleven songs were played by an electric band—a "rock 'n' roll" band.

Wilson had reassembled the same players for this date. Frank Owens was on piano, Al Gorgoni was the rhythm guitarist, Joe Macho Jr. was on bass, and Bobby Gregg was behind the trap set. Owens was an Erroll Garner–style jazz pianist who had been Johnny Mathis's musical director. Gorgoni had played guitar on innumerable pop records, including hits by the Four Seasons, Shangri-Las, and Dixie Cups. Bassist Macho backed Chubby Checker in the early 1960s and would later work with jazz pianist Les McCann and vibist Freddie McCoy. Gregg had recorded a number of pop singles with his own band and had released an album of dance instrumentals on Epic.

Of the four sidemen, only Bobby Gregg and Joe Macho could be called rock 'n' roll players. As an ensemble, the quartet lacked the "edge" that Bob Dylan was looking for. He had heard his friend young John Hammond talk about recording an album of electric blues a year earlier—his *So Many Roads* sessions—and Bob had been excited by the idea. Since the arrival of the Beatles and their British compatriots, the sound of pop music had shifted increasingly toward groups that played a combination of rock and blues. The era of acoustic folk music performed by a single musician was rapidly receding. For Dylan, the trend offered a possible escape from his increasingly confining role as folk's wunderkind, as Woody Guthrie's heir. Recording with an electric band of his own would move his music more into the mainstream. That his songwriting was becoming more personal only increased his desire to escape the limitations of "the tradition."

With Tom Wilson's help and encouragement, Dylan had recorded a portion of *Bringing It All Back Home* with electric backing. While the experiment raised more than a few eyebrows in the folk music community, the album didn't really provide the clean break the folksinger was seeking. Its electric energy was raucous in places, but the songs lacked the rock 'n' roll kick typical of tunes by the Rolling Stones or even the Beatles. Dylan wanted to take his music a step further.

That's why he had brought in Michael Bloomfield.

Tom Wilson thought that Michael was just another of Bob's pals, a friend invited to watch the recording process. When the bushy-haired guitarist made for the studio door, Wilson moved to head him off. But Dylan quickly explained that Bloomfield was going to be part of the session. The producer was surprised, not expecting any other musicians for the date, but he deferred to the artist's wishes. Michael's name was added to the session information sheet.

On the trip down from Bearsville, Bob had asked Michael to run the session. The folksinger didn't want to be distracted from his music by having to explain it to the players. "Bob told me, 'You talk to the musicians, man, I don't want to tell them anything,'" Bloomfield said. Michael was willing, but he soon realized he was in over his head.

> So we get to the session. I didn't know anything about it. All these studio cats are standing around. I come in like a dumb punk with a guitar over

> my back, no case, and I'm telling people about this and that, and this is the arrangement, and do this on the bridge. These are like the heaviest studio musicians in New York. They looked at me like I was crazy.

Despite Bloomfield's growing misgivings, he gamely tried to outline to the others what Dylan wanted. He went over the chords he and Bob had worked out in Bearsville, described the shape of the tunes, and demonstrated tempos. Watching from the control room, Al Kooper was impressed by Bloomfield's composure. He thought the guitarist handled the session with aplomb, given the circumstances.

The session got under way a little before 3:00 p.m. The first tune the band attempted was "Phantom Engineer," a variation on the blues with an unusual I–I^7–VI–V–I turnaround. At first, Michael deferred to the studio players, letting Gorgoni take the lead part while quietly playing rhythm. But by the sixth take, Bloomfield had taken over and was adding steely lead fills between Dylan's verses, giving the tune a raw, aggressive feel. By basing his rhythm riff on John Lee Hooker's "Boom, Boom," Michael shifted the song's initial two-beat rhythm to a fast shuffle. At the start of the session, he had plugged his Telecaster into one of the studio's rented Ampegs, a Gemini I, an amplifier originally intended for jazz players. But Michael soon turned it up, giving his guitar a hard, overdriven sound. *Here* at last was the edgy quality Dylan was looking for.

The musicians worked through nine mostly incomplete takes as Bob fussed with the lyrics and phrasing—the song was apparently unfinished. Bloomfield could see how the musicians were trying to give the folksinger what he wanted, but he was surprised at how disorganized the session was. His few times in the studio had been models of efficiency compared to this. Michael blamed the man in the control room.

"The producer was a *non*-producer—Tom Wilson," Bloomfield later told an interviewer. "He didn't know what was happening. I think they wanted rock 'n' roll. We did twenty alternate takes of every song, and it got ridiculous."

Al Kooper agreed with Mike's evaluation but was more generous toward Wilson. From where he sat during the recording process, he was privy to the subtle politics playing out in the control room.

"The *Highway 61 Revisited* sessions were a complete mess, but I don't know if it was anybody's fault," Kooper said. "Albert Grossman didn't get along with Wilson, and nobody had told Tom what to expect."

One of the few African-American producers on Columbia's staff, Tom Wilson came to the label with an impressive track record. A graduate of Harvard University, he had started his own jazz record label right out of college, putting out recordings by Sun Ra, Donald Byrd, and Cecil Taylor. He then produced albums for United Artists and Savoy Records before joining Columbia in the early 1960s. In 1964 Wilson scored a number-one hit single with Simon and Garfunkel's "The Sound of Silence" by adding drums and electric instruments. A year earlier, he had taken over producing Bob Dylan after John Hammond and Albert Grossman had a falling out. He had been in the studio guiding the folksinger's three previous albums and a portion of a fourth. A true visionary and progressive music enthusiast, Wilson was a canny innovator in the studio.

But his June 1965 sessions with Bob Dylan were largely out of his control, and they would be his last for Columbia.

Dylan next tried a one-chord blues with stops on the turnaround called "Sitting on a Barbed Wire Fence." Michael punched out chords on the second beat and third offbeat of each measure while Frank Owens, on organ, accented the fourth beat. As the takes progressed, Dylan began to fill the breaks between his vocals with harmonica riffs while Bloomfield backed him with increasingly aggressive lead lines. His energized, razor-sharp sound was frequently the loudest thing in the room. During one take, Michael dropped in a long searing solo, and Dylan laughingly improvised a verse in tribute. It then became part of the song.

> I got this woman in LA, she makes the sweat run down my brow
> I got this woman out in LA, she makes the sweat run down my brow
> Well, she's good all right, but she ain't as good as this guitar player
>   I got right now!

After half a dozen run-throughs of "Sitting on a Barbed Wire Fence," the musicians took a break. They had been at it for several hours, the studio wall clock reading a little past 5:00 p.m. But Dylan wanted to keep going. He wanted to work on "Like a Rolling Stone."

Michael Bloomfield knew that tune would be a challenge. Dylan had composed half a dozen verses for it, culled from a ten-page story/rant he had written a few weeks earlier at Grossman's place in Bearsville. A story told with withering scorn and condemnation, it was something he later described as a piece of "vomit." The song's form was long and unusual too—it wasn't the typical three- or four-chord rock 'n' roll ditty. It consisted of a thirty-two-bar A part for the verses followed by a twenty-four-bar B part for a repeated chorus. Dylan had sketched it out in simple chords, but Michael had arranged it with a series of elaborate substitutions and embellishments. The musicians had all been given basic lead sheets for the session, but "Like a Rolling Stone" would require considerable work if it was to be played the way he and Dylan had worked it out.

Frank Owens now took over directing the musicians. The keyboardist noted repeats, set tempos, and counted off each tune as the musicians worked through take after take. A studio veteran, Owens knew his business, and at one point he tried to exclude the newcomer by suggesting that Michael lay out. But Dylan, aware that Bloomfield's sound was an essential ingredient, cut Frank off, saying, "He *knows it*, man, he knows it!" Michael continued to play.

The group struggled through five takes of the tune, with Owens patiently reviewing chord changes after each faltered effort. Bob had originally worked the song out in 4/4 time, but prior to the session he switched its tempo to waltz time. The change gave the piece an odd "um-pah-pah" feeling, and because Dylan was most comfortable with the black keys on piano, he had everyone play in C-sharp. That further complicated the performance, but the musicians valiantly tried to find a groove.

By the fourth take of "Like a Rolling Stone," Bob's voice was showing the strain. He had been singing for nearly three hours and he was beginning to sound raspy and parched.

"The voice is gone, man," he complained. But he wanted to make one more attempt before ending the session. There was another false start, and then Owens counted it off again, "*One*-two-three, *two*-two-three, *three*-two-three, *four* . . ." This time the group navigated the changes for several verses without a problem, but then the final take of the day also broke down. The song, though, despite its being in 3/4 time, was beginning to come together. Dylan felt good about it, and the musicians filed into the control room to hear a few of the afternoon's tunes played back.

The following day, Wednesday, June 16, Bob Dylan decided to concentrate solely on "Like a Rolling Stone." The session got under way a little after 2:30 p.m.

Back in the studio with Dylan and Mike Bloomfield for the second day were Gorgoni, Macho, and Gregg. Frank Owens, who was unable to be there, was replaced by keyboardist Paul Griffin. Griffin was another studio veteran who had recorded with Dionne Warwick, the Isley Brothers, Chuck Jackson, and Jimmy Witherspoon. Also joining the group was guitarist and percussionist Bruce Langhorne, a frequent participant in Columbia sessions and a fixture on the Greenwich Village folk scene. He had been Dylan's first electric guitarist, having played tasteful lead on the electric portion of *Bringing It All Back Home*. For this session, he was equipped with a large Turkish frame drum, a tambourine-like instrument that was his trademark. It had been the inspiration for Dylan's "Tambourine Man."

The group tried a few run-throughs of "Like a Rolling Stone," warming up for the taping and allowing the new players to familiarize themselves with the tune. Overnight, the piece had reverted to standard time and was no longer an awkward waltz. In addition, the key had mercifully been lowered from C-sharp to C to make it easier to play on guitar.

Overnight, too, Michael Bloomfield had decided to back off his role as the date's "music director." Feeling his position had largely been usurped by Frank Owens during the previous session, he now let the studio professionals work things out themselves. Other than a few asides to Bob, he said little during the taping and concentrated instead on his guitar playing. It was Bobby Gregg who counted off the various takes.

Tom Wilson wanted to hear piano on the song, so he suggested that Paul Griffin move from organ to that instrument for the recording. As Griffin got up from the Hammond B3, Al Kooper, who was again sitting in the control room, saw his chance. He asked Wilson if he could play the organ for the taping of "Like a Rolling Stone." "Tom said, 'Al, you're a *guitar* player,'" Kooper recalled. "I said, 'Yeah, but I got a really great part for this—I can play it,' which was total BS. And right then, someone came and told him he had a phone call."

Kooper, not one to pass up an opportunity, hustled into the studio and hunkered down behind the big instrument. "Tom didn't say I could . . . but he also didn't say I *couldn't*," Al reasoned. When Wilson returned, the group was in the middle of another run-through with Kooper's organ tentatively complementing the piano-guitars-bass-drums instrumentation. It was only after Wilson suggested over the intercom that they try recording a take that he noticed Al seated at the organ.

"What are *you* doing there?" he asked. Kooper laughed nervously and looked from Wilson to his fellow musicians, a guilty smile on his face. The affable producer just shrugged and smiled back. "Okay, stand by."

The group ran through fifteen separate takes of "Like a Rolling Stone" that afternoon. Some were brief false starts; others were lengthy attempts that eventually broke down. Only one take was completed to the satisfaction of all involved—the fourth. For that six-minute period, the musicians achieved an extraordinary ensemble sound, blending perfectly and imbuing Dylan's biting lyrics with an authority that transcended the personal and made his words ring with universal truth. The music set the mood for the songwriter's vitriol, giving it an all-knowing, ageless quality that seemed somehow to combine youthful swagger with timeless wisdom. Though none of the participants knew it at the time, the song was destined to become one of the most highly regarded pop music releases of all time.

Michael Bloomfield's contribution was pivotal. His arrangement gave the tune its harmonic beauty, and his guitar part, with its repeated variations, added hooks that listeners could hang on before being buffeted by another gritty episode in the life of Dylan's "rolling stone" heroine. Bloomfield's lines were a departure from his usual approach—for the first time, he wasn't charging out front and "leading." Instead of thinking in terms of licks, he concentrated on harmony, on blending. Here was none of that "B. B. King shit." His guitar embellishments—along with Al Kooper's serendipitous organ flourishes—established the musical character of the song, playing a tempering counterpart to the cynicism of Dylan's uncompromising lyrics.

Pop music history had indeed been made, and Michael Bloomfield had been one of its primary shapers. For once, he was unquestionably at the center of where things were happening.

In July, Elektra was preparing to release the Paul Butterfield Blues Band's debut recording. The label had ordered ten thousand copies—which exceeded its usual initial pressing—in anticipation of brisk sales. Paul told Michael he was expecting the record to be out by the end of the month. Bloomfield had hoped that by midsummer he, too, would have a record release pending, but Epic continued to be silent on the topic. Nonetheless, Michael was happy to be part of Paul's impending success.

He was now playing regularly with Butterfield's group at Big John's. Though he still didn't consider himself an "official" member of the band, he liked playing with the harp player and was beginning to feel more at ease around him. Paul, too, had begun to warm to the flamboyant guitarist. The combination of Butterfield and Bloomfield in the front line was unbeatable as far as the club's patrons were concerned.

As his twenty-second birthday approached, Michael Bloomfield was feeling pretty good about himself. He had reason to be: he had a featured spot on what would be the first electric blues album by a group of young white bluesmen, and he had just recorded music for another album with one of the most talked-about stars in the pop music world. With any luck, he would hear from Epic soon regarding his own recording career. Things were looking up.

His buoyed spirits boosted his already hyper energy level. Michael seemed to be everywhere at once, running from one venue to another, one party to a second or third, sitting in here and jamming there. An endless stream of friends and acquaintances stopped by the Sandburg Village apartment to hear about Dylan, listen to the latest releases by soul singers like Joe Tex and Otis Redding, and maybe play a few tunes. Fred Glazer, Roy Ruby, Barry Goldberg, and Charlie Musselwhite were regulars, but Michael and Susan's guests often included old high school friends, fans from the Fickle Pickle, aspiring musicians, and other assorted characters. Joel Harlib was around, too, though he had been less involved in Bloomfield's career since the guitarist had gotten the call for a second Epic session. And whenever a crowd gathered at the apartment, someone invariably produced a baggie of grass. Visits were often an occasion to pass around a few joints.

Without question, Michael loved pot. He had been smoking marijuana since high school, and it was his preferred recreational drug. He hardly touched alcohol. But Bloomfield's experience with Roy Ruby in New York had introduced him to a new sensation—one that superseded all others. Nothing eased his mental and emotional mania like heroin.

He didn't use it very often. But when he did, he usually could find an accommodating supplier just a few blocks from his apartment. His friend Tommy Walker mostly dealt grass, but he sometimes also sold the harder stuff. There was a reason for that, though he kept it from his clientele—Walker himself was a user. Over time he had become addicted, and when Michael first approached him to buy a quantity of the drug, he became alarmed.

"When I found out he was using, I kicked his ass!" Tommy said. "I said to Mike, 'Have you lost your motherfuckin' mind?' Man, I knew what that stuff could do to you because I was strung out on it myself. Nobody knew, but I was an addict for nine years."

Despite his disapproval, Tommy Walker occasionally helped Bloomfield use the narcotic. They would sometimes indulge in the Sandburg Village apartment—but only when Susan was out.

"We'd have the stuff and the works spread out all over the kitchen table," recalled Walker. "And when Mike's wife would come home, we'd grab everything and hide it quick. He didn't want her to know he was doing it."

Whether Susan knew about her husband's drug use was beside the point. Michael's attraction to heroin wasn't so much about partying; it had more to do with his ongoing need to downshift his overdriven consciousness. It could do that better than anything he had ever tried, and he wasn't about to let the possibility of addiction prevent him from taking advantage of heroin's palliative effect.

The second week in July, the Paul Butterfield Blues Band played a benefit at the theater on North Wells Street operated by the comedy improv group Second City. At the party following the show, Paul told Michael that Elektra had arranged for the band to appear at the Newport Folk Festival later that month.

Butterfield was eager to have Bloomfield in the front line when the group took the stage at the folk music showcase so they would sound their best. He was hoping to impress an industry bigwig who was going to be at the festival and who was thinking of taking the band on. He was the same guy who managed Bob Dylan—Albert Grossman.

Michael congratulated Paul on his good luck, saying he thought Grossman would be a real asset for the band. He had seen the manager in action during the *Highway 61 Revisited* sessions, and it was obvious Albert could be a formidable advocate for his clients. Bloomfield also said he would be more than happy to play with the group at Newport.

The request came as a pleasant surprise to Mike Bloomfield. Dylan had mentioned that he would be at Newport again this year, and Michael had seen the ads for the festival in *Sing Out!*, but he really hadn't thought about going himself. Now he was excited by the prospect. To go to Newport to perform modern blues, the kind of music he had been playing almost exclusively for the last year, would be a real thrill. It would be an opportunity to show off his skills. But he wondered how Butterfield's group, an electric band with drums, had managed to get invited to a festival that traditionally featured acoustic music.

Butterfield's Newport slot had indeed taken some doing. Paul Rothchild had introduced Paul to Albert Grossman when the harmonica player had been in New York recording. The manager had picked up on Rothchild's enthusiasm for the band and thought they might make a good addition to his roster of clients. He already had one successful blues act with John Lee Hooker, and he suspected a white blues player of similar caliber might have even broader appeal. He told Rothchild he wanted to see Butterfield perform for an audience of knowledgeable listeners so he could gauge the reaction. If the response was good, he would take Butterfield on. The Newport Folk Festival seemed like the perfect venue to hold the audition.

Albert Grossman had helped festival founder George Wein organize the original Newport Folk Festival in 1959, and his artists had been prominently featured at every festival since then. Though he was viewed with suspicion by some members of the festival's board because of his commercial interests, he nonetheless exerted considerable influence over the annual event. He also had an emissary on the board in the person of Peter Yarrow, one-third of Grossman's highly successful folk trio, Peter, Paul and Mary. The twenty-seven-year-old singer, the board's youngest member, was an enthusiastic supporter of the Butterfield Band and was more than willing to plead their case. The fact that the group played electric instruments caused several board members to object to their inclusion on the festival's roster. But Yarrow, with Grossman's backing, lobbied hard to get Butterfield a slot.

Pressure was applied from another quarter too. Jac Holzman, the owner of Elektra Records, had also been involved with the festival from the beginning. Two of its board members—Oscar Brand and Theodore Bikel—recorded for Elektra, as did many other artists who regularly appeared at Newport. Holzman was well respected by the festival's management and was seen as someone who really understood and appreciated the music. The board trusted his judgment and was receptive when he went to bat for his label's latest find. With Yarrow advocating upfront and Grossman pulling strings behind the scenes, Holzman succeeded in getting the board to okay an appearance by the Paul Butterfield Blues Band. For the first time, the Newport Folk Festival would feature a modern Chicago blues band with big electric amplifiers, drum kit and all.

CHAPTER 9

PLUGGING IN AT NEWPORT

NEWPORT, 1965

Paul Butterfield was excited about his impending Newport debut. But, as had been the case with his trip to New York in March, he was also anxious about it. Having to appear before a huge audience in the company of some of folk music's biggest celebrities intimidated him. Paul had performed only in clubs during the four or five years he had been playing professionally, and most of those had been small neighborhood taverns on Chicago's South Side. Newport would be an entirely new experience for him. For moral support, he asked a few friends to accompany the band to Rhode Island. Nick Gravenites would sing a few of his songs, and Barry Goldberg was going to sit in with the quintet on piano.

In the late afternoon on Wednesday, July 21, the Butterfield entourage's two cars departed from Hyde Park for points east. One, bearing Michael, Susan, Nick Gravenites, and Barry Goldberg, had driven down from Old Town to meet up with the second, a car driven by Paul Butterfield with Elvin Bishop, Jerome Arnold, and Sam Lay. The plan was to retrace the route the caravan had taken to New York in March, but then to continue on through Connecticut and into Rhode Island. The trip would take about twenty hours, and by driving through the night they hoped to arrive in Newport before noon on Thursday. The band was scheduled to perform at a festival workshop on Friday, so they had plenty of time to get there and get settled.

Thursday dawned clear and pleasant with temperatures in the low sixties. It promised to be a beautiful day. The travelers had taken turns at the wheels of their respective vehicles overnight, and by the time the sun was well up in the eastern sky, they were crossing the Jamestown Bridge to Conanicut Island in Rhode Island's Narragansett Bay. Traffic was already heavy with concertgoers converging on the festival site at the north end of town, less than a half mile from the bridge. The location, a large tract of vacant land between Connell Highway and Girard Avenue, was new, having been selected after the previous year's site, Freebody Park, was deemed too small to handle the expected crowd. The sloping open area had been christened, aptly enough, "Festival Field."

Paul Butterfield and his crew eventually made it to the Connell Highway parking lot, where they were directed to the parking area for performers. There they were met by producer Paul Rothchild, who had been keeping watch for them. Rothchild was surprised to see that Butterfield had brought along a few friends, but he busied himself with helping the musicians unload their things. He then took them to check in at the festival office, where they were given their housing assignments. Most of Newport's big-name performers—primarily those managed by Albert Grossman—had rooms in the Hotel Viking, an imposing brick edifice located in the center of town. But nearly all the other musicians were lodged in one of seven "dormitories," private homes that had been rented by the organizers. Butterfield and his band were assigned rooms in a house a few blocks from the field.

Once they had stowed their gear, the Chicagoans hiked back to Festival Field. Though tired, they were too excited to think about sleep. Festival workers were hustling about, gearing up for the opening concert that evening. Crews were setting up rows of chairs, checking lighting and sound systems, and stringing power to food concessions. Among the throng near the main stage were dozens of folk music celebrities. Pete Seeger was in the crowd, and Joan Baez strolled by, barefoot and radiant in the afternoon sun.

It wasn't long before Paul Rothchild came over with Albert Grossman in tow. The portly manager greeted the members of Butterfield's band and then was introduced to Barry and Nick. After a few pleasantries, he said he was very much looking forward to hearing Paul and the group and that he was especially pleased to see Michael Bloomfield. "When Bobby arrives tomorrow, I'll be sure to tell him you're here," Grossman quietly said to the guitarist, referring to Bob Dylan.

Michael and Susan wandered around the festival grounds, stopping to look at the wares offered in the vendor tents and picking up programs with the festival's four-day schedule. Bloomfield was thinking about what Albert Grossman had said to him. Was the manager implying that Bob Dylan might want Michael to perform with him? Bloomfield hadn't heard anything from Dylan since the sessions in June, but Columbia had just issued "Like a Rolling Stone" as a single and it seemed to be getting lots of airplay. They had heard it on the car radio repeatedly during the trip from Chicago. The record sounded good to Michael—much better than he remembered it sounding in the studio. Whoever had mixed it—Bob himself?—had done a great job. Maybe Dylan wanted to play the song at Newport? Michael could help him re-create it.

"Like a Rolling Stone" had been getting airplay since July 15 and had been commercially released on July 20, the day before Butterfield's caravan departed Chicago for Newport. The song had almost been shelved after Columbia's sales department objected to its length, declaring it too long to be marketable. By chance it had been rescued from certain obscurity when a member of the company's production team took an acetate copy of the song to a Manhattan discotheque. There it proved so popular that Columbia overruled its marketing team and decided to put the tune out—all six minutes of it. It entered *Billboard*'s Hot 100 at number ninety-one on July 24 and would peak six weeks later on September 11 at number two. Everyone at Newport was talking about it.

There was also talk about the band that was coming from Chicago to play the blues—modern *electric* blues. Paul Rothchild and Peter Yarrow had been spreading the word about Paul Butterfield, and Fritz Richmond had been raving about the harmonica player to his Boston friends ever since he had seen Butterfield at Big John's. A sizeable group of folk insiders was eager to see what this Windy City outfit could do. Some had even heard that Dylan's new electric guitarist was going to be playing with them.

But there was another reason the Chicago blues band's Newport appearance was notable. The quintet was the folk festival's only interracial group that year. In fact, they were the first racially mixed working band to appear at the festival since 1963. For all its advocacy of civil rights and its politics of inclusiveness, the only integrated acts the Rhode Island festival had presented, until the Paul Butterfield Blues Band arrived with its controversial amplifiers and drums, were the Gateway Singers and the Tarriers. It wasn't really the fault of the organizers—it was simply that there were very few racially diverse groups at the time. While jazz had long since broken the color barrier by the mid-1960s, nearly all popular music groups, regardless of the music they played, were still either all white or all black. The Butterfield Band made no issue of their diversity; Paul Butterfield simply hired the best musicians he could find. But in 1965, the integrated blues band from Chicago represented something of a social breakthrough.

Mike Bloomfield could sense a possible breakthrough of his own that weekend at Newport. Here was a real opportunity to display his skill as a guitar player and demonstrate his knowledge of American traditional music. Many eyes would be on him when he performed with Paul, and he intended to make the most of it. As he and Susan walked down the gently sloping portion of the field that led to the stage, Bloomfield was pleased to see that some of the other musicians knew who he was. A few even came over to say hello.

One who did was Peter Yarrow. Yarrow had been appointed stage manager for the evening concerts and would be acting as emcee for the shows whenever he wasn't performing with Peter, Paul and Mary. He was also organizing some of the daytime workshops, and he asked Bloomfield if he would be willing to cohost one of them. It was scheduled for Friday morning and was called Blues

Guitar. Peter was confident that Michael would be interested, especially since the players included Mississippi John Hurt, Rev. Gary Davis, and Lightnin' Hopkins. The guitarist was happy to oblige, agreeing to introduce the players and help keep things moving along and on schedule.

The rest of the afternoon was filled with pleasant meanderings around the festival grounds, greeting old acquaintances and making new ones. Michael was pleased to see that Willie Dixon was in Newport and that he was slated for several workshops and an appearance on the main stage. The two swapped stories, laughing and trading mock insults—doing the "dozens"—much to the amusement of a small crowd that gathered around them. Michael was in his element, eager to perform for anyone within earshot. With his sharp wit and extravagant way with a story, Michael could be exceedingly funny. His good humor was contagious, and those who had never met him before were overwhelmed by his outsized personality. Word quickly got around that Bloomfield was a live wire—and he supposedly could really play guitar too.

Thursday night's opening concert was set to begin at 8:00 p.m., and nearly everyone was going. Folk diva Joan Baez was the night's headliner, but country music matriarch Maybelle Carter was also scheduled to appear, and both Son House and Rev. Gary Davis would be doing sets of country blues. In the second half of the show, the Chambers Brothers promised to liven things up with a set of soul and blues tunes, and then a new chap originally from Scotland who had been described as the "English Dylan," a nineteen-year-old folksinger named Donovan, would do a set of original songs.

A few of the Chicagoans opted to turn in, exhausted after the long, mostly sleepless trip from Illinois and a day of roaming around in the sunshine and salty ocean air. Mike Bloomfield, though, wanted to see everything and everybody, so he and Susan headed off to the field. There they joined a throng of thousands of other music fans as the Newport Folk Festival set an opening night record for attendance. The music began under the last of the summer day sun with the Blue Ridge Mountain Dancers performing wildly energetic square dances to music by Texas fiddler Eck Robertson and members of the New Lost City Ramblers. A radiant sunset illuminated the darkening western sky out over Narragansett Bay just as the Rev. Gary Davis was being introduced by emcee Pete Seeger. A breeze off the bay dropped temperatures into the lower sixties, causing many in the audience to pull on jackets and sweaters. But the huge crowd of nearly ten thousand was held transfixed by many of the performances and "was relaxed and even subdued," as reported by the *Newport Daily News*. After Joan Baez's show-closing performance of half a dozen songs, Seeger wished everyone a good night and invited them all back for Friday morning's workshops. By a little past midnight, the vast field was empty, illuminated only by the festival's overhead floodlights and a crescent moon.

Friday dawned hazy and a bit warmer. Mike Bloomfield was up by 9:30, too restless to sleep any longer. He quickly dressed, grabbed a fast breakfast downstairs in the dining room, and then headed over to Festival Field. He arrived at the site for the morning workshop fifteen minutes before its scheduled 11:00 a.m. start. The organizers, expecting good-size crowds for the blues programs, had reserved a large open area to the right of the main stage, calling the location "Bluesville." So that everybody could see, a pair of plywood platforms had been brought in to serve as a makeshift stage. Like all of the festival's workshops, Blues Guitar was more an informal series of short performances than a hands-on workshop. Festivalgoers were free to attend any of the five being held that morning, and many wandered between workshops, sampling musical styles and getting a closer look at some of Newport's legendary players.

Cohosting Blues Guitar was another white blues enthusiast, a thirty-four-year-old from Houston, Texas, named Robert McCormick. McCormick, who went by "Mack," was credited with reviving Lightnin' Hopkins's career in 1959 and had a reputation as a musicologist with an extensive knowledge of traditional blues players and styles. He explained to Michael that the workshop was to run to 1:00 p.m., and the featured players were Hopkins along with Mississippi John Hurt and Rev. Gary Davis. Representing the younger generation of bluesmen was Spider John Koerner, the twenty-six-year-old traditionalist from Minneapolis who had recorded a series of albums for Elektra with his partners, harmonica player Tony Glover and guitarist Dave Ray.

McCormick handled most of the introductions, but Bloomfield asked if he could bring on Lightnin', saying that the Texan was a personal favorite. Mack agreed and suggested that Hopkins close the workshop. Things proceeded slowly, and it wasn't until a little after 12:30 p.m. that Bloomfield stepped up on the riser and took a microphone. The workshop was threatening to run late, and he had to get Lightnin's set started.

"Of all the blues singers that I know, I've got one favorite that typifies what I feel is the blues," said Michael. "This is Lightnin' Hopkins—he's comin' up next." Bloomfield finished his brief paean with the ultimate compliment. "This is my favorite blues singer. I think he's the *king* of the blues—Lightnin' Sam Hopkins!" Hopkins took the stage and played a few numbers to resounding applause from the audience. Too soon, though, the workshop was out of time, and Hopkins closed with "Trouble in Mind," only the fourth tune he played.

Paul Rothchild was in the Blues Guitar crowd, and as the workshop drew to a close, he sought Michael out. He told Bloomfield he had been talking to Paul Butterfield, and Butterfield mentioned that Nick Gravenites and Barry Goldberg were going to play with the band. Rothchild suspected that might have been the idea when he first met Nick and Barry on Thursday afternoon, and now he told Michael that he had decided against it. The group would be a quintet as originally planned. The producer especially did not want keyboards with the Paul Butterfield Blues Band.

Rothchild asked Michael to pass the word along to Barry. Bloomfield knew the news would be upsetting, so he immediately went looking for his friend, and the keyboard player was indeed devastated by the decision. He had expected to be rehearsing with the band that afternoon, but instead he found himself sitting dejectedly in the performers tent behind the main stage. He was thinking about catching a bus home.

Following lunch, the members of the Paul Butterfield Blues Band gathered for a brief run-through of the tunes Paul wanted to play. They were scheduled to make their festival debut at the close of the afternoon blues workshop, a program called Blues: Origins and Offshoots. Butterfield wanted to feature "Born in Chicago," Nick Gravenites's tune, because Elektra was thinking of releasing it as a single in support of the band's album. But Paul Rothchild said it would be better to hold the song until the group made their main stage appearance on Sunday afternoon. Butterfield decided instead to open the afternoon's set with Little Walter's rollicking instrumental "Juke," a tune certain to get the audience moving.

The workshop began right on time at 3:30 p.m. Acting as host was fifty-year-old folklorist and musicologist Alan Lomax, son of the famed music collector John Lomax. The Lomax family had been largely responsible for creating a huge archive of traditional music and artist interviews for the Library of Congress during the 1930s and '40s. Since then, Alan had collected folk songs in the American South and in Europe, Mexico, and the Caribbean, producing numerous important folk albums from his field recordings. Recognized as one of the world's foremost traditional music authorities, his influence over the philosophy and programming of the festival was formidable. That he was also a member of Newport's governing board further served to enhance his prominence.

Lomax planned to preface each performance with remarks that would establish a historical context for what followed. He wished to track as closely to the workshop's "origins and offshoots" theme as possible, pointing out where each style fit historically and how one had developed from another. His was a pedantic take on the role of emcee.

Opening the workshop was a quartet of fife-and-drum players from Mississippi. Led by Lonnie and Ed Young, brothers whom Alan Lomax had first recorded in 1959, the group was an unscheduled addition to the workshop and an example of the lingering influence of African tradition on the music of southern blacks. They were followed by a group of former chain gang prisoners from Ramsey State Prison Farm brought up from Texas by Mack McCormick. They performed a brief set of authentic work songs.

The workshop progressed through the acoustic blues of Mississippi legend Eddie "Son" House and the dance reels of Mance Lipscomb to the definitive bluegrass sounds of Bill Monroe's band and the Grand Ole Opry stars Sam and Kirk McGee. Lomax's lengthy introductions attempted to demonstrate how the blues tradition had a strong effect on the music of white country players too.

From there, Lomax brought on the more modern blues of bassist Willie Dixon with pianists Lafayette Leake and Eddie Boyd. Their Chicago-based rhythms got the crowd clapping along, and Willie's double-time, bass-slapping solos drew repeated cheers. The workshop's audience had grown larger with each successive act and now filled the entire Bluesville area. Anticipation was high for the final performance of the afternoon, but readying the makeshift stage caused a twenty-minute delay in the action. The piano first had to be lifted off the risers and placed on the ground, and then drums, amps, and mics had to be carted in, hooked up, and arranged. The equipment was necessary because the workshop's final group was that new outfit from Chicago—the electric quintet called the Paul Butterfield Blues Band.

Paul Rothchild was standing to one side of the stage, watching Butterfield and his men set up while surveying the crowd. He was amazed by the number of people waiting to see the band. "At workshops they only expected a few hundred people to show up, and *thousands* of people showed up. The whole area was packed," he said of the experience.

While the audience wasn't nearly as large as Rothchild remembered, it was indeed big. Word had spread about the young bluesmen from the Midwest who played in the modern style. Their appearance marked the first time—as far as anybody could remember—that a heavily amplified group with drums would play at the Newport Folk Festival. It was true that the Chambers Brothers played electric guitars, and they had been backed during their Thursday evening appearance by drummer Sam Lay, but the Chicago outfit was *loud* electric. This was stretching the definition of folk music for some, graying the sacrosanct boundaries between traditional forms and crass commercialism. For others, amplified music was a welcome inclusion, a natural outgrowth of rural styles becoming urbanized. Nearly everyone, regardless of their position on electricity, was curious to see what would happen.

"The big buzz of the year was that [Albert Grossman] had brought the wonderful Paul Butterfield band to the festival," said Maria Muldaur. Muldaur was a folksinger from Greenwich Village, formerly part of the city's Even Dozen Jug Band, who in 1963 had become the featured singer with Jim Kweskin's Jug Band. She had recently married that band's guitarist, Geoff Muldaur, and was making her second appearance at Newport with the group. Because Kweskin was also managed by Grossman, she had heard all about the Chicago blues band's successful assault on the festival's non-amplified tradition. "The first time I set eyes on Michael and Butter was at the infamous blues workshop in the afternoon, where Alan Lomax [made] disparaging remarks."

For emcee Lomax, the final act for the Blues: Origins and Offshoots workshop wasn't just controversial. The Paul Butterfield Blues Band, with all its equipment and its thuggish-looking leader and flamboyant, long-haired lead guitarist, struck Alan Lomax as disingenuous at best. Lomax wasn't against amplified music—he had famously presented a rock 'n' roll band during a folk music concert he produced at Carnegie Hall in 1959—but it had to be an *authentic* part of a tradition. As far as he could see, Butterfield and his band had no real connection to the long-standing tradition of Chicago blues. They were just a bunch of ill-mannered white kids aping the most superficial aspects of the music of Muddy Waters, Howlin' Wolf, and the other Chicago masters.

Then there was the fact that the Butterfield Band was Albert Grossman's latest prospect. Lomax had been against the group's inclusion from the start, arguing that inauthentic music—electric or otherwise—had no place at a folk festival, but he had been outvoted by the board in the weeks leading up to Newport. He felt strongly that Grossman was subverting the festival's integrity to serve his own commercial interests. Newport had greatly benefited other Grossman properties—most notably Bob Dylan and Peter, Paul and Mary—and now he was about to repeat the process with what might be nothing more than a loud, amateurish imitation. In his introductory remarks, Lomax intended to make it clear that he had no confidence in the concluding act's ability to play blues with the authenticity of the workshop's previous performers—if they could play blues at all. Of course, he had never actually *heard* the group, but that didn't alter his opinion.

While the Chicagoans were getting their gear set up, Lomax addressed the huge crowd. The audience was expecting another musicology lesson, and many paid little attention to the bearded scholar. But those who listened heard the folklorist offer a challenge.

"Lomax was loaded for bear," said Paul Rothchild. "After the traditionalists and ahead of the Butterfield set, he got up and said something like, 'Today you've been hearing music by the great blues players, guys who go out and find themselves an old cigar box, put a stick on it, attach some strings, sit under a tree and play great blues for themselves. Now you're going to hear a group of young boys from Chicago with electric instruments. Let's see if they can play this hardware at all.'"

Jac Holzman, Elektra's owner, was also in the audience. He was distressed by Alan's comments. "Lomax was so condescending. I was embarrassed for him."

There was another listener in the audience who wasn't embarrassed by the folklorist's words—he was enraged by them. Albert Grossman, Lomax's nemesis, was standing at the side of the stage, waiting to hear his latest clients perform. He had decided the night before that he would take the group on as their manager, and he was eager to see how the crowd received them. When Alan all but accused the group of being poseurs, Albert saw it as not only an attempt to sway listeners but also a direct attack on himself.

The band had just finished setting up as Lomax wound up his ten-minute speech. "I understand that this present combination"—here he indicated the musicians behind him—"has not only caught up but has passed the rest. That's what I hear—I'm anxious to find out whether it's true or not." He concluded by blandly introducing the other band members from notes he had penciled on the back of a program. In the process, he described Alabama native Sam Lay as being from Ohio, a state where his family lived but he did not.

"Mike Bloomfield on piano and guitar—uh, guitar, at the moment. Sam Lay from Toledo on drums; Jerome Arnold, bass; Elvin Bishop on guitar, from Oklahoma." The emcee paused to survey the band's formidable array of amplifiers, microphones, and drums. "Anyway," he said, turning back to the packed field, "This is the new blues from Chicago, play on. We all talked about them—"

Without waiting for Lomax to finish, Paul Butterfield swung into the band's first tune, "Juke."

The sound of Little Walter's signature instrumental hit the vast crowd like an aural tsunami. Butterfield's electrified harmonica, supported by amplified guitars, bass, and drums tightly meshed in an infectious Chicago shuffle beat, was exhilarating. The crowd let out a collective gasp, and then some began to bob to the rhythm while others stood rooted, staring wide-eyed and open-mouthed. A few began to laugh out loud, and more than a few turned to their friends and exclaimed with glee. Butterfield, with his Ray-Bans and slicked back hair, his harmonica and microphone cupped firmly to his mouth, looked like a blues hit man. Behind him, Michael, Elvin, and Jerome swayed back and forth together as they played, a visual manifestation of the beat. Pushing that beat forward was big Sam Lay, hunched over, intense, his straightened hair tousled by the stiff breeze.

After Butterfield ran through the tune's melody, he soloed for two choruses, staking out his musical turf. Here was a whole new sound, and many in the workshop audience were amazed that such a small, seemingly insignificant instrument could produce such music. Nearly everyone in the crowd was unprepared for the power of an amplified harmonica.

And they were equally unprepared for what followed. After Paul's solo, Mike Bloomfield stepped up. He unleashed a fusillade of notes, burning through three choruses filled with his characteristic blend of South Side riffs and rock 'n' roll licks. Michael was so hyped up that he began to jerk from side to side as he played, digging into his Telecaster with his pick, eyes wild and manic. His gyrations shook the makeshift stage, causing his Guild Thunderbird amp's reverb unit to emit repeated crashes as its spring jogged up and down. In the middle of Michael's solo, Paul Rothchild, standing to the right of the stage, shouted something to Jerome Arnold. "Tell Mike to turn it up!" he appeared to say, and Arnold, leaning over toward Michael, repeated the mandate. But there was no need for the guitarist to boost the volume. His lines were the loudest thing on the festival's three-acre site at that moment.

Butterfield returned for two more choruses and then went into "Juke's" theme. As the harp player brought the rocking number to a close, the crowd erupted in applause, many hooting and whistling their approval. "Thank you very much," Paul said into his vocal mic, obviously pleased at the response from the sea of listeners. Until the Chicagoans' appearance, the workshop had been almost exclusively an acoustic event, amplified only by stage mics. Now, with four large amplifiers and a set of drums onstage, it became something else altogether. The band's sound, big and brash—and *loud*—transformed what had been a staid, respectful, and even academic workshop program into a raucous house-rent party.

Many people in the audience had never heard real Chicago blues. And very few had ever seen harp played the way Butterfield played it. A harmonica at Newport was an acoustic instrument, held in cupped hands and amplified only at a respectful distance from a microphone. But this guy put his harmonica right *on* the mic—and held *both* to his lips. And the sound he got—it was nothing like Sonny Terry's or Hammie Nixon's, or even Mel Lyman's. It was just as expressive, but *much* bigger. It soared over the other instruments, commanding attention like some bluesy horn of Gabriel. People cheered simply because they were astonished that harmonica could be played in such a way.

As Mike Bloomfield retuned his guitar to an open E chord, the audience quieted down, waiting to hear what the Paul Butterfield Blues Band would play next. Paul looked at Sam Lay, got a nod from Michael, and quickly counted off another tune. The band launched into "Look over Yonders Wall" with Bloomfield repeating Elmore James's classic guitar lick with an intensity that transformed the song into a runaway freight train. His amplifier's reverb unit was turned way up, giving James's famous two-bar slide phrase a seismic feel. Butterfield sang the lyrics and added rhythmic embellishments here and there on harp, but the tune was nearly all Michael's. He took a searing solo chorus, splitting the twelve bars between slide and fretted notes, and then backed Paul's vocal lines with wailing bottleneck phrases. On his second chorus, Butterfield switched from his harp mic to a stage mic, leaving his vocal largely inaudible. He repeated the opening verse, straining to be heard, and then signaled the band to play the tune out. As quickly as it had begun, "Yonders Wall" came to an abrupt end. Despite the technical difficulties, the crowd once again roared.

"Whoa, *whoa*!" said Paul, perplexed by the failure of his microphone. But there was no time to chase down the PA's gremlins. It was approaching 5:30, and it was clear the workshop would run over its allotted time. But no one in the vast crowd stirred—except to the music.

After another quick tuning session, Paul began Little Walter's "Blues with a Feeling" with a four-note pickup as the band fell in behind him on the downbeat. A few audience members near the stage screamed in delight as the medium-tempo blues began with a call-and-response exchange of riffs between harmonica and Bloomfield's ringing Telecaster. Paul sang the first verse through his harmonica mic, hoping to at least be heard. But the gain on his big Epiphone Futura amplifier heavily distorted his words, making them hard to understand as the band surged along behind him. When the band hit the stops following Paul's two choruses, Bloomfield switched to slide and bolstered the leader's unintelligible singing with sympathetic countermelodies.

Then it was Michael's solo. He fired off a flurry of fretted notes, starting low on the neck and working upward with biting aggression, switching fluidly between slide and fretted notes. Those watching now got to see the rangy guitarist in full flight as he spun out lines with an intensity that was breathtaking. The majority of Newport's performers simply stood and played, with an occasional nod or dip to the music. But not Michael. The copiously coiffed lead player cradled his instrument like it was a raging newborn, mouthing wordless lullabies to it while bobbing like a davening Hassid at a Blue Monday Shabbat. His hands were all over the Telecaster, nervously shooting up its neck, alternately shaking and caressing it. At times he nearly bent double, appearing at one moment to topple over into the crowd, tipping backward the next toward the striped curtain behind the stage. The Thunderbird continued to spit out periodic reverb crashes as the guitarist contorted and shook his way through two hot choruses. Nobody in the audience had ever seen anything like this.

Michael's solo led into another set of stops, and now it was clear that Paul's harp mic had also failed. His words were completely unamplified, picked up only by the stage mics. But the leader was undaunted. He took up the gauntlet and played a chorus of call-and-response with Bloomfield's raging Telecaster. Though he was largely inaudible, Butterfield aggressively answered Michael's phrases and sent them back at the guitarist. For those close enough to hear the exchange, it was a thrilling moment. Paul sang another unheard chorus and then took two more for an unamplified harp solo before going into a third set of stops and bringing "Blues with a Feeling" to a close with a walk through the turnaround. More wild applause, laced with shouts, hoots, and whistles. Several festival volunteers frantically dodged through the crowd, checking the mic cables in an effort to repair the PA. One fan a short distance from the stage shouted out the obvious—"We can't *hear* you, Butterfield!"

But even with the equipment failure, the Paul Butterfield Blues Band was creating a sensation. Booming blues improvisations resounded across the field that late Friday afternoon, drawing more and more people. Attracted by the commotion, they gathered around the perimeter of the Bluesville area, craning their necks to see the band. *Who's that?* they all wanted to know. *That's Butterfield*, came the reply. Word spread quickly that Chicago blues—*modern* Chicago blues—had arrived at Festival Field.

Without letting up for a moment, Butterfield kicked off "Mellow Down Easy," the band's third Little Walter cover of the afternoon. Whereas the original version had an easy rumba-style vamp leading into a twelve-bar shuffle, Paul's arrangement was *all* muscular vamp. The stagehands had momentarily revived Butterfield's harp mic, and his phrases, though not loud, were sufficiently audible. Sam Lay backed the leader's wailing harmonica with a rocking martial beat, whacking a cowbell on the off-beats, while Elvin and Jerome established the underlying riff. Bloomfield dropped high-note screeches and raw bass rumbles in between Butterfield's bursts of harmonica. The band had warmed up by now and was beginning to cook. Their performance was pure musical aggression and swagger, a hard-rocking riposte to Alan Lomax and anybody else who dared question their blues credentials.

"To the folk community, rock 'n' roll was greasers, heads, dancers, people who got drunk and boogied," Bloomfield later commented. The Paul Butterfield Blues Band was all about those uninhibited moments. "That was always the highlight of the evening—when people could get up and boogie."

People were boogying, all right—or at the very least moving to the beat. "Mellow Down Easy" was a juggernaut of excitement as Butterfield grabbed the mic and began to sing. But the PA, now working, had been set too low for his words to be heard. It mattered little, though, and Paul turned to Michael with a shout—"Go ahead!" The guitarist cranked up his Fender and for a dozen bars squeezed off volleys of raw sound before Butterfield joined in, holding warbling notes for whole breaths, toying with the bass line and counterpunching Lay's beat. After a minute or so, he settled into a repeated riff and grew steadily quieter before signaling the band and blowing a final closing phrase. Applause burst out all over the field and, for just moment, it seemed like Newport had become a rock 'n' roll festival.

Sensing he needed to tone things down just a bit, Butterfield told the raucous crowd, "We're gonna slow down here." Bloomfield laughed and shouted, "Yes, yes, *yes*!" as Paul continued, "We're gonna do a slow one. Nice, slow . . . *easy*."

Counting off the beat, Butterfield brought the band in on the turnaround as Bloomfield served up spiky fills. The leader then stretched out with a three-chorus solo filled with long, graceful phrases leavened with saxophone-like glissandi and rumbling tremolos. The PA fluctuated, becoming louder and then softer as the sound man fiddled, but Butterfield's harmonica could be heard throughout. His lines offered a colorful contrast to Bloomfield's pointed bursts and busy runs.

After Butterfield's three, Michael took two choruses for himself. He exhibited both speed and control as he alternately fretted up and down the neck and then paused for dramatic high-note bends. At the start of his second chorus, he played a two-note stretch similar to one used by Chuck Berry in "Johnny B. Goode"—but Michael repeated it for a two whole bars. Though the tempo was languid and the tune a standard South Side slow blues, the dynamic tension created by the lead guitarist's notes was exhilarating. The music was just as hot and just as exciting as some of the more up-tempo tunes had been. When the slow burner sounded its final chord, the audience rewarded the band yet again with unrestrained approval.

Butterfield was just about to start the band's final selection when Paul Rothchild caught his eye and signaled time by drawing a finger across his throat. The workshop, now thirty minutes over its two-hour limit, had to close so the field could be cleared for the evening concert. Butterfield thanked the audience and turned to his men, explaining that they were done. As the band members set about packing up their equipment, more than a few listeners came up and told Paul how much they enjoyed the music.

Alan Lomax suddenly reappeared at the right of the stage and reached over to shake the harp player's hand, congratulating him on the band's triumphant set. Though the musicologist had given the Chicagoans a disparaging introduction, damning them with faint praise, their clear ability to play had impressed him. Butterfield distractedly thanked him, and then Lomax took the PA mic and began making a few closing announcements as the audience dispersed. A couple of soundmen strolled over and began unplugging mics and collapsing stands, and Lomax passed his mic over to them after concluding his remarks. Satisfied that the afternoon workshop had been a success, the burly emcee began making his way through the crowd, heading toward the performers tent and a bit of refreshment before the evening concert.

It was then that something entirely unexpected happened.

A scuffle suddenly broke out to the right of the stage. Two big men were grappling with each other, each trying to land punches. Those close enough were shocked to see who the combatants were—Alan Lomax and Albert Grossman!

"Alan Lomax, the great folklorist and musicologist, gave us some sort of introduction—that I didn't even hear but Albert found offensive—and Albert went upside his head," Bloomfield said. "The next thing we knew, right in the middle of our show, Lomax and Grossman were kicking *ass* on the floor in the middle of thousands of people at the Newport Folk Festival. Tearing each other's clothes off and pounding—kicking ass! We had to pull 'em apart. We figured, Albert, man, *there's* a manager!"

After his closing remarks, Lomax had walked right by Grossman at the side of the workshop stage. The gray-haired manager blocked the musicologist's way, clearly angry. The two men faced off, and Lomax later described the ensuing melee.

> I had been on stage for over three hours and I was hot and tired. At this point I wasn't emceeing—I was talking about the blues. When I came off stage there was Al Grossman and he said to me, "That was the worst job of emceeing I've ever heard in my life." And I said, "It was no worse than some of the things you've done in your life." Then he said something like, "I ought to belt you in the nose." I pushed my chest up against his and invited him to try it. I don't remember swinging but there he was, stretched out on the ground. Then he jumped up and grappled me around the waist and we were both down, rolling around. By that time people pulled us apart. That was all there was to it. It couldn't have lasted more than thirty seconds.

Sam Lay, seeing the two men grappling in the dirt, instinctively stepped off the riser and into the fray. Physical disputes in the audience were not an unfamiliar occurrence for the South Side veteran, and he knew what to do.

"They got into it," said Lay, "but I separated them." The big drummer pulled Grossman and Lomax apart as those in the surrounding crowd stepped back to make room. The two men, still infuriated and not a little embarrassed, dusted themselves off and went to neutral corners. Lomax quickly retreated, leaving Grossman by the stage, the victor for the moment.

"I was cheering. I said, 'Kick his ass, Albert,'" said Bloomfield. "Wow. Albert put his body on the line to defend our right to boogie and rock 'n' roll anywhere." Michael was outraged as well by what he later learned were Lomax's comments. "We played amplified music very expertly, but when we showed up at the workshop, [he] gave us a really bad introduction. It was like, 'Well, Newport's finally reduced to bringing this sort of stuff to the stage.'"

Word of the fight went around like a shot. Albert Grossman and Alan Lomax had *slugged* each other! *Grossman* and *Lomax*! No one could believe it, and everyone who knew anything of the two titans loved it. The story was repeated again and again, with each teller adding his own spin. There was an innate sense that the conflict wasn't a dispute only between two middle-aged men, that it signified a much deeper and growing rift between what Newport had been and what contemporary music was becoming—between the old and the new.

That evening, everyone was talking about the Butterfield Band's set, and about the Grossman-Lomax tussle. Those who hadn't been there couldn't believe it, and those who had actually seen the two men come to blows made sure to affirm every lurid detail. Everyone knew that Butterfield and his men were the cause, and nearly everyone had heard the band playing, regardless of whether they had been at the Bluesville workshop. The group had been that loud. According to the festival's program, Butterfield was scheduled to appear at a second workshop on Saturday afternoon. No one wanted to miss that performance.

With, perhaps, one exception. Alan Lomax was still smarting from his very public disagreement with Albert Grossman, and he was determined to get redress. Following dinner, he hastily convened a meeting of the festival board members who were present and recounted the abuse he had suffered at the hands of the burly manager. Though all the board members had heard of the incident, Lomax's dramatic exegesis drummed up a good measure of sympathy. When he demanded that the board have the manager banned from the festival grounds, they were inclined to agree that some punitive action was needed. Grossman represented the antithesis of Newport's mission in the eyes of Pete Seeger and several other board members, and it seemed more than appropriate to remove him. But then, George Wein—with a businessman's acumen—pointed out that if Albert were to be booted, he would probably take his clients with him. That would leave Newport without Peter, Paul and Mary, Richard and Mimi Farina, Ian & Sylvia, Odetta, the Kweskin Band, and—most importantly—Newport's star attraction, Bob Dylan. Wein said he wasn't sure the festival could survive such a loss. The board, thus enlightened, weighed the consequences and reluctantly agreed. They voted to allow Grossman to stay, despite Lomax's strong displeasure.

It would be a pivotal decision.

* * *

The Friday evening main stage concert featured an unwieldy fourteen acts, concluding with the hugely popular Peter, Paul and Mary. Following the concert, there were jam sessions at many of the locations where performers were staying. Most musicians brought out instruments and began swapping songs, playing and singing while passing a jug of wine and an occasional joint. Michael found himself at a raucous jam that was being run by famed bluegrass artist Bill Monroe. He had met Monroe at the Blues: Origins and Offshoots workshop that afternoon, and he got someone to lend him a banjo so he could join the breakdown. His skills were such that he fit in easily, leaving little doubt that he was a gifted player—even on an instrument nobody knew he could play. When Bloomfield finally went up to his room, he was too energized to sleep. He sat out on the little porch at the end of the hall, quietly picking a rag on his Telecaster and breathing in the cool salt air.

Saturday dawned sunny and a bit more humid. After a quick breakfast, Michael and Susan headed over to Festival Field to take in a few of the scheduled morning workshops. He had the early part of the day free, but that afternoon the Paul Butterfield Blues Band was scheduled to appear at a second workshop in the Bluesville area. They were again to give the closing performance in a program that was slated to run from 3:00 to 5:00 p.m. Called simply Harmonica, the workshop was intended to present the varieties of harmonica styles within the various blues traditions. Curiously, the festival program listed Mike Bloomfield and the Butterfield Band separately, assigning Michael to an earlier portion of the workshop. The listing didn't really matter, though, because everyone expected the Butterfield Band to be the same group that had created such a stir on Friday.

A full day of blues presentations was scheduled for the Bluesville location, beginning at 11:00 a.m. with a traditional workshop called The South. That would be followed at 1:30 p.m. by The City, featuring younger acoustic blues players, and then the day would conclude with Harmonica. In addition to the Butterfield Band, the artists performing included nearly every other blues musician at the festival. Almost everyone attending the festival that day had one or more of the Bluesville workshops on his or her list of music to see.

Michael spent the afternoon drifting between the other workshops, enjoying the virtuosic penny whistle solos by South African musician Spokes Mashiyane during Folk Wind Instruments and tapping his foot to the bluegrass stylings of his new friends Tex Logan and Bill Monroe at Fiddle and Mandolin. In the early afternoon, he strolled over to "Area II" at the back of Festival Field to join a huge crowd that had gathered for one of the songwriter workshops.

At a little after 1:00 p.m., Newport's biggest star gave a brief performance as a participant in the Contemporary Songs workshop. Bob Dylan had arrived at the festival the night before, and the Saturday workshop was his first Newport appearance. Bloomfield stood at the back of the throng and heard a little of Bob's set. The folksinger sang a few familiar originals, accompanying himself on guitar and harmonica just as he had always done. As he watched, Michael realized his hope that Dylan might want to perform with an electric band was probably just a fantasy. When he saw Bob in the performers tent later, he would ask him about his Sunday concert plans, but it looked like the folksinger was sticking with folk.

Paul Rothchild made sure the Butterfield Band's equipment was at the Bluesville stage well in advance, ready to be set up whenever the program reached the last act. He didn't want a repeat of Friday's delay, a pause in the action that had cut into the band's performance time and annoyed the emcee. Sam Lay's kit was stacked on the back of the riser for much of the workshop, with Elvin Bishop's big Ampeg B-12 amplifier right next to it. Rothchild was also eager to avoid a repeat of technical troubles, so he arranged for there to be a backup vocal microphone. Butterfield had said that Nick Gravenites was going to sing a few tunes, and he wanted to be sure his friend would be heard.

To accommodate the larger audience that was expected after record numbers showed up for the previous day's workshop, organizers had removed the striped curtain from behind the stage. That way, the overflow could watch the performers from behind as well as from out front. The wisdom of that decision was soon evident—by 3:30 p.m., the crowd was standing four and five deep at the back of the risers.

As Spider John Koerner and Tony Glover worked through their set of country blues, hollers, and rags, Paul Butterfield and his men began to gather at the side of the bandstand. Geoff Muldaur and Jim Kweskin took the stage briefly to run through a few ragtime blues, and for their final number they were joined by Mel Lyman on harmonica. The diminutive jug bander, sporting a white fedora and owlish dark glasses, looked like an itinerant Dust Bowl preacher as he cupped his harp and swayed to Kweskin's bouncy banjo picking.

It was soon time for the Butterfield Band to perform. There was another delay as the group's equipment was positioned and mics were hooked up, but Paul Rothchild's planning worked as intended. The pause was brief, and soon the band was ready to go. There were no disparaging comments this time—Mack McCormick, the host of Harmonica, simply introduced the band and got out of the way. Applause rippled as Paul counted in the downbeat and the band launched into its first blues salvo. The capacity crowd held its breath.

The opening tune was an instrumental, a piece Elvin Bishop had worked up, appropriately titled "Elvin's Blues." A medium-tempo shuffle that took inspiration from the work of guitarist Freddie King, "Elvin's Blues" kicked into gear with two choruses from Michael. Again Bloomfield assailed his instrument, bending notes and running through licks with a hard-edged, jacked-up virtuosity. Then Butterfield wailed through two of his own, backed by Bloomfield's slide, before Michael moved in again with a blistering three-chorus solo. His playing was so intense that at one point it elicited screams from more than a few frenzied audience members. Paul returned for another chorus and then gave a nod to Elvin.

The rhythm guitarist, the band's original lead player, had been second fiddle to his more flamboyant colleague all weekend, and now on his own composition he had a chance to shine. Bishop began his solo, cranking up his red Gibson ES-345, but before he had played more than a few notes, Bloomfield suddenly charged in and took the spotlight. The lead guitarist soloed for another two choruses, unaware—or unconcerned—that he had stolen Elvin's moment. But no one noticed. Butterfield simply played the melody and brought "Elvin's Blues" to a close. The audience hooted its approval as Sam Lay ended with a press roll and a splash of sound from his ride cymbal.

The band sounded tight and aggressive, at the top of their game. The audience, now knowing nearly to a person what to expect, was completely with them, hanging on every note. But the PA was still giving the stage hands trouble. Squeals of feedback had been heard repeatedly as they struggled to find the right mix for the mics.

There was nothing to do but charge ahead. Next up was Arthur "Big Boy" Crudup's "That's All Right." It was an interesting choice, because the tune had launched Elvis Presley's career only a decade earlier and had played a pivotal role in the birth of rock 'n' roll. That the band would choose to play it at a folk festival, given the attendant controversy surrounding electric music at Newport, clearly spoke of their desire to make a statement. Mike Bloomfield may well have suggested it and, after Paul's vocals and a single twelve-bar solo, it was Bloomfield who was featured. He and Butterfield played one chorus together, intertwining their lines with canny precision, and then Paul shouted, "*Play* it!" As if to drive home the point, Michael soloed like a man possessed, again gyrating left and right, his face contorted with emotion, eyes alternately wide and wild, then pinched shut in apparent agony. Here was the worst of rock 'n' roll's excesses.

But the crowd ate it up. They whooped and whistled at the tune's raucous conclusion. Many in the back had gotten up and were dancing to the music, clearly blowing off steam after a long day of traditional performances. The mood was not unlike that found in a typical South Side tavern on any given Saturday night—play the blues good and loud, and let the good times roll!

Coming around from behind the stage and joining Paul Butterfield on the ground in front of the band was Nick Gravenites. Paul tried to introduce his friend, attempting to explain that Nick would do his own composition called "It's About Time," but the vocal mics were now so low that it was difficult to hear him. He quickly gave up and passed the microphone to Gravenites. "Ready?" said Nick. Sam Lay counted off the beat.

It was Bloomfield who played the pickup phrase to start the tune. The band came in on the downbeat, and after a few moments it became apparent to those listening that this was not another twelve-bar. Here was the one-chord vamp that Michael and Nick had worked up earlier in the year when they had a group that briefly gigged at the End in Chicago. The tune would evolve over the next twelve months, and the Butterfield Band would record a greatly expanded version of it for their second Elektra album. By then it would become a revolutionary instrumental named "East-West." But that epic recording would share the same pickup phrase that Michael now used to spark Nick's guest appearance at the "Harmonica" workshop.

As the band established a groove over Sam Lay's variation on a shuffle rhythm, Gravenites squared himself before one of the vocal mics, warming to the first verse. The burly Chicagoan, dressed in black and inscrutable behind dark sunglasses, looked like the band's muscle, a capo who would twist arms as readily as sing the blues. Even though they were hard to hear, the words to his song seemed to support that impression:

I used to go out drinkin' most every night
Well, I used to get so drunk I'd almost lose my sight.
I'd get home at four, wake up at six
I'd work a five-day week on an eight-hour shift.
It's about time, it's about time,
It's about time I quit hurtin' myself.

Those who could hear him were not a little surprised that Gravenites was an excellent singer—a fine blues baritone, in fact. He sang his lyrics with an intensity that added gravity to the band's performance, growling at times like a bear with a crew cut. The drama of his presentation set the scene for Bloomfield's solo.

Whenever Nick and Michael played "It's About Time," Bloomfield had used it primarily as a vehicle for experimentation. But the few times they had done it with Butterfield, the guitarist usually restrained himself, not wanting to deviate too far from the leader's insistence on blues purity. This time was different. Michael was onstage before a receptive audience, and the band had been accused of being amateurs, incapable of playing their instruments. He held nothing back.

Again Bloomfield grimaced and contorted himself. But this time his notes weren't restricted solely to the standard pentatonic blues scale. He dropped in jazzy flat seconds and fifths, moved in and out of relative keys, and ran modal phrases over the one-chord drone laid down by Elvin and buoyed by Jerome's ostinato bass line. Nick, too, joined in, adding a wordless vocal part to the steamrolling wall of sound. This wasn't exactly blues, nor was it rock or even jazz. It was a fusion of all those forms, something altogether different.

But as quickly as Michael had piloted the tune into uncharted territory, he brought it back. The beat coalesced around Paul as he came in with his harmonica, playing a few exotic-sounding runs of his own, and then Michael was back for another brief solo. Sam Lay began playing accents on his cow bell and beating a tambourine resting on his floor tom-tom with his right hand.

After a few moments, Bloomfield brought the ensemble to heel and quieted the tune. Butterfield moved in and blew a few phrases and then brought "It's About Time" to a close with a final descending riff. Gravenites acknowledged the wave of applause with a few nods and a boyish grin.

Nick remained front and center for a second number, another tune he had written called "It's True." A moderately paced ballad, the form of the song resembled "It Hurts Me Too," the Elmore James hit. It, too, was not a conventional blues. Nick sang three choruses with the band in restrained accompaniment and then brought the tune to a quick end. "Thank you," he said while the crowd cheered and clapped.

As the guitars tuned and Butterfield blew a few notes on his harp, Mack McCormick told the band, "Last one!"

To wind up the set, Paul again played Little Walter's "Juke." He started the tune with Walter's lick, and as the band picked up the beat and joined in, some who had been in the audience the day before recognized what they were hearing and began to sway. Soon nearly everybody in back was standing too, and many were again dancing to the insistent Chicago beat. After Butterfield's two solo choruses, Michael took three, climbing higher on the neck with each ensuing chorus. Someone in the audience shouted, "Play *out*, man!" and there was a burst of applause as he concluded his solo. Butterfield ran through the melody for two more choruses and then brought "Juke" to a resounding close. The response was immediate.

"Thank you very much," Butterfield said as the crowd roared. "We're gonna turn it back over to the emcee, whoever that may be—"

"No! *No!* Do another one!" someone shouted. There were cries of "More!" all over the field. But the Paul Butterfield Blues Band was done for the afternoon.

The festival's schedule wouldn't tolerate encores. The band members began packing up.

For nearly everyone attending the workshop, Butterfield and his men had scored a victory. The question of whether electric instruments had a place in folk music seemed, for the moment at least, happily resolved. Amplified blues could be loud and could rock, but folk fans clearly appreciated the music and freely expressed their approval.

"What we played was music that was entirely indigenous to the neighborhood, to the city we grew up in," Bloomfield said. "There was no doubt in my mind that this was folk music; this was what I heard on the streets of my city, out the windows, on radio stations and jukeboxes in Chicago and all throughout the South, and it was what people listened to. And that's what folk art meant to me—what people listened to."

Many of the younger musicians at the festival agreed. One in particular made a decision based on the Butterfield Band's reception that would set his career on a new path.

At the evening meal, Michael Bloomfield was told that Albert Grossman was looking for him. The guitarist sought the manager out at Festival Field and found him in the performers tent chatting with Bob Dylan. Bob warmly greeted Michael and after a little friendly conversation, made a request of the blues guitarist.

"Dylan asked me to play with him," Bloomfield said. The possibility of doing an electric set with the folksinger had seemed remote only the day before, but now it appeared to be precisely what Bob had in mind. For his Sunday performance, Dylan said he wanted to re-create the music they had just recorded for Columbia. Would Michael be willing to assemble an electric group for him? Bloomfield didn't have to be asked twice.

As they were discussing details, Al Kooper wandered into the tent. He had come to the festival as an audience member, and Dylan had recruited him for his backup band as well.

"I went every year to the festival, bought tickets and went to see all the concerts," Kooper said. "That year, though, I bumped into Grossman and he said, 'We've been calling you. Bob wanted to know if you would play with him tomorrow night.'" Without a moment's hesitation, Al agreed. It seemed to him that the electric band idea had only recently occurred to the folksinger. "Dylan may have hatched the idea the night before," said Kooper.

Albert Grossman cautioned them that the plan should be kept quiet. He was concerned that some of the festival organizers might not appreciate an electric band on the main stage—especially behind Bob Dylan. He was also secretly eager to get back at Alan Lomax and those on the Newport board who saw him as a pernicious influence on the festival. What better way to tweak noses than to trot out Newport's folk champion and have him plug in?

Paul Rothchild was brought in on the scheme and was tasked with convincing George Wein to lend his mansion to the musicians for rehearsals. Wein rented a Newport home every summer as the jazz and folk festival's headquarters, and that July he had taken one, a grand residence called "Nethercliffe," on prestigious Ruggles Avenue. Located half a mile from the center of town, the huge home had a spacious living room that would be ideal for organizing and rehearsing the band. After Wein agreed, Rothchild took charge of moving the necessary equipment from Festival Field down Bellevue Avenue to Nethercliffe, and Michael set to work finding additional musicians to complete the group.

Bloomfield quickly realized after a review of all the other players at Newport that he really had few options for Dylan's band. Sam Lay was the only trap drummer at the festival, and of the few bass players present, only Jerome Arnold and George Chambers of the Chambers Brothers played electric instruments. Because Sam and Jerome were used to playing together, Arnold was the better choice. So Butterfield's men would have to be pressed into service for Dylan's Sunday night set. There was one other musician that would fit perfectly with the ensemble, and Michael knew he was available. The guitarist suggested to Dylan that Barry Goldberg play piano, and Bob agreed. Goldberg, delighted to be asked, readily assented. By 10:00 p.m. everything was in place, and Michael took charge of the rehearsal. He knew Dylan's tunes and had a clear idea of how they should sound. Bob, as was his habit, said little and simply concentrated on his singing.

"Michael was, essentially, the leader," said Nick Gravenites. "He's the guy that selected the band. He figured that these guys could cut it and do it." Nick came along to watch the rehearsal and to help out wherever he could. Albert Grossman was there, too, keeping a watchful eye on Dylan and making sure the musicians had whatever they needed. The music, however, was proving to be a challenge. Despite Bloomfield's direction and the talents of the musicians involved, Dylan's tunes weren't easily learned. The group struggled through the songs as the hours slowly passed, repeating each one over and over again.

"We stayed up all night rehearsing at George Wein's place," said Al Kooper. "We did three of Bob's tunes, and after a while it was clear the drummer and bass player weren't really up to it." Kooper began to have his doubts about Dylan's plan. "It was excruciating for me, but I kept my mouth shut. I was embarrassed for them. And I think Michael was upset too."

"We were all at Newport," Bloomfield told an interviewer, still distressed over the music a decade later. "Kooper, me, Barry and this *schwartze* Jerome from the Butterfield Band playing bass, and he can't play and he's fucking up everything." Michael's use of a derogatory Yiddish term in describing Arnold was just how he talked; he had deep respect for the bassist as a player of Chicago-style blues changes and rhythms. It was just that when it came to the irregular rock-oriented chords of Dylan's tunes, Arnold was struggling. But the sextet worked through the long night to master the songs, and by first light they felt they had gotten close enough. Bob seemed satisfied, though he said little. To Michael, he appeared to be "uptight." "He was uncomfortable. I think he knew this was a much more serious thing than I did."

At the conclusion of the rehearsal, the equipment was broken down and loaded into a van for the trip back to Festival Field. The Sunday sunrise was warming the eastern sky as the musicians piled into several cars and headed up the island to their accommodations and a few hours of sleep before the start of the day's events.

The Paul Butterfield Blues Band wouldn't be making their final appearance at Newport until late in the afternoon, but a sleepy Sam Lay had reason to be at the field early. Sam had to set his drums up on the main stage before the sound checks for the afternoon concert could begin. Butterfield's sound check was scheduled for 1:00 p.m., but Lay's duties didn't end there. Once the band had completed its run-through, he had to break down his kit and move it to a pair of risers in front of the main stage. The makeshift bandstand was being used for the Chambers Brothers' afternoon appearance, and George Chambers, impressed by Lay's big sound, had asked Sam to once again back the quartet during their set.

The midday concert, one of the most anticipated presentations of the four-day festival, was cleverly titled New Folks. It would be a showcase for new folk talent, and it would give many in the audience a first look at some of the exciting young artists who were new to the scene. New Folks would also give those artists who had appeared only in workshops an opportunity to perform for a much larger audience. Paul Butterfield was both excited and nervous about appearing in the main stage's spotlight. The band's workshop sets had been casual affairs, almost like club appearances, even though the crowds had been big. The New Folks concert would be the first time the harp player had ever gigged on a formal stage in front of an audience of thousands. It had him more than a little rattled, and that had been a reason why he hadn't offered to join Bob Dylan's backup band. He wanted to put all his energies into his own performance. Albert Grossman, he knew, was counting on the band to wow the crowd.

Mike Bloomfield arrived at Festival Field a little before 1:00 p.m. Up on the main stage, Peter Yarrow was busily setting up mics in front of the band's amplifiers. Yarrow was acting as the afternoon program's stage manager and emcee, and he wanted the Butterfield Band's equipment levels to be set and ready to go. Other musicians, having had their turn before the mics, milled around onstage, chatting with one another and packing up their instruments. A few stagehands were struggling to lift a piano onto the stage while others were adjusting lights and running power cords from the stage's junction box. Every few minutes, Yarrow would shout instructions to an assistant at the soundboard on a platform several dozen rows from the stage out in the audience. A few photographers snapped photos from the pit in front of the stage.

By half past one, the harried stage manager was ready for Butterfield's sound check. He had placed a mic in front of Michael's amp, boomed one in over Sam Lay's drums, and used another for Elvin and Jerome. Butterfield was blowing harp through his big Epiphone amp and singing over the festival's powerful PA. The Paul Butterfield Blues Band was definitely going to be heard in the field's back row seats.

When his men were all in place onstage, Paul counted off "Juke" and did a quick run-through of the tune. Yarrow tried hand signals—shouting was useless—to direct his sound man but, after repeated futile gestures, gave up and clambered down off the stage and out through the rows of chairs. The only way to mix the electric band's huge sound, he realized, was to do it himself from the soundboard. A few more quick takes, interrupted by instructions shouted by the beleaguered stage manager, and the levels seemed to be under control. Yarrow took pains to impress upon the band that they needed to leave their amps set just as they were. Any fiddling with knobs would throw the whole mix irreparably out of whack. With the difficult stage-to-soundboard communications, there would be no way to fix it once the band's performance started.

The afternoon was warming up, becoming more humid under a high hazy sun. The breeze that had been constant for the past two days seemed to have relented, leaving the air feeling close and heavy. On the western horizon, out over the bay, a front of billowy clouds was building. Those out in the open soon sought the shade of one of the craft tents or a convenient stand of trees. The Narragansett Beer kiosks were suddenly doing a brisk business.

Though the afternoon performance was still hours away, Mike Bloomfield felt himself getting more and more restless. He wasn't too worried about the afternoon show with Butterfield—playing blues is what he did, and it was Paul who was responsible for the band. Michael just had to show up and play. But the set with Dylan was a different situation altogether. It was Bloomfield who had organized the group. He was the one who explained the music and led the rehearsals. Bob would be depending on him to hold the band together, to make the music sound good—to make Dylan sound good. But when he thought about the previous night's practice session, Bloomfield wasn't too sure anything could improve the sound of Dylan's pickup band. He decided there was only one thing he could improve, and that was his mental state. He went looking for Barry Goldberg, a couple of joints in his shirt pocket.

The two musicians took the edge off their jitters with Michael's dope and then meandered over to the main stage, where New Folks was just getting under way. It was half past 2:00 p.m., and the sea of wooden chairs facing the stage was occupied by a huge throng of enthusiastic folk fans. Many wore sunglasses to filter out the afternoon glare, and nearly as many sported hats or kerchiefs. The mood was lighthearted and upbeat—it was the final day of the festival, and anticipation was high. The best was yet to come.

Michael watched father-and-son fiddlers Lou and Byron Berline play through a short set of sprightly bluegrass tunes, and he was amused by the folk duo Kathy and Carol, a pair of comely twenty-year-old folk artists who had just released their debut album on Elektra. The Chambers Brothers held his attention with their rocking R&B harmonies and foot-stomping rhythms, all powered by Sam Lay's sinewy beat. But as one male folksinger followed another, Michael's attention began to wander. By the time the Charles River Valley Boys were picking their way through a few Cambridge-inflected bluegrass numbers, Bloomfield had gone off in search of some shade. The sky had clouded over, and it had grown warmer, the air still and thick. It felt like rain.

Michael was under a beer kiosk's awning when the sky suddenly opened up. A cool summer rain began falling straight down, and Bloomfield stepped in a little closer. He could see the main stage over the heads of others who ducked in out of the downpour, and there were Dick and Mimi Farina, accompanied by sister Joan Baez and washtub bassist Fritz Richmond. Some people in the seats at the back of the field were heading for cover, but the Farinas were still playing and most of the crowd was staying put, covering their heads with newspapers, blankets, and festival programs. In a minute or two, Michael could see Peter Yarrow and a few stage hands scurrying about behind the Farinas, covering the Butterfield Band's equipment with sheets of plastic. The rain was sheeting down now, and people were splashing by the kiosk as they searched for a bit of cover. The music was coming even more insistently from the stage, and Bloomfield noticed that some in the crowd down front were standing and dancing, their wet hair and clothes broadcasting spray as they moved. A few distant rumbles of thunder punctuated Dick Farina's words as he sang "Hard Loving Loser." It looked to Michael like the Paul Butterfield Blues Band might be the losers if the rain kept up.

* * *

Near the conclusion of the New Folks concert, the sky brightened and the rain stopped. The sun was making a half-hearted attempt to break through the clouds as Bernice Johnson Reagon took the mic and sang songs from the civil rights movement. Behind her a few stage hands were trying to sweep pools of water off the stage. Everything was dripping.

Michael found Paul Butterfield standing with Albert Grossman in the wings of the main stage. They had decided to cancel the band's New Folks appearance. With everything onstage thoroughly soaked, the risk of shock from their electrified instruments was too great. But Albert had rescued the situation by convincing Peter Yarrow that the band could do a brief set to open the evening concert while people were finding their seats. It wouldn't be the best time slot, but the band would be part of the prestigious closing night show and get heard by an even larger audience than had been present at the afternoon concert.

Michael wasn't terribly disappointed by the cancellation. He was happy the band would get a chance to play that evening, but his mind was on his appearance with Bob Dylan. He hadn't seen Bob since they had left Nethercliffe that morning, and he knew they had to do a sound check soon. He wondered what Dylan was thinking about his electric band plan now.

Peter Yarrow was also thinking about Dylan's set. The folk star had requested that the field be cleared before he did his sound check, and that meant Yarrow had to begin moving people out immediately following the New Folks concert. As soon as Bernice Johnson Reagon finished her last song, he took the mic and announced that because of wetness of the stage, the Butterfield Band's performance would be postponed until the evening concert. He then marshaled a dozen festival volunteers to sweep through the seats and escort stragglers off the field. The stage manager also had sound checks to run on the evening concert's other artists, and it was now just after 5:00 p.m. If Newport's gala closing event was going to open with Paul Butterfield's group a bit earlier than its scheduled 8:00 p.m. start time, there was much to do.

CHAPTER 10

ELECTRIFYING DYLAN

NEWPORT, 1965

A little after 5:30 p.m., Bob Dylan arrived at the performers tent. The folk superstar was strikingly out of costume. Gone was his conservative garb from Saturday's workshop performance. Instead, he was wearing a green polka-dotted shirt, tight dark pants, Beatle boots, and sunglasses. He looked for all the world like a fey British pop star.

Dylan quickly sought out Albert Grossman, and the two sat together, conferring in earnest about the evening concert. Grossman explained to Bob that he and the band would be going on midway through the night's lineup, right after banjo player and singer Cousin Emmy. Bob was alarmed—he had assumed that as the festival's star attraction, he would be going on last. He wanted to debut his new sound at the end of the show, at its highpoint. Not somewhere in the middle.

But it was too late to change the arrangement. The order of performers had come directly from Alan Lomax, and all the musicians had been given a copy. Peter Yarrow knew about the odd scheduling arrangement, and he knew Dylan wouldn't like it.

"Alan had decided to equalize the focus on performers," said Yarrow. "He wanted those who were least known to receive the same attention as those everybody knew. So he just made up an arbitrary order and dropped Dylan into the middle of it." Lomax had to know the placement would rile the manager and his famous client. "It was all tied up with that fight with Grossman," Yarrow added. "And Dylan was fuming, absolutely irate at not being at the end of the program. *Really* pissed off!"

Bob angrily walked over to the main stage and watched from the lighting booth as the sound checks proceeded. A few minutes later Mike Bloomfield strolled up, and as the two greeted each other, the guitarist sensed that Dylan was upset. What's up? Bloomfield wanted to know. The folksinger complained bitterly about the band's place in the middle of the program's order, but Michael was unperturbed. It didn't bother him when they played, just so long as they played. Bob's fans would love him no matter when he went on.

Before long, the other members of the Butterfield Band appeared at the side of the stage. Al Kooper arrived, followed soon afterward by Barry Goldberg. The musicians made small talk as the few remaining sound checks were completed, then Yarrow signaled to them. Stage hands were shoving a big Hammond B3 organ into place as Bob Dylan's backup band took the stage and began setting up. It was nearly a quarter after six.

With the arrival of the festival's favorite son, the bandstand suddenly became crowded. What had been mostly purposeful activity prior to Dylan's ascent quickly became a confusing scrum as a dozen workers, producers, and curious onlookers crisscrossed the stage. Yarrow flitted about, issuing orders like some frazzled second lieutenant sporting a hipster goatee. He supervised the placing of microphones, testing each in turn with a brisk "One-two, *one-two*" while shushing those onstage so he could hear what the sound man was shouting back at him. Peter knew that the festival's soundboard wasn't really capable of handling amplified instruments, and he feared the worst.

"We weren't really set up to handle electric," Yarrow said. "Drums drown out vocals, and everybody had to have very, *very* specific settings on their amps or everything could easily get too loud and out of balance."

The stage was cleared of everyone but the musicians for the sound check. Dylan started up "Maggie's Farm" and the band dropped in behind him, taking their cues from Bloomfield. Bob sang a few choruses while Yarrow adjusted microphones and tried to read the hand signals from the soundboard out front. The mix seemed to be working. The sound man gave Peter a "thumbs up" sign, and the stage manager began to breathe easier. He called for the band to try another tune.

Once more Dylan started the song, setting the beat before the others joined in. Michael finger-picked a pretty counter melody over Bob's simple chords, and Kooper laid down a seamless base of harmony. As Dylan began to sing, it became apparent that the tune was "Like a Rolling Stone." Its rhythm was different, more of a slow march than the solid 4/4 rock beat of the studio recording. Sam Lay was clearly struggling to find the right groove. As the band finished the first verse and chorus and moved into the next, Jerome Arnold suddenly got lost. "Like a Rolling Stone" sputtered to a halt.

The bass player had wrestled with the song's chords all through the previous night's rehearsal, finally writing them out on a scrap of paper so that he would have something to refer to during the performance. But though the crib sheet was on the stage floor between his feet, he still could not feel the changes. Dylan looked dismayed.

"I can play the bass part," Al Kooper suggested. "Put Barry on the organ and I'll play bass."

Though he wasn't happy to do so, Jerome surrendered his instrument to the organist, and Goldberg moved over to the Hammond. Dylan started the tune again and this time the changes went smoothly. Arnold stood to one side, his hands on his hips, now glumly watching the group.

"All right, that's it, gentlemen. Thank you," shouted Yarrow after another thumbs-up from the soundboard. "We've got to get the Butterfield Band—the *rest* of the Butterfield Band—set up onstage because the evening concert's about to start."

Dylan unplugged his Stratocaster and headed for the stage stairs. Al Kooper and Barry Goldberg followed, skirting around Elvin Bishop as he climbed up the steps.

It was now half past seven.

"Most of you have heard them at some time or other during the weekend," Peter Yarrow intoned into the center stage microphone. "They have been accompanying everybody; they have been involved with the festival as a whole, which is a credit to each of them. However, they are not sidemen, although they will be seen later this evening accompanying Bob Dylan. They are tonight accompanying themselves and the person who is, in fact, the leader of the group. Ladies and gentlemen, please welcome with us—with *me*—Paul Butterfield!"

With that, Yarrow brought the Chicago blues band onto the main stage to start the Newport Folk Festival's Sunday evening concert. A smattering of applause came from those in the audience who had managed to get to their seats all the way down front. The gates had just opened, and people were streaming onto the field from the gentle slope at the rear of the concert site. They were carrying blankets and extra clothing, anticipating a cool evening ahead, and some even had umbrellas. The sky was still overcast, though the air was much less humid. Lights were coming on all over the field as the Butterfield Band began their first tune.

Paul's harmonica kicked off "Blues with a Feeling," and the band dropped in on the downbeat for their second festival performance of the Little Walter classic. This time the PA worked perfectly, and Butterfield's harmonica and vocal choruses meshed clearly with the group's sound. Though Elvin Bishop and Jerome Arnold—and their amplifiers—were positioned behind Dylan's piano and organ, they could still be clearly heard. The performance was more restrained than it had been at the Friday Blues: Origins and Offshoots workshop, but the rhythm section was tight and fluid, and Bloomfield's fret-and-slide embellishments nimbly complemented the leader's singing and harmonica fills. This time—now that his mic was working—Butterfield took the first solo and demonstrated his ability to create clean, melodic lines with uncanny precision. Michael shadowed his phrases on slide, adding silvery punctuation to the leader's commentary. "Aw, *yeah*!" Bloomfield repeatedly shouted as Paul worked through his two choruses and into the first set of stops. Then Michael stepped up, launching his solo with a series of bright slides up the Telecaster's neck. After a flurry of fretted notes and a single chorus, Paul returned to sing a final verse and—catching Elvin Bishop off guard—abruptly ended the tune with a stop and a final turnaround. The performance, while not dramatic, was a nearly flawless example of classic Chicago-style electric blues. But Butterfield was hurrying the set along, determined to get in as many tunes as possible before Peter Yarrow signaled time.

"Thank you, thank you," Paul said as the crowd—now considerably larger—hooted and cheered. Many of the cheers came from beside the stage as other festival performers expressed their enthusiasm for the band. Bloomfield began tuning his guitar, but Butterfield wasn't waiting. Cupping harp to mouth, he blew the opening lick of "Mellow Down Easy," and Sam snapped the downbeat on his snare to bring in the group. As the leader spooled out the driving vamp's melodic phrases, Michael was right there answering them with off-the-beat bends and low-note groans.

Butterfield was clearly trying to get the audience going as more and more people filed in, filling the field and searching for their seats. He sang the opening verse through twice and then shouted "Go ahead!" to Bloomfield. The guitarist tore into a brief solo, all fast runs and low-note bends, and Paul followed with a remarkable improvisation that concluded with a ten-bar riff played in 3/4 time against Sam Lay's insistent shuffle rhythm. Bloomfield let out a joyful scream as Butterfield resolved his statement into the melody line, and the two of them dropped back into the vamp's opening call-and-response. Paul sang the final verse and the band grew progressively quieter until he brought "Mellow Down Easy" home with a final commanding phrase. The applause was instant and deep. It was after 8:00 p.m. and most of the audience had arrived, many now in their seats. More than a few were searching through their programs for the name of the electric band onstage. Those who had seen Butterfield and his men at their workshops were pleasantly surprised to encounter them again.

Next up was "Look over Yonders Wall"—it seemed like the Butterfield Band was going to replay its entire Friday afternoon set. After quickly tuning to an E chord, Michael charged into the opening slide lick. But this time his sound was less dominant. It mattered little, though, as the band sallied into the tune and Butterfield sang the first two verses, took two strong choruses on harp, and then sang a third. Michael followed, leaning on the Elmore James lick, repeating it ferociously for his first chorus and working up the neck as he soloed for a second. After two more verses from the leader peppered with Bloomfield's slide fills, the band hit a stop and Butterfield ended the song.

As Bloomfield retuned his guitar, Paul checked the wings for any sign of Peter Yarrow. The stage manager was nowhere in sight, so Butterfield decided he could fit in one more tune before the set closer. He intended to play something different—an minor blues instrumental called "Work Song."

By the mid-1960s, "Work Song" was a staple of Chicago club repertoire. It was commonly played in blues taverns on the South Side and in jazz bars on the North Side. Paul had recorded a version of it for Elektra during his first sessions for the label back in March, but it had been dropped in favor of more standard Chicago fare. Now he had an opportunity to play it, and he was going to take it. "Work Song" would demonstrate the group's ability to play more sophisticated material and show off Butterfield's talents as soloist. It would also do the same for Bloomfield and Bishop.

In that respect, the Butterfield Band was much like a typical jazz group. Solos were an essential part of the music that Paul, Michael, and the band played, and instrumentals were all about solos. Of the fifteen tunes they performed over the four days they were at Newport, five of them had no vocals, and one was even played three times. That set them apart from nearly all the other performers at the festival. Folk music was most commonly a music that included singing, its words shared from one musician to another. There were exceptions, most notably in bluegrass music. But for the most part, tunes without vocals were largely within the purview of jazz. So the Paul Butterfield Blues Band was not only infiltrating the Newport Folk Festival with the taint of rock 'n' roll, but also subtly infusing it with aspects of jazz.

"In my opinion, Butterfield is the finest blues harmonica player in the world," Bloomfield told an interviewer later that weekend. "He has taken it so far out of the realm of folk blues, it is a jazz instrument."

As "Work Song" concluded, the audience roared its approval. The band had turned the festival into something of a rock 'n' roll party the day before, and now they made it seem like the crowd had mistakenly come to the Newport Jazz Festival.

Before the applause died down, Butterfield launched into the band's closer—"Born in Chicago." The band played a chorus as the leader stated the melody and then continued the backing riff as Butterfield sang the first two verses. Michael dropped in strident accents between Paul's phrases and then laid out as the harp player went into a two-chorus solo. Two more vocal choruses led into a short duet between Bloomfield and Butterfield, with the guitarist duplicating Paul's lines. A final vocal chorus led into another harp-guitar duet and then to a resounding coda played by Butterfield and Bloomfield together.

"Thank you very much," said the leader, clearly pleased with the performance and the huge audience's enthusiastic response. The quintet gathered up its instruments and filed offstage as Peter Yarrow stepped into the spotlight and called for another round of applause. "The Paul Butterfield Blues Band!" he intoned.

Albert Grossman was satisfied with the band's performance and more than satisfied with their reception. He knew that he had made the right decision in taking Butterfield on as a client, and he sought Paul out backstage to congratulate him. The harmonica player was feeling expansive after the band's successful set, and he chatted amicably with his new manager. Standing nearby was Mike Bloomfield. He was uncharacteristically quiet, distracted by thoughts of Bob Dylan. He was acutely aware that his time on Newport's stage wasn't over yet.

The Butterfield Band was followed in quick succession by other performers, including bluesman Mance Lipscomb, folksinger Eric Von Schmidt, and the Beers Family. The capacity audience was attentive throughout the first portion of the concert, applauding generously at the conclusion of each performance and even enjoying Peter Yarrow's commentary between sets. But there were few calls for encores. Everyone was excitedly waiting to see the man described as the "voice of his generation." No one was sure when Bob Dylan would appear—his name was only one among the program's list of performers—but nearly everyone was expecting him to close the show.

At about 9:30 p.m., Cousin Emmy took the stage. She was joined by Mike Seeger's trio, the New Lost City Ramblers, and they accompanied her while she fiddled, played harp and banjo, and sang. A talented musician and comedienne, the Kentucky native soon had the audience cheering and clapping along. At the high point of her set, she beat out "Turkey in the Straw" on her cheeks.

Cousin' Emmy's folksy humor and lively playing put everyone in a good mood. As she ended her set, there was much applause interspersed with laughter and cheering. She waved to the crowd and blew kisses as Peter Yarrow came back out to announce the next act. When some in the audience noticed a stagehand switching on the amps that had been sitting unobtrusively onstage, more than a few cheers were heard. Was Dylan playing next? So soon? And were those really *amplifiers*?

The crowd didn't have to wait long to find out. As mics were moved into place and last minute equipment adjustments were made, the stage lights went down. Yarrow stepped into the spotlight and up to a microphone.

"The person that's coming up now . . . is a person who has, in a sense, changed the face of folk music to the large American public . . . because he has brought to it a point of view . . . of a poet," said Peter, distracted by the shadowy figures of band members emerging from the darkened wings. There were bursts of static as instruments were plugged in. "The person that's going to come up now," Yarrow continued, "has a limited amount of time"—great cheers arose as many in the audience recognized the famous folksinger coming in from stage left—"His name is . . . *Bob Dylan*!"

The crowd was instantly on its feet, cheering uproariously for its hero. But as the stage lights went up, it wasn't a single folksinger with an acoustic guitar that was revealed. Standing onstage were six musicians, some holding electric instruments. Dylan himself was dressed in a bright shirt and dark leather jacket. Even more surprising was the thing slung over his shoulder—the evil-looking Stratocaster.

As the cheering continued, there was more static followed by a startling blast from the organ. Mike Bloomfield plugged his Telecaster into Paul Butterfield's big Futura and then shouted to a stagehand, "Put that up, man. Give Bob a little more volume on that amp." To Dylan he said, "You want it louder?" as Bob strummed a few chords through Michael's Thunderbird. Dylan and Bloomfield were both playing electric guitars. Al Kooper was behind the big Hammond, wearing Dylan's polka-dotted shirt from the afternoon sound check. At the piano was Barry Goldberg, a red handkerchief tied around his forehead, and behind him was tall Jerome Arnold with his long Fender Precision Bass. In the rear was Sam Lay, a resolute bulldog behind his silvery set of Gretsch drums.

This was something completely unexpected.

"I was wearing Levis, a button-down shirt and a sports coat. The black guys from the Butterfield Band were wearing gold shoes and had processes," Bloomfield said, recalling the impression the group made. "Dylan wore rock 'n' roll clothes: black jacket, yellow tie-pin shirt without the tie. And he had a Fender Stratocaster. He looked like someone from *West Side Story*."

Dylan had decided to open with "Maggie's Farm." He had recorded the song in January, releasing it on *Bringing It All Back Home*. It seemed like a fitting first tune because electric instruments and drums had been used on the original, and many in the audience would already know it. But the studio version featured unobtrusive, restrained lead by Bruce Langhorne. What Bob was about to foist on his unsuspecting fans would be anything but restrained.

The folksinger set the tempo by strumming his Stratocaster, hammering on a D chord. Jerome Arnold and then Sam Lay picked up the beat as Bloomfield shouted, "Let's *go*!" and charged ahead with a two-bar rhythm part. A variation on the bass line to the Butterfield Band's version of "Shake Your Money Maker," Michael's riff cut through Dylan's tentative chords like a crapshooter's straight razor. Al Kooper joined the fracas, and Barry Goldberg pounded out syncopations with a strong right hand. Within a few seconds the sound was overwhelming, beyond loud. Three big amplifiers, a chest-high Leslie speaker cabinet, piano and drums miked through the PA—there had never been such firepower at Newport before.

Dylan tried blowing a few notes on the harmonica in the rack around his neck but quickly surrendered. He looked at Michael and then back at the rest of the band. He seemed not to know what to do. His shoulders gave an involuntary jerk. He approached the microphone again, and this time he began to sing. But his voice couldn't be heard in the audience immediately out front above the roar of the band. It was obvious that the mix was way out of balance. Peter Yarrow rushed back out onstage.

"I would traditionally mix the whole festival when I wasn't onstage singing," Yarrow said. "But with Dylan, I couldn't hear *anything*. Anything coherent or clear, that is." Yarrow could certainly hear the rest of the band. He hastily checked Dylan's mic cable, wiggling connections while Bob sang the tune's first verse. Then he tried turning down Bloomfield's amplifier. But nothing helped.

Out front, things were equally confused. Many in the massive crowd were stunned by the aural onslaught. Nearly everyone was expecting the Dylan they knew and loved, the self-effacing bard whose poignant poetry and caustic social commentary had reinvigorated folk music. Here instead was a loud, crass rock 'n' roll band whose tirade was obliterating the one thing Dylan fans most wanted to hear—his words. Worst of all was the guitarist who kept interjecting furious flurries of notes in between the few lyrics they could hear.

That guitarist was only doing what he did best. Michael Bloomfield was filling the spaces in the tune with exciting lead, just as he had done for Dylan in the studio back in June. His lines came after each of Bob's phrases and at the conclusion of each verse he soloed with growing intensity. He combined blues bends and rock riffs with startling ferocity, his Telecaster cranked and blistering.

After each verse, Dylan stepped back from the microphone as though it were a viper about to strike. Bloomfield's guitar sallies swarmed around him like angry hornets. Though the folksinger seemed dazed, he had no alternative but to press on. He stared straight ahead and sang.

"It might have been old acoustic Bob, old Ramblin' Bob, the way he ignored the musicians," said Michael, sensing Dylan's disconnection. "It could have been the Stones behind him. At most, he'd tighten his jaw and move just a little."

Bob finally turned and looked at Michael after five verses, signaling to the guitarist that the tune was finished. Bloomfield caught the eyes of the rhythm section and brought "Maggie's Farm" to a close with a final emphatic riff. The lights onstage went up.

And the field erupted. "Thank you," said the singer, slightly off mic.

In the huge outcry from the audience, it was unclear what was being expressed. Some fans were lustily cheering, that was obvious, but others in the crowd were undoubtedly booing just as loudly. The only thing not in question was the powerful effect Bob Dylan's new music was having.

"A buzz of shock and amazement ran through the crowd," said Joe Boyd. Boyd, a twenty-two-year-old producer who worked for George Wein, was helping run the festival's sound. "There were shouts of delight and triumph, and also of derision and outrage."

Some who were outraged were backstage. Festival board members Alan Lomax, Theodore Bikel, and Pete Seeger—Dylan's close friend and erstwhile mentor—had been listening by the stage steps and were now fuming. Seeger was particularly distressed that Bob's words were unintelligible. Lomax, caught off guard by the secretly arranged electric performance, felt he had been assaulted a second time by the thug Grossman. Bikel simply demanded that Joe Boyd do something to repair the sound—*now!*

But there was little that could be done. The soundboard was fifty feet away, surrounded by hundreds of audience members and cordoned off by several rows of fences. At its controls, Boyd could see, was Elektra's Paul Rothchild, grinning from ear to ear.

"I was at the console, mixing the set, the only one there who had ever recorded electric music," said Rothchild. "From my perspective, it seemed like everybody on my left wanted Dylan to get off the stage, everybody on my right wanted him to turn it up. And I did—I turned it up."

While Dylan seemed to sense immediately that his electric experiment was getting a decidedly mixed reception, he also knew instinctively that there would be no turning back. He pivoted and faced his musicians, striving to gain control of the situation. Al Kooper moved center stage to take the bass from Jerome Arnold as Barry Goldberg slid into place behind the organ. Bloomfield checked his tuning and watched Dylan expectantly. After a moment, Bob began strumming a C chord, establishing a rhythm for the next piece. It was the challenging "Like a Rolling Stone."

The audience settled down as Michael joined Bob, picking a pretty countermelody over the folksinger's strumming. After the aggressive imbalance of "Maggie's Farm," Bloomfield's guitar now blended quite well with the rest of the band. Barry entered with a single held chord, and the tune began to pick up steam. The band vamped, waiting for Bob to begin the song, but the singer seemed to hesitate. He approached the mic, opened his mouth, but then quickly stepped back. A second attempt proved successful, and as Dylan sang the first line, there were cheers of recognition from out front. People had clearly been listening to the radio in the days leading up to the festival.

The song proceeded with only a few tentative moments as the band's ensemble sound gelled and the instruments blended well. Though Sam Lay's martial beat was more than a little stiff, Barry Goldberg's re-creation of the original organ part deftly complemented Bloomfield's tasteful, elaborate embellishments. The overall performance convincingly evoked the hit single, and the audience gradually grew less restive despite the fact that Dylan's words were still difficult to make out. But the refrain was familiar enough that many in the crowd could sing along.

After he had worked through the song's four verses, Dylan again turned around, this time to signal to the band that the piece was finished. Holding a final G chord, the rhythm section faltered to a stop as Michael forced a coda with a series of licks and a final chord. Again the audience was on its feet. But this time there were fewer cries of dismay. The sound mix seemed to be under control, and the rock 'n' roll extremes of "Maggie's Farm" had abated. For the moment, anyway.

Onstage, Bob Dylan had begun to sweat. He was eleven minutes into his set, and the band had only one more tune to play. It was one that the folksinger had repeatedly attempted in the studio during his June sessions for Columbia, but without much success. It would be completely unfamiliar to the audience.

"I told Bobby it was a mistake when he said they were only going to do three songs," Peter Yarrow remembered. "He should have explained what he was doing—you know, told the audience, 'This is my new music, we're trying it out.' But instead, he did three quick songs and left. Nobody knew what was happening."

Dylan knew what was happening, though it was not happening the way he had expected. He was determined to finish the set. There would be time enough later to sort it all out. He began strumming the rhythm to "Phantom Engineer." The song, a one-chord blues with a turnaround, was one he and Michael had worked on, and it would later be titled "It Takes a Lot to Laugh, It Takes a Train to Cry." But at Newport, it was still evolving. Bloomfield had revamped its studio arrangement during the previous night's rehearsal, and now he dug into it.

Alternating between chords and a riff from John Lee Hooker's "Boom Boom," Michael's guitar part was pure blues-rock. He jacked up the volume, giving his Telecaster a raw, over-driven sound that threatened to overwhelm the performance. Kooper, now back on the organ, joined him, playing an on-the-beat organ part copped from the Ad Libs' R&B hit "The Boy from New York City." Arnold, playing bass once again, struggled to feel the song's changes, while Sam Lay droved the ensemble more convincingly than he had on the previous two tunes. The whirlwind of sound that had engulfed "Maggie's Farm" was back.

Between each of Dylan's verses, Bloomfield cranked out rocking solos that sometimes reached twenty-four bars in length. There seemed to be no stopping him, even though Bob shouted, "No solo, *no solo*!" after the second verse. Following the third and last verse, the guitarist fired a final salvo that culminated in an intense eight-bar repetition of a single G in eighth-note rhythm. The tune ground to a halt moments later. It had taken a little over three minutes to play it.

Sixteen minutes after it began, Bob Dylan's long-awaited, much-anticipated set at the 1965 Newport Folk Festival was over.

"Let's go, let's go, man," said the folksinger to his accomplices, and the band hurriedly left the stage. The audience, on its feet throughout the entire tune, now roared in response. The noise was deafening. Some were cheering, others were bellicosely booing. Most were crying out, "More! *More!*"

The emcee had also been hoping for more. A rattled, anxious Peter Yarrow stepped up to the center stage mic and was clearly at a loss. He was unsure what Dylan's fans wanted.

"The audience was mortified," Peter recalled. "The only thing running through my mind at the time was *They are really,* really *pissed off*!"

"It was like being in the eye of a hurricane," agreed Joe Boyd. "All around us people were standing up, waving their arms. Some were cheering, some booing, some arguing, some grinning like madmen."

Yarrow didn't know what to do. He polled the audience. "Would you like Bobby to sing another song? I don't know—"

Screams erupted. "*More*!"

"He's coming," Yarrow said. To appease them he added, "He's gotta get an *acoustic* guitar."

In a matter of minutes, Dylan was back out onstage, having been convinced to leave the performers tent by manager Albert Grossman. He asked Peter to get him a Martin to replace the big Gibson acoustic someone had handed him backstage, and then, clearly upset, he sang "It's All Over Now, Baby Blue," making a statement, and then "Mr. Tambourine Man," making amends. He then left the stage and did not return despite repeated cries for more.

Though no one—not even Dylan himself—understood at the time the full import of the electric set performed at Newport that Sunday evening, everyone agreed it was controversial. There were those who loved it—the music's raw energy, its big beat and loud, exciting swagger. They were tired of folk music's rigid orthodoxy and were eager to explore other musical forms unfettered by imposed notions of "authenticity." Many in the Boston folk community were energized by Dylan's new music.

"It was God awful loud," said Maria Muldaur. "But to me it was exciting. It was interesting and new."

For others, it was only loud. "Just where is Bob Dylan going? Where does all this terminate? By this I mean electric guitars, drums, organs, and rock 'n' roll," wrote one distressed reader in a letter to *Sing Out!* magazine. People had been upset because the sound was so distorted and unbalanced.

To folk traditionalists, Dylan's three electric tunes were an affront—a kind of betrayal. Though Peter Yarrow was a fan of Bob's new sound, he understood the feelings of those who heard it as disrespectful.

"The article of faith was that we were building a better world, breaking with prejudice and injustice, creating a cultural revolution," Yarrow said. "Playing folk music meant, 'I am for this change.' Electric instruments meant you were going 'commercial.' So the fact that their hero, their poet, had gone commercial, had 'sold out,' was like breaking a sacred trust for them, even though they might have liked the music."

At the heart of the controversy, pro or con, was electricity—in the form of an electric guitar. But not just any electric guitar. It was true that Dylan played a lurid, voluptuous Stratocaster that night. But if it had been Bruce Langhorne quietly accompanying him, very few would have cared what instrument Bob carried out onstage. It was Michael Bloomfield's Telecaster that provided the wattage the night Dylan "went electric." Bloomfield's extroverted, exuberant accompaniment turned the short set into a statement, a gauntlet thrown in the face of rigid folk tradition. Michael wasn't concerned with politics, with parsing the definition of commercialism or safeguarding the sensibilities of traditionalists. He went onstage that night to play Dylan's music to the best of his ability, regardless of what anybody might think. The result? Dylan had no choice but to adopt that attitude himself. The folksinger was acutely aware of the expectations fans, critics, and colleagues had of him, and it took Michael Bloomfield's searing licks to free him from having to meet those expectations. As painful as it would be, following Newport the only expectations Bob Dylan would meet would be his own.

Bloomfield later said as much in a short piece he wrote about the experience.

> The Newport establishment—Theo Bikel, Odetta, Pete Seeger—felt betrayed. These people had embraced Bob as a prophet, and when his music no longer reflected their kind of social content, they felt politically and personally betrayed. His audience was just small-minded and rigid. You know why? Because they were more interested in idolatry than music. Many people who went through very poignant life changes used Dylan's music as a background track for their lives. They said, "You

show us the way." But he probably was just a poet making product, and when his way differed from their concept of "The Way," they were angry. Dylan should have just given them the finger and said, "Hey, this is what I do. It's all over now, baby blue."

Mike Bloomfield was the middle finger of Dylan's Newport gesture. The irony, of course, was that Michael knew the folk tradition—and many of its originators—as well or better than most of the musicians and self-appointed "experts" at Newport that weekend. He had an unwavering love for its artists and their artistry. But he also knew and loved electric blues and rock 'n' roll. He had spent years playing in bars and clubs, working in show bands and dance combos, jamming in ghetto taverns, and playing on street corners. His music was unerringly honest and direct. He gave it his all, and it never occurred to him that he should confine himself to what the audience expected to hear.

It was that fearless integrity that played a large part in unlocking the door to Bob Dylan's future and freeing him from his role as the "voice of his generation."

After Dylan's calamitous performance, the Moving Star Hall Singers took the stage for a short set of gospel songs, closing out the first half of the concert. The audience settled down, but the excitement that pervaded earlier portions of the show had been lost. And at the end of each selection, there were cries to bring back Dylan.

Backstage, Mike Bloomfield was genuinely surprised to learn that Bob thought their performance had been ill-received. "I thought we were boffo, smasheroo. When it was over, I said, 'Bob, how do you think we did?' And he said, 'They were booing. Didn't you hear it?' I said, 'No, man, I thought it was cheers.' He didn't seemed pissed, he seemed perplexed. He was a guy with a hit single, and they were booing him." Michael found it hard to understand how the folksinger's fans could turn on him so easily, especially when all he was doing was playing his new music—which was getting plenty of radio airplay.

The second half of the concert forged ahead with appearances by half a dozen folk performers, including a set from Peter, Paul and Mary and a sing-along led by Joan Baez. At the conclusion of the evening, George Wein sat at the piano and played "When the Saints Go Marching In" while many of the festival's artists crowded onstage to join in on the raucous lyrics. But the merriment felt forced to many, and backstage the mood was somber. Bob Dylan's performance had created a palpable tension between those who supported his new music and those who were appalled by it. Dylan himself was nowhere in sight.

As a gesture of appeasement, Pete Seeger arranged for Mel Lyman to play solo harmonica over the PA system while people were leaving Festival Field. Lyman blew dozens of choruses of "Rock of Ages" while sitting on the edge of the stage in the dark, thus creating a moving farewell to the Newport Folk Festival of 1965.

The after-festival party was an all-night affair held at Nethercliffe, the festival's headquarters. While nearly all of the younger generation of musicians attended, few of the older players joined in the festivities. The elaborately catered event felt more like a victory celebration than a reaffirmation of the traditions that had originally inspired Newport. Once things got rolling, though, Sam Lay and Jerome Arnold set up and began to play for anybody who wanted to jam. The Chambers Brothers did several sets, and the mood soon lightened as the party got wilder and wilder. By dawn, it was still going strong.

Before he left Newport, Michael Bloomfield met with Albert Grossman. The music power broker wanted to discuss Michael's future. What, he asked, would the guitarist like to do? Was he interested in joining Bob Dylan's touring group, or would he rather become an official member of the Paul Butterfield Blues Band? Grossman was planning a tour for Dylan's new folk-rock ensemble in support of his forthcoming Columbia release, and Bob would need a good electric guitar player. Since Bloomfield already knew the music and had helped create its sound, he was the perfect candidate.

The question caught Mike off guard. He hadn't expected to be asked about his preferences. He assumed that his future would be determined by management, especially when Albert Grossman was involved.

"Albert had just signed Butter, so I figured he'd make the choice," said Bloomfield. "Now, I was already in Butter's band and Dylan asked me to play with him. Here's where we misunderstood each other. I figured Albert would tell me who to play with, where I'd be most effective, but he left the choice up to me. I said, 'OK, man, I'm a blues guitar player and I have an obligation to Butter, so I have to play with Butter.'"

Dylan wanted Michael to play on the remaining sessions for his Columbia album, and he naturally assumed that Bloomfield would be in his touring band. He liked the guitarist's energy, wicked sense of humor, and willingness to try anything. He also thought Michael was the best guitarist he had ever heard. When Grossman told him that Bloomfield had decided to join Paul's band, Bob was surprised, disappointed—and even a little hurt.

"I could even see then that Bob was sort of real thrilling," said Michael, more than a little conflicted over his choice. "But I just thought I wouldn't get a chance to play enough music—licks, actually—seriously, move my fingers enough." With Butterfield, the guitarist knew he would be given more than ample opportunity exercise his fingers—and to do so as a featured soloist. He hated to decline his friend's offer, but Bloomfield opted for the blues. The Butterfield Band was where he felt most at home—and it would be where he would hone his prodigious musical talents over the next seventeen months, developing into America's first great guitar hero.

Before Mike Bloomfield left Newport on Monday, he had one more obligation to fulfill. That morning he was interviewed by a film crew that was making a documentary about Newport. The movie's director, thirty-eight-year-old Murray Lerner, had been shooting performers at the festival since 1963 at the behest of George Wein. He and his cameramen had been at both blues workshops and had caught the Butterfield Band's rocking performances, along with their impromptu main stage appearance on Sunday, on film. Bloomfield was such a dynamic player, both aurally and visually, that Lerner asked him to go on camera expressing his views about the blues. Michael was only too happy to share his observations, and he found the film crew in a sunny spot just inside the Bluesville location, to the right of the main stage. The guitarist, wearing a white T-shirt, his hair frizzy and cowlicked from whatever sleep he had finally gotten, squinted into the camera as Lerner asked him a few questions about himself and about music. What was Michael's approach to the blues?

"Every time I play, you know, you start and then you get into the music, you reach a point within yourself where it's you and the music," Bloomfield told the filmmaker. "They're two separate entities, and when they come together and you're completely into it, and you get into that music, man, and that music becomes you. . . . You play blues with all of you—not just your hands, all of you. Every bit of you is part of that music."

Lerner asked about race and whether that mattered when it came to playing the blues. It was a prickly topic that Alan Lomax's introduction at the Friday workshop had raised by implication, and one that would later irritate Bloomfield whenever it would come up in interviews and reviews. But for the camera he turned on his boyish charm.

"I'm not born to blues, you know, it's not in my blood, in my roots or my family. Man, I'm Jewish, you know," Michael said, smiling broadly. He added with a chuckle, "I've been Jewish for years."

The filmmaker asked what the guitarist thought about the great Son House, and Bloomfield replied that because he was white, he hadn't suffered the indignities that are too often the fate of African Americans like House. But he affirmed his ability to also play the music.

"Man, my father's a multimillionaire, you know? I've lived a rich, fat, happy life," Michael said. "Man, I had a big bar mitzvah, you know? I'm not Son House. I *can* play blues, and I can feel it, in a way. Man, those guys are a different story." He went on to praise Paul Butterfield, saying there was "no white bullshit" with the harmonica player. "If he was green, it wouldn't make any difference. If he was a planarian, a tuna fish sandwich, Butterfield would be into the blues."

He was clearly enthused about his decision to become a permanent member of the Butterfield Band. "I'll tell you, man, you hear this band after this two-month tour," he said, referring to a series of gigs Albert Grossman had set up for Butterfield, "and there won't be a blues band in the history of the world that's gonna come near this band. . . . I'm really sold on this group!" Michael's initial dislike of the harmonica player had clearly begun to temper.

During the fifteen-minute interview, Bloomfield talked in a relaxed and easy manner. He freely shared his opinions, tilting his head as he spoke to avoid the glare of the morning sun. He came off as an engaging and earnest young man, guileless in his love for the music and forthright in expressing his enthusiasm for it. The camera liked him, and he was clearly comfortable in front of it. His grade school ambition to be a "dramatics teacher" wasn't simply a childhood impulse. As Joel Harlib had observed, Michael Bloomfield was a natural performer.

Michael and Susan drove back to New York City on Monday afternoon with the rest of the Chicago crew. Bloomfield had thoroughly enjoyed his long weekend in Rhode Island and had reveled in the attention he received as the Newport Folk Festival's resident electric guitarist. His appearance with Bob Dylan had established his musical credentials with the Boston and New York folk contingents, and he was now perceived not only as a gifted guitarist but as someone with access to pop music's inner circle. That he was also the lead man for the thrilling Paul Butterfield Blues Band was icing on the musical cake.

Michael had good reason to get back to New York that afternoon. He had recording sessions with Dylan scheduled for Thursday, Friday, and the following Monday, and Albert Grossman wanted the material completed so that Dylan's next Columbia album could be released by the end of the month. "Like a Rolling Stone" was climbing *Billboard*'s Hot 100 chart and looked like it might reach number one. Grossman wanted the album to benefit from its airplay and sales.

There was also a reason that the Butterfield Band had to be back in New York City. Paul Rothchild had arranged for them to do a week at the Cafe Au Go Go, a basement club that had opened eighteen months earlier at 152 Bleecker Street in Greenwich Village. The band was starting Tuesday night and playing through to Sunday, all so that Elektra could record them in live performance. Rothchild had broken the news to Butterfield at Newport that he had decided to scrap the album they had recorded in March and April. The reason? Rothchild felt strongly that though the studio sessions had been very good, they still lacked the excitement the band created in live performance. He convinced Elektra's owner, Jac Holzman, to dump the ten thousand copies of the Butterfield LP that were waiting in a warehouse, boxed and ready to ship.

"With better recording techniques, I knew we could capture the enormous energy I had felt when I first heard the Paul Butterfield Blues Band at Big John's," Rothchild said. That energy had been present at Newport, and Rothchild was determined to re-create it at the Cafe Au Go Go. With Mike Bloomfield now a full-fledged member of the band and its other dynamic soloist, the producer was confident that a live recording would do the trick.

Elektra brought in a mobile recording truck, ran cables down the stairs into the Cafe Au Go Go, close-miked everything, and proceeded to record four of the six nights the band played at the club. Though the Butterfield Band was sharing the bill with veteran folksingers Bob Gibson and Barbara Dane, the café placed ads in the *New York Times* giving the Chicago group top billing and touting them as "Direct from Newport."

Bloomfield was spending his afternoons recording with Dylan before coming to the café to play with Paul. In the studio were many of the musicians who had participated in the June dates, including Al Kooper. The newly minted organist was only too happy to comply with Bob's request that he play on the album's remaining tunes. In marathon sessions spread over the three days, the musicians recorded endless takes of nine separate Dylan compositions. Michael reprised his role as Bob's instrumental counterpart, lending melodic support to the folksinger's lyrics and creating ornamental filigree to enhance his chords. In "Tombstone Blues," one of the first tunes they recorded, Michael managed to drop in edgy, aggressive fills, recalling his hopped-up contributions during Dylan's Newport set. But during one take of the tune, following a particularly wild break that broke the singer's concentration, Bob laughingly told an engineer, "You gotta put a wall up over him, man!"

In redoing "Phantom Engineer," now retitled "It Takes a Lot to Laugh, It Takes a Train to Cry," early takes with Bloomfield's loud, raw lead were abandoned in favor of a much more genteel arrangement. Michael took the hint and toned his playing down for the remainder of the session. He did get in some restrained slide work on the forthcoming album's title song, but for the most part his contribution was relegated to unobtrusive accompaniment. The only solo instrument was Dylan's harmonica, heard occasionally in brief interludes between his verses. Michael was, practically speaking, just another session player.

He was anything but a session player at the Cafe Au Go Go. With the band back in a familiar club environment after their alfresco experience at Newport, they felt comfortable stretching out, and both Paul and Michael soloed repeatedly. While Elvin Bishop occasionally took the spotlight, it was Bloomfield's lead that dominated. His animated, emotive stage presence coupled with his wildly expressive solos excited audiences and took the music to a new level.

At the same time, though, Butterfield was acutely aware that much of what they played was being recorded. He wanted the material to be the absolute best, and he exerted tight control over the performances. He knew that things still had to be sorted out—it was, after all, the band's first working gig as an official quintet—but he insisted on strict adherence to his orders. Bloomfield had played with Paul many times and had always enjoyed working with the harmonica player. But now, as a formal member of Butterfield's band, he was obliged to follow the leader's directives. *That* was a new experience for the star guitarist.

Following the Cafe Au Go Go gig, Paul Rothchild took the tapes of the band's performances back to the studio for editing and sequencing. The small budget for the rerecording had been forced into the red when, midway through the week, a representative from the musicians union appeared at the club and protested that he hadn't been informed of the sessions. The resulting fines and fees quadrupled the cost of the project, and Jac Holzman wasn't very happy. But Rothchild was confident that he had finally captured the true sound of the band.

On Monday, August 2, Albert B. Grossman Management—ABGM, as Grossman's agency was known—held a press party for the Paul Butterfield Blues Band. The news media was invited, and bottles of champagne were uncorked as the manager officially introduced the group as his newest clients. Albert touted their debut album, saying it would soon be released on Elektra, and talked about the band's recent triumphant appearance at Newport. As an added attraction for the reporters, Grossman had his superstar, Bob Dylan, attend the event. Bob clowned with Paul and Michael as the band members quaffed champagne and Sam Lay's wife filmed the event with Sam's Super-8 movie camera.

While they were celebrating, Michael noticed Robbie Robertson, his friend from the Hawks, standing and chatting with Dylan. Bob had hired the Toronto guitarist to replace Bloomfield in his touring electric band. When Bloomfield came over to say hello, Bob interrupted him before he could say anything.

"I walked over to him and he introduces me to Robbie, who I already knew, and Bob says, 'Hey, Mike, I want you to meet the best guitar player in the world.'" Bloomfield was taken aback. "Prior to that Newport thing, he was always introducing me to his friends as 'the best guitar player in the world.' It was sort of funny."

Bloomfield felt that Dylan's redirected compliment was a way of conveying his dissatisfaction with the guitarist's decision to join Butterfield. He could feel his friend pulling away from him, but Michael remained convinced that he had made the right career choice. That very afternoon he had been in the studio, recording the final tunes for Bob's upcoming album, and it would be his last session as "Dylan's guitarist."

The following week, the Paul Butterfield Blues Band hit the road. Grossman and ABGM had booked the band on the strength of its Newport performances for two months of gigs, beginning with a short tour of New England. The management company bought a used Ford Econoline van to haul the band's equipment and a few of the band members to their gigs. The others followed in rented cars.

Their first stop was in Ipswich, Massachusetts, where they did three nights at the King's Rook, a popular local coffeehouse, starting on Thursday, August 5. From there they went to the Moon-Cusser Cafe in Oak Bluffs on Martha's Vineyard. During their stay at the Moon-Cusser, the Butterfield Band was so loud, reverberations shook the wall across from the bandstand violently enough to cause a huge plate glass mirror in the drug store next door to crash to the floor.

The trip concluded with three nights at Cambridge's best-known folk coffeehouse, Club 47, on Palmer Street in Harvard Square. The band was squeezed into the venue's busy schedule, playing there Monday through Wednesday, August 16 to 18. Jim Rooney, Club 47's manager, had seen Butterfield at Newport and wanted to present the band to the Cambridge folk community. He arranged to hire them at what seemed an astronomical price—one hundred dollars per night.

Following their shows in Cambridge, the Butterfield Band headed back to New York City. They were appearing again at the Cafe Au Go Go the following week, and Paul was eager to get back so he could hear the results of Elektra's live taping sessions from their previous gig at the club. Bloomfield was looking forward to returning the city, too, but for a different reason.

Michael's frequent bouts of insomnia were a nuisance, but he could cope with the problem as long as he remained at home. Once he began to travel, however, his sleepless nights increased. The band's tour, though it had lasted less than two weeks, was long enough to exacerbate his periods of wakefulness. He found he couldn't sleep at all—sometimes for days at a time. Without his books, records, and other distractions of his home life, Bloomfield was left with nothing to do but stare at motel room walls. That only made it more difficult to calm his restless mind. After thirteen days on the road, he was desperate to get back to New York so he could rest. He and Susan had rented a small basement apartment in the West Village at 10 Christopher Street. They had decided they needed a permanent place to stay whenever they were in the city, and when they got home Thursday afternoon, Michael went right to bed.

His sleepless tour experience, as incidental as it seemed at the time, was a harbinger of things to come.

To celebrate its fifteenth anniversary—and to promote its artists to a wider audience of potential buyers—Elektra Records decided to issue two budget-priced sampler albums. One was on their Nonesuch label and featured selections from the company's classical catalog; the other, released on Elektra itself and called *Folksong '65*, offered a dozen performances by an equal number of folk artists. Opening Side 2 of the sampler was the Paul Butterfield Blues Band's rendition of "Born in Chicago." The tune stood out as the album's only selection by an electric band with drums, and it immediately caught the attention of buyers. Thousands of them plunked down a dollar for the LP when it was released during the second week of September. Sales of "Folksong '65" were brisk, and soon they far exceeded what the company had anticipated for the promotional LP.

"Jac [Holzman] got on the phone and called the stores to ask what the hell was going on," Paul Rothchild said. "He finds out that people have been asking for the record with 'Born in Chicago' on it."

Both Holzman and Rothchild realized that they had a potential hit record on their hands—if they could just get the Butterfield album finished. But there was another problem, Rothchild confessed to his boss. He had been editing the recordings of the band from the Cafe Au Go Go and had reluctantly come to a disturbing conclusion. The tapes didn't have "30 consecutive seconds of good music," he told the chagrined Holzman. The live recordings, he said, were a dismal failure. But, he asserted, if he could bring the Butterfield Band back into the studio one final time, he was convinced that he could finally get it right.

Holzman was livid, but there was nothing he could do. He gave the determined producer permission to record the group one more time.

The Butterfield Band spent the first weeks of September perfecting additional material for the album during their Cafe Au Go Go gig. During those weeks, Mark Naftalin came by frequently to hear the band and to hang out. He was amazed by the quintet's power. The addition of Michael Bloomfield gave the band a whole new sound.

"I thought the band was *screaming*!" Mark said. "The effect of Paul and Mike mixing and matching leads was dizzying." Butterfield seemed to agree that Bloomfield's playing had taken the band to a new level. Despite his misgivings about Michael as a person, he no longer questioned Bloomfield's ability to play blues. "I remember sitting with Paul at the Bitter End, across Bleecker Street from the Cafe Au Go Go," said Naftalin. "He told me that there was no guitarist in the country he'd rather have with him than Mike Bloomfield."

The second week in September, Paul Butterfield and his men returned to Mastertone Studios in Times Square for their third try at creating an album. This time, though, Mike Bloomfield didn't touch the piano. He was featured on guitar, just as he had been at Newport. He and Paul shared solo duties.

Their first session included a remake of Willie Dixon's "Mellow Down Easy." In the original March recording, Butterfield had been the only soloist with accompaniment by Michael and Elvin. But Paul Rothchild thought Bloomfield's lead contribution had intensified the tune during the band's Rhode Island performances, so he had them redo it. This time, Bloomfield's fills snaked in and out of Butterfield's phrases with practiced precision, and his solo, following Paul's two vocal choruses, was a nearly flawless barrage of eighth notes peppered with hair-raising string bends. The band's initial recording of the tune had been an impromptu, spontaneous collaboration, created largely on the spur of the moment. By contrast, the new version of "Mellow Down Easy" sounded tight, carefully arranged, and—as a result—far more exciting. Here was the sound Paul Rothchild and Elektra were looking for.

The new sound of the band was also partly the result of recent technological advances. In the group's March and April sessions, Mastertone's engineers had used a standard three-head recording machine. But in the months since then, Ampex Corporation had developed a four-head system that greatly expanded studio mixing capabilities. Mastertone had one of the new machines and could now record the Butterfield Band with greater separation and clarity. Jerome Arnold's bass part was suddenly much more audible since it could now be isolated from Sam Lay's drum track.

The group also did a version of "Last Night," another of Little Walter's hits, with Paul and Michael splitting solos. A majestic slow blues, the tune featured Bloomfield's florid fills behind Butterfield's vocal as well as a buzzy, jangling single chorus of lead guitar. The band's ensemble sound had clearly benefited from the weeks of steady work leading up to the session, and Michael no longer sounded like the "guest soloist."

On Thursday afternoon, September 9, Paul Butterfield was back in the studio for another session. The rest of the band soon arrived and began setting up. Joining them was Mark Naftalin, there to hang out and watch the recording process. He was also hoping to get a chance to play on a tune or two.

"I showed up at one of the band's recording sessions," Naftalin recounted. "Elvin was late to the session, so Paul invited me to play on a song. He put me on Hammond organ." The instrument was new to Naftalin, but he was willing to try. "They put me on Elvin's track, and we played an instrumental in the key of A."

The tune, a collaborative effort cooked up in the studio by Butterfield and Bloomfield with Naftalin's help, was later named "Thank You Mr. Poobah." Though he was inexperienced, Mark gamely took the plunge. "I had never played Hammond organ before that moment . . . but they threw it over to me for a solo and I made it through and they seemed to like it, so they invited me to stay on organ."

After Elvin arrived, he and Mark shared a recording track and the band continued as six pieces. The session lasted for a full nine hours, and the group, now augmented by Naftalin on keyboards, got seven more tunes on tape. They recorded a new version of "Our Love Is Driftin'," the Bishop and Butterfield tune that had originally inspired Paul Rothchild to have Michael Bloomfield sit in with the band when they first recorded it back in March. The song then had been a simple, single-chord blues, but now Butterfield added a fourth verse and had the band play it as a standard slow blues in twelve-bar form. He also structured it as a solo feature for Michael, and the guitarist backed Paul's vocals and then made the tune his own with a chorus of burning lead. The quintet also did Bloomfield's arrangement of Tampa Red's 1937 recording "Love Her with a Feeling." Paul sang the slow blues with real conviction, but the soloist again was Michael.

They then did Little Walter's "Blues with a Feeling," re-creating the excitement the tune had generated at Newport with Michael's fret-and-slide leads and Paul's commanding tone. A tune that Bloomfield had played since his high school days, "Mystery Train," was next. A hit for Junior Parker, the song in the Butterfield Band's rendition evoked a highballing flyer as Bloomfield and Bishop tightly intertwined their guitar parts with Lay's driving polyrhythms.

Michael reprised Scotty Moore's guitar riff from the Elvis Presley cover of the song and then shared a solo chorus on slide with Paul.

Bloomfield also provided an original instrumental titled "Screamin'." Using a bass line taken from a tune Michael had often heard Junior Wells play called "Snatch It Back and Hold It," "Screamin'" lived up to its name as he and Paul stated and restated the theme, traded solos, and then soloed together. Next it was Sam Lay's turn as Butterfield gave the drummer the vocal part for Muddy Waters's "Got My Mojo Working." The burly percussionist hammered out the beat as he growled his way through the lyrics, goading the rest of the band to join in on the refrain, "Got my mojo working!" and then backed the leader's wailing harp solo. But in the control room it was clear that Sam's drumming was distorting his vocal, so the engineers had the group redo the tune as an instrumental and then overdubbed Lay's singing on a separate track.

Paul's reworking of Elmore James's "Shake Your Money Maker" gave Michael the solo spot again. After the vocal, the guitarist recapped James's classic slide licks and then expanded on them by repeatedly twanging an open E, the lowest note on his Telecaster. For the turnaround, he rumbled through a brace of deep notes and then walked chromatically up to the tonic. It was a striking moment, one that Rothchild accentuated in the final mix, making Bloomfield's open-E "bombs" a prominent part of the performance. The phrase demonstrated Michael's talent for fusing popular music styles, because it came straight from 1950s rockabilly vernacular. Bloomfield later confessed to a friend that he had copped the lick from one of his early idols, Cliff Gallup, Gene Vincent's guitarist. Now it was part of an Elmore James blues classic.

Of all the tunes Butterfield and the band recorded that evening, the remake of "Born in Chicago" was perhaps the most important. The original version of the song was driving sales of "Folksong '65," Elektra's budget-priced sampler, but Paul Rothchild wanted an updated recording for the album. He was certain that a four-channel taping would result in an improved mix, and it was obvious that over the last six weeks the band had tightened its arrangement of the song. Butterfield and Bloomfield had learned to blend their sounds with uncanny precision, trading riffs and playing off one another while the rhythm section charged ahead.

The band took the song at a slightly elevated tempo with Sam Lay ticking off the beat in eighth notes on his high-hat. The addition of Mark Naftalin's organ rounded out the sound of the rhythm section and gave Elvin a little more freedom with his guitar part. Butterfield sang two verses and then took twelve bars for a solo. After a third verse, instead of soloing a second time as he had in the original recording, Paul passed the lead to Michael. Bloomfield sparked his way through a chorus and then Butterfield returned to sing a final verse.

Both he and Michael soloed together, playing the same lead line in places, for three more choruses before the engineers in the booth signaled that they had enough for a fade in the final mix. The new version of "Born in Chicago" was two choruses longer than the original, giving listeners an extra helping of Paul and Michael in duet. Rothchild was right—the improved studio equipment did enhance the band's sound. The remake of "Born in Chicago" was a winner.

At one point late in the marathon session, Paul Butterfield took Mark Naftalin aside and asked him if he would like to join the band. Mark was elated by the offer. His studies at Mannes suddenly took a back seat to being a member of the Paul Butterfield Blues Band. Michael Bloomfield seemed to have thought so too. "Mike later told me that, during the session, he told Paul something to the effect of, 'You didn't hire Barry,' referring to Barry Goldberg, 'so you'd better hire this guy,'" Naftalin said. Butterfield complied, and the band was now a sextet.

To Elektra's great relief, the Butterfield Band's taping sessions at Mastertone proved successful. Paul Rothchild now had the sound he was looking for. He worked during the last weeks of September to mix the material and sequence it, doing nearly all the work himself. The band was preoccupied with performing and had no real interest in postproduction. They were happy enough to leave those duties to the professionals. Elektra's professionals, of course, had never produced an album by a loud electric band before. Rothchild and his assistant, Mark Abramson, were learning as they went along.

One thing Rothchild was experienced in was presenting groups. His Chicago musicians were all highly talented performers, but visually they were a motley crew. ABGM had arranged for the band to make a triumphant return to Big John's in the Windy City, a six-week stay timed to coincide with the release of their Elektra album. Rothchild felt they needed to have a more professional look, now that they were the rising stars of electric blues, so he took the band to Orchard Street on Manhattan's Lower East Side and got them all matching Continental suits. Butterfield, as the band's leader, was outfitted with one in green.

"Our jackets were cat-shit brown, as Mike described them," said Mark Naftalin with a laugh. "I remember trying the suit on and Jerome Arnold taking one look and saying, 'What insurance company do you work for?' We also got Beatle boots, and Michael's didn't fit, and he wore them only once—open and flapping when he walked."

Their haberdashery suitably upgraded, the members of the Paul Butterfield Blues Band loaded the van with their equipment and departed for Chicago the first week in October, forming a caravan with the Econoline and several cars. Back in their hometown, they settled into Big John's, the place where the Paul Butterfield Blues Band had begun a year earlier. Playing five nights a week to sold-out crowds, their shows generally consisted of four or five sets beginning around 9:00 p.m. and winding up at 4:00 a.m., or 5:00 a.m. on Fridays and Saturdays. Repertoire consisted of standard Chicago blues, a few originals including "Born in Chicago," and many of the tunes the band had recorded for Elektra. The interplay between Butterfield and Bloomfield added a new dimension to the group's sound, further impressing fans who had first heard the band as a quartet. One of those who came to the Old Town tavern on North Wells Street to hear the group was Michael's brother, Allen. It had been a long while since he had seen Michael, and he had never heard Paul play before.

"I was a freshman in college, and they were at Big John's," said Allen. "It was amazing! I sat really close and was just knocked out by Paul's playing. I had never seen or heard anything like what he was doing with the harmonica. Mike was there too, a part of it, and he sounded great, but it was seeing Butterfield play that got to me. The whole band was amazingly woven together, loud and tight, right within the form. . . . I was so inspired, I started playing harp myself—just like a thousand other kids after seeing Paul."

Now that his brother was playing with Paul, Allen suddenly saw him in a new light. He and Michael hadn't seen much of each other since Michael left home after graduating from Central Y in 1961. Their adolescent rivalry had blossomed into a deep antipathy that kept them apart. Harold's fervent disapproval of Michael's pursuit of music had strongly affected Allen, and the younger Bloomfield scion opted to pursue a career in business as a way to curry his father's favor. That choice seemed to underscore the brothers' differences. But now they began to find common ground. Michael's musical success was one reason, but there was another.

Allen had moved with his parents to North Lake Shore Drive after they sold the Glencoe house in 1963. But he had never felt at home there. The high-rise residence also felt less than homey due to the growing tension between Harold and Dottie. Their numerous differences had hardened to such a degree that by 1964 they were each leading entirely separate lives. The final straw came a year later when Harold revealed that he had fallen in love with a woman in the accounting department at Bloomfield Industries and that he had decided to move in with her. He and Dottie separated soon afterward, and Harold left Chicago for Hinsdale, a suburb ten miles west of the city, to join his new love.

The news of their parents' separation and subsequent divorce did not really surprise either of the Bloomfield brothers. They had seen it coming.

Allen continued to work for his father at the Cicero plant when he wasn't in school, but he stayed in the apartment with his mother. Michael had always been closest to Dottie and, after years of enduring his father's disapproval, now saw very little of Harold. It didn't matter to him where his father was living. Only when he visited Harold's new home did the implications of the change take on a more serious nature.

"His dad had this other family," said Fred Glazer. "Harold was never home when Michael was growing up, and lots of times he was with his girlfriend and her family. He eventually introduced Michael to them."

While the Butterfield Band was in Chicago playing at Big John's, Michael got invited to Hinsdale. He drove out to his father's new suburban home for dinner one evening and was shocked to learn that Harold's new life included another extended family. Michael's future stepmother was from Hinsdale, and many of her relatives lived there, too. Harold was now a part of her family, and it seemed that he fully intended to become a parent again with his wife-to-be. The image of his father starting over with another family was too much for Michael. It felt like a complete rejection.

"When he came back from dinner, he was horribly depressed," recalled Glazer. "Michael said Harold was much nicer to them than he was to his real family. He was physically ill—really pissed off!"

The dissolution of his parents' marriage served only to further alienate Michael Bloomfield from his already distant and judgmental father. The traumatic discovery in Hinsdale seemed to confirm that he was unloved. It did have one positive effect, though. It helped forge a bond between the two brothers. Following the split of their parents, Allen and Michael grew closer and in time became good friends as well as good brothers. "We got close, and it was really good," said Allen. "I'd put on a Lenny Bruce record, and I'd hear Michael start laughing in the other room. Sharing things like that was great."

The third week of October, while the Butterfield Band was appearing at Big John's, Elektra released the group's debut album. Called simply *The Paul Butterfield Blues Band*, the long-awaited LP offered eleven tight, exciting examples of Chicago-style blues with commanding solos from the leader and the band's lead guitarist, Mike Bloomfield. On the cover was one of the pictures taken by Elektra art director Bill Harvey during the band's Maxwell Street photo shoot, and another by Leonard Heicklen showing the original Butterfield quartet performing at the Village Gate. The album's front cover had been designed for Elektra's original Butterfield release and thus omitted Mark Naftalin, who had only joined the band in September. But Naftalin was shown on the flip side of the jacket in a photo with Michael and Paul onstage during a performance at the Philadelphia Folk Festival.

Nearly all the tunes on the album had been recorded during the first weeks of September. Of those selections from the earlier version of the record, only Junior Parker's "Mystery Train" and Elmore James's "Look over Yonders Wall" made the cut. Rothchild had decided that the four-track recordings were far superior to the initial three-track efforts. They made up the rest of the LP and included the two Little Walter tunes "Blues with a Feeling" and "Last Night"; a second by Elmore James, "Shake Your Money Maker"; Muddy Waters's "Got My Mojo Working"; and a Willie Dixon song written for Little Walter, "Mellow Down Easy." There also were the three originals by the band, "Thank You Mr. Poobah," "Screamin'," and "Our Love Is Drifting." Leading off side 1 was Butterfield's signature tune, Nick Gravenites's "Born in Chicago." The whole album was no-nonsense Chicago fare, expertly performed, hard-driving and exciting.

The record's liner contained extensive notes by Michael's friend and music guru Pete Welding. Addressing the obvious issue, Welding tendered a long essay on the validity of whites playing black music. Paul Butterfield, Pete asserted, was unimpeded in his blues by questions of race because he was "one white bluesman . . . for whom these obstacles do not exist." In other words, Paul and his music were the real thing. Welding also mentioned the other members of the group, describing Michael as "an extraordinarily agile and inventive blues guitarist." But he said little about the music on the album. Pete's notes had been written for the first record, and those tunes had nearly all been jettisoned.

Also included on the back of the album was a note thanking Columbia—not Epic—for allowing Bloomfield to perform, and another touting Hohner harmonicas as Butterfield's instrument of choice. But boxed and prominently displayed was a suggestion that no one who purchased the record could fail to miss. It seemed to contradict the unerringly respectful and reverent attitude Elektra usually adopted toward the music it released. Buyers were urged to "play this record at the highest possible volume to fully appreciate the sound of the Paul Butterfield Blues Band." This was not to be an intimate folk music experience—it was instead an invitation to party, to get up and dance. Paul Rothchild's hand was clearly evident in the note's inclusion, for he was determined that listeners should experience Butterfield the way he had when he first encountered the band at Big John's. But that single sentence also pointed toward the future of pop music. The meaning was clear. Loud, assertive, big-beat music was no longer fare fit only for "greasers, heads, dancers, people who got drunk and boogied," as Bloomfield had characterized them. It was now music that everyone could enjoy.

The album was given a "Spotlight Review" in *Billboard* magazine on November 13, with the trade publication characterizing it as a "hot discotheque item," a "rockin' and wailing package of well-done performances of pulsating blues tunes." Two weeks later *The Paul Butterfield Blues Band* was chosen as a "Breakout Album" by the magazine, designating it as one "reported to be getting strong sales action by dealers in major markets." The following week the LP entered the *Billboard* Hot 100 chart at number 133 with a bullet.

Of course, the Butterfield album was more than just a "hot discotheque item." It was that, but it was also something much more revolutionary. It was a visionary fusion of elements from largely distinct musical styles: folk, rock, jazz, and blues.

The Paul Butterfield Blues Band played folkloric music, but they did so using amps and drums—tools common to the pop music world. Since the mid-1950s, nearly every commercial hit used some form of percussion and amplification. And since the Beatles crossed the ocean in 1963, electric guitars and rock 'n' roll had become synonymous. Butterfield and crew had all the trappings of a lightweight pop group—Alan Lomax implied as much during his introduction at Newport. But there was nothing superficial about the music they made.

Coming out of Chicago's black electric blues tradition, Butterfield and his men understood that the ability to *play* was central to their music. On the band's album, mastery of that contemporary blues imperative was demonstrated by the two primary soloists. Both Butterfield and Bloomfield took multiple choruses that were authoritative and competent, improvising very much in the manner of jazz soloists. Michael's embellishments were also loud and exciting, expanding on those qualities he heard in the music of rock 'n' roll players like Chuck Berry, Scotty Moore, and Cliff Gallup.

But rock 'n' roll soloists nearly always played a subordinate role—their contribution was usually secondary to that of the singer. In blues, the solo was an extension of the singer—often *more* expressive than the singer. In the music the Butterfield Band played, the roles of singer and soloist were reversed. It didn't matter so much how well Paul sang; it was how well he played harmonica that was more to the point. Butterfield's record may have sounded like rock 'n' roll suitable for a "discotheque" to the popular music establishment, but that was only one aspect of its impact. It was nothing less than an extraordinary amalgam of tradition found in folk music combined with the improvisational skills characteristic of blues and jazz, all presented with the pop sensibilities of good-time rock 'n' roll.

As such, *The Paul Butterfield Blues Band* opened a whole new world of possibilities. It was what rock 'n' roll would become.

PART II

HIS HOLY MODAL MAJESTY

CHAPTER 11

ON THE ROAD WITH BUTTER

NEW YORK, BOSTON, CHICAGO, AND SAN FRANCISCO, 1965–1966

The profound effect *The Paul Butterfield Blues Band* album would have on 1960s popular music would become evident over time. But in early November 1965, things remained largely unchanged for the band. Even though they had a record on the charts, they still were playing multiple sets at Big John's five nights a week, setting up and breaking down their own equipment. Though they were making steady money, no one was getting rich. The routine could be a grind, but it was not without its small pleasures.

As the two most recent additions to the band, Mike Bloomfield and Mark Naftalin gravitated toward one another. The slight, studious keyboard player could not have been less like the extraverted guitarist outwardly, but the two shared a mischievous, quirky sense of humor, and both were intellectuals with a scholarly interest in music and the blues. They frequently discussed music while strolling up and down Wells Street near Big John's during breaks between performances. More often than not, their interlocutions were fueled by a shared smoke.

"On this gig, Mike and I developed the ritual of walking a certain route during our set breaks, smoking joints," Mark said. "This we referred to as our 'Wells Street Promenade.'"

As the Big John's engagement drew to a close, ABGM informed the Butterfield Band that their next job was back on the East Coast, this time in Boston at a club called the Unicorn Coffee House. On Tuesday, November 9, the members of the band loaded up their van, said farewell to their Windy City friends, and headed east. The weeks in Chicago had been both a triumph and a trial for Michael Bloomfield. He had seen the release of the Butterfield Band's album, the first record to feature him as a soloist, and had played to wildly appreciative and packed houses at Big John's. But he had also discovered that his father had a new family. The emotional ups and downs had served only to exacerbate his already mercurial temperament.

The band made the journey to Massachusetts in two long days. Michael, Mark, and their wives rode with Sam Lay and spent the night in Cleveland at Sam's family's home. The group opened at the Unicorn two days later on Friday, November 12, and advertisements touted them as "the sensation of the Newport Folk Festival." The coffeehouse, across the Charles River at 825 Boylston Street in Boston's Back Bay neighborhood, was a comfortable, dark room with exposed brick walls, risers for a stage, and a unicorn coat of arms and tapestry backdrop with scalloped casements for decor. The club presented folk acts as many as seven nights a week; though the Butterfield Band's music was a departure from its usual acoustic offerings, the response to the group was beyond enthusiastic.

By now, many in Boston's folk music community had heard about Bob Dylan's controversial set at Newport, and most knew that Mike Bloomfield had been his guitarist. They had also heard about the band from Chicago that was preaching the blues in a new way and were eager to see the harmonica player who amplified his harp so that it sounded like a saxophone. The combination of Butterfield's sonorous lines and Bloomfield's furious lead was so overwhelming, people said it had to be experienced to be fully appreciated.

Onstage, the two soloists could not have been more different. While Butterfield generally stood and played, darkly intense but largely stationary, Bloomfield was as restive and hyper as ever. The voluble guitarist was as animated onstage as he was off it, and his playing had an astonishing fervor. One evening, his restlessness led him to amaze the audience with a skill no one suspected he had. During an unusually long pause in a set, Michael got fidgety and began picking Merle Travis's "Walkin' the Strings" on his Telecaster. The crowd, momentarily stunned, roared with delight in response to the bluesman's unexpected virtuosity. Michael was not only a master blues player; he could play hot country too!

While performing at the Unicorn, Bloomfield met another Boston guitarist, a blues player who was becoming interested in country music himself. His name was John Nuese, and he was playing a bright gold Gibson guitar—a ten-year-old Les Paul he had purchased that August.

"I got it from a guy in Providence for $125 with a case," said Nuese. But John found that the heavy guitar wasn't very good at producing the twangy tone preferred by country players, so he was looking for a Fender Telecaster. The Les Paul, called a "Goldtop" because of its metallic patina, immediately caught Mike Bloomfield's eye—it was the instrument Freddy King, John Lee

Hooker, Howlin' Wolf's guitarist Hubert Sumlin, and even Muddy Waters had played at one time or another.

"When Michael saw that I had a Goldtop, he tried it and said, 'I'll trade you right now!'" Nuese remembered. John was eager to get a Telecaster, so he agreed to switch guitars. Though he was delighted with Bloomfield's Fender, Nuese did feel as though he had gotten the shorter end of the bargain.

"Mike's Tele didn't even have a case, and it was so dirty you could grow potatoes on it!" John remarked, laughing.

Bloomfield was soon playing Nuese's vintage Gibson onstage at the Unicorn, and the instrument added a whole new dimension to his sound. Michael had owned a Les Paul, a black Custom, as a teenager, but the Goldtop had a much fatter, hotter sound. The guitar's tone and sustain allowed him to hold and bend notes with extraordinary fluidity. Though it was a small guitar, about an inch shorter than the Telecaster, the Gibson was far heavier. The guitar's density—it was essentially a block of solid mahogany—coupled with its single-coil pickups, known as "P-90s," gave the Gibson a remarkably meaty sound. Michael found that if he turned his amp's volume, midrange, and treble tone controls up to "10," their highest settings, and turned down the bass, he could get incredible sustain on held notes. He could even use the resulting feedback to create exciting new effects.

If Bloomfield's playing had been loud before, with the Goldtop it was louder than loud.

But volume for Michael wasn't just an indulgence. It did put him center stage, giving him a dominant voice in the music. But it was also a tool he used to convey emotional complexity. He explained it one evening to a friend at the Unicorn. "You know why I play so loud?" Bloomfield said. "So they can hear the subtleties."

They were hearing the subtleties and then some at the Unicorn. The group had never sounded tighter and more exciting. Butterfield was a consummate leader, calling the shots and taking his role very seriously. He demanded focused, professional performances from his men, and had the band frequently rehearse in the afternoons before the club opened. He worked up careful set lists for their shows and insisted that one tune follow another with a minimum of delay. And everyone had to wear the matching jackets Paul Rothchild had purchased for them.

For Michael, this was a new experience. His own band, the Group, rarely if ever rehearsed. He seldom gave a thought to what they would play until the band was onstage. Tunes might run three minutes or thirty, depending upon Bloomfield's mood. And the pause between them could be equally as long. Michael's approach to leadership was, needless to say, casual to a fault.

Paul's was just the opposite, and sometimes his authoritarian approach could be overbearing. Whether the band was working up arrangements of new material or going over familiar pieces, Paul was an exacting taskmaster. He tolerated nothing less than complete commitment, and if he felt that one of the band members wasn't giving his all, he was quick to respond—sometimes physically.

"I've known Butterfield to hit [Elvin]," said Sam Lay. "I didn't see him do it, but he said he did and I take his word for it." Lay recalled that Paul would sometimes call a tune that Bishop didn't know. "He expected Elvin to know it, and that would piss him off."

Paul's wrath sometimes extended to Michael. The guitarist's penchant for speaking his mind could provoke Butterfield, especially when Bloomfield felt things weren't right. He would challenge Paul's authority, and the harmonica player would get angry.

"That cat, man, he didn't want nothing to go wrong with us. Anything he thought was wrong, he was right on it," Lay said of Bloomfield's finely honed sense of fair play. "Him and Butterfield would get into it . . . get ready to rumble-in-the-jungle, you know what I mean? He'd come flyin' to me. If I was in the dressing room, you'd see that dressing room door fly open. 'Bloomfield, man, what's the matter?' 'Butterfield's goin' crazy—he's threatening to bust my damn guitar over my head!'" Sam was the band's peacemaker, a big, calming presence when tempers flared. He seemed to be the only one who could talk Paul down.

"It's a funny thing," Lay said. "As temperamental as Paul was . . . when I talked to him, I would settle him down right there on the spot. He would just listen to me."

The formula seemed to work. Whenever squabbles broke out in the group, whether they involved physical threats from the leader or were protests over treatment from the sidemen, Sam managed to restore the peace. As a result, Butterfield's rigorous demands were tolerated and usually met, and the group grew closer musically and socially. Mark Naftalin described the Butterfield Band at the time as feeling like "a warm family." A family that was tearing up the club circuit with its fiery brand of Chicago blues, that is.

Over the five weekends the Paul Butterfield Blues Band appeared at the Unicorn, they worked on their repertoire, adding new tunes and honing those they had been playing for nearly a year. Crowds regularly packed the club, and the band's reception was beyond expectations. Albert Grossman was pleased, particularly because he had scheduled a major concert in New York City to showcase the band and promote their Elektra release just as it was breaking into *Billboard*'s Hot 100 listings. ABGM had rented prestigious Town Hall, a 1,500-seat auditorium just off Times Square. Appearing with Butterfield would be two other Grossman acts: folksinger Gordon Lightfoot, who was making his New York City debut, and the Jim Kweskin Jug Band, the evening's headliners.

On Saturday, November 27, the members of the Butterfield Band loaded up and drove down to New York from Boston for their Town Hall appearance. They would miss a night at the Unicorn, but they would be back in plenty of time for their Sunday show. The concert began at 8:30 p.m. with a folk set by Lightfoot. The Canadian singer was well received, but the real excitement began when the scrappy-looking blues band from Chicago took the stage. Some in the audience had seen Butterfield at the Cafe Au Go Go when the band was a still a quintet, and a few had even seen them at Newport. But many were experiencing the electrified sound of Chicago blues for the first time. With an arsenal of new Fender Twin and Super Reverb amplifiers, recent upgrades over the band's initial hodgepodge of equipment, the Butterfield Band provided an aural experience unlike anything that most of the crowd had ever heard. The press was in attendance, and they duly reported the effect of so much firepower.

Billboard observed that the band was "a hit with teenagers at Town Hall" and was "supported by lots of electric wattage." The publication went on to say, "The six-man group came on with the new type of rocking-blues that is becoming more and more popular these days—and they did it with extreme dynamic expression." Acknowledging the Butterfield Band's unique ability to fuse styles, *Billboard* noted that "the blues feeling was there, but also a sense of jazz."

Robert Shelton, music critic for the *New York Times* and a fan of Butterfield's playing, acknowledged that "the Paul Butterfield Blues Band, aided now with an electric piano and more vocals by Sam Lay, the drummer, was strong and swinging." Sam was now regularly featured as the vocalist on "Got My Mojo Working."

The show was over by 11:00 p.m., and by midnight the Chicagoans had packed up their gear and retired to a nearby watering hole for a nightcap. Michael and Susan spent the night at Christopher Street before heading back to Boston in the morning. The return trip took nearly four hours and required another hour to unload and set up the equipment. By the time it was done, all Michael wanted to do was curl up in bed with a good book. But the band's first set was just hours away, and they wouldn't be finished until after 1:00 a.m.

* * *

Along with the revolution in popular music ushered in by the Beatles, Bob Dylan, and—in a not insignificant way—the Paul Butterfield Blues Band came a concurrent change in the attitude toward recreational drugs. Marijuana use among pop and folk artists and their fans had been growing over the past decade, and by 1965 pot smoking was pervasive. Joints were nearly as common as alcohol at hip parties and gatherings. Hard drugs, though, were still rarely seen. Mike Bloomfield and a few friends occasionally indulged in heroin, but they were the exception. Where narcotics were concerned, white middle class values prevailed. But a new class of drugs was rapidly gaining acceptance—and altering minds in the process. Chief among them was a concoction first synthesized in 1938 and called lysergic acid diethylamide, or LSD.

Originally marketed in 1947 by a Swiss pharmaceutical company as a psychiatric medication, LSD soon began to attract attention for its strong hallucinogenic properties. Experiments with behavior modification, expanded self-awareness and creativity, and impulse control followed. Then, in 1963, as patents expired and the drug's formula entered the public domain, several noted academics began experimenting with LSD's "psychedelic" effects. One prominent researcher was a Harvard psychology professor named Timothy Leary. The outspoken educator's inquiries into LSD led to a curiosity about the drug among his students, an interest that soon extended to the larger community. By 1965 Leary had been fired from Harvard and "acid," as LSD was commonly called, was being used around Cambridge and elsewhere as a recreational drug. People were beginning to "tune in, turn on, drop out," as Leary would later characterize the psychedelic experience.

Mike Bloomfield had heard about LSD and, always game for a new sensation, soon tried some. He and Mark Naftalin were staying just a few blocks from Harvard Square while performing at the Unicorn, and it wasn't difficult to find someone who had a few hits of Leary acid to share. The two musicians spent the night marveling at the visions and sensory stimulation the drug triggered, and they experienced a feeling of expanded consciousness. For Bloomfield, the "trip" resulted in a musical awakening.

"Later on, after dawn as I remember, we got together in the kitchen of my half of the house and we were smoking jays, trying to keep the buzz going," Mark said. "Mike told me he had been listening to Indian music over in his part of the house in the meantime, and that he had had a revelation into the workings of Indian music. Now he understood it. Almost immediately after that, he started to work up the song 'East-West.'"

Bloomfield had first heard Indian ragas after his friend Roy Ruby played him some of sitarist Ravi Shankar's records in the summer of 1959. The boys were both still in high school, and Ruby had heard Shankar play with tabla master Ali Akbar Khan at Windsor Mountain, his prep school. Shankar made annual trips to the school to visit friends, and while there he would perform for the students at evening meals. Pete Welding had also played Indian music recordings for Michael during their jazz listening sessions in Old Town as a way to explain some of the things saxophonist John Coltrane was attempting to do. Bloomfield was drawn to the tonal and rhythmic complexity of the ragas, seeing in Indian classical music possibilities for expanding his own playing.

"I drew upon the fact that you could improvise for a long, long, long time on certain modes and themes, you know, and just don't play the straight blues," Michael said. "You could play a lot of other things and they would fit, too."

Bloomfield had been playing Nick Gravenites's "It's About Time" for nearly a year, first in the band he and Nick had organized in early 1965 and then occasionally with Butterfield whenever Nick would sit in. When the Butterfield Band did it at Newport, Michael soloed using scales other than the conventional pentatonic blues scale. Similar to an Indian raga because it used a single chord played as a drone, "It's About Time" left a lot of room for improvising. With his newfound insight into Indian music, Bloomfield was determined to build on the musical freedom Gravenites's tune afforded him. He talked Paul into regularly playing something like "It's About Time" with the group.

"The band started working it up with Michael, and there was a process to it," Naftalin remembered. "The structure of it was provided by Mike as he went through these various modes." Bloomfield created a series of different moods using a variety of scales, each section in the series partitioned off from the others by a brief crescendo. For lack of a better name, he called the piece "The Raga."

The second week in December, Paul Butterfield and his group headed back to Chicago for another ten days at Big John's. The Windy City's harsh winter season was just beginning, and the combination of bitter cold temperatures and lake-effect precipitation made getting around town difficult. More often than not, the band would have to trudge home after the gig through newly fallen snow, bundled up against the "almighty hawk"—the city's legendary gale-force wind. Sam Lay had picked up what he thought was a case of bronchitis in Boston, and it only got worse once the band arrived in Chicago. He was experiencing shortness of breath and extreme fatigue on the bandstand, so one afternoon he visited Cook County Hospital. A doctor examined him and told him his bronchitis was actually a case of pneumonia that had caused his chest cavity to fill with fluid, resulting in a dangerous condition known as pleural effusion. Because the fluid had become infected, the physician immediately checked the drummer into the hospital.

"Sam became ill," Mark Naftalin said of Lay's malaise. "He used to come offstage at the Unicorn and go outside without a jacket, which concerned me at the time, and rightly so, because he ended up in the hospital. Mike and I visited him on the ward, and it was quite grim. But he could no longer be in the band."

The loss of the Butterfield Band's powerful drummer was a devastating blow. Sam's superb blues timekeeping, done in the quintessential Chicago style, was a key factor in the band's success. Paul knew he had to find a replacement who was as good—and he had to find that person soon. Between them, the members of the band knew nearly every blues drummer in the city, and among the possible candidates they came up with was a veteran player who had just recorded a well-received album with harpist Junior Wells. His name was Bill Warren, and he was a thirty-six-year-old former jazz drummer who was a regular on Maxwell Street and at Theresa's. His drumming style was flashier than Sam's, but Paul decided to ask him to sit in with the band for the rest of the Big John's gig. With Lay's kit still onstage at the club, all Bill had to do was show up and play.

The band finished up the week at Big John's with Bill Warren providing the beat. Because much of the group's repertory was standard Chicago fare, Bill was already familiar with many of the tunes. But to help him adapt to the group's hard-driving style, Paul held afternoon rehearsals at the club, going over arrangements and working on unfamiliar material. The drummer worked hard, but his sound was very different from Sam Lay's.

The final week of December, the band hit the road again for a week in Detroit at the Chessmate, a folk music coffeehouse at Livernois Avenue and West McNichols Road. Patronized primarily by University of Detroit students, the club was a dark and cavernous venue with high ceilings and good acoustics. But as the week progressed, it became clear that Bill Warren was not the right drummer for the Paul Butterfield Blues Band. Though they were all trying to make it work, Bill's style was just not a fit for the band's brand of blues. With heartfelt regret, Butterfield decided to let Warren go at the end of the week. While the drummer loaded up his kit for the ride back to Chicago, Paul, Michael, and the rest of the band stowed their gear in the van and packed for a different destination. The Butterfield Band was headed west for its first visit to California, an extended stay in Los Angeles.

But first, the group had to find a drummer.

While jamming with Junior Wells one night at Theresa's the previous April, Michael Bloomfield had been impressed by another of the harp player's drummers. The man's timekeeping had a jazzy feel to it, a swing that implied the beat rather than spelled it out. He was Billy Davenport, a thirty-four-year-old veteran trap set player whose jazz chops were the real thing. He had played in Chicago jazz groups since the late 1940s, backing greats like saxophonists Sonny Stitt and Leo Parker and bassist Slam Stewart. With jazz's decline in popularity in the late 1950s, Davenport had been gigging with Otis Rush, Howlin' Wolf, James Cotton, and other blues players on the South Side to pay the rent.

Davenport had been Bloomfield's first choice to replace Sam Lay, but Billy was making steady money with guitarist Fenton Robinson's group at Pepper's and he declined the offer. When Bill Warren didn't work out, Bloomfield was on the phone again with Davenport in an effort to convince him to become a member of the Butterfield Band. But Billy was hesitant. The issue of race was on his mind, and in 1965 an integrated band was often an invitation for trouble. It was only when Paul got on the phone and promised Billy that the rest of the group wouldn't go anywhere the drummer couldn't go that Davenport relented. The next day, Billy packed his drums and with his wife drove to Michigan, where they met up with the members of the band. On Monday, January 3, the Paul Butterfield Blues Band caught a flight out of Detroit, bound for Los Angeles. The sextet, with its new drummer, was off to bring the blues to California—making music history in the process.

The Butterfield Band debuted in the City of Angels on the Sunset Strip at a nightclub called the Trip. Located in the basement of a building at 8572 Sunset Boulevard, right next door to the ten-story Playboy Club, the Trip was a showroom with a seating capacity of nearly one thousand that featured contemporary pop bands and targeted a young, hip clientele. Its management favored music acts with records that were getting lots of airplay, thus ensuring strong receipts at the door and at the bar. With its size and commercial thrust, the Trip wasn't at all like the coffeehouses and folk clubs the Butterfield Band had been playing.

Beginning Wednesday, January 5, the group began a month-long stand at the Trip. For the first two weeks, they opened for the Byrds, the local folk-rock band that had scored a number-one hit with Bob Dylan's "Mr. Tambourine Man" and was currently riding high on the popularity of their second big single, "Turn! Turn! Turn!" Michael Bloomfield knew the band's leader, Jim McGuinn, from Chicago, back when the singer was part of the city's folk movement. They had met as teenagers at the Old Town School of Folk Music, and McGuinn later remembered showing Michael how to bend strings. The Byrds had a huge following of fans that packed the club each night, eager to dance to the rock rhythms and close harmonies of the charismatic quintet. With their Beatle haircuts, capes, ankle boots, and granny glasses, the Byrds looked like LA's answer to the Fab Four. Their music, though, drew more from the folk music revival than from the 1950s rock 'n' roll that inspired the Beatles. Both McGuinn and band member David Crosby played electric guitars, but the emphasis was on harmonious singing rather than soloing.

The Butterfield Band's aggressive, solo-laden blues was the antithesis of the jangly, melodious folk-rock of the Trip's headliners. Though Butterfield's music was danceable, the patrons weren't ready for their loud, heavy, backbeat-driven rhythms. They were more attuned to the Strip's go-go and twist beats, the "groovy" sounds commonly heard on TV dance programs like *American Bandstand*. They just didn't get the music of the Paul Butterfield Blues Band.

The mixed reception, though, didn't matter much to Butterfield and his men. They were excited to be in California and on the Sunset Strip, a place of legend, movie stars, and famous names, renowned for its clubs, restaurants, and attractions. The band was lodged in the Colonial West Motel on Sunset Boulevard, a hostel that frequently provided rooms for visiting celebrities appearing on the Strip. Because the Colonial was less than a quarter mile from the Trip, it was an easy walk to and from the gig, and there was plenty to see along the way. Crowds of fashionable people strolled up and down the boulevard, pretty girls and flashy cars were everywhere, neon lights gaudily hyped diversions of every variety, and the sound of music was pervasive. It was like Rush Street in Chicago but on a much grander scale. The only difference was that Hollywood clubs closed earlier than their counterparts in the Windy City. That left little for Mike Bloomfield to do following the band's sets at the Trip other than to return to the motel. As a consequence, he and Mark Naftalin spent many late evenings hanging out together at the Colonial.

"Mike and I used to spend the hours after the show smoking joints in our motel room," said Mark. "We'd go into the closet and light up there, naively thinking that way nobody would smell it. We would talk for hours, and we became pretty good friends during that period." Mark began to notice how difficult it was for Michael to shut down. There were some nights when the guitarist never went near a bed.

While the band was working at the Trip, Michael Bloomfield began seriously developing "The Raga." With Billy Davenport now in the band, new rhythmic possibilities presented themselves. Sam Lay was a top-notch blues drummer, but for "The Raga" to achieve the complexity Michael envisioned for it, the piece would require a variety of other rhythms. As a jazz drummer, Billy was proficient in swing, bop, and Latin drumming styles, and he moved easily between them and straight blues. He and Bloomfield experimented with these different beats, trying one pattern after another to find the one best suited to each movement of the instrumental. Eventually, Davenport hit upon a rhythm that combined elements of Latin cha-cha and Brazilian bossa nova with the syncopation of jazz swing, a hybrid ideal for Bloomfield's extended solo experiments. "The Raga" began to take shape as an amalgam of Eastern and Western influences with vast spaces for open-ended improvisation—"pseudo jazz," as Bloomfield later characterized it.

The last two weeks in January, the headliner at the Trip was one of Atlantic Records' star soul singers. Wilson Pickett and his revue took over the top spot, playing music that was more in sync with what the Butterfield Band was doing than the Byrds' folk-rock had been. But the soul singer's act was geared toward show lounge audiences, with choreographed steps, rehearsed gestures, and carefully coordinated arrangements. Paul, Michael, Elvin, Mark, and Jerome didn't do dance routines when they performed. They were more like jazz musicians, cool and focused, hardly moving—Bloomfield was the exception—as they worked through their blues repertoire. Crowds at the Trip remained largely indifferent to the Chicago sextet, preferring instead to save their enthusiasm for Pickett's stylish R&B.

Probably at Michael Bloomfield's urging, the Butterfield Band may have picked up one thing from Wilson Pickett's crowd-pleasing performances. To bring on the soul singer, Pickett's band often played a brief instrumental medley of his hits. The musical introduction served to fire up the crowd and allowed Wilson to make an exciting entrance. Thinking that something similar might help grab the audience's attention at the start of their sets, Paul, along with Michael and the rest of the band, worked up a medley of familiar blues and R&B phrases. Abrupt tempo changes and short solos gave the brief introduction an exciting edge. It announced the band as the tight, no-nonsense professional unit they were. Paul was soon opening every one of the band's sets with the medley.

Once the gig at the Trip ended, the Paul Butterfield Blues Band moved down the Strip for several weekends at Hollywood's premier nightclub, the Whisky a Go Go. The Whisky was the inspiration for many other dance venues around Los Angeles, with go-go dancers suspended in cages from the ceiling, multiple bands performing, DJs filling in between sets, and continuous dancing. Butterfield was billed as the Whisky's headliner those weeks, opening on Friday, February 4. The band's reception was better than it had been at the Trip, and they were held over for a third weekend, running through Sunday, February 20.

While they were playing the Whisky, Elektra released a single from *The Paul Butterfield Blues Band* album. "Born in Chicago" would have been the logical choice, but the company instead issued "Mellow Down Easy" backed with "Got My Mojo Working." Jac Holzman reasoned that the Nick Gravenites tune had already appeared on record twice—once on the sampler "Folksong '65" and again in an updated version on the full LP—and he wanted to get some of the group's other material out for possible radio airplay. The album did make the playlists of many college stations around the country, and though Elektra reported that it seemed to have peaked on *Billboard*'s charts, hanging on at number 130, it was selling very well in record stores near college campuses. The expectation was that the single would also appeal to a college audience, and not long after its release, "Mellow Down Easy" came to the attention of a young critic who was a student at Swarthmore College. Paul Williams had just started *Crawdaddy*, a magazine that would become the first serious rock 'n' roll publication, and the February issue, his first, contained a review of the Butterfield single.

"It's a great song," Williams enthused about "Mellow Down Easy." "Butterfield's singing and harmonica are fantastic here, as is Mike Bloomfield's electric guitar. . . . Butterfield definitely has the best sound of all the blues groups, including the Stones." While the Rolling Stones were hardly a "blues group" in the Chicago sense, comparing Butterfield favorably to the hugely successful British quintet was high praise indeed.

Elektra was also keen to release a second single, preferably one featuring some of the band's new material. Jac Holzman wanted to get Butterfield into the studio while the band was in Los Angeles for a few quick sessions. But the recording process had been complicated by the fact that the band's producer and chief supporter, Paul Rothchild, had been arrested for drug possession in the late fall of 1965. In the growing crackdown on marijuana use, the producer was given a two-year prison sentence in his home state of New Jersey and had begun serving time in November. Rothchild would obviously be unavailable to oversee the sessions, forcing the company to depend on a local production team.

Despite the risks, Holzman went ahead and arranged for the band to go into RCA Studios at 6363 Sunset Boulevard for several afternoons of taping. The engineers there had recorded the Rolling Stones in 1965, so they were experienced in dealing with electric instruments and drums. To make sure the sessions would succeed, Holzman hired an independent producer named Barry Friedman. Friedman was working with the Byrds and a new group called Buffalo Springfield, and he had a reputation for hip experimentation in the studio. In mid-February, the Butterfield Band joined him in RCA's recording facilities, intent on producing a commercial single.

Friedman suggested the band try something original for the next single release, reasoning that it might be good to have a backup if "Mellow Down

Easy" and "Got My Mojo Working" failed to break into the charts. Elvin Bishop had written a tune called "If I Had My Way," and they decided that the group would work up an arrangement and record it.

Straying from their blues roots, the band next recorded a three-minute version of Bloomfield's "The Raga." Condensing his twenty-minute exercise in improvisation down to fit the Top 40 format may have appealed to Michael's puckish sense of humor, but he doubtless thought the piece would have a novel appeal. He talked Friedman into recording it, and Barry crafted an arrangement that used, oddly enough, a violinist and two soprano singers. They harmonized in an unorthodox manner as the band played "The Raga," adding startling dissonance to its already unusual sonorities. "Whoever assigned them the flatted-second degree scales, sung and played in unison, I don't know," said Mark with a laugh. "*I* didn't do it."

Finally, Butterfield and his men jettisoned the blues altogether and recorded a true pop song. One of the bands Friedman had been working with was a quartet recently assembled for the NBC TV program called *The Monkees*. Michael Nesmith, a songwriter, guitar player, and singer, was one of the four musicians selected for the pop group, and he penned a number of originals for the Monkees to perform. Barry thought one of those tunes would work well with Butterfield's sound and suggested the band try it. Called "Mary, Mary," the song was given a muscular arrangement that included backup vocals, overdubbing, fuzz-tone effects, and dramatic stops. Paul got in a short harmonica solo in the middle of the tune, and Michael added a flurry of hot licks for a fade at the end, but the three-minute number was clearly intended for Top 40 airplay. Its danceable beat was enhanced in one take by the addition of sonorous percussion. Friedman brought in jazz pianist, vibes player, and percussionist Victor Feldman to overdub a kettledrum part. Feldman, who had worked with Cannonball Adderley and Miles Davis, was earning a living as a studio player in Los Angeles at the time.

But when the tune was finally released on the Butterfield Band's second album in August, Feldman's contribution on timpani had been removed. "I guess the drums didn't pass muster with Rothchild," Mark surmised, laughing. Paul Rothchild, who would be paroled from prison in July, returned to Elektra in time to supervise the record's final mix. The rumbling percussive effect on "Mary, Mary" would prove to be a little too much for him.

Though the Butterfield Band was solid musically and functioned onstage as a close-knit, cohesive unit, there were still occasions of conflict. With all the pressures of performing, tempers could grow short. Butterfield, in his role as leader, could sometimes push his men too far, and more than once they revolted. Without Sam Lay there to mollify Paul, things easily escalated. They came to a head one afternoon while the group was still in Hollywood.

"Paul had this old sort of domineering relationship, like Howlin' Wolf would have with his sidemen," said Bloomfield. "He was the stone leader. He took all the bread and all the things. And we were contributing as much as we could. So we had this revolution, and we all quit on him in the middle of this gig in LA." Michael threatened to reorganize the band and sign them with Greif-Garris Management, a Los Angeles agency he had heard about from Barry Friedman. They managed the New Christy Minstrels and Stan Kenton's big band, among others. That pushed Butterfield over the edge, and he took a swing at Michael.

"He punched me—and I *really* quit for good then," Bloomfield professed. But with Albert Grossman's assistance, cooler heads eventually prevailed, and the Paul Butterfield Blues Band did not become the rhythm section for the New Christy Minstrels. "I was on my way to the airport, and they pulled me back. We got it together then and made it an equal organization." Butterfield got the message and eased up on his musicians, giving them more of a say in decisions regarding band matters. He was learning that Michael's sense of fair play was a force not to be trifled with.

From the Whisky, ABGM sent the band some twenty miles down the coast to Huntington Beach for several weeks at a small jazz club. The town, a large beach community renowned for its miles of sandy strand and excellent surfing, was a far cry from the glitz and glamour of the Sunset Strip. But its laid-back, bohemian denizens were more open to the hard-charging, solo-driven blues played by the Chicago sextet. Life on the beach also suited Butterfield and his men. They were getting tired of living out of suitcases, of motels and bad food, of the constant traveling. Afternoons spent on the beach enjoying the sun and sea breezes were a tonic.

But fatigue was becoming an issue, and Butterfield agreed to give the group Mondays off whenever possible. For Bloomfield, the road was especially difficult because of his chronic insomnia. But even without sleep, he was always able to perform, often inspiring the rest of the band with his intense energy.

"A lot of times, we'd get to the gig and maybe a couple of us were not feeling so good. We'd open up with a number and by the time Bloomfield would get through with his solo, everybody was up," said Billy. "You know, he was just that type of guy. He'd throw that feeling into the band. If you were feeling bad, by the time he'd get through working, man, you were all right!"

Even though they might sometimes be tired, the band's music just kept getting better and better. Playing three and four sets a night, five or six nights a week, for the past six months had served to tighten their ensemble sound to the degree that Paul and Michael seemed to know intuitively what the other would play. Whenever Elvin got a chance to solo, his improvisations added an exciting counterpart to Bloomfield's lead. With Naftalin, Arnold, and Davenport providing a solid rhythmic foundation, there was no other group in America in 1966 that could rival what the Paul Butterfield Blues Band was doing with modern blues.

As a consequence, word was getting around. Despite the band's lukewarm reception in Los Angeles, college radio stations were playing their record and people in the music community were talking them up. One promoter who heard about the Chicagoans was named Chet Helms. A California native who had grown up in Texas, Helms had returned to San Francisco in the early 1960s and eventually began organizing dances and managing bands for the city's growing counterculture community. Friends had told him how exciting the Butterfield Band was, and he decided—without ever hearing them—to bring the group to San Francisco. With his partner, John Carpenter, Chet had contracted with Albert Grossman to have the Butterfield Band perform for three nights at an aging dance hall on the edge of the city's blighted Fillmore District. The hall, fittingly called the Fillmore Auditorium, was leased by another promoter, a transplanted New Yorker named Bill Graham. Helms and Graham had an arrangement to use the hall on alternate weekends, with Chet producing his shows under the rubric "the Family Dog." For Butterfield's appearance, Helms's third concert collaboration with Graham, Bill was a reluctant cosponsor. The band was unknown to him, and Helms and Carpenter had struggled to talk him into backing the Chicagoans' appearance.

The Family Dog agreed to pay the band $2,500 for the weekend at the Fillmore. The sum was far more than the promoters had ever laid out for a single group, and they decided to fly to Los Angeles to see if the band was really as exciting as Chet's friends claimed. They visited the venue where the Butterfield Band was playing, a place called the It Club on Washington Boulevard in Lafayette Square, and were shocked to find the bar nearly empty. Normally a jazz nightclub, the It Club was located in a predominantly black neighborhood, and its usual patrons weren't interested in Chicago-style blues. Michael said of their reception that the room was "just empty," and he acknowledged that the Butterfield Band bombed with the It Club's black audience. Helms and Carpenter, though, weren't aware of the booking error, and they returned to San Francisco in a bit of a panic. They immediately called everyone they knew, urging them to come out to the Fillmore to see the new blues band from Chicago. Those last-minute efforts at promotion, coupled with the growing buzz around the Butterfield Band, succeeded beyond the producers' wildest expectations.

On Friday, March 25, the sextet from the Windy City debuted at the Fillmore Auditorium, playing the first of three nights of dance concerts put on by the Family Dog. Opening for the group was a local band with the whimsical name Quicksilver Messenger Service, a first hint that something different was happening in San Francisco. Even though the big hall was already crowded, more people continued to stream in. Many were dressed in colorful costumes—the women in billowy Indian print dresses with flowing silk scarves and colorful headbands, the men wearing army surplus jackets over paisley-patterned shirts, strings of beads around their necks and suede moccasins on their feet. Some in the audience were even wearing colorful face paint. It was standing room only, as there were no seats, and the vast open floor provided ample space for dancing.

The focus of the auditorium was a long stage with a three-story-high wall behind it that served as a colossal backdrop. Spotlights in balcony booths around the room provided illumination, highlighting the performers onstage while playing over dancers on the floor. A special "light show" run by artist Bill Ham projected wild, amorphous images on the wall behind the bands, adding a surreal quality to the performances as colors and shapes moved and changed with the music. Blacklights around the room gave those wearing white an ethereal, ghostly cast, further underscoring the hall's fantastic tableau. This was an environment that had nothing in common with the glitzy jacket-and-tie venues on the Sunset Strip, the beachcomber hangouts on Huntington Beach, or even the studied hipness of folk coffeehouses back east. The Fillmore and its patrons were an entirely new experience for the Butterfield Band. They took it all in as Quicksilver Messenger Service ran through its brief set and the crowd continued to grow. Despite the cold temperatures outside, the hall was close and warm, fragrant with bodies, patchouli oil, and the pungent smell of marijuana.

"Was there a different vibe at the Fillmore? No kidding!" Mark Naftalin exclaimed, laughing.

The Butterfield Band had played for large crowds before, so they weren't fazed by the sea of faces staring at them as they came out onstage. They knew their business, and they were intent on giving the best performance they could. What was unnerving, though, was how quiet the big auditorium was.

"When we got to the Fillmore, it was frightening," said Billy Davenport. "We went onstage and nobody said nothing. The place was packed. They were just standing there looking."

The band launched into its medley opener, and as the music built to a climax and reached a pause, Paul Butterfield shouted, "1, 2, 3, 4!"

In a heartbeat, the Chicagoans ripped into the opening changes to "Look over Yonders Wall" and then got out of the way as Bloomfield's slide, again quoting Elmore James, tore the roof off the Fillmore. Butterfield grabbed a mic, tilted his head to one side, closed his eyes and began to sing. There was a look of intense emotion on his face, an expression as serious as your life.

Look over yonder's wall,
Hand me down my walking cane
I got myself a woman,
Yonder come your man.

The great hall was no longer quiet. It was filled with the power of amplified blues, with sound booming around the cavernous space, bouncing from one wall to another. And now there were other sounds. The erstwhile silent crowd had begun to cheer, hooting and whistling after every guitar solo, every harmonica break. They had come alive too, undulating to the beat, dancing with abandon, arms waving, hair and beads flying, jumping, twisting, gyrating. At the center of all the commotion was the band from Chicago, six determined musicians preaching Chicago-style blues gospel. The music rose to a fevered pitch, and then "Look Over Yonders Wall" came to a thunderous close.

The Fillmore erupted.

"Man, when we got through, the people were like they went crazy," said Davenport. "We were surprised, because up till then it seemed like that nothing was working. But after we played that one number, man, from there on the Fillmore was our place."

The audience, thrilled by the tight, uncompromising music of the Butterfield Band, crowded the stage and let out a storm of whoops and cheers at the end of every number. Though there wasn't any room to spare, everyone was dancing, caroming about in wildly exuberant displays of kinetic frenzy. People weren't doing the Frug, the Watusi, the Twist, or any of the other dance steps common to go-go clubs and show lounges—they were simply improvising their movements to the pulse of the music.

As the Chicagoans worked through their set, they watched the sea of bobbing heads with growing amazement. They were used to the sit-down audiences of coffeehouses and the carefully choreographed dancing of neatly dressed club patrons. San Francisco's dance concert crowd was something altogether different. And it wasn't just their dress and frolicking that set them apart.

"Michael was amazed to see a couple making love under the stage that first night at the Fillmore," Chet Helms remarked, laughing at the memory. "He was giddy, ecstatic about it."

San Francisco was undergoing a cultural shift in 1966. Young people were openly experimenting with sex, drugs, and rock 'n' roll; questioning their parents' choices; and challenging restrictions imposed by authority. In a decade when civil rights, the war in Vietnam, gender roles, and social norms were being reevaluated by a growing number of people across the nation, the young residents of San Francisco were in the vanguard of the search for alternatives to the established order. Thousands of teenagers and young adults had moved to the city over the past year, seeking a new sociopolitical paradigm—a way of life based on peace, love, and justice. They had taken Timothy Leary's edict, "Tune in, turn on, drop out," to heart. In the City by the Bay, these long-haired immigrants found an accommodating political climate and a welcoming populace. They also frequently found free rent, free food, free love—and plenty of drugs, free or otherwise.

It was an eye-opening experience for the tough, streetwise musicians from the Windy City. Used to hustling or being hustled, Paul, Michael, Elvin, and the rest of the band were struck by the innocence and openness of San Francisco's residents. They found themselves drawn to the "love" ethos, the relaxed and accepting atmosphere that pervaded the city. It would soon begin to change them.

San Francisco would be changed by the Chicagoans as well. The Fillmore's patrons loved the music of the Paul Butterfield Blues Band. While the group had been well received in most of the other venues they had played, at the Fillmore they felt like real stars for the first time. "We were the biggest thing in town!" said Naftalin. "We weren't expecting that at all—we thought it was going to be just another gig. But every time we played there, people flocked to see us." The *Berkeley Barb's* ED Denson tried to put into words what it was like to experience the Butterfield Band for the first time.

> As a blues band they are fine. . . . At the opposite end of the stage from Butterfield stands Bloomfield, the furthest out of the band musically, doing things with the electric guitar that the southside never dreamed of. These two alternate the lead, which is also occasionally taken by the fine organist, and the rhythm half of the band lays a concrete bottom. They have more drive and generate more excitement than any group I have seen since the Animals were here.

The success of the Butterfield Band's first night at the Fillmore brought even more people to the group's Saturday and Sunday shows. Chet Helms estimated that nearly seven thousand people attended the weekend's performances, grossing about eighteen thousand dollars for the partners. He and John Carpenter were elated. So was Bill Graham.

An experienced and hard-nosed businessman, Graham saw an opportunity. He got up early Saturday morning and put through a call to ABGM and Albert

Grossman. Would Albert give him exclusive rights to present the Butterfield Band in the Bay Area over the next two years? he asked. After a bit of New York–style negotiating, Grossman and the promoter reached an agreement. Bill Graham would be the sole presenter of the Paul Butterfield Blues Band in San Francisco. It was the beginning of a fruitful relationship.

It was also the end of Graham's relationship with the Family Dog. The loss of the act Helms had brought to San Francisco angered the producer. It was true that he had far less business experience and fewer resources than his erstwhile partner, but he nevertheless felt tricked by the former New Yorker. As a result, Helms never again put on a show at the Fillmore Auditorium, and the venue became the home base of Bill Graham Productions. Graham wanted the Butterfield Band back at the auditorium as soon as possible, but first the group had to return to Huntington Beach for two weeks at another beachfront venue. This time they played the blues at a restaurant and folk music club dating back the late 1920s called the Golden Bear.

Located at 306 Ocean Avenue, the Golden Bear, with its fanciful Moorish facade, faced the vast azure expanse of the Pacific Ocean across the street and was frequented by a revolving crowd of beach habitués, tourists, and folk music fans. The band performed at the club from April 1 to April 10 while staying in the Compass Motel nearby. Their shows were a hit, and they played to audiences nearly as enthusiastic as they had been at the Fillmore. "The Raga" was now a part of the band's regular repertoire, and Michael Bloomfield was continuing to develop its exotic sound, extending the piece and taking it in new directions.

"The house was usually packed," said Mark Naftalin. "And when we would play that tune, the Golden Bear crowd exploded!" At this early stage in its development, "The Raga" was largely a vehicle for Bloomfield's virtuosic guitar work. After short solos from Paul and Elvin, Michael would take over and guide the rhythm section through as many as five distinct sections, each with a different mood and each climaxing in a thunderous crescendo. The piece frequently was the band's set closer, because its twenty-minute-plus duration often left the audience too overwhelmed to hear anything more.

The second week in April, the Butterfield Band drove north to San Francisco to do another weekend at the Fillmore. When they arrived at the hall on Friday, April 15, Bill Graham was on the stage barking orders, shoving equipment around, and checking cables while simultaneously taking phone calls. His frenetic, harried demeanor right away caught Mike Bloomfield's attention.

"I remember Mark Naftalin and me gazing at this insane guy on the stage, just at a sound check, no one in the place, but still freaking out," said Michael. It didn't take long for Bloomfield to recognize in Graham a drive and business savvy that reminded him of his father, Harold. Though Bill had a volatile temper, Michael wasn't threatened by his tirades. Instead, Graham's intensity brought out the adolescent prankster in Bloomfield, and he amused himself by provoking the older man. Graham, in turn, soon understood that the guitarist was someone he couldn't bully, an artist who wasn't afraid of the producer's bravado and bluster and who would say what he thought. Bill Graham respected Michael's honesty, and the two soon became good friends.

For that weekend's shows, Graham paired the Butterfield Band with another up-and-coming San Francisco group with a surreal name. The Jefferson Airplane, as they called themselves, had been together for about seven months—a bit longer than the sextet from Chicago—and their music was a blend of folk, rock, and blues with an emphasis on harmonized vocals. With two excellent lead singers—Signe Anderson and leader Marty Balin—the band was fast becoming one of the most popular in the Bay Area.

Billed as a "Blues-Rock Bash," the shows were split between the Fillmore Auditorium and the Harmon Gymnasium on the Berkeley campus of the University of California. The Jefferson Airplane was quite popular among the university's students, but when Michael heard them he was unimpressed. Their singing was admittedly very good, but their ability to play their instruments struck him as rudimentary. Like many of the players in other Bay Area bands, the members of the Airplane had been acoustic musicians until recently, and playing amplified folk rock was something new for them. They and other San Francisco bands were still learning how to do it. But Bloomfield had no patience for inadequate musicianship.

"We heard the music in San Francisco and thought it was just utter garbage," Michael said. "Completely unprofessional, obviously folkies that had picked up electric instruments about a year ago and were no way rooted. . . . I was very disillusioned about the music scene here."

The Butterfield Band's second Fillmore appearance was an even bigger success than their first. Bill Graham was delighted with the proceeds from their three nights and was determined to have the group perform at the Fillmore as often as possible. But Elektra was eager to get the band back into the studio to begin work on a second album, and ABGM had arranged to bring them back east for an extended tour. Bill Graham would not get a chance to present the group again until late September.

Mike Bloomfield saw that Graham genuinely liked the band's tough, Chicago-style blues, and he took Bill aside one night and told him that if he liked what the Butterfield Band was doing, he should hear some of the great blues masters that he, Paul, and Elvin had learned from. The producer, the guitarist said, should bring some of the legendary black players out to San Francisco to perform at the Fillmore. Butterfield might not be back for six months, but Bill didn't have to wait. He could get the real thing with Muddy Waters, Otis Rush, James Cotton, Magic Sam, or Buddy Guy. Michael was particularly enthusiastic about his idol, B. B. King. Graham definitely had to hire King, Michael said, because he was the best blues guitarist in the world. The producer listened and was impressed. He wouldn't forget Bloomfield's recommendations.

The Butterfield Band flew to New York the third week in April, and on Sunday, April 24, they headlined at a spring break show for Penn State University, sharing the stage with the British pop band the Searchers. From there they went to Stony Brook University on Long Island, opening a show for the folk duo Simon and Garfunkel. For both performances, the Butterfield Band again featured selections from their Elektra release, including "Blues with a Feeling," "Thank You Mister Poohbah," "Mellow Down Easy," and "Born in Chicago." But Paul had also begun letting his sidemen perform a few tunes. Elvin took center stage at one point and, with a cigarette dangling from his lip, sang a mournful soul ballad titled "Never Say No," written by singer Percy Mayfield. Bishop's pleading delivery, subtly backed by Butterfield's moaning harp and Naftalin's sanctified organ, was a hit with the audience, offering a brief respite from the band's otherwise intense presentation.

The following day, the Chicagoans packed up and headed to Detroit for two weeks at the Living End. Located on John C. Lodge Drive in New Center, the city's scruffy business district, the venue usually featured folk artists like Odetta, Judy Henske, and Gordon Lightfoot. The club's small bandstand had just room enough for the band as long as one member—usually Paul—stood on the floor. The place, very much like Big John's in Chicago, had tables with checkered tablecloths and a small dance floor that was opened up whenever necessary. There was usually plenty of dancing when the Butterfield Band hit the stage.

The group opened on Tuesday, April 26, and appeared at the Living End through May 8. Crowds thronged to the venue each night, excited by the new sounds of the blues and thrilled by Paul's and Michael's soloing. A reviewer for the *Detroit Free Press* described the band as "tearing audiences apart . . . with some of the grooviest sounds I've heard," and went on to single Bloomfield out as the band's star attraction. "You won't believe the sounds that come out of Bloomfield's guitar. While he plays, he talks to the guitar and shakes his head. It's like he's encouraging a person to do what he wants."

From Detroit, Butterfield and the group headed back home to Chicago. They were expecting to play at Big John's for several weeks, making a triumphant return after successfully touring the West Coast. But ABGM sent them instead to a recently opened venue called Poor Richard's, a nightclub housed in a former church at 1363 North Sedgwick Street. The Butterfield Band opened there on Thursday, May 12, and played nightly through May 22. Once again, crowds packed the venue. One evening, to everyone's delight, Sam Lay, now fully recovered, came by and sat in with the band.

With their growing reputation as one of Chicago's hottest groups playing the new blues, the Butterfield Band was beginning to garner national attention. One evening, a reporter from the venerable entertainment weekly *Variety* showed up to review a performance. The writer came away suitably impressed, describing the band as being "in the forefront in the resurgence of what is known locally as Chicago style blues." He went on to characterize the experience of seeing them live. "Butterfield's six-piece group dishes up big beat blues at its best. The sound, definitely not for the delicate of ear, is at times almost overwhelming in sheer volume. The band's three electric guitars, drums, organ and Butterfield on harmonica, play with considerable intensity, yet never degenerate into becoming merely noise."

The showpiece of the evening was Michael Bloomfield's mash-up of Eastern and Western influences. "Outstanding in the turn was a throbbing treatment of 'The Ragga' [*sic*], an instrumental heavily influenced by the music of India."

"The Raga" had started out as an experimental piece built around extended solos by Bloomfield. But by the time the Butterfield Band arrived back in Chicago, the instrumental had evolved into a lengthy group collaboration. It now comprised a series of improvisations that stretched beyond the limits of blues, rock, or even jazz. Bloomfield still had the lion's share of solo time, but Paul and Elvin also made formidable contributions. The piece was never the same twice, with each performance following a basic outline while generating variations depending upon discoveries made along the way as the soloists improvised. The rhythm section ebbed and flowed according to the mood of each of the disparate sections, and accompaniment varied from a tambura-like drone to impromptu duets and trios.

On a typical evening at Poor Richard's, the Butterfield Band would close out the last show with "The Raga." Elvin Bishop would begin the piece, taking the first solo, and then Butterfield would improvise over Billy Davenport's Latin-tinged drumming, establishing a bluesy mood before building to the instrumental's first crescendo. Bloomfield would then work furiously through the next section, using the flatted seconds and sixths commonly found in traditional Indian morning ragas to create a quasi-Eastern tonality. Following a second crescendo, the guitarist would improvise airy melodies before bringing Elvin and Paul back in for a concluding ensemble statement. A final crescendo would close the piece with breathtaking intensity.

In performance, "The Raga" would typically last thirty minutes or longer. At its thunderous conclusion, spontaneous gasps and cries would invariably erupt around the room as the audience rose to its feet for a vociferous ovation. Because the Butterfield Band's frontline players favored loud Fender Twin and Super Reverbs—Bloomfield himself used two of the amps daisy-chained together—the piece's dramatic coda produced not only a release of musical tension for the audience but also a moment of real physical relief.

While the Butterfield Band was working at Poor Richard's, they continued to add new tunes to their playbook. Along with Elvin Bishop's version of "Never Say No" were several others by Percy Mayfield, including "River's Invitation" and "Danger Zone." Butterfield sang both "Get Out of My Life Woman" by New Orleans songwriter Allen Toussaint and "One More Heartache" by Marvin Gaye, while Jerome Arnold had the vocal on "You're So Fine," an old doo-wop tune by the Falcons, and Wilson Pickett's "In the Midnight Hour." Muddy Waters's "Walkin' through the Park" featured Paul, and Bloomfield got to sing Albert King's "Let's Have a Natural Ball" and an original titled "Feel It."

Of the new tunes, only two were standard blues—the others were drawn from soul and R&B sources. It was clear that the Butterfield Band was beginning to branch out, moving slowly away from the leader's initial preference for straight Chicago blues. Bloomfield's "The Raga" offered the most convincing evidence of the band's expanding musical horizons, but there were other examples as well. They regularly performed jazz pianist Herbie Hancock's "Watermelon Man," and "Work Song" was now an alternate set closer. The band's new cooperative structure allowed Michael and the other players to occasionally choose the tunes they wanted to perform, and frequently those tunes were not strictly blues. Paul, surprisingly, seemed to want to try other things as well.

"We hope to advance with the times," he told an interviewer. "Maybe in ten years, we'll be back with jazz or Indian or classical, but we want to progress. The blues has changed and will change and so will we." By the late spring of 1966, the Paul Butterfield Blues Band had clearly begun to change.

The new ground the Butterfield Band was breaking, in terms of both its own development and its revolutionary deconstructing of pop music tropes, attracted a growing following of fellow musicians. More and more, wherever the band performed, it was Michael Bloomfield's contribution that garnered the most attention. The flamboyant guitarist's furious solos, his seemingly unlimited ability to improvise without repetition, his boundless energy and charismatic personality—coupled with a wicked sense of humor—were beginning to win

Bloomfield a cult following. The fact that he was friendly and outgoing and thus easy to approach only increased his popularity.

For young guitarists across the country, hearing the Butterfield album was an ear-opening experience. For those who saw Michael play in person, the experience was life changing. With the growing interest in blues and blues-oriented rock, many young pop music fans were picking up guitars and trying to play the sounds they heard on Rolling Stones, Animals, and Yardbirds records. But when they heard the Paul Butterfield Blues Band with Michael Bloomfield, it was like a door opened. By the end of the year, *Hit Parader* magazine's editor, Jim Delehant, would write that Michael "is the most influential guitarist in pop music as evidenced by the hundreds of lead guitarists in minor bands learning from him."

CHAPTER 12

EAST-WEST

CHICAGO, SAN FRANCISCO, AND NEW YORK, 1966–1967

Jac Holzman and Elektra Records were anxious to get the Butterfield Band back into the studio to begin work on a second album. The group's first release hadn't been a hit record, but it had made the *Billboard* charts, and sales continued to be steady. Critical reaction was universally positive, and the album was reportedly a favorite at campus parties. Holzman was certain that a second release would be profitable, perhaps even more so than the band's first effort. But with the Butterfield Band constantly on tour, it had been difficult to find time to get the group into Mastertone Studios in New York. The delay had been further complicated by Paul Rothchild's incarceration. Without Rothchild to plan and coordinate the sessions, the second Butterfield Band album had stalled.

But Holzman and assistant producer Mark Abramson had an idea. Since the Butterfield Band was in Chicago, the home of the blues, Holzman suggested they record at Chess, the place where the best Chicago blues records had been made. The group was amenable, and while they were at Poor Richard's, they spent afternoons during the second and third weeks of May at 2120 South Michigan Avenue—Chess's Ter Mar Studios—recording a series of tunes for their next album.

The label's ace recording engineer, Ron Malo, was brought in to give the band the legendary Chess sound. Malo was an expert at capturing the music of loud electric bands, and the sessions proceeded smoothly. One of the first pieces the band taped was a fully developed version of Mike Bloomfield's experimental modal instrumental. During the studio sessions, "The Raga" was officially renamed "East-West."

"'East-West' was done quickly in the studio. We just played it through," said Naftalin. He added, "It was done all in one take." There were few of the redos that had hindered the band's first sessions for Elektra.

The studio version of the extended instrumental was arranged just as it had been in the band's live performances at Poor Richard's. It retained the three-section structure and overall form, and it opened with the rhythm section comping to Billy Davenport's variation on a bossa beat. The tempo was quick and bright, and Elvin Bishop jumped right in, opening his solo with a two-bar unison. He then cast a series of angular lines, jacking up his Gibson ES-345 for maximum sustain. After soloing assertively for five minutes, Bishop passed the baton to the leader. Butterfield then reeled off a series of bold rhythmic phrases, big melodies right out of the blues tradition. He developed the lines into a brief statement and then began building toward the first crescendo, with both guitarists furiously punching out supporting chords as Bloomfield slowly ascended toward that high D. Moments later, the band hit the piece's first break.

Michael leapt into his modal solo, opening the second section with a brief tremolo between D and D♭, accompanied only by bass and drums. With the start of the guitarist's improvisation, Jerome Arnold changed his opening bass part to a line closely resembling the pattern used in saxophonist John Coltrane's seminal 1964 composition "A Love Supreme." Bloomfield spun out line after line, accenting his phrases with flatted seconds and sixths, occasionally allowing a plucked open D to drone behind improvisations. Several minutes into his solo, Michael played a series of phrases using octaves over open-string drones, giving "East-West" a raga-like sonority as he and Elvin merged in a wash of D-based overtones. Butterfield then pushed to the front with a full-blown D♭-to-D warble, signaling the start of the second section's crescendo. Jerome switched to a repeated D played in eighth note rhythm; the rest of the band followed, and the ensemble built to an intense climax. The second section ended with a breath-catching break.

The third portion of "East-West" set an entirely different mood, just as it did in the Butterfield Band's live performances. Bloomfield began with a D–E–F♯ phrase, a motive he often used to open the section. He then improvised deftly, giving his solo an open, jazzy feel that stood in stark contrast to the musical firestorm that preceded it. As Michael spun out melodic lines, the volume of his playing diminished almost to the point of inaudibility. Billy Davenport provided support with subtle high-hat accents and soft mallets on tuned drumheads. Bloomfield returned briefly to the D–E–F♯ motive, then created from it a marvelous compound phrase that twisted and turned for a full sixty seconds, resolving back to D only some forty bars after it started. In its coherence, clarity, and Bach-like motion, the passage brilliantly demonstrated the guitarist's musical virtuosity.

Bloomfield then played a quiet series of descending and ascending dyads on the downbeat. After a moment he was joined by Butterfield, and the two introduced a new theme consisting of F♯–G–A, with the A repeated in triplet rhythm. The phrase was a variation on one that opened Muddy Waters's 1956 tune "Forty Days" and formed the melody of jazz organist Jimmy Smith's 1961 composition "Back at the Chicken Shack." The riff set up the duet portion of the section, and with Butterfield blowing pedal tones, Bloomfield and Bishop created a joyous counterpoint for a full minute. Michael took the higher line and Elvin worked the middle register while Mark Naftalin shadowed them, adding a third melody to the guitars. The momentum built for sixty seconds and then the band punctuated the rhythm as a unit. The final crescendo ran for twelve bars before ending with a glorious flurry on a final concluding chord, Butterfield's harp having the last say.

It was an unprecedented performance.

In the control room, Ron Malo looked at Mark Abramson and nodded his approval. The Chess engineer had recorded jazz sessions where pieces occasionally ran to ten minutes and longer, but this was the first time he had ever taped an extended composition by a pop band. And this instrumental wasn't just extended—it was almost *fifteen* minutes long. That was nearly an entire side of a standard long-playing record. No blues band in Malo's experience had ever attempted something so audacious. The piece clearly wasn't blues and it wasn't jazz, although its solos had much in common with jazz improvisation. The beat was too sophisticated for rock, and even though the scales used in portions of the piece sounded Eastern, it certainly wasn't ethnic folk music. Malo had no idea how to describe "East-West" because he had never heard anything like it.

"East-West" was unquestionably a tour de force, a magnificent demonstration of virtuosic playing unlike anything previously recorded in pop music. A fusion of blues, rock, and jazz that incorporated Eastern and modal scales, the piece transcended the sum of its parts to become a bellwether for a new form of popular music. Bloomfield's instrumental, after its release in October, would be categorized as a prime example of "psychedelic rock."

Over the next week, the Butterfield Band recorded a number of other tunes for the album. One, "I Got a Mind to Give Up Living," was another feature for Mike Bloomfield, just as "Our Love Is Drifting" from their first record had been. Originally recorded by B. B. King in 1965 as "All Over Again," the tune was a minor blues in C with emotionally charged lyrics. Paul sang them plaintively and then stepped aside as Michael stormed through two hair-raising choruses of slow, dirge-like blues. In the ten months the band had been together, Michael's blues playing had become more nuanced. On "I Got a Mind to Give Up Living," he shaded notes with subtle bends, varied the dynamic of his attack, and implied phrases without fully stating them. In a word, Bloomfield's playing had become more "vocal."

The band also recorded another instrumental, getting the Nat Adderley composition they had been playing since Newport on tape. "Work Song" had been honed over many months into a tight demonstration of the Butterfield Band's skilled ensemble interplay, and it had become one of the group's featured tunes. They played the F-minor blues as a straight-ahead jazz number, allowing the guitars, harp, and keyboard ample space for soloing. As had been their practice since the Newport festival the previous July, the group switched from the tune's sixteen-bar structure to a standard twelve-bar format during the solos.

After Paul blew the theme on unaccompanied harp, punctuated by chords on the downbeat from the band, a lengthy round of solos began with Michael Bloomfield's fleet modal run up his Les Paul's neck. Combining blues, rock, and jazz styles with modal inflections once again, Bloomfield improvised for seven full choruses, at turns shaking out screaming high notes and then switching to Wes Montgomery-style octaves. Butterfield followed with three of his own, alternating long commanding tones with cascades of staccato notes. Mark Naftalin, who had been playing a Hohner Pianet, an early electric piano, when accompanying the other soloists, moved over to organ for his three-chorus statement. The big sound of the studio Hammond added muscle to his lines as he set the stage for Elvin Bishop's five-chorus blues improvisation. The guitarist's edgy, raw licks built to a thunderhead of intensity until, backed by Paul's harmonica, Bishop yielded to two choruses of rapid solo exchanges between all four musicians. Known in jazz parlance as "trading fours"—in this instance "twos," alternating players every two bars—the technique was commonly used to generate excitement as one soloist tried to best another in a quick back-and-forth. Around the four musicians went—Michael's ethereal, cerebral lines flowing into Mark's thoughtful runs and then Elvin's jagged, hard-edged riffs followed closely by Paul's wailing swoops. Their fleet handoffs, with one man's phrase blending seamlessly into another's, added a thrilling conclusion to the song's cascade of solos. After the exchanges, Butterfield restated the theme, and the band brought the piece to a close with a dramatic ritard of the melody's first four bars. "Work Song" was another example of how the Butterfield Band was pushing the limits of pop music by fusing together elements drawn from disparate traditions. It also served to demonstrate the individuality of each of the band's soloists.

While he was playing in his hometown, Michael Bloomfield spent what little spare time he had visiting friends and making the rounds. One afternoon Michael ran into photographer Peter Amft in Old Town. Amft was happy to see the guitarist—he always found Bloomfield entertaining.

"He was totally funny," said Amft. "He was like being onstage with Lenny Bruce." Michael's ebullient nature amused Peter. "He was always smiling. . . . [H]e was *very* effusive. He had like this terrible posture, and he'd be striding down the street like this big crazy spider, and talking to everybody! He was like the most enthusiastic person in the world."

When Michael met Peter on the street, his enthusiasm at the moment was for a visit to Tommy Walker's place. He convinced Amft to come along, and the two friends walked up North Wells Street to the corner of North Avenue. There they shouted up to Walker to throw down the key to the building's front door. Amft knew of Walker and his reputation as a drug dealer, but he had never been to the Mayor of Old Town's apartment. He went upstairs with Michael and soon understood that the guitarist's visit was more than just social. Shortly after their arrival, the works came out, and Tommy, despite his disapproval of Bloomfield's casual heroin use, began cooking up a dose. He injected Michael and then fixed himself, and for a half hour the three men chatted amicably.

But soon Bloomfield began to nod. His lips turned purple and then blue, and eventually he slumped over. Tommy saw that his friend was in trouble, and he told Peter to help him get Michael into the bathroom. There he filled the tub with cold water while quickly stripping off the guitarist's clothing. Once he was naked, the two men hefted the comatose Bloomfield into the bath. Walker began slapping his face, trying to get the star of the Paul Butterfield Blues Band to wake up. It was too much for Peter Amft.

"He was totally blue and naked in the bathtub," said Amft. "They had to put ice cubes on him. I left!" Twenty-four hours later, Peter met Michael on the street, and the guitarist acted as though nothing had happened. "The next day, he looked fine!" said the photographer, amazed at his friend's resilience. The guitarist had been lucky. That he could have died seemed not to concern him. It would not be the last time Michael Bloomfield would depend on friends to bring him back from a narcotics overdose.

In the days following their stint at Poor Richard's, the Butterfield Band recorded additional tunes at Ter Mar Studios for the new album. They waxed a variation of Muddy Waters's "Still a Fool," calling it "Two Trains Running," and one of Junior Parker's 1965 records, "These Kind of Blues," which they called "All These Blues." The former tune featured Bloomfield as its lead soloist, while Paul took the choruses on the latter. Neither was arranged as a typical Chicago blues, and "Two Trains Running" had Muddy's original sixteen-bar structure but was given a completely different treatment. Michael reeled off two choruses of steely, blues-rock lead following Paul's vocal and then the band dropped into a I–IV vamp as Bloomfield wailed until Ron Malo waved them out, signaling from the control room that he had enough to do a fade on the final mix.

The band also did a cover of "Get Out of My Life Woman," the tune that Paul had recently begun performing. An Allen Toussaint song, it had charted earlier in the year with a version by soul singer Lee Dorsey, and the Butterfield Band's rendition closely followed the original. But where Dorsey sang the tune straight through, Butterfield left space for a solo, and this time the nod went to Mark Naftalin. The keyboard player's usual role with the band was as an accompanist, but given the spotlight he turned in two convincing choruses in Toussaint's style, demonstrating a real command of the keyboard. Paul also recorded a modern version of Robert Johnson's 1936 cover of "Walkin' Blues," originally by Son House. Keeping Johnson's on-the-beat march rhythm, Butterfield sang the legendary Delta blues singer's first and fourth verses, then added two from Muddy Waters's "Country Blues," another variation of the tune. This time it was Elvin who was given the solo, and he and Paul split a chorus while Michael added accents on slide. The arrangement gave the traditional Delta tune an updated, contemporary sound, making it into a rocking electric dance number.

The Butterfield Band's final recording at Ter Mar was the pleading blues that Elvin Bishop had been singing so effectively for the past month. With Paul and Mark providing quiet accompaniment over the rhythm section's subtle beat, Elvin offered a quavering, sorrowful vocal interpretation of Percy Mayfield's "Never Say No." With no solos to interrupt the mood, the piece was all Bishop, and though he wasn't a particularly strong singer, he managed to deliver the lyrics with real pathos.

With the completion of the five additional tunes, Jac Holzman felt the band had nearly enough material for its next album. ABGM was eager to get the group back on the road, so with the studio sessions concluded, Albert Grossman had Paul, Michael, and the rest of the band pack up once again and head back east for a week at the Unicorn Coffee House in Boston. By now, the Butterfield Band was well known around the city, and the Unicorn was standing room only every night. During their week at the club, the band introduced several tunes new to the group's book. One was an exciting version of the instrumental "Comin' Home Baby." Written by jazz bassist Ben Tucker, the Butterfield Band's rendition favored meaty solos over an insistent, driving beat provided by Billy Davenport. Mike Bloomfield also contributed a new number that he had written. Called "If You See My Baby," the twelve-bar blues had a walking, New Orleans-style lilt to it, a fact that Bloomfield frequently emphasized by dedicating the tune prior to each performance to the Crescent City's Fats Domino.

Following their successful stay in Boston, the Butterfield Band returned to Chicago to spend the first weeks of June finishing up work on the album for Elektra. They then returned to the East Coast and on Monday, June 20, opened a week-long stay at Club 47 in Cambridge's Harvard Square. The band had made the long trip from Chicago to Boston for the second time that month to appear at the popular coffeehouse. It had been nearly a year since they had last performed at Club 47, and at that time very few of the club's patrons had ever heard of the blues band. Since then, everything had changed. The small venue, filled to capacity every night, was now turning away eager Butterfield fans at the door. One newspaper reported that the club was "filled to overflowing" and that midway through the evening, "managing director Jim Rooney cleared the house to let the long line outside have a turn." The band's closing number, the reporter went on to say, was "of about 15 minutes duration" and "moved to a great crashing, stomping climax which left the performers and audience limp." "East-West" was becoming an aural and emotional watershed—so much so that another reviewer experienced a musical conversion upon seeing the band at Club 47: "If there was one thing I was not before last Tuesday, it was a fan of rhythm and blues, but after one night this has all changed. Perhaps it's called blues, but to me it's a fantastically happy sound."

On Friday afternoon, *Crawdaddy* editor Paul Williams came by the club to interview the band for the sixth edition of his rock 'n' roll publication. Paul Butterfield was reluctant to talk, so his most loquacious sideman dominated the conversation right from the start. Williams, thinking of the band's recent experiments with jazz and Indian music, wanted to know if the group still thought of themselves as a blues band. "We used to be in what you would call an exclusively Chicago blues thing," said Bloomfield, acknowledging the shift. "But we've come out of it in the last few months and we're gradually working into the establishment of possibly a new idiom. Who knows?"

Hoping to get Michael to be more specific, Williams asked, "You're not moving in any specific direction, it's just what you want to do now?" "It's just what's coming out of us," Bloomfield replied. He stressed that because they all came from different backgrounds, they were interested in a variety of music. The band members were able to blend those interests when making their own music. Then Michael spoke with obvious pride.

"And I'll say this, the level of musicianship of our group is higher than almost any other group of this nature that I've heard in the country. Almost any rock band that I've heard." He went on to praise his boss. "Paul's the best in his field; there's not a person living in the world today that can cut him."

Williams again tried to get Michael to define the direction the band was taking, asking about "this new electric blues business." But the guitarist would comment only in general terms.

"I think electric music is really the music of the future," he asserted. "You'll find that all music will be amplified one day. It's a new type of musicianship. It's a musicianship of this generation."

Williams then asked about the band's new album.

"Well, there's one very long piece that I like," replied Bloomfield, speaking of "East-West." He also mentioned "Never Say No." "Elvin sings a tune I'm very fond of on the album. I like it, it's more modern than our other album, but I still don't think it's as good as us in person."

Following the interview, the editor stayed for the show and had to agree with its lead guitarist. The Paul Butterfield Blues Band was even more exciting in person than they were on record.

The next stop for the constantly touring Butterfield Band was New York City. The group had a two-week engagement at their home base in the Big Apple, the Cafe Au Go Go. For the first weekend, from July 1 to July 3, they shared the bill with Michael's old friend and mentor Big Joe Williams. Joe was a regular at the café, often appearing at its "Blues Bag" Sunday jam sessions whenever he was in town. He was delighted to see his former Chicago protégé, and he and Michael reminisced backstage, playing a few numbers together with Bloomfield picking out leads on his unplugged Les Paul Goldtop.

Also performing that weekend was a group from Greenwich Village called the Blues Project. Formed in the fall of 1965 around the talents of guitarist Danny Kalb, the Blues Project also regularly performed at the café and had even recorded their first album there. They were a popular attraction in New York, but they had also been well received in San Francisco when they appeared at the Fillmore Auditorium a month after the Butterfield Band had debuted there. Their eclectic mix of blues, jazz, folk, and rock, coupled with Kalb's busy guitar solos and bassist Andy Kulberg's flute playing, won them a dedicated following. For many, they seemed to be the Big Apple's answer to the blues band from the Windy City. Howard Solomon, owner of the Cafe Au Go Go, decided to put that assumption to the test and booked both bands back to back. It was a brilliant bit of marketing, and it brought out the crowds. It also gave the rival bands a chance to get to know each other.

Mike Bloomfield already knew one of the Blues Project members. Al Kooper had joined the group as its keyboard player not long after he had finished touring with Bob Dylan following the completion of *Highway 61 Revisited*. He not only played and sang in the band, but also wrote and arranged much of its material. He and Michael quickly renewed their friendship.

"We played this double bill together at the Cafe Au Go Go," said Kooper. "The bands would switch off playing first and second, and it was competitive, but we had a great time." He added with a laugh, "I remember Michael saying to me, 'I heard you guys were shit, but you guys are *really* good.' He would always say whatever was on his mind; he just didn't care how it sounded!"

Both bands enjoyed the friendly competition while they shared the café's stage, and each had come to respect the other's abilities. But Mike Bloomfield had been the dominating presence throughout the weekend. His extraordinary energy, ebullient personality, and ferocious soloing overwhelmed all who caught the shows, including the members of the Blues Project. One fan was impressed enough to return with a tape recorder, determined to get an interview with the animated guitarist. Jim Delehant, editor of the music magazine *Hit Parader*, had once hired Michael to interview some of Chicago's blues legends. Now he wanted to do an article about Bloomfield himself. One evening, prior to the Butterfield Band's opening set, he and Michael sat down backstage at the café and had a wide-ranging conversation.

Delehant asked the guitarist about his early days in Chicago and about discovering the blues as a teenager. Bloomfield, voluble as ever, talked of his infatuation with rock 'n' roll and how that led him to the blues of Lightnin' Hopkins, Muddy Waters, and eventually B. B. King. He recounted delving into the folk blues tradition and acknowledged his debt to Big Joe Williams. He went on to describe the call from Bob Dylan that resulted in *Highway 61 Revisited* and criticized the blues being made by English bands as "farcical." "For my money, nobody plays it but us," Michael confidently told Delehant. He then spoke frankly about the Butterfield Band's music.

> The long piece we do is not Indian by any means. It just conveys that feeling. To get emotional is the most important thing in music. If you can't get emotions out of your audience, it doesn't mean a thing. Swinging will almost always do that. Many of the blues bands don't swing. "Swinging" is an archaic term. Sometimes we don't, but we're capable of hard swing.

Jim was curious. Would the band's latest single and its upcoming album be "hard swingers"? "No," replied Bloomfield emphatically. "Our single and LP are *in drerd* so far." Delehant was unfamiliar with the Yiddish expression, and Michael explained that it meant the recordings hadn't "gotten off the ground" yet. They were still working on the mix. He added that the band was becoming "weary of putting out straight blues" and that he and Mark Naftalin were writing tunes that "weren't blues at all." Bloomfield then surprised the editor by saying he was getting interested in "electronic music."

> I don't use echo chambers and fuzz tones and machines and stuff. It's like learning to play a whole new instrument. You've got to learn how to play electricity. Maybe I will someday. It's too much right now. I'm still learning how to play music. Electric music is learning how to play

> the amplifiers, too, and the other equipment, like colors, strobe lights. It's all very groovy, a good way to make money and blah, blah, but we can still play music for a while.

Michael could sense the aural possibilities inherent in amplified music, but he had yet to really explore any of them. He was already using a degree of sustain and feedback in his performances, but his playing would remain fairly straightforward. It would be up to another guitarist to realize the full potential of plugging in. Mike Bloomfield had yet to meet that guitarist, but his prophetic observations would prove truer than even he could have suspected.

Michael concluded the interview with a few terse observations about the city of Chicago and a colorful retelling of the death of John Lee "Sonny Boy" Williamson. When *Hit Parader* published the conversation in two parts in its January and February 1967 issues, Delehant wryly headlined it, "Mike Bloomfield Puts Down Everything."

A few blocks from the Cafe Au Go Go, down Bleecker Street and around the corner on McDougal, there was a basement coffeehouse called the Café Wha? Opened in 1959, the club featured a variety of entertainment throughout the daytime and evening hours. Its casual booking policy gave stage time to amateurs and accomplished performers alike, and the fare usually included an odd assortment of comedians, ventriloquists, folk singers, poets, and anyone with a modicum of talent and a desire to perform.

Since June, one of the regular evening acts was a scruffy rock-and-blues quartet fronted by a slight and soft-spoken twenty-three-year-old black guitarist who called himself Jimmy James. Folksinger Richie Havens had gotten him the gig, and James was playing multiple nightly sets of rock 'n' roll covers, pop tunes, and blues for whatever basket money the band could make. What set him apart from other performers at the café was his flamboyant stage presence—and his entirely unique sound on electric guitar. It wasn't long before word spread that there was a band at the Café Wha? worth checking out.

"I was performing with Paul Butterfield, and I was the hotshot guitarist on the block—I thought I was *it*," Michael Bloomfield recalled. A friend told him he had to go see the new guitar player working over on McDougal Street. "I went right across the street and saw him . . . and that day, in front of my eyes, he burned me to death. I didn't even get my guitar out." Michael learned that this formidable guitarist's real name was Jimmy Hendrix and that he was from Seattle. He looked vaguely familiar, and Bloomfield soon remembered him.

"I had seen him before and not paid any attention to him," he said. "I'd seen him play with Little Richard and the Isley Brothers." Hendrix had been a sideman for the legendary rock 'n' roll singer in 1965, and he had briefly toured with the Isleys, but now he was on his own, playing six nights a week at the Café Wha? and tearing up the house. "He had a band called Jimmy James and the Blue Flames. They were obviously just pick-up musicians he had gotten to just learn a few tunes so he could do what he wanted."

From the stage, Hendrix immediately recognized the star of the Paul Butterfield Blues Band. With Bloomfield's extravagant personality and his equally extravagant swarm of bushy hair, he was hard to miss. Jimmy James decided he would make an impression on the Chicagoan.

"I walked in there and I sat down with a friend of mine, another guitar player" said Bloomfield.

> And Jimmy Hendrix watched me sit down—and I remember what he was playing, a Stratocaster, and he had a Twin Reverb amp, a Gibson Maestro Fuzztone, and he had a wah-wah pedal—and he got every sound on those that I was to hear on all his subsequent records . . .
>
> Bombs exploded! Airplanes took off! Buildings collapsed! It was a *holocaust*! Plus, you know, endless amounts of incredible playing. He just did it with a little half-assed grin on his face. I was sitting in the front row and I was just blown away. It was *no* contest.

Michael described how Hendrix spent the first part of the set "just making these unbelievable sounds and noises." Using feedback, sustain, wah-wah effects, and distortion, Jimmy created an aural collage of electronic moods. "*Then* he started playing music," Bloomfield said, laughing. The guitarist's mastery of amplified sound deeply impressed Michael, but he wondered if Hendrix could do anything else.

"I said, well, he can make all these sounds but, OK, can he really play?" Bloomfield said. "Then I heard him play, and he could play *better* than he could make sounds!"

Those few hours spent at the Café Wha? watching an unknown guitarist from Seattle reinvent the way an electric guitar was played left Michael Bloomfield deeply shaken. He had come up against other skilled guitarists—that was nothing new. On Chicago's South Side he had jammed with blues guitar masters like Otis Rush, Buddy Guy, Smokey Smothers, and Hubert Sumlin. He had even encountered expert players his own age, including Texan Johnny Winter, Canadian Robbie Robertson, and, most recently, the Blues Project's Danny Kalb. He had been impressed by their playing, and occasionally he felt his own hadn't measured up. But he had never for a moment doubted his ability as a guitarist. He knew what those other players were doing and, even if he couldn't immediately replicate their style, he understood it. But this Jimmy

James—Jimmy *Hendrix*—was doing things that were beyond comprehension. That had never happened to Michael before. He felt a tinge of insecurity, and more than a tinge of envy.

"He got right in my face with that ax, and I didn't want to pick up a guitar for the next year," Bloomfield opined.

The Butterfield Band performed at the Cafe Au Go Go through Sunday, July 10, and then returned for another two weeks at the Bleecker Street venue beginning Wednesday, July 27. Following that, they were booked into the Living End in Detroit, brought back, as the club's promotion proclaimed, "by popular demand." Then they traveled back to New York City for a Friday, August 26, appearance at the Rheingold Music Festival in Central Park's Wollman Rink, sharing the stage with folksinger Odetta.

Meanwhile, Paul Rothchild, now back at Elektra and acting again as the Butterfield Band's producer, was trying to finish up the mix for the new album. The record was scheduled to be released in August, but Rothchild's constant tinkering had pushed its shipping date back by several weeks. The band had decided to call the LP *East-West*, taking the name from Bloomfield's epic instrumental and signifying their desire to expand their repertoire beyond basic blues. The music the sextet wanted to include was representative of where they were headed, but it also posed a production problem: there was just too much of it. To fit all the tunes onto a single record, several minutes of Elvin Bishop's "East-West" solo and one of Mark Naftalin's "Work Song" choruses had to be edited out. But even with the cuts, the record timed out at more than forty-two minutes, a duration that exceeded the length of many classical recordings.

For the album's cover, Rothchild chose a photo showing the band once again posed in a Chicago location. A lineup shot similar to the one used on the first album, it had Butterfield and his men standing together on one of the porticos at the Museum of Science and Industry in Hyde Park. Flanked by two massive caryatids, the six musicians looked stern and a bit foreboding. "That's because it was late and getting cold, and the picture was taking a long time," Mark Naftalin explained, laughing. Elektra's art director, Bill Harvey, had photographed the band at the museum on a cool afternoon in May while they were in Chicago performing at Poor Richard's and recording at Ter Mar Studios.

On the back of the album, the group was shown jogging through the Lake Shore Drive underpass that led to Promontory Point, the park in Hyde Park where Michael, Paul, and Elvin had spent many afternoons playing music and hanging out in the early 1960s. Bill also took several photos of the band out on the point to use in promotional material and advertisements for the Elektra release.

The Paul Butterfield Blues Band was back at the Cafe Au Go Go for the third time in eight weeks when they got word that *East-West* had been released. The cover photo, with its powerfully symmetrical image and stylized lettering, made an excellent poster for the band when the album went on display in record stores across the country. Its liner notes, though, were the antithesis of the scholarly essay penned by Pete Welding for the first Butterfield LP. These took a flippant, off-handed tone and began with the statement, "We don't want any liner notes; we'll do our own notes, hey." In an ironic twist, the squib was attributed to Paul Nelson, a well-respected music authority and publisher of the Minnesota-based folk magazine the *Little Sandy Review*. Coming out of a journalistic tradition of rigorous documentation and historical accuracy, Nelson normally might have rivaled Welding's word count. But he largely let the band speak for itself, and his 350-word, semi-comic blurb was, for him, a definite departure. Nonetheless, its casual tone perfectly underscored the Butterfield Band's hipness, cool demeanor, and apparent disdain for establishment rules and regulations.

The music, on the other hand, was anything but casual. Fans had eagerly awaited the band's new LP, and they weren't disappointed. The two long instrumentals, "Work Song" and "East-West," were immediate favorites with listeners, but "Never Say No" and "I Got a Mind to Give Up Living" also drew high praise. Prerelease sales were brisk, and a *Billboard* magazine ad on page one of its September 17 edition stated that "advance orders for this Butterfield LP are the largest in Elektra's history. A sure hit." Accompanying the announcement was a color shot of the band standing under a tree on Promontory Point with Lake Michigan in the background. It was one of the photos Bill Harvey had taken in May, and it showed six musicians who looked cool and confident, members of what was clearly one of the leading young groups in the burgeoning blues-rock movement.

Mike Bloomfield's reputation had grown exponentially in his year as a member of the Butterfield Band. By his twenty-third birthday, he was considered by many to be one of the country's best guitarists—certainly one of its finest blues-rock players, if not *the* finest. His work with Bob Dylan on *Highway 61 Revisited* and his subsequent appearance with the folksinger at Newport had introduced him to the music industry's makers and shakers, and to tens of thousands of folk and pop music fans. The release of the first Butterfield Band album further revealed him to be an exciting and masterful soloist, and musicians across the country began to take note. Twelve months of touring had enabled many thousands to witness firsthand Michael's extraordinary skill and electrifying stage presence. And now with the release of *East-West*, it was clear that the young guitarist from Chicago was not only a thrilling blues soloist but also capable of playing far more than just blues. The *Boston Globe* called Michael Bloomfield "an extraordinarily creative musician," while the *San Francisco Chronicle*'s Ralph J. Gleason enthused that the guitarist "produces long, exciting, soaring solos that leap out over the sound of the band and come alive, whirring and snapping through the hall." Bloomfield was undoubtedly "really out of sight," as one fan aptly described him in the argot of the day.

But if Michael was aware of his growing stardom, he showed little sign of it. He continued as he always had, sitting in wherever he could, making the rounds and hanging out with friends, checking out other players, getting to know everybody and treating everyone—famous or otherwise—with the same enthusiastic deference. At home, he passed the time reading, listening to music, and practicing. Onstage, even if he hadn't been sleeping or was weary from the road, he gave each performance all he had, energizing the audience and often the band as well. Unlike many other pop music stars, he remained entirely approachable—as open and genuine as he had been back in his early Chicago days.

With Bloomfield's new celebrity came occasional opportunities for studio work. In September, he participated in a session with an old friend. Barry Goldberg had moved to New York City after the breakup of the Goldberg-Miller Blues Band, a group he had formed in 1965 with guitarist Steve Miller and Michael's close friend Roy Ruby. Goldberg was doing session work in the city with Carmine Riale, the bass player from Robby and the Troubadours, and Riale was putting together a new band with Barry on keyboards. They were going to record for a label called DynoVoice, and Carmine was looking for a guitarist to go into the studio with them. Barry immediately suggested Michael, and Bloomfield was only too happy to make a little extra money in addition to his regular Butterfield Band pay.

On the day they were to record, Michael arrived at the studio, guitar in hand, and was greeted by the session's producer, Bob Crewe. Crewe, a highly successful songwriter and record executive who had written and produced many of Frankie Valli's hits with the Four Seasons, was regarded as something of an innovator in the studio. His use of ambient sounds, pumped-up arrangements, backup voices, and overdubbing had created a signature sound for groups like Mitch Ryder and the Detroit Wheels. Under Crewe's direction, Ryder scored several top-ten hits. The producer was hoping to do the same for the Chicago Loop, Riale's new group.

"The day Michael came in and met Crewe for the first time, we were planning to cut this song called '(When She Wants Good Lovin') She Comes to Me,'" said Goldberg. "Michael and I both knew the song, because it had been recorded by the Coasters." The producer went over the arrangement he had in mind for the tune and then handed Bloomfield a set of headphones and asked him to set up at some distance from the other musicians. He explained that he wanted to be able to isolate Michael's playing so that he could control it in the final mix. Bloomfield was intrigued—it was the first time he had ever recorded using headphones. He and Norman Dayron had done some amateur overdubbing years ago, but he had never used the technique in a professional studio setting.

"Michael was used to playing 'live' in the studio, with no overdubbing," Barry recalled. "But this wasn't the way Bob Crewe produced a record. And because we knew how many hit records he'd already made, we just shut up and listened to what he wanted us to do."

At one point during the session, Crewe told the guitarist he could take a break. As Michael found a seat in the control booth, the producer rolled tape on the group's rhythm section, having them play the song by themselves. Once he was satisfied with the rhythm track, Bob sent Bloomfield back into the studio and had him play his guitar parts over it while listening on headphones. The guitarist executed the overdubbing masterfully, and Crewe was delighted with the results. The song, when mixed and released in early October, eventually reached number thirty-seven on *Billboard*'s Hot 100 chart. Because Crewe added the sounds of a raucous crowd in the background—replete with bottles breaking, girls squealing, and guys laughing—the tune had a unique "party" sound. It was so successful that in 1967 it was used as the music for a Macleans toothpaste commercial.

The encounter with Bob Crewe had a profound effect on Bloomfield. He was fascinated by the way the producer worked, using the studio itself as a kind of musical instrument. Michael closely observed the techniques Crewe used to enhance the music's sound and made mental notes on where he placed microphones and how he separated the players. Bob seemed undaunted by loud electric instruments and clearly knew how to capture them without diminishing their effect. The guitarist thought Elektra could benefit from a few lessons with DynoVoice's visionary head man.

In mid-September, the Paul Butterfield Blues Band flew out to California. They were eager to get back to the West Coast's sunny weather and sunnier attitudes after New York's heat, humidity, and urban grime. San Francisco impresario

Bill Graham was also eager to get them back into the Fillmore, exercising his option with ABGM as the group's exclusive presenter to once again fill his auditorium to capacity. First, though, the band had to make a stop at a seaside resort community several hours south of the City by the Bay.

Monterey, a city that was home to many artists, musicians, and writers, had long been a community associated with the arts. Since 1958, it also had been the location for a musical extravaganza called the Monterey Jazz Festival. Modeled on the Newport Jazz Festival, the annual three-day event presented stars of contemporary and traditional jazz at the Monterey County Fairgrounds on the city's east side. In the eight years of its existence, the event's roster had rarely strayed far from the mainstream. But in 1966, Jimmy Lyons, the festival's creator and producer, had been talked into presenting electric pop groups on Monterey's stage. One of those groups was the Paul Butterfield Blues Band.

For much of the decade, jazz singer Jon Hendricks, a member of the highly successful vocal trio Lambert, Hendricks & Ross, had presented a blues program at Monterey. For the 1966 event, the afternoon presentation was titled Blues All the Way, with Hendricks narrating a "history of the blues" while festival musicians provided musical examples. This time, he wanted to include two contemporary groups that he felt represented the new wave in blues development. San Francisco's most popular band, the Jefferson Airplane, suggested by Ralph J. Gleason, was one of them; Butterfield's sextet was the other.

Blues All the Way opened at 1:30 p.m. on Saturday, September 17, with Hendricks seated onstage, surrounded by a group of small children. The singer began by reading a poem he had written, addressing it to his diminutive audience.

I have a story to tell, and I want to tell it to you,
Because in your youth, you are wiser by far than adults are.

He went on to describe the development of rhythm and music in colorful, homespun language, pausing every so often to allow the musicians onstage behind his little story circle to offer a musical example. Also performing that year as part of Hendricks's aural history were Muddy Waters and his band, Big Walter Horton, blues shouter Big Mama Thornton, swing vocalist Jimmy Rushing, and pianist Memphis Slim. As the program progressed, Hendricks's narration interrupted the music less and less, and eventually Muddy and Big Mama were able to do full sets. Then the Jefferson Airplane came out and played two songs of their own. To finish up the presentation, Hendricks brought on Paul Butterfield and his men.

The sextet sailed through a brief set, playing a Chicago-style shuffle and "Never Say No," then concluding with a truncated version of "East-West," a clear indication that modern blues was headed in a new direction. The band cranked up their amps, striving to fill the vast arena with electric sound, and Mike Bloomfield's fiery solos rang out with a clarion brilliance. The performance stood in stark contrast to the rest of the weekend's acoustic offerings and, just as at Newport the previous year when Bloomfield backed Dylan, some jazz purists in the vast audience were not pleased. One who was particularly displeased was the venerable jazz critic Leonard Feather. His review of the afternoon's performance, published two days later in the *Los Angeles Times*, was headlined "Hard Rock Stones Sweet Sound of Monterey Festival." He dismissed the Butterfield Band for their excessive sound, ignoring the fact that the group offered the afternoon's only example of true contemporary blues.

Others on the fairgrounds that afternoon were unperturbed by the addition of amplified music to Saturday's blues program. Jimmy Lyons, Monterey's founder, called the performance "stirring" and seemed to genuinely appreciate the inclusion of the new sound on the festival roster. Respected jazz critic Whitney Balliett expressed more annoyance with Jon Hendricks's narrative interruptions than with anything else about the program. In his review of Blues All the Way for the *New Yorker*, Balliett presciently linked Bloomfield's "East-West" with jazz's "new thing"—a reference to the music of John Coltrane and other purveyors of jazz's freewheeling avant garde. "The Butterfield group includes two Negros and four whites . . . who worked their way through three numbers, the last of which was a ten-minute collective free-for-all blues that had much in common with some of the new-thing scrambles. . . . The electric din was terrific, but the music it amplified stayed afloat."

Balliett endorsed the fusion of jazz with elements of blues and rock, stating that "a merger would be welcome and edifying." He and Mike Bloomfield seemed to be thinking along the same lines, and the guitarist's visionary exercise in extended improvisation and stylistic amalgamation seemed to be, for the erudite critic, an indication of things to come.

For the Butterfield Band, their appearance at a prestigious festival like Monterey was a real validation. Sharing the stage as equals not only with some of their blues idols but also with many of America's jazz greats spoke of their acceptance as accomplished bluesmen and musicians. Playing coffeehouses and taverns, night clubs, and dance halls was one thing, but successfully winning over an attentive and critical audience of jazz fans was something else. The Saturday afternoon crowd had clearly been roused by the Butterfield Band's performance. Their applause and loud cheers as the group concluded the afternoon with its revolutionary instrumental felt like a real endorsement.

* * *

Toward the end of the month, the Paul Butterfield Blues Band headed up to San Francisco for a series of gigs starting on Friday, September 23. It had been five months since they had performed in the City by the Bay, and there was great excitement over their return. Impresario Bill Graham, expecting a record turnout, arranged to rent a hall on the corner of Post and Steiner Streets, several blocks from the Fillmore Auditorium. Called the Winterland Ballroom, the facility had been designed in 1928 as a skating arena and was larger than the Fillmore, with a capacity of nearly 5,500. To ensure a sellout crowd, Graham arranged for the Jefferson Airplane to open for the Chicago blues band. He also brought in Muddy Waters, acting on Michael Bloomfield's suggestion from the previous April. Since Muddy was already in California, Graham wouldn't have to cover the expense of bringing his group out from Chicago and could try them out essentially risk free. The Friday and Saturday shows would be at the Winterland; the final day, when the crowd was expected to be smaller, the performances would move to Geary Street for an afternoon show at the Fillmore. Bill titled the weekend series the Blues-Rock Bash II.

It was a reunion of sorts. All three bands had been onstage together the week before in Monterey, performing for the jazz festival. Those appearances had been highly structured, though, with time limits and program restrictions intended to accommodate a jazz audience that was older and more conservative. Now all three bands would get a chance to stretch out and play their music however they wished for a crowd of youngsters that was more than ready to boogie.

For opening night, Mike Bloomfield had a special stunt planned. While the group had been recording in Los Angeles in February, producer Barry Friedman amazed Michael with a trick he had learned as a performer with the circus when he was a teenager. He showed the guitarist how to soak a wand in white gas, ignite it, and insert the flaming torch into his open mouth. It was the age-old fakir feat of "eating fire," and Bloomfield quickly mastered it. He decided he would perform it onstage right in the middle of "East-West," when the piece was at its most intense. The Butterfield Band's fire-breathing guitarist would become quite literally that. The showman in Michael couldn't resist the high drama of such a moment, and the prankster in him knew he would probably blow more than a few chemically altered minds in the audience. He brought his fire-eating paraphernalia with him that evening and stowed it onstage behind his amps.

On Friday night, the immense ballroom was completely filled. Everybody was talking about the Butterfield Band's new record, and every guitarist in town wanted to hear "East-West" live. The Jefferson Airplane had also just released an album, their first on RCA, and it was selling out in local record shops. UC

Berkeley students, back from summer break and eager to catch both groups on the same stage, crowded into the Winterland. As soon as the music started, a carnival atmosphere pervaded the ballroom. Long-haired kids in full hippie regalia pirouetted and cavorted wherever there was room to dance, and others in the seats passed around joints while bobbing to the electric beat booming from the stage. Here and there, a few suede-clad hipsters discreetly handed out tabs of LSD.

After a forty-five-minute set from the Airplane, there was a short intermission while the stage was reset for the legendary blues master from Chicago's South Side. Muddy Waters had played for large crowds before—most notably at the Newport, Chicago, and New York folk festivals—and he had entertained white audiences on the North Side of Chicago and at venues in the Northeast like the Cafe Au Go Go in New York and Club 47 in Boston. But this free-wheeling San Francisco crowd was something entirely new. If Muddy was apprehensive about how his band would be received, he showed no sign of it. Following Bill Graham's introduction, the band roared into "Chicken Shack," an instrumental that was frequently Muddy's opener, and harp player George "Harmonica" Smith took the lead. His big, wailing sound brought everyone in the packed auditorium to their feet almost immediately. The young, mostly white audience was dancing and clapping along, enthusiastically cheering on the blues septet.

As Muddy wound up the group's performance with a rocking version of his closer, "Got My Mojo Working," the audience again rose to give him an ovation. An enthusiastic Bill Graham grabbed a mic and encouraged the crowd to call the bluesman back. "Ladies and gentlemen, Muddy Waters and his band. *Mr. Muddy Waters*!" After a few moments, the group returned and fired up a redux of "Mojo." The crowd roared with delight as Waters finished the rollicking shuffle by moving center stage and breaking into an impromptu two-step.

Another intermission followed with stagehands shifting equipment and rearranging mics, then Bill Graham walked back out onstage. "Thank you for waiting," Graham intoned into a microphone. A few cheers and a smattering of applause rippled through the hall. "It's been a good night, and it's going to get even better. I want to introduce . . . the members of the next band . . . to you. On drums, Mr. Billy Davenport." The crowd, listening now, began to clap. "On bass, Mr. Jerome Arnold." More applause and cheers. "On keyboards, Mr. Mark Naftalin." A cascade of applause. "On guitars, Mr. Elvin Bishop and Mr. Michael Bloomfield. Ladies and gentlemen, please welcome . . . Paul Butterfield and the Paul Butterfield Blues Band!" The house erupted in joyous appreciation as Bloomfield counted off the group's first number and Billy Davenport kicked in the downbeat with a pickup on his snare.

The band's hour-long set included tunes from their first and second albums as well as a few new numbers they had recently added to their repertoire. One was an original by Paul and San Francisco songwriter Tucker Zimmerman called "Droppin' Out," an up-tempo march with a quirky two-bar interlude in waltz time. Played so fast that Butterfield had trouble getting in all the lyrics, "Droppin' Out" failed to swing in the way that most of the band's material did. But it featured Elvin Bishop's fuzz tone-enhanced rhythm guitar and a furious solo by Michael that touched on the modal sonorities used in "East-West." Paul also sang "Mother-in-Law Blues," a lament that Junior Parker had recorded in 1956. "Willow Tree," a shuffle played at a moderate tempo, was an original that drew lyrics from Papa Charlie Jackson's "She Belongs to Me Blues" and a few other sources. Paul and Michael took turns soloing in between the verses on "Willow Tree," and Elvin Bishop grabbed a few choruses as well.

In recent months, Elvin had begun to assert himself, taking more time in the spotlight. With his raw tone and uncomplicated lines, he was a perfect foil for Bloomfield's virtuosic intensity. In performance, the two guitarists usually occupied opposite ends of the bandstand—Michael standing stage right while Elvin took stage left. When they traded solos, staring at one another across the expanse of the stage, it almost seemed as if they were dueling. The impression given the crowd was of two musicians who had squared off, each attempting to outdo the other, which served to ramp up the excitement. That there may have been more than a modicum of truth to this impression only increased the drama of the moment.

For the band's opening night at the Winterland, Bloomfield and Bishop had taken their customary corners on the bandstand. Anticipation out in the audience for the band's closing number was high, because nearly everyone in the house expected it to be "East-West." With the two guitarists at opposite ends of the stage, flanking the band's leader, the scene seemed to be set for a guitar competition. It was true that few pop bands had a lead guitarist of Bloomfield's caliber, but it was also true that *no* other band had *two* lead guitarists. "Battling" soloists were a long-standing tradition in the jazz world, with tenor rivalries dating back as far as the 1930s in classic recordings by Count Basie stars Lester Young and Herschel Evans. But this was something new to popular music, made possible in large part by the Butterfield Band's emphasis on solos and by the supreme competence of the musicians who played those solos. It was yet another way that the band had become a crucible for the merging of previously disparate musical styles.

"We're gonna take it out right now, with a tune we recorded for our new album," Paul Butterfield announced from center stage. "It's called 'East-West.'" The crowd responded with cries of "Yeah!" and spontaneous applause as

Michael checked his tuning and Jerome Arnold ran through a few bass riffs. After a moment the harp player counted off the beat, and Bloomfield launched into the epic instrumental's rhythm riff with Arnold and Davenport in close support. Elvin was first up, soloing for a full five minutes to get the piece rolling. Butterfield followed and then, after the first crescendo, Michael took up the challenge and roared into the "Eastern" portion of the piece. The audience had been animated, grooving to the beat of the music, but now they stared transfixed, focused solely on the grimacing, gyrating figure onstage. As Bloomfield's lines grew in intensity and it seemed that he could get no hotter, he suddenly left off in mid-phrase and quickly circled around behind his amps. He bent over for a moment, then came back out front holding what looked like a drum mallet. The crowd was caught off guard—had the guitarist blown out his amplifiers? Was something wrong?

The music continued unabated. Suddenly the stage lights went down and a single spotlight picked out Bloomfield. He held up his left hand. In it was the "mallet," and with his right hand he quickly flicked a cigarette lighter. In an instant, the mallet was alight, its evil-looking yellow-orange flame spiraling upward and giving off ribbons of inky black smoke. Elvin began playing a drone on an open D, adding fuzz-tone distortion to his accompaniment, while Paul dropped in emphatic embellishments on harp. The music became louder, more insistent. After a moment, the band began building to another crescendo.

Bloomfield let the flaming stick become fully engulfed. He then slowly tipped his head back and raised his left arm. The crescendo gained in momentum. The guitarist angled the burning mallet down toward his mouth. It hung there in the air for an instant as the band's accompaniment roared. Then, just as the crescendo entered its final moments, Michael plunged the torch into his gaping mouth and blew out a rooster tail of gaudy flames. Billy Davenport accented the feat with a huge crash of his ride cymbal and then the Butterfield Band hit the second of the piece's three stops. The stage went dark.

The audience shrieked in amazement. Did Bloomfield really do *that*? Did he breath fire? *Too* cool! But before the house could regain its composure, the spotlights came up and Michael was again cradling his Les Paul. Billy Davenport reestablished the beat, now playing softly behind Jerome's new, major-sounding bass line. Michael began to solo, playing sweet melodies over their jazz-like accompaniment. "East-West" had moved into its melodic section. The crowd applauded in delight.

"If you can imagine a bunch of people being stoned on acid—I mean, it was enough of a spectacle to see this weird looking blues band, and then for a guy to start up doing some stuff like *that*," recalled Elvin Bishop, laughing. "I don't know . . . they must have had to carry a few people out!"

The piece lasted more than half an hour. Even Jerome Arnold was given a solo spot. When the final notes of "East-West" sounded and the band concluded its set, it was a little after 10:00 p.m. Everyone was spent and drenched with sweat. The group did a brief encore, playing "Got My Mojo Working" in tribute to Muddy Waters, and left the stage as the Winterland echoed with cheers and applause. It had been an exhilarating sixty minutes, but there was still a second set to play. And then they would have to do it all over again the next night.

The Winterland/Fillmore performances were so successful that Bill Graham arranged with ABGM to do three more weeks of shows with the Butterfield Band headlining. Graham decided to hold most of the programs at the Winterland, fearing that the Fillmore might too easily sell out. The Friday, Saturday, and Sunday shows for the weekend of September 30 again opened with the Jefferson Airplane and Muddy Waters, but on Saturday, a racially charged police shooting in the neighborhood caused Graham to move the remaining performances to the smaller venue. The following week Graham arranged for the band, in addition to their Winterland and Fillmore stints, to perform across the bay in Berkeley, this time at the University of California's Basketball Pavilion. Only the Butterfield Band and the Airplane appeared, as Muddy Waters had gone back to Chicago, but the performances were inspired, and Bloomfield even jammed with the Airplane during their set using Jorma Kaukonen's guitar.

To complete the October 7 and 8 Winterland billing, Graham added a quintet of former folk players that was becoming increasingly popular with San Francisco's counterculture movement. Called the Grateful Dead, the group played a healthy cross section of American musical styles from folk to country, blues, and rock, but they often did so in a less-than-polished manner. Michael Bloomfield wasn't impressed with their blues playing, calling them "amateurs," but that mattered little to the hometown crowd. Each of the three bands had their fans, and when combined on the same stage, Butterfield, the Airplane, and the Dead were a pop music trifecta. The weekend's final show, a Sunday matinee back at the Fillmore, drew another capacity crowd and provided a memorable afternoon of music for thousands of cheering San Franciscans.

The Butterfield Band nearly always closed their sets at the Winterland or the Fillmore with one of their long instrumentals—either "East-West" or Nat Adderley's "Work Song." When the choice was "East-West," Mike Bloomfield could be counted on to dazzle the audience right from the start with his virtuosic technique and furious soloing—whenever he wasn't eating fire. It was the same with "Work Song," except that Bloomfield would often do something strikingly different to launch his solo on the minor jazz blues. As far back as the band's performances at Poor Richard's in Chicago, Michael had been setting up a sonic framework for his "Work Song" improvisations by playing a series of whole- and half-note tones for as many as four full choruses. That portion of his solo came across as a sparse, almost meditative statement, standing apart from the onslaught that followed. It was an odd contrast, and one that intrigued more than a few fans in the audience. But Mark Naftalin knew exactly what his friend was doing.

"He was setting a mood," said Mark. "Establishing a sonority. He was trying out the notes he planned to use during his solo." Those notes sometimes included an A♮, the third pitch in the F-major scale. Because "Work Song" was in the key of F-minor, the A sounded particularly jarring. But Bloomfield was experimenting, playing a major third against a minor chord, in which the third is minor. That his probing, exploratory notes could sometimes sound odd or "wrong" seemed only to inspire Michael to emphasize them. "There was a certain amount of repetition when he did that," commented Naftalin. "He was creating an exotic flavor, hearing how the notes fit together and changed depending upon the accompaniment."

The guitarist was setting up possibilities, listening closely to what he was playing and then building on what he heard—and on the *implications* of what he heard. Unorthodox notes merely served to extend the scope of his musical understanding, to suggest other possibilities. The technique was one frequently used by jazz musicians, particularly those who were committed to pushing boundaries. John Coltrane often began his solos with a series of held notes or repeated phrases, sometimes extending the process over multiple choruses. He would create a framework and then build his solo from it, a method he began using while still a member of Miles Davis's band. Michael had seen Coltrane with Miles in 1959, a period of intense experimentation for the tenor saxophonist, and had heard Coltrane many times since. He had been greatly inspired by the legendary jazz man, and while he may not have been directly imitating Coltrane's method, Michael's approach was essentially the same. It was a way to open up new possibilities, to tap into the very essence of creativity in music.

The Butterfield Band did one more weekend for Bill Graham, this time playing all three shows at the Fillmore Auditorium. The Airplane again shared the bill, but now the third act was Big Mama Thornton, the blues belter who had nearly stolen the show at Monterey during Jon Hendricks's Blues All the Way program. It was another great weekend of contemporary blues and rock in the City by the Bay.

* * *

The month spent in San Francisco was a pleasant one for Michael Bloomfield and the rest of the Butterfield crew. They had been the first blues-rock band from out of town to be hired by local promoters, and because they arrived with a degree of professionalism and experience that most San Francisco bands lacked, they were admired by nearly everyone who heard them. Musicians watched the band closely, observing how they structured their performances, how they used their electric instruments—working with dynamics, sustain, and feedback—and how they integrated exciting solos into the tunes they performed. Guitarists in particular studied the group, copping licks, fingering techniques, and chord substitutions from Bishop and Bloomfield. Because Michael was so approachable, they frequently sought him out, asking for tips and a quick lesson or two. The gregarious guitarist relished sharing his knowledge—and his unbridled enthusiasm—with whoever asked. Word soon spread that Bloomfield was not only an extraordinary player but also a very friendly guy, someone who would talk with anyone about music. He had lots of opinions, it was true, but he knew what he was talking about, and he could back up whatever he said with his guitar. It wasn't long before everybody seemed to know who Michael was. People began stopping him on the street, calling his name from passing cars, waving as they went by. San Francisco began to feel just a little like home.

"I loved the ambience, and I loved the neighborhood," Bloomfield enthused years later about the City by the Bay. "I loved this area of the country, I loved the whole Haight Street scene, I loved taking acid, I loved all that pussy." For the first time since his days in Old Town, Michael began to feel comfortable in himself. And for the first time, he began to feel like a real celebrity. He liked the feeling.

CHAPTER 13

BLUES TO BRITAIN

LONDON, 1966

Immediately following the matinee show at the Fillmore on Sunday, October 16, their final gig for Bill Graham, the six members of the Paul Butterfield Blues Band boarded a plane at the San Francisco International Airport for a fourteen-hour flight to Heathrow Airport in London. They were off on their first overseas tour.

For the past month, Albert Grossman had been working with Elektra Records on a deal with Radio London to bring the band to England as part of a concert package. British pop star Georgie Fame was headlining a review that included rock and blues singer Eric Burdon and the New Animals; Rolling Stones cover artist Chris Farlowe; and soul shouter Geno Washington and his R&B backup ensemble, the Ram Jam Band. The four groups were heavily featured in Radio London's daily rotation, and the station, a "pirate broadcaster" with its transmitter located on a former US Navy minesweeper moored three miles off the English coast in the North Sea, had organized a series of sixteen nationwide concerts. The program would also include several lesser-known local bands, with the Paul Butterfield Blues Band added almost as an afterthought.

The American group was largely unknown outside of London, and they had received very little airplay over Radio London, despite the fact that, in anticipation of the tour, Elektra had released "All These Blues" backed with "Never Say No" as a single in England. The push was on to generate European sales for *East-West*, and the company was hoping that by pairing Butterfield with some of Britain's top performers, the band would be able to connect with thousands of pop music fans across the country. The tour would be an intense eighteen days of traveling to venues, setting up, playing short sets, breaking down equipment, reloading, and then getting back on the bus for the return trip to London. It would be strenuous, but both Elektra and ABGM saw the junket as the best way to expand the Butterfield Band's popularity and promote sales in a new market.

The band members were largely unconcerned. It was the first time any of them had been out of the country, and the first time they had ever been part of an official "tour." Nearly everyone was excited, looking forward to meeting some of their British contemporaries and checking out London's blues scene. The prospect of four weeks of hard traveling did little to dampen their enthusiasm. But there was one exception—Mike Bloomfield was dreading it.

Sleep on the road continued to be a constant problem for Bloomfield. He knew that any long stretch of time away from home and familiar surroundings could exacerbate his chronic wakefulness. Going abroad, with its attendant time change, would almost certainly worsen the condition. He would have to cope the best he could, but he knew it wouldn't be easy.

On the long flight over to London, Michael read while the rest of Butterfield's party did their best to sleep. The plane flew through the Arctic night over northern Canada and Greenland and on into the European dawn and day, touching down at Heathrow at 4:00 p.m. local time. For the travelers, it was a groggy 8:00 a.m. back in San Francisco. They sleepily ambled off the plane and across the tarmac to the terminal building, where they collected their luggage and caught taxis for the sixteen-mile ride into downtown London. It was nearly time for afternoon tea.

Albert Grossman arranged a press conference for the Butterfield Band at Ronnie Scott's, London's famous jazz club, shortly after their arrival at Heathrow. Though the rest of the band was visibly combating jet lag, Bloomfield, accustomed to sleepless nights, was as animated as ever. During the meet-up with the media, he did most of the talking. Responding to a question about the band's impressions of London, Michael described his surprise at the reception they had received from the public.

"I've spent the day driving around London ever since we got in," Michael said, "and I realized that musicians and blues fans have been buying our records and talking about us, but that we're not known among the general public."

Michael had anticipated a different response from people he met on the street. Bob Dylan had told him stories about being mobbed at his 1965 London concerts and not being able to leave his hotel room without attracting a crowd. Bloomfield had also seen *A Hard Day's Night*, with its mad chase scenes as the Beatles fled from their crazed fans. He wasn't expecting the Butterfield Band to be greeted at the airport by hordes of hysterical, screaming teenagers, but he fully expected to be recognized by more than a few passersby on Carnaby Street. Michael sounded almost disappointed that no one seemed to know who he was.

But he went on to respond with real enthusiasm to a reporter's question about the British blues scene, offering unqualified praise. His low opinion of

London's blues bands had changed since his interview for *Hit Parader* in July, largely because of the talents of one guitarist. That player he singled out as on a par with no less a talent than B. B. King. "Eric Clapton, he's one of the best guitarists," Michael said. "I just haven't got words to describe him. Man, I'm jealous—I wish I could play like that."

Bloomfield had heard Clapton's groundbreaking guitar work with John Mayall on Mayall's *Blues Breakers*, an album of raw electric blues that had been released in July. Clapton also appeared on an Elektra sampler, another of Jac Holzman's budget LPs that had come out in August. Titled *What's Shakin'*, the record featured five selections by the Butterfield Band from its first aborted album and included three tunes by Eric with a group called Powerhouse. Bloomfield could hear that the Englishman fully understood the blues idiom and was a gifted soloist. He said he was eager to meet Eric while the Butterfield Band was in England.

Butterfield himself then managed to quietly answer a few questions about his blues influences before a query about *East-West* brought Bloomfield charging back into the discussion. According to one reporter, the star guitarist was so animated he "bubbled." "You've *got* to see us live, man," Bloomfield enthused. "It's nothing like on the record. We're moving forward all the time and really working on modern, electronic and progressive blues."

The first chance London got to hear a few members of the Paul Butterfield Blues Band live was several days later. The Americans spent all of Tuesday resting up, trying to recoup the hours they had lost on the flight over, but on Wednesday, October 19, they paid a visit to the Scotch of St. James, a small club located at the back of a courtyard off Duke Street St. James's in the center of London. Performing that night with his new band was the guitarist that Michael had praised so enthusiastically. Eric Clapton was appearing with Cream, a collaborative trio he had formed with drummer Ginger Baker and bassist Jack Bruce after leaving Mayall. They were gigging around London while recording material for their second album. It was Bloomfield's first opportunity to see Clapton play, and he was as impressed by the British guitarist in person as he had been with Clapton's recordings. He and Paul got up and jammed with the trio on a few blues numbers, and Eric was equally impressed by his American counterpart. After the show, the two sat and talked about music, the blues, and the American and British scenes. Michael was more hyped up than usual, operating on pure adrenaline after nearly two days without sleep, and he overwhelmed the Englishman with his ideas and opinions.

"His way of thinking really shocked me the first time I met him and spoke to him," said Clapton of the voluble Chicagoan. "I never met anyone with so many strong convictions."

Two years Michael's junior, Eric Clapton had grown up in Ripley, Surrey, a small village some twenty-five miles southwest of London. While in secondary school, he had been given a guitar and by age fifteen had mastered the basics of the blues. Like Bloomfield, Eric learned by listening to records and practicing long hours, working to get every lick or chord progression just right. Michael's access to the real thing on Chicago's South Side gave him a distinct advantage, but Clapton had somehow managed to absorb the music and become a proficient player simply by listening. Now in their early twenties, both guitarists were devoted to the blues, and both were acknowledged in their respective countries as exciting and talented players.

But there the similarities ended. The two musicians' personalities could not have been more different. Where Bloomfield was impulsive and outgoing, Clapton was polite and reserved, almost shy. Michael's sense of humor was broad and mischievous; Eric's could be cutting and sarcastic. While Bloomfield had become a more disciplined and professional musician since joining Butterfield, Clapton had been playing in organized bands since age seventeen. He had come up through the British club system, working regular gigs in venues around the country with bands that dressed neatly, started and ended on time, and could be depended upon to play a proper set of popular tunes. Groups on the circuit had managers, booking agencies, rigorous schedules—and, in some cases, recording contracts. Clapton's half decade of club work not only allowed him to hone his skills as a guitarist but also gave him a thorough schooling in how to be a professional musician.

In 1963 Eric joined a London-based R&B group called the Yardbirds. At a time when Mike Bloomfield was still playing the occasional University of Chicago twist party, jamming in South Side clubs, and playing for spare change on Maxwell Street, Clapton was performing nightly at the Crawdaddy Club, where the Yardbirds had been hired to replace the Rolling Stones. By the end of 1964, Eric had recorded three singles with the group for Columbia, and one of them—"For Your Love"—had sold over a million copies. His subsequent work with John Mayall cemented Clapton's reputation as a star blues guitarist, and by the time he and Michael met at the Scotch of St. James, the Englishman's six-string prowess was being extolled on walls across the country with the slogan "Clapton is God."

By comparison, Mike Bloomfield's musical career seemed haphazard and largely serendipitous. His mercurial nature, his inclination to push boundaries and buck authority—the "rock 'n' roll rebel" in him—precluded the discipline necessary for the sort of organized, steady ascent Clapton had attained. The American popular music scene also lacked the cohesion found among British venues, a de facto circuit that provided steady employment for hundreds of local bands. England had what amounted to a "farm system" for its popular musicians, while in the States performers were left to their own devices. That doubtless suited Michael's freewheeling nature, but it had in some ways limited his career choices—at least until he joined the Butterfield Band. Paul was a paragon of discipline, and under his leadership Bloomfield got his musical life on track and began receiving the national attention his astonishing talent merited. Had he remained on his own, he might not have achieved even a portion of the status Clapton enjoyed. After all, Columbia still had done nothing with the nine tunes he recorded for them two years earlier.

Despite these differences, Michael very much liked the British bluesman. He marveled at Clapton's technique, his ability to play all tempos with equal agility, to build solos that ranged over the entire neck and incorporated an arsenal of exciting blues licks. He was also impressed by Clapton's seemingly limitless knowledge of classic blues tunes. "I knew that he couldn't play the far out way that I could play, like on 'East-West' and stuff like that," Bloomfield later said. "But as far as straight blues, he was as good as they got. . . . [H]e was just *so* good." Clapton's virtuosity didn't intimidate Michael. He understood completely what the English guitarist was doing and appreciated it fully. Jimmy Hendrix's highly original and unorthodox guitar technique had left Michael at a loss, but what Eric was doing was as familiar to the Chicagoan as his own blues playing.

Bloomfield was also awed by Clapton's sound. "His tone was exquisite. He had a kind of vibrato that was like Itzak Perlman. Just a slow, exquisite vibrato, very languorous, melodic and soulful." Clapton was playing a striking, flame-red Les Paul Standard guitar, a model that was introduced by Gibson in 1958 as a replacement for its Goldtop line. Sales had been disappointing, and the company had dropped the model, affectionately known as the "Sunburst," in 1960. But the instrument had always been popular with blues guitarists because of its warm tone and exceptional sustain capabilities. Les Paul Sunbursts were fitted with pickups called "humbuckers," an improvement over the noisier single-coil versions on Goldtops. The new hardware reduced the Les Paul's buzzy hum and gave the Standard model its characteristic clean, full sound. Clapton had mastered the Sunburst's tonal capabilities and used them brilliantly in creating blues-rock versions of Robert Johnson's "From Four until Late" and "Cross Road Blues," as well as Skip James's "I'm So Glad" and numerous blues-based originals by Cream.

Michael knew the Les Paul Sunburst well. It had been the guitar he originally had in mind when he met John Nuese in Cambridge the previous November and swapped his Telecaster for Nuese's Goldtop. In the spring of 1965, he had become friendly with John Sebastian, the guitarist and harmonica player for the folk-rock group the Lovin' Spoonful, while staying at the Hotel Albert in New York. The Spoonful rehearsed at the Albert, and Sebastian had a Sunburst that he occasionally used. Bloomfield played it whenever he could.

"He loved that guitar," Sebastian said. "Michael was always asking to borrow it, but I never did let him take it. I knew better!" Bloomfield's reputation for abusing instruments was well known by then.

But now that he heard what Clapton could do with a Sunburst, Michael was determined to get one for himself. He wanted that beautiful tone. His Goldtop had a raw, powerful sound, but it wasn't as clean as the Sunburst's, and it tended to get muddy when he played chords at high volume. And then there was the fact that Michael's Les Paul, after a year on the road, was in less than ideal shape. Somewhere along the way, the guitar had lost its rhythm pickup tone knob and the screws fastening its plug jack had stripped and fallen out. Bloomfield taped the jack back in, but it had a tendency to pop out whenever he got too animated onstage. It was definitely time for a new instrument, and Michael decided it would be a Sunburst.

The next day, Thursday, October 20, the Georgie Fame tour kicked off its three-week road trip with a gala appearance at the Astoria Theatre in Finsbury Park, north London. Seven acts performed, including the four headliners. Chris Farlowe's backup band, the Thunderbirds, did their own set following the Butterfield Band and a quintet called Eyes of Blue, the show's openers. In between groups, DJs from Radio London kept up a steady stream of hip patter, promoting the station, its sponsors, and the recordings of whatever band was up next. Each group had a new single to hype during their set, thus limiting whatever else they could play, and sets were kept brief in order to keep things moving. Right away, the Butterfield Band ran into trouble.

"We didn't have but fifteen minutes on the stage, so we really couldn't play 'East-West,'" remembered Billy Davenport. The band also couldn't get their equipment to work. English wall sockets wouldn't take American plugs, which was fortunate because the local grid put out 220 volts—enough to fry the group's 120-volt Fender amplifiers. As a result, the Butterfield Band limped along with borrowed equipment for the first week of the tour. Until they could get their own amplifiers modified, they weren't at all happy with their sound.

But that first night was a chance to hear some of London's top performers, and Paul Butterfield thought Georgie Fame was very good. Mike Bloomfield was impressed by Chris Farlowe's guitar player, Albert Lee. Geno Washington's group, the Ram Jam Band, rocked hard and used horns effectively, and Eric Burdon's keyboard player, Dave Rowberry, won Paul's approval. The audience packed the three-thousand-seat theater and cheered the familiar acts, and even though Eric Burdon, who was backed up by a new edition of the Animals, was heckled by a few in the crowd, *Melody Maker* declared the evening a "great show."

In the vast audience that night was one familiar face, at least to the Americans. Guitarist Jimmy Hendrix—now *Jimi* Hendrix—had arrived in London just three weeks before the Butterfield Band. While playing at the Cafe Wha? in New York City that September, the flamboyant guitarist had connected with former Animals bass player Chas Chandler, and Chandler, signing on as Hendrix's manager, had brought him to England in search of a record contract. Hendrix hastily assembled a trio, and the group had just returned from a week of gigs in France, their first-ever performances. He and Chandler stopped by the Astoria to catch the review and hobnob with some of Britain's biggest pop stars. The new manager was taking every opportunity to introduce the unknown American to as many musicians and music industry people as possible, getting his name out and touting him as a major new talent. For his part, Jimi was eager to see the Butterfield Band—and especially Michael Bloomfield—in a review with a sampling of London's best groups. When the Chicagoans took the stage early in the show, Hendrix was amused to see Michael hamstrung by having to play through a mid-sized Klemt Echolette, a German-made amplifier belonging to the Ram Jam Band's guitarist, Pete Gage.

But the blues band from Chicago sounded tight, and Paul's electrified harmonica wowed many in the audience—few had seen or heard the instrument played in that fashion. The band charged through a short set that included "All These Blues," their current single, and closed with a rousing rendition of "Got My Mojo Working" in an arrangement by jazz organist Jimmy Smith. The applause at the end was spirited, but nothing like the response the group had inspired at the Fillmore only a week earlier. The Finsbury audience was waiting for current hit makers Chris Farlowe, Eric Burdon, and especially Georgie Fame, whose recently released version of Bobby Hebb's "Sunny" was one of Radio London's top-five records.

"I don't think we were a fairly raving success," Elvin Bishop said, remembering the band's cool reception while with the tour. "I don't think they knew what to make of us. . . . [T]here were a lot of rock acts on the bill and that's who was gettin' over."

It was going to be a long three weeks for the Paul Butterfield Blues Band.

* * *

The next morning, the tour entourage boarded several chartered buses for a two-hour drive to Birmingham. Instruments and gear were stowed in the buses' lower luggage compartments, and the thirty-three musicians, along with assorted Radio London personalities, roadies, and technicians, found seats and settled in for the trip. They were headed for the Odeon Theatre in the center of Birmingham, England's second largest city. Radio London and its partners had contracted with the Gaumont-British Picture Corporation, owner of nearly 350 movie theaters, to present the tour's performances in sixteen different picture palaces across the country. Variously named "Gaumont" or "Odeon," the theaters featured super-sized screens, multitiered seating for thousands, and wide proscenium stages. They were perfect for musical reviews of the sort Radio London was offering with big draws like Georgie Fame, Eric Burdon, and Chris Farlowe.

The buses arrived in the early afternoon at the downtown theater. While the support crew hauled in the equipment; set up amps, drums, and microphones; and tested the PA, the musicians wandered off in search of food and refreshment. They were scheduled to play two complete shows that evening, and no one had eaten since breakfast. By late afternoon, the tour's managers were running sound checks, arranging microphones, and setting levels as each band in quick succession took the stage and ran through a number or two. Outside, the sun was setting and evening was coming on, and fans were already queuing up at the theater's box office.

The show began promptly at 6:00 p.m., opening as it had in Finsbury Park with Eyes of Blue. The house was nearly sold out, and the audience was as enthusiastic as it had been the night before, cheering the headliners and standing for much of the show. Geno Washington got them going with a few driving soul numbers, including his latest hit, "Que Sera Sera," a tune originally recorded by pop singer and movie star Doris Day that Washington recast as an R&B stomper. Eric Burdon followed with a set that culminated in a wild, rollicking vamp on "Help Me Girl," his latest single. By the time Chris Farlowe and then Georgie Fame took the stage, the girls in the crowd were nearly drowning out the music with their screams. Fame, with his boyish good looks, elicited frenzied shrieks whenever he gestured toward the audience or executed a few dance steps.

The Butterfield Band played their tunes at the start of the show and once again were politely received. There were no screams when they came out onstage, and no one clapped in recognition as they began their songs—few in the audience had ever heard them before. When Michael and Elvin soloed, it was hard to hear what they were playing over the sound of Billy Davenport's drums in the cavernous theater. Because none of the other guitarists in the review played real solos, the stage hands had set the volume on the amplifiers to a conservative level. As a consequence, it was difficult for Michael to get the sustain and dynamic range he normally used with the band. The audience also wasn't prepared for long blues solos—they were there to hear songs they knew from the radio sung live by some of their favorite pop singers. The review format worked well for that purpose, but it wasn't really suited to music that frequently emphasized long improvisations over vocals—just the sort of music the Butterfield Band played. In a roster filled with cheery Beatle-coiffed lads in matching suits and go-go boots, Butterfield's men stood out like stevedores at a poetry reading.

Their brief set was over well before 7:00 p.m., and that meant Paul, Michael, and the rest of the band had a couple of hours to kill before they went onstage again for the second show. They milled around backstage, went out for food, chatted with the review's other band members, and tried not to watch the clock. Following Georgie Fame's final encore, the house was cleared and the stage reset for the next run through. After thirty minutes, the late show audience began taking their seats, and this time the theater appeared to be sold out. The program started right on time, at 8:40 p.m., with Radio London's DJ Mark Roman welcoming the crowd, hyping the acts, and talking up the station. Then the performances began again. When the Butterfield Band appeared, there seemed to be louder applause and even a few cheers—obviously there were more blues fans in the audience for the second show.

The review finished up at a little past 11:00 p.m. It took another hour for the roadies to pack up and load all the equipment. Many of the performers were already in their seats on the buses, and some were sleeping while others were playing cards or reading. It was after midnight when the caravan pulled out and headed southeast on M6, and it was almost 2:00 a.m. when the buses pulled into downtown London. The passengers roused themselves, gathered their instruments and belongings, and headed off into the night. The Butterfield Band caught taxis to their hotel and beds.

So ended their first full day on the road with the Radio London Georgie Fame package tour.

Over the next sixteen days, the Butterfield Band would be on the road constantly, traveling to towns like Doncaster, Manchester, Liverpool, Bristol, and Southampton, and even venturing as far north as Newcastle and Glasgow in Scotland. When it wasn't practical to return to London following a show, the bands would spend the night in a local hotel or—for those who wanted to save money—on the buses. Though the musicians were given a day off each week to recover from their travels, the tour quickly became an ordeal for Michael Bloomfield.

During one of the tour's off days, Bloomfield gave an interview to *Melody Maker*, sharing his views on the British pop music scene and discussing the state of blues back home in Chicago. The reporter was amused by Michael's animated demeanor, describing him as "gesticulating madly as he puts a point over" and equating his "dynamic" personality with his volatile guitar playing.

In the interview, Michael again praised Eric Clapton and lauded guitarist Jeff Beck, whom he had met in Los Angeles in January when the Yardbirds were touring the States. "They wouldn't know what hit them if those cats went over to America and started sitting in around Chicago," he declared. But Chicago's blues scene, Bloomfield sadly noted, was in decline. "The truth is that blues isn't really making it in America. American white people don't know what it's about," he said. What about the Butterfield Band? the interviewer asked. "Well, I think it's very good!" the guitarist enthused. But he added, "Our tastes are changing and our band's getting kind of amorphous. Personally, I'm interested in how bands with horns play—I mean bands all the way from Don Redman to Gil Evans." Skipping over Michael's coy reference to two great jazz arrangers, the reporter touched on the complex issue of race and music. Could whites really play blues as well as blacks? It was a question Bloomfield had been answering since his early days sitting in on the South Side, and he replied unequivocally:

> I think that anybody with a knowledge of the idiom knows if you're playing good blues—if you're putting something down. I agree with what Paul Butterfield says about this: that the only cats who put white blues down are people with bad racial attitudes in the first place. I don't care whose throat the sounds are coming out of. It sounds the same to me if it's pleasing to my ears.

In a telling moment, Michael told the interviewer that even though the Butterfield Band had plenty of gigs, he wasn't too happy about it. "There's a lot of work, although personally I hate going on the road. I prefer to stay right in Chicago." Unfortunately, staying anywhere for more than a day was the one thing he couldn't do while in England.

The Chicagoans wound up their three-week road trip with final performances with the revue at the Odeon Theatre in Leicester on Sunday, November 6. Though the Radio London tour had been a taxing experience, the Butterfield Band's British sojourn was hardly over. ABGM had set up two additional weeks of club gigs in and around the city to showcase the band to London's musical elite while promoting *East-West* for Elektra.

Following a day off, the group opened at a club in Kensington on Tuesday evening, playing to a packed house of musicians, hipsters, dancers, and scene-makers of every stripe. Called Blaises, the small venue was located in the basement of the Imperial Hotel on Queen's Gate and was one of the city's most popular nightclubs. The crowd, described as "riotous" in one report, was there to see the American blues band with its harp-playing leader and its virtuoso lead guitarist. They had heard the Butterfield Band's albums and they had read about Paul and Michael, but they wanted to see for themselves if the Chicagoans were as good as their press. Everyone on the scene in London knew that Eric Clapton was the world's greatest blues-rock guitarist, but many said Mike Bloomfield was as good. Plus, Bloomfield played some pretty far-out stuff on the latest Butterfield Band release. The question on the minds of many in the audience at Blaises that Tuesday was a simple one: Who's better, Clapton or Bloomfield?

It was a query that the music publication *Disc* extended to the guitarists' respective bands. Because Cream, Clapton's trio, was playing at the Marquee Club in Soho that same night, the magazine had "a unique opportunity to judge the best of what's happening here and across the Atlantic." *Disc*'s reporter caught shows by both groups, and though he credited the Chicagoans with the more authentic blues background and cited Bloomfield and Elvin Bishop as "two of the best guitarists in the country," he preferred the hometown team. "Clapton's guitar work is unbelievable, at times sounding like a horn," he enthused. The Butterfield Band was good, "but they could not do any better than a couple of tracks off their last album." Cream was also superior in volume, a harbinger of popular music's future. The reporter noted that the trio "produced enough noise—good noise—to blast out everyone's eardrums down at the Marquee." Clapton's huge Marshall amp could indeed be deafening.

But Paul, Michael, and Elvin were not without serious firepower of their own. Midway through the tour, Butterfield road manager Mark Dorinson had managed to retrofit the band's Fender amps with transformers and new plugs so they would work on English current. The muscular Twin Reverbs were brought back into service for the remainder of their British sojourn, and they added a much-needed boost to the Butterfield Band's sound.

On Wednesday, Michael paid a visit to Olympic Studios on Church Road in West London. The Rolling Stones were recording there for their next album, and Bloomfield was curious to meet the group considered by most American listeners to be a "blues band." He wanted to see if they really knew anything about blues at all. When he got there, Michael talked his way into the studio and was pleased to discover that the Stones knew who he was. Guitarists Keith Richards and Brian Jones welcomed their American colleague, taking a break from the overdubbing they were doing for a tune that Richards had written called "Ruby Tuesday." They asked Bloomfield about the scene in Chicago and told stories of their recording sessions at Chess Studios in the summer of 1964. Michael was surprised to discover that Brian Jones knew nearly as much about the music as he did. The two got into a deep discussion of obscure blues artists and rare recordings, comparing favorite tunes and players. Singer Marianne Faithfull, Mick Jagger's girlfriend, was also in the studio that afternoon, and she remembered Jones making a musical connection that Bloomfield had never considered.

"Brian was obsessed by his notion of a hybrid of Elizabethan lute music and Delta blues," wrote Faithful, "and would hold forth on the essential similarities between Elizabethan ballads and Robert Johnson to anyone who would listen—a bemused Michael Bloomfield or an incredulous Jimi Hendrix, for instance."

Bloomfield came away from the session with a new respect for England's top blues-rock band. His talk with Brian Jones convinced him that there was more substance behind the Rolling Stones' output than he had originally thought. He still considered their music derivative and their musicianship suspect, but he recognized in Jones, at least, a fellow traveler, a musician whose interest in blues, like his own, went far beyond the latest fad or trend.

The following day, it was the Butterfield Band that headlined at the Marquee, and then the band traveled north for two shows later in the week in Manchester. On Sunday they were back in town to perform at the RamJam Club in Brixton, then on Monday they appeared in North London at the Cooks Ferry Inn, the country's oldest jazz club. There, between sets, they were interviewed by the *International Times*, a newly launched "underground" newspaper based in London. The question of race was again raised, and the reporter pointedly asked: "The blues is basically a negro form. Can the white man really play it?"

"You have ears, don't you? You heard Paul play," retorted Michael Bloomfield. He then added, "I think an important thing though to be playing blues, if you're white, and why most cats fuck up and can't do it, is because they only hear it on records." With that observation, Michael casually dismissed most of England's blues players. Though he sincerely admired Clapton, Beck, and many of the country's other blues-rock guitarists, he was not above pulling rank when it came to authenticity. When asked about the Butterfield Band's future, Bloomfield replied, "We don't really know where we're going." He then elaborated on the group's development over the last year:

> We still play blues, but so many other things also. When we started this group each of us were fairly good musicians but nothing too special, but since that time we have improved vastly, man, vastly. All of us have learned much more about music, from Coltrane to Dixieland. And all that is coming out in our playing. . . . It has completely evolved naturally, nothing has been planned at all. We've tightened up the group, we've gotten tighter, cleaner, sharper arrangements. Things are worked out a little better. Nobody is planning on going anywhere. It evolves, man, it's a natural evolvement, like a crystal growth. Any sound they hear, they're going to say, "unmistakably the Butterfield Band."

Once again, Bloomfield dominated the conversation. Paul, Elvin, and Mark got in a few comments, but it was primarily Michael who spoke for the group. The reporter concluded the interview by asking how African American listeners responded to the Butterfield Band.

"Depends on the individuals," said Bloomfield. "Some cats are jealous and up-tight because they are assholes. And some cats are not up-tight." Did some blacks say whites can't play the blues? "Sure," quipped Michael. "And then we cram it down their fucking throats. All right, watch *this*, motherfucker!" The "can-whites-play-blues" question had come up often enough over the last sixteen months that the guitarist's patience had worn thin. Gone was the generous, self-effacing attitude Bloomfield evinced for filmmaker Murray Lerner at the Newport Folk Festival. In its place was an apparently unshakable confidence in his own ability as a blues player and a mature sense of his worth as a musician. His race was irrelevant. Good blues playing was good blues playing, period.

On Tuesday, the Butterfield Band went to Associated-Rediffusion Studios, a large television facility in Wembley. There the group was taped for a television appearance, a segment for the popular Friday evening TV program *Ready Steady Go!* The thirty-minute show aired over the ITV network and featured popular music acts and dancers performing for an enthusiastic audience of young fans. Unlike many music shows of the day, *RSG!* allowed its artists to play full versions of their hits, and by 1965 it was having groups perform live. The show aired nationwide and regularly presented top British acts like the Beatles, the Rolling Stones, the Who, and the Dave Clark Five as well as American stars like Otis Redding, James Brown, and the Beach Boys.

The Butterfield Band and the show's other performers had to arrive early in the afternoon so the program's technical staff could block out their performances in advance and prerecord whatever accompaniment was needed. Each group in turn rehearsed a few numbers while *RSG!*'s cameramen circled their huge floor units around, seeking the best spots for catching the action. Appearing on that Friday's program along with the blues band from Chicago were the American vocal quartet the Four Tops; Dusty Springfield's backup singers, the Breakaways; British mod group the Small Faces; and the Butterfield Band's former touring mate Eric Burdon.

That week, Elektra was scheduled to release the band's second *East-West* single in both the United States and England. Bloomfield's searing interpretation of "I Got a Mind to Give Up Living," a tune that had been included in the album, formed the new 45's B-side. The A-side, however, featured a song that was being released for the first time. An original Paul had written with Michael and Elvin called "Come On In," the song was a high-energy R&B-style tune that had little to do with the blues. Sung by Butterfield, it was the logical choice for the band to play on national television, at least from a marketing perspective. But Butterfield decided instead to do "Droppin' Out," an original the band had been playing for a few months but had not yet recorded.

Once preparations were complete, the *RSG!* studio audience was brought in and dancers positioned themselves around the set. On cue, emcee Cathy McGowan introduced the program as the audience moved to the sounds of the Supremes' "You Keep Me Hanging On," and then she brought on the Small Faces. When it was the Butterfield Band's turn, Paul sang and played live while Michael and the rest of the band mimed to a rhythm track they had recorded earlier. The segment featured tight shots of the leader and close-ups of Bloomfield grimacing as he re-created his earlier guitar solo at the end of the tune. In ten minutes the taping was completed, and in fifteen minutes the band was on its way to its next performance. They would have to see the rest of the show when it aired on Friday evening.

The Butterfield Band's Tuesday night gig was in a club situated in a quintessentially British locale. The band was scheduled to perform in the middle of London's famed Thames River.

"The place was on Eel Pie Island," said Mark Naftalin. "It was known as a haunt of the Stones, so we were told." Located nearly twenty miles upriver from the center of London, the small river island was home to several dozen residents, a hotel, and a cavernous, members-only rock club called Eelpiland. Opened in the 1950s, the eccentric venue had become a favorite hangout not only of the Rolling Stones but also of Eric Clapton, John Mayall, the Yardbirds, and many other British musicians.

"The place was memorable because in order to get your equipment into the club you had to wheel it over some kind of narrow footbridge," Naftalin said with a laugh. The Butterfield Band moved all their gear over the walkway above the river and into the Eel Pie Hotel, in whose large, dingy ballroom Eelpiland was located. Though it was only Tuesday, a sizeable crowd turned out to see the American blues band, dance, and quaff Harp lager. The Butterfield Band did two raucous sets with a couple of local bands opening for them, and they might even have sampled the hotel's specialty—meat pies generously stuffed with the island's namesake.

The Chicagoans then finished out the week with two shows in Birmingham and one in the Golders Green section of London. On Friday afternoon, Paul Butterfield joined John Mayall and his band, the Bluesbreakers, in a studio in West Hempstead, North London, for a recording session Elektra had arranged with Mayall's label, Decca. The four tunes that resulted, all featuring Butterfield's powerful harp, were later issued under Mayall's name on an EP. It would be the only recorded evidence of Butterfield's trip overseas.

On Saturday night, November 19, a dance concert in Lewes officially brought the Paul Butterfield Blues Band's tour of Great Britain to an end. The group had been abroad for thirty-four days, played twenty-nine venues, and given nearly sixty performances. They had logged over three thousand miles traveling around the country in buses and vans, staying in a variety of hotels and hostels, sleeping wherever possible, and grabbing something to eat whenever there was a moment. They had met scores of musicians, played with most of them, and heard many more; had been interviewed and written up in the London press; and had performed for thousands of enthusiastic British rock and blues fans. They had been largely unknown when they arrived in London in mid-October, but now English groups were attempting to play some of their signature tunes. Two singles had been released while they were in the country, and their latest album had started getting airplay. By any measure, the trip was a resounding success. While the Butterfield Band's reception hadn't approached anything like the hysteria that greeted Bob Dylan when he made his controversial visit to England earlier in the year, Albert Grossman and ABGM were satisfied that the Chicagoans had increased their fan base and had been very well received. Elektra, too, was happy with the band's record sales. Everyone was pleased.

Everyone, that is, except Michael Bloomfield.

With his chronic insomnia profoundly aggravated by the band's nonstop performing and constant traveling, the twenty-four-year-old guitarist was physically exhausted. As the Butterfield entourage filed into the gate at Heathrow Airport on Sunday afternoon and queued up to board the flight home, Michael collapsed into a seat by the check-in counter. For once, he had very little to say. He was simply worn out. While he had consistently given extraordinary performances and managed to cope without sleeping for days at a time, he was emotionally spent. His usual ebullience and boundless enthusiasm were at a low ebb. And even though he was headed home, he knew the Butterfield Band was still going to have to travel. It was left to Susan to check their bags and get their boarding passes.

At least they weren't going all the way to California. The flight back to the States was only eight hours because the band's destination was New York City. Albert Grossman had arranged for the Paul Butterfield Blues Band to play a triumphant return engagement at Town Hall on West Forty-Third Street. The Thanksgiving show was set for Saturday, November 26, giving the Chicagoans five full days to rest up.

Back in the United States, the members of the Butterfield Band checked into rooms at the familiar Hotel Albert in the Village and, despite the place's grime and questionable clientele, were glad to be back home. Mike Bloomfield, as tired as he was, had an additional reason to be pleased. At one of the newsstands around Washington Square, he picked up a copy of *Crawdaddy*, the New York–based rock 'n' roll publication that had interviewed the Butterfield Band in Boston that summer. The October issue contained a lengthy transcription of the interview as well as an in-depth review of *East-West*. Bloomfield was featured prominently in both, and as he read through the issue stretched out on the bed in the hotel room while Susan unpacked their bags, he gradually came to a realization.

"I always knew I was good, and took it for granted," Michael later told an interviewer.

> There were always good people around me, or *better* people, and I always wanted to play like them. I never knew about [my own virtuosity] until I read a review in *Crawdaddy* . . . when I had done the Butterfield *East-West* album. They were talking about rock 'n' roll guitar in America and putting it in a sort of folkloric perspective that I had always put music into, but had never really looked at myself in that way. And then I knew I was *really* hot shit.

The reviewer, Jon Landau, seemed unable to decide whether he really liked *East-West*. He praised the group, describing it as "happening" and acknowledging that "live, of course, everybody raves about the kind of excitement this band creates when it's having a good night." But in a piece that ran to nearly 1,700 words, Landau took the album apart tune by tune, comparing those that were covers to the originals, analyzing arrangements and the recording production, and singling out each band member, parsing their contributions and enumerating their shortcomings. It was a review unlike any other the band had yet received, and it treated the music with a respect, a "folkloric" seriousness that, while not terribly complimentary, clearly implied that *East-West* was a work of historical and cultural merit.

Accordingly, Landau was unsparing in his criticism. He denigrated each band member's contribution in turn, coolly enumerating their shortcomings. The album's saving grace, he then asserted, was its lead guitarist. "Mike Bloomfield is the outstanding musician of the group," Landau wrote. "In fact, I consider Mike the best lead guitarist I've heard in any rock band, even though I'm basically a rock addict and the music here is mostly blues." He went on to proffer praise that must have brought Michael a rush of pleasure: "His technique, his phrasing, his timing, and his taste are all extraordinary. The only one who can come close is Jeff Beck, but Jeff hasn't yet recorded anything that compares to what Bloomfield has done."

Having just returned from London, where he encountered blues players who were every bit as good as any in Chicago, and having seen himself compared to them in the British press, Bloomfield must have found Landau's reference to Jeff Beck particularly satisfying. Michael had been greatly impressed by Beck's playing when he first saw him with the Yardbirds earlier in the year, and he readily acknowledged to anyone who asked that the Brit was a master. But Bloomfield's competitive nature, coupled with a curious insecurity about his own playing, often compelled him to overly praise those he found more than a little intimidating musically. As his friend and former manager Joel Harlib said, Michael was "this incredible egotist who really enjoyed attention," but he was also "very insecure." When Bloomfield felt someone else's talent merited attention, he would give it as a way to deflect the obvious comparison with his own. That Landau placed him above Jeff Beck—and didn't even *mention* Eric Clapton—could have only sent Michael's self-esteem through the roof.

The critic concluded the review by all but dismissing the album's title selection. But even as he took "East-West" to task, he once again lauded Bloomfield. "The cut could more appropriately have been titled 'Fooling Around with Indian Sounds,' because that's all that really happens. Bloomfield provides us with the only playing of any real note (it seems that he can make anything sound good)."

Landau's article was a serious piece of music criticism published in the first serious publication concerned with contemporary rock 'n' roll. It confirmed

Mike Bloomfield's status as one of the best—if not *the* best—guitarists in the world of popular music. Michael realized that he was important, that his artistry and what he did with it mattered. It gave him a new sense of confidence and purpose. As he candidly said after reading *Crawdaddy*, "I knew I was *really* hot shit."

On Saturday, November 26, the Paul Butterfield Blues Band played its first gig in America in over a month. The group was by now well rested and eager to get back onstage, and newspaper ads for their appearance at Town Hall listed the show as "standing room only." Tickets were going for as much as $4.50 each, a premium price for a blues-rock act in 1966, and anticipation for the band's return appearance at the Midtown concert hall was undoubtedly high.

As was the case when they played Town Hall in 1965, there were several other unrelated performances going on throughout the day at the West Forty-Third Street venue. A Gilbert and Sullivan operetta occupied the space from 11:00 a.m. to early afternoon, and a classical piano recital went through the dinner hour and into the early evening. The Butterfield Band had to wait until nearly 7:00 p.m. before they could begin setting up their equipment onstage, and it was almost 7:30 before they were able to do a sound check. Fans waiting out in the lobby got a foretaste of the performance through the closed house doors as the group ran through a few tunes while warming up and setting levels. Stagehands set up extra seating on either side of Town Hall's wide stage during the sound check in order to accommodate the sellout crowd, and at 8:00 the audience began streaming in. The *New York Times*' Robert Shelton was among the concertgoers.

"The Paul Butterfield Blues Band blasted its way into Town Hall Saturday night," read Shelton's lead for his review of the performance in the *Times* the following Monday. While the critic was no stranger to amplified music and an early supporter of the blues band from Chicago, he felt assaulted by their volume. "Even the concert manager was trying, in vain, to get the Butterfield Band to turn its amplifiers down."

Playing through new Fenders, replacement amps for the gear that had been modified for the British tour, Paul, Michael, and Elvin filled the vast hall with a wall of sound. Butterfield and Bishop were both playing through Twin Reverbs, and Bloomfield had daisy-chained a Twin and Super Reverb together. Mark Naftalin was powering his Hammond organ through a big Leslie speaker unit augmented by a second Fender amp, and Jerome Arnold had upended his Fender Bassman to better project its rumbling sound. All the amps, as well as

Billy Davenport's drums, were miked directly into the hall's PA. The sound of the band was indeed impressive.

Shelton claimed he had to seek the relative quiet of the foyer after a few tunes because the music was so loud. But despite his discomfort, he readily acknowledged that the harp player and his lead guitarist were extraordinary musicians. "Mike Bloomfield's wild electric guitar solos are among the best to be heard, and Mr. Butterfield's harmonica is indeed a magic flute."

The band opened with Sonny Boy Williamson's "Help Me" and then Bloomfield switched to slide for "Mystery Train." "Shake Your Moneymaker" was next, then Michael and Paul traded solos on "Walking by Myself," an eight-bar blues by Jimmy Rogers that the band played in standard twelve-bar format behind the solos. Because there would be only a single set, and because they were playing to a packed house in New York's prestigious Town Hall, the band included both "Work Song" and "East-West" in the show, closing with the latter. Their extended performance of the epic instrumental, driven by Bloomfield's explosive guitar, shook the walls of the theater and left the audience stunned and amazed. Robert Shelton missed its pyrotechnics, but another reviewer did not. *Billboard*'s reporter managed to remain in his seat throughout the entire performance. For him, the piece was clearly the concert's highlight.

> "East-West," the title tune of the group's latest album, is a production-plus number and was, without doubt, the hit of the night. The number, featuring blues variations of Eastern music themes, in part, ranges from the softly melodic in tempo to the crashing psychedelic. The record company reports that the album is selling at a rate of 10,000 to 15,000 a week and, after hearing this number, it's easy to see why.

The article, when it appeared in *Billboard* a few weeks later, was accurately titled "Butterfield & Blues Band an Impact Act." In the same issue, the Top LPs chart listed *East-West* at number ninety-eight. Though the record hadn't been a runaway hit, it had managed to remain on the charts for three months, a clear indication of the strong sales mentioned in the review. *East-West* would eventually reach a respectable number sixty-five and would remain on *Billboard*'s charts for another four months, through April 1967.

A week after their successful Town Hall appearance, the Butterfield Band was back at the Cafe Au Go Go on Bleecker Street in the Village. They opened on Tuesday, December 5, and played there nightly through the weekend. Enthusiastic crowds filled the club each night, having heard selections from *East-West* and the band's latest single, "Come On In," on college radio stations around New York. Nearly everyone had heard of Mike Bloomfield, the Chicago guitar virtuoso who had played with Dylan and was now doing some really far-out stuff with Paul Butterfield. Word was that he had to be seen in person to be believed.

On Friday, December 16, Butterfield took the band up to New York University's Bronx campus for a show at the school's historic Gould Memorial Library in University Heights. The group also appeared at a dance put on by a fraternity affiliated with Columbia College, part of Columbia University. The performance was nothing out of the ordinary, except that the band was filmed by an ABC-TV camera crew. The network was producing an hour-long documentary about the process involved in creating a popular music hit. Called *The Songmakers*, the program intended to show composers and musicians working on and performing material they had written. One of the upcoming bands to be featured was the Paul Butterfield Blues Band, and the filming was not without a few gremlins.

"The power went out repeatedly, leaving only the sudden sound of drums and unamplified harmonica!" said Mark Naftalin, recounting how the band's power draw, combined with that of the TV cameras and their lights, blew fuses throughout the evening's performance, leaving band, dancers, and cameramen in near total darkness. But despite electrical bugs, the crew managed to capture the raw excitement of a Butterfield Band performance, showing Paul singing intensely and blowing harp while Elvin bobbed and swayed and Michael gyrated wildly while soloing. When the special aired on February 24, it included numerous pop stars and icons of American song, including the Mamas and the Papas, Dionne Warwick, Simon and Garfunkel, and the Byrds as well as Burt Bacharach and Johnny Mercer. Following a segment profiling their East Coast rivals, the Blues Project, the Butterfield Band was shown in a brief, exciting clip doing "Born in Chicago."

Over the holidays, the Butterfield Band continued to gig around the New York area. Toward the end of the first week of the new year, the band's frequent Fillmore partners arrived in New York City for a special event hosted by their record company. The Jefferson Airplane made its East Coast debut on Sunday, January 8, in the ballroom at Webster Hall on East Eleventh Street in Manhattan. The label had organized an exclusive concert and party to introduce music industry bigwigs and the media to San Francisco's most popular rock band. Mike Bloomfield joined the Airplane onstage following the formal presentation of the band's music for the highlight of the evening—a psychedelic jam session. With Barry Goldberg added on organ, the quintet attempted to re-create Michael's "East-West," but without much success. Though the critics and music executives loved it, the chaotic nature of the Airplane's psychedelic instrumental clearly demonstrated how skilled the Butterfield Band was at collective improvisation. Their "East-West" never lost its cohesion and musical direction, and even though it was often top-heavy with flamboyant and virtuosic solos, the piece was always a collaboration, a creation of the entire ensemble. In that way, Michael, Paul, Elvin, Mark, Jerome, and Billy were like jazz musicians. They listened and responded to each other without getting in the way—not an easy thing to do.

The following weekend, the band drove up to Boston for concerts with the Otis Rush Blues Band at the New England Conservatory's Jordan Hall. Billed as the "blues show of the year," the performances packed the auditorium with wildly enthusiastic blues fans. A week later, the sextet was back on the road. ABGM had arranged for Butterfield to fly to San Francisco for another series of shows for Bill Graham at the Fillmore Auditorium. Graham was going to use the band's popularity to gauge whether the Fillmore audience would be receptive to jazz. He had hired saxophonist Charles Lloyd and his quartet to open for the Butterfield Band for the three days of shows, knowing the Chicago blues band would almost certainly fill the hall.

The Butterfield Band played Friday, Saturday, and Sunday, January 20 to 22, to capacity crowds at the Fillmore, and Charles Lloyd was given a standing ovation by the rock 'n' roll audience. The response was so positive that Atlantic Records, Lloyd's label, brought in San Francisco audio engineer Wally Heider to record the jazz quartet in performance during a second weekend of shows. The result would later be issued as *Love-In* by the Charles Lloyd Quartet. The popularity of the Paul Butterfield Blues Band had helped create a whole new audience for the progressive jazz saxophonist, and Bill Graham would soon go on to successfully present Rahsaan Roland Kirk, Gary Burton, and other jazz artists at the Fillmore.

Michael Bloomfield was glad to be back in the City by the Bay, with its relaxed, tolerant attitudes, thriving music scene, and burgeoning counterculture. But he was growing increasingly weary of having no real place to call home, no regular routine, and no relief from the chronic insomnia and anxiety those deprivations caused. Drugs, both legal and illegal, further exacerbated his condition. Sleeping pills were a frequent palliative for his wakefulness, and marijuana was a daily indulgence that took the edge off his increasingly agitated mental state. LSD, now pervasive in contemporary music, provided a welcome and entertaining escape from reality. But it was heroin that gave Michael palpable relief. While he didn't use it all that often, whenever he did, his problems simply faded away and his mind became quiet.

Lately he had been having greater difficulty quieting his mind, and some of that difficulty stemmed from the Butterfield Band itself. The constant traveling and performing had worn Michael down physically, but he was also beginning to chafe at the stylistic limitations imposed by playing in a blues band—even one as progressive as Paul's. Bloomfield had been interested for a while in working with reeds and brass, in "how bands play with horns" as he explained during one of his interviews with *Melody Maker*. B. B. King played blues with a horn section, as did Ray Charles and Bobby "Blue" Bland. Soul singers like Otis Redding, Jackie Wilson, and James Brown were all backed by horns. The addition of saxophones, trombones, and trumpets could open up a whole new range of possibilities for music-making.

"You know, for a long time all of us in Paul's band had wanted horns," Michael later explained. "All of our blues records, or many of them, other than the Chicago stuff and stuff that came out of the South and Detroit, had horns. . . . [A]s a guitar player, I really wanted to hear that sound of the guitar interacting with horns." Bloomfield began to think about what he might do if he put together a band of his own, one that included horns.

There was another issue with the group, one that wasn't so much musical as personal. The original Paul Butterfield Blues Band had been a quartet, with Elvin Bishop as its guitarist. Elvin had initially played both lead and rhythm, but with Michael's arrival that changed. Bishop had been relegated to second guitar status, frequently only playing chords while Bloomfield took all the solo spots. Even though Elvin eventually became a second soloist—and a good one—it was Michael who was considered the Butterfield Band's star. That had to bother the guitarist from Oklahoma, and even though Bishop said very little about it, Bloomfield thought he could sense Elvin's resentment. It made Michael uncomfortable and, while he loved the spotlight, he felt his celebrity was unfairly standing in the way of Bishop's career.

With thoughts of getting off the road, starting his own group, and passing the torch to Elvin, Michael told Mark Naftalin he was thinking about quitting the Paul Butterfield Blues Band.

But leaving Butterfield was something Bloomfield hadn't really thought through. What would it mean to suddenly be without a steady gig? His reputation was built on his playing with Butterfield, but what would happen if he suddenly disappeared from public view?

Things as usual were moving rapidly for the blues band from Chicago, and Michael had little time for charting a future other than the one directly ahead.

On January 28, following their two weeks at the Fillmore, the group packed its gear for a short hop to Palo Alto and an afternoon performance at Stanford University's Tresidder Union. The college crowd packed the hall and cheered the band on as they worked through a quick set. The Chicagoans were such a hit that they got their picture on the front page of the university newspaper the following Monday. It ran with the flattering headline, "Tell It Like It Is, Baby."

But there was no time to savor the applause. Immediately following the Stanford show, Butterfield and his men headed down the coast to Huntington Beach for two weeks of performances at the Golden Bear. The club was one of the group's favorite West Coast venues, and they were looking forward to playing there. But its relaxed, convivial atmosphere did little to allay thoughts of departure for Mike Bloomfield. Though he continued to play with the band to the best of his ability, he was still thinking seriously about leaving.

In the weeks since they had returned from England, the Paul Butterfield Blues Band had added new material to its book. Most of the tunes were standard blues, songs they had learned in Chicago, often from the artists who had composed them. The band's featured number, though, remained "East-West." By February 1967, the instrumental had evolved into a nuanced, episodic improvisation, a work no longer just a vehicle for Michael Bloomfield's virtuosity, but a stunning musical effort by the entire ensemble. Performances generally lasted half an hour, and on some nights ran to a full hour and beyond. While "East-West" continued to be a three-part composition with distinct sections separated by dramatic crescendos, the shape of those sections, their various motives and rhythms, varied from performance to performance. By listening closely and responding to each other, the members of the band were able to recompose parts of the piece each time they played it. That fluid quality kept everything fresh.

Toward the end of the third section, following Bloomfield's melodic solo, the band would begin the familiar "Chicken Shack" quote. But now they stretched it out and emphasized it, playing it in three-part harmony supplied by Paul, Michael, and Elvin. The beauty of those notes, woven together with a delicacy that contrasted with the mad deluge that preceded them, completed the merging of East and West and created a kind of harmonic convergence. From there, Michael and Elvin would launch into their duet, building toward the final crescendo and the piece's club-shaking conclusion. But now, Mark Naftalin, the one member of the band always in the background quietly supporting the lead voices, would move to the forefront. With all the stops open and the volume cranked on his Hammond B3, Naftalin would play the opening melody to the traditional Christmas hymn "Joy to the World" over the thundering crescendo.

"I usually played the first iteration of the melody in octaves and the second one in up to quadruple-octaves," said Mark. "Following that there was a slight vamp on a plagal or IV-I 'amen' cadence."

With the hymn's final chords, "East-West" would be brought to a joyous close.

The Golden Bear engagement lasted through Sunday, February 12. Another road trip across the country followed and the Butterfield Band eventually found itself back in Boston the last weekend in February. Far from the warm sea breezes and clear skies of sunny southern California, the sextet was now slogging through wet snow and slush, braving temperatures in the low thirties and bundling up against icy winds off Boston Harbor and the gray Atlantic. They were in town to play another college gig—but this time it wasn't to be just one quick set. ABGM had arranged for the group to perform not at one school, but at three—and all on the same day.

The first show was in Cambridge at the Massachusetts Institute of Technology, a concert given for the start of the school's Interfraternity Council Weekend. Beginning at noon and running until 4:00 p.m., the Butterfield Band along with the Jim Kweskin Jug Band, the other group on the bill, were to do multiple sets for toga-clad Hellenophiles and their dates. Then the Chicagoans were to load up and head across the Charles River for an early evening set at the Commonwealth Armory on Commonwealth Avenue in Boston, right next to Boston University. Their final appearance of the day was at the university itself, in BU's compact Sargent Gym, adjacent to the river. That show was to begin at 8:30 p.m. and would open with two local bands, thus pushing Butterfield's set back to nearly 10:00.

When the band arrived at the armory for the first of two shows, it was clear they were nearly spent. Only after the producer bribed them with a case of beer and an ounce of grass did the sextet agree to do both sets. Though the refreshments helped revive them, Butterfield and his men still had to move on to the university's gym for their final show of the day. It was a grueling ten hours, the result of a serious case of overbooking by ABGM.

Those who were there remember Michael Bloomfield playing with characteristic virtuosity, and one fan said the guitarist was so hyper he appeared to be thoroughly enjoying himself. But whether Mike Bloomfield was exuberant or exhausted onstage that evening may have been difficult to tell from the audience. Whatever his mood at the moment, Saturday's performance marathon served to force the issue. In his mind, the question of his membership in the blues band from Chicago had been resolved.

Michael Bloomfield quit the Paul Butterfield Blues Band, effective that very evening.

It was not an entirely rational moment, as Michael himself later admitted: "The reason I split from the band is that I went crazy. I flipped out over Christmas and went nuts." It may have been more than a little crazy to want to leave a band that seemed poised to break into the mainstream, but Michael wasn't thinking in commercial terms. The urge to jump ship had been festering over the holidays, and Saturday's triple-play finally tipped the scales. The constant traveling, recurrent insomnia, and pressures of performing had become intolerable. Strengthening Bloomfield's resolve to move on was the desire to try other musical things, to add horns, to have a real group of his own to use as an incubator for his many ideas. When the Butterfield Band got back to New York City on Monday, Michael made it official. He told Paul he was through as a member of the band.

"That's where it went down, that he said he was leaving. It was in the Albert hotel," said Kathryn Butterfield, Paul's wife. "It was *very* upsetting. It was really hard, and it was a big loss." Her husband was hit particularly hard by Bloomfield's decision, Kathryn said. "It was really a blow to Paul. He felt like he'd lost a brother." Other members of the band were distraught too.

"I was really brokenhearted," Billy Davenport said candidly. For him, the whole dynamic of the music changed. "The band wasn't the same."

Mark Naftalin thought his friend's timing was all wrong. "I wasn't too happy about his leaving at the time because it seemed like things were just starting to happen for us. I thought we had a chance to become the equivalent of the Rolling Stones, in a commercial sense. I knew Mike wanted to try some things on his own, but I do wish he'd stayed a little longer."

There was no staying longer. In March, when the Paul Butterfield Blues Band left New York for a series of concerts through the Midwest that culminated in an appearance at the University of Wisconsin in Madison, Michael Bloomfield was not with them. Advertisements for the band still featured him prominently, and press releases referred to him as Butterfield's star lead player. But when fans arrived, they were disappointed to see that Bloomfield wasn't there. For the first time in nearly two years, America's finest blues-rock guitarist was without a gig.

CHAPTER 14

HOISTING THE FLAG

NEW YORK AND SAN FRANCISCO, 1967

Mike Bloomfield hunkered down in New York City and pondered his next move. He was more than happy to finally be off the road and to have time to read and visit with friends, catch some music around town, and maybe even get some uninterrupted sleep. But he was also thinking hard about the future. He was still under contract to Epic Records, at least as far as he knew, and he believed he still had a manager. Albert Grossman hadn't been too pleased by Michael's decision to leave the Butterfield Band, but he seemed open to retaining the talented twenty-three-year-old as a client. Bloomfield had built a reputation as one of the finest guitarists in the country—even *Playboy* magazine acknowledged that fact. Its annual jazz poll, just out in the February issue, ranked him number thirteen among the world's best guitarists. The question now before Michael was a simple one: How should he best utilize these advantages?

There was one advantage that Bloomfield still lacked. He hadn't forgotten about the guitar he had seen Eric Clapton playing with Cream when the Butterfield Band had been in England. A quick search hadn't turned up a Les Paul Standard while he was in London, but now that Michael was back home and on his own, he was determined to find one. It suddenly occurred to him that he knew someone who had just such a Les Paul—a beautiful, fire-red 1959 Sunburst. His name was Dan Erlewine, a guitarist from Ann Arbor whom Michael had gotten to know when the Butterfield Band first played in Detroit. He hadn't seen Erlewine since the band had last played the Motor City in September, but Michael remembered seeing his Ann Arbor friend playing the guitar with his group, the Prime Movers Blues Band. Dan had kept in touch, and Bloomfield had his phone number. He called him up right away.

"Michael told me he was looking for a Les Paul like mine," said Dan. "For some reason, he didn't want the Goldtop anymore, he wanted the cherry-red one." Bloomfield's Goldtop had been Erlewine's inspiration for purchasing the Sunburst, and now Michael suggested they trade instruments. Hadn't Dan really wanted a Goldtop anyway? "He said, 'Oh, man, I *gotta* have your guitar.'

I'd have done anything Michael said, so I said, 'Well, you know, we can work something out.' So he gave me his Goldtop—and $100."

The 1959 Les Paul Standard arrived a few weeks later via Railway Express, shipped from Ann Arbor direct to Bloomfield's apartment on Christopher Street in the Village. Its warm luster and woody, polished smell greeted Michael when he unpacked it and opened the guitar's plush case. He plugged it into a small practice amp, cranked up the volume and ran a few scales followed by several bluesy licks. *There* it was—the tone he was looking for. The guitarist was thrilled.

With his days now largely free, Michael was soon spending much of his time with his friend Barry Goldberg. Barry had moved into the Hotel Albert, just a few blocks from Michael and Susan's apartment, and following a brief stint with the Chicago Loop was working sporadically as a session player while writing and hustling songs. Like Michael, he, too, was looking toward the future, hoping to make a solid career for himself in the music business. The two friends talked about possibilities, and Bloomfield brought up his desire for a band of his own, a new type of rock band—one that would include horns.

"He had told me, long before this, of his idea for a 'dream band' that he wanted to build and organize," said Barry. "It was going to be an 'American music band' . . . [,] one that would encompass all the different types of music that we loved: blues, jazz, R&B, rock 'n' roll, soul . . . in this one entity." Now that his time was once again his own, Michael realized his dream could well become a reality. With Albert Grossman's backing, he could make it happen. And Barry could help.

In mid-March, Bloomfield got a chance to put his ideas about horns into practice. Harmonica player James Cotton was recording his first album as a leader, and Michael was brought in by Albert Grossman to help produce it. Grossman had become Cotton's manager at the urging of Bloomfield and Paul Butterfield, and now that the guitarist was a free agent, Albert wanted him to direct the sessions for Muddy Waters's former harp man. Michael asked Barry to go with him to Chicago to help with the recording, and he also got his friend Norman Dayron involved. Norman was teaching at Northwestern University in Evanston, just north of Chicago, and was also engineering recording sessions whenever he could. He had recently produced dates by bluesmen Floyd Jones and Eddie Taylor for Testament Records.

On their arrival in Chicago, Michael and Barry had dinner at Dorothy Bloomfield's apartment on Lake Shore Drive. Susan joined them, having come to Chicago earlier to visit her family. During the meal, Michael discussed his plans for the new band. It would be based in San Francisco, the guitarist said, where they were open to new ideas. He described how the band would have a horn section, how its material would be drawn from all genres of American music, and how it would merge jazz, blues, rock, and even country into a new and exciting hybrid. He also explained that he wanted to use the recording studio as a musical element in itself, playing with the mix, adding effects and using it to shape the band's sound. As he laid out his vision, he got more and more excited. His enthusiasm was contagious, and soon Susan was caught up in it.

"Michael and Barry had just come back from wherever they were, and they said, 'We're gonna go form this new band. . . . [Y]ou gotta come; we can't do it without you,'" recalled Susan. "I was so moved that they couldn't do it without me! I went against my better judgment at the time, because I didn't really want to go."

On March 15, Bloomfield, Goldberg, and Dayron joined James Cotton and his band in a studio at Universal Recording on East Walton Street in the Windy City's Rush Street neighborhood. Michael was pleased to see Sam Lay there—his former Butterfield bandmate was now working regularly with Cotton. As they busied themselves setting up equipment and microphones, other musicians began arriving. With Norman's help, Michael had arranged for a full horn section of one trumpet, two trombones, and three reeds to be present. He wanted to re-create the big band sound of recordings by B. B. King and Bobby "Blue" Bland for the harp player's album. The six musicians he had hired included jazz trumpeter Paul Serrano and saxophonist Gene Easton, and all were seasoned session men, well versed in jazz, R&B, soul, and blues. They easily put together arrangements to back the blues and R&B tunes Cotton and Bloomfield had selected to record.

With Michael coaching James and Barry directing the musicians while Norman monitored the sound from the control room, the ensemble successfully recorded eleven songs, nine of which included the horns. The big sound of the band, fronted by James's vibrant vocals and soaring harmonica, and complemented by guitarist Luther Tucker's stinging solos and Sam Lay's driving beat, gave Cotton's traditional Chicago blues a contemporary updating. The combination worked beautifully, and everyone was satisfied—especially Mike Bloomfield. He wanted to hear what horns would sound like with a modern blues band, and the Cotton date had shown that electric instruments and brass could work together very well. When *The James Cotton Blues Band* LP was released in May on Verve/Folkways, *Broadside* magazine's reviewer wrote, "This is an excellent album; some of the cuts are the best I've heard of Chicago blues. . . . Cotton and his band play cleanly with considerable polish." In a few months' time, those observations could easily be made about Michael Bloomfield's own brass blues-rock band.

On the trip back to New York, Michael and Barry began seriously thinking of musicians they would like to include in the new group. Bloomfield also planned to talk to Albert Grossman about footing the bill, at least in the beginning, because bringing together seven or eight professional players and keeping them together would require a substantial investment. But even that seemed doable, and Bloomfield was soon thinking of his new band in terms of "when" rather than "if."

Toward the end of the month, Mike Bloomfield was hired as a sideman for veteran jazz alto player Eddie "Cleanhead" Vinson on a BluesWay Records session. Vinson was known for his jump blues novelties and clever lyrics, and jazz producer Bob Thiele, the guiding force behind Impulse Records, had been brought in by parent company ABC to manage BluesWay, its new imprint. Thiele was tasked with giving older jazz and blues artists a more contemporary sound, thus introducing them to the younger generation of blues enthusiasts. Those listeners all knew Mike Bloomfield, and the producer hoped the guitarist could give Vinson's swinging, jazzy approach to blues a modern electric inflection.

The session took place one evening at Capitol Record's New York studios on West Forty-Sixth Street. The band recorded five medium-tempo numbers during its three-hour session, all of them blues vocals in the key of B-flat. For the first time, Bloomfield used his new Les Paul, trying out its various pickup and tone settings. But instead of asserting himself in his best Butterfield style, Michael kept his volume low and added only respectful fills. He took no solos and was content simply to back Cleanhead's singing with tasteful licks. If Thiele was hoping for a more dynamic contribution from the young guitarist, he was doubtless disappointed. But Bloomfield knew Vinson's long history in jazz and blues, starting in the early 1940s with trumpeter Cootie Williams's big band and later with Kansas City's Jay McShann and Johnny Otis's pioneering rock 'n' roll review. Out of deference to the older musician, Michael refused to lead and instead played a sympathetic, supporting role.

It was something he would often do when working with older blues masters. And it would be a habit that would frequently confuse his producers and sometimes disappoint his fans.

Bloomfield was anything but reticent at another recording session, his third that month. Barry Goldberg got a call from the singer on whose 1966 hit "Devil with a Blues Dress On" he had played. Mitch Ryder was going into the studio to try something different on the recommendation of his producer, Bob Crewe. He was going to record an album without his usual backup band, the Detroit Wheels—a solo effort that would be part romantic ballads, part up-tempo party tunes. Ryder wanted Barry to play keyboards on the party half, and Goldberg suggested he use Michael Bloomfield for the guitar parts.

In a long session at Mira Sound Recording Studios on West Forty-Seventh Street in Manhattan, Barry and Michael played on the five up-tempo tunes that Ryder planned to use on the album. Bloomfield once again closely watched the way Bob Crewe used the studio to create the sound he wanted for the singer. Just as he had with the Chicago Loop date back in September, the producer used multiple tracks and overdubs to create a complex, layered audio collage. This time, though, he seemed to hold nothing back. Crewe had the horns and backup singers weave in and around Ryder's vocals to build a wild, frenetic wall of sound. Abrupt stops and frequent key modulations only intensified the music, giving it a chaotic thrust. He instructed Bloomfield to play as loudly and aggressively as possible—the guitarist usually heard the opposite request from producers—and Michael complied by unleashing a flood of fast, over-driven licks wherever possible in each tune. The resulting song masters would require extensive mixing, but that was just how Bob Crewe worked, using a studio's postproduction capabilities to craft appealing, catchy tunes that were more than the sum of their parts. Often so much more that they became hits.

But that was not to be the case with Mitch Ryder's solo album. *What Now My Love* was released on Crewe's DynoVoice label in November and failed to make the charts. The party side of the album had Bloomfield's contribution so far down in the mix that he was often hard to hear, and the overly busy arrangements made Ryder's tunes difficult to decipher—and just plain noisy. The singer soon reorganized the Detroit Wheels and forgot about going solo. But Michael benefitted from the experience by getting another opportunity to watch the innovative Bob Crewe at work. The guitarist would apply some of Crewe's techniques to his own recording sessions in upcoming months.

As the spring of 1967 approached, Michael Bloomfield was spending much of his time with his friend Barry Goldberg. Even when they weren't working the same freelance gig, the two were together often enough that Michael began spending nights at Barry's place in the Hotel Albert. Because they frequently were out late, the guitarist explained that it would be easier to stay there rather than go back to Christopher Street and possibly disturb Susan. But Barry thought there were other reasons Michael was avoiding going home—and avoiding Susie.

"Their relationship had been going through a lot of changes, and she and Michael had a lot of issues to work out," said Goldberg. Bloomfield's growing fame had altered the dynamic of his marriage. He had become the person people were interested in, the person everyone wanted to know and talk to. Susan was often sidelined, excluded from the conversation. People frequently didn't even know who she was or that she was Michael's wife. Pop stardom held an appeal for fans of all sorts—and female fans were particularly drawn to charismatic rock musicians. Bloomfield was no exception, and there were many temptations on the road and in the concert halls. Trust had become an issue between husband and wife, and Michael felt he and Susan needed some space to sort things out.

Bloomfield wasn't the only one with troubles. Barry was also working through a difficult relationship. While leading the Goldberg-Miller Blues Band with guitarist Steve Miller, he had met a young woman from Brooklyn and had fallen in love. But the romance had soured after Barry had a run-in with her disapproving father. The keyboard player was hit hard by his girlfriend's eventual departure and, feeling depressed and dispirited, sought solace in the numbing effects of drugs. He was a regular pot smoker like everyone else, but now he wanted something stronger.

"My curiosity about heroin had been in the back of my mind for years," Barry said. "But now I told myself that I had no reason *not* to try it." With the help of a few musician friends who were users, Goldberg began using the drug whenever he could afford it. Knowing that Michael occasionally indulged, he saw no reason to hide his use. It was just another interest the two friends shared. Goldberg sought to assuage his problems with an intermittent fix, and in their weeks together at the Albert, Mike Bloomfield undoubtedly joined him.

But their days and nights weren't spent only gigging around town and scoring the occasional high. Michael Bloomfield had a band to organize. Albert Grossman had given the project a green light, offering to cover expenses until the group was up and running, and agreeing to manage them with Bloomfield as the leader and star attraction. Michael and Barry began rounding up musicians they thought would work well in the American Music Band, as they initially called it. Their first choice was suggested by Barry. Because Bloomfield had asked him to pick the horn players, Goldberg chose Peter Strazza, his former bandmate from Robby and the Troubadours.

Strazza, a twenty-four-year-old native of Greenwich, Connecticut, played tenor and baritone sax and doubled on flute. He had worked briefly as a hairdresser before joining the Troubadours in New Haven and then went with them to Chicago in 1962 for their extended engagement at the Playboy Club. Peter was an aspiring jazz player whose favorite musician was John Coltrane.

A guitarist from Galveston, Texas, provided Bloomfield with a second horn player. Larry Coryell was in town performing at the Cafe Au Go Go as a member of jazz vibes player Gary Burton's quartet, and he suggested Michael recruit a trumpet player he had worked with in his college days named Marcus Doubleday. A twenty-four-year-old Seattle native, Doubleday had played with pop acts like Bobby Vinton, Jan and Dean, and the Drifters, but Coryell knew he was looking for more challenging work. Doubleday's bright, ringing tone and ability to play a variety of styles impressed Bloomfield, and Marcus—or Mark as he was more commonly known—was enlisted for the band.

Michael then signed up a bass player he had met during Dylan's *Highway 61 Revisited* sessions. Born in Manhattan and raised in Queens, twenty-three-year-old Harvey Brooks was a close friend of Al Kooper's, a busy studio musician, and a familiar face around Village clubs and coffeehouses. He wasn't very experienced as a blues player, but Michael had heard good things about Harvey since they had worked with Dylan. Though he was hesitant at first, the bassist agreed to leave the security of the studios and join the new band.

Both Michael and Barry had been impressed by Billy Mundi, a drummer they had seen with guitarist Frank Zappa's band, the Mothers of Invention. They were planning to talk to him, but Harvey Brooks urged them to first check out an amazing young drummer he had seen backing soul singer Wilson Pickett. His name was George Miles, but everyone called him "Buddy." He was performing with Pickett at an extravagant review that week, and Harvey said they should go see him.

Staged by radio and TV personality Murray Kaufman—known professionally as "Murray the K"—the star-studded show was curiously titled *Music in the Fifth Dimension*. It was held at the grandly ornate RKO Theater on Fifty-Eighth Street and ran for nine days beginning on Saturday, March 25. Bloomfield and Goldberg went one night when Pickett's band was there.

"We walked into this theater, and the whole theater was rocking to this massive drum beat. We were just mesmerized," recalled Goldberg. "It was Buddy Miles, who was Wilson Pickett's drummer."

Both Michael and Barry already knew about Miles because he was supposed to have been the drummer for Ryder's recording sessions with Bob Crewe. But he had been replaced by Bernard Purdie after it was discovered that Miles couldn't read music. That didn't matter to the two friends—they were interested only in Buddy's sound, and it was more than impressive.

A nineteen-year-old African American man from Omaha, Nebraska, Buddy Miles had joined Pickett in 1965 after a year on the road with the vocal group the Delfonics. A gifted singer and natural showman, the young drummer was eager to move into the spotlight, and when Michael and Barry found him backstage after Pickett's set, he agreed to go back to the Albert with them so they could discuss plans for the new band in detail. Along the way, Michael stopped into a corner grocery and bought a package of Oreo cookies—the drummer's favorite. When they got to Barry's rooms, Michael explained that they were thinking of basing the group in San Francisco and then regaled Miles with stories of the beautiful girls he would meet there. With each new detail, he fed Buddy more cookies. Then they asked Buddy to sing something for them.

"Buddy sang *great*!" said Michael. "We knew then that he was just dynamite." In short order, the friends got a commitment from Miles to join them in the new band. Though he finished the RKO gig with Wilson Pickett and even did a few shows with him at the Apollo Theater in Harlem, Buddy soon gave notice. When he did, the soul singer was enraged that someone would steal his drummer. Both Bloomfield and Goldberg were worried that Pickett, who was known to have a hot temper and a fascination with guns, might come after them, so they advised their new drummer to stay out of sight until they were ready to head to California.

The new band still needed a vocalist. Though Buddy was an excellent singer, Michael also wanted a lead singer who could front the band. Their recent session with Mitch Ryder had convinced Bloomfield that Mitch's would be the perfect voice for the new group. But when asked, Ryder declined the offer, feeling his career would be better served by remaining with the Detroit Wheels. Bloomfield then realized he knew another fine vocalist who was available, and who was also a good friend. He called Nick Gravenites, his former bandmate from their days in Old Town, and asked him if he would like to be part of the new group.

Nick, who had moved back to San Francisco in 1966 and was spending his days working in a car repair shop, was more than happy for the opportunity to get back into music. The twenty-eight-year-old was living with another Chicago friend, a former restaurant owner named Ron Polte. Polte was managing Quicksilver Messenger Service, the rock band that had opened for the Butterfield Band at the Fillmore back in March, and Gravenites was helping out.

"Michael called me from New York, saying he was quitting Butter," Gravenites said. "Grossman was gonna back him and he was putting a band together, and he wanted to know if I wanted to be the singer. I said, 'Sure.' He says, 'Well, you're out there, go rent a house. I'll start shipping people out to you.'"

Gravenites began looking around for something suitable for a group of seven musicians. Houses were more affordable outside of San Francisco, and suburban Marin County, just across the Golden Gate Bridge, seemed like the ideal place. In no time, he found a modern ranch-style house with three bedrooms in the foothills of Mt. Tamalpais. The residence was located on a quiet cul-de-sac called Wellesley Court in the picturesque town of Mill Valley. It seemed like the perfect place for band members to get to know each other, and to have the space to practice and work out musical ideas. Nick sent the rental details to ABGM and had them pay the deposit and the first month's rent. Then he called Michael in New York and told him he had a house—all it needed was musicians.

Bloomfield was pleased that Nick had found a home for the new band, at least for the first few months while they were working on material and rehearsing. But Michael knew there was more to building a band than simply providing a place for its members to sleep and safely store their equipment. He was going to need help with the logistical details, with all the things that needed keeping track of, the duties and responsibilities that came with running a successful music group. Michael had seen Paul Butterfield grapple with them, and there had been many times when he was glad he wasn't the leader of the Paul Butterfield Blues Band. But now he would be in charge, and he knew he was going to need assistance.

One evening, Bloomfield walked over to the Garrick Theater on Bleecker Street to catch a late set by Frank Zappa and the Mothers of Invention. He wound up in the projection room following Zappa's performance, and there he got to talking with the technician who was running the Garrick's light show. An affable, outgoing twenty-year-old from Canada, his name was Chris McDougal. Bloomfield took an immediate liking to him.

"We smoked a few joints together," said McDougal. "Michael said, 'I've played my last gig with Butterfield, and I'm putting together a band. I need somebody to help me. Are you interested?' I said I was, and he said, 'OK. You work for me.'" Bloomfield explained that his manager, Albert Grossman, would be hiring the band's road crew and other operations people, but Michael wanted his own person, someone he could trust who worked only for him. "Mike said he would pay me out of his own pocket."

McDougal, the son of an RCMP commissioner, had come to New York City as a roadie and driver for the Toronto band the Paupers. While the group was performing at the Cafe Au Go Go as the opening act for the Jefferson Airplane, McDougal had been hired to run the Garrick's light show. He explained to Michael that he would have to work until the theater found a replacement, but then he would come out to San Francisco and go to work for the guitarist. They shook on the deal, and Michael invited his new assistant up to the Apollo Theater in Harlem to hear Buddy Miles play his last gig with Wilson Pickett.

* * *

By mid-April, Michael Bloomfield was collecting his new band members and getting ready to head west to California. He was energized by the thought of the new group, by the music it would create, and by the new ground it would break. A rock band with horns—it would be something altogether different. As far as Michael knew, it had never been tried before. And with the new band would come a fresh start, a chance to make a statement that was truly his own.

He and Susan packed suitcases and closed up the apartment. The second week in April, they flew out to San Francisco and began setting up house at 404 Wellesley Court. A few members of the group had already arrived in Mill Valley, shuttled there by Nick Gravenites. Barry, who was afraid of flying, drove out from New York with Peter Strazza, and Mark Doubleday flew in from Seattle with his wife, Vickie.

By mid-April, all the members of the new band were in Mill Valley and getting to know one another. Susan set up the kitchen and did her best to organize meals, taping a few "House Rules" posters to the wall in the dining area. "THIS IS YOUR HOME" one sign proclaimed, urging everyone to clean up after themselves and take out their garbage. Accommodations were Spartan, but the house was light and airy, and the occupants quickly established a routine.

They soon had an unexpected visitor. Actor Peter Fonda, son of Hollywood icon Henry Fonda, had come to San Francisco in search of a band to provide music for a movie he was working on. When he heard that Mike Bloomfield was in town putting together a new group, Fonda immediately got directions to the house in Mill Valley. The twenty-seven-year-old actor knew Michael from the Butterfield Band, having met him when the group was performing on the Sunset Strip in 1966. He had been greatly impressed by Bloomfield's playing and was eager to hear his new band. He was also eager to persuade the guitarist to create the soundtrack for his next film project, a provocative ninety-minute exposé on drug use called *The Trip*.

Bloomfield was intrigued when he heard the actor's proposal. Peter said the film was going to be a state-of-the-art examination of a counterculture phenomenon and thus needed a score that was edgy and adventurous. Michael was more than a little amused when Fonda told him the film would attempt to simulate a trip on LSD.

"The band had just formed, and local word had gotten around that we were a hot band," said Michael. "Peter Fonda came around with *The Trip* movie, just to sort of hang out with us, and he showed it to us. I was delighted to do the soundtrack, but I thought it was a really absurd movie." Bloomfield told the actor that he and the band would be happy to create the soundtrack for his "acid movie," but first Fonda needed to talk to Albert Grossman. ABGM handled all of the group's engagements, even though there were none to speak of at the moment. Peter said he would have the producers contact the agency.

Albert Grossman himself soon paid Wellesley Court a visit. As was his practice, he had the band members sign personal management agreements with ABGM as well as individual recording contracts. He also insisted they agree to have his company, Albet Music Corp., publish any original material they wrote for the band. Nick Gravenites, who was experienced with music publishing, balked at that requirement. But the usually enigmatic Grossman was direct in his response. If Gravenites didn't sign, he was out. The singer reluctantly signed.

Albert then explained that he had been approached by American International Pictures, producers of *The Trip*, and had arranged for Bloomfield's American Music Band to create its soundtrack. The director, independent filmmaker Roger Corman, had requested the band on Peter Fonda's recommendation, and Grossman said that Michael and the group would be heading to Hollywood to begin recording the soundtrack the following week.

Michael's personal assistant, Chris McDougal, arrived just as the band was preparing to depart for Los Angeles. He had driven out from Chicago in a big blue fifteen-passenger Chevrolet van that Bloomfield was going to use to ferry the band members around town. But for the present, it wouldn't be needed. McDougal parked the van and, with all the beds at the house occupied, took a room in a nearby motel. The last weekend in April, the band flew to LA for the start of what promised to be a very exciting musical career.

Accommodations for the band in Los Angeles had been arranged by Albert Grossman and his partner, producer John Court. They rented a private home in the Hollywood hills on a winding, serpentine lane named Glendower Avenue. A striking Moorish-style structure, the house had an observation tower, multiple balconies, a cathedral-ceiling living room and 5,500 square-feet of habitable space. Its owner, actor John Law, called it "the Castle." For Michael Bloomfield and the band, the residence would provide a trippy, surreal backdrop for their work on *The Trip*.

"It was a crazy place—it was Hollywood. It was stucco, *musty* stucco," Nick Gravenites recalled, laughing. "It had all kinds of different rooms. I stayed upstairs in a big circular room, all glass windows—I was being the 'sensitive songwriter,' you know. But down in the basement . . . what do they have? An opium den. A genuine Chinese opium den—red-and-black lacquered bunks, you know? This room was built for opiates!"

Barry Goldberg took a room in the Castle's lower level. "It was almost like sleeping in a dungeon," he remembered. One night, he awoke to find a statuesque blond standing at the foot of his bed. "She just kind of barged in and startled me awake, and I was a little freaked out. 'Who the hell are you?' I said.

'I am Nico, superstar.'" Goldberg's nocturnal visitor was one of Andy Warhol's actresses, the German model and singer Nico. She had lived in the Castle while Warhol was filming *Imitation of Christ* earlier in year and remained behind when the pop artist returned to New York. She was only one of many exotic visitors to the Castle while the American Music Band was in residence.

"We all moved into there during our recording sessions," Nick said. "And, of course, the entourage would show up. Runaway girls would show up—*bizarre* things happened there! Michael had that intangible quality called charisma. People just wanted to be around him, like Jesus, you know—'touch the hem of his garment.' They just were magnetized by this guy."

"I remember there was this sort of semi-circle, C-shaped driveway," said Norman Dayron. The professor, taking a break from teaching at Northwestern, had come west to visit his friend and watch the band record. "Over it was this portico over the front door, and Michael's room was above it, and he could walk out his window and sit on that roof. I was wandering about stoned one evening, and I looked up and here he was, sitting cross-legged in a yoga position, with his shirt off and his giant electric hair, grinning beatifically like some demented Jewish Buddha presiding over the world's most insane rock 'n' roll circus!"

The day after the band arrived in Hollywood, Michael and Nick visited director Roger Corman to discuss *The Trip* and sign contracts for the soundtrack job with American International Pictures.

Corman explained how he wanted the film to be a serious exploration of the effects of LSD, both negative and positive, and talked about how his production team was hard at work creating special visual effects that would closely approximate the sensory experience of a drug-induced trip. The director said he had researched the subject thoroughly before embarking on the project, even taking LSD himself so that he would experience its effects firsthand. The music, Corman said, would be an extremely important part of the movie. He wanted it to underscore the visual impact of the film, which he characterized as innovative and visionary. Because nearly all of the *The Trip* narrative would take place while Fonda's character was under the influence of LSD, the soundtrack would have music in almost every scene. Composing the accompaniment for so many different moments and moods would pose a real challenge, Corman acknowledged, but he had been told Michael Bloomfield and his band were more than capable of tackling the job.

The forty-one-year-old filmmaker's gentle demeanor and quiet sincerity—and his earnest enthusiasm for his "acid movie"—charmed Bloomfield. He was completely taken with the director, even though he had misgivings about the merits of the film's subject matter and its likely exploitation at the box office. He assured Corman he had nothing to worry about—the group would do a great job for him. That pleased the director because the band he had originally hired hadn't really been equal to the task. They had also been recommended by Peter Fonda—a quartet calling themselves the International Submarine Band.

Michael recognized the name, remembering that the ISB was the group his friend John Nuese and songwriter Gram Parsons had formed in Cambridge before moving to New York City in 1966. That was not long after Nuese traded his Goldtop Les Paul for Bloomfield's Telecaster. Michael was delighted to learn that John was in town, and more than a little chagrined that his band would be replacing Nuese's for *The Trip* soundtrack. But Corman said he thought the ISB's music was too conventional for the film's controversial topic and experimental visuals. The soundtrack job was now Michael's, and Peter Fonda was excited to be working with him.

"I hung out with Michael while the band was recording the music for *The Trip*. Fonda was there in the studio a lot, and Dennis Hopper would come by, too," said John Nuese. Actor Hopper was one of the film's leads along with Fonda. "He was the *craziest* motherfucker I ever met!" John said, laughing.

They were all in crazy LA, enjoying the warm weather, the celebrities, and the glitzy eccentricities of Hollywood. For Mike Bloomfield, creating music for *The Trip* would tap all his skills as a musician, incorporating innovation and improvisation with his knowledge of styles and techniques. It would also involve wild parties, drugs, and indulgences of every kind before the job was completed. And the new band was just getting started.

Scenes for *The Trip* had been shot at various locations in and around Los Angeles over a fifteen-day period during the first three weeks of April, and Roger Cormon and his editors were busy cutting them together and creating special effects. They prepared rushes of scenes that needed music so Bloomfield and the rest of the group could watch the action, gauge the mood, and get a sense of time requirements. The soundtrack recording sessions were held at United Artists Studios, a complex of sound stages and film studios on the corner of Santa Monica Boulevard and Formosa Avenue in West Hollywood.

"Mike had them project the film on the wall—there was no screen," said Chris McDougal. "Lots of times, they just created the music while watching." Bloomfield encouraged his players to try things, often demonstrating what he wanted and then coaching each musician in turn.

Many of the scenes requiring music involved Fonda wandering about in dream-like environments, hiking through shadowy forest glades or dodging surf along rocky shorelines while pursued by mysterious hooded riders or pike-wielding bandits. To enhance the altered-consciousness aspect of the action, the music obviously needed to have an ethereal, otherworldly quality. Bloomfield was familiar with the sound experiments of New York's free jazz players and knew well the groundbreaking aural excursions of Chicago's Sun Ra and the avant garde collective called the Association for the Advancement of Creative Musicians. He knew he could get the band to create free-form collages of atmospheric sounds using their conventional instruments. But he wanted something more, something that could add an entirely new dimension to the music. He wanted sounds that had never been heard before—because that was just what LSD did. It took the user to new and hitherto unknown levels of consciousness.

There was a musician who frequently worked on film soundtracks at the Santa Monica Boulevard studios, usually providing special effects for low-budget science fiction and horror movies. He started his professional career as a jazz organist but, like so many musicians in Los Angeles, had found steadier work in the film studios. He was fascinated by electronic instruments like the theremin, a tone oscillator frequently used in film, and had even created some sound devices of his own. His name was Paul Beaver.

"He was a really serious electronic musician at a time when nobody else was doing it," said Norman Dayron of the forty-one-year-old Beaver. "I believe he had the first Moog synthesizer other than Robert Moog himself."

During the 1960s, New York inventor Robert Moog had developed a keyboard-based electronic instrument he called a "synthesizer." By 1967 he had produced a portable version and, hoping to get musicians interested in using it, hired Paul Beaver as his West Coast sales representative. Beaver had just demonstrated the instrument at the Audio Engineering Society convention in Los Angeles in April and thus had one of Moog's cumbersome devices on hand. Michael had heard about the synthesizer, and when he discovered that Beaver had one, he enlisted the keyboardist's services for the soundtrack. The Moog machine could easily provide that missing otherworldly element for much of *The Trip*'s background music.

"Everybody was talking about it in 1967, but nobody could play the Moog—the original instrument looked like an old Bell Telephone switchboard with cables and plug bays everywhere," Dayron said. "You really had to know what you were doing to get music out of it, and Beaver had that skill."

With Paul Beaver now involved, the improvised sound segments were worked out right in the studio. The musicians set up and watched whatever scene they were to score. Then, with Michael's direction, parts were worked out and combinations tried. Usually, several run-throughs were recorded and then played back, allowing the musicians to select the best take. The moods of the pieces varied—some sounded sinister, others playful and sprightly, and still others were hypnotic drones. Bloomfield had the musicians use whatever they could find around the studio in addition to their own instruments, augmenting the mix with acoustic guitars, a harpsichord, timpani, bells, wood blocks, a tambourine, and a harmonica. Michael used his electric guitar to create wails of feedback, playing with its volume knob to get eerie vocal effects. Barry switched from piano to organ and then to harpsichord while Harvey Brooks anchored each piece, providing a bass line for the others to improvise over. Weaving in and out through each collage were the synthesized sounds of Beaver's Moog—hisses, hums, pops, gurgles, and other electronic noises that were as much a part of the music as any of the sounds produced by the more conventional instruments. The mood in the studio bordered on the surreal as film clips played on the wall with lights low, and the music evoked a pastiche of darkly suggestive thoughts and semi-lucid dreams. More often than not, the band drew inspiration from whatever drug was on hand.

"We'd work at night, and then we'd all go out to Shoney's Big Boy for breakfast," said McDougal. He was impressed watching Bloomfield work in the studio. "Mike understood sounds as music—just like Hendrix did. He would hear squeaks and rattles and say, 'That's music.'"

Nearly half the music required for *The Trip* supported the main character's hallucinogenic experiences and thus was mostly improvised in the studio. The remainder of the soundtrack required set pieces composed by Michael, Barry, Nick, or all three together. Though Bloomfield would receive composer's credit for nearly all the material recorded for Roger Cormon's film, the music was jointly created.

Recording sessions for those tunes were a bit more conventional. One sequence early in the movie required Peter Fonda's character to turn on the TV and hear music from a commercial coming over the set. Gravenites tackled the scene, writing a characteristically sardonic tune that puffed "Psyche Soap," a product that "makes you clean inside." Sung to comic, mock-Dixieland accompaniment, Nick's lyrics admonished the viewers to "clean up or flip out." Mark Doubleday's brisk lead trumpet drove the piece while Barry's ragtime piano embellishments added an appropriately hokey touch. Nick's vocal was even compressed, making it sound as though he were singing through a megaphone in classic Rudy Vallée style. The soap commercial would be the only non-instrumental on the soundtrack.

Another composed piece was a lovely evocation of Mexican mariachi music called "Green and Gold." It also featured Doubleday's trumpet, and the horn man's warm tone lifted the melody over contrapuntal harmony provided by Bloomfield on electric guitar. For a scene in which Fonda's character is interrogated by Dennis Hopper's hippie judge, Michael provided a calliope-like waltz, replete with a whistling pump organ, orchestra bells, a harmonica, and various vocal sounds. Mark was again featured, this time playing the trilling melody on fluegelhorn.

A piece by Barry called "Home Room" evoked the sort of club music the keyboardist once played with Robby and the Troubadours, while a hard-driving piece, doubtless created by Bloomfield and appropriately titled "Peter Gets Off," was a one-chord jam that was a solo feature for Peter Strazza's husky tenor. Buddy Miles got to demonstrate his thunderous power on "Flash, Bam, Pow," a runaway train of sound used behind Peter Fonda's terror-filled dash down Sunset Boulevard during the paranoid portion of his trip. "Senior Citizen," another Dixieland-inspired romp by the entire ensemble, lacked only a ringing banjo to complete its send-up of "moldy-figge" jazz re-creationists.

Michael Bloomfield got to display his guitar skills on the two longest instrumentals the band recorded for the soundtrack. One, called "Fine Jung Thing," was an up-tempo blues with an inverted turn-around that was much rockier than anything Michael had ever played with Paul Butterfield. It opened with a few choruses by Goldberg on organ and then Michael cranked up his newly acquired Sunburst and loosed a torrent of brilliant licks, building each new line on the preceding one with increasing intensity for nearly sixteen full choruses. It was almost as though he had returned to his glory days with the Group at Big John's, where a jam blues could last as much as half an hour.

The other tune that featured Bloomfield would accompany the film's concluding scene. A slow, grinding, riff-based blues featuring Brooks's heavy bass doubled by Strazza's growling baritone and Miles's pounding drums, the piece sounded much like an updated version of Muddy Waters's 1954 hit "Just Make Love to Me." Michael reeled off a half dozen choruses of aggressive, Chicago-style lead as the horns and Barry's organ complemented his lines. The raw, seductive music would provide a virile pulse as Fonda's character makes passionate love to the film's elusive female lead, played by Salli Sachse. The tune would be not-so-subtly titled "Gettin' Hard."

For the central theme of *The Trip*, the leitmotif that would play under the opening and closing credits and at pivotal points throughout the film, Bloomfield, Goldberg, and Gravenites created an exotic-sounding anthem that was an unusual thirteen bars in length with three subsections and a four-bar introduction. They wanted a distinctive sound for its melody, something that would set the theme apart from the rest of the music in the movie, and Michael found it in the rich tones of Bobby Notkoff's amplified violin.

Notkoff, a twenty-six-year-old Los Angeles native, was a violinist who had performed with the LA Philharmonic but also played rock and blues. His excellent intonation and ability to improvise made him a popular addition to local jam sessions. He was living in Laurel Canyon, and Michael met him through

John Nuese. The violinist had an electrified fiddle that was a modified acoustic instrument. "It was a regular violin with some sort of Rube Goldberg pickup stuck on it," said Norman Dayron.

The addition of Notkoff's plugged-in violin provided the unique sonority Bloomfield was looking for. Bobby played a brief flourish to open "Peter's Trip"—as the theme was called—and then trilled over Miles's drum beat and Beaver's tick-tocking Moog to create the tension-building introduction. He then launched the piece's Eastern-sounding melody as Barry accompanied him, adding baroque ornamentation on harpsichord. The entire ensemble supported the melodic line through the piece's three subsections, with Bloomfield providing counterpoint on electric guitar and the horns creating rich harmonies behind Notkoff's lead. The complete form was repeated four times without solos, building slightly in intensity with each run-through until it concluded on the downbeat with a gong-like tag from Buddy's ride cymbal. Beaver's synthesized tick-tocks then finished the piece just as they had opened it.

It took the band ten days to record and mix the music for *The Trip*. All told, Bloomfield and his musicians watched a rough cut of the movie a total of six times through before they were done. When the sessions were completed, they had created a rich tapestry of musical sounds, some immediately recognizable, others new and exotic, and still others that more than stretched the definition of "music." Michael Bloomfield's creative use of sound was both innovative and clever, and the way he, Barry, and Nick skillfully arranged the instruments gave the resulting pieces an impressive range. Elements of rock, blues, jazz, and country were brought together with freely improvised, impressionistic audio collages. The use of electric violin was entirely novel. Though the amplified instrument had been used in country music and jazz for some years, its inclusion as a lead voice in a contemporary pop music setting was something completely new.

Also new was the contribution by the revolutionary instrument called the Moog synthesizer. Though Paul Beaver was already working on his own electronic music album with his partner, Bernie Krause, that record wouldn't be completed until much later in the year. His recordings with Mike Bloomfield were some of the first with the new synthesizer. There would soon be dozens of albums featuring the Moog, recordings by everyone from the Monkees and Beatle George Harrison to esoteric groups like the United States of America and San Francisco's Fifty Foot Hose. But *The Trip* soundtrack was one of the very first to pioneer the new technology, and in creating it, Bloomfield used the Moog's sounds not as gimmicky effects but as fully realized musical elements.

Roger Corman was more than pleased with the music Michael and his group created for *The Trip*, and he used nearly all of it in the film's final edit. He realized that his use of rapid cutting and special effects would be difficult to orchestrate, and he thought the American Music Band succeeded admirably.

"The music I think is *very* good," said Corman. "It really helps interpret scenes much more than most musical scores do. . . . The music constantly changes with the scenes, and because so many of them were so short, it was a tough score for the composer to make."

Peter Fonda, too, was delighted with Bloomfield's soundtrack. "The group covered the realm of music," he told an interviewer on the eve of the film's release. "There are three R&B numbers, a disco-dance sequence, and the last love scene is into heavy rock. There is some straight jazz and some symphonic effects. They're not into one bag." With more than a bit of pride, he added, "And we didn't just have a bunch of studio cats playing; we had a bunch of cats *creating*."

All told, Michael Bloomfield and his new band spent nearly three weeks in Hollywood working on the soundtrack for *The Trip*. When they weren't in the studio on Santa Monica Boulevard, they were visiting friends in Laurel Canyon, cruising the Sunset Strip, or hosting get-togethers at the Castle. Because word had spread that Bloomfield and his musicians were in town, more than a few fans dropped by the imposing residence on Glendower Avenue. Personalities of all sorts, appearing at all hours of the day or night, created a continual parade of the famous and near-famous. Life in the Castle soon resembled a freewheeling, unending party.

"People wanted to be around Michael," said Nick. "They wanted to follow him around. Wherever he went, they went[;] wherever he lived, they would show up. It got to be an entourage. Half of them would be guys who would be copping for the band, you know, and other half hangers-on, some friends from Chicago—it just got to be ridiculous!"

"There were a lot of people in and out while we were there," said Chris McDougal. "There was a girl who called herself Pandora—she was related to the famous Los Angeles defense lawyer Harry Weiss. Skippy Diamond was there too. He was an LA drug dealer who had been a pro wrestler."

Drugs were as much a part of the party as their purveyors.

"We had all kinds of drugs—it seemed like everybody was on acid all the time," said Norman Dayron. He remembered a special feature of the Castle's property that catered to expanded consciousness. "Someone had painted day-glow footsteps on the stone pathways in the garden out behind the house, and they guided you to amazing views if you were stoned. Obviously someone had been there before and had found the great views to look at if you were tripping!"

Psychedelics, especially LSD, were a requisite, given the time and place—and, coincidently, the topic of the movie that brought the band to Hollywood. But harder stuff was also in play. Barry Goldberg had begun using heroin casually at the end of 1966, and now he was regularly fixing. He was not alone.

"Mike's shooting junk . . . the trumpet player, Mark Doubleday, *he's* shooting junk, Peter Strazza, the sax player, *he's* shooting junk," Gravenites said. "We had this half junked-out band!" Bloomfield's use was still occasional, but Doubleday had joined the band with a well-established habit. Both he and his wife were users, having started in Seattle, where, he later told a friend, "everyone did it." Peter Strazza was still an infrequent user, but he, too, would join the others in Barry's basement quarters when he felt the need. No one was incapacitated—heroin was still largely a recreational indulgence. But the other members of the band were troubled by its presence. Especially Harvey Brooks.

"I didn't realize how different I was from these fellows. A lot straighter," said Brooks. He was not accustomed to such tolerant attitudes when it came to controlled substances. "There was a lot of drugs, a lot of heroin. Reefers were like cigarettes."

"It was a crazy scene," agreed John Nuese. "Drugs, nudity, jamming, blues—nonstop revelry!"

"The trip that we were on," said Norman Dayron, "had you filmed that, you would have had a *real* trip movie."

While they were still in Los Angeles, word came from Albert Grossman that ABGM had booked the band into a big festival that was in the works for the fairgrounds in Monterey. It would be held in the same outdoor arena as the Monterey Jazz Festival, but this weekend of concerts would be a celebration of pop music. It was rumored the Beatles would be there along with Bob Dylan, the Beach Boys, the Mamas and the Papas, and dozens of the best rock 'n' roll bands from both coasts and England. An industry showcase, it was going to be called the Monterey International Pop Festival and was scheduled to take place June 16 through 18, less than a month away.

Even though he was focused on finishing up the music for *The Trip*, Michael Bloomfield quickly realized the band would have to work fast to be ready in time for Monterey. In the month they had been together, the group had sketched out a few original tunes and had worked up arrangements for several covers, but they had nothing resembling a repertoire. The pressure only increased when

Grossman quietly let Michael know he was going to use the festival to present the band to the major record labels. If the companies liked what they heard, the manager said, he would negotiate a very favorable record deal with the one that made the best offer. But that was only if the companies liked what they heard.

With that in mind, Michael decided to see how well the band performed onstage. He had played the Whisky a Go Go on Sunset Boulevard numerous times with Paul Butterfield, and he knew the club sometimes presented unbilled acts along with those that were on the marquee. Through ABGM, Bloomfield arranged for the American Music Band to do one quick set at the Whisky with no publicity or fanfare. To prepare, they held a few quick rehearsals at John Nuese's place in Laurel Canyon and worked up several blues and a half dozen standards that everybody in the band knew.

Shortly before they finished work on *The Trip*, the American Music Band played for a surprised audience at the Sunset Strip dance club. The music wasn't very challenging, but it gave the group a chance to hear themselves in performance and to try out a few things. It also served to reassure Michael that with work they would be able to pull off an appearance at Monterey. That would be their *next* gig.

By the third week of May, the American Music Band and its leader were back in Mill Valley, busily woodshedding. The house on Wellesley Court didn't have room for the group to set up all its equipment, so Bloomfield rented rehearsal space in nearby Sausalito. Only fifteen minutes from the house, the rental was in a two-story frame building on the harbor, a structure called the Heliport. Though its primary business was providing seaplane and helicopter tours of the bay, the Golden Gate Bridge, and the city, the facility had empty rooms on its second floor that it rented out to local bands. Because many of the spaces were windowless, they were largely soundproof and thus perfect for loud practice sessions. Bloomfield and the band began rehearsing there regularly.

"Each day I would drive the big blue van over to pick up the guys and take them down to the Heliport," said Chris McDougal. "I'd go to Gate 6 Road and drop them off." The American Music Band wasn't alone at the Heliport. Quicksilver Messenger Service had a room there, as did pop singer Gale Garnett and several other bands, including the Freedom Highway and the Sons of Champlin.

The band began to work on its repertoire with several of the originals whose arrangements and parts they had already begun. One was a song called "Groovin' Is Easy," written and sung by Nick Gravenites. Built on an eighteen-bar AABC form with an eight-bar opening fanfare and interlude, the tune had a catchy mid-tempo melody and timely lyrics urging a lover to pursue "whatever you're cravin'." The song had nothing to do with the blues and everything to do with pop music, but as Michael and the band put its sections together, it soon became clear that "Groovin' Is Easy" was an exceptionally groovy tune.

"We worked out all the parts, but we never played it as a band 'til we had every part worked out," Michael later explained. "I said, 'OK, now we're gonna play this song from beginning to end.' And the sound just blew our minds. All of a sudden, we knew we had a dynamite band. And, man, it was a fantastic feeling."

It was fantastic because the band worked together so well musically, but also because Bloomfield knew Grossman was expecting them to produce music that was commercially viable. The innovative stuff for *The Trip* was fine, but a hit record was, as far as ABGM was concerned, infinitely preferable.

"Groovin' was the thing for a pop record, groovin' all over the place," said Bloomfield, explaining why he decided to concentrate on the song. "I figured, well, we got a pop record. In my opinion, 'Groovin' Is Easy' is a really great pop record, a really pop record from beginning to end." The arrangement the band had put together for Nick's song left no space for solos, though Michael did supply a brief bagpipe-like cadenza during the interlude following the second verse. The tune, however, fit right in with the sort of commercial music being produced in the spring of 1967.

A second original the band worked out was one written by Michael and Barry together. Titled "Over-Lovin' You," the tune was a soul scorcher that gave Buddy Miles the vocal spot. Constructed around a repeated four-bar progression with an eight-bar bridge, the song made full use of the horns and Bloomfield's complementary rhythm guitar fills. Barry Goldberg's electric harpsichord, added to the introduction and bridge over Miles's rumbling, timpani-like tom-toms, framed the tune with hints of classical continuo. But it was Buddy's vocal that dominated "Over-Lovin' You." The big drummer's ringing tenor, clear and confident, delivered the lyrics with an assurance that belied his nineteen years. He was unquestionably the band's soul powerhouse.

Though the band was making steady progress, rehearsing new and familiar material in preparation for the June festival wasn't without its moments of tension. *The Trip* sessions had been a relaxed, creative effort composed of opened-ended experimentation with no objective beyond making music suitable for the film. It was the way Michael Bloomfield liked to work, and he thoroughly enjoyed the process. But now, with the date of the Monterey festival approaching and pressure coming from Albert Grossman for a performance good enough to reel in one of the industry's top record companies, Michael was feeling the weight of the responsibilities that come with leadership. There were expectations that had to be met, and *he* was the one who had to meet them. That put him on edge.

"I saw a different side of Michael during the first weeks after we'd returned from LA," said Barry Goldberg. "He would run the rehearsals, and it was not uncommon for him to start yelling at the guys in the band if they weren't getting something quickly enough. He would berate any and all of us, including Nick and me, if he thought we were screwing up." Time for preparation was running out, and word was beginning to spread about the festival that was coming to the seaside town of Monterey in just a few weeks. It was going to big—bigger than any music festival that had ever happened.

The Monterey International Pop Festival had been on the drawing board since March 1967, when organizers Alan Pariser and Ben Shapiro put together a one-day popular music concert to be held at the Monterey County Fairgrounds. Pariser had attended the Monterey Jazz Festival at the fairgrounds the previous September and had seen the Jefferson Airplane and the Paul Butterfield Blues Band perform as part of Jon Hendricks's Blues All the Way production. Impressed by the crowd's response to the amplified bands and by the legitimacy imparted to the performers by the festival's artistic standing, Pariser hoped to do something similar for pop music. He hooked up with producer Ben Shapiro and the two began recruiting bands to perform at the fairgrounds. When they approached John Phillips hoping to enlist the Mamas and the Papas as one of the concert's headliners, Phillips was intrigued by the pop festival idea and brought it to the band's manager, Lou Adler. Presenting rock, soul, and blues as forms with artistic merit held strong appeal for both men, and Phillips and Adler soon maneuvered to take over as directors of the festival. By May, Shapiro was out and the event had evolved into a three-day pop music summit, a major showcase for new rock talent as well as established stars.

To document the proceedings, a deal was struck with ABC-TV allowing the network to film the shows and broadcast them later in a television special. Respected filmmaker D. A. Pennebaker was hired to make the movie. His documentary of Bob Dylan's 1965 British concert tour had just been released in May to critical acclaim.

Word quickly spread through the industry that a watershed event was about to take place in Monterey, and no one wanted to be left out. Reporters and photographers clamored for press passes. Managers pitched their clients for inclusion in the burgeoning list of performers. Record company executives hoped to discover emerging stars and sign promising acts. The acts themselves recognized a once-in-a-lifetime opportunity to gain access to a vast new audience. That audience saw a chance to catch on one stage all the groups they knew from records and radio, as well as hear dozens of new bands that were on the cutting edge of pop music. Ticket sales by the end of May were brisk.

The roster for the three-day festival favored West Coast rock bands, but there were also a fair number from New York and Chicago, as well as from London. The lineup included a healthy mix of rock 'n' roll, folk-rock, blues, and folk performers, including established stars like the Beach Boys, the Association, Johnny Rivers, Simon and Garfunkel, the Byrds, and Eric Burdon. Rumors went around that the Beatles, who had just released *Sgt. Pepper's Lonely Hearts Club Band*, would be making a surprise appearance.

Though the Fab Four were not officially on the bill, up-and-coming rock acts like Buffalo Springfield and the Jefferson Airplane were. Soul music would be represented by jazzy club singer Lou Rawls, songwriter Laura Nyro, and Memphis powerhouse Otis Redding. Among the lesser-known bands were Canned Heat from Los Angeles and the Paupers from Toronto. They would be joined by five San Francisco groups—the Grateful Dead, Quicksilver Messenger Service, Country Joe and the Fish, Moby Grape, and Big Brother and the Holding Company—all courtesy of producer Bill Graham. Blues performers included the Paul Butterfield Blues Band and the Steve Miller Blues Band. The English group the Who, little known in the States, would try to win converts to its brand of mod rock. The festival's international status would be affirmed by the presence of South African trumpeter Hugh Masekela and the Indian classical sitar master Ravi Shankar. In a category by himself would be the American with a British band, guitarist Jimi Hendrix.

It was into this maelstrom of talent, ambition, and industry brinksmanship that Albert Grossman sent the American Music Band. The group had only just patched together a set's worth of material before Chris McDougal had to pack the blue van with their equipment and get ready for the three-hour drive down to Monterey. The band was scheduled to close the festival's Saturday afternoon program, capping off a presentation of bands forging the new sound of contemporary blues-rock.

Mike Bloomfield's fans had read that he was assembling a new group, and more than a few knew he would be bringing it to the Monterey festival. Many in the music business, both musicians and executives alike, also were eager to hear what Paul Butterfield's former lead guitarist would do on his own. Bloomfield was unquestionably a star, considered by many to be the greatest young guitar player in America, and all eyes were on his next move, on this band he was debuting at the fairgrounds. In a little over two months, Michael Bloomfield's dream of an American music band had gone from being a casual, late-night

Hotel Albert fantasy to a highly anticipated, seven-man-strong musical reality, a dream real enough to be featured at perhaps the greatest popular music festival ever held. Anticipation was high, and expectations were higher. What would Bloomfield's new "big band"—as any band with horns was described in 1967—sound like? What kind of music would they play? Could their music be more amazing than what Michael had played with Paul Butterfield?

One more question. What was the band's name?

In the rush to create music for *The Trip* and then get ready for Monterey, no one had bothered to give the new group an official name. Bloomfield simply referred to his septet as the American Music Band, and when *The Trip* would be released in August, American International Pictures would obligingly bill the group as such. But that wasn't a *name*; it was a description—one that apparently hadn't even reached Monterey's front office in the weeks leading up to the festival, because they knew the band only as "Mike Bloomfield's thing." And so the group was billed in the festival's press releases: the Mike Bloomfield Thing. It was one more indication of how quickly the new band had been minted and thrust into the spotlight.

CHAPTER 15

MUSIC, LOVE, AND FLOWERS

MONTEREY, 1967

Norman Dayron had gone back home to Chicago after Michael and the band finished up work on the soundtrack for *The Trip*. But only a few weeks later, Bloomfield invited his friend back out to California for the big festival that had everyone talking. The college professor had heard about Monterey too, and he flew out to the seaside town just before the festival's start. He was amazed by what he saw when he arrived.

"I got on a plane and I booked right into Monterey—I had gone right from the San Francisco airport on one of these little planes, right into the Monterey airport," said Dayron. "As I was halfway down the ramp, I look down and it was like the *Wizard of Oz*. I mean, it was like the plane had landed in *Alice's Adventures in Wonderland*! I never saw so many people wearing these amazing costumes, these handmade, incredibly colorful and unusual outfits. You know, they were the natives of another country, and it was like I had washed ashore in a DC-3."

A former fishing village, the quiet town of Monterey had a population of about twenty-five thousand. Residents were accustomed to annual music festivals, having hosted the Monterey Jazz Festival since its inception in 1958. They knew there would be a large influx of people toward the end of each summer, with crowds for the jazz festival roughly doubling the town's population for three or four days. But these were well-mannered adult fans for the most part who rented hotel rooms and had money to spend. This pop music festival was something altogether different. Its attendees were younger, drug users instead of drinkers, unconcerned where they slept, and often short on funds. The newspapers called them "hippies," and town authorities eyed them with suspicion. It didn't help matters that they began arriving in large numbers several days before the festival was scheduled to begin.

But fears that there would be trouble were unfounded. The "flower children," many of them with actual flowers in their hair, comported themselves in a peaceful manner, professing love for one another and even for the local cops who patrolled the festival's perimeter. Flowers were everywhere, adding fragrant color to the festivities and underscoring Monterey Pop's slogan, "Music, Love, and Flowers." The event received a huge publicity boost when a song written by codirector John Phillips and sung by his friend Scott McKenzie reached number four on *Billboard*'s charts after its release in May. While not specifically about Monterey or the festival, "San Francisco (Be Sure to Wear Flowers in Your Hair)" seemed to provide the weekend of performances with its dress code and emotional compass.

Those who came to Monterey Pop got the message. As Dayron observed, the attire was eye catching, and the people wearing it were exotic, long-haired, and beautiful. It was a scene derived from some fantastic children's fairy tale. With their numbers approaching thirty thousand as the first day of the pop festival approached, the hippies seemed to be everywhere. Many without formal accommodations simply set up camp wherever they could find space. There were tents of all kinds and even a few teepees, and cars and vans lined the streets and filled the parking lots. A hint of marijuana could be detected every so often in the gentle breezes coming in off the bay while impromptu music jams provided homespun accompaniment for those perusing craft stalls, sampling cuisine from food vendors, or looking for someone hawking tickets. The prevailing mood was one of acceptance, serenity, and genuine brotherhood.

Into this huge counterculture gathering with its music industry underpinnings came the Mike Bloomfield Thing. Only now the band had an actual name. In the weeks leading up to their appearance at Monterey, an official moniker had finally been selected. At one point, Michael jokingly told a reporter the band was the "Royal Zoo," and he had seriously considered calling the group The Sound, or maybe Thee, Sound. But the final decision was ultimately a serendipitous one. The band's name was taken from a patriotic apparatus that struck all the members, especially Michael Bloomfield, as comical.

"The reason we chose the name 'Electric Flag' was because of Ron Polte, a tough buddy of Nick's from Chicago who became our resident manager," said Barry Goldberg. "Ron had this little motorized American flag that lit up and waved when you'd plug it in."

"There was this base with a motor in it and a pole with holes and a flag," Harvey Brooks said. "The motor would blow air through the pole and wave the flag."

Polte found the motorized flagpole in some high school or American Legion hall in San Francisco and, thinking it an amusing novelty, acquired it. Through Nick, Ron had gone to work for the band as its on-site manager, making travel arrangements and coordinating gig dates for ABGM. When he brought his plug-in flag over to the Heliport one afternoon while the band was rehearsing,

Michael Bloomfield asked for a demonstration. Seeing the device in action cracked the band up, and Bloomfield decided they had to use it during their performances.

"I would set it up on top of Barry's Leslie speaker cabinet," said Chris McDougal. "We rigged it up so he could turn it on with the organ's tremolo switch. That's where the band's name came from."

Mike Bloomfield's Thing was now officially the Electric Flag.

The Electric Flag arrived in Monterey several days before the start of the International Pop Festival. Michael and Susan, not wanting to drive, caught a flight down to the seaside town from San Francisco. They were pleasantly surprised to be joined on the small aircraft by another musician who was headed to the festival.

"Ravi Shankar was on the same plane," said Susan. "We were so awestruck that I curtsied and Michael bowed!" For Bloomfield, it was a real thrill to meet the Indian sitar virtuoso, the man whose music he had first heard with Roy Ruby back in Chicago a decade earlier. He told Shankar that he had been inspired by the sitarist's playing to create a raga-like piece of his own and that he tried to use some of the scales common in Indian classical music in his own soloing. The master listened politely, smiling at the animated young man who was so earnest about music. He couldn't help but be charmed by Michael. For Bloomfield, the chance meeting felt like a good omen.

A suite of rooms had been reserved for the Flag in a motel on Fremont Street, a four-lane thoroughfare just a block north of the Monterey fairgrounds. The festival had rented rooms for performers there and in several other motels along the busy street. After settling in, Michael and the other Flag members wandered up and down the halls, visiting with musicians they knew and getting acquainted with those they didn't. Then it was a trip up to the fairgrounds to check out the scene at the festival. Preparations were well under way, with crowds of workmen hanging lights, moving audio equipment, setting up chairs and cyclone fences, hanging banners, and finishing craft vendor stalls. There was activity everywhere, and everywhere there was the thrum of excitement.

The festival's music performances would take place in the big arena on the fairgrounds. It was an enclosed rectangular space, about half the size of a football field, with a packed dirt floor and an elevated stage at one end. With hundreds of rows of folding chairs set up on the main floor, the arena could provide seating for some 6,500 patrons. During most of the Monterey festival, every one of those seats would be taken.

Back at the motel, more groups were arriving. A few of Michael's friends had also appeared. On Bloomfield's invitation, John Nuese had come up from

Laurel Canyon and was camped out in one of the Electric Flag's rooms. Joel Harlib, Michael's first manager and Old Town cohort, made the trip from Chicago to see his friend and catch the new band's performance. Norman Dayron, too, had found his way to the Flag's motel. The colorful characters he had seen at the airport were only a preamble. Once again, it seemed to Norman, the circus was in town. But this wasn't a Barnum & Bailey sideshow. It was more like the Cirque du Soleil.

"I went to Mike's motel and met all these people," said Dayron. "There were lots of people there who played at the festival, and they were meeting each other and feeling each other out. But it wasn't like when we were in LA for *The Trip*. This experience was surprisingly free and lighthearted, and people were really just looking and listening with open ears."

For Michael Bloomfield, the prefestival revelries were like a grand reunion. Of all the musicians at Monterey, he was the one who knew many of the players on the festival's roster personally. He had shared a stage with most of the bands from San Francisco, worked with the Byrds in Los Angeles, jammed with the Blues Project in New York, opened for Simon and Garfunkel on Long Island, knew Canned Heat's Al Wilson from Boston, toured with Eric Burdon, and traded licks with Jimi Hendrix. He was intimately familiar with the Chicago groups, having been part of the Butterfield Band and having worked in the same clubs as Steve Miller. It seemed like Michael knew everyone and everyone knew him. It also seemed like everyone wanted to know what the country's hottest blues-rock guitar player was going to do with his new band.

"Everyone was talking about Michael and the Electric Flag," said Dayron. "I mean, that was the mystery band; that was the group that everybody wanted to hear. Everybody would be dropping by and paying homage to Michael."

Among those who came by was one well-known San Franciscan who wasn't a musician. His name was Augustus Owsley Stanley III, a thirty-two-year-old one-time ballet dancer, sound technician, and amateur chemist who in 1965 began producing massive quantities of LSD for general consumption. Since that time, Owsley, as he was commonly known, had become the West Coast's chief supplier of psychedelic drugs, both familiar and experimental. He was in the habit of offering doses to local rock bands and their fans, and that was his reason for coming to the festival. He had concocted a new batch of LSD that he called "Monterey Purple" in honor of the occasion and was passing out free tabs at the motel on Fremont Street.

Drugs were just as much a part of the scene at Monterey as they had been in the Hollywood Hills when Bloomfield had been working on *The Trip*. Due mostly to Owsley's largess, acid use over the weekend was rife both backstage and out front in the audience. For nearly everyone in attendance, the drug's mind-expanding qualities enlarged the musical experience while concurrently bathing the festival in a rosy glow of communal epiphany. That mystical commensality had been missing in Hollywood, but it soon became the central theme of the Monterey Pop experience. Even Michael Bloomfield was not immune to its aura of brotherhood and good will. For the guitarist, the welcoming, nonjudgmental acceptance he felt at Monterey was a real, tangible thing. It readily overwhelmed the streetwise, cynical side of his nature and seemed to rework his long-held image of himself as a tough rock 'n' roll greaser. At Monterey, Mike Bloomfield became—if only for a weekend—a flower child, a newly minted hippie.

The first round of sound checks for Monterey Pop's schedule of concerts was held Friday morning. The day dawned hazy and cool with temperatures hovering in the upper fifties. A slight fog coming in off the bay was gone by noon as the sun made a half-hearted attempt to break through the clouds. In the arena at the fairgrounds, activity was clustered around the stage as a succession of groups plugged in and took their places behind mics for a quick run-through. The untried sound system was also being taken for a test drive, with its huge "Voice of the Theatre" horns and speaker cabinets flanking the stage. Stage hands arranged mics and positioned amplifiers, noting their placements and settings while Al Kooper, called into service as the festival's assistant stage manager, ushered each band on and off the platform. Kooper had recently parted ways with the Blues Project and was working at Monterey while hobnobbing with musician friends and generally taking in the scene.

The plan was to get all the bands slated for the Friday evening and Saturday afternoon shows onstage so that levels could be set, the mix could be mastered, and lighting could be adjusted. In quick succession, starting with the Friday performers, Kooper brought up each group for a few minutes in front of the mics. The big PA speakers boomed out over the empty arena with snippets of familiar tunes as engineers in the sound booth at the back of the facility adjusted volumes and tightened the mix. Workmen were still busy hanging signs and decorations, adjusting lights, and running cables.

Once the Electric Flag's turn onstage came, mics were positioned and checked, and equipment was hooked up. With the big amps provided by the festival buzzing behind them, the Flag played a few choruses of one of their tunes. The engineers in the booth at the back of the arena made adjustments and then signaled they had the levels set. Michael Bloomfield counted off the tune again, a bit faster than the first time, and the band charged into its introduction. The tune was a blues, a fast shuffle based on a 1946 jump blues by Granville "Stick" McGhee called "Drinkin' Wine, Spo-Dee-O-Dee." In the wings, several stagehands began nodding to the beat. One executed a few quick steps in mock-jitterbug fashion, laughing with pleasure as the music took off. The Electric Flag's sound was tight, their arrangement meshing with the precision of a well-rehearsed dance routine. Following Nick's vocal came a dramatic break and then Bloomfield took the lead and blew through two choruses, leaving no doubt who was in charge. Al Kooper smiled knowingly from his vantage point at the side of the stage. If Michael's performance at the Flag's sound check was any indication, America's greatest blues-rock guitarist was clearly going to steal the show at Monterey.

Back at the motel on Friday afternoon, Michael Bloomfield corralled a few of his men and organized a band rehearsal. He wanted to play through the tunes they were planning to do yet again, making sure that each musician knew his part. The Flag's arrangements, he knew, had to be as tight as possible for the band's debut to be impressive. Though the band had worked up a dozen possible tunes in preparation for the festival, Bloomfield was completely satisfied with only four of them. There were the two originals they had put together in Mill Valley, "Groovin' Is Easy" and "Over-Lovin' You," and the tune they had played at their sound check, Stick McGhee's "Wine." The remaining song was "The Night Time Is the Right Time," an old R&B number done by numerous artists over the years. The Flag re-created Ray Charles's 1959 hit version of the song, with Buddy Miles taking both Charles's and Margie Hendricks's vocal parts. With only four tunes prepared, the band's set would be short, but Michael was hoping the Electric Flag's intensity, formidable musicianship, and unique sound would more than make up for the brevity of their appearance.

The entire band was excited about their billing as the featured group on Saturday afternoon, and Bloomfield was especially keyed up. He had good reason to be. Albert Grossman arrived at the festival that afternoon with his wife, Sally, and soon appeared at the Flag's motel. He told Michael that CBS's top man, Goddard Lieberson, would be attending the festival along with Columbia Records' new president, Clive Davis. Davis, Albert said, was on the lookout for rock 'n' roll talent and had expressed an interest in Bloomfield's new group. Atlantic Records would also have its chief producer and head A&R man, Jerry Wexler, in the audience scouting for new acts throughout the weekend of performances. The shrewd Grossman saw an opportunity to pit one company against the other, creating a bidding war for Bloomfield's Electric Flag and securing the band a lucrative recording contract. For the plan to work, though, Saturday's performance would have to be a showstopper. Michael hastily reassured him that the band was ready and was sure to impress. The silver-haired manager seemed satisfied but offered only the slightest of smiles in reply. What was beginning to impress Bloomfield was just how stressful being the leader of a band could be.

But there was no time to dwell on the pressure. The motel was crowded with musicians, their friends, and scores of fans, and there was a constant parade of people through the Flag's suite of rooms. "Everybody would come by and pay homage," said Norman Dayron. "They would find out what room Michael was in and timidly knock at the door, come in, and say a good word. Literally, everyone who was on the festival. We were all in these motel rooms, this big complex of interlinked motel rooms, like this spectacular beehive, and Michael was the king bee. That's what it looked like to me."

The Monterey International Pop Festival officially began at 9:15 p.m. on Friday evening with codirector John Phillips welcoming the crowd from the stage and then bringing on the pop vocal group the Association for the first set of the first concert. Some eight thousand fans crowded into the arena, and hundreds more peered over the amphitheater's fences or climbed on nearby rooftops to get a view. The day had cooled, and temperatures at show time dropped into the upper fifties. Many in the audience were bundled in sweaters and coats or wrapped in blankets, but the mood was warm and friendly, and the atmosphere was charged with anticipation.

The festival's first night of performances featured well-known pop acts with only a few new names. The Association was a safe bet to launch the concert series with their comfortable harmonies and familiar melodies. The group's recent single "Windy" was climbing the charts on its way to becoming number one, and they sang it as well as the two other top-ten hits they had scored with previous releases. They were followed by one of Albert Grossman's recently acquired bands, the Paupers. The largely unknown Canadian group, Chris McDougal's former employers, had been included in the festival's roster at Grossman's insistence. An innovative quartet with, at times, three of its members playing drums, the Paupers' set was unfortunately hampered by equipment failure and a few doses of Owsley's potent Monterey Purple.

Next came soul singer Lou Rawls, who treated the huge outdoor amphitheater as though it were an intimate supper club in Chicago's Loop. Backed by the festival's house band, he sang standards and narrated his way through his two hard-times hits, "Dead End Street" and "Tobacco Road." He was followed by Paul Simon's erstwhile girlfriend, English folksinger Beverly Kutner, known simply as Beverly. Her three songs, including one written for her by Donovan, went by almost unnoticed. Pop-rock singer Johnny Rivers opened his set with the Beach Boys tune "Help Me, Rhonda" and finished up with his 1966 hit "Secret Agent Man," covering Lead Belly, the Four Tops, Chuck Berry, and others in between.

The first inkling of what was to come at the festival arrived onstage with British superstar Eric Burdon. Backed by a coruscating San Francisco–style light show, his newly formed edition of the Animals played gutsy blues-rock and featured long, psychedelic renditions of Donovan's "Hey Gyp" and the Rolling Stones' "Paint It Black." It was the festival's first taste of contemporary rock 'n' roll performed by a headlining act, and its trippy excess was well received by the crowd. Burdon's salty vocal intensity was followed by the sweet harmonies of Monterey's Friday-night closers, Simon and Garfunkel. Their seven originals, all penned or adapted by Paul Simon, ended the evening on a smart, literary note, sending the vast audience off at midnight humming the duo's pretty melodies.

Michael Bloomfield caught the shuttle van back to the Flag's motel after the show. Susie was asleep, having spent the day in bed nursing a case of the flu, so the guitarist went into the lounge, where he found other members of the band. Sleep was out of the question—Bloomfield was too keyed up to even sit still. He wasn't alone.

"I didn't even sleep the night before," said Harvey Brooks. He had gotten used to Michael's nocturnal habits and wasn't surprised to see Bloomfield. "There would be times where I would hear him in the middle of the night playing. It would be real quiet, but it would be real intense." A wakeful night, though, was something unusual for Brooks. It was a measure of how pumped up the band was.

Saturday morning dawned clear and brisk, with temperatures hovering around fifty degrees. After a big breakfast in the motel's restaurant, Mike Bloomfield headed to the fairgrounds. The Electric Flag's performance wasn't scheduled until late Saturday afternoon, but he wanted to get to the festival to talk with Albert Grossman about the band's prospects and learn the manager's plans for it following Monterey. He also had to be there because he was scheduled to give a guitar workshop with the Byrd's Jim McGuinn, now known as Roger, in the seminar building on the fairgrounds. McGuinn was going to talk about folk guitar styles, and Michael, being the country's top blues-rock guitarist, would demonstrate blues techniques.

When the shuttle van let him off behind the stage at the arena, Michael found Albert and Sally Grossman there. While they were talking, the Grateful Dead's Jerry Garcia arrived, soon followed by an exotic-looking Jimi Hendrix. The three musicians, arguably the best guitarists in contemporary rock 'n' roll, chatted amicably for a few minutes, sharing gossip about the festival and critiquing the Friday night performances. Of the three, Michael Bloomfield was the national figure. Very few fans outside of San Francisco had ever heard of Garcia, and Hendrix was completely unknown. By the end of the weekend, though, that would dramatically change. And only Jimi Hendrix knew how dramatically it would change.

Both Hendrix and Garcia also had a good reason to get to the festival early—their bands were scheduled to do sound checks that morning in preparation for the Sunday evening show. Other groups were there for that purpose too, and the backstage area soon became crowded with musicians, both famous and near-famous. As the morning progressed, assistant stage manager Al Kooper brought up one band after another to get their levels set and their setup notated. Last to take the stage was Hendrix. His big Marshall amplifier and its cabinets, brought over from London, were carried out and stacked in front of the festival's smaller Fenders. After a few moments' delay while waiting for his bandmates, Hendrix plugged in to the big amp, powered up, and launched into a blues, just playing a mix of chords and lead. The volume was overwhelming and the empty arena echoed with sound. Kooper could see that the former Jimmy James had become someone altogether more formidable.

"I had seen Hendrix in the Village," said Al. "But this was something else."

Michael Bloomfield missed the Seattle guitarist's moment onstage because he was busy getting ready to teach festivalgoers about the blues at Monterey's guitar workshop. He already knew what Hendrix could do, and, as impressive as it was, it didn't really concern him. It wouldn't be until Sunday evening that the full impact of Jimi Hendrix's artistry would affect him.

Gates to the arena opened at 1:15 p.m., and the facility was soon filled with eager concertgoers. Those who had no tickets again boosted themselves up on the wall at the back of the arena, hoping to see at least some of the afternoon concert. The fairgrounds had been crowded since midmorning with thousands of people wandering about, perusing the exhibits, visiting the various craft and instrument booths, and sampling offerings in the food court. Children frolicked in a special playground created just for them, and couples lounged together on blankets in the grassy picnic area next to a giant statue of the Buddha. Clothing was even more colorful and imaginative than it had been in the days leading up to Monterey's opening, and it seemed as if the huge festival had become a vast medieval pageant. Everyone who passed through the festival's main gate was given a flower, and there were orchids everywhere. The air was alternately sweetened by the floral bouquet and by joints passed among the blooming throng.

Monterey's constabulary had been told to stand down, and many of the city's cops were sporting boutonnieres. There would be no pot busts that afternoon.

Following his workshop, Mike Bloomfield made his way through the crowd. He could hear the afternoon concert's first group, Canned Heat, working through Muddy Waters's "Rollin' and Tumblin'" as he passed into the backstage area and joined other musicians waiting in the dressing rooms beneath the main stage. A TV monitor showing the performance caught Michael's attention for a few moments, but he soon got into an animated conversation. Harvey Brooks, who had also come over to the festival early, listened in.

"Michael and I were in a room with Brian Jones, who was an incredibly nice person and very much into the blues," said Brooks. "He and Michael could really talk shop."

Bloomfield and Jones renewed their acquaintance and, recollecting their discussion at Olympic Studios in London last November, resumed talking as though they had just left off the day before. The two were a study in contrasts. Bloomfield, conservatively dressed in Levis, a light blue Oxford shirt, and a short-waisted safari jacket, was a head taller than the diminutive Jones. His single concession to sartorial embellishment was the white silk scarf he wore around his neck and tucked into his coat. The Rolling Stone, layered in paisley-patterned silk shawls, lace scarves, and love beads, resembled an eccentric viscount sporting a unisex pageboy. Michael was emphatic, talking fast and underscoring his points, as was his habit, with broad gestures and repetition. Jones, looking slightly dazed, spoke softly and smiled frequently. But he was clearly enjoying himself. The two talked about everything from recent blues releases to the extraordinary scene at Monterey.

Before long, though, their attention and that of nearly everybody in the room was drawn to the stage monitor. Performing was the first of the San Francisco groups, Big Brother and the Holding Company. Bloomfield thought that they, like most of the other bands from the City by the Bay, were hardly more than amateurs. But he very much liked the power and intensity of their twenty-four-year-old singer, Janis Joplin. Joplin was singing the Big Mama Thornton hit "Ball and Chain," and it was obvious, even on the small black-and-white screen, that something was happening. She looked wild, stomping and shaking, singing with a passion that went beyond anything yet seen at the festival. Bloomfield and several others crowded through the door at the far end of the room and out into a small stagehand pit to the left of the stage, where they could watch Joplin in action. She was truly astonishing. Shrieks, cries, feints, and moans, all backed by loud, distorted blues-rock.

Bloomfield could see that the crowd was right with her, cheering Joplin on, and she was responding, seeing how far she could go with them. It was a moment like many he had seen in clubs on Chicago's South Side, where the audience had been just as much a part of the performance as had the players. But this was on a scale unimaginable in a ghetto tavern. When the band brought the slow blues to a crashing finish, a huge roar went up from the audience, and for the first time Michael turned to look out over the main floor in the amphitheater. He was staggered by the size of the crowd. There were people as far as he could see, people in bleachers on both sides of the arena, people on roofs and on fences at the back. People were everywhere, and they were all on their feet, cheering and applauding. The audience had been big at Newport two years earlier, but this one suddenly seemed much larger. Michael could feel himself getting more than a little nervous.

The afternoon was beginning to warm as the sun shone down on the fairgrounds. People in the arena were wriggling out of their sweaters and shedding coats, stowing blankets under their seats. In the dressing rooms below the stage, the air was becoming hot and stuffy. The members of the Electric Flag loitered backstage or in the alleyway behind the arena, or they wandered out into the audience to watch the other performances. Country Joe and the Fish followed Big Brother, playing an appropriately psychedelic set while enjoying the effects of Owsley's Monterey Purple. Next came Al Kooper, shirking his stage manager duties to do a twenty-minute set with Elvin Bishop, Harvey Brooks, and Billy Davenport. By the time the Paul Butterfield Blues Band took the stage, it was nearly 4:00 p.m., and there were still two more bands to go before the Flag.

Michael went out to the wings to watch his old employer's set. Butterfield had expanded the band after Bloomfield's departure by adding two horn players, ironically replicating the instrumentation Michael had selected for the Electric Flag. As the guitarist watched, Paul worked through a set that included many of the numbers Michael used to do with the band, and the addition of horns filled in the sound nicely. The harp player concluded his performance with a beautifully nuanced version of "Driftin' Blues," playing a portion of his solo acoustically. It was a masterful demonstration of blues, and Bloomfield applauded enthusiastically along with the rest of the audience at the conclusion of Butterfield's performance. But his pleasure was tempered by growing feelings of insecurity. Michael was beginning to worry about how the Electric Flag would be received.

"I was jacked up on adrenaline. It was the end of a long afternoon, and we were scared shitless. Everybody we saw were old friends of ours, and it was their greatest hour," Michael later said. "Then Butterfield came on. He had horns! He was better, he was just—we couldn't follow *any* of them."

After the Butterfield Band came Quicksilver Messenger Service, the third group from San Francisco to appear that afternoon. Ron Polte was still managing the popular quintet despite his recent affiliation with the Flag, and he had helped Quicksilver build a reputation for long, blues-tinged guitar jams. But it was approaching 5:00 p.m. and time was running short, so the group could offer only a truncated set of tunes that would later appear on their first album. After the breakup of the Goldberg-Miller Blues Band, guitarist Steve Miller had relocated to San Francisco, and the group he put together in the intervening months was next on the afternoon's roster. Called the Steve Miller Blues Band, they played a mixture of blues and psychedelic rock featuring Miller's thick, fuzz-toned lead. For his appearance at Monterey, the guitarist added prerecorded sound effects, and though they weren't as effective as he had hoped, the audience gave the band's short set a rousing ovation. It was almost 5:45.

The last act to appear on Monterey's Saturday afternoon program was giving its first official performance. Still listed in the program simply as the Mike Bloomfield Thing, the newly minted septet waited nervously backstage as mics were moved into position and the drum kit and Hammond B3 were wheeled out onto the stage. The press pit in front of the proscenium was suddenly crowded with photographers elbowing for the best vantage point while reporters, determined to get the inside story on the new band fronted by America's hottest young guitarist, pulled out their notepads. The wings on both sides of the stage quickly filled up with festival personalities including Al Kooper, the Jefferson Airplane's Paul Kantner, producer Chet Helms, Paul Butterfield, Mark Naftalin, Quicksilver's David Freiberg, and the Byrds' David Crosby. Joining the throng was Susie Bloomfield, wearing a high-waisted peasant dress and wrapped in a fringed yellow shawl to ward off the late afternoon chill. She was still recovering from the flu, but she was determined not to miss the debut of her husband's band.

Chet Helms had introduced the San Francisco bands throughout the afternoon concert, but now he yielded the microphone to a representative of the Los Angeles contingent. David Crosby, a friend of Michael's since the Butterfield Band first shared a stage with the Byrds in 1966, insisted on doing the honors. Stylishly clad in pegged Levis and a brushed-suede jacket, his beaver-fur hat pulled down seductively over his eyes, Crosby enthusiastically brought on the final act of the afternoon concert.

"You're going to hear a man whom I think is one of the two or three best guitar players in the world," said Crosby, provoking cheers and applause. "And you are going to hear some people that he thinks are one of the best bands in the world—and I do too. You're going to hear an awful lot of it, and it's called the Electric Flag."

The audience applauded warmly, but many in the vast amphitheater were suddenly confused. Who was this "Electric Flag"? Wasn't the band supposed to be Michael Bloomfield's new group? The program said nothing about a band called the Electric Flag, and Crosby hadn't mentioned Bloomfield. It was only when the members of the Flag ambled out onstage that many in the crowd recognized Michael. His explosive tangle of unruly black hair was a dead giveaway.

There was, however, one member of the audience who definitely knew whose band the Electric Flag was. A reporter sitting next to Cass Elliot described her enthusiastic reaction in breathless terms.

> Mama Cass glanced at her program to see who was on next, and went into a frenzy of excitement. "This is it," she yelled at us. "This next group is it!" The Electric Flag—the group she was so excited about—came on and knocked us out of our tiny skulls. They were an incredibly talented group, playing unbelievable music to a background of Cass appreciatively screaming, "Yeah, yeah!"

The band took a few moments to ready itself, and then Bloomfield faced his musicians, cradling his beautiful new Les Paul Sunburst. The moment of truth had come.

Michael's opening harmonic was embellished by a fanfare from the horns as Harvey Brooks's descending bass line ushered in the piece's initial chords and melody. It was Nick Gravenites's "Groovin' Is Easy," the first original tune the Electric Flag had worked up following *The Trip*. The band sounded tight, with Buddy Miles punctuating the horns' phrases with press roles and ride cymbal splashes. After the ten-bar introduction, Mark Doubleday and Peter Strazza punched the downbeat and the Flag kicked the tune into tempo. It sounded a bit rushed, but that was no surprise considering all the adrenaline onstage at the moment.

Nick sang two verses with the horns offering crisp support and Bloomfield providing fills, though his Les Paul was turned down so low that he was more felt than heard. He cranked up for the eight-bar guitar interlude that split the verses, and the audience got their brief first taste of "one of the two or three best guitar players in the world." Michael plucked the interlude's raga-tinged melody over a bagpipes-like drone from the horns, organ, and bass, then ended the section by stretching up to a high A. Gravenites returned for one more verse and then, sounding a bit breathless, overreached his range with repeated cries while the band thundered along behind him. In later performances of "Groovin' Is Easy," Bloomfield would answer the singer's vocal embellishments and then would extend the vamp with an intense solo of his own. But for Monterey, he merely comped for the vamp's sixteen bars and then brought the piece to a close with another fat-sounding string bend—this time up to a high D. Holding the screaming note as Buddy pounded out a thunderous roll and the horns tagged the melody, Michael brought the Les Paul up over his head and then slammed it down for the coda.

This time, the audience responded with unequivocal cheers and applause. "Thank you, thank you," mumbled Nick, clearly relieved. Bloomfield began tuning his guitar but then abruptly stopped and stepped over to a microphone. He grabbed its stand and hunched over it, clearly intending to address the huge crowd.

"When we'd play in San Francisco—that was our hometown—he used to get on the mic and speak for maybe ten minutes to the people," said Peter Strazza, remembering Michael's penchant for addressing audiences during the Flag's shows. "He'd say, 'This is my home, I love it here,' blah, blah. Then he'd start playing, and everybody would just go *berserk*!" It was important to Michael that those out front knew just what was happening with the band, and especially with himself. He wanted to be certain that listeners understood what the group was trying to convey. A natural talker, he saw no better way to do that than by simply telling them himself.

"Man, we're really nervous, man," Michael began, grimacing for emphasis and rocking back and forth. "This is like our first gig, you know, and we're *really* nervous. But we *love* you all, man, 'cause this is very groovy, man—Monterey is *very* groovy, man. This is *something*, man! This is our generation, man. All you people, we're all together, man! It's groovy and dig yourselves, 'cause it's really groovy." The excitement and tension of the moment—compounded by more than a little backstage partaking of the substances being passed around—rendered Michael somewhat less than articulate. The crowd began to giggle, but the guitarist's sincerity delighted and touched many.

"We were pumped," said Harvey Brooks. "Bloomfield kept using the word 'groovy' in all its variations, in his excitement to describe the scene that was set out before us. We played in the afternoon, so we were able to see people dancing and the expressions on their faces as we played. Their feedback was *amazing*. The band was nervous and tense, but once we started performing, and the audience accepted us, we relaxed enough to play a decent set."

"I remember Bloomfield talking to the audience exactly as if he were talking to one or two of his friends," said music writer and Country Joe manager ED Denson. Denson was in the audience, and he was impressed by Michael's candor. "I had never seen anyone have that kind of ease on the stage, that kind of intimacy. Because, of course, he wasn't talking to one or two of his friends, he was talking to one of the largest audiences that had ever gotten together to watch this kind of music."

Redoubling his effort to make himself understood, Bloomfield introduced the next tune.

"And now, listen—now hold on, hold on, wait a minute—no, cool it, no, c'mon," Michael said, laughing, trying to get his amused listeners' attention while focusing his own. "I'll tell you . . . we're going to do a song now, uh, that's our single, and it's called 'Over-Lovin' You.' And we're gonna do it now. So."

With that, Bloomfield unstrapped his Les Paul, passed it to a stagehand and picked up a new Telecaster that was leaning against the Hammond B3. He wanted the soul tune that he and Barry had written to have an authentic R&B sound, so he opted for a guitar that was Stax guitarist Steve Cropper's favorite. He plugged in, checked the Tele's tuning, and then gave a nod to Buddy. The big drummer, perched behind his kit like a human earthquake held in check by a taut black suit, slapped a one-note pickup and brought the band in on the downbeat.

A four-bar introduction with Bloomfield playing arpeggios that alternated between D and E♭ chords set up the rhythm for the tune, with Nick beating it out on conga and tambourine while Harvey Brooks clapped his hands over his head. Then Miles came in with the vocal, and "Over-Lovin' You" switched into high gear. The formidable drummer, his hot-combed pile of hair falling forward like a licorice waterfall, sang with complete control even as he drove the beat. The entire band seemed suddenly caught up in a musical whirlwind of their own creation. Buddy sang two verses and then, following a stop, brought on a four-bar interlude with Barry playing an organ trill while Harvey took a brief solo break. A third verse followed and then a bridge that stretched to eight bars, giving Bloomfield another opportunity to display his skills. Running up the neck in a flurry of notes and grimacing with intensity, he ended on a tremulous high A. The tune then fell into a vamp that lasted for thirty full bars while Buddy moaned, groaned, and shouted, leaving the audience rocking and rolling in their seats. Michael and Barry brought "Over-Lovin' You" to a conclusion with a brace of arpeggios around a surreal-sounding G^{sus2}, nailing the coda on the downbeat with a final press roll from the Flag's big drummer.

The audience erupted, rising to its feet, cheering, hooting, and whistling. Buddy Miles's performance electrified the entire arena. Critics would later say that after a long afternoon of white blues performers, Monterey finally got "the real thing" from Miles. But Buddy wasn't really a blues singer. He was an excellent soul singer who could handle modern blues and an exciting spectacle behind the drums. He was a part of the much-anticipated Mike Bloomfield Thing, and the audience was ready to be thrilled and amazed. Buddy was nothing if not thrilling and amazing.

The Electric Flag was warmed up now. Without pausing, Peter Strazza kicked off "The Night Time Is the Right Time," re-creating altoist Hank Crawford's introduction to the Ray Charles hit with a gritty, chorus-long tenor solo and then riffing with Doubleday while Buddy again took the vocal. The slow blues chugged along on Harvey Brooks's walking bass line, with Michael and Barry comping over Miles's stomping drum beat. Buddy sang two choruses with Gravenites, Brooks and Bloomfield backing him with the "night-and-day" refrain, and then took a third, singing "Baby!" in a call-and-response duet with Michael. The guitarist, having switched back to his Les Paul, echoed the drummer's cries with righteous bends, shaking the instrument as though he were a South Side bartender setting up a blues cocktail. That potent concoction was then poured out over the next two choruses as Bloomfield took his first real solo of the afternoon. "The Night Time Is the Right Time" was in the key of D, which allowed for easy bends high on the guitar's neck, and Michael exploited that advantage to its fullest. His two choruses were a mix of flashy runs and high-note bends, pushing the Les Paul to its limit.

The audience hooted and applauded as Bloomfield finished. Buddy then returned, improvising a vocal chorus that began "I'm so proud," a candid acknowledgment of his delight at finding himself the center of so much attention. He flailed away at his drums, sticks a blur, his upper torso rocking back and forth, his hair standing on end. From the audience it looked like he was trying to destroy his drum kit.

The band bore down for the last chorus as Miles again moaned and shouted, this time with Bloomfield comping in the spaces, and after a final turnaround, the band walked up to the tonic and ended the tune with one last stretch from Michael—again all the way up to a high D.

Again the audience went wild. Buddy Miles was momentarily overcome, stunned by the sound of eight thousand cheering people. People cheering *him*. After years of toiling in the shadows, backing other soul stars in countless clubs across the country, he suddenly was no longer anonymous. Buddy was the star now. It was intoxicating.

"It was a total get-off! Are you kidding me? I'd never done anything like that before in my life," Miles later confessed about Monterey. "To be up there, this big guy in this Beatles-type suit I had made with a paisley tie on, and you couldn't tell me I wasn't Dapper Dan!"

There was no time to savor the moment, though. The Electric Flag was fifteen minutes into its set and had played three-quarters of its prepared material, but the crowd was primed for more. Bloomfield mouthed a tempo to Nick, and the burly singer counted off "Drinkin' Wine, Spo-Dee-O-Dee," jacking up the beat. The audience, caught up in the energy of the moment, started to cheer as the band steamrolled into the jump blues. Michael primed the pump with a single held note, and then the horns jumped in, riffing furiously as Gravenites worked through the first verse. Turning to Michael, he broke out in a big smile as he pointedly sang,

You got a nickel and I got a dime,
Let's get together and buy some wine.

Bloomfield and Brooks repeated "wine, wine, wine" as Nick belted out the refrain and then sang a chorus enumerating a variety of vintages.

Elderberry, port, or sherry,
Sweet Lucy, Thunderbird wine.
Hey, buddy, pass that bottle to me!

Following Gravenites's request for a taste, the band came to a series of stops and then powered up to the four on Buddy Miles's staccato kick drum, launching Mike Bloomfield's solo into the stratosphere. Bending up to a held A, Michael began with a chorus of facile licks and then, to open his second twelve bars, stretched a high G up to an A, holding and shaking the note for nearly four bars, his right arm extending above his head with repeated strikes. It was a classic Bloomfield move, a moment of breathtaking intensity, and the crowd was visibly stirred. Michael then alternated between licks high and low on his Gibson's neck, creating a moment of call-and-response with himself. A third chorus brought a barrage of runs that created counterrhythms to the song's meter and then closed his statement with a second bend from G up to A.

Nick came back in, repeating all three verses as the band developed a ferocious, driving beat behind him. Buddy Miles hammered his drums mercilessly, his mouth wide in a silent cry as his entire body rocked. Barry Goldberg raked his keyboard, and Harvey Brooks arched backward, his Fender Jazz Bass nearly vertical. A stop followed the last turnaround as Gravenites shouted, "Hey!" and the horns executed a slow climb up to the tonic while cutting the tempo in half. Michael let loose one final fusillade of notes as Buddy pounded his bass drum, both arms extended above his head and ready to end the tune on one final, massive downbeat. And then down they came, crashing on snare and tom-tom, nailing "Drinkin' Wine, Spo-Dee-O-Dee" and concluding the Electric Flag's contribution to the 1967 Monterey International Pop Festival.

Or so it seemed.

The crowd was again on its feet—jumping, clapping, cheering, laughing. "More, *more*!" came the cries from all over the arena. Michael, all smiles, bowed to the cheering throng, unstrapped his guitar, and, along with Barry, Nick, Harvey, and Buddy, quickly exited stage right. Peter and Marcus, gazing out over the main floor and gauging the audience's overwhelming response, stayed put, fully expecting to do an encore. Susan had been seated on the edge of the stage, all the way over by the lighting board, but now she was up and cheering, overjoyed to see that Michael and the Electric Flag were such a hit.

As the band clustered in the wings, Bloomfield grabbed a stagehand and asked him to do something about the backup vocal mic—he wasn't sure it had been working when he and Harvey were singing. He had to shout to make himself heard over the noise of the crowd, and it soon became clear that the band would have to do an encore. But they had nothing prepared beyond the four tunes they had played, and Buddy, looking dazed and spent, was unsure what to do. It was left to Susan, caught up in the excitement of the moment, to turn the big man around and affectionately shove him back out onstage. Seeing Miles emerge from the wings, the audience redoubled their cheers, and he was quickly followed by the rest of the Flag. After a minute, the band fired up "Wine" again, having no other material to choose from. But it mattered little. The audience, letting loose at the end of a long afternoon, clapped along and danced at their seats. Susan, along with the band's road manager Ronnie Minsky and half a dozen other festival insiders, moved out onto the stage and began dancing too, clapping and laughing as they gyrated to the beat. On the other side of the stage, David Crosby stood cheering, fists in the air. The excitement was contagious. When the band brought the tune to a finish with another grand flourish, the crowd refused to let them leave the stage until they had run through "Wine" a *third* time.

As the members of the Electric Flag filed offstage to another wave of applause, Susie hugged each in turn. Michael, one of the last into the wings, was greeted like a conquering hero, with friends and fellow musicians slapping him on the back and offering their congratulations. It was a triumphant moment, and members of the band were giddy with relief. Their debut had been successful, and they were deeply gratified by the band's enthusiastic reception. For Buddy Miles, the Electric Flag was the hit of the festival.

"We were all nervous, 'cause it was our debut into the world," said Miles. "But people loved us. People went *crazy* over the band."

Barry Goldberg also was happy with the group's performance. "It wasn't one of our best gigs, and I wouldn't say it was our worst, but even at maybe 50 percent of what we could do, we still blew minds. People there never saw anything quite like it. . . . [I]t was pretty much unheard of at that time to have a horn section with a band that had a rock 'n' roll format." That, combined with the strength of the Flag's players, made the group exceptional in Goldberg's mind. "We had these guys that could really play and put on a show—and when Buddy got going, I don't think there was anyone who could touch us."

"Everybody was talking about them," said Norman Dayron, recalling the Flag's reception. "They were *the* hot topic of conversation."

A review published in the Los Angeles underground paper *World Countdown* seemed to capture the overall response to the Electric Flag's performance that Saturday afternoon.

> They were the Electric Flag, and as introduced by one of the Byrds [had] "the scariest drummer in the world" with the "second greatest guitarist in music." And they were so alive. The lead guitarist lived up to his introduction. He was happily out of his mind and into your head. This band is going to cause a lot of disturbance in music circles. It is Mike Bloomfield's latest labor of love, and there was great applause complete with the first standing ovation of the Festival.

It seemed that the only person in the arena that afternoon who was at all critical of the Electric Flag's performance was the leader of the band himself. Despite resounding approbation from nearly every quarter, Michael Bloomfield felt something wasn't right. The Flag had pulled off its first gig with real finesse and had thrilled thousands of listeners, but musically the band hadn't really broken any new ground. It wasn't like it had been when they had created music for *The Trip*. In the rush to cobble together a set for Monterey and woo industry bigwigs, innovation and risk-taking had been sidelined in favor of conventional song forms and covers. The band's choice of material had been effective—there was no doubt about that—but Michael's original reason for creating the Electric Flag seemed to have gotten lost along the way. Those misgivings were compounded by the guitarist's feeling that his own playing, while very good, had fallen short of what he knew he could do.

But these concerns were quickly subsumed by the hoopla that followed the band's twenty minutes on Monterey's stage. Attention directed at the group backstage was largely focused on Bloomfield, and though he felt it was unwarranted, he couldn't help but enjoy it. As Michael had confessed to his friend Charlie Musselwhite, there was nothing he liked better than to be in a room full of people with "all of them looking at me." Still, Norman Dayron could tell that his friend wasn't entirely happy.

"I think he was, in some sense, disappointed that Monterey didn't live up to his vision of what the Flag should have delivered, what he wanted for the group, what his dream of it was," said Dayron. Norman could see, too, that his friend was overwhelmed by all the unconditional praise. "I think he was completely blown away by the energy and the reception they got. I think he was quite surprised, like a lot of people are when they get a completely unequivocal, one hundred percent acceptance of what they do, even when they think it's no good."

Still, there was no doubt that by early Saturday evening, Michael Bloomfield was one of the stars of the Monterey International Pop Festival.

The festival was scheduled to resume at 9:00 p.m., and the arena gates were opened a little after 8:00. Once again the arena was filled to capacity, with the back wall and the roofs over the bleacher seats commandeered by hundreds who didn't have tickets. The mood was celebratory and lighthearted. The "peace, love, and music" theme of the festival was partly responsible for the vibe, but so too was the pervasive use of Monterey Purple, marijuana, and other recreational substances. After the parade of hip rock acts that afternoon, the crowd was primed for even more excitement from Saturday night's program of new and name acts.

First to appear was a new band from San Francisco called Moby Grape. The creation of Skip Spence, the Jefferson Airplane's former drummer, the group was one of the few from the City by the Bay that Michael Bloomfield thought competent. Their lead guitarist, Jerry Miller, impressed him as an excellent all-around musician who could play nearly any style. Michael got to the arena early because he didn't want to miss their set.

There was another reason Bloomfield had to be prompt. The Byrds were scheduled to perform early in the evening, and David Crosby had asked Michael to return the favor by introducing the band. But first, Hugh Masekela played a set of South African jazz. The trumpet player's group was augmented by conga drummer Big Black, and lengthy solos from everyone onstage caused Masekela's performance to last for nearly an hour. It was almost 10:30 p.m. before the Byrds were up.

Comedian Tommy Smothers had been emceeing, but now he brought Michael Bloomfield out onstage to introduce the star quintet from Los Angeles. Michael, still caught up in the spirit of the Summer of Love, gave the Byrds a fittingly poetic welcome.

"The musicians that are playing rock 'n' roll, they know where you're at, where your minds are at, and they're playing *for* you, *to* you," said Bloomfield. "And like the Beatles, and other groups, you know, their music will get to you and reach you, and the colors will flash and the sounds will embrace you. And it's beautiful—it's the Byrds." Though he managed to refrain from punctuating his thoughts with expressions like "man" and "groovy," Michael was still clearly smitten by Monterey's paradigm for the new world order.

The Byrds, suffering from internal conflicts and on the verge of breaking up, turned in a less than satisfactory set. But of the many things said by David Crosby during the band's performance, probably the least controversial was his comment about his guitarist friend's new band. "Man," the singer quipped, "if you didn't hear Mike Bloomfield's group, man, you are out of it, so far out of it."

Following the Byrds' performance, the Paul Butterfield Blues Band made a return appearance, substituting for the Beach Boys, who were a last-minute no-show. After their unscheduled set came New York singer-songwriter Laura Nyro. She sang several songs from her recently released album and, fronting a show band with backup singers, failed to connect with the audience. She left the stage after only four tunes, reportedly in tears.

It was up to the Jefferson Airplane to get things back into the Monterey groove, and the best of the San Francisco bands succeeded handily. Their tight harmonies and blues-tinged accompaniment, augmented by a trippy light show, delivered their current hit "White Rabbit" and other tunes from their latest record with a psychedelic rush. A light rain had begun to fall by the end of the Airplane's set, but the crowd was undeterred, rising to its feet and shouting for an encore as the band left the stage. The Saturday night concert was fast running out of time, though, and midnight was approaching, so the sextet did not return.

Instead, it was soul singer Otis Redding and his band of Stax veterans who appeared. Booker T. and the MGs warmed up the crowd with a few instrumentals, and then Redding took the stage by storm, leaping into Sam Cooke's "Shake" and bringing the audience to its feet. He delivered more of the same with "Respect" and then slowed things down with a steamy version of "I've Been Loving You Too Long," addressing his rapt listeners as "the love crowd." By the time Redding ended his twenty-minute set with a wrenching rendition of "Try a Little Tenderness," the twenty-five-year-old rising star of the Chitlin' Circuit had gained a whole new audience. He left the stage to a massive standing ovation, Monterey's second of the day after the Electric Flag, and would soon be acknowledged as one of the surprise stars of the festival.

Michael Bloomfield was eager to see the soul singer because he very much admired Redding's guitar player, Memphis session man Steve Cropper. Cropper's brand of Telecaster-fueled R&B had become a Stax/Volt trademark, and Bloomfield wanted to see him in action. But once Otis Redding came out, Michael got caught up in the excitement right along with everyone else. The crowd reacted to Redding just as it had to Buddy Miles earlier in the day, but the Memphis soul singer was able to take their enthusiasm to an entirely new level. Bloomfield was impressed, and he was not alone. Buddy Miles, watching from the wings, took serious mental notes as Redding whipped all of Monterey into a frenzy. The big drummer felt he was seeing his future.

The third day of the Monterey International Pop Festival dawned gray and rainy. The temperature was no warmer than it had been the previous two days, and it looked like the final day of concerts might be a wet one. But the rain never amounted to much more than a misty drizzle, and volunteers worked their way down the hundreds of rows of folding chairs in the arena, wiping puddles off the seats in preparation for the afternoon show. It was again a sellout.

The sole performer for the 1:30 p.m. program wasn't by any standard a pop musician, though his music had achieved a startling level of popular acceptance by 1967. Indian sitarist Ravi Shankar was known throughout the world as one of the great soloists on his instrument, and he had been coming to the United States to play Indian classical ragas since the 1950s. But it was only when the Beatles and other pop superstars began using sitars in their music and promoting Shankar that the general listening public discovered Indian classical music and its leading virtuoso. The festival organizers, wanting the Sunday afternoon concert to be a meditative, spiritual experience for the listeners, gave its scheduled three hours entirely over Shankar and his accompanists, tabla player Alla Rakha and tambura player Kamala.

Shankar's performance began a little late, following a protracted period of tuning, but once he and Rakha began their series of ragas, the audience was held in rapt attention. The only sound heard in the packed amphitheater was that of sitar and hand drums in intimate conversation.

Having met the Indian master on the flight to Monterey, Mike Bloomfield was not going to miss Shankar's performance. The guitarist caught the shuttle to the arena and entered the backstage area, greeting other festival musicians who were also there to see the sitar virtuoso. Peter Strazza was there too, and he and Michael made their way to the pit at the left of the stage for an unobstructed view of the Indian masters. Once the music started, Bloomfield was transfixed.

"We were standing near the stage," remembered Peter Strazza. "I said, 'Man you're *really* into this!'" One of Pennebaker's cameraman caught Bloomfield staring at the performers, his jaw slack and eyes wide, looking as though he had gone into a trance. The music clearly had an overpowering effect on him.

Shankar's set ran through five lengthy pieces, including a stunning drum solo from Rakha, and culminated in a furious exchange of riffs between sitarist and drummer. The concert lasted until nearly 5:00 p.m., and when Shankar finally brought it to a conclusion, the entire arena rose up. The exhausted crowd cheered and applauded, as much from appreciation of the performance as from relief that it had ended. Mike Bloomfield was in a state of bliss. He had heard all of Shankar's recordings, but this was the first time he had seen the classical sitarist up close.

With three hours to kill before the start of the evening show—Monterey's final concert—Michael headed back to the motel. He was supposed to meet with Albert Grossman to discuss the Electric Flag's future, and he wanted to get something to eat. When the burly manager appeared, they agreed to talk over dinner.

Grossman had been busy negotiating. He told Michael that the band's performance had been so effective that both Columbia and Atlantic were ready to sign them. He was inclined to have them go with Clive Davis and the venerable music giant because he felt that Atlantic's business practices were questionable. He also didn't care for the flinty, often abrasive Jerry Wexler. Michael protested that the Flag's music would be more appropriate for Wexler's label, a company well known for producing jazz and R&B artists. But Albert was firm. The band would become part of Columbia's roster, provided the money was right. He told Michael he was asking Davis for a huge advance. It would be an offer the guitarist couldn't refuse, Albert wryly added.

For his part, the president of Columbia Records, after catching their afternoon set, was completely sold on the Electric Flag. It seemed the hefty advance would not be a problem. "[Bloomfield] was a musician that everyone in the know was watching, and the Electric Flag, a tough, hard-hitting blues band powered by a torrid horn section, was his latest move," said Clive Davis. "The Electric Flag hit with gale force, and I was determined to sign them that day."

The evening program was scheduled to begin a bit earlier than the previous night's shows, starting at 8:00 p.m. Opening were the Butterfield Band's old rivals the Blues Project. Their set included a lengthy, psychedelic re-creation of "Flute Thing" with tape-delay sound loops and other special effects enhancing Andy Kulberg's flute improvisations. But without Al Kooper, their former keyboardist and guiding light, the Blues Project sounded tentative and unfocused. The crowd was also distracted, waiting eagerly for Big Brother and the Holding Company and their wildly emotive singer. Word had gone around that though the band was not listed in the program, they would be doing a repeat of their Saturday performance. Nearly everyone had heard about that show, and those who hadn't been there wanted to see what all the fuss was about.

Joplin had time for only two numbers, but she made the most of them. Concluding with "Ball and Chain," she once again shouted, moaned, pleaded, and cajoled her way through the lyrics, backed by the distorted, manic lead guitar of James Gurley and the crashing drums of Dave Getz. The singer deftly controlled the dynamics of the song, moving from ear-splitting cacophony to near silence in a heartbeat, and conveyed the raw emotion of her words with a conviction that was utterly convincing. She stomped so hard during one of the tune's stops that her ankle bracelet broke and lay on the stage for the remainder of the performance. But Joplin had the audience completely with her once again, and they cheered her every cry and whimper. At the conclusion of the tune, the singer skipped off the stage to a massive ovation, clearly delighted with herself and with the overwhelming response.

No one could follow Big Brother after such an electric performance, and it was almost no one who did. Festival director John Phillips's friends Cyrus and Renais Faryar were folk musicians who occasionally played around Los Angeles and San Francisco. They had put together an eclectic ensemble to perform at the Mt. Tamalpais Magic Mountain Festival in Mill Valley the previous weekend, and Phillips generously gave them a slot at Monterey. Prophetically calling themselves the Group with No Name, their appearance was brief, underrehearsed, and almost unnoticed by an audience still recovering from Joplin's pyrotechnics.

Buffalo Springfield, minus Neil Young but buoyed by the addition of Byrds renegade David Crosby, recaptured the audience's attention. Kicking off their set with "For What It's Worth," their hit from earlier in the year, the LA-based quintet-plus-one worked through a half dozen tunes and got the festival back on the contemporary rock 'n' roll track. It was a good thing, because a serious helping of rock was next on Monterey's menu.

One of England's most popular groups, the Who, was slated to come near the end of the evening's performances—perhaps as the last act before Monterey's closers, the Mamas and the Papas. But Pete Townshend, the quartet's guitarist, had shared a stage with Jimi Hendrix at London's Saville Theatre in January when the Experience opened for the Who, and he knew what the incendiary guitarist was likely to do onstage.

"He went on and did his thing," said Townshend, remembering the earlier show. "He knocked the amplifiers over, he practically smashed it up . . . and I went on afterwards and I just stood there and strummed." Townshend didn't want a repeat of that experience, and he didn't want his band to have to follow what was doubtless going to be a show-stopping performance.

Pete found Jimi in the dressing rooms beneath the stage, and they decided they would flip a coin to determine who would go on first. Hendrix lost the toss; he would have to follow the English rockers. Though he wasn't happy about it, he seemed to take his follow-up status almost as a challenge.

"Jimi said, 'If I'm gonna follow you, I'm gonna pull out all the stops,'" recalled Townshend. But he was satisfied, and not a little relieved that the Who would not have to contend with an audience that had just been amazed by Hendrix's extraordinary playing.

Eric Burdon introduced his countrymen, warning the audience that the Who would "destroy you completely in more ways than one." Though the group was well known in England with a string of top-ten hits to their credit, their fame had yet to spread to the United States, and few in the audience knew what to expect. Starting out with "Substitute," one of their UK hits, the band worked through a half dozen tunes from their mod art-rock repertory, no song lasting longer than five minutes and each executed with a precision that was foreign to many of the American acts. The Who's material featured English choirboy harmonies over a heavy rock 'n' roll beat and, unlike nearly all the music heard at Monterey that weekend, had little to do with American blues or R&B. Dressed in multicolored suits with ruffled shirts, hair poofed and permed, they presented a visual departure from the festival's hippie couture as well.

By the end of their set, the Who had won over the huge crowd. Cheers and applause greeted each of their tunes, and when Townshend announced their final number, "My Generation," many in the audience applauded in recognition. What few anticipated was the way the Who would end the tune. "Auto-destructive art," an aesthetic movement Townshend had learned about in art school, had been part of the band's act for several years. The guitarist and the group's drummer, Keith Moon, would destroy their instruments at the conclusion of each set, thus making what they felt was an artistic statement. The band's Monterey performance was no exception, and as the song reached a climax, Townshend cranked up his Fender Stratocaster and began sliding its neck over a nearby mic stand. Feedback and distortion filled the arena as Moon flailed at his drums and bassist John Entwistle slashed a slew of cascading notes and chords. Lead singer Roger Daltrey stepped aside as Townshend flipped his Stratocaster over his head, grabbed its neck and brought it crashing down on the stage floor. In moments, the heavy electric guitar was in splinters and smoke bombs were exploding behind the drums, obscuring the stage in a real purple haze. The noise was deafening as stagehands rushed out in an effort to rescue mics and stands from the whirling Townshend. The crowd, momentarily stunned, rose to its feet, wildly cheering and applauding the spectacle.

What Michael Bloomfield thought of the Who's theatrics has gone unrecorded. He doubtless recognized their value as a kind of entertainment, but trashing instruments and setting off explosions had nothing to do with music—*real* music—as far as he could see. A truly great artist wouldn't need to resort to such tactics; the music would suffice. Michael respected Pete Townshend's playing and saw him as a competent rock 'n' roller. But the Who's smash-and-crash, their "auto-destructive art," seemed like nothing more than a calculated act, an obvious gimmick grafted on to an otherwise conventional rock performance. Such antics would have been greeted with howls of derision on Chicago's South Side.

Providing an antidote to the Who's raucous finale was the Grateful Dead, another of San Francisco's favorite groups. They were up next, and there was nothing pretentious about their music, and certainly nothing artificial. Though they performed only four tunes, guitarist Jerry Garcia's lengthy solos turned each into a mini-jam. Opening with "Viola Lee Blues," the Dead soon had the crowd up and moving, and by the end of their set, Monterey had become a huge, San Francisco-style dance party.

It was Brian Jones, the aristocratic peer of Monterey's rock 'n' roll realm, who strolled out onstage following the Grateful Dead. He had asked to introduce the next act, and he now did so sotto voce, describing the psychedelic gypsy waiting in the wings as "the most exciting performer I've ever heard." With that, the Jimi Hendrix Experience took the stage.

Right away it was clear that something different was about to happen. A slight black man suddenly appeared onstage wearing a pink feather boa, a mustard yellow ruffled shirt, bright-red bell bottoms, and a multicolored jacket festooned with hand-painted eyeballs. His unruly tangle of hair was held back by a paisley scarf tied in headband fashion around his forehead, and he carried a jet-black Stratocaster strung upside down. With him were two equally hirsute white men, one in a striped morning coat and the other in pink ruffles. Though there were scores of players watching from the wings, there were only three musicians on the wide stage. The Jimi Hendrix Experience would be the only electric band to perform at Monterey as a trio. They wouldn't need anyone else.

Hendrix plugged into his tall Marshall stack and twisted a few knobs on its head. Then he abruptly turned, faced the audience, and began furiously strumming the opening riff to an arrangement of Howlin' Wolf's "Killing Floor." The lights came up as bass and drums joined in, and the band was off and roaring.

Very few in the audience knew who Jimi Hendrix was, and those who did knew his music only from the Experience's version of "Hey Joe," released as a single in the States in May. The guitarist from Seattle via London was determined that his ten thousand listeners would leave Monterey without any question in their minds as to who Jimi Hendrix was. He plowed through "Killing Floor" at an aggressive tempo, singing a few verses and then stepping back from the mic to solo at an ear-splitting volume for a few more. Alternating between holding notes to the point of feedback, left arm extended above his head, and hammering out slithery tremolos, tongue extended and wagging lewdly, Hendrix drew open-mouthed stares from many in the audience and cries of delight from many more. Ending the tune on one last tremolo and a final squelch of feedback, the Experience was rewarded with a showering of applause, whistles, and cheers. This was something entirely new.

"Yeah, what's happening, brother?" Jimi said into the mic as the crowd quieted down, waiting for whatever was next. He was vigorously chewing a wad of gum and squinting from the glare of the spotlight. "We got a little thing called 'Foxy Lady.' My fingers will move, as you see, but you won't hear no sound. Yeah, but dig this . . ." The guitarist slowly turned up the volume on his Fender and a sirocco of electric wind blew through the arena. He then began the original tune's opening riff, while the rhythm section fell in behind him. Singing and dancing around the stage, gesturing to the audience, playing guitar with one hand, Hendrix was constantly in motion as he performed. His movements were completely fluid, at one moment elegant and graceful, the next suggestive and vulgar. All eyes were on him—no one could look away. He was a magnificent spectacle, a rock 'n' roll cataclysm.

In the middle of the song, Jimi suddenly swung his left leg up and over the Stratocaster, pulling its long neck up between his legs and forming a phallus with the guitar's distinctive headstock. He stroked it vigorously, adding a tremolo for emphasis. Some in the audience—and even a few journalists in the pit in front of the stage—were shocked. It was only the beginning.

For forty minutes, the Jimi Hendrix Experience played intense, primitive, loud, uncompromising rock music on Monterey's stage. The guitarist's revolutionary use of feedback and distortion was a revelation. No one had ever played guitar like that. And no one, it seemed, had ever played with such finesse and ease. His timing and coordination were flawless. It was almost as though the instrument were an extension of Hendrix's body.

Then there was the guitarist's act. He played the Stratocaster behind his back, over his head, with his teeth. He did a backward somersault while playing. He pranced, shook his hips, slithered his hands up and down the Fender without missing a beat. He moved from crashing waves of sound to supper-club volume with a control that was as exciting as it was startling. He talked sweetly to the audience between tunes, wooing them with a self-effacing coyness that stood in marked contrast to the visceral assault of his music. His performance was an act of seduction, enticing the crowd into his embrace, forcing it to yield to his sonic caress. It was, in short, pure sex.

Mike Bloomfield watched Jimi Hendrix from the wings, standing back in the shadows behind the crush of gaping musicians, stagehands, managers, promoters, and groupies. The doings onstage were familiar to him. He had seen Hendrix's guitar tricks many times on the South Side, used by guitarists in the gritty bars and taverns of Bronzeville, and over on the West Side in countless dives and roadhouses. He had even mastered a few of them himself, amazing his high school bandmates by playing behind his back or with his teeth. But tricks were just that—tricks. Buddy Guy used them sometimes, but he had often been criticized for "shucking" too much, for using too many gimmicks to get over. Guitar stunts, Michael knew, were little more than a cheap way to impress an unhip audience.

Hendrix's suggestive bit was also nothing new. Sex was an essential part of any blues performance. Many times on the South Side, Bloomfield had seen the music used as a prelude to coitus. He had watched dancers simulate the sex act, inspired by the bump and grind of the blues. He had seen women hike their dresses, exposing themselves to the musicians and anybody else who cared to look. He had come upon patrons entwined in the restroom or behind the stage or outside the bar on a park bench. The blues was all about love—especially carnal love. The audience at Monterey may have found Hendrix's gestures shocking, but for Michael they were as familiar as the changes to a twelve-bar.

But Bloomfield was beginning to feel uneasy.

There was something about what was happening on Monterey's stage at that moment that went beyond mere gimmickry and sexual innuendo—something that was substantive and transforming. What Jimi Hendrix was doing exceeded anything Michael Bloomfield had ever seen on the South Side. It exceeded anything he had seen in clubs and on concert hall stages across the country. It transcended the role of the performer, as far as Michael understood it. It was something entirely new. Bloomfield had been unable to comprehend what Hendrix was doing when he first saw him at the Cafe Wha? in 1966, and now he was again at a loss.

Onstage, Jimi Hendrix was making another speech between tunes, telling the audience how much he loved them and how he wished he could just grab them and kiss them. "I'm gonna sacrifice somethin' right here that I really love," he told them, making an offering to the sea of faces before him. "I'm not losing my mind, this is just for everybody here—this is the only way I can do it."

Jimi had exchanged his black Stratocaster for a white model, one he had decorated the night before with painted red-and-black hearts and ornate arabesques. Backing slowly away from the mic, he turned up the guitar's volume and created a hum of feedback. Pointing to his ears and then out into the crowd, the grinning guitarist seemed to say, "Loud? Watch *this*!" He then grabbed the Stratocaster by its waist and turned it upside down, using the motion and the guitar's tremolo bar to change the shape and intensity of the escalating feedback. Banging the instrument against his hip created even more varieties of sound—ominous rumblings, crackling explosions, distant thunderheads. Sliding his pick down the coils of the Fender's E string produced a wailing siren, and then Hendrix slapped the strings while hitting a fretted tremolo with his right hand and jerking the tremolo bar with his left. The sound had gone from raw noise to an undulating, throbbing pulse, an orgasmic murmur from some distant god of amplification. Then . . . silence.

Suddenly, the storm broke. Hendrix slammed into the opening chords of "Wild Thing," lurching with the beat, crouching into it as he chopped out the rhythm and the bass and drums followed. Urging the audience to sing along, he coursed through the verses to the simple tune, a number-one hit in 1966 for the English pop band the Troggs. After a few verses, Hendrix suggestively quoted the melody from Frank Sinatra's "Strangers in the Night" and then stepped back to the row of amps behind him and turned the volume all the way up on the festival's big Fender Dual Showmans. He had daisy-chained them together from his Marshall stack, anticipating the need for more amplification than even the huge British amp could supply. Playing his guitar behind his back, Jimi sang the song's final verses and then stepped away from the mic, tentatively bowing to his listeners. He turned and faced the wall of amplifiers, set himself, and then charged the Marshall, ramming himself into it and pressing his Stratocaster against its grill. After repeatedly thrusting his pelvis into it, he backed away and dropped to the floor. It was time for the sacrifice.

What happened next has become a staple of American popular culture. Jimi Hendrix set his freshly painted Stratocaster on fire.

Kneeling onstage, he humped the prone ax while spasmodically jerking its tremolo bar, causing the three amps behind him to roar in protest. The guitarist bent down and gave his tortured instrument a farewell kiss, and then he squirted it with lighter fluid, almost as though he were urinating on it. In an instant, it was alight. The result was pandemonium. Drummer Mitch Mitchell and bassist Noel Redding assaulted their instruments furiously as the din onstage reached unbearable levels. As the flames rose, so did Hendrix. He grabbed up the burning instrument, swung it like an ax through the air, sending mic stands flying, and then brought it crashing down on the stage repeatedly. Bits of guitar hung by splayed strings as Jimi tossed them into the audience, a cord wound like a talisman around his neck. In less than three minutes, the guitarist's act achieved climax.

Hendrix sauntered off the stage to the biggest ovation the Monterey International Pop Festival had yet seen. The audience of thousands rose as one to cheer what they instinctively knew was a performance of historic merit. The rock 'n' roll arsonist was mobbed by well-wishers as he made his way into the wings, a conquering hero home from the culture wars. After years of defeat, victory was, at last, Jimi's.

* * *

Monterey's closing act on Sunday evening was codirector John Phillips's hit-making vocal group the Mamas and the Papas. Their performance was a pleasant pop confection despite being somewhat underrehearsed and uneven. But no one cared or even noticed. The big news, the story on everyone's lips, was the wild playing and wilder stage antics of the unknown guitarist from London—or was he from New York? It seemed he had come out of nowhere and, in a single extraordinary set, had established a new standard for rock 'n' roll performance. Jimi Hendrix had to be seen to be believed.

The critics were of two minds regarding Hendrix. Robert Christgau, writing for *Esquire*, famously derided the guitarist as a "psychedelic Uncle Tom," noting that he "played what everybody seems to call 'heavy' guitar; in this case, that means he was loud." For Christgau, the "shuck" factor overwhelmed everything else. *Newsweek*'s Michael Lydon first reacted to the Experience with alarm: ". . . end of everything . . . decay . . . nothing louder exists." Later, he seemed to change his mind, stating that Hendrix's "act became more than an extension of Elvis' gyrations[;] it became an extension of that to infinity, an orgy of noise so wound up that I felt that the dynamo that powered it would fail and fission into its primordial atomic state."

Rock reviewer Barry Hansen reported on the festival for *Down Beat*. His take on Hendrix was less visceral, and he placed the guitarist squarely in context by mentioning the rock world's two star players:

> This was the American debut of [Hendrix's] English group and quite possibly the major event of the festival. Hendrix's roots are deep in blues and soul; yet he has learned all the best licks and tricks from the white blues and psychedelic guitarists: Bloomfield, Clapton and all the rest—an unprecedented and very likely unbeatable combination. His tone and phrasing on the guitar, which he plays left-handed, are amazing.

Bloomfield—along with his English counterpart, Eric Clapton—was the gold standard by which all other pop music guitarists were measured in the summer of 1967. Hansen rightly observed that Jimi's playing melded the best of black and white styles, effectively reversing the formula so successfully applied by Elvis Presley. Contrary to the usual cultural flow, it was Michael Bloomfield who was a source for Jimi Hendrix.

Bloomfield may not have realized that at the time—at least not literally. What he couldn't help noticing was Jimi's choice of material. Of the nine tunes Hendrix performed—more than any other Monterey artist with the exception of Johnny Rivers—there were two blues, four originals, and three covers. One of the songs he covered was Bob Dylan's "Like a Rolling Stone." It received a respectful, almost reverent treatment, as Jimi was a devoted Dylan fan. He even introduced the tune, making sure that all his listeners knew what he was about to play. Bloomfield then watched as Hendrix re-created the song, playing through its complex chord structure effortlessly, adding embellishments, making it all his own. As he finished the refrain following the first verse, Jimi dropped in a distinctive lick taken from the original. Michael recognized it immediately—it was one he had created for Dylan after the folksinger ruled out any "B. B. King shit." Now Hendrix was playing Michael Bloomfield shit, and playing it better than Michael had. The leader of the Electric Flag, America's star blues-rock guitarist, felt the sting of humiliation, and not a small amount of anger.

And perhaps a little surprise too. When he first heard Jimi Hendrix play, Michael Bloomfield was as impressed as everyone else. He readily acknowledged that the former Chitlin' Circuit guitarist was an extraordinary player as well as a master manipulator of amplified sound. But offstage, Michael found Hendrix less than impressive. The black guitarist was shy, even awkward. He didn't say much, and when he did talk, he spoke too softly and mumbled. When he was nervous, he tended to giggle. To Michael, he seemed sweetly innocent and even a little naïve. That Jimi Hendrix could be a calculating, ambitious, and driven artist, willing to use people and situations to his own advantage, seemed inconceivable.

Until Monterey, that is.

Despite his flap with Townshend about the order of Sunday's performers, Hendrix had planned all along to do exactly what he did during his set. He didn't burn his guitar in response to Pete's "auto-destruction" routine; he was going to ignite his Stratocaster regardless of when he went on or what Townshend did or didn't do. He had already spent part of Saturday preparing a special Fender for sacrifice and had wandered around the town of Monterey Sunday afternoon looking for lighter fluid, hoping to repeat a fire stunt he had first tried in May at a concert in London. He had instructed a roadie to brace his Marshall amp from behind so it wouldn't topple over when he threw himself at it, and he asked another to have a wet towel handy in case his burning-ax gambit started a more serious conflagration. What appeared onstage to be a spontaneous offering to the gods of rock 'n' roll was instead a well-planned and strategically executed play for maximum attention and notoriety.

It was also a message to Pete Townshend, part of whose act Jimi had adopted as his own. By outdoing Townshend, Hendrix made it clear that there was a new gun in town. That message was also directed at Michael Bloomfield. By commandeering the tune that had helped make Michael's career, Jimi let the country's top guitarist know that he was no longer in charge. Hendrix's performance was geared to elevate his own status, but it was also engineered to put his competitors in their place.

Michael Bloomfield felt the put-down acutely. Though he said nothing about Hendrix's set, he got the message. Two years earlier at the Newport Folk Festival, he had been the guitarist leading the way. His searing performances with Paul Butterfield and his fifteen electric minutes behind Bob Dylan helped to radically reshape popular music. Michael Bloomfield's playing made old men out of Newport's established musicians that summer. The song that had provided leverage for the transition was Dylan's "Like a Rolling Stone." Now it was Jimi Hendrix who was leading the way, and "Like a Rolling Stone" was again a harbinger of a new direction in pop music. This time, though, it was Mike Bloomfield who was the old man.

After Hendrix's Sunday night spectacle, the Electric Flag's performance suddenly felt staid and dated. Bloomfield had repeatedly rehearsed his men, carefully arranging the Flag's tunes and tightly structuring parts so that nothing would be left to chance. The band's original material was crafted to sound like the pop music everyone knew from commercial radio, and their covers were essentially re-creations of the originals. Michael's solos were unscripted, but they, too, were constrained by the rigidity of the Flag's musical conception.

In contrast, Jimi's music felt loose and largely improvised. The flamboyant guitarist seemed to make it up as he went along, doing whatever came into his head, following the music wherever it led him. His songs were obviously rehearsed, and his set was clearly planned, but the guitarist's act had a spontaneity that gave it an edge, made it fresh and exciting. No one knew what Hendrix would do next, and that made him both fascinating and more than a little frightening. It gave him power.

It was the same power Mike Bloomfield had exhibited at Newport those two summers ago, when he was confident of his skills and unconcerned by what anyone thought of him. His playing was loud and aggressive, and what he played shocked and amazed people. He gyrated and contorted himself as he performed, and no one had ever seen anything like him.

But now, everyone knew Bloomfield. They knew what to expect when he played, and they expected to be amazed. Bloomfield had to fulfill those expectations—not only for the listening public but for his manager, concert promoters, producers, and even his band members. It was a growing burden, one that could dampen his creativity and sap his self-confidence. Hendrix had no expectations to meet and thus was free to do as he wished. After Sunday night, Michael suddenly felt he was a captive of his own celebrity.

Then there was the fact that Jimi was not only an extraordinary player but also a skilled and willing entertainer. He knew how to put on a show. He had no qualms about acting the fool if it served his purpose. Bloomfield realized he could never do that. He could engage with people offstage, make them laugh and entertain them, but tomfoolery had nothing to do with his music. As his friend and former manager, Joel Harlib, observed about Michael, "He always considered himself to be an artist and a musician—and *not* a performer." Bloomfield's fire-breathing routine, while undoubtedly a bit of showmanship, was really nothing more than a stagey practical joke. He would never have considered using it during the Electric Flag's performance Saturday afternoon. It would not even have occurred to him.

As the crowd exited the arena and left the fairgrounds that Sunday evening, the consensus was that Monterey had been a huge success. The generally peaceful vibe, the sense of community and sharing, the free use of drugs, and the exciting music all made the Summer of Love seem like something more than mere media hype. It really felt like the culture was entering a new era. The Monterey International Pop Festival was just the first magnificent stop along the psychedelic way forward.

But for Michael Bloomfield, Monterey was ultimately a confusing jog in the road. He arrived there as America's most celebrated blues-rock guitarist, someone whose influence was pervasive, a virtuoso whom all young guitar players strove to emulate. As such, he was sought out by other musicians and fans at Monterey and given the deference and respect accorded a star soloist. Michael knew the Electric Flag's performance wasn't as good as it could have been, and he felt that the standing ovation the band received was partially due to the excitement of the moment—"festival madness," he would later call it. But he remained secure in the belief that he was regarded as *the* guitarist, the player by whom all others were judged.

In the space of twenty-four hours, though, all that seemed to change. By Monday morning, Michael Bloomfield felt like the *other* guitar player, the one who didn't set his instrument on fire.

CHAPTER 16
GROOVIN' IS EASY

LOS ANGELES, BOSTON, AND NEW YORK, 1967

There was no time to dwell on the ramifications of Monterey. Albert Grossman informed Michael that he had come to an agreement with Clive Davis and that the Electric Flag would indeed be recording for Columbia. The company was offering the band a five-year contract, with ten thousand dollars paid upon signing and additional payments of thirty thousand and twenty thousand after one and two years. Columbia would further advance the Flag forty thousand dollars against royalties once their album was completed.

Though it wasn't the most money paid to a rock band in 1967, the contract was by any measure quite generous. Grossman could see that Clive Davis was determined to get Columbia into contemporary rock music, and he knew the company's huge financial resources would work to the Flag's advantage. He told Michael he wanted to get the band into the studio as soon as possible so that they could begin work on a few singles in preparation for releasing an album. To that end, he had arranged for the band to fly to Los Angeles for sessions at Columbia's studios at 6121 Sunset Boulevard in Hollywood. They were scheduled to begin the last week in June.

After a brief stopover in Mill Valley, the Electric Flag traveled to Los Angeles and took up residence in a motel a few blocks down Sunset Boulevard from Columbia's Hollywood studios. Michael planned to record "Groovin' Is Easy" and the song he had announced from the stage at Monterey as the band's single, "Over-Lovin' You." He believed both tunes had real commercial potential, a quality that would appease Albert Grossman, since Columbia wanted radio airplay in order to generate interest in the Flag's forthcoming album. A hit single, Bloomfield knew, would do that very nicely.

The Electric Flag's sessions at Columbia went slowly. When Michael and the band had last been in the studio, recording the soundtrack for *The Trip*, they had largely been given free rein to work as they pleased. Now they had to contend with Columbia's bureaucracy of studio managers and unionized engineers as well as the facility's busy schedule and inflexible hours. Most of the engineers were veterans from the days of live radio—the Sunset Boulevard facility had originally been built for radio broadcasts—and they knew nothing about the innovative techniques Bloomfield had seen Bob Crewe use during Mitch Ryder's sessions the previous fall. Albert Grossman dispatched his partner, John Court, to LA in an effort to move things along, but Michael found Court more of a hindrance than a help. John, a former jazz drummer, had been co-owner with Grossman of Chicago's folk nightclub the Gate of Horn and had briefly managed the city's Playboy Club prior to joining ABGM.

Though Court had some experience as a producer, Bloomfield felt he really knew nothing about the new music. Chris McDougal agreed with his boss. "One day this guy showed up and I didn't like the vibe," McDougal remembered. "He was John Court. All of a sudden, the fun part of making music was not like it had been before." But Court was Grossman's man, and he was there to keep an eye on things, making sure that the Flag focused on the task at hand. He would be involved in the recording process from start to finish, whether Bloomfield liked it or not.

Over the course of several weeks in July, the band recorded the various sections for "Groovin' Is Easy," overdubbing Barry Goldberg's organ in places and adding a second guitar track for Michael's brief lead embellishments. One afternoon, Cass Elliot dropped by the studio to visit with Michael and watch the band record. Mama Cass had been deeply impressed by the Flag's performance at Monterey, and as she watched Nick Gravenites record the vocal track for the song, she suddenly volunteered to sing a harmony part. A microphone was set up, and the pop superstar briefly became part of the Electric Flag as a guest vocalist.

The band next recorded tracks for "Over-Lovin' You," with Buddy singing the lead vocal just as he had at Monterey. For the four-bar introduction and the breaks throughout the song, Barry switched from organ to an electric harpsichord. The baroque instrument gave the tune a bright, sprightly feel and, coupled with Miles's ebullient singing, cast "Over-Lovin' You" as a soulful bit of rhythm and blues with clear pop potential. Driving the tune was Harvey Brooks, his bass line meshing tightly with Bloomfield's guitar part. In the song's interlude, Harvey got to drop in a few fills that displayed his skill on the instrument. The horns were busy throughout the piece, riffing behind Buddy and playing out the vamp that closed the song. Though the band had extended it in performance at Monterey, in the studio Columbia's engineers ended the tune with a board fade.

In August the Electric Flag was back in Mill Valley working on material for its first concert performances. ABGM had arranged with Bill Graham to have the band do three stints at the Fillmore Auditorium, the first running from

Tuesday, August 8, to Sunday, August 13. In the six weeks since Monterey, the Flag had managed to put together a respectable repertory of soul and blues covers. They were also working on several new originals, including Barry Goldberg's "Sittin' in Circles" and Nick Gravenites's "She Should Have Just." Both tunes were once again solidly in a pop vein, and both featured Nick's clear baritone. The group spent much of its time at the Heliport in Sausalito preparing for their San Francisco debut, but when they weren't working they found other, more pleasurable diversions. Young Buddy Miles was especially susceptible.

"One night at Wellesley Court, Mike got a call," said Chris McDougal. "He woke me up and said Buddy was in the hospital and would I go down and check on him." The surprised McDougal was groggy with sleep, but he got dressed, climbed into the Flag's blue van, and drove into San Francisco. "When I arrived, there was Buddy in a hospital gown, asleep in a wheelchair!" A nurse told Chris that the drummer had gotten food poisoning and had to have his stomach pumped. He was sedated for the ordeal and was now dozing peacefully, sleeping off the effects of the medication.

"It turned out he had gone to a barbecue at Owsley's place," McDougal said, laughing. "The steak Buddy had eaten had been soaked in LSD. The next day he was OK and playing, but he had suddenly gone psychedelic! He got a blow-out hairdo and started wearing these wild, custom-made clothes."

Owsley wasn't dosing just his cookout guests with LSD. San Francisco's resident psychedelic chemist frequently visited the Heliport with samples of his latest mind-altering concoctions, and the Electric Flag's rehearsal space soon became a favorite stop. He would pass out tabs of his latest acid batch, or of a new hallucinogen called STP, or whatever other psychotropics he might have on hand. The band members would often swallow whatever they were handed without giving much thought to what they had just ingested. Owsley was, in essence, conducting laboratory trials on his unsuspecting subjects. But it was the summer of 1967 and a new era was dawning, one in which drugs and heightened consciousness were all part of the equation. The Flag, along with the other bands at the Heliport, willingly participated in Owsley's field research. It was, in effect, expected of them.

By early August, with their newly expanded repertory, the Electric Flag was ready for their first Fillmore show. Bill Graham billed them as the headliners, expecting to sell the house out on the strength of Michael's reputation. Though the Fillmore's dancers had never heard the Flag, Graham was confident they would turn out to see what America's top blues-rock guitarist was doing with this new group. Personally, though, he had reservations about the Flag. The producer had been distressed when he learned that Bloomfield had left the Butterfield Band, and he felt Michael's new band was more of a commercial venture. But Graham was a businessman, and Bloomfield undoubtedly was good business. When the Electric Flag made its debut at the Fillmore on August 8, they would be the featured group.

For the first three nights of shows, Moby Grape opened for the Electric Flag. They were replaced by the Steve Miller Blues Band for the remaining three. Also on the bill was a group from Chicago led by Mike Bloomfield's old friend Charlie Musselwhite. Called the Southside Sound System, the band included Chicagoan Harvey Mandel on guitar, and Bloomfield entertained them backstage with stories about Monterey and his adventures with the movie crowd in Hollywood. With the addition of Steve Miller's band, the Fillmore suddenly felt like a Big John's reunion. The Electric Flag was well received and fans packed the auditorium throughout the week, but Bill Graham remained unenthusiastic about Bloomfield's new brass rock band. He still preferred the sound of Michael's guitar with the Butterfield Band.

The following week, the Electric Flag was scheduled to fly to Los Angeles for an appearance at a gala concert that the Mamas and the Papas leader John Phillips had organized on the heels of his overwhelming success at Monterey. Mama Cass, remembering how well received the Electric Flag had been at Monterey—and probably more than a little infatuated with Michael—talked Phillips into having Bloomfield's band be their opening act.

When Michael learned that the Flag was to appear at the Hollywood Bowl, he immediately had misgivings. The Bowl, as the West Coast's premier performance venue, had long epitomized the interests of the Los Angeles music industry. Its concerts traditionally featured mainstream acts of the most commercial sort. It had none of the hip gloss of Monterey and was associated with pop singers like Johnny Mathis and Barbra Streisand, and with Top 40 groups like the Monkees. It attracted well-heeled, middlebrow audiences with little or no appreciation for the kind of music the Electric Flag performed. It was, in short, the squarest of square places to perform in 1967.

"Blues is a language, and when I speak the language, I expect a response at the appropriate moments because they know the language," Michael said, characterizing his ideal audience. He felt strongly that those in the seats at the Mamas and the Papas concert wouldn't be conversant. He went on to say of the Flag's music, "I want to tell it to ears that understand what we're talking about. White people just don't know."

Clueless white people may not have been the only reason Michael was reluctant to bring the Flag to the Hollywood Hills. The man who had reinvented the electric guitar at Monterey would also be onstage at the Hollywood Bowl, right along with the Electric Flag. Papa John, mindful of the groups that had been a hit at Monterey, had enlisted the Jimi Hendrix Experience as the show's other opener. But this time, Hendrix wouldn't be stealing Pete Townshend's act. It would be Bloomfield's thunder he would usurp. Or so it may have felt to Michael. It was a prospect that tapped directly into the insecurity that sometimes overwhelmed him. He was known as America's top blues-rock guitarist, and the thought of getting cut at a Mamas and the Papas concert in front of an uncomprehending audience was more than he could bear.

On the afternoon of August 18, as the show's performers congregated at the Hollywood Bowl for sound checks, Mike Bloomfield and the Electric Flag were not there. John Phillips was surprised to learn that ABGM had canceled their contract at the last minute. The cancellation may have been the result of contractual differences between Grossman and Adler, but it's likely that Bloomfield's dissatisfaction with the venue and his wariness of Hendrix were key to the band's disaffection. Whatever the cause, Lou Adler hastily replaced them—with a classical string quartet. He had them play Mozart in between the concert's sets.

Though Michael Bloomfield was reluctant to have a comparison drawn at the Hollywood Bowl between himself and the flashy guitarist from Seattle, a similar juxtaposition would be unavoidable at the Electric Flag's next Fillmore gig. The band was scheduled to perform at the auditorium from August 29 to September 3, and this time they wouldn't be the headlining act. They would be opening for the hottest new group from London. Cream was in town, and their volatile brand of heavy blues-rock was winning converts all around the Bay Area. The trio had been the warm-up act for Paul Butterfield the week before, making their West Coast debut at the Fillmore. But after the wildly enthusiastic response they received, Bill Graham decided to move them to the top slot for their second week. Eric Clapton, Jack Bruce, and Ginger Baker were such a powerful combination that the promoter felt they would outdraw even America's top blues-rock guitarist.

Bloomfield had nothing but admiration for Clapton's blues playing, and he very much liked the modest Englishman as a person. But in his present state of mind, Michael felt acutely uncomfortable sharing the stage with yet another virtuoso player. To make matters worse, the Gary Burton Quartet would also be on the bill, and Burton's guitarist, Larry Coryell, was a rising star in the emerging world of jazz-rock. For San Francisco's music fans, it would be an exciting opportunity to catch three great guitarists on the same stage in one week. But for Michael Bloomfield, it was a billing that set expectations high—*too* high.

One person who was definitely expecting a lot from the Electric Flag's guitarist was Michael's bandmate Barry Goldberg. Barry knew of Clapton's reputation, and he had heard the Brit's records with Cream and with John Mayall. But he had never met Eric, and he couldn't believe anyone could outplay Bloomfield. The prospect of going toe to toe with three pasty-faced Englishmen had him pumped up.

"We were all ready to wipe the Cream off the stage, 'cause we felt we could," said Goldberg. "We felt that Michael could burn Clapton right back to England."

"Everybody wanted to do it," Peter Strazza agreed. "Except for Mike. He got intimidated by Clapton, and we kept tellin' him, 'Man, he's *not* gonna cut you down at all!' . . . but his ego couldn't deal with it."

When the Flag came out for their first set at the Fillmore on Tuesday, Bloomfield surprised everyone—especially those in his band—when he grabbed a microphone.

"He made a speech before we went on, telling everyone that Eric Clapton was the greatest guitar player that ever lived. That Eric Clapton was where it's at, not him," Barry said, feeling disappointed. "We wanted him to come out and say, 'We're gonna *kick your ass*,' you know? But then, it was like Michael was very strange sometimes, when it came to that."

Praising Clapton at that moment may have indeed seemed like a strange thing to do, even to some in the audience. Michael Bloomfield was known to many as the country's finest blues-rock player, and yet there he was, touting the skills of another while denigrating his own. Was he just being modest? Humble? Those who knew Bloomfield from his Chicago days might not have recognized the guitarist they remembered as highly competitive and even a bit egotistical. It was no wonder Barry Goldberg and the rest of the band were confused.

But Bloomfield's self-confidence had been profoundly shaken in the last month. It had dissipated like the fog rolling in off the bay that Monday morning following Monterey Pop. There was a reason he told an interviewer, "When Eric plays the blues, it's all over, Jack—that's the best you can get," or described Jimi Hendrix as "one of the best guitarists I've ever heard in my life." It gave Michael an out. If his own playing didn't measure up, if it fell short of what was expected—well, hadn't he himself said that Eric, or Jimi, or whoever, was the best? Meaning *he* was not? It was a way to lower expectations, to relieve the pressure to outperform everyone else—especially when he wasn't sure he could.

Despite his insecurity, Michael did deliver extraordinary performances that week at the Fillmore. His playing was fluid and commanding, the new Les Paul supplying a tone that was warmer and more vocal than he had been able to get with his Goldtop or Telecaster. Buddy Miles continued to drive the band, both as its drummer and as its exuberant vocalist. The horns gave the Flag a distinctive sound, and Peter Strazza took occasional tenor solos that bridged the gap between rock and jazz in a way that pointed to the future. For those in the audience, the Electric Flag seemed to fuse the jazz of the Burton quartet with the hard rock of Clapton's trio. And then there was the blues.

Both Cream and the Flag relied heavily on the blues for inspiration and material. But there were clear differences in how each band approached the form. While the Electric Flag favored tight arrangements and solos generally lasting only two or three choruses, Cream indulged in half-hour jams and cranked out lengthy improvisations that could reach a fever pitch. And though the Flag could be loud when both Buddy and Michael dug in, Clapton and Jack Bruce, with their dual Marshall stacks, and Ginger Baker, with his two bass drums, were earth-shakingly loud. The Flag seemed to be following the Stax model in all but the way they dressed. Cream, on the other hand, was exploring territory that Bloomfield had originally mined with "East-West," but they were taking it to extremes never imagined by the Butterfield Band. Their version of the blues was visceral, muscular, and raw. The Fillmore audiences loved them. For nearly everyone in the big hall, Clapton's trio was a rock juggernaut, a musical powerhouse of overwhelming intensity. The Electric Flag ran a close second, but the Brits were dominant.

There were other problems too. Mike Bloomfield's insecurity may have taken the edge off his playing, but at least he was onstage. There were some evenings when one or another of the Flag's members didn't even make the gig. Mark Doubleday was unable to perform on opening night and had to be replaced by another horn player. Barry Goldberg became ill midway through the week, forcing the band to cancel that night's performances. Though nothing was said, it was likely the missed shows were the result of drug use. By mid-August, half the Electric Flag was regularly using heroin. What had started in Hollywood as occasional chipping was now becoming a regular habit.

"Buddy, Nick, Harvey, and myself were the only ones *not* doing heroin," Chris McDougal said. "Barry was a mess, and Mark Doubleday was a hardcore junkie."

"There were a lot of hard drugs in the band, you know, there were junkies—people with real bad hard drug problems," said Nick Gravenites. "They were just exacerbated by the lifestyle." With Owsley delivering regular doses of psychedelics and with pot, hashish, pills, and other substances being shared freely by everyone else on the scene, heroin may have seemed like just one more drug among many.

"It was a real problem," said Peter Strazza. "But everybody could have still done their thing, because nobody was being real super abusive about it." The one exception was the band's trumpet player. "Marcus was pretty messed up, as far as doing his stuff," Strazza acknowledged.

Doubleday's drug problem was acute enough that the band members decided they needed to add a third horn player, someone who could fill out the sound as well as cover for Mark whenever he was unable to play. Buddy Miles suggested a musician he knew from his days in Omaha, a multi-instrumentalist named Herbie Rich. A veteran of numerous Omaha R&B bands, Herbie was not only a talented reed player but also a gifted singer and organist. Buddy had only to vouch for him to get Rich hired as the Flag's new tenor man. The horn parts, and if needed, the keyboards, would now be covered if any problems should arise on future gigs.

Herbie Rich arrived just after the Electric Flag concluded its shows at the Fillmore and was preparing to head back to Los Angeles for more recording. Columbia wanted the band to begin working on material for their album. "Groovin' Is Easy" and "Over-Lovin' You," the songs the Flag had completed in July, were scheduled for release in late September as a single, and the company was hoping to quickly follow it with the band's debut LP. They were expecting Bloomfield and company to spend a few weeks in the studio recording and then one or two more editing what they had recorded. With luck, the Electric Flag's first album would be out in time for the Christmas rush.

But Michael Bloomfield wasn't in any hurry.

Back in Los Angeles, Bloomfield and the rest of the band resumed their Hollywood recording routine. They spent their days at Columbia's studios on Sunset Boulevard, working on arrangements, getting the parts on tape, doing overdubs, and refining the mixes. The process was slow and exacting because Bloomfield was determined to get each tune just right. He wanted to use some of Bob Crewe's innovative editing techniques and maybe some of the effects pioneered by legendary producers like Phil Spector and Dave Hassinger. He was also thinking about using some of the tape manipulations the Beatles had incorporated into their most recent releases. But the process was complicated by the fact that Columbia's engineers remained uninterested in tinkering with their recording methods. Michael was on his own if he wanted to experiment. As a result, the Flag's September sessions comprised tunes that wouldn't require much beyond the standard production treatment—at least, not at first. There were the two songs the band had already been working on—"She Should Have Just" by Nick Gravenites and "Sittin' in Circles" by Barry Goldberg—and a new one by Michael himself called "You Don't Realize."

Michael's tune took inspiration from the soul music that was coming out of Memphis at the time. "You Don't Realize" was intended as an homage to the soul singer who had caused a sensation at Monterey, Stax's Otis Redding, and to Redding's frequent guitarist Steve Cropper of Booker T. and the MGs. A slow ballad, it was perfect for Buddy Miles, and he sang the song with an affecting intensity. The horn section, now with Herbie Rich, was featured prominently, and its trumpet-and-two-tenors blend carried the melody along while soulfully complementing Miles's clear tenor. Barry Goldberg offered support with sustained organ chords and overdubbed piano ornamentation. The composer himself remained uncharacteristically in the background, preferring to limit his guitar playing to quiet fills and subtle embellishment. Michael was undoubtedly thinking of Cropper's own accompanying style and trying to respectfully re-create it.

Nick's "She Should Have Just" was, on the other hand, derived from an entirely different sector of the American musical landscape. An elaborate composition squarely in the pop music category, the tune's complex structure was based on a repeated twenty-bar AABB form with an eight-bar interlude. Introduced by a harpsichord-and-piano duet by Barry, the song featured four choruses sung by Nick in his rich baritone that were separated by a contemplative trumpet solo from Mark Doubleday. Played with a Harmon mute, Doubleday's brief improvisation sounded not unlike something from Miles Davis, giving the song an unexpected and fleeting jazzy feel.

With this tune, Michael began in earnest to use the studio creatively. The song's basic parts were recorded first, and then Bloomfield added additional layers, overdubbing backup vocals behind Nick's lead, threading in snippets of solo guitar around the lyrics, and dropping in subtle rhythmic accents with, of all things, castanets. Bloomfield also incorporated a tambourine, thumb cymbals, and even a gong-like crash cymbal—the latter serving to conclude the introduction and launch the tune proper. The song's final moments became a sixteen-bar vamp divided between Peter Strazza's free-jazz tenor solo and Michael's own intense, bluesy lead.

As if those enhancements were not enough, Bloomfield also got his former collaborators from *The Trip* sessions, violinist Bobby Notkoff and keyboardist Paul Beaver, to contribute. Notkoff added a flowing countermelody on electric violin to Goldberg's four-bar introduction while Beaver used his Moog synthesizer to give Doubleday's trumpet interlude a background of sounds resembling waves breaking on an ethereal shore. By the time Michael finished editing "She Should Have Just" and had mixed the song to his satisfaction, he had turned Gravenites's pop tune into a minor rococo masterpiece. He even used the mix's stereo separation to cause the various solos to swing back and forth between left and right speakers, giving the song a subtle psychedelic touch.

Nick was again the vocalist for Barry Goldberg's "Sittin' in Circles," another medium-tempo pop tune. Described by Barry as having a "nice, romantic feel," "Sittin' in Circles" had an unusual twenty-eight-bar structure, alternating verses and chorus with a four-bar introduction and vamp. Michael and Barry worked together on its arrangement, writing lush horn parts that used Herbie Rich's baritone to anchor the trumpet and tenor harmonies. In the vamps between Nick's vocals, Bloomfield added heavy blues-rock guitar, jacking up the volume on his Les Paul for maximum sustain as he soloed.

As he had done with "She Should Have Just," Michael again layered the tune's mix with additional parts. For the introduction, he had Nick play twelve-string guitar behind his own quiet electric lead and an overdubbed third part, weaving the three lines together to form a delicate counterpoint. To the verses and chorus, he added orchestra bells, giving the chord changes a tinkly, bright sound. He used castanets again for percussive emphasis, and this time Michael augmented them with maracas. Midway through the song, he dubbed in novel accents created by manipulating his Les Paul's volume. By striking a note with the volume down and gradually turning it up, Bloomfield could simulate the sound of a violin. By shaking the string, the note would take on an unearthly tremolo. The technique would later become known as "volume swelling," and something like it had been used by George Harrison on several early Beatle recordings. But the Beatles' lead guitarist had used a volume pedal to achieve the effect; Michael simply fingered his guitar's knob while playing the note.

The final number the Electric Flag worked on during its September stay in Los Angeles was a languid blues, a version of St. Louis Jimmy's "Goin' Down Slow." Michael had first recorded it for John Hammond with the Group back in 1964, but this time he decided to concentrate on soloing and leave the vocal to Gravenites. There was just time to lay down rhythm tracks with Buddy, Harvey Brooks, and Barry on piano. Horn arrangements would have to wait, because the Flag had to be back in San Francisco for their third appearance at the Fillmore. Michael played the tune as a straight-ahead blues, peppering Nick's three vocal choruses with biting six-string asides and then firing off two of his own filled with masterful licks.

While the Electric Flag was in Hollywood, ABGM arranged for the band to do four nights at the Whisky a Go Go on the Strip, just a mile down Sunset Boulevard from Columbia's studios. The band opened on Thursday, September 7, and played through the following Sunday, trying out new material and tightening up the rest of their book. Albert Grossman had advised Bloomfield that he wanted the group to do a tour of the Midwest and Northeast beginning in mid-October, and Michael knew the Flag's live show would have to be ready. Their performances at the Fillmore had been a success, but they had been before a sympathetic hometown crowd; in New York and Boston, the band might not find audiences so accommodating. So that he could hear what the Flag actually sounded like, how well the instruments blended, and whether the arrangements worked, Michael had Grossman hire a professional engineer to record a few of their Whisky sets.

On the Flag's final evening at the famed nightclub, the first and second sets were captured on tape. The band was suitably tight and energized, and among the new tunes played were a version of Otis Redding's "I'm Sick Y'all," a slow blues by Michael titled "My Baby Wants to Test Me," and a rousing remake of Howlin' Wolf's "Killing Floor." Buddy sang the Redding and Wolf numbers with his customary élan, and Nick did Bloomfield's tune with its quirky lyrics in his best South Side manner. Michael soloed on both songs, tracking Nick's lines on "My Baby Wants to Test Me" with startling intensity and then taking a solo that was a breathtaking confirmation of the Chicagoan's reputation as the country's most dynamic blues-rock guitarist.

Listening back to the evening's performance, Michael Bloomfield had to have been pleased with the way the band sounded. The recording's mix fluctuated and was uneven at times, but the Flag was clearly well rehearsed and exciting, and the horns meshed smoothly with the rhythm section. Michael's own playing was as dynamic as ever, and much of it was extraordinary. With a few more gigs, the Electric Flag would undoubtedly be ready to take its show on the road.

But something was bothering Bloomfield. He was troubled by the group's reception at the Whisky a Go Go. Though he had played there many times and had even arranged for the nascent Flag to do a pre-Monterey warm-up on the Whisky's stage, something was not right. The club's audience was appreciative, even effusive, but the crowd wasn't really in sync with the band. He had noticed a similar disconnection at the Fillmore while opening for Cream. When a writer from the magazine *GQ Scene* showed up to interview him after a set at the Whisky, Michael unburdened himself, taking pains to explain just what was on his mind.

"You know what I'd really like to do, man? I'd really like to play in places with colored people in them," he told the interviewer. "I'm so sick of working in front of honkies, man, I just can't stand it anymore." With candor unusual even for him, Michael decried the way white audiences seemed incapable of creating the requisite give-and-take between listener and musician. It was the same deficiency that had been partially responsible for his reluctance to perform at the Hollywood Bowl, and now he gave it a full airing. "White people just don't know, they just don't know about anything. They suck entirely," Bloomfield opined, overlooking the inherent irony. He seemed to be characterizing the fervent response Cream had inspired with its loud, frenetic rock at the Fillmore when he went on to dismiss groups "freaking out people." "I'm glad that they're freaked out, I'm glad they're enjoying themselves, but that's not where I would like to be, you know." Michael wanted to perform for *knowledgeable* audiences. When he gave his listeners a solo like the one he played during "My Baby Wants to Test Me," he wanted them to know how good it was and why, and to respond in a way that inspired him and the rest of the band to even greater heights. There was nothing superficial about that sort of exchange, no "freaking out" of the listeners. He then offered his philosophy on making music.

> Musicians have to satisfy themselves with their art. If we're artistically satisfied, then we make it. I don't care if the audience drops dead because we're good. If we turn each other on, that's the secret, you know. If we know we're really wailing—if we know we're really cooking and playing beautiful music—that will turn us on. If we can keep this groove between ourselves, then the audience will pick up on it. Then you've got it made and that's what you've got to do.

It was a surprisingly mature observation for a twenty-four-year-old rock star to make, but Michael Bloomfield had clearly thought long and hard about what it meant to be a musician. His perspective was more that of an artist because, as he himself said, "I ain't no entertainer."

Bloomfield went on to lament the passing of one of his inspirations, the great jazz saxophonist John Coltrane. He called Coltrane, who had died of liver cancer in July, a "living, breathing genius of the highest caliber." That set the usually apolitical guitarist off on a tirade against Lyndon Johnson, then president of the United States. He chastised the chief executive in the most unflattering terms, calling him a "stinking lousy fucking cracker" for neglecting to acknowledge Coltrane's death. Such vehemence was unusual for the guitarist, but Bloomfield may have been motivated by the difficult position he himself was in. Wasn't there a lack of understanding for what he was trying to do with the Electric Flag? With their music? Lyndon Johnson, white audiences—weren't they all the same? Know-nothings with all the power and none of the awareness?

"Right in the music thing, it's the same thing, because the language we are speaking will never get across to the people who are supposed to hear it. It's just going to get worse and worse."

"That's really sad," was all the interviewer could manage in reply.

Portions of the interview were published toward the end of the month in the *Los Angeles Free Press*, and those excerpts quoted Bloomfield verbatim. The article was headlined "Honkies Can't Dig Soul Music" and read like a caustic broadside on race relations and the music business in America. A sanitized version of the complete interview would appear in *GQ Scene* in November, but the unedited excerpts clearly conveyed Michael Bloomfield's growing dissatisfaction with the music world and his role in it. And, as he himself said, it was only going to get worse.

On Thursday, September 14, the Flag opened at the Fillmore Auditorium for three nights of performances. The shows were once again a sellout, and the addition of Herbie Rich in the horn section gave the band a fuller sound and added another excellent soloist. The star of the band, though, remained its guitarist, and Bloomfield's solos were the high point of every set. Buddy Miles was also beginning to attract attention with his outsized stage presence, animated vocals, and showy theatrics. During his numbers, he often exhorted the crowd to "Clap your hands!" frequently coming out from behind the drums and grabbing a stage mic. The Brobdingnagian drummer, dressed in an American flag shirt, his hot-combed hair like an exclamation point above his contorted features, would attempt to turn the hippie rock palace into a steamy tent revival. Bloomfield at first found his drummer's grandstanding amusing, but after repeated instances of Miles's exaggerated showmanship, he began to have his doubts. Still, the band's live show was really starting to cook, and when the Flag was on, as Barry Goldberg said, "nobody could touch us."

During their weekend stint at the Fillmore, the Electric Flag introduced a tune new to their repertory, one written by Nick Gravenites and arranged by Michael. Called "Another Country," the song's lyrics voiced sentiments popular at the time about escaping the lies and fear endemic to America during the Vietnam War era, about finding a safe place to hide—an escape to "another country." Bloomfield's treatment turned the tune into an episodic commentary, with separate sections that followed Nick's vocal that included jazz passages, intense solos, and more than a few minutes of prolonged dissonance—a sort of mini-suite meant to characterize the distressed state of the country in 1967. "Another Country" amazed the Fillmore crowd with its startling changes and its epic scope, and it was yet another example of the musical range and creativity of the Electric Flag.

Toward the end of September, Capitol Records' subsidiary, Sidewalk, released the soundtrack to American International Pictures' motion picture *The Trip*. With nearly forty minutes of music and eighteen selections, the album contained all but a few moments of the material Mike Bloomfield, Barry Goldberg, and Nick Gravenites had created for the film. The band was billed on the jacket with its full name, "The Electric Flag, an American Music Band," and the album was given a "Soundtrack of Special Merit" seal by *Billboard*. The publication's brief review declared that the band "managed to capture the unusual excitement of the motion picture which centers on LSD."

Other reviewers were equally impressed with the recording. *Hullabaloo* magazine's reporter wrote, "'The Trip' is one of the best soundtrack LPs I've heard. And the Electric Flag would seem to be a great deal more than promising." *Teenset* said, "This is not just a collection of goofy noises. On the contrary, and to Bloomfield's credit, the natural tendency toward too much electricity and not enough music was skillfully checked." A newspaper columnist raved, "'The Trip' is a movie no one who sees it will forget. Much of the shaking impact of the movie lies in the music. [This] is an album you won't want to miss[,] . . . an album of many moods and many emotions."

Michael Bloomfield himself was very happy with the record. He felt it was an excellent representation of the range of music the Flag could play, and he regarded several of his own solos as some of his best to date. "On 'The Trip' album. My best blues playing is on that. . . . There's some really good blues guitar on a track called 'Getting Hard,'" he told *Hit Parader* magazine.

The movie itself, which opened across the country in mid-August, received decidedly mixed reviews. But the soundtrack to *The Trip* offered a first glimpse of what the Electric Flag could do. The range of influences—from experimental to hard rock, folk, jazz, and ethnic—showed the band's command of musical genres and its willingness to creatively expand upon them. It was easily one of the most adventurous soundtracks of the year, and certainly the best created by a pop music band. The film failed to achieve the artistic status Peter Fonda had envisioned for it, and its controversial subject had an impact on the album's sales and distribution. But those who heard the record were intrigued by the new band and its music.

The Electric Flag was back in Columbia's Hollywood studios the last week in September, working on the material they had recorded earlier in the month. Michael spent four days refining mixes, recording additional parts, and redoing those he was dissatisfied with. Then, on Friday, September 29, the Flag opened a two-weekend stint at the Golden Bear in Huntington Beach, putting the finishing touches on their live show in preparation for their upcoming tour. By all accounts, the band was ready.

"The Flag really tore it up at the Golden Bear," said Chris McDougal. "The place was packed every night, and the guys sounded great. They loved playing there." The group was staying at the Huntington Beach Inn just a few blocks down Ocean Avenue while they were performing at the beachfront restaurant and nightclub. After the show, most band members would stroll back to the motel and relax in their rooms for several hours before turning in as dawn was breaking. Typically, several of them would gather to talk over the evening's performance and listen to music—something they were doing on Saturday, September 30. But as the night hours waned, the postperformance confab proved to be anything but typical.

At 3:30 Sunday morning, a call came into the Huntington Beach police station complaining of loud music coming from the Huntington Beach Inn. A pair of officers were dispatched to the motel, where they roused the night manager. As the two cops explained the situation, they could plainly hear music coming from a room on the motel's second level. The manager offered to intercede, but the officers said they were required to investigate and proceeded up the stairs to room 12. A knock on the door was answered by a bushy-haired young man whom the officers later identified as Michael Bloomfield. While informing Bloomfield of the noise complaint, one officer—qualified to detect the "odor of burning marijuana"—noted a tell-tale smell wafting from within the motel room. He noted, too, that another of the room's occupants was "having difficulty maintaining his balance" and that "his speech was slurred and his eyes were bloodshot and watery with the pupils dilated." Suspecting that a narcotics violation was in progress, the cops entered the room and proceeded to search for drugs.

By 4:30 a.m., Mike Bloomfield, Harvey Brooks, Nick Gravenites, and Barry Goldberg—the occupant with "bloodshot eyes" and the Flag member to whom room 12 was registered—were all at the Huntington Beach police station being booked for narcotics possession.

The drug-certified cop had taken Barry into the suite's bedroom and there discovered a "marijuana cigarette" in an ashtray on the nightstand next to the bed. That single reefer would be the officially acknowledged reason for the bust, with half the Electric Flag being hauled in and charged. All four band members were held in the department's lockup until bail could be arranged by ABGM later that morning. Michael knew the arrests could have serious consequences for the future of the band and for his own future, because he knew marijuana was the least of their offenses.

It's unlikely that even a cursory search of a Flag member's motel room would have failed to turn up some evidence of heroin use—especially if that room were Barry Goldberg's. "Barry would leave needles lying around, his arms all bloody," said McDougal. "He and Ronnie Minsky were what we called 'heat scores,' meaning they attracted the authorities because they were always strung out and procuring dope." The police undoubtedly uncovered more than just a single joint in their search of room 12, but in the end only the marijuana violation made it to court. Albert Grossman had bailed the four band members out, and he likely used whatever influence he had to reduce the charges. He had a lot invested in the Electric Flag, and he protected his investments.

Michael, Harvey, Nick, and Barry were arraigned in front of a judge that morning and given a hearing date of Friday, October 20. They were ordered not to leave the state or they would forfeit bail. That meant that the band's tour, scheduled to begin the second week of October, would have to be delayed by several weeks. When the bust was reported in the first issue of a new San Francisco–based underground semimonthly, a newspaper called *Rolling Stone*, Nick Gravenites, making a veiled reference to heroin use, was quoted as saying of the bust experience, "We're in the hands of fate. It's a whole different scene: lawyers, police, the government. The whole Lenny Bruce riff."

The Electric Flag finished out its second weekend at the Golden Bear without additional mishap. The band's performances remained strong and attendance was good. But Michael Bloomfield was beginning to feel more than a little paranoid. He had come close to getting caught up in a serious narcotics bust, and he knew that the members of his band, the musicians whose livelihoods depended on him, were being placed at risk every time he or anyone else in the Flag used heroin. The drug's pleasures often overrode his better judgment, but the stress it caused him was just one more burden that he, as the band's leader, had to bear.

With their court date taking precedence, the Electric Flag was forced to cancel the first few gigs of their extended tour. When the four band members appeared in Orange County court later that month, charges against Michael, Harvey, and Nick were dismissed. But the judge read out a single charge of "marijuana possession" against Barry and ordered him to appear for a jury trial at a date to be determined. Michael Bloomfield was greatly relieved, but his friend was less sanguine. "I took the rap, because it was my room," said Barry. But the organist also acknowledged that his drug use had caused a problem—not only for himself but for the whole group. His entanglement with the law and the courts would continue for nearly two years before the case would finally be resolved. For the present, though, Goldberg was released on his own recognizance.

Two days later, the Electric Flag set off on its debut tour as a working band. Their first stop was the Factory on West Gorham Street in Madison, Wisconsin, where they played a one-night stand on Wednesday, October 25. After a stopover in Chicago, they flew to Boston and drove to Worcester for a show at Holy Cross College. In a brief interview with the school newspaper before the performance, Michael again complained about contemporary audiences and their lack of musical knowledge. "You should want to study the way I want to play guitar," he admonished the student reporter. The band's Worcester appearance unnerved Michael, and not just because the crowd was uninformed. "You know what really put me uptight?" he later said. "I played Holy Cross and there was nothing but *goyim*. That really put me uptight. It was wrong, I didn't see any Jews." Though he was not observant religiously, Bloomfield had a deep affinity for his Jewish heritage, and there were times when the cultural differences he felt with some Christians could make him more than a little uncomfortable.

He was more at ease at the band's next stop.

On Tuesday, October 31, the Electric Flag began a series of shows over a ten-day period at a newly opened Boston club called the Psychedelic Supermarket. Located in an alley behind 590 Commonwealth Avenue, just off Kenmore Square, the venue had been a basement parking garage until George Papadopoulos, owner of the Unicorn in Cambridge, commandeered it in September for a week of performances by Cream. Since then, Papadopoulos had brought in other bands on an irregular basis, frequently selling out the concrete-and-cinder-block cavern to the Boston University students who lived nearby.

After numerous warm-up performances over the past months and two weeks of hard gigging on the road, Michael Bloomfield's Electric Flag was ready to take a major eastern American city by storm. The group was sounding loud and aggressive, its tight arrangements and intense soloing calculated to overwhelm audiences. With a solid mix of covers and originals combining blues, jazz, soul, and psychedelia, the Electric Flag was indeed electrifying.

The press seemed to agree. One night, a reviewer for *The Heights*, Boston College's weekly newspaper, caught one of the Flag's sets. "People wandering around, dazed, muttering meaningless words of wonder and praise, or simply nodding their heads in silent approval. This was the reaction to the first Boston appearance of the Electric Flag," he began his article. The author went on to say:

> From the perspective of one writing in the fall of 1967, I would say that the Electric Flag represents the zenith of electric blues music. If this is true, then it is also true that lead guitarist Mike Bloomfield has reached the greatest heights of artistry yet achieved in this "bag" (though Bloomfield is also accomplished in all other forms of music in which a guitar is used). While watching him, one is completely absorbed in his genius—his intricate fingerwork, his contorted face, his unbelievable sound. Bloomfield has been playing professionally since he was 14 (he

> is now 24) and has ingrained himself with a vast collection of sounds and notes produced by his Negro predecessors. He draws freely from this source but the ultimate sound is distinctly his own. I think it is this great depth of talent and knowledge which may give Bloomfield a slight edge over other great guitarists like Eric Clapton and Jimi Hendrix. Clapton, for example, can probably do a few things better than Bloomfield, but his range and overall excellence are just as probably inferior to Bloomfield's.

The reviewer's prescient observations were born out by recordings the band made of several of their sets during their Psychedelic Supermarket stay. Just as he had done at the Whisky a Go Go two months earlier, Bloomfield had tapes made of the Flag's live presentation so he could once again hear how the arrangements worked, assess the order of the tunes, and critique his own soloing. The recordings revealed the band's music in all its unvarnished glory, showing the group to be infused with Bloomfield's kinetic energy and Buddy Miles's ebullient showmanship. One set included ten tunes and lasted for nearly an hour; the other had eight and ran almost fifty minutes from start to finish. More than a few of the performances were extraordinary, and several revealed the dynamic between the group's various personalities.

One of the songs captured on tape that night was a new one to the Flag's repertory. Mike and Nick had done it in the band they briefly had together in Chicago back in 1965, but now Junior Wells's "Messin' with the Kid" had a whole new sound with the addition of horns. Its arrangement was volatile and tricky, with subtle rhythmic shifts and an energizing chromatic walk up to the four in the third chorus. The Flag's version of Wells's tune was taken at a much faster tempo and came off like the original's sleeker urban cousin.

When the band launched into its signature tune, "Groovin' Is Easy," the audience's response was immediate and enthusiastic. The song—originally scheduled to be released as a single with "Over-Lovin' You" by Columbia on September 26—had finally been issued only a week before the Flag arrived in Boston. "Groovin' Is Easy" was doubtless getting some airplay, as many in the crowd seemed to recognize it, but the Electric Flag's music in November 1967 was known to very few outside of San Francisco and Los Angeles. Aside from *The Trip* soundtrack, the single was their only available record. Though many in the audience had no doubt read about Mike Bloomfield's new band and most knew of his reputation from his many visits to Boston with the Paul Butterfield Blues Band, practically no one had actually *heard* the Electric Flag. That the band was so well received at the Psychedelic Supermarket was yet another testament to the group's exciting stage presence and fine playing.

The audience had no idea what to expect, however, when Bloomfield counted off "Another Country." The song's opening moments with composer Nick Gravenites singing its two verses were conventional enough. But then, with the words "I'm gonna find another country," the band launched into a cacophonous section of free improvisation. Intended to represent the turmoil expressed by the singer, the noise featured moans from Nick; a firestorm of notes, slurs, and slides from Michael; a fists-and-elbows keyboard barrage by Barry; and shimmering cymbal work from Buddy. The horns, too, were going full tilt, improvising squawks, squeals, and honks with unrestrained abandon.

This went on for over a minute. The crowd doubtless stared wide-eyed, unsure what they were hearing or where the band was going. While collective improvising was common in jazz by 1967—and even had its own category under the rubric "free jazz"—it was not something that pop bands did. For the Flag to insert "noise" into an upbeat horns-and-rhythm anthem like "Another Country" was something quite radical, and it was another example of Bloomfield's determination to push limits. The band had played the piece at the Fillmore, and there, too, audiences had been startled. Boston was not San Francisco, however, and experimenting before a potentially more conservative crowd was risky business. But the experiment seemed to work.

Buddy Miles signaled the end of the cacophony and a return to tempo with a series of triplets, and Michael launched into his jazzy guitar-and-rhythm solo. Following the abrupt change, the crowd showered the band with a warm round of applause, clearly enjoying the delightful release the transition provided. Bloomfield soloed breezily for some forty-four bars before Miles, with a flourish, kicked in a heavy rock beat backed by the horns. Michael continued for another sixty-four bars, building his solo in intensity and drive until the tension became almost unbearable—an electrifying performance. As the opening drone of the piece returned, the audience applauded wildly. Nick then came back for a final verse, and the piece ended with a rhythmic shift and tag. The audience immediately rewarded the band with loud applause and cheers—even though most had just heard the piece for the first time.

Also caught on tape was a stunning example of the Electric Flag's versatility—and a revealing demonstration of Buddy Miles's theatrics. The band had added a medley of familiar blues and soul tunes, using a clever arrangement to pay tribute to various influences in rapid succession. The Butterfield Band, at Bloomfield's urging, had done something similar as a performance opener, but the Flag's medley went way beyond the blues band's brief introduction.

The medley began with the horns playing the riff from the film *The Magnificent Seven* and then kicked into Arthur Conley's current hit "Sweet Soul Music," sung with gusto by Buddy. He must have enjoyed the irony that his former employer—the cantankerous Wilson Pickett—would be first mentioned in the tune's roster of soul greats. Then, after a drum flourish, the arrangement moved on to Little Richard's 1957 hit "You Keep a-Knockin'," and classic rock got a nod as Peter Strazza soloed on tenor for two choruses backed by Barry Goldberg's piano. After Buddy returned with the refrain, the tempo shifted again, and the Flag dropped down into Guitar Slim's languid 1954 shuffle blues "The Things that I Used to Do."

Goldberg switched to organ and Bloomfield offered masterful fills, shadowing Miles's screaming, rococo interpretation of Slim's lyric. Michael then soloed intensely for two choruses before peppering Miles's final verse with more searing fills. As the band moved into the blues' final turnaround, they held the five, about to launch into what sounded like James Brown's "Papa's Got a Brand New Bag." In an instant, though, the medley resumed with Buster Brown's rollicking rocker "Fannie Mae" from 1959, with Bloomfield's guitar screaming over the cascading beat. Gravenites sang the lyric, followed by furious lead from Michael, and then the tumult came to an abrupt halt on the downbeat of another chorus—and suddenly the opening theme from "Sweet Soul Music" returned. The twelve-minute medley had come full circle. There was another coda and a pause during which a few members of the audience gamely began to applaud, and then Buddy kicked in a final massive flourish with a drum roll to finish the performance. The musical concatenation was a prime example of the Electric Flag's desire to dazzle its audience, to put on an extraordinary show.

The band then introduced several other new tunes, and one was a cover of a slow soul torcher called "Good to Me," recorded by Otis Redding in 1966. Curiously, it was Michael who took the vocal, and the guitarist hewed closely to Redding's singing style, straining his voice to effectively deliver the soul singer's characteristic shouts, melismas, and vibrato. Buddy Miles would have been the obvious choice to deliver a convincing version of "Good to Me," but Bloomfield felt confident enough of his own singing now that he decided to take on the challenge himself. Though it was a stretch, he carried it off—at least in the opinion of one Flag member.

"We went to a radio station to do an interview while we were in Boston," said Peter Strazza. Following their performance one evening, the band was interviewed on DJ Dick Summer's *Nightlite Show* on WBZ. "They played the song 'Good to Me,' and I said, 'Who's *that*?' and he said, 'That's you guys. That's Mike.' Michael had more like a talking voice, but his singing sounded *really* good!" The station had gotten a copy of the Psychedelic Supermarket tape and had aired Bloomfield's Otis Redding impersonation. It had been good enough to fool one of the musicians who had helped create it.

* * *

While they were in Boston, Michael and Nick Gravenites visited a few local musicians they had heard about from a fan while the Flag was performing at Holy Cross College in Worcester. Guitarist John Geils and his two roommates, harmonica player Richard Salwitz and bassist Danny Klein, shared an apartment a few blocks away from Kenmore Square. On one of their nights off, the Electric Flag's leader and lead vocalist stopped by to introduce themselves to the three musicians who would later become the nucleus of the J. Geils Blues Band. Geils knew of Bloomfield from his recordings with the Butterfield Band, and he was delighted to meet Mike and Nick in person. The five talked late into the night about music, bands, and the blues while doing a little jamming and having a grand time. It was only when a neighbor called to complain about the noise that Geils noticed Bloomfield's mood suddenly changed.

"Mike was completely freaked out," John said. "He had been busted not long before, in California, or he'd had a run-in with the law somewhere." Bloomfield, mindful of his tussle with the authorities in Huntington Beach, did not want a repeat of the experience. There was no telling what damage a second arrest would do to his career and to the Flag's chances for success. With that in mind, he and Nick said good night to their new friends. But before they left, they invited Geils and his roommates to sit in with the Flag during one of their sets at the Supermarket the following night.

"We went down there and, I don't know, two-thirds of the way through their set, Mike had everybody get off the stage except the rhythm section," said Geils. "We went up there and did two tunes. The place loved it, he loved it, and we had a great time."

Michael Bloomfield indeed seemed to have a great time at the Psychedelic Supermarket, despite its industrial interior and its limitations as an acoustic space. He always liked performing in Boston, in part because he found the audiences there to be particularly hip to the blues. Though he had repeatedly complained about the uninformed crowds that turned out to see the Electric Flag, he expressed a different view to an interviewer from the city's *Vibrations* magazine. Boston audiences, he said, "a lot of them, seem to know what we're doing—I like people who can dig us this way." But since his experience with the Huntington Beach cops, Michael's general outlook had darkened. The paranoia that John Geils sensed in Bloomfield was increasingly real. The sentiments advanced in "Another Country" seemed right in line with Michael's own misgivings about the fabric of American society. The rosy future of peace, love, and tolerance promised by Monterey only a few months earlier had given way to a harsher reality.

"I've appeared here a million times and dug it, but now it's changed. . . . [T]he police are like Gestapo," Bloomfield explained in another interview. Laying out his views while backstage at the Psychedelic Supermarket, he went on to say, "In the last six months, the country, including Boston, has changed. It's hostile territory. Everyone is starting to get uptight and I have no idea what's coming. You just walk through the streets and you've really got cause to worry."

Of course, in the last six months, Michael himself had changed. He had left the Butterfield Band, started his own group, scored music for a major motion picture, created a sensation at Monterey, and landed a lucrative recording contract with America's premier record company. He was not only the country's best-known blues-rock guitarist, but also the leader of pop music's first brass-rock group. He had gone from being an unencumbered sideman to being the man in charge, responsible for the well-being of a dozen or more people, obliged to meet their expectations as well as those of his manager, his record company, and countless promoters, agents, and club owners. The change in his circumstances had been, in a word, extreme.

Adding to the stress was Michael's chronic insomnia. Since leaving San Francisco in mid-September, he had slept only sporadically, sometimes going for days without closing his eyes for more than a quick catnap. Fatigue altered his mood and clouded his judgment, and he sought solace wherever he could find it. Drugs, both legal and illegal, were often his only recourse. With those that were unsanctioned, though, came the disquieting possibility of another entanglement with the law. Knowing how frequently he and those in his band used serious drugs, Bloomfield felt another bust was imminent—it was only a question of time. In his manic state, paranoia infused his outlook. It only added to the stress.

Still, Michael was unguardedly candid on the subject. When asked by the *Vibrations* interviewer if he himself ever used drugs, Bloomfield replied, "Yes and no. I smoke grass, everyone does, and I took acid and other stuff, like mescaline and psilocybin, but I don't do it now so much. It was a thing to do, to see what it's like—it was a groove." When asked if he ever played "stoned," the guitarist said, "Not usually, but others in the band do—it's their own thing." Heroin was not mentioned, but it was there between the lines, part of the band's "own thing."

Michael Bloomfield's life had become vastly more complicated since starting the Electric Flag, and those complications—and the habits acquired along with them—were beginning to exact a toll. But there were shows to play and a record to complete. The guitarist had no choice but to press on.

CHAPTER 17

ANOTHER COUNTRY

NEW YORK AND SAN FRANCISCO, 1967–1968

The Electric Flag played their final show in the converted parking garage just off Commonwealth Avenue on Sunday, November 12. The band was due in New York City later that week to continue work on its album in Columbia's Fifty-Second Street studios. The company had recently relocated its facilities from Seventh Avenue to the Midtown address, and Mike Bloomfield was hoping to lay down tracks for "Another Country" and several other new tunes in a final push to complete the record. He was also hoping to secure the services of an engineer more adventurous than those he had encountered in Los Angeles. His plans for several of the new songs would require more than just a few simple overdubs and a standard mix.

The band was also going to New York to make its official East Coast debut. The Bitter End Cafe on Bleecker Street, a world-renowned nightspot that featured top names in music and comedy, booked the Flag for two weeks beginning Thanksgiving weekend. The cafe ran numerous ads in the city's papers, taking reservations for three shows nightly and counting on Bloomfield's reputation and reports of the band's formidable music to sell out the room.

There were other blues bands appearing in the city that first weekend too, making it a "Blues Week in New York," according to one newspaper columnist. The Paul Butterfield and James Cotton bands were hosting a Blues Bag session at the Cafe Au Go Go; Blood, Sweat & Tears, Al Kooper's new rock band with horns, was heading a Thanksgiving blues jam at the Scene on West Forty-Sixth Street; and Muddy Waters's Chicago blues band was at the Electric Circus on St. Marks Place in the Village. The timing was excellent for the premiere of guitar wizard Mike Bloomfield's new brass-rock band, and the Flag was the one group everyone wanted to see.

On Wednesday, November 22, the Electric Flag: An American Music Band opened at the Bitter End, making its New York debut. As the lights went down in the sold-out club, a single spotlight focused on the band's namesake perched atop Harvey Brooks's big Fender Bassman amp. The electric flag slowly began waving in its artificial breeze and then, as the spotlight pulled back, an ear-splitting sound filled the room.

"Michael wanted to get everybody's attention when the Flag started the show," said Chris McDougal. "So he had me find a fire siren to play at the beginning of the set. It would make people duck under the table—they thought the cops were raiding the place!"

The band opened with "Killing Floor," a fanfare from the horns introducing Buddy Miles's drum roll to get the medium-tempo shuffle steamrolling. Nick sang Howlin' Wolf's lyrics with frightening intensity, his head lolling from side to side between phrases, his eyes tightly shut, the microphone cupped before his mouth. Then it was Michael's turn. The guitarist burned through three solo choruses, wrestling with his Les Paul as though it were a thing alive. He shook it, cradled it, pricking notes, slapping them, his right hand shooting up over his head between bouts. His expression told a tale of passion and pain as he wordlessly mouthed the sound of his licks, rolling his eyes and wagging his bushy mane. Harvey Brooks, standing directly opposite, became the guitarist's partner in a blues *pas de deux*, the big men moving in graceful sync with the pounding beat. Between them sat Buddy Miles in his flag shirt, a patriotic blur behind his kit as he thrashed his snare, tom-toms, hi-hat, and cymbals.

Through three long sets, the Electric Flag performed with an intensity that left each of their audiences limp. The club was filled to the walls for each show, and the crowds were wildly appreciative. After the last chord had sounded and the final straggling patrons were buttoned into their coats and up the café's steps and out the door, Bloomfield and his men fell back into the Bitter End's dressing rooms, exhausted. Albert Grossman was there waiting for them, and he was, for once, all smiles. Here was an investment that he had little doubt was about to pay off.

Over the next four days, the Electric Flag played to overflowing crowds at the Bitter End Cafe on Bleecker Street. Friends and musicians dropped by to see the band perform and to pay their respects. Mark Naftalin was in the audience one evening, and Michael's good friend John Hammond sat in with the band on Saturday night, playing harmonica for several numbers. Friday's edition of the *New York Times* ran an effusive article about the band, calling Bloomfield "probably the flashiest electric guitar player in the country" and describing the Flag as a "commercialized pop version of the old big-band sound." It went on to say:

> When Mr. Bloomfield performs, it's in a ballet with his guitar as he pumps his body, grimaces with the physical torment of the hummingbird speed of his fingers and sings his guitar parts out loud while he plays them. His guitar becomes so much a part of him that its sound seems to be coming out of his mouth rather than out of his amplifier.

The article simply confirmed what everyone already knew. Michael Bloomfield was the country's greatest blues-rock guitarist, a soloist unequaled in pop music, unquestionably a superstar. His new band had to be seen to be believed, and everybody in New York, it seemed, wanted to see it. Lines snaked out from under the Bitter End's blue awning and down Bleecker Street for nearly every show. Most of those waiting to get in knew Mike Bloomfield and had his records with Dylan and Butterfield. But there were also many who had simply heard everyone talking about the exciting new band in town. The Electric Flag's East Coast debut was an undeniable success, and it seemed all but certain the band was destined for great things.

But the problem that had first appeared in Huntington Beach was still there—and was becoming acute.

While the band was in New York City, Michael and his musicians roomed at the Hotel Chelsea, a storied hostelry on Twenty-Third Street. Known for the many famous artists and musicians who had called it home over the years, the complex had been awarded landmark status by the city in 1966. But it was dark and dingy and, like the Hotel Albert, populated by legitimate residents as well as transients and other unsavory characters. Chief among those were drug dealers who made regular rounds, going from floor to floor servicing their clientele. Some of their visits were to members of the Electric Flag, and those transactions chiefly involved heroin.

It wasn't long before the drug began to affect the band's playing. By the end of their first weekend at the Bitter End, the Flag's performances had become uneven. One reviewer caught their third set on Sunday night, expecting to be amazed. He was not.

"The word's been out that the Flag was fantastic," he wrote. "And how could they miss? Mike Bloomfield on lead guitar made it a success *a priori* and with jazz coming in, the trumpet and two saxes shouldn't hurt." But he went on to say:

> Out they came, poorly dressed (my friend Barry said they looked like they had been sleeping in their clothes for six weeks) and as "unprofessional" as can be. . . . [T]o me, it looked like, and more important, sounded like, a loose hodge-podge that was playing some pretty good blues, but that's all. Bloomfield couldn't be bad, but I've never heard him worse. . . . The horns were a mess and they were by far the sloppiest part of the band. It's unfortunate, because I felt that this would be the most exciting thing to hit rock since Jim Morrison.

The Electric Flag was unquestionably an exciting band, and its configuration was indeed new and innovative. But the combination of intemperance and, in Michael's case, extreme fatigue was enough to dilute whatever excitement the Flag usually generated. That several of the band's members were sometimes having difficulty even playing their instruments was becoming a real issue. The reviewer noted as much, singling out one band member in particular. "I've heard Barry Goldberg play organ like nobody plays organ—with his own band in Chicago and with Charlie Musselwhite at the Go Go, but last night I wasn't sure if his organ was even plugged in or not."

It was clear that Barry's drug use had reached a critical point, and the organist himself realized that something needed to be done. Following the band's appearances at the Bitter End, he met with Albert Grossman and told him of his increasing dependency on the narcotic. But the manager seemed unconcerned. He simply told the keyboardist to deal with his drug problem himself. Goldberg felt he was left with no alternative—he had to quit the Electric Flag.

"I called Michael and told him I was out," Barry recalled. "I said, 'Just replace me, man. I have to quit. I'm really sorry.'" By the end of November, Michael Bloomfield's collaborator, musical partner, and close friend was gone from the band they had cofounded some seven months earlier. Barry would head back to San Francisco and then on to Los Angeles, where he would enter the drug treatment program at the Los Angeles Free Clinic. It would be a long struggle back to sobriety for the twenty-five-year-old keyboardist, but his decision to leave the Electric Flag was, in the end, the right one. It very likely saved his life.

The Electric Flag had a week before they had to be back in San Francisco for another round of shows for Bill Graham, and Michael Bloomfield wanted to get the band into Columbia's studios before they left New York. There were the tunes he wanted to begin recording for their album, but there was also a new assignment from the band's manager. Albert Grossman told Michael that his client Peter Yarrow was producing a film about the counterculture movement, and Yarrow wanted Bloomfield's band to contribute to the soundtrack. The movie, called *You Are What You Eat*, was going to feature Haight-Ashbury hippies, eccentric personalities, iconic locales, and random footage in a stream-of-consciousness collage of sixties hipness. The closing scenes were to be a montage of dancers cavorting at the Shrine Auditorium in Los Angeles, and Peter, having seen *The Trip*, thought the Flag's music would be an excellent fit for the psychedelic chaos of the film's concluding images.

Michael readily agreed to contribute to Yarrow's documentary, but there was a problem: the band had lost its keyboard player. They would need to find a replacement quickly, not only to record music for *You Are What You Eat* but also because their next Fillmore gig was less than two weeks away. Whoever

The striking Dorothy Klein in an early 1940s studio shot by the famed Chicago celebrity photographers Maurice and Seymore Zeldman, known professionally as "Maurice Seymour." Dorothy would soon become Mrs. Harold Bloomfield, and Michael, the first of her two sons, would be born in 1943. Twenty years later, Maurice Zeldman's son, Danny Seymour, would briefly be Mike Bloomfield's housemate on Carmelita Avenue in Mill Valley. Photo courtesy of Allen Bloomfield.

Thirteen-year-old Michael Bloomfield lights the candles on the cake at his bar mitzvah with assistance from his grandmother Ida Bloomfield at North Shore Congregation Israel in Glencoe. One of the presents he received was a small transistor radio, a gift that opened a whole new world of music to the young guitarist. Photo courtesy of Allen Bloomfield.

Michael Bloomfield, about to be throttled by brother Allen, clowns for the camera with other friends at Bishop's Lodge, a resort ranch in Santa Fe, New Mexico, where the boys spent the summer in 1957. Photo courtesy of Allen Bloomfield.

Boogie-woogie pianist Vince Viti had a special drumhead made for his band in the summer of 1960, when they performed at PG's Club 7 in Highwood, Illinois. Michael Bloomfield was the group's lead guitarist. "He'd make you look good—man, could he *play*!" said Viti. Photo courtesy of Vince Viti.

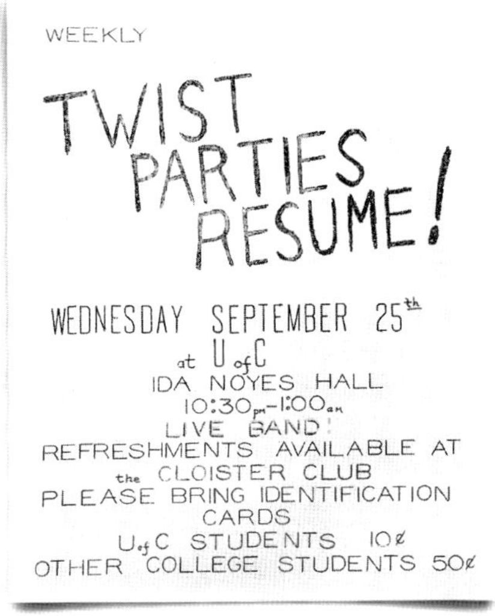

Begun in 1961 as mid-week "coffee hours," the Wednesday evening gatherings at the University of Chicago in Hyde Park soon became sock hops known as "twist parties." By 1963, live bands were providing the music, and Paul Butterfield and Elvin Bishop were regular performers. When Mike Bloomfield sat in, his dynamic lead lines, a blend of rock 'n' roll and blues, added real excitement. Flyer from author's collection.

During a recording session in Norman Dayron's Hyde Park apartment, Michael Bloomfield plays a vintage Martin 00-21. The photo may have been taken on the evening in January 1964 when Michael made a demo tape that Joel Harlib, his manager, took to New York and played for producer John Hammond. Photo courtesy of the Norman Dayron Archive.

Michael Bloomfield plays piano in *Down Beat* editor Pete Welding's apartment in Chicago in the summer or fall of 1963. Welding was a close friend and mentor to the young guitarist, giving him a crash course in the history of jazz. In the background, Big Joe Williams's nine-string Silvertone guitar can be seen leaning up against the wall; the man himself is on the right. Photo by George Mitchell.

Michael Bloomfield explains things to producer John Hammond in Columbia's Chicago studios during the guitarist's first recording session for Hammond on December 8, 1964. Photo by Mike Shea, courtesy of Rene Aagaard.

Warming up the Group during his first Columbia recording session, Michael Bloomfield solos using an old Fender Duo-Sonic that he purchased from his grandfather's pawn shop. Playing rhythm is Mike "Gap" Johnson. Photo by Mike Shea, courtesy of Rene Aagaard.

Michael Bloomfield explains an arrangement to harp player Charlie Musselwhite, left, while Paul Butterfield listens in. Butterfield had come along to Bloomfield's Columbia session to observe the recording process in preparation for his own date with Elektra Records a few days later. Photo by Sandy Speiser; courtesy of Sony Music Archives.

For Michael Bloomfield's second recording session for John Hammond on March 1, 1965, in New York, the guitarist brought along his new 1963 Fender Telecaster. He waxed three songs, using a rhythm section that included Sam Lay and Jerome Arnold from the Butterfield Band. Photo by Sandy Speiser; courtesy of Sony Music Archives.

On June 15, 1965, Bob Dylan began recording songs for his sixth album, *Highway 61 Revisited*, in Columbia's Manhattan studios. He was looking for a more "electric" sound for his new music, and he brought in Michael Bloomfield expressly for that purpose. He and Bloomfield worked out arrangements in Bearsville prior to the session, and Bob asked Michael to act as the session's music director. From left, Bobby Gregg, Al Kooper (who soon moved to the control room), Al Gorgoni, Bloomfield, Frank Owens, Joseph Macho Jr., and Dylan. Photo by Don Hunstein; courtesy of Sony Music Archives.

NO SMOKING
IN STUDIOS

The Paul Butterfield Blues Band with guest guitarist Mike Bloomfield runs through a blues at their sound check prior to the New Folks concert at the Newport Folk Festival on Sunday, July 25, 1965. From left, Jerome Arnold (behind Bloomfield), Bloomfield, Sam Lay, Butterfield, and Elvin Bishop. Photo courtesy of Dr. John Rudoff.

Michael Bloomfield makes a point during Dylan's *Highway 61 Revisited* sessions. Michael used his Telecaster for most of the afternoon's taping, but here he can be seen playing Bob's Stratocaster. Photo by Don Hunstein; courtesy of Sony Music Archives.

The Butterfield Band appeared at the Monterey Jazz Festival on September 17, 1966, during an afternoon presentation called Blues All the Way. Their reception at the prestigious event inspired producer Alan Pariser to create a similar showcase for rock music. Less than a year later, both Butterfield and Bloomfield would appear on the same stage, performing for the Monterey International Pop Music Festival with their respective bands. From left, Mark Naftalin, Elvin Bishop, Billy Davenport, Bloomfield, Butterfield, and Jerome Arnold. Photo courtesy of Sony Music Archives.

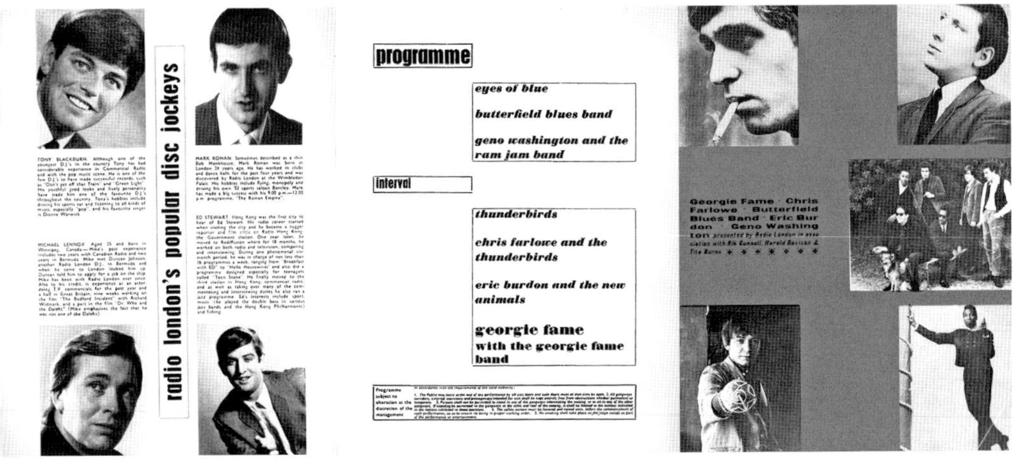

Radio London's program for its 1966 Georgie Fame tour included a little-known group from America called the Paul Butterfield Blues Band. Photo from the author's collection.

Michael Bloomfield mimes to a solo he had recorded earlier for *Ready Steady Go!*, the popular BBC music program. The Butterfield Band made a guest appearance on the show on November 15, 1966, toward the end of their tour of Great Britain. Pictorial Press Ltd./Alamy Stock photo.

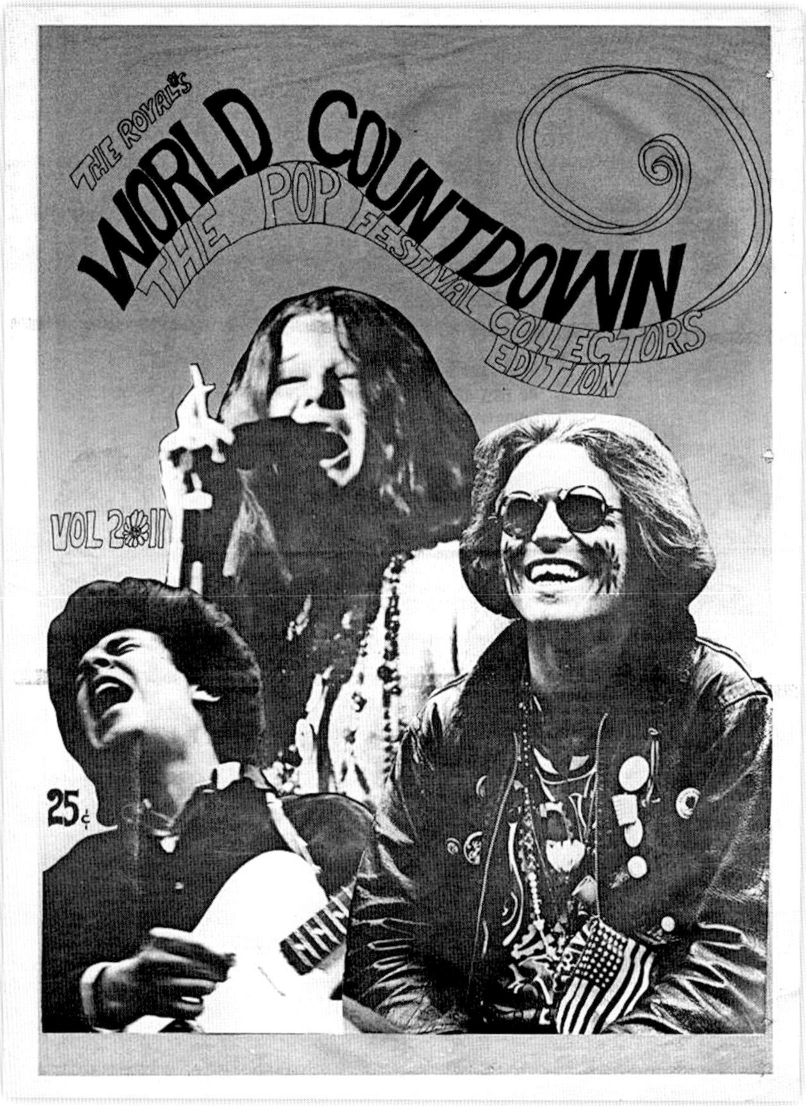

The Electric Flag made its debut at the Monterey International Pop Festival on June 17, 1967, and received a standing ovation from an audience of thousands. Michael Bloomfield was featured on the cover of *World Countdown*, a Los Angeles underground paper sold at the festival, attesting to his status at the time as the country's star guitarist. Photo from the author's collection.

Almost entirely unknown in America prior to his appearance at the Monterey International Pop Festival, Jimi Hendrix left the stage following his Sunday evening set a superstar. His antics, coupled with his revolutionary guitar playing, set a new standard for pop music entertainment that Bloomfield knew he could not—and would not—meet. Pictorial Press Ltd./ Alamy Stock photo.

On Saturday morning at the Monterey International Pop Festival, three of America's greatest rock guitarists congregated in the alleyway behind the fairgrounds stage. Of the three—Jerry Garcia, left; Jimi Hendrix, center right; and Mike Bloomfield, center—only Bloomfield was nationally known. Michael's manager, Albert Grossman, is standing to Bloomfield's right. Photo from the author's collection.

In April 1967, keyboardist, band leader, and composer Al Kooper became a record producer. His first project: a "jam session" album with his friend Michael Bloomfield for Columbia Records. It seemed like a hassle-free way to make a record. Phillip Harrington/Alamy Stock photo.

The great illustrator and Americana painter Norman Rockwell, a friend of Columbia Records art director Bob Cato, was brought in to create a cover portrait of Al Kooper and Mike Bloomfield for Kooper's live *Super Session* album. Here, the "blues singers," as Rockwell called Al and Michael, pose with the artist in Columbia's photo studio in October 1968. Photo by Bob Cato; courtesy of Sony Music Archives.

Michael Bloomfield, Paul Butterfield, and Mark Naftalin perform at the reopening of the Fenway Theatre in Boston, a partial reunion of the Paul Butterfield Blues Band that Albert Grossman arranged in December 1971. The two nights of concerts received laudatory reviews in *Rolling Stone*, the *Boston Globe*, and other papers, and fans hoped the group would become Butterfield's new working band. Alamy Stock photo.

On the road, Michael Bloomfield and Friends perform at the Rivoli Theater in Indianapolis. With Michael are drummer Dave Bartlett and bassist Bob Heberman; Mark Naftalin, unseen, was the keyboardist. Photo by Steve Rusin.

Michael Bloomfield and Buddy Miles on stage at the Bottom Line in New York during an appearance by the reconstituted Electric Flag in September 1974. Though the band received favorable reviews, it split up after only four months. Lewton Cole/Alamy Stock photo.

The most successful of the Butterfield Band reunions occurred on February 23 and 24, 1973, at the Winterland Ballroom in San Francisco. Here, Michael Bloomfield solos during an opening set by his Friends group. Later, he, Elvin Bishop, Mark Naftalin, and Jerome Arnold joined Paul Butterfield in re-creating several of the seminal blues band's original tunes—including a stirring version of "East-West." Photo by Jonathan Perry.

Michael Bloomfield, wearing his "Guitar King" T-shirt, solos with slide on his Fender Stratocaster during a gig at the Old Waldorf on October 26, 1978. Photo courtesy of the Norman Dayron Archive.

The guitarist in repose: Michael Bloomfield gets comfortable in Mill Valley in the late 1970s. Photo courtesy of the Norman Dayron Archive.

The intensity of Mike Bloomfield's playing comes across in his facial expression during a gig at Tulagi in Boulder in August 1972. The guitarist was one of the first rock stars to exhibit wildly emotive body language when soloing. Photo by William Lulow.

Though he was a big star by the late 1960s, Michael Bloomfield was always approachable, happy to discuss music and anything else with whoever was interested. This picture, taken in the mid-1970s, shows the affable guitarist at the wheel of his car. Photo by Leonard Trupin.

A wistful Michael Bloomfield poses during a photo shoot for the cover of *The Live Adventures of Mike Bloomfield and Al Kooper*, a follow-up recording to the hit record *Super Session*. Photo by Bob Cato; courtesy of Sony Music Archives.

Roy Ruby with a friend in Jenner, California, in 1970. Photo by Leonard Trupin.

Barry and Gail Goldberg in 1975. Photo by Leonard Trupin.

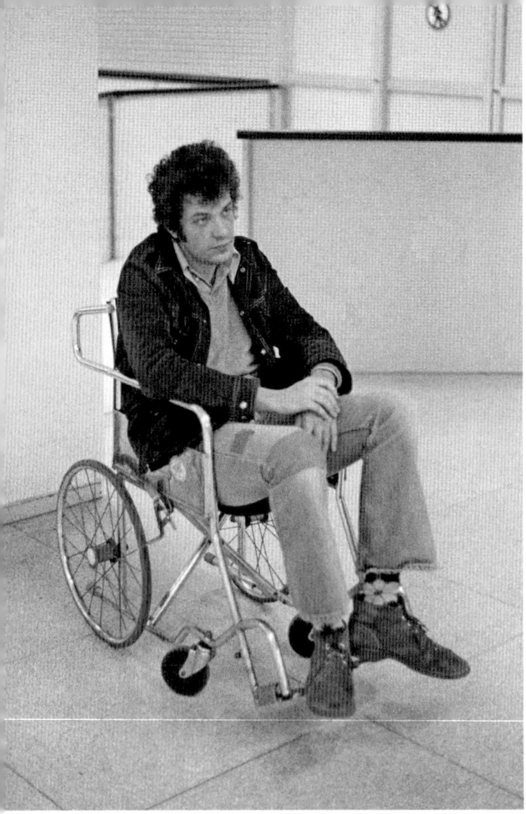

Susan Beuhler.
Photo by Leonard Trupin.

While en route east for a brief concert tour in November 1971, Michael Bloomfield commandeers a wheelchair on a whim in the airport lounge and sits in it until the band boards the plane. Photo by Mark Naftalin; © Mark Naftalin.

Mike Bloomfield makes a few calls from his desk in the Carmelita Avenue house in January 1971. Photo by Mark Naftalin; © Mark Naftalin.

would fill Barry Goldberg's spot would have to be a quick study—as well as an excellent musician.

Buddy Miles knew of one such player. He had met Michael Fonfara, a classically trained keyboardist from Ontario, when Buddy was touring with Wilson Pickett and Fonfara was with a band from Toronto called Jon and Lee and the Checkmates. Most recently, Fonfara had been gigging in New York with another Canadian, a singer named David Clayton-Thomas, but Clayton-Thomas had been deported for working without a visa. That left the keyboardist without a gig, and the twenty-one-year-old Fonfara was only too happy to join the Electric Flag when Buddy contacted him.

The band, with its newest member, congregated at Columbia's Fifty-Second Street studios during the last week in November to record a number of instrumentals for Peter Yarrow's movie. In quick succession, Michael and his men put together a number of up-tempo vamps featuring his own frenetic soloing as well as fiery contributions from Strazza and Rich on saxophone. The overall sound of the pieces closely resembled several they had done for *The Trip*, and Bloomfield was pleased with the results. But the time it took to create the instrumentals had run out the clock. Michael had intended to begin work on the remaining tunes for the Flag's album, but the band was due back in California. The album would have to wait.

The record was becoming a problem. It obviously would not be ready before the upcoming holidays, and the band had already used up the thirty-five hours of studio time allotted them by their Columbia contract. Albert Grossman and ABGM were responsible for any additional studio charges, and Bloomfield was already running a tab with his manager. The sooner he and the group could finish the Flag's album, the better it would be for everyone. "Michael had been given a budget of twenty-five thousand dollars for the record, but it wound up costing more like fifty thousand to produce," Chris McDougal recalled. "Albert had to make up the difference."

The Electric Flag was due back in San Francisco the first week in December for three days of gigs at the Fillmore Auditorium. Michael, again weary of the road, was looking forward to getting home. He was hoping to catch up on his sleep and get a few days away from the band's ever-present entourage of managers, roadies, fans, groupies, and hangers-on. Chief among that last group were the drug dealers. There seemed to be more of them now than ever.

It had also been six weeks since the guitarist had seen his wife. In the last year, the couple had been together only sporadically, with Michael busy organizing the Flag and traveling between San Francisco and Los Angeles while recording and performing. Susan had been in Chicago with her family for part of the year and had moved out to San Francisco only to keep house for the band. In the intervening time, she had come to appreciate her new home and her newfound friends. She had decided not to go on the road with her husband for the tour east, preferring the comforts of Mill Valley and home. But the truth was, Susan and Michael had grown apart, particularly since Monterey. With Bloomfield's newly assumed responsibilities as a bandleader, his obligation to travel, and his growing celebrity, there seemed to be less and less time for his wife of five years. The couple's relationship had begun to suffer, and there was often friction between them. Bloomfield's insomnia frequently soured his mood, making him irascible and argumentative. But there were other reasons that the marriage was increasingly strained.

"Michael seemed to feel entitled to do whatever he wanted to do, and for a long time now he had not acted like a guy who was married," Barry Goldberg said. The temptations that went along with rock stardom included excesses of all sorts, and Michael's indulgences weren't limited only to drugs. Since the early days of rock 'n' roll, female fans had pursued their musical idols. But with the arrival of the Summer of Love and the liberalization of attitudes toward morality and sex, even lesser-known rock bands were besieged by legions of "groupies"—young girls who made a game out of collecting dalliances with as many group members as were willing. Bloomfield, considered to be the country's greatest blues-rock guitarist, was an especially enticing target. More often than not, he acquiesced.

It was a situation that didn't escape Susan's notice, and her husband's liaisons served only to push the two further apart. For Michael, their growing estrangement was just one more element making his life difficult. "During the Flag, it was such a hype scene," he later said. "All the stuff was getting me down, and I couldn't sleep, and my marriage was getting cruddy."

Bloomfield had little time, though, to dwell on his domestic problems. The Electric Flag flew back to San Francisco a few days prior to their Fillmore gig, and on Thursday, December 7, the band began three days of shows that featured the Byrds as headliners. Also on the billing was one of Michael's idols, the great hero of modern blues B. B. King. Michael had been largely responsible for getting Bill Graham to book the master bluesman, and King was making only his second appearance at the auditorium since Graham had taken over its lease. Bloomfield was delighted to share the stage with the man he called "the last word" in the blues. His respect for B. B. was so great that when he learned the veteran guitarist was scheduled to be the opening act, he insisted the Electric Flag go on first. That gave Michael the opportunity to introduce B. B. to those in the audience who had never heard of the great blues player.

"I was scared. All those young white people, and I didn't think they knew who I was," said King, referring to his first set on Thursday night. "Mike

Bloomfield introduces me and says, 'Ladies and gentlemen, the greatest blues guitar player in the world—the Chairman of the Board—B. B. King!' And they all stood up. I couldn't believe it. My first white audience and my first standing ovation in my whole life."

It was an urban blues extravaganza for the Fillmore's patrons that weekend. With B. B. King and his blues band with horns, and the Electric Flag with Mike Bloomfield and its horns, the three nights of shows featured some of the best blues guitar playing San Francisco had yet heard. The headlining group, the Byrds, was in a period of transition with the loss of David Crosby, and their performances paled in comparison to B. B.'s rocking big-band blues and the blues-rock intensity of Michael and the Flag.

Bloomfield fans were treated that first night to a new blues that Michael and Buddy Miles had written, a languid twelve-bar called "Texas." The tune began quietly with Michael soloing gently over rhythm accompaniment for two choruses. The horns then entered, introducing Buddy as he sang in a plaintive, dolorous tone.

> I just got in from Texas, babe, you didn't even know I was around, girl
> I just got in from Texas, you didn't even know old Buddy was around
> And when you saw me walkin' on the street, baby
> You looked at me like I was a Ringling Brothers clown

Michael's fills between Buddy's lines set up a call-and-response dialogue that was stunning in its casual precision—neither musician rushed the other, and neither got in the other's way. The guitarist and the singer succeeded in making a notoriously difficult musical trope look as easy as a lover's smile. At one point, Buddy sang a word in heady falsetto and Michael immediately replicated it, using his trick with the Les Paul's volume knob to give the note an uncanny vocal quality. Then, after Buddy's two verses, Bloomfield moved into the spotlight.

The star guitarist launched into a double-barreled solo, soaring through one chorus and then taking another. After its first four bars, the band suddenly dropped out, creating the sort of musical break often used by blues guitarist Albert King for dramatic effect. Michael punched out a cluster of notes low on the neck, accompanied only by Miles's bass drum triplets, and then carried the intensity of the moment into the next six bars as the band came back in. With the Flag waving briskly behind him, Bloomfield ran through a flurry of notes that culminated in a repeated high D. As the chorus concluded, the band dropped way down and Michael used his guitar's volume control to bring his solo in for a gentle landing.

The Fillmore crowd was instantly on its feet, cheering its guitar hero. Two more verses from Buddy brought the blues to a full stop, and as the Flag came in on the coda, Michael tossed off one last volley. The applause was immediate and flooded with cheers of delight. It had been a masterful performance, even to those whose knowledge of the blues extended only to a few covers by the Rolling Stones.

The Electric Flag performed three other new tunes that weekend, adding to its book Stevie Wonder's 1966 R&B hit "Uptight" and a funky blues released earlier in the year by Albert King called "Born under a Bad Sign." As a tribute to the other star guitarist on the Fillmore stage for the weekend of performances, Michael sang B. B. King's "Rock Me Baby"—a song he had been playing since his teen years.

Bill Graham was pleased by the turnout and encouraged by the response B. B. King and his band received. But he still did not particularly like the Electric Flag. The group put on an exciting show, and Mike Bloomfield was as dynamic as ever, but Graham noticed that several of the band's members seemed to be out of it, and Michael himself wasn't always together. The promoter was running a business, and even though he was presenting rock 'n' roll, he expected his bands to be dependable and on time. Bloomfield was never very punctual, and now he seemed even less interested in schedules.

"Bill used to call me 'Bloomfield's schlepp,'" said Chris McDougal. "Whenever he'd see me moving the band's equipment up the Fillmore's two flights of stairs, he'd say, 'Well, *you're* here at least. Is the rest of the band coming?'"

Though he could be petulant and condescending, Graham still greatly admired the star guitarist and valued their friendship. He knew Michael would always tell him the truth. He just wasn't sure the Electric Flag was the right fit for Bloomfield's prodigious talent. And Michael seemed far more distracted and harried than he had ever been when he was with the Butterfield Band.

Following the Flag's shows for Bill Graham, Michael Bloomfield decided he needed to get in another round of recording sessions before the holidays. That meant the band had to fly to Los Angeles because Columbia had no facilities of its own in San Francisco, and company policy did not allow artists to record in non-company studios. Though he had been home only a week and had no desire to get back on the road, Bloomfield was feeling pressure to complete the album. It was already behind schedule, and there were still half a dozen tunes the band needed to get on tape.

The Flag arrived in Los Angeles during the second week of December and went to work at Columbia's Sunset Boulevard studios creating tracks for the new songs. They again found accommodations in Hollywood, this time on

Santa Monica Boulevard at the Tropicana Motel. Like the Albert and Chelsea hotels in New York, the Trop also had its share of shady characters, and it was regularly visited by Los Angeles cops looking for drug dealers, hustlers, and prostitutes. While the Electric Flag was busy recording, the LAPD made one of its sweeps of the motel and netted a few suspects, including one member of the band. Mike Fonfara was found to be in possession of a small quantity of marijuana and was taken into custody.

Bloomfield contacted ABGM and explained the situation to his manager, fully expecting Albert Grossman to once again work his magic. But Grossman, tired of drug-related hassles caused by his rock 'n' roll charges, decided instead to cut Fonfara loose. Though the keyboardist had joined the band only a few weeks prior to his bust, he was Canadian and not an American citizen. That circumstance would greatly complicate any effort to get the charges dropped, and the manager wasn't about to expend time and capital on a quixotic struggle with the Los Angeles authorities. Besides, didn't the Electric Flag already have another organist? Couldn't Herbie Rich easily take over the keyboards? The band would still have two horn players.

For Grossman, the decision was an easy one. Herbie Rich became the organist for the Electric Flag, and Mike Fonfara's brief tenure with the band was brought to an abrupt end. The Canadian consequently stayed behind in Los Angeles to deal with his legal troubles when Bloomfield and the rest of the band headed back to San Francisco for the holidays.

Back in Mill Valley, Michael Bloomfield was facing troubles of his own. The tension with Susan had reached a point where it could no longer be ignored. The couple knew they had to sort it out, and over Christmas weekend they sat down together.

"We had a long, tearful talk," Susan said, "about how our marriage was over. I had my own life. He had his own life. It seemed silly to be married." She had tired of the music world and its excesses, of traveling from gig to gig, of keeping irregular hours and living nowhere, of being seen only as the wife of a rock star—when she was seen at all. Susan felt trapped, and she had decided she wanted to be free to find her own way in the world. Michael, for his part, had little time for the work required to nurture and grow a successful marriage. Much as he disliked it, he was now married to his duties as a bandleader and musician. Those obligations made it all the more difficult to maintain the continuity and fealty essential to a healthy marriage. The guitarist simply wasn't around enough to fulfill the role of a husband, and even when he was at home, he was often distracted by the demands of his career.

The couple decided they would separate. Michael was headed back to New York in January anyway, so they were already going to be apart. There was no reason to make other living arrangements, at least for the moment. They talked of divorce, but neither was willing to take that step just yet. Their marriage, though, definitely felt like it was over. Despite the hesitancy, divorce seemed like the only way forward.

"Susan was Mike's great love," said Chris McDougal. Bloomfield's personal assistant could see how deeply the guitarist was affected by the separation and by Susan's eventual departure. "He loved her only, and I remember how excited he was when she was coming out to Mill Valley to keep house for us. He never got over it when she left."

After the New Year, Bloomfield flew back to New York with the Electric Flag. He was determined to complete the sessions for the band's album and get on with mixing and mastering it. He was feeling pressure from both Columbia and ABGM to get it finished. And while the guitarist was uncertain when that would be, he was sure of one thing. His marriage to Susan Smith was unquestionably finished.

The Flag again took up residence in the Hotel Chelsea in Manhattan and spent the next two weeks working every day in the studio. They concentrated on four tunes—two covers and two originals—that were part of their standard live set, songs they had developed in performance specifically for the album and had begun recording in Los Angeles. There were three blues—"Killing Floor," "Wine," and "Texas"—and the band's rock anthem "Another Country." The Flag had been playing them long enough now for all the kinks to be worked out and the arrangements tightened, the solos all fluid and inspired. All they needed to do was get them completed on tape.

As he had done in Los Angeles, Mike Bloomfield again had the sections recorded separately and then overdubbed whatever additional parts were needed. He started with "Killing Floor," laying down a rhythm track that included himself on guitar, Herbie Rich now playing organ, Harvey Brooks's walking bass, and Buddy Miles's steadfast shuffle drumming. He worked out a jazzy introduction using bass and guitar, then added the horns, kicking in the rhythm with a stop and a harmonized lick punctuated by Buddy's floor toms.

The muscular, medium-tempo shuffle got rolling with a chorus of overdubbed lead from Michael, and then Nick sang two verses, spotted by the guitarist's salty fills. The horns riffed behind the vocal, using Hubert Sumlin's guitar part from the original Howlin' Wolf recording to accentuate the beat. Michael next took three choruses, one without the horns. Coming in as Bloomfield sailed into his second chorus, the horns built tension with a staccato riff borrowed from Albert King's "Crosscut Saw." Michael himself paid tribute to Albert when, in his third chorus, he played a phrase that King had used prominently in "Crosscut Saw."

After two more verses from Gravenites, "Killing Floor" suddenly morphed into a vamp while Peter Strazza soloed on tenor. Following a brief turnaround, the band then dropped back into the blues form, and Nick sang one more verse with Michael overdubbing a second rhythm guitar part. A final turnaround and a hard stop brought the tune to an abrupt but powerful close. The unusual coda may well have been a serendipitous product of an engineering oversight.

"On 'Killing Floor,' at the end of the tune the tape ran out," wrote Harvey Brooks. "The producer was furious at the recording engineer, the band was furious with the producer because it was *the* take. But then John Court, the producer, said, 'Hey, great ending!' He was right."

The Electric Flag's version of "Killing Floor," as Bloomfield crafted it in the studio, was a straight-ahead example of classic urban blues. Played at a more aggressive tempo than Wolf's version, the song was geared to appeal to rock audiences as well as to listeners who knew the original Chess recording. Michael added no exotic instruments, no synthesized sounds or effects. His only concession to embellishment was the superimposition of handclaps on off beats throughout the tune.

It was no different with Stick McGhee's "Wine." Bloomfield took a similar approach, recording the rhythm tracks with Nick's vocal first and then adding the horns and his lead guitar. The band's arrangement was nearly identical to the one they had used onstage at the Monterey Pop Festival seven months earlier, with Bloomfield and producer John Court overdubbing exuberant backup vocals. For the studio version, though, Gravenites added a satirical commentary during the final choruses:

You ever hear of Janis Joplin? You know Janis Joplin.
She'll tell you all about that wine, baby! Whoa, wine!
Well, I can't do much more without that wine, baby.
Nothin' at *all* without that wine.

The mention of Big Brother and the Holding Company's star singer was a topical reference that gave the rollicking jump blues a contemporary edge.

The arrangement for "Texas" once again featured a straightforward rhythm section backed by horn embellishments. The style was classic slow blues, evoking the sound of the Ray Charles orchestra from a decade earlier. A triplet from Buddy Miles brought in the downbeat and a lush ninth chord from the three horns—Mark Doubleday's bright trumpet and the two tenors of Peter Strazza and Herbie Rich. Rich was doing double duty, playing piano on the rhythm tracks and then filling out the horn section with a third voice, making possible the subtle chordal shadings needed to give the accompaniment a necessary robustness.

Just as it had been in concert, the studio version of "Texas" was primarily a duet between Michael and Buddy. The drummer sang through two verses as the guitarist hovered, his Les Paul stinging the air between the singer's declamations. As the horns wove a sultry framework around the soloists, Harvey Brooks's booming bass moved the action resolutely forward. "Texas" had a sound as big and expansive as its namesake.

Michael's fills led seamlessly into his solo. Without pausing for breath, the guitarist smoked his way through twelve bars, making his notes sing as he bent and shook them while enveloped in the harmonic wash of the horns. It was stellar Bloomfield—intense, commanding, and tough—and just what his fans expected. But the solo lasted only a single chorus before Buddy was back with a third and fourth verse. In concert, Bloomfield opened the slow blues with several choruses and took as many as three for his main solo. But in the studio, Michael limited himself to a single twelve bars and omitted the exciting break he had used to thrill the crowd at the Fillmore.

Last to be tackled by the Flag in the early weeks of January was Nick Gravenites's epic musical landscape "Another Country." The three tunes already recorded by the band had fairly uncomplicated arrangements, but "Another Country" was an altogether different musical construct. Based in its initial verses on a rhythmically complex twenty-bar AAB structure with an eight-bar bridge, the piece, as Michael and Nick arranged it, required each musician to learn a specific part. The charts for the horns meshed tightly with Bloomfield's rhythm guitar lines, and Harvey Brooks's bass succinctly rooted their harmony while complementing Miles's percussive support of the melody. The band had played the piece often enough in live performance to have mastered its complexities, but getting them on tape was no easy task. This time Michael may have recorded the rhythm section and Nick's vocal together with the horns, ensuring the parts for the piece's opening section would be rhythmically tight. That meant everything had to be played perfectly or the take would have to be redone.

To add an exotic touch to the opening portion of "Another Country," Bloomfield used the talents of someone he had met on his first visits to New York back in the early 1960s. Folksinger Richie Havens was in Columbia's Fifty-Second Street building one afternoon, and Michael asked him to play sitar. Havens dutifully plucked the single note, adding a sinister-sounding buzz to the first two choruses of the piece. His inclusion in the session was typical of the way Bloomfield worked—while the arrangement was carefully constructed with detailed parts for all the musicians, Michael was not above allowing a chance encounter and a moment's inspiration to contribute to the plan.

Serendipity also played a part in the recording of the middle segment of "Another Country," its jazz-inflected instrumental section. Bloomfield wanted the rhythm to have a Brazilian feel, evoking the nimble lilt of a samba or bossa nova. When the Flag played the piece live, Buddy drove the section with a steady 4/4 beat using a modified cha-cha-cha pattern. For the recording, though, Michael had Buddy sit out altogether after establishing the downbeat and enlisted other members of the band to continue the tempo with small percussion instruments. They used a clave, guiro, woodblocks, and shakers to create a light, effervescent rhythm. All that was missing was the sound of classic Brazilian guitar and, while he knew he could probably dub in suitable accompaniment himself, Michael also knew where he could find the real thing. The legendary Brazilian singer, accordion player, and guitarist Sivuca was living in New York City and working as a session player in the studios and as a solo performer. Bloomfield had met him in 1965 when the Brazilian was working with Oscar Brown Jr. and Brown and the Butterfield Band were sharing the stage at the Cafe Au Go Go. Michael arranged to have Sivuca play his gut-stringed acoustic guitar for the section, comping along with the percussion ensemble and establishing an appropriately sultry mood. The addition of Brooks's bass and Rich's open organ chords gave the passage a solid harmonic foundation.

Over this ensemble, Mike Bloomfield soloed freely for sixty bars, using an A-minor scale and spinning out a delicate tracery of melody while creating a sound that was neither jazz nor rock nor blues, but a combination of all three. It was a sound characteristically Bloomfield, one no other guitar player had. Following this breezy interlude came a short melody stated first by Michael's guitar and then picked up by the horns. That brought in Miles's drums, and the section kicked into rock mode, the horns riffing repeatedly as Bloomfield took another forty-four bars, his Les Paul now cranked and wailing.

The section concluded with a single bar of repeated triplets leading into the horn fanfare and a return of the piece's original form. Richie Havens again sounded his single sitar note, this time backed by tablas—perhaps played by producer and former drummer John Court—and then Nick sang the final verse. "Another Country" was brought to a conclusion with a vamp, and as Gravenites expressed his desperate hope that "there must be someplace, people, someplace I can rest my weary head," the horns riffed while Harvey and Buddy pressed the beat. To this formidable rolling coda, Michael added Mark Doubleday playing a muted trumpet solo, Herbie Rich hammering out eighth notes on piano, and himself playing an aggressive fuzz-tone guitar solo. In live performance, the band had an elaborate ending worked out for "Another Country," but in the studio the engineers simply executed a board fade as the vamp continued. But before it became completely inaudible, Michael dubbed in a whistler who provided the melody to "America the Beautiful" through his teeth. The puccolist was probably Nick, offering a final commentary on his composition's dire message.

With the musical portions of "Another Country" completed, Michael Bloomfield tackled the piece's sound collage. In concert, the Flag created the section by putting up a wall of noise using their instruments. But for the album, Bloomfield had different ideas. He wanted the passage to be more than just a collective banshee wail. Taking inspiration from the work of Bob Crewe and Dave Hassinger, the tape effects used on the Beatles' recent albums, and even the audio experiments Frank Zappa had included in some of his releases with the Mothers of Invention, Michael decided he would use ambient sounds, spoken words, audio manipulations, sundry musical snippets, and whatever else caught his ear to make a musical statement with the collage. In Los Angeles, he had used Paul Beaver's Moog synthesizer to incorporate different sounds into the music for *The Trip*. This time, though, he would create the aural effects using the studio itself as an instrument.

But first he had to find a Columbia engineer who was willing—and able—to help him. He had had no luck in LA. Maybe it would be different now that he was in New York.

"I was real lucky," Bloomfield said. "After we recorded that album, a guy named Roy Segal, an engineer for Columbia—we mixed it in New York, and he was just very open. It was mixed in a little room called the 'Mixing Room.' You couldn't record in it—it was just a little room—and he was just very open, and whatever engineering things I wanted to pull off on that record, he allowed me to pull 'em off."

One thing the guitarist wanted to pull off was a political statement of some kind. The civil rights movement had spread from peaceful marches against the flagrant discrimination of the South to rampaging riots over the de facto segregation of the North, the Vietnam War was killing nearly a thousand Americans every month, and college campuses were hotbeds of student protest and growing radicalism. The country was beginning to feel like it was at war with itself, with nearly every aspect of daily life carrying a political charge. Though he had never had much interest in politics, Bloomfield had little tolerance for injustice and was not immune to the outcry that surrounded him. He had railed against President Johnson's perceived racism in an interview the previous fall and had experienced firsthand the oppressive tactics of the police during the band's drug bust. Now he was ready to make his views known, and a song like "Another Country" seemed the right place to do it.

With Roy Segal's assistance, Bloomfield began constructing the piece's audio collage. They started with a single track, a recording of Michael playing a rapid tremolo on an open D. To that the guitarist added lead licks, using a fuzz-tone effect to distort them. Cranking up the volume, the studio reverberated with sound.

"When we were recording 'Another Country' for the first Electric Flag album, we filled the studio with amplifiers and recorded the feedback," said Harvey Brooks. "The regular sound engineers were not happy, saying, 'It sounds like noise,' and the producer was saying, 'Do whatever they want.' Bloomfield's idea was to use the feedback as a setup for his guitar solo. Brilliant effect!"

For a melodic element, Bloomfield had Mark Doubleday record a mariachi-like trumpet part using a mute and then had him overdub a second line to create a pinched harmony. Columbia had a bullpen of excellent studio musicians, string players who were classically trained, and Michael had one come in and record a snippet of a solo violin piece. The fiddler chose the fugue from Bach's Violin Sonata in G minor, and it became another melodic element added to the mix.

A spoken-word selection was next. Bloomfield wanted to be unequivocal about the political nature of the collage, so he was determined to use something from President Johnson. CBS Radio had offices in the building on Fifty-Second Street, and Segal suggested Michael look through their tape archive of the president's speeches. He would probably find something suitable there. As a Columbia engineer, Roy had access to the archive and could pull any recording Michael wanted to use.

A few hours of digging through the CBS Radio vault turned up a tape Michael thought might work for his purposes. It was Johnson's landmark speech on the Voting Rights Act, his so-called "We Shall Overcome" address, given to Congress on March 15, 1965. In it, the president spoke of race and civil rights, of injustices and the righting of wrongs, taking a brave stand against the prejudice and inequality rife in American society. The content of the speech and its subsequent political ramifications squarely challenged Michael's characterization of Johnson as a "stinking lousy fucking cracker," but the guitarist was unconcerned. The collage was going to be about larger issues, and excerpts from the president's speech would be fine for that purpose.

Bloomfield also wanted other words that spoke directly to the alienation and paranoia expressed in Nick's lyrics. He found a text that seemed to address those issues without literally doing so. It had the stilted language of a rough translation, something that sounded distinctly foreign. Michael's friend Norman Dayron remarked upon hearing the text that it reminded him of something the French Symbolist poets might have written. "Maybe something by Paul Verlaine, from the period when he'd gone mad and was living on the street," said Norman. Whatever its source, the text was recorded using a compression filter, making it sound as though it were being spoken through a megaphone. The effect made the words sound otherworldly, mysterious:

> Mine is the life of the street. Oh, so well that I was turned on. I continued to grow, but away from the overt madness, the blind futility. And one by one there faded away from me the shades of hate. Until I met with only one criminal presence. I was turned on. I was criminal in compassion. My mind was against the law. If I could just keep my head from breaking open and blurring my reality in criminal love, I might make it to another country.

With these elements in place, Bloomfield hunkered down in the mixing room with Roy Segal and went to work assembling the collage. A rumbling drone was created by layering the guitar ostinato, and its ominous undertones were spiked with flashes of fuzz-toned lead. The trumpet melody, sounding very much like a sad vaudeville number played on an old Victrola, was repeatedly faded in and out as the drone progressed. So, too, was the lone violinist's plaintive Bach melody, played and then replayed amid the growing swirl of electric sounds.

Into this musical mélange Bloomfield inserted snippets from Johnson's speech. "There is cause for hope, and for faith, in our democracy," the president intoned as the trumpets provided a maudlin setting for his words. The speech continued for a few moments and then sped up, making Johnson sound like one of the Chipmunks from the popular cartoon series. After a few seconds, the president was back, speaking in an unaltered cadence and stating, "There is no Negro problem." The assertion was repeated and then again sped up. Bloomfield was turning Johnson's serious statements into comic relief, using them to lead into the alienation text. That came next and was nearly inaudible at times due to the confluence of other sounds. But phrases that emerged from the chaos—"the overt madness," "the blind futility," "my mind was against the law"—served to make the point.

There were other snippets of dialogue. One brief comment Michael inserted came from one of the takes of "Another Country" in which producer John Court could be heard to say over the studio intercom, "Thank you, gentlemen." A more serious locution came later in the collage when an aggressive male voice said, "We gotta get this son of a bitch Johnson." That left no question about the song's ideological bias.

When it was all done, the collage ran for more than a minute and a half and was unlike anything that had previously been recorded for use in a conventional pop music tune. Bloomfield and Segal added the innovative sound segment to other portions of the piece and carefully mixed them so the music flowed convincingly from one section to the next. To grab listeners' attention—and to sound an alarm about the need to escape contemporary society—Bloomfield added a clip of the police siren he had been using in the band's live performances. Placing it at the start of "Another Country" and introducing its piercing wail with a single guitar note held to the point of feedback, he effectively set the stage for the drama that was about to unfold.

At almost nine minutes in its finished form, "Another Country" was very much another country musically, infusing its pop landscape with elements of rock, jazz, and blues as well as Brazilian and experimental styles, and doing so while incorporating superb solos and serious political commentary. The piece's message was delivered not only through its lyrical content but also via its musical elements, with the discord of the sound collage, portraying the world as chaotic and inhospitable, yielding to the safety and comfort of the samba section's new terrain. The answer to Gravenites's question, "Don't you think I might find someplace to rest my weary head?" seemed, at least musically, to be a reassuring yes.

With all the music for the Electric Flag's debut album now on tape, mixing each tune's tracks was Mike Bloomfield's next task. He and Roy Segal tackled the job, working with John Court to establish balances, set levels, and, where necessary, redo parts that needed work. As they were going through the takes of the various songs, Michael decided one would benefit from additional accompaniment. "Sittin' in Circles," Barry Goldberg's pretty pop melody, still sounded too sparse. It had gone through a number of revisions when the band originally recorded it back in September, and hearing it again, Bloomfield realized he still was not satisfied with its sound. What it needed was strings, he reasoned. The Beatles had used classical string quartets and octets to enhance many of their most memorable melodies, and Michael thought violins might do the same for Barry's tune. John Court was amenable to the suggestion, and a quartet of Columbia's best studio fiddle players was assembled to play arrangements that Bloomfield worked out with help from other Flag members. The violin quartet parts, once added to the mix and blended with the horns, gave "Sittin' in Circles" a much bigger presence, almost as though a full orchestra were backing the band on the tune's refrain.

But Michael still wasn't finished with "Sittin' in Circles." To create a mood, he decided to add ambient sounds to the opening of the song. From Columbia's effects library he selected a recording of a spring rain storm with gentle rumblings of thunder and mixed it into the opening chorus. The steady patter of raindrops enhanced the romantic mood of the tune, and that, along with the addition of strings, satisfied the guitarist that "Sittin' in Circles" had at last fulfilled its potential.

There was one other song that Michael felt could benefit from an added element. Musically, he thought "Killing Floor" worked well, but its title suggested other possibilities. President Johnson had just returned from Vietnam at the end of December and, while surveying the US troops, had stated confidently that the enemy had "met his master in the field." But to a growing number of Americans, the nearly half million young men serving in the Southeast Asian country were no more than cannon fodder caught in a meaningless conflict. Their country had done little more than send them to the slaughter, to the "killing floor" of Vietnam. Though Howlin' Wolf's "Killing Floor" referred to a romantic liaison gone wrong, Bloomfield thought a literal interpretation of the tune's title might offer a biting commentary on the president's war and, more fittingly, on his cavalier disregard for the lives it was costing. He listened again to the tape of Johnson's voting rights speech and was immediately drawn to the president's opening statement.

"I speak tonight for the dignity of man, and the destiny of democracy," Johnson began. Bloomfield sensed the irony—there was nothing dignified about dying in a rice paddy half a world away. He had Roy Segal add the president's words to the opening of "Killing Floor" and then, to underscore his point, dubbed in a crowd laughing uproariously and applauding. The song took off from there, with the president's voice trailing off in the background and all but overwhelmed by the music. It wasn't a subtle juxtaposition, but the inclusion of Johnson's words more than made Bloomfield's point: the president was sending the Love Generation off to be killed in Southeast Asia.

There was one final tune that Michael wanted to include along with those he had selected for the album. It was a brief solo number, a blues over a relaxed, walking bass line he had created by overdubbing a rhythm guitar part. Bloomfield had recorded it almost as an afterthought during the January sessions, and now he decided the instrumental might make a good closer for the album. With Roy Segal's help, he edited it down to slightly less than a minute in duration; then, thinking of the John Lee Hooker recordings he loved as a teenager, Michael added the sound of a foot tapping out the beat on a wooden plank. The piece, with its casual, down-home feel, evoked the image of a backwoods porch on a warm summer's evening. To enhance that impression, Bloomfield had Segal again mix in the sound of falling rain, complete with a distant rumble of thunder. When finished, the tune seemed to offer a glimpse into America's musical origins, providing an antecedent that foreshadowed all the other music on the album. By placing it at the conclusion of the record, Bloomfield allowed it to function as a reminder to listeners: *this* is where all this music began. Whether it was blues or ragtime, spirituals, bluegrass, country reels, or church hymns, American music at one time or another was played on porches; in parlors or sanctuaries, bar rooms or bordellos; and by field hands, school teachers, preachers, prisoners, roadhouse roustabouts, choirs, and street corner beggars. It was music made by people for people, for friends and family, for lovers and dancers and fighters. It spoke to the fabric of American culture.

That was a lot for one fifty-second musical snippet to convey, but the short blues succeeded handily. For a title, Michael selected a phrase common in traditional blues parlance, two words that signified not only the unhurried, self-assured composure of a backroads rambler on the prowl but also the compliant virtue of a willing and experienced lover. Both Blind Lemon Jefferson and Tampa Red had created blues with the phrase in the title, and Bessie Smith, Ma Rainey, Joe Turner, Lightnin' Hopkins, and countless other blues singers had used it in song lyrics. The phrase was largely unknown in the world of contemporary rock, but in a little more than a year it would enter the counterculture lexicon with a reinvigorated meaning that far exceeded its original scope. Bloomfield was the first of his generation to use it. He called his little musical codicil "Easy Rider."

The mixing and mastering of the ten selections Mike Bloomfield wanted to include in the Electric Flag's first release for Columbia Records was finally finished on Thursday, January 18. Michael had been working on the music nearly every day for the past three weeks, the final push to complete a project the star guitarist had begun back in July, nearly eight months earlier. He felt a great weight lift from his shoulders when the masters were finished. He was satisfied with the results, and though he thought his own playing could have been better in places, the overall sound of the Flag's recordings approximated what he had envisioned for an "American music band." There were elements of blues, jazz, rock, pop, and soul throughout the music, and the tunes were exciting, melodic, and listenable. They weren't as adventurous as those the band had produced for *The Trip*, but Michael thought—even hoped—there might be a Top 40 hit among them. The sequence of the album's selections was quickly worked out and the tapes were then packed up and shipped to Columbia's plant in Terre Haute for pressing into vinyl.

That same week, Columbia and ABGM began a media campaign in anticipation of the release of the Electric Flag's album. An interview with Michael was arranged with Columbia Features, an independent newspaper syndication service, and it was obvious the guitarist was feeling upbeat.

"We're seven dedicated musicians, all brought up in America, and every one of us wants to present the best music we know how," Michael told the reporter. He explained that the "American Music Band" tag had come about "because we've all listened to American music all our lives and that's what we play." He mentioned the Flag's album for the first time by name—*A Long*

Time Comin'—and said, "It took us four months to get our music ready for recording. . . . [W]e wrote some of the numbers and some are traditional. Our music is rock, but it's a new sound."

The interview, along with a promotional photo of the band, appeared in as many as 150 newspapers around the country during the last week in January. It appeared most often on the features page in the "Under Twenty" column, thus ensuring teenagers across the nation would read about the band, its outspoken leader, and its soon-to-be-released album. The industry campaign to hype the Flag and to sell records was just getting under way.

Production of *A Long Time Comin'* was also getting under way. Its cover featured a comely flower child surrounded by a collage of photos of the band members, pictures taken during the group's November appearance at the Bitter End. Columbia's art director, Bob Cato, created a "psychedelic" logo from the Flag's name, and it, along with the album's title, appeared across the top of the jacket. The reverse carried an extensive list of credits down one side of a big black-and-white photo showing the Flag posed in a tight grouping with Michael perched above them. The picture had been taken one warm afternoon during the first week in February by Jim Marshall, one of Columbia's regular freelancers. Marshall talked the band into going down to the Sausalito waterfront, not far from their Heliport rehearsal space, and had them pose amid the reeds and other debris, using a massive brick viaduct as a backdrop. His wide-angle lens gave the octet a monolithic appearance, and their dour expressions—no doubt the result of a growing impatience with the photographer's process—radiated attitude. There was no flower power here—just a formidable brass-rock/soul/blues band, ready to kick ass musically and otherwise. But printed beneath this intimidating image were sentiments that offered a more nuanced take on the group's artistry. Mike Bloomfield had written a brief paragraph in which he gave voice to his original vision for the Electric Flag, stating in simple, elegant words his musical philosophy: "The Electric Flag is an American Music Band. American music is not necessarily music directly from America. I think of it as the music you hear in the air, on the air, and in the streets; blues, soul, country, rock, religious music, traffic, crowds, street sounds and field sounds, the sound of people and silence."

On January 25, the Electric Flag flew from New York back to San Francisco for another trio of appearances for Bill Graham. It was another long cross-country flight for the Flag, their third in six weeks.

When Michael arrived at 404 Wellesley Court in Mill Valley, he found the house dark and locked up. It didn't take him long to realize that Susan had moved out. She had gone to live with a friend, making it clear that her separation from Michael was more than a passing impulse. The guitarist was distraught, half expecting that things would work out, that they would go on as before, leading their own lives while remaining husband and wife. But it was not to be. Susan told him she was moving back to Chicago and was going to file for divorce. Tempers flared and they argued, but Michael's protestations changed nothing. The marriage was over.

Though his personal life was coming apart, Michael Bloomfield had no time to sort things out. He was the country's foremost blues-rock guitarist, and fans wanted to see him play his guitar. As the leader of the Electric Flag, he had no other choice. The show had to go on.

There were other issues, too. Following the Flag's New York debut at the Bitter End, Albert Grossman let it be known that he thought the band might benefit from a more appealing presentation. The members of the group were all male, and some of those males were quite large—they hardly looked like rock stars. Albert reasoned that an attractive female vocalist could compensate for the group's otherwise dowdy presence. He was particularly distressed at how disheveled Nick Gravenites looked at the Bitter End and suggested Michael think about finding a new lead singer.

Bloomfield had no desire to replace his longtime friend, but he again felt pressured. He quietly approached a few of the better female vocalists he knew and asked if they would be willing to join the Flag. His first choice was Tracy Nelson, a vocalist he had first met in Chicago when Tracy was dating Charlie Musselwhite. He had always thought of her as a strong singer, and her work with her new band, Mother Earth, had deeply impressed him. But Tracy was enjoying some success with the group—they had just signed with Mercury Records—and she wanted to stay right where she was. Debbie Danilow, a pretty young vocalist from Fort Worth who was turning heads in San Francisco, also declined Michael's offer, preferring to remain in the Bay Area. Bloomfield then considered asking Janis Joplin, but he knew she was thinking of starting a solo career and would be unlikely to sign on with another band if she decided to leave Big Brother.

The guitarist's search eventually faltered, and even though he continued half-heartedly looking—a newspaper gossip columnist reported that Cass Elliot, who had just left the Mamas and the Papas, was considering joining the band—Michael found no takers. Gravenites remained the Flag's lead man, even though his tenure at times was tenuous.

"He was firing and hiring Nick all the time," said Harvey Brooks. "Nick was a great vocalist, but he wasn't a pop icon. Michael was getting pressure about 'pop.' A band has to, you know, have somebody to look at."

There were other personnel issues, too. Now that Herbie Rich was behind the organ, the Electric Flag was down a horn player. The arrangements called for three instruments, and that meant Herbie would have to be replaced in the section for the band to sound complete in live performances. Buddy Miles immediately suggested another of his friends, an alto player he knew from his early days gigging around Omaha named Harold Stemziel Hunter. Known as "Stemsy," Hunter was an excellent soloist and section player, and he was also a competent singer. Michael readily agreed to hire him, and Buddy called Stemsy and told him to meet the band in Mill Valley. If he could get there in time, Hunter could join the band onstage at the Fillmore.

The Electric Flag, despite its various distractions, managed a successful run at the auditorium and then, with Stemsy Hunter on board, played the following weekend at the Avalon Ballroom on Sutter Street and opened for Janis Joplin and Big Brother at the Earl Warren Showgrounds in Santa Barbara. They then returned to Los Angeles on Saturday, February 10, for a big show at the opulent Shrine Auditorium on Jefferson Boulevard, next to the University of Southern California. For that appearance, the Flag shared the stage with the Jimi Hendrix Experience—for the first time since Monterey.

"Jimi Hendrix was headlining, and the lineup also included the Soft Machine and Blue Cheer," said Dave Pearson, a then-seventeen-year-old aspiring guitarist from nearby Palos Verdes. Pearson attended the concert with members of his high school rock band. "I was there because of Michael Bloomfield. Hendrix was a draw for us, too, because we had the UK edition of *Are You Experienced?* and loved 'Red House.'"

The Flag and several other bands were opening for Hendrix, and early that afternoon, they gathered at the auditorium for sound checks and lighting cues. While waiting for their turn onstage, Michael and Jimi sat together in one of the dressing rooms. With their instruments in hand, they naturally began to play.

"We were backstage fooling around with our guitars," said Bloomfield. "Hendrix was playing with his toggle switch, tapping the back of the neck and using vibrato, and it came out like a sirocco, a wind coming from the desert." Michael again was awed by the Seattle guitarist's ability to create musical sounds with his instrument's electronics. They jammed briefly, but then the Flag was called to the stage. When it came time for the Experience's sound check, Hendrix remained onstage and Harvey Brooks, Buddy Miles, and David Crosby—who had come by to watch the show—joined him in an impromptu jam. Bloomfield, preferring to avoid a friendly cutting session, watched from the wings.

But when show time came that evening, Mike Bloomfield was primed and ready. The Electric Flag's set was dynamic and exciting, and Bloomfield's playing, along with Buddy Miles's theatrics, delighted the audience. For Dave Pearson, the band's performance was a revelation.

"We were young guys who thought we already knew—boy, were we surprised," he said.

> The Flag stole the show—even in the opinion of the Hendrix aficionados we knew. Their stage presence—set sequencing, lighting, and transitions with the spotlighted, windblown flag and Buddy in his American flag shirt performing various feats—seemed almost choreographed. When Michael played a solo, the spot was on him alone. It was *very* theatrical. His hair was puffed up into a natural almost like Herbie Rich's, and his facial expressions while playing were of the sort that became legendary with LA musicians. Some even copied them. It was so good, we were all exhausted by the time Jimi got out there!

Pearson thought the Experience look tired by comparison. Even though Hendrix concluded his set by tossing his Stratocaster into the screen behind the stage in what one critic called a "cataclysmic-volcanic-orgasmic finale," the precision and professionalism of the Electric Flag left a lasting impression on those who saw the show, and the Flag received the night's only standing ovation. "Their sound was the most balanced of the four acts," recalled Pearson. "It was this slick professionalism that blew us away at first. They had the Memphis thing but with much flashier playing. We thought the stagy elements made it. We were wrong—it was the music."

Following the concert, the bands traveled to Peter Tork's house in the Hollywood Hills for a wild party that lasted until dawn. The next day, the Flag flew back to San Francisco. Though the band was due to head back east at the end of the week, Mike Bloomfield had an important date to keep in the City by the Bay. He was scheduled to be interviewed by *Rolling Stone*.

With only five editions issued since the San Francisco–based underground publication launched in November 1967, *Rolling Stone* had already become the nation's foremost rock music and counterculture publication. Its subscriber base was still small, but its influence was impressive and its articles were well written and authoritative. With the paper's insightful and provocative commentary on the war, civil rights, drugs, and sex, as well as interviews with pop superstars like Bob Dylan, George Harrison, Pete Townshend, and Donovan, *Rolling Stone* was setting new standards for alternative journalism. That the paper treated contemporary music as a subject worthy of intelligent criticism was a fact not lost on its readers. A positive review in the *Stone* was generally the imprimatur that could ensure an album's commercial success.

The paper's editor, Jann Wenner, called Michael Bloomfield seeking to get the guitarist to talk about himself and his music for publication, and they had set up an interview for the third week in February. Wenner knew the Flag's debut recording was going to be released sometime in March, and he knew a feature on Bloomfield would be timely. He usually assigned interviews to other writers, but this one he wanted to do himself.

"At that time I was a real fan of guitar playing," said Wenner. "I thought, 'Here's a white Jewish kid playing guitar like I wish I could play.' I was quite taken with Michael—he was a *brilliant* guitar player."

The editor drove up to Mill Valley one afternoon during the second week in February, bringing with him the magazine's editor of photography, Baron Wolman. While Wenner asked questions, Wolman planned to take candid shots of the guitarist to go along with the interview. They eventually found their way to the house on Wellesley Court, and Michael welcomed them in. While the editor set up his tape recorder, Bloomfield went into the kitchen to make coffee.

Once the interview started, Michael was as animated as ever, eagerly sharing his views with the editor on any and all topics. Wenner began by asking him about contemporary guitar players and then dug into Michael's early days in Chicago, his experiences with Bob Dylan and Paul Butterfield, and his thoughts about his current band, the Electric Flag. Throughout their conversation, Bloomfield was candid and loquacious, readily offering observations and opinions on a variety of subjects. Wolman took multiple pictures as Michael answered Wenner, capturing the guitarist gesturing broadly while making a point, laughing at his own witticisms, and smiling coyly as he recalled a long-forgotten episode. The interview lasted nearly two hours, and by the time they had finished, Wenner knew he had more than enough material for an excellent piece on the country's best blues-rock guitar player.

Michael, too, was satisfied. He had been interviewed before, but this was his first opportunity to really talk in depth about himself, his experiences, and his ideas about music and musicians. *Rolling Stone* was a serious periodical, and to be an artist featured in its pages was no small thing. Bloomfield also knew that Albert Grossman would appreciate the publicity coming at the time when the Flag's album was about to be released.

By the end of the week, Michael Bloomfield and the Electric Flag were on the road again, making their way back to New York City for a two-week stint at the Cafe Au Go Go in March. They arrived in New York on Monday, February 19, and the following day Michael was in the studio with bluesman James Cotton, helping Cotton record material for his second Verve Forecast release.

John Court was producing the sessions this time, but Cotton wanted Michael there to make sure the music was recorded properly. This time there were no horns present because Cotton had decided to use his regular working quintet for the album, and the harp-plus-rhythm combination gave the music a traditional Chicago sound. But Bloomfield felt it was a little thin in places, so he added an organ part to guitarist Luther Tucker's "Fallin' Rain" and played rhythm guitar behind Tucker on St. Louis Jimmy's "I Remember." For Cotton's rocking instrumental "The Creeper," Michael took the guitar part himself and added driving support to James's no-holds-barred blowing.

On Friday and Saturday, February 23 and 24, the Electric Flag performed at the Anderson Theater near the corner of Second Avenue and Fourth Street. Like the Village Theater, the Anderson had been a venue for Yiddish plays and movies when the Lower East Side was a Jewish enclave. Now it featured dance performances and pop music concerts, and the headliner for Friday night was to be rock 'n' roll legend Chuck Berry. Bloomfield was delighted to learn that he would be sharing the stage with one of his idols.

Music critic Robert Shelton caught the Friday show and reserved most of his praise for Berry. But he was no stranger to Bloomfield and his skill with a guitar, and he was unequivocal about the Flag. "The seven-man soul and rock group, led by Mike Bloomfield, was vexed with technical problems, but some excellent guitar flashes by the leader and generally excellent arrangements broke through the static." The Flag turned in exemplary performances for two shows on both nights, despite the fact that, as Shelton inadvertently indicated, the octet was shy one musician.

Nick Gravenites had not made the trip east with the band. The Flag's vocalist had decided to remain in San Francisco, telling one reporter that he would no longer travel with the band but would continue to write and record with them. That may have been true, but it was also likely that Bloomfield, on orders from Albert Grossman, had asked Nick to skip the tour, "firing" him temporarily. Grossman did not want the burly singer fronting the Flag while they were in New York at a time when their album was about to be released. There would be press coverage, and the manager felt the band needed to look its best. For the four weeks the Electric Flag would be on the road, Buddy and Stemsy Hunter would cover Nick's vocals.

Following the weekend gig at the Anderson, Bloomfield dropped by Columbia's Fifty-Second Street studios to pick up a few promotional copies of the Flag's new album. Advance pressings had been created for DJs and reviewers, and a number of them had been set aside for ABGM and members of the band. As soon as he learned they were available, Michael laid claim to a stack for himself. He was generally pleased with the way the album looked and sounded, but when, he wanted to know, would it be in record stores? The Flag's LP, he was told, was scheduled to be released Wednesday, March 13, a full four months after Columbia originally planned to put the record out. But even that new date was somewhat tentative. The release might have to be delayed a bit longer to allow more time for advance orders. The title *A Long Time Comin'* seemed more appropriate than ever.

While he was at the studios, Michael was invited to join several members of Moby Grape in an impromptu jam session. The San Francisco quintet was in New York finishing up their second album for Columbia, and they had decided to make it an unusual two-record set. The second LP would comprise largely improvised, unrehearsed performances issued under the wry title *Grape Jam*. Guitarist Jerry Miller asked Bloomfield to sit in on piano, giving the guitarist an opportunity to demonstrate his skills at the keyboard. He and Miller, along with bassist Bob Mosley and drummer Don Stevenson, played a languorous, slow blues with the lion's share of soloing given to Michael's piano. Five minutes into the steady-rolling groove, Miller tried to bring the blues to an abrupt close, but Bloomfield, unwilling to quit, restarted the beat with a new riff, and soon the quartet was back into it.

The piano jam, when it was released in April as part of Moby Grape's two-record set called *Wow/Grape Jam*, would be titled "Marmalade." It would feature some robust playing by Bloomfield and a few flashes of Miller's guitar work, but it would primarily be an unadorned instrumental blues, competent but nothing special. It would, however, serve to introduce many die-hard Bloomfield fans to the fact that their favorite guitar player was also a capable pianist.

While playing the session, Bloomfield ran into Al Kooper. Kooper had been invited to sit in with Miller, Mosley, and Stevenson on another instrumental jam, and though he and Michael didn't play on the same tune, they had a chance to catch up. They talked over their experiences as bandleaders, trading road stories and other misadventures, and Al told Michael about the month he had spent recording Blood, Sweat & Tears. He described using special effects and tape tricks on several selections and how much fun they had had creating them with the help of Fred Catero, another of Columbia's more innovative engineers. The album had been released the previous week on February 21, and Kooper offered to get Michael a copy. But Bloomfield told him not to bother—he had bought one already, and he thought it was great. As the guitarist got up to leave, Al told him they should stay in touch.

"I've got your number, Michael," said the keyboardist. "I'll give you a call sometime."

CHAPTER 18

SHUCKS AND SESSIONS

NEW YORK, LOS ANGELES, AND SAN FRANCISCO, 1968

On Tuesday, February 27, the Electric Flag traveled to Philadelphia for three nights of shows at the Second Fret on Sansom Street. The band spent the entire week in the city, also performing at the Trauma on Arch Street the following Friday and Saturday nights. They played to big, enthusiastic crowds all five nights, and everyone wanted to know when the Flag's album would be out.

The official release of the album, though, was still several weeks away. Back in New York the first week in March for a stint at the Cafe Au Go Go, Bloomfield was a guest on DJ and producer Murray Kaufman's freewheeling radio show on WOR-FM. Murray the K, as Kaufman was known, listened as Michael talked enthusiastically about Blood, Sweat & Tears, candidly saying that he felt the production on their album, *Child Is Father to the Man*, was superior to that of the Flag's forthcoming release. When Murray asked Michael about guitar players, Bloomfield sang the praises of Jimi Hendrix, recounting how amazed he was when he first heard the Seattle guitarist at the Cafe Wha? back in 1966. Kaufman played selections from an advance copy of *A Long Time Comin'* throughout the interview, and New York radio fans got a taste of what they could expect from the Electric Flag's debut record.

The band's March appearance at the Cafe Au Go Go had originally been timed to coincide with the March 13 release of *A Long Time Comin'*. But word from Columbia was that the album might not be out until the week following the gig's closing. By then the group would be on the road, heading back to the West Coast. It would be a missed opportunity, but even without the record in store bins, the Cafe Au Go Go shows would almost certainly generate good publicity.

The run at the Cafe began on Thursday, March 7. Though the club usually offered double billings, featuring an opening act along with a headliner, the Electric Flag had the Cafe's bandstand all to themselves for the entire two weeks. They were, after all, superstars with a new record about to hit the charts, and Howard Solomon, the club's owner, was confident the band could fill the basement venue for multiple shows each night. He was not disappointed.

Playing tunes from the album along with their usual repertory of dynamic soul and blues covers, the Electric Flag overwhelmed the club's audiences. Michael's incendiary guitar, Buddy's histrionic vocals and powerhouse drumming, and Herbie Rich's squalling organ, all punctuated by the three horns and anchored by Harvey Brook's rumbling bass, flooded the brick-walled room with sound night after night. The band's performances were inspired, doubtless due in no small part to their excitement over the imminent release of *A Long Time Comin'*. While the *New York Times* did not send Robert Shelton to cover the shows, several other critics from lesser publications did print glowing reviews. Albert Grossman got some of the publicity he was looking for.

"At the Flag's debut at the Cafe Au Go Go last Thursday, they presented a new side of their talent," wrote a reviewer for the *New York Free Press*, a recently launched underground tabloid. "Breaking out of the soul syndrome, they added wild jazz pieces, raga runs, hard rock rhythms and old blues renditions." He went on to praise the band's new album. The record's deft blending of musical styles greatly impressed him, and he lauded the Flag's treatment of soul.

> The Electric Flag seems to be transcending this tradition on record. Their first Columbia album is a new dimension in soul. For the first time, someone has used the form while excluding the clichés. Each of the guitar runs (Bloomfield) is done with originality and verve, while the organ riffs (Barry Goldberg) and bass runs (Harvey Brooks) are searchingly inventive. Buddy Miles on drums also presents a genuinely talented voice, used with a sensitivity for its astonishingly wide range. The horn section . . . frequently reaches for jazz and Dixie runs, emerging out of the hack vamping role usually relegated to soul horn men.

The reviewer singled out one tune in particular for high praise. "Buddy Miles sang the definitive version of 'Hey Joe,' tearing into each chorus with a delicacy and drama which had the audience in hysterics by the time the last chord rolled in."

New to the Electric Flag's book, "Hey Joe," a song that had been a hit single in England for Jimi Hendrix a year earlier, was undoubtedly brought to the band by Buddy Miles. He had jammed on the tune often enough with Hendrix to appreciate its dramatic potential, and he soon decided he wanted to do his own version with the Flag. But "Hey Joe" wouldn't be just another cover tune. Given the song's association with the superstar from Seattle, a rendition by the Electric Flag would establish a direct comparison between Hendrix and Bloomfield. That had to make Michael more than a little uncomfortable. Since Monterey, he had gone out of his way to avoid sharing a stage with the flamboyant guitarist, and even though some of his own band members took every opportunity to jam with Jimi, Bloomfield seldom did. Hendrix's cover of "Hey Joe" had made the tune his own, and his version was on tens of thousands of turntables across the country. Why would Michael want to compete with that?

But in the last few months, Buddy Miles had begun to take a more dominant role in the Electric Flag. With his grandstanding showmanship and unbridled ambition, he frequently made himself the center of attention during the band's performances. Soon he was calling the shots offstage, too. That annoyed Bloomfield, but the guitarist, weary from bouts of insomnia and worn down by the constant stress of being the Flag's leader, often yielded to the drummer's demands. In time, he even came to accept Miles's vision for band.

"The band sort of fell into the bag of a soul band because of Buddy's dominant personality," Michael told editor Jann Wenner during his *Rolling Stone* interview. "I kinda didn't dig it, but now I really dig it. The band has become an extremely good soul band."

Buddy was less circumspect about his role. "If you're a lead singer, if you're anything in a band, you gotta stand up in there, in front of those people, you gotta stand up in there and *take* yours. If you want to be it, you don't talk about it. You *do* it." Miles was doing it, and audiences generally loved him for it. He soon talked Michael into playing "Hey Joe," and the band debuted its arrangement of the song at the Trauma in Philadelphia the week before their Cafe Au Go Go shows.

The Electric Flag's version of the Billy Roberts composition was entirely unique. It bore little resemblance to earlier interpretations of the song recorded by the Leaves and the Byrds, and, most tellingly, it was nothing like Jimi Hendrix's "Hey Joe." The Flag played the song at an achingly slow tempo, framing Buddy's emotive vocal with Michael's open-string guitar pluckings and lush harmonies from the horns. The arrangement was undoubtedly a collaboration between Bloomfield and Miles, but the saxophone and trumpet parts had a Spanish tinge that likely was Mark Doubleday's doing. The song's tale of a crime of passion ending in an escape to Mexico was fittingly underscored by the mariachi-like charts, with Doubleday's clarion trumpet lines recalling his "Green and Gold" contribution to *The Trip* soundtrack.

The arrangement was nothing less than stunning. The Flag's treatment of "Hey Joe" turned the song into a dynamic melodrama, a three-act mini-opera with singer and guitarist as its protagonists. It was no surprise that the critic for the *New York Free Press* called it the "definitive version."

* * *

On Friday, March 15, the start of the Electric Flag's second weekend at the Cafe Au Go Go, members of the band were interviewed backstage between sets by a reporter from a new pop culture magazine. Called *Charlie*, the publication was scheduled to be launched in May, and its editors hoped to appeal to the younger generation by featuring one of the prominent bands from what it called the "new rock circus." As the reporter chatted briefly with Harvey Brooks, Buddy Miles, and Mike Bloomfield, the musicians made light of most of the questions, treating them as an opportunity to have a little fun. Brooks described the "newest things happening in rock" as "extreme admittance to insanity," and Bloomfield compared contemporary pop to the music of John Philip Sousa. But when asked about the Flag's songs, Michael gave an answer that revealed as much about his growing dissatisfaction with his role as leader of the band as it did about the group's material. "I don't want to do those tunes anymore, man. I'm just sick of them. . . . I don't usually get this sick of songs."

In another telling moment, Buddy teasingly chided Michael for not coming to band rehearsals. When Bloomfield sheepishly said he would make the next one, Miles challenged him, "OK, practice tomorrow, then. Tomorrow at two o'clock." But Michael begged off, suddenly remembering that he had something else to do. The exchange made it obvious that the leader of the Electric Flag was disengaging from the band he had created. Prior to Monterey, and for a long time afterward, Michael had been a stickler for rehearsals, running the group through each song until the parts were played flawlessly. Now, he claimed he couldn't even remember what the songs were. "Well, let's see. . . . [R]eally, I can't call the tunes right now," he told the reporter. He wasn't entirely serious, but it was clear his fatigue with the whole band business was.

Another of the Flag's problems was hinted at during the course of the twenty-minute interview. "What is the greatest source of friction in the group?" the reporter wanted to know. Bloomfield responded stiffly, saying, "I can't tell you. I *can* tell you, but I'm not going to." "Artistic or personal?" the reporter pressed. "Neither," Michael replied. "I can't tell you about it. I just can't tell you in an interview what our latest hang-up is." The guitarist then deflected the question to the issue of the band's finances, claiming that the Flag was in debt and that the band members were having trouble supporting themselves. While that may have been true, it was likely not the "hang-up" he initially had in mind. Money was something he was clearly willing to discuss.

What he couldn't mention was the one thing that was a serious, ongoing issue for the band: its drug use. Barry Goldberg had left the group because of heroin, but Marcus Doubleday, Peter Strazza, and, increasingly, the leader himself, continued to use it. Several members of the band's road crew were addicted, and crew chief Ronnie Minsky was not only using the narcotic but dealing it.

"Half the band was junked out," said Nick Gravenites. "The other half wasn't. . . . [I]t drove Michael nuts."

"The problem in the band was totally drugs," agreed Harvey Brooks. "We could not control it. The arrangements were good, the songs were good, when we rehearsed them they were good. A lot of times the performances were good, and a lot of times they weren't. More often than not it depended on if the guys were able to score or not. What was on their minds—you know, to play music well, you have to have the music on your mind."

The division between the Flag's hard-drug users and those who favored marijuana and psychedelics had grown to a chasm in the last few months. The narcotic users ran with an entirely different crowd than the acid heads, and those differences generated friction. Instead of growing together over time, forming tighter relationships and bonding through their music, the members of the Electric Flag seemed to be splintering into cliques. There were factions in the band that spent their offstage hours in entirely different pursuits.

"It had to do with the lifestyle," Brooks said. "It was all based around the drugs."

Despite the group's growing difficulties, the Electric Flag continued to give exceptional performances. They finished out their two weeks of shows at the Cafe Au Go Go on Sunday evening with a final dynamic set, then treated the audience to an extended jam session. Joining members of the Flag onstage were Paul Butterfield, Elvin Bishop, and, just back from a gig in Maine with the Experience, Jimi Hendrix. The Seattle guitarist very much admired the Flag, and he was always eager to sit in with Buddy, Harvey Brooks, Herbie Rich, and the Flag's horn players. As was his habit whenever Hendrix was around, Michael Bloomfield retired backstage and didn't participate. He was increasingly reluctant to go toe to toe with Jimi, and seeing players from both his current and previous bands crowding the stage to jam with Hendrix must have been more than Michael could deal with. Prone to insecurity at the best of times, Bloomfield could do little more than remove himself from the field of battle.

Following their Cafe Au Go Go gig, the Electric Flag packed up and hit the road. They flew to Detroit for a one-nighter on Monday, March 18, and then, the next morning, found themselves the victims of a holdup. The robbery was reported in a music industry tabloid with a story headlined "Gunmen Rob Pop Stars in Motel." Its lede described a lurid scene.

> Pop musician Peter Strazza opened the door of his motel room . . . and found himself staring into the muzzle of a loaded revolver. Two gunmen pushed Peter, tenor sax player with the Electric Flag, back into the room of the Detroit motel and closed the door behind them. One of the men put his gun to Peter's head and demanded that he hand over his watch.

The armed robbers then moved to the room next door, tying up Herbie Rich and Stemsy Hunter after having relieved them of their cash. They did the same to road manager Gary McPike, and then banged on the door to the room Mike Bloomfield and Buddy Miles were sharing. When they failed to rouse the two sleeping musicians, the thieves, fearing additional noise might attract unwanted attention, made good their escape, taking with them the band's valuables.

After untying Rich and Hunter, McPike summoned the police and filed charges, explaining how the band's lives had been threatened and all their money stolen. He next called the offices of ABGM in New York and told them what had happened, saying he didn't have enough money to get the Flag to its next destination. Albert Grossman had his assistant, Vinnie Fusco, wire cash to Detroit to rescue his stranded clients. The manager, though, was not happy. He knew there was probably more to the story.

What really happened was never acknowledged. But the "robbery" was almost certainly a drug deal gone sour. Once the gun-toting pair left, Gary McPike cleaned up the scene and called the cops. He was angry enough over the thefts to risk the drug connection coming to light. Fortunately, that did not happen—probably because the authorities decided to overlook the obvious.

The last week in March, *A Long Time Comin'* was finally released. The Electric Flag's debut album shipped to stores across the country and was introduced to the industry in a capsule review on *Billboard*'s "Album Review" page on March 30. "The group consists of eight outstanding instrumentalists who know how to work as a team through a grab-bag that covers rock, blues, soul, country or whatever possesses them," the blurb asserted. The album entered the magazine's "Top LPs" chart several weeks later at number 123, and the following week it had risen to 108 with a star, indicating it was moving rapidly up in rank. Columbia took out ads in publications around the country and even bought generous space in underground newspapers. The label's full-page promos touted the Flag's rock-and-soul sound as well as its two great soloists—Mike Bloomfield and Buddy Miles. The long wait for the record's release was over, and fans everywhere were eager to hear it.

Reviewers were too. They soon offered their assessment of the inaugural effort by Michael Bloomfield's American music band, and they generally applauded. The *Washington Post* declared, "The Electric Flag has a volcanic sound. It's a blues band that moves with the velocity and power of a diesel train." The review went on to say: "The Flag's first album, *A Long Time Comin'*, is full of unabashed energy. The band rocks on 'Killing Floor' like there won't be any music to follow. The song starts with the recorded voice of President Johnson, speaking 'for the dignity of man.' It is abruptly interrupted by one of the wildest, raucous openings conceived by a rock group."

Another article, published in the *Chicago Tribune*, also praised the record. "Few groups have ever shown more versatility, more awareness of a whole spectrum of influences," the paper's critic observed. He had high praise for Bloomfield, clearly a hometown favorite: "Another article would be necessary to discuss the high degree of musicianship found in this group. Bloomfield's guitar work alone is somewhere beyond perfection and lends a moving and fitting last cut, a calming 50-second solo of 'Easy Rider.'"

Of the tunes on the album, the *Tribune*'s reviewer singled out "Another Country" as "among the best psychedelic sounds around." He concluded by characterizing the record as "blues mixed with soul, country and even happy, upbeat sounds throughout."

Some critics, though, were less impressed. On the West Coast, the *Los Angeles Times* dismissed the LP, saying, "It should have been a great album because of the band's reputation and the time it took to record, but it is a disappointment." It continued:

> Their sound is similar to that of the Paul Butterfield Blues Band and Blood, Sweat & Tears, both blues groups now toting brass sections, but less individual and less exciting than either group. Most of the songs are routine, as are the vocals. Although the band includes some top musicians, they seem good only as individuals, not as a band.

The most pointed criticism came not from a rock reviewer but from the *New York Times*' jazz critic John S. Wilson. In an article about the growing trend toward mixing rock and jazz, Wilson cited the Electric Flag's album as evidence that "rock and blues musicians are so fundamentally unaware of the potentials of horns and reeds that they are having trouble thinking of anything to do with them aside from having them present."

The one review that probably counted more than any other was the one that appeared in *Rolling Stone* on May 11. To the reviewer, the record was a mixed bag. "Nobody who's been listening to Mike Bloomfield—either talking or playing—in the last few years could have expected this," he began. "This is the New Soul Music, the synthesis of White Blues and Heavy Metal Rock." It was an amalgamation that, despite some very fine performances, seemed to him only moderately successful.

> The album is not spectacular. It's good, truthful. The Flag are honest imitators as well as innovators. Nothing they do can be attributed to any one singular source. Nick Gravenites sings to himself, but it's OK. The band isn't as tight as expected. I get the feeling Bloomfield's not quite sure if the group is kosher like this: he senses there can be no dualism in music or anything else. "A Long Time Comin'" is suspended in a blues-soul limbo, working feverishly to figure itself out.

The writer went on to praise "Over-Lovin' You," calling it a "beautiful, driving screamer," and described "Sittin' in Circles" and "You Don't Realize" as the highlights of the album. The sound-collage portion of "Another Country" he felt was unnecessary, but he described Bloomfield's lengthy solo as "magnificent." Like several other reviewers, the writer found the final tune on the record to be the album's most enticing: "The last fifty seconds are devoted to a sweet, willowy, unaccompanied Bloomfield rendering of 'Easy Rider' that is absolutely beautiful. I would have loved to hear him go on with it."

But the record, as far as *Rolling Stone* was concerned, was less than the sum of its parts. The reviewer had expected more and was left wanting.

Many Bloomfield fans were also underwhelmed by *A Long Time Comin'*. They had last heard Michael on record with the Butterfield Band, and most were expecting more of the Bloomfield from "East-West" and "Work Song." The Flag's album, with its carefully crafted studio sound, highly arranged material, and obvious commercial aspirations, seemed the antithesis of the freewheeling, fiery improvisation and visionary innovation that had previously characterized the star blues-rock guitarist's work. There were great solo moments on *A Long Time Comin'*, to be sure, but what happened to Bloomfield the Guitar God?

There also were little inconsistencies with the album that many sharp-eyed fans noticed. While Barry Goldberg was a founding member of the Flag and was listed as one of the group's keyboardists, he was absent from the band photo on the back of the jacket. Stemsy Hunter *was* in the picture, but his name appeared nowhere in the credits. Quicksilver Messenger Service manager Ron Polte, who had briefly worked as a road manager for the band, was given composer credit for all the tunes Nick Gravenites had written. It seemed that the Flag was in flux, and rumors soon surfaced that several of its members might be leaving the band. Some even whispered that Mike Bloomfield himself was about to quit.

* * *

But the leader of the Electric Flag was too busy to pay much attention to what was being said or not said about his band and its new album. Following gigs in Miami and Rochester, Bloomfield and the Flag flew to Chicago and then on to San Francisco. Once back home in Mill Valley, Michael got a call from ABGM. Albert Grossman wanted to speak to him.

The Electric Flag's manager came on the line and told his client that he was very unhappy with what had transpired in Detroit. He said that he was no longer interested in cleaning up whatever drug-related messes Michael and his bandmates got themselves into. Grossman told the guitarist he saw real potential for the Flag now that its album had been released, but only if the band could get its act together. That wouldn't be possible, he said, unless the drug problem was addressed. There was only one way to do that. "I want you to fire the horn players—get rid of Strazza and Doubleday," the manager ordered.

Michael demurred. The two musicians were an important part of the Flag, he protested. They helped to define the band's sound, and they had been with the group from the very beginning. "They're my *friends*," Bloomfield added, feeling indignant.

But Grossman was adamant. "I'm not asking, I'm telling. Fire them."

"For some reason, they didn't want to use horns anymore," remembered Peter Strazza, still unsure what precipitated his and Doubleday's departure. "All of a sudden, they call us in and they say, well, we're just gonna have four pieces. Mike was gonna be part of the four pieces, along with Herbie, Buddy and Harvey."

The new, slimmed-down version of the Electric Flag would also no longer use the services of newcomer Stemsy Hunter. Though Stemsy had no part in the band's drug problems, there was no way a single horn player could play the Flag's three-part arrangements. As Albert Grossman commanded, the band would be horn free, no longer an innovative brass-rock powerhouse. The Electric Flag would continue as little more than a conventional blues-rock band.

The remaining members of the Flag had mixed feelings about the forced reorganization. The division between those who used hard drugs and those who didn't had already created a de facto split in the group, and it was a relief to see the heroin users go. With them in the band, the threat of a bust was constant.

But everyone also knew that the horns were what made the Flag special, and both Strazza and Doubleday, despite their habits, were excellent musicians. Without them, the band would lose the element that made it special. There was also the fact that the Flag's leader was occasionally using heroin. Did Grossman want to get rid of Michael too?

Needless to say, morale in the Electric Flag was at a low ebb. Even though the group had just played to packed houses in New York and now had an album climbing the charts, they seemed to be coming apart. That didn't concern Albert Grossman, though. The Flag had a problem, and he saw a simple way to fix it. Now that it was fixed, there were gigs scheduled right through the summer, and the band could play them just as easily as a quartet. In fact, more easily.

The next week, the Electric Flag had shows to do at the Cheetah in Santa Monica and a weekend appearance at Santa Barbara's Earl Warren Showgrounds. They were the headlining act for the Santa Barbara concert, along with a new band from England called Traffic, a quartet that also played blues, rock, and soul. The British band mirrored the new horn-free edition of the Flag, and the similarity only underscored the fact that Michael's band was now no different than most other rock bands.

That fact was not lost on the concert's producers. Where, they wanted to know, were the Electric Flag's horns? Wasn't the group a rock, blues, and soul band with a trumpet and two saxophones? Didn't the contract call for *seven* pieces?

"They got rid of the horns and all the bookings went down the tubes," recalled Peter Strazza. "Nobody wanted the band without horns. . . . [M]ost of the clubs dropped the band. So they brought us back again."

It was soon evident that Grossman's solution to the Flag's drug problem created a problem of another sort, one that threatened the band's very existence. Promoters wanted the group specifically because it was a "big band," a brass blues-rock band. They were less interested in the Flag if it no longer had the element that made it a marketable attraction. As far as the majority of club owners and concert producers were concerned, no horns, no gigs. That quickly became apparent to Albert, and within a week, Strazza, Doubleday, and Hunter were reinstated.

But the shake-up in the band's personnel served only to increase its fractiousness. The divisions between the Flag's various members were exacerbated, and whatever unity the group had achieved during its eleven months of existence was lost in the chaos. It felt like no one was at the helm.

"It was like anarchy," said Harvey Brooks. "We were out of control." For the leader of the band, taking control seemed no longer an option. "If you're gonna lead a band, you either have to completely depersonalize it—they're your sidemen, they can just go die in their spare time, they can go to hell, you don't care what they do—or they're gonna be like a big family to you," said Bloomfield. "But nothing in between." Michael was finding that he could do neither, especially with the financial and commercial pressures the Electric Flag was under now that its album was out. He knew the band would probably have to tour in support of the record, and he was dreading having to make another extended road trip.

And then there was Buddy Miles.

A force to be reckoned with right from the start, Buddy had effectively taken over the band by April 1968. Michael had acknowledged the drummer's increasingly dominant role during his interview with *Rolling Stone*, but in the ensuing months, Miles had begun acting as though he were the leader of the band. Two good friends from Omaha had joined the Flag on Buddy's recommendation, and, with Nick Gravenites frequently sidelined, it was the drummer who was singing most of the group's songs. Many of those tunes were covers that Buddy had selected. More and more often, he would take over the band's performances with his theatrics. His stage routine was built around the Chitlin' Circuit antics he had learned with Wilson Pickett and other soul shouters, and he loved nothing more than to whip the audience into a frenzy with vocal feints and histrionics, false endings, "clap-your-hands" interludes, and impromptu call-and-response moments. He would leave the drums in mid-performance and cavort around the stage, mic in hand, improvising lyrics and generally taking over. While audiences were usually thrilled by Buddy's showboating, Michael had begun to dislike it intensely. Not only did it distract from the integrity of the music, putting the emphasis instead on corny shtick, but it also made Michael feel like nothing more than a sideman in a Buddy Miles soul extravaganza.

It was at this difficult moment in the Electric Flag's mercurial career that *Rolling Stone*'s interview with Mike Bloomfield hit the newsstands.

Printed in the April 6 issue of the San Francisco–based publication, the conversation with Michael Bloomfield ran a full five pages and featured Baron Wolman's candid shots of the guitarist as he answered editor Jann Wenner's queries. The article led off with a half-page photo showing Michael soloing intensely during one of the Flag's appearances at the Fillmore Auditorium in December, and what followed was a rollercoaster ride of Bloomfield's ideas on music, race, blues, rock 'n' roll, and his own place in their evolution. The interview was so long that a note at its conclusion promised a second installment in the magazine's subsequent issue. The article was as extensive as any yet published in *Rolling Stone* except for its interview with Bob Dylan. Michael came off as highly animated, a larger-than-life savant whose opinions were hard edged and legion. His respect for his antecedents and his disdain for musical wannabes—especially those in San Francisco—were offered with unqualified and assured candor. It was the world according to Michael Bloomfield.

He told of his days sitting in with Muddy Waters on Chicago's South Side, of putting together the Group, and of starting the blues scene at Big John's in Old Town. He praised Paul Butterfield, saying, "Whatever I didn't like about Paul as a person, his musicianship was more than enough to make up for it. He was just so heavy, he was so much. Everything I dug in and about the blues, Paul was." Displaying an authoritative knowledge of the genre and its masters—many of whom he had known and worked with personally—Bloomfield explained how his enthusiasm for blues bands with horns had led to the creation of the Electric Flag. Though his original vision for the American Music Band had evolved since forming the group in 1967, he expressed admiration for the talents of Buddy Miles. He also praised the artistry of Eric Clapton and Jimi Hendrix, calling the latter "monstrous. Really talented cat, super together cat." He spoke passionately about all sorts of music, especially gospel. "That's my favorite music today in the whole world. I think that's the most happening thing in the world now."

But Michael also talked about race in America and—as he had done six months earlier in the *Los Angeles Free Press*—complained about white audiences' reaction to black music. "You gotta know what's going down. In an Indian thing you've got to know when a cat played a good way. If you were at a fuck-a-thon, you'd have to know when a good fuck went down to know what's happening. These kids don't know."

He then offered strong opinions on the prickly subject of whites playing black music, seemingly unaware of how his own position vis-à-vis the topic might raise questions for those unfamiliar with his deep experience with and commitment to black music. "It's really hard to put into words what the real blues is and what it isn't. . . . [Y]ou're not studiously trying to cop something, you're not listening to a Robert Johnson record and trying to sound like it, you are merely playing the most natural music for you." Butterfield was an exemplary white blues player because, as Michael put it, Paul had transcended his race and learned the blues "by adapting himself to that environment, that he turned over, that he transformed, changed, and anything that's in his background . . . is completely dissolved." In other words, anything less than total commitment from whites was just imitation—bad imitation.

West Coast rock came in for some of Bloomfield's harshest criticism. About the local scene, he said, "I think San Francisco music isn't good music. Not good bands. They're amateur cats." The Grateful Dead, Michael asserted, "don't have a good beat. I can't explain it. It's not the real shit, and it's not even a good imitation." In quick succession, he dismissed Country Joe, Quicksilver Messenger Service, and Big Brother. "There's no real heavies out here at all," Bloomfield declared. When he took aim at the city's foremost progressive group, he may have crossed a line for the *Rolling Stone*'s editor. "I don't dig the Airplane. I think they're a third rate rock 'n' roll band."

Wenner took exception, pointing out that while the City by the Bay had its share of mediocre bands, it had also produced some excellent groups. But twenty-four-year-old Michael Bloomfield was resolute, the authority in all things. "You know, man, it's a fraudulent scene. I don't think that many good bands have come out of San Francisco."

The Electric Flag *was* a good band that had come out of San Francisco, and now they were back in the city, gearing up for a week of performances for Bill Graham. On Sunday, April 21, they did an impromptu set at the Carousel Ballroom, a large second-floor dance hall located at the intersection of Van Ness Avenue and Market Street that Graham had been using occasionally as an alternative to his Fillmore and Winterland venues. The Flag kicked off the evening show with a freewheeling semi-jam that included well-known Bay Area jazz saxophonist Virgil Gonsalves. The enlarged group opened with Stevie Wonder's "Uptight," played a few tunes from the Flag's regular repertory, and then ventured into jazz territory with Miles Davis's "The Theme," playing it as a twelve-bar blues.

The action then moved to the Fillmore Auditorium on the following Thursday for three nights of shows that featured the Flag as the headliner. On Sunday, April 28, the band appeared at San Francisco State College's annual folk festival and, according to one report, "left a dazzled audience dancing in the aisles." They also appeared at San Diego State University on May 3, giving a good show despite being hampered by technical problems. The performance received a standing ovation, proving that the Electric Flag, even with its drug issues and its leader's growing disaffection, could still "blow minds."

From San Diego, the Electric Flag traveled up the coast to Santa Monica for a weekend at the Cheetah. Once again, the group was at its best, and Michael Bloomfield, in particular, seemed inspired. He had good reason to be. Eric Clapton, on a break from Cream's rigorous touring schedule, was in Los Angeles for a few days, and on Friday, May 10, he caught the Flag's late set at the club on the Santa Monica pier, visiting with Michael briefly backstage. The band played material from its album and other familiar tunes from its repertory, and Buddy Miles entertained the packed room with extroverted versions of "Higher and Higher" and "Drivin' Wheel." But then, almost as an afterthought, Michael suggested they do Nick Gravenites's "It's About Time."

The band had worked up an arrangement for the piece but seldom played it, thinking it preferable to feature "Another Country" from the album as their lengthy jam number. But Michael was in a mood to hold nothing back, and "It's About Time," following Nick's vocal, was essentially a one-chord, open-ended platform for free improvisation. Bloomfield had used it for exploring the limits of tonality ever since he and Nick developed it back in 1965 with their group at the Trip in Chicago's Old Town, and that Friday night at the Cheetah, he didn't want to be limited by the band's constricting arrangements. He was going to show the enthusiastic crowd—and especially his British friend and colleague—what he could do.

Bloomfield counted off the tempo, and the rhythm section came in on the downbeat, building momentum around Harvey Brooks's two-bar bass line. The horns began to vamp in harmony while Gravenites sang the opening lines.

It's about time, it's about time
It's about time I quit hurtin' myself

Michael underscored the singer's phrases with aggressive fills, his Les Paul cranked and menacing. Nick sang through two verses, repeating the opening phrase as the vamp built steadily behind him, Buddy Miles pounding out the beat on his bass drum and toms with the force of a rock-and-soul pile driver. Michael turned and faced the band, conducting them with both hands as Gravenites began to moan and shout. An audience member, a young woman down front, shouted back, exhorting the Flag with ecstatic cries. Buddy suddenly double-timed the beat, creating a thunderous roll, and the horns, too, doubled their riff, building a tremor of sound that shook the entire building. For a moment, there was only the relentless pulse of "It's About Time." Then Mike Bloomfield fired off an opening salvo.

His first run employed a favorite Bloomfield conceit, one that he alone among rock guitarists used. Because "It's About Time" was in C minor, his first phrase, built around an E-flat major scale, established the relative-minor relationship. But it also suggested G minor, the piece's dominant chord. Thus, with a single flashy lick, Michael placed "It's About Time" in three separate but related keys, giving it a jazzy, exotic sound and opening its musical landscape to a wide variety of solo approaches. He then proceeded to exploit that breech with hair-raising ferocity.

Using dissonance, extended harmonies, and a variety of unusual scales, Michael Bloomfield soloed for four seemingly unending minutes without pause. He was like a virtuoso gone mad, playing out the world's fiery end as though his notes were its last chance for salvation. Bloomfield was known for astonishing performances, but this was beyond anything most fans had ever heard. It certainly beggared anything he had ever done in the studio. It was a cataclysm, a revelation, the apocalypse.

The guitarist built passages of raga-like melodies and then tore them apart with careening rock licks, only to rebuild them seconds later with even greater speed and precision. He moved from consonant arpeggios to dissonant microtonal bends without concern for musical convention, his notes conveying an unending cascade of extravagant ideas. Toward the end of his epic display, Michael left off phrasing altogether and began bending and shaking his notes in an evocation of some wailing blues banshee in the throes of an unearthly passion. Nothing like it had ever before been heard in American pop music. It came to an end only when Bloomfield, physically spent, played a slow, descending scale, ending on a final resounding low note.

But the piece wasn't done yet. Peter Strazza immediately took center stage with his tenor and soloed effectively for another two minutes, eventually clamping down on his reed and creating shrill notes far above his horn's standard range while Doubleday and Hunter riffed behind him. Then Bloomfield returned, echoing the saxophonist's altissimo statements with a repeated, piercing high note.

The guitarist, refreshed and now less volatile, continued soloing in his Les Paul's upper register for another minute and a half, creating the blues-rock lines that were familiar to "East-West" fans everywhere. As the Flag's rhythm section dropped back into the piece's opening vamp, Nick began singing the refrain. Michael again shaded Gravenites's words, using his volume control trick with two- and three-note clusters to create an ethereal chorus. After a single verse from the singer, Herbie Rich, still behind his Hammond, picked up his baritone sax and began to solo using his right hand while accompanying himself on organ with his left. But without a microphone, the big horn was all but inaudible over the roar of bass and drums, and after several attempts, Rich put the sax aside and began soloing instead on organ. Bloomfield was right there with him, repeating the organist's opening phrase note for note.

What followed was a full-blown duet between the guitar player and his keyboardist, a freely improvised counterpoint that wove in and around a harmonic center. Bloomfield would riff on a line from Rich, and then the organist would embellish Michael's phrase with his own variation. They danced musically for a full four minutes, and at one point Herbie even imitated the sound of highland pipes. Through it all, Buddy Miles kept up a relentless beat, as unstoppable as a runaway locomotive. As the duet ended, the drummer put down his sticks and pounded out the rhythm using only his foot pedal and bass drum. Then a remarkable thing happened.

Michael hung on a single note, bending it slowly in and out of tune. Peter Strazza joined in, playing a second dissonant note on his tenor to create an eerie, otherworldly sound. Mark Doubleday added a third tone, a Harmon mute giving his trumpet a squeaky, childlike tonality. Nick Gravenites began to moan as feedback from Bloomfield's Sunburst created yet another ethereal effect. "It's About Time" had suddenly become a Halloween night prank, with ghosts and goblins cavorting in an aural graveyard. It had evolved into the midnight howl of fright-night apparitions.

It was up to Buddy Miles to disperse these nocturnal haunts. With a flourish of triplets on his snare, the big drummer focused his unruly bandmates and returned the Flag to the original "It's About Time" vamp. A moment later, Miles launched the piece's final crescendo, stomping the beat for a full sixteen measures as Michael played ascending chords with ever greater intensity. The band came to a full stop as members of the audience screamed from delight and utter exhaustion, and then the Electric Flag completed the coda with a final flourish. Bloomfield fired off a last fusillade of notes as Buddy brought "It's About Time" to a resolute conclusion with a thunderous crash on his kit. There was a blink of silence and then the stunned audience was on its feet, cheering, shouting, applauding. Michael Bloomfield, his face glistening with sweat, smiled appreciatively.

It was an extraordinary performance from a band that did indeed "blow minds." The quality of improvisation, the tight ensemble work, the innovative harmonies and melodies, the powerhouse sound—these all were a testament to the Flag's superior musicianship. But it was Mike Bloomfield's unparalleled performance that set the piece apart. It was a moment when his musical gifts—his skill as a guitarist, his knowledge of musical styles, his understanding of music theory, his willingness to take extravagant risks, his prowess as an innovator—were all vividly on display. It was a wild twenty-minute exploration of musical territory that was neither rock nor blues nor jazz, but a fusion of all three, another country overlorded by an extroverted, brilliant, benevolent monarch named Michael Bloomfield. It's not known what Eric Clapton thought of Bloomfield's playing that night, though later he famously described his friend as "music on two legs." Michael, however, seemed to know how remarkable his performance of "It's About Time" at the Cheetah had been. He kept a tape of the night's show for many years, recording over much of the Flag's set but always carefully preserving that one piece.

The next day, Saturday, May 11, the latest issue of *Rolling Stone* hit newsstands. In a bit of serendipity, its cover story was an interview with Bloomfield's guest from the night before, Eric Clapton. In the piece, Eric mentioned Michael as one of his two greatest influences as a person—Bob Dylan being the other. He described being overwhelmed by Bloomfield's personality when they first met, a claim many of Bloomfield's friends and acquaintances could also make.

The tribute from the other great master of the blues-rock idiom had to please Michael. But that satisfaction was quickly overshadowed.

There was another article in the tabloid that caught Michael Bloomfield entirely by surprise. The publication's cofounder, and San Francisco's preeminent music critic and columnist, Ralph J. Gleason had devoted his "Perspectives" column to the leader of the Electric Flag. It was headlined "Stop This Shuck, Mike Bloomfield" and could in no way be construed as a tribute.

"No matter how long he lives and how good he plays," Gleason began, "Mike Bloomfield will never be a spade." The critic had read Michael's April 6 interview and clearly had been irked by some of the guitarist's more outspoken observations. Gleason felt some comeuppance was in order, and he decided to take Michael to task over an issue around which he thought the guitarist was most vulnerable—his race. Despite all his talent, the critic asserted, Bloomfield had become little more than a white musician trying to sound black.

> The trouble with it all is that Bloomfield is a fine musician. But he will always be a Jewish boy from Chicago and not a black man from the Delta. There are a lot of people who think he is black, but then they also think that the song is "Parchment Farm" and don't even know that the name of the prison farm is Parchman.

Gleason cited examples of white jazz players over the decades who he felt had tried to sound black but wound up being nothing more than pale copies. "Tragically enough, the better they were at sounding black, the less they were themselves and the more obviously they were an imitation," he caustically observed. The Electric Flag, Bloomfield's band, was a case in point. "They ought to sound original and ought to be a gas but they are really only a good white band playing black music."

San Francisco bands, by comparison, made no pretense about being anything other than what they were. Bloomfield may have called them "amateurs," Gleason noted, but they made no apologies for their whiteness—"the first American musicians, aside from country & western players, who are not trying to sound black." He saw the city's rock bands as an encouraging development. Unlike Michael's group, they did not sound like anybody else.

The critic concluded his column with a veiled reference to minstrelsy. "It won't rub off. You can't become what you are not and it's not for sale. Play your own soul, man, and stop this shuck."

The piece was a demeaning and offensive broadside, and it caught the guitarist completely off guard. Coming from someone as important to the San Francisco scene as Ralph J. Gleason, a writer of national and international prominence, the column wasn't just an opinion piece; it was a pronouncement. Michael Bloomfield had been exposed once and for all as a talented poseur, a wan copy of the kind of musician he could never hope to be. Unoriginal, an imitation. Worse—a disappointment.

The critic's words stung and embarrassed Michael. He felt exposed, publicly humiliated. Musicians and friends alike all saw the column, and they now knew America's greatest blues-rock guitarist was little more than a phony. At least, that's how it felt. And while Bloomfield was more than willing to debate the race issue with anyone who had the temerity to raise it, there was little he could do to effectively respond to Gleason. The critic's highly respected status in the world of music journalism made his observations all but unimpeachable.

In truth, though, there was perhaps more to Ralph J. Gleason's attack than his words let on. Though he had begun his career as a jazz critic, Gleason also wrote favorably about folk and blues and was an early supporter of 1960s pop music. He championed many San Francisco rock bands in his *Chronicle* columns and was particularly impressed with the Jefferson Airplane and the Grateful Dead. He had promoted both bands vigorously, investing his own credibility in the merits of their music and in their importance as musicians and artists of stature. And then, in his *own* publication, an outsider named Michael Bloomfield dismissed the entire San Francisco popular music scene, saying it "isn't good music" and pronouncing the city's bands "not good bands." That may well have irked Gleason. When Bloomfield went on to call the Airplane a "third-rate rock 'n' roll band" and condemned the Dead's blues as "not the real shit, and . . . not even a good imitation," the critic must have felt that he had to respond. Those declarations were a personal affront, not only a challenge to Gleason's status as the city's cultural arbiter, but also an unprecedented questioning of his judgment. That was too much.

Then there was the prickly issue of race. Gleason was, of course, himself a white man with a background not unlike Bloomfield's. He had grown up in wealthy Westchester County, in the hamlet of Chappaqua, some thirty miles north of New York City. While his family wasn't rich, young Ralph had a comfortable and privileged childhood and was able to attend Columbia University in Manhattan after graduating from high school. His interest in jazz came from the music he initially heard over the radio, and after dropping out of college, Gleason and two friends started a four-page weekly newsletter called *Jazz Information*. It was one of the first serious publications dedicated to the music, and twenty-two-year-old Ralph wrote many of its articles and record reviews. That he was a white man writing about what he himself readily acknowledged was fundamentally a black man's art seemed not to trouble him. He also made no distinction between white and black jazz—the music was either good or it was not. Were white players imitators? The question never came up. What about young Gleason's views on jazz? Were they invalid because he would always be an Irish boy from New York's segregated suburbs and not a black man from Harlem? That, too, seemed not to be an issue.

Yet the critic made race an issue in his attack on Michael Bloomfield. It was a measure of just how annoyed he was with Bloomfield's condemnation of the music Gleason found so praiseworthy. His desire to strike back at the guitarist blinded him to the potential irony of his own position as a white critic of black jazz.

Of course, those who knew Mike Bloomfield well knew there was little substance to many of Gleason's charges. The guitarist was no mere imitator; that accusation was entirely absurd. As for originality, there were few guitarists in rock—in any type of music, for that matter—who were as innovative and original as Michael Bloomfield. And "play your own soul"? There was no way the guitarist could do anything *but* play his own soul. No shuck involved.

One reader felt Ralph J. Gleason's accusations could not go unanswered, regardless of the critic's vaunted status. *Rolling Stone* gave Nick Gravenites space in its May 25 edition to write a response, and Bloomfield's no-nonsense, streetwise friend and bandmate forcefully rebutted some of the critic's more outlandish claims. Nick pointed out that many of Gleason's statements amounted to Crow Jim racism. "Mike is from Chicago," Gravenites asserted. "Chicago has over one million black Americans living there and . . . it is virtually impossible to live in the city and not become a little black in your heart and soul. It's not so unnatural to play blues in Chicago." In his article, pointedly titled "Stop This Shuck, Ralph Gleason," the singer noted that blues was part of the musical environment for *all* Chicagoans—not just those from the black community—and that Bloomfield had been playing as an equal with black musicians for most of his musical life. It was a straightforward and eloquent reply, one that inspired numerous letters to the editor in support. Gleason had clearly crossed a line, and Gravenites had successfully redrawn it in Michael Bloomfield's favor.

But valiant as the piece was, it failed to answer one of Gleason's salient criticisms. The Flag had largely become a soul-and-blues cover band by the late spring of 1968, and Bloomfield knew it. The critic said as much, pointing out that there had been a de facto change in the group's leadership. "It's Buddy Miles' Electric Flag, not Mike Bloomfield's Electric Flag, which is a tragedy and which shows you where it's at," he wrote. The tragedy, in Gleason's opinion, was that the group had failed to fulfill its potential as an American music band. Aware that his original vision for the Flag had long been sidetracked, Bloomfield had to acknowledge that the critic was right.

Ralph J. Gleason's "Perspectives" column could not have come at a more critical moment in Michael Bloomfield's career. Things, it seemed, were coming to a head. The guitarist was weary of his responsibilities as a bandleader, exhausted from months of touring and performing, and creatively drained from his efforts to produce *A Long Time Comin'*. The album had started strong on *Billboard's* charts and was still doing well after four weeks, having risen to number 36, but Michael was dreading the tour that would be required to support the record. The band's recent drug troubles had also left him fearful of further entanglements with cops and unscrupulous dealers, knowing that Albert Grossman was unlikely to bail out the band a third time. And now he had been called on the carpet by one of the most respected critics in contemporary music. To Gleason, Michael was a disappointment, a failure. For the guitarist, that was an all-to-familiar experience. It was a judgment his father, Harold Bloomfield, had also repeatedly made.

However ambivalent Michael Bloomfield felt about continuing with the Electric Flag, Ralph J. Gleason's column only hastened the day of reckoning. The guitarist now wanted nothing more than to step out of the spotlight, forego whatever status he had as a rock star, and retire to the anonymity of Mill Valley and the comfort of his bedroom. There, with his books, records, and TV, he could escape the music industry's unceasing demands and the expectations of his fans. There he could quiet his mind.

Following the shows at the Cheetah, the Flag played four nights at the Whisky a Go Go. While there, Michael put in a call to Albert Grossman in New York. The manager had to know what was coming—he, too, had read the Gleason piece—but he didn't want to hear it. Michael was unwavering, though. He told his manager that he couldn't do it any longer, that he was through being the leader of the Electric Flag. There was silence on the line, and then Grossman told his star guitarist that there were shows coming up, and then he wanted the band to do something for Bill Graham in New York. He said Michael would have to play those, and then they would talk about the future.

One show coming up was a huge outdoor rock extravaganza in Santa Clara at the city's fairgrounds. Billed as the Northern California Folk-Rock Festival, the two-day event promised over twenty bands headlined by the Jefferson Airplane and the Doors. The Electric Flag appeared mid-afternoon on Sunday, and they were also booked into the Carousel Ballroom in San Francisco for three nights beginning that Friday, so it was a busy weekend for the band. Sharing the stage with the Flag at the Carousel was the Don Ellis Orchestra, a progressive jazz big band that was experimenting with rock rhythms and electric instruments, among other things. The leader himself was playing what he called an "electrophonic" trumpet, using a pickup to feed the sound of his horn through a tape-delay machine called an Echoplex. Ellis had first met Bloomfield in 1966 when the Butterfield Band performed at the Monterey Jazz Festival, and when Michael mentioned that he was leaving the Flag, the trumpeter right away asked him to join his big band. Unlike most jazz orchestras, Ellis's group had no guitar player, and Bloomfield's adventurous work with the Butterfield Band and with his own horn band seemed well suited to the direction Ellis's orchestra was taking. But Michael, wanting nothing more than the comforts of home, wasn't ready for a new challenge. He was flattered by the bandleader's offer and said he would think about it.

Later that week, the Electric Flag made its third trip to Southern California in a little more than a month. The band flew into Los Angeles and then drove up to Santa Barbara on Friday, May 24, for an appearance at UC Santa Barbara's Robertson Gymnasium. They were scheduled to open for Cream, one set only, and then had to make the trip back to Los Angeles, where they were the headliners for another show at the Shrine Auditorium that same night—making it a very long night for the band.

Word had gotten out about Michael Bloomfield's disaffection with the music industry, and rumors had begun to spread about the impending breakup of the Electric Flag. Many of the college students at the Robertson Gym and fans at the Shrine that evening expected to see an abbreviated version of Bloomfield's band onstage. But the *Los Angeles Times* reported that the members "were all there, joyfully active." If they were at all tired from the day's arduous travels, it was not apparent. Michael was especially animated. "He bounces around the stage in a perpetual state of excitement, seemingly too in love with the sounds of his guitar to remember to face the audience," the *Times* enthused. "Bloomfield has few peers in the rock field." The publication also praised Nick Gravenites and Buddy Miles, and it reported that the Flag "worked most of the Shrine crowd to their feet at the end of the Friday concert, a sure proof of excitement."

The excitement—and the traveling—continued the following day, Saturday, as the band headed north to Fresno for a show at the Selland Arena, a huge sports palace, where they were the opening act for Frank Zappa's Mothers of Invention. In a repeat of Friday's schedule, the band then quickly boarded a plane for the short flight back to LA and a second night at the Shrine Auditorium. If Albert Grossman hoped to convince his star client to stay with the Electric Flag, scheduling him to play four shows in three separate venues over two nights was probably not the way to do it.

* * *

Back in San Francisco, Mike Bloomfield got a call from another friend. It was keyboardist Al Kooper on the line, and he had a proposition for the guitarist: Would Michael be interested in going into the studio to make a record? Not a typical record, Al said, but a jam session. He was going to play on it, and he was also going to produce it. He had left Blood, Sweat & Tears, Kooper told Bloomfield, and was now working as a producer for Columbia Records. He had been given an office and a secretary, and all he lacked was something to produce. That's when the idea for a jam LP came to him.

"I was sitting around the office with nothing to do," said Al. "I had the album cover from Moby Grape's *Grape Jam*, the record that had both Michael and me playing on it, and I was looking at it, and I suddenly thought, 'Let's make a *real* jam album.'" A long-standing tradition in the jazz world, impromptu studio sessions with skilled musicians had produced some of the tradition's greatest recordings. Why not try the same concept with a few rock stars? Kooper thought it might just work. Especially if he could get a musician of Mike Bloomfield's caliber into the studio. He knew what Michael could do, having jammed with him many times when the Blues Project and the Butterfield Band shared the stage at the Cafe Au Go Go. *That* Bloomfield had never been captured on record, and Kooper thought a relaxed jam setting might allow Michael the psychological space to open up musically.

Bloomfield was less sanguine about the idea. The last thing he wanted to do in his current mental state was go back into the recording studio. He still had gigs to do with the Electric Flag, and Grossman wanted the band to make another trip to the East Coast. One more obligation might be more than Michael could handle. But Kooper was persuasive, and he made the date sound like the casual, easygoing get-together he intended it to be. The guitarist reluctantly agreed, but he asked that they record on the West Coast so he wouldn't have to travel as far.

"I didn't want to make that record too much," Bloomfield said. "It was just a favor for Al Kooper."

The producer was delighted that Michael was willing to participate in his "jam session" project, and he suggested that they "make it fair" by each selecting a sideman to form a quartet. Al chose his old friend Harvey Brooks as the session's bass player, and Bloomfield, having spent the last twelve months playing with Harvey, was fine with that. But Michael's choice for the group's drummer left Kooper confused.

"He said he wanted Eddie Hoh, the drummer with the Mamas and the Papas," Al recalled. "I didn't understand that at all. I had never heard of this guy. I told him I didn't know this guy's playing at all, but I would trust him on it."

Hoh may have seemed like an odd choice, but the drummer was someone Michael knew from Chicago. Eddie had grown up in Forest Park, one of the Windy City's western suburbs, and had gigged around Rush Street as a teenager, where he had picked up the nickname "Fast Eddie" because of his speed and accuracy. Bloomfield met him when the guitarist briefly was a member of Robby and the Troubadours and Eddie was the twist band's drummer. They reconnected at Monterey when Hoh backed the Mamas and the Papas, and Michael would occasionally see him around Los Angeles, where the drummer was a session player for the Monkees and for folksingers Donovan and Tim Buckley. Bloomfield knew the twenty-three-year-old was an excellent rock percussionist who could easily handle Chicago-style blues as well as more complex jazz rhythms because he had played with him many times. In fact, Bloomfield and Hoh had participated in a recording session only a month before. On that date, Michael's good friend Barry Goldberg had been the leader.

"Michael came to LA to play with me," Goldberg said. Since leaving the Flag in November, Barry had been living in Los Angeles, getting his health back and organizing his own band. He had gotten a recording contract and he asked his guitarist friend to help him record a few tunes. "The concept was supposed to be Michael and myself. But I was on Buddah Records, and Columbia wouldn't let us use Michael's name. The album was 'Barry Goldberg and . . . ,' but it was supposed to be 'Barry Goldberg and Michael Bloomfield.'"

While the Flag was in Los Angeles killing time before its May 10 and 11 appearances at the Cheetah, Bloomfield spent an evening at LA's Paramount Studios with his friend and former bandmate. Barry had invited Eddie Hoh to the session, and the three musicians, with the addition of a bass player, recorded a number of tunes for Goldberg's album.

Al Kooper knew nothing of Michael's friendship with Eddie Hoh, and it wasn't surprising that he was perplexed by the guitarist choice of a drummer for their studio jam session. But he was willing to trust Bloomfield's judgment, and a date for the recording session was set for the last week in May. The quartet would meet in Los Angeles and spend several relaxed evenings in the studio, jamming on a few tunes, playing some blues and whatever else appealed to them in the moment. The plan was as simple and uncomplicated as Al could make it.

Nothing, though, was uncomplicated in Michael Bloomfield's life in the late spring of 1968. The guitarist's emotional state was in turmoil. He was quitting his band, the record he had spent half a year creating hadn't produced a hit, he had been publicly humiliated by one of the nation's most respected critics, and his marriage had failed—all within the span of a few months. Complicating his mood was his exhaustion from years on the road and countless sleepless nights. His attempts to find relief through drugs provided him with only a few hours' respite, and they, too, came with complications—ones Michael may have been trying to avoid by choosing Eddie Hoh for Al Kooper's date.

Hoh was himself a heroin user. He had begun using drugs as a teenager in Chicago when he was part of Robby and the Troubadours. Drugs eventually broke up the Troubadours, but Hoh landed on his feet and found success in LA's studios. Michael knew he was still a user, and that may have played a role in his selecting the drummer for Kooper's recording date. Because Eddie was a local guy, he would certainly have a connection. That would mean one less complication for the troubled guitarist.

On the surface, Al Kooper's plan to capture a rock jam session on record seemed inspired. Nothing could be simpler—or cheaper—to produce. And even if the results were not stellar, the record was bound to sell enough copies to turn a tidy profit. What could go wrong? Nothing. Nothing, except that Kooper had unwittingly hitched his wagon to a rock star who was about to implode.

On Tuesday, May 28, Harvey Brooks and Michael Bloomfield joined Al Kooper in a large, comfortable home in the Hollywood Hills. Al had arrived a few days earlier, flying into LA from New York to make sure all was ready for his first big assignment with his new employer. The house had been rented for the month by another young Columbia producer, David Rubinson, who had been working on blues singer Taj Mahal's second album. With Mahal's sessions completed and the house available, Kooper took advantage of the remaining time on the rental to provide luxury accommodations for his players. The place even had an in-ground pool in the backyard.

When Michael showed up, he was less concerned with the house's amenities than he was with an infected toe that had been bothering him for several weeks. "He arrived with an ingrown toenail, which he kept insisting was gangrene," Al recalled with a laugh. The guitarist had played the Flag's recent gigs barefooted because it was too painful to wear shoes for very long, and Kooper recalled that Bloomfield immediately filled an expensive crystal bowl with hot water so he could soak his afflicted foot. While the guitarist sought relief, the trio chatted amicably and Kooper shared his thoughts about the session. Al said the idea was just to do a little open-ended jamming, come up with some tunes, and see what resulted. He suggested they might try a few improvised blues pieces to feature Michael's guitar, and then maybe a Dylan tune and one or two soul numbers that he thought would work well. The guitarist and bass player were intrigued by the concept. Using valuable studio time to make music without a specific plan or objective was a radical idea. But simply going into the studio to *play*, without lead sheets, arrangements, or rehearsals, appealed to Michael, despite his initial reluctance to participate. It was an approach that was the antithesis of the one he had taken with *A Long Time Comin'*, and he was curious to see how it would work.

That afternoon, Michael, Harvey, and Al drove to Columbia's studios on Sunset Boulevard in Hollywood. There they met Eddie Hoh, and while they were setting up their equipment, Barry Goldberg arrived, having been invited by Michael to watch the session and maybe play on a tune or two on piano. Al was surprised to see the keyboardist, and he didn't really know Barry, but he was willing to let Goldberg play if it was what Michael wanted. The date was, after all, supposed to be a jam session.

The studio's engineers spent the better part of an hour arranging sound barriers between the players and positioning microphones in front of amps and around the drums. Once preparations were complete, the quartet warmed up with a slow blues in G, beginning with the turnaround. Michael took the lead and soloed in languorous style for a chorus, then opened up and began building in typical Bloomfield fashion, only to drop down at the beginning of his third chorus for twelve bars of understated, intimate phrases. With the fourth chorus, Michael began aggressively pushing the beat and then holding it back, building once again as he switched to his Les Paul's fuller-sounding neck pickup. In the fifth chorus, he hung on a high C for two full bars in the turnaround and then brought the piece to a close in the sixth with a furious display of virtuosity. No one else got a chance to solo, but Kooper didn't mind. It was clear that his star guitarist was in excellent form. *This* was the Bloomfield Al remembered from live performances.

"While we were playing the blues, I was thinking, 'This is so great! He's playing beautifully, he's totally comfortable!'" Kooper said. "I knew then that I could get the best out of him."

Though the engineers in the control booth were already running tape, Kooper suggested that the group try an actual take, a version of the blues they just did but this time in the key of C. He said Michael could take the first solo, but then he wanted a few choruses for himself on organ. Harvey Brooks wasn't happy with the walking bass line he had used, so he switched to a more open style, playing the root on the first beat of each measure and then walking down from the octave. Bloomfield counted the instrumental off, this time having the musicians start right in on the chorus rather than the turnaround.

Again Michael took the lead, playing sensuous lines at first and toying with the beat, and then pumping up the volume and becoming aggressive. This time though, he ended his solo after only two choruses, and then it was Kooper's turn. Al followed Michael's lead, building his phrases as he worked through one chorus, making brief melodies and then answering them with chords and flurries of notes. Midway through his second chorus, he dropped down into the Hammond's lower register, creating a basso stutter that rumbled its way through the turnaround. Then Bloomfield was back, his guitar softly purring as he held single notes for a measure or more, playing again with the beat and the piece's tonality as he stretched his notes in and out of tune. The effect was uncanny for its vocal-like quality. But in his next chorus, the tune's last, Bloomfield reared back and loosed his Les Paul's full power, taking the blues down the home stretch with a volley of licks high on the neck. The band then walked through the turnaround as a unit and ended with a I–V–I coda.

Everyone seemed satisfied with the take as they listened to the playback, and as they were discussing what to play next, photographer Jim Marshall walked into the studio. With him was Linda Ronstadt, the lead vocalist for a folk-rock group called the Stone Poneys. She was making a name for herself in the Los Angeles area as a strikingly talented—and strikingly attractive—singer. She took a seat off to the side in the big room and quietly watched the musicians work as Marshall loaded his Leica cameras with film. The photographer frequently provided Columbia with images for their record covers, and Kooper wanted to be sure his jam session recording date would be well documented.

"Jim would get information from me about music that was happening, and he would go photograph it. I asked him to come by to take some pictures of us as we played," Al said. He added with a laugh, "Linda came with him—she was there to advance her career."

The musicians decided to try another blues in G, a shuffle this time, with Barry Goldberg joining the jam. An electric piano was set up and miked, and the group, now a quintet, launched into a relaxed shuffle. Michael introduced it with a two-beat pickup, and then, as the rhythm section came in on the downbeat of the turnaround, he began to solo. After only a few bars, it was clear Al Kooper was right. The guitarist was entirely at his ease, his notes and phrases coming with a fluidity and command that was striking. Michael wasn't holding back, and he wasn't swinging for the fences, either. He was simply playing definitive electric blues, three full choruses worth, with licks and phrases that evoked B. B. King, Albert King, Otis Rush, and other greats of the tradition but that also were wholly his own. It was thirty-six bars of the *Michael Bloomfield sound*, with all its bends, shakes, feints, tonal slurs, and tempo pulls. There was none of the skittery excess that sometimes flooded the guitarist's solos in earlier years, no overplaying, no rush to the exit. Here was the mature Michael Bloomfield showing them all how it should be done—no mere imitation, just the man playing his own soul.

Kooper followed, offering a melodic rejoinder to the sweet-and-salty preaching of the guitarist's three choruses. The organist built three of his own around easy, single-note phrases punctuated with fat chords and tremolos, and on the turnaround to his last twelve, Bloomfield, unable to resist, trotted back in and soloed out the chorus. Michael then took the blues home with two more, his last twelve bars a kind of call-and-response between lush held notes and tough, staccato riffs. When he tagged the coda with a run up to another high C, everybody knew the performance was a winner.

That blues would later be named "Albert's Shuffle," a teasing tribute to Bloomfield's ursine manager and his ambling gait. As Kooper had hoped, the performance captured, for nearly the first time, Michael's distinctive sound and style in a studio setting. He had tried to create an environment in which his guitarist friend would feel at ease, and it looked very much like he had succeeded.

"I think he didn't really ever do well with producers," Al said of Bloomfield's studio experiences. "They could make Michael uptight, and I consciously tried not to do that with him."

While the musicians took a break, Jim Marshall hovered, snapping candid shots of Harvey Brooks and Michael Bloomfield kidding around, the guitarist's much-abused Les Paul lying on the studio floor next to him. After a moment, Al joined them, kicking off his boots and sitting cross-legged on the floor as they talked over what to play next. Barry sauntered over and got into the discussion, and in a few minutes the musicians had decided to try a tune called "Stop." Recorded by soul singer Howard Tate earlier in the year, the song had been a hit on *Billboard*'s R&B chart. But with an involved AABB, sixteen-bar structure, a bridge, and three vocal choruses, it soon became obvious that working up a full rendition of "Stop" was going to take too much time. So Kooper had the group play just the opening eight bars, the AA section, repeating them to create a funky instrumental.

He began the tune with an organ-and-guitar vamp, the rest of the group joining in on the second four bars. Michael then stepped up and soloed, his Sunburst turned up to give his notes a muscular sustain. Played in the key of E major, the simple three-chord progression allowed Bloomfield to solo up on the guitar's neck, centering his lines around the notes E, D, and F♯, and using bends and slurs to give them a bluesy inflection. His playing was rock merged with blues, heavy on the beat and forcefully stated, reminiscent of his contributions to Dylan's *Highway 61* sessions. Once again, Kooper's organ followed, spinning out convincing melodies, simple constructions that emphasized the changes and backbeat, while Bloomfield accompanied with damped chords and bass riffs built around an open E chord. As Al finished, Michael dropped in a series of clusters on the changes and then outlined them with a few bars of folk-style fingerpicking. The quintet then fell into a groove on the progression, playing it out as an ensemble. In Kooper's final edit of the piece, "Stop" would fade out at this point.

Once the musicians had completed their variation on the Tate tune, it was nearly 5:00 p.m. and time for an official break. "Columbia had a very strict recording policy in those days," Al Kooper remembered. "Their artists could only record in their studios, and only with their engineers. Sessions were three hours long—no longer—and each session had to be followed by a one-hour break. I used to call it the 'engineers' break.'" Union regulations mandated time off for members, and at the three-hour point in Kooper's session, all activity in the control booth ceased for the allotted sixty minutes. To the musicians, it seemed like a good time to go out for food, or maybe just take a walk and smoke a joint.

When things got started again a little after 6:00, the piece the group attempted next had been suggested by the producer. Al Kooper had a Curtis Mayfield song in mind. "'Man's Temptation'—that was really the only tune I brought to the session," Al said. "Everything else we just figured out right there in the studio." The song, written by Mayfield, had been a minor hit for soul singer Gene Chandler in 1963, and Kooper thought it would make an effective vocal number. As he ran through the changes for the rest of the musicians, Barry dropped out, preferring instead to sit with a young lady he had brought with him to the session. "While Michael, Harvey and Eddie proceeded to cut several more tracks with Kooper, I got busy with this cute surfer chick who I think had been an Electric Flag fan when I first met her," Goldberg later wrote. His infatuation with the comely blond effectively sidelined the pianist, ending his participation in the session. But the quartet carried on as originally planned, and they soon had an arrangement of "Man's Temptation" worked out. Michael jotted down the chords on a lead sheet and placed it on a music stand so that both he and Harvey could refer to it.

Hoh kicked off the tune, and as the band came in on the introduction, Kooper began to sing. Accompanying himself on piano, the producer worked through three verses without pause, his high tenor straining for soulful effect. Bloomfield tracked his phrases, adding fills and subtle embellishments to complement the melody with striking precision. "Michael was one of the best accompanists I ever played with," said Al. "He knew just what to do—we never had to work anything out. When we played together, it all just fit. We had a really good musical relationship that way, he and I." Though they were only four pieces, the ensemble managed to fill out the sound, and when Kooper would later add horns, he simply had them double many of Michael's ornamentations.

By the time "Man's Temptation" was completed to everyone's satisfaction, it was approaching 8:00 p.m. The question of what to play next was resolved once again by the date's producer. Kooper had his eye on an odd keyboard instrument that was sitting on a table next to the piano. "There was an Ondioline in the studio, and I wanted an excuse to use it," said Al. "I wanted to make it sound like a soprano sax, so I told Bloomfield we should do a modal thing." The Ondioline was a small electronic instrument with a three-octave keyboard, a kind of early synthesizer that had been invented by a Frenchman, Georges Jenny, in the early 1940s. Played through an amplifier, it was able to convincingly simulate a wide variety of instruments, from violins and cellos to banjos and trombones. Because its keyboard was mounted on a spring system, a player could create vibrato and dynamic effects unavailable on other electric keyboards. Kooper had used the instrument on recordings with his other bands, the Blues Project and Blood, Sweat & Tears, and he very much liked its sound. As he played with the Ondioline's settings to get the right saxophone effect, Michael and Harvey worked up a 6/8 pattern in G major, a two-bar descending line that moved between octaves in a G–F–C progression. The guitarist added harmony using clusters that incorporated an open G string, and with Eddie Hoh keeping straight time on his ride cymbal, kick drum, and snare, the three soon had a suitable background for Kooper's mock soprano.

But Michael wanted something a little freer to improvise on, so Eddie shifted the beat to a polyrhythmic pattern, opening up the tempo. Bloomfield also suggested that they transposed the key to E minor, the relative minor of G, so that he could solo using both G-major and E-minor scales with the option of using open G and E strings as drones. That gave the piece a modal, jazzy feel.

That jazzy feel was wholly intentional. With Kooper "blowing" soprano sax to open the piece and then sharing solos with Bloomfield on a one-chord vamp in syncopated waltz time, everyone was thinking of jazz saxophonist John Coltrane. Coltrane's "My Favorite Things," recorded seven years earlier, was a jazz waltz famously played on soprano over a vamp-like piano figure in E minor. The similarities were striking, but the session's modal piece wasn't inspired only by the great saxophonist's reinvention of the Rodgers and Hammerstein hit. For Bloomfield, it obviously harkened back to "East-West" with the Butterfield Band and to other freewheeling jams, most notably his recent epic re-creation of Nick Gravenites's "It's About Time" from the Electric Flag's Cheetah show earlier in the month. That performance had unquestionably stretched the boundaries of blues-rock. Now Michael would use his skills to attempt the same thing with jazz, creating jazz-rock—"pseudo jazz," in the guitarist's parlance.

The musicians soon had the piece mapped out and ready to go, but it was nearly 9:00 p.m. and time for another mandated break. The engineers went out for coffee while Kooper and his men sampled the night air on Sunset Boulevard, watching as the passing parade headed toward the Strip and its nocturnal amusements.

After an hour, recording activity in the studio resumed. When the musicians were in place and ready, Mike Bloomfield began the modal piece at a moderate tempo, playing the G progression for two bars by himself. Brooks and Hoh joined in on the next two, and then Kooper entered on Ondioline, playing a simple melody that echoed Michael's pattern. The keyboard instrument's reedy sound had some of the qualities of a soprano—it could convincingly slur and bend notes—but it clearly wasn't a saxophone. Its curious timbre lent a spacey quality to Al's lines as he briefly soloed, having fun with the Ondioline's vibrato and pitch-altering capabilities. The effects gave the sound a bagpipe-like quality as Kooper spun out clusters of notes over the rhythm section's pleasant drone. After a few moments, he climbed up to a high C and held it for nearly nine measures as Bloomfield joined him. Then Harvey Brooks walked the bass line down to a repeated E, and Michael duplicated that note, shifting the tonal center. The key change ushered in the new tempo as Eddie Hoh moved from straight time to a jazz 6/8, keeping the beat on ride cymbal and snare. After a few more melodic phrases, Al began soloing again, his lines this time busy and fleet.

"I had to BS my way through that modal piece," Kooper later confessed, adding with a laugh, "I cut out a lot of my solo when I edited the session."

After Al had his say, it was Michael's turn, and the guitarist started his statement by briefly outlining an E-minor chord. From there, he stepped off into modal space as he incorporated flurries of notes into his characteristic rolls, moving between scales in E and G, sliding from note to note, creating motives and repeating them, shaking out old phrases while inventing new ones. Harvey Brooks, listening closely, followed Michael's lead, hanging on an E one moment and running riffs up to a G the next, complementing the guitarist's licks with lines of his own. The bass player's months with Bloomfield in the Electric Flag had clearly given him a deep understanding of the guitarist's volatile soloing style. For eighty-two bars, Bloomfield explored the tonal landscape, erecting spires of auditory ornamentation, populating space with ambulatory sound, moving from one improvised edifice to another. Then, after satisfying his musical curiosity, he dropped back into a rhythm pattern. The producer, now on the more familiar Hammond B3, reentered.

Kooper soloed, displaying his skill at creating simple but effective melodies. Beginning on F♯, the organist played a series of descending and ascending phrases that were variations on the piece's opening theme. Resolving the series up to an A, he held that note, providing a drone as he played additional lines, building for twelve bars and then breaking into chords that rose to one crescendo and then another. He played a second sustained A, moving up to a bright B before loosing one final, resolute chord. With that, all instruments but the drums suddenly dropped out. Eddie Hoh was left to vamp alone for four bars.

It was a moment that echoed the dramatic second crescendo in the studio recording of "East-West." As had happened in the Butterfield Band's signal instrumental, Michael Bloomfield began quietly soloing. Beginning on an E, the guitarist wove lines that rose and fell with an engaging simplicity as Kooper's B3 burbled and Brooks's bass anticipated. The quartet was now tightly synced, working together with the ease of a seasoned jazz combo. Nineteen bars into Michael's solo, the guitarist played an ascending E-minor scale that both Al and Harvey caught and played right along with him. Eddie picked up their eighth-note run and redoubled it on his snare. There was nothing "pseudo" about the moment.

Bloomfield continued to riff, becoming more aggressive as Kooper played chord inversions behind him and Hoh pressed the beat. The quartet built a wave of sound as the organist played a series of ascending chords and Eddie added splashy accents on his cymbals. But then Bloomfield stopped soloing and plucked, first an open E string and then a commanding Em^{7} chord. The wave began to crest as the guitarist's Twin Reverb suddenly squealed with feedback and Harvey repeatedly thumped a high E on his bass. Al slowly eased off the Hammond's volume pedal as Michael struck several more Em^{7} chords, the last tagged by Hoh as the drums then fell silent. Harvey sounded a few more pedal tones, and Kooper hung on a hushed E-minor chord. The stage was set for a closing cadenza from the guitarist.

With his Les Paul's volume down to nearly acoustic level, Michael began picking out notes, sketching the tonality, offering a spacey summation of the piece. He rolled up to a high C♯ and then to a higher F♯, rolling down again while plucking open B and G strings, almost as though he were fingerpicking a trippy bluegrass breakdown that had broken down. Brooks provided support by sounding a few high Gs, and then Bloomfield sallied one final run, a delicate ascent up to a high B while plucking an open B. From there, he played a series of descending clusters in ritardando, finally concluding his commentary with a last Em^{7}. He let its sound decay until the big room was completely silent.

The musicians looked at each other and smiled. Eddie Hoh quietly murmured, "Far out!" Everyone laughed. The piece was long—nearly ten minutes long—but it contained some of the session's most adventurous playing. It also qualified as the jam's only true original, created entirely in the studio and dependent wholly on the players' abilities as improvisers. Al Kooper was thoroughly satisfied, knowing that though his own solos were probably going to need editing, he had succeeded in getting his friend on tape at his exotic best. The instrumental—Al would later name it "His Holy Modal Majesty"—wasn't a groundbreaker like "East-West" or an experimental epic like "Another Country," but it did show off Mike Bloomfield's skill as an blues-rock improviser of singular merit, an original voice with few equals. No one else played the "far out" way that Bloomfield did, because no one else could. "The tune worked simply because it was a great vehicle for Michael's talent," Kooper said.

By the time the modal piece was completed, it was after 11:00. The producer decided to call it a day, thanking his tired men for a productive session and proposing they head home for a possible nightcap and then bed. They would meet at the studios again the next afternoon to complete the date. All agreed, and Eddie Hoh headed home to his apartment in Los Angeles while Al, Harvey, and Michael drove back to the rented mansion in the Hollywood Hills. With another long day in the studio ahead of them, the three musicians decided to retire to their rooms without further delay. There would be time enough for other pleasures once Kooper's jam session date had been completed.

Columbia's newest producer was very happy with the day's efforts. Everything had gone smoothly, with the musicians working well together to create music that sounded fresh and spontaneous. Kooper's chief concern—the mood of his guitarist friend—had faded as the afternoon progressed. Bloomfield had not only seemed relaxed and engaged during the session, but played with the uninhibited verve and creativity that so often characterized his live performances. Al was certain the jam date had captured Michael Bloomfield's playing as no other studio session had. And Michael himself seemed satisfied, even pleased, with his performance. He had been animated throughout the date, his usual ebullient self—joking and telling stories, full of hyper energy, just the way he always was. Kooper had every reason to expect Wednesday's session would be even better. He went to sleep, confident that his first job as a producer for Columbia Records would be an unqualified success.

Several rooms away, the session's star guitarist felt no such confidence. Michael Bloomfield sat on the edge of his bed, staring at the wall. He was wide awake. Sleep was out of the question. His exuberance had vanished, gone like a jilted lover's smile. In its place, he felt a deepening depression, a yawning chasm of self-doubt and anxiety. The manic high of the day's activities had dissipated, and the creative effort expended during the session, the pressure to perform and meet expectations, had taken a toll. Now Michael was exhausted, but he couldn't quiet his mind. He was used to struggling with insomnia, but this was something worse. Much worse.

He had anticipated trouble when Al Kooper first proposed the recording session. It was one reason why he had arranged for Barry Goldberg and Eddie Hoh to be there with him. There was some comfort in knowing that if he needed to resort to opiates, there would be friends who would understand and could help. But Barry left the recording session early with his surfer girlfriend, and Eddie was at home in the city, unreachable. Neither Al Kooper nor Harvey Brooks were heroin users, and Kooper didn't even know about the guitarist's involvement with the narcotic. That left Michael all alone with his condition, and the helplessness he felt only exacerbated it.

He suddenly became panicked.

He *had* to leave. It was all he could think of. Breathing rapidly and sweating, he got up and walked out of the room. He felt his way down the darkened hallway, found the stairs, and went in search of a telephone. In twenty minutes, he was on his way to the airport, sitting sprawled across the back seat of a cab, the Les Paul and his overnight bag at his feet on the floor. As irrational as it seemed, getting home to Mill Valley and the safety of his room was his only recourse. Now that he was on his way, he began to breathe more easily. He could relax a little, but that only gave more emotional space to his feelings of depression. In addition to all his other troubles, he was now leaving his friend in the lurch. It was one more thing to feel bad about. Al Kooper would have to find someone else to finish the session. But it couldn't be helped. Michael had to leave.

At least he had left the producer a note of apology.

It was that note that Kooper found in Michael's empty bedroom the next morning. He had been awakened from a deep sleep by the ringing of a telephone a little before 9:00 a.m. When he managed to find and answer it, the voice on the line had a question for him.

"Some girl was calling from the airport in San Francisco," Kooper remembered. "She said, 'Did Michael make his plane?' I said, 'Oh, no—that can't be right. He's here; he's in the next room sleeping.' And she said, 'Well, I'm supposed to pick him up at the airport.' So I told her to hold the line." Kooper went down the hall and peeked into Bloomfield's room. The unslept-in bed gave him a shock. "He was gone, and there was a note on the pillow that said, 'Dear Alan, Couldn't sleep, went home. Sorry.' *That* was a terrible way to wake up!"

In a panic, Kooper quickly went through his phonebook, calling every guitar player that he knew on the West Coast, hoping to find someone who could cover for Bloomfield at the last minute. "I wasn't going to fuck up this date, my first big project as Columbia's resident hippie producer," Al said with a laugh. "I had studio time reserved, a fancy house rented, musicians booked, and half a record completed." Kooper put in calls to the Grateful Dead's Jerry Garcia, to Steve Miller, to Spirit's Randy California, and to Stephen Stills from Buffalo Springfield. "Stills was the only one who called me back," Al said. "I had his number because the Buffalo Springfield guys would always come see Blood, Sweat & Tears whenever they'd come east, and our bassist, Jim Fielder, had played with them. Steve said it sounded like fun and he'd do it, and he saved my ass."

With a replacement found, Kooper's jam-session recording date proceeded as planned, minus its star player. But Stills proved to be a competent substitute, and the quartet went on to complete material for the album with four more "jams," one of which would become its de facto hit.

Back home in Mill Valley, Michael Bloomfield was finally able to sleep. Once he arrived at Wellesley Court, his body simply shut down. Weeks of accumulated stress had finally overwhelmed his perpetually overdriven constitution. Without sleeping pills or any other medication, Bloomfield slept through the day and into the night. When he awoke the next morning, he still felt exhausted, emotionally drained. If he let himself think about it, he also felt guilty for leaving Al Kooper. It was true, though, that he had warned his friend that there could be a problem. "I have insomnia, and I told Kooper that," Bloomfield later explained. "I said I probably won't be able to cut this record." For Kooper, the guitarist's departure had less to do with sleeplessness than with his involvement with drugs. "I think he just couldn't score in Los Angeles," Al said in retrospect. "Therefore, he could not sleep. He just went nuts—he said, '*Fuck* this!' and made phone calls over the course of the evening until he got himself out of there."

Mike Bloomfield's heroin use undoubtedly played a role in his failure to complete the jam-session date. He had expected to have access to the narcotic, and when that option failed, his anxiety soared. But the drug wasn't the cause of his anxiousness. He wasn't an addict, fearful of suffering painful withdrawal symptoms. Heroin was a medication he used to ease his mania, to quench the "fire burning in his brain," as brother Allen described it. More and more, too, the narcotic was helping to keep a deepening depression in check. The painful events of the past six months threatened to overwhelm Michael's fragile sense of well-being with self-doubt, insecurity, and fear. Kooper's Los Angeles session had been the event that burst the dam of Michael's psyche. He had suffered what in contemporary terms might be described as a full-blown panic attack.

"I had just finished with the Flag and was really depressed," the guitarist said in a later interview. "I didn't want to play any gigs at all. Nothing. All I wanted to do is sit around and read." In his bedroom on Wellesley Court, Bloomfield could keep the world at bay. He could be safe from the demands of stardom, from the expectations of fans, from the assessments of critics and colleagues. But most importantly, in his bedroom he could be safe from himself.

Even so, Michael Bloomfield wasn't finished with the Electric Flag. Not yet, anyway. The band had a series of shows to play on the East Coast beginning on Friday, May 31, and Albert Grossman was expecting him to be onstage with them. The Flag was booked for three nights into a recently opened club in Philadelphia called the Electric Factory, a converted tire warehouse on Arch Street. From there, they were to play a return engagement at the Psychedelic Supermarket in Boston's Kenmore Square, and then on to New York City to do a weekend for Bill Graham. San Francisco's rock impresario had decided to open a venue in the Big Apple and had commandeered the Village Theater on Second Avenue, reopening it in March as the Fillmore East. It was the Fillmore appearance that Grossman was most concerned about. The *New York Times* and several other publications were going to cover it, and the resulting publicity could help drive sales of the Flag's album. Even though *A Long Time Comin'* had reached number 31 on *Billboard*'s Top LPs chart by June 1, its momentum was slowing. The manager wanted the full benefit of Bloomfield's celebrity while the guitarist was still in the band, hoping to revive the album's prospects. For that reason, the normally undemonstrative Grossman insisted that Michael perform.

Bloomfield was in no mood to go anywhere, let alone fly to the East Coast for a week of gigging on the road. But he was in debt to ABGM for advances and for the extra studio charges the Flag had accumulated while working on their record. He saw that he had no choice—he had to go. Though it was widely rumored he was leaving the band, the Flag's viability still depended largely on its star guitarist. Fans wanted to see *Michael Bloomfield's* Electric Flag.

The Flag's players all knew that Michael was leaving, and they, too, were not pleased. Buddy Miles, in particular, was upset about the leader's imminent departure. "Michael didn't want to go on any further than we went, because it scared him," the drummer said. He attributed Bloomfield's defection to drug use. Nick Gravenites felt the drummer himself bore some responsibility for Michael's defection. "Buddy was a success-oriented guy," Nick said. "He wanted to be famous, successful. Michael didn't give a shit about that. He hated it." Miles's stage antics and desire to be the center of attention, in Gravenites's estimation, simply rubbed Bloomfield the wrong way, and the guitarist had had enough. Peter Strazza, on the other hand, never really understood why Michael left, especially when the band had a record on the charts and was poised to break through to a much larger audience. "Mike started drifting out of it," Strazza said. "And then we wound up with another guitar player, and then it got all messed up."

The Electric Flag played its final concerts with its star guitarist at Bill Graham's new rock palace, and the *New York Times* was indeed there for one of the performances. The paper's brief review was again written by Robert Shelton, and this time the critic managed to remain in his seat for the entire show. "Mike Bloomfield, who organized the Electric Flag, was making his final appearance with that group," Shelton wrote. "Mr. Bloomfield's farewell to the nine-member jazz-rock band was a sentimental moment and crossroads event, for the band was just coming into its own as a cohesive unit."

Despite his unhappiness with having to perform, Michael rose to the occasion. He doubtless had real regrets about leaving the group that had been his dream, a band he had created and then developed into one of contemporary rock's most dynamic, exciting groups. Though Buddy Miles dominated the Fillmore shows, many in the theater were thrilled by Bloomfield's performance. "Mike came out onstage barefoot, and he killed," reported one fan. "It was one of the best displays of guitar playing I had ever heard up to that point." *Cash Box* magazine, in its review of the Fillmore show, acknowledged that Michael was the evening's big draw: "The major attraction for most of the audience was not the Electric Flag, but the group's organizer—lead guitarist Mike Bloomfield. Since his days with the Paul Butterfield Blues Band, Bloomfield has become an underground superstar, and the possibility of his non-appearance (rumors have been flying) kept the audience in suspense. But Bloomfield was there."

Following the Flag's final show on Saturday night, the audience was treated to an impromptu encore set. Members of the band remained onstage, and out from the wings, as the audience cheered, came Jimi Hendrix. In a surprise appearance, the Seattle superstar spent the better part of an hour jamming with Buddy Miles, Herbie Rich, and Harvey Brooks, playing blues and a variety of other tunes to the delight of the packed house. Michael Bloomfield, though, was nowhere in sight. He left the stage following the Electric Flag's final number, his swan song with the band, and did not return. That Hendrix swept in and took his place, if only just to jam, seemed to complete the transition that had begun a year earlier at Monterey. The country's top electric guitarist, its rock superstar, was no longer the brash, fearless kid from Chicago who had taken disparate elements of American music and infused them into the pop vernacular. The music was changing, and so was Michael Bloomfield. The industry was becoming more interested in the player and less interested in the playing, and Bloomfield was discovering he had little interest in either.

PART III

KNOCKIN' MYSELF OUT

CHAPTER 19

ENTERTAINER NO MORE

PHILADELPHIA, NEW YORK, AND SAN FRANCISCO, 1968

By mid-June 1968, the Electric Flag was back in California for a three-day stint at the Golden Bear in Huntington Beach. It was the first time the band had returned to the club since their bust the previous September, and this time there was no trouble with the law. But Michael Bloomfield was not onstage with them. Fans who crowded into the seaside venue were disappointed to discover that the leader of the group, its star guitarist, was nowhere in sight. Word soon spread that Mike Bloomfield had quit his own band, and though it was just as quickly rumored that he might return, that possibility proved to be nothing more than wishful thinking. At subsequent Flag shows in San Diego and Sacramento, at the Fillmore and the Newport Pop Festival in Costa Mesa, Michael was a no-show. It was clear that he really was gone.

The Flag did several recording sessions for Columbia in Los Angeles, getting a number of new songs by Nick Gravenites on tape in preparation for a second album. But without Bloomfield, the band's sound just wasn't the same, and Columbia's support soon wavered. By the end of September, despite half-hearted efforts to keep the American Music Band together, the Electric Flag had been lowered. The pioneering blues, rock, and soul horn band was no more.

When the Electric Flag finally folded, the straight media took little notice beyond a few mentions by syndicated music columnists. Curiously, though, there was even less acknowledgment from the paper that had devoted a half dozen pages to Michael Bloomfield and the Electric Flag over two of its editions in April. *Rolling Stone* had nothing to say about the fortunes of the rock star it had called "one of a handful of the world's finest guitarists." Ralph J. Gleason's spleen had apparently morphed into editorial policy, and as far as pop music's leading critical publication was concerned, Mike Bloomfield was persona non grata.

What the public did learn about the Flag's breakup was that it had largely resulted from Buddy Miles's desire to lead his own group. The *Chicago Seed* quoted Nick Gravenites as saying, "Basically, Buddy wanted to do his own thing. He wanted to be pretty much out front into a soul review type of thing, so he split." Miles hired lawyers to break his contract with Albert Grossman and ABGM, proving that he was in fact underage when he signed them. After successfully severing ties with the manager, Miles moved to Los Angeles and began assembling a new band. By October, his new soul band, the Buddy Miles Express, was opening for the Jimi Hendrix Experience at the Winterland Ballroom in San Francisco. The Electric Flag was a distant memory.

But Michael Bloomfield had finally gotten his wish. His time was his own. He could spend all day sleeping and all night reading if he wanted to. He didn't have to go anywhere; he was obligated to no one. He could pass his days at home, lying in bed, fingering his unplugged Les Paul or one of his Telecasters, playing along with the music on the commercials while he watched TV. He could invite friends over, hang out, play records, and jam, whenever he felt like it.

But he was finding he *didn't* feel like it. For the first time in two years, Michael Bloomfield had nowhere to be. No rehearsal to make, no recording date to arrange, no gig he was rushing off to. But instead of relief, he mostly felt numb. It was a numbness that served to keep depression at bay. But Michael Bloomfield was, in fact, deeply depressed.

Since his late teens, he had wanted nothing more than to be a great guitar player. He had put in untold hours practicing, working whenever and wherever he could with anyone who would let him play. In time, he had achieved a level of skill and musicianship unparalleled in pop music, and he had mastered a folk form—the blues—reinvigorating it with the excitement of rock 'n' roll and the sophistication of jazz. His desire to be recognized had ultimately been achieved. He was acknowledged as one of the great guitarists of his generation.

But along with that recognition came all the trappings of stardom that, as far as Michael was concerned, had nothing whatsoever to do with music or artistry. There was the objectifying adulation that fans lavished on their pop star heroes, the uncritical attention that made any kind of real interaction all but impossible. There were the temptations of life on the road—an endless diet of sex, drugs, and booze. There was the day-to-day grind of performing, of playing the same material over and over and *over* again. Those aspects of celebrity were hard enough to deal with. But for Mike Bloomfield, there was also another dimension to stardom that he had been unprepared for, one that he found even more onerous.

He hated being treated like a product.

The pop music business was a business like any other. Its practitioners made and sold a product in order to make money. That the product was music often was incidental to that objective. The industry's workers—its musicians—were frequently little more than a means to an end. Because that end could be exceedingly profitable, a great deal of effort went into selling the product. That the musicians who produced it were often highly skilled and gifted artists was frequently irrelevant. They were part of the sale.

Michael Bloomfield resented being sold. He didn't like being told he had to fire musicians because of the way they looked or didn't look. Or that he had to travel great distances under difficult circumstances, sometimes playing shows in two or more venues on the same night, just because someone in the front office saw a way to maximize profits. Or that industry hype could project an image of him that had nothing to do with who he really was, solely as a marketing ploy. Or that his artistry was controlled largely by men who had no understanding of music because they never listened to it, nor even liked it.

"There's things about the pop music industry that I found highly offensive," Michael candidly told an interviewer not long after leaving the Electric Flag. "And there were things about my life that I found highly offensive. I find it offensive to travel, to be in motel rooms, and to deal with people who consider me a commercial product as opposed to an artist. Or feel that I am an artist because I have the powers of producing capital through my music—capital for another person."

But it wasn't just the corporate side of the music business that offended Michael Bloomfield. There was another reason for his disaffection. He would not be—indeed, *could* not be—an entertainer. The growing appeal of "the show," of audiences' enthusiasm not just for musical artistry but for spectacle, was increasingly disconcerting to the guitarist. He had seen crowds in London dazzled by acts like the Who when he was there with the Butterfield Band, and then he had watched Jimi Hendrix redefine rock 'n' roll performance with his pyrotechnics at Monterey. In recent months, his own band, the Electric Flag, had begun incorporating theatrics into their performances. Buddy Miles, in his increasingly dominant role, turned much of what the band played into routines for working the crowd. To Bloomfield, that had nothing to do with making music, and he found it increasingly distasteful. He was not about to dress in outlandish outfits, lewdly prance about, destroy his equipment, or engage in other staged shenanigans just to get a rise out of the audience.

"I also know, as the Flag got more and more on—let's say—a star level, that it put me more and more uptight," Michael said. "Because people were accepting music that was more show than music, and I really wasn't accepting that myself."

Of course, music-as-entertainment and music-as-business had long been inextricably intertwined. Since the days of sheet music and parlor pianos, novelty acts had been driving pop music sales. Rock 'n' roll was especially dependent on the formula. Without exciting, crowd-pleasing stage routines, stars like Elvis Presley, Jerry Lee Lewis, Little Richard, and countless others would have had far less impact. As a teenager, Bloomfield himself had been thrilled by Chuck Berry's duck-walk bit, and he knew that the "show" was a large part of the rock 'n' roll experience. Michael was also the son of a kitchen supply magnate, a millionaire merchandiser, and having grown up in a family of shrewd and pragmatic businessmen, he was certainly no stranger to the ways of commerce. As a young guitarist just starting out, he was not averse to selling himself in order to secure a recording contract. With Butterfield, and then again with the Flag, Michael readily complied with efforts to produce a pop hit. He knew that commercial success was an essential part of the pop music formula and that it required compromises. He had been willing to make them.

But now Bloomfield was disparaging the business behind making music and the onstage exhibition that frequently supported it. His restiveness, he said, came from the realization that those aspects of pop music had nothing to do with art—that they, in fact, frequently stood in the way of making good music. The truth, though, was more complex.

Bloomfield certainly felt his artistry had been hampered by the commercial demands of mid-level managers and record label accountants, and he disdained the artificiality of "entertaining." But he also sensed that he, too, was part of the problem. Deep down, he knew he lacked the ability to be a consummate pop music showman, to both play *and* entertain the way Jimi Hendrix so easily could. Or the way Chuck Berry did. Or, for that matter, the way his former bandmate Buddy Miles so often did. Since Monterey, it had become increasingly apparent that the very best musicians were not only extraordinary players but also artists who could put on a bang-up show. Bloomfield knew he would fall short if audiences expected entertainment, and audiences—as well as music critics, managers, and industry bigwigs—seemed more and more to be expecting just that. The inability to meet those expectations was a growing source of insecurity for the star guitarist.

It was that insecurity, coupled with a genuine aversion to the music business and the concomitant insularity of rock stardom, that suffused Michael Bloomfield's mood as he lay in bed at 404 Wellesley Court on a sultry June afternoon. For the first time in his career, he was unsure what to do next. He felt stuck, immobilized, unable to move forward. He was America's superstar blues-rock guitarist, but at the moment he didn't feel like a star. All he felt was numb, which was the only thing between him and a crippling depression.

* * *

To distract himself, Mike Bloomfield went to see his mother. Toward the end of June, the guitarist flew to Chicago and stayed with Dorothy Bloomfield in her apartment on Lake Shore Drive. While in the Windy City, Michael visited friends and made the rounds of his old haunts. Big John's had closed in December of 1966, but Mother Blues was still going strong and there was a new Fillmore-style venue called the Electric Theater in Uptown, the Chicago neighborhood where Michael and Susan had first lived after getting married. While he was in the city, Michael did an interview with the city's underground newspaper, a tabloid that had debuted in 1967 called the *Chicago Seed*. Like *Rolling Stone* and many other alternative papers, the *Seed* published articles on politics and the emerging counterculture while reporting on the pop music scene. The paper devoted several pages to the interview.

The interviewer's first question concerned Michael's status with the Electric Flag. He quickly confirmed that he was no longer with the group, though he described the Flag as a "good band" and said that he was "extremely gratified and pleased with the band's sound and development." But, he candidly added, "because I just don't think I'll ever be able to cut getting too famous, I split." Asked about his plans for the future, Michael said he didn't really have any, though he was "still going to be playing music." He mentioned the offer to join Don Ellis, adding that he would also like to play with Ray Charles and that he might form a duo with keyboardist Mark Naftalin, his former Butterfield bandmate. Naftalin had just left Paul's group and was now living in San Francisco. The interviewer then brought up the "Stop This Shuck" column in *Rolling Stone*, asking if Bloomfield would like to respond to Ralph Gleason. "No. Well, no," the guitarist said. But then he added,

> He's a good man. A little unenlightened (as is Frank Kofsky and the older hierarchy of jazz critics who jumped on the bandwagon this year to regain the fountain of youth, to hang around the teeny-boppers, to, you know, yuk it up with the young folks—who finally realize that there are people who are not playing jazz or classical music who are intelligent musicians) for an old fart who finally, you know, hopped on what's happening. They're all right. They're beautiful.

The question clearly irked Michael, and his mood seemed to abruptly change. His answers became sarcastic, almost as though he were putting the interviewer on. What direction did Bloomfield think contemporary music was taking? "The scrotum of the Lord. Modern music is becoming more ornate," came the reply. Michael then added, "Ornate sound is coming back. Whether it's produced by instruments, tape recorders, horns, synthesizers or computers is basically irrelevant. A large sound with many things to arrest your attention. Kinetic charisma. Whatever you want to call it. But a large sound."

Who were Bloomfield's favorite guitar players? Michael mentioned Clapton, Hendrix, and Jerry Garcia as well as blues masters B. B., Freddie, and Albert King; Earl Hooker; Albert Collins; Otis Rush; and Buddy Guy. Jazz players Wes Montgomery, George Benson, Sonny Sharrock, and Larry Coryell also got a nod. Then Michael began toying again with the interviewer, improvising predictions for the future of pop music while upending Gleason's chief complaint about the guitarist himself.

> I think there is going to be a huge movement in negative soul. People are going to be as unsoulful as they can. They're going to say all the square, unsoulful things. Matter of fact, soul will become a completely un-negro property and it will really become un-any ethnic group. No ethnic group will have soul. The soul movement will be taken over by white protestant teenagers from Moline and Cicero. And that is where the soul of the country is going to reside. Everyone else will be too busy getting their thing together and leaving.

Midway through the conversation, Michael was asked about his recent recording session with Al Kooper. The guitarist responded seriously, acknowledging the date and saying, "We came down there and I jammed with him in the studio and recorded some sides and was supposed to record the next day, but I was ill and left." In a prescient moment, he then enthusiastically added, "What we jammed was some of the best playing that I've ever had on record. Certainly not the best playing I've ever done in my life, because I don't play well in the studio. But better than anything else on record."

Mike Bloomfield could not have known how right that statement would prove to be.

Back in Mill Valley toward the end of the month, Mike Bloomfield settled into a life out of the public eye. In the space of three weeks, he had gone from a chaotic routine of constant traveling and gigging while dealing with managers, booking agents, club owners, and countless supernumeraries to spending quiet afternoons and evenings watching TV and reading. Though he was still brooding over the tumultuous events of previous months, the trip to Chicago provided a much-needed change of scenery, and he had returned to Wellesley

Court refreshed. At the end of June, Michael even received a bit of good news. In the June 27 edition of *Down Beat* magazine, the legendary Miles Davis expressed unqualified praise for one of the tunes on *A Long Time Comin'*. Leonard Feather subjected the jazz trumpet player to a two-part "Blindfold Test," the critic's regular column for the magazine wherein he played recordings for jazz musicians and got their reactions. Not a fan of contemporary rock, Feather slipped in the Electric Flag's "Over-Lovin' You," doubtless expecting Davis to dismiss it. But the trumpeter told Leonard to "leave that record here[;] it's a nice record."

> It's a pleasure to get a record like that, because you've got to know they're serious no matter what they do. . . . I liked the rhythm on that. I mean, if you're going to do something, *do* it. You know what I mean? If you're going to play like that, play like that—*good*—but don't jive around.

Davis seemed in a few brief sentences to refute Ralph J. Gleason's accusations that the Flag's music was nothing more than imitation. The compliment, coming from an artist of such renown, could only have pleased Michael. But he was no longer with the Flag and had no interest in playing with any band, at least for the time being. He was at home, busy being a homebody and nothing more.

On the Fourth of July, Bill Graham produced his last show at the venerable Fillmore Auditorium. The music he was presenting had finally outgrown the storied hall's 1,100-person capacity, and he needed a larger space to keep his productions profitable. He had been using the Winterland whenever he thought a show would sell out, but it was the Carousel Ballroom that he took over as a permanent home for his productions. He planned to open the new venue, which he renamed the Fillmore West, with a gala concert on July 5 featuring the Paul Butterfield Blues Band and the English blues-rock quartet Ten Years After. Also performing would be numerous guests, making it an exhilarating evening of freewheeling blues jams. Graham invited Elvin Bishop, Fleetwood Mac's Peter Green, Buddy Miles, and Janis Joplin to sit in, and he then put in a call to Mike Bloomfield. He knew the guitarist would likely be available now that his time was his own.

Michael was glad to hear from his friend, and he and Graham spent a few moments running the dozens on each other before Bill asked him to come down to the old Carousel and help christen the new Fillmore. Bloomfield said he would have to think about it, that maybe he would. "But I'm retired now, you know, Bill," the guitarist told the producer. Graham just laughed. "I'll see you on Friday, Bloomers," he said.

But Graham didn't see Michael for his opening celebration. Bloomfield decided to stay home, watching *F Troop* and *Star Trek* instead and then, after the news, catching comedian George Kirby on the David Frost Show. For the time being, Michael Bloomfield would rather be entertained than be the entertainment.

Throughout the remainder of July, Mike Bloomfield stayed home. His days were filled with books, records, and TV. Friends came by to visit, some camping out in the house's empty bedrooms for extended stays. They would smoke dope and listen to music, go out to eat, and maybe drive into San Francisco to catch Albert King or Magic Sam. More and more often, Michael would cop a few bags of heroin and get high with the help of his housemates. It was a pleasant summer, quieter than any the guitarist had known since his childhood. The only thing to disrupt his extended reverie was the news that Al Kooper's jam session record was out. On July 22, Columbia announced the release of the album, with Michael Bloomfield featured on one side and Steve Stills on the other. All three musicians were pictured on its cover, their names prominently displayed above the title. It was the title that caught Michael's attention. *Super Session*? What could be "super" about a casual jam session? He hadn't even stayed to complete the date. More music industry hype, Bloomfield thought.

He put the record on and played it for his friends. Everyone seemed to like it. Michael thought his playing was as good as he remembered it being, even on that long, jazzy confabulation they had cooked up in the studio—"His Holy Modal Majesty," as it had been grandly titled. But he could hear places where Kooper had judiciously edited the performances, and he was surprised that horns had been added to some of the tunes. The whole thing sounded carefully planned, even though Bloomfield knew it had really been just a crapshoot, a make-it-up-as-you-go patchwork of blues, soul tunes, and comping. The other side, the one with Stills, sounded more produced, with studio effects and additional overdubbing. But everyone he played the record for thought it was great. "Let's hear 'Season of the Witch' again!" they would often say.

Al Kooper had spent much of June editing and mixing the jam session's reels, working to turn his rock experiment into a cohesive, marketable whole. The keyboardist's keen ear for what would and wouldn't work musically led him to hire Joe Scott, a former jazz pianist and successful New York studio arranger who had scored TV commercials and worked with a variety of performers, including the Four Seasons and comedienne Phyllis Diller. Scott teamed with Kooper to create horn parts that effectively filled out the performances, making them sound in places like outtakes from a Blood, Sweat & Tears or Electric

Flag session. By the end of the month, the record had been completed—all except for its title.

"We were in a production meeting in New York," recalled Kooper. "It was Bruce Lundvall who came up with a name for the record. He said, 'You should call it "Super Session."' I *never* would have thought of that." Lundvall was head of marketing for Columbia, a dedicated jazz fan, and a rising star in the company. His suggestion was an immediate hit, and the name stuck. "I think we might have been the first to use the word 'super' in that way," said Al. Excluding Andy Warhol's use of the term "superstar" to describe his motley film entourage, and the NFL's recently created Super Bowl, Kooper may well have been right.

While "super" might not have been the best way to describe Kooper's casual jam sessions, it aptly described the album's sales. Within a few weeks of its release, *Super Session* was selling briskly around the country and was climbing up *Billboard*'s Top LPs chart as a starred entry. The producer himself was surprised to discover that his maiden effort for his new employer looked like a runaway commercial success.

"I was back in L.A. the day it was released, and ambled into Tower Records to see the initial reaction," Al later wrote of *Super Session*. "I swear they were sailin' 'em over the counter like Beatles records!" A moment of inspiration, a few days in the studio, and several weeks of editing and mixing were apparently all it took to create a successful product. Kooper was chagrined. "I never dreamed we'd have a *hit* record. I thought we'd go into the studio, have some fun, and maybe make a little money. But that was it," Al said. "When I saw what was happening, I couldn't believe it!"

Columbia backed up *Super Session*'s strong sales by heavily promoting the album with smart ads in newspapers and on radio around the country. "Have your mind jammed by experts," one promotion proclaimed. The ad went on to tout the album as the real thing, using the hip argot of the period. "It was recorded late at night when everyone was feeling loose, on and ready. The result is not a hype, not a put-on, but a beautiful jam—a 'Super Session.' It'll mess your mind over!" Word quickly spread among Al Kooper's Blood, Sweat & Tears fans that here was another excellent album from the keyboardist featuring a rock ensemble with horns, and Buffalo Springfield followers were excited to hear Stills in a new setting. But it was Mike Bloomfield's fans who were most enthusiastic about *Super Session*. Kooper was right—he had captured the guitarist's playing as no other producer had. Here were nearly thirty minutes of music that featured Bloomfield's guitar. His solos were dynamic and adventurous, and his Les Paul's tone was full and electric. There was nothing "processed" about the music's sound. Even though Al had carefully edited and mixed the original tapes, working in the studio to clean them up, Michael's playing retained a loose, live feel that very much mirrored his style in performance. It was a first opportunity for many listeners to hear Bloomfield's virtuosity unconstrained by busy arrangements, flat production, or commercial concerns. For young guitarists, *Super Session* was a revelation. Players across the nation began woodshedding, honing their chops, and trying to cop Michael's licks. Suddenly, every guitarist in a blues band was looking for a Les Paul Sunburst.

Meanwhile, *Super Session* continued its climb up the charts. The album would eventually reach the number twelve position and would earn Al Kooper, Steve Stills, and Michael Bloomfield each a gold record from the Recording Industry Association of America. It would post over one million dollars in retail sales over the next year.

Mike Bloomfield was only vaguely aware of the commotion at Columbia surrounding Al Kooper's jam session album. The record was OK, and it was nice that it was selling well, but he really wasn't interested. He was thinking instead about getting out of town. The constant parade of people through the house on Wellesley Court was getting out of hand. Friends were one thing, but Michael's star status also attracted an assortment of characters, hangers-on, and oddballs, and his reputation as a user had dealers knocking on the door at all times of the day and night. The easy availability of drugs—especially heroin—meant he was high much of the time, and he was seriously out of it with increasing regularity. His responsibilities as the leader of the Electric Flag had necessarily tempered his drug use, but now he was free to do as he pleased. What he found himself doing was shooting heroin. He knew he needed to change that growing habit, and the only way to do that was to remove himself from temptation. He would have to leave Wellesley Court and Mill Valley. It was the only way he could get clean.

In August, Michael Bloomfield packed his belongings into the blue Electric Flag van and drove north on Route 101 to Sir Francis Drake Boulevard, following the winding two-lane highway out past San Anselmo and Fairfax to Lagunitas. A small forested community with a population of a few hundred, Lagunitas had a general store, a post office, and one service station. The unincorporated village seemed like an ideal place for America's top blues-rock guitarist to hide. But the northern reaches of Marin County had appealed to San Francisco's musicians since the early 1960s, and both the Grateful Dead and Big Brother and the Holding Company had spent time in Lagunitas's redwood hills. Quicksilver Messenger Service briefly had a place up the road in nearby Olema. By the time Michael decided to seek the solitude of rural Marin, it was well known as a region where San Francisco's bands could find cheap rents, ample space for rehearsals, and plenty of quiet time for bonding. Bloomfield wasn't interested in woodshedding, though. He wanted to get away from heroin before it became something he wouldn't be able to escape.

The guitarist arranged through a friend to rent space in a modern bi-level complex of three apartments located on Arroyo Road, just around the corner from the post office and near an old Girl Scout camp that had served as the Grateful Dead's compound in 1966. Though the apartments all shared a single deck, the other two were empty and Michael had the place to himself. He could keep his irregular hours, play music whenever he wished, and come and go without disturbing anyone. With a small TV and a set of rabbit ears for catching late-night television broadcasts from San Francisco, the arrangement seemed well suited for a period of rehabilitation. Bloomfield would have only to resist the urge to cop. That would be a struggle.

In late August, Michael's solitude was interrupted by a visitor from back east. Allen Bloomfield paid an unexpected visit to his brother. The young men hadn't seen much of each other since Michael's marriage and departure from the family home in 1963, and in the intervening time, their paths had sharply diverged. While the guitarist had gone on the road with Paul Butterfield as a professional musician, Allen had attended college and then worked for his father in Bloomfield Industries. Always the more responsible of the two Bloomfield boys, Allen decided to win their father's approval by going into the family business, a formula that worked for a time. But he had grown restless, wanting to find something of his own to do, and had moved to New York City in search of other employment.

"I came to New York to find my way, and New York is a fairly demanding environment. My first go 'round wasn't too successful," Allen recalled with a laugh.

> A very good friend of mine said, well, why don't you go pay your brother a visit? So I got into my Mustang, packed everything up . . . and drove for at least three days. On the fourth day, I called my brother and said, "You've got company!" and he said, "OK, come on down." I hung out with Michael for like three months.

Allen drove his new Ford Mustang, a gift from Harold, out to Lagunitas and parked it in the carport under the apartment on Arroyo Road. He found his famous brother warm and welcoming, but he was surprised that Michael was doing little more than reading and watching TV. "He was pretty much goofin'," said Allen. "We hung out together and he didn't do much of anything."

Michael didn't mention his effort to wean himself from heroin and Allen didn't ask. They spent pleasant days together, and the few times Michael went into the city to play, Allen would go along. "I would pick up chicks, and I'd see him in the morning and he'd say, 'Stop bringing them over to the house!'" the younger Bloomfield recalled, chuckling. "I'd say, 'What are you, Dad, man? Whadda you mean, stop bringing them over to the house?' Then he'd have a look at them and he'd try to get *me* out of the house!"

While Allen was staying with Michael in Lagunitas, there would often be another visitor to the Arroyo Road apartment. "Michael's wife, Susan, had found another house in Mill Valley, but she was over quite a lot," Allen remembered. Susan was back in California after finding Chicago not to her liking and, though they were now divorced, she and Michael were still friends. She would check on him periodically to make sure he was OK. "We'd have family dinners," said Allen. "The nights were long and leisurely, and when Johnny Carson came on, or one of those insane programs like *Sanford and Son* came on, man, we were into that. Hilarious!"

Even so, there were occasions when Michael faltered in his effort to clean up. Every so often, the guitarist went into San Francisco in search of a fix. Allen sometimes drove and waited in the Mustang while his brother made a connection. The trips were usually uneventful, with Allen driving Michael back to Lagunitas while the guitarist nodded in the passenger seat. One time, though, Michael had an experience that shook him to his core.

"He found himself in a predominantly black neighborhood," said Allen.

> And he was recognized by a black kid who directed the criticism at him, "You can't play, you ain't worth shit. You'll *never* be B. B. King. You, as far as I'm concerned, are *jive*, motherfucker!" This was a kid—this was not a critic or anything, just a kid mouthing off—but it took Michael by the throat. He took it as his worst haunting nightmare—is it *possible* that this is true? It devastated him!

The deep-rooted insecurity that Bloomfield secretly harbored about his ability as a guitarist was inflamed by those few cutting remarks. Allen was astonished that his brother, America's acknowledged blues-rock master, could be so affected by a trash-talking adolescent. "It was something most people would just dismiss, coming from a kid like that. But he didn't—he took it to heart. I think he even believed it!"

It was a painful experience for Michael Bloomfield. Ralph J. Gleason had criticized him for being an imitator, for trying to pass himself off as a "spade." But Gleason had no more credibility on the issue of race and music than did any other white critic. But this kid on the street—that was different. There was no denying *his* credibility. He spoke with the authority afforded him by his race, and there was no defense against that. If he called Michael an imitator, he *was* an imitator, end of story. A "jive" imitator, at that. His words made Bloomfield feel like someone who had no right to play African American blues, like a white usurper. It was the one accusation Michael could not refute, no matter how well he played. He was nothing more than an exploiter, after all.

At least, that's how it felt. Michael Bloomfield wasn't black, never would be black—that was true. But culture is a fluid thing, and no one community has exclusive rights to it. Intellectually, the guitarist knew that. But he couldn't shake the gnawing feeling that he was an interloper expropriating a music he was not entitled to. How could he play blues after that?

But then, Mike Bloomfield wasn't doing much playing. Whatever conflicts the street kid's comments planted in the guitarist's mind, they had little effect on his day-to-day existence in Lagunitas. He continued to hang out with his brother and with a growing circle of friends in the San Geronimo Valley. He seldom indulged in anything stronger than marijuana, and when he did use heroin, he seemed to have it under control. Michael began to look healthy and rested, and his sleep patterns, while still erratic, improved. The country retreat was accomplishing its purpose.

Allen, on the other hand, began to feel run-down and achy. By early November, he was running a low-grade fever. "It turned out I had picked up a case of hepatitis, probably from one of the girls I brought home," said Allen. "So I decided I'd better head home and take care of it."

Michael drove his ailing brother to the airport, saying he would look after Allen's car until he was well enough to retrieve it. The siblings said goodbye at the terminal building, giving each other a farewell hug, and then the guitarist headed back north in the Mustang. Allen caught a flight to Chicago, and when Dottie Bloomfield and her mother met him at the arrivals gate in O'Hare, they were shocked.

"Grandma Phyllis fainted when she saw me," Allen recalled with a chuckle. "I was so yellow from the hepatitis, I looked like a banana! I was in the hospital for three weeks recuperating. And *that* was my trip to visit Michael."

The last week in August, not long after his brother arrived in Lagunitas, Michael got a call. It was one that he had been half expecting and half dreading. Al Kooper was on the line, and he had another proposition.

"I got a bad case of commercial fever and decided to cut a follow-up to our quasi-hit," Kooper later wrote, referring to the unexpected success of *Super*

Session. He told Michael he wanted to re-create the album onstage in front of an audience, presenting the jam session in a live setting and recording it for release on Columbia as a sequel. "I called Bloomfield and he said sure, I owe you one, for when he snuck out of the first album." Al had no idea that Michael was in Lagunitas, dealing with the issues that had led to his departure in May. He thought it would be an easy gig for both of them—they would play a few tunes from the record, do a half dozen new numbers of their choosing, and, of course, solo on a sampling of blues. The performances would have a jam feel even though they would rehearse everything well in advance, and once the shows were over, that would be it. No group commitment, no touring, just a one-weekend deal. It would be another fun, hassle-free way to make a record.

"I figured on ten days of rehearsal in Marin County, where Michael lived," Kooper wrote. "I booked Wally Heider's remote truck to record the proceedings, and got the budget OK. Things were looking good." Al left it up to Michael to find a space for rehearsals, and then he put in a call to Bill Graham. Would Graham allow them to do a live version of *Super Session* at the Fillmore West—and record it? Graham said he would, quite pleased with the idea. Kooper began making the arrangements, confident that his plan would produce another successful album.

Michael Bloomfield wasn't so sure. He hadn't really wanted to do the first recording session, and now "jamming" in front of a live audience, even though he had agreed to it, was the last thing he felt like doing. "I don't dig gigging live," he opined to an interviewer years later. "It's not a question of intellectually digging it or not, I just don't react to it well." Coming from a guitarist who as a kid would climb out his bedroom window to go sit in on Chicago's South Side, the claim sounded oddly disingenuous. Mike Bloomfield, the ebullient, extroverted rock star, uncomfortable with performing live? No one would have believed it. But Bloomfield's growing antipathy was a measure of just how profoundly he had been affected by the events of the last few months. Those experiences triggered bouts of insecurity that, combined with his chronic insomnia and drug use, produced in the guitarist what might be described as a condition of "existential stage fright." Whatever it was, it meant Michael really did not want to get up onstage to jam.

There may have been another reason behind Bloomfield's reluctantly accepting Al Kooper's offer to do another *Super Session* album. He felt obligated to Kooper because he had left the producer hanging during the first recording session, but he was also obligated to Albert Grossman. Michael owed his manager for the extra studio hours the Electric Flag had accrued while working on their album, and for expenses the band accumulated while touring. There were also legal fees from the Flag's various entanglements with the law. Grossman had footed the bill, and he wanted to be paid back. He was considering taking his star guitarist to court over the matter.

"Albert tried to sue Mike after the band broke up," said Chris McDougal. As McDougal understood it, the manager was behind Bloomfield's participation. "He forced Mike to play those Super Session shows. He hated doing them." Whether Grossman was directly involved or not, Bloomfield was certainly aware of his debt to the manager—a debt that would have to be repaid. "I never feel that it is really worth it," Michael later said of performing, "other than to make the bread." The live Super Session gig would make some "bread," hopefully enough to placate Albert Grossman for a while.

Al Kooper flew into San Francisco on Thursday, September 19, to begin the rehearsals for the three days of performances at the Fillmore West. He had suggested to Michael that they each once again pick another musician to make up a quartet, and Al had selected a drummer he met at the Monterey Pop Festival named Skip Prokop. A member at the time of the Canadian rock quartet the Paupers, Prokop had recently left the group to form the rock orchestra Lighthouse. "I had played on one of Skip's albums," Kooper said. "That's how I picked him. I thought he was just a great drummer." Prokop met up with Kooper in San Francisco on Friday morning, and the two musicians drove up to Sausalito. Bloomfield had arranged to use one of the practice rooms in the Heliport for rehearsals, and he met Kooper and Prokop there after driving down from Lagunitas. With him was his choice for the group, a bass player named John Kahn, whom he had met at a jam session in Novato. A resident of Sausalito, the twenty-one-year-old Kahn had started out as a jazz bassist, and after studying for several years at the San Francisco Conservatory of Music, had started doing session work for local rock groups. Bloomfield very much liked Kahn's ability to play a variety of styles, and he thought John would be an excellent fit for Kooper's jam band.

Michael and Al spent five days picking songs, working on arrangements, and having the band play them through as they rehearsed. Though the practice time was only half of what was originally planned, Kooper was satisfied that the band had gotten together enough material for the shows and for the subsequent album. By Thursday, he felt that they were ready. After a final run-through, the musicians packed up their instruments and drove to the Fillmore West. Though the rehearsals had gone smoothly and the musicians got along well, Mike Bloomfield was increasingly uneasy. All week he had been battling insomnia.

"I had stage fright," Michael later declared. "I couldn't sleep. I was up for days." His months out of the limelight, away from the music scene in San

Francisco and secluded in the forested hills of Lagunitas, had quickly drained the stress from the guitarist's life. Now it flooded back in, making him feel panicky. True, he had played a few gigs in the city since fleeing to Marin County's woodsy northern reaches, but those had been casual performances with friends. There was nothing casual about this Super Session show, despite Al Kooper's best efforts to make it hassle free. The "super" jam group was the featured act, and it would be Michael's first publicized appearance since leaving the Electric Flag. With the success of the album—it reached number forty-seven with a star on *Billboard*'s chart that week—there was real excitement about the show, and Bill Graham was expecting a sellout. That all three nights were going to be recorded for a follow-up *Super Session* record on Columbia only made things more stressful. In the span of a week, Mike Bloomfield had gone from semiretirement right back to superstar status, and it was no wonder he was agitated.

Backstage at the Fillmore, Michael paced around, talking nonstop. He had plenty of people to talk to—the room was crowded with musicians and their friends, groupies, managers, and assorted Fillmore people. No one was surprised at his loquaciousness—the guitarist was known for his friendly ebullience, ability to hold forth on any topic, and wicked sense of humor. But tonight Bloomfield seemed particularly animated, and it was only when he sat down, falling suddenly silent and gazing blankly up at the scores of posters stapled to the ceiling, that some in the room took notice. What's up with Bloomfield? they wondered. Al Kooper, too, was watching his star bandmate with increasing concern. He was counting on Michael to rally once they got onstage. The success of their performance—and of the follow-up album—depended largely on the protean guitarist.

It was a little before 10:00 p.m. when Skip Prokop, John Kahn, Al Kooper, and Michael Bloomfield took the stage for the Super Session quartet's first set. Kooper circled around stage right and sat behind his chocolate-colored Hammond B3, facing the rest of the band across the proscenium. Long dark ringlets of hair framed his narrow face, giving him the look of a hip Borscht Belt Hasid in Ray-Bans. He was staring at Skip Prokop. The drummer sat behind his kit, sticks aloft, ready for the downbeat. John Kahn stood to Prokop's left, his Fender bass held perpendicular to the stage as if it were a bass violin. Kahn's short hair and Fu Manchu moustache seemed a better fit for a Midwestern trucker than for a rock musician. He was watching Bloomfield.

Mike Bloomfield's two Twin Reverbs were stacked stage left, piled on the other side of the bassist. But Bloomfield wasn't in position in front of them. He was stepping across the stage toward one of the vocal microphones. His Les

Paul hung on a twisted strap around his neck, its cord in his right hand. With his left, he reached out and grabbed the mic just as Bill Graham was about to introduce the band.

Gazing out into the lights and squinting in an effort to make out the crowd in the cavernous performance space, Bloomfield began to address the audience. He spoke in a sweet, halting voice, almost as though he were gently explaining the facts of life to a group of small children.

"Uh, listen here. Now, here's what. . . . This is where it's at. This is the thing of this gig, and here's . . . here. . . . I'll tell you about it now," he said, struggling to express himself. The crowd suddenly fell silent, knowing what to expect. Most had heard Bloomfield's speeches before, but what was he going to say this time?

"Uh, a while ago Alan Kooper, my friend, called me on the phone and said, 'Let's make this gig . . . uh, an LP, in Los Angeles, and we'll jam together and we'll see what will happen . . ."

Michael took a breath and charged ahead, determined to set the audience straight on what they were about to hear. He explained the quartet's brief history together and described the material they had prepared, hoping the crowd would be receptive without expecting too much. Then, feeling that he had put everything properly into perspective, Bloomfield smiled and demurely added, "OK?"

With the speech over, the audience burst into amused applause. Bloomfield stepped back from the mic.

Kooper, unfazed, caught Prokop's eye and counted out the beat. The Hammond organ roared to life, filling the concert hall with muscular chords. Bloomfield, now plugged in, caught the organist's downbeat accents with a series of ascending chords as Prokop hammered out staccato quarter notes on his kick drum, introducing the quartet's first tune. The sound swelled, and the audience cheered. And then, following a robust chordal flourish, the music's volume and tempo suddenly dropped back.

"Slow down, you're way too fast," Kooper intoned in his nasal tenor. Here was the first surprise of the evening. The band's opener wasn't a rocking blues or a jazzy instrumental, something everyone expected. Instead, it was an unlikely folk-rock number, a tune written by Paul Simon of Simon and Garfunkel that had reached number thirteen on *Billboard*'s singles chart the year before in a version by the bubblegum band Harpers Bizarre. "You've got to make, yeah, the morning last," the organist continued, beginning the first verse of "The 59th Street Bridge Song," or, as everyone knew it, "Feelin' Groovy."

It was an odd choice to play with a blues-rock firebrand like Mike Bloomfield. But Kooper's arrangement was inventive and dynamic, and with solid support from Kahn and Prokop, the song sounded more like a rock anthem than it did a Top 40 ditty.

As the quartet warmed to the tune, Bloomfield deftly filled the spaces between the organist's lyrics with subtle runs and three-note clusters. The Hammond swelled to full-throated glory on the refrain, then dropped back to a hushed whisper for the second verse. Again Michael salted Kooper's words with inventive ornamentation. His D string slid out of tune momentarily, but he brought it back to consonance with a quick twist of its tuning peg while simultaneously comping. Kooper finished the second verse and another refrain. It was time for Michael's first solo of the night.

The guitarist began on a languid note, hewing closely to the song's melody. It was only when Al opened up the organ on the refrain that Bloomfield dished up a slew of bluesy licks. His Les Paul sang with its distinctive vocal tone—the Bloomfield tone. But then, just as the guitarist was beginning to take off, he dropped down and returned to his role as accompanist. Kooper then improvised for a chorus and sang a third verse before comping on the refrain to give Michael space for a few more exuberant licks. "C'mon! *C'mon, Michael,*" he urged as Bloomfield wailed. "I don't know how you feel, but I feel . . . *groovy*!" For twelve full bars, the quartet soared behind Michael's robust lines, and then, on the downbeat of the thirteenth, came to an abrupt stop. All that could be heard was an airy A^{sus2} chord, held by Bloomfield. The audience, caught off guard, sat in stunned silence. But then the cheers began and the big room gradually filled with boisterous applause as everyone realized the band had finished "Feelin' Groovy." Al Kooper's *Super Session* redux appeared to be off to a good start.

But some in the audience were surprised—and even a little disappointed. Mike Bloomfield playing a pop tune? And only taking a single chorus for his solo? This wasn't the Guitar God that everyone knew. Maybe the rumors about Bloomfield's quitting the Electric Flag because he had burned himself out were true? Many decided to reserve judgment, waiting to see what came next.

"We had six tightly worked-out tunes," Kooper later wrote of the quartet's repertory, "and about ten frameworks for jam situations." The "frameworks" included a healthy number of blues, and on those Bloomfield displayed the virtuosity he was known for. One of those came next in the quartet's set, and Michael's fans were quickly reassured that their guitar hero was in full command of his legendary abilities. But they were in for another surprise—it looked like Bloomfield was going to sing!

Michael began Ray Charles's "I Wonder Who," a slow drag originally recorded in 1953, with two solo choruses, quietly singing the blues with his Les Paul. But then he stepped over to a mic and began to croon.

I wonder who gon' be your sweet man when I'm gone?
I wonder who, now baby, gon' be your sweet lovin' man when
 I'm gone?
I wonder who, baby, goin' to carry my lovin' on?

Taking inspiration from Charles's original, Bloomfield sang in a husky, intimate voice, frequently ornamenting his phrases with a tremulous vibrato. Unlike Brother Ray's vocalizing, though, Michael's sense of pitch was at times almost as shaky as the quavering tags he added to his lines. But there was a sincerity in his voice that transcended its limitations, and his sympathetic guitar accompaniment more than made up for his singing's shortcomings. He worked through two verses and then launched into his first real solo of the night, taking multiple choruses while Kooper and the rhythm section swelled in support behind him. Each new twelve-bar volley eclipsed the last as the guitarist worked his way up the neck, the Sunburst sounding increasingly electric, the ripeness of its tone imparting a singular righteousness. *Here* was the Mike Bloomfield his fans were eager to hear, and they roared their approval as the solo concluded. Al followed with a chorus of his own, and then Michael returned for two more verses, closing the slow blues out to a storm of cheers and applause. The crowd was jazzed—Bloomfield could *sing*! Nearly everyone knew of his guitar prowess, but few imagined the legendary leader of the Electric Flag could also vocalize. Granted, he wasn't the strongest of singers—at least, judging by this single performance—but his heart was in it, and he sang with real feeling. How could Bloomfield do otherwise?

Of course, Mike Bloomfield had been singing almost since he had picked up the guitar all those years ago in Glencoe. He had sung at his audition for John Hammond, at Big John's with the Group, on the road with the Paul Butterfield Blues Band, and even as recently as concert performances with the Electric Flag. He had never *not* sung when he was onstage. It was just that he hadn't ever sung on record, and that was how most of his fans knew his music. With the release of the live Super Session date, that would all change. But for the moment, Michael Bloomfield as vocalist was something entirely new for many fans.

Ray Charles was one of Bloomfield's idols, especially when it came to vocalizing, and Michael couldn't resist singing another of his compositions later in the show. As he had done on "I Wonder Who," the guitarist opened Charles's 1956 hit "Mary Ann" with a solo, this time serving up a subtle, three-chorus primer on blues phrasing and dynamics. Kooper backed him with restrained riffs while Prokop created an engaging rhythmic tension with a cha-cha-like pattern on his toms. Following his solo, Michael eased into his second vocal of the evening, doing two verses in a coy, seductive tone while accompanying himself with plaintive lead.

> Oh, Mary Ann, can I go home with you?
> Whoa, Mary Ann, can I go home with you?
> I'll give you all that lovin'—anything you want me to do

As he often did, Bloomfield supplied his own version of the lyrics, using Charles's original simply as a framework. He may not have even remembered the actual words, but it didn't matter. The lyrics fit the mood of the song perfectly, and his singing was breathily effective. Two more solo choruses over the Latin beat followed, each with a flirty, pleading tone, and then Michael kicked the rhythm into an aggressive shuffle. Kooper, Kahn, and Prokop drove the solid-four tempo as Bloomfield opened up the Sunburst and burned through two more searing choruses before the quartet dropped back into the cha-cha beat. The guitarist then repeated the first verse and soloed quietly for twelve bars before shouting over to Al, "One loud one!" As Kooper leaned on the big Hammond and the band roared, Bloomfield brought "Mary Ann" home with a final chorus of his trademark fat electric lead. The audience was on its feet once again, cheering, whistling, and applauding their blues-rock champion. It was turning out to be a good night.

That evening and the next, the Super Session quartet did a number of covers in addition to Michael's blues. They played an instrumental version of the Band's "The Weight," with Kooper taking the melody and Bloomfield improvising for a chorus in a combination of country and blues styles. Al sang an effective version of Frank Wilson's "Together 'Til the End of Time," a tune recorded by Motown's Brenda Holloway and by Stevie Winwood with the Spencer Davis Group. Kooper also sang Winwood's "Dear Mr. Fantasy," a simple three-chord song in G that the British singer had released with his group, Traffic, a year earlier. Super Session's version incorporated a jazzy interlude following Al's vocal, giving Michael space to freely solo in the relative minor. As Skip Prokop switched to a fast 4/4 tempo, "Dear Mr. Fantasy" took on aspects of "His Holy Modal Majesty" from the studio session—no surprise because both pieces shared the same key, chord progression, and structure. Michael riffed aggressively through sixty-four bars, playing pentatonic runs peppered with his characteristic rolls and bluesy bends, and then brought the band back to the original tempo with a two-bar phrase that ushered in Kooper's vocal. After a single verse, Al introduced a new melody with wide-open chords on the Hammond—it was the refrain from the Beatles' "Hey Jude," the current number-one single. He followed that with a solo on the Ondioline, the curious keyboard instrument he had used in the studio to evoke the sound of John Coltrane on "His Holy Modal Majesty." Michael briefly restated the Beatles' theme, and then Kooper closed the performance with a final vocal chorus. It was an adventurous arrangement, and the quartet brought it off convincingly—except that during the final verse, Kooper's mic came unplugged and his singing was all but inaudible for the remainder of the song.

Other selections included a muscular, gritty version of "Green Onions," Booker T. and the MGs' R&B hit from 1962. Michael made no attempt to re-create Steve Cropper's guitar solo, transforming the riff blues instead into a robust demonstration of his own six-string capabilities. Arthur "Big Boy" Crudup's "That's All Right," the song that had been Elvis Presley's first hit in 1954, was also given an exciting treatment by the quartet. Bloomfield took the vocal, shouting the lyrics over Al's gutsy organ and his own guitar fills, clearly enjoying himself. "Aw, you *know* it's all right!" he cried as he began a solo chorus, his Les Paul bristling. After a second verse, the band eased into a rocking vamp and Michael exhorted them to "stay there! *Stay there*!" What followed was a suggestive exchange between guitarist and guitar. "Is that *all right*?" A single bent note mimicked a lover's reply. "That's all right *too*!" The note again. "*Ooooo*!" And again. "*Yeah*, mama—well, *play* it for me!" Over the vamp, Bloomfield punched out a series of intense runs and then settled on a repeated barre A chord with an octave high on the neck. That brought "That's All Right" to a climax and then to a hard stop on the downbeat. Bloomfield's call-and-response routine had clearly been rehearsed, but it nonetheless felt spontaneous and provided a thrilling moment for the audience. They rewarded the quartet with whoops and cheers.

One other instrumental also took inspiration from "His Holy Modal Majesty" and was later titled "Her Holy Modal Highness," making the connection more than clear. Played in 6/8 time too, the piece consisted of the middle portion of the original with an out-of-tempo bass solo from John Kahn accompanied by Bloomfield's spacey chordal accents. Kooper soloed on Ondioline to open and close "Highness," and Michael offered a pastiche of "East-West"-style motifs for his solo contribution. The Fillmore crowd throughout the show had been boisterous and rowdy, but now they quieted down and politely applauded each solo as though they were in an intimate jazz club. They clearly knew the proper response for a piece like "Her Holy Modal Highness," having seen artists like Charles Lloyd, Gary Burton, and even Thelonious Monk at the Fillmore.

On Friday night, an old bandmate was in the audience, and toward the end of the second set, Michael invited him to sit in. Elvin Bishop had just left the Butterfield Band and was in San Francisco working on organizing a group of his own. He was more than happy to be called up onstage to play some blues.

But Michael, exhausted from nights without sleep, took Bishop's guest appearance as an opportunity to slip backstage for a few moments of rest. Left on his own, Elvin played a steamy version of Sonny Boy Williamson's "No More Lonely Nights," drawing out the performance to nearly thirteen minutes while Al Kooper, mindful of the Fillmore's closing time, tried valiantly to bring the tune to an end.

One of the most masterful performances of the first two nights of shows came during another tune that featured Bloomfield's singing. "I hope y'all can dig some blues, 'cause here's some blues," Michael said, by way of introduction. There obviously wasn't a fan in the house who wouldn't "dig some blues," and the guitarist counted off a slow burner in B-flat, beginning with the turnaround. Taking a chorus to warm up, Michael served up sweet blues declamations, subtly shading his pitches and slurring his phrases with the seductiveness of a practiced lover. The tempo was indeed slow—agonizingly so—but bass and drums handled it without faltering. Kooper's organ provided the perfect foil for Michael's guitar commentary, bridging the gap between phrases with uncanny intuition. At the end of the first chorus, Bloomfield stepped up to a mic. "Hey, baby," he intoned. "Don't throw your love on me so strong." It was the Albert King blues by the same name, originally recorded in 1962.

As he sang, Michael adroitly filled the spaces between lyrics with come-hither lead. There were traces of Albert King in his playing, and B. B. King too, but the phrasing, choice of notes, and their inflection were pure Bloomfield. After years of playing, studying the masters, learning from them, and gigging with them while working to perfect his technique, the guitarist had developed his own sound. Here it was in all its glory.

Following a second verse, Bloomfield signaled Kooper, and the rhythm section ramped up the volume for his solo. Michael took the first four bars with characteristic intensity, firing off fierce runs peppered with vocal-like bends, building to a climax. That moment came with the downbeat of the fifth bar—and everything stopped. It was the dramatic effect he had first begun using when playing slow blues with the Electric Flag, the trick that Albert King often resorted to. Usually, the guitarist would fill the sudden silence with a torrent of notes, but this time Bloomfield simply laid out. "Whoa! Have mercy, have *mercy*!" he shouted as the crowd began to cheer. Kooper, Kahn, and Prokop accented the downbeat of the sixth bar as Michael struck and held a tremulous B♭ to the point of feedback, and then the band came back in on the seventh bar. Michael played out the chorus with a furious dispatch of licks that had the crowd on its feet, expecting even greater pyrotechnics. But the guitarist again surprised them. He caught Kooper's eye, and the organist dropped the volume to a whisper. Michael continued soloing, but quietly now, playing understated lines low down on the Sunburst's neck. "Yeah!" he said, pleased with the sound as his playing took on a sweetly melodic tone. The guitarist's awareness of dynamics, and his control in imparting them through his playing, were a hallmark of every authentic blues performance—and one of the genre's most difficult techniques to master. Mike Bloomfield made it look easy.

At the end of the chorus, Michael repeated an insistent C♯-to-B♭ phrase, prompting the band to ramp up the volume as he sailed into a third twelve bars. But after the first four, the band again stopped, and this time it was Al who filled the void with a spiky run on his Hammond. He soloed out the remainder of the chorus, and then it was three more verses from Bloomfield. As he accompanied himself he couldn't help singing along with his lead fills out of sheer enthusiasm. Some of the words he sang were his own and not those of King's original, but it didn't matter. Here was Bloomfield doing his thing, the thing he was known for, celebrating the blues and relishing his role as a purveyor of them. He brought the tune to a close after a final turnaround and a flurry of licks over Kooper's held tonic chord, and then the Fillmore fans were once again standing, loudly cheering the quartet.

To close each performance, Kooper and Bloomfield had worked up a brief instrumental they called "Refugee." They ended the second set on Friday night with it, and as the band played a final flourish on its concluding chord, Michael hit one last high G—and then released his guitar strap, letting his much-abused Gibson crash to the Fillmore's stage floor. Its highly amplified impact created a cacophonous roar, an aural confusion of distressed strings and feedback that stopped only when the guitarist grabbed the instrument by the neck, picked it up, pulled its plug, and strode offstage. The dramatic gesture seemed to capture Michael's ambivalence toward the whole Super Session project. It could also serve as a harbinger of what was about to befall Kooper's jam session redux.

CHAPTER 20

LIVE ADVENTURES

SAN FRANCISCO AND BOSTON, 1968

Al Kooper woke on Saturday morning around 11:00 a.m. He had slept well and was feeling well rested. As he ordered coffee from room service, he thought back over the last week with some satisfaction. He had managed to organize and promote a live jam session as a concert presentation, something that hadn't really been done before in pop music. He had also convinced a major label to record it, and succeeded in getting the volatile Michael Bloomfield on tape before an enthusiastic audience. He was certain that some of those tunes featured Bloomfield's best playing yet, and he was pretty sure he had enough material for the live *Super Session* album. That evening, Al decided, they would repeat a number of the songs to create alternate takes, thus ensuring that he would have the best possible performances for the record. It looked very much like the novice producer had once again pulled off an improbable, innovative recording date.

Then the phone rang.

It was Susan. "She says, 'I had to put Michael in the hospital. They're putting him to sleep. Sorry, but he can't play tonight,'" Kooper recalled with chagrin. "I couldn't believe it. He'd done it to me again!"

Susan had been staying in Lagunitas at Michael's place on Arroyo Road, watching with dismay as her former husband became more and more exhausted. Saturday night had been the last straw. Michael's fatigue and his inability to lull himself to sleep had driven him to the point of delirium. In a panic, Susan drove Michael to San Francisco and checked him into a hospital.

"He was miserable; he couldn't sleep," said Susan. "I was thinking, 'Oh my god, this *so* terrible!' But the doctors said, 'No—we'll give him a Seconal now, and then an hour later we'll give him another Seconal.' It was like nothing, I guess, to them to knock him out. But that's what he needed." She knew that once Michael was sleeping soundly, he would be out for the rest of the day and a good portion of the night—possibly right through to Sunday morning. That meant performing at the Fillmore that evening was out of the question. Back in Lagunitas, Susan realized it was up to her to pass the word along. She called Al Kooper first and then late in the afternoon broke the news to the Fillmore's manager.

Graham had already heard the news. Kooper had gone directly to the Fillmore's offices after speaking with Susan, knowing that the irascible Graham would have to be mollified once he learned the headliner for that night's concert would be a no-show. Al also knew he would have to find a replacement for the star guitarist—no easy task with fewer than ten hours to showtime. As anticipated, the Fillmore's impresario did not take the news of Bloomfield's cancellation well.

"I was very upset that Michael was a no-show," Graham later said. "I don't think we could find him. And then somebody said that they did find him, and he was in no condition to perform."

Nonetheless, the show had to go on, and Kooper and Graham—once he cooled down—worked the phones trying to enlist a replacement for the recumbent Bloomfield. By late afternoon, Al had gotten commitments from guitarist Steve Miller and from a young player named Carlos Santana, the leader of an increasingly popular Bay Area rock band. Santana's group was pioneering a fusion of Latin rhythms and blues-rock, but he had started out playing strictly blues and recently had even been taking lessons from Mike Bloomfield in Lagunitas. He was happy to sit in and offered to bring along his bass player, David Brown. With the guest roster for his Super Session jam now complete, Kooper once again had a real jam session on his hands.

That evening, as the Fillmore's patrons filed in through the lobby, they were greeted by ushers holding up signs that read, "Mike Bloomfield has been hospitalized and will not appear tonight." At the start of the first set, Al Kooper came out and solemnly explained the situation.

"I flew out here last Thursday, and we all met the next day at Michael's house," said Kooper to the audience. "Michael informed me that, as usual, when he's working he doesn't sleep—he's sort of an insomniac, if you can dig that. And up 'til last night, since that Thursday, he had not, in fact, slept." Al went on to reassure Bloomfield's fans that Michael was all right but regretted that Michael would be unable to play that evening. Instead, Kooper promised to bring up "people that you know of" to perform in the guitarist's place. "It's a lot like the other Super Session, where more or less the same thing happened, and Steve Stills joined us."

By Monday, Michael Bloomfield was back in Lagunitas, fully rested and restored to his former amiable, animated self. He and Al Kooper hadn't spoken since Friday evening, but the guitarist had heard that his friend managed to pull off two successful sets Saturday night, first with Steve Miller and then with Carlos Santana subbing on guitar. Though he felt a twinge of guilt for leaving the organist in the lurch a second time, Michael was greatly relieved that he was finally finished with this Super Session business. He was also more than a little amused at the thought of Al's rehearsed "jam session" taking on aspects of the real thing, and he savored the irony that Carlos Santana, his student, should be selected to take his place.

Al Kooper had flown back to New York on Sunday with Wally Heider's tapes from Super Session's three nights at the Fillmore West. He was focused on salvaging what he could from the six shows and putting together a viable follow-up to his million-seller. He hadn't called Michael, and he was more than a little peeved that the fickle guitarist had walked out on him once again, but Al knew his friend was probably OK. He was also quite certain that Michael, in spite of his acute exhaustion, had turned in some of his best guitar playing ever. With luck—and a bit of judicious production work—this new record might just eclipse the first, and the producer was eager to tackle it.

Though he had fully recovered from his acute bout of insomnia, Michael Bloomfield began to have second thoughts about Lagunitas. It was an idyllic spot—quiet, secluded, and far from the distractions of the city. Its isolation had helped him cut back on his drug use. But Lagunitas was maybe *too* remote. It was lucky that Susan had been there Friday night to help him. If no one had been around, Michael had no idea what he would have done. He was beginning to think it might be better to move back to Mill Valley. If nothing else, help—if he ever needed it—would be close by.

There was also the fact that Albert Grossman was pressuring Michael to take on studio work for ABGM as a way to pay down his debt. James Cotton had a session for Verve/Forecast coming up in a few weeks in New York, and Grossman wanted Michael to produce it. Getting to the airport from Lagunitas, Bloomfield knew from experience, could be a hassle. But from Mill Valley, the trip was less than an hour. A house of his own in the sleepy San Francisco suburb might be just the thing if he were frequently going to be flying out of the city at Albert's behest. And Michael knew a house that was available.

Harvey Brooks had eventually rented an older two-story home on Carmelita Avenue in Mill Valley after he had come out to California in 1967 to join the Electric Flag. It had been his residence for the year he played with Bloomfield and the band, but with the final disbanding of the group in August, Harvey was thinking about returning to New York. But then, in September, he had gotten a call from Cass Elliot. She had left the Mamas and the Papas and was planning to launch a solo career with an extravagant stage show in Las Vegas in mid-October. She wanted Harvey to organize the band for the show, and that meant he would have to move to Nevada right away to begin rehearsals. It also meant his house would be vacant, and if Mike Bloomfield wanted it, Brooks said, Mike was welcome to it.

By the end of the first week of October, Bloomfield was back in Mill Valley, having settled into his former bass player's place on Carmelita, just off Blithedale Avenue, in the heart of town. The three-bedroom home had a full basement and six rooms on two floors, plus a sizable backyard and patio. It was a considerable improvement on the apartment in Lagunitas and was roomier than his home on Wellesley Court. Michael set up house, taking one of the bedrooms for himself and even bringing in a piano. The other bedrooms he offered to whoever dropped by or was in town for a visit. In the driveway, he parked the Flag's van and his brother Allen's Mustang.

It wasn't long before word got out that Mike Bloomfield was back in town, and soon his new household on Carmelita Avenue was an increasingly busy place. The star guitarist's reputation for generosity and openness, coupled with his ever-increasing celebrity on the heels of the unexpected success of *Super Session*, brought many admirers to his front door. Some of those who came by never left. Henri Napier, a young woman who had been working at *Rolling Stone* as a receptionist, took one of Michael's upstairs bedrooms and quickly became the guitarist's de facto housekeeper. Mark Naftalin introduced Bloomfield to Andy Boehm, a high school friend from back in Minneapolis, and it wasn't long before Boehm, too, was a resident of 35 Carmelita Avenue. The interlopers seemed not to bother Bloomfield. He was happy to have people around, and he wasn't terribly concerned about who they were or how they had arrived on his doorstep. He enjoyed them for whatever diversion they could provide.

Roy Ruby, too, was a frequent guest. He had spent a year in Mexico before returning to California in the fall of 1968 and was shuttling between Berkeley and Los Angeles. He eventually moved into an apartment in LA with Mark Naftalin's younger brother, Dave. But Mill Valley was one of his regular destinations, and he could often be found picking guitar on the couch in Michael's living room. The shingled house on Carmelita Avenue was rapidly becoming a nexus for San Francisco's hip elite, with the ebullient Michael Bloomfield at its center.

One visitor, though, wasn't part of the growing counterculture scene in the city across the Golden Gate Bridge or an old pal from Michael's colorful past. He was a neighborhood kid, a fifteen-year-old sophomore at Mill Valley's Tamalpais High School named Toby Byron. Though he had seen Bloomfield with the Paul Butterfield Blues Band at a Fillmore Auditorium matinee in 1967, it was when he went to an Electric Flag show at the Winterland Ballroom in

January 1968 that Toby was truly impressed by the guitarist. "That's when Michael *really* knocked me out," Byron recalled. "They were monsters, and he was fantastic!" When he learned that Bloomfield was living nearby, Byron screwed up his courage and, taking a friend along for moral support, paid a visit to Carmelita Avenue.

"We knocked on the door and woke Michael up," Toby said with a laugh. "He came to the door in a yellow T-shirt and nothing else! This was well into the afternoon, and he didn't appreciate being woken up—but he still invited us in." The teenagers visited with the guitarist for several hours, talking about music and listening to records. "Michael was the first famous person I'd ever met—he was a *real* rock star. He was really eye-popping with his hair and his behavior, and he was *so* articulate."

Byron had been booking his friends' bands and occasionally working with established local groups, arranging gigs at Brown's Hall on Miller Avenue. He was planning a benefit show at his high school to raise funds for the Republic of Biafra, a newly formed country that at the time was fighting a disastrous civil war with Nigeria, and he decided to ask Mike Bloomfield to be the headliner. To his surprise, Bloomfield agreed. "I hired Michael and the band for all of $150," Toby said, smiling. "That seemed like a lot of money at the time. We had a light show with gels, just like the real thing, and two other groups. The concert was great, but the sound was terrible because we did it in the gym." The high school appearance by the famous blues-rock guitarist took place on November 11, a Monday evening when Bloomfield just happened to have a free night.

In mid-October, Albert Grossman had Mike Bloomfield produce James Cotton's third album for Verve/Forecast during a week of sessions in New York. A few weeks later, Grossman called with another task for his guitarist client. ABGM had taken on the management of Otis Rush's career, hoping to bring the legendary Chicago bluesman's music to a more mainstream audience. Rush was about to record a new album for the Cotillion label, and Grossman wanted Michael to produce the sessions, just as he had done for Cotton. Bloomfield was honored to work with Rush, one of his great guitar idols, but he wanted to do more than just organize the session's musicians and oversee the recording process. He wanted to create a body of original material for the brilliant guitarist as a way to introduce him to the vast new audience for blues-rock. To do that, Michael enlisted the help of one of the best songwriters he knew—Nick Gravenites.

The second week in November, Michael and Nick flew to Chicago with nine new songs they had created for the Otis Rush date. They wanted to show the music to Otis and go over the arrangements they thought would work well. The tunes, though, were a definite departure from the legendary bluesman's usual material. Only three of them were in the standard blues form; the remaining six were bluesy R&B or soul-tinged compositions, mostly played with a funky boogaloo-style backbeat.

What Otis Rush thought of them is unclear. But the bluesman was willing to let his two young producers take control of his sessions if it meant he would reach a wider audience and thus take his career to another level. He had seen how being discovered by white listeners had revitalized B. B. King's career, and Otis was hoping for a similar outcome by following Michael and Nick's advice. He was also not a little influenced by the excellent advance payment the two producers had secured for him. But he was surprised to learn that the album's sessions wouldn't be in Chicago.

Michael had decided that the best way to give Otis Rush a more contemporary sound was to have him record in a small facility far from Chicago—and away from the music industry's epicenters of Los Angeles and New York. Named Florence Alabama Music Enterprises after its original 1950s location, the place was more commonly known as FAME Studios, and by 1968 it could be found outside the small city of Muscle Shoals, Alabama. Starting in the early 1960s, a string of R&B hits had been produced there, and soon soul artists including Joe Tex, Etta James, Wilson Pickett, and Aretha Franklin were making records at FAME. What made those recordings from Muscle Shoals stand out was the tight, soulful accompaniment the studio's staff musicians could provide. Their concise, funky backing had become known as the "Muscle Shoals sound," and Mike Bloomfield thought Otis Rush's singing and playing could benefit from it. He had Albert Grossman rent studio time at FAME and, toward the end of the month, headed there to produce the legendary bluesman's crossover album.

"Mike flew down and I rented a car in Chicago and drove Rush down," said Gravenites. "Now, I knew Otis was a quiet cat, but I didn't know how quiet. He put a matchstick between his teeth in Chicago when we set out, and it was still in his mouth when we got to Muscle Shoals, I don't know how many hours later. He kept it in his mouth and hardly said a word the whole trip."

Despite his tight-lipped demeanor during the ten-hour ride to Alabama, Rush rose to the occasion once in the studio and seemed to enjoy working with the southern musicians. Bloomfield again invited Mark Naftalin along for the date, and as he had for James Cotton a month earlier, Naftalin backed the guitarist with tasteful accompaniment. Mark enjoyed the sessions, in part because he was happy to work with skilled musicians, such as FAME guitarist Jimmy Johnson, keyboardist Barry Beckett, and drummer Roger Hawkins.

The session players also included a young guitarist named Duane Allman, a blues aficionado from Nashville who had just celebrated his twenty-second birthday. Allman had played a few sessions for FAME earlier in the year, but he had become a full member of the staff only that month. His enthusiasm for the music and skill as a soloist impressed Michael enough that he used Duane as Rush's accompanist on several of the performances and featured his lead on "Reap for What You Sow." In only a few short years, Allman's playing would be celebrated as some of the best in blues-rock after he and his brother, Gregg, formed the Allman Brothers Band.

Michael and Nick worked out arrangements for the studio's horn section and added them to their original material. Rush also wanted to redo several of his earlier records, so the producers created charts for his 1950s hits "It Takes Time" and "My Love Will Never Die." They also put together a version of B. B. King's "Gambler's Blues," a tune that Otis liked to do. For those, Bloomfield and Gravenites essentially re-created the original versions, appeasing the guitarist by giving him something familiar to work with. The remainder of the songs were new, and Rush did his best to make them work.

Bloomfield and Gravenites spent the better part of a week in Muscle Shoals producing the sessions for Otis Rush's Cotillion album. When it was released in August 1969, the record, titled *Mourning in the Morning*, would feature the blues legend playing nontraditional material, mostly over a funky, boogaloo-style backbeat, with prominent horn arrangements throughout and only a few instances of the bluesman's dynamic guitar lead. Blues fans would be disappointed, rock audiences would be unimpressed, and the few critics who reviewed the record would damn it with faint praise. Michael and Nick's effort to introduce Otis Rush's music to a vast new audience would fall short of the desired outcome. But both producers returned to San Francisco confident in the knowledge that, if nothing else, they had gotten their friend and mentor properly recorded in an excellent studio and had made sure he was well paid for what would be his first full-length album release.

It was Al Kooper who next required Mike Bloomfield's services. The guitarist had been back in Mill Valley for little more than a week when the phone rang and, once again, it was his producer friend on the line. Al had been working on the production of their live Super Session performances at the Fillmore and was convinced that the music was good enough to warrant the release of a two-record set. He was going to try to talk Columbia into making the album a twofer, and he also was thinking it might be good to have more material to bolster his argument. For that reason, he had arranged with Bill Graham to have the Super Session quartet do a couple of weekends at the Fillmore East in New York during the holidays, and he would get the record company to record them. The *New York Times* had given a glowing review to *Super Session* at the end of September, calling the record "one of the few good jams available" and praising its music as "loose and lucid, spontaneous and immediate." With the *Times*' imprimatur and *Super Session*'s steady sales, Kooper was certain Columbia would approve the plan. The shows would undoubtedly sell out, and the music would likely be inspired.

Once again, Michael was unenthusiastic. But once again, he couldn't refuse. He still owed Albert Grossman, and, as Bloomfield told a friend, "Alan gets *really* great bread. I don't know how he does it, man—big bucks for both of us. Very cool." But the guitarist balked when Kooper suggested he come a few weeks early so that they could play a Sunday warm-up set during the Cafe Au Go Go's weeklong Blues Bag series. Instead, Michael agreed to fly in a few days ahead of the first Fillmore show so they could rehearse. This time, it would be up to Al to select the bass player and drummer.

When he informed his manager that he would be doing yet another round of Super Session gigs, Albert Grossman was pleased. But he, too, had a request. ABGM's star client, Janis Joplin, was going to leave Big Brother and the Holding Company. Her departure had been in the works since midsummer, but prior commitments and other complications had delayed the launch of her solo career. Now Janis was ready, and after her final appearance with Big Brother on December 1, she was going to put together an entirely new group—a soul band with horns. Grossman felt Michael Bloomfield would be the perfect person to organize it for her, and Michael was only too happy to oblige. He knew Janis was a great talent, and he didn't think much of the other musicians in Big Brother. Organizing the new backup band for the Texas blues shouter would be a pleasure.

But first, Michael had to fly to New York for the first of the Super Session shows at the Fillmore East. On Wednesday, December 11, the guitarist joined Al Kooper in the city for two days of rehearsals, giving them a chance to break in the ad hoc group's new members. Kooper had recruited bassist Jerry Jemmott, a session player who had worked with Ray Charles, Wilson Pickett, and Aretha Franklin, and jazz drummer John Cresci, whose recording credits included dates with singers Lena Horne, Helen Merrill, pianist Cy Coleman, and trumpeter Joe Wilder. Their credentials were beyond reproach, and they would doubtless provide solid backing for Bloomfield's adventurous improvisations. Michael already knew Jerry, because the bassist had been part of Otis Rush's Muscle Shoals sessions for Cotillion in November. To give more depth to the group's sound, Al also hired a friend from Queens, a pianist named Paul Harris. With his thorough knowledge of blues and gospel styles, Harris was an accompanist who could also contribute as a convincing soloist. The Super Session crew, now a quintet, looked like it couldn't miss, and Kooper was sure the dates would result in some excellent music.

The band first went over some of the tunes Kooper and Bloomfield had performed at the September Fillmore West shows. The rhythm section was soon up to speed on "The 59th Street Bridge Song," "That's All Right," "Together 'Til the End of Time," "Green Onions," "The Weight," and "Don't Throw Your Love on Me So Strong." To these, they added Fats Domino's "I'm Ready," the New Orleans pianist's 1959 hit, and "One Way Out," an Elmore James composition made popular by Sonny Boy Williamson. Michael also brought along several originals he wanted to perform. One was "(Please) Tell Me Partner," a highly personal slow blues he had asked James Cotton to record in October, and the other was a country-and-western foxtrot, a typical tale of a fallen woman called "For Anyone You Meet." Finally, instead of trying to create another variation on "His Holy Modal Majesty," Kooper talked Bloomfield into doing an arrangement of "Season of the Witch," the Donovan song from the Steve Stills side of *Super Session* that was helping to drive sales of the album. Michael disliked the tune, but Al joked that it could be their "psychedelic jam," and Michael begrudgingly agreed.

The Fillmore East was packed for the show's opening night. In the seats were many soul music fans there to see the headliners Sam and Dave. But just as many in the audience were dedicated Bloomfield followers who were eager to catch the New York debut of Super Session. The album had reached the number-thirteen position on *Billboard*'s Top LPs chart that week and was unquestionably a hit record, a potential million-seller. Columbia had agreed to Al Kooper's request to record the shows, and with the enthusiastic crowd spurring them on, Kooper was certain he and Bloomfield could improve upon some of the material they had recorded at the Fillmore West in September.

After the opening act, Kooper's quintet took the stage and the house lights dimmed. Bill Graham stepped up to the mic, intending to introduce Super Session, but once again Mike Bloomfield got there ahead of him. Mike Bloomfield's speeches, it seemed, were becoming a regular feature of Super Session shows.

"Hello . . . Uh, I wanna tell you all about the nature of this Super Session gig here," Bloomfield haltingly began. "Now, the history of the Super Session gigs is this." For a full minute and a half, Michael again recounted the Super Session story and explained what the audience was going to hear. He summed up his exegesis by introducing the members of the group himself, leaving Graham with nothing to say beyond, "It's a gas for us to bring on Michael Bloomfield, Al Kooper, and their friends." With that, Kooper kicked off the introduction to "The 59th Street Bridge Song," and the band roared into the first number of its first set.

Right away, it was obvious that Mike Bloomfield was in excellent form. His accompaniment meshed fluidly with the organist's singing, and his lead licks snapped with the crack of a bull whip. This was not the insomnia-slogged Bloomfield, the sleepless rock star flying solely on an adrenaline rush. There would be no vanishing act, no late-night flight home, no hospital visit. Michael was rested and confident, in command, fully himself.

The band's second tune was "I'm Ready." Fats Domino had originally done it using a rock 'n' roll variation on the basic New Orleans second-line march beat, but Michael opted to play it with more of a straight rock feel, taking the vocal himself. As usual, Michael's singing had more feeling than it had finesse. But he sang with conviction, clearly enjoying himself, and it worked. Something else, though, wasn't working. The tune had started out with drummer John Cresci emphasizing the fourth beat, moving the song along by tagging each measure while setting up the next. But very quickly he began accenting the second and fourth beats equally, and the song acquired a two-beat, "um-pah" feel. The forward motion essential to shuffle blues, the "swing," evaporated, and "I'm Ready" began to sound more like "I'm Stuck."

Undeterred, the band moved right into the next tune. It was a slow blues, creating a dramatic contrast, and it opened with a single sultry chorus from Bloomfield's Les Paul. Michael then stepped up to a microphone and began the lyrics to his blues "(Please) Tell Me Partner." After two verses, he stepped back, cradled the Gibson, closed his eyes and gritted his teeth while wagging his head from side to side, and sailed through two masterful choruses. For the third, he and Kooper exchanged phrases, Al going first and Mike answering, echoing the organist's lines. Before they had even finished, many in the audience were already cheering, caught up in the excitement of the blues call-and-response. Bloomfield concluded the slow drag with two more verses, continuing the dialogue with his guitar, using the Les Paul to embellish and underscore his oddly personal lyrics. He then brought the tune to a close with a stop and I–V–I coda ornamented with a final burst of licks. The crowd thundered its approval. Al Kooper couldn't help smiling. Michael was *wailing*!

The quintet next played "Together 'Til the End of Time" and "Green Onions," with the audience clapping along on the latter tune and Michael playing with staggering intensity, shaking his battered Sunburst as though he would shake it to pieces. His performance of the Booker T. tune was superior even to the version the guitarist had created during the September Fillmore shows. Its only flaw was the heavy, stilted accompaniment provided by John Cresci. The jazz drummer seemed unable to find a groove with the quintet's blues material and reverted to simplistic offbeat accents that gave the tempo a turgid, unfunky feel.

Michael's country-and-western-style original "For Anyone You Meet" was next, and Al Kooper strapped on a guitar to play rhythm. Bloomfield affected a hillbilly twang as he sang the poignant lyrics, and for once Cresci's two-beat backing worked with the music. What startled many of Bloomfield's fans was the fact that the blues-rock master was also—of all things—a master of country and western. A brief reprise of "The Weight" followed, eliciting cries of delight as the Fillmore crowd recognized the Band's hit tune. Then, as Bloomfield intoned into a mic, "Last one, this is the last one," the quintet launched into a roaring rendition of "That's All Right." In an effort to keep to Graham's rigorous schedule, the performance was truncated, but Michael got in his "Stay there, *stay there*!" routine and jacked the intensity and volume to an ear-splitting level. When it was all over, Al Kooper's Super Session quintet received a standing ovation, and cries of "More! More!" could be heard all over the house. More, though, would have to wait until the second set.

Friday's second set also had its share of surprises. Chief among them was one that came right after the opening tune, Elmore James's "One Way Out." As the ebullient crowd cheered the performance, Mike Bloomfield grabbed a microphone and struggled to get their attention. "We got a cat sitting in," he said breathlessly, "a cat that I met a long time ago when I was playing like twist joints and this cat was on the road, he was playing in Chicago. He's from Texas and, man, this is the baddest *motherfucker*, man—" Here the crowd nervously laughed and hooted, jazzed to hear a word everyone knew but still considered shocking in 1968. Bloomfield chuckled and brought guitarist Johnny Winter out from the wings.

Though Winter was completely unknown to the Fillmore audience, Michael knew the albino whirlwind would certainly amaze them. Because he respected Winter's skill as a guitarist, he was excited to present him to his own fans. It was typical of Bloomfield's generosity—he was happy to share the spotlight with anyone whose talent merited it. And Johnny Winter had plenty of talent. The Texan came out and played "It's My Own Fault," the tune B. B. King had first recorded for RPM in 1952.

Winter's style was a departure from Bloomfield's. Where Michael's tone was fat and horn-like, Johnny's was edgy and bright. His notes were profuse and fleet—played with dazzling speed and precision. The tune quickly acquired a sinewy feel as he infused blues licks with a rocker's aggression. No question about it, Winter's solo was a stunning—and unexpected—display of virtuosity.

But his ferocious attack also lacked some of the fluid, vocal quality of Bloomfield's. Winter tended to play on the beat, and his lines frequently had a rhythmic predictability that grounded them in mid-flight. When Michael got wound up, he pulled and pushed the beat, animating it in the manner of the best jazz soloists. By comparison, Johnny Winter sounded dry, almost academic. The difference between the two bluesmen mattered little to the audience, though—they were enthralled by the exotic newcomer.

Bloomfield followed Winter's two solo choruses with two of his own, building his lines with ever-increasing intensity and eventually reaching a ringing high D—the highest note fretable on his Les Paul. Winter then sang a final verse and then executed a coda routine that he had performed many times over the years. This time, though, he had the attention of a national audience, and scatting with his lead licks and incorporating a call-and-response exchange between guitar and voice had the desired effect. The crowd went wild and applauded uproariously as he finished, thrilled by the dramatic conclusion of "It's My Own Fault." Johnny Winter left the stage in triumph, and within days he was signed to Columbia for an astronomical six-figure advance. It turned out that a few of the label's executives had been in the Fillmore audience that Friday night, and they, too, had been suitably impressed.

The Saturday night Super Session shows were as successful as Friday's. Al Kooper was pleased with the effort, relieved that for once there had been no complications. Even though the accompaniment had at times faltered, Al was confident they had captured much material that was release-worthy. Michael, too, seemed satisfied, and he actually appeared to enjoy himself onstage both nights. But he headed straight for the airport right after their final set on Saturday and was home in Mill Valley by early Sunday morning. He had to be in San Francisco for a mid-week organizational session with Janis Joplin and her newly minted backup band, but first he wanted a few days to unwind.

Personnel for Joplin's group had been selected by Grossman's office in New York, and by the first week of December, musicians were gathering in San Francisco to start rehearsing Janis's material. The only holdover from Big Brother was guitarist Sam Andrew, included because Joplin wanted at least one familiar face in the new band. They all congregated in the vacant synagogue next door to the Fillmore Auditorium on Geary Boulevard and were working fitfully on the few songs Janis had suggested. Then, toward mid-month, Grossman called to say he had gotten Janis an invitation to premiere the new group in Memphis—at the annual Stax/Volt holiday showcase. The record company was going to present its roster of artists in a gala called the Yuletide Thing.

Appearing would be Carla Thomas, Rufus Thomas, Booker T. and the MGs, Johnnie Taylor, the Staples Singers, and many other soul stars. Suddenly, the pressure was on for Joplin to get her new band up to speed.

On Wednesday, December 18, Mike Bloomfield came to the rescue. He dropped by the Geary Boulevard rehearsal space, Les Paul in hand, ready to work with the group. They jammed on a slow blues at first, and then Joplin suggested they try "Piece of My Heart." After a few false starts, the group managed to get through an acceptable rendition of the singer's hit single, and Bloomfield seemed satisfied with the performance.

But the singer, well known for her proclivity for drugs and alcohol, was feeling the stress of suddenly being on her own. With Big Brother, she had been just another member of the band. But now, she alone was responsible for whatever was happening with her career. To relieve the anxiety, she turned increasingly to her favorite restorative, a spices-and-whiskey-flavored liqueur called Southern Comfort. She also resorted to narcotics.

"She was a drug-fiend alcoholic," Michael said of Janis, speaking with characteristic candor. Though he had a great deal of respect for Joplin's talent, Bloomfield knew the singer's foibles all too well. Some of them he himself shared. "I shot much dope with her," Michael explained. "I sat in her apartment and got high with her *countless* times." Now that the guitarist was working with the singer, ostensibly helping to get her new band together with Grossman's blessing, there would be plenty of opportunities to get high. But even with these distractions, the group managed to work up arrangements for a dozen tunes. Though he had only one day to work with them before their Memphis sojourn, Bloomfield did his best to get the band sounding suitably soulful. Then, on Thursday, December 19, the Janis Joplin Revue—as the singer's new backup band was hastily named—flew to Memphis for their first gig. Mike Bloomfield went along too.

On Saturday, the Janis Joplin Revue made its debut in front of a mixed audience at the huge Memphis Mid-South Coliseum on the city's fairgrounds. Equipment gremlins and an inadequate sound system, coupled with the fact that most of the audience was there to see Johnnie Taylor and Eddie Floyd, left Joplin struggling to connect with her listeners. In the end, though the band played well, she received only polite applause. The singer left the stage feeling dejected and more than a little embarrassed.

Mike Bloomfield, watching from the wings, felt the problem lay with the singer herself. Harkening back to statements he made regarding white audiences in his 1967 *Los Angeles Free Press* interview, he attributed Joplin's lackluster reception to her unfamiliarity with black musical traditions. "I don't think Janis was real well versed in that language of call-and-response, which is so necessary to get it on with black people, or with any sort of indigenous, ethnic music," he said.

The next morning, the members of the Revue packed up and headed off to the airport. They would take a break over the holidays and then reconvene to continue working with Joplin on new material in preparation for touring and recording. Mike Bloomfield wouldn't work with them again until Janis's studio sessions for Columbia in New York the following summer. For now, though, his obligation to Albert Grossman had been fulfilled, and the guitarist caught a flight to Chicago. He was going to spend the holidays with his family.

Michael Bloomfield's Windy City sojourn was a brief one. He had to be back in New York City later in the week for the second of Al Kooper's Super Session shows at the Fillmore East. But because they would be playing with the same quintet, there was no need for rehearsals and no need for Michael to arrive early. He booked a flight out of Chicago's O'Hare Airport for Friday morning, expecting to arrive at the Fillmore by late afternoon, well before the first set. Mother Nature thought otherwise.

"Bloomfield called me," Kooper said, recalling the first day of the weekend gig. "He says, 'I'm stuck in a snowstorm in Chicago. I don't know if I can get a plane out of here.'" Once again, it looked like the organist would have to play a Super Session gig without his star guitarist. "You'd think I'd get smart by now!" Al said, laughing. But Bloomfield had a valid excuse—a belt of snow, sleet, and freezing rain was moving across the Great Lakes and toward the Northeast, closing stretches of highway and causing delays and cancellations at affected airports. O'Hare was locked in by fog and freezing rain.

The ever-resourceful Kooper quickly came up with a scheme to save the show—and save himself from another Bill Graham tongue-lashing. B. B. King was in town playing at the Village Gate in Greenwich Village, and Kooper hastily made arrangements to have the legendary bluesman sit in for the Friday Super Session performances. Kooper and the rhythm section would play a few tunes, and then they would bring B. B. out. His surprise appearance would undoubtedly appease disappointed Bloomfield fans in the audience—and would also appease the querulous Mr. Graham.

The Fillmore's roster that weekend included the Crazy World of Arthur Brown, a psychedelic novelty act from Britain with a number-one hit, and the Paul Butterfield Blues Band. Butterfield was headlining and Super Session was scheduled to open. When the house lights dimmed at 8:00 p.m. for the first set, Kooper and company filed out onstage and took their places behind their instruments. The now-familiar vamp to "The 59th Street Bridge Song" resounded through the theater as the quartet began its portion of the show. Pianist Paul Harris did his best to cover Bloomfield's part, and the tune came off well despite the star guitarist's absence. The audience responded warmly, and as the applause died down, a spotlight focused on Kooper behind his Hammond B3. This time it was the organist who made a speech.

After introducing the band, Al said, "I have to apologize to you. You were all expecting to see Michael Bloomfield up here with us tonight, and I was too. But you can see that the weather outside"—the winter storm had reached New York—"is a problem. Michael called me this afternoon to say he's in Chicago, snowed in, and can't make tonight's show." Groans of disappointment filled the house. "Yeah, I know, I know" Kooper said. "But we've arranged for another guitar player to join us for the rest of the show, and we hope you'll like our substitute—Mr. B. B. King!"

Out from the wings strode the great bluesman, a borrowed guitar under his right arm, waving to the cheering crowd with his left. He rounded the stage, plugged into an amp, and after smiling broadly at the delighted audience, kicked off his 1964 hit "How Blue Can You Get." The stage went dark and a spotlight picked out the stout guitarist as he sang, creating a dramatic effect. What happened next seemed like a stunt conjured up by a Hollywood script writer—except that it actually occurred.

"We were sitting pretty close to the stage," said one member of the audience. "Suddenly we noticed a figure appear in the wings, wearing a leather jacket and jeans, and carrying a guitar case. The figure took off his jacket, plugged in his guitar, and began playing along with B. B. and the rest of the Super Session band. We turned to each other [and asked], '*Who* is that?'"

After a few notes, it was obvious. The mysterious guitarist was none other than the snowbound Michael Bloomfield. A spotlight found him, and the crowd went crazy as they recognized the costar of Super Session. Somehow, he had managed to catch a late flight into LaGuardia Airport in Queens and had taken a cab to the theater in time for the band's opening set. He and B. B. traded solos and licks throughout the remainder of the show, creating a blues barrage that thrilled the Fillmore crowd. Al Kooper, too, was amazed. "Michael was always full of surprises," he said. "That night I was just happy he was there, and that I got to play with him *and* B. B."

Following the Fillmore East shows, Michael Bloomfield headed back to San Francisco and Mill Valley for the New Year. As 1968 drew to a close, the blues-rock star got the news that *Super Session* had achieved gold record status for sales in excess of 450,000 copies. He now had the first official hit record of his career, and the Recording Industry Association of America would soon ship him a plated and framed copy of the LP as proof of the achievement. But Michael didn't really care. He was just glad that his involvement with *Super Session* and its related projects seemed to have reached a conclusion. He had no interest in performing endless variations of "Season of the Witch," regardless of how successful the gigs were or how well they paid. He was thinking instead about his contract with Columbia and its option for two more records. Albert Grossman was thinking about it too, and he was urging his client to put together a band and begin working on a new record. Michael still owed ABGM for the cost overruns incurred during his Electric Flag days, and the only way to pay it back was to make records and perform.

Michael thought he might kill two birds with one stone. He had played live shows with Al Kooper, shows that were going to be released as an album. Why couldn't he do that with a live session of his own? Instead of spending long hours in the studio recording and rerecording parts, mixing tracks and editing takes, why not organize a band, record a few of their gigs, and issue the results as a "jam" album? Simple and relatively painless, he thought. An excellent way to fulfill his contractual obligations to Columbia while earning hard cash for Albert. In November, the *New York Times* had published an article about the growing popularity of rock jam sessions, and the reporter had even quoted Michael saying, "They're the easiest thing in the world to do and as soon as the record companies recognize this, there will be jam albums all over the place." The moment seemed right for Bloomfield to make good on his own prediction.

At one of the jam sessions he had attended in Novato, the place where he had met bassist John Kahn, Michael had been impressed by a twenty-one-year-old drummer named Bob Jones. Jones and Kahn were part of a group called the T&A Rhythm and Blues Band, and Bob excelled at Stax-style accompaniment. It was that quality in his playing that attracted Bloomfield's attention at the Novato session.

"I had learned to play drums just like Al Jackson, and I had learned to sing, pretty much note-for-note, every song Otis Redding had ever recorded," Jones said. "So, I was doing 'Cigarettes and Coffee,' and this guy with this 'fro stuck his head around the corner when I was finished and said, 'Man, I thought it was Otis Redding singing and Al Jackson playing drums!' He brought his Les Paul into the room, plugged in and started playing, and he was absolutely *phenomenal*!"

Bob had never heard of Michael Bloomfield, but he, too, was impressed. Jones had originally been a guitarist and singer with a pop group called We Five. They had scored a top-ten hit with "You Were on My Mind," a folk-rock ballad that featured Bob's electric twelve-string guitar. But Jones was looking for more challenging music, and in 1968 he left We Five to concentrate on playing soul drums.

Bloomfield right away proposed that they work together. He explained that he was assembling a band to do a few gigs at the Fillmore West, and that those shows would be recorded and issued as an LP. "I think he was extremely frustrated with Columbia," said Jones. "He looked at the live jams as the easiest way to fulfill his album commitment under his contract. I think he had done all of the fighting he was going to do about the Flag, and at this point he was trying to get the best record he could get without hassling too much."

Throughout the month of January, Bloomfield enlisted musicians for his jam band and worked on the tunes he wanted to perform. The group he created hewed closely to the Electric Flag formula, using a basic rhythm section supported by a full complement of horns. In addition to Bob Jones, there were pianist Mark Naftalin and bassist John Kahn. Ira Kamin, Michael's friend from Chicago, added a second keyboard as the organist. The horns included tenor player Noel Jewkes and trumpeter John Wilmeth, both members with Jones and Kahn of the T&A Rhythm and Blues Band, and Gerald Oshita and Cornelius "Snooky" Flowers on baritone saxophones. Nick Gravenites reprised his role as the band's vocalist and songwriter, and helped with the arrangements.

Rehearsals were held at the former synagogue next to the Fillmore Auditorium, the place where Bloomfield had first worked with Janis Joplin's new band. Organizing ten musicians, arranging tunes, assigning parts, and learning new material in just a few weeks posed a challenge. Though Michael knew how he wanted the music to sound, he was often less than completely organized. Nick ably assisted, but the practice sessions were sometimes unfocused and chaotic. "The rehearsals weren't really well organized," Bob Jones remembered. "There may have been only two or three, and I don't think the horn players were always there." Michael later lamented that he didn't get all the horn parts finished in time, leaving Wilmeth, Jewkes, Oshita, and Flowers to come up with riffs of their own onstage during the performances. "You really learn to improvise in situations like that!" Jones said, laughing.

The Fillmore West shows were scheduled for the last weekend in January and the first weekend in February. The band for both appearances was billed collectively as Mike Bloomfield, Nick Gravenites, Mark Naftalin and Friends, and the January 30 through February 2 shows were appropriately titled "The Jam." For that weekend, Michael planned to invite local musicians up to sit in during the last set of each night, effectively re-creating the live Super Session experience. This time, though, the guests would be joining Bloomfield onstage rather than replacing him.

Columbia once again arranged to have Wally Heider bring in his remote unit to record all seven nights of Michael Bloomfield and his friends. Bill Graham expected an excellent turnout for the shows, having brought in rock legend Chuck Berry as the headliner for the first weekend and filling out the second with the Byrds and a new rock-and-soul group from Los Angeles called Pacific Gas & Electric. With the success of the *Super Session* LP and the excitement generated by the live Super Session re-creations, expectations were high for Bloomfield's jam shows and for the commercial potential of the resulting album. Easy to make, cheap to produce—those features of "jam" recordings very much appealed to the executives in the front office at Columbia.

On Thursday, January 30, Michael and ten friends crowded onto the Fillmore West's stage for the first set of the evening. Added to their number was conga player Reinol "Dino" Andino, brought in by Bloomfield to give a Latin sound to some of the arrangements. Several of those included adventurous reworkings of two Nick Gravenites standards, "It's About Time" and "Born in Chicago." Both were given funky vamps that utilized conga and Bob Jones's soul drums, and both had clever release riffs on their refrains. With their intricate horn parts, it was clear that those two tunes were among the ones the band had thoroughly rehearsed. A number of other Gravenites originals, newly penned by the singer for his own Columbia album, included "Moon Tune," "Holy Moly," "Killing My Love," "Work Me Lord," and "Gypsy Good Time." Michael contributed "Oh, Mama," a Ray Charles-inspired ballad, and "Carmelita Skiffle," a spritely jump blues named for the guitarist's new digs in Mill Valley. Covers of tunes by other artists included Arthur Conley's 1967 song "Love Got Me," a vocal feature for Bob Jones, and a version of Otis Rush's "It Takes Time," an up-tempo shuffle blues Nick had frequently done with the Electric Flag. Bloomfield himself sang "When My Heart Beats Like a Hammer," a blues that had been a hit for B. B. King in 1954.

There were original blues as well. Nick sang two of his own, "Wintry Country Side" and "Blues on a Westside," while Michael did the vocal on "Young Girl Blues," a cautionary tale he had written about underage females, also known as "San Quentin Quail." For comic relief, Bloomfield and the band created a blues variation on the theme from a TV commercial for Ajax cleanser, calling it "Stronger than Dirt," the kitchen product's slogan.

The sets went off well, and Michael was in top form, contributing multiple choruses of bracing blues-rock guitar on tune after tune. His playing, especially on Nick's "Killing My Love" and "Moon Tune," was as forceful and intense as anything he had done with Al Kooper. The crowd, thrilled by Bloomfield's fiery virtuosity, cheered every solo. Though the horns were occasionally less than together, Noel Jewkes contributed fine tenor and soprano solos on several of the blues. Mark Naftalin's solo piano introduced "Wintry Country Side" with multiple choruses rendered in solid South Side style, while Ira Kamin added a jazz feel with his occasional solos on organ. The rhythm section, built around Kahn's imperturbable bass lines and Jones's sparky funk beat, powered each tune and provided the soloists with an ample framework for their improvisations. Here was a fine blues, rock, and R&B horn band, a group fronted by a superstar guitar player. It was almost as though the Electric Flag had been reunited—except that someone forgot to invite Buddy Miles.

There were other musicians who were invited. For the jam portion of the shows, Michael brought in several San Francisco players, including a few who were already under contract to Columbia Records, thus eliminating the need to obtain releases. Among the guitarists who joined the jam were the Sons of Champlin's Terry Haggerty, and Jerry Miller from Moby Grape may have also played a few tunes. But prominently featured was a twenty-six-year-old blues singer who had emigrated from rural Massachusetts to Los Angeles in the early 1960s and had just released his first album of blues covers on Columbia. Henry Fredericks, known professionally as Taj Mahal, sang several smoky blues in a raspy baritone while Bloomfield seeded his phrases with azure fills. Mahal even played a few choruses of chromatic harmonica on James Cotton's "One More Mile," giving his performance an earthy, down-home feel. On "If I Ever Get Lucky," a slow blues that Taj improvised onstage, his regular guitarist, Jesse Ed Davis, got in a few licks following Bloomfield's solo. The feeling was relaxed and casual, almost as though the shows were real jam sessions taking place after hours in some North Beach hipster bar. That fact was driven home by Nick Gravenites, who placed a rocking chair onstage and sang more than a few songs seated, comfortably rocking along with the beat. Everyone was encouraged to contribute, including the horn players, and Snooky Flowers was the featured soloist on several tunes and the vocalist for B. B. King's "Sweet Little Angel." Michael even invited members of the audience to get involved.

"We've been recording every night of this gig," Bloomfield announced midway through the second set one evening. "For people who want to do something on the record, well, now's your night. Later on, in the middle of the thing, anyone that has something they think is valid and pertinent enough to be on a Columbia record, you can come up here and say it or do it." Bloomfield the prankster then added with a smirk, "Think carefully, 'cause you want it to be, you know, pretty groovy to be on the record there. . . . Just come up; take over!" Over the course of the weekend, a number of local musicians took Michael up on his offer, causing things to occasionally become chaotic and disorganized.

Under those circumstances, the music generally suffered. But Bloomfield didn't mind—he usually left the stage before the amateurs "took over."

The first week in January, Columbia released the second Super Session album. Accurately titled *The Live Adventures of Mike Bloomfield and Al Kooper*, the LP was a twofer, a specially priced two-record set, just as Kooper had requested. It featured some of the best moments from his collaboration with Michael at the Fillmore in September, as well as several fine selections by Bloomfield's replacements, Elvin Bishop and Carlos Santana. But the most striking thing about the album was its cover. It had no title and no lettering or identifying logo of any sort, just a painting of the LP's two stars—and, in bright red lettering, the painter's signature: "Norman Rockwell."

Columbia's art director, Bob Cato, knew the famous illustrator well, having encountered Rockwell while working in the magazine industry prior to joining the record company. Cato mentioned to Al that if Kooper, as a Columbia producer, would like to use Rockwell's talents for an album cover, he could arrange it. Al dismissed the offer at first, unable to see how Rockwell's traditional Americana style would ever be appropriate for the sort of music he intended to produce. But then, one afternoon, it occurred to him that using a conservative icon like Norman Rockwell to create the cover for the live Super Session album might be delightfully ironic.

"I was lying in bed one Sunday, watching a football game on TV, just like everybody else in Middle America," Kooper said. "Except that I'm this hippie musician with long hair and funny clothes. And I suddenly thought, why not have the guy who paints Middle America paint Michael and me for the record jacket? I thought, 'Wow, that's a *great* idea!'"

Kooper had Cato arrange a meeting with Rockwell in October at Columbia's Seventh Avenue headquarters, and Michael Bloomfield, in town at the time working on James Cotton's latest album, joined them. Cato took photos of each of the musicians separately and then took several group shots with the avuncular illustrator. Bloomfield was effusive with the bemused Rockwell, inviting him out to San Francisco to paint the city's colorful counterculture denizens. According to Al, Michael's enthusiasm was inspired in part by the pills he had found in the pocket of his coat and had just taken. "Bloomfield was smashed out of his mind," Kooper recalled with a smile.

The final painting showed the musicians standing together, though they had been photographed separately. It arrived at Columbia's offices in New York in a garish, gold-leafed frame with a bill for five thousand dollars. But it was a striking portrait, and the resulting cover of the "blues singers," as Rockwell called them, made *Live Adventures* stand out on record racks across the country. And the music inside was even more inspiring. To record buyers, all the tunes were new, and several—especially "Mary Ann" and "Don't Throw Your Love on Me So Strong"—featured superb playing by Mike Bloomfield as well as the guitarist's first recorded vocals. The novel arrangement of "The 59th Street Bridge Song," with vocal harmony added in the studio by its composer, Paul Simon, was a winner, and Columbia was considering releasing "The Weight" as a single. Elvin Bishop's "No More Lonely Nights" was an added bonus, and "Sonny Boy Williamson" introduced guitarist Carlos Santana to blues-rock fans everywhere. The strains of "Her Holy Modal Highness" could soon be heard emanating from dorm rooms on college campuses throughout the nation.

But perhaps the most intriguing thing about *Live Adventures* was the drama surrounding Michael Bloomfield's collapse during the last day of the Fillmore shows. His disappearance from the original Super Session date hadn't been mentioned with the release of that album. But *Live Adventures* not only acknowledged Bloomfield's failure to complete the gig, but publicized it. Al Kooper's speech to the Fillmore audience on the Saturday that Michael failed to appear, attributing his absence to insomnia and reporting that he had been hospitalized, opened side three of the album. His liner notes described the stressful week leading up to Bloomfield's malaise and explained that Bishop and Santana had been brought in as substitutes. Michael's fans suddenly learned that their favorite guitarist, an American icon and a pioneer of the new blues-rock idiom, was prone to sleeplessness so severe it could leave him incapacitated. It was a condition, it seemed, that made him undependable when under pressure. Here was a side of Michael Bloomfield that, until the release of *Live Adventures*, very few outside of the guitarist's immediate circle were familiar with. It would, however, become something very much a part of Bloomfield's public persona going forward.

The album also afforded fans a glimpse of another side of Michael's complex personality. Starting off the record was the opening-night speech that the guitarist had given to the audience letting them know what they were about to hear. Kooper had included his entire introduction, and it gave record buyers a moment with Mike Bloomfield that was engaging, humorous, and not without a certain unvarnished charm. Bloomfield sounded like a regular guy, which is exactly what, in many respects, he was.

The release of *Live Adventures*, combined with the overwhelming response to the first weekend of Bloomfield's jam shows, convinced Bill Graham to give Michael and his friends top billing for their February 6–8 Fillmore West appearances. Bloomfield's playing was again transcendent, particularly when the band performed "Born in Chicago." During his extended solo, usually following Noel Jewkes's Coltrane-inspired statement, Michael encouraged the horns to improvise as an ensemble behind his own wildly extravagant phrases, effectively creating a free-jazz-style tsunami of sound. Gravenites's lament to his hardscrabble early years in Chicago, the tune that had first brought the Paul Butterfield Blues Band to the attention of a new generation of blues fans, would evolve onstage into an amalgam of avant-garde jazz, blues, rock, "East-West," "Another Country," and whatever else inspired Bloomfield in the moment. Even the song's composer, long accustomed to the guitarist's virtuosic displays, could be impressed. "I *hear* you, Michael," Nick intoned after one such performance.

But things did not always go smoothly. Michael may have missed one of the Friday sets, and it often took quite a bit of discussion between tunes to decide what the band would play next. At times it seemed as though no one onstage was actually in charge, and Bloomfield's casualness toward the band's presentation seemed to infect several of its other members. Nick Gravenites attributed the lack of organization to one thing. "Well," he said many years later, "Michael was junked out. A lot of people were junked out. It was just one of those things."

Since he returned to Mill Valley from his retreat in Lagunitas, Michael Bloomfield had resumed the life of a rock star. He was once again shuttling around the country, producing sessions, playing gigs, making records, and answering to managers and company executives. His home life was crowded with hipster housemates, old friends seeking stardom of their own, comely women and hangers-on attracted by fame, and transients of every sort. Many of Michael's guests were coping with intemperate habits of their own, and it was not uncommon to find a variety of drugs at 35 Carmelita Avenue. Bloomfield soon found he couldn't resist the temptation. With the renewed pressures of his career came a return of the anxieties and insecurities that had plagued him during his last months with the Electric Flag. He had resorted to heroin then to ease the stress, and now he found himself falling back into that familiar routine. His use wasn't sufficient to hook him physically, but the need was frequent enough to cause what the guitarist later described as a "psychological addiction." In the weeks following his Fillmore West jam sessions, Michael Bloomfield became increasingly inactive, enjoying the pleasures of home and friends—and the frequent peace of mind conferred by narcotics-induced euphoria.

Still, Michael's days in early 1969 weren't entirely without musical projects. The tapes from his Fillmore shows were being edited and mixed in Columbia's studios, and Bloomfield had decided to let the label assign them a producer rather than taking on the task himself. The album was supposed to be a live jam, so there was no need for extensive edits and overdubbing, and thus no real need for Michael's participation in its final mastering. Instead, Bloomfield turned his attention to planning his next record for Columbia, one he hoped would fulfill his contractual obligations to the label.

This final album, Bloomfield decided, would be a studio production. It would be a solo effort, featuring all original material created in collaboration with musical friends and associates. The more he thought about it, the more Michael felt compelled to use the record to make a grand statement. He would celebrate all the varieties of music that he loved while paying tribute to the many artists who had inspired him. The album would be a summation of his career and of his contribution to American popular music. The idea excited and energized him—when he was feeling confident and focused. There were times, though, when the prospect of another album—especially one with such grand ambitions—seemed beyond his capabilities.

But those misgivings were easily kept at bay. There were a variety of distractions in the house on Carmelita Avenue, and Michael could avail himself of them whenever he felt the need. Throughout February, he worked on new songs for the album, putting words to music in diverse styles, singing them for his housemates, and gauging their reaction. Some of the songs were comic, but most were personal—a few profoundly so. The majority were pop tunes; only two were conventional blues.

While working on material for the new album, Michael was surprised one afternoon in early March to hear again from Al Kooper. The producer had a familiar request. Because *Live Adventures* was selling steadily and climbing *Billboard*'s Top LPs chart, Columbia was keen to have the Super Session stars do a mini-tour in support of the album. Would Michael be willing to play a couple of concerts later in the month, just to appease the company's promotional department? Kooper promised it would be the last time they would have to take their "jam" on the road. "I know I originally said we'd just go in the studio and play, with no commitments, no obligations," Al told his guitarist friend. "But who knew we'd have a hit record?" Ever mindful of his indebtedness to Albert Grossman, Bloomfield once again acquiesced. Kooper told him he would arrange a few shows in the Northeast for mid-month.

Michael made note of the gigs and went back to working on material for his solo album. For the recording sessions, he intended to use many of the same musicians who had participated in the Fillmore West jams. That would be convenient, because most of them lived right in Mill Valley—and some were his housemates. But work on the new record was soon interrupted again. Albert Grossman called to say Kooper's Super Session band was scheduled to appear that weekend at the Rock Pile in Toronto and in Boston the following day at a huge hockey rink called the Boston Arena. It was going to be an arduous trip, and the guitarist found himself dreading it. He would have to fly out of San Francisco, change planes in Chicago, and then fly on to Toronto for the band's Friday evening performance. Grossman told him there would be three shows, with the final set not beginning until nearly 2:00 a.m. Then the band would have to catch a red eye into Boston's Logan Airport for the Saturday show at the Arena. Michael would be back in Mill Valley late Sunday, but that was little consolation. He would doubtless not close his eyes for more than fifteen minutes during the entire weekend.

That decided it. He wouldn't go.

At least, not to Toronto. It was winter, and Toronto was cold. Michael would tell Grossman he was getting over the flu and didn't want to risk being out in the freezing Canadian air. As a consolation, Bloomfield promised to make the Boston show. He wouldn't leave Kooper entirely in the lurch.

The guitarist's manager was not happy with Michael's decision. But there was nothing he could do, other than accommodate his temperamental client. The March 14 Super Session appearance at the Rock Pile was canceled. The next day, Bloomfield flew as promised to Boston for the appearance at the Boston Arena. Though he was late getting to the Back Bay venue and was a reluctant participant, the guitarist, once onstage, rose to the occasion. One audience member remembered being amazed at how animated Michael was, jerking from side to side while soloing. Another called him "*very* energized." A review of the show in Tuesday's *Boston Globe* complained of the facility's poor acoustics, but reported that "it wasn't until organist Al Kooper, guitarist Mike Bloomfield and drummer Skip Prokop, 'Super Session,' began to play, with 'Feelin' Groovy,' that the quality of the music began to get ahead of the decibels bouncing off the ceiling."

Following the performance, Mike Bloomfield seemed almost pleased to have made the trip. As he was packing up behind the stage, he chatted amicably with a few admirers. "He was really buzzed," said one fan. "Big smile, wide-open and warm, big black eyes. I felt we were instant friends, like he was my older brother." Regardless of his mood, Bloomfield was always approachable. He may have even been feeling energized enough to head over to the Ark, a recently opened rock venue on Lansdowne Street, for a post-concert jam session with Buddy Miles and members of the Buddy Miles Express. His good friend, Chicago blues pianist Otis Spann, was also there, and they took over the bandstand and jammed into the early morning hours. Michael just made it to Logan Airport in time for his flight back to San Francisco.

Later that week, *The Live Adventures of Mike Bloomfield and Al Kooper* reached number eighteen on *Billboard*'s Top LPs chart.

CHAPTER 21

MICHAEL'S LAMENT

SAN FRANCISCO AND CHICAGO, 1969

Back in San Francisco, Mike Bloomfield continued to work sporadically on material for his solo album. Columbia had tentatively assigned the LP an August release date, and the production schedule required Michael to complete all recording sessions by the end of May. Rehearsals for the dates would have to wait until April, though, because Michael Bloomfield and Friends, as the guitarist's band was now called, had another series of shows to do for Bill Graham. This loose aggregation, with Nick Gravenites, John Kahn, and drummer Bob Jones, played four nights of shows at the Fillmore West beginning Thursday, March 27, and reprised many of the tunes they had performed for the "jam" shows, plus a few of Bloomfield's new compositions. The Paul Butterfield Blues Band headlined the weekend of concerts, and Michael delighted the audience by inviting his former boss to sit in on several of the Friends' tunes.

The following week, Bloomfield flew to Chicago to visit his family during the Passover holiday. While there, he had his photographer friend Peter Amft take a few studio portraits, thinking they might be useful for the new album. The guitarist posed in a black leather jacket and dark turtleneck, seated against a professional backdrop of seamless gray paper. He stared impassively at the camera, cradling his iconic Les Paul Sunburst with its various dings and scratches, on his lap. Amft took a dozen shots, including a few close-ups of Michael's hands on the Gibson's neck, and captured a side of Michael Bloomfield that would have been unfamiliar to most blues fans. The perpetually ebullient, outgoing blues-rock star, normally clad in a button-down Oxford shirt and Brooks Brothers sport coat, now looked almost menacing. Dressed like a back-alley hoodlum from an earlier era, the guitarist wore an expression that seemed to issue an unspoken challenge to the viewer. Here was Bloomfield the leather-jacketed greaser, the rock 'n' roll gangster threatening mayhem, wielding a six-string electric switchblade. It was Michael's adolescent image of himself made all too real.

Whether the guitarist intended to present another side of himself to Amft's camera, he didn't say. Peter simply obliged his friend by taking several striking large-format portraits and promised to send a few prints to Michael once the film was developed. But Bloomfield wasn't interested only in photos—he was hoping the photographer could help him with the album itself.

"I had a graphic studio that I started with my friend Don Wilson, an illustrator, and the name of it was Daily Planet," said Amft. "Michael told me he was going to put out an album, and he wanted us to create the cover art for it. He said it was going to be called 'With a Little Help from My Friends,' and it was going to be a double LP. He said the sky was the limit for whatever we wanted to do with it." Daily Planet had done several album covers for Chess Records, but the studio had never worked for a major label and certainly had never been given an open-ended budget. Peter told Michael that he and Don would get right to work on a proposal and that he would come out to San Francisco in a few weeks to show him mock-ups and take additional photos for the album jacket's inside spread.

While in Chicago, Michael visited Norman Dayron. Norman had left Northwestern University and had taken a full-time position as an assistant engineer at Chess Records. He was happy to see his friend, and as they talked, Bloomfield described his plans for his new record. He said he was thinking of paying tribute to all the great artists that had inspired him, that he wanted to acknowledge the "fathers" of the blues. "I'm just like Muddy's son," Bloomfield told Dayron. "Musically, that's just what I am." Norman thought the idea was an excellent one, and he suggested the tribute concept might merit an album of its own. Why not record a special LP that brought together younger white blues players with the music's elder black masters? A collaborative effort that would honor those who inspired a new generation of bluesmen? "Yeah, that's groovy, and you can call it 'Fathers and Sons,'" quipped Michael.

The more they talked, though, the more Norman couldn't help noticing that the guitarist seemed out of sorts. Bloomfield was as animated as ever, but he seemed down, almost depressed. Probably fatigue, Dayron thought, and he tried to cheer Michael with his own experiences at Chess, where he was doing everything from working the board to cleaning up after musicians and sweeping the place out. The guitarist listened distractedly and then interrupted Norman. Would it be OK if they went over to the Chess studios? he asked. Michael said he felt like playing and wanted to record a few of the tunes he had written for the new record.

Two hours later, the guitarist and the assistant engineer were in one of the new Ter Mar studios in the Chess building at 320 West Twenty-First Street.

Grabbing a few hours of free studio time for his friend didn't worry Norman—he knew that his boss, chief engineer Ron Malo, wouldn't mind, if only because he wasn't there. Who was there was another friend of Michael's, an amateur pianist named Jonathan Cramer. Bloomfield had met Cramer through Barry Goldberg after Cramer married Barbara Goldberg, Barry's cousin and the daughter of famed justice and United Nations envoy Arthur Goldberg. Jon was a blues enthusiast and could play convincing Chicago-style piano, and he had eagerly joined the impromptu recording session after getting the call from Michael. The duo ran through a few slow blues instrumentals as Bloomfield played some sultry slide, again sounding more than a little like the legendary Robert Nighthawk. Cramer occasionally got lost in the chord changes outlined by Michael's improvisations, but for the most part he provided solid accompaniment and even took a few convincing solos himself.

After about an hour, Michael sat down at the piano. He felt his way through Ray Charles's "Come Rain or Come Shine," singing the lyrics in a raspy, halting voice as he played. Then he sang one of his own compositions, a mournful tune he had created for his new album called "Michael's Lament." Its melancholy lyrics spoke to the depressed mood Norman had observed in his friend, and as he played and sang, Bloomfield seemed to grow more morose. He tried a version of "Young Girl Blues," a song he had performed during the Fillmore West "jam" shows, and then improvised two blues as he cycled through the changes at the keyboard. One he called "No Rest Blues."

I'm feelin' so sick, I haven't slept for many long days
I'm so sick, people, you know I have not slept for days
Yes, when my mind starts to ramblin', it won't take my troubles away
When your head is on, and it will not let you rest
When your head is on, it will not let you rest
Yes, it starts to ramblin' like the wild geese in the west

He followed that with "My Old Friends," a somber tribute to all his Chicago acquaintances.

I'm so glad, so glad to be with my old friends again
Say I'm glad to be with my old friends again
You know I only see them sometimes, people, you know it's
sometimes now or then
Since I lost my baby, you know my friends are the only ones I have
Since I lost my baby, darlin', you know my friends are the only ones
I have

They keep me easy when I'm sick, people, when I'm down they can
make me laugh

He wound up the unscheduled recording session by singing a bit of "My Melancholy Baby," telegraphing his mood, if it weren't already obvious enough. At one point, Bloomfield paused and said, "Lemme see, what are a few more I could sing to satisfy my mind, let it be cool for a while?" He then murmured, "I won't even record 'em—I'm just too tore up to do 'em any sort of good justice." By the time Michael had played through enough music to "satisfy" his mind, he had filled two ten-inch reels of tape. Norman labeled them and packed them up, unsure what to do with them. "Keep them for me," Michael told him. "Maybe I'll want dubs later." That weekend, Bloomfield flew back to San Francisco and the comfort of his home in Mill Valley.

In the weeks since Bloomfield's visit, Norman Dayron had grown more excited about the "fathers and sons" album idea. Not long after his conversation with Michael, the assistant engineer took the concept to Marshall Chess, and Marshall told him that Bloomfield had mentioned the idea to him too. Because he was interested in developing an audience for the company with younger rock listeners, Marshall convinced his father, Leonard Chess, to approve the project. The business logic behind a collaborative album was compelling. By recording a few blues-rock superstars with several of Chess Records' legendary masters, the company could introduce rock fans to the classic urban blues that made up much of the Chess catalog. A fathers and sons album would also drive sales of current releases by those master bluesmen. The elder Chess gave the go-ahead for his son and Norman Dayron to arrange whatever musician permissions would be needed and told them to set up session time at Ter Mar. Muddy Waters, it was decided, would be the recording's featured Chess artist.

When Norman called Michael to tell him that Leonard Chess had OK'd the fathers and sons project and that he had to be part of it, Bloomfield surprised Dayron with a less-than-enthusiastic response. The guitarist said he was working on material for his own album and wasn't sure he would have time for a session in Chicago later in the month. But Norman was insistent, and when he explained that it would be a chance for Bloomfield to record with his old friend and mentor Muddy Waters, Michael brightened. "OK, I'll do it," he said. "But you'll have to clear it with Albert and Columbia first."

Dayron and Marshall Chess quickly secured the services of Paul Butterfield, who was delighted to participate, and got Sam Lay to agree to play drums for the sessions. Muddy Waters requested that his longtime accompanist, pianist Otis Spann, be included, and Dayron thought Chess session guitarist Phil Upchurch would be the right choice for group's bass player. But Marshall wanted to bring in additional talent from outside the label's roster of artists, so he enlisted Memphis bassist Donald "Duck" Dunn from Booker T. and the MGs. For additional support, Norman invited harp player Jeff Carp and guitarist Paul Asbell to the dates, a move that pleased Sam Lay. Both Carp and Asbell had been working with Lay in the drummer's quartet Home Juice. By mid-April, the producers had succeeded in securing top talent for the fathers and sons sessions and were ready to record.

On Saturday, April 19, Mike Bloomfield flew to Chicago for three days of taping at Chess Records. But he wasn't going into the studio only for the fathers and sons date. Added to the project was a hastily arranged concert with all the participants from the collaborative sessions, a live benefit for a Wheaton, Illinois–based academy loftily named the Phoenix Fellowship of Cultural Exploration and Design. The show, curiously billed as the "Cosmic Joy-Scout Super-Jam," was going to be held at the Auditorium Theater on Congress Parkway, a venue more commonly used for dance performances and Broadway musicals. The concert was intended to conclude a full week of star-studded blues in the Windy City, capping off the Chess recording sessions with a live version featuring Muddy Waters backed by the date's powerhouse team of white and black bluesmen. It would be a great way to spark local interest in the forthcoming record release.

As was frequently his habit when he came to Chicago, Michael stayed at his grandmother Ida Bloomfield's place in the Belmont, a majestic apartment building with sweeping views of Lake Michigan at 3172 North Sheridan Road. On Sunday morning, Mrs. Bloomfield invited the entire family to brunch because both her grandsons were in town. By coincidence, Allen Bloomfield had come to Chicago that weekend too. He was working as Al Kooper's assistant while the keyboardist was in town for a gig, and he brought Kooper along to the family gathering. When they arrived, Al was happy to see Michael—and was more than impressed by Mrs. Bloomfield's opulent digs.

Dottie Bloomfield was also there, and she charmed Kooper, striking him as a "typical Jewish mother." It was only Michael's father who appeared a bit odd to Al. Harold Bloomfield stood apart from the gathering, leaning up against the fireplace and glowering. "He was completely separate," remarked Kooper. "He hardly said anything, and he didn't eat anything. He didn't have anything to do with the rest of us. He just stood there—and he was wearing jodhpurs!"

Michael's father, an enthusiastic horseman, had come to the brunch right from his Sunday morning ride at a stables in the Loop and hadn't expected to see his former wife at the table. He was fuming at the awkwardness of the situation and refused to participate. But Michael managed to ease the tension with a tale about his recent bout of insomnia. Al recalled him saying he had just left a hospital where he had gone for a sleep cure because they had put him in the psychiatric wing. "He said he was up all night watching all the crazy things the patients were doing," Kooper reported, laughing. "There was no way he could sleep with all that going on. So he just packed up and left." For the keyboardist, brunch with the Bloomfields was one of the more memorable noshes he would ever have.

Monday, April 21, was the first day of sessions at Chess's Twenty-First Street studios. Now officially called *Fathers and Sons* after Bloomfield's suggestion, the album was going to be a two-record set with one LP containing studio selections and the other offering excerpts from the concert. Material for the studio sessions had been carefully selected by Norman Dayron from among Muddy Waters's classic Chess recordings. "I went through everything in the vaults, trying to find things I thought would inspire the musicians and would really work well with a more modern sound," said Dayron. "Muddy was really pleased with the selections, and I think everybody else was too."

In the studio that afternoon, a reunion of sorts was under way. Paul Butterfield had flown in from New York, where his band had just played two nights at the Fillmore East, and he happily greeted Muddy with an uncharacteristic hug. Duck Dunn, just in from Memphis, introduced himself around with the gentility that came natural to a son of the South. Sam Lay brought Jeff Carp and Paul Asbell over to chat with Otis Spann and joked with Marshall Chess about the company's new upscale facilities. Only Mike Bloomfield seemed less than energized. The guitarist talked briefly with Muddy and Spann, and acknowledged Butterfield, but he said little to anyone else and seemed unusually subdued. There was clearly a lot of enthusiasm for the project, but something about it was not right for Mike Bloomfield.

Norman Dayron thought his friend might have been cowed by the collective virtuosity of the gathered ensemble. "Michael went in there, and he was intimidated," Dayron said emphatically, convinced of the guitarist's insecurity. "Butterfield loved it—he was like a duck in water. Just sat right down in a very craftsman-like way, went to work, didn't stop, didn't let up for one minute. But the band was just too awesome for Michael to deal with, and he freaked out."

Whatever the cause of Bloomfield's reticence, the session soon got under way with Dayron acting as producer and head engineer Ron Malo rolling tape in the control room. With both Butterfield and Carp in the studio and ready to go, Norman suggested they try "All Aboard," a two-harp tune with a shuffle rhythm that evoked the sound of a southbound flyer making up time. Muddy had originally recorded it in 1956 with Little Walter playing chromatic harp and James Cotton blowing the train whistle on a Marine Band. For the remake, Jeff Carp was given Walter's part, playing the melody and soloing, while Paul, who never played chromatic, re-created Cotton's lonesome whistle effect. It was that sound that began the tune, and then Muddy shouted, "All aboard!" and made the hissing sound of air escaping from the engine's brake cylinders. Over Sam Lay's rolling beat, Muddy sang the lyrics with gusto, faithfully re-creating the sound and feel of the original recording. There was one unmistakable difference, though—the guitar part was missing. In the 1956 version of "All Aboard," guitarist Jimmy Rogers had added a "chugga-chugga" effect to the rhythm. For the *Fathers and Sons* update, only the harmonicas, bass, and drums were used. Muddy simply sang, his red Telecaster still in its case, with Michael Bloomfield, his Les Paul cradled on his lap, impassively watching.

Two more songs were recorded that afternoon before the guitarist could be cajoled into joining the ensemble. The group did the tune that was originally released as the flipside to "All Aboard," Muddy Waters's "Forty Days and Forty Nights," and "Sugar Sweet," first done in 1955 with Big Walter Horton playing harmonica. Both remakes featured wailing solos from Butterfield, clearly inspired by the proceedings, and some solid rhythm guitar from Paul Asbell, but again nothing from Michael. When Bloomfield finally did plug in, Norman had him play slide on "Oh Yeah," an up-tempo shuffle Muddy recorded in 1954. The *Fathers and Sons* version of the song was taken at a slower pace, and Michael played fills and soloed in Waters's slide style, essentially taking the bluesman's place on guitar. But even in the solo spotlight, Bloomfield sounded like he was holding back.

When the session finally ended, everyone was more than satisfied with the results. It had been a productive afternoon, and Muddy was pleased that the new versions of his old hits seemed as good as or better than the originals. The musicians chatted with one another as they packed up, reminiscing about the old days at Chess and gossiping about the label's other blues stars. Michael Bloomfield, though, didn't linger. He was out the door and gone, guitar case in hand, before anyone noticed that he had left. When Norman realized Bloomfield was no longer there, he made a mental note to check on his friend. Something was definitely not right with the *Fathers and Sons* star guitarist.

Wanting to thoroughly document Chess Records' historic collaboration between the blues masters and their protégés, Dayron had asked his girlfriend, Jo McDermand, to photograph the sessions. McDermand had snapped pictures of the action throughout the afternoon, but now Norman had another task for her. He asked her to go after Michael and find out what was troubling him. "Jo was this beautiful Marilyn Monroe look-alike and a good friend of Michael's," said Dayron. "If anybody could find out what was bugging him, I knew she could."

Jo immediately called Ida Bloomfield. Was Michael there? No, came the answer, because he had just left for the airport. Mrs. Bloomfield said her grandson was on his way to O'Hare to catch a flight home to San Francisco. McDermand quickly hailed a cab and headed to the world's busiest airport.

"She got there just as he was heading to the gate," Norman recalled.

> It was really crazy—there he was, all set to cut out on *Fathers and Sons*, the project that had originally been his idea and something he had wanted to do. So Jo just grabbed him and dragged him back to the city. She could be very persuasive when she wanted to be, and the next day he was back in the studio.

The means McDermand used to abort the volatile guitarist's decision to leave is up for speculation, but it was clear that Bloomfield felt uncomfortable standing in for his friend and mentor. Acting as Muddy's substitute may have skirted too close to the charges leveled by Ralph J. Gleason a year earlier—here was Bloomfield trying to be a "spade" once again. There was also the fact that Paul Butterfield had asserted himself musically right from the session's start, playing with real finesse and dominating many of the performances. Michael had grown unaccustomed to working with another strong soloist, and that may have sapped his enthusiasm for the project. But it's likely, too, that his attempted escape was partially motivated by the same demons that caused him to flee the first *Super Session* date. Fear, insecurity, anxiety—these coupled with the guitarist's "psychological addiction," his need to self-medicate and the possibility that he might not be able to do so, triggered panic and caused an overwhelming desire for security and the safety of home.

Those concerns seemed to recede over the remaining two days of recording. Jo McDermand's efforts succeeded in restoring Bloomfield's self-confidence to a level that allowed him to contribute more than mere accompaniment as Muddy redid many more of his hits from the 1950s. Waters himself played keening lead slide on "Mean Disposition," a song he had done for Aristocrat in 1948, and on "Country Boy," one of his earliest recordings issued on Chess. But all the other guitar solos fell to Michael, and while his playing was respectful, there were more than a few moments of the Bloomfield fire. "You Can't Lose What You Ain't Never Had" and "Walkin' thru the Park" both featured strong solos from the guitarist, and on "I'm Ready," a Waters song that had reached number four on *Billboard*'s R&B chart in 1954, Butterfield even shouted his approval as

Michael soloed intensely in the final choruses. For "Blow Wind Blow," a 1953 Waters composition, Paul and Michael split a solo chorus, re-creating the excitement of the first Butterfield Band, and the guitarist subtly backed Muddy's vocal with tasteful fills on 1963's "Twenty-Four Hours." On Willie Dixon's "I Love the Life I Live," Butterfield took the solo, but Michael again backed Muddy's singing, this time using extravagant string bends and vocal-like vibrato.

By the time the *Fathers and Sons* sessions had wrapped, the musicians had also recorded "Trouble No More," "Sad Letter Blues," and "I Feel So Good," all tunes from the 1950s. In a departure from Muddy's usual hard Chicago blues material, the group also did a re-creation of a gospel-style song the singer had recorded in 1962, backed by a female quartet of sanctified singers. Dayron had come across the obscure recording, called "I Wanna Go Home," in the Chess vaults and thought it would be a treat to have Waters do an updated version. He brought in one of the label's gospel groups—probably the Meditation Singers—to sing backup and had a Chess studio reeds player provide the tune's saxophone solo. Michael added subtle fills and rhythmic embellishments, but for the most part, he and Butterfield remained in the background. Then Norman suggested that Muddy do a second take without the sax, giving Bloomfield the solo spot. "There were two takes—one with the sax and one with Michael," Dayron said. "Michael did this *amazing* solo." By 1969 gospel music had become one of the guitarist's favorite genres, and his enthusiasm for it—and for Muddy's willingness to take on the style—clearly showed in his playing.

The Fathers and Sons concert was scheduled for Thursday, April 24. Despite receiving only minimal publicity, the Cosmic Joy-Scout Super-Jam concert had sold 2,600 tickets, nearly filling the house, and there was much buzz about the reunion of Butterfield and Bloomfield as well as their collaboration with Muddy Waters. Other enticements announced on flyers posted around town included a guest appearance by Buddy Miles and the addition of harp player James Cotton. Norman Dayron, the show's coordinator, had enlisted the services of Nick Gravenites, and Nick, who was working with the reorganized Quicksilver Messenger Service, booked them for the show too. To open the evening's program, Gravenites had his friend Ron Polte bring in the Ace of Cups, the all-female group that Polte was managing. The women were good friends with Michael, and Nick thought their band would benefit from the exposure. It would be an eclectic show, but undoubtedly an exciting one.

By 8:00 p.m., the huge theater was filled, with paid admissions crowding the orchestra, ground floor, and first balcony seats while several hundred additional guests packed into the upper balconies. The crowd was restive and loud, clearly ready for a good time and expecting nothing less. Soon the house lights dimmed and into the spotlight at center stage stepped the Phoenix Fellowship's founder, JoAnna Guthrie Smith. Smith, originally a member of the quasi-religious Theosophical Society, had formed the fellowship to "create new approaches to ethics, religion, philosophy, art and science." She explained at length to the increasingly bewildered audience that the fellowship was on a mission to reconnect mankind with the "Creator" and that a new age would soon be dawning. What that had to do with Chicago blues was unclear, and fans in the packed theater soon let it be known with catcalls and general restlessness that they would rather hear some music.

The curtain finally went up, and there stood the Ace of Cups. A five-woman psychedelic band from San Francisco, the Aces had been the first group to rent rehearsal space at the Heliport, and their house in Mill Valley had provided an early practice space for Bloomfield's newly formed Electric Flag. Since that time they had earned a reputation as a competent rock band that often featured vocals rendered in five-part harmony. What generally set them apart was their gender—they were the Bay Area's only all-female group. What set them apart on the auditorium stage that evening was their music. The audience was expecting muscular Chicago blues, and the Aces' brand of San Francisco hippie folk-rock was anything but that. The quintet completed only four tunes before catcalls drove them from the stage.

The Ace of Cups were followed by Nick Gravenites fronting the Quicksilver Messenger Service. With him were guitarist John Cipollina, bassist David Freiberg, and drummer Greg Elmore. The trio had been working with Gravenites on his forthcoming album for Columbia, and Nick sang a number of tunes he had written for the LP. The singer also played guitar and took a few convincing solos, and Quicksilver ran through a few of their standard numbers. The set went over well, and an inspired "Who Do You Love?" brought rousing cheers from the audience. Then it was time for the main event.

Starting the blues portion of the show were Paul Butterfield, Mike Bloomfield, Duck Dunn, and Buddy Miles. The quartet was augmented by keyboardist Ira Kamin, in Chicago to perform at the benefit at Michael's request. Kamin took his place behind the Hammond B3, and then Bloomfield, after taking a moment to tune, counted off "Young Girl Blues." The slow blues, by now a staple in Michael's repertory, featured his quavering, strained vocal, which for many of his listeners was an acquired taste. But when it came to his solo, the restrained guitar player of the previous three days was nowhere in sight. Bloomfield contorted his way through three choruses of superb lead, building in intensity after each turnaround. This was what the fans in the voluminous theater had been waiting for.

Butterfield was next to be featured. He sang Ray Charles's dramatic minor blues "Losing Hand," soloing with the mic cupped to his harp for one chorus and then playing it acoustically, using only a vocal mic to amplify his improvisation. The crowd loved it, and Bloomfield, obviously inspired, made his Gibson sing for another two choruses. Then the two former bandmates traded licks in a call-and-response chorus that had the crowd on its feet. Butterfield sang the final verse and then ended the tune with an unaccompanied falsetto declamation that brought down the house.

Buddy Miles quickly kicked off another blues, this time an up-tempo shuffle that brought more fine solos from the two frontmen, and then the big drummer, resplendent in a flamboyant purple jumpsuit, shifted the beat to a boogaloo vamp and began to sing "Funky Broadway." After a few verses, Buddy switched from the tribute to his one-time employer to his collaboration with Mike Bloomfield and—with all the stops, cries, and feints from the Flag days—sang a thrilling version of "Texas." For once, Michael seemed energized by Miles's theatrics, and the two traded vocal and lead lines like a pair of entwined lovers. By now, the audience was delirious with excitement.

Suddenly Otis Spann and Sam Lay were onstage, and as Buddy Miles made for the wings, out strode the star of the show. Dressed in an iridescent sharkskin suit and dark turtleneck, the legendary Muddy Waters acknowledged the roar of shouts and cheers that greeted his entrance with a broad smile. Then he plugged in, turned to the mic, and reeled off the opening phrase of "Hoochie Coochie Man." The rest of the band, sparked by Sam Lay, joined in, and Muddy sang the first verse to his 1954 hit. The bluesman postured, shook his head, and stabbed the air with a finger as he sang Willie Dixon's lyrics with full braggadocio.

Waters next offered a languid version of "Long Distance Call," a tune he had first recorded for Chess back in 1951. At the song's conclusion, the singer indulged in a bit of melodrama he had added to the tune over the years he had performed it. After the final turnaround, the band stopped and Muddy continued alone, playing out a tawdry tale of infidelity repeatedly punctuated with the phrase "Another *muuuule*!" When he finally completed the sentence by singing, "Another mule . . . is kicking in your stall!" the theater rocked with cheers and applause.

The set continued with "Honey Bee" and Big Joe Williams's "Baby Please Don't Go," and then Muddy launched into his closer from 1957, "Got My Mojo Working." If the theater had been rocking before, now people stood in their seats and danced to the booming shuffle beat. It was Otis Spann who introduced the tune and Butterfield whose harmonica complemented Muddy's vocal, but on the refrain the entire theater joined in—"Got my mojo working!"

After a raging solo by Butterfield, Waters brought the tune to a close and then called Buddy Miles back onto the stage to join Sam Lay on drums. Spann again hammered out the introduction, and this time Waters stretched "Mojo" out, giving solos to both Butterfield and Bloomfield. The rocking beat, with two drummers pounding it out, became massive. The entire auditorium was moving and singing along as one. Waters himself was so energized that, following Michael's brief chorus, he cake-walked across the stage, creating near hysteria. When the tune finally ended and Muddy Waters had left the stage after several curtain calls, the applause continued for ten solid minutes. "Hey, Muddy Waters . . . and a lot of his old friends!" announced Nick Gravenites as the curtain descended.

The Fathers and Sons concert, though it wasn't billed under that rubric, was a huge success. Chess brought in San Francisco engineer Reice Hamel to tape the performances, and within a few weeks production of the *Fathers and Sons* album was under way. Daily Planet was hired to design its cover, and mid-August was targeted for a release date. The concert itself was reviewed favorably in *Rolling Stone* by Don DeMichael, who called Muddy's performance a "triumph" and said "it was indeed his night, his week. It's like will seldom come again." Norman Dayron and Marshall Chess were pleased with the entire week's efforts, and they had little doubt the resulting two-record set would be a huge commercial success.

It had all been Mike Bloomfield's idea, but he took little credit for it. Despite his earlier misgivings, the guitarist had warmed to the recording sessions and had even enjoyed the live concert. It had been a real pleasure to spend time with Muddy and to play with him. But Bloomfield had other things to think about. He had his own album to produce, with new songs to write and others to finish, and he had rehearsals and recording sessions to organize. Complicating the matter was his growing ambivalence toward the music industry and his role in it. The thought of going back into the studio left him feeling enervated and depressed.

Now that he was back in Mill Valley, Mike Bloomfield had another project to tackle before he could resume work on his next Columbia release. While in Chicago, Michael had gotten a call from a relative, Haskell Wexler, with an offer to create music for a film Haskell was directing. A highly regarded cinematographer by 1969, the forty-seven-year-old Wexler was Harold Bloomfield's cousin, the son of Sam Bloomfield's sister, Lottie. Wexler was completing work on his first feature-length movie, and he needed incidental music for several of its scenes. Tentatively titled *The Concrete Wilderness*, the film followed the experiences of a TV news cameraman and a young Appalachian boy living in the impoverished neighborhood of Uptown in Chicago. Haskell wanted music that reflected the various cultures he was portraying on the screen—traditional old timey tunes for the clips with rural whites, and blues and R&B for the scenes in the black ghetto on the city's South Side. He knew his cousin's son was a gifted guitarist, capable of playing in a variety of styles, and he also knew Michael had created film music before—for *The Trip* with the Electric Flag. He asked Bloomfield to provide him with a dozen original selections that were distinctive but unobtrusive enough to function as backgrounds for the action. Michael agreed, and when he returned to Marin County, he rented studio time at Coast Recorders on Bush Street in San Francisco and assembled a group of friends for several days of sessions. When 16 mm sample reels of the film arrived, the musicians got to work.

With his encyclopedic knowledge of classic folk and country styles, Michael created authentic-sounding reels and fiddle tunes, the kind of music he had played in his years as a "folkie" at the University of Chicago and at the Old Town School of Folk Music. He also improvised moody acoustic guitar interludes and even added a whistled melody to one of them. For several acoustic blues, he invited Paul Butterfield in to blow some unamplified harp, giving the music a convincing down-home feel. When the various selections were completed, they were nearly as diverse as those the Flag had recorded for *The Trip*. This time, though, Michael concentrated on more traditional sounds in an effort to complement Wexler's subject matter.

When the completed film was released in August, it was retitled *Medium Cool*, taking inspiration from the work of media theorist Marshall McLuhan, and its focus had shifted from the plight of the young boy and his mother to the power of images and the cameras that capture them. Dramatic footage of protests during the city's 1968 Democratic Convention was intertwined with the film's fictional narrative, giving the movie a documentary feel and drawing high praise from critics. The music for its opening sequence was provided by the Los Angeles rock group Love, and the Mothers of Invention contributed two songs that were heard during sequences filmed in Chicago's Electric Theater and at Grant Park. But Mike Bloomfield's incidental music was used subtly throughout the movie, and the guitarist's name was prominently featured in the opening and closing credits. He had enjoyed re-creating the sounds of traditional acoustic music for his cousin's film, and the experience would, in coming months, inspire him to begin recording classic pop, blues, and country tunes for his own amusement.

* * *

As April 1969 gave way to May, Michael Bloomfield knew he needed to begin recording material for his solo album. To help with the record's production, the guitarist enlisted two trusted friends. One was his bandmate and frequent collaborator Nick Gravenites. The other was another friend from Chicago, someone he had known since they were both students at New Trier High School in Winnetka.

"He asked his friend Nick the Greek and me to produce the album for Columbia," said Michael Melford, referring to Gravenites by his nickname. Melford had gone on to become a music producer and audio engineer for the advertising and movie industries, and over the years, whenever he needed a guitar player, Melford would use Bloomfield. "During the late '60s, I worked with Mike in studios in Chicago and in the Bay Area, recording music for film scores, and for radio and TV commercials. For Mike's album, Nick functioned as a sort of social director, trying to keep everybody calm, while I looked after the music and the business details."

Work on Michael Bloomfield's Columbia album officially began on Thursday, May 15, at Golden State Recorders on Harrison Street in San Francisco's Mission District. The studio had been opened in 1964 by veteran sound engineer Leo de Gar Kulka and was considered one of the better facilities in Northern California. So that he could commute from home to the sessions each day, Bloomfield managed to talk Columbia into making an exception to their usually iron-clad recording policy. "Ours was one of the first LPs CBS permitted to be recorded outside of Columbia's own studios in New York, Nashville, and Los Angeles. Although Leo and his assistant were first-rate recording engineers, the record company required us to have two union engineers present. They flew up from LA," said Michael Melford. "The engineers still had a strict union contract with the major labels in those days, and all they did was turn the tape recorder on and off. They also took the master tapes with them every night."

Melford came out from Chicago and stayed with Michael for the duration of the recording sessions, finding a spare bed wherever he could in the Carmelita Avenue house. The producer's first task was to help his guitarist friend select material for the record. Because the original plan to release a double album had been scuttled in favor of a single LP, Bloomfield had more tunes than he needed. Deciding which to include and which to shelve was a challenge. The more Melford heard those tunes that Bloomfield wanted to record, the more the producer began to have his doubts. "I felt the repertoire was not strong. We disagreed about what should go on the record. For example, he was determined to do one he had written called 'Assholes' that I knew was not going to win him any friends."

For the sessions, Michael used the rhythm section from the band he had assembled for his Fillmore West jam performances. Mark Naftalin, John Kahn, and Bob Jones provided the musical framework for most of the tunes Bloomfield and Melford ultimately agreed to record. Michael then added other musicians as he and John Kahn worked out arrangements, selecting from a pool of more than a dozen players, several of them close friends and frequent collaborators. Ira Kamin and Roy Ruby both played organ parts, while Denise Kaufman and other members of the Ace of Cups provided backup vocals. The Fillmore horn section—Noel Jewkes, Gerald Oshita, and John Wilmeth—was reassembled and augmented by trumpeter Mark Doubleday and San Francisco saxophonists Mark Teel and Ron "Rev" Stallings. The coproducers themselves contributed, with Mike Melford playing mandolin on a few tunes and Nick Gravenites occasionally singing harmony. Newcomers included accordion player Richard Santi and pedal steel guitarist Orville "Red" Rhodes, an LA studio musician Bloomfield had first heard about from a member of Johnny Rivers's band at the Monterey Pop Festival.

All of the tunes Michael planned to record were originals, with one exception. Little Junior Parker's 1956 hit "Next Time You See Me" was an up-tempo shuffle blues with smart lyrics and several tricky stops. It was just the sort of tune Bloomfield might have done with the Electric Flag, and the arrangement, with a full horn section, was very much in the Flag style. Michael sang its lyrics with gusto and soloed for two choruses with his usual brio, clearly having a good time. A rollicking, kick-in-the-pants twelve-bar, "Next Time You See Me" was exactly what Michael Bloomfield fans were expecting to hear on an album by the blues-rock superstar.

But what they got was largely something else. Of the twelve tunes Bloomfield recorded for the record, only five were blues. The others ranged in style from gospel to ragtime to country—especially country—and only a few featured his vaunted lead playing. None ventured into experimental territory, and none could be construed as "jams." But each song—they were all, with one exception, songs—featured Michael Bloomfield's singing. Lots of it.

"Why did Mike do so many vocals on his own weak compositions? Because he had something he felt he had to say. It never occurred to him that it might be painful for listeners," explained Michael Melford.

Michael Bloomfield did indeed have something to say. Since forming the Electric Flag two years earlier, touring the country as a leader, seeing his celebrity rise to superstar status, and scoring a hit record while being ranked among the world's top pop guitarists, he had achieved what originally had been only an adolescent fantasy. He really *was* that lanky, luxuriously coiffed rock 'n' roll outlaw he had always imagined himself to be. He had an international reputation, thousands of fans, scores of groupies, an entourage—all the trappings of rock stardom. But in those two years, he had also learned a lot about himself. He learned that he didn't really like being in the spotlight, having to meet expectations night after night, and that he hated traveling and managing others while being managed himself. He had learned, too, that the music industry was a business like any other, that it thrived on money, novelty, and hype and seemed not the least bit interested in music, only in music product. Most of all, Michael Bloomfield hated being treated like a product.

But the guitarist's core concerns went even deeper. Emotionally, Bloomfield was exhausted, spent. The failure of his marriage, the dissolution of his brass-rock band, the anxiety caused by *Super Session*, his on-again, off-again struggles with drugs—all these had pushed the guitarist to the brink. He felt profoundly depressed, desperately lonely, deeply misunderstood, and wracked by insecurities. Even the distractions of his busy household provided only temporary relief. Michael wanted to tell his troubles to the world. He wanted to explain himself fully through his music. He had originally intended his solo album to be a tribute to those artists who had inspired him and to the varieties of music he loved, a record created "with a little help from my friends." But now, as his anxieties and unhappiness grew, he decided he would use the record to bare his soul to all who would listen and thus purge himself of his demons. That those listeners might fail to understand seemed not to have occurred to Michael.

"Michael's Lament," the song that Bloomfield sang during his impromptu recording session with Norman Dayron at Chess's studios in April, was one of the originals he recorded at Golden State. He gave it a gospel treatment, using Ira Kamin's organ to set a sanctified mood while the Ace of Cups evoked a church choir on the choruses. The lyrics spoke of Michael's loneliness, adding a hint of paranoia with the refrain, "And it seemed like it had to be planned." The song was unsettling, but its dour mood was mild compared to some of the others Bloomfield chose to record.

"Far Too Many Nights," a slow blues of the sort Bloomfield loved to play, featured two choruses of fat lead fired off with the guitarist's usual bravado. He was ably supported by Naftalin's piano and Kamin's organ, and the horn section seeded his choruses with energizing riffs. But the words Michael sang belied the music's swagger. With lyrics similar to those a depressed Michael Bloomfield improvised to create "No Rest Blues" for Norman at the April session, "Far

Too Many Nights" laid out the guitarist's struggle with insomnia—and then ominously suggested its possible resolution.

> You know it's far too many nights and I have not got no rest
> You know if it was all over tomorrow, whoa, maybe that would be
> the best.

Loneliness again was the impetus behind "The Ones I Loved Are Gone." A soulful ballad with swelling horns and an angelic chorus, the song showcased Michael's singing at its rawest as he shouted, moaned, and even howled his way through the lyrics. Again, it was obvious the singer was in distress. "People die and life goes on," Michael intoned. "Some will live, while some are gone. Oh, I'm so all alone and the ones I love are gone." The pain Michael still felt over the loss of Susan was overwhelming, judging by the song's words. It was almost as though he were mourning her death. That, coupled with the departure of his "best friend," left the singer feeling totally abandoned in a world where change, and especially mortal change, was a constant. All that remained, Bloomfield's only consolation for his suffering, were the memories his loved ones had left him. For a three-minute pop tune, this was high drama of a very personal nature.

But perhaps the most disturbing of the guitarist's compositions was one that would eventually provide a new title for the album. "It's Not Killing Me," a slow, sweet-sounding country-style ballad, comprised three verses and a refrain, all sung by Michael alone, with no solos. Over sympathetic accompaniment by the rhythm section, this time without horns, the guitarist told the story of his emotional life. In the other songs, Bloomfield focused on single issues that troubled him—his loneliness, his insomnia. But with "It's Not Killing Me," he seemed to suggest those problems were only part of a life that had been irreparably damaged and had now run its course. To Michael's friends, he was "a mess," a condition resulting from the fact that "something must be wrong in your life." That life, the life of a rock star, had played itself out—"it's all done"—and Bloomfield wasn't even sure it had been worth it—"was it fun?" In the final verse, he complained of nagging self-doubt and a kind of emotional paralysis. As he sang "It's Not Killing Me," it sounded like Mike Bloomfield was giving up. His life, while not lethal, was nothing but continual pain.

> Oh, I sit and twitch, Lord, I itch and bitch
> Over some small mental mistake
> I don't know whether it's fine or if it's not
> Well, I'm starting to rot
> It's not killing me, but it sure is hard to take.

It wasn't all doom and gloom, though. There were other less dire songs that Michael had the ensemble record. One was a wistful narrative about an elusive elder, a visionary savant who spoke little but imparted weighty truths when he did engage. Called "Good Old Guy," the old-timey country tune told a story that seemed inspired in part by the Beatles' "The Fool on the Hill" and by Bob Dylan's surreal talking blues. Bloomfield arranged the tune in an unusual manner, starting his vocal accompanied only by his acoustic guitar and Roy Ruby's organ. With each ensuing verse, another instrument was added, building to a wall of sound as bass, drums, piano, electric guitar, mandolin, banjo, and accordion each joined the evolving ensemble. The song's "good old guy," as characterized by Michael, was a wise, insightful, and kindly sage, a mystical father-like figure who was nothing like the taciturn, judgmental Harold Bloomfield. The old guy doubtless embodied traits Bloomfield would have wanted in his own father. But this idealized paternal character in the end seemed to be more a reflection of the singer, saying that he, like Michael, was also unsure of himself. In the final verse, years had passed and the singer had moved on, but the old guy "had not changed." The song concluded with Bloomfield's observation that it was "all so strange," returning his mood to one of doubt and uncertainty.

Also recorded was Michael's country-and-western original "For Anyone You Meet," the tune the guitarist had debuted during the Super Session shows at the Fillmore East. The operatic tale was given a conventional Nashville-style treatment, with Bloomfield re-creating his twangy, pedal steel-style fills on his Les Paul while Michael Melford added high harmony on the vocal refrain.

One of the last tunes Bloomfield recorded was starkly different from all the others—and from nearly every other pop tune, past or present. Its mood was an abrupt departure from the anxiety and pain that drove many of the guitarist's other compositions. It instead expressed the anger and frustration Mike Bloomfield had lately felt toward anyone who antagonized him, criticized him, or tried to tell him what to do. It was a not-so-subtle rant against those who made his life more difficult than it already was, and it was almost certainly aimed at music industry managers and agents, critics, and promoters. It was the tune that Michael Melford had tried to dissuade the guitarist from recording, the one Bloomfield called "Assholes." On Monday, May 19, Michael went ahead and recorded it anyway.

With its hard-driving rock beat augmented by the guitarist's tart lead fills, "Assholes" was a marked departure from the moderate tempos and easy sonorities of much of Michael's other material. The guitarist sang the lyrics with an aggressive swagger, making it clear he knew he was pushing limits and thoroughly enjoying doing so. Here was Bloomfield the prankster, the adolescent rebel thumbing his nose at the establishment. Michael certainly knew the obscenity he used for the song's title and that word's repeated use in the lyrics would prevent Columbia from releasing "Assholes." But he didn't care. He was going to tell everybody off, regardless of the consequences.

Assholes are all the people I don't like
You know, those assholes are everyone who puts me uptight
Don't tell me what I should do—I'm me, you're you.
Assholes are all the people I don't like
Assholes are everyone who puts me down
Assholes, I don't want 'em comin' around, no, no, no.
If they think I like 'em, then they're out of luck
You know—they suck!

Having plainly stated his case, Michael then shouted insults at the offenders, trading epithets in rapid-fire fashion with Roy Ruby over a staccato vamp provided by the rhythm section.

Butt kissin'!
Pool pissin'!
Ass kickin'!
Nose pickin'!
Crap writers!
Uptighters!
Back biters!
Incense lighters!
Bum trippers!
Odd hippers!
Ego rippers!
Art drippers!
Stall cleanin'!
Back teasin'!
Old geezers!
Young greasers!
Bad mothers!
Bad brothers!
Loose lovers!
Any others!
Whaaaaah!

As if the message weren't clear enough, Bloomfield drove his disdain home with one last obscenity. This time, though, it wasn't garden-variety profanity. It was one of the most offensive phrases in the English language, certainly in 1969.

> Assholes can be your mama herself, yes she can
> You know, assholes can be anybody else
> If you ask me 'bout you, I will tell you true
> Don't think you're green when you smell like blue
> Assholes, you can dig it—FUCK YOU!

The song then ended with a quick I–V–I turnaround and a hard stop, tagged with a surreal shout from Michael, a kind of harsh bark delivered with echo chamber–like reverberation. With its "dozens" ethos, unapologetic use of taboo language, and aggressive attitude, "Assholes" easily ranked as one of the most unusual pop songs of the 1960s. Had it been released as part of Mike Bloomfield's solo album, it would certainly have made history of a sort as one of the first instances—if not *the* first—of direct profanity used on a major label record release. It would also have made it clear that Michael Bloomfield, rock superstar and American guitar icon, wasn't going to take it anymore.

But Bloomfield wasn't done with all of his antagonists, not just yet. He decided he would record a sixty-second tag to "Assholes" that would serve to close out the album with a personal message. He created a background by soloing on guitar over a bluesy, two-chord shuffle played by organ, piano, bass, and drums, and then he overdubbed himself speaking directly to his listeners.

> This is the, uh, this is the fade-out of my record fadin' in. Soon it will fade out for good, and I hope that all of you who have spent your money for this record have enjoyed it. Now, it's time to say a few words about a friend of mine. I wanna say thank you to good, sweet ol' Ralph, every musician's friend, and give my regards to Tricky Dick. I want y'all to remember that whatever you may be, you're you and I'm me. Later . . . so long . . . after a while . . .

Still smarting from Ralph J. Gleason's *Rolling Stone* "shuck" column from a year earlier, Bloomfield couldn't resist taking a poke at the critic and lumping him in with Richard Nixon, who had just completed the first one hundred days of his presidency. Knowing Nixon was deeply unpopular with the counterculture movement, associating Gleason with "Tricky Dick" made clear Michael's true feelings about "every musician's friend." And then, to underscore his independence, Bloomfield restated the "I'm me" line from "Assholes." The short farewell, delivered with the guitarist's usual candor and affability, provided a kind of folksy benediction to what would undoubtedly be, when the album was completed, an unsettling listening experience for many of his fans.

"Mike was deeply depressed at the time," said Michael Melford. "He was making a half-hearted attempt to quit using heroin, and he had a lot of demons. This must be apparent to anyone who listens to the album." Bloomfield's songs portrayed the guitarist as a pained and tortured soul, but they also showed him to be in command and confident when he played the blues and, in the case of "Assholes," assertive to the point of outright aggression. It was a contrast in personality traits that lay at the heart of Michael Bloomfield's psychological makeup, a disconnect that his brother Allen described as evidence of bipolar disorder. His swings between emotional highs and lows, between mania and depression, had become acute by the late spring of 1969. His desire for relief found expression in the material he was recording for his record, but it also expressed itself in an increasing impulsiveness that could make him unpredictable. Michael Melford did his best to keep his friend focused and on track.

"A friend of mine, John Jordan—we called him 'Crash'—served as Michael's driver during the recording sessions," explained Melford. "He picked Mike up at his house in the morning and took him to his psychiatrist in the city." Bloomfield had started seeing a therapist in an effort to sort out his emotional issues. "From there, John brought him straight to the studio. After work, he drove him home. The idea was to keep Mike away from his drug connections. Even so, he managed to get off a couple of times."

With Nick Gravenites keeping the peace in the studio and making sure everyone was where he was supposed to be, and with Melford helping Bloomfield organize sessions and paying the bills with advances from ABGM, the recording dates at Golden State were completed by the third week of May. But the more he listened to the unmixed tapes, the more the guitarist felt dissatisfied with the results. Consequently, Bloomfield spent Tuesday, May 27, at Columbus Recording, another independent studio in San Francisco, creating new vocal tracks for eight of the eleven songs he had recorded earlier at Golden State. On the majority of those, he also reworked his guitar parts. But Michael Melford felt the guitarist's efforts did little to improve the performances. Bloomfield's singing continued to be a problem.

The first week in June, Melford flew to New York to mix and master his friend's completed session tapes. Bloomfield wasn't interested in wrangling with

Columbia over the material he wanted to include in his album, so he remained behind in Mill Valley, trusting Melford's editing skills and judgment. But anxiety over the process frequently got the better of him, and he repeatedly checked in with the producer.

"Michael would call every day to find out what was happening," said Melford. "He wanted to hear the rough mixes as soon as we finished them." Bloomfield also talked Al Kooper into acting as his advocate during the editing process. Kooper was back in New York, putting in regular hours as a staff producer for Columbia, and the guitarist knew he had influence with label's management. Michael thought Al could help him keep the label from cutting some of the record's more controversial material.

There was one tune even Kooper could not get reinstated. Columbia would not release "Assholes," even though Michael tried to convince the company's executives that they were hearing the lyrics incorrectly. "When people would say, 'You can't say "assholes,"' he'd say, 'I'm not saying "assholes," I'm saying "hassles,"'" Melford explained. The ruse fooled no one, and "Assholes" remained in the can.

With the masters finally approved, preparations were made to have Michael Bloomfield's first solo LP pressed at Columbia's Terre Haute plant in August. The process was routine, but the guitarist's obsession with the release had complicated its production unnecessarily. Michael Melford felt his friend's emotional state, as exemplified by the songs he had recorded and by his behavior during and after the sessions, had reached a crisis state. "His life was really falling apart at that point," he said. "He had a severe problem with drugs, he was going to a psychiatrist every day to try to keep himself together, and he was quite depressed—and, I think, paranoid. He thought various people were out to get him; if you listen to the lyrics of some of his songs, that's the gist of them." In Melford's assessment, Bloomfield was frustrated by his record company, angry at those critics who had been unsympathetic to his music, and feeling abandoned by those who loved him. But that wasn't all.

"He felt that his career was waning at that point," said the producer.

It's unlikely that Michael Bloomfield's career was actually on a downward slide in the spring of 1969. The first and second *Super Session* albums were still on the charts, the guitarist's own jam session LP and first solo record were about to be released, and he was still regarded by many fans and critics as America's greatest blues-rock guitarist. But Michael Melford was right about one thing—his friend was struggling with deep and persistent emotional problems that were largely rooted in his past but that had been exacerbated in recent months by drugs and the demands of his career. Whatever the cause, it was clear that Michael Bloomfield's life was undergoing a painful transition. He would survive, but it would not be pleasant. As he put it in his song, "It's not killing me, but it sure is hard to take."

For the week of June 15, Michael flew to New York to help Janis Joplin record her first solo album. Both Joplin and Albert Grossman wanted Bloomfield there to make sure her group, now called the Kozmic Blues Band, performed her material convincingly. Grossman was eager to follow up on the stunning success of *Cheap Thrills*, Joplin's breakout album with Big Brother and the Holding Company, but her performances with the Kozmic Blues Band had been getting mixed reviews ever since the group made its debut in Memphis. One critic had even suggested the singer should go back to Big Brother. With Bloomfield in the studio, Grossman reasoned, the musicians would have an experienced and sympathetic adviser who could, when needed, plug in and play the guitar parts himself. The canny manager also knew he would not have to pay for Bloomfield's services, since the guitarist was still working off his debt.

Michael worked with Joplin and the band through the week, striving to tighten arrangements while experimenting with a variety of rhythms and trying out different accompaniment combinations. On four of the tunes Joplin had selected for the album, Bloomfield did indeed contribute guitar parts. He played rhythm behind guitarist Sam Andrew on "To Love Somebody" and provided tasteful fills throughout "Maybe." "Work Me, Lord," a tune written for Janis by Nick Gravenites, featured a somber guitar interlude by Michael over a brass choir that he had probably arranged. On Joplin's slow blues "One Good Man," the guitarist couldn't resist asserting himself. He backed the singer's verses with ringing slide, soloed for one fiery chorus, and then took the tune out with an intense volley of bluesy licks. Janis was in excellent voice during the sessions, and the material the Kozmic Blues Band recorded, while quite different from the raw psychedelic rock of Big Brother, sounded tight and professional. Joplin's solo album would be a departure for the rock diva, a combination of rock, soul, and R&B with an added dash of blues, all done with horn accompaniment. Michael's influence was evident in much of the music, and Albert Grossman was doubtless satisfied with the results.

But Michael wasn't just playing A&R man for Joplin's recording date while in New York City. His personal problems came with him on the trip east, and hanging out with Janis after a day in the studio provided ample opportunity to get high. "He was having problems himself," said Sam Andrew of Bloomfield. "He and I and Janis were always going out to buy heroin. It was a real, real confused time." Despite his misgivings about his own drug use and his desire to quit heroin altogether, Michael found it hard to pass up the pleasurable relief the narcotic provided. Having two friends who were habitually fixing made the temptation to join them impossible to resist. His week in New York was productive in the studio, but it was often given over to intemperate excess after hours.

While he was working with Joplin at Columbia in New York, Michael listened again to the final mixes of the songs that were to be included on his own album. Hearing them anew caused him to again find fault with several of his vocals, including a few he had already rerecorded. Using his formidable powers of persuasion, the guitarist managed to talk the company's production department into delaying the pressing of the record so that he could redo the vocal parts yet again and have new mixes made. It would have to be done quickly, because the album was scheduled to be released in August.

Bloomfield was back in San Francisco by the end of June, and on Wednesday, July 3, he spent the afternoon with Leo Kulka at Golden State, redoing the vocal tracks on three of his songs. It took numerous takes until he was satisfied, but eventually the guitarist completed "The Ones I Loved Are Gone" and "For Anyone You Meet." He also reworked "Michael's Lament," which he had taken to calling "Portnoy's Lament" after reading the novel by Philip Roth that had been published in January. Michael was still insecure about his singing, but there was little else he could do. He was never going to sound like Ray Charles no matter how hard he tried, and the time allotted for revisions had more than run out.

One other thing Bloomfield did want to do was record a replacement for the vetoed "Assholes." His tag to the Electric Flag's album, the brief instrumental "Easy Rider," had won universal praise from reviewers and fans alike, so the guitarist decided he would do something similar for his solo LP. With Ira Kamin joining him on piano, Michael played a slow, easygoing eight-bar blues through a studio reverberation unit. The echo gave his Les Paul a mournful, bell-like tone, and with Kamin's gospel-tinged piano, the short piece took on a hymn quality. It seemed like a fitting way to conclude an album that, for the guitarist, was a raw and revealing emotional statement. In a moment of ironic humor, Michael gave the new instrumental the title "Goofers." The next day, the finished tapes were packed up and shipped to New York.

The summer months passed quickly. Michael Bloomfield spent July and much of August at home on Carmelita Avenue, doing little more than visiting with friends, watching TV, playing piano, and reading. He hardly touched his guitar, and he played no gigs. He was frequently awake through much of the night and asleep—when he could sleep—until early afternoon. The house had a constant parade of guests, musicians, fans, and assorted characters, many craving Bloomfield's attention. Some wanted help with a project, some wanted assistance with their careers, and some just wanted to meet the famous guitar player. Some arrived looking for drugs, while others came with drugs to share. It was, for most of the residents of 35 Carmelita Avenue, a pleasant, carefree existence. But for their host, the languid drift of days created a crippling inertia. Inactivity fed Michael's depression and exacerbated his anxieties about his career, his music, and even his health. Easy access to drugs only compounded the problem. In the weeks following his departure from the Electric Flag, Bloomfield had allowed himself to retreat into a similar haze of drugs and lethargy—it was the reason he had sought the solitude of rural Lagunitas. The change of scene had allowed him to clear his head and shake off his dependency on drugs. But now Michael seemed incapable of freeing himself from the numbing distractions of his Mill Valley home life. It was at this difficult moment that the guitarist's jam album was released by Columbia.

Given the literal title *Live at Bill Graham's Fillmore West*, the album was shipped on August 6 and promoted with a full-page ad in the August 23 edition of *Billboard*. The LP, though, was curiously low-key. Its cover featured a blurry montage of photos showing Bloomfield and his Sunburst flanked by Nick Gravenites and Taj Mahal. Because his image was dominant, it seemed that Columbia CS 9893 was Michael's album. But the legend on the cover listed all the participating musicians, with Bloomfield just one among those being "featured." There was no mention of the fact that the live sessions were intended to be jams, and there were no liner notes at all to explain what listeners were hearing. Unlike Kooper's annotated *Super Session* releases, *Live at Bill Graham's Fillmore West* simply presented the music without providing context or photos other than the front cover images. The grainy picture of the album's venue on the back cover gave record buyers the impression the LP was more about the Fillmore West and Bill Graham than about Michael Bloomfield and his music. The music, too, was an eclectic mix, a combination of blues and soul tunes featuring vocals by Taj Mahal, drummer Bob Jones, Nick Gravenites, and Michael himself. The one constant was Bloomfield's guitar, and his playing was as powerful and impressive as it had been during the two weeks of jam performances at the Fillmore. But the record gave no indication that the project was Michael's or that he was the reason for its release. Listeners could easily assume that Taj Mahal was intended to be the featured artist or that the album was just a collection of tunes put out by Columbia using artists who were signed to the label. And in Michael's case, that was largely what *Live at Bill Graham's Fillmore West* was.

Included in the release were Nick's "It's About Time" and "Blues on a Westside," and his version of Otis Rush's "It Takes Time." Michael sang "Oh Mama," and Bob Jones did "Love Got Me." Taj performed "One More Mile," the LP's longest selection, and "Carmelita Skiffle," Bloomfield's blues instrumental, concluded the album. While the horn players were occasionally adrift, the performances were generally very good, and Bloomfield's soloing easily equaled his work on Super Session's *Live Adventures*. Michael's dedicated fans were doubtless happy with their purchase.

But other record buyers likely found *Live at Bill Graham's Fillmore West* to be something of a hodgepodge with no clear objective beyond promoting music one might hear on any typical Saturday night in a San Francisco ballroom. Nothing remarkable, just some blues and other stuff. Take it or leave it. Many listeners did leave it.

The critics, too, were indifferent. One of the very few reviews the album received came months after its release in the November 15 edition of *Rolling Stone*. "The band is ragged, the singing is bad, Bloomfield's guitar is frequently out of tune," wrote the reviewer. Though those harsh judgments were inaccurate and unwarranted, the observation that *Live at Bill Graham's Fillmore West* was "more of the same" was a fair assessment. Album buyers had already heard Bloomfield live at the Fillmore—with Al Kooper on *Live Adventures*. The new album seemed like little more than a less-successful rehash.

In that same review was an evaluation of Nick Gravenites's debut album, *My Labors*. Gravenites had struck a deal with Columbia to use some of the material performed during Bloomfield's Fillmore jam sessions for his own LP. Consequently, five of the eight selections on *My Labors* were tunes Nick had sung with Michael at the Fillmore. Each featured lengthy and powerful solos from the guitarist, solos that were even stronger than many of those on *Live at Bill Graham's Fillmore West*, with some exceeding Bloomfield's best work on *Live Adventures*. *Rolling Stone*'s reviewer begrudgingly acknowledged as much, describing "Moon Tune," one of the selections from the Fillmore, as "Gravenites at his best." But the critic also complained that the "subtleties of [Gravenites's] phrasing often get smothered in the horns and clatter of Bloomfield's arrangements." In the end, the writer dismissed both releases as "embarrassing." "They are *so* bad," he wrote. "The music is flat, unimaginative and badly played."

Michael Bloomfield didn't much care what people thought about *Live at Bill Graham's Fillmore West*. The release had accomplished its purpose, which for the guitarist was fulfilling one of his album commitments under his Columbia contract. It was his solo album that Michael was anticipating. Though its original release date had been August 26, the last-minute reworking of several vocals had again delayed its delivery.

It wasn't until mid-September that Columbia finally shipped Michael Bloomfield's first solo record, called *It's Not Killing Me* after the song that concluded side one. The company promoted the album with a half-page ad that read, "Michael Bloomfield: lead guitar, vocals, piano, acoustic guitar, words, music. No other album can make that statement," running it in *Rolling Stone*, a few other underground newspapers, and *Billboard* magazine. The promo's claim was driven home by images of Bloomfield playing guitar, fingering piano keys, and singing. But the only indication of the record's title was in a small photo of its cover. It was almost as though the executives in Columbia's promotion department were uncomfortable mentioning it.

Whatever misgivings Michael may have had about *It's Not Killing Me*, he was determined to celebrate its debut. One warm September night, the blues-rock superstar invited friends over to Carmelita Avenue for a record-release bash. "Michael had a big party for the album when it first came out," said Toby Byron, Michael's teenaged neighbor and fan. "He was being real effusive, praising it and saying how much he loved it." The guitarist's behavior struck Byron as unusual enough that he suspected Michael was on drugs. "I never really saw or knew Michael to be using heroin," Toby said. "But that night he definitely seemed high to me." In all likelihood, the party's host was feeling no pain. Michael may have simply wanted to indulge because he was in a celebratory mood. But he may also have been feeling insecure about the reception the intensely personal *It's Not Killing Me* would likely receive. A shot of dope would take care of his anxiety—for the duration of the party, anyway.

But Michael probably knew the album's reception would not be good. There weren't many reviews in the weeks following its release, and those that did appear were largely negative. The critique that ran in *Rolling Stone* was perhaps the most damning. In the same November review that had taken *Live at Bill Graham's Fillmore West* and *My Labors* to task, a few paragraphs summed up *It's Not Killing Me*. If the first two records had come in for harsh treatment, the guitarist's solo album fared even worse. The review called Bloomfield's LP a "specimen of boring exhibitionism." It described Michael's playing as "a caricature of itself; it sounds stale, full of instrumental mannerisms and little else." Homing in on the guitarist's greatest weakness, the reviewer said, "Bloomfield's singing should never have been released—he has a terrible voice." Curiously, he accused the material of being "largely empty of the emotion it pretends," saying that most of the songs "are built from musical clichés—and sound it."

But not all the critics were unsympathetic. One reviewer heralded Bloomfield's arrival as a solo performer, calling him "probably the most talented blues guitarist alive." Describing the record as "country-rock," the writer noted that while it "does not approach Bloomfield's best," the LP was the guitarist's "most relaxed album to date." Unlike his *Rolling Stone* counterpart, the reviewer picked up on Bloomfield's mood right away. "The songs are simple and sad," he wrote. "They deliver the thoughts and feelings of lost love and confused depression." But, he concluded, country music was not really a fit for the guitarist; he should stick with the music of his earlier experience. "Almost as much as the great Negro performers of the city sound, Bloomfield is the blues," the reviewer asserted.

"When the record started out, it had pretty good initial sales," said Michael Melford. The producer followed *It's Not Killing Me* after its release, curious to see how it would perform in the market and whether his friend's introspective, painful compositions would find an audience. "Then it tailed off quickly. There was nothing on there that could get played as a single, and Michael was not in any kind of shape to go out and tour in support of the release of the album. It didn't do that great." Bloomfield's solo debut never made it onto *Billboard*'s charts, and the guitarist did nothing to promote it. The songs he had written for the album, songs that he had labored over for months, crafting them to be deeply personal and meaningful, were never performed in public. In later years, Michael even seemed embarrassed by them, describing the record as "pretty bad." "Columbia was nice enough to release it," Bloomfield said, essentially apologizing for *It's Not Killing Me*. The label soon realized that the record was a commercial flop and discontinued it within a year of its release. In 1971 the album was reissued on the label's budget imprint, Harmony, in an effort to recoup the company's initial investment. Michael Bloomfield, in record industry parlance, had become a "stiff."

There was, however, one fall release featuring Mike Bloomfield that was an unqualified success. Chess Records issued its *Fathers and Sons* twofer during the first week of September to nearly universal critical acclaim. *Billboard* touted the album as sure to "thrill blues buffs," saying "Muddy's style is as dramatic as ever." *Rolling Stone* praised it, and reviewers in both the underground and mainstream press offered positive assessments. One syndicated writer described *Fathers and Sons* as a "dream set for blues fans," concluding that the album was "an authentic masterpiece." Though his name was prominently featured on the cover, Michael's contribution was largely in the background. Few of the released tunes featured solos by the guitarist; of the "sons," it was Paul Butterfield who dominated.

Still, in the fall of 1969, it seemed to many Michael Bloomfield fans that the guitarist was everywhere. He was the leader or a prominent sideman on four major record releases in the span of six weeks, and *Super Session*, both the studio and live editions, could regularly be heard on FM radio across the country. He toured with Al Kooper, produced Janis Joplin, and had given important concerts at the Fillmores on both coasts. The guitarist seemed to be more active than ever, both in the studio and out, and his playing, when it was featured, had achieved a level of maturity that ranked him as one of the true masters of American blues. The pop music world waited to see what Michael Bloomfield would do next.

It would be a long wait.

CHAPTER 22

STONED LEISURE

MILL VALLEY, 1969–1972

In the fall of 1969, Nick Gravenites found a small corner bar on Vallejo Street in the North Beach section of San Francisco that he thought had potential. Its owner, Freddy Herrera, occasionally presented music, but more often he featured topless dancers, hoping to attract customers. Nick liked the joint's seedy atmosphere and its Bohemian location, and he thought it would make a great place to play. He approached Herrera and offered to bring in a band for a few weekends to see what would happen. The venue, named Keystone Korner, reminded him of Big John's in Old Town.

"Michael told me he hated the Fillmore audiences," Gravenites said. "They just wanted bands to get it on—you know, 'rock out.' But Michael really wanted to play in a small bar like in Chicago. So I found Freddy's place, and we started playing there."

Beginning on Friday, September 19, Michael Bloomfield and Nick Gravenites began a three-day trial run at the Keystone, performing with a band that included Mark Naftalin, John Kahn, and Bob Jones. The gig, promoted only with flyers and by word of mouth, quickly filled the little bar with thirsty, music-loving patrons, and Herrera and Gravenites agreed to make the arrangement permanent. The Bloomfield/Gravenites group would regularly appear, and Nick would bring in other San Francisco bands as well.

"Nick was really comfortable playing at the Keystone," said Bob Jones. "Michael, too. We would try stuff out, playing a kind of Stax/Volt thing. After a while it was always crowded, and it became a real scene."

As word spread about the new club in North Beach where Mike Bloomfield and his friends could be seen for a few dollars at the door and a couple of drinks, the Keystone Korner began to develop a hip following. For Bloomfield, it was like going home again. The parallels to Old Town and Big John's from earlier in the decade were striking. At the Keystone, he could play the music he loved for people who appreciated and understood it, and he could work with musicians who were his friends in an intimate setting just a short drive from home. No touring, no managers or promoters, no cavernous amphitheaters or boomy ballrooms. Best of all, no hype. Just the music, played for people who really listened to and appreciated it.

"You know, by 1970 in San Francisco, the vast majority of people were into the psychedelic rock thing. They'd go to hear bands that would drop acid and could barely play, noodling around for hours on a single tune," Bob Jones said. "But there was a select group of people who wanted to hear serious blues and R&B, that knew the music, and they would go to the Keystone. It was a *great* feeling to play for a crowd like that!"

Bloomfield, Gravenites, and the crew performed at the Keystone Korner through September and into October and November, eventually alternating weekends with the bands of Elvin Bishop, Charlie Musselwhite, and others, including Bob Jones's own group, Southern Comfort. On occasion, Buddy Miles would stop by, and then Michael would perform tunes from the Electric Flag days. Offstage, the burly drummer was just as much a performer as onstage. "I remember between sets Buddy and Mike would get into a contest," Jones said, laughing. "They'd try to outdo each other to see who could tell the biggest whopper."

Michael Bloomfield mostly enjoyed playing at the Keystone Korner, and at first he regularly joined Nick, Mark, John, and Bob whenever it was their weekend. He generally let Gravenites or Jones do the singing, but occasionally he would step up to the mic to perform reggae singer Desmond Dekker's "The Israelites" or "Dyin' Flu" by bluesman Albert Collins. But as the weeks passed, Bloomfield began not showing up for some of the nights the band was scheduled to perform. Sometimes he would skip the weekend altogether. Regular Keystone patrons quickly learned that an appearance by Mike Bloomfield was never a definite thing. The music would go on but often with another guitarist sitting in. Sometimes Michael would arrive late, walking in during the first set. He would greet a few friends at the bar, make the rounds of the tables, and then join the band onstage for the second set. Or he might leave without playing at all. It all depended on his mood.

Appearances at the Keystone Korner and occasional gigs with Nick at other venues in San Francisco and the surrounding area were all that occupied Michael Bloomfield's days as 1969 gave way to 1970. There were several additional recording sessions, too, but nothing of any consequence. Norman Dayron called him in December with an oddball project that he and Marshall Chess had cooked up in the wake of the success of *Switched-on Bach*, Columbia Records' album of classical pieces played entirely on Moog synthesizer. Chess wanted to do the same for blues, creating an album of synthesized boogie-woogie instrumentals. Dayron thought the idea was ridiculous and turned the project into a parody. He got Bloomfield into a studio in Berkeley and had him overdub solos on "Fireball Boogie" and "Angel's Dust Boogie." When the record was released in the spring, the guitarist was credited as "Fastfingers" Finkelstein.

Another recording date was a more serious endeavor. Michael Brewer and Tom Shipley were a folk singing duo from Los Angeles, and Nick Gravenites had been hired to produce their debut album for Kama Sutra Records. On several of the songs the pair recorded, Gravenites had the members of Southern Comfort and a few other musician friends back them. "Pigs Head," one of those tunes, featured Bloomfield playing some bluesy slide guitar.

Mostly, though, Michael Bloomfield stayed home. In the Carmelita house, his TV, books, and piano were his solace, and his room was his cave. The guitarist's emotional state and internal equilibrium were in constant flux. Drugs took the edge off his anxiety, but their palliative effect was only temporary, and repeated use simply exacerbated his troubles. Friends provided a distraction, but they were largely unaware of Bloomfield's inner turmoil. Even therapy failed to get at the root of the guitarist's malaise. The last two years of Michael's public life had exacted a heavy toll, and now, with the failure of his solo album—the album he had hoped would make a statement about his struggles as an artist, friend, and lover—he seemed to have lost interest in music altogether. The blues-rock superstar, the flamboyant, innovative guitarist who had set the standard for guitar players across the country and around the world, had gone to ground. He wanted no longer to be a rock star, and in time he would get his wish.

In the early fall of 1970, a California Highway Patrol officer pulled over a car that was being driven erratically on Route 101 near San Rafael in Marin County. When he had the driver step out of the vehicle for a sobriety test, the patrolman noticed there were fresh needle marks on one of the man's arms. After failing the test, the man produced his license, identifying himself as Michael B. Bloomfield of 35 Carmelita Avenue in Mill Valley.

It was Mike Bloomfield's first run-in with the authorities over drugs since his Electric Flag days. After being booked and charged, Bloomfield was released on $1,200 bail and ordered to return at a later date for an appearance in the county's Municipal Court on a charge of driving under the influence of narcotics. As it was his first offense and no drugs were found in the car, the famed guitarist would likely, with the help of a good lawyer, be let off with just a fine. But the episode was a clear indication that Bloomfield was still wrestling with one of his demons—heroin. It was a struggle he was not winning.

In the year since the release of *It's Not Killing Me*, Michael had worked sporadically, performing at Keystone Korner with Nick and occasionally appearing at other small clubs around San Francisco. There were several gigs at the Fillmore and one long weekend in Honolulu with John Lee Hooker, the Elvin Bishop Band, and guitarist Boz Scaggs's group. But Bloomfield had no plans to put a permanent band together, no desire to make another record, and definitely no interest in taking his music on the road. Manager Albert Grossman found his client's reticence perplexing, and he repeatedly urged Michael to come out of hibernation. If the guitarist would only agree to work more and would use the Electric Flag name—which Grossman owned—the manager could get more money for the band and find them better gigs. But the last thing Bloomfield wanted was a return of the Flag with all the hype that would entail, so he almost always declined Grossman's requests. He played as few shows as possible and stayed home. What lay ahead, he couldn't say.

In the summer of 1970, *Rolling Stone* had reported as much. "Mike Bloomfield Just Doesn't Know" read the headline to a blurb that ran in the August 6 edition of the pop culture publication. In it, Bloomfield was quoted as saying, "I just can't do it. The whole commercial music scene really has me down. I don't see any gigs worth playing." What Michael *was* doing, he said, was making "multiple track recordings" on his own equipment at home, recordings that were "great stuff." But, he added, his home recordings couldn't be released by Columbia, his record label, because of the company's insistence on using its own union engineers. The magazine also mentioned that Bloomfield's "old lady had a baby just last week," giving the impression that the guitarist had started a family, another reason for him to stay home. Though he wasn't interested in performing, Michael did express a desire to someday work with Ray Charles and, in a revelation that would have brought cheers from blues fans across the country, declared he would "love to play again with Paul Butterfield."

It sounded like the star guitar player was biding his time, enjoying family life while actively recording new material and weighing his career options. Though the article characterized him as uncertain about the future, it said Mike Bloomfield was still making music, still playing enough to keep his hands "in shape." It wouldn't be long before the public would hear from him again.

In truth, the situation was something quite different. The "multiple track" recordings Bloomfield was making were little more than amateur overdubs made in his bedroom on Carmelita Avenue. Michael created them using a big Teac 4-track reel-to-reel recorder, a machine Norman Dayron had gotten for him. Recording his vocal on one track while accompanying himself on guitar or piano, and then adding lead guitar improvisations on a second track, Bloomfield created numerous duets with himself playing traditional jazz and country tunes. While the recordings had a certain verve and were similar to the selections he had created for the film *Medium Cool*, their quality was such that Columbia would never have considered releasing them, regardless of their engineering restrictions.

Also, Bloomfield's domestic situation wasn't quite what the article made it seem. His "old lady" was actually his housemate Kathy Moore, an attractive young dancer who had moved into the Carmelita house in the fall of 1969. While she and the guitarist may have had a causal relationship, Moore's baby wasn't Michael's, and she and the child would soon head off to New York City to join her lover, filmmaker Danny Seymour. Bloomfield's "family life" was little more than a temporary communal arrangement.

Michael's existential quandary—"I just don't know"—was largely the product of his deep depression, a condition brought on in part by anxiety, sleeplessness, and drug use. He wasn't just sitting at home planning his next move. He was hunkered down on Carmelita Avenue, primarily because he *couldn't* move. Psychological inertia, coupled with a thorough disdain for the music industry, had succeeded in removing Bloomfield from the scene and taking him out of the public eye. Ironically, it may have been just those conditions that saved his life. Two famous musician friends weren't so lucky.

On Friday, September 18, Jimi Hendrix died in his sleep in a London apartment. A little more than two weeks later, on Sunday, October 4, Janis Joplin died in a seedy motel room in Hollywood. Both succumbed to drug overdoses, Hendrix from barbiturates, Joplin from heroin. Both were international rock stars at the height of their fame, and both had enjoyed extraordinary success. What they hadn't been able to do was escape their own celebrity. The constant touring, the relentless demands of managers and record company executives, the pressure to meet or exceed fans' expectations—these had worn Jimi and Janis down, just as they had Michael. But unlike Bloomfield, Hendrix and Joplin had been unable to withdraw from the entertainment world's pernicious cycle. The creature comforts that often accompanied rock 'n' roll stardom—sex, drugs, and alcohol—were made even more prevalent by the pop stars' newfound wealth. In the end, their fame had overwhelmed them, killing both Hendrix and Joplin at age 27. Michael Bloomfield was also 27, a fact that did not escape his notice. It was just one more reason to stay home.

But staying home also had its drawbacks. It wasn't only Albert Grossman who was concerned about Mike Bloomfield's inactivity. Michael's mother, Dorothy Bloomfield, viewed her son's reluctance to perform with growing alarm. She was one of Michael's biggest fans, having created a huge scrapbook filled with clippings about her famous son. She followed his career as though it were her own, and when she learned he had been arrested for using narcotics, she felt she had to do something. One way she thought she might reach Michael was through someone her talented son deeply admired.

Mrs. Bloomfield decided she would go see B. B. King.

The master bluesman was doing a two-week stint in September at Mister Kelly's, an upscale Chicago nightclub at the intersection of State and Rush streets, and one night an attractive middle-aged woman approached him between sets. "I wrote a note, and I said, 'Dear Mr. King, Would you mind if I come backstage? I must talk to you'—and I underlined 'must,'" said Dottie. She signed the note "Dorothy Bloomfield, Michael Bloomfield's mother" so there would be no misunderstanding. When she was brought back to B. B.'s dressing room, the former actress and beauty queen explained that she hoped the legendary guitarist could do something to rouse her son from his musical lethargy.

"I was in Chicago, and his mother came out and said, 'My son likes you. He idolizes you,'" remembered King. "She said, 'If you would talk to him, I'm sure that would help him out.' And I thanked her, and I did." B. B. took Michael's phone number, and when he had a moment, he made good on his promise. He called Michael and gave him a pep talk.

Mike Bloomfield was surprised—and not a little embarrassed—to get the call from his idol. It was one thing to run into B. B. backstage at the Fillmore and chat with him about blues and the music scene. But to have the legendary guitarist telephone expressly for the purpose of motivating Michael, of getting him out of his room and back onstage—that was almost too much. And then to have the call instigated by his *mother*! Bloomfield felt ashamed for allowing his talents to languish, and for putting B. B. King in the position of having to call him out on it. For the first time in months, Michael began to think about cleaning himself up and getting back to performing.

But though he was moved by the legendary bluesman's intercession on his behalf, he did little at first to alter his routine. He still played occasional gigs with his Friends collective, often sharing the billing with Nick Gravenites or Mark Naftalin and almost always appearing at clubs close to home. In December, Michael participated in a recording session for guitarist Jim Murray, a former member of Quicksilver Messenger Service, and on New Year's Eve, he joined saxophonist Eddie "Cleanhead" Vinson onstage at the Ash Grove in Los Angeles. As 1971 began, Michael contributed to several recording sessions as favors to other musician friends. In January, he played wah-wah guitar on two selections for keyboardist Merl Saunders, and then he added a rocking series of solos to a funk instrumental by his old colleague and Moog player Paul Beaver in February. There were also several appearances at the Swing Auditorium in San Bernardino and another weekend at the Keystone. But for the most part,

Michael continued to stay home in Mill Valley. The vast majority of his playing took place in the solitude of his room on Carmelita Avenue.

Whenever Mike Bloomfield felt the urge to play guitar or run the ivories on the piano in his room, he usually flipped on his Teac reel-to-reel. He put a blank reel of tape on the machine and recorded himself playing and singing whatever tunes came to mind in a sort of stream-of-consciousness medley of American popular music. He might start with Hank Williams's "A Tramp on the Street" and then follow that with "Release Me," a big hit for pop singer Engelbert Humperdinck, only to veer off into "Let's Go Get Stoned" by Ray Charles and then croon George Jones's "I Cried Myself Awake." His knowledge of lyrics was uncanny—he seemed to know not only all the chords to an extraordinary number of songs, old and new, but also all the words to all the verses. Once the reel on the machine was filled, he wound it back and added a second channel of electric guitar, playing lead behind his singing and filling in the piano accompaniment with additional chords and harmony.

These were the "multiple track" recordings Michael mentioned in the *Rolling Stone* article, and as the weeks and months went by, they began to pile up. By early 1971, there were dozens of them, stashed in boxes piled high on the piano and around the room. Their technical quality was uneven, with occasional distortions, dropouts, and volume problems, and Bloomfield frequently stopped and started whatever he was singing, jumping from one tune to another. But taken as a body of work, they displayed the guitarist's astonishing knowledge of popular music from all genres and from every era. What was also striking was that of the scores of songs Bloomfield recorded, there were only one or two repeats. He would sing a song and then move on to something else. Songs such as the spiritual "Steal Away to Jesus," country singer Jim Reeves's "Put Your Sweet Lips Closer to the Phone," Elvis's "Are You Lonesome Tonight," Patsy Cline's "Honky Tonk Merry Go Round," or Hoagy Carmichael's "Georgia on My Mind"—it seemed there wasn't a pop tune that Bloomfield didn't know. He would sing each one once, almost as though he were working his way through a bound anthology of America's favorite songs.

It was not surprising that many of Michael's home-recorded selections were country tunes. Country music's sentimental, often maudlin narratives seemed to suit his depressed mood. It would have amazed blues fans to learn that their favorite blues-rock guitarist was spending his private moments playing lachrymose weepers like Porter Wagoner's "Green, Green Grass of Home." But Bloomfield had always enjoyed pretty ballads, romantic airs, and frivolous show tunes. He loved the expository melodies of "Oklahoma" and other

Broadway musicals that he heard as a child in the Bloomfield household, and he had even played many of those songs for Harold Bloomfield in rare moments of father-son closeness. The sweet nostalgia they induced was a balm to the guitarist's soul, even as an adult. He was the leather-jacketed greaser, the rock 'n' roll rebel of his adolescent fantasies, to be sure, but he was also a tender-hearted, emotional man who felt deeply. It was just another instance that proved, as Michael's first manager and friend Joel Harlib put it, "whatever you could say about him, you know, you could also say the opposite about him."

In March, Bloomfield was interviewed at home on Carmelita Avenue by staff writer Michael Brooks for *Guitar Player*. A specialty publication that was launched in 1967, the magazine catered to players of the instrument with articles on technique, equipment, and musical styles as well as in-depth interviews with leading guitarists from every musical genre. Over the course of an afternoon, Michael talked freely with Brooks about his life in music and shared his thoughts on everything from instrument manufacturers to other guitarists he admired, past and present. He recounted his early days learning to play, his discovery of the blues and jamming on Chicago's South Side, his playing with Dylan and then with Butterfield, and his mixed feelings about the Electric Flag and his dates for Super Session. It was Bloomfield's first major interview since talking with Jann Wenner for *Rolling Stone*, and it was clear that Michael had matured in the intervening three years. He was much less assertive, more open and candid. The "street smart" Bloomfield of the *Rolling Stone* piece, quick to judge and prone to condemn, had been replaced by a more introspective and thoughtful musician. Michael, it seemed, no longer needed to impress his interlocutor.

As their conversation concluded, Brooks asked the guitarist about his plans for the future. Michael's answer came as a surprise, considering his ongoing reluctance to perform and his mixed feelings about the music industry. He revealed that he intended to record a new album for Columbia, one that would be his "best guitar playing record of all." It would be an LP of duets between himself and a close friend and frequent musical partner. "Mark Naftalin, the best piano player I know, will be making the album with me," said Bloomfield. "I'm going to make it with him and I hope there's going to be a 50/50 dialogue between us in musical interaction." It may have been B. B. King's phone call that caused Michael to eventually consider another foray into the studio, or it may have been the fact that Columbia had extended his contract for one more album. Whatever the reason, the guitarist and his pianist friend were intent on producing a record that would "incorporate all the early sounds that

I liked so much." "It will all make sense if we get it together right," Bloomfield declared. "But mostly I want it to be long periods of time, 20–30 minutes of meaty chunks of playing."

In the spring of 1970, Columbia Records, wishing to accommodate their San Francisco artists, decided to open a studio facility in the City by the Bay. That meant Mike Bloomfield would no longer have to haggle with the label over permission to record in San Francisco. He was pleased that his duets project could be taped close to home in an officially sanctioned facility, and on Monday, May 3, he and Mark Naftalin met at Columbia's new studios on Folsom Street for the first of what would be six separate recording dates.

Over the course of several three-hour sessions, they recorded a dozen tunes, of which eight were originals. Of those, three were blues improvised as warm-ups in the studio—"Jam in A," "Blues in C," and "Bouncing Boogie." They also did Willie Nelson's "Night Life," a jazzy rendition of "Sweet Georgia Brown," and the Big Maceo tune that had been a hit for B. B. King, "Worried Life Blues." Michael contributed an original called "Skies Are Blue," and Naftalin provided a piece appropriately titled "Mark's Tune." Both players collaborated on two instrumentals named "Fast in B" and "Drone," and then they wound up the session with a version of Big Joe Williams's "Baby Please Don't Go" and a feature for Mark on accordion aptly titled "Accordion Tune." It was an eclectic mix of material, and while none of the tunes recorded approached a half hour in length, there was plenty of soloing from both musicians and some fine interchanges between them. Michael Bloomfield seemed serious about fulfilling his promise that the forthcoming LP would be his "best guitar playing record of all."

The spring of 1971 also brought other changes for Michael. Not only was he back in the studio working on another record, but in late April he decided to move out of the house on Carmelita Avenue. Intent on making a fresh start with his music, he also thought a new living environment might help restore his emotional equilibrium. The lease on the Carmelita house was up in May, and Bloomfield chose not to renew. Instead, he asked his friend and one-time assistant Chris McDougal to help him locate a new place. Chris checked newspaper classifieds, visited a few realtors, and quickly came up with a suitable home available from Vail and Associates, a local realty company.

"I went to look at the house with Mrs. Vail first," said McDougal. "And then I took Mike over to see it, and that's when I noticed all the doors had handles made for people in wheelchairs—the place had been some kind of rest home for old folks!" Bloomfield was immediately taken with the modern, ranch-style house located up a steep, curving driveway on a wooded hill overlooking Miller

Avenue, one of Mill Valley's main thoroughfares. "Mike said the door handles were cool, because *this* was the place he wanted to call home," McDougal recalled, laughing. The lease was signed with the realty company, and Michael Bloomfield became the tenant of a single-family, five-bedroom residence with a possible apartment on its unfinished lower level. The new house was located at 9 Reed Street, and Michael was soon settled in with all his books, records, instruments, and other possessions. To outfit the new kitchen, he reached out to Bloomfield Industries.

"A call to his dad, Harold, got us a whole lot of kitchen supplies," Chris said. "Every pot and pan you could think of!"

Throughout the month of May, Bloomfield continued to record at Columbia's Folsom Street studios with Mark Naftalin. Over a two-week period, the duo added nineteen tunes to those they had already taped, bringing the total to more than thirty selections. Most were original compositions, but they also did a pair of gospel songs, "Sinner's Prayer" and "Were You There (When They Crucified My Lord)," as well as Ray Charles's "Hit the Road Jack" and "Walk on By," the pop hit for Dionne Warwick. Several of their collaborations were gentle parodies—a version of James Brown's "Hot Pants" was one—while other tunes, including "Bongo Breakdown," were semi-comic improvisations. One original was unlike any of the others Michael and Mark recorded.

"We did a lot of different stuff. There was one tune, 'Jewish Song,' that was really experimental," said Naftalin. For that performance, Bloomfield brought in a rhythm section to back his guitar and Mark's piano. Naftalin later wrote about the piece, describing it wryly as "an unendurably long and lugubrious minor-key dirge, where the bass player played nothing but keening upper-register glissandi, and Mike's overdubbed slide guitar parts moaned with the tribal *schrei* of our ancestors." Some of their time in the studio was spent pushing the limits of what could conventionally be called music, but neither Michael nor Mark were concerned with limits. They were trying things.

During the summer months of 1971, Michael settled into his new home. With its panoramic view of the valley, the house provided a picturesque environment for its inhabitant. Though it was just off one of the main roads to town, the place's hillside location, surrounded by trees and bushes, gave it a secluded feeling. Its porches caught the morning sun and cool evening breezes, and the lower floor, bermed into the property's steep embankment, provided an ideal space for practice sessions. Bloomfield felt right at home, and he took a bedroom down a hallway off the kitchen. Comfortably cluttered with his piano, guitars, books, and music, it became his refuge from the outside world.

But it wasn't long before the outside world discovered 9 Reed Street. Visitors soon began making the perilous ascent up the driveway, looking for Michael, and many who came stayed for days and weeks. One who dropped by frequently was Bloomfield's best friend, Roy Ruby. Ruby had moved from LA to Jenner, a coastal village several hours north of San Francisco, in 1969. He was living there along the Russian River with a few friends, hoping the quiet seclusion of California's northern coastal landscape would provide inspiration for his music and poetry. He was also hoping it would help him overcome his growing dependence on heroin. But by 1971, Roy had tired of Jenner's remoteness, and despite its scenic vistas, sun-bleached beaches, and salty sea breezes, he was thinking of moving back to the city. To help him make the transition, Michael offered to let Roy stay at 9 Reed Street, and the would-be poet was soon camped out in one of the house's spare rooms. It wasn't long before the two roommates became a triumvirate with the arrival of their friend Fred Glazer.

Fred had gone off to Europe following his stab at married life, and after several years he had returned to Chicago in poor health. His condition was such that he spent part of 1969 recovering in an institution. "When I came back, I was in the nuthouse for a while," Glazer candidly recalled. Fred had come out to Mill Valley to visit his friends and was thinking about moving to the West Coast. For Michael, having both his childhood friends stay with him was like a perpetual Glencoe reunion. The three enjoyed swapping stories and reliving their adventures on Chicago's South Side, seeing who could top the others' comic anecdotes. One afternoon, they got a chance to share their experiences with a larger audience.

Dan McClosky, a programmer at KPFA-FM in Berkeley and host of a weekly jazz program called *McClosky's Got a Brand New Bag*, came to Reed Street to interview America's greatest blues-rock guitarist. McClosky had met Michael through Roy Ruby when Roy suggested Bloomfield could help with questions for a series of blues interviews Dan was planning to produce for his show. He and Michael struck up a friendship, and after talking to B. B. King, John Lee Hooker, and Bobby "Blue" Bland, McClosky surprised the guitarist by asking if he could interview Bloomfield himself. Michael agreed, and on Monday, May 17, Dan set up his tape recorder in Bloomfield's bedroom and spent several hours chatting with Michael about his life in music. The conversation mirrored the guitarist's recent interview for *Guitar Player* magazine, but because the twenty-one-year-old McClosky was a friend, Michael was much more at ease and talked freely and in greater detail about his early days and about Butterfield and the Electric Flag. He told stories about his experiences growing up and his adolescent forays into the city's South Side blues scene, about working with Butterfield, and about the Flag's drug problems. He also spoke frankly for the first time about his deep discomfort with his rock star celebrity and the adulation it engendered.

"All of a sudden I realized it was the name that was being sold; the hype was being sold," said Michael emphatically, describing the workings of the music industry.

> Cats were applauding the idolatry. I think they were just there to get off, to get their satisfaction in seeing that record image in person, live, seeing the flesh and blood, the mystique, being real. And sometimes it got very confused with quality and non-quality. Man, this seemed like a very jive thing to me at that time, and it still does in a way.

Bloomfield also relished telling McClosky colorful tales about his musical experiences without allowing their questionable veracity to spoil a good story. One involved Harold Bloomfield's disapproval of his son's obsession with music. "My father used to break my guitars," Michael claimed. "He used to call them 'fruit boxes,' and he'd just take them and break 'em up." Another story illustrated the ghetto's dangers with a horrific scene he witnessed on the South Side. "I remember a time I was playing in a bar, and a guy walked in and took a woman's head and slammed it on the bar top," Michael confided. "He said, 'Bartender, give this bitch a beer!'" Neither of these claims had any basis in fact, but they served Michael's desire to entertain and amaze his interviewer. Toward the end of the session, Roy and Fred joined the conversation, sharing anecdotes about Big Joe Williams, Lightnin' Hopkins, Howlin' Wolf, and other aspects of the blues life in Chicago. The interview quickly devolved into a hilarious confab between three friends, each displaying his love for the music and for each other.

"Well, let's adjourn," said the guitarist at the conclusion of their conversation with McClosky. "Take the tape off, pack up the gear, and let's smoke some grass."

In June, Bill Graham announced, to the surprise of many in the rock music community, that he was shutting down the Fillmores East and West. The business of rock music and its burgeoning costs had grown beyond the clubs' capacity for paying patrons, and Graham could no longer afford to keep them open, despite packed houses and top acts. As a farewell gesture, though, he planned a gala week of final shows at both venues, featuring favorite groups and free-for-all jams. The closing night for the Fillmore West took place on July 4, and Graham extended an open invitation to any San Francisco musician who wished to sit in. The scheduled performers included Santana, Creedence Clearwater Revival, and Tower of Power, but dozens of other musicians showed up to participate in the closing ceremonies. Bill made sure to invite his friend Mike Bloomfield, and Michael drove into the city to see the show but had no desire to actually perform. He ran into Graham in the lobby, and because Bill was being followed around by a film crew documenting the venue's last days, he got Michael to mug for the camera as he teased him about the time Dorothy Bloomfield came to see her son perform and Michael told Graham, "Tell her I'm not here."

As the two laughed over the story, the impresario insisted that Bloomfield play something before the night was through. Michael reluctantly agreed and, using a borrowed Les Paul Custom, climbed onstage for the ballroom's final jam, a forty-five-minute vamp that featured guitarists Carlos Santana and John Cipollina, jazz pianist Vince Guaraldi, vocalists Van Morrison and Lydia Pense, and various other members of the Fillmore musical family. Despite his reticence, Bloomfield's soloing was masterful, and his contribution helped give form to what was largely a chaotic mélange of riffs and rhythms. Fifteen minutes into the jam, the stage was crowded with dozens of musicians vying for a little solo space, and after trying unsuccessfully several times to bring the performance to a close, Michael unplugged and quietly exited. As the Fillmore's farewell instrumental roared on behind him, the guitarist disappeared backstage, where a gala party was just beginning.

Among the revelers was a girl that Bloomfield knew, a sixteen-year-old named Christina Svane whom Michael had first met at the Fillmore several years before. The two felt a strong mutual attraction, and the guitarist suggested they find a quieter place where they could talk. The teenager agreed but brought along her brother as a chaperone, and Bloomfield drove them over the Golden Gate Bridge, into Marin County, and up to the summit of Mt. Tamalpais.

"We saw the sunrise, and it was very romantic," Christie remembered. "We really fell in love right there, watching the sunrise on that kind of historic moment." Though he was nearly a dozen years Svane's senior, the guitarist was smitten with the comely high school student. He asked to see her again and drove up the next day to the town of Davis, where she was living with her mother. Christie, too, was infatuated, finding the attentions of the charismatic rock star more than a little flattering. But she was still a student, a young girl living at home with a lifestyle quite different from Michael's, and there was no way she was ready for a serious relationship—especially with someone as mercurial as the famed guitar player. The two saw each other whenever they could, but Christie soon graduated and headed off for travels in Europe before going on to school in Vermont. "I went away to college," Svane said. "And I'd see him in the summer or at Christmas." For Mike Bloomfield, though, the chance meeting with young Ms. Svane at the Fillmore's closing would grow into a relationship that he would pursue right up until his final days.

Christie Svane, however, wasn't to be the only woman in Mike Bloomfield's life in 1971. In September, Michael got a call from his mother—one that both surprised and pleased him. Dottie Bloomfield told her son that she was sending his ex-wife out to Mill Valley, hoping that Susan could move in with him and look after things. Mrs. Bloomfield was still concerned about her son's well-being, and when Susan came to visit her in Chicago, she saw an opportunity to stabilize Michael's home life and perhaps revive his interest in his career.

"I called Michael and told him about Susie," said Dottie. "He said, 'Send her right out here!'"

Susan had gone to Europe after finalizing the divorce in Chicago in 1969, and she was abroad for several years before returning home to the Windy City. She moved back in with her family, but life in the Smith household was complicated by the reason for her return. While in Europe, Susan had become pregnant, and in August she gave birth to a son.

"I had a baby, Toby, independent of Michael," said Susan. "When my son was two months old, Michael's mother said, 'Please go out to California.'" Susan was eager to escape Chicago, where she felt she was "suffocating," and when Mrs. Bloomfield offered to buy her a plane ticket to San Francisco, she was only too happy to accept. She flew out to California and by October had moved into Bloomfield's home on the hill. "I kept house for Michael. I just lived there and took care of things. That was a very wonderful period of time, when we were all living in Michael's house on Reed Street."

Though they were no longer married, Michael and Susan resurrected a kind of partnership once they were again sharing a living space. They still very much cared about each other and had the intimacy of friendship, but the amorous aspect of their relationship had long been over. Though there was no real possibility of renewing their marriage, the former husband and wife benefitted from each other's presence. And just as Dottie Bloomfield had hoped, Susan's return to Mill Valley soon provided the stability her son's life had lacked since the divorce.

But even with Susan now looking after things, Michael still made little effort to resume the arc of his once-brilliant career. He continued to play sporadic gigs, mostly around San Francisco, and took the occasional studio session if the money was good. But he had no desire to organize a working band beyond the loose collective of friends he pulled together whenever he had to perform.

His ambitious plan for a Columbia album of "meaty" guitar-and-piano duets with Mark Naftalin seemed to have stalled over contract issues, and watching Johnny Carson and the *Tonight Show* was frequently the only thing Michael *really* wanted to do. Too often, he would watch while doing drugs.

Heroin use was still an issue for Michael Bloomfield. Though he was not an addict, recreational indulging sapped his motivation for other things and the sedation often consumed many hours that could have been spent more productively. The feeling of well-being induced by the narcotic brought welcome relief for Bloomfield's emotional pain, but the cost was sometimes steep. "Heroin takes up a lot of time," Michael explained. "When you get high, you're stoned for like fourteen, fifteen hours, and then you're *hors de combat*; you're out of it for a long time." Though he was feeling fit and healthy now that his ex-wife was looking after things, he still felt the pull of the needle whenever his anxieties and insecurities overwhelmed him. In those moments, he was as likely to fix as not. "Heroin is the best thing in the world," the guitarist once asserted. "It's better than sex."

In November, Albert Grossman called Bloomfield and told him he was organizing a show for the reopening of what was likely to be an important new music venue in Boston. The Fenway Theatre, a historic performance space on the corner of Massachusetts Avenue and Boylston Street, had been fully refurbished, and its management was planning to celebrate its return as a music hall with an ambitious concert series in December. They had asked Grossman to supply an exciting act for the series opener, and the manager promised to arrange a special reunion of a band that had been extremely popular in Boston. For a premium fee, he would reassemble the original Paul Butterfield Blues Band, Mike Bloomfield included.

Mindful that he still was in debt to Grossman, Michael agreed to appear for the two nights of performances, and he was secretly happy to get a chance to play with Paul again. Putting the band back together for a weekend and playing the old tunes also sounded like it might be fun. The shows were scheduled for Friday and Saturday, December 10 and 11, and other members of the original group were soon contacted. Mark Naftalin heard from the leader himself. "Butterfield called me up and asked me to play," said Mark. "So I flew in a few days early and stayed at his place up in Woodstock." Soon, though, the reunion concept faltered. Elvin Bishop was working with his own band that weekend and was unavailable, and efforts to locate Sam Lay and Jerome Arnold in Chicago proved unsuccessful. With only three of the original six members attending, the reunion had to be reconfigured as "the Paul Butterfield

Blues Band reunited with Mike Bloomfield." To substitute for Arnold and Lay, Michael suggested bassist John Kahn and drummer Billy Mundi. Paul agreed, and both musicians were quickly enlisted.

Advance publicity for the Fenway performances had generated real excitement around town, in part because many media outlets had inaccurately touted the performers as "the original Butterfield Blues Band." The details, though, mattered little to most of the group's fans. The news that "Butter and Bloomers" would be playing blues together again, if only for two nights, was like a dream come true. The theater's 1,600 seats quickly sold out for both nights and all four shows. The reunion of "the two Bs" was newsworthy enough that reviewers from *Rolling Stone*, *Crawdaddy*, and other underground papers, as well as reporters from the *Boston Globe* and *Boston Herald*, found seats in the audience. Grossman himself arrived with an entourage that included Hollywood character actor Michael Pollard. WBCN's popular morning show host Charles Laquidara acted as the concerts' emcee. With the theater's new sound system, elaborate stage lighting, curtains, and backdrops, the presentation and acoustics would doubtless be first rate. The only people with any misgivings about the shows were, ironically, the musicians themselves.

Paul Butterfield was annoyed when he learned that the band's lineup had been promoted as the one that made music history back in 1965. According to one backstage account, the harp player turned to John Kahn and said, "John, you better start looking black. In a hurry." Michael, too, was uneasy, saying he hoped the crowds weren't expecting to hear "East-West" re-created onstage. The quintet planned to do some of the original group's signature numbers, but nobody was prepared to attempt something as demanding as Bloomfield's fiery instrumental. So it was with some apprehension that the five musicians took their place onstage behind the heavy house curtain at the start of Friday's shows. But they needn't have worried.

"They had a scrim hanging in front of the band with backlighting, so all you could see were their silhouettes," said Allen Bloomfield. He had driven up from New York because he, too, was excited to see his brother and Paul share the same stage again. "When the music started, the lights came up and the scrim was raised—it was *fabulous*!" The Fenway crowd was primed and ready, just as the audience had been in Chicago for the Fathers and Sons concert, and they cheered loudly as the band launched into its first tune. The music was somewhat uneven that first evening as the five musicians worked to find a common groove. Michael spent a good portion of the show turned away from the audience and focusing on Kahn and Mundi, conducting their performances with nods and gestures so they wouldn't miss a cue or get lost. Butterfield did nearly all of the singing, and his harmonica playing was as sharp as ever. But the leader seemed oddly disengaged, almost as though he were a sideman at his own gig. The group played a number of familiar tunes, introduced a few new selections, and then closed the first show with a rocking version of "Born in Chicago" that had the whole audience on its feet. As the band left the stage, cries for more devolved into rhythmic clapping and stomping, but the quintet did not appear again until their second set. It, too, had the house cheering in appreciation even though the band was still somewhat unfocused.

By Saturday night, things seemed to have coalesced. Michael was more relaxed, and though he continued to direct the rest of the band, his playing was more assertive and confident. Paul sang and played with real feeling, though at times he appeared irked by the accompaniment. The audience was again effusive, warmly applauding the tunes they didn't recognize and loudly cheering the ones they did. Of those, the band played "Mystery Train" and "Shake Your Money Maker," and they even pulled off a fine version of "Work Song" with the three original members trading off solos at the instrumental's conclusion, just as they had in the glory days. Michael was featured on B. B. King's "I've Got a Mind to Give Up Living," a slow minor blues from the Butterfield Band's second album that was a particular favorite of Bloomfield fans, and Paul sang "Ball and Chain," paying tribute to Big Mama Thornton and the late Janis Joplin. Midway through the second set, both the leader and the guitarist took turns at the piano, with Paul singing an effective version of Bobby Charles's "Homemade Songs" and Michael belting out "What Am I Living For," a Chuck Willis hit. Bloomfield took multiple choruses of weeping slide on Elmore James's "The Sky Is Crying" and then shared powerful solos with Paul on "Nobody's Fault but Mine," a dark gospel moan by Blind Willie Johnson. Michael even called Boston folksinger Geoff Muldaur up to share the vocal on one tune.

By the end of the evening, the audience was on its feet and dancing in the aisles, cheering the "two Bs" and yelling for more. A rumor quickly spread that the "reunion" group would be making a record, and some fans said the quintet was probably going to be the new Paul Butterfield Blues Band. The media were more guarded in their optimism, but the reviews were all favorable, and one correspondent asserted that if the quintet stayed together, it would be "the comeback of the decade." Some members of the group, too, were hopeful. "We're just kind of playing it by ear," John Kahn said in reply to questions about the band's future. "We'll stay together if it works out and we're digging it." Though Michael Bloomfield had said he would like to play with Paul Butterfield again, the guitarist was not digging it. He was happy to have performed with his former bandleader, but he definitely was uninterested in anything more permanent. He flew home to Mill Valley the day following the shows and quietly resumed his reclusive routine.

* * *

By the winter of 1971, Columbia Records, under the leadership of Clive Davis, had become a formidable player in the hugely profitable world of contemporary music. It not only had hit albums by pop icons like Bob Dylan, the Byrds, and Paul Simon, but also issued highly successful releases by brass rock groups like Chicago and Blood, Sweat & Tears. It had moved into the R&B market with sophisticated soul acts like the O'Jays and Harold Melvin and the Blue Notes, and had enabled crossover jazz artists like Miles Davis and Weather Report to find huge new audiences. Powerhouse guitarists Jeff Beck, Johnny Winter, Carlos Santana, and John McLaughlin all recorded for Columbia, and the company's stable of up-and-coming acts included groups as diverse as New Riders of the Purple Sage, Argent, Dr. Hook and the Medicine Show, and Blue Oyster Cult.

It was a company that had changed radically since producer John Hammond brought a young guitar player from Chicago to New York for an audition. But it was the Columbia that had Michael Bloomfield under contract, and it was the company he would have to deal with if he wanted to get his album of duets with Mark Naftalin released. Having been down that road before, Michael was less than motivated, and he deferred to Mark.

"I worked hard with our attorney to design a contract which was so favorable to us that it ultimately stuck in the craw of the Columbia legal department," wrote Mark. "On the eve of signing, we were told, a Columbia attorney popped up from somewhere and said that the company had never signed a contract like that before and wouldn't do it now. And then—unexpectedly, and despite thousands of dollars already spent—the plug was pulled on the project!"

The rejection by Columbia came as a surprise to Mark—and a disappointment. He and Michael had spent hours in the studio working up nuanced versions of familiar tunes and creating distinctive, unusual originals, striving for the purity of sound found in recordings by early piano-guitar partnerships like Leroy Carr and Scrapper Blackwell. Summarily shelving their efforts over supposed contractual details seemed disingenuous, and Naftalin thought Columbia had another reason. "I had heard somewhere in the halls of the Columbia studios that label chief Clive Davis had said, 'I want three minutes of music, not ten minutes of music,' by which he would have meant that he wanted a hit record, not meandering, nearly formless 'jams,'" wrote Mark. The pianist could understand why Davis, if he had heard a selection like the duo's shrill "Jewish Song," might have preferred something shorter.

Bloomfield, on the other hand, seemed unperturbed by the cancelation. In the intervening months, he had largely lost interest in the project and no longer cared about releasing the album he had initially claimed would be his "best guitar playing record of all." Though he had made an earnest attempt to create an LP of honest, direct music that was both traditional and experimental, Michael later distanced himself from the effort and spoke of his duets with Naftalin disparagingly. "We jacked around in the studio for six weeks or so and didn't come up with anything," Bloomfield said of the sessions. "We really just chucklefucked around."

If Michael Bloomfield's fans were wondering by 1972 where their guitar hero had gone, they were not alone. Many of San Francisco's star guitarists were also concerned about his disappearance from the popular music scene.

When Michael first came to San Francisco with the Butterfield Band, those he most impressed were the city's musicians. The Chicagoan's command of his instrument, the skill and verve he displayed as a soloist, and his wildly inventive improvising were qualities that, when coupled with his absolute mastery of electric blues, had sent ripples through the city's community of guitar players. Everyone began listening to Bloomfield, watching the way he played, copping his licks, and studying his technique. They had thrilled to Michael's adventurous work with Butterfield and soulful sorties with the Electric Flag, and they even admired his Super Session outings. But that Michael Bloomfield, the visionary guitarist who set the standard for every other player, seemed to have disappeared. Some of his former protégés thought they knew the reason, and they felt compelled to do something about it.

"I would go over to Michael's all the time and bug him about drugs," said Terry Haggerty, guitarist for the Sons of Champlin. He was concerned about Bloomfield's continued heroin use, something he had observed as far back as when the Sons and the Flag both had rehearsal spaces in the Heliport. "For Marin County, IV drug use, all that shit, that was unheard of."

"Somebody told me he wasn't doing that well, that he wasn't playing. He was just watching TV," said Carlos Santana. The guitarist deeply admired Bloomfield and had first talked with him about drugs when he visited Michael for a few lessons in Lagunitas. "I always felt that if God gave you a gift, you should progress with it . . . and it was sort of like Michael was on hold. Musically, I felt that he was stagnant, that he'd hit a wall." Santana wasn't alone in feeling that Michael had abandoned his life's purpose, that he was allowing his great gifts to languish. There were others, too, who braced Bloomfield over his dissolute ways. But America's star blues-rock guitarist was unconcerned.

"I just said, hey, I'm not into that anymore," Bloomfield later recalled telling his visitors. "I'm into watching 'The Tonight Show' and shooting dope. I'm into stoned leisure."

But Michael's determined friends refused to let the drug issue die. His mother had been the first to raise it, and she had gotten B. B. King to confront her son. Now some of the best musicians in San Francisco were hassling him over it. Their resolve, combined with their own talents as guitarists, eventually touched Bloomfield and began to shake him out of his lethargy.

"That those guys would do that, to come down on me so hard, to get the balls to do that . . . ," Bloomfield later said, "it so moved me that these people wanted to see me playing again[;] it affected my heart tremendously."

But though he was moved, Michael remained mostly at home, immobile. In the first six months of 1972, he gave only one live performance—an afternoon of piano-and-guitar duets at UC Berkeley. Bloomfield did a set of tunes by jazz pianists James P. Johnson and Fats Waller, teaming up with twenty-nine-year-old ragtime-and-stride pianist Mike Lipskin, himself a student of Willie "The Lion" Smith. The April 22 performance was part of a weekend concert series titled "Classic Ragtime and Harlem Stride Piano," whose featured artists were legendary jazz pianists Earl Hines and Eubie Blake. Michael couldn't pass up an opportunity to play traditional jazz while getting to meet two of the art's great practitioners, so he happily took the job. But on all other work, the guitarist took a pass.

"I have perfected the art of laying around. I can do it forever," Bloomfield said. "And I read a million books, and watch TV from eight o'clock to three in the morning every day of my life. I can tell you the whole line-up for Saturday. First there's 'All in the Family,' then 'Bridget Loves Bernie,' 'Mary Tyler Moore Show,' and 'The Tonight Show' reruns. And I play guitar all the time I'm watching." Michael was so enamored of television that he composed a paean to its glories, a sanctified tribute devotedly titled "TV Hymn."

There may have been another reason why Michael Bloomfield remained reluctant to perform. His bouts with emotional pain, his insomnia, and his disdain for the road and for the business of music—those issues were formidable enough to keep him shut away in his room with the television blaring. But Michael may have also chosen not to play simply because he didn't have to. He now had enough money to pay most of the bills, thanks to his family.

"Our grandfather set up a trust fund for his four grandchildren when we were kids," explained Allen Bloomfield. Sam Bloomfield had set aside a generous sum of money for Harold's boys, Michael and Allen, and for his brother Daniel's two children. "It was divided up so each of us got 25 percent. When we reached a certain age, we could receive payments at the option of the trust's executor."

By his twenty-eighth birthday, Michael Bloomfield had begun receiving payments. He had elected to have checks drawn on the fund's interest income paid to him on a quarterly basis. "I decided to have my portion reinvested, but Michael took the payments," said Allen. "It wasn't a lot of money, but it was enough to give him a real cushion, and it was probably detrimental in a way. He didn't have to keep his nose to the grindstone." The payouts amounted to a modest annual income, and they took the pressure off Michael to earn a basic living. The money covered essentials and allowed the guitarist to remain inactive for weeks and even months at a time. If there was any cash left over, he was free to spend that however he wished.

In the late spring of 1972, Mike Bloomfield wished to see Europe. He had gone to England in 1966 with the Butterfield Band, but the rigors of the band's performance schedule left little time for sightseeing. This time, the guitarist wanted to go abroad as a tourist. He wouldn't take a band with him, and he wouldn't book any gigs—he would simply travel, visit the great cities and historic sites, and see the world. With no shows to do, he could move around at his leisure, sleep whenever he needed to, and pace the trip to accommodate his often manic moods. With the extra money from his trust fund, Michael could afford to stay abroad for the better part of a month, with the option to return home whenever he felt like it. All he needed to make the trip complete was a sympathetic traveling companion.

His best friend, Roy Ruby, now in Los Angeles, had just taken a job in a bookstore to supplement his own monthly trust fund check, so he was unavailable for the overseas junket. Fred Glazer was back in Chicago and had no wish to return to Europe. But Jonathan Cramer, Barry Goldberg's cousin-in-law and the pianist who had accompanied Michael during his impromptu session at Chess studios, was living in San Francisco and playing in a band with guitarist Joe Louis Walker, one of Bloomfield's protégés and a former Carmelita Avenue housemate. Jon was free to go on an extended journey because he, too, was being supported by his wealthy family. With Michael's help, Cramer could afford to tag along, and he was more than happy to do so.

While making arrangements for the trip, Michael decided he needed someone to look after the Reed Street house in his absence. The place's steady stream of colorful visitors might pose a problem while he was away, especially with Susan there all by herself with baby Toby. Having another person around to keep an eye on things would doubtless be a good idea, and Michael knew just the fellow for the job.

"He asked me in the most tender manner to move into Reed Street, mostly because he was concerned about Susan," Toby Byron said. The nineteen-year-old had graduated from high school in January of 1971 and was living on a horse ranch while booking local bands and running a coffeehouse with a friend and former classmate named Bonner Beuhler. Bloomfield could see that Byron was a responsible, no-nonsense young man who would take his caretaking duties seriously, someone whose judgment Michael could trust. The fact that Toby was a devoted Bloomfield fan only enhanced his qualifications. The teenager accepted the offer and soon was living at 9 Reed Street. "I moved into the house's lower level that spring," said Toby. "It was unfinished, but it was like a separate apartment, and it was fine for me."

For much of May, Bloomfield and Jon Cramer traveled around Europe. On his return, Michael got a call from Nick Gravenites. Hollywood needed their services.

While the guitarist had been away, Nick had been busy. He and his band, Blue Gravy, had been playing occasional gigs for a troupe of comedians based in San Francisco. Called the Committee, the improv group was composed primarily of former Second City members, and they regularly performed satirical anti-war skits in coffeehouses around the country with actress and activist Jane Fonda. The group's founder, Alan Myerson, was a friend of Gravenites, and whenever the Committee needed music, Myerson would use Blue Gravy.

In the spring of 1972, Alan Myerson was hired to direct a movie. Warner Brothers was eager to cash in on the success it had enjoyed with Fonda and Donald Sutherland in *Klute*, and Myerson had been enlisted on the actress's recommendation to create an edgy, hip feature film follow-up. Alan was going to use performers from the Committee as the film's cast and thought a soundtrack of classic jazz and blues recordings would work perfectly with his script—a tale that involved eccentric outcasts rebuilding an old airplane so they could fly off to a better world. But the studio refused to pay for licensing and insisted that the film's score be entirely original material. That's when Myerson called Nick.

"The studio wanted to hire the Band, but Myerson insisted I do it," said Nick. "It was a lot of fun. He and Jane Fonda were having an affair at the time, and they decided they wanted to do a movie together. So he used the guys from The Committee and hired a neophyte—me—to do the music." Gravenites needed a collaborator, and Mike Bloomfield was the one other person he knew who had scored films. When the guitarist learned that Nick was going to create movie music in the style of Bessie Smith, Tampa Red, and Fats Waller, he enthusiastically joined the effort. Here, he thought, was an opportunity to write music in the traditional styles he had been recording in his bedroom over the past two years.

Bloomfield and Gravenites set to work composing a variety of songs, keying the lyrics to the action on screen with help from the screenplay and selected film clips. Because Nick had a real budget to work with, he was able to hire his good friend Paul Butterfield as well as Maria Muldaur, the blues chanteuse from the Jim Kweskin Jug Band. Other players included keyboardist Merl Saunders, bassist John Kahn, and Butterfield's drummer, Chris Parker.

Recording sessions began on Monday, June 26, at Golden State Recorders with Leo Kulka at the board, and by mid-July Bloomfield and Gravenites had completed nearly twenty selections with multiple alternate takes. Using both acoustic and electric instruments and overdubbing vocal and instrumental parts, they created a variety of songs in styles ranging from jug band hokum and hard-edged Chicago blues to country hoedowns and even a doo-wop finger-snapper. Michael attempted to sing a few of the numbers himself, but he was dissatisfied with the results and had Gravenites redo them. He did get in a few strong solos on acoustic and electric guitar, but for the most part he remained tastefully in the background. The resulting music had a relaxed, good-time feel, and it was clear the musicians enjoyed making it. "Even Butterfield took a serious part in it—he wasn't just there to get paid," Nick recalled, laughing.

When Myerson's movie was released as *Steelyard Blues* in January 1973, it received mixed reviews. Most critics wrote favorably of Sutherland and Fonda but thought the film's whimsical counterculture plot was unworthy of their talents. "Their presence gives it more importance than the material warrants," wrote Vincent Canby in the *New York Times*. The music Gravenites and Bloomfield created for the movie, on the other hand, was deemed strong enough by Warner Brothers to be released as a soundtrack album in February. It was well received, with reviewers calling the record "uniformly excellent" and declaring that "it may be destined to become the most listened-to soundtrack since Curtis Mayfield's blockbusting 'Superfly.'" Even *Rolling Stone* had kind words.

"On the whole, a good soundtrack, and a pretty decent album," declared the underground paper's review. "There are at least five songs you'll want to hear a lot of." The critic noted that the record marked the "reemergence of Mike Bloomfield on wax after a long absence" and went on to claim, "Bloomfield plays just the right riffs in the right places." While most of the praise was reserved for Maria Muldaur, it seemed like *Rolling Stone* was offering the guitarist something of an olive branch.

CHAPTER 23

REED STREET

MILL VALLEY, 1972–1974

On July 28, Michael Bloomfield turned twenty-nine. It had been many months since he had performed regularly, and he suddenly was feeling the urge to play again. He didn't want to be a rock star—that part of his life was over. But that didn't mean he couldn't play with his friends in clubs around the Bay Area. He was a musician, after all, and musicians made music. His drug use was under control, and he was feeling healthier than he had in a long time. Susie had moved in, bringing stability to his home life. The trip to Europe had been reinvigorating and had given him a fresh perspective on his music. Maybe, Michael thought, it was time to start really working again.

There were other reasons why the guitarist was considering getting back onstage. The trip abroad had depleted his trust fund cushion, and there were bills to pay. The soundtrack job with Gravenites had paid nicely, but Bloomfield still owed Albert Grossman a substantial sum, and lately he had been receiving official-looking letters in the mail—letters from the Internal Revenue Service. He had tossed them out without opening them, but he knew they probably meant trouble. It seemed like a good idea to start earning a real income.

The household at 9 Reed Street now consisted of Michael, Susan and baby Toby upstairs, and Toby Byron downstairs. The Mill Valley native had done a conscientious job taking care of the house in Bloomfield's absence, and Michael could see that he was dependable. He also saw that Byron was booking gigs for other bands around the area. Why couldn't he get gigs for Michael Bloomfield and Friends? The guitarist liked Toby and knew he could trust him to take care of business, and Toby had often expressed an interest in reviving Bloomfield's flagging career. Plus, he lived right downstairs. It seemed like a perfect arrangement, and Byron agreed to take Michael Bloomfield on.

"I just did whatever needed to be done," Toby said. "I'd get gigs, organize equipment, haul stuff to shows, and set things up." But he added with a laugh, "Michael was pretty much an unmanageable person. He'd take these spontaneous gigs, do recording sessions, whatever he wanted. I remember around that time he took me to a Polydor recording session for Link Wray, and he wound up playing with Link on the record. That was just the way Michael did things!"

Throughout the fall and winter of 1972, Toby went to work arranging appearances for Michael Bloomfield and Friends. He soon had the band performing in small clubs like the Lion's Share in nearby San Anselmo, the Inn of the Beginning in Cotati, and a newly reopened venue called the Keystone Berkeley on University Avenue in Berkeley. Freddy Herrera, owner of the original Keystone Korner, had purchased the New Monk, a pizza-and-beer joint for college students with music on the weekends, renamed it the Keystone Berkeley, and begun presenting name bands four and five nights a week. With a steady stream of UC Berkeley students as patrons, the Keystone Berkeley quickly became Bill Graham's main competition in the Bay Area.

In addition to performing, Bloomfield's emergence from hibernation included a stint in academe. He agreed to contribute to a course being taught at the New College of California. True to its name, the college, located in Sausalito, had opened its doors only in 1971, and one of its newest faculty members was Michael's friend Norman Dayron. Norman had moved to Mill Valley following the death of Leonard Chess in 1969 and the sale of Chess Records to General Recorded Tape, or GRT, several years later. Despite producing a number of very successful albums for the company, including *Fathers and Sons* and *The London Howlin' Wolf Sessions*, Dayron found himself out of a job after GRT moved the label to New York in 1971.

"I suddenly had nothing to do, and there was nothing happening in Chicago," said Dayron. "Everybody I knew was living in or around San Francisco by that time, and the Bay Area music scene was humming. So I bought a ticket." Norman taught an innovative New College course in audio engineering and record producing, one of the first of its kind, and to give his students the musician's perspective, he invited Mike Bloomfield to host several sessions. Given the mock title "Distinguished Visiting Lecturer," Michael held the class in thrall with firsthand accounts of working with master producers like Bob Crew and recording with superstar musicians like Bob Dylan. A natural storyteller, the guitarist could hold forth on any subject with erudition, and he loved sharing his enthusiasm for music with an audience. His manner of speaking was unadorned and direct, and his insights were often laced with penetrating humor, making his presentations highly entertaining. The young engineers-in-training thoroughly enjoyed Professor Bloomfield's guest lectures.

Then, in February 1973 Michael got a call from an old friend. Blues singer John Hammond was going to record a new album for Columbia, and in a moment of inspiration, he decided that he would do it with Mike Bloomfield. "I asked him if he wanted to record with me again, and he said, 'Yeah,'" Hammond recalled. "I got Dr. John involved, too, and we flew out to San Francisco to work on the tunes and rehearse." Hammond originally planned to use Capricorn Sound, a studio in Macon, Georgia, for his sessions, but at Michael's request, he moved them to California. In mid-February, the trio got together in a small studio on Folsom Street and, with the help of a rhythm section and a few horn players, began selecting and arranging material for the date.

Michael was happy to comply with his friend's request, thinking the session would be as dynamic as when they had recorded together in 1965. But the music, despite their best efforts, refused to come together. "They had many rehearsals at Studio Instrument Rentals, right across the street from Columbia's studios, and Michael loved Dr. John (Mac Rebennack). But John's health was not good," said Toby Byron. Dr. John and Bloomfield got along well, and Rebennack came over to Reed Street to visit a few times, but after a week of unproductive rehearsals, the "Night Tripper" tripped back home to Los Angeles. Hammond persisted, though, and convinced Dr. John to return for another attempt. This time, Rebennack brought along his own rhythm section. With the addition of bassist Chris Ethridge, a former member of the Flying Burrito Brothers and Los Angeles session player, and Fred Staehle, Dr. John's drummer from New Orleans, the music suddenly seemed to jell. The last week in February, the quintet finally began to record, holding multiple sessions at Columbia's San Francisco studios.

The group's material was evenly split between blues and New Orleans rhythms. They recorded three originals by Dr. John, a Big Easy–style R&B number called "I Yi," a Professor Longhair–inspired march titled "Louisiana Flood," and "Sho Bout to Drive Me Wild," a funk groove with gritty guitar fills from Michael. Dr. John also paid tribute to his hometown with Art Neville's "Cha Dooky Doo" and King Floyd's "Baby Let Me Kiss You." The five blues selections Hammond chose for the sessions included Little Walter's "Last Night," John Lee Hooker's "Ground Hog Blues," Elmore James's "It Hurts Me Too," B. B. King's "Rock Me Baby," and "Just to Be With You," the Muddy Waters hit Michael had originally recorded with Paul Butterfield back in 1965. For good measure, Hammond added "Pretty Thing," a Bo Diddley rocker, curiously replacing the harmonica part played by Billy Boy Arnold on the original with an ocarina blown by Dr. John.

Once the basic tracks were completed, Hammond had the tapes shipped to Los Angeles, where background vocals and horns were added. In the final mixes, Michael's contribution was muted and much of his playing was relegated to rhythm accompaniment. But he did get in fine solos on "Rock Me Baby," "Just to Be with You," and "Cha Dooky Doo." Columbia scheduled a June release date for the album, titling it *Triumvirate*, and though it was officially his record, John Hammond shared the billing equally among the three principals. To underscore that fact, he posed with Michael and Dr. John for the album's cover in Jim Marshall's photo studio shortly before heading to Los Angeles. When the record was released that summer, its jacket showed the three musicians grouped together under its title and larger type that read "Bloomfield-Hammond-Dr. John." It was a trio that radiated confidence and maturity, and the three veterans looked very much like the masters they were.

John Hammond thought it was a trio that could very possibly be big. He told Michael and Dr. John he was going to arrange a series of concert appearances once the album came out, and that Columbia intended to promote the record heavily. An appearance on ABC TV's popular *In Concert* variety show had already been scheduled for a May taping, and the *Triumvirate* trio would be provided with a full band, complete with horns and backup singers, for the tour. John was excited about the collaboration, seeing it as an opportunity to reshape his career. "It was a big deal," he said. "It was like things were just about to pop."

Michael Bloomfield, however, wasn't thinking about the possibilities that lay ahead for *Triumvirate*. He had more immediate concerns. Albert Grossman had called earlier in the month with the news that there was going to be another reunion of the Paul Butterfield Blues Band. This time, though, it really *would* be the original band that would perform, and Grossman was planning to have Butterfield, Elvin Bishop, and Michael open the two nights of shows with sets by their respective groups. The official billing would list the three bands separately, with reunion "jams" to follow. The manager was also going to have the concerts taped, thinking the performances might make an excellent album release. Even if the resulting record sold only modestly, it would still provide a return on Grossman's hefty investment in the Chicagoans.

With his growing need for cash, Michael was in no position to refuse Grossman's request. An opportunity to play with Paul was always welcome even though the guitarist knew the shows would probably be hyped mercilessly. The best thing about them was that Albert had arranged with Bill Graham to hold the concerts in the Winterland Ballroom, just a short drive from Reed Street. At least Michael wouldn't have to travel.

The first night of the "official" Paul Butterfield Blues Band reunion took place on Friday, February 23. As expected, the Winterland was packed with fans eager to hear Paul, Michael, and Elvin reunited for the first time since they had last appeared together on a San Francisco stage nearly six years earlier. Michael Bloomfield and Friends were scheduled to open the show, and they would be followed by the Elvin Bishop Group and then Butterfield's Better Days. At about midnight, "the three Bs" would return to the stage with Mark Naftalin and Jerome Arnold for a re-creation of the original group. The only member missing would be Billy Davenport, who at the time had retired from music. But Better Day's drummer Christopher Parker would remain onstage behind his kit, sitting in as Billy's able substitute.

When Bloomfield came onstage with Mark Naftalin, John Kahn, and drummer Rick Schlosser a little after 8:00 p.m., the response was deafening. The Winterland was ready to party, and the Friends band was ready to accommodate their rowdy audience as Michael tore into a version of "Hesitation Blues," sharing the vocal with Mark and soloing with abandon on a recently acquired Fender Telecaster. The quartet followed that with rocking renditions of Fats Domino's "Goin' to New Orleans" and Dr. John's "Lights Out," giving a nod to Michael's recent *Triumvirate* collaborator. The set continued for forty-five minutes, drawing cheers and hoots at the conclusion of each song, and even included two country-and-western selections. The party was just getting under way.

"It was shortly after midnight when Butterfield was joined onstage by the Blues Band alumni," wrote a reviewer for *Rolling Stone*. "The sound was a little ragged at first, but after a few minutes of a 12-bar blues jam, Bishop cued a change in tempo, rocked into 'Won't You Light on Me,' and Winterland jumped again." Though he garbled the title of Chuck Berry's "Don't You Lie to Me," the writer, too, was jumping right along with everyone else in the huge auditorium. The veteran Chicago bluesmen worked their way through a set that included a redux of "Born in Chicago," a tune about which Butterfield quipped, "We used to play this so much that we all grew to hate it," and even attempted a re-creation of Bloomfield's seminal "East-West." As sated fans filed slowly toward the ballroom exits following the show, it had been a near-perfect night of blues and memories.

On Saturday night, the bands, more relaxed now that they knew what to expect, played with real confidence and verve. The Winterland's 5,500 seats were filled with joyful, vociferous fans ready for a second night of electrifying blues-rock. Michael Bloomfield and Friends again opened the show, reprising "Hesitation Blues" to start the set and getting the vast crowd moving. The quartet also did "Mary Ann," a Bloomfield favorite, and a medley of "Baby Let Me Kiss You," a tune from the *Triumvirate* collaboration, and the Meters' 1969 hit "Cissy Strut." Michael's playing was inspired, and he, too, seemed caught up in the evening's celebratory mood. "It's so nice to play here," he gushed into a mic at one point. "Y'all are just . . . nice tonight, man. It's comin' out good!"

At the conclusion of the quartet's set, the audience was on its feet and cheering. The applause, stomping, and calls for more went on unabated for nearly three minutes before the Friends reemerged from the wings and plugged back in. After a moment's hesitation while Naftalin warmed up his Hammond B3, Michael roared into the bass line from the Ritchie Valens hit "La Bamba." "Yi, yi, yi, *yiii*!" shouted Naftalin, and the whole house was up and rocking. Bloomfield soloed frantically over the three-chord vamp, moving from blues to rock to "East-West" pseudo-jazz and back again, as the rhythm section followed his lead and the crowd did "la bamba" all over the ballroom. In five minutes, the rush of rock 'n' roll ebullience was over, and above the roar of applause Michael shouted, "Thank you very much. The show will be right on—Elvin's up next!" After a few minutes, Bill Graham walked out from stage left and grabbed a mic. "Let's hear it again, please. One of the great ones—*Michael Bloomfield*!"

Even with all the guitarist's demons, there was no denying the truth of that statement.

Three weeks later, Michael Bloomfield received a profound shock. News reached him that his best and closest friend, a person he had known since grade school and had shared many formative experiences with, was dead. Roy Ruby succumbed to an overdose of heroin on March 9.

"Roy died, apparently on a Friday," said Ruby's friend Dave Naftalin. "But he was only found on Monday." Dave—Mark Naftalin's brother—was a filmmaker and editor, and he had met Roy in Los Angeles in 1968, not long after Ruby had returned from Mexico. Because they both shared an interest in music and poetry, they became friends and had roomed together for a while. "At the time of his death, Roy was living in this old Angeleno stucco apartment rising up over Echo Park Lake," said Dave. The lake was located in the Edendale neighborhood of Los Angeles, and Roy had been living there for some months while working in a neighborhood bookstore. His drug use had spiked in recent months, and it finally caught up with him that weekend. The young poet and musician was just a few months shy of his thirtieth birthday.

"Roy and Mike were real close—they had a special relationship," said Dave. "I knew when Roy died, it hit him pretty hard."

Michael Bloomfield was deeply distressed by the sudden loss of his good friend. He had known Roy for nearly twenty years. They had grown up together sharing a deep love of music and literature, and they had learned much from each other along the way. Ruby's intelligence, good humor, and kindness were greatly appreciated by all who knew him, but it was with Michael that he shared a special bond. His untimely passing stunned Bloomfield. And yet, the news wasn't entirely unexpected.

"I remember Roy and Mike had a bet about who would die first," said Dave Naftalin. "It was one of those things, just joking around, but they didn't think they'd reach thirty." Fatalistic humor aside, both Michael and Roy knew that using narcotics entailed certain risks—ones that could have lethal consequences. Those consequences were made all too real when Roy overdosed. Though his death was tragic, such tragedies had become common by the 1970s, as drugs increasingly claimed the lives of the famous and not-so-famous. For Michael Bloomfield, however, the death of his childhood friend was a severe blow, a personal loss that left him devastated. It was a bet he never intended to win.

Throughout the spring and summer, Michael Bloomfield continued to work with increasing regularity. With Toby Byron's help, he gigged at the Keystone Berkeley and the Lion's Share, gave a concert of duets with Mark Naftalin over KSAN radio on Easter Sunday, and traveled to Los Angeles for an appearance with John Hammond and Dr. John at UCLA's Royce Auditorium, the show that was videotaped for Don Kirshner's *In Concert*. The TV program would broadcast excerpts of their set in August, right after Columbia planned to release *Triumvirate* and the band would begin its promotional tour.

Reviving his performing career wasn't the only thing on Michael Bloomfield's mind in the spring of 1973. That April, it came to light that he hadn't paid his 1971 taxes. In fact, he hadn't paid any income tax at all since leaving the Electric Flag and coming off ABGM's regular payroll in 1968. Susan had begun looking after the household finances, and as tax time approached, she asked Michael to help her do them. That's when the notifications from the IRS came up. Susan quickly realized the problem was much bigger than anything she could handle. They needed a good tax accountant, and they quickly found one in San Francisco named Maya Lit. She and Susan set to work untangling the mess. One thing was obvious, even before they started—Michael was going to need a substantial amount of money to make restitution with the feds.

His tax troubles meant the guitarist was going to have to work even more than he recently had been. The upcoming tour to promote *Triumvirate* promised to bring in a good amount, and Bloomfield was gearing himself up for an ordeal of weeks on the road, but then John Hammond called. Columbia's president, Clive Davis, was being investigated by the FBI for embezzlement, Hammond said, and CBS had just fired him. All of the label's projects were on hold indefinitely, including all the promotion that had been planned for *Triumvirate* and the trio's extensive concert tour. John said he was sorry, but he was scuttling the trio and going back to working as a single. Michael was secretly relieved, but the cancellation left him without an expected source of revenue. He still needed to raise cash.

At the end of May, Bloomfield arranged through the San Francisco Booking Agency to go on a ten-day concert tour of his own. Beginning on May 31, the Friends quartet flew to Vancouver, and then on to Chicago, Indianapolis, and Louisville. The trip concluded with a five-day stint in Milwaukee at a storefront club on East Locust Street called Humpin' Hannah's. The band planned to drive up to the gig from Chicago, saving money by using a car borrowed from Michael's father. When the guitarist arrived at his dad's home in Hinsdale on the morning of June 5, he was expecting to be given a company car. Instead, Harold lent his son his shiny new Bentley. "How can I go to a joint called Humpin' Hannah's in a *Bentley*?" Michael observed wryly when he picked up the rest of the band.

Several days before his thirtieth birthday, Michael Bloomfield got a call from another old friend. Bob Dylan's agent was on the line, and she told Michael that Bob wanted to come by with a few of his new songs. Dylan thought they could play them together, the agent said, and then maybe Bloomfield could help Bob record them for his next album. Michael said he would be delighted to have his friend visit and that he looked forward to playing with him. But then the agent mentioned certain conditions.

"I got phone calls—'No one can be here! Make sure there was *no one* here at all!'" Bloomfield later said. Dylan's people wanted to be sure that only Michael would be present, a demand that struck Bloomfield as a symptom of the folk-rock poet's extraordinary celebrity. Dylan needed to protect himself from the public, a fact that was confirmed for Michael when Bob arrived at 9 Reed Street one afternoon in late July. "The guy I used to know, I just couldn't reach him, because I guess he figured everybody wanted something from him, or I guess he'd been hit on so many times it was just impossible to get the real guy out there again." Bob's distant, guarded demeanor made the guitarist very uncomfortable. And then they started to play.

"He pulled out his guitar, and he started playing the songs, one after another," Michael said. "I said, 'Hold on, man, you don't even have to sing 'em—just let me tape the chord changes so I can learn these things.'" But Dylan ignored his friend's request and continued without pause. Michael did his best to follow along, but it was clear things were not going well. In the end, Bloomfield summed the experience up in three words: "We didn't jell." The guitarist later attributed his difficulty to the fact that Dylan used odd tunings, making it hard to discern the chords he was playing. Michael also blamed his own guitar, an acoustic model with a cutaway that had recently been custom built for him by Mill Valley luthier Ove Beggerby, saying that it hadn't been set up properly. Whatever the reason, the guitarist failed the "audition," and Dylan found other guitar players to record his songs. The tunes would be released in early 1975 on the album *Blood on the Tracks*, a record that would eventually be regarded as one of Dylan's best—on par with *Highway 61 Revisited*, the album that Michael did get to play on.

Throughout the summer of 1973, Susan worked with Maya Lit, Michael's accountant, to untangle the complex history of the guitarist's income. Bloomfield had always left it to Albert Grossman and ABGM to look after his tax obligations, and he never bothered with receipts, W-2 and 1099 forms, or any other essential paperwork. As a result, re-creating his work history since leaving Grossman's management posed a nearly insurmountable challenge. If Michael's expenses could be accurately tallied, the amount the IRS said he owed in back taxes could be substantially reduced. But even if those outlays could be ascertained, Bloomfield still had hefty payments to make. Added to those were the penalties and compounded interest that had accrued. The guitarist obviously needed to generate even more income.

In September, Bloomfield again went on tour. The Friends quartet opened at My Father's Place in Roslyn on Long Island on Friday, September 7, and then played a show in the small Catskills resort town of Woodbourne. From there, they flew to Halifax, Nova Scotia, for a one-nighter at Dalhousie University and then on to Birmingham, Alabama, to appear at the Graham Mountain Music Festival in Woodland. The next stop was back up north, in Boston for a weekend at Katy's in Kenmore Square and a concert at the Orpheum Theater. The tour's last show was all the way north again, a performance at the six-thousand-seat Bangor Auditorium in Bangor, Maine, on Saturday, September 22. Toby Byron went along as road manager, making sure that everyone got to where they were going with luggage and instruments intact, setting up accommodations, checking on flights and rental cars, and collecting payments for services rendered. While the band was in Boston, Toby recalled an instance in which Bloomfield put his creativity with the truth to good use. "We went to this fancy seafood place on Long Wharf, but we weren't dressed properly and they wouldn't let us in," Toby recalled, laughing. "So Michael took the maître d' aside and explained that we were reps from the Levi-Strauss Company. We got a table right away!"

Back in California at the end of the month, Mike Bloomfield had little time to recover from his travels. On October 2, he was scheduled to perform for a benefit at the Winterland Ballroom, and then, a few days later, he was to appear at a "Sound Experience" expo staged by the audio retail chain Pacific Stereo. He also had decided to become a homeowner.

In sorting through Michael's financial situation, the guitarist's accountant had observed that one way to keep the IRS from placing a levy on whatever funds he had was to invest that money in real estate. The feds, it seemed, were reluctant to confiscate a delinquent taxpayer's home. So she suggested that Michael consider buying the Reed Street house. The guitarist thought that was an excellent idea, and before he left on tour he set the deal in motion with the home's owner, Mill Valley realtor Mildred Vail, using an advance from his trust fund account. The closing took place right after Bloomfield's return, and on Friday, October 5, Michael became the owner of the two-story ranch-style house located at 9 Reed Street. At least now the IRS wouldn't get everything.

In October, two new musicians joined Michael's regular Friends group. George Rains, former drummer for Mother Earth, Boz Scaggs, and the Sir Douglas Quintet, began supplying the beat for the quartet. A big, burly bass player named Roger Troy had moved to San Francisco from Cincinnati that summer, and he was soon filling in for John Kahn, who had left to join Jerry Garcia's new bluegrass band. The twenty-seven-year-old Troy, known affectionately as "Jellyroll," had been a bandleader and session player for many years in his hometown, working for both the King and Jewel record labels, backing James Brown, and touring with Alan Freed rock 'n' roll shows. He was not only an excellent soul, blues, and R&B bass player, but also a fine singer who inspired comparisons with Bobby "Blue" Bland. With these powerful new players in the Friends' rhythm section—and with Troy's soulful vocalizing—the sound of Michael Bloomfield's group improved significantly.

It was this band that Bloomfield took on yet another road trip in November. This time the quartet performed one-nighters in Toronto, Buffalo, Roslyn, and Boston, and then finished up the sojourn with a weekend at Tulagi, in Boulder. On the second night at Tulagi, Michael brought up his high school friend Bob Greenspan to sing a few songs. Greenspan, who was living in Utah, had come to Boulder to see his friend and former bandmate, and Bloomfield insisted he perform. They had both come a long way in the thirteen years since they played together with Vince Viti and Them, and Greenspan, too, had continued to perform and write songs. Michael, offering encouragement, invited Bob out to San Francisco, where the guitarist promised to introduce him around.

Back in Mill Valley following the tour, Bloomfield continued to perform locally throughout December. On the first weekend of the month, Bill Graham staged yet another Butterfield Band "reunion" at the Winterland, repeating the three-band formula that had worked so well in February. The hall was again packed for both nights, and the shows were just as successful, with the *Berkeley Barb* describing Bloomfield as having "a nice set of grimaces, head bobs and spastic movements to accompany his technically excellent, usually superb guitar work." For the jam portion of the show, Nick Gravenites made a guest appearance and sang one of his latest blues compositions, a dystopian lament humorously titled "Love Me or I'll Kill Ya."

The New Year and the start of 1974 brought more shows at the Keystone Berkeley and a trip up the coast for appearances with Michael Bloomfield and Friends in Washington and Vancouver. The guitarist also participated in a recording session for English singer Mike D'Abo, former vocalist for the Manfred Mann group. D'Abo was working on his third album as a single, and Michael added tasteful guitar to several of the songs he recorded. Then, in February, an ominous letter from the Internal Revenue Service arrived. Bloomfield was distressed to learn that on January 4, the feds had placed a lien on 9 Reed Street for unpaid taxes and penalties owed for the years 1968 through 1970. The amount due was based in part on income earned from the guitarist's *Super Session* collaboration with Al Kooper, a substantial amount of money. The lien comprised a significant portion of the value of the house, and Michael could be forced to sell if he didn't start making payments. Maya Lit began working with the IRS to set up an installment plan to forestall any effort by the government to levy the property. The pressure was now even greater on Bloomfield to make money.

In the Bay Area that spring, there was an easy way to make quick cash. It wouldn't require Michael to tour, nor would he even have to perform. He would just have to spend a few afternoons in the studio, recording short instrumental clips and background music. Two brothers in San Francisco were hiring musicians to compose music for a series of short films they were producing. Michael first met them in 1969, not long after they opened the O'Farrell Theatre, the city's first upscale X-rated movie house. Since that time, Jim and Artie Mitchell had become kingpins of San Francisco's adult entertainment world and producers of big-budget pornographic films. They had started by creating "nudie loops," erotic clips of cavorting females, for use at the O'Farrell, and by 1972 they had scored a huge financial success with *Beyond the Green Door*, one of the first feature-length hard-core movies to be distributed nationally. Now the brothers were planning to create a new series of shorts under the rubric "Ultra-Kore," a name taken from one of the themed rooms in the O'Farrell, and intended to convey an erotic experience that went beyond hard-core. To further their objective of producing high-quality, "artsy" pornography, the

Mitchells decided to hire local musicians to create original music for the films' soundtracks.

Michael Bloomfield became the first nationally known musician to work for the Mitchell brothers. The money was good, and he liked the fact that the Mitchells had a reputation for challenging establishment norms. He also was attracted to the illicit nature of their business and the fact that Artie and Jim frequently collaborated with shady characters, were usually in trouble with the law, and basically cared little for convention. Michael booked time at Golden State Recorders and asked Norman Dayron to help him with the recording sessions.

"We would go into the studio with a guy from the Mitchell brothers," recalled Norman. "He would describe the action in each scene and use a stopwatch to determine lengths. He'd say she's prancing around in a G-string here, and I'd say, 'Hillbilly?' and Michael would say, 'No, country.' And Michael would play for fifty-three seconds, or however long the scene was."

In short order, Bloomfield created music for a number of Mitchell shorts, including a torrid interlude titled *Marzoff and Day*, a graphic send-up of the Third Reich in *Hot Nazis,* and a campy romp in oral hygiene of a different sort named *Rampaging Dental Assistants*. The music was period Americana and cabaret-style novelties, brief instrumentals not unlike the things Michael had been recording at home in his bedroom, and how they fit with the action on the screen was sometimes less than clear. But the action on the screen was the point—very few viewers paid attention to the score playing under the utterances and undulations of the actors. The music, though, was important to the brothers because it allowed them to claim that their productions weren't simply gratuitous "depictions of sexual acts intended to arouse sexual excitement" (pornography as defined by the legal authorities) but were erotic narratives with real artistic merit. To prove that fact, they were careful to add production credits to the end of each of their Ultra-Kore shorts and even included credits in newspaper advertisements for the movies. These weren't typical "nudie loops" because they had real directors, actors, producers, and crews. Composers, too.

When the Ultra-Kore series hit adult screens in San Francisco and Los Angeles in November, Michael Bloomfield's name was prominently displayed as one of the contributing composers. It wasn't long before the national press picked up on the collaboration, reporting it with thinly disguised distaste. The implication was that the guitarist's stardom had faded to such a degree that he was forced to work for pornographers in order to make ends meet. The truth, of course, was that Michael didn't care about his celebrity, and he liked the cachet of being associated with antisocial activity. If the establishment was shocked, so much the better; their squeamishness only underscored the guitarist's image of himself as an outlaw. But he wasn't just thumbing his nose at convention and making quick money—he was also doing something he really enjoyed. *Melody Maker* quoted the guitarist as saying he "sure would be happy doing nothing but that forever." The publication added that Artie and Jim had hired Bloomfield to compose as many as fifty more soundtracks, making it appear that he would indeed be doing nothing but that forever.

Even so, the $3,600 he was paid for each hour of film music he created for the Mitchells did not meet Michael's deepening financial obligations. To do that, he would need a project that would pay upward of five figures.

In April, Michael went on the road again, this time taking his Friends band to New York for weekend shows at a newly opened venue called the Bottom Line. Al Kooper and Barry Goldberg were guest keyboardists both nights, and John Hammond sat in for one set, singing and blowing harmonica on several blues. While in town, Michael and Al were interviewed on *Speakeasy*, a syndicated music-and-talk TV series hosted by Chip Monck, the lighting designer for the Monterey and Woodstock music festivals. They were joined by guitarist Alvin Lee, leader of the British blues-rock band Ten Years After, for a discussion of music and the music business with the program's host. The trio then improvised several blues, with Michael playing both guitar and piano, and then, on a dare from Monck, Bloomfield closed the show by demonstrating his old fire-eating routine. Kooper played the jazz standard "What's New" as Michael deftly inserted and withdrew the flaming wand several times without even singeing his new mustache. Monck was impressed—and not a little relieved that his famous guest hadn't immolated himself on camera. The guitarist took a few mock bows as Kooper jokingly played the Mexican waltz "Sobre las Olas" to conclude the show.

From New York, Michael Bloomfield and Friends traveled to Connecticut for shows in Waterbury and Ellington, and they then flew to Florida to appear at the armory in Tampa and at the University of Miami in Coral Gables. At the university, doo-wop singer Dion opened for the Friends and then joined the quartet for a re-creation of his big hit, "Teenager in Love." Midway through the set, when fans began shouting for "Season of the Witch," Michael did not mince words.

"That song makes me wanna puke," the guitarist barked. "I *hate* that song. I wouldn't play that song if it were my mother's dying request, man!"

The increasingly common calls Michael was getting for *Super Session* material—especially for a tune he *hadn't* played on—were beginning to try the guitarist's patience. To appease the rowdy crowd, though, Bloomfield fired off a frantic version of "Work Song" from the Butterfield days, replete with two-bar solo exchanges between himself and Mark Naftalin in its final choruses. The audience cheered the tune and the rest of the set, but fan requests were quickly becoming another reason why Mike Bloomfield did not enjoy performing.

Back in Mill Valley, Michael's Reed Street household had gained another member. Bonner Beuhler, Toby Byron's high school friend and former business partner, had become romantically involved with Susan. They first met right after Toby moved in and Bonner, returning from a five-month stay in Europe, came by to visit his friend. The nineteen-year-old felt an immediate attraction the moment he saw Susan, and he soon was spending much of his time at Reed Street. The couple's relationship quickly became serious, and by the spring of 1974, Bonner had essentially moved in. If Michael was bothered by his former spouse's new relationship, he showed no sign of it. He liked the easygoing, articulate Beuhler, and he was always happy to have another engaging personality under his roof. Reed Street's four adults and one child soon took on all the characteristics of an actual family, with everyone caring for the household and for each other in ways that felt entirely natural. For Bloomfield, it was the home life he had never had growing up in Glencoe.

Because he was the charismatic doyen of the house on the hill, life tended to revolve around Michael. His schedule and interests often dictated everyone else's daily routine. The guitarist usually awakened in the early afternoon, breakfasted, and then began making calls to friends, agents, club owners, and anyone else he needed to speak to. Other friends would stop by for a few minutes or for the entire afternoon, entertaining Bloomfield with stories, requesting help with one project or another, listening to music, or picking a few tunes on one of the guitars lying about. The evening meal would almost always be a family dinner, and guests were frequently invited. On holidays, Reed Street would be the scene of large gatherings, big joyous parties with plenty of food and drink for dozens of revelers. Drummer George Rains remembered one soirée he attended that spring.

"Michael invited me to his Passover seder," said Rains.

> I didn't know anything about Passover, but I went, and Ira Kamin was there and all these Chicago guys. There were kids running all around, and everybody was having fun, doing the ceremony sort of tongue-in-cheek. At one point, I remember Mike taking a fistful of gefilte fish and squishing it through his fingers. It was really a wild time—Passover with the Bloomfields!

Though Michael rarely went to temple and wasn't at all religious, his Jewish heritage was a large part of his identity, and holiday rituals were an infrequent but important part of life at 9 Reed Street.

Evenings in the Bloomfield household continued to be given over to television, with *All in the Family*, *M*A*S*H*, and *Sanford and Son* a few of the house favorites. "It was a whole lot of watching TV, just hanging out," said Toby of their days on Reed Street. "Michael would be on the couch, running scales on his Les Paul and laughing at whatever Norman Lear show was on the screen." Life for Mike Bloomfield was, for much of 1974 and the years that immediately followed, a scene of domestic tranquility. Despite his money worries and the temptations involving drugs, he was truly enjoying home life for the first time since leaving Chicago and Sandburg Village. He was healthier than he had been in years, too, with his diet greatly improved by Susan's cooking and his narcotics use down to a minimum. "Michael never used heroin in the house when I was there," Byron stressed. "He was strictly a pot smoker in those days. He might use Placidyl or Valium—but only as sleeping pills, because his sleep was a problem. But he wasn't drugging."

Despite the emotional turmoil that lay beneath the surface of Michael Bloomfield's animated persona, he now seemed content with life. Outwardly, at least, he appeared to have found a formula for happiness. "See, my habits are now to work enough to pay the rent for a couple of months, live good for as long as I can stretch it, then go out and work as little as I can to stay not-working as long as possible," Michael explained to an interviewer. "It makes for a very pleasant life, you know?"

That pleasant life took an abrupt detour in May. Bloomfield got a call from Barry Goldberg, and Barry had a concrete proposal for an idea he had been kicking around for several years. He told Michael they now had real backing for a return of the Electric Flag. The keyboardist had just released an album in March on the Atco label, an effort coproduced by Jerry Wexler and Bob Dylan. Dylan had introduced Goldberg to Wexler and had brokered the record deal, and Wexler, while working with Barry, got to talking about his missed opportunity to sign the Electric Flag with Atlantic Records back in 1967. Barry told him Michael Bloomfield was available and might still be interested in doing something.

"Just pondering Mike Bloomfield, and knowing that he was anxious to play, I said to Barry, 'Do you think there's a chance of maybe putting the Flag together?'" recalled Wexler. "I didn't know how Buddy would stand on it, so we started making phone calls." Barry's first call was to his old friend from Chicago, but soon he was making other calls. Nick Gravenites was interested, and the idea was pitched to Debbie O'Brien, Buddy Miles's manager. Michael, as expected, was reluctant at first, fearful of being trapped once again into the "superstar" role he had struggled so long to escape. But when nobody rejected the idea outright and it looked like a reunion might actually happen, Bloomfield agreed to participate. The Flag had been an innovative group in its day, and critics and fans alike lamented its passing. It had never lived up to its potential—that's what they always said about the first brass rock band. Maybe this time, Michael thought, it might. And if it did, the rewards wouldn't be only musical. With any luck, the financial return might free him from his remaining debts to the IRS—and to Albert Grossman.

With four of the former Flag members on board, and everyone located on the West Coast, rehearsal sessions were organized in San Francisco. Harvey Brooks was in New York, working with his own band, the Fabulous Rhinestones, and might have been interested in joining the reunion, but Bloomfield suggested they use Roger Troy instead. Jellyroll was an excellent bassist, and his ability to sing gave him an advantage over Brooks. Roger also had extensive studio experience and could assist in the album's production if needed. Tom Dowd, Atlantic Records' ace recording engineer, flew in from Miami to oversee the sessions, and by the third week in May, the nascent Electric Flag was working on new material at Marin Recorders in San Rafael, a studio just fifteen minutes from Mill Valley. All five musicians contributed original compositions, and the emphasis was on soul music and funky blues-rock. It was a promising beginning.

In June, the members of the reconstituted Electric Flag, their wives, partners, and even a few children flew to Miami on Atlantic Records' corporate jet for several weeks of intense recording under the direction of Jerry Wexler and Tom Dowd. Despite protestations from Mike Bloomfield and several others, Wexler insisted on doing the taping in Florida. He and Dowd had been using Miami's Criteria Studios in recent years for all their Atlantic record dates, and the producer felt he would get better results in a familiar facility. Michael reluctantly agreed, but he wasn't happy about having to camp out in a motel for days on end. To make the stay feel more like home, he talked Susan into coming—and bringing little Toby along. They all checked into the Thunderbird Motel in Miami Beach after landing at Miami International, and session work began the next day.

Right away, there was trouble. The first morning in the studio, Tom Dowd was busy setting up mics as the musicians were coming in. When Buddy Miles saw how the engineer had miked his drum kit, he wasn't happy. He and Dowd argued, and by the time Jerry Wexler arrived, the disagreement had escalated to a shouting match. "Somehow, Buddy got excited and said, 'Who is this *asshole* that's telling me how to set up my drums?'" Wexler remembered. Miles got so incensed, he came out from behind his kit and tried to grab Tom. That was enough for the taciturn Dowd, and he walked out, leaving Wexler to deal with the petulant drummer. It was only the first of many blowups.

"Buddy used to get so excited that people in the Flag had a way of calming him down," Jerry said with a laugh. "They used to rub his arms and pat him down to soothe him." Before long, Miles began acting as though he were in charge of the recording sessions, giving orders and making demands. "He used to get all worked up, and suddenly he'd come out to the middle of the floor," said Wexler. "He'd say, 'Get me a marimba, somebody!'"

"The only thing everybody could agree on during those sessions was killing Buddy!" Mike Bloomfield exclaimed. The guitarist was amazed one afternoon to see Miles rolling around on the floor, having a full-blown temper tantrum. Michael was so turned off by the discordant atmosphere in the studio that he kept his contribution to a minimum. Wexler was frustrated by the guitarist's apparent reluctance to do anything other than play rhythm. "I couldn't get Michael to play solos, couldn't get him to play any real lead," Jerry said. The producer finally talked Michael into overdubbing a few solos on several of the tunes after the sessions had been completed.

Despite the friction, the newly hoisted Flag managed to record nearly twenty tunes while at Criteria. Additional musicians were brought in to fill out the band's sound, including Richard "King Biscuit Boy" Newell on harmonica, keyboardists Albhy Galuten and Richard Tee, and session guitarist George Terry, who was occasionally called upon to take solos for the recalcitrant Bloomfield. With three strong vocalists now in the band, there was no need for backup singers. Nick, Buddy, and Jellyroll each took turns singing lead and then sang harmony wherever needed. The addition of horns, brought in later by Jerry Wexler, gave the performances a final polish, with several of the arrangements written by Jellyroll Troy.

Of the songs the group recorded, the majority were written by Michael, either by himself or in collaboration with other band members. One was a quirky blues that Bloomfield had originally penned for Otis Rush called "I Was Robbed Last Night," a tale based on a break-in at Norman Dayron's apartment. It was one of the few selections recorded at Criteria that featured extensive lead by Michael. He also wrote "I Found Out," a gospel-tinged rocker effectively sung by Jellyroll Troy, and shared composer credits with Jellyroll on "Sweet Soul Music." With Miles, he created "Talkin' Won't Get It," a slow soul vamp that had effective harmonica fills from harpist Newell behind Buddy's preachy vocal. "Losing Game," written with Barry, featured Goldberg's low-key singing over a bass line created on Mellotron by Muscle Shoals' Barry Beckett and some fine slide work from Michael.

The guitarist also had the group record "The Band Kept Playing," a novelty number he had originally hoped to do with John Hammond. Echoing the style of classic Bluebird recordings by Tampa Red and Big Bill Broonzy, the song told of the misdeeds of "bad man" Peetie Wheatstraw. The real Wheatstraw, known as the "Devil's son-in-law," was a blues artist named William Bunch, who recorded for Decca. But in Michael's telling, Wheatstraw was a gun-toting miscreant who created mayhem while "the band kept playing." The tune culminated in a dirge-like recitation of the first line from the traditional hymn "Nearer My God to Thee," making it by far the most elaborate composition recorded by the new Flag.

Nick Gravenites authored two blues-inflected rockers, "Earthquake Country" and "Doctor Oh Doctor (Massive Infusion)." The former featured George Terry's slide guitar and a brief solo from Michael, while the latter showcased Bloomfield using a wah-wah pedal. Jellyroll Troy sang his own composition "Never Be Lonely" and gave the lead vocal to co-composer Buddy Miles on "Every Now and Then," a soulful dance number with a bright melody created by Beckett on a Moog synthesizer. With Barry, Miles cowrote "Make Your Move," a funky boogaloo that featured Buddy singing an overdubbed duet with himself in its final chorus.

The Flag also recorded several originals by non-band members. Jellyroll sang "Inside Information," an R&B tune he had been doing for years that had been written by a bandleader and A&R man he had met at King Records named Sonny Thompson. Bloomfield suggested "Lonely Song," a ballad by Mark Naftalin, and Buddy sang it sweetly, supported by fills overdubbed later by the guitarist.

As the Criteria sessions wound down, the tension in the studio seemed to recede. The musicians, with their different personalities, opinions, and expectations, began to find common ground. While there were disagreements, those conflicts no longer threatened to scuttle the project. Once all the material had been recorded, the finished tapes were shipped to Atlantic's offices in New York for mixing and editing in June. Their overall sound was clean and professional, the product of seasoned musicians working with one of the finest production teams in the country. The tunes were well conceived and convincingly performed, and while there may not have been a Top 40 hit among them, they all had commercial appeal. Unlike the material recorded by the original Electric Flag for its debut album, the new songs had a homogeneous feel to them. There was a coherence that was lacking the first time around.

But the new recordings were not without problems. Exciting elements that had been there in 1968 were noticeably missing. Most conspicuous among these was Mike Bloomfield's protean guitar work. The guitarist was still present, but not as the dynamic, fearless innovator he had originally been. His contributions were muted and controlled, almost as though he were a session player on his own record. Buddy Miles's drumming was also an issue. On many of the performances his playing was rudimentary, and on all of them it was down in the recording mix, depriving the music of the bottom necessary to give it weight. During the sessions, some of the Flag members began to grumble that the querulous drummer seemed to have forgotten how to play.

It was, of course, too late to try to correct those deficiencies. The mastering and mixing proceeded apace, and cover art and liner notes were created. The album was given the apt title *The Band Kept Playing*, taking a cue from Michael's tune of the same name, and was scheduled for release the first week in November. Because Bloomfield and Miles were under contract to Columbia, and Goldberg and Gravenites were affiliated with Warner Bros., Atlantic struck an unusual deal with Columbia to share distribution rights as well as costs and profits from all records produced by the Electric Flag. Atlantic would issue the first LP, and plans were already being made for a second to be released on Columbia in 1975.

Plans of a more immediate nature were also being made for appearances by the reconvened Flag, both onstage and on television. Buddy Miles's manager, Debbie O'Brien, agreed to take on management of the group, and the band's first gig would be in July. They would debut before a festival crowd numbering in the tens of thousands, not unlike what had occurred with the original band in 1967. Though Michael Bloomfield had assiduously avoided performing for huge audiences since leaving the Electric Flag in 1968, it seemed the return of the brass-rock band meant a return to the spotlight for him.

Back home in Mill Valley following the Electric Flag sessions, Mike Bloomfield began thinking about resolving his contractual obligations to Columbia. He was still obliged to produce a final LP for them under the terms of the contract he had signed in 1968, and the experience in Miami had revived his interest in songwriting. He decided he would create as many original tunes as he could for his next album, and this time they would have real commercial potential. He had composed most of the material on *It's Not Killing Me*, his first solo record, but those songs had been highly personal. Michael now wanted to see if he could write music that would appeal to the listeners. He thought he might even be able to finally compose a hit song.

In July, Mike Bloomfield scheduled recording time at Columbia's Folsom Street studios and assembled many of the Friends regulars for several weeks of sessions. The group was essentially the revived Flag with George Rains replacing Buddy Miles and Mark Naftalin added on keyboards. Additional sidemen included pianist Howard Wales and Chicago guitarist Jimmy Vincent, both of whom had been working with Jerry Garcia. John Wilmeth, trumpeter for Southern Comfort and several of Bloomfield's other projects, headed up a horn section that included his bandmate Rev Stallings on tenor and a number of studio players. Hart McNee, a baritone saxophonist from Chicago and a friend of Christie Svane's, was one of them. It was an ensemble of musicians that Mike Bloomfield knew well and would undoubtedly feel comfortable with.

After a few quick rehearsals, Bloomfield and his men gathered in the studio on Wednesday, July 10, and began laying down tracks for the new album. Over the course of eight separate sessions, Michael would record twenty-five original compositions, most of them his own. As with past composing efforts, the songs' styles varied from blues to gospel, soul and R&B to country. But this time the guitarist labored to make each tune as accessible as possible, getting the best performances out of his players and himself while giving most of the lead vocals to Jellyroll Troy or Nick Gravenites. Though he eventually sang five of the selections himself, Michael was mindful of his limited vocal range and tried to keep his pitch and vibrato under control. His soloing, however, he did not restrain. On his last two recording sessions—those for Triumvirate and the Electric Flag—Bloomfield had held back, keeping his lead work to a minimum. But now, knowing that fans expected to hear him play, Michael took multiple choruses whenever he could. He strove to solo at his "hottest," a term he often used to describe his best lead, and his playing on several selections easily reaffirmed his status as one of the country's best blues-rock guitarists.

Though he fully intended to write songs that anyone could relate to, Bloomfield couldn't help creating a few that had personal significance. "Midnight on the Radio" told of the transistor radio Michael received at his bar mitzvah and how it changed his life by exposing him to a whole new world of music. Another tune, "Lord Take Me Fast," addressed Bloomfield's sense of his own mortality. It was written during a time when he was regularly using heroin and had developed an abscess on his arm that he feared might prove fatal. A third autobiographical number was one the guitarist had first performed with Mark Naftalin in their duet session over KSAN radio in 1973. Called "TV Hymn," it was a gospel-style tune whose quirky lyrics said much about Bloomfield's outlook on life—and his affection for the "idiot box."

There were other tunes that would unquestionably please his fans. One, a Bobby "Blue" Bland hit from 1962 called "Your Friends," featured a powerful vocal by Jellyroll and equally powerful blues soloing from Michael. Troy was also the vocalist for a well-crafted gospel piece by Michael called "When I Get Home." Patterned after the traditional music of black gospel groups like the

Swan Silvertones, the song featured a sanctified chorus backed by church-style organ and piano, all in support of Jellyroll's soaring vocal. Michael even added guitar embellishments to the accompaniment, using his amp's vibrato effect to convincingly evoke the sound of Pop Staples. "When I Get Home" could easily have found a home in the rotation of a WVON or WGES gospel broadcast.

A third song, neither blues nor gospel, was a Bloomfield original titled "When It All Comes Down." A brilliant pop confection, the tune featured Nick's rich baritone coursing over a catchy melody while Bloomfield's acoustic guitar and Mark Naftalin's marimba provided accents to its sprightly Latin beat. Michael played a short cadenza between Nick's verses, adding to the tune's light, south-of-the-border feel, and a smart arrangement seamlessly propelled it all along at a danceable tempo. "When It All Comes Down" was an ideal candidate for release as a single, and with proper promotion from Columbia, it might make its way up the charts. With luck, it could be the hit song Michael Bloomfield was hoping to write.

While he was in the middle of recording for Columbia, Mike Bloomfield also had an important date to make in Chicago. WTTW, the Public Broadcasting System affiliate in the Windy City, was planning to launch a national series of music programs called *Soundstage* in November, and its debut show was scheduled to tape in mid-July. That program, titled "Blues Summit in Chicago," would be a special tribute to the music and artistry of the city's great bluesman, Muddy Waters. Muddy and his band were going to perform for a studio audience, and then they would be joined by a number of special guests, one of whom would be Mike Bloomfield. The show's producer, Ken Ehrlich, especially wanted Bloomfield included because of his pivotal role in bringing Waters's music to a national audience, and because of his reputation as the country's first great blues-rock guitarist. Nick Gravenites was also invited as one of the pioneers of Chicago's white blues scene, and Johnny Winter, a devoted Muddy fan who had become a superstar in the rock world, readily agreed to appear. A fourth white player, Dr. John, was an odd candidate for a Chicago blues "summit," but Mac Rebennack also loved Muddy's music—and was a big name that would draw viewers. Another curious choice for the tribute was Buddy Miles, but with two other members of the reunited Electric Flag making an appearance, Ehrlich decided the drummer should be included, too. With additional local guests like Willie Dixon, blues singer Koko Taylor, and Junior Wells, the hour-long special promised to be a delight for blues fans.

On Wednesday, July 17, Bloomfield, Gravenites, and Miles flew to Chicago, and the next afternoon they congregated at WTTW's studios on North St. Louis

Avenue. There Muddy Waters and his band were running through a few tunes on the set's stage-in-the-round while Johnny Winter and Dr. John stood off to one side. During a break, with cameras rolling, the guests climbed onstage and greeted Muddy, producing a genial moment that would later be edited into the program. The musicians' brief tête-à-tête set the mood for the rest of the taping session as everyone relaxed and focused on Muddy and the music. Right from the start, Mike Bloomfield took charge.

"Michael was real, real responsive to making the show really for Muddy," said associate producer Eliot Wald. Wald saw Bloomfield—and Nick Gravenites—as the "emotional center" of the tribute. With an audience of several hundred Chicago blues fans seated around the stage and three cameras on dollies circling, the tribute got under way. Nick acted as emcee, and following an opening performance of "Blow Wind Blow" by Waters's working band, he introduced each guest musician in turn. First up was Bloomfield, and he remained onstage getting cues from Muddy and directing the other players throughout the remainder of the session.

Though the guitarist was indeed energized and enthusiastic, he didn't really play with his usual verve. His reticence largely grew out of respect for his mentor, much as it had during the *Fathers and Sons* sessions five years earlier, and he purposely toned down his playing. But it mattered little. Muddy Waters was obviously pleased with the music as the show progressed, and Bloomfield clearly enjoyed himself, too. The group worked through "Five Long Years," "Long Distance Call," "Messin' with the Kid," and other classic blues as Nick called up Junior Wells, Johnny Winter, and Dr. John in quick succession. For "Wang Dang Doodle," Gravenites brought out Willie Dixon and Koko Taylor and then introduced guitarist Phil Guy, Buddy Guy's brother, and bassist Rollo Ranford from the Siegel-Schwall Blues Band. Buddy Miles was the featured vocalist and drummer for "Down by the River," the only non-blues of the session, and then everyone returned to the stage for a rousing rendition of "Got My Mojo Working." As Muddy often did at the conclusion of "Mojo," the legendary bluesman got off his stool and broke into a jig as the music roared. The studio audience was on its feet and cheering as the tune came to an end, and after a moment's hesitation, Bloomfield bounded across the stage and threw his arms around his idol. Muddy was beaming, clearly delighted with the response. "You don't know how happy I am. . . . It's the thrill of my life, man. Just to think that the kids didn't forget me," he told a reporter from *Rolling Stone*. The "Blues Summit in Chicago" taping, everyone agreed, had been an unqualified success.

* * *

The three members of the Electric Flag didn't have time to linger in Chicago following the *Soundstage* taping. They were due in Sedalia, Missouri, the following afternoon for an appearance by the reconstituted Flag at the Ozark Music Festival—the band's first live show. The festival, like the watershed 1969 Woodstock concert it was modeled after, was a three-day extravaganza featuring more than thirty top-name rock acts as well as camping, food, crafts, and a "no hassles guaranteed" environment.

Michael Bloomfield, Nick Gravenites, and Buddy Miles flew to Kansas City on Friday morning, July 19, caught a connecting flight to Sedalia Memorial Airport, and arrived at the festival a little after 1:00 p.m. There they met up with Barry Goldberg; Jellyroll Troy; and the band's newly acquired horn men, trumpeter Tom Bray, saxophonist Steve Lawrence, and trombonist Kenny Walther. The Electric Flag was scheduled to perform at 3:00 p.m., but it wasn't until half-past five that the band finally filed out onto the festival's vast stage.

"Yes, indeed! With us here we have some superstars of rock," emcee and radio DJ Wolfman Jack growled into the microphone as the crowd began to cheer the performers onstage. "It looks like it's gonna be a nice night, and we gon' rock 'n' roll! We got Mike Bloomfield! Nick Gravenites! Barry Goldberg! Buddy Miles! The Electric Flag, baby, back together after seven years! *The Electric Flag, everybody!*"

Buddy's kick drum and high-hat set the beat, and then Barry added electric piano. Jellyroll's bass thundered in as the horns began to repeat a funky riff. "All right, y'all. Everybody clap your hands. *Everybody!* Let's make some noise!" Miles exhorted the huge crowd over the surging vamp. Following a brief crescendo and horn riff, Nick launched into his composition "Doctor Oh Doctor," and the new Electric Flag was suddenly a reality.

The octet sounded tight and in command. The horns played cleanly and in tune. Barry rocked his organ, switching seamlessly between it and his electric and acoustic pianos. Jellyroll's bass anchored the music with rumbling, earth-shaking authority. Even Buddy Miles's drumming was inspired. The revived Electric Flag sounded even more forceful and exciting than the original. Though Michael was drained from what had probably been a sleepless night following the *Soundstage* taping with Muddy Waters, the music quickly revitalized him, and after the first tune his lead lines were prominent. The spark of energy that the Flag's Miami recording sessions seemed to lack was now present in full. So, too, was Buddy Miles, the Flag's relentless showman.

"I want you to start out by clapping your hands," Miles commanded the audience as he began the band's second number. "C'mon, *everybody* clap your hands!" He went on to repeat the command a full five times before starting

"Every Now and Then." It was clear to Michael and the rest of the band that Buddy's desire to be the center of attention, to put on a show, hadn't abated in the years the band had been apart. If anything, it had gotten worse. Throughout the entire set, Miles worked the audience, getting them to clap repeatedly or engage in call-and-response shouting matches. His presence, even on those tunes where he wasn't the lead singer, was so domineering that the local paper inaccurately described the band as "Buddy Miles and his Electric Flagship," saying that Miles played selections from his new album to be released "in a month." That record, in truth, was the Electric Flag's, due out in November.

The band turned in an energetic set and did perform many of the tunes from *The Band Kept Playing*. Their big sound and exciting bravura brought the massive audience to its feet more than once and merited a standing ovation at the end of the set. Buddy Miles, drenched in sweat, thoroughly enjoyed himself, and the rest of the group seemed satisfied with the performance. For his part, Michael Bloomfield was simply relieved the show was over. He was thinking only of Mill Valley and of getting back to the comfort of his Reed Street bedroom. But he had played well, and though he hadn't dominated the performance as he so often did in the Flag's early days, he exhibited moments of characteristic dynamism and breathtaking intensity. The new Electric Flag's debut at the Ozark Music Festival seemed as successful as the original band's had been at Monterey in 1967. It was an auspicious start.

The first week in August, Mike Bloomfield finished up the sessions for his next solo LP in Columbia's Folsom Street studios. He recorded a jumping version of "Lights Out," a tune he regularly performed live, and featured Jellyroll Troy on "Shine on Love," an original by the bassist, and "Let Them Talk," another soul ballad by King Records' Sonny Thompson. "I've Been Treated Wrong," a blues written by Washboard Sam, was given a straight Chicago twelve-bar treatment with fine solos by Michael and some solid harp playing from Mark Adams, one of Toby Byron's friends. Bloomfield also recorded three additional originals, one an old-timey sixteen-bar blues variation called "Baby Come On" and another an AAB ballad titled "Tomorrow Night" that featured Michael's slide guitar, Mark Naftalin's accordion, and Hart McNee's growling baritone sax. The tune the guitarist chose as the album's title selection was his "Try It Before You Buy It," a funky soul number sung by Rev Stallings. With cautionary lyrics, a catchy turnaround, and a danceable beat, the song had a complex arrangement with a full horn section and backup vocals by Jellyroll and Nick Gravenites. Stallings was not a strong singer, but his lead vocal was reminiscent of Archie Bell's singing with the Drells, and it gave the tune a casual appeal that would draw listeners in. "Try It Before You Buy It" would be right at home on *Billboard*'s Hot Soul Singles chart.

After redoing a few of the selections he wasn't satisfied with, Mike Bloomfield finished up the recording sessions for his next Columbia release by mid-August. He was particularly pleased with the way the music turned out and was convinced the album would sell. He had worked diligently to produce music that had integrity but also had commercial appeal. The tapes were mixed and mastered by one of Columbia's staff engineers at the Folsom Street facility, and it looked like the album was a go.

But then nothing happened.

Columbia never scheduled a release date, and it did not proceed with the LP's production. The mastered tapes for *Try It Before You Buy It* were put on a shelf in the label's San Francisco vault, and there they sat. Nothing was said to Bloomfield about them, but it was clear that as far as his next solo album was concerned, Columbia had tried it and they were *not* buying it. The guitarist was deeply disappointed that he had lost the company's support, especially because he believed the record would have been a success. But he also understood why the front office was hesitant to take another chance on him. "That was a really good album," he later said. "It's a shame it never came out, because I think that Columbia would have definitely recouped their investment. But they lost a lot of money on me, and you can't blame them when you think about it."

Toward the end of the month, Michael Bloomfield and the Electric Flag hit the road for the band's first extended tour. In quick succession, the Flag played gigs in Decatur, Illinois, on Cape Cod in Massachusetts, and in New York City, Toronto, and Allentown, Pennsylvania. When they played at the Nassau Coliseum on Long Island, Michael's brother, Allen, caught the show.

"The Flag was opening up for the Band," said Allen. "That was a tough gig. Buddy started right in with his shtick, 'Everybody clap your hands!'—you know, that whole bit. The audience wasn't into it, of course—they were there to see the Band. Michael was just embarrassed by all his showboating." The conflict that had developed between the guitarist and his drummer back in 1968 still resonated six years later.

"I'll tell you one difference between Buddy and me—his ambition is to be a musician forever," Michael told an interviewer that summer.

> *I* only want to make enough money to get out of the business—yesterday would be too late. . . . The applause and the smell of the greasepaint is

not my incentive. I like to have a good time playing with the musicians and communing on that level—that's important to me, not the money. I'm not interested in anything else about it.

Despite his disdain for Buddy's antics, Bloomfield soldiered on. He had committed to performing live with the Flag in support of the band's upcoming Atlantic release—and he needed the money.

The Coliseum show was an exception. Most of the Electric Flag's live appearances were resounding successes. When the group did four nights at the Bottom Line in New York beginning Wednesday, September 4, they were enthusiastically received by capacity crowds. Though Bloomfield, Gravenites, and even Buddy Miles were largely seen as musicians from an earlier generation by the mid-1970s—as stars of the progressive rock era of the 1960s—the Electric Flag, especially Mike Bloomfield, had a huge following in the Big Apple. That following packed the Bottom Line and cheered the guitarist and the band on, responding unhesitatingly whenever Buddy shouted, "Clap your hands!"

From New York, the band flew to Los Angeles for an appearance on *Don Kirshner's Rock Concert*, a newly expanded version of the syndicated TV show *In Concert*. The taping took place before a studio audience at Metromedia Television's huge Hollywood complex, and the band did several selections from their forthcoming album, including "Sudden Change," and finished the short set with "The Band Kept Playing." When the program aired in October, just prior to the release of their Atlantic LP, the Flag shared the hour-long broadcast with the British folk-rock group Steeleye Span and Irish hard-rock guitarist Rory Gallagher. Also included was one of Michael's favorite comedians, Robert Klein. But of the three bands, the Electric Flag would seem the least contemporary. While their music was engaging and well played, to younger viewers it harkened back to an earlier era. The novelty of combining horns with a rock group had long since faded, and funky soul music had become commonplace with mainstream audiences following the advent of a highly danceable form known as "disco." By the mid-1970s, the popularity of rock music built around lengthy guitar improvisations was waning and being replaced by artfully superficial songs with melodic hooks that were sung by androgynous twenty-somethings sheathed in spandex. This latest trend in pop music was described accurately as "glam rock" for the sartorial glamour of its star practitioners. The Electric Flag, for all its musical prowess and formidable physical presence, would never have been considered glamorous.

When the band appeared at the Winterland Ballroom for Bill Graham in November, a review in a local college newspaper brought home the point. Bloomfield, Miles, Gravenites, and Goldberg, it implied, were refugees from a bygone era. "'Twas nostalgia night for Winterland patrons as they flocked to hear the reformed Electric Flag and New (Moby) Grape relive the Sixties," read the reviewer's lede. San Francisco, of course, was where the sixties began, and the audience had no problem with delving into the past, especially when it involved Mike Bloomfield. If the Electric Flag's music was outdated, it mattered little to them. The guitarist, feeling right at home, reciprocated with characteristic virtuosity, and the reviewer noted that Bloomfield "settled down for some extraordinary jamming on 'Killing Floor.'" But it was Buddy Miles who drew the "screams" from the Winterland's audience. Toward the middle of the set, the drummer took over and once again engaged the crowd. "As is his style, every song which Buddy harmonized was saturated with pleas for 'putting your hands together,'" the reviewer reported. "When this line finally failed to get a response, Buddy resorted to searing drum solos and claps resounded once more." Doubtless Mike Bloomfield's patience for his bandmate's overbearing stage routine was growing thinner by the gig. In fact, at one point late in the set, when Miles came out from behind his drum kit to implore the audience once again, Bloomfield simply unplugged his guitar and stalked offstage. He didn't return, and the band completed the show without him.

Even though he was devoting most of his time to the Electric Flag, Bloomfield still worked occasionally with his Friends band. Toby Byron continued to book gigs for Michael, including a date at the Edgewater in Oakland, an appearance on KSAN radio, and a duet with Mark Naftalin at Stanford University. One of the Friends shows was in Vancouver for a week-long stint at a Hornby Street nightspot called the Cave. A supper club famous for its cave-like interior with rocky walls and a stalactite-encrusted ceiling, the venue featured top stars like Lena Horne, Liza Minnelli, the Supremes, and Sonny and Cher. By the mid-1970s, its new owner, Stan Grozina, was showcasing rock acts, and Michael Bloomfield and Friends were scheduled to appear November 12 through 16. The guitarist flew up from San Francisco with Mark Naftalin, Jellyroll Troy, and George Rains, but when they arrived in Vancouver, Michael wasn't thinking about the gig. "The only thing Mike would talk about on the flight was some TV show," remembered George Rains. "He just kept talkin' about how he wanted to see it." It was a show Bloomfield wanted to see because he was in it.

The premiere broadcast of PBS's *Soundstage*, the tribute to Muddy Waters called "Blues Summit in Chicago," was scheduled to air the second week in November on public television affiliates around the country. Bloomfield had read that some stations planned to carry it on November 12, his first night at the Cave, and he was hoping to find a TV that could pick up the broadcast from Seattle or possibly tune it in on local cable. When the band checked into the Blue Horizon Hotel on Robson Street, Michael searched through the TV listings and discovered that Vancouver's Channel 9 would be carrying the program. But though he fiddled at length with the set in his room, it would not get the channel. The frustrated guitarist eventually made his way over to the Cave, arriving just fifteen minutes before the start of the first set, and then rushed through the evening's performance so he could get back to the hotel. During a break, he told a reporter for the *Vancouver Sun* how distressed he was to miss the program. "To think there are people here tonight who *have* seen it," Michael complained bitterly. The reporter complimented the guitarist's playing despite his preoccupation, saying, "People go to hear Bloomfield and he clearly dominates with the sharp bursts of funky resonance that few white artists have been able to achieve, and if Muddy Waters wanted him for his television program, surely that indicates his success."

But Michael continued to have no success when it came to seeing "Blues Summit in Chicago." By early Wednesday morning, he was thoroughly disgusted, and he made a decision. As he had so often done before, Bloomfield simply packed up and went home. In San Francisco, he knew he would be able to catch the show, and his job at the Cave was really of no consequence. The guitarist didn't like playing there and he didn't like the club's owner, and it really didn't matter whether he showed up or not—to Michael, anyway.

It was mid-afternoon before Mark Naftalin, George Rains, and Jellyroll Troy learned that they were without a leader—and without a gig. The Thursday edition of the *Vancouver Sun* bemusedly reported Bloomfield's defection, saying that Jellyroll "got the word from the switchboard operator," a message scrawled in pencil that read, "Roger, I know you will hate me, but I hate this gig and I is splitting. Perhaps you can talk Stan into keeping you and Mark and George, but I is gone. Please take my axes home for me. Sorry, sorry. Bye-bye, Love, Michael."

"We couldn't believe he would do that!" said George Rains. "That was the only time I ever got mad at Mike." The guitarist left his sidemen stranded in Vancouver and hadn't even paid his own hotel bill. "We had to have money wired from San Francisco so we could get home," Rains recalled. "I heard that Mike told them at the airport he had a sick child and he had to get on a flight right away. He was a great guy, very funny, but it was just like him to do something like that."

Club owner Stan Grozina was not amused. He threatened to file a complaint with the musicians union over Bloomfield's breach of their contract. But then he realized he had a better option. Michael's guitars and amp were sitting in the Cave's office, stored there for safekeeping while the Friends were appearing at the club. Grozina decided he would keep the instruments until Bloomfield made restitution for the venue's lost business. Later in the week, Stan secured the services of Barbi Benton, the *Playboy* Playmate who was attempting a second career as a country singer. She replaced Michael Bloomfield and Friends, and Bloomfield's guitars were quietly moved into storage in the Cave's basement.

When he abruptly departed Vancouver in mid-November 1974, one of the instruments Michael Bloomfield left behind was a blue Fender Telecaster, a late 1960s model that he had acquired in 1973. It had been custom painted by Pandora Welland, the teenage daughter of a Chicago friend, with African figures, serpents, and fantastic shapes, giving it a uniquely amorphous look. The other guitar stowed in the Cave's basement was an instrument that had been associated with Bloomfield since the Monterey Pop Festival in 1967. It was his 1959 Gibson Les Paul Standard, the Sunburst he had gotten from his friend Dan Erlewine.

That tiger-striped guitar had appeared on the covers of *Super Session* and *Live at Bill Graham's Fillmore West*, and had figured prominently in Columbia's print ads for those albums. It was there in Bloomfield's *Rolling Stone* and *Guitar Player* interviews, and with him on the cover of *Down Beat*. He had done some of his best work using it, and fans from San Francisco to New York and Boston associated its fiery patina and classic shape with the "Bloomfield sound." Though only 1,700 Sunbursts had been made between 1958 and 1960, when Gibson discontinued the guitar for lack of sales, English blues rockers Eric Clapton, Jeff Beck, and Peter Green each had one. But it wasn't until Mike Bloomfield acquired his Sunburst that American players really took notice. Since then, Gibson's Les Paul Standard with the flamed finish had become the most sought-after instrument in rock music. Prices had increased tenfold and more for a good used one—if one could be found—because every blues player wanted the sound that Bloomfield had. The Sunburst had become the quintessential blues-rock guitar because, in the eyes of his fans, the guitar was quintessential Michael Bloomfield.

But the guitarist had no interest in his "brand." One guitar was pretty much as good as another, as far as he was concerned. He loved the Les Paul for its tone, sustain, and responsiveness, but he also liked his blue Telecaster and was even fond of an old Fender Stratocaster he had recently purchased. By 1974, Bloomfield's Sunburst was showing the effects of seven years of hard touring and rough treatment, and Michael had begun dismissing it as a "wreck." Its headstock had been split more than once, the back of its neck was pitted and black, its tailpiece was scaly with rust, and the control knobs were mismatched.

The whole instrument was crusty with years of sweat and grime, and after it was taken hostage by the Cave's management, Bloomfield thought it was probably no great loss. He made no effort to get it back and rarely spoke of it again. Various stories of how he had lost it circulated among his friends, but nobody except the band really knew what happened. All they did know was that Mike Bloomfield was suddenly without his iconic, tiger-striped powerhouse guitar, the instrument that had defined his sound for a significant portion of his remarkable career.

CHAPTER 24

LOVING THESE BLUES

MILL VALLEY AND SAN FRANCISCO, 1974–1977

The first week of November saw the release of the Electric Flag's Atlantic album *The Band Kept Playing*. While *Billboard* touted it as the "long-awaited reunion LP of one of rock's more popular bands" and described it as "well worth waiting for," the record was visually lackluster with a drab, cartoonish cover depicting the band hoisting Old Glory, an image based on the famous Iwo Jima flag-raising photo from World War II. The picture on the back, taken while the group was in Miami, showed five somber-looking musicians staring suspiciously at the camera—five big men who more resembled middle-aged tourists than they did rock stars.

The record's music, though, was very well produced and generally well received. "As a contemporary rhythm-and-blues album, 'The Band Kept Playing' is solid stuff," proclaimed one reviewer. *Rolling Stone*, having forgotten its enmity for Michael Bloomfield, was magnanimous, even flattering in its assessment. "*Mirabile dictu*, every lick is in place, the vocals are restrained and to the point, nothing is overblown or pretentious," wrote the reviewer. Much praise went to Jerry Wexler for creating a "brilliantly executed, incredibly believable illusion . . . well within the Atlantic tradition." The review concluded by stating, "As far as Bloomfield, Goldberg, Gravenites and—possibly—Miles are concerned, this is their finest hour. They've all blossomed into versatile songwriters, their egos are sublimated for the time being to creating a group image and they have found in Wexler the perfect producer for what they're trying to do."

It might not have been entirely accurate, however, to proclaim a sublimation of egos among *all* the members of the reunited Electric Flag. Buddy Miles's insistence on taking over every performance with his attention-grabbing "clap your hands" routine had sown seeds of discontent right from the band's first gig. Now everyone—especially Mike Bloomfield—had reached their limit. With only two more appearances scheduled for the Flag—one in Lake Tahoe and the other on Maui in Hawaii—Bloomfield announced he was quitting the group. Within a week, Buddy himself let it be known he would no longer tour with the band, preferring instead to go on the road with his own group. Barry Goldberg was willing to record, but he also would not tour, citing his aversion to flying. A newspaper columnist reporting on the de facto breakup of the band noted that Mike Bloomfield preferred to make "soundtracks for pornographic movies." Another report quoted Michael as saying he was planning to open a chain of "massage parlors" catering exclusively to women. Though he was serious about severing ties with the Flag, Michael could not resist having a little fun with the story.

By February 1975, the Electric Flag had been furled once again. There would be no tour to promote *The Band Kept Playing*, no second album on Columbia, and no hit song penned by Michael Bloomfield. The guitarist went back to working local gigs with the Friends, many of whom were also former Flag members. Often the only difference between Michael Bloomfield and Friends and the Electric Flag was the band's name—and the absence of Buddy Miles.

Throughout the late winter and early spring, Michael Bloomfield played fewer than a dozen gigs. With the cushion from his trust fund arriving every twelve weeks, the guitarist could afford to work only when he wanted to. He still owed the government a substantial amount in back taxes, but the regular checks took his mind off his debts. Toby Byron had been booking performances for Michael Bloomfield and Friends for more than two and a half years, but now that the guitarist was performing less often, Toby began looking for other work. "I tried to arrange something with Bill Graham," Byron said, "but that didn't work out. There really was nothing happening in the Bay Area at the time. It was dead for me." Bloomfield's frequent road manager began thinking about relocating, possibly heading to Los Angeles or even the East Coast.

In May, the Mitchell brothers came to Michael with another film project. This time they wanted him to create an elaborate soundtrack for a huge production they were planning, a ninety-minute sex epic based on the biblical stories of Sodom and Gomorrah. The guitarist was intrigued by the proposal, seeing it as an opportunity to explore ethnic music in a historical context. "I did a whole lot of research on Middle Eastern music and Bible music," Bloomfield said. "I checked out a lot of Turkish music, got Folkways records, real ethnic sorts of things."

Despite the Mitchells' often campy attitude toward filmmaking and their casual disregard for coherent plots and credible acting, Bloomfield again took the assignment seriously. He assembled a group of friends that included Barry Goldberg, jazz reed player Bert Wilson, violinist "Steamin'" Freeman Lockwood, and drummer Carmine Appice, a former member of Vanilla Fudge, at Golden State Recorders. Over the course of three days, they recorded dozens of short instrumentals for use as backgrounds and several longer pieces for scene transitions and credit sequences. Using a variety of hand drums, wooden flutes, and string and reed instruments, Michael created atmospheric music that evoked the arid plains of the Negev, the bustle of a Sumerian marketplace, and the sensual pleasures of King Herod's banquet hall. He also arranged fully orchestrated selections that used piano, guitar, bass, drums, and a horn section to establish regal or martial moods. The film's main theme featured the rhythm section with a vocal and chorus, and Bloomfield brought in Mill Valley singer Anna Rizzo, a close friend of Norman Dayron's, to sing the lyrics. With a melody reminiscent of the Four Tops' 1967 hit "Reach Out," the theme seemed to suggest pleasures of a more platonic sort than those portrayed in the Mitchells' footage. But Bloomfield's soundtrack music was well played and convincing—and stylistically a real departure from his other film scores. Had he created it for a "legitimate" film studio, he would undoubtedly have received critical acclaim for its inventiveness.

Though *Sodom and Gomorrah: The Last Seven Days* was heavily promoted in the press when it was released in September, it was a critical and commercial flop. Reputed to have cost the Mitchells nearly half a million dollars, the film was a peculiar blend of oddball science fiction, Cecil B. DeMille pageantry, Keystone Cops slapstick, and gross-out copulation. The one thing it wasn't was sexy, and porn fans stayed away in droves, nearly driving Jim and Artie Mitchell's adult entertainment empire into bankruptcy. The only part of the biblical skin flick that succeeded was its musical soundtrack. Mike Bloomfield's score was, for those who stayed past the first reel, the most enjoyable part of the experience. But it would be the guitarist's last collaboration with the Mitchells, and the brothers would never again attempt a feature-length production.

Money was still a problem for Michael Bloomfield. Even though he had managed, with his accountant's help, to secure a release of the IRS lien on his house, the balance remaining on his unpaid taxes for 1971 and 1972 was considerable. His trust fund checks covered only his day-to-day expenses, and the payment he had received from the Mitchell brothers, as generous as it was, went mostly to studio time and musician fees. Michael also had medical bills. In June, he had gone into the hospital for surgery to remove a painful bone spur from his hand, and those payments were coming due soon. So it was no surprise that Bloomfield was receptive when Barry Goldberg said he had a manager friend who might be interested in working with them. Since the demise of the reformed Electric Flag, both Barry and Michael had been looking for a way to keep the remnants of the band together, and it was with that objective in mind that Goldberg had approached Elliot Roberts. As cofounder of Asylum

Records and the manager of star singer-songwriter Neil Young, Roberts had extensive connections in the music industry and had played a prominent role in developing the careers of more than a few pop music stars. He thought he might be able to do the same for Michael and Barry, and he arranged a meeting to discuss possibilities. Right away, though, Elliot made it clear that he didn't want anything to do with the former Flag.

"Nobody knew who the guys were in the band that Barry and I had been playing with previously," said Michael. "So the manager said we needed *names*." Roberts's plan was to assemble a "supergroup" around the guitar player and keyboardist, a band that comprised marketable names that would appeal not only to record buyers but to record companies. "He said to me, 'Look, man, we've got Ric Grech to play bass in this new band. We've got a *name* drummer—Carmine Appice.' I told him I wasn't interested in playing with these guys. 'Are you crazy?' I said. But he said, 'We'll clean up.'"

Once again, Michael reluctantly went along with someone else's vision for his music. This time it felt even more like a violation, because Roberts eventually secured a contract with MCA Records, a conglomerate that owned Decca, Kapp, and numerous other smaller labels. The company favored pop music with a commercial emphasis, and their stable of artists included mainstream superstars like Elton John, Neil Diamond, and Olivia Newton-John. MCA's executives were hard-nosed businessmen, corporate managers who were more interested in moving product than they were in music, and Bloomfield sensed the disconnect right away. "All these execs who came to see us looked the same: pinky ring, leisure suit, shirt open to the tits, fabulous complexions, and blow-dried hair," the guitarist opined. "We were a product, we were hula hoops, we were skateboards. We got a record deal, though."

In June, MCA's latest supergroup assembled in Los Angeles to rehearse and work up material for their debut album. Along with Bloomfield and Goldberg were the promised Grech and Appice, plus an LA-based jazz-and-rock vocalist who had previously worked with Michael named Ray Kennedy. They got along well enough at first, but Bloomfield soon realized that the members of the group had no real connection beyond their shared MCA contract. Ric Grech was an Englishman who had played bass with Family and had been part of the supergroup Blind Faith with Eric Clapton. Carmine Appice had been a member of the hard rock quartet Vanilla Fudge, and more recently had been part of Jeff Beck's power trio. He had played briefly with Bloomfield on the *Sodom and Gomorrah* soundtrack but only as a session player. Of the five musicians, it was Barry and Michael who were friends with similar musical backgrounds; it made sense for them to play together. But there was no natural reason why they should join up with Kennedy, Grech, and Appice.

"I began to realize the meaning of the word 'band'—meaning to band together, to congregate for some coherent meaning, whether it be religious, or they're all gay, or they're all black, or whatever," Bloomfield said. "In KGB, there was no real reason to congregate at all."

Underscoring the artificial nature of the quintet was its name. Management had elected to call the supergroup KGB after the Russian spy agency, implying that the initials stood for Kennedy, Goldberg, and Bloomfield. But there really was no more logic to the band's moniker than there had been behind the selection of its personnel. KGB's raison d'être may have been dubious, but its five musicians were nonetheless professionals. Whatever their differences, they set to work in the studio and within a week had recorded nearly two dozen tunes.

It was no surprise, then, that the music the quintet created was cleanly played and tightly arranged. Ray Kennedy's vocals were strong and effective. Barry Goldberg's keyboard work was tasteful and dynamic. Ric Grech and Carmine Appice provided a solid foundation for each the selections. Only Michael Bloomfield was subdued. He primarily played rhythm, with occasional lead fills here and there. As with the Electric Flag sessions in Miami the previous year, the guitarist refused to assert himself. He once again was little more than a sideman in his own band. It was only after the guitarist returned to Mill Valley and the recordings had been completed that he agreed to overdub a few solos in a local studio, adding his distinctive sound to several of the tunes.

Of the ten songs selected for the album, two were written by Michael and Barry together. "Baby Should I Stay or Go" was a sentimental ballad with a fine vocal by Ray Kennedy and a harmonizing chorus, but their "Working for the Children" was a standout. Built around the funky Jamaican rhythms of reggae, "Working for the Children" opened with an atmospheric solo on acoustic guitar by Michael and then dropped into an infectious dance beat provided by Grech and Appice. To close the song, Bloomfield overdubbed frenetic lead on electric guitar, making one of his few solo statements and doing so with characteristic passion. The tune was one of two on the record to feature a driving beat; the other, written by Barry alone, was "It's Gonna Be a Hard Night," a soul romp powered by the keyboardist's organ and Bloomfield's wah-wah guitar. An overdubbed solo from Michael concluded the tune, giving it a bluesy tag. On "High Roller," a mid-tempo ballad by songwriter Daniel Moore, Bloomfield played sonorous slide, using his Fender Stratocaster to get a sound that was brighter than his abandoned Les Paul would have produced. The Stratocaster would soon become his main guitar, and he would often play it with slide.

The remaining selections for the group's album were mostly mainstream pop tunes, light rock confections that sounded like they were intended for the

FM radio market. Taken together, KGB's music was a journeyman effort—competent, innocuous, and nothing special. There were no prominent players, no star soloists. The musicians worked together like cogs in a well-oiled machine, each playing his part and no one overshadowing anyone else. The result was well crafted—and more than a little dull. But the front office at MCA was satisfied, and plans were made for a post-holiday release scheduled for the first week in February. Discussions began for Elliot Roberts, who would manage KGB, to set up a concert tour in the spring to promote the album.

Just when it seemed he had gotten his tangled finances somewhat under control, Michael Bloomfield received a surprise birthday present. The day after his thirty-second birthday, the guitarist got a notice that the Internal Revenue Service had placed a second lien on his Reed Street house. The feds had run out of patience. They were now demanding payment in full for the balance of back taxes, penalties, and interest still owed by the guitarist. If payment were not forthcoming, Bloomfield would lose his house.

To compound his troubles, Michael's resident booking agent, the earnest and hardworking Toby Byron, decided to pull up stakes. In early August, he drove with Barry Goldberg and Barry's wife, Gail, from San Francisco to Los Angeles. From there, Byron hooked up with manager Mark Meyerson through Atlantic's Jerry Wexler and went to work for jazz fusion players George Duke and Billy Cobham. With Toby's departure, Bloomfield had not only lost a member of his Reed Street family, but also lost someone he could count on to hustle up gigs for his Friends band whenever he wanted to perform. With the IRS breathing down his neck, Michael needed to perform more than ever.

The guitarist was also exploring other income possibilities. Since childhood, he had always enjoyed writing and making up stories. He was a voracious reader and deeply admired authors like Bernard Malamud, Philip Roth, Bruce Jay Friedman, and Patrick Dennis, and he particularly enjoyed the ribald low-life fiction of Charles Bukowski. Bloomfield thought he, too, might become a writer. He had told a French interviewer as early as 1970 that he was planning to write short stories for the Grove Press, and though that hadn't happened, Michael still had the desire to put pen to paper. He mentioned his ambition to Norman Dayron one afternoon, and Norman, thinking of his friend's glib and easy way with spoken words, suggested that instead of writing them out, Michael could dictate his stories into a tape recorder. From there, they could be transcribed and edited as necessary and then submitted to a publisher. The narratives could even be turned into screenplays for movie treatments. The idea intrigued Bloomfield, and a recording session was quickly set up.

"We sat around my dining room table one evening with a reel-to-reel," said Dayron, "Michael told a story I'd heard many times before. But this time he told it with a rhetorical brilliance that was pure Bloomfield—he made it into a comic masterpiece." For nearly an hour, the guitarist recounted his adventures with his friend and mentor Big Joe Williams, retelling in florid hipster argot the saga of their trip to East St. Louis on that hot Fourth of July weekend. The junket, in Michael's telling, became a young musician's coming-of-age tale, an epic as humorous and insightful as it was unflinchingly candid. By the time he concluded the narrative, he had created a vivid picture of the chasm between white and black cultures and of his well-intentioned attempts to bridge it.

Dayron was deeply impressed. His girlfriend, Sally Moses, volunteered to transcribe the recording. "I wasn't sure what they were going to do with it—maybe a screenplay for a movie? I don't think they even knew themselves," said Moses. "But I could type and I was happy to do it." The story, when finished, ran to thirty-four pages and was titled "Me and Big Joe, a Reminiscence by Michael Bloomfield." Over the next few weeks, Michael recorded other stories, fictional tales he largely improvised on the spot.

One was titled "King Ivory." "It was about this cantankerous old blues guy who was real domineering and demanding with his sidemen," said Norman. "Michael based him on Howlin' Wolf, and he has the guy get into a fight with one of his musicians. The musician, a much younger guy, kicks his ass and then feels really bad about it. In the end, the band gets back on the bus, deciding to stay with King Ivory and keep the music going." Another recording was intended to serve as the basis for a screenplay and involved the demise of a stand-up comedian. "That one was called 'M.O.R.,'" Dayron continued. "It was the story of a talented truth-teller comic—think Lenny Bruce or Richard Pryor—who was pure, honest, and hysterically funny. It's about how he was slowly corrupted by his wife and eventually sells himself out."

Sally Moses transcribed those stories as well as Michael's other narrations. "There were six or seven of them that he eventually recited into the tape recorder," said Norman. Though the tapes and manuscripts were eventually put aside and Bloomfield's literary ambitions remained unfulfilled, it was clear that the guitarist was a natural storyteller, a raconteur who was as gifted with words as he was with a guitar.

Michael Bloomfield continued to work sporadically throughout the final months of 1975, playing shows with Mark Naftalin, Nick Gravenites, and the Friends at UC Berkeley, the Savoy in San Francisco, the Santa Rosa Fairgrounds, and the Family Light Music School in Sausalito. Though he no longer had Toby

Byron's help, Bloomfield managed to set up gigs whenever he needed them. His accountant was managing his finances with Susan's help, and the money from the KGB sessions that they sent to the IRS seemed to appease the feds. But things came to a head one afternoon in December when a government agent appeared at the front door of 9 Reed Street.

"Michael had to come up with fifty grand," said Bonner Beuhler. "I remember the revenue guy walkin' right up the driveway!" The agent demanded immediate payment of the balance of Bloomfield's back taxes or, he said, the government would take possession of the premises, evict the guitarist and his housemates, and put the place up for immediate sale. Michael had ten days to come up with the cash or be out of the house—time for negotiating had run out. The guitarist, realizing he was out of alternatives, did what he had often done in similar situations—he called Harold. "His pop helped bail him out," said Bonner.

"When my dad got involved, that's when all of Michael's tax problems got cleared up," remembered Allen Bloomfield. "Susie and the accountant did the best they could, but Harold brought in 'professional talent' to fix things." Stories circulated that Michael's friends had to lend him money so he could keep his house, and a few may have contributed, but it was Harold Bloomfield who ultimately resolved his son's obligation to the government. By January 30, the lien on Reed Street had officially been released, and all back taxes and penalties had been satisfied. Michael had humbled himself by going to his estranged father, but now he was, after years of hassling, finally clear of debt. Harold, for his part, strongly admonished his son to *never* ignore paying taxes again.

With the arrival of 1976 came a new place for Michael Bloomfield and Friends to play. Located at 2801 California Street, near the corner with Divisadero Street in the Pacific Heights neighborhood of San Francisco, was a small bar. The watering hole, owned by a music fan and former bail bondsman named Jeffrey Pollack, occasionally had music on the weekends. Bloomfield knew Pollack from Jeffrey's brief stint as a partner in the Matrix, and the guitarist stopped by one evening when he was in the city to check the new place out. Right away the Old Waldorf reminded him of Big John's in Chicago, and Michael quickly made Pollack an offer.

"The Old Waldorf was like an old, rancid sailing vessel that was floating in a sea of stale Anchor Steam Beer," Norman Dayron recalled, laughing. "Every ounce of wood in that place was old and soaked in the liquor of one hundred years of history. It was *funky*!" Bloomfield told Pollack that he would organize music for the club on a weekly basis, just as he and Nick Gravenites had done at Keystone Korner. "He went up to the owner and said, 'Listen, I've got this band, and if you let me play here, we can split it,'" Dayron recalled. "Pollack figured he had nothing to lose and Michael would bring people in." Bloomfield offered to play for whatever money was collected at the door, and Jeffrey could keep the food and bar receipts. Within a few weeks, Michael Bloomfield and Friends were appearing regularly at the Old Waldorf, and business began to pick up. Norman thought it might be a good idea to document the band's performances, just as he had with the Group a decade earlier in Chicago, and he was soon making recordings whenever he could at the Old Waldorf. The tapes captured the guitarist in a relaxed setting, performing with his friends in front of a sympathetic audience. It was the way Bloomfield loved to make music, and the cache of recordings would later provide material for records Michael and Norman would produce together.

In mid-February, MCA released KGB's eponymous album. The label launched the record with a big promotional party in Hollywood, with refreshments served by waiters dressed in Cossack outfits with knee-high boots and tall sheepskin hats. The company announced that the band would soon be doing an extensive tour to promote the record with dates around the nation and in England.

"The material is good on the album," Barry Goldberg was quoted as saying in an MCA press release. Michael Bloomfield, though, wasn't so sure about the project. Faced with an exhaustive tour of as many as fifty cities—so Michael later claimed—he gave an interview to the *Los Angeles Times* in which he shared a litany of complaints about MCA, KGB, and superstar groups in general. With his usual candor, Bloomfield ripped into what he saw as a typical music industry charade. "I'm no hype artist," he told the reporter. "MCA would like me to say that the members of the group were meant to play together and that we love each other and that lots of record companies were clamoring to get us. Unfortunately, none of that is true." He continued, "We're a bunch of strangers. . . . [S]ome of the guys are people I would not choose to play with for various reasons." One of those guys was Ric Grech. The bassist, who had severe drug and alcohol problems, had been a target of Bloomfield's wrath during the band's recording sessions. Now he suggested that Grech would have to be replaced for the band to tour. And that wasn't all.

"I think the supergroup thing is really a scam and a hustle," Michael declared. When asked why he had agreed to join KGB, the guitarist unhesitatingly replied, "Money. Last year I owed a lot of money to the IRS and I have a family to support. I would have done anything to get some money. I don't have the slightest interest in pandering to the tastes of 14-year-olds, which is what KGB does. I had to join this group—or do something worse." The article concluded by implying that the famed guitarist preferred making music for pornographic movies to working with KGB. The Mitchell brothers didn't pay as much as MCA, but at least their projects provided the guitarist a "challenge to try and make these foul little movies a little bit more interesting."

When the *Los Angeles Times* published the article on February 22, Mike Bloomfield was distressed that so many of his disparaging comments had been included. He regretted being so outspoken to the reporter and later said, "I can't really explain why I told him all that. . . . I was just being dumb." But the damage was done. The executives at MCA were outraged by what they saw as the sabotaging of KGB even before the band had a chance to get started. They had invested a substantial amount of money into creating the group and producing the record, and now their efforts had been publicly derided as a "scam" by one of KGB's leaders. Michael saw he had no recourse but to resign from the band, something he truthfully was only too happy to do. He wrote a two-page letter to Elliot Roberts stating he was backing out of KGB and reiterating his complaints about the artificial nature of the project. He readily acknowledged that he should never have accepted the deal in the first place. "I was wrong to take the money," he wrote. "I was wrong not to walk out of your office the first or second time I met you and you referred to me as a loser and those people I play with as losers." He even offered to reimburse MCA for their losses.

Bloomfield's all-too-public departure from the band he had agreed to organize, a major-label supergroup that had been promoted as an exciting collaboration between some of contemporary rock's greatest musicians, sealed his fate with the music industry. He already had a reputation among certain record executives as a temperamental artist who could be both unpredictable and undependable, and now word spread that he was also prone to shooting his mouth off whenever he had a complaint. Those qualities, coupled with the fact that his most recent albums hadn't charted or even recouped their costs, were enough to make Mike Bloomfield into music industry poison. The superstar guitarist, once one of the business's hottest properties, was now seen as a problem, a risk not worth taking. "The big labels won't sign me because I won't work," Bloomfield said, acknowledging the fact that his disinclination to tour was a drawback. But the real issue was with the guitarist's attitude. He didn't like the music business, and now the business didn't like him either.

But while Michael Bloomfield was severing ties with the record industry, he was also going through what he later described as "an intense period of musical self-awareness." The guitarist felt he had finally come to terms with his celebrity and had accepted himself for who he was as an artist and a person. He now understood that he was so much more than the virtuoso guitarist who recorded *Super Session* or fronted the Electric Flag, that his interest in music and art far exceeded the industry's definition of "musician." The rock star "persona" had nothing to do with the Michael Bloomfield who read books, delved into American music history and styles, appreciated movies and television, loved comedy, and savored good food. It was all right, Michael realized, to be the musician *he* wanted to be, to play the music *he* wanted to play the way *he* wanted to play it. It had been a long time coming, but now, in the early spring of 1976, Bloomfield finally felt the burden of his stardom lift. He no longer felt obliged to be anyone other than who he was.

"I knew what I wanted to do," Michael said. "All of my diverse inputs were sort of coming together and solidifying. It was coming out in the way I wrote prose, painted pictures—the same aesthetic value was brought to everything, and I thought that it was valid." The guitarist understood that he could practice his art in whatever way suited him, even if that meant doing it entirely on his own.

"It was a realization," Michael explained in an interview with *Rock-N-Roll News* that spring. "A few months ago I realized I was an eclectic guitar player. I had so many styles, was into so many different forms of American music. I could just play in front of an audience a whole variety of music, just by myself." Michael had discovered the work of guitarist Ry Cooder, an artist whose music encompassed a wide variety of styles, including blues and rock but also country, old-timey, Latin, and traditional jazz. Bloomfield right away recognized a kindred spirit and was impressed by the way Cooder worked at his art, playing the music he loved on his own terms without concern for success as defined by the music industry. Michael saw that he could do that, too. "I realized everything was coming together for me in an artistic sense. I was developing a set of 'Bloomfield criteria.' I realized that I have a way of seeing the world, and everything was filtered through this certain aesthetic mechanism."

As Michael was going through this period of growth and change in his musical life, his home life was also undergoing a major change. Susan and Bonner Beuhler had been romantically involved for several years, and in the spring of 1976, they decided they had to move out. With a home of their own, the couple felt, they could begin a life together, and little Toby, now a thriving six-year-old, could have his own room. Their Reed Street experience had been a gratifying one, but it was Michael's house and the focus was invariably on him. The closeness of the daily routine had begun to chafe, and Susan and Bonner were eager to create a life together. For Susan, it was a difficult decision, because she still cared deeply for Michael and they had been together on and off for so many years. But her love for Bonner took precedence, and her growing concern for her impressionable young son's welfare was a strong motivator. "I had to get out of the house," said Susan. "Michael was into the drugs and things. I had a child. I had to get out."

The family at 9 Reed Street was suddenly a family of one. Michael Bloomfield found himself frequently all alone in his hillside retreat—a condition he had rarely experienced. Without Susan, little Toby, Bonner, and Toby Byron, though, the place didn't feel the same. Even though there continued to be a steady stream of friends and acquaintances dropping by, the house on the hill above Miller Avenue frequently felt empty.

In June, Mike Bloomfield flew to New York City for an appearance at the Newport Jazz Festival. He had been invited to play in a late-night program titled "Blues at Midnight," opening for Muddy Waters, Bobby "Blue" Bland, and Fats Domino. For the performance, he assembled an edition of his Friends band that included keyboardist Ira Kamin, bassist Doug Kilmer, and drummer Bob Jones. To open the set, though, he planned to do something different. In keeping with his recent revelations about music and his desire to play only what conformed to his own aesthetic, Michael decided he would begin the show with a few acoustic numbers. He would do several classic blues all by himself, picking and singing them in a traditional style, just as though he were sitting at home in his room.

On Friday night, June 25, the concert's emcee introduced Michael Bloomfield to the wildly appreciative blues crowd that had packed Radio City Music Hall for opening night of the Newport Jazz Festival. Many in the audience were surprised, however, to see the guitarist amble out from the wings with an acoustic instrument and take a seat on a chair downstage. Bloomfield then invited his friend Mike Michaels up to sit in on harmonica, and after introducing Michaels, he launched into a rendition of country blues singer Jim Jackson's 1927 tune "Kansas City." Fingerpicking the song's rhythm and lead parts while Michaels embellished the melody on harp, Bloomfield won the crowd over with his own clever rewrite of Jackson's lyrics.

> Just like the Arab told the Jew
> You don't like me, I don't like you
> Move 'em out, move 'em out
> Move 'em out to Kansas City
> People, where they don't 'low you!

Very few members of the audience that night had ever seen Michael Bloomfield play traditional blues on an acoustic guitar, and those who had certainly wouldn't have expected him to do so in an ostentatious setting like Radio City Music Hall. But there he was, the blues-rock master who had sparked the Paul Butterfield Blues Band, powered the Electric Flag, and supercharged *Super Session,* sitting hunched over on that vast art deco stage, plucking out a country blues as though he were entertaining a few closing-time patrons in a Greenwich Village coffeehouse. The novelty of the acoustic performance jazzed the crowd, and they responded vociferously when Michael concluded "Kansas City." But not everyone in the hall was pleased. "There were some rowdy guys in the front row," Mike Michaels remembered. "I could hear them shouting out for 'Albert's Shuffle.'" It was the increasingly familiar request for a tune from *Super Session*, and Bloomfield, as usual, ignored the hecklers. He jumped right into "Big City Woman," a ragtime number by Wilton Crawley with bawdy lyrics that elicited whoops and cheers, and then moved on to "Death Cell Rounder Blues," a slow drag inspired by the duet recordings of Leroy Carr and Scrapper Blackwell. Joined by Mike Michaels and now by Ira Kamin on piano, the guitarist sang of a murderer's rendezvous with the gallows, giving the lyrics a dramatic flourish. Michael was clearly enjoying himself.

But the audience was growing restless. Their surprise at seeing the guitarist play traditional folk blues had begun to fade, and now they wanted the Mike Bloomfield they all knew. As if sensing the change in mood, the guitarist brought out Doug Kilmer and Bob Jones, then plugged in a Gibson Marauder Deluxe, a new line of guitars that Michael had agreed to promote. After tuning up and adjusting mics, he counted off "Big Chief from New Orleans," his version of a Professor Longhair blues that featured ringing slide, and then rocked into Albert King's "I've Made Nights by Myself," an up-tempo shuffle that he peppered with biting, frenetic lead. Despite sound problems with Kamin's keyboards, the raucous crowd cheered the band on, and even the few catcalls for *Super Session* left Michael unperturbed.

"Lemme tell you about this song. This is a very *strange* song," the guitarist said, introducing the next tune. "In these days now of bisexuality and overts, and ambi-sexuality, whatever you want to call it, twenty years ago they had the same thing, but just the name was different. And this dude wrote a song about it." The song was "Bad Girl Blues," a novelty number about lesbian love by Willie Borum of the Memphis Jug Band. But Michael announced it as "Women Lovin' Each Other," eliminating any question about its subject matter. The quirky, suggestive lyrics appealed to the guitarist's fascination with the aberrant, and the verses he sang might have raised more than a few eyebrows in the house. But the blues, played with the piano now audible, had a raw electric vitality that was just what Newport's Bloomfield fans wanted to hear, and they responded with unbridled enthusiasm. For the remainder of the set, the guitarist stayed plugged in and played Chicago-style blues, including a stinging version of "Mary Ann," and closed the show with a rocking rendition of Big Joe Turner's "Shake, Rattle, and Roll." The audience was delighted and stood for an ovation as the guitarist and band walked offstage.

But some in the seats for "Blues at Midnight" found Michael Bloomfield's appearance less than satisfying. A review in the *New York Times* the following Sunday chided the guitarist for playing a long set and thus depriving Muddy Waters, Bobby Bland, and Fats Domino of more time onstage. The review went on to say that while Bloomfield's "enthusiasm for a variety of old blues styles can't be denied," his acoustic numbers seemed irrelevant given the rest of the concert's urban sensibilities. It was a telling observation about the new direction Michael was taking, especially with his live performances. Playing the music he wanted to play in the manner he wanted it played was not going to appeal to those listeners who expected him to be a rock star. There would likely be a price to pay for doing things his way. But Mike Bloomfield didn't care about critics, or even about what his fans might say. He was finding his way back to his roots, back to those aspects of music that had first inspired him before he had become a music industry "product." If a few noses were put out of joint because of that, it was none of his concern.

While in New York City, Michael visited with someone he had known since the Butterfield Band made its West Coast debut at the Trip in Hollywood back in 1966. Now a highly successful twenty-nine-year-old fashion designer, Tere Tereba had been a teenager when she and Bloomfield began their friendship, and from the start she had been drawn to the charismatic guitarist's outsized personality and exciting music. She was also a friend of pop artist Andy Warhol, and after moving to New York to work in the fashion industry, she had contributed articles to Warhol's pop culture magazine, *Interview*. She told Michael the artist was about to begin shooting his latest movie, a satire called *Andy Warhol's Bad*, and that she was going to play one of its characters. The production team, she added, was looking for someone to create the soundtrack, and Tere had suggested Michael.

"When it came to selecting the person for the score, many people were lobbying for it," said Tereba. "Lou Reed, of course, very much wanted to be doing the score. People like Rod McKuen said he'd do it for free." Tere knew Michael might be a long shot for the job, but she was able to convince the crew that Bloomfield was the man for the job. "At the end of the day—Jed Johnson was the director, and with Andy's final approval—Michael Bloomfield was picked and did the score for *Andy Warhol's Bad*."

Michael met with the famous artist on several occasions to discuss the film and get Andy's ideas for the soundtrack. The encounters might tactfully be described as interesting. Warhol, by 1976, was a strikingly odd-looking man, with his pasty, haunted visage framed by clear, horn-rimmed glasses and topped with a white fright wig. Bloomfield, candid to a fault, couldn't help commenting on the artist's appearance and demeanor. Such candor might have resulted in a social fiasco, but the guitarist's charm won Warhol over. "Michael was such an unusual person that he was able to make these truths—and they were nothing but truths—turn into something very positive," Tere said of Bloomfield's observations. "By the end of the meeting, Michael had turned what seemed like it was going to be a debacle into something where everybody was feeling very good about themselves."

"Michael called me from New York," said Norman Dayron. "He said he was hanging out with Warhol, and Andy wanted him to do the *Bad* soundtrack, and he, Michael, wanted me to produce it." The guitarist was enthusiastic about the project and knew he could count on Norman's help with the soundtrack's recording and mixing. His initial plan was to use Irving Berlin's 1929 song "Marie" as the movie's theme, but when rights to the classic tune proved prohibitive, Bloomfield decided to go in a completely different direction. After he returned to California, he set to work creating an entirely original theme in the style of contemporary dance club music. It was something he had been thinking about doing for a while, and now he had the opportunity. For *Bad*'s title music, Michael composed and arranged a disco tune.

"I'm dying to cut disco singles under the name Count Talent and the Originals," Bloomfield enthusiastically told an interviewer at the time. The Warhol movie provided an excellent chance to experiment with the popular genre, and Michael came up with an elaborately scored dance track that he called "Andy's Bad." Combining a synthesized chordal background with wah-wah guitar rhythms and a funk bass bottom over shakers and fatback drums, the theme had all the characteristics of a typical disco single. To give it an unusual twist, Bloomfield then added himself playing the tune's melody—on slide guitar. The effect gave the theme an uncanny vocal-like quality, almost as though Michael were singing through his instrument. "Andy's Bad" would undoubtedly be the only disco tune ever to feature blues-style bottleneck.

The remainder of the soundtrack's material was created using the technique Michael and Norman had developed for scoring the Mitchell brothers' films. Even though Warhol's production crew sent a copy of *Bad* out to Mill Valley, the guitarist and his producer had to resort to the film's script. "One day I came home to find a crate of thirteen film canisters—one-inch wide 35 mm film reels—on my doorstep!" Dayron said, laughing. "We had no way of watching them, so Michael said we'd get a synopsis of the scenes and their lengths, and 'make shit up.' We never actually *saw* the film."

Even without viewing any of the movie's 105 minutes, Bloomfield managed to produce a score that fit perfectly with its campy, bad-taste ethos. In addition to the main theme and other incidental disco music, the guitarist created rock instrumentals for barroom and street scenes, moody minor vamps for suspenseful sequences, and catchy melodies for comic interludes. When he shipped the completed soundtrack tapes to New York in July, *Bad*'s director, Jed Johnson, was delighted with the music—and so was Warhol.

Michael, too, was satisfied with the music. His first attempt at creating a convincing disco dance track had more than succeeded, and he hoped that soon he would be able to release his own club music as his pop music alter ego, Count Talent, with the Count's review, the Originals.

While he was working on the movie soundtrack for *Andy Warhol's Bad*, Mike Bloomfield was also quietly completing a project he had started for MCA in the early summer. As part of the deal for signing the KGB contract, Michael was given an option to do a solo album for the company. The executives no doubt were hoping the guitarist would produce a saleable pop-oriented record, but Bloomfield had other plans. The disgust he felt over his involvement with the company's manufactured supergroup left him with a deep desire to make music that was more meaningful. "I felt this overwhelming urge to do something with integrity," Michael acknowledged in an interview with *Guitar Player* magazine. The revelations he had recently experienced regarding the merits of his own artistic vision and the wealth of influences that had shaped it gave Bloomfield an idea. He decided he would record an album that highlighted those influences and that would serve as a resource for other guitar players. It would be, simply put, an instructional record.

But after his blow-up with KGB, MCA was in no mood to release anything by the problematic guitar player—certainly not an "instructional" album. They were in the business of making and selling pop records, not educating listeners. But Michael had already begun work on the album and had rented time at Blossom Studios, a small basement facility in San Francisco that had been set up as a recording and rehearsal space by musician and engineer David Blossom. It was the same studio Michael used to record the soundtrack for *Bad*, and many of the same musicians were involved. With MCA no longer interested in the guitarist or in rescuing his integrity, Bloomfield's instructional LP was temporarily on hold while he turned his attention to the Warhol project. But once that had been completed, Michael found another label for his how-to album—one that was in the business of putting out "learning materials."

In 1976 *Guitar Player* magazine formed Guitar Player Records, a company dedicated to issuing albums for "the complete guitarist." The label was planning to release LPs by guitarists Larry Coryell and Herb Ellis, records that would demonstrate jazz and blues styles and would include explanatory booklets. Michael Bloomfield had long been on *Guitar Player*'s advisory board, and when he learned that the magazine's publisher, Jim Crockett, was going into the instructional record business, he asked them to take on his unfinished MCA project. It was a serendipitous moment, and Guitar Player Records readily accepted the guitarist's offer. A deal was worked out with MCA that limited distribution to mail-order only, and the corporation was only too happy to be rid of Michael Bloomfield.

For the first time in his career, the blues-rock virtuoso had complete control over his "commodity," as he described it. He wasn't creating music for a major record label. There were no pinky-ringed executives involved, no A&R men or meddlesome producers. No one was expecting him to write a hit song or sell records. The recording studio, engineers, musicians, and production people were all of his choosing. So, too, was the music. He had been in charge of various aspects of his creative output before, but this time Bloomfield wasn't working *for* anyone. He was free to make the music he wanted to make in the way he wanted to make it. With that freedom came real inspiration.

The record, Michael decided, would present blues through a wide variety of styles and techniques. It would have folk and country blues, urban and Chicago-style blues, and white blues and black blues. He further determined that he wouldn't slavishly re-create the original tunes that had inspired him but instead would work up his own compositions in the style of each artist he was illustrating. Using Friends regulars Ira Kamin, Doug Kilmer, Roger Troy, Rev Stallings, and Hart McNee, and also drummers Tom Donlinger and Dave Neditch as well as pianist Eric Kriss, Guitar Player Records' founder, Bloomfield scrupulously re-created the styles of nearly a dozen blues greats. Using combinations of acoustic and electric instruments, the guitarist recorded and rerecorded parts for each tune until he got the desired results. He was determined to make them as accurate as possible.

Over the course of several weeks, Bloomfield taped tributes to B. B. King, T-Bone Walker, Lonnie Johnson, Scrapper Blackwell, Blind Blake, Blind Lemon Jefferson, Jim Jackson, John Lee Hooker, Guitar Slim, Eddie Lang, and the "Singing Brakeman," Jimmie Rodgers. He also recorded two original tunes as a general homage to the music, pieces he described as "gospel-type blues." One, titled "If You Love These Blues," was meant as an introduction to the album. Done in the urban style of B. B. King and Ray Charles, it featured masterful lead guitar, sanctified organ, and a voice-over by Bloomfield explaining the record's mission: "I'm glad to have the chance to pass on what I have learned by listening to records, to radio, and to so many great bluesmen. You know, blues is America's musical legacy to the world, and if you love these blues, play 'em as you please." The other original, intended as the album's closer, was called "Altar Song" and featured a haunting melody played with a slide as the guitarist recited the names of those artists he felt indebted to. In a little more than two minutes, Michael acknowledged more than 115 singers and players who had inspired him throughout his career. It was a striking testimonial from a young white blues superstar.

Of the acoustic selections Michael recorded, several were standouts. "Blue Ghost Blues," a piece based on the Lonnie Johnson tune also known as "Haunted House Blues," was played on guitar with additional guitar and banjo parts overdubbed. Using a shifting twelve-bar form and repeated tempo doublings, the song demonstrated Bloomfield's skill at fingerpicking intricate syncopated patterns. Another impressive performance was his original instrumental "Thrift Store Rag." Meant to evoke the early recordings of Blind Blake, the piece was played "piano style" on a single guitar with Michael executing tricky contrapuntal rhythms and a mid-piece modulation. Bloomfield also recorded two of the acoustic numbers he had played at the Newport Jazz Festival. "Kansas City" lacked Mike Michaels' sinewy harmonica accompaniment in the studio version, but Bloomfield sang and played the ragtime toe-tapper with the same good-humored virtuosity. For "Death Cell Rounder Blues," pianist Ira Kamin was replaced by Eric Kriss, and though Kriss's style was rudimentary by comparison, Michael's dexterous guitar work more than compensated for the deficiencies.

Of the four electric blues Bloomfield recorded, "WDIA," a mid-tempo shuffle named for the radio station in Memphis that Michael listened to in his early teens, was inspired by B. B. King. Faithfully re-creating the sound of King's early RPM records, the instrumental showcased Michael's string-bending skills as he built exciting tension by playing slightly ahead of the beat. "City Girl" was the guitarist's recasting of T-Bone Walker's "Glamour Girl," an urban-style blues that was one of Michael's early favorites. Using the full band with horns, Bloomfield sang the castigating lyrics and then soloed in Walker's dense, arpeggiated style, evoking the Texas bluesman with uncanny precision. He did the same with Eddie "Guitar Slim" Jones, again using the horn band on "Death in the Family," an original slow blues. Based on Slim's "The Story of My Life" and "The Things That I Used to Do," Michael effectively mimicked the New Orleans guitarist's laconic approach but then soloed in his own style, leavening the twelve-bar with a bit of Bloomfield verve. Making a guest appearance, Nick Gravenites contributed "Mama Lion," an original vamp blues played with the raw aggression typical of recordings by John Lee Hooker. Nick sang the cautionary tale and played rhythm while Michael threw in stringent asides on slide and then bore down for a razor-edged solo. It was a two-fisted, up-from-the-Delta roadhouse blues that varied from its 1950s progenitors only in the quirky poetry of Gravenites's lyrics.

When the sessions for the Guitar Player instructional record were completed in early August, Michael gave Norman Dayron the task of mixing the tapes. Dayron prepared the selections, mastered them, and then shipped them to Takoma Records, an independent folk-and-blues label in Santa Monica that had agreed to press and distribute Guitar Player Records releases. Michael was very pleased with the results, feeling that he had achieved exactly what he had set out to do.

"I was striving to get the sounds of various old records, and that came through," Bloomfield later said in an interview. "I was trying to look at not just the different guitar styles, but also the whole setting, the feel, the persona, the ambience of certain musics—sort of a musicological period movie." He planned to write explanatory notes for each of the album's tunes so that listeners would know their origins and the artists associated with them and then could learn to play them themselves. After years of unsatisfying musical "scams," Michael Bloomfield felt he had finally produced an album he could be proud of. He later affirmed as much, saying, "I know it's my best record, me at my hottest."

On Saturday, August 7, Michael Bloomfield re-created his Newport Jazz Festival performance a little closer to home—at the San Francisco Blues Festival in the city's John McLaren Park. Beginning his set with a few solo numbers just as he had at Radio City Music Hall, Bloomfield opened with "Kansas City," picking the Jim Jackson classic on his Beggerby acoustic guitar with a jury-rigged pickup taped into its sound hole. Michael then moved over to piano to pound out a jump blues before bringing on Ira Kamin, Doug Kilmer, and Bob Jones for a wildly exuberant version of "Women Loving Each Other." The quartet worked through half a dozen other tunes with Bloomfield alternating between wailing slide and frenetic fretted lead while singing with carefree abandon. The audience in the outdoor amphitheater responded vociferously, picking up on the guitarist's enthusiasm and sparking the music with an energy of their own. Michael was clearly enjoying himself.

The set, with its split between solo and group performances, would become the new format for Mike Bloomfield's live appearances. He had tried it successfully at Newport in New York, and now, with the good response at home in

San Francisco, he decided that solo blues numbers, played on guitar or piano or both, should be part of every gig. It was music he wanted to play, an aesthetic he wished to explore, regardless of what record label executives, managers, club owners, and even his fans thought. The music he had recorded for his Guitar Player album was music that was important to him, that represented who he was and what mattered to him, and that going forward he was determined to play. He was going to put his "Bloomfield criteria" into practice.

In the early fall, Bloomfield took his quartet on the road for several gigs up north. The band appeared as part of a concert series called Blues in Alaska, opening for John Lee Hooker in Anchorage and Fairbanks. They also performed at the other end of the country, in Austin, Texas, at a blues club called Antone's, which had opened in 1974. Each appearance featured Michael singing and playing a few solo tunes before bringing on the full band. Reaction was mixed, at least until the quartet appeared, because few fans were aware that Bloomfield was anything other than a plugged-in blues-rocker. Michael seemed unperturbed, though, and he enjoyed playing the traditional blues just as much as he did his electric material.

In October, 9 Reed Street received another house guest, this time from out of town. Bob Greenspan came for an extended visit, taking Michael up on his offer of hospitality made at Tulagi. Almost immediately, Bloomfield arranged a gig for his friend. "Mike was playing at the Old Waldorf, and he had me open up for him," said Greenspan. "I'd get up and play solo before Naftalin, Jellyroll, Bob Jones, and those guys would come on." The performances gave Bob a chance to work on his material in preparation for the demo he planned to make with Michael's help. Sometimes, though, Greenspan wouldn't get around to singing. "Back in those days, I was drinking some whiskey," Bob recalled, laughing. "I was in the club's back room one time, and I had a bottle of Wild Turkey, and I downed the whole damn thing, just like that! I went out and I never sang one song—all I did was tell jokes!" The audience, there for music, wasn't prepared for a comedy act, especially one that was none too sober, and people soon began to leave. Bloomfield, watching Bob from the side of the stage, found the situation hilarious even though the crowd was making for the door. When Greenspan finally wound up his routine and came offstage, Bloomfield, still laughing, praised his friend. "He goes, 'That was one of the funniest things I've ever seen. Man, you're as funny as Steve Martin!'" Bob said. "He just loved it! He didn't give a shit whether his people left. That's just the kind of guy he was—he loved comedy and loved to laugh. If it was off-the-wall crazy enough, because *he* was off-the-wall crazy, he thought it was just great."

* * *

In mid-December, Guitar Player Records began promoting *If You Love These Blues, Play 'Em as You Please* by Michael Bloomfield. The album cover featured a photo of an acoustic guitar with a pickup taped over its sound hole in imitation of Bloomfield's Beggerby rig, and stuck in its strings was an engaging snapshot of the guitarist that Susan had taken. The record's liner contained notes on each of its thirteen selections, detailed listings of the musicians involved, and an explanatory statement from the guitarist. "I was lucky enough to grow up in Chicago when you could hear blues on seven or eight radio stations," Michael's blurb began. He went on to say that he was indebted to all the great musicians who had taught him, and the Guitar Player record was one way of paying them back. He would pass on what he had learned to future players, sharing his knowledge of the blues in all its varieties. "Listen carefully," he advised the buyer, "imitate what you can, add your own creative energy, and you'll be on your way."

The music on the record was as varied as Bloomfield's cover note promised. It ranged from classic blues played on acoustic guitar to the big sound of urban blues performed with electric instruments by a full rhythm section with horns. Most of the tunes were originals by Michael, and all successfully evoked the playing styles of one or another of the music's greatest artists. Between the selections, Bloomfield included spoken-word introductions that provided historical details and shared information about keys, instrumentation, and techniques. For those who wanted to know more, there was a card that could be mailed in for a booklet Michael had written that contained additional information and instructions. *If You Love These Blues, Play 'Em as You Please* was a serious scholarly effort, an instructional recording that was also an overview of one musician's journey through the genre known as the blues.

The January 1977 issue of *Guitar Player* magazine contained a full-page ad for the record, touting it as "a whole new kind of educational recording," one that "people who take music seriously can *enjoy* as well." For those who wanted to learn to play blues, Michael Bloomfield's latest opus could serve as a comprehensive primer. But for those who just wanted to listen, the record could also stand on its own as a fine blues album. Unlike most other instructional LPs, *If You Love These Blues* eschewed the usual step-by-step pedagogy and presented its tunes as complete, uninterrupted performances. Students could pick up progressions, patterns, and techniques the same way Michael did when he was starting out—by repeated listening. The only difference was that Bloomfield had included helpful tips with each tune. The magazine ad had a coupon that buyers could fill out and mail in to the company's Saratoga, California, headquarters to obtain a copy of the album. It was only available through mail order.

Also in January, Mike Bloomfield learned that *If You Love These Blues* had been nominated for a Grammy Award. Because the awards had no separate category for blues recordings in 1976, the album was in the running for the year's "Best Ethnic or Traditional Recording." Other nominees included blues guitarist Hound Dog Taylor, actor Chief Dan George, a Scottish bagpipe band, and folksinger John Hartford. Though Hartford was the eventual winner, Michael Bloomfield was justly proud of his nomination. "The Guitar Player record I really like to hear over and over again," the guitarist later said, confirming that as far as he was concerned, it was a winner.

With the arrival of 1977 and the start of a new year, Michael Bloomfield continued playing weekends at the Old Waldorf. But the club that had reminded him of Big John's was no longer located on California Street. Owner Jeffrey Pollack, finding the original space too small for the growing crowds, had moved the Old Waldorf to a much larger venue at 444 Battery Street in San Francisco's Financial District. The new room, on the second floor, had a much larger stage and could accommodate as many as 750 patrons. It was undoubtedly an improvement over the first Old Waldorf, but for Michael the new space lacked the funky charm of the original. Nevertheless, he still enjoyed its casual atmosphere and liked working for Pollack, so he continued to perform there, playing both acoustic and electric sets.

One afternoon in March, Norman Dayron dropped by Reed Street with a proposition for his friend. He had been listening to some of the recordings he had made of the Friends band over the last months at the Old Waldorf, and he thought they had potential. "I told Michael I thought we could release some of the Waldorf stuff on our own, you know, find a label and put it out. It was that good," said Dayron. "But Michael wanted to go a step further. He told me he wanted to produce his own records, that he was through dealing with the major record companies and wanted complete control over whatever records he was going to make." Bloomfield had experienced that control while producing his Guitar Player album, and he was determined to keep it. He also knew that there was little chance any major company would be interested in recording him after the KGB debacle, so he had nothing to lose by doing it all himself. Norman readily agreed, and the two friends decided they would form a production company.

On March 10, Norman's friend Sally Moses took out a legal notice in the *Marin County Court Reporter*, to be published on consecutive Fridays in April. It announced the formation of a new company called C.T. Productions, with herself as secretary and Michael Bloomfield and Norman Dayron as its principal partners. "We based C.T. Productions out of my apartment on Millwood Street in Mill Valley," said Dayron. "C.T. was for 'Count Talent,' and we published Michael's songs under 'King David Music.' He was under contract to Warner Brothers at the time, and he didn't want them to get his publishing. Right away we started looking for a label to release whatever albums we were going to produce." The obvious choice was Takoma Records, the small company in Santa Monica that was handling the distribution of Bloomfield's *If You Love These Blues*. Perhaps they would be interested in releasing other recordings by Michael Bloomfield.

Later in the month, Bloomfield received an invitation to the premiere of *Andy Warhol's Bad*. The film was opening in Los Angeles the last week in March, and its costar Susan Tyrrell was throwing a huge party at her mansion in Hancock Park for Warhol, the people involved with the movie, and nearly every celebrity in Hollywood. Michael agreed to go, but only if pianist and singer Randy Newman would be there. He greatly admired Newman's gift for writing clever, intelligent songs, and he was eager for a chance to meet him. That Newman often featured Ry Cooder on his albums also appealed to the guitarist. In Bloomfield's mind, both musicians were artists who remained true to their own aesthetic despite popular trends. Newman was invited to the *Bad* party, and Michael arrived hoping to meet him. But his attention was caught by another guest at the event, and he never got around to introducing himself to Newman. Michael spent most of the party talking instead to the oddest-looking person in the room—gigantic Arnold Schwarzenegger, just off the bodybuilding circuit.

The movie itself was unfavorably reviewed by the mainstream media in ensuing weeks, with most critics put off by its unapologetic, amoral cynicism. "The problem is that it is not outrageous, it is revolting," the *New York Daily News* declared, while the *New York Times*' Vincent Canby cautioned that the film "is not a movie I would recommend to anyone without a warning." The film quickly assumed cult status and was relegated to art movie houses when it was shown at all, but the music was perhaps its most palatable aspect. Bloomfield's score helped lighten the film's darker moments, and moviegoers often hummed the *Bad* theme as they exited the theater while the credits rolled.

With his new approach to performing now firmly established, Michael Bloomfield made a special concert appearance in Santa Monica on April 13. The guitarist brought a quartet to McCabe's Guitar Shop, a music retailer on Pico Boulevard that specialized in acoustic and electric guitars. The shop had a small performance space with room for an audience of 150, and on weekends the owners would bring in guest guitarists to perform. The intimate setting appealed to Michael because playing there felt very much like playing in his living room at home. The shop also was capable of making professional-quality tapes for its performers, thanks to a remote recording facility set up by a record company that had its offices next door. That company, coincidentally, was Takoma Records, and Michael, seeing an opportunity, approached general manager Jon Monday and asked if he would be interested in working with C.T. Productions to issue future Bloomfield recordings. Monday said the company would be, and suggested they roll tape on Michael's show at McCabe's for possible release as a live album. Takoma had already put out several LPs recorded at the guitar shop, and if Bloomfield was happy with his performance, perhaps it, too, could be issued. Michael agreed and passed the word on to the band.

The band for the McCabe's gig didn't consist of Michael's usual Friends players. Mark Naftalin had come with him from San Francisco, but his bass player and drummer were local players from Santa Monica. Buell Neidlinger was a classically trained bassist who had been a member of jazz pianist Cecil Taylor's seminal quartet in the 1950s and had played in the Houston Symphony Orchestra in the 1960s. Drummer Russell "Buddy" Helm had played with Frank Zappa and folksinger Tim Buckley before becoming a session player in LA's television and film studios. Both musicians were thoroughly schooled in the blues, and though Bloomfield's material was not the sort of music they usually played, they were capable accompanists.

Michael opened the Wednesday evening show with an acoustic set, picking traditional blues and ragtime tunes on his big Beggerby guitar. He began with the familiar "Kansas City" but then performed a number of tunes that were new to his repertory. "Some of These Days" and "Darktown Strutters Ball" were both by the Vaudevillian entertainer Shelton Brooks and from the early 1900s. In the latter tune, he amused the crowd by inserting saxophonist Louis Jordan's jump novelty "Mop-Mop" and then tossed in a few lines from the traditional rag "Black Dog." He sang Jimmie Rodgers's version of "Frankie and Johnny," adding his own lyrics and picking its syncopated melody and rhythm with impressive agility. Two gospel selections were also part of the set. One, "Lo, I Am with You Always," a variation on the Rev. Gary Davis song, took the form of an eight-bar blues. The other, "Great Dreams from Heaven" by the Bahamian guitarist and singer Joseph Spence, was a moving instrumental that Michael had heard Ry Cooder play. To complement the Christian bent of those selections, the guitarist sang a blues titled "I'm Glad I'm Jewish," a variation on Barbecue Bob's 1928 song "Chocolate to the Bone." The new lyrics were classic Bloomfield, and the first verse brought down the house with peals of laughter.

I'm glad I'm Jewish, I'm glad I'm Jewish
Hebrew to the bone, lord, lord
I'm glad I'm Jewish, Hebrew to the bone
You know the Christian girls
Just can't leave little Jew boys alone.

The guitarist closed out the set with a lyrical guitar improvisation that fell into tempo and then became a fleet version of the traditional blues "Stagger Lee," which Michael sang using R&B singer Lloyd Price's familiar lyrics. "Thank you very much!" he said breathlessly over the cheers and applause, and then he headed up the stairs at the back of the stage for a fifteen-minute intermission.

Following the break, Michael brought out Mark Naftalin to play several selections as a piano-and-guitar duet. Plugging in his Stratocaster, the guitarist kicked off the first tune by fingerpicking an insistent rhythm, vamping steadily as the pianist joined in. With a rocking tempo established, Bloomfield began "My Father Was a Jockey," John Lee Hooker's double-entendre boogie from 1950, and then added lyrics from Hooker's "Boogie Chillen'." Michael and Mark worked the boogie riff, driving the performance with a syncopated hocketing of the rhythm. "Hi-yo, hi-yo Silver!" the guitarist exuberantly shouted as he brought the one-chord foot-stomper to its conclusion. As the audience whooped and cheered, Bloomfield abruptly changed the mood and eased into a slow blues, an instrumental in B-flat that intertwined his fluid phrases on slide with Naftalin's strong left hand and fleet-fingered countermelodies. Switching to fretted lead for his solo, Michael toyed with the beat, one moment pushing it forward and the next lagging seductively behind as Mark echoed his phrases. The pianist's solo featured a dramatic series of rumbling runs in the bass clef, and then Bloomfield returned to close the performance with more languid slide work. Mark called the piece "Groundskeeper's Blues," a dedication to the legendary blues pianist Jimmy Yancey, who for years made a living tending the field at Comiskey Park for the Chicago White Sox.

The remainder of the set was performed by the full quartet. Michael brought the rhythm section on with B. B. King's "Eyesight to the Blind" and then slid into his current favorite, "Women Loving Each Other." Both Neidlinger and Helm displayed an uncanny ability to intuit keys and tempos with little more than a nod from the leader or a cue from Naftalin. With no rehearsal and Bloomfield's habit of starting a tune with no information beyond the mention of a title—if that—lesser musicians would have stumbled. But the bass player and drummer meshed seamlessly with their San Francisco compatriots, and the performance went off without a problem. Bloomfield played Chuck Berry's

"Don't You Lie to Me" and "Wee Hours," engaging in a wailing duet with Naftalin on the latter tune, and then bore down for a stunning solo on "Cherry Red," the eight-bar blues by Big Joe Turner. Mark introduced a riff instrumental that sounded inspired by King Curtis's "Soul Serenade," and Michael indulged in a bit of "East-West"-style improvisation before closing the set with a quirky tune by Randy Newman. Called "Uncle Bob's Barrelhouse Blues," the song, in its original version, was a dyspeptic whine whose lyrics used blues tropes to create a surreal parody. Newman ended the tune by intoning the refrain "We love you" over and over, and Michael did, too, but then he added a tag at the song's end, coyly declaring to the audience, "We hope you love us, too!" Judging by the applause as the guitarist led the band offstage, the audience did indeed love them.

The McCabe's show was a milestone in Michael Bloomfield's career. It caught the guitarist at his very best—relaxed, confident, and in complete command of his considerable musical talents. His acoustic performances were stunning—a revelation to many in the audience. His singing was controlled and convincing, the perfect complement to his playing. When joined by the band, the more familiar Bloomfield emerged, and the guitarist's electric lead was brilliant. But it was also denser, more complex, played with greater urgency. Here was the mature Michael Bloomfield, the seasoned pro who had nothing to prove and everything to share. He was in his element, playing the music he loved in an intimate setting without pretention or artifice. The two-and-a-half-hour concert was a tacit summation of Bloomfield's life in music, running the gamut from his early fascination with Chuck Berry-style rock 'n' roll, to his folkloric immersion in traditional rags and blues, to his love for B. B. King and the urban sound, and finally to his own blues-rock, a melding of all those forms that came to define 1960s pop music. The McCabe's concert demonstrated that the guitarist's "Bloomfield criteria" not only had personal validity but could work as a holistic presentation. Michael's artistry, coupled with his easy humor and considerable charm onstage, won over the audience without reservation. There were no catcalls for "Season of the Witch" that night. No one in the room was living in the past. It was Michael Bloomfield's present that mattered.

CHAPTER 25

COUNT TALENT

MILL VALLEY, NEW YORK, 1977–1980

Back in Mill Valley, Michael told Norman Dayron about his conversation with Jon Monday of Takoma Records. He said the company was interested in working with C.T. Productions and that his appearance at McCabe's Guitar Shop had been recorded for possible release on the label. But, he added, he wanted his next album to be a studio effort. He felt the complete control he had exhibited while recording his Guitar Player LP had made the music as good as it was, and he intended to repeat the process for his next release. Norman agreed but said they should get copies of the McCabe's tapes anyway because they might want to do something with them in the future. He also said he would contact Monday, work out the details with Takoma, and find a studio for the guitarist's sessions. The two friends shook on it, and C.T. Productions was suddenly a reality.

"The Takoma albums were $1,500 to $2,000 tops, everything but the artwork," said Dayron of their financial arrangement with the company. With Takoma's limited funds, the label generally split the budget for an album evenly between recording sessions and postproduction. Bloomfield was accustomed to more generous terms when making a record, and he quickly realized he wouldn't be able to pay for studio time and hire musicians on Takoma's modest advance. But one way he could save money was to play all the instruments himself. That would make scheduling easier, and with Norman's help he could keep the additional studio time for overdubbing to a minimum. In April, C.T. Productions went to work producing Mike Bloomfield's next album.

Norman booked time for the recording sessions at American Zoetrope, an excellent sound studio that was owned by filmmaker Francis Ford Coppola and located on Kearny Street in the North Beach section of the city. Michael got to work recording the initial tracks for the tunes he planned to do, bringing in an arsenal of stringed instruments. He had decided the album would be primarily acoustic, taking inspiration not only from traditional blues recordings but also from recordings he had heard of early popular music groups. "I used to have records of these old string bands," Michael said. "They'd play rags, quadrilles and schottisches, and they'd take music that was usually played by horns and do it with strings." He wanted to re-create the sound of those bands on several of the album's selections using a variety of acoustic instruments.

With that in mind, the guitarist laid down tracks for five instrumentals, tunes that would consist of solos accompanied by other stringed instruments. One was a tribute to the classic blues duets that guitarists Eddie Lang and Lonnie Johnson recorded for Okeh back in the late 1920s. Called "Mr. Johnson and Mr. Dunn," using the segregation-era pseudonym Lang adopted, the bright-tempo blues featured Michael comping in traditional swing style behind an extensive single-string solo he then overdubbed. His lead phrasing had more in common with contemporary styles than it did with Lang's on-the-beat improvisations, but the tune faithfully re-created the feel of the earlier collaborations.

Michael's favorite gospel group, the Swan Silvertones, provided inspiration for another instrumental. "At the Cross" had been recorded by the quintet in 1963, its melody carried by Claude Jeter's extraordinary falsetto. The guitarist evoked the singer's fluid vocalizations with his Stratocaster by using a slide, then backed them with overdubbed piano, organ, and bass. The drums he left to Bob Jones, knowing an actual drummer could better handle the song's slow tempo.

Michael did play drums himself on "Mood Indigo," Duke Ellington's classic instrumental. In keeping with his string band aesthetic, he substituted guitars for Ellington's clarinet, trumpet, and trombone choir, playing the tune's melody in unison using slide. By adding tinkling piano, he gave the selection a honky-tonk feel, and occasional instances of rubato, intentional or otherwise, made the music sound a bit wobbly.

Bloomfield's rhythm was rock steady, though, on another instrumental he recorded. A solo guitar piece of his own composition, "Effinonna Rag" opened with a series of chordal flourishes and then fell into steady 4/4 beat. Played piano-style with an alternating bass line and fingerpicked lead, the rag was an impressive eight-bar blues variation with a bridge. It had much in common with tunes Michael had played at McCabe's, and it bore some resemblance to "Kansas City" and "Thrift Shop Rag" from the guitarist's Guitar Player LP.

The final instrumental, another Bloomfield original, was unlike anything the guitarist had yet recorded. Called "Hilo Waltz," Michael created it by overdubbing a Western guitar, ukulele, and bass with a tiple, a guitar-like instrument of Colombian origin with a varying number of often doubled strings (this one had 10), and a Hawaiian Hilo guitar with a hollow neck and raised strings, meant to be played with a slide. Using an um-pah-pah rhythm, Bloomfield strummed chords, thumped the bass, and plucked the melody, all while creating slippery counterharmonies on the Hilo and tiple. He occasionally used slide on both guitars, and their slightly out-of-sync lines gave the tune a fractured sonority.

With so many stringed instruments busily filling the aural space, "Hilo Waltz" sounded more than a little like a child's music box on a bender. It was quite a departure from the blues.

But Bloomfield also recorded a number of conventional blues and vocals during his Zoetrope sessions. He sang "Frankie and Johnny," accompanying himself on acoustic guitar just as he had when he played it at McCabe's. "Big 'C' Blues," another of Michael's originals, was a slow Chicago-style shuffle played with a full band created by overdubbing guitar, piano, organ, bass, and drums. The song was a grim cousin to "Goin' Down Slow," with Bloomfield singing fatalistic lyrics about the effects of cancer and backing them with some intense soloing. In a different mood altogether was Michael's "Peepin' an a-Moanin' Blues," a semi-comic number about voyeurism, inspired by what the guitarist described as "a whole school of *double entendre* tunes" from the 1930s and 1940s. The song successfully captured the burlesque feel of those early Bluebird records with its "red hot mama" tempo and the guitarist's bluesy accompaniment on acoustic guitar and piano.

A final selection recorded for the Takoma album was an ensemble effort. "Analine," sung by its composer, Nick Gravenites, featured a rhythm section that included Mark Naftalin, Jellyroll Troy, and Bob Jones. Michael played rhythm guitar, adding quiet fills between Nick's phrases and subtle ornamentation to the song's melody. To create a fuller sound, he then overdubbed himself on mandolin and organ, and had Mark play accordion. Singers Anna Rizzo and Marcia Ann Taylor joined Nick on the song's refrain, turning it into a kind of anthem that swelled and intensified with each succeeding chorus. The tune was a standout, not only because it featured other musicians and was at variance with Bloomfield's folkloric string band aesthetic, but because it had a more contemporary sound than any of the other material. "Analine" didn't refer back to anything—it was a song all on its own.

Michael completed the tapes by the end of the month and turned them over to Norman for editing and mixing. Dayron worked on them at Xanda Recording Company, a studio on Geneva Avenue in San Francisco, and then, with Bloomfield's approval, shipped them off to Takoma Records in Santa Monica. The album, they decided, would be named *Analine* after Gravenites's tune, and Norman took a few photos of Michael and all his string instruments on Reed Street's back patio for use on the album cover. The label scheduled the record's release for early August.

Analine would be Michael Bloomfield's first commercial release that was entirely under his own control. The music, the personnel, the recording studio, even the cover art, were all of his choosing. It would be his first release that conformed wholly to his own "set of criteria" and that was not constrained by some other vision. The Columbia albums, with their emphasis on commercial viability, and even the Guitar Player record with its educational imperative had been shaped to a greater or lesser degree by outside expectations. Not so for *Analine*. The album was whatever *he* wanted it to be, regardless of what promoters, distributors, retailers, managers, fans, or anyone else thought.

But even with Bloomfield in control, *Analine* was not without problems. Some were technical. There were extraneous sounds on some of the tunes—a peculiar "thunk" in the middle of "Hilo Waltz," guitar box noises during "Effinonna Rag." Other glitches were musical, as when Michael stumbled on the lyrics to "Frankie and Johnnie," when he dropped a beat on drums at the end of "Big 'C' Blues," and when his guitar went out of tune on "Hilo Waltz." The overdubbed selections tended to sound cluttered, with too many instruments vying to be heard and none of them really standing out.

Most of these issues could have been easily corrected, but for some reason they weren't. Part of the problem may have been the budget. With the money C.T. Productions had for studio time, there was a limit to how many retake sessions were financially feasible. Too many fixes could have sent the project into the red, so Michael and Norman may have decided to make do with what they had. But there were other complications, too, that doubtless affected the recording process. "We were all doing a lot of drugs at the time," said C.T.'s secretary Sally Moses. "Marijuana, speedballs, and heroin. We'd all be high in the studio, and sometimes Norman would have to run out for more drugs. Michael, though, was very functional." Functional or not, Bloomfield's drug use had increased since Susan's departure from Reed Street a year earlier. His home life had lost much of the structure she had provided, and drugs, including heroin, were more and more often part of his regular routine. There were times when they undoubtedly affected his judgment, and the imperfections of *Analine* may have been one result. But there were also times when more than judgment was at stake.

"I was with Michael one time when he overdosed and turned blue. He was comatose—it was pretty frightening, really," said Bob Greenspan. Michael had just come out of his room, and they were watching television together. Bob noticed that his friend seemed increasingly unresponsive and became concerned.

> He was sitting on the couch, and I didn't know he'd shot any heroin. But I went up to him and said, "Mike?" and he goes, "I'm alright, I'm alright," but I could see him start to slump over, so I shook him a few

times, and he fell asleep. He was breathing and all, so it wasn't a severe thing, but I didn't know what the hell to do.

In 1975, Mike Bloomfield candidly told an interviewer that despite the pleasures of heroin, he no longer used the narcotic—"I outgrew it," he declared. That was wishful thinking. There were long periods when the guitarist abstained, but by 1977 he was fixing with greater frequency. Many of his friends and musical associates were also users, and some were outright addicts. Heroin was a part of his day-to-day life, and the opportunities to shoot up were plentiful. Bob Greenspan's unnerving experience with his friend's drug use was a harbinger of things to come. Before long, a Bloomfield overdose would be an unpleasant occurrence that nearly all the guitarist's close friends would have to contend with.

Through the late spring and summer months, Michael Bloomfield continued to work sporadically. He played weekends at the new Old Waldorf; made another appearance at McCabe's; took the band on the road to Seattle and Eugene, Oregon; and did shows at Freddy Herrera's new venue, the Keystone Palo Alto. He also started work on a short story with a writer friend from his Chicago days.

Scott Summerville first met Bloomfield at Big John's, and he, too, had moved to the San Francisco area in the late 1960s. "I would see Michael around Marin County off and on, and then one day he was complaining that he didn't have a good place to practice—he was disturbing the neighbors," the thirty-four-year-old Summerville said. "So I built a little soundproofed studio in his basement for him." Knowing that Scott was a writer, Michael mentioned that he had several stories and screenplays he was hoping to eventually publish. Perhaps Summerville would help edit them? Scott said he would, and within a few weeks he was hard at work tightening up Michael's pages.

"We started to work on a screenplay," Summerville recalled. "Then he said, 'Why don't you take a look at this?' and he gave me thirty-four pages of material that he said he'd spoken into a tape recorder." It was the transcript of Bloomfield's narrative about his trip to East St. Louis with Big Joe Williams. Summerville was immediately taken by the story's gritty candor, its stark clash of cultures, and its broad humor, and he eventually winnowed the manuscript down to twelve pages. He then sent it off to *Rolling Stone*, hoping to publish it in the periodical, which was now a monthly magazine. The editors, unfortunately, weren't interested.

"They had just made the changeover from counterculture magazine to Peter Framptonesque fanzine of pop culture, and they rejected it," Scott wryly observed. But he was not discouraged. He told Michael he would find some other publisher for the piece, and in the meantime they could work on other stories. As the summer progressed, though, it got harder and harder to interest Bloomfield in working on the manuscripts, and Summerville eventually stopped coming by.

"I just couldn't get him to work on anything," said Scott. "He'd be up and around, but his mind would just be *way* elsewhere. Finally I gave up after several months of trying. We had a bunch of outlines for movie scripts, plot ideas, and I wanted to work on those. But it became impossible to get him to do anything, and that all fell by the wayside."

On July 28, Michael Bloomfield turned thirty-four. That same week, *Analine* was released by Takoma Records. Its cover featured a colorful close-up of the guitarist thoughtfully contemplating his mandolin, while on the reverse side was a Norman Dayron photo of the instruments used on the record and another he had taken with a timer showing him posing with Michael in look-alike leather jackets and sunglasses. Also on the back was a picture of a smiling Bloomfield cradling a student-model parlor guitar while sitting in his favorite Reed Street seat, a vintage rattan wheelchair. The guitarist looked self-assured and comfortable in the photos, as well he might have been, having just produced his own album with his own production company. C.T. Productions—and his partner, Norman Dayron—were prominently credited in the LP's notes.

Though *Analine* received very little promotion from Takoma, it was reviewed positively by the publications that gave it a listen. *Stereo Review* praised Bloomfield's overall contributions to the blues and described the album as "a sort of busman's holiday," declaring that Michael "obviously enjoyed his working vacation, and we can enjoy its fruits." A syndicated newspaper column described the guitarist as "a colorist with a fine sense of humor [who] doesn't take too much seriously," saying that *Analine* was "a warm personal album, and modestly announces that Bloomfield's talent hasn't disappeared at all." But the mainstream media largely ignored the LP, and it even failed to get a mention in *Billboard*. The silence was due in part to Takoma's limited promotional resources and to the noncommercial nature of the album's music. But it was also a measure of just how far Michael Bloomfield's star had fallen. With no real major label release to showcase his talents as a blues-rock guitarist since *Live at Bill Graham's Fillmore West* nearly a decade earlier, Bloomfield had largely faded from pop music's collective memory. Anonymity and the freedom that came with it had been a goal, one of Michael's "criteria," and with *Analine* he seemed to have achieved it. His control over his artistry, as far as he was concerned, was now truly complete.

* * *

In the fall, Michael Bloomfield and Friends acquired a new member. David Shorey, a thirty-year-old guitar player from Concord, Massachusetts, had come out to Mill Valley in 1976 by way of Salt Lake City and Lake Tahoe. Not long afterward, he met Bloomfield and, because Shorey had a truck, he began helping Michael haul equipment to and from the guitarist's local gigs. "I was living with Bob Jones, and I sort of became their chief gofer," said Dave. "I would give them equipment, drive them around, repair stuff, things like that. After a while, I started playing bass and rhythm guitar with the band." Bloomfield had begun using Mike Kappus of the Rosebud Agency in San Francisco to book the group, and he gave Shorey the task of coordinating whatever gigs Kappus arranged. But other times, Michael would simply agree to perform somewhere and not tell Dave. Already known as a reluctant performer, Bloomfield began to develop a reputation for not showing up.

Throughout the remainder of the year, Michael and the band played casual gigs in San Francisco at the Other Café on Cole Street and the Coffee Gallery on Grant Avenue, and did shows at the Bodega in Campbell and up the coast at Humboldt State University in Arcata. There was also a weekend in Santa Monica at the Starwood and a return engagement at McCabe's Guitar Shop. While Bloomfield didn't work steadily, he did perform often enough to pay the bills and keep the band together. C.T. Productions, though, was working on a new recording project that promised to make the company some serious money.

"Norman did the deals with the record companies," said Dave Shorey. "He dealt with Takoma, and he also set up the Count Talent record." Mike Bloomfield's desire to record an album of disco music had inspired Dayron to reach out to the company that was one of the major purveyors of the genre, having scored huge hits with KC and the Sunshine Band and other groups in the mid-1970s. TK Records, a label created by producer Henry Stone, was riding high on the disco craze, and Dayron was able to sell them on the idea of releasing a Bloomfield album. "TK wanted to get into rock 'n' roll, and they thought Michael was the way to do it," said Norman. "So Henry Stone was expecting a real rock 'n' roll album." Unlike Takoma, TK Records had real money to invest in the project, and Dayron was able to negotiate an impressive deal for C.T. Productions and Michael Bloomfield. "They gave us a completely atypical fifty thousand dollars for the production budget!" said Norman, still impressed by the amount.

In December, Dayron scheduled studio time at Xanda Recording, and Michael began organizing recording sessions with his usual Friends sidemen. Despite his best efforts, though, the guitarist could not get a satisfactory performance on tape. "I had a real trip with that record," Michael said. "For three weeks in the studio it just didn't happen. Night after night we didn't get a take. So I had to junk three weeks of work and three weeks of paid studio time." Dave Shorey, who played bass on several of the date's selections, thought some of the difficulty lay with the leader himself. "Michael had this habit of charging ahead without really explaining anything, without talking the music through," Dave recalled. "He'd get angry when it didn't go the way he heard it, even though we were all trying. He would just go off in all these different directions at once."

Included in the sessions was a core group of musicians Michael had worked with over the years; they were augmented by a revolving cast of newcomers. Regulars Nick Gravenites, Mark Naftalin, Jellyroll Troy, and Bob Jones were joined by singers Anna Rizzo and Marcia Ann Taylor. Soma Marshall, Bob's girlfriend, played bass on several tunes, as did Dave Shorey. A four-piece horn section, members of a San Francisco funk band called Rubicon, was brought in, as was a second group of studio horn players, nicknamed "the Scabs" by Bloomfield because they were moonlighting. These musicians, in various combinations, struggled to get the sound Michael was looking for. He remained dissatisfied and eventually decided to use even more players.

Added to the sessions were bassist Jack Blades from Rubicon, blues pianist Clay Cotton, and studio players Thaddeus Reece and Ted Ashford. While Michael redid a number of the tunes with the new players, he didn't rerecord everything. On most of the selections, he simply overdubbed additional parts that he himself played. Three tunes, though, were entirely remade with the guitarist playing nearly all the instruments, just as he had done for *Analine*. Those and the other new versions were an improvement, but Michael was still not entirely happy with the performances. There was no time for additional tinkering, though, and he and Norman hastily mixed and mastered the tapes. By the middle of January 1978, they had shipped the reels off to TK Records.

The executives at the company were shocked by what they heard.

"When we sent them the masters, they didn't like it," said Dayron. "They had some kind of conception of what contemporary rock 'n' roll was, and this wasn't it." Of the ten tunes C.T. Productions had produced for Michael Bloomfield's new album—the LP that would launch TK Records' new rock imprint Clouds—none sounded even remotely like the music currently on *Billboard*'s Hot 100 chart. Contemporary rock 'n' roll was Fleetwood Mac, Rod Stewart, and the Eagles—not this. "We thought they maybe had a good point," Norman said with a laugh.

The tunes were, in fact, a mix of funky dance tracks, oldies rock, honky-tonk blues, and soul grooves. Of the ten selections, seven were Bloomfield originals.

Perhaps the most engaging of those was a shuffle blues with a bridge, a song inspired by the entertainer and Rat Pack member Sammy Davis Jr. Michael had seen Davis perform on countless late-night TV talk shows and had come to admire the diminutive actor's many talents. He wrote "Sammy Knows How to Party" as a tribute and had Anna Rizzo sing it while he provided busy guitar fills and a brief solo. Remembering what producer Bob Crew had done with Mitch Ryder's "What Now My Love" sessions, Michael added crowd noise to the song to give it a party feel and then had the revelers back Rizzo on the refrain.

Jellyroll Troy was the vocalist on Bloomfield's "You Was Wrong," a song with a 1950s rock 'n' roll tinge augmented by the guitarist's dense soloing. Troy's powerful baritone gave the tune's accusatory lyrics a plaintive, soulful inflection and transformed it into a lover's plea. For Michael's moody minor vamp "Bad Man," Nick Gravenites was the singer. With Shorey and Jones keeping the beat, the guitarist overdubbed himself playing organ, piano, and Fender Rhodes as he backed Nick's vocal with Wes Montgomery-style octaves on guitar. The song differed from the others on the album in its overall restraint, and the overdubbing, for once, sounded entirely natural. The one tune that came closest to the popular light rock of the day was "You're Changin'," a feature for vocalist Marcia Ann Taylor. While the melody and tempo were pleasant enough, Taylor's airy head voice lacked the heft necessary to carry the song all by itself, and "You're Changin'" began to drag long before its five minutes were up.

Michael also contributed two solid dance originals. One, a 1950s Jerry Lee Lewis rocker called "Saturday Night," he sang himself. With its doo-wop backup singers and high-octane tempo, the song recalled the good-time rock 'n' roll of Bloomfield's youth, and he responded by reeling off one of the "hot licks" solos from his teen years between its verses. Bob Jones sang the other upbeat tune, a party manifesto titled "Let the People Dance." With its insistent rock beat, clever lyrics, full-throated chorus, and big horn section, the song was an all-out celebration of the joys of rhythm and movement.

Perhaps the most unusual of Bloomfield's originals was the honky-tonk blues "Peach Tree Man." Played with a barrelhouse-style rhythm section that backed Michael's vocal and slide guitar, the song told the story of a transgender female's unfulfilled romance. It was another example of the guitarist's fascination with unconventional sexuality and "overts"—and it stemmed from personal experience. "'Peach Tree Man' was about this mulatto transvestite named Stanley who fell in love with Michael and tried to seduce him," said Norman. "He failed because Michael wasn't interested. But a 'peach tree man' wasn't something Michael made up—it's a part of black culture, an expression for a person who cross-dresses." Sung by the guitarist in a vocal style reminiscent of Randy Newman, the song traced the title character's transition from "Stan" to "Peaches" and his infatuation with "Michael," declaring in the refrain that "Peaches never was so sweet!" Bloomfield played effective slide throughout, shouting "Tell on it!"—a favorite Bloomfield expression meaning "speak truthfully"—as he began his solo. The tune, despite its unconventional subject matter, had an engaging, good-time feel.

The three other selections recorded for the album were by other composers. Bob Jones contributed a funk tune called "Love Walk," a dance number that featured the composer's driving vocal backed by slide guitar from Michael. "I Need Your Loving," an R&B hit from 1962 by Don Gardner and Dee Ford, was sung by Jellyroll Troy and Anna Rizzo in a faithful re-creation of the original. The only instrumental on the album was an arrangement of a pop song that had hit number one for several weeks in May. "When I Need You" by Leo Sayer had the kind of sentimental lyrics and lush melody that appealed to Michael, and he re-created the song as a vocal-less feature for his slide guitar. Backed by the bass and drums of Soma and Bob Jones, Bloomfield played gospel-style piano and then overdubbed the melody, his slide sounding much the way it did on "Andy's Bad." Mark Naftalin added strings and chimes on synthesizer to fill in the background, and the completed song had a much more soulful feel than the original.

TK Records, though, wasn't interested in soul. They wanted contemporary rock. The company demanded that Bloomfield and Dayron come to their studios in Florida to work with their engineers to improve the mix. C.T. Productions' two partners obliged and spent several days at TK's recording studios in Hialeah working with the label's chief producer, trying to reshape the music's sound. In the end, though, their efforts seemed to make little difference. TK threw in the towel and simply sent the masters on to their production facility. Michael Bloomfield's new "disco" album was scheduled for release in June. It would be called *Count Talent and the Originals*, just as Michael had planned, and it would feature music that was strikingly different from his recent folkloric releases on Guitar Player and Takoma. As far as Bloomfield was concerned, the differences were inconsequential—it was *all* good music, music that he liked, all American music. For his fans, though, the incongruities would be hard to reconcile. One thing was definitely clear: the Mike Bloomfield who was the guitar superstar of *Super Session*, had by 1978 become little more than a faded memory.

Through the winter months and into the early spring, Mike Bloomfield continued to work irregularly. His trust fund check arrived in January, and the money allowed him to coast for a while. He stayed home and busied himself with reading, recording tunes in his bedroom, and indulging in marathon sessions of late-night TV. There were always friends dropping by, some staying for an afternoon, others for a few days. There were drugs, too, and they brought another kind of visitor. Bloomfield's reputation for generosity was well known throughout the Bay Area, and he was always willing to help a friend out with a meal, a place to stay, spending money, or whatever was needed. When those kindnesses were drug related, they only encouraged others who were desperate for a fix or a handout. As a consequence, narcotics were increasingly part of the environment at Reed Street.

In April, Michael took a large group to Boulder for a weekend appearance at Tulagi. In anticipation of the release of his TK Records album, he had the band introduced as Count Talent and the Originals, and much of what they performed was material from the record. The Originals included Mark Naftalin, Jellyroll Troy, Bob Jones, and singers Anna Rizzo and Marcia Ann Taylor—most of the principal players from the TK sessions. The addition of three horns stretched the group to nine pieces, the largest ensemble Bloomfield had ever taken on the road.

The leader and his band weren't Count Talent and the Originals in name only for the Friday and Saturday shows at Tulagi. They looked the part, too. Instead of his usual T-shirt and jeans, Michael wore a white suit, a *Saturday Night Fever* special with wide lapels, high-waisted flared pants, and a tailored fit. The rest of the band did likewise, and for a few nights, Michael Bloomfield and Friends became a revue with choreographed horns, attractive female singers, and coordinated lapels. Though no one in the club was familiar with the band's repertory, everyone seemed to enjoy the music. They were amused by this new Michael Bloomfield.

While he was in Boulder, Michael had a good time, too. Backstage one night, he met Betsy Rice, a striking young woman who seemed to know a lot about the blues and even more about his music. The guitarist was instantly attracted to the comely twenty-five-year-old and, after spending the evening with her, invited her out to Mill Valley for a visit. She said she would think about it and promised to keep in touch.

In May, Takoma Records asked Michael to contribute a few seasonal tunes to a Christmas record they planned to release in December. He agreed but decided to keep things simple, using only one other musician and overdubbing whatever additional instruments would be needed. David Shorey was enlisted, and one afternoon he and Michael recorded a number of holiday favorites in the living room at Reed Street. "I played bass and accordion," said Shorey. "We did it at Michael's house, and we recorded 'Auld Lang Syne,' 'Go Tell It on the

Mountain'—tunes like that." Bloomfield played a variety of instruments just as he had for *Analine*, creating the string band sound that he found so appealing. But after they had completed the tapes, the record label abruptly abandoned the project. "Takoma went, 'Look, we ain't gonna put out a Christmas record, but we'll give you the money that we were going to give you, and you can go make a record of your own choice,'" said Shorey. "That's when we recorded the *Michael Bloomfield* album."

Once again, Norman Dayron made the arrangements, scheduling sessions at a little studio on West California Avenue in Mill Valley called Tres Virgos. And once again, Bloomfield played nearly everything, overdubbing himself on piano, organ, and a variety of stringed instruments while he sang and played lead guitar. For most of the selections, he had Shorey and Bob Jones record the basic rhythm tracks and then added his own parts to them. Most of the tunes were blues, as the guitarist, having gotten Count Talent out of his system, was returning to his roots.

"Guitar King," a tune Tommy McClennan had recorded for Bluebird in 1941, was a song Michael had heard on Maxwell Street in Chicago, and he had lately been performing it as part of his regular club set. For the Takoma album, he recorded himself playing piano over Dave's bass and Bob's drums and then added distorted rhythm and lead guitar parts to create raw electric accompaniment for his forceful vocal. "Michael would always open with that tune whenever he wanted to kick some ass," Bob recalled, laughing. "I always knew it was going to be a hot show when he'd play that one."

With a touch of sardonic humor, Michael taped a version of Lil Green's "Knockin' Myself Out," a novelty number from 1941. With its jivy viper lyrics and good-time shuffle tempo, the song was a perfect example of the hip folkloric blues Bloomfield loved to play. That its drug references and praise of excess mirrored aspects of his own life only made it more appealing, and he added his own comic verses to underscore the similarities. In a similar vein, the guitarist did "You Took My Money," a traditional honky-tonk blues with original lyrics by Michael. Its funky beat and reverb-laden sonority fit perfectly with the tune's "dozens" posturing, and Bloomfield's ringing solo on slide cut through its grease like a hot knife through butter. Mill Valley trombonist Kraig Kilby's tailgating fills were added to give the tune a suitable jazz inflection.

Michael also featured his slide on the melody of a gospel-style instrumental that Norman composed. Called appropriately enough "The Gospel Truth," the guitarist played piano, organ, bass, and even Moog synthesizer in addition to electric guitar, leaving only the drums to be covered by Bob Jones. After the melody, Bloomfield switched to fretted lead and soloed passionately over the swelling, sanctified accompaniment. In a completely different mood was "My

Children, My Children," a soul vamp written by Dr. John and recorded by New Orleans soul singer Jessie Hill in 1967. It was another tune the guitarist regularly played in live performance, and he re-created Hill's halting, shouted vocal with faithful exuberance while Dave and Bob chanted the refrain. A slide solo and additional verses completed the song with a busyness that bordered on happy anarchy.

The most unusual arrangement Bloomfield recorded during the sessions was a version of Blind Lemon Jefferson's "See That My Grave Is Kept Clean." Michael played guitar, piano, accordion, and tiple over Shorey's bass and Jones's drums, and he sang the funereal lyrics in a quavering, exaggerated voice awash with studio reverb. It was a treatment that gave the tune an otherworldly sound, almost as though the guitarist were singing from beyond the grave. The layering of the acoustic guitar and tiple parts contributed a spacey clutter, like so many aural insects buzzing around the singer's words. It was a striking and somewhat odd performance. "I learned it from Blind Lemon Jefferson a long, long time ago," said Bloomfield of "See That My Grave Is Kept Clean." "It seems like I've known it all my life."

The Tres Virgos sessions went well, but before he had enough material to complete the new Takoma record, Bloomfield's enthusiasm for the project began to wane. "Mike struggled to get that album out," said Robin Yeager, one of the studio's owners. "I got the feeling that it was more Norman's idea than Mike's." To move things along, Dayron suggested they fill out the album with a few tunes from the performances he had recorded at the Old Waldorf. That was fine with Michael, and they selected "Women Loving Each Other," an obvious choice, and "Sloppy Drunk," a paean to intoxication by Muddy Waters's guitarist, Jimmy Rogers. Both tunes were enthusiastic performances played by Bloomfield's Friends quartet for a rowdy Waldorf bar crowd, and their inclusion added to the album's bluesy flavor. By the end of the month, sessions for the Takoma record were complete, and Dayron went to work mixing and mastering the tapes.

It was right around this time that Mike Bloomfield acquired a new house guest. One afternoon he answered a knock at the front door, and there stood the attractive young woman he had met in Boulder. Betsy Rice had arrived at Reed Street, suitcases in hand, intending to pay him an extended visit.

"I only met Betsy once, at dinner over at Michael's," said Leonard Trupin, a friend who had been introduced to Bloomfield by Roy Ruby. "I knew nobody liked her, but she seemed nice enough to me. In some ways, I think she was good for Michael—she didn't lay any trips on him."

The guitarist's new live-in girlfriend never questioned his behavior, never judged the choices he made—that was certainly true. If Michael wanted to do drugs, if he needed a fix, that was his business. She didn't stand in his way or lecture him. Her laissez-faire attitude made things easy. But Bloomfield could see that it was an attitude that most likely stemmed from her own sobriety issues.

"Betsy was a nice enough person sober," said Norman Dayron. "But when she'd had a few drinks, she could get pretty volatile. She'd get revved up, go off on someone, and all hell would break loose. I think that really amused Michael."

"Mike found her enormously entertaining," agreed Bob Jones. "He would take her places and use her as a 'psychological guided missile.' He would sort of 'aim' her at people and then sit back and watch the fireworks."

The guitarist found his new partner's penchant for confrontational drama very funny, especially when its victims were caught off guard. Betsy's alcohol-fueled tirades created situations that were, for Bloomfield, just like the time Bob Greenspan decided to tell jokes at the Old Waldorf. People were unprepared for what happened, and the results could be hilarious. The guitarist's home life, with the addition of its riotous new member, soon took on an added dimension of craziness.

Chet Helms, San Francisco's legendary promoter and founder of Family Dog Productions, ended a five-year hiatus from the Bay Area music scene in October 1978 with a "potluck picnic and dance," a re-creation of the Family Dog's annual hippie gatherings called "Tribal Stomps." Helms felt the need to revive the 1960s counterculture spirit with a multifaceted celebration of the era's music and arts, and he enlisted a number of San Francisco's best-known bands to perform at the day-long event. Appearing would be Country Joe and the Fish, It's a Beautiful Day, Big Brother and the Holding Company, and several others. Headlining the gala concert would be the Paul Butterfield Blues Band, the group that gave Helms his start as a serious producer back in 1966. But it wouldn't be the harp player's current band the Tribal Stomp would showcase—Chet arranged with Albert Grossman to present the original Paul Butterfield Blues Band.

It would be another Butterfield reunion, the fourth since Bloomfield left the band in 1967, and this one would again include five of the original six members. For the first time, Sam Lay would be behind the drums, rejoining Butterfield, Bloomfield, Bishop, and Naftalin onstage to re-create some of the band's trademark Chicago blues. Only Jerome Arnold would be absent, replaced by Jellyroll Troy.

Though he had no desire to play for a huge festival crowd, Mike Bloomfield agreed to participate. A single set of familiar tunes was manageable enough, and the show was going to take place right across the bay at UC Berkeley's Greek Theatre, so no traveling was involved. Plus he was looking forward to seeing Sam again, and he always liked playing with Paul.

The Tribal Stomp took place on Sunday, October 1, and when the Paul Butterfield Blues Band was introduced late that evening by Chet Helms, the vast crowd in the amphitheater roared. The Butterfield alumni charged into a rousing rendition of "Born in Chicago" and then played "Our Love Is Drifting," "Everything's Gonna Be Alright," "Shake Your Money Maker," and other blues standards from their original repertory. Despite a few initial sound glitches, plenty of the old magic was there, and the sextet sounded tight and exciting. But as the set progressed, Elvin Bishop began to take center stage, his guitar cranked and his wide-eyed "Pigboy Crabshaw" persona on full display.

"Elvin wanted to do his thing," said Naftalin. "He was putting himself out there. Paul and Mike just sort of faded. I have this image of Mike hunkered down in some corner of the stage by a stack of speakers." Bloomfield, hunched over his black Stratocaster, stood offstage right, out of the spotlight. His playing became more frenetic as the performance progressed, and as Elvin got louder, it became harder to hear Michael. When Bishop launched into a tune of his own called "You've Got to Pay the Price for Feeling Nice," he essentially turned the reunion into the Elvin Bishop show. The audience ate it up, but from that point on it was clear who was in charge.

A rollicking rendition of "Got My Mojo Working," sung by Sam Lay, and an extended encore with guest vocalist Maria Muldaur joining Elvin on "Don't You Lie to Me" ended the set and concluded the Tribal Stomp festivities. The audience whooped and hollered as Butterfield and his sidemen filed offstage, memories of the band's former glories disappearing into the night air with them. "And a good time was had by all!" shouted a jubilant Bishop into a mic as the lights came up. "Take it easy folks! Thank you, bye-bye!"

It had been a memorable show, and the audience loved it. But not everyone had a good time—not onstage, at least. "Paul said something interesting to me after the gig," Naftalin remarked. "He said, 'Remind me never to stand between those two guys again—they don't like each other.'" While Naftaln had never sensed any real enmity between the two guitarists in the band's heyday, the old hierarchy had been upended. Instead of Michael Bloomfield dominating the stage as the fire-eating guitar superstar, it was Elvin Bishop's extroverted hayseed who was the main attraction. That he had been upstaged by the band's one-time rhythm guitarist surprised Michael. He had expected the dynamic to be much as it had been in 1967, but Elvin had grown as a performer and was a confident and talented leader himself. He had also scored a top-ten hit in 1976 with "Fooled Around and Fell in Love," and its popularity made him a national star. Many people had forgotten about Michael Bloomfield in the intervening years, but Elvin Bishop was a name everybody knew. It was further proof that Bloomfield's quest for anonymity had succeeded, although its success was, at times, a double-edged sword.

The last week in October, Michael Bloomfield and Friends flew to New York for appearances at My Father's Place in Rosalyn and at the Bottom Line in the Big Apple. With Bloomfield were Mark Naftalin, Dave Shorey, and Bob Jones, and the trip was short enough that it wasn't too difficult for the guitarist. Michael was playing well, and most of his sets were performed on his Stratocaster with the full quartet. After his humiliating Butterfield reunion experience, Bloomfield felt the need to reassert himself as an electric guitarist and took every opportunity reassure his audience—and himself—that he was still a masterful player. One tune in particular, new to the band's repertory, was clearly meant to demonstrate his skill as an improviser. That it was not a blues only underscored the fact that Bloomfield could play anything with virtuosity.

"Maria Elena" was a pop song that Michael had heard in his teen years, a hit from 1962 by a popular Mexican guitar duo known as Los Indios Tabajaras. The guitarist had rediscovered the instrumental when he heard it on a Ry Cooder album a decade later, and he had grown so fond of its melody that he had eventually worked out an arrangement of his own. For the shows at My Father's Place and the Bottom Line, Bloomfield inserted "Maria Elena" in between hard-edged blues like "Women Loving Each Other" and "Guitar King," creating a palpable shift in the continuity of the band's sets. Fans were often momentarily confused, not sure where the guitarist was going. But as Bloomfield navigated the tune's complex changes, the audience watched with growing amazement. By the end of "Maria Elena," they were cheering him on.

At the Bottom Line, Michael's playing was especially inspired. He always enjoyed performing at the club on West Fourth Street, and his New York City fans were some of the most dedicated. But he had other reasons to want to play his best. His friend John Hammond came by to see one of the band's shows, and between sets on Sunday night, Johnny Winter appeared backstage. Bloomfield clearly wanted to impress them both when he went onstage.

Michael also had another reason to be energized. Backstage was his former girlfriend, Christie Svane. She had been thinking about him, and when she discovered his band was appearing in New York, she came to the show. Though they hadn't really communicated in years, Michael was delighted that she had come, and she, too, had strong feelings. "We were just over the moon to see each other," Christie said. With the spark rekindled, the twenty-four-year-old

Svane went with Bloomfield back to his hotel room following the show, and together they made up for lost time. It was a very romantic interlude, but not without its complications, because both Michael and Christie were involved with other people. But the guitarist had clearly been thinking about love and its consequences earlier in the evening at the club when he acknowledged a tabloid tragedy that had played out several weeks earlier.

"Michael opened the show saying, 'I'm dedicating this to Sid and Nancy,' and he started playing 'Frankie and Johnny,'" Svane said. The guitarist was referring to punk rocker Sid Vicious and his slain girlfriend, Nancy Spungen. "He did the most incredible version," said Christie.

Back in Mill Valley, Michael's domestic life was beginning to unravel. Betsy's drinking was increasingly a problem, and often the focus of her inebriated ire was the guitarist himself. Her outrageous behavior had ceased to be amusing and had become a liability. People didn't like being around Bloomfield when his unpredictable girlfriend was with him, and Michael began leaving her home whenever he visited friends.

In January 1979, he left her home to go on yet another tour. As usual, he had no desire to take a band on the road, but Dave Shorey and Bob Jones needed the work, and the guitarist felt obliged to help them out. Leaving the details to Bob, Michael booked a week-long series of performances for his Friends quartet in several cities back east. But the gigs weren't on the usual New York-to-Boston circuit. For some reason, it was arranged for Michael Bloomfield and Friends to appear in venues across southeastern Canada—in the dead of winter. The guitarist was not happy, and it was only through the efforts of Bob Jones that he made the trip.

"Michael had become notorious for not showing up," said Bob. "I would always make sure he'd make the gig, because I'd go get him and his equipment and drive him to the airport." But even with Bob's help, the trip was an arduous one, with complex travel connections, harsh weather conditions, and rustic accommodations. Bloomfield, anticipating a lengthy bout of insomnia, brought along plenty of medication—pills he had been taking since the late 1960s to help him get to sleep. By 1979, though, Placidyl wasn't just a sleep aid for Michael. It had become a habit.

"Michael's use of Placidyl was *not* recreational," said Shorey. "He was just trying unsuccessfully to get to a calm, quiet place." Years of using the sedative, however, had created a dependency that frequently extended into the guitarist's waking hours, making him groggy and unresponsive. For the Canadian tour, that condition became acute. The band played multiple shows in Ottawa, Rouyn, Toronto, and finally Montreal. By that time, Bloomfield was in bad shape.

"When we got to Montreal, he was so full of Placidyl . . . he had no idea where he was, and he was sort of a blithering idiot," Jones remembered. Despite his soporific condition, Michael still managed to perform well, relying largely on reflexes. If audiences noticed that the guitarist wasn't his usual dynamic self, they didn't show it. The band was enthusiastically received wherever they went, with Bloomfield's Canadian fans grateful just for a chance to see the legendary guitarist in the flesh. But Michael was miserable.

"One day we traveled 17 hours to play 40 minutes," he later complained to an interviewer, describing the trip to Rouyn. Though he exaggerated, it was clear the journey hadn't been pleasant. He went on to sum up his aversion to touring: "Doing a solo gig within driving distance is sure a lot easier than going on the road with a band."

Solo gigs *were* easier, and following the Canadian sojourn, they were increasingly the guitarist's preference. It was much simpler to load a few instruments into the car and drive to the club, do a few sets, and then drive home. In March, he did a week just like that at the Boarding House, an upscale nightclub on Bush Street in San Francisco that regularly featured name rock and comedy acts. For the shows, Bloomfield sang, played a variety of acoustic guitars in various tunings, and even did entire sets on piano. His material ranged from the traditional blues and gospel tunes with which he had been opening his performances with his Friends band to country favorites, jump jazz novelties, pop standards, and even 1950s rock 'n' roll. Occasionally, he would accompany himself by soloing along with a tape recording that he had made earlier. The solo format allowed the guitarist the freedom to play whatever came to mind on whatever instrument struck his fancy. It was, for Mike Bloomfield, exactly like playing at home and thus entirely within his comfort zone.

For audiences, though, it could be a mixed bag. Over the course of several sets, the guitarist would play what amounted to an encapsulated survey of American popular music. But because Michael rarely announced the tunes he played or said anything about their history, only those listeners who shared his enthusiasm for musicology would recognize the selections and appreciate the logic behind his presentation. Everyone else was on his or her own, trying to figure out what the guitarist was doing. There was the added complication that many were expecting the old Super Session razzle-dazzle. When confronted with a solitary Bloomfield seated onstage with two or three acoustic instruments and nothing else, the audience was apt to be disappointed. That's when the "Season of the Witch" requests would begin.

But the patrons at the Boarding House were too polite to heckle the guitarist, and some were aware of his acoustic routine, having seen it before. The shows went well, with polite applause following each number, and Michael even told a few jokes. The performances were very much like those he had given fourteen years earlier at Mother Blues in Chicago—with the exception that the guitarist no longer needed Joel Harlib to drag him to the gig.

A few weeks later, Bloomfield was interviewed by associate editor Tom Wheeler for *Guitar Player*'s April edition. As Wheeler listened, Michael reminisced about his career, recapping his early days in Chicago, his stint with Butterfield, and his rock-star period with the Electric Flag. He once again dismissed Super Session as a cynical commercial ruse and decried his involvement in for-profit projects like the reunited Flag and KGB. He also shared his ideas about music and the industry, and he even spoke candidly of his drug use—although only in the past tense. When Wheeler asked about Bloomfield's latest recordings, the guitarist confessed that he had no idea if they were selling but expressed frustration that his Guitar Player album, his Grammy-nominated overview of the blues, was so hard to get. "Everywhere I go, man, *everywhere*, someone asks me where they can get that record," the guitarist complained. "I'm not that big a seller, but that album would be my biggest of all time, no doubt about it." Ironically, *If You Love These Blues* would go entirely out of print by the time Bloomfield's interview would be published.

Wheeler, a noted guitar expert and a longtime Michael Bloomfield fan, gave the guitarist ample space to express himself on a range of topics. But he also offered insights of his own into the guitarist's career and artistry—and Michael's validity as an authentic blues master. The editor described Bloomfield as a direct link to the postwar urban blues that so profoundly shaped contemporary popular music. Michael not only was an exponent of that tradition, but was also its most enthusiastic supporter and promoter. As such, he played a pivotal role in mapping out the direction modern rock took as it matured as an art form. Bloomfield's knowledge of American music, and his ongoing examination of its various styles and genres as a performer, set him apart from many of his contemporaries. That was one reason why *Guitar Player* titled the interview "Michael Bloomfield: Barroom Scholar of the Blues."

Photos that accompanied the *Guitar Player* interview showed Michael in his Reed Street bedroom surrounded by an arsenal of instruments. There was his Harmony archtop, the Hilo Hawaiian guitar, a mandolin, the Telecaster and black Stratocaster, and several others. Missing, though, was the Beggerby guitar, one of two that had been custom made for Bloomfield by the Mill Valley luthier Ove Beggerby. The big Western-style dreadnought wasn't there because it had been damaged.

"Mike told me over the phone one night that his girlfriend broke his guitars," said Bob Greenspan. "She got pissed off about something and smashed them up and threw them off the balcony at Reed Street."

Bloomfield's relationship with Betsy Rice had, by early April, become tempestuous. She had discovered the guitarist's feelings for Christie Svane when she read postcards Christie had sent him, and her jealous rages, fueled by drugs and alcohol, could be fearsome. Michael, frequently addled by Placidyl, was powerless to stop her whenever she became agitated, and one afternoon she exacted her revenge on the one thing she knew was important to him—his guitars. The wounded Beggerby went over the balcony railing at Reed Street and tumbled down the hill toward Miller Avenue, its handmade sound box crushed. For once, Michael was not amused.

There was nothing amusing about the guitarist's condition, either. Though he was often alert and able to function normally, just as often now he was unresponsive and out of it. Christie discovered as much when she called him in April. "He sounded almost unintelligible," she recalled with alarm. "I said, 'Michael, what's wrong?' He said, 'Placidyl. I'm strung out on Placidyl, and I need help.'" Though Svane offered, Bloomfield told her there was nothing she could do. It was professional help that he needed, and it would be up to him to seek it. The only problem with that was it was much easier to stay home and do nothing. Michael did nothing until mid-May, when an old friend paid him a visit.

"I was managing this Dixieland band in Vancouver, and they had a gig in San Francisco," said Chris McDougal. "I drove the band down and then went to see Michael at Reed Street. I was shocked—he looked real skinny, pale, and bad. I said, 'You're coming back to Vancouver with me right now!'" When the guitarist refused, McDougal insisted on taking his friend to the hospital. "I drove him there and got him checked in. I made sure they would keep him for a while so he could get himself cleaned up. He was looking that bad."

It was a timely intervention. Bloomfield had used heroin for many years without becoming addicted, but he had been unable to avoid developing an acute dependency on the sedative. Without McDougal's help, he may never have gotten treatment. But his hospitalization enabled him to overcome his addiction under proper medical supervision. It also inadvertently addressed another of Michael's problems—his irascible girlfriend. With the guitarist away for the foreseeable future, there was no reason for Betsy Rice to remain at Reed Street. It was time for her to go. "With Michael out of it, his friends packed her up and drove her to the airport," remembered Leonard Trupin. "They had an opportunity to get rid of her, and they took it." The young woman flew back to Boulder and out of Mike Bloomfield's life for good.

The guitarist spent a full month recuperating. McDougal had taken him to Ross General Hospital, fifteen minutes from Mill Valley in the town of Ross. The hospital was a modest-size institution with 240 beds, but it had added a treatment facility for the care of alcoholics and patients with drug problems in the early 1970s, and it specialized in rehabilitation. In Michael's unit were patients with a variety of mental disorders and chemical dependencies, and many were heavily drugged. It was a depressing scene, but Bloomfield soon felt right at home. The guitarist was entirely comfortable trusting in medicine once he had been admitted. Coping with symptoms of withdrawal, the peculiarities of his fellow patients and the tedium of convalescence was possible as long as Michael had a team of doctors focused on his well-being. It was an extension of his fascination with medical oddities and abnormalities, and not unrelated to his obsession with his own health. "Michael was a bit of a hypochondriac," said Norman Dayron.

When Bloomfield was finally released from Ross General, the first thing he did was send a telegram to Christie, asking her to call him. She was in Boulder, having left New York to spend a few months as a guest dance instructor at the Naropa Institute. When she talked to Michael and learned that Betsy was gone, she decided to fly to San Francisco and stay with him for a while. They both wanted to give their relationship a chance. But when she got there, she found he was not alone in the house.

"There was a friend of his, a psychiatrist, who had moved into Reed Street with him," Svane said. "He was a pill doctor who had had his license taken away from him, I think twice, for overprescribing. He had a plan to keep Michael off Placidyl." The plan, Christie discovered, was for the psychiatrist to mimic Michael's behavior, a tactic that was intended to provide the guitarist with a mirror image of himself. When he acted in self-destructive ways, Bloomfield would see the consequences played out by the therapist. That tableau would disgust the guitarist, and thus provide a deterrent to future bad behavior.

It was a novel approach, but one without any real efficacy. What it meant, Christie soon learned, was that instead of coping with one person high on drugs, she had to deal with two. Because Michael's own method for avoiding Placidyl involved substituting straight gin or vodka for the drug, he was now often drunk. That meant the psychiatrist was frequently inebriated too. To complicate matters further, because Svane had come to live with Michael, the therapist had his girlfriend, a prostitute from Los Angeles, move in as well.

Life at Reed Street took on a surreal quality, and the situation quickly became untenable.

It was in the middle of this domestic chaos that Mike Bloomfield decided to record another album. This time, though, the sessions would be simple and direct—no overdubbing, no rhythm section or horns, and no expensive studio time. The record was going to be a series of guitar duets, and Norman Dayron suggested they do the taping right in the living room of his apartment. Michael planned to record some of his favorite gospel songs as guitar instrumentals, and accompanying him would be a twenty-six-year-old formally trained guitarist from New York named Woody Harris.

Harris had studied classical music at Mannes College in the early 1970s before developing an interest in blues, ragtime, and folk forms. Inspired by the innovative work of guitarist John Fahey, Woody developed his own amalgam of American musical styles, compositions he played using a variety of finger-picking techniques and patterns. He moved to San Francisco to record his first solo album in 1976 and had done several others since then. Though he had seen Mike Bloomfield in performance a few times, Harris had never met him.

It was Norman who brought the two guitarists together. While in California, Woody occasionally played gigs with Mark Naftalin, and Mark had appeared on Harris's latest record in a selection engineered by Dayron. Thinking that Michael might appreciate Woody's playing, Norman suggested the two guitarists meet. When Harris came to the Old Waldorf one evening and sat in, Bloomfield very much liked his clean, precise sound, and the idea of recording a gospel duets LP was born. "Bloomfield generally doesn't like to work with other guitar players," Dayron later wrote in the album's liner notes. "Michael told me that Woody had a pure classical style of playing that would beautifully complement his own style."

On Thursday, July 19, Michael and Woody brought their instruments over to Norman's apartment on Millwood Street. For the next four days, the living room would serve as C.T. Production's recording studio while Dayron engineered multiple takes of the various gospel tunes the two guitarists worked out. Norman set up mikes, monitored levels, and rolled tape, just as he had in 1963 when he and Michael made the guitarist's first demo in his Hyde Park apartment. That recording had launched the guitarist's career, and his collaboration with Harris was, in a way, an epilogue to its momentous arc. The gospel performances would distill all the soulfulness of the man's artistry and spirit into seven brief duets and one solo performance.

The two guitarists started the session by playing a number of tunes finger-picked on acoustic guitars. Michael took the lead on "I'll Overcome," an earlier version of the 1960s civil rights anthem that the guitarist had first heard at

Maxwell Street, and then played rhythm while Woody picked the melody to "I Must See Jesus," a song Bloomfield had learned from a Snooks Eaglin record. Michael played lead on "I Am a Pilgrim," a traditional gospel tune that he had first heard Merle Travis play, and then played harmony behind Woody's interpretation of "Have Thine Own Way," switching to slide for the song's last chorus. For the Joseph Spence hymn "Great Dreams from Heaven," Michael put down his guitar and let Woody fingerpick the piece by himself. Harris's rendition was so effective, Bloomfield couldn't help shouting an encouraging "Yeah!" on his second chorus.

Later in the week, Bloomfield switched to amplified guitar, and the duo recorded Blind Willie Johnson's "You're Gonna Need Somebody on Your Bond" with Michael playing the melody and improvising with slide. His lines had a pulsating, spacey quality that was created by his amplifier's vibrato and reverb effects. For "Just a Closer Walk with Thee," Bloomfield stated the theme and then soloed for repeated choruses, again with slide, spinning out variations on single strings while Harris played syncopated rhythm. The two guitarists used a similar arrangement for "Farther Along," a song Michael had first encountered at one of the University of Chicago folk festivals. He kept it uncomplicated by simply repeating the song's powerful melody throughout the performance with only a few embellishments.

The final selection recorded for the album was the only one to use overdubbing. After the duet sessions had concluded, Michael recorded a solo rendition of "Peace in the Valley," the traditional hymn that had been a staple of church choirs since the 1930s when Mahalia Jackson first sang it. For his version, Bloomfield took inspiration from a recording of the song by one of his earliest influences—Elvis Presley. "He plays piano; just singing while sitting at the piano playing those simple, beautiful chords," the guitarist wrote of Elvis in his song annotations. To re-create that feeling, Michael first played the piece's basic chords and then overdubbed slide guitar for its melody. He again used the amp's vibrato, but this time he set the effect's pulse rate to its widest interval, giving his lead an odd "wah-wah" quality. Michael later said he tried to evoke the sound of a cornet, but the treatment only made "Peace in the Valley" seem pleasantly intoxicated.

Following the completion of the taping sessions, Norman Dayron spent several days editing and mixing the nine selections. He had arranged with Kicking Mule Records, a small label owned by producer, manager, and music journalist ED Denson, to release the album in the late fall. When he delivered the finished masters to Kicking Mule, Norman also included dozens of photos he had taken during the sessions for the album's cover. Several pictures showed a relaxed, healthy-looking Bloomfield chatting amicably with Harris, while others captured him intently playing guitar. There were even a few shots of Christie. She had come to all of the sessions and had been deeply moved by the music.

On July 28, Mike Bloomfield turned thirty-six. He celebrated by having a few drinks, something he rarely did in the past but now did with increasing frequency. But it wasn't just alcohol that had become a problem. Hard drugs, too, had come back into Michael's life. Many of his friends were users, and some were severely addicted. Their constant presence at Reed Street contributed to his own habit, which was then mimicked by his doctor friend. The psychiatrist was also periodically dosing Michael with MDA, a psychedelic similar to ecstasy, in an effort to keep him from drinking. The craziness of the situation got to a point where Christie Svane could no longer stand it. "I remember taking a butcher knife one night in the kitchen, just slamming it down on the butcher block and saying, 'That's it! All of you guys out of here!'" Svane said. "Everybody looked so shocked and hurt, like I was saying, 'No more fun.'"

Christie's ultimatum worked for a while, and she even succeeded in evicting the pill doctor and his lady friend. But she was left alone with Michael, who was sliding back into a pattern of dissipation, and she had no idea how to help him. Nor did any of his close friends. "We all could see that Michael was struggling," said Leonard Trupin. "But we really didn't know what to do about it, and I'm not even sure he would have accepted any help." Feeling overwhelmed, Christie told the guitarist she was going back to New York to resume her career as a dancer. She had come to Mill Valley to see if she and Michael could restart their relationship, but the weeks at Reed Street had proven too chaotic and surreal. She needed to distance herself from the experience and clear her head. By mid-August she was gone, and Michael Bloomfield was suddenly all alone again in the house on Reed Street.

"Mike was always looking for the 'big rush,'" said Bob Jones. The drummer had reluctantly decided to stop playing with Bloomfield following their Canadian tour. The effort required to get the guitarist to the few shows he agreed to play, coupled with his drug use and now his drinking—it had all become too much. It seemed like Bloomfield was on a destructive path, and Bob didn't want to be around to witness it. He had already seen more than enough.

> One time he OD'd in my apartment—turned blue—and I got really scared. I didn't know what to do. We eventually put him in the bathtub

> with ice and were able to bring him back. But that's when I said, "I'm done doing this with you." Michael always wanted to have the whole thing, to dance closer to the edge. I couldn't do that, and I had to quit.

By the fall of 1979, Michael Bloomfield was largely on his own. Many of his old friends had also begun avoiding him. Nick Gravenites wouldn't work with him, because he never knew if Michael would show up. Even Mark Naftalin, one of the guitarist's closest friends and his favorite musical partner, had started working with other players. Though Dave Shorey was distressed by Michael's decline, he still tried to keep the guitarist working. "I worked with Mike Kappas, his agent, to keep him going," said Shorey. "We were talking about a tour of Europe—doing clubs in France—and Michael said he'd go. But then he backed out. His reluctance came from scary shit, mental issues—they were not understandable. He was just incomprehensible at the time."

The risk of a fatal overdose was increasingly a part of Bloomfield's life. Though he now tempered the urge to shoot heroin with copious amounts of gin and vodka, he still got off, especially when his user friends would drop by. Because the guitarist always insisted on doing the whole dose, his turning-blue routine had become a regular occurrence. It was frequent enough that whoever was with him when he began to OD now knew just what to do. "The Mill Valley Fire Department would get the 'Bloomfield call,'" Shorey said. "They would get calls to come up and resuscitate him." EMTs were habitually dispatched to Reed Street, and they would revive the guitarist and anyone else needing assistance. An emergency call was just one more aspect of the craziness that now permeated Mike Bloomfield's life.

In October, Kicking Mule Records released *Bloomfield/Harris*. The album cover featured a jovial picture of the two guitarists, each smiling broadly and posing with their instruments. Bloomfield, though, was wearing a hospital shirt from Ross General, a hint that at the time of the recording, he had been dealing with other more serious issues. The album's liner notes were by Norman, and annotations from Michael accompanied each of the record's nine selections. The music was simple, straightforward, and tasteful. Though Bloomfield occasionally overplayed during his solos, and though his slide sounded too spacey in places, it mattered little. The soulfulness of the performances was pervasive and genuine. Though there were only thirty minutes of music on the record, it was a satisfying half hour for lovers of acoustic guitar and traditional gospel.

Kicking Mule sent around a press release informing reviewers about the album, but without funding for advertising, *Bloomfield/Harris* went largely unnoticed by the record-buying public. For most fans, anyway, acoustic gospel music was not what they wanted to hear from Michael Bloomfield. Despite the guitarist's recent albums featuring traditional blues and rags, most listeners still knew his playing only through his recordings with Butterfield and Kooper. They expected more of the same, not some folky collaboration with another guitarist they had never heard of. But as luck would have it, later in the month another Bloomfield album was issued that was more to their liking.

Between the Hard Place and the Ground, released by Takoma Records the last week in October, was a compendium of no-nonsense electric blues. Its cover featured photos of Mike Bloomfield taken in the spring and winter of 1965 that showed the guitarist playing with the group he briefly had with Nick Gravenites and then with the Butterfield Band. Norman Dayron had taken the photos, and it was he who had assembled the music for the record. Of the seven selections on *Between the Hard Place and the Ground*, four were raw, bare-knuckled performances Dayron had taped of Michael's quartet at the Old Waldorf between 1976 and 1977. They featured the guitarist fronting a rhythm section of Friends regulars and performing blues for a happy, vociferous crowd. Alternating between slide and fretted lead, Bloomfield sang "Big Chief from New Orleans," Sleepy John Estes's "Kid Man Blues," "Juke Joint" by Big Joe Turner, and the title tune, one of his own compositions. Michael's playing was exuberant and, driven by Bob Jones's stomping drums, displayed more than a few moments of the old fire. Here was the Mike Bloomfield his many fans craved.

The three remaining selections on *Between the Hard Place and the Ground* were from a different source. Although the liner notes claimed all the tunes on the LP were recorded at the Old Waldorf, "Lights Out," "Orphan's Blues," and "Your Friends" were all studio dates. They had been recorded in July 1974 at Columbia Studios in San Francisco and were originally intended for Bloomfield's unreleased solo album, *Try It Before You Buy It*. Norman had gotten the album's masters, and because Columbia clearly had no intention of releasing them, he had discreetly added the tunes to the Takoma album's Waldorf selections. C.T. Productions wasn't too concerned about permissions because it was unlikely anyone in Columbia's legal department would notice—or even care. "We were more interested in getting Michael's music out," said Dayron. "Corporate control of his artistry was a thing of the past as far as I was concerned."

Norman worked out a deal to have *Between a Hard Place and the Ground* released by Takoma, and the record was selected by *Billboard* as one of its Top Album Picks. "[Bloomfield] returns after a long absence," the magazine's blurb declared, "with seven blues cuts in the traditional mold, backed by a capable quartet, and proves he can still bend those notes." The *Boston Globe* had high praise for the album, saying, "There's a studied informality to the record . . . that suggests Bloomfield just walked in, picked up his axe, and proceeded to set yet another standard for urban blues guitarists to emulate." The record showcased the guitarist's first live recordings since his *Live at Bill Graham's Fillmore West* LP in 1969, and it was his first all-electric blues release in nearly as long. That it was readily available in record stores gave it an advantage over the Guitar Player album, Michael's other recent blues effort. For those fans who bought the Takoma album, Bloomfield was indeed back.

But the truth was that the selections on *Between a Hard Place and the Ground* were from an earlier period, a time when Michael was in transition. By 1979 Bloomfield was more likely to give solo performances, often playing as much piano as guitar during a set and including country, pop, and ragtime tunes along with traditional blues. The Takoma album had been Norman's project, and the guitarist had very little to do with its production. He was much more interested in the gospel music he and Woody Harris had played together on their Kicking Mule release. That was one reason why he agreed to do a concert with Woody to promote the duet album.

On Friday, October 12, Michael Bloomfield and Woody Harris appeared at McCabe's Guitar Shop in Santa Monica, their first public appearance together. They each did a few solo numbers and then finished the set as a duo, re-creating the songs on the album and adding a half dozen more, including a number of blues. The audience was appreciative, and Michael even called a few members up to sing the refrain to "John, John on the Battleground," his variation on the Mardi Gras Indian chant "Corrine Died on the Battlefield." The show was a success, and Michael's playing was inspired.

But it wasn't always so. In November and December, Bloomfield did a number of gigs, again appearing solo at the Boarding House in San Francisco and performing with his band at the Catalyst in Santa Cruz and at several other venues. One of those was the Sleeping Lady Café on Bolinas Road in nearby Fairfax. Michael Bloomfield and Friends were scheduled to appear there one weekend evening, but when Mike arrived, he was in no condition to play. He sat at the piano, fingered the keys while singing to himself, and paid no attention to the audience. When the crowd began to get rowdy, shouting the usual requests, Michael got angry and shouted back. Not knowing what else to do, the band left the stage, causing many in the café to demand their money back. Others just walked out. Michael already had a reputation for being unreliable, but now people around the Bay Area were starting to say that even if he did show up, he might not be able to play.

"He was drinking Stoli by emptying the bottle into a saucepan, and he'd put the pan in the freezer. He wouldn't even keep the bottle," said Dave Shorey. "He'd bring the saucepan out and drink the whole thing right out of the pan." Michael's drinking had become, by the end of 1979, a serious problem.

He had begun quaffing alcohol as a way to curtail his Placidyl and heroin use following his stay at Ross General, but now the deterrent had itself become an issue. Never a drinker before, Bloomfield suddenly became a sloppy drunk. On those days he felt the need to get intoxicated, he would start very early in the morning. "He'd get up at 4:00 a.m. and drink vodka and orange juice," remembered Leonard Trupin. "I'd hide the bottle, but he'd demand it until I gave it back to him."

It was in this condition that Michael Bloomfield left Mill Valley and moved to New York City. Toward the end of December, he surprised Christie Svane by showing up at her apartment in the city. He had decided they should live together, and he had come to move in with her.

They had tried living together in New York once before. Not long after Christie left Mill Valley in August, Michael followed her east, and for a time they had shared her small apartment. But the guitarist's drinking quickly became a problem, one that she was not willing tolerate. "That was the deal," Christie said. "If you're going to stay with me this time, we can't do this drunken thing. So he went back to San Francisco." But Bloomfield had returned, eager to try yet again to make their relationship work. By odd coincidence, he wasn't the only person close to Christie who arrived unexpectedly.

"My mother got in a drive-away car in San Francisco and drove alone cross-country in the snow," Svane said. "She also descended on my doorstep. So I had these two people in my life who I didn't want right then." The dancer had recently joined a dance company and was busy performing. She felt her career was taking off, and she didn't have time to devote to two needy persons, no matter how much she cared for each of them. "I rented an apartment in the Village and installed them both there," she said. "Actually, Michael paid the rent on the place. It was $400 a month, bathroom in the hallway."

Two failed attempts at rekindling their on-again, off-again romance had left the dancer leery of a third try. But she had strong feelings for the troubled guitarist and was willing to have him in her life if they each had their own spaces. The arrangement was acceptable to Michael, but having Mrs. Svane as his roommate made it more than a little unorthodox. Nonetheless, the odd couple moved into the apartment on Prince Street and seemed to get along well despite the potential awkwardness of the situation.

While he was in New York, Michael sat in with country-and-western singer Kinky Friedman several times at the Lone Star Café and did a solo gig at the Ear Inn on Spring Street. But for the first months of 1980, he was largely inactive. He hung around the Greenwich Village apartment reading and watching TV, just as he did at home on Reed Street—and, just as he did at home, he continued to drink. The only difference in his saucepan-and-vodka routine was that he now had a partner. "He and my mom, for breakfast, would sit there drinking it in coffee cups," Christie said of Bloomfield's freezer cocktail.

By the end of February, Mike Bloomfield was back in Mill Valley. His relationship with Christie seemed to have stalled once again, and he missed California and the comforts of home. He also had unpaid bills to take care of and a house to look after, so he flew back to San Francisco, intending to stay at least until the weather warmed up. While there, Michael started playing with a new band.

With most of his former musical associates working with their own groups or simply avoiding him, Bloomfield had to find other musicians to back him whenever he needed a group. As was his habit, the guitarist simply enlisted friends, and two were players he had known since his early days in Chicago. Jack "Applejack" Walroth had been part of the South Side's blues scene in the early 1960s, working with Smokey Smothers, Sam Lay, and many others, and had moved to San Francisco in 1968 to join Elvin Bishop's group. Recently, though, Walroth had been playing with his own group, a septet called Chicago Blues Power that he had formed with fellow Chicagoan Ron Butkovich. Ron, who also knew Michael from Chicago, was the band's guitar player. He had originally approached Bloomfield about using Chicago Blues Power as his backup band, and that spring the guitarist took him up on the offer. "Ron wanted to get Michael back into playing," said the group's bass player, Steve Mallory. "I think that was the main reason he put the band together with Applejack." Mallory had met Bloomfield in 1979 through Hart McNee, who, along with Ben "King" Perkoff, was part of Chicago Blues Power's horn section.

The group was ideal for Michael's purposes. A competent blues band whose veteran players had an easygoing, relaxed attitude, Chicago Blues Power could provide Bloomfield with suitable accompaniment for whatever he felt like playing. That he knew nearly all the band's players well, and knew they would hustle up work while handling the logistics, made the arrangement even more appealing. On March 8, Michael Bloomfield and Chicago Blues Power traveled up to Petaluma for their first performance together at the Phoenix Theater on Washington Street. Also on the bill was a British blues-rock singer that Bloomfield had toured with in England back in 1966.

"Ron had this old hearse that he used for hauling around the band's equipment, and we drove that to the gig. We opened for Eric Burdon and his band," said Mallory. "It was a great show, and Jellyroll Troy sat in, joining Michael for some amazing blues." As was frequently the case, when the guitarist was inspired and focused, he could perform with breathtaking virtuosity. But those times were becoming the exception. Too often, Michael simply went through the motions, refusing to solo or opting only to play piano. Sometimes, he wouldn't show up at all.

"He'd be a no-show, and we'd just wind up playing as Chicago Blues Power," said Steve. "He was having a lot of trouble sleeping, and occasionally he'd sleep right through the date. That happened a few times when we played at Sweetwater." The Sweetwater Café was downtown Mill Valley's foremost night-spot, featuring name bands and rising stars. It was just minutes from Michael's house, but unless Ron Butkovich stopped by Reed Street to pick Michael up, the band was never sure whether the guitarist would appear.

CHAPTER 26

LAST CALL

MILL VALLEY, NEW YORK, SAN FRANCISCO, ITALY, AND SCANDINAVIA, 1980–1981

In April, Michael flew back to New York to play a few dates with Woody Harris. Woody had returned to the East Coast following the duo's appearance at McCabe's and was living in Chester, Connecticut. He had been giving classical concerts with his partner, cellist Margaret Edmondson, and it occurred to him that Maggie might make an excellent addition to the music he had been playing with Michael. Through his agent, Harris arranged for the trio to play a series of shows over several days. The first would be in a college town outside of Philadelphia.

The Main Point was an intimate coffeehouse on Lancaster Avenue in Bryn Mawr, a favorite nightspot for students from nearby Bryn Mawr and Haverford Colleges and Villanova University. The Bloomfield-Harris-Edmondson trio did two shows there on Saturday, April 5, playing to a room packed with Bloomfield fans who were eager to see the reclusive guitarist in person. But, as so often happened whenever he appeared outside the Bay Area, many in the coffeehouse were surprised to see Michael without his iconic Les Paul. "The audience was somewhat shocked by the absence of electric instruments—after all, his electric work earned him accolades from contemporary music writers and critics, including the 'Encyclopedia of Pop, Rock and Soul,' which called him 'America's answer to Eric Clapton,'" one newspaper review stated. That superstar persona was by 1980 a relic of the distant past, and any association with the English blues-rock giant was nowhere in evidence as Michael picked his way through traditional blues and rags, played old rock 'n' roll and New Orleans marches on piano, and harmonized with Woody and Maggie on a half-dozen gospel selections. But the Main Point crowd warmed to the new acoustic Bloomfield as the evening progressed, and the show was well received.

The following Monday and Tuesday, the trio appeared at New York City's Bottom Line. Bloomfield again opened each set, playing both piano and guitar, and then introduced Harris and Edmondson. Following their duet, he joined them onstage, and they finished the show as a trio. The first night, a portion of Michael's performance was filmed. A French TV crew was in the city doing an overview of New York's music scene for France 2's pop culture program *Chorus*, and they had decided to tape one of the Bottom Line's shows. They weren't quite sure what to make of Michael's acapella opener, a brief ditty of his own creation that went, "I got loaded last night, then I pissed on the floor; cleaned it up with my toothbrush, don't brush my teeth much anymore." But they also caught Bloomfield singing the classic Porter Grainger song "Prescription for the Blues" and Randy Newman's "A Wedding in Cherokee Country" while sitting at the piano.

The cameras then followed him as he switched to guitar and amused the crowd with a rendition of the all-too-pertinent "Knockin' Myself Out." The mood then changed, and the guitarist played a powerful version of "In My Time of Dying" based on Josh White's original recording, and then he finished the set with a soulful interpretation of Robert Johnson's "Come On in My Kitchen," both played with slide. The New York audience, already familiar with Bloomfield's enthusiasm for traditional acoustic music, wasn't caught off guard by his solo performance. They cheered and applauded each tune, and French TV's footage clearly showed the guitarist enjoying himself. He was in excellent form, not only because he was being filmed, but also because his one-time rival and former Blues Project guitarist Danny Kalb had come to see the show, and Michael was determined to impress him. As an encore, the guitarist again had members of the audience come onstage to sing the refrain of "John, John on the Battleground." When the Bottom Line segment was broadcast on *Chorus* in May, French television watchers got a preview of the music that America's great blues-rock guitarist was now playing. In a few months, other Europeans would get a chance to experience it firsthand.

Bloomfield remained in New York following the Bottom Line gig for a few weeks, but by May, he was back in Mill Valley. Ron Butkovich had gotten Chicago Blues Power another gig at the Catalyst, and on May 30, Michael fronted the group, playing with a brilliance that surprised even his bandmates.

Then, in June, Mike Bloomfield became a published author. Scott Summerville had succeeded in finding a publisher for "Me and Big Joe," and a limited edition of the guitarist's blues saga was issued as a forty-eight-page chapbook by RE/Search Publications. "We had a thousand copies printed up," said Summerville, "and I think only about four hundred got sold." The little book, with its black cover and title in blocky white type, was a modest product. But its text recounted Bloomfield's Fourth of July sojourn those many summers ago in vivid and entertaining prose. Summerville had polished Michael's language and syntax, but the guitarist's affection for his subject, canny insights, and exuberant humor came across undiluted. The book had cut-and-paste photos of some of the veteran blues artists mentioned in the story, a back-page picture of Big Joe, and a frontispiece of Michael, taken in 1971. In all, the little volume was an unassuming and engaging portrait of an uneasy comingling of cultures and a young man's coming of age.

But Mike Bloomfield may not have even been aware that *Me and Big Joe* had been released. "I was living down in LA at the time," said Scott. "Michael was on his final descent, and it was too sad—I just couldn't stand it. I was staying away from him, and I just gave the material to the company and they published it." The guitarist's drinking, combined with bouts of drug use, had proven too much for Summerville. He, like many of Michael's other friends, had distanced himself from the guitarist. But Bloomfield seemed unconcerned. In July, he was back in New York City.

Over the Fourth of July weekend, the guitarist appeared at the Other End coffeehouse in Greenwich Village. The club had formerly been known as the Bitter End—the same venue that had hosted the New York debut of the Electric Flag nearly thirteen years earlier. But it was a very different Michael Bloomfield who now took the stage and did two nights of solo shows, playing and singing traditional American music while accompanying himself on acoustic guitar and piano. The crowds were nothing like they were in 1967, but the audience was respectful and appreciative, caught up in Bloomfield's enthusiasm for the music and amused by his occasional wry asides. Though he appeared to be slightly intoxicated, his playing remained largely unaffected.

That wasn't the case several weeks later when Michael did four nights at the Greene Street Café. Three days after his thirty-seventh birthday, the guitarist split a gig at the Soho supper club, playing several nights on his own and then working as a trio with Woody Harris and Maggie Edmondson. On one of his solo nights, a member of the audience repeatedly heckled him with the usual requests. Felix Cabrera, a blues harmonica player and a dedicated Bloomfield fan, was in the audience and remembered Michael's reaction. "He was playing acoustic, and a fellow was shouting 'Super Session! Super Session!' in between tunes. Bloomfield got up and started screaming at the guy, saying, 'What the *fuck* is the matter with you? Do you see any drums? Any horns? Keyboards?'" Cabrera said everyone in the club was embarrassed, unsure how to react. "He went crazy on the man, screaming and pointing at the guy, and his face was all puffed up from heavy drinking." Normally, the guitarist would ignore those few in the audience who insisted on bringing up his past glories. But his drinking sapped his patience just as much as it hampered his playing, and that night he had had enough.

* * *

In September, Woody Harris's agent arranged an overseas tour for the Bloomfield-Harris-Edmondson trio. The group had eight shows scheduled in Italy, with stops in Rome, Milan, Venice, Turin, and several other cities. There was also the possibility of additional appearances in Sweden, Finland, and Denmark. The idea of spending a few weeks on the road in a foreign country was unnerving to Michael, so much so that he had backed out of the French tour Dave Shorey had organized. This junket would be even longer, and that would mean many more sleepless nights paired with just as many stressful days. But the idea of seeing Italy, with its legendary cities, magnificent art and architecture, and historic piazzas, all while indulging in its gourmet food and drink, was not without appeal. The guitarist decided he would go, but only if Christie Svane would come with him. When she agreed, the contracts were signed and the details were finalized. Michael Bloomfield was going to perform abroad for the first time since his trip to Great Britain with the Butterfield Band, nearly a decade and a half earlier.

The first week in September, Michael, Christie, Woody Harris, and Maggie Edmondson flew to Milan to begin a ten-day tour of northern and southern Italy. During the six-hour flight, Bloomfield made a game of sneaking shots of gin off the beverage cart every time it went by, and soon he was drunk enough that he peed in his pants. But the flight otherwise was without mishap, and the four travelers were met at the airport by their Italian host, the tour's producer. Because no one could remember his name, they gave him a nickname. "We called him 'the Trout,'" Harris recalled, laughing.

The trio's first show was on September 8 in Florence, several hours south by car. The concert was held at the city's Cascine Park in an outdoor amphitheater, and the crowds were huge. But not everyone was there to see Mike Bloomfield and his two accompanists, as the group soon learned. A good portion of the tour had been booked to coincide with an annual Italian political event, a countrywide celebration originally sponsored by the Communist Party that was called the Festa de l'Unità. There were amusements, games, dancing, and other activities, plus vendors and food concessions, all happening concurrently throughout the huge park. Though many in the trio's audience had come to see the legendary American guitarist, just as many had wandered in out of curiosity. As a result, the crowd was noisy and restive, with much coming and going in the back seats. But the trio's performance went well, and their ninety-minute set presented many of the selections they had played at the Bottom Line, plus a dozen new ones.

Following an introduction by the Trout, Woody Harris started the show with a few solo instrumentals. Maggie Edmondson then joined him, and they played several more wordless tunes as a duo. Mike Bloomfield then strode onstage and sat at the piano. He was wearing his bright white Count Talent suit coat, a T-shirt, flared-leg Levis and work boots. He also was sporting a pair of prescription wire-frame glasses with stylishly tinted lenses. He looked more like an extra from a *Miami Vice* episode than a Chicago bluesman, but with a coy "*Buonasera*!" Bloomfield launched into a solo version of Lefty Frizzell's "She's Gone, Gone, Gone," bouncing on the piano bench as he played and sang. Those in the audience who knew the famous guitarist's recordings were expecting *Super Session* guitar wizardry, but they clapped and cheered anyway, caught up in the exuberance of Michael's performance.

After a few more tunes on piano, Bloomfield moved to center stage, sat down, and picked up a Yamaha acoustic. He played several solo selections, beginning with "Frankie and Johnny," and then brought out Woody and Maggie for the trio portion of the show. They performed the gospel tunes from the Kicking Mule album and did a few blues, and then Michael finished the set by himself with "Motorized Blues," a Nick Gravenites original. Though there were a few cries for *Super Session* as the trio left the stage, most of the crowd applauded enthusiastically. It was a good first night.

"Michael was received really, really well," said Woody. "People brought albums he had done backstage and had him sign them. He was just incredibly happy."

Other shows for the Unità festival followed on successive nights. The trio played for a huge crowd of fifteen thousand in Pisa and then did performances in Rome, Naples, Venice, Verona, and Milan. The mood was generally relaxed, and the trio's sets had a casual feel, as though Michael, Woody, and Maggie were entertaining a few friends in an intimate Greenwich Village coffeehouse. But Bloomfield's drinking often affected his performance, and the group's shows could appear disorganized and chaotic when he had drunk too much before going onstage. Frequently, though, his inebriation was not entirely his own fault.

"The Italians are so attached to the mythos of the alcoholic blues guy that they would sort of taunt Michael every step of the way," said Christie. "They'd have drinking contests with grappa." Never one to pass up a competition, Bloomfield would do shots of the potent local brandy with his hosts and would soon be besotted. Under those circumstances, his playing could become sloppy and his mood combative, especially when the audience was unreceptive. The trio's appearance in Naples proved difficult for just those reasons.

A faulty sound system marred the first portion of the show, causing the audience to become restless. When Michael took the stage following Woody and Maggie's duet, shouts of "Go home!" could be heard out front. More delays only soured the mood, and when people began shouting for *Super Session*,

Bloomfield barked back, "Hey! I don't tell you all how to suck cock! Don't tell me what to play!" Edmondson tried to get the guitarist to cut the performance short, hoping to get off the stage, but Michael refused to surrender to the crowd. He insisted on playing the entire set all the way through to the bitter end.

Naples wasn't the only difficult concert the trio gave. In Milan, there again were long delays between tunes, and the audience was noisy and distracted. Bloomfield tried repeatedly to quiet them so they could hear the subtleties as he played "Come On in My Kitchen," but to no avail. He finished his portion of the show with "Motorized Blues," introducing the song with a dismissive, "*Only* one more, y'all." Though most in the crowd were respectful and clapped enthusiastically at the conclusion of each number, there also were derisive whistles and occasional catcalls. The trio performed well, but Michael had clearly been drinking and things could easily have gotten out of hand. As it was, the group was called back for an encore. But then Bloomfield spent ten minutes wandering through the audience and trying to get a few people up onstage to sing "John, John on the Battleground." That effort interrupted the performance's flow for yet another lengthy delay.

During their ten days in Italy, Mike Bloomfield seemed relaxed and content to Woody Harris, more so than he had ever been in the short time they had played together. But Christie got the opposite impression. She saw how the crowds, expecting electric blues, sometimes taunted him and were abusive, and how it affected him. Underneath his genial demeanor, his anything-goes façade, she could see there was a man who was deeply depressed. "This will sound arrogant, Christie, but it isn't. It's the truth," Michael said to her. "I've seen it all, and I've done most of it, and I'm on my way down." There were just two things he wanted to do now, he told her—go home and marry her.

That second desire caught the young dancer by surprise, and though she was in love and enticed by his proposal, she knew that marriage to Michael would only be possible if he made some real changes. The thought of sharing a life and possibly having a child with a partner whose drug use might prove fatal at any time frightened her. She demurred, but she didn't give the guitarist a definitive "no." When she left the tour after its first week and headed to Amsterdam and London for a series of dance workshops, Michael asked her to think seriously about his proposal.

Italian blues fans finally got a chance to hear Bloomfield play the music he was famous for when the trio did its last show, a performance at the Palasport Stadium in Turin. When they arrived, the Trout informed them that a blues band would be playing the opening set—and then he made a request. "When we got to Turin, the presenter dropped this Treves Blues Band on Michael like a lead shoe," said Woody. "He said those guys would be the warm-up band, and wouldn't Michael play with them? They were an absolute group of deadbeats. Michael was really pissed!" Fabio Treves, a harmonica player from Milan, had organized the country's first Chicago-style blues band in 1974, modeling it on the Paul Butterfield Blues Band. Michael met Fabio earlier in the tour and had invited him to sit in as a guest soloist at a few of the trio's concerts. But Bloomfield had no idea that Treves's band would be sharing a stage with them, and he certainly had no desire to jam with them. The Trout, sensing Michael's reluctance, quickly sweetened the deal by saying the blues band's portion of the show would be recorded and issued as an album, and that Michael would be paid for his participation. The details were worked out, a Stratocaster was quickly found, and for the first time on the tour, Mike Bloomfield would plug in and play electric blues.

The guitarist began the opening set on piano with the Treves Blues Band, playing "Shake, Rattle, and Roll." He then switched to guitar for Muddy Waters's "Five Long Years," Chuck Berry's "Don't You Lie to Me," and his own variation on Champion Jack Dupree's "Junker's Blues." Though they weren't the equal of their American counterparts, the Treves Blues Band was better than Woody Harris gave them credit for, and Michael suddenly seemed inspired. He sang with happy abandon and played furious lead for multiple choruses, sharing solos with Fabio's wailing harp. He seemed to be relieved to shed the constraints of the trio's acoustic format, if only for a few tunes. But he unplugged for the second set and, along with Woody and Maggie, entertained the crowd in the vast arena with the traditional blues, rags, and gospel tunes he had originally planned to perform.

While the trio was in Italy, Bloomfield, Harris, and Edmondson stayed in local hotels. There Michael was often joined by other musicians and fans, and he frequently played music with them throughout much of the night. Marco Bonino, a singer who had been hired as the tour's sound man and road manager, remembered those late-night jams well. "After the concert, we'd come back to his room and we'd pass the night playing and singing together with all our friends," Marco said. "We played tunes by the Beatles and Randy Newman—Michael's favorite—and lots of blues and country." But after Christie's departure, the guitarist was finding it harder than ever to close his eyes. "Every night he was looking for a way to go to sleep," said Marco. "He was doing a lot of wine and pills. He would say, 'Please don't leave me alone!'"

As always when he was away from home, sleep for Mike Bloomfield was an elusive commodity. In Italy, it was a constant struggle. Drinking made him drowsy, but he frequently only dozed when under the influence. Sleeping pills helped, but they were nothing like the powerful sedative Placidyl and so were of limited efficacy. The only thing Michael could do was drink even more than he already was—to "obliterate his mind." He was desperate for relief by the third week of September, just as the trio flew to Sweden, Finland, and Denmark for the tour's remaining shows.

"He drank himself absolutely *wild* in Scandinavia," remembered Woody Harris. "Maggie smacked him around a lot, trying to keep him in line. It wasn't easy!" The group played shows in Stockholm and Uppsala in Sweden and then flew across the Baltic Sea to Finland for an appearance in Helsinki. All the while, Michael was seldom sober. But maintaining his alcoholic haze was difficult, because liquor was available only in state stores, and only in limited quantities. "Everybody would buy something and hide it under the seats in the car, and we'd ration it out to him," said Woody. "It was his substitute for drugs."

It was a poor substitute for obvious reasons, but booze provided the guitarist with the only relief available. His mood was such that, following the trio's appearance in Helsinki, he responded to a reporter's question about his withdrawal from the music scene by saying, "I am an old man. . . . In California, I've alienated all my friends, and so I'm just doing this stuff as a hobby." He went on to say that he was making his living "as a carpenter," a shocking admission from someone who was still considered to be one of the world's great blues-rock guitarists. Even in his depressed state, though, Bloomfield could not help bristling when the reporter asked about requests for *Super Session*. "How do those idiots think I can make the trio sound like 'Super Session' when we don't even have drums or bass—not to mention horns?" the guitarist angrily replied.

The Bloomfield-Harris-Edmondson trio played its final show in Copenhagen at the end of the month, and the next day the three musicians flew home to New York City. When the plane landed at Kennedy International Airport in Queens, Bloomfield bypassed the baggage claim, leaving his luggage and guitars behind, and headed straight for the taxi stand. He had been drinking heavily on the flight, and in his sloshed condition he instructed the cab driver to drive him to the one place he knew he could find the relief he so desperately needed. "He just got out of the plane and came out to visit a friend that we had in Connecticut," said Woody Harris. "He paid $300 for a taxi to take him from JFK up into Connecticut. And he was so drunk that he threw up all over the inside of the cab!"

As soon as Michael Bloomfield had recovered from his three-week ordeal abroad, he left his friends in Connecticut and flew home to San Francisco and Mill Valley. It had been nearly three months since he had left Reed Street, and he was relieved to be back. In his absence, friends kept an eye on the place, and some had stayed there for weeks at a time. A guitarist named Perry Lederman, a thirty-eight-year-old master of a variety of traditional fingerpicking styles, was one part-time resident, and so was Jon Cramer. Joining them was John Finn, a thirty-four-year-old mathematician and carpenter whom Bloomfield had met when Finn was doing work on a house nearby. John had also been making some repairs for Michael, working with Leonard Trupin's cousin, Bob Trupin. "Bob was a master carpenter," said Leonard. "Michael hired him to do some work on Reed Street, and they were all hanging out there together." The guitarist intended to work with Trupin and Finn on the fixes, an ambition that had doubtless inspired his career-change comment to the Finnish magazine reporter. But not long after his return, Michael was doing something other than hammering nails.

"John Finn got him back into dope," said Leonard. It wouldn't have taken much convincing to get Michael Bloomfield involved with heroin again, because everyone hanging around the house—Lederman, Cramer, Finn, and even Bob Trupin—was using. Despite his desire to marry Christie, and his awareness that only a real commitment to sobriety would make that happen, Michael couldn't help himself. The temptation was too great—and so was the pressure from friends and acquaintances, and even from people he hardly knew. Woody Harris had observed that pressure while the two guitarists were working on their Kicking Mule album. "It was patently obvious to me that there were an awful lot of people in the Bay Area who were hitting on Michael all the time," said Woody. "He was so manipulatable, that if some friend came around and said, 'Let's do this,' he'd just do it."

Meanwhile, C.T. Productions was working on a deal with Takoma Records to put out a fourth Michael Bloomfield album. Norman Dayron had gotten the go-ahead and an advance from the company, and in October he scheduled time at Wally Heider's former studios on Hyde Street in San Francisco. Norman found the place to be less than ideal, describing it as a "dark, suffocating little studio," but the price was right, and he quickly began organizing the recording sessions. Bloomfield, back home at Reed Street, was largely uninterested in the project.

"Michael had started using drugs again, and he wasn't in very good shape," admitted Norman. "Those sessions turned out to be very difficult, painful really, partly because the musicians we used were this very odd assortment of people." Because many of Bloomfield's regular musical partners had stopped working with him, Dayron had to find other players to record the parts Michael couldn't overdub himself. San Francisco veteran Henry Oden, who had worked with Freddie King and Mark Naftalin, was hired to play bass while Anna Rizzo's brother, Tom, was enlisted as the date's drummer. Rizzo was a novice player whose limitations soon became evident. "He really had no idea how to play blues," said Dayron. "I asked him to play brushes on one song and he didn't even know what brushes were!"

To further complicate matters, Michael insisted on using his friend Jon Cramer as the sessions' pianist. Cramer was a passable keyboardist and knew how to play blues, but he wasn't in Mark Naftalin's league, and Norman was concerned that he wouldn't be up to the task. But Dayron also realized that Michael was trying to give his friend some work, so he reluctantly agreed to include Cramer in the sessions.

Recording for Michael's next Takoma release began on Monday, October 27, with the guitarist and the rhythm section taping basic tracks for the various songs he and Dayron planned to include in the album. Only two of them were Bloomfield originals, but one, destined to become the album's title tune, had lyrics that for Michael were unusually aggressive. Called "Cruisin' for a Bruisin'," the song was a funky rocker that railed against "black-shaded pimps," "white boys with long hair," "two men suckin' tongue," and other undesirables who "put their shit up in my face." The guitarist threatened to "put your ass away" but growled and mumbled his words to such a degree that much of what he sang was unintelligible. It was as though "Cruisin' for a Bruisin'" were a barfly's drunken rant, delivered on a street corner after being tossed out of a favorite watering hole.

The other Bloomfield tune was an instrumental called "Papa-Mama-Rompah-Stompah." A tight funk vamp with a bridge, the tune was smartly arranged and featured a lengthy solo from the composer. Curiously, though, Michael's guitar was routed through an effects device that gave his lead a compressed, filtered sound, quite unlike its usual tone. His soloing, though, was effective, and the tune, with its opening chords evoking the beginning of Steppenwolf's "The Pusher," had an infectious dance beat.

Bloomfield overdubbed lead and piano on both his compositions, using only Oden and Rizzo for the rhythm section. A trio of horns, consisting of saxophonists Hart McNee, King Perkoff, and Derrick Walker, was then added to the mix to fill out the sound and support the solos.

Over the next few weeks, Bloomfield and his musicians recorded "Junker's Blues," with an arrangement attributed to Dr. John; Nick Gravenites's "Motorized Blues," with Derrick Walker blowing harp; "It'll Be Me," a country rocker originally recorded by Jerry Lee Lewis; and an instrumental shuffle called "Midnight" that was a variation on "Chicken Shack." Hart McNee was the vocalist on an obscure doo-wop tune originally recorded by Cookie and the Cupcakes called "Mathilda," and he sang a spirited duet with Bloomfield's lead. Michael also recorded "Linda Lu," a song he had featured in live performance for more than seven years, dubbing a fine guitar solo over Jon Cramer's attempt at barrelhouse piano.

Cramer was the pianist on three other selections the ensemble recorded, including one that was his own composition. A minor-key dirge called "Snowblind," the song had oblique lyrics that seemed to describe being caught in a blizzard but also may have alluded to cocaine addiction. Michael changed its original refrain, "I'm snowblind, snowblind, that's all I can figure out," to "I was snowbound, couldn't find my way to higher ground," making the song literally about being caught in a freak snowstorm. Cramer's lyrics mentioned Blind Lemon Jefferson, the legendary blues singer who was said to have died in the snow on a Chicago street, using his death to extend the song's drug metaphor. But Bloomfield's rewrite made the snow itself the lethal element and transformed Cramer's song into a lament for the great 1920s blues guitarist. Norman Dayron hated the song, but Michael insisted on including it in the album.

The ensemble then recorded a final instrumental with just the rhythm section and Bloomfield's lead. Written by Norman Dayron, "Winter Moon" was the album's only selection without horns, and its most complex musically, with a forty-bar AABC structure. The tune gave the guitarist an opportunity to stretch out over non-blues chord changes, and he soloed cleanly for its entire five-minute duration, demonstrating that he was still a formidable improviser.

Sessions for the Takoma release, tentatively titled *Cruisin' for a Bruisin'*, were finally completed on Saturday, November 29, more than a month after they began. The logistics of scheduling various ensembles of musicians for multiple recording and overdubbing sessions, coupled with Bloomfield's health issues and general apathy, had slowed the recording process. For Norman Dayron, producing Michael's next LP had been a real struggle, but he was satisfied with the results. "Those were very strange sessions, very strained," Dayron later said. "But Michael really pulled them off—whatever happened to work was Michael triumphing over all the problems, really, not me."

While he was working on *Cruisin' for a Bruisin'*, Michael Bloomfield had a surprise visitor one Friday evening at Reed Street. He was lounging on the couch in his bathrobe, watching TV in the living room, when there was a knock at the front door. Though the guitarist wasn't expecting anyone, he hopped up and went into the foyer. When he opened the door, there stood singer Maria Muldaur, smiling shyly. Completely surprised, Bloomfield invited her in, happy to see her. But what, he wanted to know, was she doing there? "I said, 'I've got somebody here who wants to see you,'" Muldaur recalled. "So I motioned to Bob to come up and said, 'Look who's here. Look who I've got here.'"

Stepping out of the darkness and into the light of the living room was Bob Dylan. Michael was delighted to see his old friend, and he gave the folk-rock superstar a warm hug. Dylan, in San Francisco for two weeks of shows at the city's Warfield Theatre, had been visiting Muldaur in Mill Valley, and he had asked the singer to take him to see his guitarist friend. The two musicians hadn't seen each other since Bob played selections from *Blood on the Tracks* for Michael in that same room back in 1973. Much had changed since then, and Michael and Bob sat on the couch reminiscing, laughing about other musicians they knew, the music business, and their days together in New York. It was like old times, and after half an hour, Bob told Michael he had to come down to the Warfield and sit in. The guitarist quietly declined, saying he wasn't into performing much anymore. But Dylan insisted, replying that Jerry Garcia was going to play a few tunes on Sunday and Maria was going to join him onstage later in the week. The folksinger again urged his friend to come, and Michael said he would try.

The next afternoon, Mike Bloomfield called Norman Dayron to explain that he wouldn't be able to work on *Cruisin' for a Bruisin'* that night. When Norman asked why, Michael replied that Dylan had paid him a visit and asked him to play a few numbers at the Warfield. Dayron, knowing Bloomfield's casual relationship with the truth, laughed and asked for the real reason. No, Michael replied, Dylan really had been there and really had asked him. But the guitarist said he wasn't really sure he would go. "He was going to blow it off!" said Norman. "But I didn't care what he wanted to do—I had to see him onstage with Dylan again. So I told him he was *definitely* going!"

On Saturday evening, November 15, Michael Bloomfield and Norman Dayron drove to the Warfield Theatre on Market Street in downtown San Francisco. They found their way to the theater's box office and, after hassling with security, were finally admitted backstage. Bloomfield was carrying his Stratocaster in its well-worn gig bag and was dressed in torn jeans, a T-shirt, and a funky leather jacket. He looked like the neighborhood bad boy—down to his ankles, at least. On his feet he wore bedroom slippers. "He came to Dylan's show wearing these old scuffs, a pair of slip-ons he'd wear around the house," Norman recalled, laughing. "Michael had to be comfortable!" They found their way to the dressing rooms, and Dylan was delighted to see Bloomfield. Michael introduced Norman, and the three chatted for a few minutes about the show. Bob said that he would get things started, and then Bloomfield should come on after the second tune. Dylan would do an introduction, giving Michael time to plug in, and then they would play "Like a Rolling Stone."

* * *

Bob Dylan was in the middle of his "Musical Retrospective Tour," a follow-up to his two controversial gospel tours, but he was still working with a backup choir and still doing his Christian material. Accordingly, he opened the show with "Gotta Serve Somebody" and followed that with "I Believe in You." Then there was a brief pause. As the organist improvised quietly on a C chord, the lights went down. A single spotlight found Dylan standing center stage and strumming his Stratocaster. He stepped up to a microphone and addressed the audience in the packed theater.

"I was playing in a club in Chicago, I guess it was about 1960, and I was sitting in a restaurant. I think it was probably across the street or maybe part of the club; I'm not sure. But a guy came down [and] said that he played guitar," Bob began.

From the wings, a shadowy figure emerged and rounded the row of amps at the back of the stage. As Dylan continued, the figure crouched down and plugged in the guitar that was slung over his shoulder.

"So he had his guitar with him, and he begin to play—"

Here the figure slid a steel cylinder over his little finger and began to play subtle, bluesy slide.

"I said, well, what can you play? And he played all kinds of things—I don't know if you ever heard of a man, does Big Bill Broonzy ring a bell? Or Sonny Boy Williamson, that type of thing?"

Many in the audience started to cheer and whistle.

"Anyway, he just played circles around anything I could play, and I always remembered that. Anyway, we were back in New York, I think it was about 1963 or 1964, and I needed a guitar player on a session there I was doing, and I called up—I even remembered his name—"

The slide runs became more pronounced, following Dylan's words.

"And he came in and recorded an album at that time. He was working in the Paul Butterfield Blues Band."

More cheers and applause from the audience. The slide began to sweetly sing.

"Anyway, he played with me on a record, and I think we played some other dates. I haven't seen him too much since then—anyway, he played on 'Like a Rolling Stone,' and he's here tonight. Give him a hand—"

The band stirred to life. The crowd began to applaud. Older Dylan fans knew what his next words would be.

"Michael Bloomfield!"

With the force of a dam breaking, the opening chords to "Like a Rolling Stone" surged out from the stage and washed over the cheering house. The lights went up, revealing a leather-clad guitarist hunched over a grimy black Stratocaster. It *was* Bloomfield!

The folksinger began to sing the words to his folk-rock masterwork, the tune that had launched a revolution fifteen years earlier. Michael fell in with the band, deftly backing the leader's vocal, but then asserted himself at the end of each line with the familiar fills he had devised all those years ago. His playing was nearly flawless, and though he missed a chord in the first verse, causing Dylan to chuckle as he sang, the performance's energy was breathtaking. With each succeeding chorus, Bloomfield's embellishments became more adventurous, more assured. The gospel choir's soulful intensity lifted Dylan's challenge "How does it feel?" to heights unachieved in the original and caused him to invest the song's caustic lyrics with renewed conviction. As he sang, he caught Michael's eye and smiled broadly. In reply, the guitarist fired off another lead phrase that was none of that "B. B. King shit."

In five minutes, the song was completed. In less time than it took to play the original, "Like a Rolling Stone" had once again become a landmark. Bob Dylan and Michael Bloomfield had revisited a moment in time that had proven to be a turning point in both their careers, and they had reinvigorated it by reuniting their protean talents.

Not everyone in the theater that night understood the gravity of what they had witnessed, but everyone felt the excitement. The crowd was on its feet as the song came to an end, clapping and hooting, cheering for the tune they all recognized and for the disheveled, bushy-haired guitarist who had played with such intensity and who was now shambling offstage with a sheepish grin on his face.

"Michael Bloomfield!" Dylan shouted to the house as his friend headed for the wings. With no recent accomplishments to cite in the reclusive guitarist's favor, Bob simply added, "Y'all go see him if he's playing around town."

Later in the show, Dylan called Bloomfield to the stage once again to play on a new song called "The Groom's Still Waiting at the Altar." The guitarist had tried to leave following the triumph of "Like a Rolling Stone," but he and Norman were still backstage, and when Michael heard that Bob was calling for him, he unpacked his Stratocaster. Joining the band on the tune's second verse, Bloomfield plugged in and began playing. This time, though, his lead had a frantic, noisy sound. He switched to slide for a second solo, and his phrasing improved, but his contribution remained more chaotic than controlled. The performance evoked that moment at Newport in 1965 when Bloomfield's furious soloing threatened to derail Dylan's "Phantom Engineer." This time, though, the singer was unfazed by his friend's aggressive accompaniment, and the song was brought to a successful conclusion. "Michael Bloomfield!" Bob shouted once more as the crowd stomped and cheered.

Though his second appearance onstage had been anticlimactic and had largely dissipated the magic of "Like a Rolling Stone," Michael Bloomfield was happy with his overall performance. Unsure whether he would be able to play at all, he had not only played but played well on the tune that really mattered. Dylan was pleased enough that he made a point of thanking his friend after the show, expressing his gratitude in a touching scene that Dayron remembered clearly. "He said, 'God, I had forgotten what a difference your playing made in my music, and how important it was to me, and how much I had missed it."

When Michael got home, he called Christie Svane to tell her that he had played with Bob Dylan. She was back in New York, having returned from Europe after giving dance workshops in Amsterdam and London, and she was unsure whether to believe her storytelling lover. But Bloomfield told her it was really true, that Dylan had invited him to sit in and that he had actually gone and performed. "I played fantastic," Michael proudly proclaimed. He added with satisfaction, "It was great to see him, and he didn't have his character armor anymore. He's a much sweeter guy."

The second week in December, Mike Bloomfield flew back to New York City to see Christie Svane. He also had a couple of shows to play. Woody Harris had gotten the trio a gig in Washington, DC, and another just down the road from his home in Chester, Connecticut.

The show in the nation's capital took place on Thursday, December 11, at a small club in the city's DuPont Circle called the Childe Harold. Woody remembered their performance as one of the group's worst. "It was absolutely an abysmal evening," he later said. Author Jan Mark Wolkin saw the show and thought Michael played well, though he did notice moments of tension. "At one point, Maggie said something in a patronizing tone about 'how great Michael sounds tonight,'" Jan said. "But Mike played great, as I remember it."

The trio did their usual set, playing individually and in different combinations, and at one point Michael did a tune in response to a request from the audience. "A woman asked him to play a Beatles song in memory of John Lennon," Wolkin recalled. The former Beatle had been murdered in New York five days earlier. "Mike politely declined, saying he didn't really have any Beatles songs prepared. But then he played a nice version of 'Amazing Grace,' dedicated to John."

The next evening, the trio appeared at the historic Meeting House in Chester. A Colonial-era structure, the landmark hall was a former church that had been repurposed as a community center. Its period stage and wraparound balcony gave it an intimate feel, and a small but appreciative crowd gathered for the trio's seventy-minute performance. Bloomfield started out on piano, even doing a version of "Women Loving Each Other" at the keyboard, and then fingerpicked a few blues on guitar. He was in excellent form, playing with astonishing dexterity and verve, and the crowd hung on every note. In the second part of the show, Michael and Woody did an adventurous version of "Somewhere Over the Rainbow," one of Bloomfield's favorite songs from childhood, and then to conclude the evening's program, all three musicians burned through a rocking version of an instrumental they had created as a feature for Michael's bright slide called "Finger Fat." It was an excellent show.

Michael spent the weekend at Woody's place and then returned to New York City for a few days. While there, he again raised the possibility of marriage with Christie. She remained hesitant, largely because Michael's condition had not improved as far as she could see, and because she was focused on another exciting project. She had been offered the "chance of a lifetime," an opportunity to go on a teaching and performing dance tour of Europe, all expenses paid, for three full months. The tour was scheduled to depart in February, and she was busy preparing for it. She cared deeply for Michael and wanted to be with him and help him overcome his self-destructive habits, but at the moment she needed to concentrate on her career. She told him it would be best if he went home, and when she returned at the end of April, they could decide what to do. In the meantime, she said, she would call him every day. For Bloomfield, her willingness to consider marriage felt like a tacit "yes," and he headed back to Mill Valley feeling hopeful.

"He had apparently worked the whole thing out that they would get married," said Woody Harris. "He was really in love with Christina."

Life at 9 Reed Street had long since lost its homey appeal for Michael Bloomfield. Friends were around—John Finn was frequently there, as were Jon Cramer and Perry Lederman—but too often their visits involved drugs and alcohol. Any effort to complete the repairs Bob Trupin had begun on the house in the fall had been abandoned when Bloomfield ran short of cash. The place had taken on a messy, unkempt look as housekeeping duties were neglected during the guitarist's long absences. Often there was nothing in the kitchen to eat and nothing clean to wear. Reed Street's domestic chaos only added to the unsettled way Michael was feeling.

But mostly what Mike Bloomfield was feeling was alone. "He would get very lonely, and he'd come over to my place," said Norman Dayron. "He'd sit on the couch and play guitar for hours. Many times he'd set up a tape recorder and just record. I've got stacks of reels, and I don't even know what's on them." Despite his daily calls from Christie and the real possibility of marriage, the guitarist was distressed that she would be gone for so long. Sometimes he would go over to Susan and Bonner Beuhler's house in search of solace. His ex-wife and their former housemate had gotten married at the end of 1977, but Michael was still close to them, and Susan could see that he was distraught. "He was very unhappy," she said. "He would come here and lie down on the bed, just curl up and cry and moan." She and Bonner knew Michael was anxious to marry Christie, but they also knew he had been hanging around with people whose bad habits were reinforcing his own. "He did like nutty people," said Susan. Bonner agreed, "Yeah, they seemed to flock around him." Most of them, nutty or not, were harmless. But one of Bloomfield's new friends was of a different order.

"Michael would brag about this guy he'd met, someone named Jerry who lived on Divisadero near the Castro," said Norman. "He said the guy was a 'bad guy,' a real criminal. I met him once, and I think he'd been busted for armed robbery or something like that." Jerry was in the business of dealing drugs, and Bloomfield would drive into the city with friends to buy heroin from him. He liked being around Jerry, because the dealer was an "outlaw," someone he believed had committed real crimes. "Michael was really attracted to people like that," Dayron said. "Gangster-types, guys who were 'dangerous.' I think they made him feel like he was one of them too." Bloomfield's adolescent fantasy of himself as a greaser, a "hood," still had strong appeal for the guitarist, even at age thirty-seven.

"He told me about Jerry," said Leonard Trupin. "Mike said he'd turned in these guys who'd robbed a bank in New York, and he'd used the reward money to set himself up as a dealer in the city. But I think the guy was really just a punk dope dealer."

Punk or not, Jerry was someone in Mike Bloomfield's vast circle of acquaintances who was unlike his other friends. Jerry didn't know anything about the guitarist's habits when it came to drug use, nor did he care. For that reason alone, he was indeed dangerous.

Over the holidays, Michael continued to struggle with depression, and with drugs and alcohol. He spent Christmas with Susan and Bonner at Bonner's parents' home in Mill Valley and was in good spirits. But a week later, on New Year's Eve, a different Mike Bloomfield attended Ira Kamin's birthday party. "He was really messed up," said Ira. "Two of his friends carried him in, they carried him to my piano, and he played piano all night. Then they carried him out." The guitarist celebrated the arrival of 1981 doing his "sloppy drunk" routine at the keyboard. It was not a great start to the New Year.

But then, in January, his mood began to lighten. Michael had hit upon a plan that would allow him to tag along with Christie when she left for Europe at the end of the month. He would simply set up a tour of his own to coincide with hers, and they could meet up in Europe.

Michael called his friend Al Kooper with the idea. Al had moved to England following a very successful run as the producer of the Southern rock band Lynyrd Skynyrd, and he was living in a small house in London. He was surprised to hear from the guitarist and delighted to hear what Bloomfield had in mind. "His girlfriend was coming to Europe and he was coming with her, so he wanted me to book some gigs for us to play in London," said Kooper. "I said, 'Wow! That's great. Let's do it.'" The keyboardist said he would get to work setting up dates, but he first wanted to be sure Bloomfield would really show up. "Knowing Michael, I asked him how he was doing," Kooper said. "He told me he had quit drinking and wasn't doing drugs, that he had cleaned himself up. He even said he'd been working out regularly, getting in shape, though whether that was really true . . ." But Al was suitably reassured, and within a few weeks, he had booked Michael and himself into the Venue, a small club on Victoria Street. He was looking forward to working with the mercurial guitarist again.

Bloomfield's claims, for once, were actually true. The guitarist had suddenly stopped drinking and was making a real effort to curtail his drug use. The possibility of joining his lady love overseas was inspiration enough to pull himself together, but his resolve had been reinforced by Christie herself. "I said to Michael that I was really, really lovesick and heartsick," she later confessed. "I said, 'When I come back from this trip, all I want to do is be with you, and we'll take it from there.'" That was what Michael had been hoping to hear, and he was determined to make it happen. He began taking care of himself, refusing to drink with friends when they came over and doing nothing stronger than pot. Christie's mother also provided him with an excuse to curtail friends' visits. Mrs. Svane had taken Bloomfield up on his offer of Reed Street as a place to stay when she returned to San Francisco, and because she suffered from migraine headaches, he would explain that she wasn't feeling well and that everyone had to leave. That way, Michael could avoid temptation.

"He sort of turned his life around," said Bonner Beuhler. "He looked good and had plans. He'd gotten his alcoholic phase behind him."

Bloomfield was soon feeling well enough that he began doing solo performances. The last Saturday in January, he opened for Doug Sahm's quintet at the Catalyst in Santa Cruz and then sat in with Sahm, playing electric guitar on a few blues, including Dylan's "Just Like Tom Thumb's Blues," a song he had recorded with Bob in 1965. Bloomfield also did sets in the student unions at San Jose State University and San Francisco University, and he agreed to fly down to San Diego later in February to appear with Bob Greenspan at the Belly-Up Tavern in Solanas Beach.

"It's ironic how Mike did his first professional gig with me," Greenspan later said. "And his last show was going to be with me too."

On Friday afternoon, February 13, Michael Bloomfield was interviewed at home on Reed Street by Tom Yates, former program director at KSAN, and his coproducer, Kate Hayes, for a radio series they were creating called *Guitar: A Rock Episode*. Consisting of thirty-six hour-long programs that would feature music and interviews with scores of rock's top guitarists, the production was scheduled to begin airing on major FM stations around the country in September. Yates was a big Bloomfield fan, and though the guitarist's stature had declined since the 1960s, he gave Michael a full sixty minutes to talk about his career and about other guitarists who had been important in the development of blues-rock.

Bloomfield was relaxed and engaging, offering candid insights into his own music and its evolution while providing a detailed history of rock 'n' roll and blues. His knowledge of popular music was impressive, and so were his observations regarding contemporary players and trends. He analyzed the styles of Robert Johnson and Eric Clapton, and he parsed Jimi Hendrix's technique while describing him as one of the music's true innovators. When Yates questioned Michael's dismissal of his Electric Flag and *Super Session* recordings, the guitarist responded with familiar criticisms about commercialism and scams. But he did add the observation that, for listeners, even music that might be tainted in his eyes could be valid.

"As you know, the music you listen to becomes the soundtrack of your life," Bloomfield told the interviewers.

> It may be the first music you made love to, or got high to, or went through your adolescence to, or whatever poignant times in your life. Well, that music's going to mean a lot to you. It's going to take on much more import than just the sound of the notes, because it's become the background track for your existence.

Of his recent work, Michael said, "I'm content, and have been musically, in the direction I'm going, for about five or six years now." The best example of his playing, the album that truly represented all his influences, he said was *If*

You Love These Blues, his LP for *Guitar Player* magazine. "For me on record, that's it. That's the best I've ever played on record."

By the time the interview concluded, Mike Bloomfield had delivered what amounted to a candid assessment of his remarkable career. Here was a mature artist sharing his views on music and examining his role in it. Yates and Hayes were clearly impressed. "Your awareness of yourself and your image is probably the highest I've ever seen," said Tom. "I'm a musicologist as much as a player," Bloomfield replied. "You have to be able to look at it clearly as a historian. Take yourself right out of it and put yourself in it in a musicological-historical perspective. It gives you a clear view of where you lie in music history as it unwinds."

History was indeed unwinding for Michael Bloomfield. He did not know it, but his conversation with the two radio producers would amount to his valedictory, a farewell to the popular music world that he had done so much to alter and shape.

Later that evening, Michael and Norman Dayron went to see Stefan Grossman at the Great American Music Hall on O'Farrell Street in San Francisco. Grossman was a traditional blues player, a thirty-five-year-old guitarist from New York who had studied with the Rev. Gary Davis in the early 1960s and was a master of numerous country blues styles. He was in town, opening for English guitarist John Renbourn, and Bloomfield wanted to talk with him about a project they had first discussed in September.

"We were making plans to do a recording of guitar lessons and an acoustic blues album, and maybe do a tour too," said Grossman. He was impressed by how Bloomfield's condition had improved since the last time he had seen him. "Mike was in a great mood, totally spot-on, healthy," he said.

ED Denson, Stefan's partner in Kicking Mule Records, the company that would release the proposed albums, was also there, and he remembered Bloomfield extending an invitation to Grossman. "We were in the dressing room, and Michael invited Stefan to come over to his house after the show, presumably to play music all night." But Grossman had an appointment in northern California the next day, so he declined, saying they would get together another time.

"I came down Sunday night to fly out, and we were going to make plans to rehearse and do the recordings," said Grossman. "At the airport motel, I called up my folks to say hello, and they said, 'Oh, did you read about Mike Bloomfield?'" Before Grossman could reply, they shared the news. He was stunned.

"They told me Michael had died the night before."

* * *

Sunday, February 15, dawned clear and cold in San Francisco. By 11:30 a.m., the sun was warming the air with a hint of spring. It was going to be a beautiful day.

On a tree-lined street in Forest Hill, one of San Francisco's residence parks, a dramatic tableau was unfolding. An ambulance and several police cars, lights flashing, were nosed in at the curb. They formed a perimeter around a beat-up Mercury, blocking one side of the street and creating a bottleneck as passing motorists slowed for a look. Half a dozen cops were working on the Mercury, a rust-brown 1971 Montego sedan, while two emergency services medics were hauling a gurney out of the back of the San Francisco Fire Department ambulance. All the activity appeared to be focused around the person sitting in the front seat of the car.

The call to emergency services had come a half hour earlier from a man who identified himself as Ted Ray. He said he lived at 572 Dewey Boulevard, near the traffic circle, and that there was a man in a vehicle parked in front of his house who might need medical help. Ray said he had noticed the car earlier, and the guy sitting in it hadn't moved all morning. He went out to check on him, and the man didn't respond when he tapped on the car window and tried to speak to him. Officer Joseph Cotta of SFFD Emergency Services took the call, and he sent an ambulance and notified the San Francisco Police Department. By 11:30 a.m., officials were on the scene.

The man in the Mercury was clearly unconscious. All four car doors were locked, but one officer managed to wedge an arm through a partially opened rear window to pop the lock button. The vehicle's occupant was "observed to be unresponsive," and the medics quickly determined that he was not breathing and his skin was cold to the touch. It would require a physician to make the official pronouncement, but the man in the Montego was obviously dead.

There was no evidence of physical trauma. A search of the vehicle yielded an empty prescription bottle for Valium, found in the pocket of a leather jacket lying on the back seat, and it was assumed the deceased had overdosed on the drug. But an autopsy would be needed to determine the actual cause of death. In removing the body from the car, rigor was observed, suggesting that the occupant died late Saturday evening. Mr. Ray couldn't say how long the car had been parked in front of his house, only that he had noticed it that morning.

The deceased carried no identification, and no note was found in the car. But as the body was being placed in the ambulance, an officer retrieved the car's documentation from the glove box. The Mercury was registered to a resident of Mill Valley, a person by the name of Michael Bloomfield.

* * *

The county coroner's office began looking for the next of kin that afternoon. They had Michael's name and his Reed Street address, and an official soon had Christie Svane's mother on the phone. Before long, he reached Susan and Bonner Beuhler, and the couple was shocked to hear the news. But the official said they weren't certain yet that the deceased was actually Michael, because they still needed someone to positively ID the body. Would Susan be willing to do that?

It fell to Michael Bloomfield's ex-wife to confirm that the body lying in the San Francisco morgue with a "John Doe" tag was actually that of the former blues-rock superstar. Once the identity had been positively established, the official suggested that Susan contact the immediate family with the news. She phoned Allen.

"It was such a complete shock," said Allen about receiving Susan's call. "I just had to go sit by myself and process it—that Michael was gone and I would never see him again." The younger Bloomfield booked a flight to San Francisco for that night. His next call was to his father.

Harold Bloomfield was living with his family in La Jolla, having moved from Chicago to California in 1977. He received Allen's news with characteristic taciturnity. "I remember when the call came," said half-brother Randy. "We were in the living room, and my mom was sitting with my dad. He showed little or no emotion, and I was really amazed by that."

Susan also called Norman Dayron. Norman, too, was stunned. "I couldn't believe it," said Michael's friend and partner. "We had just been together on Friday night, and we were supposed to go to a show on Saturday. But I never heard from him." Bloomfield's death upset Dayron not only because he had lost his closest friend, but also because their various C.T. Productions projects were suddenly in limbo. "I remember Norman was really shaken, crying," said Dave Shorey. "We were all really upset."

Al Kooper learned of his friend's death one evening later in the week when he noticed an obituary in the local newspaper. "I guess nobody knew how to reach me, and I only found out when I happened to see a notice in the paper," Kooper recalled. "I was completely shocked and shaken. We had this gig coming up later in the month, and I was really looking forward to playing with him again." The keyboardist celebrated his friendship with the blues-rock guitarist the best way he knew how. He pulled a copy of *Super Session* off the shelf and put the album on the turntable. "I just played that record all night," Al said.

Despite everyone's shock and grief, there were things that had to be done. Susan told Norman that Michael's car had been towed to a Shell gas station on the corner of Lincoln Way and Nineteenth Avenue in San Francisco's Taraval police district and that they had to go claim it. "We drove down there and got Michael's Mercury, one of those junkers he bought at a police auction. He called it his 'narcotics officer car,' meaning it was plain, old and inconspicuous," said Norman. "When we picked it up, I saw that his leather jacket was lying on the back seat—that's when it *really* got to me."

Dayron drove his friend's car back to Reed Street, parked it on the hill, and went inside the house. "Mrs. Svane was staying there, but when I walked in, the place was totally deserted. I didn't see any of Michael's guitars, which was unusual because there were usually one or two lying around," Norman remembered. The producer was struck by how empty the house felt without its ebullient proprietor.

On Monday morning, the Bloomfield family gathered at the morgue to view the body. Allen Bloomfield remembered the difficult experience vividly. "My dad was there, having flown in, and I was there, and my mom with her new husband," he said. When the assistant coroner pulled back the curtain over the window in the viewing room, the sight of Michael's outstretched body on the gurney was too much for Dottie. "My mom passed out," Allen said. "I had to get her to a couch so we could revive her." Harold remained stoic and took charge of the situation, but he, too, was shaken. The family quickly departed and drove north out of the city, crossing the Golden Gate Bridge into Marin County.

"We went up to the house in Mill Valley," said Allen. When they arrived, they, too, found the place empty. Allen had never been to Reed Street, and as he walked through the house, he was struck by the meagerness of his brother's possessions. It was when he walked into his brother's room that he was overwhelmed with sorrow.

> I looked into Michael's closet, looking at his clothes—clothes that I had seen him wear since he was like eighteen—and I realized he lived like a camper. . . . He had nothing—absolutely *nothing*. There was an impermanence about everything in the house, all the material things connected to him. He never cared for material things, and here was proof.

Christie Svane received the news of her lover's passing from her mother. She had left New York for France earlier in the week and had been traveling for several days. When she finally reached Paris on Sunday evening, the phone in her hotel room rang. It was a brief conversation that left her devastated. Michael's death filled her with such overwhelming pain and regret that throughout the weeks of the tour and the ensuing months, she struggled to overcome the desire to join her departed partner. In a twist that added a bittersweet poignancy to her loss, Christie realized that Michael had very likely died on Valentine's Day.

On Tuesday, February 17, an afternoon funeral service for Michael Bloomfield, America's first great blues-rock guitarist, was held at Mt. Sinai Memorial Chapel on Divisadero Street in San Francisco. Nearly all of his friends and acquaintances from the Bay Area attended, and many offered condolences to Allen and Harold and shared tearful hugs with Dottie. At the front of the chapel, on a wheeled bier, was the guitarist himself, enclosed in a bulky, ornate silver coffin. His parents had hastily organized the service in accordance with Jewish rites, and they intended to give their son a formal Jewish funeral. As dictated by tradition, the coffin lid was closed.

San Francisco cantor Martin Feldman presided over the service and delivered the eulogy. "I know that so many people present could speak of Michael's talents and accomplishments far better than I," the cantor began. Many in the seats agreed, wondering why a man who had probably never heard of Mike Bloomfield until the day before had been asked to offer a tribute. Feldman did his best to cite the guitarist's many achievements and outstanding qualities, but eyes rolled as he sometimes got it wrong. The cantor mentioned the guitarist's success "at Woodstock," described how he identified with the "soul music" of Chicago's South Side, and how "it was Michael alone who brought about a renaissance of the blues," giving B. B. King and Muddy Waters "hope" and bringing them "to national and international prominence." The eulogy wound up with a flowery recounting of Michael's Jewish qualities, describing him as a loving and dutiful son who had enriched the lives of all those who knew him. Though well intended, Cantor Feldman's encomium left many in the chapel feeling that the Michael Bloomfield they had known was nowhere in evidence.

But Michael was indeed there, sealed in his casket. Following the service, friends asked that the gaudy enclosure be opened so that the mementos a few mourners had brought could be placed in the coffin with the deceased. The request was granted, and photos, guitar pics, strings, copies of Bukowski novels, and other ephemera were deposited with the recumbent guitarist to ease him along on his journey through eternity. The simple parting gestures provided a few moments of authenticity in what otherwise felt like the last rites for a stranger.

The next evening, the vibe was entirely different. Bill Graham threw a gala farewell party for his friend Michael Bloomfield at the new Old Waldorf on Battery Street. The entire Bay Area community was invited, and hundreds turned out to enjoy music and refreshments, courtesy of the former Fillmore impresario. Because Michael always said he wanted a New Orleans–style send-off rather than a conventional funeral, the reception was given a Big Easy theme. *Always for Pleasure*, Berkeley filmmaker Les Blank's documentary celebrating New Orleans bands and traditions, was shown, and Blank himself wandered among the partygoers, filming their remembrances. A few bands played, and the atmosphere was mostly celebratory and festive. But the Bloomfield family was there, too, and there were more tearful embraces and heartfelt condolences. The one Bloomfield who would have thoroughly enjoyed the party wasn't present. Michael's remains were en route to Los Angeles for a second funeral and interment.

On Friday, February 20, a final ceremony commemorating the life of Michael Bloomfield was held at Hillside Memorial Park, a Jewish cemetery in Culver City renowned as the resting place for numerous artists, musicians, and entertainers. Dottie had selected Hillside so that her son would be close to her now that she was living in Los Angeles with her new husband, Bill Shinderman. The service was primarily for the family and a few close friends, but those in attendance included Bloomfield's former manager Albert Grossman. Barry Goldberg and his wife, Gail, were also present, and Barry delivered the eulogy. "Michael, it's me, Boris," Goldberg began, using the nickname the guitarist had given him back when they were teenagers. He went on to speak of his twenty-year friendship with Michael, creating a heartfelt portrait of the great guitar player, and his comments had a veracity that stood in sharp contrast to the euphemistic sentiments expressed in San Francisco earlier in the week. Following a few words from the rabbi and a final prayer for the deceased, the service concluded with the family accepting condolences from attendees as they all moved toward the door.

Not long afterward, the big casket containing the remains of Michael Bernard Bloomfield was eased into a berth in the Sanctuary of Meditation Crypt in the Courts of the Book Mausoleum complex at Hillside Memorial Park. A slab of white marble was placed over the opening and sealed. With his final resting place secured, it would take only one kind favor to see that Michael's grave was kept clean.

Reports of the passing of Michael Bloomfield flooded the news media in the days following the discovery of his body. The wire services ran daily updates throughout the week, and the *San Francisco Chronicle*, *Examiner*, *Chicago Sun Times*, *Chicago Tribune,* and hundreds of other newspapers across the country printed profiles of the blues-rock guitarist. The alternative press, led by *Rolling Stone*, noted Bloomfield's passing with full-page assessments of his impact on contemporary music and lengthy excerpts from earlier interviews. *Time* and *Newsweek* magazines carried obituaries, and FM radio stations broadcast musical tributes. Bloomfield was described as a "brilliant but tortured guitarist," a "pivotal figure in awakening white audiences to the urban blues style of Chicago blacks," a "blues scholar," and a "blues guitarist extraordinaire."

The circumstances surrounding the guitarist's death also made the news. On Tuesday morning, the papers reported that San Francisco's deputy coroner had ruled Michael Bloomfield's death "accidental." That surprised no one who knew him, because the guitarist had seemed happy and engaged at the time. He was enthusiastic about upcoming projects, and he was in love, hoping to marry Christie Svane after she returned from Europe. Michael had no reason to take his own life.

But later in the week when the results of the coroner's autopsy were released, Bloomfield's friends were puzzled. The report stated that the deceased had expired from a "drug overdose," which was expected. But the overdose was due to "cocaine and methamphetamine poisoning." Everyone knew Michael hated cocaine and studiously avoided stimulants like meth. "I never knew Michael to use anything like that," said Norman Dayron. "He was always trying to slow things down. That's why he liked heroin, that's why he drank. He didn't need to speed things up—he was already operating at an elevated level." The mysterious cause of Bloomfield's death generated suspicions, and friends speculated about what must have really happened that Saturday night in Forest Hill. A police investigation was said to be under way, but when no report appeared, that, too, seemed suspicious. People said the cops weren't really interested in uncovering the truth—the victim to them was just another dead junkie, and good riddance. Others said Michael had been slipped a hot shot at a party so that thieves could rob his house. One friend was convinced that the guitarist had been eliminated because he owed the notorious Mitchell brothers a slew of money.

Michael's mother, Dottie, was certain her son had been poisoned—"rat poison" was what she said the autopsy showed.

But the truth was undoubtedly less sensational. Bloomfield and Norman Dayron had talked about going to hear music on Saturday evening, but they hadn't made any real plans, and when Norman didn't hear from his friend, he thought nothing of it. For whatever reason, Michael decided he would go into the city instead. Though he had given up drinking and had been conscientiously avoiding narcotics, he might have felt like celebrating. His new Takoma album, *Cruisin' for a Bruisin'*, was coming out at the end of the month, he was going to record and tour with Stefan Grossman, and he would soon be joining Christie overseas and gigging with Al Kooper in London. He was feeling healthy, and he was even sleeping better. Why not find a party to go to?

Michael rang up John Finn and asked if he would like to go into San Francisco to cop. Susan Beuhler remembered Finn telling her about the call. "He phoned John and asked him to go along, but he didn't go," she said. "John was very unhappy about that because he felt if he'd been along, Michael would still be alive." When Finn was uninterested and calls to other friends produced no takers, the guitarist decided to go by himself. That was something he rarely ever did. "He would never one-on-one jump in his car and go *anywhere*," said Dave Shorey. Shorey knew, because he had been Michael's driver countless times. But this time may have been an exception.

What is known for certain beyond this point is that Bloomfield did go into the city. Where he went and what he did once he got there remain largely a mystery. But one likely scenario was suggested by Norman Dayron. When he looked into the circumstances of Bloomfield's death in the months following the funeral, Dayron came to the conclusion that his friend had gone to see Jerry, the dealer who lived on Divisadero Street. "He was dangerous, not only because he was a gangster, but because he wasn't a user himself," Norman said. "He had no idea what was in the stuff he was selling, and if you bought from him, you had no idea what you were getting." Dayron further speculated that because the autopsy report found no real evidence of opiates in Bloomfield's system, he must have been given a "designer drug." "Something like synthetic morphine, that might not show up in the coroner's tests," Norman said.

Here, then, is what probably happened on that Saturday night:

Michael knew where he was going as he drove into San Francisco that evening, because he had been there more than a few times. It was a straight shot across the Golden Gate, into the city on Lombard Street, and then a quick right onto Divisadero. A few blocks from the Castro, he parked the Montego at the curb in front of a nondescript apartment building in the middle of a row of storefronts, and then he pressed the buzzer to Jerry's basement apartment. In a moment, the door opened and the guitarist disappeared inside. The party was already under way.

How long Bloomfield was there before he ran into trouble is unknown, but it likely was not very long. He got off right away, having someone administer whatever concoction Jerry was offering. The drug took effect quickly, and within thirty minutes Michael was beginning to turn blue from lack of oxygen. Because he had come to the party by himself, no one was looking after him, and none of the other guests paid much attention to his worsening condition.

"Michael had a heroin habit, but he didn't know how to inject his own drugs," said Ira Kamin. "So the thing that saved his life all those years when he would take way, *way* too much was that somebody was around him who would oversee what he was doing."

But not this time. When people finally did notice that the bushy-haired guy on the couch was really out of it, they did what they could to bring him around. "One of Jon Cramer's girlfriends was at the party that night," said Leonard Trupin. "She said they did manage to wake Michael up, but then he just passed out again." By the time they tried to rouse the comatose guitar player a second time, it was too late. "That's when they injected him with cocaine," said Norman, "a last ditch effort to wake him up, but that didn't work either. And then they panicked."

Jerry had to get the moribund Bloomfield out of his apartment. With his criminal activities, he couldn't risk being connected to a fatal drug overdose, so he had the guitarist carried out to his car. But the Montego was parked right in front of the building, and having Bloomfield found there was almost as bad. So he tossed Michael's leather jacket in the back seat, propped the guitarist up on the passenger side of the front seat, slid in behind the wheel, and keyed the ignition. The dealer drove the Mercury down Castro Street to Market, through Corona Heights to Portola Drive, around Woodside Avenue, and onto Dewey Boulevard. A second car from the party followed close behind and pulled to the curb in back of the Mercury as Jerry parked it in front of 572 Dewey. The Forest Hill neighborhood was a quiet bedroom community of two-story family houses, and the street at that hour was deserted. It was an ideal place to dispose of a drug casualty, and it was also five miles away from the dealer's apartment on Divisadero.

Jerry switched off the Mercury, cut the headlights, and then gave his motionless passenger a shake. When Bloomfield didn't respond, the dealer shrugged, reached over to lock the doors, and climbed out of the car, leaving the keys in the ignition. If Michael did wake up, at least he would be able to drive himself home. Jerry looked up and down the darkened street and, seeing no one, stepped around to the passenger side of the chase car, got in, and told the driver to go. The vehicle cruised down the hill to the traffic circle and made a right onto Montalvo Avenue, its red tail lights disappearing around the corner.

It was a few minutes before midnight. Michael Bloomfield sat motionless in the moonlight, his mind quieted at last.

EPILOGUE

GREAT GIFTS FROM HEAVEN

A month after Michael Bloomfield's tragic death, his Takoma album *Cruisin' for a Bruisin'* was released. A second LP, on the small Minneapolis-based Waterhouse label, was also issued. Both were produced by Norman Dayron, and the latter, called *Living in the Fast Lane*, was a compendium of Bloomfield material dating from the mid-1970s that Norman described candidly as "a bunch of leftover shit I hadn't used." Both records had a cut-and-paste feel to them, and though there were moments of brilliance on each, the albums were largely dismissed by critics. "As epitaphs go, [they] barely hint at Michael Bloomfield's true greatness," *Rolling Stone*'s reviewer observed. He was right.

Mike Bloomfield's greatness could not be conveyed by a few recordings. The measure of his contribution could not be taken from a few club performances or concerts. His legacy could not be observed and understood from the critical vantage point of a few months—or even a few years. It was just too vast.

The obscurity Bloomfield longed for in his last decade he achieved posthumously with stunning success. *Rolling Stone* published a special twentieth anniversary edition six years after Michael's death, and nowhere in its three-hundred-plus pages was the guitarist mentioned. Guitar polls invariably ranked Jimi Hendrix and Eric Clapton at the top, and they often included lesser talents like Lindsey Buckingham, Gram Parsons, and Lou Reed. But not Michael Bloomfield. He never made the cut. His records were soon relegated to the cut-out bins, and most of them eventually disappeared altogether. Within a decade, the guitarist had become little more than a footnote to Bob Dylan's appearance at Newport.

But the Newport Folk Festival of 1965 provides an excellent prism through which to refract the white light of Michael Bloomfield's musical and cultural luminations.

Bloomfield's solos with the Butterfield Band that weekend were a signpost for every serious musician. His careening improvisations said to every guitarist: *this* is how you must be able to play. In the decade that followed, all credible rock guitarists had to solo. They had to demonstrate competency as musicians, not just as entertainers. That was one aspect of Mike Bloomfield's legacy.

Another was revealed when he performed with Dylan. They had created folk-rock together in the studio, but his raw interjections at Newport flooded Bob's lyric imagery with a gravitas it might have otherwise lacked, and suddenly rock 'n' roll ensemble playing had real *guts*. In those fifteen minutes, Michael demonstrated the extraordinary power of the electric guitar. It was a power central to Chicago's blues aesthetic but largely unknown in the pop world before June 1965. Bloomfield shredded pop music's naughty schoolboy sensibilities and replaced them with a bluesman's life-and-death swagger and aggression. Those were qualities that had the ring of truth, that could release any music from its tethered politeness. They were qualities that Dylan would remember, and they, too, were part of Bloomfield's legacy.

There were many other contributions in the years after Newport.

Michael not only played a central role in introducing white audiences to urban blues, but also was largely responsible for bringing great black blues artists to those audiences. His instrumental experiments with exotic scales and modes gave rise to countless "psychedelic jams" and created a whole new genre of music. His band with horns blended blues, jazz, and rock in a fusion that pointed the way for many other brass-rock aggregations. He helped to revive interest in American musical traditions at a time when contemporary pop music was looking to the British Isles for inspiration, and his encyclopedic knowledge of those traditions set a benchmark for those musicians who were serious about their art.

Then there was the sound Bloomfield could get from a guitar. It was immediately recognizable, and so was his instrument. The Gibson Les Paul Standard, with its distinctive sunburst finish, was the Michael Bloomfield guitar. An instrument that had been discontinued after only two years of production because of poor sales, that languished in music shop showrooms and could be bought used for a few hundred dollars, was suddenly the most sought-after guitar in the world. Clapton, Beck, Green, and Page all had Sunbursts, but in America its popularity soared only after Bloomfield began playing one. Gibson, responding to the overwhelming demand, reintroduced the guitar in 1968, and it has continued to be the company's most popular—and profitable—model ever since. Bloomfield's imprimatur was all that was needed.

Michael Bloomfield was, of course, more than a rock star guitar virtuoso. He was also a scholar and educator, a brilliant autodidact who taught seminars on American music in both formal and informal settings. He would share his enthusiasm for the music and its history with anyone who was interested, citing musicians—many of whom he knew personally—and their recordings with a thoroughness that rivaled that of any tenured professor. His voracious appetite for the printed word meant he was better read than many PhD candidates, and his encyclopedic memory enabled him to be conversant with nearly any topic that might arise. He repeatedly astonished his listeners with the depth and extent of his knowledge, and more than a few felt he was the most brilliant person they had ever met.

But Mike Bloomfield was also a vibrant, ebullient personality. His humor, unflagging energy, charisma, and irresistible charm all conflated within his rangy frame to make the guitarist a character of extraordinary magnitude. Those who knew him well readily acknowledged his influence on their lives.

"Mike was a very dear friend of mine. We had a close friendship, and also a close musical relationship," said Mark Naftalin. "As far back as the '60s, we would just play, the two of us, at his house or my house or at a party, and we really had a wonderful simpatico. I miss him every day."

"I loved playing with him," said Al Kooper. "I had the experience with him that I've never had with any other musician—that is, we never discussed the music. We just played, and we both knew how to play behind the other person. I treasure that experience, because it's so rare. He was truly special that way."

"I played with Mike for ten years, and I miss him as a person," said Bob Jones. "He was funny, incredibly intelligent, and immensely talented. It is the single biggest blessing of my life that I got to play and hang out with him for a decade."

"Michael had all this charisma. That's something people don't talk about, but he had charisma," said Nick Gravenites. "He'd walk into a room, and things would perk up. Things would get snappy—people would start laughing. It was almost mystical the way people were drawn to him."

"One of the chief things that I'll always remember about Michael was his ability to draw in and hold the attention of those in his company," said Toby Byron. "He was simply one of the most engaging and magnetic individuals *ever*."

"He was a smart dude, Michael was. He knew a hell of a lot about music," said Woody Harris. "He was an incredibly smart dude, and *incredibly* well read. *Outrageously* well read! I'd turn him on to some author, and he'd just go out and buy everything the guy wrote."

"Bloomers was always for stretching the limits and trying different things," said Elvin Bishop. "He was into everything . . . bluegrass, soul, jazz, old standards, anything."

"Michael was so gone into the music! Anybody else would sanitize it," said Dave Shorey. "If you gave him that one special block of brevity, within the channel of the fuckin' Red Sea just as it parts, Michael will just stroll on through, and he will tell you some A-200 [a lice treatment] flea story about how to get grits out of your konk. And he would think that that was the fuckin' *one*, man. And he wouldn't let it go—the thing would be a paragraph of Kerouac that would be like twenty-nine sentences that would have fuckin' fifty footnotes. *That* was Michael."

"I was probably the person closest to Michael in the last years of his life," said Norman Dayron. "I could see how he suffered, but I also saw his brilliance, both as a musician and as a human being. Without question, he enriched my life, and the lives of everyone who knew him. But he also changed the music, and in that way he touched the lives of people everywhere."

"There is no person on earth I'd rather hang with than Michael," said Allen Bloomfield. "If you took J. D. Salinger and added a pinch of Bukowski, a dash of Terry Southern, and a sprinkle of Oscar Levant—you would have an approximation of what he was like. A wit like Lenny Bruce and the persona of a gangster with a rose tattoo. The kid from Glencoe who played the blues and made them his own."

NOTES

PROLOGUE

For the dramatization of Michael Bloomfield's first meeting with Bob Dylan, I used Bloomfield's essay "Impressions of Bob Dylan" from *Hit Parader*, June 1968, and his interview in *Guitar Player*, June 1971. Descriptions of the club come from *Chicago Scene*, April and June 1963; *Down Beat*, June 6 and August 15, 1963; and contemporary newspaper advertisements. I also used Bill Keenom's interviews with Fred Glazer, Ron Butkovich, and Peter Amft.

3 "Weirdness accompanied by Holy Rollers": *Chicago Scene*, Apr. 1963.
4 "He could just flat out play": Bob Dylan, *Rolling Stone*, May 2009.
4 "I didn't relate": Michael Bloomfield, *Guitar Player*, Apr. 1979.

CHAPTER 1: SOCIAL MISFIT

The dramatization of Bloomfield's first trip to Pepper's comes from Dan McClosky's interview with him and Roy Ruby. My own interviews with Allen Bloomfield, Bob Greenspan, and Fred Glazer were the basis for the description of Bloomfield's difficult school years. Bill Keenom's interviews with Allen Bloomfield and Dorothy Shinderman (Michael's mother) were also used, as was Dan McClosky's interview with Bloomfield, Roy Ruby, and Fred Glazer.

12–13 Re-creation of the trip to Pepper's Lounge was based on Bloomfield and Roy Ruby's interview with Dan McClosky, 5/17/1971.
14 Bloomfield's problematic social status in Glencoe came from Allen Bloomfield, author interview, 2/19/2008.
15 Dorothy Shinderman's explanation of Bloomfield's truancy came from her interview with Bill Keenom, 1996.
15 "It knocked me out": Michael Bloomfield, interview with Dan McClosky, 5/17/1971.
15 "He wanted to be this": Allen Bloomfield, author interview, 6/12/2008.

CHAPTER 2: NORTH SHORE HOTSHOT

My description of New Trier High School comes from personal experience. Information about the Place came from Mike Henner, a musician who played there. The basis for much of this chapter was my interviews with Fred Glazer, Bob Greenspan, Gerry Pasternack, Roy Jespersen, Michael Melford, Horace Cathcart, Vince Viti, Jim Pauly, and Nicole Bloomfield. Bill Keenom's interviews with Fred Glazer, Michael Melford, and Bob Greenspan were also used.

16–18 Descriptions of Bloomfield's first band, their demo recording, and their talent-show appearance came from Roy Jespersen, author interview, 11/30/2011.

18 Description of Bloomfield's early drug use came from Fred Glazer, interview with Bill Keenom, 1996.

18, 19 Description of drug use on the North Shore came from Michael Melford, email to the author, 1/7/2013.

19, 20 "[Mike] sat in": Roy Ruby, interview with Dan McClosky, 5/17/1971.

20 Description of playing with Bloomfield came from Horace Cathcart, email to the author, 5/20/2009.

20 Lack of integrated bands on the North Shore came from Fred Glazer, interview with Bill Keenom, 1996.

20 "I'd get Mike to come": Gerry Pasternack, author interview, 2/25/2013.

20 Description of playing with Bloomfield on Rush Street came from Gerry Pasternack, author interview, 2/25/2013.

20 "Small, wiry and introverted": from "A Bird in the Hand," an unpublished story by Michael Bloomfield, ca. mid-1970s, courtesy of Norman Dayron.

20, 21 Description of the Bloomfield brothers' difficult relationship with each other and their father came from Allen Bloomfield, author interview, 2/19/2008.

21 "The teacher would ask": Allen Bloomfield, author interview, 2/19/2008.

22 "There was this story": Fred Glazer, interview with Bill Keenom, 1996.

22 Study hall incident re-creation based on Gerry Pasternack, author interview, 2/25/2013.

23 Description of Cornwall Academy came in part from Rei Reynolds, Cornwall alumnus, email to the author, 6/27/2013.

23–24 Description of Bloomfield's Cornwall Academy experience came from Fred Glazer, interview with Bill Keenom, 1996.

25 Bloomfield's purchase of a Les Paul Custom came from a posting on gibson.com/Products/Electric-Guitars/Les-Paul/Gibson-Custom/Michael-Bloomfield-1959-Les-Paul-Standard.aspx by John A., 10/11/2015.

25 Details of the Gala Holiday Show at the Regal Theater came from *Down Beat*, 2/28/1960; description came from Michael Bloomfield and Roy Ruby, interview with Dan McClosky, 5/17/1971.

26 Description of Bloomfield playing in Highwood came from Bob Greenspan, author interview, 1/19/2012.

27 "Mike could really play": Vince Viti, author interview, 4/20/2013.

27 Playing at PG's Club 7 description came from bandmate Jim Pauly, author interview, 5/19/2014.

27 "We had a piano": Gerry Pasternack, author interview, 2/25/2013.

27 Description of recording a demo at Lyon & Healy came from Gerry Pasternack, author interview, 2/25/2013; Jim Pauly, author interview, 5/19/2014.

28, 29 Description of Bloomfield at Maxwell Street came from Fred Glazer and Mick Weiser, interviews with Bill Keenom, 1996.

28, 29 Description of Maxwell Street came from author's personal experience, 1977–1982.

29 Description of Bloomfield at Muddy Waters's house came from Michael Bloomfield, interview with Dan McClosky, 5/17/1971.

29 Description of Bloomfield playing with Otis Spann came from Michael Bloomfield on Spann's death in *Rolling Stone*, 5/14/1970.

29 "Muddy Waters, he was": Michael Bloomfield, interview with Dan McClosky, 5/17/1971.

30 Bloomfield drunk at school episode came from Fred Glazer, interview with Bill Keenom; partially confirmed by Michael Melford, email to the author, 4/28/2013.

30, 31 Bloomfield being committed to Northwestern University Hospital came from Michael Melford, emails to the author, 9/29/2006 and 4/28/2013.

31 Bloomfield family history of depression came from Nicole Bloomfield, author interview, 11/1/2014.

32 "I think our dad": Allen Bloomfield, interview with Bill Keenom, 1995.

32 Bloomfield's possible bipolar disorder evaluated by Steven Silverstein, PhD, director, Division of Schizophrenia Research, UMDNJ–University Behavioral HealthCare, email to the author, 5/29/2013.

32 "I remember my brother": Allen Bloomfield, interview with Bill Keenom, 1995.

33 Central Y high school description came from Fred Glazer, interview with Bill Keenom, 1996.

33, 34 Description of meeting Bloomfield, attending Central Y, and going to Silvio's came from Barry Goldberg, interview with Bill Keenom, 1995; *Two Jews Blues* by Barry Goldberg and Steven Roeser, St. Paul Books, 2012.

34 "They were going up": from "A Brother's Words: Allen Bloomfield Remembers Michael" by Allen Bloomfield, *Vintage Guitar Magazine*, Aug. 1997.

35 "Mike decided to live alone": Dorothy Shinderman, interview with Bill Keenom, 1995.

CHAPTER 3: FOLK FANATIC

My brief overview of the 1950s folk revival and the University of Chicago Folk Festival was taken from a variety of sources, including Ronald D. Cohen's *Rainbow Quest: The Folk Music Revival and American Society, 1940–1970*; his book with Bob Riesman, *Chicago Folk*; issues of *Sing Out!* from 1962 to 1966; and issues of the New York *Broadside*, 1963 to 1965. Information about the Fret Shop came from my interviews with Norman Dayron, Mike Medina, and Mike Michaels. The description of Bloomfield's relationship with Susan Smith was taken from Bill Keenom's interviews with Susan Beuhler, from my interviews with Norman Dayron, and from *Michael Bloomfield: If You Love These Blues*. Information about the Jazz Record Mart and Bob Koester came from delmark.com/delmark.history.htm and from personal knowledge; data on Koester's Blind Pig shows came from issues of *Down Beat* magazine. Descriptions of the UC "twist parties" came from my interviews with Mike Michaels and Mark Naftalin. An essay describing Bloomfield's trip to Memphis to see Elvis Presley was sent to me by its author, Sid Scott.

37 "There was a time": Michael Bloomfield, interview with Walter Rimler, summer 1975.

38 "I'd heard about the festival": John Hammond, author interview, 7/22/2014.

38 "He seemed to know everybody": John Hammond, author interview, 7/22/2014.

39 "One day I went": Norman Dayron, author interview, 7/7/2007.

39 "I had heard great": Norman Dayron, author interview, 7/7/2007.

39 Description of Nick Gravenites's childhood and schooling came from "Bad Talkin' Bluesman," *Blues Review*, July/Aug. 1995.

39 "I was a pistol-packin' tough guy": Nick Gravenites, *Michael Bloomfield: If You Love These Blues*, Miller Freeman Books, 2000.

40 "Most people could": Nick Gravenites, *Sound Waves* magazine, Aug. 2015.

40 "I met Bloomers": Elvin Bishop, *Michael Bloomfield: If You Love These Blues*, Miller Freeman Books, 2000.

40 "I didn't know much": Elvin Bishop, *New Straits Times*, 4/12/1981.

40 Description of Uncle Max's Buy & Sell came from Allen Bloomfield, author interview, 6/12/2008.

41 "He told us this crazy story": Susan Beuhler, *Michael Bloomfield: If You Love These Blues*, Miller Freeman Books, 2000.

41 "There weren't too many": Susan Beuhler, interview with Bill Keenom, 1996.

41, 42 Description of Bloomfield's first date with Susan Smith came from *Michael Bloomfield: The Rise and Fall of an American Guitar Hero*, Cherry Lane Books, 1983.

42 "Michael said, 'Well'": Susan Beuhler, *Michael Bloomfield: If You Love These Blues*, Miller Freeman Books, 2000.

42 "This was the strangest thing": Susan Beuhler, *Michael Bloomfield: If You Love These Blues*, Miller Freeman Books, 2000.

42 Description of Bloomfield trading his Les Paul Custom for two acoustic guitars comes from Mick Weiser, interview with Bill Keenom, 1995.

44 "That was the first time": Fred Glazer, interview with Bill Keenom, 1995.

45 Description of Paul Butterfield's early years came from Kathryn Butterfield, interview with Bill Keenom, 1996.

45 Description of Butterfield's relationship with Nick Gravenites came from "Bad Talkin' Bluesman," *Blues Review*, July/Aug. 1995.

45 "One balmy spring night": Mike Michaels, email to the author, 12/17/2008.

46 "I watched him playing": Mark Naftalin, author interview, 6/15/2008.

46 "He said we should": from "Michael, Matt and Me," an essay by Sid Scott, provided by Scott, 2/9/2016.

46 "He made up hilarious songs": Sid Scott, author interview, 2/12/2016.

46 "We couldn't find anything": Sid Scott, author interview, 2/12/2016.

46 "We stood outside the gates": Sid Scott, author interview, 2/12/2016.

47 "Bloomfield had his guitar": Sid Scott, author interview, 2/12/2016.

47 Description of Bloomfield's performance with Rev. Gary Davis's guitar came from Peter Amft, interview with Bill Keenom, 1995.

47–48 Description of Bloomfield moving in with Norman Dayron came from Norman Dayron, email to the author, 1/22/2012.

48 "I know my father used": Susan Beuhler, *Michael Bloomfield: If You Love These Blues*, Miller Freeman Books, 2000.

48–50 Description of Bloomfield's trip to Colorado came from Fred Glazer, author interview, 10/10/2007.

49 "Boulder was just developing": Fred Glazer, *Michael Bloomfield: If You Love These Blues*, Miller Freeman Books, 2000.

49 Information about Warner Logan came from Joe Loop, interview with John Ivey, emailed to the author on 1/4/2012.

50 Description of the Sink gig came from Fred Glazer, interview with Bill Keenom, 1995.

50 "It was like Big John's": Fred Glazer, *Michael Bloomfield: If You Love These Blues*, Miller Freeman Books, 2000.

50 "Mike walked in": Joe Loop, interview with John Ivey, emailed to the author on 1/4/2012.

50, 51 Description of Judy Roderick's audition for Leon Bibb came from Joe Loop, interview with John Ivey, emailed to the author on 1/4/2012.

50 "They performed 'Come Back Baby'": Joe Loop, interview with John Ivey, emailed to the author on 1/4/2012.

51 "We met this black guy": Fred Glazer, *Michael Bloomfield: If You Love These Blues*, Miller Freeman Books, 2000.

51 "It was a little heavier scene": Fred Glazer, interview with Bill Keenom, 1995.

51 "I was from a very rich family": Michael Bloomfield, interview with Walter Rimler, summer 1975.

52 "[I]n this fucked up country": Michael Bloomfield, "Michael Bloomfield: Honkies Can't Dig Soul Music," *Los Angeles Free Press*, 9/22/1967.

53 "Harold": Susan Beuhler, interview with Bill Keenom, 1995.

53 "I remember being": Fred Glazer, *Michael Bloomfield: If You Love These Blues*, Miller Freeman Books, 2000.

53 Description of Fred Glazer's wedding came from Fred Glazer, author interview, 10/10/2007.

CHAPTER 4: MARRIAGE, THE PICKLE, AND BIG JOE

My description of Bloomfield's marriage to Susan Smith came from *Michael Bloomfield: If You Love These Blues*, from Bill Keenom's interviews with Susan Beuhler, and from my interviews with Allen Bloomfield and Fred Glazer. Allen Bloomfield also told me about his parents' reaction to his brother's nuptials. Data on Charlie Musselwhite's friendship with Bloomfield came from *Michael Bloomfield: If You Love These Blues* and from my email correspondence with Charlie. Information on Pete Welding and Testament Records came from Welding's essay at bluesworld.com/PWTestessay.html and from *Down Beat* magazine. Descriptions of Bloomfield's first trip to New York came from my interview with Fred Glazer and from Bill Keenom's interviews with him. The sessions for Yank Rachell's Delmark record were recalled in Bill Keenom's interview with Bob Koester. Descriptions of the Fickle Pickle and the Blues Night shows came from my interviews with Joel Harlib and George Mitchell, and from *Michael Bloomfield: If You Love These Blues*. Norman Dayron spoke with me about recording the Fickle Pickle shows and allowed me access to his tapes of them. George Mitchell shared with me his recollections of his and Bloomfield's trip to East St. Louis with Big Joe. Additional information came from a transcript of Bloomfield's taped recounting of the junket and from Walter Rimler's interview with him. Descriptions of the Bear and Bloomfield's first meeting with Bob Dylan came from *Hit Parader*, *Rolling Stone,* and *Guitar Player* interviews as well as *Chicago Scene*, *Down Beat,* and newspaper ads.

54 “I felt like”: Susan Beuhler, *Michael Bloomfield: If You Love These Blues*, Miller Freeman Books, 2000.

55 “We sat in the boat”: Fred Glazer, *Michael Bloomfield: If You Love These Blues*, Miller Freeman Books, 2000.

55 The gardener telling Bloomfield’s parents about his marriage came from Susan Beuhler, *Michael Bloomfield: If You Love These Blues*, Miller Freeman Books, 2000.

56 “There was a huge blowout”: Allen Bloomfield, author interview, 2/19/2008.

56 “I bawled my husband out”: Dorothy Shinderman, interview with Bill Keenom, 1996.

56 “That was the weird thing”: Allen Bloomfield, author interview, 2/19/2008.

56 “That was the way it was”: Allen Bloomfield, author interview, 2/19/2008.

56 “We took a stab”: Susan Beuhler, *Michael Bloomfield: If You Love These Blues*, Miller Freeman Books, 2000.

56, 57 Description of Bloomfield returning wedding gifts came from Fred Glazer, interview with Bill Keenom, 1995.

57 “He really didn’t *do* anything”: Susan Beuhler, interview with Bill Keenom, 1996.

57 “We were children”: Susan Beuhler, *Michael Bloomfield: If You Love These Blues*, Miller Freeman Books, 2000.

57 “One day I was standing”: Charlie Musselwhite, *Michael Bloomfield: If You Love These Blues*, Miller Freeman Books, 2000.

59 “Jim was living there”: Fred Glazer, interview with Bill Keenom, 1995.

60 Bloomfield’s leaving a demo at Folkways Records came from Fred Glazer, interview with Bill Keenom, 1995; Joel Harlib, author interview, 7/22/2007.

60 “I remember we went”: Fred Glazer, interview with Bill Keenom, 1995.

60 “Jim Cain was this writer”: Fred Glazer, interview with Bill Keenom, 1995.

61 “He was telling me”: Fred Glazer, interview with Bill Keenom, 1995.

61 “Mike loved it”: Fred Glazer, interview with Bill Keenom, 1995.

62 Description of Yank Rachell session at Bloomfield’s apartment came from Bob Koester, interview with Bill Keenom, 1995.

62 “Bloomfield soon had to look”: Bob Koester, liner notes from *Mandolin Blues*, Delmark 606, 1963.

62 “John, Hammie and Yank were supposed”: Bob Koester, *Michael Bloomfield: If You Love These Blues*, Miller Freeman Books, 2000.

63 “Larry Fleischman told me”: Joel Harlib, author interview, 7/22/2007.

64 “I had fantasies”: George Mitchell, author interview, 3/3/2014.

64 “He invited me up”: George Mitchell, author interview, 3/3/2014.

65 “I was really into”: Michael Bloomfield, interview with Walter Rimler, summer 1975. Bloomfield mistakenly attributes “I’m Gonna Move to the Outskirts of Town” to Washboard Sam; the tune was composed and originally recorded by Casey Bill Weldon.

65 “Kokomo’s big hit”: Michael Bloomfield from his original taped narrative “Me and Big Joe,” transcribed by Sally Moses, ca. 1975.

65 Bloomfield’s gift of a guitar to Kokomo Arnold came from George Mitchell, author interview, 3/3/2014.

66 Bloomfield getting Mike Royko to write about the Fickle Pickle came from a comment posted by Tom Parmenter on facebook.com/MichaelBloomfieldLegacy/.

66 "He was bigger than life": Joel Harlib, author interview, 7/22/2007.

67 "One way Bloomfield came up": George Mitchell, author interview, 3/3/2014.

67 "He was so good": George Mitchell, author interview, 3/3/2014.

67 "I had an ancient Telefunken": Norman Dayron, author interview, 10/28/2011.

68 List of artists recorded by Norman Dayron at the Fickle Pickle came from Dayron's archive of tapes as cataloged by the author, Oct. 2011.

68 Bloomfield's jamming with Johnny Winter came from *Raisin' Cain: The Wild and Raucous Story of Johnny Winter*, Backbeat Books, 2010; Mick Weiser, interview with Bill Keenom, 1995.

69 "His first album": Michael Bloomfield, interview with Walter Rimler, summer 1975.

69 "When I got there": Michael Bloomfield, "Impressions of Bob Dylan," *Hit Parader*, June 1968.

69 "Here was this genius cat": Michael Bloomfield, "Impressions of Bob Dylan," *Hit Parader*, June 1968.

70 "We stayed up": Peter Amft, interview with Bill Keenom, 1996.

70 "Big Joe had said": George Mitchell, *Michael Bloomfield: If You Love These Blues*, Miller Freeman Books, 2000.

71 "We all got in the car": Michael Bloomfield from his original taped narrative "Me and Big Joe," transcribed by Sally Moses, ca. 1975.

71 "Joe was the type": Michael Bloomfield, interview with Walter Rimler, summer 1975.

72 "Big Joe didn't drink": George Mitchell, author interview, 2/16/2014.

72 "Chicago has such funky tenements": Michael Bloomfield, interview with Walter Rimler, summer 1975.

72 "When we got to her place": Michael Bloomfield from his original taped narrative "Me and Big Joe," transcribed by Sally Moses, ca. 1975.

72 "My God, it was hot": George Mitchell, author interview, 3/3/2014.

73 "On the way down": George Mitchell, author interview, 2/16/2014.

73 "I knew that": Michael Bloomfield from his original taped narrative "Me and Big Joe," transcribed by Sally Moses, ca. 1975.

73 "Joe said, 'Well'": Michael Bloomfield from his original taped narrative "Me and Big Joe," transcribed by Sally Moses, ca. 1975.

74 "Man, I got sick": Michael Bloomfield from his original taped narrative "Me and Big Joe," transcribed by Sally Moses, ca. 1975.

74 "Mike and I crashed": George Mitchell, author interview, 2/16/2014.

74 "Mike and I found": George Mitchell, author interview, 2/16/2014.

75 "I woke up": Michael Bloomfield from his original taped narrative "Me and Big Joe," transcribed by Sally Moses, ca. 1975.

75 "He was holding": Michael Bloomfield from his original taped narrative "Me and Big Joe," transcribed by Sally Moses, ca. 1975.

75 "It was so hot": George Mitchell, author interview, 2/16/2014.

75 "Me and Mitchell went out": Michael Bloomfield from his original taped narrative "Me and Big Joe," transcribed by Sally Moses, ca. 1975.

75 "When we got back": George Mitchell, author interview, 2/16/2014.

75 "Joe was just crazy": Michael Bloomfield from his original taped narrative "Me and Big Joe," transcribed by Sally Moses, ca. 1975.

76 "She said, 'You can't'": Michael Bloomfield from his original taped narrative "Me and Big Joe," transcribed by Sally Moses, ca. 1975.
76 "It was hot as hell": George Mitchell, author interview, 2/16/2014.
76 "I said, 'Joe'": George Mitchell, author interview, 2/16/2014.
76 "Well, now we're gonna": Michael Bloomfield from his original taped narrative "Me and Big Joe," transcribed by Sally Moses, ca. 1975.
77 "He was really like putting": Michael Bloomfield, interview with Dan McClosky, 5/17/1971.
77 "It looked like they": Michael Bloomfield from his original taped narrative "Me and Big Joe," transcribed by Sally Moses, ca. 1975.
77 "This famous blues singer": Michael Bloomfield from his original taped narrative "Me and Big Joe," transcribed by Sally Moses, ca. 1975.
77 "We recorded Joe": George Mitchell, author interview, 2/16/2014.
77 "He just would saw off": Michael Bloomfield from his original taped narrative "Me and Big Joe," transcribed by Sally Moses, ca. 1975.
78 "The first thing I see": Michael Bloomfield from his original taped narrative "Me and Big Joe," transcribed by Sally Moses, ca. 1975.
78 "I took one look": Michael Bloomfield from his original taped narrative "Me and Big Joe," transcribed by Sally Moses, ca. 1975.
78 "Inside the apartment": Michael Bloomfield from his original taped narrative "Me and Big Joe," transcribed by Sally Moses, ca. 1975.
78 "Whatever radical chic pretensions": Michael Bloomfield, interview with Walter Rimler, summer 1975.
78 "I said, 'Joe, pack up'": Michael Bloomfield from his original taped narrative "Me and Big Joe," transcribed by Sally Moses, ca. 1975.
78 "The sad truth was": Michael Bloomfield from his original taped narrative "Me and Big Joe," transcribed by Sally Moses, ca. 1975.
79 "He got madder": Michael Bloomfield from his original taped narrative "Me and Big Joe," transcribed by Sally Moses, ca. 1975.
79 "I kicked him": Michael Bloomfield, interview with Dan McClosky, 5/17/1971.
80 "We felt real bad": Michael Bloomfield from his original taped narrative "Me and Big Joe," transcribed by Sally Moses, ca. 1975.
80 "No, go on": Michael Bloomfield from his original taped narrative "Me and Big Joe," transcribed by Sally Moses, ca. 1975.
80 "I said, 'Big Joe'": George Mitchell, author interview, 2/16/2014.
80 "He said, 'These people'": George Mitchell, author interview, 2/16/2014.
80 "I was scared": Michael Bloomfield from his original taped narrative "Me and Big Joe," transcribed by Sally Moses, ca. 1975.
81 "We had us a time": Michael Bloomfield from his original taped narrative "Me and Big Joe," transcribed by Sally Moses, ca. 1975.

CHAPTER 5: OLD TOWN

My description of Bloomfield's daily routine came from my interviews with Joel Harlib, George Mitchell, Tommy Walker, Fred Glazer, and Norman Dayron; from Paul Petraitis's interview with Joel Harlib; and from my email correspondence with Charlie Musselwhite. Bloomfield's move to Sandburg Village was described to me by Joel Harlib, Norm Mayell, and Sidney Warner. Joel Harlib also told me about managing Bloomfield and his first gigs at Mother Blues. Information about Bloomfield's stint with Robby and the Troubadours came from Barry Goldberg's autobiography, *Two Jews Blues*; from Bill Keenom's interview with Mick Weiser; from my email correspondence with Chicago music researcher Mike Medina; and from Bloomfield's interviews in *Hit Parader*. Descriptions of Bloomfield's sleep issues came from his interviews in *Guitar Player* and *Rolling Stone*; from Dan McClosky's interview with him; from *Michael Bloomfield: If You Love These Blues*; from Bill Keenom's interviews with Susan Beuhler, Nick Gravenites, Dorothy Shinderman, and Allen Bloomfield; and from my interviews with Allen Bloomfield and Norman Dayron. The creation of Bloomfield's demo was described to me by Joel Harlib and Norman Dayron. Audio files of the demo were provided to me by Norman Dayron. Information about Paul Rothchild's offer to record Paul Butterfield came from *Follow the Music: The Life and High Times of Elektra Records in the Great Years of American Pop Culture*. Bloomfield's quitting the Fickle Pickle was recounted by waitress Dorothy Weiss in an interview with Bill Keenom. Information about Bloomfield's appearance with Big Joe Williams at the UC Folk Festival came from *Chicago Folk* and from photos by Raeburn Flerlage. Joel Harlib told me of his meeting with John Hammond.

82 "I could play as good": Michael Bloomfield, interview with Walter Rimler, summer 1975.
83 "Mike was always": George Mitchell, author interview, 2/16/2014.
83 "I considered him": Joel Harlib, author interview, 7/22/2007.
84 "Mike and I would": Joel Harlib, author interview, 7/22/2007.
84 Information about Tommy Walker came from Tommy Walker, author interview, 3/1/2014.
85 "He was a real showman": Joel Harlib, author interview, 7/22/2007.
86 "He didn't like being": Joel Harlib, author interview, 7/22/2007.
86 "Mike was so charismatic": Joel Harlib, interview with Bill Keenom, 1995.
86–87 Harold Bloomfield's purchase of the Sandburg Village apartment building came from Sidney Warner, author interview, 9/2/2010.
87–88 Description of Bloomfield's trio with Michael Melford and Ira Kamin came from Michael Melford, email to the author, 4/28/2013.
89 "Michael was never": Dorothy Shinderman, interview with Bill Keenom, 1996.
89 "It's always been my theory": Susan Beuhler, interview with Bill Keenom, 1995.
90 "We decided we had to": Joel Harlib, author interview, 7/22/2007.
91 Poor attendance at Fickle Pickle shows was reported in *Down Beat*, 1/2/1964.
91 "He said, 'Oh, by the way'": Dorothy Weiss, interview with Bill Keenom, 1996.
92 "Something Michael made up": Norman Dayron, author interview, 10/28/2011.
93 "We started overdubbing": Norman Dayron, author interview, 10/28/2011.
95 "I decided I might as well": Joel Harlib, author interview, 7/22/2007.
95 "I cold-called him": Joel Harlib, author interview, 7/22/2007.
96 "I said to him": Joel Harlib, author interview, 7/22/2007.

CHAPTER 6: AUDITIONING FOR HAMMOND

Negotiations with John Hammond and his subsequent heart attack were described to me by Joel Harlib; information also came from *An Autobiography: John Hammond on the Record*. My re-creation of Bloomfield's audition for John Hammond came from my interview and email correspondence with Joel Harlib and from audio files provided by Al Kooper and Paul Thompson. Some of the dialogue during the session was taken from those recordings; the remainder was created by myself. Information about Columbia and Epic came from *The Label: The Story of Columbia Records*; details about Bloomfield's contract with Epic came from documents supplied by Bruce Dickinson. A description of Sleepy John Estes's Delmark recording session came from Bill Keenom's interview with Bob Koester and from Koester's liner notes for the album. Bloomfield's days at the Old Wells Record Shop were described to me by Charlie Musselwhite in our email correspondence; information also came from *Michael Bloomfield: If You Love These Blues*. My description of Bloomfield and Paul Butterfield jamming at Theresa's was taken from photos supplied to me by Norman Dayron. Guitarist John Hammond's electric blues recording session was described to me during my interview with John Hammond and in my email correspondence with Charlie Musselwhite. Additional information came from *Across the Great Divide: The Band and America* and from the discography *60 Years of Recorded Jazz, 1917–1977*. Charlie Musselwhite emailed me the story of performing at Big John's with Big Joe Williams and Bloomfield, and Donna Koch Gower described the club to me and recounted seeing the Group perform there. Dates for performances came from issues of *Down Beat*. Norm Mayell, Mike Johnson, Sidney Warner, and Brian Friedman shared their experiences playing in the Group in interviews with me. Norman Dayron described Bloomfield's participation in Mike Shea's Maxwell Street documentary project; additional information came from the liner notes to *And This Is Maxwell Street* and Pete Welding's Chicago Blues News column in *Blues Unlimited*. Dayron also told me about recording the Group at Big John's.

97 John Hammond telling his father about Bloomfield came from John Hammond, author interview, 7/22/2014.

98 Bloomfield to record for Epic came from John Hammond, letter to Michael Bloomfield, 11/5/1964, provided by Bruce Davidson.

99 "Good playing, Mike": audio clip from *From His Head to His Heart to His Hands*, Sony Legacy CD box set, 2014.

100 "That was the end": Joel Harlib, author interview, 7/25/2007.

101 Details of Bloomfield's Epic contract came from Columbia Artist Card, provided by Bruce Davidson.

102 Description of Butterfield's appearance at Old Town North came from *Hootenanny*, May 1964.

103 "John said he was going": Charlie Musselwhite, email to the author, 10/26/2014.

103 "I was amazed": John Hammond, author interview, 7/22/2014.

104 "John loaned me a mic": Charlie Musselwhite, email to the author, 10/26/2014.

104 "He wasn't about to": Charlie Musselwhite, email to the author, 10/26/2014.

105 Bloomfield being replaced by Donald Cook came from the discography *60 Years of Recorded Jazz, 1917–1977*.

106 Information about Chicago clubs came from issues of *Chicago Scene*, *Down Beat*, and newspaper ads.

106 "The owners of the bar": Charlie Musselwhite, email to the author, 10/26/2014.

106 "I remember it was": Charlie Musselwhite, email to the author, 10/26/2014.

107 "That was the very beginning": Charlie Musselwhite, email to the author, 10/26/2014.

108 "Michael was standing there": Norm Mayell, author interview, 1/20/2011.

108 Description of Erwin Helfer playing with Bloomfield at Big John's came from *Down Beat*, 9/24/1964.

109 "After a while": Mike Johnson, author interview, 10/24/2007.

109 "You could hear them": Donna Koch Gower, author interview, 12/13/2017.

110 "Mike Bloomfield was our connection": Gordon Quinn, "This Was Maxwell Street," *Wall Street Journal*, 7/31/2008.

110 Information about the duration of filming for *And This Is Free* came from Pete Welding's column in *Blues Unlimited*, Sept. 1963.

111 "They say in the future": audio clip from *And This Is Maxwell Street*, Rooster Blues Records CD set, 2000.

111 "Michael was so frenetic": Norm Mayell, author interview, 1/20/2011.

111 "When I first met him": Brian Friedman, author interview, 10/10/2013.

112 "We never practiced": Mike Johnson, author interview, 10/24/2007.

112 "One day I was walking": Sidney Warner, author interview, 8/14/2010.

112 "Mike brought me up": Sidney Warner, author interview, 8/14/2010.

113 "On our best nights": Norm Mayell, author interview, 1/20/2011.

113–114 The tunes played by the Group and recorded by Norman Dayron at Big John's on Oct. 15, 1964, were "Blues for Roy," "Country Boy," "Intermission Blues," and "Gotta Call Susie." They were released on a CD that accompanied *Michael Bloomfield: If You Love These Blues*, 2000.

114 "I remember we'd sometimes": Sidney Warner, author interview, 8/14/2010.

CHAPTER 7: BIG JOHN'S AND THE GROUP

Descriptions of the Group's months at Big John's came from my interviews with band members Norm Mayell, Mike Johnson, Sidney Warner, and Brian Friedman, and from Norman Dayron; additional information came from *Down Beat* magazine. The Group's stint at Magoo's came from my interviews with Sidney Warner, Joel Harlib, and Norm Mayell; Donna Koch Gower described the club's physical layout and Bloomfield's last night there. Bloomfield recounted convincing Paul Butterfield to take the Group's place at Big John's in his *Rolling Stone* interview. Butterfield shared his thoughts about Bloomfield in a *Down Beat* interview. Bruce Dickinson provided me with John Hammond's letters regarding his plans to record Bloomfield. The Group's Chicago recording session was recalled by members of the band and by Joel Harlib in my interviews with them. Other information was provided by Mike Shea's photos of the session, shared with me by Peggy McVickar and René Aagaard. Descriptions of Bloomfield's band with Nick Gravenites came from Gravenites's email to the author, from his article "Bad Talkin' Bluesman" in *Blues Review*, from Bill Keenom's interviews with him, and from photos taken by Norman Dayron. Bloomfield's purchase of a 1963 Telecaster came from comments he made in *Guitar Player* and *Rolling Stone*; the dialogue is my own creation. Paul Rothchild's signing of the Paul Butterfield Blues Band came from *Follow the Music*. Bloomfield's second recording session for Columbia was described to me by Fred Glazer and in emails from Charlie Musselwhite; additional information came from Columbia Tape Identification Data cards provided by Bruce Dickinson. Information about Bob Morgan came from *The Label*.

116 "The crowds at Big John's": Sidney Warner, author interview, 8/14/2010.

116 "Paul Butterfield and Elvin Bishop": Mike Johnson, author interview, 10/24/2007.

116 Barry Goldberg sitting in with the group was recalled by Norm Mayell, author interview, 1/20/2011.
116 "The group is built": Pete Welding, *Down Beat*, 12/3/1964.
117 "When I started": Sidney Warner, author interview, 8/14/2010.
117 "The McGovern boys were": Sidney Warner, author interview, 8/14/2010.
117 "It was a gangster hangout": Sidney Warner, author interview, 8/14/2010.
118 "Mike hated playing there": Sidney Warner, author interview, 8/14/2010.
118 The Group's weekly schedule at Magoo's came from Mike Johnson, author interview, 10/24/2007.
119 "He just sort of thought": Michael Bloomfield, *Rolling Stone*, 4/6/1968.
119 Butterfield's schedule at Big John's came from *Down Beat*, 12/3/1964.
119 "I talked to your mother": John Hammond, letter to Michael Bloomfield, 11/5/1964.
119 "This kid is a tremendous": John Hammond, memo to Bob Morgan, Len Levy, and Sol Rabinowitz, 11/5/1964.
120 "We were basically a jam band": Mike Johnson, author interview, 10/24/2007.
121 "Hammond came into the studio": Norm Mayell, author interview, 1/20/2011.
121 Bloomfield's Duo-Sonic guitar is described in Michael Brooks, "Michael Bloomfield: Straight Stone City Blues," *Guitar Player*, June 1971.
124 "We were really excited": Sidney Warner, author interview, 8/14/2010.
124 "We were kind of deflated": Norm Mayell, author interview, 1/20/2011.
124 "We made wild music": Michael Bloomfield, *Rock & Folk* (translated from the French by the author), May 1981.
125 "Silver Sid would switch to guitar": Norm Mayell, author interview, 1/20/2011.
125 "That's it!": description of Bloomfield's quitting the Group's gig at Magoo's came from Donna Koch Gower, author interview, 12/13/2017.
125 "I went to the McGoverns": Sidney Warner, author interview, 8/14/2010.
125 "After a while": Mike Johnson, author interview, 10/24/2007.
126 "After Sid left": Norm Mayell, author interview, 1/20/2011.
126 "Big John's was my first": Nick Gravenites, "Bad Talkin' Bluesman," *Blues Revue*, July/Aug. 1995.
127 "I had a lot of fun": Nick Gravenites, "Bad Talkin' Bluesman," *Blues Revue*, July/Aug. 1995.
129 "We was looking": Sam Lay, interview with Bill Keenom, 1996.
130 "Paul was really nervous": Nick Gravenites, interview with Bill Keenom, 1996.

CHAPTER 8: BUTTERFIELD BLUES

Information about the Butterfield Band's appearance at the Village Gate came from my interviews with Mark Naftalin and John Hammond, from *Michael Bloomfield: If You Love These Blues*, from Robert Shelton's profile of Butterfield in the *New York Times*, and from newspaper ads. Descriptions of the band's recording sessions for Elektra came from my interviews with Fred Glazer, Norman Dayron, and David Gedalecia; from emails to me from Charlie Musselwhite; from Bill Keenom's interviews with Fred Glazer; from Bloomfield's interview in *Guitar Player*; and from Mark Abramson in *Follow the Music*. Bloomfield's activities while in New York and his drug use were described to me in emails from Charlie Musselwhite; information also came from Bill Keenom's interviews with Fred Glazer. Roy

Ruby's drug use was described to me by Tommy Walker. My re-creation of the Butterfield Band's photo shoot for Elektra was inspired by Nick Gravenites's comments on facebook.com/MichaelBloomfieldLegacy and by additional photos taken by William Harvey. Bloomfield's recording *Highway 61 Revisited* with Bob Dylan was described by Bloomfield in his *Rolling Stone* and *Guitar Player* interviews and in his *Hit Parader* article. He also spoke of the sessions in Dan McClosky's and Walter Rimler's interviews with him. Dylan commented on the sessions in *Rolling Stone* and in Martin Scorsese's film *No Direction Home*. Additional information came from Bloomfield's observations to Larry Sloman in *On the Road with Bob Dylan*. Al Kooper shared his recollections of the sessions with me in several interviews. Recording details came from Sony Legacy's *The Cutting Edge, 1965–66 Bootleg Series, Vol. 12*. The facts surrounding Bloomfield's drug use in Chicago were relayed to me by Tommy Walker. The politics behind the Butterfield Band's Newport Folk Festival appearance came from my interview with Peter Yarrow and from *Follow the Music* and *Dylan Goes Electric!*

136 Dates for the Butterfield Band appearances at the Village Gate came from ads in the *New York Times*, 3/2/1965–3/4/1965.

137 "The talk of musical circles": Robert Shelton, "Beatles Backlash Spurs Modern Blues," *New York Times*, 3/11/1965.

137 "Has been brought to New York": *Billboard*, 3/6/1965.

138 "Paul asked me": Michael Brooks, "Michael Bloomfield: Straight Stone City Blues," *Guitar Player*, June 1971.

139 "I do remember one time": Charlie Musselwhite, email to the author, 10/26/2014.

139 "Oh, Mike had a tremendous": Charlie Musselwhite, email to the author, 10/26/2014.

140 "We'd buy cough syrup": Charlie Musselwhite, email to the author, 10/26/2014.

140 "He came in": Tommy Walker, author interview, 3/1/2014.

140 "We were in somebody's apartment": Fred Glazer, interview with Bill Keenom, 1996.

140 "I *dug* it!": Michael Bloomfield, interview with Walter Rimler, summer 1975.

140 "We needed it": Fred Glazer, interview with Bill Keenom, 1996.

141 "Until further notice": *Down Beat*, 4/8/1965.

142 Elektra's difficulties recording the Butterfield Band came from comments by Mark Abramson, *Follow the Music: The Life and High Times of Elektra Records in the Great Years of American Pop Culture*, FirstMedia Books, 2000.

143 Description of Butterfield Band back at Big John's came from *Down Beat*, 4/22/1965.

144 "For a while": Michael Bloomfield, *Michael Bloomfield: The Rise and Fall of an American Guitar Hero*, Cherry Lane, 1983.

145 "That's it, boys": Nick Gravenites, comment on facebook.com/MichaelBloomfieldLegacy.

146 "[Paul] was the white guy": Michael Bloomfield, interview with Walter Rimler, summer 1975.

146 "He was an expert player": Bob Dylan, *Rolling Stone*, May 2009.

146 "He could outplay anybody": Bob Dylan, *No Direction Home*, Spitfire Pictures, 2005.

146 "Then I saw him again": Michael Bloomfield, "Michael Bloomfield Puts Down Everything," *Hit Parader*, January 1967.

147 "I knew he was, like": Michael Bloomfield, interview with Walter Rimler, summer 1975.
148 "The first thing I heard": Michael Bloomfield, "Impressions of Dylan," *Hit Parader*, June 1968.
149 "All on the black keys": Michael Bloomfield, interview with Larry Sloman, *On the Road with Bob Dylan*, Three Rivers Press, 1978.
149 "I didn't recognize Albert": Michael Bloomfield, interview with Larry Sloman, *On the Road with Bob Dylan*, Three Rivers Press, 1978.
149 "We used to call him": Michael Bloomfield, KSAN interview, San Francisco, ca. 1974.
150 "I used to hang out": Al Kooper, author interview, 9/16/2014.
150 "I realized then": Al Kooper, author interview, 9/16/2014.
151 "So we get to the session": Michael Bloomfield, "Impressions of Dylan," *Hit Parader*, June 1968.
152 "The producer was a non-producer": Michael Bloomfield, interview with Dan McClosky, 5/17/1971.
152 "The *Highway 61 Revisited* sessions": Al Kooper, author interview, 9/16/2014.
154 "He knows it": Bob Dylan, studio comment from *The Cutting Edge, 1965–66 Bootleg Series, Vol. 12*, Columbia Legacy CD box set, 2015.
155 "Tom said, 'Al'": Al Kooper, author interview, 9/16/2014.
155 "Tom didn't say I could": Al Kooper, author interview, 9/16/2014.
155 "What are you doing there?": Tom Wilson, audio clip from *The Cutting Edge, 1965–66 Bootleg Series, Vol. 12*, Columbia Legacy CD box set, 2015.
157 "When I found out": Tommy Walker, author interview, 3/1/2014.
157 "We'd have the stuff": Tommy Walker, author interview, 3/1/2014.

CHAPTER 9: PLUGGING IN AT NEWPORT

Information for my narrative of the Butterfield Band's appearances at the Newport Folk Festival came from festival documents and audio recordings in the Library of Congress; from the films *Festival* and *The Other Side of the Mirror: Bob Dylan at the Newport Folk Festival 1963–1965* as well as additional footage; from Bloomfield's interviews in *Rolling Stone* and *Guitar Player*; from Barry Goldberg's autobiography, *Two Jews Blues*; from Nick Gravenites's "Bad Talkin' Bluesman" articles in *Blues Review*; from Bloomfield's article in *The Sixties*; from reports in the *Newport Daily News*; from *Dylan Goes Electric!*; from *Follow the Music: The Life and High Times of Elektra Records in the Great Years of American Pop Culture*; from *Baby, Let Me Follow You Down: The Illustrated Story of the Cambridge Folk Years*; from *Michael Bloomfield: The Rise and Fall of an American Guitar Hero* and *Michael Bloomfield: If You Love These Blues*; from Bill Keenom's interviews with Nick Gravenites and Sam Lay; from Jan Mark Wolkin's interview with Maria Muldaur; and from my own interviews with Al Kooper and Peter Yarrow.

161 Information on the release of "Like a Rolling Stone" came from "The Hit We Almost Missed" by Shaun Considine, *New York Times*, 12/3/2004.
163 Opening-night attendance numbers and performers came from the *Newport Daily News*, 7/23/1963.
164–166 Workshop schedule came from the festival program in the Library of Congress.

164 Festival layout came from photos by David Gahr, Dr. John Rudoff, and others; the films *Festival*, 1967, and *The Other Side of the Mirror: Bob Dylan at the Newport Folk Festival 1963–1965*, 2007, both by Murray Lerner; Lerner's additional footage.

164 "Of all the blues singers": Michael Bloomfield, audio clip from *Lightnin' Hopkins Live at Newport*, Vanguard LP, 1965.

165 Barry Goldberg's exclusion from the Butterfield Band performances described in Goldberg's *Two Jews Blues*, St. Paul Books, 2012.

165–174 Description of the Butterfield Band's first workshop was taken from audio recordings in the Library of Congress; the festival's program; the films *Festival*, 1967, and *The Other Side of the Mirror: Bob Dylan at the Newport Folk Festival 1963–1965*, 2007, both by Murray Lerner; Lerner's additional footage.

166 "At workshops they only": Paul Rothchild, *Baby, Let Me Follow You Down: The Illustrated Story of the Cambridge Folk Years*, University of Massachusetts Press, 1994.

167 "The big buzz": Maria Muldaur, interview with Jan Mark Wolkin, 1995.

168 "Lomax was loaded": Paul Rothchild, *Follow the Music: The Life and High Times of Elektra Records in the Great Years of American Pop Culture*, FirstMedia Books, 2000.

168 "Lomax was so condescending": Jac Holzman, *Follow the Music: The Life and High Times of Elektra Records in the Great Years of American Pop Culture*, FirstMedia Books, 2000.

168 "I understand that": Alan Lomax, audio clip from the Library of Congress.

171 "To the folk community": Michael Bloomfield, "Dylan Goes Electric," *The Sixties*, Random House/Rolling Stone Press, 1977.

173 "Alan Lomax, the great": Michael Bloomfield, KSAN interview, San Francisco, ca. 1974.

173 "They got into it": Sam Lay, interview with Bill Keenom, 1995.

174 "I was cheering": Michael Bloomfield, "Dylan Goes Electric," *The Sixties*, Random House/Rolling Stone Press, 1977.

175 Bloomfield jamming on banjo with Bill Monroe reported by Sam Lay, interview with Bill Keenom, 1995.

176–180 Description of the Butterfield Band's second workshop was taken from audio recordings in the Library of Congress; the festival's program; the films *Festival*, 1967, and *The Other Side of the Mirror: Bob Dylan at the Newport Folk Festival 1963–1965*, 2007, both by Murray Lerner; Lerner's additional footage.

179 "Thank you very much": Paul Butterfield, audio clip from the Library of Congress.

180 "What we played": Michael Bloomfield, *Michael Bloomfield: The Rise and Fall of an American Guitar Hero*, Cherry Lane Books, 1983.

180 "Dylan asked me": Michael Bloomfield, "Impressions of Dylan," *Hit Parader*, June 1968.

180 "I went every year": Al Kooper, author interview, 9/16/2014.

181 Bloomfield getting Barry Goldberg to play with Bob Dylan reported by Goldberg in *Two Jews Blues*, St. Paul Books, 2012.

181 "Michael was, essentially": Nick Gravenites, *Michael Bloomfield: If You Love These Blues*, Miller Freeman Books, 2000.

181 "We stayed up all night": Al Kooper, author interview, 9/16/2014.

181 “We were all at Newport”: Michael Bloomfield, interview with Larry Sloman, *On the Road with Bob Dylan*, Three Rivers Press, 1978.

182 “He was uncomfortable”: Michael Bloomfield, interview with Larry Sloman, *On the Road with Bob Dylan*, Three Rivers Press, 1978.

182–185 Description of the Butterfield Band’s sound check and the New Folks concert came from photos by David Gahr and others; audio recordings in the Library of Congress; *Positively 4th Street: The Lives and Times of Joan Baez, Bob Dylan, Mimi Baez Fariña and Richard Fariña*, Picador, 2001; *Baby, Let Me Follow You Down: The Illustrated Story of the Cambridge Folk Years*, University of Massachusetts Press, 1994; *Dylan Goes Electric!*, Dey Street Books, 2015.

CHAPTER 10: ELECTRIFYING DYLAN

For my re-creation of Bob Dylan’s Newport Folk Festival appearance, I used festival documents and audio recordings in the Library of Congress; the films *Festival* and *The Other Side of the Mirror: Bob Dylan at the Newport Folk Festival 1963–1965* as well as additional footage; Bloomfield’s interviews in *Rolling Stone* and *Guitar Player*, and his article on Dylan in *Hit Parader*; Barry Goldberg’s autobiography, *Two Jews Blues*; Nick Gravenites’s “Bad Talkin’ Bluesman” articles in *Blues Review*; Bloomfield’s article in *The Sixties*; reports in the *Newport Daily News*; issues of *Sing Out!* magazine; Bill Keenom’s interviews with Nick Gravenites; and my own interviews with Al Kooper and Peter Yarrow. Additional information came from the following books: *Dylan Goes Electric!*; *Follow the Music; Baby, Let Me Follow You Down: The Illustrated Story of the Cambridge Folk Years*; *White Bicycles: Making Music in the 1960s*; *Michael Bloomfield: The Rise and Fall of an American Guitar Hero*; and *Michael Bloomfield: If You Love These Blues.* My description of the Butterfield Band’s Cafe Au Go Go appearances came from *Follow the Music* and the liner notes to *The Paul Butterfield Blues Band: The Original Lost Elektra Sessions*. Information on Bob Dylan’s final recording sessions for *Highway 61 Revisited* came from *The Cutting Edge, 1965–66 Bootleg Series, Vol. 12* CD box set and from my interview with Al Kooper. Details of the Butterfield Band’s third round of recording sessions for Elektra came from liner notes to *The Paul Butterfield Blues Band: The Original Lost Elektra Sessions*; from my interviews with Mark Naftalin; and from Naftalin’s personal history, sent to Bill Keenom. The Butterfield Band’s return to Big John’s was described to me by Mark Naftalin and Allen Bloomfield. Bill Keenom’s interview with Fred Glazer provided me with Bloomfield’s reaction to his parents’ separation.

186 “Alan had decided to”: Author interview, 2/23/2015.

187 “We weren’t really set up”: Peter Yarrow, author interview, 2/23/2015.

187 “I can play the bass part”: Al Kooper, author interview, 9/16/2014.

188 “Most of you have heard them”: Peter Yarrow, audio clip from the Library of Congress.

188–191 Description of the Butterfield Band’s Sunday performance came from audio recordings in the Library of Congress; the films *Festival* and *The Other Side of the Mirror: Bob Dylan at the Newport Folk Festival 1963–1965*; additional footage.

190 “In my opinion”: Michael Bloomfield, interview with Murray Lerner, 7/26/1965.

191 “The person that’s”: Peter Yarrow, audio clip from the Library of Congress.

192 “Put that up”: Michael Bloomfield, audio clip from the Library of Congress.

192 "I was wearing Levis": Michael Bloomfield, "Dylan Goes Electric," *The Sixties*, Random House/Rolling Stone Press, 1977.

193 "I would traditionally mix": Peter Yarrow, author interview, 2/23/2015.

193 "It might have been": Michael Bloomfield, "Dylan Goes Electric," *The Sixties*, Random House/Rolling Stone Press, 1977.

194 "A buzz of shock": Joe Boyd, *White Bicycles: Making Music in the 1960s*, Serpent's Tail, 2006.

194 "I was at the console": Paul Rothchild, *Follow the Music: The Life and High Times of Elektra Records in the Great Years of American Pop Culture*, FirstMedia Books, 2000.

195 "I told Bobby": Peter Yarrow, author interview, 2/23/2015.

196 "The audience was mortified": Peter Yarrow, author interview, 2/23/2015.

196 "It was like being": Joe Boyd, *White Bicycles: Making Music in the 1960s*, Serpent's Tail, 2006.

196 "Would you like": Peter Yarrow, audio clip from the Library of Congress.

197 "It was God awful loud": Maria Muldaur, *Baby, Let Me Follow You Down: The Illustrated Story of the Cambridge Folk Years*, University of Massachusetts Press, 1994.

197 "Just where is Bob Dylan going?": Letter to *Sing Out!* magazine, Nov. 1965.

197 "The article of faith": Peter Yarrow, author interview, 2/23/2015.

197 "The Newport establishment": Michael Bloomfield, "Dylan Goes Electric," *The Sixties*, Random House/Rolling Stone Press, 1977.

198 "I thought we were boffo": Michael Bloomfield, "Dylan Goes Electric," *The Sixties*, Random House/Rolling Stone Press, 1977.

199 "Albert had just signed": Michael Bloomfield, "Impressions of Dylan," *Hit Parader*, June 1968.

199 "I could even see": Michael Bloomfield, KSAN interview, San Francisco, ca. 1974.

200 "Every time I play": Michael Bloomfield, interview with Murray Lerner, *Festival*, Patchke Productions, 1967.

200 "I'm not born to blues": Michael Bloomfield, interview with Murray Lerner, *Festival*, Patchke Productions, 1967.

201 "Man, my father's": Michael Bloomfield, interview with Murray Lerner, *Festival*, Patchke Productions, 1967.

201 "I'll tell you": Michael Bloomfield, interview with Murray Lerner, extra footage, 7/26/1965.

202 Paul Rothchild's decision to rerecord the Butterfield album is described in *Follow the Music: The Life and High Times of Elektra Records in the Great Years of American Pop Culture*, FirstMedia Books, 2000.

202 "With better recording": Paul Rothchild, liner notes to *The Paul Butterfield Blues Band: The Original Lost Elektra Sessions*, Elektra Traditions, 1995.

202 "You gotta put": Bob Dylan, audio clip from *The Cutting Edge, 1965–66 Bootleg Series, Vol. 12*, Columbia Legacy CD box set, 2015.

203 Elektra being fined by the union is described by Paul Rothchild in *Follow the Music: The Life and High Times of Elektra Records in the Great Years of American Pop Culture*, FirstMedia Books, 2000.

204 "I walked over": Michael Bloomfield, "Impressions of Dylan," *Hit Parader*, June 1968.

204 Description of the Butterfield Band's volume causing a mirror to fall to the floor came from Geoff Muldaur, interview with Bill Keenom, 1995.

204 Description of the Butterfield Band's gig at Club 47 came from Jim Rooney, *Baby, Let Me Follow You Down: The Illustrated Story of the Cambridge Folk Years*, University of Massachusetts Press, 1994.

205 "Jac [Holzman] got": Paul Rothchild, *Follow the Music: The Life and High Times of Elektra Records in the Great Years of American Pop Culture*, FirstMedia Books, 2000.

205 Paul Rothchild deciding to rerecord the Butterfield album a third time is described in *Follow the Music: The Life and High Times of Elektra Records in the Great Years of American Pop Culture*, FirstMedia Books, 2000.

206 "I thought the band": Mark Naftalin's personal history, sent to Bill Keenom, 1996.

206 "I remember sitting": Mark Naftalin's personal history, sent to Bill Keenom, 1996.

207 "I showed up": Mark Naftalin, author interview, 6/15/2008.

207 "I had never played": Mark Naftalin, author interview, 6/15/2008.

208 Bloomfield's use of a Cliff Gallup phrase on an Elmore James tune came from Bob Greenspan, author interview, 1/19/2012.

209 "Mike later told me": Mark Naftalin's personal history, sent to Bill Keenom, 1996.

209 "Our jackets were": Mark Naftalin, author interview, 6/15/2008.

210 "I was a freshman": Allen Bloomfield, author interview, 2/19/2008.

210 Allen Bloomfield moving to Chicago with his parents came from Allen Bloomfield, author interview, 2/19/2008.

211 "His dad had": Fred Glazer, author interview, 10/10/2007.

211 "When he came back": Fred Glazer, author interview, 10/10/2007.

211 "We got close": Allen Bloomfield, author interview, 2/19/2008.

CHAPTER 11: ON THE ROAD WITH BUTTER

My description of the Butterfield Band's weeks in Chicago at Big John's came from my interviews with Mark Naftalin and from Mark's personal history sent to Bill Keenom. Information about the band's stint in Boston at the Unicorn came from my email correspondence with David Gedalecia and Nick Nicolaisen. Bloomfield's trading his Telecaster for a Les Paul Goldtop was described to me by John Nuese. The description of occasional strife in the Butterfield Band came from Bill Keenom's interview with Sam Lay and from Dan McClosky's interview with Bloomfield. The band's appearance at Town Hall was described in reviews in the *New York Times* and in *Billboard*. Information on LSD and Timothy Leary came from Wikipedia; Bloomfield's first experience with the drug was described to me by Mark Naftalin. Fred Glazer recalled Roy Ruby introducing Bloomfield to the music of Ravi Shankar in an interview with Bill Keenom. The creation of "The Raga" was described to me by Mark Naftalin; additional information came from Dan McClosky's interview with Bloomfield. Mark also told me about Sam Lay's illness, his departure from the band, and the attempt to replace him with Bill Warren. Billy Davenport described joining the band in Bill Keenom's interview with him, parts of which appeared in *Michael Bloomfield: If You Love These Blues*. Information about the Butterfield Band's first trip to the West Coast came from my interviews with Mark Naftalin and from Bill Keenom's interview with Billy Davenport. Data about the band's club appearances came from newspaper listings and ads. The story of the band's first appearance at the Fillmore Auditorium came from my interviews with Mark

Naftalin, from *Michael Bloomfield: If You Love These Blues*, from Dan McClosky's interview with Bloomfield, from Bill Keenom's interviews with Billy Davenport and Chet Helms, and from a review in the *Berkeley Barb*. Information on the development of "East-West" and the Butterfield Band's shift away from blues came from my interviews with Mark Naftalin, from Bloomfield's interviews in *Hit Parader*, and from various newspaper reviews of the band.

217 "On this gig": Mark Naftalin's personal history, sent to Bill Keenom, 1996.

218 Bloomfield's playing "Walkin' the Strings" came from David Gedalecia, email to the author, 3/8/2010.

218 "I got it from a guy": John Nuese, author interview, 1/10/2010.

219 "When Michael saw": John Nuese, author interview, 1/10/2010.

219 "Mike's Tele didn't": John Nuese, author interview, 1/10/2010.

219 "You know why": Bloomfield quoted in Nick Nicolaisen, email to the author, 3/26/2009.

220 "I've known Butterfield": Sam Lay, interview with Bill Keenom, 1995.

220 "That cat, man": Sam Lay, interview with Bill Keenom, 1995.

221 "The six-man group": *Billboard*, 12/11/1965.

221 "The Paul Butterfield Blues Band": *New York Times*, 11/29/1965.

222 "Later on, after dawn": Mark Naftalin, author interview, 6/15/2008.

223 "I drew upon the fact": Michael Bloomfield, interview with Dan McClosky, 5/17/1971.

223 "The band started": Mark Naftalin, author interview, 6/15/2008.

224 "Sam became ill": Mark Naftalin, author interview, 6/15/2008.

224–225 The description of Billy Davenport joining the Butterfield Band came from *Michael Bloomfield: If You Love These Blues*, 2000.

226 "Mike and I used": Mark Naftalin, author interview, 6/15/2008.

227 Butterfield's use of a medley introduction came from recordings of 1966 performances and from set lists provided by Mark Naftalin.

228 "It's a great song": *Crawdaddy*, 2/2/1966.

228–229 Description of the Butterfield Band sessions produced by Barry Friedman came from Mark Naftalin, email to the author, 6/3/2015.

229 "Whoever assigned them": Mark Naftalin, email to the author, 6/1/2015.

229 "I guess the drums": Mark Naftalin, email to the author, 6/1/2015.

230 "Paul had this old": Michael Bloomfield, interview with Dan McClosky, 5/17/1971.

230 "He punched me": Michael Bloomfield, interview with Dan McClosky, 5/17/1971.

230 "A lot of times": Billy Davenport, interview with Bill Keenom, 1995.

231 Bloomfield mentioned the band's disastrous appearance at the It Club in "Michael Bloomfield Puts Down Everything," *Hit Parader*, February 1967.

232 "Was there a different vibe": Mark Naftalin, email to the author, 8/25/2015.

232 "When we got to the Fillmore": Billy Davenport, *Michael Bloomfield: If You Love These Blues*, 2000.

233 "Man, when we got through": Billy Davenport, *Michael Bloomfield: If You Love These Blues*, 2000.

233 "Michael was amazed": Chet Helms, interview with Bill Keenom, 1996.

234 "We weren't expecting": Mark Naftalin, author interview, 6/15/2008.

234 "As a blues band": ED Denson, *Berkeley Barb*, 3/1/1966.

235 "The house was usually": Mark Naftalin, author interview, 6/15/2008.

235 "I remember Mark Naftalin": Michael Bloomfield, interview with Dan McClosky, 5/17/1971.

236 "We heard the music": Michael Bloomfield, interview with Walter Rimler, summer 1975.

236, 237 Bloomfield's urging of Bill Graham to bring in black blues players came from Nick Gravenites, interview with Bill Keenom, 1996.

237 "You won't believe": *Detroit Free Press*, 4/29/1966.

238 "Butterfield's six-piece group": *Variety*, 6/1/1966.

238–239 Descriptions of "The Raga" came from recorded examples on *The Paul Butterfield Blues Band: East-West Live*, Winner CD, 1996.

239 "We hope to advance": Paul Butterfield, *Melody Maker*, 3/19/1966.

240 Bloomfield's approachability was described by Michael Erlewine, author interview, 5/21/2015.

240 "Is the most influential guitarist": *Hit Parader*, Jan. 1967.

CHAPTER 12: EAST-WEST

Information about recording the Butterfield Band's second album for Elektra came from *Follow the Music* and from my interviews and emails with Mark Naftalin. My analysis of "East-West" came from my essay "Beyond the Blues: A Critical Look at 'East-West.'" Bloomfield's heroin use while in Chicago came from Bill Keenom's interview with Peter Amft and from my interview with Tommy Walker. The Butterfield Band's appearance at Poor Richard's was described to me by Michael Erlewine. Information about the band's return to Club 47 came from several newspaper reviews and from *Crawdaddy*'s interview with them. Descriptions of their gigs at the Cafe Au Go Go with the Blues Project came from my interview with Al Kooper, from Bill Keenom's interview with Danny Kalb, and from newspaper ads. Additional information about the Butterfield Band came from Bloomfield's interview in *Hit Parader*. Bloomfield's first encounter with Jimi Hendrix came from his article in *Guitar Player* and from Tom Yates's interview with him. The final production work and release of "East-West" was taken from comments by Paul Rothchild in *Follow the Music* and from my emails with Mark Naftalin. My description of Bloomfield's recording session with the Chicago Loop and Bob Crewe came from Barry Goldberg's autobiography, *Two Jews Blues*. Information about the Butterfield Band's appearance at Monterey came from *Down Beat*, the *Los Angeles Times*, the *New Yorker*, and Jimmy Lyons's history of the festival, *Duke, Dizzy, the Count and Me*. Additional information came from Jon Hendricks's Columbia album *Evolution of the Blues Song* and from Jim Marshall's photos. My re-creation of Bloomfield's fire-eating stunt at the Fillmore came from my emails with Mark Naftalin; from a clip of Bloomfield doing the trick on *Speakeasy*, sent to me by Peggy McVickar; and from a review in the *Berkeley Barb*. The band's set list was taken from recordings of their Fillmore performances. Bloomfield's affinity for the San Francisco area came from Walter Rimler's interview with him.

241 "'East-West' was done": Mark Naftalin, email to the author, 6/1/2015.

245 "He was totally funny": Peter Amft, interview with Bill Keenom, 1995.

245 "He was totally blue": Peter Amft, interview with Bill Keenom, 1995.

247 "Of about 15 minutes": *The Boston Globe*, 6/26/1966.

247 "If there was one thing": *The Fitchburg Sentinel*, 6/28/1966.

247 "We used to be": Michael Bloomfield, *Crawdaddy*, Nov. 1966.

247 "And I'll say this": Michael Bloomfield, *Crawdaddy*, Nov. 1966.
247 "I think electric music": Michael Bloomfield, *Crawdaddy*, Nov. 1966.
248 "We played this double bill": Al Kooper, author interview, 9/16/2014.
249 "The long piece we do": Michael Bloomfield, *Hit Parader*, Jan. 1967.
249 "I don't use": Michael Bloomfield, *Hit Parader*, Feb. 1967.
250 "I was performing": Michael Bloomfield, "Hendrix Remembered," *Guitar Player*, Sept. 1975.
250 "I had seen him": Michael Bloomfield, interview with Tom Yates, 2/13/1981.
251 "I walked in there": Michael Bloomfield, interview with Tom Yates, 2/13/1981.
251 "Then he started": Michael Bloomfield, interview with Tom Yates, 2/13/1981.
252 "He got right in my face": Michael Bloomfield, "Hendrix Remembered," *Guitar Player*, Sept. 1975.
252 "That's because it was late": Mark Naftalin, email to the author, 6/1/2015.
254 "Produces long, exciting": Ralph J. Gleason, *Hit Parader*, Oct. 1966.
255 "The day Michael came in": Barry Goldberg, *Two Jews Blues*, St. Paul Books, 2012.
255 "Michael was used to playing": Barry Goldberg, *Two Jews Blues*, St. Paul Books, 2012.
256 "I have a story": Jon Hendricks, lyrics from *Evolution of the Blues Song*, Columbia LP, 1961.
257 Leonard Feather's critical review of electric bands at the Monterey Jazz Festival came from the *Los Angeles Times*, 9/19/1966.
257 Jimmy Lyons's comments on the Butterfield Band came from *Duke, Dizzy, the Count and Me*, California Living Books, 1978.
257 "The Butterfield group includes": Whitney Balliet, *New Yorker*, 10/1/1966.
260–262 The Butterfield Band's set list for the Fillmore's Blues-Rock Bash II was taken from Fillmore soundboard recordings of the band from 9/30/1966 and 10/14/1966.
260 Bloomfield and Elvin Bishop as dueling guitar players came from Bill Keenom's interview with ED Denson, 1996.
261 Description of Bloomfield's fire-eating stunt came from ED Denson's review of the show, *Berkeley Barb*, 3/1/1966.
261 "If you can imagine": Elvin Bishop, interview with Bill Keenom, 1996.
263 "He was setting a mood": Mark Naftalin, author interview, 4/2/2013.
263 "There was a certain amount": Mark Naftalin, author interview, 4/2/2013.
264 "I loved the ambience": Michael Bloomfield, interview with Walter Rimler, summer 1975.

CHAPTER 13: BLUES TO BRITAIN

The Butterfield Band's flight to London was described to me in emails from Mark Naftalin. Information about the band's British tour came from Bill Keenom's interviews with Elvin Bishop and Billy Davenport; from my interviews and emails with Mark Naftalin; from reviews and interviews in *Melody Maker*; from *The Ultimate Complete Michael Bloomfield Discography*; from *Jimi Hendrix: The Ultimate Experience* and *Strange Brew: Eric Clapton and The British Blues Boom 1965–1970*; from the Radio London tour program; and from newspaper reviews, interviews, ads, and audience members' emails to me. Bloomfield's realization that he was a star came from Walter Rimler's interview with him; the review that prompted that awareness appeared in *Crawdaddy*. Information about the Butterfield Band's concert at Town Hall came from reviews in the *New York Times* and *Billboard*, and from photos of the show. My description of *The Songmakers* TV program came from newspaper reviews and TV listings, from my emails with Mark Naftalin, from Bill Keenom's interview with Billy Davenport, and from a clip of the band's segment sent to me by Bob Sarles. Information regarding Bloomfield's guest appearance with the Jefferson Airplane in New York came from photos of the event and from an audience recording. My description of Bloomfield's desire to leave the Butterfield Band came from his interviews in *Rolling Stone*, *Guitar Player*, *GQ Scene,* and *Hit Parader*; from Dan McClosky's, Walter Rimler's, and Tom Yates's interviews with him; and from my interviews with Mark Naftalin. My description of Bloomfield's final gigs with the Butterfield Band came from newspaper ads and listings, from emails from producer Peter Casperson and audience member Frank Richards, from Bill Keenom's interviews with Kathryn Butterfield and Billy Davenport, and from my interviews with Mark Naftalin.

265, 266 Description of the Butterfield Band's flight to London came from Mark Naftalin, emails to the author, 7/30/2015.

266 "I've spent the day": Michael Bloomfield, *Melody Maker*, 10/2/1966.

267 "Eric Clapton, he's one": Michael Bloomfield, *Melody Maker*, 10/2/1966.

267 "You've got to see": Michael Bloomfield, *Melody Maker*, 10/2/1966.

268 "His way of thinking": Eric Clapton, *Rolling Stone*, 5/11/1968.

269 "I knew that he couldn't": Michael Bloomfield, interview with Tom Yates, 2/13/1981.

270 "He loved that guitar": John Sebastian, comment to the author, 10/4/2014.

270 "We didn't have": Billy Davenport, interview with Bill Keenom, 1995.

271 Jimi Hendrix's presence at the Butterfield Band's first British tour performance came from *Jimi Hendrix: The Ultimate Experience*, Thunder's Mouth Press, 1999.

271 "I don't think we were": Elvin Bishop, interview with Bill Keenom, 1995.

274 "I think that anybody": Michael Bloomfield, *Melody Maker*, 10/29/1966.

274 "There's a lot of work": Michael Bloomfield, *Melody Maker*, 10/29/1966.

275 "Clapton's guitar work": *Disc*, 11/14/1966.

276 "Brian was obsessed": Marianne Faithfull, *Faithfull: An Autobiography*, Cooper Square Press, 2000.

276 "You have ears": Michael Bloomfield, *International Times*, 11/14/1966.

276 "We don't really know": Michael Bloomfield, *International Times*, 11/14/1966.

277 "We still play blues": Michael Bloomfield, *International Times*, 11/14/1966.

277 "Depends on the individuals": Michael Bloomfield, *International Times*, 11/14/1966.

278 "The place was": Mark Naftalin, email to the author, 6/3/2015.

278–279 Description of Eel Pie Island came from the story "From a British King to Rock 'n' Roll: The Slippery History of Eel Pie Island," npr.org, 2012.

279 "The place was memorable": Mark Naftalin, email to the author, 6/3/2015.

280 "I always knew": Michael Bloomfield, interview with Walter Rimler, summer 1975.

281 "Mike Bloomfield is": Jon Landau, *Crawdaddy*, Nov. 1966.

281 "His technique": Jon Landau, *Crawdaddy*, Nov. 1966.

282 "The Paul Butterfield Blues Band blasted": *New York Times*, 11/28/1966.

283 "Mike Bloomfield's wild": *New York Times*, 11/28/1966.
283 "'East-West,' the title tune": *Billboard*, 12/10/1966.
284 "The power went out": Mark Naftalin, email to the author, 6/3/2015.
285 Description of the Charles Lloyd Quartet's reception at the Fillmore came from the liner notes to Lloyd's album *Love-In*, Atlantic Records, 1967.
286 "You know, for a long": Michael Brooks, "Michael Bloomfield: Straight Stone City Blues," *Guitar Player*, June 1971.
287 "Tell It Like It Is, Baby": *The Stanford Daily*, 1/30/1967.
287 "East-West" running as long as an hour came from Mark Naftalin, author interview, 6/15/2008.
288 Bribing the Butterfield Band to do two sets came from Peter Casperson, invasiongroup.com/casperson.html.
288 Bloomfield's demeanor during the Boston University appearance was described by audience member Frank Richards, email to the author, 2/20/2010.
289 "The reason I split": Michael Bloomfield, *GQ Scene*, Oct. 1967.
289 "That's where it went down": Kathryn Butterfield, interview with Bill Keenom, 1996.
289 "I was really brokenhearted": Billy Davenport, interview with Bill Keenom, 1995.
289 "I wasn't too happy": Mark Naftalin, author interview, 6/15/2008.

CHAPTER 14: HOISTING THE FLAG

My description of Bloomfield's days in New York after quitting the Butterfield Band came from Barry Goldberg's autobiography, *Two Jews Blues*; from my interviews with Norman Dayron; from Bloomfield's interviews in *Rolling Stone* and *Guitar Player*, and his interview with Dan McClosky; and from the recordings Bloomfield made with James Cotton, Eddie "Cleanhead" Vinson, and Mitch Ryder. Bloomfield's acquisition of a 1959 Les Paul Standard was described to me in email correspondence with Dan Erlewine. *Two Jews Blues* also provided me with background on Bloomfield's desire to form his own band, as did his interviews in *Rolling Stone*, *Guitar Player*, and *Hit Parader*, and Dan McClosky's interview with him. Additional information came from Bill Keenom's interview with Susan Beuhler and from *Michael Bloomfield: If You Love These Blues*. My description of the formation of the Electric Flag came from Bloomfield's *Rolling Stone*, *Guitar Player,* and *Hit Parader* interviews; from *Two Jews Blues*; from Bill Keenom's interviews with Harvey Brooks and Nick Gravenites; from Jan Mark Wolkin's interviews with Peter Strazza and Buddy Miles; and from *Michael Bloomfield: If You Love These Blues*. Information about the Flag's first days in Mill Valley came from Bloomfield's *Rolling Stone* interview; from Bill Keenom's interviews with Nick Gravenites and Susan Beuhler; from my interviews with Norman Dayron, Chris McDougal, and Denise Kaufman; from the video "A Special Tribute to Michael Bloomfield," produced by Marty Balin; and from photos provided by Norman Dayron. Information on the Flag's time in Los Angeles creating the soundtrack for *The Trip* came from Bill Keenom's interviews with Nick Gravenites, Harvey Brooks, and Chet Helms; from Jan Mark Wolkin's interview with Peter Strazza; from my interviews with Norman Dayron, Chris McDougal, and John Nuese; from selections on *The Trip* soundtrack album; from articles about the movie in the *Los Angeles Times* and the *New York Times*; and from photos of the Castle. Information about the Flag's preparations for their Monterey Pop Festival debut came from Bloomfield's interviews in *Rolling Stone* and Dan McClosky's interview with him, from my interviews with Chris McDougal and John Nuese, and from *Two Jews Blues* and *Michael Bloomfield: If You Love These Blues*.

290 "Michael told me": Dan Erlewine, email to the author, 1/5/2007.
290 "He said, 'Oh, man'": Dan Erlewine, email to the author, 1/5/2007.
291 "He had told me": Barry Goldberg, *Two Jews Blues*, St. Paul Books, 2012.
292 "Michael and Barry had just": Susan Beuhler, interview with Bill Keenom, 1996.
292 "This is an excellent album": *Boston Broadside*, vol. 6, 1967.
295 "Their relationship had been": Barry Goldberg, *Two Jews Blues*, St. Paul Books, 2012.
295 "My curiosity about heroin": Barry Goldberg, *Two Jews Blues*, St. Paul Books, 2012.
296 "We walked into this theater": Barry Goldberg, *Michael Bloomfield: If You Love These Blues*, Miller Freeman Books, 2000.
297 "Buddy sang great!": Michael Bloomfield, interview with Dan McClosky, 5/17/1971.
297 "Michael called me": Nick Gravenites, interview with Bill Keenom, 1996.
298 "We smoked a few joints": Chris McDougal, author interview, 9/14/2013.
299 "The band had just formed": Michael Bloomfield, interview with Walter Rimler, summer 1975.
300 Albert Grossman's insistence that every band member sign their publishing over to him came from Nick Gravenites, *Michael Bloomfield: If You Love These Blues*, Miller Freeman Books, 2000.
300 "It was a crazy place": Nick Gravenites, interview with Bill Keenom, 1996.
300 "It was almost like": Barry Goldberg, *Two Jews Blues*, St. Paul Books, 2012.
301 "We all moved into": Nick Gravenites, interview with Bill Keenom, 1996.
301 "I remember there was": Norman Dayron, author interview, 7/7/2007.
301–302 Bloomfield's meeting with Roger Corman was described by Nick Gravenites, interview with Bill Keenom, 1996.
302 "I hung out with Michael": John Nuese, author interview, 1/10/2010.
302 "Mike had them project": Chris McDougal, author interview, 9/14/2013.
303 "He was a really serious": Norman Dayron, author interview, 7/7/2007.
303 Description of Paul Beaver's Moog demonstration at the 1967 Audio Engineering Society convention came from *Electronic and Experimental Music: Technology, Music, and Culture*, Routledge, 2012.
303 "Everybody was talking": Norman Dayron, author interview, 7/7/2007.
304 "We'd work at night": Chris McDougal, author interview, 9/14/2013.
305, 306 Bloomfield meeting Bobby Notkoff through John Nuese came from John Nuese, author interview, 1/10/2010.
306 "It was a regular violin": Norman Dayron, author interview, 7/7/2007.
306 Bloomfield watching footage from *The Trip* six times while creating the soundtrack came from Peter Fonda's interview in the *Los Angeles Times*, Sept. 1967.
307 "The music I think": Roger Corman, commentary on *The Trip*, MGM DVD, 2003.
307 "The group covered": Peter Fonda, interview in the *Los Angeles Times*, Sept. 1967.
307 "People wanted to be": Nick Gravenites, interview with Bill Keenom, 1996.
307 "There were a lot": Chris McDougal, author interview, 9/14/2013.

307 "We had all kinds": Norman Dayron, author interview, 7/7/2007.
308 "Mike's shooting junk": Nick Gravenites, interview with Bill Keenom, 1996.
308 "I didn't realize": Harvey Brooks, interview with Bill Keenom, 1996.
308 "It was a crazy scene": John Nuese, author interview, 1/10/2010.
308 "The trip that we were on": Norman Dayron, author interview, 7/7/2007.
309 "Each day I would drive": Chris McDougal, author interview, 9/14/2013.
310 "We worked out": Michael Bloomfield, interview with Dan McClosky, 5/17/1971.
310 "Groovin' was the thing": Michael Bloomfield, *Rolling Stone*, 4/6/1968.
311 "I saw a different side": Barry Goldberg, *Two Jews Blues*, St. Paul Books, 2012.

CHAPTER 15: MUSIC, LOVE, AND FLOWERS

The scene at the Monterey International Pop Festival was described to me by Norman Dayron, Al Kooper, and Chris McDougal. Information on the three-day festival came from *A Perfect Haze: The Illustrated History of the Monterey International Pop Festival* and *Monterey Pop, June 16–18, 1967*; from *The Complete Monterey Pop Festival: The Criterion Collection* DVD set and additional footage of the Flag's performance shared with me by Toby Byron; and from photos by Jim Marshall, Henry Diltz, Elaine Mayes, and many others. My depiction of the Electric Flag's appearance came from Bloomfield's interviews in *Rolling Stone* and *Guitar Player*, and Dan McClosky's interview with him; from selections of their set on *Old Glory: The Best of the Electric Flag* CD; from *Two Jews Blues*; from Bill Keenom's interviews with Barry Goldberg, Susan Beuhler, and ED Denson; from Jan Mark Wolkin's interview with Peter Strazza; from Harvey Brooks's interview in *20th Century Guitar*; and from *Michael Bloomfield: If You Love These Blues*. Information on the Flag's signing with Columbia came from Clive Davis's autobiography *The Soundtrack of My Life*. My re-creation of Jimi Hendrix's Monterey appearance came from *Jimi Hendrix: The Ultimate Experience* in addition to the sources mentioned above. Reviews of the festival came from *Esquire*, *Newsweek*, and *Down Beat*.

314 "I got on a plane": Norman Dayron, author interview, 7/7/2007.
315 Possible name for the Electric Flag came from the *Berkeley Barb*, 5/19/1967.
315 "The reason we chose": Barry Goldberg, *Two Jews Blues*, St. Paul Books, 2012.
316 "I would set it up": Chris McDougal, author interview, 9/14/2013.
316 "Ravi Shankar was": Susan Beuhler, interview with Bill Keenom, 1996.
317 "I went to Mike's motel": Norman Dayron, author interview, 7/7/2007.
317 "Everyone was talking": Norman Dayron, author interview, 7/7/2007.
319 Description of Bloomfield's motel room rehearsal of the Electric Flag came from Norman Dayron, author interview, 7/7/2007.
320 "Everybody would come by": Norman Dayron, author interview, 7/7/2007.
321 "I didn't even sleep": Harvey Brooks, *20th Century Guitar*, Sept./Oct. 1994.
322 "I had seen Hendrix": Al Kooper, author interview, 9/16/2014.
323 "Michael and I were": Harvey Brooks, *20th Century Guitar*, Sept./Oct. 1994.
324 "I was jacked up": Michael Bloomfield, interview with Dan McClosky, 5/17/1971.
325 "You're going to hear": David Crosby, audio clip from Monterey Pop Festival, 6/17/1967.
326 "Mama Cass glanced": *Go-Set* (Australian magazine), 7/12/1967.

327 "When we'd play": Peter Strazza, interview with Jan Mark Wolkin, 1996.

327 "Man, we're really nervous": Michael Bloomfield, audio clip from Monterey Pop Festival, 6/17/1967.

327 "We were pumped": Harvey Brooks, *Bass Musician*, 3/20/2011.

327 "I remember Bloomfield": ED Denson, interview with Bill Keenom, 1996.

328 "And now, listen": Michael Bloomfield, audio clip from Monterey Pop Festival, 6/17/1967.

329 "It was a total get-off!": Buddy Miles, interview with Michael Buffalo Smith, swampland.com, Feb. 2006.

331 "We were all nervous": Buddy Miles, *Michael Bloomfield: If You Love These Blues*, Miller Freeman Books, 2000.

331 "It wasn't one": Barry Goldberg, interview with Bill Keenom, 1996.

332 "Everybody was talking": Norman Dayron, author interview, 7/7/2007.

332 "They were the Electric Flag": *World Countdown*, 7/19/1967.

332 "I think he was": Norman Dayron, author interview, 7/7/2007.

333 "The musicians that are playing": Michael Bloomfield, audio clip from Monterey Pop Festival, 6/17/1967.

334 "Man, if you didn't hear": David Crosby, audio clip from Monterey Pop Festival, 6/17/1967.

335 "We were standing": Peter Strazza, interview with Jan Mark Wolkin, 1996.

336 "The Electric Flag hit": Clive Davis, *The Soundtrack of My Life*, Simon & Schuster, 2013.

337 "He went on": Pete Townshend, *Jimi Hendrix: The Ultimate Experience*, Thunder's Mouth Press, 1999.

337 "Jimi said, 'If'": Pete Townshend, *Jimi Hendrix: The Ultimate Experience*, Thunder's Mouth Press, 1999.

338–342 Descriptions of performances by the Who and Jimi Hendrix are based on *The Complete Monterey Pop Festival: The Criterion Collection* DVD set, 2017.

343 Robert Christgau's comments on Hendrix's set came from "Anatomy of a Love Festival," *Esquire*, Jan. 1968.

343 Michael Lydon's comments on Hendrix's set originally came from *Newsweek*, reprinted in *Flashbacks: Eyewitness Accounts of the Rock Revolution, 1964–1974*, Routledge, 2003.

343 "This was the American debut": Barry Hansen, *Down Beat*, 8/10/1967.

CHAPTER 16: GROOVIN' IS EASY

Details of the Electric Flag's contract with Columbia Records came from documents supplied to me by Bruce Dickinson. Columbia's interest in the new pop music was described in Clive Davis's autobiography *The Soundtrack of My Life* and in *The Label: The Story of Columbia Records*. Information on the Flag's first recording sessions came from Bloomfield's interviews in *Rolling Stone* and Dan McClosky's interview with him; from my interview with Chris McDougal; and from master takes on *A Long Time Comin'*, the band's Columbia LP, and alternate takes on *Old Glory: The Best of the Electric Flag*, a Columbia CD. The band's drug use was described in *Two Jews Blues*; in Bill Keenom's interviews with Nick Gravenites and Harvey Brooks; and in my interview with Chris McDougal. Data on the Flag's Fillmore shows came from the website chickenonaunicycle.com. Information about their canceled

Hollywood Bowl concert came from Bloomfield's interview with the *Los Angeles Free Press*, from my interview with Chris McDougal, and from John Phillips's *Papa John: An Autobiography*. My description of the Flag's Fillmore appearance with Cream came from Bloomfield's interview in *GQ Scene*, from Bill Keenom's interview with Barry Goldberg, and from Jan Mark Wolkin's interview with Peter Strazza. Information on heroin use by band members came from Jan Mark Wolkin's interview with Peter Strazza, from my interview with Chris McDougal, from Bill Keenom's interview with Nick Gravenites, and from *Michael Bloomfield: If You Love These Blues*. Bloomfield's efforts in the recording studio were described in Tom Yates's interview with him. Information about the sessions also came from *Two Jews Blues* and my interview with Chris McDougal. Master takes on *A Long Time Comin'* and alternate takes on *Old Glory: The Best of the Electric Flag* provided the basis for my analysis of the recording process. Selections recorded by the band at the Whisky a Go Go were provided to me by Norman Dayron. Bloomfield's critique of white audiences came from his interview in the *Los Angeles Free Press*. Reviews of the Flag's soundtrack for *The Trip* came from *Billboard*, *Hullabaloo*, *Teenset*, and *Hit Parader*. The description of band members' arrests on drug charges came from my interview with Chris McDougal, from comments by Nick Gravenites and Barry Goldberg in *Rolling Stone* from *Two Jews Blues*, and from the Huntington Beach police report. The schedule for the Flag's first tour came from newspaper reviews and ads; my re-creation of the band's performance at the Psychedelic Supermarket came from a recording from one night of the gig. Bloomfield's visit with J. Geils came from *Michael Bloomfield: If You Love These Blues*. Bloomfield's growing paranoia was taken from his interviews in *Vibrations* and the *Boston Broadside*.

347 Details of the Electric Flag's recording contract with Columbia Records came from Artist Contract Cards supplied to the author by Bruce Dickinson.

348 Bloomfield's opinion of John Court came from Bloomfield's interview in *Rolling Stone*, 4/6/1968.

348 "One day this guy showed up": Chris McDougal, author interview, 9/14/2013.

349 "One night at Wellesley Court": Chris McDougal, author interview, 9/14/2013.

349 "It turned out": Chris McDougal, author interview, 9/14/2013.

349 Description of Owsley's providing the band with drugs came from Barry Goldberg, *Two Jews Blues*, St. Paul Books, 2012.

350 Bill Graham's dislike of the Electric Flag came from Graham, interview with Bob Sarles, ca. 1985, provided by Bill Keenom.

350 "Blues is a language": Michael Bloomfield, *GQ Scene*, Winter 1967.

352 "We were all ready": Barry Goldberg, interview with Bill Keenom, 1996.

352 "Everybody wanted to do it": Peter Strazza, interview with Jan Mark Wolkin, 1996.

352 "He made a speech": Barry Goldberg, interview with Bill Keenom, 1996.

352 "When Eric plays": Michael Bloomfield, *GQ Scene*, Winter 1967.

353 "Buddy, Nick, Harvey, and myself": Chris McDougal, author interview, 9/14/2013.

353 "There were a lot of hard drugs": Nick Gravenites, *Michael Bloomfield: If You Love These Blues*, Miller Freeman Books, 2000.

354 "It was a real problem": Peter Strazza, interview with Jan Mark Wolkin, 1996.

354 Bloomfield's interest in producers like Phil Spector and Dave Hassinger was described in Tom Yates's interview with him, 2/13/1981.

356 "Nice, romantic feel": Barry Goldberg, *Two Jews Blues*, St. Paul Books, 2012.

357 "You know what I'd really like": Michael Bloomfield, "Honkies Can't Dig Soul Music," *Los Angeles Free Press*, 9/22/1967 (this interview was split between the *Los Angeles Free Press* and *GQ Scene*).

357–358 "White people just don't know": Michael Bloomfield, "Honkies Can't Dig Soul Music," *Los Angeles Free Press*, 9/22/1967.

358 "Musicians have to satisfy": Michael Bloomfield, *GQ Scene*, Winter 1967.

358 "Right in the music thing": Michael Bloomfield, "Honkies Can't Dig Soul Music," *Los Angeles Free Press*, 9/22/1967.

360 "Managed to capture": *Billboard*, 9/16/1967.

360 "'The Trip' is one of the best": *Hullabaloo*, Nov. 1967.

360 "This is not just a collection": *Teenset*, Fall 1967.

360 "'The Trip' is a movie": Penny Baker, "The In Beat," King Features Syndicate, 9/16/1967.

360 "On 'The Trip' album": Michael Bloomfield, *Hit Parader*, Apr. 1968.

360 "The Flag really tore": Chris McDougal, author interview, 9/14/2013.

361, 362 Description of the Flag's drug bust came from a Huntington Beach police report, 10/1/1967.

361 "Barry would leave needles": Chris McDougal, author interview, 9/14/2013.

362 "We're in the hands": Nick Gravenites, *Rolling Stone*, 11/9/1967.

362 "I took the rap": Barry Goldberg, *Rolling Stone*, 2/14/1974.

363 "You should want": Michael Bloomfield, *The Crusader*, Holy Cross College, 11/2/1967.

363 "You know what really put": Michael Bloomfield, *Rolling Stone*, 4/27/1968.

363 "From the perspective of one": *The Heights*, Boston College, Nov. 1967.

366 "We went to a radio station": Peter Strazza, interview with Jan Mark Wolkin, 1996.

367 "Mike was completely freaked out": J. Geils, *Michael Bloomfield: If You Love These Blues*, Miller Freeman Books, 2000.

367 "We went down there": J. Geils, *Michael Bloomfield: If You Love These Blues*, Miller Freeman Books, 2000.

367 "[Audiences here], a lot": Michael Bloomfield, *Vibrations*, Dec. 1967.

368 "I've appeared here": Michael Bloomfield, *Boston Broadside*, Dec. 1967.

368 "Yes and no": Michael Bloomfield, *Vibrations*, Dec. 1967.

CHAPTER 17: ANOTHER COUNTRY

My description of the Electric Flag's New York debut came from my interview with Chris McDougal; from newspaper articles, reviews, and ads; from Don Paulsen's photos; from Ira Schneider's film footage of their opening night; and from audience members' emails to me. Barry Goldberg's departure from the band was described in *Two Jews Blues*, in his interview with Bill Keenom, and in *Michael Bloomfield: If You Love These Blues*. Information about *You Are What You Eat* came from my interviews with Peter Yarrow and John Simon. The circumstances behind Michael Fonfara's joining the band came from my email correspondence with Nick Warburton and from my interview with Prakash John. A description of Bloomfield's studio cost overruns came from my interview with Chris McDougal. Bloomfield's marital troubles were described in Dan McClosky's interview with him and by Barry

Goldberg in *Two Jews Blues*. My re-creation of the Flag's Fillmore gig opening for B. B. King came from newspaper articles and from recordings of one of the band's shows. Information regarding Michael Fonfara's departure from the Flag came from researcher Nick Warburton. The dissolution of Bloomfield's marriage was described by Susan Beuhler in Bill Keenom's interviews with her and in *Michael Bloomfield: If You Love These Blues*. My description of the Flag's final New York recording sessions came from Tom Yates's interview with Bloomfield; from Bill Keenom's interviews with Nick Gravenites; from Harvey Brooks's interviews in various publications; and from the Flag's Columbia Recording Cards, provided to me by Bruce Dickinson. Master takes on *A Long Time Comin'* and alternate takes on *Old Glory: The Best of the Electric Flag* provided the basis for my analysis of the recording process and for my examination of the sound collage on "Another Country." Norman Dayron provided me with insight into the collage. Bloomfield described his collaboration with engineer Roy Segal in Tom Yates's interview with him. Albert Grossman's urging Bloomfield to hire an attractive singer for the Flag was described to me by Chris McDougal. My description of the band's appearance with Jimi Hendrix at the Shrine Auditorium came from audience member Dave Pearson and from *Jimi Hendrix: The Ultimate Experience*. Bloomfield's *Rolling Stone* interview was described by Jann Wenner in Bill Keenom's interview with Wenner and by photos taken by Baron Wohlman. The Flag's appearance at the Anderson Theater in New York was reviewed in the *New York Times*, and Al Kooper described to me his and Bloomfield's participation with members of Moby Grape in a session that resulted in *Grape Jam*.

369 "Blues Week" in New York was described in the *Bucks County Courier*, 12/14/1967.

370 "Michael wanted to get": Chris McDougal, author interview, 9/14/2013.

370 "When Mr. Bloomfield performs": *New York Times*, 11/24/1967.

371 Drug dealers in the Hotel Chelsea were described by Bloomfield in *High Times*, June 1983.

371 "The word's been out": *The Statesman*, Stony Brook University, 12/12/1967.

372 "I've heard Barry Goldberg": *The Statesman*, Stony Brook University, 12/12/1967.

372 "I called Michael": Barry Goldberg, *Two Jews Blues*, St. Paul Books, 2012.

373 "Michael had been given": Chris McDougal, author interview, 9/14/2013.

374 "Michael seemed to feel": Barry Goldberg, *Two Jews Blues*, St. Paul Books, 2012.

374 "During the Flag": Michael Bloomfield, interview with Dan McClosky, 5/17/1971.

374 B. B. King was described as the "the last word" by Michael Bloomfield, *Rolling Stone*, 4/6/1968.

374 "I was scared": B. B. King, *Deseret News*, 8/30/1984.

376 "Bill used to call me": Chris McDougal, author interview, 9/14/2013.

377 "We had a long, tearful talk": Susan Beuhler, *Michael Bloomfield: If You Love These Blues*, Miller Freeman Books, 2000.

378 "Susan was Mike's great love": Chris McDougal, author interview, 9/14/2013.

379 "On 'Killing Floor,'": Harvey Brooks, blues.gr, 7/31/2013.

382 "I was real lucky": Michael Bloomfield, interview with Tom Yates, 2/13/1981.

383 "When we were recording": Harvey Brooks, blues.gr, 7/31/2013.

383 "Maybe something by": Norman Dayron, author interview, 10/28/2011.

387 "We're seven dedicated musicians": Michael Bloomfield, interview with Kurt Lassen, Columbia Features, 1/25/1968.

389 Debbie Danilow's refusal to join the Electric Flag came from debbiedanilow.com.

389 "He was firing": Harvey Brooks, interview with Bill Keenom, 1996.

390 "Jimi Hendrix was headlining": Dave Pearson, email to the author, 3/30/2008.

390 "We were backstage": Michael Bloomfield, *Jimi Hendrix: The Ultimate Experience*, Thunder's Mouth Press, 1999.

391 "We were young guys": Dave Pearson, email to the author, 3/30/2008.

391 "Their sound was": Dave Pearson, email to the author, 3/30/2008.

392 "At that time I was": Jann Wenner, interview with Bill Keenom, 1996.

393 "The seven-man soul": Robert Shelton, *New York Times*, 2/24/1968.

393 Decision that Nick Gravenites would no longer tour with the Flag came from the *Chicago Tribune*, 7/18/1968.

394 Description of the Moby Grape jam session came from Al Kooper, author interview, 9/16/2014.

CHAPTER 18: SHUCKS AND SESSIONS

The Electric Flag's week in Philadelphia was described to me in emails from Paul Lerman. Information about Bloomfield's appearance on Murray the K's radio show came from listener Peter Stone Brown. The actual release date for *A Long Time Comin'* came from Columbia Recording Cards provided to me by Bruce Dickinson. Data on the Flag's Cafe Au Go Go shows came from a review in the *New York Free Press*. Buddy Miles's dominance of the band was described by Bloomfield in his *Rolling Stone* interview, by Nick Gravenites in Bill Keenom's interviews with him, and by Buddy Miles in Jan Mark Wolkin's interview with him. My description of the Flag's ongoing drug problems came from the band's interview in *Charlie*, from Nick Gravenites's comments in the Mill Valley Film Festival's "A Special Tribute to Michael Bloomfield," and from Bill Keenom's interview with Harvey Brooks. Information regarding the armed robbery of Flag members came from an article in *Go Magazine* and from *The Mansion on the Hill*. Albert Grossman's firing of the band's horn section and their subsequent rehiring was described by Peter Strazza in Jan Mark Wolkin's interview with him. Critical reviews of *A Long Time Comin'* came from *Billboard*, the *Washington Post*, the *New York Times*, the *Chicago Tribune,* and other newspapers as well as *Rolling Stone*. Bloomfield's life story, his observations about music, and many other opinions came from his *Rolling Stone* interview. I discovered Bloomfield's extraordinary performance of "It's About Time" among dubs of his personal recordings sent to me in digitized form by Bob Andres. Excerpts from Ralph J. Gleason's column critical of Bloomfield came from *Rolling Stone*, as did quotes from Nick Gravenites's column in reply. Bloomfield's reaction to Gleason's broadside was shared with me by Chris McDougal. My description of the Flag's appearance at the Northern California Folk-Rock Festival came from comments by audience members, from film clips of the festival, from an audience recording, and from photos by Jim Marshall and others of the band in performance. Al Kooper told me about his *Super Session* project and Bloomfield's participation in it. Additional information came from his interview in *20th Century Guitar*; from Bill Keenom's interviews with Barry Goldberg and Mick Weiser; from Michael Bloomfield's interview in *Guitar Player*; from the master takes on *Super Session*, the original Columbia LP, and alternate takes on the remastered Columbia CD; and from photos of the session by Jim Marshall. My surmise that Bloomfield suffered a panic attack following Kooper's recording session was based in part on information in *The American Psychiatric Publishing Textbook of Anxiety Disorders*. My description of Bloomfield's last gig with the

Flag at the Fillmore East came from reviews in the *New York Times* and *Cashbox*, and from comments posted by an audience member.

395 Bloomfield's appearance on Murray the K's radio show came from listener Peter Stone Brown, email to the author, 12/15/2013.
396 "At the Flag's debut": *New York Free Press*, 3/14/1968.
396 "The Electric Flag seems": *New York Free Press*, 3/14/1968.
396 "Buddy Miles sang": *New York Free Press*, 3/14/1968.
397 "The band sort of fell": Michael Bloomfield, *Rolling Stone*, 4/6/1968.
397 "If you're a lead singer": Buddy Miles, interview with Jan Mark Wolkin, 1996.
398 All band quotes from the Electric Flag interview in *Charlie*, May 1968.
399 "Half the band was junked out": Nick Gravenites, "A Special Tribute to Michael Bloomfield," Mill Valley Film Festival video, 1983.
399 "The problem in the band": Harvey Brooks, interview with Bill Keenom, 1996.
399 "It had to do": Harvey Brooks, interview with Bill Keenom, 1996.
400 "Pop musician Peter Strazza": *Go Magazine*, 3/22/1968.
400 "The group consists of": *Billboard*, 3/30/1968.
401 "The Flag's first album" *Washington Post*, 3/5/1968.
401 "Another article would be": *Chicago Tribune*, 3/18/1968.
401 "It should have been": *Los Angeles Times*, 5/5/1968.
401 "Rock and blues musicians": *New York Times*, 4/7/1968.
402 "The album is not": *Rolling Stone*, 5/11/1968.
402 "The last fifty seconds": *Rolling Stone*, 5/11/1968.
403 "For some reason": Peter Strazza, interview with Jan Mark Wolkin, 1996.
404 "They got rid": Peter Strazza, interview with Jan Mark Wolkin, 1996.
404 "It was like anarchy": Harvey Brooks, interview with Bill Keenom, 1996.
404 "If you're gonna lead": Michael Bloomfield, interview with Dan McClosky, 5/17/1971.
406–407 All quotes are by Michael Bloomfield, *Rolling Stone*, 4/6/1968.
407 "Left a dazzled audience": *San Mateo Times*, 4/29/1968.
407 Description of Eric Clapton visiting Bloomfield backstage at the Cheetah came from *Strange Brew: Eric Clapton and the British Blues Boom*, Outline Press, 2007.
408–410 Description of "It's About Time" came from a recording originally in Bloomfield's personal collection, sent by Bob Andre, 3/16/2009.
410 Bloomfield's influence on Eric Clapton came from Clapton's interview in *Rolling Stone*, 5/11/1968.
411 All quotes from Ralph J. Gleason, "Stop This Shuck, Mike Bloomfield," *Rolling Stone*, 5/11/1968.
412, 413 Information about Ralph J. Gleason's early days as a jazz critic came from *Jazz Information*, 1939–1940.
413 Nick Gravenites's response to Gleason's column came from *Rolling Stone*, 5/25/1968.
413 "It's Buddy Miles' Electric Flag": Ralph J. Gleason, "Stop This Shuck, Mike Bloomfield," *Rolling Stone*, 5/11/1968.
415 "He bounces around": *Los Angeles Times*, 5/27/1968.
416 "I was sitting": Al Kooper, author interview, 9/16/2014.

416 "I didn't want": Michael Brooks, "Michael Bloomfield: Straight Stone City Blues," *Guitar Player*, June 1971.
416 "He said he wanted": Al Kooper, *20th Century Guitar*, Sept./Oct. 1994.
417 Information about Eddie Hoh came from Bill Keenom's interview with Mick Weiser, 1995.
417 "Michael came to LA": Barry Goldberg, interview with Bill Keenom, 1995.
417, 418 Information on Robby and the Troubadours came from Bill Keenom's interview with Mick Weiser, 1995; Mike Medina, emails to the author, 3/4/2015.
418 "He arrived with": Al Kooper, author interview, 9/16/2014.
418–427 Details about the *Super Session* recording date came from the Al Kooper, author interview, 9/16/2014; photos of the session by Jim Marshall.
419 "While we were playing": Al Kooper, author interview, 9/16/2014.
420 "Jim would get": Al Kooper, author interview, 9/16/2014.
421 "I think he didn't": Al Kooper, author interview, 9/16/2014.
421 "Columbia had a very": Al Kooper, author interview, 9/16/2014.
422 "'Man's Temptation'—that": Al Kooper, author interview, 9/16/2014.
422 "While Michael, Harvey, and Eddie": Barry Goldberg, *Two Jews Blues*, St. Paul Books, 2012.
422 "Michael was one": Al Kooper, author interview, 9/16/2014.
422 "There was an Ondioline": Al Kooper, author interview, 9/16/2014.
424 "I had to BS": Al Kooper, author interview, 9/16/2014.
425 "The tune worked": Al Kooper, author interview, 9/16/2014.
427 "Some girl was calling": Al Kooper, author interview, 9/16/2014.
427 "I wasn't going": Al Kooper, author interview, 9/16/2014.
427 "Stills was the only one": Al Kooper, author interview, 9/16/2014.
428 "I have insomnia": Michael Brooks, "Michael Bloomfield: Straight Stone City Blues," *Guitar Player*, June 1971.
428 "I think he just couldn't": Al Kooper, interview with Bill Keenom, 1995.
428 "I had just finished": Michael Brooks, "Michael Bloomfield: Straight Stone City Blues," *Guitar Player*, June 1971.
429 "Michael didn't want": Buddy Miles, *Michael Bloomfield: If You Love These Blues*, Miller Freeman Books, 2000.
429 "Buddy was a success-oriented guy": Nick Gravenites, *Michael Bloomfield: If You Love These Blues*, Miller Freeman Books, 2000.
429 "Mike started drifting": Peter Strazza, interview with Jan Mark Wolkin, 1996.
429 "Mike Bloomfield, who organized": *New York Times*, 6/10/1968.
430 "Mike came out onstage": comment by audience member, thegearpage.net.
430 "The major attraction": *Cash Box*, 6/22/1968.

CHAPTER 19: ENTERTAINER NO MORE

My description of Bloomfield's departure from the Electric Flag and his attitude toward the music industry came from Dan McClosky's, Walter Rimler's, and Tom Yates's interviews with him; from his interviews in *The Chicago Seed* and *Guitar Player*; from *Michael Bloomfield: If You Love These Blues*; and from various newspaper reports. Miles Davis's praise for the Flag and "Over-Lovin' You" came from *Down Beat*. The production of *Super Session* and the record's unexpected success was described to me by Al Kooper. Additional information came from Kooper's autobiography, *Backstage Passes and Backstabbing Bastards: Memoirs of a Rock 'n' Roll Survivor*; from *Billboard*; and from newspaper ads. Bloomfield's retreat to Lagunitas was described in my interviews with Allen Bloomfield and Paul Lerman. Information on his stay there also came from Bill Keenom's interviews with Allen Bloomfield and Susan Beuhler. Al Kooper told me about arranging the Super Session gig at the Fillmore West and another at the Fillmore East; additional information came from *Backstage Passes and Backstabbing Bastards: Memoirs of a Rock 'n' Roll Survivor*, from the liner notes to *The Live Adventures of Michael Bloomfield and Al Kooper*, from Tom Yates's interview of Bloomfield and his interview in *Guitar Player*, from Bill Keenom's interview with Susan Beuhler, and from audience member Brent Pellegrini.

434 "Basically, Buddy wanted": Nick Gravenites, *Chicago Seed*, Nov. 1968.

435 "There's things about": Michael Bloomfield, *Chicago Seed*, July 1968.

435 "I also know": Michael Bloomfield, *Chicago Seed*, July 1968.

437 "He's a good man": Michael Bloomfield, *Chicago Seed*, July 1968.

437 "The scrotum of the Lord": Michael Bloomfield, *Chicago Seed*, July 1968.

438 "I think there is": Michael Bloomfield, the *Chicago Seed*, July 1968.

438 "We came down": Michael Bloomfield, *Chicago Seed*, July 1968.

439 "It's a pleasure": Miles Davis, *Down Beat*, 6/27/1968.

441 "We were in": Al Kooper, author interview, 9/16/2014.

441 "I was back in L.A.": Al Kooper, *Backstage Passes and Backstabbing Bastards: Memoirs of a Rock 'n' Roll Survivor*, Backbeat Books, 1998.

441 "I never dreamed": Al Kooper, author interview, 9/16/2014.

443 "I came to New York": Allen Bloomfield, interview with Bill Keenom, 1995.

443 "He was pretty much goofin'": Allen Bloomfield, interview with Bill Keenom, 1995.

444 "Michael's wife, Susan": Allen Bloomfield, interview with Bill Keenom, 1995.

444 "He found himself": Allen Bloomfield, interview with Bill Keenom, 1995.

445 "It turned out": Allen Bloomfield, interview with Bill Keenom, 1995.

445 "Grandma Phyllis fainted": Allen Bloomfield, interview with Bill Keenom, 1995.

445 "I got a bad case": Al Kooper, *Backstage Passes and Backstabbing Bastards: Memoirs of a Rock 'n' Roll Survivor*, Backbeat Books, 1998.

446 "I figured on ten days": Al Kooper, *Backstage Passes and Backstabbing Bastards: Memoirs of a Rock 'n' Roll Survivor*, Backbeat Books, 1998.

446 "I don't dig gigging": Michael Bloomfield, *Guitar Player*, June 1971.

447 "Albert tried to sue": Chris McDougal, author interview, 9/14/2013.

447 "I never feel": Michael Bloomfield, *Guitar Player*, June 1971.

447 "I had played": Al Kooper, author interview, 9/16/2014.

447 "I had stage fright": Michael Bloomfield, interview with Tom Yates, 2/13/1981.

448 Bloomfield's restlessness backstage came from *Backstage Passes and Backstabbing Bastards: Memoirs of a Rock 'n' Roll Survivor*, Backbeat Books, 1998.

449–455 Tune descriptions were taken from selections on *The Live Adventures of Michael Bloomfield and Al Kooper*, Columbia LP, 1969.

449 "Uh, listen here": Michael Bloomfield, audio clip from *The Live Adventures of Michael Bloomfield and Al Kooper*, Columbia LP, 1969.

450 "We had six": Al Kooper, *Backstage Passes and Backstabbing Bastards: Memoirs of a Rock 'n' Roll Survivor*, Backbeat Books, 1998.

CHAPTER 20: LIVE ADVENTURES

Al Kooper told me about Bloomfield's failure to appear for the third night of Fillmore performances. Bill Keenom's interviews with Susan Beuhler also provided information, as did Bob Sarles's interview with Bill Graham from *Sweet Blues: A Film about Michael Bloomfield.* My description of Bloomfield's return to Mill Valley came from Bill Keenom's interview with Harvey Brooks; Mark Naftalin and Toby Byron told me about the people who were his housemates. Toby also told me about producing a concert with Bloomfield at Tamalpais High School. Information on Bloomfield's production work with Otis Rush for Albert Grossman came from Bill Keenom's interviews with Nick Gravenites; from *The Best of the Blues: The 101 Essential Albums*; from *Michael Bloomfield: If You Love These Blues*; from my interviews with Mark Naftalin; and from master takes on *Mourning in the Morning*, Rush's Cotillion LP, as well as alternate and unused takes that were supplied to me by Norman Dayron. Al Kooper's Fillmore East Super Session shows were described by Kooper in my interview with him. Additional information came from Paul Lerman; from *Fillmore East: The Lost Concert Tapes 12/13/68*, Columbia Legacy CD, 2003; and from an audience member's recording of one of the shows. My description of Bloomfield's efforts to organize Janis Joplin's new band came from Walter Rimler's interview with Bloomfield and from keyboardist Bill King's blog. Information on the second weekend of Super Session shows at the Fillmore East came from my interview with Al Kooper; additional information came from an audience member's comments on mikebloomfield.com. Bloomfield's live jam shows at the Fillmore West were described to me by Bob Jones; additional information came from master takes from *Live at Bill Graham's Fillmore West*, the original Columbia LP, as well as numerous outtakes shared with me by Bill Keenom and Peggy McVickar; from Bill Keenom's interviews with Nick Gravenites; and from *Michael Bloomfield: If You Love These Blues*. Information on the release of *The Live Adventures of Mike Bloomfield and Al Kooper* came from my interview with Al Kooper and from *Billboard*. Descriptions of Bloomfield's last live Super Session appearance came from my own recollections of the show, from the *Boston Globe*, and from emails from an audience member.

456 "She says, 'I had'": Al Kooper, author interview, 9/16/2014.

456 "He was miserable": Susan Beuhler, interview with Bill Keenom, 1996.

457 Susan Beuhler calling Bill Graham to tell him Bloomfield could not perform came from Beuhler, interview with Bill Keenom, 1996.

457 "I was very upset": Bill Graham, *Sweet Blues: A Film about Michael Bloomfield*, Ravin Films, 2014.

457 "I flew out": Al Kooper, audio clip from *The Live Adventures of Mike Bloomfield and Al Kooper*, Columbia LP, 1969.

458, 459 Bloomfield moves into the Carmelita Avenue house formerly rented by Harvey Brooks came from Brooks, interview with Bill Keenom, 1996.

460 "That's when Michael": Toby Byron, author interview, 4/28/2016.

460 "We knocked on the door": Toby Byron, author interview, 4/28/2016.

460 "I hired Michael": Toby Byron, author interview, 4/28/2016.

461 "Mike flew down": Nick Gravenites, *The Best of the Blues: The 101 Essential Albums*, Penguin Books, 1997.

463 "One of the few": *New York Times*, 9/29/1968.

463 "Alan gets really great bread": Michael Bloomfield, "How I Met Michael Bloomfield," Paul Lerman, mikebloomfieldamericanmusic.com, 2010.

463 Bloomfield's low opinion of Big Brother came from his interview in *Rolling Stone*, 4/6/1968.

464 "Hello . . . uh": Michael Bloomfield, audio clip from *Fillmore East: The Lost Concert Tapes 12/13/68*, Columbia Legacy CD, 2003.

466 "We got a cat": Michael Bloomfield, audio clip from *Fillmore East: The Lost Concert Tapes 12/13/68*, Columbia Legacy CD, 2003.

468 Description of Bloomfield rehearsing Janis Joplin's new backup band and then accompanying them to Memphis came from keyboardist Bill King, billkingmusic .blogspot.com.

468 "She was a drug-fiend": Michael Bloomfield, interview with Walter Rimler, summer 1975.

468 "I don't think Janis": Michael Bloomfield, interview with Walter Rimler, summer 1975.

469 "Bloomfield called me": Al Kooper, *Michael Bloomfield: If You Love These Blues*, Miller Freeman Books, 2000.

470 "We were sitting": Audience member comment, mikebloomfield.com.

470 "Michael was always": Al Kooper, author interview, 9/16/2014.

471 "They're the easiest thing": Michael Bloomfield, *New York Times*, 11/5/1968.

471 "I had learned to play": Bob Jones, author interview, 4/21/2011.

472 "I think he was": Bob Jones, author interview, 4/21/2011.

472 "The rehearsals weren't": Bob Jones, author interview, 4/21/2011.

474 "We've been recording": Michael Bloomfield, audio clip from Fillmore West jam sessions, 1/30/1969 or 1/31/1969.

475 "I was lying in bed": Al Kooper, author interview, 9/16/2014.

475 "Bloomfield was smashed": Al Kooper, *Michael Bloomfield: If You Love These Blues*, Miller Freeman Books, 2000.

477 "Well, Michael was junked out": Nick Gravenites, *Michael Bloomfield: If You Love These Blues*, Miller Freeman Books, 2000.

479 Another called him "*very* energized": Audience member Andrew Shiff, email to the author, 3/16/2013.

479 "It wasn't until": *Boston Globe*, 3/18/1969.

479 "He was really buzzed": Audience member Andrew Shiff, email to the author, 3/16/2013.

CHAPTER 21: MICHAEL'S LAMENT

Photos of Bloomfield taken by Peter Amft came from *Michael Bloomfield: If You Love These Blues* and from images sent to me by Bill Keenom. The description of Bloomfield's plans for his solo Columbia album cover came from Bill Keenom's interview with Peter Amft. Bloomfield's impromptu recording session at Chess was described to me by Norman Dayron; Dayron also gave me access to the recordings Bloomfield made during that session. Norman described Bloomfield's idea for a fathers and sons album and told me about setting up and producing the sessions for it. My description of brunch at Bloomfield's grandmother's apartment came from my interview with Al Kooper. Harold Bloomfield's enthusiasm for horseback riding was shared with me by Randy Bloomfield. Information about the Fathers and Sons concert came from my interview with Denise Kaufman; from emails to me from audience member Paul Petraitis; from Don DeMichael's review in *Rolling Stone*; and from the selections on *Fathers and Sons*, the resulting Chess album. Information on Haskell Wexler and *Medium Cool* came from *VideoHound's Golden Movie Retriever 2017: The Complete Guide to Movies*; my description of Bloomfield's soundtrack came from *Medium Cool* on DVD. The recording and production of Bloomfield's solo LP *It's Not Killing Me* was described to me in emails from Michael Melford; additional information came from Bill Keenom's interview with Melford and from Artist Contract Cards supplied to me by Bruce Dickinson. My analysis of Bloomfield's songs came from selections on the original album, from alternate takes on the Japanese reissue, and from unreleased tunes shared with me by Bob Andres. Janis Joplin's recording session in New York with Bloomfield acting as producer was described by Sam Andrew in Bill Keenom's interview with him. Information about the release of *Live at Bill Graham's Fillmore West*, *It's Not Killing Me*, and Nick Gravenites's *My Labors* came from *Billboard*, from *Rolling Stone*, and from newspaper ads and reviews. Toby Byron told me about Bloomfield's release party for *It's Not Killing Me*. Information about the release of *Fathers and Sons* came from *Billboard* and from newspaper reviews.

481 "I had a graphic studio": Peter Amft, interview with Bill Keenom, 1996.
481 "I'm just like Muddy's son": Norman Dayron, author interview, 10/26/2011.
482–483 Lyrics from Bloomfield's Chess studio recordings were supplied by Norman Dayron.
483 "Lemme see, what": Michael Bloomfield, audio clip from Chess studio recordings, 4/4/1969.
483 "Keep them for me": Norman Dayron, author interview, 10/26/2011.
484 "He was completely separate": Al Kooper, author interview, 9/16/2014.
485 "He said he was": Al Kooper, author interview, 9/16/2014.
485 "I went through everything": Norman Dayron, author interview, 10/26/2011.
485 "Michael went in there": Norman Dayron, author interview, 10/26/2011.
487 "Jo was this beautiful": Norman Dayron, author interview, 10/26/2011.
487 "She got there": Norman Dayron, author interview, 10/26/2011.
488 "There were two takes": Norman Dayron, author interview, 10/26/2011.
489 The Electric Flag using the Ace of Cups' house in Mill Valley as an early rehearsal space came from Denise Kaufman, author interview, 9/5/2016.
489 The Ace of Cups being driven from the stage after only four songs came from audience member Paul Petraitis, email to the author, 1/12/2010.
490–491 Description of tunes was taken from *Fathers and Sons*, Chess LP, 1969.
491 "It was indeed his night": Don DeMichael, *Rolling Stone*, 5/31/1969.
493 "He asked his friend": Michael Melford, email to the author, 4/28/2013.
493 "Ours was one": Michael Melford, email to the author, 4/28/2013.
493 "I felt the repertoire": Michael Melford, email to the author, 4/28/2013.
494 "Why did Mike": Michael Melford, email to the author, 4/28/2013.
495–500 Description of selections recorded came from master takes on *It's Not Killing Me*, the original Columbia LP release; alternate takes from the Japanese reissue; unreleased selections shared by Bob Andres.
500 "Mike was deeply depressed": Michael Melford, email to the author, 4/28/2013.

500 "A friend of mine": Michael Melford, email to the author, 4/28/2013.
501 "Michael would call": Michael Melford, interview with Bill Keenom, 1996.
501 Bloomfield soliciting Al Kooper's help in getting some of his more controversial tunes included on *It's Not Killing Me* came from Al Kooper, interview with Bill Keenom, 1995.
501 "His life was really falling": Michael Melford, interview with Bill Keenom, 1996.
501 "He felt that": Michael Melford, interview with Bill Keenom, 1996.
502 Description of selections recorded came from Janis Joplin's *I Got Them Ol' Kozmic Blues Again Mama!*, Columbia LP, 1969.
502 "He was having": Sam Andrew, *Michael Bloomfield: If You Love These Blues*, Miller Freeman Books, 2000.
503 Bloomfield's reworking of several selections from *It's Not Killing Me* came from Artist Contract Cards supplied by Bruce Dickinson.
505 "The band is ragged": *Rolling Stone*, 11/15/1969.
505 "Subtleties of [Gravenites's] phrasing": *Rolling Stone*, 11/15/1969.
506 "Michael had a big party": Toby Byron, author interview, 4/28/2016.
506 "Specimen of boring exhibitionism": *Rolling Stone*, 11/15/1969.
507 "Probably the most talented": *The Record*, Troy, NY, 10/11/1969.
507 "When the record started": Michael Melford, interview with Bill Keenom, 1996.
507 "Columbia was nice enough": Michael Bloomfield, *Guitar Player*, Apr. 1979.
507 "Muddy's style is": *Billboard*, 8/16/1969.
507 "Dream set for blues fans": *Fergus Falls Daily Journal*, 10/2/1969.

CHAPTER 22: STONED LEISURE

Information about Keystone Korner came from my interview with Bob Jones and from Bill Keenom's interview with Nick Gravenites. Norman Dayron told me about recording the "Moogie Woogie" album for Chess. Bloomfield's arrest for driving under the influence of narcotics was reported in the local San Rafael paper. Bloomfield's ambivalence about music and the music industry was expressed in a *Rolling Stone* article. Dorothy Bloomfield's concern about her son's lethargy and her contacting B. B. King was described in Bill Keenom's interview with her; King's response was taken from *Sweet Blues: A Film about Michael Bloomfield*. Bloomfield's reaction to his mother's interceding came from Dan McClosky's interview with him. My description of Bloomfield's home recording routine came from dubs supplied to me by Bill Keenom and Bob Andres. Bloomfield's observations on his life and career, and his ambivalence toward the music business, came from his interview in *Guitar Player*. Information about his duet recordings with Mark Naftalin came from Bloomfield's interview in *Guitar Player* and from my interviews with Mark Naftalin. Additional information came from a satirical story on the recordings that Naftalin wrote and shared with me. Bloomfield's move to the house on Reed St. was described to me by Chris McDougal. Information on Roy Ruby's time in Jenner came from my interviews with Leonard Trupin; Ruby's move to Reed Street with Fred Glazer was taken from Dan McClosky's interview with them. Bloomfield's attending the closing of the Fillmore West was captured on film in *Fillmore: The Last Days* and in an audio broadcast over KSFX. His relationship with Christina Svane was described by Svane in Jan Mark Wolkin's interview with her and in *Michael Bloomfield: If You Love These Blues*. Susan Smith's return to Mill Valley and Reed Street was described in Bill Keenom's interview with her and in *Michael Bloomfield: If You Love These Blues*.

Bloomfield's observations about heroin use came from Walter Rimler's interview with him. The Butterfield Band's semi-reunion at the Fenway Theatre was described to me by Mark Naftalin. Additional information came from my interview with Allen Bloomfield, from a video of the performance by Bob Lewis, from *Crawdaddy*, and from other newspaper reviews. Inspirational visits to Bloomfield by Carlos Santana and Terry Haggerty were described in Bill Keenom's interviews with them and in Bloomfield's interview in *Guitar Player*. Information about Bloomfield's trust fund came from my interviews with Allen Bloomfield and Chris McDougal; additional information came from Bill Keenom's interview with Bonner Beuhler. Bloomfield's trip to Europe with Jonathan Cramer was described to me by Toby Byron; Toby also told me about moving into the Reed Street house at Bloomfield's request. Recording the soundtrack for *Steelyard Blues* was recounted by Nick Gravenites in Bill Keenom's interview with him. Additional information came from selections on the original *Steelyard Blues* album, from unreleased soundtrack tunes provided to me by Bob Andres, and from newspaper reviews.

509 "Michael told me": Nick Gravenites, interview with Bill Keenom, 1995.

509 "Nick was really comfortable": Bob Jones, author interview, 4/21/2011.

510 "You know, by 1970": Bob Jones, author interview, 4/21/2011.

510 "I remember between sets": Bob Jones, author interview, 4/21/2011.

511 Bloomfield's arrest for driving under the influence of narcotics came from the *Daily Independent Journal*, San Rafael, Oct. 1970.

512 Albert Grossman's urging Bloomfield to use the Electric Flag name for his Friends band came from Phil Brown, interview with Bill Keenom, 1995.

512 "I just can't do it": Michael Bloomfield, *Rolling Stone*, 8/6/1970.

514 B. B. King's appearance at Mister Kelly's came from *Billboard*, 9/6/1970.

514 "I wrote a note": Dorothy Shinderman, interview with Bill Keenom, 1995.

514 "I was in Chicago": B. B. King, interview with Bob Sarles, *Sweet Blues: A Film about Michael Bloomfield*, Ravin Films, 2014.

515–516 Description of Bloomfield's home recordings came from dubs sent by Bill Keenom and Bob Andres.

516 "My best guitar playing record": Michael Bloomfield, *Guitar Player*, Aug. 1971.

516 "Incorporate all the early": Michael Bloomfield, *Guitar Player*, Aug. 1971.

517 "I went to look": Chris McDougal, author interview, 9/14/2013.

518 "A call to his dad": Chris McDougal, author interview, 9/14/2013.

518 "We did a lot": Mark Naftalin, from his satirical story "Waldy Boy," provided by Naftalin.

519 Roy Ruby's retreat to Jenner was described by Leonard Trupin, author interview, 1/30/2017.

519 "When I came back": Fred Glazer, interview with Bill Keenom, 1995.

520 "All of a sudden": Michael Bloomfield, interview with Dan McClosky, 5/17/1971.

520 "My father used to": Michael Bloomfield, interview with Dan McClosky, 5/17/1971.

520 "Well, let's adjourn": Michael Bloomfield, interview with Dan McClosky, 5/17/1971.

521 Bill Graham's anecdote about Bloomfield wanting to avoid his mother came from *Fillmore: The Last Days*, 20th Century Fox, 1972.

521 "We saw the sunrise": Christina Svane, *Michael Bloomfield: If You Love These Blues*, Miller Freeman Books, 2000.

522 "I called Michael": Dorothy Shinderman, interview with Bill Keenom, 1995.

522 "I had a baby": Susan Beuhler, *Michael Bloomfield: If You Love These Blues*, Miller Freeman Books, 2000.

523 "Heroin takes up": Michael Bloomfield, interview with Walter Rimler, summer 1975.

523 "Heroin is the best thing": Christina Svane, *Michael Bloomfield: If You Love These Blues*, Miller Freeman Books, 2000.

523 "Butterfield called me up": Mark Naftalin, email to the author, 1/20/2011.

524 "John, you better start": *Boston Globe*, 12/13/1971.

524 "They had a scrim": Allen Bloomfield, author interview, 1/2/2017.

525 "The comeback of the decade": *Crawdaddy*, Jan. 1972.

525 "We're just kind of": *Crawdaddy*, Jan. 1972.

526 "I worked hard": Mark Naftalin, from his satirical story "Waldy Boy," provided by Naftalin.

526 "I had heard somewhere": Mark Naftalin, from his satirical story "Waldy Boy," provided by Naftalin.

527 "We jacked around": Michael Bloomfield, *Guitar Player*, Apr. 1979.

527 "I would go over": Terry Haggerty, interview with Bill Keenom, 1996.

527 "Somebody told me": Carlos Santana, interview with Bill Keenom, 1996.

527 "I just said, hey,": Michael Bloomfield, *Guitar Player*, Apr. 1979.

528 "That those guys would": Michael Bloomfield, *Guitar Player*, Apr. 1979.

528 "I have perfected": Michael Bloomfield, *Crawdaddy*, May 1973.

528 "Our grandfather set up": Allen Bloomfield, author interview, 1/2/2017.

529 "I decided to have": Allen Bloomfield, author interview, 1/2/2017.

529 "He asked me": Toby Byron, author interview, 4/28/2016.

530 "I moved into": Toby Byron, author interview, 4/28/2016.

530 "The studio wanted": Nick Gravenites, interview with Bill Keenom, 1996.

531 "Even Butterfield took": Nick Gravenites, interview with Bill Keenom, 1996.

531 "Their presence gives": *New York Times*, 2/11/1973.

531 "Uniformly excellent": *Pasadena Star-News*, 3/4/1973.

531 "It may be destined": *Syracuse Post-Standard*, 3/3/1973.

531 "On the whole": *Rolling Stone*, 5/24/1973.

CHAPTER 23: REED STREET

My description of Bloomfield's home life on Reed Street came from my interview with Toby Byron, from Bill Keenom's interviews with Susan and Bonner Beuhler, from Bloomfield's interview in *Guitar Player*, and from *Michael Bloomfield: If You Love These Blues*. Toby Byron also told me about booking gigs for Bloomfield and about touring with his Friends band. Norman Dayron recounted his move to Mill Valley and his using Bloomfield as a guest lecturer in his music production course in my interviews with him. Information about John Hammond's *Triumvirate* sessions came from my interview with Hammond; from my interview with Toby Byron; from selections on *Triumvirate*, the original Columbia release; and from *Michael Bloomfield: If You Love These Blues*. My description of the Butterfield

Band's reunion shows at the Fillmore came from a review in *Rolling Stone* and from a recording of one of Bloomfield's sets supplied to me by Norman Dayron. Facts about Roy Ruby's death came from Bill Keenom's interview with Dave Naftalin; additional information was provided to me by Leonard Trupin. My description of Bloomfield's tax troubles came from Bill Keenom's interviews with Susan and Bonner Beuhler, from my interview with Allen Bloomfield, and from *Michael Bloomfield: If You Love These Blues*. Information about Bob Dylan's visit to Reed Street came from Bloomfield's interview with Walter Rimler, from Bill Keenom's interview with Bonner Beuhler, and from *Michael Bloomfield: If You Love These Blues*. Bloomfield's purchase of the Reed Street house came from Marin County real property records. George Rains told me about joining Bloomfield's Friends band and attending a Passover seder at Reed Street. Information about Bloomfield's performance schedule came from my own research, from my interviews with Toby Byron, and from Toby's contributions to my Bloomfield website. Accountant Maya Lit's efforts to sort out Bloomfield's tax issues were described in Bill Keenom's interview with Susan Beuhler. Information on the Mitchell brothers came from the website brightlightsfilm.com, from Bloomfield's interview with Walter Rimler, from my interviews with Norman Dayron, from Bill Keenom's interviews with Dayron, from *Michael Bloomfield: If You Love These Blues*, and from a digitized version of an Ultra-Kore short. The resurrection of the Electric Flag was described in Bloomfield's interview in *Guitar Player*, in interviews with the band members in *Zoo World*, in Bill Keenom's interview with Jerry Wexler, and in *Michael Bloomfield: If You Love These Blues*. Additional information came from *The Band Played On*, the Flag's original album on Atlantic, and from unreleased material supplied to me by Norman Dayron. Data on Bloomfield's *Try It Before You Buy It* sessions came from Columbia Artist Contract Cards supplied to me by Bruce Dickinson and from selections intended for the original album. Additional information came from Bloomfield's interview in *Guitar Player*; from my interviews with Toby Byron, Mark Naftalin, and George Rains; and from Bill Keenom's interview with Bonner Beuhler. My description of Bloomfield's participation in the PBS tribute to Muddy Waters came from the Rhino video "Soundstage: Blues Summit in Chicago" and from Jan Mark Wolkin's interview with Eliot Wald. My description of the Electric Flag's appearance at the Ozarks Music Festival came from ads and listings in *Billboard*, from newspaper reports and reviews, and from a recording of the band in performance. Information about the Flag's East Coast tour came from my interview with Allen Bloomfield. My description of Bloomfield abandoning his band and his instruments in Vancouver came from newspaper reports, from my interview with George Rains, and from *Vintage Guitar* magazine.

532 "I just did whatever": Toby Byron, author interview, 4/28/2016.

533 "I suddenly had nothing": Norman Dayron, author interview, 10/28/2011.

533 "I asked him": John Hammond, author interview, 7/22/2014.

534 "They had many rehearsals": Toby Byron, author interview, 4/28/2016.

535 "It was a big deal": John Hammond, *Michael Bloomfield: If You Love These Blues*, Miller Freeman Books, 2000.

536 "It was shortly": *Rolling Stone*, 3/29/1973.

536 "It's so nice": Michael Bloomfield, audio clip from Fillmore performance, shared by Norman Dayron.

537 "Thank you very much": Bill Graham, audio clip from Fillmore performance, shared by Norman Dayron.

537 "Roy died": Dave Naftalin, interview with Jan Mark Wolkin, 1996.

537 "I remember Roy": Dave Naftalin, interview with Jan Mark Wolkin, 1996.
537 "Roy and Mike were": Dave Naftalin, interview with Jan Mark Wolkin, 1996.
539 "How can I go": Bob Welland, interview with Bill Keenom, 1996.
539 "I got phone calls": Michael Bloomfield, interview with Walter Rimler, summer 1975.
539 "He pulled out": Michael Bloomfield, interview with Walter Rimler, summer 1975.
540 "We went to": Toby Byron, author interview, 4/28/2016.
542 "A nice set": *Berkeley Barb*, 12/14/1973.
542–544 Information on the Mitchell brothers and their films came from John Minson, "Before the Green Door: The Mitchell Brothers, the Counterculture, and Hardcore's Beginnings," *Bright Lights Film Journal*, 8/1/2007, brightlightsfilm.com/green-door-mitchell-brothers-counterculture-hard-cores-beginnings/#.Wl4nlKinHIU.
543 "We would go": Norman Dayron, interview with Bill Keenom, 1996.
544 "Sure would be happy": *Melody Maker*, 12/7/1974.
544 "That song makes me": Michael Bloomfield, audio clip from concert recording, shared by Peggy McVickar.
545 "Michael invited me": George Rains, author interview, 2/4/2017.
546 "It was a whole lot": Toby Byron, author interview, 4/28/2016.
546 "Michael never used": Toby Byron, author interview, 4/28/2016.
546 "See, my habits are": Michael Bloomfield, *Zoo World*, 8/1/1974.
546 "Just pondering Mike Bloomfield": Jerry Wexler, *Zoo World*, 8/1/1974.
547 "Somehow, Buddy got": Jerry Wexler, interview with Bill Keenom, 1996.
548 "Buddy used to get": Jerry Wexler, interview with Bill Keenom, 1996.
548 "The only thing everybody": George Rains, author interview, 2/4/2017.
548 "I couldn't get": Jerry Wexler, *Michael Bloomfield: If You Love These Blues*, Miller Freeman Books, 2000.
553 "Michael was real": Eliot Wald, interview with Jan Mark Wolkin, 1996.
553 "You don't know how happy": Muddy Waters, *Rolling Stone*, 11/21/1974.
554 "Yes, indeed!": Wolfman Jack, audio clip from a recording of the Electric Flag's performance, youtube.com/watch?v=GSEn1bfnblA.
554 "I want you to start": Buddy Miles, audio clip from a recording of the Electric Flag's performance, youtube.com/watch?v=GSEn1bfnblA.
556 "That was a really": Michael Bloomfield, *Guitar Player*, Apr. 1979.
556 "The Flag was opening": Allen Bloomfield, author interview, 2/19/2008.
556 "I'll tell you one": Michael Bloomfield, *Zoo World*, 8/1/1974.
558 "'Twas nostalgia night": *Sacramento Community College Express*, 11/7/1974.
558 "The only thing Mike": George Rains, author interview, 2/4/2017.
559 "To think there are people": *Vancouver Sun*, 11/13/1974.
559 "People go to hear": *Vancouver Sun*, 11/13/1974.
559 "Roger, I know you will": *Vancouver Sun*, 11/14/1974.
559 "We couldn't believe": George Rains, author interview, 2/4/2017.
559, 560 Stan Grozina keeping Bloomfield's equipment as reimbursement for damages came from John Picard, "A Sunburst Mystery," *Vintage Guitar* magazine, June 2011; email correspondence with Chris Okey, 2014–2016.
560 Bloomfield's effect on the vintage guitar market came from guitar dealer and expert George Grunn, "How to Buy a Vintage Guitar," Homespun Tapes, 1991.

CHAPTER 24: LOVING THESE BLUES

My description of the Electric Flag's album *The Band Kept Playing* came from the original release on Atlantic and from reviews in *Rolling Stone* and other newspapers. The band's breakup was also described in various newspapers. Toby Byron told me about his departure from Mill Valley in my interview with him. Bloomfield's creating the soundtrack for the Mitchell brothers' *Sodom and Gomorrah* was recounted in Walter Rimler's interview with him. Additional information came from a digitized version of the film supplied to me by Peggy McVickar and from the *Bright Lights Film Journal* website. Bloomfield's involvement with KGB came from Barry Goldberg's autobiography, *Two Jews Blues*; from Bloomfield's interview in *Guitar Player*; from selections on *KGB*, the original release on MCA; and from the press release for the album. Data on the IRS lien on Bloomfield's house came from Marin County real property tax records. Bloomfield's dictating "Me and Big Joe" and other stories was described in my interviews with Norman Dayron and Sally Moses; Sally Moses also shared her original transcript of the "Big Joe" story with me. The resolution of Bloomfield's tax problems was explained to me by Allen Bloomfield. Additional information came from Bill Keenom's interview with Bonner Beuhler. Norman Dayron told me about Bloomfield's performing at the Old Waldorf. Bloomfield's disgust with *KGB* was expressed in his interview in the *Los Angeles Times*; in his interview in *Guitar Player*; and in his resignation letter to the producer, reprinted in part in *Michael Bloomfield: The Rise and Fall of an American Guitar Hero*. In *Guitar Player* and *Rock 'n' Roll News*, Bloomfield described going through "an intense period of musical self-awareness" after his KGB experience. Susan Beuhler described her decision to leave Reed Street in Bill Keenom's interviews with her and in *Michael Bloomfield: If You Love These Blues*. Bloomfield's appearance at the 1976 Newport Jazz Festival was described by Mike Michaels in my interview with him. Additional information came from a recording of Bloomfield's performance supplied to me by Michaels and from a review in the *New York Times*. Tere Tereba told me about her efforts to get Bloomfield involved in creating the soundtrack for *Andy Warhol's Bad*. Additional information came from my interview with Norman Dayron; from Tereba's video "Michael Bloomfield, Andy Warhol: Tere Tereba Tells All"; and from Bloomfield's interview in *BAM*. Bloomfield talked about his instructional record *If You Love These Blues, Play 'Em as You Please* in an interview in *Guitar Player*. Information about Guitar Player Records came from *Billboard*, from press releases, and from advertisements. My description of the selections recorded came from the original release; from the CD on Kicking Mule; from Bloomfield's liner notes; and from the album's mail-order booklet, shared with me by Bill Keenom. Bloomfield's amusement at Bob Greenspan's comedy routine at the Old Waldorf came from Bill Keenom's interview with him. Information on Bloomfield's nomination for a Grammy Award came from the Grammy Wikipedia page. Norman Dayron told me about forming C.T. Productions with Bloomfield, and Sally Moses sent me information about its incorporation. My description of Bloomfield's attending the party in Hollywood for *Andy Warhol's Bad* came from Tere Tereba's video "Michael Bloomfield, Andy Warhol: Tere Tereba Tells All." I used the many CD releases of the concert to describe Bloomfield's appearance at McCabe's.

562 "As a contemporary": *Lincoln Nebraska Journal*, 12/11/1974.
562 "*Mirabile dictum*": *Rolling Stone*, 1/2/1975.
563 "I tried to arrange": Toby Byron, author interview, 4/28/2016.

563 "I did a whole lot": Michael Bloomfield, interview with Walter Rimler, summer 1975.
565 "Nobody knew who": Michael Bloomfield, "Barroom Scholar of the Blues," *Guitar Player*, Apr. 1979.
565 "All these execs who": Michael Bloomfield, "Barroom Scholar of the Blues," *Guitar Player*, Apr. 1979.
566 "I began to realize": Michael Bloomfield, "Barroom Scholar of the Blues," *Guitar Player*, Apr. 1979.
568 "We sat around": Norman Dayron, author interview, 10/28/2011.
568 "I wasn't sure": Sally Moses, author interview, 1/13/2013.
568 "It was about": Norman Dayron, author interview, 10/28/2011.
568 "There were six": Norman Dayron, author interview, 10/28/2011.
569 "Michael had to come up": Bonner Beuhler, interview with Bill Keenom, 1996.
569 "When my dad got involved": Allen Bloomfield, author interview, 1/12/2017.
569 "The Old Waldorf was": Norman Dayron, author interview, 7/7/2007.
570 "I'm no hype artist": Michael Bloomfield, *Los Angeles Times*, 2/22/1976.
570 "I think the supergroup thing": Michael Bloomfield, *Los Angeles Times*, 2/22/1976.
571 "I can't really explain": Michael Bloomfield, "Barroom Scholar of the Blues," *Guitar Player*, Apr. 1979.
571 "I was wrong to take": Michael Bloomfield, *Michael Bloomfield: The Rise and Fall of an American Guitar Hero*, Chicago Review Press, 2016.
571 "The big labels won't": Michael Bloomfield, *Daily Camera*, Boulder, Colorado.
571 "An intense period": Michael Bloomfield, "Barroom Scholar of the Blues," *Guitar Player*, Apr. 1979.
572 "I knew what I wanted": Michael Bloomfield, "Barroom Scholar of the Blues," *Guitar Player*, Apr. 1979.
572 "It was a realization": Michael Bloomfield, *Rock-N-Roll News*, 6/11/1976.
572 "I realized everything": Michael Bloomfield, "Barroom Scholar of the Blues," *Guitar Player*, Apr. 1979.
572 "I had to get out": Susan Beuhler, *Michael Bloomfield: If You Love These Blues*, Miller Freeman Books, 2000.
573 Lyrics from the concert recording were provided by Mike Michaels.
574 "There were some rowdy guys": Mike Michaels, author interview, 12/15/2008.
574 "Lemme tell you about": Michael Bloomfield, audio clip from concert recording, provided by Mike Michaels.
575 "Enthusiasm for a variety": *New York Times*, 6/27/1976.
575 "When it came to selecting": Tere Tereba, "Michael Bloomfield, Andy Warhol: Tere Tereba Tells All," youtube.com/watch?v=ckir4c8FgUc&t=68s, 2016.
576 "Michael was such": Tere Tereba, "Michael Bloomfield, Andy Warhol: Tere Tereba Tells All," youtube.com/watch?v=ckir4c8FgUc&t=68s, 2016.
576 "Michael called me": Norman Dayron, author interview, 10/28/2011.
576 "I'm dying to cut": Michael Bloomfield, *BAM*, June 1976.
576 "One day I came home": Norman Dayron, author interview, 10/28/2011.
577 "I felt this overwhelming urge": Michael Bloomfield, "Barroom Scholar of the Blues," *Guitar Player*, Apr. 1979.
580 "I was striving": Michael Bloomfield, "Barroom Scholar of the Blues," *Guitar Player*, Apr. 1979.

580 "I know it's my best": Michael Bloomfield, "Barroom Scholar of the Blues," *Guitar Player*, Apr. 1979.

581 "Mike was playing": Bob Greenspan, interview with Bill Keenom, 1995.

581 "Back in those days": Bob Greenspan, interview with Bill Keenom, 1995.

582 "I was lucky enough": Michael Bloomfield, liner notes to *If You Love These Blues, Play 'Em as You Please*, Guitar Player LP, 1976.

583 "The Guitar Player record": Michael Bloomfield, "Barroom Scholar of the Blues," *Guitar Player*, Apr. 1979.

583 "I told Michael": Norman Dayron, author interview, 10/28/2011.

584 "We based C.T. Productions": Norman Dayron, author interview, 10/28/2011.

586, 587 Lyrics and commentary came from *Between the Hard Place and the Ground*, TKO Magnum Midline CD; *I'm with You Always*, Benchmark CD; other releases of the McCabe's show.

CHAPTER 25: COUNT TALENT

Information about Bloomfield's arrangement with Jon Monday and Takoma Records was provided to me by Norman Dayron. Norman also told me about their deal with the label to record *Analine* and described the recording sessions. Additional data came from Bloomfield's interview in *Guitar Player*, from Norman Dayron's interview in *Tape Op* magazine, and from my interview with Sally Moses. My description of the selections recorded came from the original release of *Analine* on Takoma Records. Bloomfield's increasing use of drugs was described by Bob Greenspan in Bill Keenom's interview with him. My description of Bloomfield's efforts to get "Me and Big Joe" published came from Bill Keenom's interview with Scott Summerville. Reviews of *Analine* came from *Saturday Review* and several newspapers. David Shorey told Bill Keenom about meeting Bloomfield and joining the guitarist's band; he also described numerous gigs that the Friends band played. The recording, mixing, and remixing of Bloomfield's album for TK Records, *Count Talent and the Originals*, was described by Norman Dayron in Bill Keenom's interview with him. Additional information came from Keenom's interview with David Shorey, from Bloomfield's interview in *Guitar Player*, and from Norman Dayron's interview in *Tape Op*. My description of the selections on *Count Talent and the Originals* came from the original album release. Bloomfield's appearance at Tulagi with his Count Talent band was shared with the author by audience member John Ivey. Bloomfield's aborted Christmas record for Takoma was recalled by David Shorey during Bill Keenom's interview with him. Keenom's interviews with Shorey and Norman Dayron also provided information about recording *Michael Bloomfield* for Takoma. My description of the selections on the record came from the original album release. The arrival of Betsy Rice at Reed Street was described to me by Norman Dayron, Bob Jones, and Leonard Trupin. The Tribal Stomp appearance by the reunited Paul Butterfield Blues Band was recounted in my interview with Mark Naftalin; additional information came from a video of the band's performance provided to me by Peggy McVickar and from a review of the reunion in *Rolling Stone*. My discussion of Bloomfield's "Maria Elena" came from my essay "Mike Bloomfield's Lost Masterpiece" and from concert recordings provided to me by Bob Andres and Peggy McVickar. Bloomfield's reuniting with Christina Svane was described by Svane in Jan Mark Wolkin's interview with her and in *Michael Bloomfield: If You Love These Blues*. The Friends band tour of Canada was recounted in my interview with Bob Jones, in Bill Keenom's interview with David Shorey, in Bloomfield's interview in *Guitar Player*, and in *Michael Bloomfield: If You Love These Blues*. Additional information came from concert recordings provided to me by Bob Andres. Bloomfield's interview with Tom Wheeler for *Guitar Player* was excerpted throughout much of this chapter and several previous chapters. The destruction of Bloomfield's Beggerby guitar was described by Bob Greenspan in Bill Keenom's interview with him. Chris McDougal told me about taking Bloomfield to the hospital to recover from his addiction to Placidyl. Bloomfield's home life after his hospitalization was described by Christina Svane in Jan Mark Wolkin's interview with her. The recording of *Bloomfield/Harris* was described by Norman Dayron in my interview with him and in his liner notes to the album. My description of the selections on the record came from the original Kicking Mule release. The alienation of Bloomfield's friends was related to me by Bob Jones and Leonard Trupin; additional information came from Bill Keenom's interview with David Shorey. Norman Dayron told me about producing *Between a Hard Place and the Ground*. Reviews of the album came from *Billboard* and the *Boston Globe*. David Shorey told Bill Keenom about Bloomfield's drinking problem, and additional information came from my interview with Leonard Trupin. Bloomfield's months in New York with Christina Svane were described by Svane in Jan Mark Wolkin's interview with her; additional details came from *Michael Bloomfield: If You Love These Blues*. My description of Chicago Blues Power and their gigs with Bloomfield came from my interview with Steve Mallory.

588 "The Takoma albums were": Norman Dayron, "Norman Dayron on Recording Michael Bloomfield," *Tape Op*, 9/1/2001.

588 "I used to have": Michael Bloomfield, "Barroom Scholar of the Blues," *Guitar Player*, Apr. 1979.

591 "We were all doing": Sally Moses, author interview, 1/13/2013.

591 "I was with Michael": Bob Greenspan, interview with Bill Keenom, 1996.

592 "I outgrew it": Michael Bloomfield, interview with Walter Rimler, summer 1975.

592 "I would see Michael": Scott Summerville, interview with Bill Keenom, 1996.

592 "We started to work": Scott Summerville, interview with Bill Keenom, 1996.

592 "They had just made": Scott Summerville, interview with Bill Keenom, 1996.

593 "A sort of busman's holiday": *Stereo Review*, Aug. 1977.

593 "A colorist with a fine": *Montreal Gazette*, 1/13/1979.

594 "I was living with": David Shorey, interview with Bill Keenom, 1995.

594 "Norman did the deals": David Shorey, interview with Bill Keenom, 1995.

594 "TK wanted to get": Norman Dayron, interview with Bill Keenom, 1996.

594 "They gave us": Norman Dayron, "Norman Dayron on Recording Michael Bloomfield," *Tape Op*, 9/1/2001.

595 "I had a real trip": Michael Bloomfield, "Barroom Scholar of the Blues," *Guitar Player*, Apr. 1979.

595 "Michael had this habit": David Shorey, interview with Bill Keenom, 1995.

595 "When we sent them": Norman Dayron, interview with Bill Keenom, 1996.

596 "'Peach Tree Man' was": Norman Dayron, interview with Bill Keenom, 1996.

598 "I played bass": David Shorey, interview with Bill Keenom, 1995.

599 "Michael would always": Bob Jones, author interview, 4/21/2011.

600 "I learned it": Michael Bloomfield, "Barroom Scholar of the Blues," *Guitar Player*, Apr. 1979.

600 "Mike struggled to get": Robin Yeager, author interview, 2/20/2016.

600 "I only met Betsy": Leonard Trupin, author interview, 9/15/2016.

601 "Betsy was a nice": Norman Dayron, author interview, 10/28/2011.
601 "Mike found her": Bob Jones, author interview, 4/21/2011.
602 "Elvin wanted to": Mark Naftalin, author interview, 4/2/2013.
602 "And a good time": Elvin Bishop, audio clip from concert recording, provided by Peggy McVickar.
602 "Paul said something": Mark Naftalin, author interview, 4/2/2013.
603 "We were just": Christina Svane, interview with Jan Mark Wolkin, 1996.
604 "Michael opened the show": Christina Svane, interview with Jan Mark Wolkin, 1996.
604 "Michael had become": Bob Jones, author interview, 4/21/2011.
604 "Michael's use of Placidyl": David Shorey, interview with Bill Keenom, 1995.
605 "When we got to Montreal": Bob Jones, *Michael Bloomfield: If You Love These Blues*, Miller Freeman Books, 2000.
605 "One day we traveled": Michael Bloomfield, "Barroom Scholar of the Blues," *Guitar Player*, Apr. 1979.
606 "Everywhere I go": Michael Bloomfield, "Barroom Scholar of the Blues," *Guitar Player*, Apr. 1979.
607 "Mike told me": Bob Greenspan, author interview, 10/19/2012.
607 "He sounded almost": Christina Svane, *Michael Bloomfield: If You Love These Blues*, Miller Freeman Books, 2000.
607 "I was managing": Chris McDougal, author interview, 9/14/2013.
607 "With Michael out": Leonard Trupin, author interview, 9/15/2016.
608 "Michael was a bit": Norman Dayron, author interview, 10/28/2011.
608 "There was a friend": Christina Svane, interview with Jan Mark Wolkin, 1996.
609 "Bloomfield generally doesn't": Norman Dayron, liner notes to *Bloomfield/Harris*, Kicking Mule Records, 1979.
611 "I remember taking": Christina Svane, *Michael Bloomfield: If You Love These Blues*, Miller Freeman Books, 2000.
611 "We all could see": Leonard Trupin, author interview, 9/15/2016.
611 "Mike was always": Bob Jones, author interview, 4/21/2011.
612 "I worked with": David Shorey, interview with Bill Keenom, 1996.
612 "The Mill Valley Fire Department": David Shorey, interview with Bill Keenom, 1996.
613 "We were more interested": Norman Dayron, author interview, 10/28/2011.
613 "[Bloomfield] returns": *Billboard*, 10/29/1979.
613 "There's a studied informality": *Boston Globe*, 11/1/1979.
614 "He was drinking": David Shorey, interview with Bill Keenom, 1996.
615 "He'd get up": Leonard Trupin, author interview, 9/15/2016.
615 "That was the deal": Christina Svane, *Michael Bloomfield: If You Love These Blues*, Miller Freeman Books, 2000.
615 "My mother got": Christina Svane, *Michael Bloomfield: If You Love These Blues*, Miller Freeman Books, 2000.
616 "He and my mom": Christina Svane, interview with Jan Mark Wolkin, 1996.
616 "Ron wanted to get": Steve Mallory, author interview, 3/22/2012.
616 "Ron had this old hearse": Steve Mallory, author interview, 3/22/2012.
617 "He'd be a no-show": Steve Mallory, author interview, 3/22/2012.

CHAPTER 26: LAST CALL

Information on gigs Bloomfield and Woody Harris played came from Jan Mark Wolkin's interview with Harris. The review of their Main Point show with Maggie Edmondson came from *ELECTRICity*. My description of Bloomfield's performance at the Bottom Line came from a video clip from the French TV program *Chorus*. The publishing of "Me and Big Joe" was described by Scott Summerville in Bill Keenom's interview of him. Bloomfield's outburst during his appearance at the Greene Street Café was described by Felix Cabrera in emails to me. Information about the Bloomfield/Harris/Edmondson trio's tour of Italy and Scandinavia came from Jan Mark Wolkin's interview with Woody Harris, from Wolkin's interview with Christina Svane, from *Michael Bloomfield: If You Love These Blues*, from *The Ultimate Complete Michael Bloomfield Discography*, from the album *Mike Bloomfield Live in Italy*, from a video of the trio's performance in Milan, and from emails sent to me by Marco Bonino. Leonard Trupin told me about Bloomfield's housemates following his return from abroad. Recording sessions for *Cruisin' for a Bruisin'* were described to me by Norman Dayron. Additional information came from Dayron's interview in *Tape Op* magazine and from the selections originally released on the album in 1981. My description of Bloomfield's guest appearance with Bob Dylan at the Warfield Theatre came from my interview with Norman Dayron, from Bill Keenom's interview with Dayron, from Jan Mark Wolkin's interview with Christina Svane, and from a recording of the performance shared with me by Bob Andres. Jan Mark Wolkin told me about seeing Bloomfield's performance at the Childe Harold, and my description of the trio's Chester concert came from a recording provided to me by Peggy McVickar. Bloomfield's depressed state in late 1980 was described to me by Norman Dayron; additional information came from Bill Keenom's interview with Susan and Bonner Beuhler. Bloomfield's drug-dealer friend Jerry was described to me by Norman Dayron and Leonard Trupin. Al Kooper told me about Bloomfield's plan to accompany his girlfriend to Europe and about his proposal that they perform together in London. Bloomfield's improved health and his abstinence from drugs and alcohol was described by Bonner Beuhler in Bill Keenom's interview with him. Additional details came from *Michael Bloomfield: If You Love These Blues*. Bloomfield's observations about his life in music, his contemporaries, and the players who had influenced him came from Tom Yates's interview with him. The description of Bloomfield's last days came from my interview with Norman Dayron and from Bill Keenom's interviews with Stefan Grossman and ED Denson. I re-created the discovery of Bloomfield's body from police report notes provided to me by Norman Dayron; from Bloomfield's death certificate, sent to me by Brent Pellegrini; and from my visit to Dewey Boulevard in San Francisco. The days following Bloomfield's death were described to me in my interviews with Allen and Randy Bloomfield and Al Kooper. Additional information came from Bill Keenom's interviews with Allen Bloomfield, Norman Dayron, and David Shorey; from Jan Mark Wolkin's interview with Christina Svane; from *Michael Bloomfield: If You Love These Blues*; and from various newspaper reports. Information on Bloomfield's funeral came from my interview with Norman Dayron, from *Rolling Stone*, and from newspaper reports. Bill Keenom shared with me Cantor Martin Feldman's eulogy. My description of Bill Graham's memorial party for Bloomfield came from Bill Keenom's interviews with Susan Beuhler, Country Joe McDonald, Barry Melton, and Bob Greenspan. Bloomfield's internment in Culver City was described in *Two Jews Blues* and by Dorothy Shinderman in Bill Keenom's interview with her. The circumstances surrounding Bloomfield's death came from newspaper reports; from my interviews with Norman Dayron and Leonard Trupin; and from Bill Keenom's interviews with Dorothy Shinderman, Susan Beuhler, Ira Kamin, and David Shorey. My re-creation of the night Bloomfield died was based on those sources and my own speculation.

618 "The audience was": *ELECTRICity*, May 1980.
619 "I got loaded": Michael Bloomfield, audio clip from *Chorus*, France 2 TV program, May 1980.
619 "We had a thousand copies": Scott Summerville, interview with Bill Keenom, 1996.
620 "I was living": Scott Summerville, interview with Bill Keenom, 1996.
620 "He was playing acoustic": Felix Cabrera, email to the author, 3/7/2007.
621 "We called him 'the Trout'": Woody Harris, interview with Jan Mark Wolkin, 1996.
622 "Michael was received": Woody Harris, interview with Jan Mark Wolkin, 1996.
622 "The Italians are so attached": Christina Svane, *Michael Bloomfield: If You Love These Blues*, Miller Freeman Books, 2000.
623 "Hey! I don't tell you": Michael Bloomfield, audio clip from Naples concert, 9/12/1980.
623 "This will sound arrogant": Christina Svane, *Michael Bloomfield: If You Love These Blues*, Miller Freeman Books, 2000.
623 "When we got to Turin": Woody Harris, interview with Jan Mark Wolkin, 1996.
624 "After the concert": Marco Bonino, email to the author, 3/25/2010.
625 "Obliterate his mind": Norman Dayron, author interview, 10/26/2011.
625 "He drank himself": Woody Harris, *Michael Bloomfield: If You Love These Blues*, Miller Freeman Books, 2000.
625 "Everybody would buy": Woody Harris, *Michael Bloomfield: If You Love These Blues*, Miller Freeman Books, 2000.
625 "I am an old man": Michael Bloomfield, Finnish rock magazine, Oct. 1980; translation by the author.
625 "He just got out": Woody Harris, *Michael Bloomfield: If You Love These Blues*, Miller Freeman Books, 2000.
626 "Bob was a master carpenter": Leonard Trupin, author interview, 4/5/2017.
626 "John Finn got him": Leonard Trupin, author interview, 4/5/2017.
626 "It was patently obvious": Woody Harris, interview with Jan Mark Wolkin, 1996.
626 "Michael had started": Norman Dayron, author interview, 10/26/2011.
627 "He really had": Norman Dayron, author interview, 10/26/2011.
628 "Those were very strange": Norman Dayron, "Norman Dayron on Recording Michael Bloomfield," *Tape Op*, 9/1/2001.
628 "I said, 'I've got'": Maria Muldaur, *Michael Bloomfield: If You Love These Blues*, Miller Freeman Books, 2000.
629 "He was going": Norman Dayron, author interview, 10/26/2011.
629 "He came to Dylan's show": Norman Dayron, author interview, 10/26/2011.
630 "I was playing": Bob Dylan, audio clip from Warfield concert, 11/18/1980.
630 "Michael Bloomfield!": Bob Dylan, audio clip from Warfield concert, 11/18/1980.
632 "I played fantastic": Christina Svane, *Michael Bloomfield: If You Love These Blues*, Miller Freeman Books, 2000.
632 "At one point": Jan Mark Wolkin, email to the author, 4/16/2007.

632 "A woman asked": Jan Mark Wolkin, email to the author, 4/16/2007.
633 "He had apparently worked": Woody Harris, interview with Jan Mark Wolkin, 1996.
633 "He would get very lonely": Norman Dayron, author interview, 10/28/2011.
634 "He was very unhappy": Susan and Bonner Beuhler, interview with Bill Keenom, 1996.
634 "Michael would brag": Norman Dayron, author interview, 10/28/2011.
634 "Michael was really attracted": Norman Dayron, author interview, 10/28/2011.
634 "He told me about Jerry": Leonard Trupin, author interview, 4/5/2017.
634 "He was really messed up": Ira Kamin, interview with Bill Keenom, 1995.
635 "His girlfriend was coming:" Al Kooper, author interview, 6/30/2016.
635 "I said to Michael": Christina Svane, *Michael Bloomfield: If You Love These Blues*, Miller Freeman Books, 2000.
635 "He sort of turned": Bonner Beuhler, interview with Bill Keenom, 1996.
636 "It's ironic how Mike": Bob Greenspan, author interview, 1/19/2012.
636–637 All quotes from Michael Bloomfield, interview with Tom Yates, 2/13/1981.
637 "We were making plans": Stefan Grossman, interview with Bill Keenom, 1996.
637 "We were in the dressing room": ED Denson, interview with Bill Keenom, 1996.
637 "I came down": Stefan Grossman, interview with Bill Keenom, 1996.
639 "It was such a complete shock": Allen Bloomfield, author interview, 1/2/2017.
639 "I remember when the call came": Randy Bloomfield, author interview, 10/7/2015.
639 "I couldn't believe it": Norman Dayron, author interview, 10/28/2011.
639 "I remember Norman was": Dave Shorey, interview with Bill Keenom, 1996.
639 "I guess nobody knew": Al Kooper, author interview, 9/16/2014.
639 "I just played": Al Kooper, *Sweet Blues: A Film about Michael Bloomfield*, Ravin Films, 2014.
640 "We drove down": Norman Dayron, author interview, 10/28/2011.
640 "Mrs. Svane was staying": Norman Dayron, author interview, 10/28/2011.
640 "My dad was there": Allen Bloomfield, author interview, 1/2/2017.
640 "We went up": Allen Bloomfield, author interview, 1/2/2017.
641 All quotes from the eulogy by Cantor Martin Feldman, sent by Bill Keenom.
642 "Michael, it's me": Barry Goldberg, *Two Jews Blues*, St. Paul Books, 2012.
643 "I never knew Michael": Norman Dayron, author interview, 10/28/2011.
643 The conclusion that her son was given "rat poison" came from Dorothy Shinderman, interview with Bill Keenom, 1995.
644 "He phoned John": Susan Beuhler, interview with Bill Keenom, 1996.
644 "He would never": Dave Shorey, interview with Bill Keenom, 1996.
644 "He was dangerous": Norman Dayron, author interview, 10/28/2011.
644 "Michael had a heroin habit": Ira Kamin, interview with Bill Keenom, 1996.
645 "One of Jon Cramer's girlfriends": Leonard Trupin, author interview, 9/15/2016.
645 "That's when they injected": Norman Dayron, author interview, 10/28/2011.

EPILOGUE

647 "As epitaphs go": *Rolling Stone*, 4/2/1981.
649 "Mike was a very dear": Mark Naftalin, author interview, 4/2/2013.
649 "I loved playing": Al Kooper, author interview, 6/30/2016.

649 "I played with Mike": Bob Jones, author interview, 4/21/2011.
649 "Michael had all this": Nick Gravenites, "A Special Tribute to Michael Bloomfield," Mill Valley Film Festival video, 1983.
649 "One of the chief things": Toby Byron, letter to Bill Keenom, shared by Keenom.
649 "He was a smart dude": Woody Harris, interview with Jan Mark Wolkin, 1996.
649 "Bloomers was always": Elvin Bishop, interview with Bill Keenom, 1996.
649 "Michael was so gone": David Shorey, interview with Bill Keenom, 1995.
650 "I was probably": Norman Dayron, author interview, 10/28/2011.
650 "There is no person": Allen Bloomfield, author interview, 2/19/2008.

BIBLIOGRAPHY

Aagaard, René. *The Ultimate Complete Michael Bloomfield Discography*. Alleroed, Denmark: self-published, 2004. http://www.the-discographer.dk/vinyl/bloomfield-disko.pdf.

Aronowitz, Al. "Revolution in His Head." In *Dylan: Visions, Portraits and Back Pages*. New York: DK Publishing, 2005.

Bacon, Tony. *Million Dollar Les Paul: In Search of the Most Valuable Guitar in the World*. London: Jawbone, 2008.

Balin, Marty, dir. "A Special Tribute to Michael Bloomfield." Video produced for the Mill Valley Film Festival, 1983.

Benarde, Scott R. *Stars of David: Rock 'n' Roll's Jewish Stories*. Waltham, MA: Brandeis University Press, 2003.

Black, Johnny. *Jimi Hendrix: The Ultimate Experience*. New York: Thunder's Mouth, 1999.

Bloomfield, Michael. "Dylan Goes Electric." In *The Sixties*, edited by Lynda Rosen Obst. New York: Rolling Stone Press, 1977.

———. "Hendrix Remembered." *Guitar Player*, September 1975.

———. "Impressions of Dylan." *Hit Parader*, June 1968.

———. "An Interview with Muddy Waters." *Rhythm and Blues*, July 1964.

———. "Me and Big Joe." Tape recording transcribed by Sally Moses, ca. 1975.

Bloomfield, Michael, and Raeburn Flerlage. "An Interview with Howlin' Wolf." *Rhythm and Blues*, February 1965.

Boyd, Joe. *White Bicycles: Making Music in the 1960s*. London: Serpent's Tail, 2006.

Braittman, Stephen. "Mike Bloomfield: Eureka! A Niche at Last!" *The Rock 'n' Roll News*, June 1976.

Branton, Michael. "Chet Helms' Hippie Reunion." *Rolling Stone*, November 16, 1978.

Brockman, Susan, dir. *The Wizard of Waukesha*. Private DVD shared with the author, 1979.

Brooks, Michael. "Michael Bloomfield: Straight Stone City Blues." *Guitar Player*, June and August 1971.

Cohodas, Nadine. *Spinning Blues into Gold: The Chess Brothers and the Legendary Chess Records*. New York: St. Martin's, 2000.

Cohen, Ronald D. *Rainbow Quest: The Folk Music Revival and American Society, 1940–1970*. Amherst: University of Massachusetts Press, 2002.

Cohen, Ronald D., and Bob Riesman. *Chicago Folk*. Toronto: ECW, 2009.

Corman, Roger, dir. *The Trip*. DVD. MGM Home Entertainment, 2003.

Cross, Charles R. *Room Full of Mirrors: A Biography of Jimi Hendrix*. New York: Hyperion, 2005.

Davis, Clive, with Anthony DeCurtis. *The Soundtrack of My Life*. New York: Simon and Schuster, 2012.

Delehant, Jim. "Michael Bloomfield Puts Down Everything." *Hit Parader*, January–February 1967.

———. "Mike Bloomfield, Leader of the Band." *Hit Parader*, April 1968.

DeMichael, Don. "Father and Son: An Interview with Muddy Waters and Paul Butterfield." *Down Beat*, August 7, 1969.

———. "Mike Bloomfield." *Melody Maker*, February 1970.

———. "Up with the Blues: Mike Bloomfield." *Down Beat*, June 26, 1969.

Dylan, Bob. *Chronicles*. New York: Simon and Schuster, 2004.

Faithful, Marianne, with David Dalton. *Faithful: An Autobiography*. New York: Cooper Square, 2000.

Flerlage, Raeburn. *Chicago Blues*. Toronto: ECW, 2000.

Gale Research. *VideoHound's Golden Movie Retriever 2017: The Complete Guide to Movies*. New York: Gale Research, 2017.

Gleason, Ralph J. "Perspectives: Stop This Shuck, Mike Bloomfield." *Rolling Stone*, May 11, 1968.

Goldberg, Barry, with Steven Roeser. *Two Jews Blues*. Kindle Edition. N.p: St. Paul Books, 2012.

Golden, Lotti. "Whatever Happened to Michael Bloomfield?" *Crawdaddy*, May 1973.

Goodman, Fred. *The Mansion on the Hill*. New York: Times Books, 1997.

Graham, Bill, prod. *The Last Days of the Fillmore*. DVD. Rhino, 2009.

Gravenites, Nick. "Bad Talkin' Bluesman." *Blues Review*, July/August 1995.

———. "Stop This Shuck, Ralph Gleason!" *Rolling Stone*, May 25, 1968.

Grissim, John. "Winterland Reunion: Butter, Bloomers and Bishop." *Rolling Stone*, March 1973.

Hajdu, David. *Positively 4th Street: The Lives and Times of Joan Baez, Bob Dylan, Mimi Baez Fariña, and Richard Fariña*. New York: Picador, 2011.

Hammond, John, and Irving Townsend. *John Hammond on Record*. New York: Penguin Books, 1977.

Hirsch, Abby. *The Photography of Rock*. New York: Bobs-Merrill, 1972.

Hjort, Christopher. *Strange Brew: Eric Clapton and the British Blues Boom*. London: Jawbone, 2007.

Holmes, Thom. *Electronic and Experimental Music: Technology, Music, and Culture*. New York: Routledge, 2012.

Holzman, Jac, and Gavan Daws. *Follow the Music*. Santa Monica, CA: FirstMedia Books, 2000.

Hoskyns, Barney. *Across the Great Divide: The Band and America*. Milwaukee, WI: Hal Leonard, 2006.

———. *Small Town Talk*. Boston: Da Capo, 2016.

Johnson, Jed, dir. *Andy Warhol's Bad*. DVD. Cheezy Flicks, 2004.

Kamin, Ira. "Playing for Nothing on a Hot Afternoon." *Rolling Stone*, September 17, 1970.

Kerby, Bill. "Michael Bloomfield: Honkies Can't Dig Soul Music." *Los Angeles Free Press*, September 22, 1967.

Kooper, Al. *Backstage Passes and Backstabbing Bastards: Memoirs of a Rock 'n' Roll Survivor*. New York: Backbeat Books, 2008.

Kubernik, Harvey, and Kenneth Kubernik. *A Perfect Haze: The Illustrated History of the Monterey International Pop Festival*. Solana Beach, CA: Santa Monica, 2011.
Kyle, Dave. "A Brother's Words: Allen Bloomfield Remembers Michael." *Vintage Guitar*, August 1997.
Landau, Jon. "Blood, Sweat & Tears/The Electric Flag." *Crawdaddy*, August 1968.
———. "East-West." *Crawdaddy*, November 1966.
Lerman, Paul. "How I Met Michael Bloomfield." mikebloomfieldamericanmusic.com, 2011.
Lerner, Murray, dir. *The Other Side of the Mirror: Bob Dylan Live at the Newport Folk Festival 1963–1965*. DVD. Columbia Legacy, 2007.
———. *Festival!* DVD. Eagle Eye Media, 2005.
Levy, Arthur. "The War Is Over: A Rock 'n' Roll Revival in Six Parts." *Zoo World*, August 1974.
Lotito, Mark, Al Kooper, Harvey Brooks, and Jimmy Vivino. "The Legendary Michael Bloomfield." *20th Century Guitar*, September–October 1994.
Lydon, Michael. *Flashbacks: Eyewitness Accounts of the Rock Revolution, 1964–1974*. New York: Routledge, 2003.
Lyons, Jimmy, with Ira Kamin. *Duke, Dizzy, the Count and Me*. Los Angeles: California Living Books, 1978.
Marcus, Greil. *Like a Rolling Stone: Bob Dylan at the Crossroads*. New York: Public Affairs, 2005.
Marmorstein, Gary. *The Label: The Story of Columbia Records*. New York: Thunder's Mouth, 2007.
Marshall, Terry. "Mike Bloomfield: I Wanna Be the Best." *BAM*, June 1976.
Martin, Peter. "Electric Flag: Bloomfield Sifts with Soul." *Pop/Rock Music*, December 1968.
McClintock, Jack. "The Electric Flag: American Music Returns." *Rolling Stone*, August 1974.
Miles, Barry. *Hippie*. New York: Sterling Publishing, 2003.
Mitchell, Artie, and Jim Mitchell, dirs. *Sodom and Gomorrah*. Private DVD shared with the author, 1975.
———. Ultra-Kore shorts including *Hot Nazis*. Private DVD shared with the author, 1974.
O'Neal, Jim, and Amy van Singel. *The Voice of the Blues: Classic Interviews from Living Blues Magazine*. New York: Routledge, 2002.
Pennebaker, D. A., dir. *Jimi Plays Monterey: The Criterion Collection*. DVD. Criterion, 2009.
———. *Monterey Pop*. DVD. Criterion, 2008.
Perry, Charles. *The Haight-Ashbury: A History*. San Francisco: Wenner Books, 2005.
Phillips, John, with Jim Jerome. *Papa John: An Autobiography*. New York: Dell Publishing, 1986.
Polizzotti, Mark. *Highway 61 Revisited*. New York: Bloomsbury Academic, 2012.
Roby, Steven, and Brad Schreiber. *Becoming Jimi Hendrix*. Cambridge: Da Capo, 2007.
Rosen, Steve. "The Bloomfield File." *International Musician*, April 1978.
Rotolo, Suze. *A Freewheelin' Time*. New York: Broadway Books, 2008.
Rowe, Mike. *Chicago Breakdown*. London: Eddison, 1973.
Santelli, Robert. *The Best of the Blues: The 101 Essential Albums*. New York: Penguin Books, 1997.
Sarles, Bob, dir. *Sweet Blues: A Film about Michael Bloomfield*. DVD. Ravin Films, 2014.
Scorsese, Martin, dir. *No Direction Home: Bob Dylan*. DVD. White Horse Pictures, 2016.
Scott, Sid. "Michael, Matt and Me." Unpublished essay shared with the author, 2014.

Selvin, Joel. *Monterey Pop*. San Francisco: Chronicle Books, 1992.

———. *San Francisco: The Musical History Tour*. San Francisco: Chronicle Books, 1996.

Shea, Mike, dir. *And This Is Free*. DVD. Shanachie Entertainment, 2008.

Shorey, David Randall. *Tell on It: Compendium of Obscurity*. San Francisco: Xlibris, 2004.

Simmons, Michael. "Michael Bloomfield: Who Is That Guitar Player?" Liner notes to CD box set. Michael Bloomfield. *From His Head to His Hear to His Hands*. Sony Legacy, 2014.

Skirboll, Aaron. *The Last Night of the Guitar Virtuoso*. Kindle Edition. Kindle Single, 2016.

Sloman, Larry. *On the Road with Bob Dylan*. New York: Three Rivers, 1978.

Sloman, Larry, and Michael Bloomfield. "Copping: Stories from a Lifetime of Getting High on the Road." *High Times*, June 1983.

Soundstage: Blues Summit in Chicago. Santa Monica, CA: Rhino Home Video, 1993.

Stein, Dan J., and Eric Hollander. *The American Psychiatric Publishing Textbook of Anxiety Disorders*. New York: American Psychiatric Publishing, 2002.

Von Schmidt, Eric, and Jim Rooney. *Baby, Let Me Follow You Down: The Illustrated Story of the Cambridge Folk Years*. Boston: University of Massachusetts Press, 1994.

Wald, Elijah. *Dylan Goes Electric!: Newport, Seeger, Dylan, and the Night That Split the Sixties*. New York: Dey Street Books, 2015.

Ward, Ed. *Michael Bloomfield: The Rise and Fall of an American Guitar Hero*. New York: Cherry Lane Books, 1983.

Welding, Pete. "Caught in the Act: The Group." *Down Beat*, December 1964.

Wenner, Jann. "The Rolling Stone Interview: Mike Bloomfield." *Rolling Stone*, April 6, 1968.

Wexler, Haskell, dir. *Medium Cool*. DVD. Criterion, 2013.

Wheeler, Tom. "Barroom Scholar of the Blues: Michael Bloomfield." *Guitar Player*, April 1979.

———. "Jammin' with the Blue Jew." *Rolling Stone*, April 2, 1981.

Winter, Johnny, with Mary Lou Sullivan. *Raisin' Cain: The Wild and Raucous Story of Johnny Winter*. New York: Backbeat Books, 2010.

Woliver, Robbie. *Hoot!* New York: St. Martin's Press, 1986.

Wolkin, Jan Mark, and Bill Keenom. *Michael Bloomfield: If You Love These Blues*. San Francisco: Miller Freeman Books, 2000.

ADDITIONAL RESOURCES

The items in the following list can serve as supplements to the biography and as additional resources for readers interested in learning more about Michael Bloomfield.

WEBSITES

mikebloomfieldamericanmusic.com

The digital companion to this biography, this redesigned website features an exhaustive Michael Bloomfield performance history and timeline, a detailed discography, and information about Bloomfield's various guitars, plus photos, videos, audio essays, and other features.

facebook.com/Mike-Bloomfield-An-American-Guitarist

This is the Facebook presence of mikebloomfieldamericanmusic.com. It offers rare music clips, additional videos, photos, and information about Bloomfield-related topics.

michaelbloomfield.com

The official website of the Michael Bloomfield estate, this site offers a biography of the guitarist and a detailed timeline of his career, as well as a collection of photos.

facebook.com/MichaelBloomfieldLegacy

The creation of Michael's friend, housemate, and onetime gig coordinator Toby Byron, this Facebook page has a wealth of rare photos, music, and information, plus commentary from Bloomfield's friends and fans.

the-discographer.dk/vinyl/bloomfield-disko.pdf

This remarkable online Bloomfield discography lists every known recording by the guitarist in every version, both domestic and foreign, with informative commentary. Compiled by music historian René Aagaard, the discography can be downloaded for personal use.

PRINT

Michael Bloomfield: If You Love These Blues, Miller Freeman Books

An oral history of Bloomfield's life and times by Jan Mark Wolkin and Bill Keenom, this book is essential reading for anyone wishing to know more about the guitarist. Included with it is a CD of rare early Bloomfield recordings.

Michael Bloomfield: The Rise and Fall of an American Guitar Hero, Chicago Review Press

Originally published in 1983 by music critic and historian Ed Ward and recently updated, this biography has been greatly expanded with new information by Edd Hurt. The book also includes Bloomfield's complete *Rolling Stone* interview from 1968.

Two Jews Blues, St. Paul Books

Musician and composer Barry Goldberg recounts his close friendship with Bloomfield in this autobiography, cowritten with Stephen Roeser. Goldberg's candid insights provide the reader with a greater understanding of the guitarist's troubled later life.

The Last Night of the Guitar Virtuoso, Kindle Single

In this short e-book, Aaron Skirboll gives a brief overview of Bloomfield's career and then speculates on what may have occurred on the night the guitarist died of a drug overdose.

RECORDINGS

Note: The following records and CDs were used as source material for *Guitar King: Michael Bloomfield's Life in the Blues*, but I also used many unreleased concert and club recordings. For a complete listing of those unreleased recordings, please visit the website Michael Bloomfield: An American Guitarist, at mikebloomfieldamericanmusic.com.

LP RELEASES (CHRONOLOGICAL)

Mandolin Blues. Yank Rachell. Delmark DL 606, 1963.
Broke and Hungry. Sleepy John Estes and the Tennessee Jug Busters. Delmark DS 608, 1964.
Folksong '65. Paul Butterfield Blues Band, various artists. Elektra S-78, 1965.
Highway 61 Revisited. Bob Dylan. Columbia CS 9181, 1965.
Newport Folk Festival 1965. Paul Butterfield Blues Band, various artists. Vanguard VRS 9225, 1965.
The Paul Butterfield Blues Band. Paul Butterfield Blues Band. Elektra EKS 7294, 1965.
So Many Roads. John Hammond. Vanguard VRS 9178, 1965.
East-West. Paul Butterfield Blues Band. Elektra EKS 7315, 1966.
What's Shakin'. Paul Butterfield Blues Band, various artists. Elektra EKS 4002, 1966.
The James Cotton Blues Band. James Cotton Blues Band. Verve Forecast FTS-3023, 1967.
The Trip: Original Motion Picture Soundtrack. Electric Flag. Sidewalk ST 5908, 1967.
Cotton in Your Ears. James Cotton Blues Band. Verve Forecast FTS-3060, 1968.
Grape Jam. Moby Grape with Michael Bloomfield, Al Kooper. Columbia MGS 1, 1968.
A Long Time Comin'. Electric Flag. Columbia CS 9597, 1968.
Pure Cotton. James Cotton Blues Band. Verve Forecast FTS-3038, 1968.
Super Session. Michael Bloomfield, Al Kooper, Steve Stills. Columbia CS 9701, 1968.
Two Jews Blues. Barry Goldberg. Buddah BDS 5029, 1968.
What Now My Love. Mitch Ryder. DynoVoice DY 31901, 1968.
Fathers and Sons. Muddy Waters, Michael Bloomfield, Paul Butterfield, and others. Chess LPS-127, 1969.
It's Not Killing Me. Michael Bloomfield. Columbia CS 9883, 1969.
The Live Adventures of Mike Bloomfield and Al Kooper. Michael Bloomfield, Al Kooper. Columbia KGP 8, 1969.
Live at Bill Graham's Fillmore West. Michael Bloomfield and others. Columbia CS 9893, 1969.

Living with the Animals. Mother Earth. Mercury SR 61194, 1969.
Mourning in the Morning. Otis Rush. Cotillion SD 9006, 1969.
My Labors. Nick Gravenites. Columbia CS 9899, 1969.
Sam Lay in Bluesland. Sam Lay Blues Band. Blue Thumb BTS-14, 1970.
Weeds. Brewer and Shipley. Kama Sutra 2016, 1970.
Brand New. Woody Herman Orchestra featuring Michael Bloomfield. Fantasy 8414, 1971.
Gandharva. Beaver/Krause. Warner Bros. WS 1909, 1971.
The Best of the Electric Flag. Electric Flag. Columbia C 30422, 1972.
Golden Butter: The Best of the Paul Butterfield Blues Band. Paul Butterfield Blues Band. Elektra 7E-2005, 1972.
Melton, Levy and the Dey Brothers. Barry Melton, Jay Levy, Rick and Tony Dey. Columbia KC 31279, 1972.
Steel Yard Blues: Original Motion Picture Soundtrack. Nick Gravenites, Michael Bloomfield, Paul Butterfield, Maria Muldaur. Warner Bros. BS 2662, 1972.
Triumvirate. John Hammond, Michael Bloomfield, Dr. John. Columbia KC 32172, 1973.
The Band Kept Playing. Electric Flag. Atlantic SD 18112, 1974.
If You Love These Blues, Play 'Em as You Please. Michael Bloomfield. Guitar Player 3002, 1976.
KGB. KGB. MCA 2168, 1976.
Analine. Michael Bloomfield. Takoma B-1059, 1977.
Count Talent and the Originals. Michael Bloomfield. Clouds 8805, 1978.
Michael Bloomfield. Michael Bloomfield. Takoma B-1063, 1978.
Between the Hard Place and the Ground. Michael Bloomfield. Takoma TAK 7070, 1979.
Bloomfield/Harris. Michael Bloomfield, Woody Harris. Kicking Mule KM-164, 1979.
Cruisin' for a Bruisin'. Michael Bloomfield. Takoma TAK 7091, 1981.
Living in the Fast Lane. Michael Bloomfield. Waterhouse 11, 1981.
Bloomfield: A Retrospective. Michael Bloomfield. Columbia C2 37578, 1983.

CD RELEASES (CHRONOLOGICAL)

A Long Time Comin'. Electric Flag. Columbia CK 9597, 1993.
Don't Say That I Ain't Your Man! Essential Blues 1964–1969. Michael Bloomfield. Columbia Legacy CK 57631, 1994.
Old Glory: The Best of the Electric Flag. Electric Flag. Columbia Legacy 57629, 1995.
The Original Lost Elektra Sessions. Paul Butterfield Blues Band. Elektra Traditions R2 73505, 1995.
Strawberry Jam. Paul Butterfield Blues Band. Winner 446, 1995.
East-West Live. Paul Butterfield Blues Band. Winner 447, 1996.
And This Is Maxwell Street. Various artists. Rooster R 2641, 1998.
Live at the Old Waldorf. Michael Bloomfield. Columbia Legacy CK 65688, 1998.
Rare Performances 1964. Michael Bloomfield. CD included with *Michael Bloomfield: If You Love These Blues*, Miller Freeman Books, 2000.
Knockin' Myself Out. Michael Bloomfield. Fuel 2000 Records 302 061 256 2, 2002.
Fillmore East: The Lost Concert Tapes 12/13/68. Michael Bloomfield, Al Kooper. Columbia Legacy CK 85278, 2003.

Super Session. Michael Bloomfield, Al Kooper, Steve Stills. Columbia Legacy CK 63406, 2003.
Michael Bloomfield: From His Head to His Heart to His Hands. Michael Bloomfield. Sony Legacy 88765476342, 2014.
The Cutting Edge 1965–1966: The Bootleg Series, Vol. 12. Bob Dylan. Columbia 88875124412–6, 2015.

ACKNOWLEDGMENTS

It was in 2004 that I decided to create a simple website that tracked the career of Michael Bloomfield. One Saturday morning, I said to my new girlfriend, "You know, Mike Bloomfield still matters." "Of course he does," she obligingly replied, having no idea who Mike Bloomfield was. "No, really, people need to know about him," I said. "I've got to do something to let them know." "I think you should," she agreed. Little did she know.

Like many people my age, I first discovered Michael Bloomfield when I was a teenager. The kids at school all loved Jimi Hendrix, and I did too. But Michael was my secret favorite. So when I heard that he was coming to Boston with Al Kooper for a Super Session gig, I had to go. Two weeks later, I waited in line outside the ticket booth at the decrepit Boston Arena with a crowd of scruffy Northeastern students, then sat through several sets of loud, boomy rock music while I took it all in. It was my first rock concert, and I was enthralled.

When Michael finally took the stage, I was impressed by his hair and his tall, rangy presence. Before he played a note, though, he made a speech to the audience, something about how "Bean Town cabbies" were being killed and how we should all be nicer to them. That seemed odd to me, but for all I knew, rock stars always started their shows with inchoate speeches.

It was when Bloomfield began playing that everything suddenly made sense. The guitarist peeled off frenetic solos that rang through the big, iron-girdered building with the sonic urgency of a fire alarm. His sound was huge, and backed by Kooper's organ, it commanded the attention of every pair of ears in the place. What struck me was the way Michael's whole body moved with the ebb and flow of his lead lines, jerking from side to side, his head wagging, arching way back one moment, lurching forward the next. He was a visual analog of the music. Everyone else just stood there, but not him.

That was the first time I saw Michael Bloomfield. It was also the last.

But his performance made a deep impression, and thousands of other kids across the country were equally impressed. We all learned to play blues guitar.

We all formed blues bands. We all knew that a Les Paul Sunburst was worth whatever ridiculous price the seller was demanding, if only because Bloomfield played one.

In time, though, Michael's star faded. He retired to Mill Valley, north of San Francisco, and spent the last decade of his life in self-imposed obscurity.

I, too, moved on. I went to college, got a job, got married, and started a family. I was living in Chicago when I heard that Bloomfield had died. John Lennon had been shot three months earlier, and a CBS radio reporter waylaid me at my L stop to get my thoughts on his tragic killing. But nobody stuck a microphone in my face when Bloomfield overdosed. He was just another rock 'n' roll drug casualty—one of many—famous long ago but now forgotten.

I was troubled that the man who had introduced blues to white America, who pioneered psychedelic rock, created brass blues-rock, and then became a scholar of American musical styles, had largely faded from view. One of the best guitar players of his generation, a musician whose soulful sound and passionate exuberance were on stunning display every time he picked up an instrument—how could he be ignored by polls, surveys, histories, and best-of lists?

I decided I had to do something to correct these oversights.

I started by creating a Bloomfield website—a chronology of all his recordings and shows, inspired by the discographies that are essential tools for all serious music listeners. In just a few years, the site grew to encompass much more. Contributions from Michael's fans added greatly to the history, and soon there were interviews, personal recollections, photos, audio clips, and videos in addition to the time line. It was through the expanded website that I met author and musician Bill Keenom, who, along with music historian Jan Mark Wolkin, had published the excellent oral history of Bloomfield's life aptly titled *Michael Bloomfield: If You Love These Blues*. One thing led to another, and one day several big boxes arrived on my doorstep. They contained all of Bill's taped interviews with Michael's family, friends, and fellow musicians—recordings that had been transcribed and used in the biography. Bill generously thought I should have them to help with the website, and I found them fascinating—in part because they contained many details that had not made it into print. Wouldn't it be great, I thought, if those facts could be made available to the many fans that Michael still had? In 2010 I began doing interviews of my own, quietly telling myself that I might want to write a critical biography of the guitarist. And after several years of amassing stories, I decided to do just that.

I began work on the biography in September 2012, using Bill and Jan's interviews as a framework. I got to know them both through my Bloomfield website, and their assistance in the writing of this book has been invaluable. I'm grateful to Jan for his insightful emails, his patience with my many questions, and his freely sharing with me his recollections and research. Though we've never met, I consider Bill a good friend, and it was his extensive conversations with Susan Beuhler, Nick Gravenites, Elvin Bishop, Barry Goldberg, Ira Kamin, and many others that got me started on the biography. He readily granted me permission to use whatever I needed to tell Michael's story, and I am indebted to him for his enthusiasm, humor, and kindness.

I myself talked to many of Michael Bloomfield's friends and family members while writing this book, and their willingness to freely share their memories helped immeasurably. When I first met Allen Bloomfield, I was struck by how much he looked and sounded like his brother. He invited me into his home, fed me, and shared with me many tales of life in the Bloomfield household in Chicago and Glencoe. His support and trust have been an inspiration throughout this project, and I am much the richer for them.

Mark Naftalin provided me with fascinating details about the early days of the Butterfield Band and about his friendship and musical partnership with Michael. Mark's intelligence, probing insights, and wry humor not only kept me on my toes but gave me a sense of what life must have been like traveling in such fast company. I greatly appreciated his hospitality and his readiness to talk about those heady days.

I spent a memorable week in Mill Valley with Michael's good friend Norman Dayron, conducting extensive interviews and cataloging a small portion of Norman's vast archive of recorded material. His kindness in bringing me into his home and allowing me access to his collection made my work that much easier. Norman deserves much credit for capturing the sound of Chicago blues in a period of transition, and for preserving Mike Bloomfield's role in it.

Al Kooper, the man who organized the session that resulted in Bloomfield's only hit record, spoke freely with me about his days with Michael, recording with Bob Dylan, performing with Dylan at Newport, and *Super Session*. His love for Michael and his appreciation of the guitarist's talent, as well as his understanding of his friend's various struggles, guided my efforts in re-creating those pivotal moments.

Other well-known musicians readily told me of their experiences with Bloomfield. John Hammond recounted meeting Michael for the first time at the University of Chicago Folk Festival and talked of recording with him, both in New York in 1964 and with Dr. John for the *Triumvirate* sessions. Peter Yarrow graciously recalled his encounters with Bloomfield at Newport when Dylan went electric and later in New York when they recorded together. My friend Charlie Musselwhite related many details of his days in Chicago with Michael, filling in more than a few blanks in the guitarist's nascent career. Charlie is a true gentleman of the old school.

I was fortunate to do several interviews with Bloomfield's Fickle Pickle partner, George Mitchell. George recounted in striking detail his trip to East St. Louis with Michael and Big Joe Williams, the fateful junket that resulted in Bloomfield's chapbook, *Me and Big Joe*. George's southern accent added real color to the tale, and his descriptions of his days organizing shows at the Pickle with Michael were priceless.

Drummer Bob Jones played with Michael throughout the 1970s, and he shared with me numerous colorful Bloomfield stories, from recording *Live at Bill Graham's Fillmore West* to touring around the country with the guitarist's Friends group. I was fortunate to have spoken with him before his untimely passing in 2013. Michael's other great drummer, George Rains, told me about the gig in Vancouver when Bloomfield ditched the band and his legendary Les Paul so he could watch his performance on the *Soundstage* Muddy Waters tribute. George's recounting of a Passover seder at Michael's home on Reed Street was a hoot.

Keyboardist Vince Viti recalled for me the summer when Michael, then a high school junior, played in his band and made everybody "sound good." Steve Mallory played bass in one of Bloomfield's last backup bands, Chicago Blues Power, and he related his experiences with Michael, confirming that even in decline the guitarist could recapture the early fire.

A true champion of the Bloomfield legacy, Toby Byron gave me critical help with my Michael Bloomfield website, not only providing visuals and information but offering sincere encouragement as well. His recollections about living and working with Michael in the 1970s were extremely helpful.

Sally Moses told me all about C.T. Productions and about working with Michael and Norman Dayron on transcribing "Me and Big Joe" and several of Bloomfield's other dictated stories. Denise Kaufman, a member of the Ace of Cups, San Francisco's first all-female rock band, recalled Michael and the Electric Flag rehearsing at her house on Autumn Lane in Mill Valley and then later sharing the stage with him and Muddy Waters at the Cosmic Joy-Scout Super-Jam. Her genuine affection for the guitarist impressed me greatly.

Pioneering R&B and blues guitarist Sidney Warner talked with me several times by phone, sharing his memories of playing bass in Michael's band the Group. Those stories helped me chart the band's progress from its initial success at Big John's to recording for John Hammond to its regrettable demise several months later. Sid's candor, humor, and generosity made interviewing him a pleasure. His life story would make a truly fascinating book; unfortunately, he passed away in 2011.

Three other members of the Group spoke with me about playing with Michael. Guitarist Mike Johnson recalled meeting Bloomfield at a Hyde Park fraternity party and then getting a call from him to join the band at Big John's. Mike regrettably passed away in 2013. The late Brian Friedman was in poor health when I spoke to him in 2012, but he graciously took the time to tell me of his experiences performing and recording with Michael. Norm Mayell, later the drummer for Sopwith Camel, patiently worked with me to get the timeline right for the Group's run at Big John's, then gave me a hilarious recollection of an LSD-fueled evening spent at the Hotel Albert with Bloomfield during the Flag days.

The late Fred Glazer gave me a lengthy interview about his close friendship with Michael, and his candid observations and humorous asides, as well as his insight into his friend's psychological complexity, furnished me with a real understanding of the guitarist's early days. Another high school friend, musician and singer Bob Greenspan, described his teen years with Michael playing in Highwood and their days together camping in Utah and gigging at the Old Waldorf. Michael Melford told me about meeting Bloomfield in Glencoe, playing rock 'n' roll and bluegrass with him, and later producing his solo album for Columbia. His observations about that problematic recording and Michael's mental state at the time were candid and revealing.

The "Mayor of Old Town," Chicago's Tommy Walker, talked frankly with me about Michael's drug use and about the guitarist's uncanny ability to win over South Side audiences whenever he sat in. The late Joel Harlib, Bloomfield's first manager, told me of the meeting he had with producer John Hammond that resulted in Michael being signed by Epic, and about the happy days he and Bloomfield spent together going to clubs, producing shows at the Fickle Pickle, and just hanging out.

In the course of my research, I also had the good fortune to locate many of Michael's other childhood friends. Drummer Roy Jespersen provided me with the real story behind Bloomfield's provocative gig at New Trier High School, a performance that nearly got him expelled, and Gerry Pasternack recalled his days playing drums with Michael around the North Shore and on Rush Street with a vividness that was both discerning and hilarious. Horace "Ace" Cathcart shared stories about his days playing bass with Michael in Highwood and later at the Fickle Pickle, and he conveyed how unusual it was for a group in those days to be integrated.

High school friend Sid Scott sent me his essay about taking an impromptu road trip with Michael to visit Elvis Presley in Memphis one weekend, a tale that was as entertaining as it sounds, and Steve Scheff added amusing details about the sojourn and about playing with Bloomfield at the Tally Ho in Highwood—on cello. Rob Jacklin gave me vivid descriptions of Michael's home life and his wildly extravagant personality with a candor that I much appreciated.

Guitarist Jim Pauly was in some of Michael's early bands, and he was very helpful with their chronology. His story about recording four selections with Michael at Lyon & Healy in the Loop was tantalizing.

Michael's closest friend from his school days, Roy Ruby, unfortunately died long before I began this project, but his half brother, John Landes, was kind enough to share with me Roy's family history and some of his personal writings. It was through Roy that Leonard Trupin met Michael, and I spoke with Leonard numerous times about his friendship with Bloomfield during the guitarist's last years. Lennie also was kind enough to give me permission to use several of his photos from those days.

The late guitarist, helicopter pilot, and lumberjack Chris Okey never met Bloomfield, but he did own Michael's famed Les Paul Sunburst for several years after Bloomfield abandoned it in Vancouver in 1974. Our email correspondence helped me understand what happened to the guitar after Bloomfield lost it. Likewise, John Picard, the guitarist known as "Mister Zero" of the legendary Canadian rock band the Kings, shared with me his research on the fate of the Sunburst and gave me a crash course in the value of vintage Gibson guitars.

The current executors of the Bloomfield estate—Michael's half brother, Randy Bloomfield, and Allen's daughter Nicole Bloomfield—have been supportive of me and the biography from the beginning. Their generosity and kindness have been a real blessing. Randy helped me better understand his father, Harold Bloomfield, and Nicole shared her memories of her grandmother, Dorothy Shinderman, during one delightful evening over dinner. Under their stewardship, Michael Bloomfield's legacy will doubtless assume its rightful place in the history of popular music.

There were numerous Bloomfield friends and fans who reached out to me over the years through my website, and they all aided my efforts in ways large and small. I can't acknowledge them all here, but David Gedalecia, Nick Nicolaisen, Corry Arnold, Don Mock, Jim Murphy, Dann Glenn, Marc Skobac, Brent Pellegrini, Ralph Heibutski, Felix Cabrera, Peter Castro, and Frank Macias are just a few whose contributions I especially appreciated. John Ivey did some marvelous research on Bloomfield's junket to Boulder in 1963, and he unearthed rare recordings the guitarist made with Judy Roderick. Donna Gower, Michael's close friend from the Big John's years, shared with me on Facebook marvelous stories of the guitarist's brotherly efforts to protect her, an attractive young woman, from the dubious intentions of more than a few of his friends. Nick Lerman and Alex Wernquest, two talented Brooklyn college students, approached me about making a video about Michael for the website, a brief documentary about Bloomfield's days in New York. It instead became a ninety-minute video biography that has now been viewed over one hundred thousand times on YouTube. Guitarist Paul Lerman, Nick's dad, allowed me to post his essay about putting Michael up in his college apartment during a Flag gig in Philadelphia and then seeing Super Session at the Fillmore East as Bloomfield's guest. Paul's appreciation for Michael's artistry is contagious, and his generosity has greatly touched me. I'm honored to be his friend.

Filmmaker Bob Sarles, creator of *Sweet Blues: A Film about Michael Bloomfield*, the excellent video included in Sony Legacy's Bloomfield box set, gave me access to some of his interviews, including one with Bill Graham. He also shared with me rare footage of the Butterfield Band's appearances at Newport in 1965, helping to clarify details of the Grossman/Lomax fracas. Guitarist Paul Petraitis shared his memories of Bloomfield's appearance with Muddy Waters at the Father and Sons concert in 1969, and he graciously sent me highlights from his interviews with Joel Harlib. Columbia producer Bruce Dickinson granted me access to the label's artist cards and other documents that aided greatly in assigning dates to Bloomfield's various recording sessions for the company. Author and editor Larry "Ratso" Sloman told me about how Michael would sleep on his couch when he was in New York, and about the time he took members of the New York Rangers hockey team to see Bloomfield perform at My Father's Place on Long Island. Discographer René Aagaard shared his extraordinary work *The Ultimate Complete Michael Bloomfield Discography* with me just as I was beginning my own efforts. He has been helpful all along, cheerfully sharing additional information whenever he uncovered it. The indefatigable Bruno Ceriotti is another discographer whose contributions I have greatly appreciated. I'm also indebted to researcher Bob Andres for sending me a trove of rare Bloomfield recordings. They have proven to be an extremely informative resource. Lastly, I must express my sincere thanks and gratitude to the doyen of all things Bloomfield, Peggy McVickar. Peggy accepted me early on as a true believer, and she has contributed immeasurably to my efforts to chronicle Michael Bloomfield's artistry for more than a decade. I could never have completed this project without her help.

Finally, let me add a few personal acknowledgments. My editor at the University of Texas Press, Robert Devens, is himself a longtime Bloomfield fan, and his enthusiastic and insightful advice throughout the writing of this book has been invaluable. Author and critic Michael Simmons, the scribe who penned the excellent notes for the Sony Legacy box set, has become a close friend and confidant. His encouragement, guidance, and good humor have been a real inspiration over the years. His skill with wordplay has also been greatly appreciated. My son, Sam Brandis-Dann, has cheerfully suffered through many years of his old man's rantings about the "Blue Jew" and even listens to a Butterfield Band cut or a Super Session track every now and then. I don't need to remind him that this book wouldn't exist had he not given me a copy of *If You Love These Blues* way back when.

Of all those who helped me with this biography, it is Laurie Knoop, my significant other, who has been my rock throughout the process. She encouraged me right from the start and has been an advocate for and a champion of Michael Bloomfield, a musician she first learned about on that Saturday long ago. She has charmed those who might have been reluctant to trust an unknown author with personal recollections, and she's read through many iterations of the text with an enthusiasm that might seem pathological were it not so sincere. I owe her a debt of love and gratitude that I can never repay.

ABOUT THE AUTHOR

DAVID DANN is a commercial artist, music historian, writer, and amateur musician who worked for many years in the news industry as a senior graphic designer for an upstate New York daily newspaper and as copublisher of an award-winning Catskills weekly. Most recently, he was the editor of *Artenol*, a radical art journal described by the *New York Times* as "a cross between *The New Republic* and *Mad Magazine*." He has also hosted a weekly jazz program on WJFF Radio Catskill for nearly three decades and has a collection of more than 8,500 jazz and blues recordings. From his extensive archive, he has occasionally supplied the Smithsonian Institution with rare recordings, and he recently provided the Museum of Modern Art in New York with vintage albums for one of its exhibits. David grew up on Chicago's North Shore and later lived in Chicago, where he hung out at Theresa's, the Checkerboard, Florence's, and other bars on the South Side as well as on Maxwell Street. He currently lives in the Catskill Mountains in New York's Sullivan County.

INDEX

D

H

I

J

N

O